The International Monetary Fund
1979–1989

Silent Revolution

The International Monetary Fund
1979–1989

James M. Boughton

International Monetary Fund

©2001 International Monetary Fund

Production: IMF Graphics Section
Cover design: Massoud Etemadi
Figures: Theodore F. Peters, Jr.
Typesetting: Choon Lee

Photo and illustration credits: p. 6—Gwendolyn Stewart; p. 8—IMF photo; p. 10—Padraic Hughes; p. 26—Joe Diana; p. 29—Denio Zara; p. 189—World Bank Map Design Unit; p. 303—AP/ World Wide Photos; p. 326—©Tribune Media Services, Inc. All rights reserved. Reprinted with permission; p. 363—Tony Cretaro, Citibank; p. 463—Landrú, *Diario Clarín*, Buenos Aires, Argentina; p. 528— Jorge Cardoso/*Correio Braziliense*; p. 700—Denio Zara; p. 910—Ernesto Bertani, "No More Funds" (acrylic on canvas), courtesy of Zurbaran Gallery, Buenos Aires, Argentina; p. 944—IMF photos; p. 969—IMF archives; p. 1055—Denio Zara.

Library of Congress Cataloging-in-Publication Data
Boughton, James M.
  Silent revolution : the International Monetary Fund, 1979–1989 / James M.
    Boughton. p. cm.
  Includes bibliographical references.
  ISBN 1-55775-971-5 (alk. paper)
    1. International Monetary Fund—History.   2. International finance—
  History. I. Title.

HG3881.5.I58 B68 2001
332.1'52—dc21   2001039540

⊗ The paper used in this publication meets the minimum requirements of the American National Standard for Information Sciences—Permanence of Paper for Printed Library Materials, ANSI Z39.48-1984.

Address orders to:
International Monetary Fund, Publication Services
700 19th Street, N.W., Washington D.C. 20431, U.S.A.
Telephone: (202) 623-7430
Telefax: (202) 623-7201
E-mail: publications@imf.org
Internet: http://www.imf.org

Contents

Foreword

The International Monetary Fund has long been in the forefront among major financial institutions in making its history available to the general public. In 1969, we published a three-volume history of our founding at Bretton Woods and our first 20 years of operations. We followed that publication with a history of 1966–71 that focused primarily on the creation of the SDR, and then with a history of 1972–78 that analyzed the switch from fixed to floating exchange rates and other turbulent financial events of the 1970s. We are proud to continue this tradition with a major new history that carries the story of the IMF through to the end of the 1980s.

These 11 years, 1979 to 1989, were even more tumultuous for the world financial system and the IMF than the preceding periods. As the major industrial countries experimented with different policies for restoring economic growth and financial stability, the IMF developed new approaches to surveillance so as to track the process and help guide it in directions beneficial to the world economy. When an international debt crisis erupted in 1982, the IMF worked with both creditors and debtors to develop and implement a strategy for putting debt and economic growth back on sustainable paths. At the same time, many countries in the early stages of independence and economic development called on the IMF for financial assistance and policy advice, and the range of issues and problems to which we had to respond expanded dramatically. Knowledge of these events is important for its own sake and for understanding how and why the IMF responded to even greater challenges in the 1990s and beyond.

To write this history, the IMF named James M. Boughton as the institution's third Historian. Having served in the IMF Research Department in the 1980s and earlier as a Professor of Economics at Indiana University, he has witnessed, participated in, and analyzed many of the events to be chronicled here. As with his two predecessors, he was given full access to the IMF archives and was able to interview many of the principal actors in this global drama. In a spirit of increasing openness and transparency, he was asked, and expected, to present the findings of his research fully and independently. Accordingly, this book represents his personal views, not the institutional views of the IMF, and he assumes full responsibility for its contents.

September 2001   Horst Köhler
                                                 Managing Director
                                         International Monetary Fund

Preface

Background

In 1965, the management of the International Monetary Fund decided to commission a history of the institution's first twenty years of operation: to record how the Bretton Woods conference came about and how it succeeded, how the key decisions were taken to make the Fund viable, and how it gradually came to play a significant if still modest role in shaping the postwar international monetary system. J. Keith Horsefield, who was about to retire as the Fund's Chief Editor, accepted the challenge and produced a three-volume set (Horsefield, 1969): his own chronicle of events (sunnily subtitled "Twenty Years of International Monetary Cooperation"), a collection of essays by Fund staff on the main issues, and a compilation of the Fund's official documents. Horsefield's primary sources, aside from his own experience and his close contacts with others on the staff, were the minutes of meetings of the Executive Board, staff papers prepared for the Board, and related documents in the Fund's archives. By design, his History focused largely on the work of the Board, as the Fund's principal decision-making body. He was not permitted to document his sources, because they were not open to public scrutiny, but he was able to quote Executive Directors by name and to open a window on how the interests and influence of member countries were manifested. Publication of his History marked the first major crack in the culture of confidentiality that had pervaded the Fund from the beginning.

Even as Horsefield was writing, the Fund was growing out of its formative stages and was assuming a more central role in the international system. Economic growth in Europe and Japan was weakening the ability of the U.S. dollar to continue to serve as the centerpiece and anchor of the system and was leading to calls for the Fund to develop a new multilateral supplement to official reserve assets. As a result, the Fund's charter—its Articles of Agreement—was amended in 1969 to permit the Fund to create "special drawing rights" (SDRs) and allocate them to member countries. Margaret Garritsen de Vries, who had first joined the Fund staff in 1946, had been the first woman to head a division, and had worked with Horsefield on his second volume, took over as Historian and wrote the story of the development of the SDR and other activities of the late 1960s (de Vries, 1976).

Once again, the history-in-progress was overtaken by events. As de Vries was writing the second History (more darkly subtitled "The System Under Stress"), the Bretton Woods system of fixed but adjustable exchange rates was collapsing under the weight of disparate policies and conditions in an increasingly multipolar world. The SDR was incapable of saving a system that was still based on gold and the U.S. dollar. Despite the best efforts of the world's finance ministers and central bank governors to build a new system of fixed exchange rates, systemic reform failed. The turmoil of the 1970s thus ushered in an age in which private capital markets would take over from official agencies as the prime financiers of international payments positions. De Vries chronicled that story in a History subtitled "Cooperation on Trial" (de Vries, 1985).

As the Fund's role expanded, its history became increasingly intertwined with the history of the world economy. De Vries's primary sources continued to be the minutes and Executive Board documents, but she also had greater recourse than Horsefield did to outside publications and to interviews with officials who had dealt with the Fund. Her two histories were as much the story of the workings of the Group of Ten industrial countries, the more global Committee of Twenty, and the C-20's successor, the Interim Committee, as they were of the Executive Board. Within the Fund, the work of the staff took on increasing importance alongside that of the Board and the Managing Director.

De Vries (1985) told the story of the Fund through 1978, when the Second Amendment to the Articles of Agreement took effect. Floating exchange rates were now the norm for the main reserve currencies, and the Fund had a mandate to exercise "firm surveillance" over the exchange rate policies of its 138 member countries. The sequel to de Vries (1985) would in large measure be a story of how the Fund exercised that mandate, of how it tried to oversee the international monetary system in the 1980s. Once again, however, new and widespread instabilities arose that further broadened the Fund's role: a final virulent burst of inflationary pressures on industrial countries, an international debt crisis centered on Latin America, and a series of payments crises arising from deep-seated structural inadequacies in low-income countries. This fourth History of the IMF therefore has three distinct but interrelated themes: the practice of surveillance in the 1980s (Part I), the strategy for coping with the debt crisis (Part II), and the shift toward lending in support of structural adjustment (Part III). It also includes, in Part IV, a more general history of the institution in the 1980s.

This History, like its predecessors, is an "insider" account, written by a staff member at the Fund. As an economist in the Research Department, I was involved in some of the events described below, and I obviously am too close to my subject to qualify as an independent observer. If I did not accept and share the fundamental objectives of the IMF, I would not have taken on this task. I nonetheless have tried to be objective and balanced, and I have drawn some conclusions that many of my colleagues may not share. Only superficially is this book an "official" history. In the selection and treatment of key events, it reflects my own professional judgments and not those of the institution.

A Note on Language

In addressing this book to readers both inside and outside the IMF (or "the Fund," which is used interchangeably throughout this book), I have tried to strike a balance between adhering to terminology that is familiar and clear to insiders and translating this often arcane language for the rest. The following are common examples of internal argot and technical language that I have retained here.

- The "authorities" of a country, in most references in this work, are the senior officials with whom the Fund staff and management discuss economic policies and conditions and who are responsible for formulating and implementing macroeconomic policies; in that context, the term is shorthand for "monetary authorities." The reader might usefully think of them as "the government," but the term applies primarily to treasury or finance ministry officials and to central bank officials who, in some countries, are independent of the government. Executive Directors at the Fund also use the phrase "my authorities" to refer to the government.

- The "management" of the IMF refers collectively to the Managing Director and the Deputy Managing Director (or, since 1994, to the three Deputies). The expression is very commonly used within the Fund; for example, it is "management" that clears staff documents for circulation to the Executive Board. Use of the term in this History is limited to cases where the Deputy acted on behalf of the Managing Director, where the two were both actively involved, or where the record is not clear as to which individual was involved.

- The Executive Board is the main decision-making body in the Fund, sitting in "continuous session" (normally meeting two or three days each week). The 22 Executive Directors who composed the Board in the 1980s represented "constituencies" of from 1 to 24 countries. Executive Directors are officers of the Fund who either are appointed by their governments for an indefinite period (in the case of the largest countries) or are elected by one or more countries for fixed terms of two years. Directors are referred to in this History by their nationality, which by tradition is always within the constituency. Each Executive Director may be represented at Board meetings by his or her Alternate or by an Advisor or Assistant who has been designated as a Temporary Alternate.[1]

- The Fund's charter, drafted at Bretton Woods, New Hampshire, in July 1944, is its "Articles of Agreement." Through 1989, the Articles were amended twice, as mentioned above.
  - The "First Amendment," which took effect in 1969, introduced the SDR both as the unit of account of the Fund and as an unconditional line of credit for participating countries. Since that time, the Fund's lending com-

---

[1] Readers seeking a more detailed introduction to the structure and governance of the Fund may wish to begin by reading the second section of Chapter 20, "Governance." For reference, that section also includes a complete list of constituencies and Executive Directors for 1979–89.

mitments are specified in SDRs, and disbursements may be made either in SDRs or in convertible currencies.[2] Initially, the SDR was defined as the equivalent of the gold value of one U.S. dollar. In 1974, it was redefined as a basket of 16 currencies; in 1981, the basket was reduced to 5. (See Chapter 18.) Because the value of the SDR fluctuates daily relative to each currency and is little known outside the realm of international finance, this History generally gives the amounts of Fund credits and loans both in SDRs and in U.S. dollars.[3]

- The "Second Amendment," which took effect in 1978, ratified what is commonly known as the "floating exchange rate system." Instead of specifying and maintaining a "par value" in terms of gold or the U.S. dollar, as before the amendment, each country specifies its own exchange rate policies, which may range from independent floating to pegging against the dollar or another currency (or group of currencies). The Second Amendment aims to promote a "stable system of exchange rates" (as distinguished in an undefined manner from stable exchange rates) through the exercise of "firm surveillance" by the IMF over each member's exchange rate policies. Article IV, which was completely rewritten for this purpose, is frequently used as a metaphor for surveillance. (See Chapter 2.)

- Each member country is assigned a "quota" that determines both voting rights and borrowing (or "access") limits. (On this and the following points, see Chapter 17.) Originally, access to Fund resources was limited to 25 percent of quota in any 12-month period and 100 percent of quota cumulatively. Those limits were expanded over time and were always subject to exceptions, but the principle of basing each country's limit on its quota was retained. When a country becomes a member or receives a quota increase, it pays in 25 percent (the "reserve tranche"; see below) of its quota or quota increase in internationally traded (convertible) currencies or SDRs. The remainder is credited as a bookkeeping entry to the country's balance in the "General Resources Account" (GRA) at the Fund. Therefore, at the moment a country joins, the Fund's "holdings of the member's currency" equal 75 percent of the member's quota. If a country has fully drawn out its reserve tranche and has not borrowed from the Fund, and if no other members have made net use of that currency in outstanding transactions with the Fund, then the Fund's holdings of the country's currency will equal 100 percent of quota.

- Starting in 1952, the IMF began referring to "tranches" of access to the resources of the Fund. Each country had potential access to its "gold tranche" (the portion of its quota that it had paid in gold) and four "credit tranches," each equivalent to 25 percent of quota. The only tranche mentioned in the Articles was the gold tranche, which was defined and given operational sig-

---

[2]Note that a statement that the Fund lends a country so many SDRs should be interpreted to imply an amount in currencies and/or SDRs equivalent to the given SDR value.

[3]From 1979 through 1989, the monthly average dollar value of the SDR ranged from a low of $0.96 in February 1985 to a high of $1.42 in December 1987. Its average value was $1.18.

nificance in the First Amendment. The credit tranches were defined and made operational only through Executive Board policy decisions on access to Fund resources. With the Second Amendment, the gold tranche was re-defined as the "reserve tranche."

- Each member country has unconditional access to its reserve tranche, easy access to its first credit tranche, and access to higher levels of credit subject to increasingly strict "conditionality" or requirements to adjust economic policies.[4] By the 1970s, when countries' indebtedness to the Fund frequently exceeded 100 percent of quota, the individual tranches beyond the first lost operational significance, and most subsequent references distinguished only between the first credit tranche and the open-ended "upper credit tranches." "Stand-by arrangements" (Fund commitments to lend specified amounts of money to member countries at specified intervals, subject to agreed condi-tions), drawings under which would raise the Fund's holdings of a member's currency above 125 percent, are referred to as upper-tranche arrangements.

- Indebtedness to the Fund is generally measured by the Fund's holdings of the member's currency in excess of 100 percent of quota. Exceptions arise when a country chooses not to draw its reserve tranche before borrowing or draws on one of the Fund's specialized "facilities"[5] in circumstances when such drawings are permitted to "float" relative to the standard tranches. For ex-ample, until 1992, if a country borrowed the equivalent of 25 percent of its quota through the Compensatory Financing Facility (CFF), it could borrow another 25 percent under the general tranche policies and still be considered as having drawn only on its first credit tranche.

I generally have eschewed expressions that are in common usage only at the IMF, whenever perfectly good substitutes are more widely understood. A problem arises with regard to the Fund's financial operations, which are uniquely structured. When a member country borrows from the general accounts of the Fund, the amount borrowed is technically a "purchase" of foreign exchange or SDRs in ex-change for the country's own currency; the subsequent repayment of the principal is a "repurchase."[6] In legal terminology, this type of financing is technically distinct from a conventional loan contract (and does not involve a contract between lender and borrower), but the economic effects are indistinguishable from a loan.[7]

---

[4]This policy was first enunciated clearly in the *Annual Report 1963* (p. 16): "The Fund's atti-tude to requests for transactions in the 'first credit tranche' . . . is a liberal one, provided that the member itself is making reasonable efforts to solve its problems. Requests for transactions beyond these limits require substantial justification." The early history of the Fund's tranche policies is reviewed in Chapter 18 of Horsefield (1969), Vol. 2, and current policy is described in Treasurer's Department (1998). Also see Chapter 13.

[5]When a financial institution lends under special conditions, the conventional jargon refers to the process as a lending "window." At the Fund, such windows are instead called "facilities."

[6]An especially elaborate piece of internal jargon is "the provision of conditional liquidity to member countries," which simply means "lending." The Fund also makes conventional loans, most notably through the structural adjustment facilities discussed in Chapter 14.

[7]Gold (1980) discusses the political as well as the legal implications of the distinction as it ap-plies to stand-by arrangements.

Here, I refer to the purchase either as a drawing (on a stand-by arrangement) or as a credit, and to the repurchase as a repayment. However, when a member country draws on its reserve tranche, which represents international reserve assets that the member has deposited with the Fund (and in effect still owns), the drawing is not a credit, and the member has no obligation to repay it.

For the sake of readability, I have generally used the familiar, colloquial names of countries. In a few cases, subsequent shifts in national boundaries may require the reader to be aware of geopolitical divisions that prevailed in the 1980s. References to Germany, for example, are to the Federal Republic of Germany, which was vernacularly known as West Germany during the period of this History. The German Democratic Republic (East Germany), which was not a member of the IMF, merged with the Federal Republic in October 1990. References to Yugoslavia are to the Socialist Federation, which was dissolved as a country in 1992 and replaced by five smaller successor states. Zaïre changed its name in 1997 to the Democratic Republic of the Congo. In several other cases, changes that occurred before 1990 are described in footnotes at relevant points.

Sources

Like my predecessors, I was given unrestricted access to the Fund's archives. In January 1996, the Fund decided to begin opening those archives to the general public. That policy shift, and a generally more open culture at the Fund, have made it appropriate for this History to include citations to the internal documents that have been its primary sources.[8] At the time of this writing (2000), unpublished Board documents are being made available when they are 5 years old, and most other internal documents (including Board minutes) are available after 20 years. Hence virtually all of the unpublished Board documents cited in this book are currently available to researchers upon application to the Fund, and most other cited documents are expected to become available during the coming decade.[9]

---

[8]Current information on public access to the archives may be obtained from the Fund's web site, www.imf.org. For researchers interested in the source documentation of Horsefield's History (1969), an internal draft entitled *Annals of the Fund* is available in the Central Files of the Fund. That draft includes footnote references to many of the Executive Board meetings mentioned in the published book.

[9]Citations to official Fund documents are in standard Fund notation: TT/yy/nn, where TT is the type of document, yy is the year of issue, and nn is the number within that year's series of such documents. The principal types of documents cited are EBD (Executive Board Documents, normally papers circulated by the Secretary for the information of Executive Directors), EBS (Executive Board Specials, usually designating staff papers for discussion by the Executive Board), ID (Informal Documents, staff papers for discussion by Executive Directors in informal sessions), and SM (Staff Memorandums, normally background staff papers providing supplementary information in conjunction with EBS papers). Minutes of Executive Board meetings are cited by EBM number except for informal sessions, which are designated by an IS number. Citations to internal memorandums and other unnumbered documents include the location of the document in the Fund archives. Items in the Central Files are listed as "IMF/CF C/country/NNN" or "IMF/CF S/NNN"; items in the Records Depository are generally listed as "IMF/RD (Accession no., Box no., Section no.)."

All quotations are from printed records unless specifically noted otherwise. With the exception of quotations from the minutes of Executive Board meetings, the most common sources are draft speaking notes and final texts of speeches. Oral remarks may have departed from the text, but in most cases no record exists of what was actually said. A more substantive issue arises with regard to the Board minutes. The minutes are prepared by the staff of the Secretary's Department from a stenographer's verbatim transcript and audio tapes.

The minute writer also attends the Board meeting and is expected to use his or her own judgment in editing the discussion for clarity and sense. The transcript is supplemented by prepared statements submitted either before or after the meeting by participants.[10] Those prepared statements might or might not have been delivered orally during the meeting, and the minutes do not distinguish the two cases. Other statements and general discussion are rendered into indirect speech and are edited into a consistent style.

Standard practice is to excise much of the stylistic flavor of the discussion, such as humorous or parenthetical remarks, so that the official record focuses as clearly as possible on the substance of the meeting. In addition, each speaker is given an opportunity to review and edit the text of his or her own remarks prior to finalization. The resulting product is an accurate reflection of what each speaker intended to say, but not necessarily of what was actually said during the meeting.[11]

A particularly important source document is the "Chairman's summing up" of an Executive Board meeting. This document, the official record of the sense of the meeting, reflects the input of the staff, the Board, and the Managing Director (or the Deputy Managing Director, in which case the document will be attributed to the "Acting Chairman"). Normally, in the period covered here, a draft would have been prepared by the staff prior to the meeting, based on anticipations of what Directors were likely to say, and the Managing Director might have offered revisions at that time. As the meeting progressed, either the Managing Director or the staff, or perhaps both, would redraft as necessary, making careful attributions to collectivities such as "a few," "some," "several," or "most" Directors and often making major alterations to the substance of the document to reflect the views being expressed.[12] At

---

[10]The audio tapes and verbatim transcripts are destroyed after the final minutes are approved.

[11]In quoting from the portions of the minutes that are in indirect speech, I have occasionally taken the liberty of restoring the presumed original form by replacing a past with a present tense. Thus, if the minutes report that a Director "remarked that markets were frequently motivated by unrealistic expectations," the speaker might be quoted here as stating that "markets are frequently motivated. . . ."

[12]Quantification of these "code words" has been avoided, because the references are shaded to reflect the large range of voting power among Directors, to avoid conveying a sense of rigidity in views, and to promote movement toward consensus. In 1983, however, the Managing Director offered the following key: 2–4 Directors are a "few"; 5–6 are "some"; 6–9 are "a number"; 10–15 are "many"; 15 or more are "most"; and 20 or more are "nearly all." (At the time, there were 22 seats at the Board.) "Several" lies vaguely between "some" and "a number." See minutes of EBM/83/11 (January 12, 1983), pp. 3–5. A special problem arises with references to the views of the United States, given that the U.S. voting power is much larger than that of any other. Occasionally, a U.S. view was described as that of "some" Directors, but on other occasions the problem was avoided by putting U.S. views in the passive voice ("the view was held that . . .").

the end of the meeting or—exceptionally—at the beginning of the next meeting, the Chairman would read the draft aloud. Directors then had an opportunity to comment and to suggest revisions. (Occasionally, further revisions would be suggested a day or two later.) A final text was then circulated and was incorporated in the minutes of the meeting. Rarely was any record retained of the various drafts or the comments made upon them. The document therefore must be interpreted as representing the views of Executive Directors, albeit with some reservations. For more background on the summing up, see Chapter 2.

The present History departs from the practice of its predecessors by giving greater emphasis to the role of the staff and by attributing staff contributions by name where appropriate.[13] This convention should not obscure the fact that much of the staff's work is performed in teams and subject to a high degree of institutional discipline. Frequent references are made to the chiefs of staff missions to member countries; it should be understood that their views and arguments as described here were to some extent developed, conditioned, and tempered by their colleagues, both on the mission teams and at headquarters. I have retained the practice of respecting the international (not just multinational) character of the institution by not identifying staff members' nationalities, except in the profiles of senior staff in the final chapter.[14] By stressing staff contributions while limiting references to personalities and backgrounds, I have tried to strike a balance between portraying the Fund as a monolithic institution driven by rational but disembodied analysis and depicting its policies as shifting by personal predilection. Either extreme would mislead, and I hope that the case studies throughout this book will convey a sense of constant tension in the development and application of Fund policies. Mission chiefs and other managers are not interchangeable cogs, but neither are they completely free agents.

In addition to the publications listed at the end of each chapter, I have relied on several general reference works for information on the political and economic developments that formed the backdrop for the activities of the Fund. I would like especially to note my indebtedness to the "Background Notes" on countries produced by the U.S. State Department and disseminated on its World Wide Web site; to *Keesing's Record of World Events* (formerly *Keesing's Contemporary Archives*; London: Longman); and to the Country Profiles published by the Economist Intelligence Unit (London).

Acknowledgements

I could not have begun to write this History without the help of my colleagues at the Fund who spoke to me about their work and who read early drafts of my

---

[13]For a statement of previous policy, see de Vries (1985), pp. 1017–18.

[14]The Fund's charter specifies that "the staff of the Fund, in the discharge of their functions, shall owe their duty entirely to the Fund and to no other authority" (Article XII, Section 4(c)). On appointment, each staff member must "solemnly affirm . . . that I will accept no instruction in regard to the performance of my duties from any government or authority external to the Fund" (Rule N–14). To an extraordinary degree, Fund staff have demonstrated an ability to operate as international civil servants without distinction as to nationality.

chapters; and of the many distinguished officials, bankers, and other individuals from around the world who agreed to be interviewed for this project. Those discussions and interviews have been conducted on a background basis. Where necessary for clarity, notes refer to interviews as the source of specific information, though without identifying the individual concerned unless a quotation is given.

The recollections of participants in the events of the 1980s have been extremely valuable, especially by helping me understand and empathize with the perspectives and problems of countries that depend on the Fund for assistance. Without the particular insights of my many interviewees, this book would have suffered much more from being written from inside the Fund. My biggest debt is to the staff of the Fund, many of whom spent a great deal of time with me and with successive drafts of this book. To them as a team, I offer my thanks and my apologies for not listing them all by name. Looking beyond their shoulders, I would like to thank the following for taking the time to talk to me and to share their memories and insights:[15]

- former IMF management and staff: Michel Camdessus, Jacques de Larosière, H. Johannes Witteveen, William B. Dale, and Richard D. Erb; Sterie T. Beza, Nigel Carter, Stephen Collins, Andrew Crockett, Margaret Garritsen de Vries, Michael P. Dooley, David Finch, Sir Joseph Gold, Jack Guenther, Nihad Kaibni, Joseph Lang, P.R. Narvekar, Jacques J. Polak, Walter Robichek, Brian Rose, Charles Schwartz, Samuel Stephens, Sir Alan Whittome, and John R. Woodley.
- from Argentina: Ubaldo Aguirre, Adolfo Diz, Alejandro M. Estrada, Ernesto Feldman, Enrique Garcia Vázquez, José Luis Machinea, and Manuel Solanet.
- from Australia: Ian McFarlane.
- from Belgium: Jacques de Groote.
- from Brazil: Luiz Carlos Bresser Pereira, Antonio Delfim Netto, Ibrahim Eris, Mailson Ferreira da Nobrega, Hernane Galveas, Michal Gartenkraut, Alexandre Kafka, Affonso Celso Pastore, Luis Paulo Rosenberg, and José Augusto Savasini.
- from Canada: Michael Kelly and Douglas Smee.
- from Chile: Carlos Francisco Cáceres, Jorge Cauas, Hernán Felipe Errazuriz, Luis Escobar, Enrique Seguel, and Hernán Somerville.
- from China: Shang Ming.
- from France: Jean-Yves Haberer, André de Lattre, Daniel Lebègue, Ariane Obelensky, and Jean-Claude Trichet.
- from Germany: Wilfried Guth, Manfred Lahnstein, Gerhard Laske, Eckard Pieske, Karl Otto Pöhl, Helmut Schlesinger, Horst Schulmann, Gerhard Stoltenberg, and Hans Tietmeyer.
- from Hungary: Ede Bakó, Péter Bod, Janos Fekete, Piroska Horvath, and István Szalkai.

---

[15]Except as noted (*), all of the individuals listed in the country groups were senior government or central bank officials. Those marked with an asterisk interacted with the Fund while working in the private sector. Executive Directors also are listed under their country.

- from India: Montek Singh Ahluwalia, Gopi Arora, Raja Chelliah, R.N. Malhotra, I.G. Patel, and Arjun Sengupta.
- from Indonesia: Emil Salim and Widjojo Nitisastro.
- from Italy: Lamberto Dini, Fabrizio Saccomanni, and Mario Sarcinelli.
- from Japan: Toyoo Gyohten, Yusuke Kashiwagi, Shijuro Ogata, Takeshi Ohta, Kumiharu Shigehara, Makoto Utsumi, and Kiichi Watanabe.
- from Kenya: Ahmed Abdallah, Manu Chandaria,* Micah Cheserem, Maurice Kanga, Christopher Kirubi,* Musalia Mudavadi, Harris Mule, Simeon Nyachae, and George Saitoti.
- from Korea: In Yong Chung, Mahn-Je Kim, Tae-Shin Kwon, Sung Sang Park, Il SaKong, and Hyung-Sup Shim.
- from Mexico: Ariel Buira, José Angel Gurria, Miguel Mancera, and Jesus Silva Herzog.
- from the Netherlands: Wim F. Duisenberg, H. Onno Ruding, André Szasz, and J. de Beaufort Wijnholds.
- from New Zealand: Murray Sherwin.
- from Pakistan: Mueen Afzal and A.G.N. Kazi.
- from the Philippines: Cesar E.A. Virata and Edgardo P. Zialcita.
- from Poland: Leszek Balcerowicz, Jan Boniuk, Zbigniew Karsz, Krzystof Krowacki, Stanislaw Raczkowski, and Zdzislaw Sadowski.
- from Saudi Arabia: Sheikh Mohammed Abalkhail, Mohammed Al-Jasser, Sheikh Abdul-Aziz Al-Quraishi, and Yusuf A. Nimatallah.
- from Senegal: Mamadou Touré.
- from Sweden: Kjell-Olof Feldt, Arne Lindå, Sten Westerberg, and Lars Wohlin.
- from Switzerland (officials of the Bank for International Settlements): Remi Gros, Alexandre Lamfalussy, Daniel Lefort, Fritz Leutwiler, and Gunter Schleiminger.
- from Tanzania: Fulgence M. Kazaura, Cleope Msuya, E.I.M. Mtei, and Charles Nyirabu.
- from Uganda: Suleiman Kiggundu and Emmanuel Tumusiime-Mutebile.
- from the United Kingdom: Christopher Brougham,* Terry Burns, Kenneth Couzens, Geoffrey Howe, Guy Huntrods, Tim Lankester, Nigel Lawson, Geoffrey Littler, Anthony Loehnis, Kit McMahon, Jeremy Morse, Brian Quinn, Gordon Richardson, and Nigel Wicks.
- from the United States: James A. Baker III, Sam Y. Cross, Charles Dallara, Michael de Graffenried,* Robert Dineen,* Peter Kenen,* Denis Lamb, R. T. McNamar, David Mulford, William Rhodes,* Jeffrey Sachs,* Anthony Solomon, Robert Solomon, Thomas Trebat,* Edwin M. Truman, Paul A. Volcker, and Walter Wriston.*
- from Venezuela: Hernán Oyarzabal.

A review panel of four leading experts in modern economic history provided generously detailed comments on the draft manuscript, which led to a significant sharpening of the text. For that help, I express my heartfelt thanks to Sebastian Edwards, Barry Eichengreen, Louis Pauly, and Richard Webb.

This work has also benefited greatly from the generous assistance of the staff of several libraries and archives, including notably the Records Division at the Fund, the Joint Library of the IMF and the World Bank, the Library of Congress, the Gelman Library of George Washington University, the Mudd Manuscript Library at Princeton University, the Jimmy Carter Presidential Library, and the U.S. National Archives. I am grateful to Andrew Crockett for access to selected historical archives at the Bank for International Settlements, and to Fabrizio Saccomanni and Giorgio Gomel for providing access to files at the Bank of Italy on meetings of the Group of Ten. I learned a great deal from Harold James, with whom I shared an office suite and many enjoyable discussions while he was researching his excellent history of postwar monetary cooperation (James, 1995). Thanks are due also to Anne Salda, whose annotated bibliography on the Fund (Salda, 1992) is an indispensable reference.

Finally, I am most grateful to Leo Van Houtven for asking me to undertake this task, for his belief in the importance of history, and for being my mentor as I set out to learn the intricacies of the history of the Fund; to Reinhard Munzberg and Shailendra Anjaria, for directing the project through to a successful conclusion; to Marta Vindiola, for greatly improving both this book and my enjoyment in writing it through years of outstanding editorial and research assistance; to Marina Primorac, for her excellent editing of the final manuscript; to my wife, Lesley Anne Simmons, who has helped me in more ways than I could list; and to Michel Camdessus for his support and encouragement and for his strong conviction that the Historian must be independent to be effective. They and all of the others mentioned here would no doubt wish that I had paid more attention, but I hope that they will be consoled by my taking full personal responsibility for everything in the pages that follow.

References

de Vries, Margaret Garritsen, 1976, *The International Monetary Fund, 1966–1971: The System Under Stress*, Vol. 1: *Narrative;* Vol. 2: *Documents* (Washington: International Monetary Fund).

————, 1985, *The International Monetary Fund, 1972–1978: Cooperation on Trial*, Vols. 1 and 2: *Narrative and Analysis;* Vol. 3: *Documents* (Washington: International Monetary Fund).

Gold, Joseph, 1980, *The Legal Character of the Fund's Stand-By Arrangements and Why It Matters*, IMF Pamphlet Series, No. 35 (Washington: International Monetary Fund).

Horsefield, J. Keith, ed., 1969, *The International Monetary Fund, 1945–1965: Twenty Years of International Monetary Cooperation*, Vol. 1: *Chronicle,* by J. Keith Horsefield; Vol. 2: *Analysis,* by Margaret G. de Vries and J. Keith Horsefield with the collaboration of Joseph Gold, Mary H. Gumbart, Gertrud Lovasy, and Emil G. Spitzer; Vol. 3: *Documents* (Washington: International Monetary Fund).

James, Harold, 1995, *International Monetary Cooperation since Bretton Woods* (Oxford: Oxford University Press).

Salda, Anne C.M., 1992, *The International Monetary Fund*, International Organization Series, Vol. 4 (New Brunswick, New Jersey: Transaction Publishers).

Treasurer's Department, International Monetary Fund, 1998, *Financial Organization and Operations of the IMF*, IMF Pamphlet Series, No. 45 (Washington: International Monetary Fund, 5th ed.).

Abbreviations

APEC	Asia-Pacific Economic Cooperation
APEF	Asia-Pacific Economic Forum
BCEAO	Central Bank of West African States (French acronym)
BEAC	Bank of Central African States
BIS	Bank for International Settlements
BSFF	Buffer Stock Financing Facility
C-20	Committee of Twenty
CCFF	Compensatory and Contingency Financing Facility
CFF	Compensatory Financing Facility
CMEA/COMECON	Council for Mutual Economic Assistance
EAC	East African Community
EBRD	European Bank for Reconstruction and Development
EAR	Policy on Enlarged Access to the Fund's Resources
EC	European Communities
ECB	European Central Bank
ECM	External Contingency Mechanism
ECOSOC	Economic and Social Council (of the United Nations)
ECU	European currency unit
EFF	Extended Fund Facility
EMS	European Monetary System
ENA	Ecole Nationale d'Administration
ERM	exchange rate mechanism
ESAF	Enhanced Structural Adjustment Facility
ETR	Exchange and Trade Relations Department
FAO	Food and Agriculture Organization
G-5	Group of Five industrial countries
G-10	Group of Ten industrial countries
G-24	Group of Twenty-Four developing countries
GAAP	Generally Accepted Accounting Principles
GAB	General Arrangements to Borrow
GATT	General Agreement on Tariffs and Trade
GDP	gross domestic product
GRA	General Resources Account
HIPC	heavily indebted poor countries

IATA	International Air Transport Association
ICM	internal contingency mechanism
ICO	International Coffee Organization
IDA	International Development Association
IDB	Inter-American Development Bank
IDRC	International Development Research Centre
IFC	International Finance Corporation
IFIs	international financial institutions
IIE	Institute for International Economics
IIF	Institute of International Finance
ILO	International Labor Organization
INS	Institute
MERM	Multilateral Exchange Rate Model
MIGA	Multilateral Investment Guarantee Agency
MYRA	multiyear rescheduling agreement
NAB	New Arrangements to Borrow
ODA	official development assistance
OECD	Organization for Economic Cooperation and Development
OPEC	Organization of Petroleum Exporting Countries
PAMSCAD	Program to Mitigate the Social Costs of Adjustment
PFP	Policy Framework Paper
PLO	Palestinian Liberation Organization
PPP	purchasing power parity
PRC	People's Republic of China
PRI	Partido Revolucionario Institucional
PSBR	public sector borrowing requirement
RED	recent economic developments (background paper)
ROC	Republic of China
SAC	Staff Association Committee
SAF	Structural Adjustment Facility
SAL	Structural Adjustment Loan
SAMA	Saudi Arabian Monetary Agency
SCA	Special Contingent Account
SDR	Special Drawing Right
SFF	Supplementary Financing Facility
SRF	Supplemental Reserve Facility
UNDP	United Nations Development Programme
WEO	World Economic Outlook

1

The Silent Revolution

THE NEED IS FOR STRONGER POLICIES AND NOT FOR ANY
complacent gradualism in adjustment efforts . . . Several countries are choosing to
go this way—a painful decision in many cases—because it offers them a prospect of
achieving sustainable growth. This "silent revolution" in attitudes in many developing countries . . . is now showing itself in the number of countries that have requested Fund help in formulating their growth-oriented adjustment programs.

Michel Camdessus
Managing Director, IMF
September 26, 1989[1]

This book is a narrative history of the coming of age of the International Monetary Fund as a participant in the international financial system. The men
who designed the framework of the system at Bretton Woods, New Hampshire, in
1944 envisaged the Fund as an independent, objective, and essentially automatic
force, subject to broad political constraints and the limits of predetermined financial resources. For more than two decades afterward, the Fund's active role was
episodic and, from a global perspective, minor. The institution's value derived primarily from its passive embodiment of the understandings and commitments that
came to be known as the Bretton Woods system. Subsequently, however, the compass for action began to expand.

As recounted in earlier histories of the IMF, world economic and financial imbalances multiplied in the 1960s and 1970s.[2] The Bretton Woods system of fixed
but adjustable exchange rates came under strain and collapsed, and a more flexible
system was negotiated. Because the new system imposed few constraints on national economic policies, the Fund was drawn into a more active "surveillance"
role in overseeing its implementation. Moreover, as the landscape of the world
economy became more precarious, the Fund was drawn into a more active lending

---

[1]IMF, *Summary Proceedings*, 1989, p. 15.

[2]The earlier histories (all published by the IMF) are Horsefield (1969), which covers the years
through 1965; de Vries (1976), covering 1966–71; and de Vries (1985), covering 1972–78. Other
major histories of the period that discuss the role of the Fund in the world economy include notably Solomon (1982) and James (1996).

role that required a deeper and more sustained involvement in the formulation of macroeconomic policies in countries facing economic crises. During the 11 years covered in this work, 1979 through 1989, a confluence of upheavals propelled the institution into a more central and pervasive role than ever before.

The primary purpose of this study is not to judge the Fund's success in carrying out this expanded role, but rather to explain how and why and in what circumstances the Fund acted and evolved during a period of great change. The limitations to the Fund's role and abilities are readily apparent, even to a casual observer of international affairs, while its strengths are more subtle and controversial. The "creditor countries" that provide the bulk of the financing for the Fund and that issue the main reserve currencies are obviously going to retain and exercise substantial control over their claims and over their own economic affairs. In less obvious ways, they may find it in their interest to submit to independent surveillance by the Fund. Countries that borrow from the Fund are obviously in a much weaker position and must sacrifice some policy autonomy in exchange for international financial assistance channeled through the Fund. The Fund thus has become, to some extent, an agent of an asymmetric and unequal distribution of economic power. Less obviously, the Fund's financial and policy (or "programming") assistance has in many cases helped restore borrowers' autonomy, reduce global inequities, and counteract the dominance of industrial power. An effort to provide a balanced explanation of these relationships is bound to focus more on the subtleties than on the surface gloss.

This opening chapter begins by examining the question of whether events in the 1980s really constituted a revolution, and it then introduces the men who led the institution through this period. The rest of the chapter gives an overview of the major developments in the world economy, the international monetary system, and the IMF from the end of the 1970s to the beginning of the 1990s. It is intended to serve as a primer to the major events, each of which is covered only briefly. The reader will find more detailed explanations and references in the chapters that follow.

Revolution or Evolution?

During the 11 years from 1979 through 1989, the world economy evolved in seemingly small but ultimately dramatic and profound ways. From a starting point at which the state was viewed as holding a primary responsibility for controlling economic development, the "third world" gradually diminished and even rejected that role in favor of privatization and reliance on market incentives. From a starting point at which central planning and international barter isolated much of the "second" or Communist world from the global market, internal reforms in China joined with the gradual enfeeblement of the Soviet empire to break down the barricades from central Europe to eastern Asia. From a starting point at which the largest industrial countries held sharply divergent macroeconomic philosophies and maintained that each country should pursue its own independent course, the "first world" took at least tentative steps toward more cooperative and mutually consistent policies. The philosophical and economic barriers between North and South and between East and West remained in place at the end of the 1980s, but the means for destroying them were nearer and more evident than ever before in history. This "silent revolution," as Michel Camdessus named it in a more specific context,[3] brought an unprecedented importance to the IMF as every region in the world struggled to keep its footing in an increasingly dynamic and global economy.

Was there a revolution in international political economy in the 1980s? History does not accept such drama readily, and the term cannot be asserted without justification. No single event gave definition to a silent revolution: no storming of the Bastille, no Declaration of Independence, no satyagraha campaign, no Long March. The Fund as an institution underwent surprisingly little structural change as it responded to the challenges of this decade. But in some dimensions, the world economy changed diametrically from the beginning of the decade to the end, and that drift ultimately wore a revolutionary cloak.

The term "silent revolution" in this book refers to a shift in the prevailing paradigm for international economic and political relations, away from tendencies toward autarky, insularity, mercantilism, and governmental planning and control over economic activity; and toward a common set of beliefs and policies based on open international trade and finance, competitive pricing and production decisions, and cooperation between countries. To a great extent, the silent revolution of the 1980s resulted from a shift in economic philosophy toward a new classical synthesis in which government has an indirect role in, but not a direct responsibility for, ensuring national economic prosperity; in which private economic activity is promoted through good governance and the development of physical and social infrastructure.[4] That shift was not born in the 1980s; in some aspects and in

---

[3]The phrase has, of course, been used in other contexts as well. Perhaps the most direct antecedent, though one with unrelated and troubling connotations, was its application to the economic reforms introduced under General Pinochet in Chile in the 1980s; see Lavín (1987). It also has been applied to Camdessus's style of leadership at the Fund; see Sparks (1988).

[4]One should not confuse the gradual shift toward economic liberalization—the focus of the silent revolution discussed here—with the political democratization that also flourished with great drama throughout much of the developing world in the 1980s. Both logically and empirically, the two developments were distinct and independent events. To take four of many possible examples, the policies initiated in India by Finance Minister Manmohan Singh in 1993 illustrate economic reform in a democracy; economic policy in Chile under Presidents Allende and Pinochet illustrate, respectively, deterioration in a democracy and reform in a dictatorship; and the Philippines under Ferdinand Marcos illustrates economic deterioration under dictatorship. For the logical argument, see McGuire and Olson (1996), where it is shown that the "invisible hand" governing market activity works similarly under autocracies and democracies, as long as the ruler or the majority has a sufficiently long time horizon. Also see Rodrik (1996), which suggests that democratic governments may not have a sufficiently long time horizon; and Williamson and Haggard (1994), which examines the broader difficulties of explaining the political preconditions for successful economic reform. Historically, as emphasized by Myrdal (1968) and analyzed by Krueger (1993), economic development has proceeded at least as rapidly under economically enlightened dictators (Krueger's phrase is "benevolent social guardians") as under populist democracies. Studies of developing countries in the modern period have generally found little or no correlation between political freedom and economic progress; for a summary and references, see World Bank (1991), pp. 50 and 132–34.

some countries, such trends had long been apparent. Nor did it occur as a complete or final revolution in more than a handful of countries. From a global perspective, the silent revolution could also be described as a Quiet Evolution. To write such an epitaph, however, would greatly understate the significance of the decade for the world economy—and for the IMF.

The upheavals of the 1980s forced the Fund to reconsider its role and its ability to guide and shape the international monetary system. Throughout the decade, the staff, management, and Executive Board of the Fund debated and struggled with policy issues that went to the heart of the nature of the institution and that continued to resonate throughout the 1990s.

- In response to expanding international private credit markets, should the Fund become less of an official financial intermediary and more of a financial and policy adviser?
- Could the Fund rely on markets to provide international finance when and where it was needed, or should it devise new ways to influence private capital flows?
- Should the Fund borrow from markets to supplement its traditional lending resources?
- In response to a shift in demand for official financing from industrial to developing countries, should the Fund get more involved in structural reforms and long-term lending, or should it reduce its own lending and defer more to the multilateral development banks?
- In a system of floating exchange rates, should the Fund attempt to influence the major countries to stabilize their rates and coordinate their economic policies, or should it concentrate its energies on smaller countries where its influence was more likely to be felt?
- Was it feasible to rebuild the international financial system around the SDR as the "principal reserve asset," as mandated by the Fund's Articles of Agreement?
- Was there a significant role for unconditional financing for developing countries, or would the Fund have to get even more deeply involved in formulating economic policies in borrowing countries?

Leadership at the IMF

An even broader theme that came to the fore in the 1980s was the potential conflict between the Fund's primary role as a monetary institution and the overseer of the international monetary system and its emerging role as a guiding force in economic development. The fifth Managing Director, H. Johannes Witteveen (from the Netherlands; in office 1973–78), guided the Fund into development-oriented activities such as lending for longer maturities and on concessional terms, but he also forcefully argued that the Fund's essence was its monetary character. Reconciling that apparent paradox became increasingly difficult in the 1980s—and even more so in the 1990s—as the Fund became more deeply entrenched in the task of helping developing countries formulate beneficial and sustainable economic policies.

To a striking degree, the story of the Fund's responses to these themes and to the silent revolution in policymaking is a story of the influence of Witteveen's successors, the two men who led the institution through the 1980s: Jacques de Larosière, who became the Managing Director some six months before the start of this narrative; and Michel Camdessus, who succeeded him in January 1987. Both French; both graduates of the École Nationale d'Administration (ENA, the prestigious academy whose graduates are familiarly known in France as "enarques" and constitute an elite corps of corporate and government leaders); both former directors of the French Treasury; one a former and one a future governor of the French central bank, the Banque de France; both holders of the same paradoxical vision of the IMF as a sound financial institution dedicated to improving the welfare of developing countries. De Larosière and Camdessus were nonetheless dramatically different in style and even in substance.

Jacques de Larosière de Champfeu was born in Paris in November 1929, was raised and educated there, and spent his entire pre-IMF career at the French treasury and finance ministry. In 1974 he was named Chef du Cabinet (chief of staff) to the minister of finance, Valery Giscard d'Estaing. When Giscard became president of France later that year, de Larosière became Director of the Treasury, the post he held until moving to Washington to head the IMF in June 1978.

De Larosière, whom *The Times* of London characteristically called "the IMF's Gallic mastermind," tackled the job of Managing Director as a technical as much as a political challenge. He understood well that each of the Fund's 134 member countries (the number when he arrived in June 1978) brought its own unique issues, problems, and pressures to the table, but he took as a guiding principle that the institution should deal with all countries in as even-handed and uniform manner as possible. In conducting surveillance over macro-economic policies, both in the public arena and in private meetings, he criticized the fiscal excesses of the United States in the same carefully structured tones that he applied to those of Argentina or Tanzania. In evaluating requests for loans, he consistently stressed that each country's economic program had to be fully financed: in the Fund's parlance, the task was to fill the "financing gap" and restore viability to the country's external accounts. The Fund was and is a political body, but the consistency and technical clarity of de Larosière's approach to problems usually prevented him from being blown far off course by strong political winds.

De Larosière's stress on technical clarity and his disciplined style led to his being widely misunderstood as a technocrat. In his first few years as Managing Director, he built on Witteveen's initiatives to greatly expand Fund lending to low-income countries and to find ways to subsidize that lending. He vigorously advocated the creation of a special lending window at the Fund to help developing countries finance food imports, and he encouraged the staff to work on issues related to the alleviation of poverty and the provision of basic human needs. Over

Jacques de Larosière, Managing Director June 1978–January 1987

the next few years, he expanded the Fund's interaction with the United Nations, including UNICEF and the UN Development Programme. In his last two years in office, he supported the reinstatement of lending on highly concessional terms to the poorest countries. For a time, he was accused of being too soft in his lending decisions, but he gradually developed a sterner reputation and that side of him became largely forgotten.

A defining personal characteristic was de Larosière's habit of reading each of the hundreds of draft documents that crossed his desk each year with painstaking care. A 30-page staff report on a loan request or a surveillance review would come back to the author after a few days with several notes penciled in the margins in the Managing Director's tidy (and tiny) handwriting, often questioning the consistency of statements or numbers in different sections of the paper or asking why footnotes did not seem to match the text or the tables. In meetings with finance ministers and central bank governors, he often knew at least as much about the details of their economic policies as they did. During day-long meetings of the Executive Board, he would work his way through fistful of pencils, meticulously writing and rewriting his summing up of the meeting until every nuance was right. He astonished all who heard him with the precision of his nearly unaccented English, and he occasionally embarrassed Executive Directors from Anglophone countries by gently interrupting to ask if they had not really meant something slightly different from the phrase they had just chosen.[5]

De Larosière viewed the Executive Board as a forum for nearly unlimited debate. During his tenure of 8½ years, the Board often met long into the night until every Director had said his piece (even though statements often were simply read from texts that had been prepared in advance). Although this practice made for a lot of weariness and was not a model of efficiency, it did create an atmosphere in which every view could be fully and fairly presented and no Director felt slighted because of difficulties of language or expression.

As Managing Director, de Larosière had little tolerance for disloyalty, and he expected both hard work and high standards from his staff. He sparked fear and respect, but he also strongly defended the staff both in the Executive Board and in outside forums. When he left the Fund in the midst of his second term, his lavish praise of the staff—for their "dedication, professional competence, integrity, and capacity for hard work and personal sacrifice in the interests of the institution"— was fairly interpreted as heartfelt, and he received a rousing farewell from the several hundred staff who gathered in the tree-lined atrium of the Fund's headquarters in Washington to see him off.

After leaving the Fund, de Larosière returned to Paris and spent 6½ years as governor of the Banque de France. Then, in 1993 at the age of 63, he moved to London and took on the challenge of rescuing the European Bank for Reconstruction and Development (EBRD) from the financial excesses of its first president,

---

[5]English is the official language of the IMF, and meetings of the Executive Board normally are conducted in English without simultaneous interpretation.

Meeting of the Executive Board, 1982

Jacques Attali. By that time he had been honored with the highest decorations from the governments of France and of a half dozen other leading industrial and developing countries. He retired in 1998.

Michel Camdessus was born in 1933 in the town of Bayonne, the historic gateway to the Pyrenees and the Basque country in the far southwest of France. He studied and earned degrees at the University of Paris, the Institute of Political Studies, and finally the ENA. As a junior officer in the French army during the war of Algerian independence, he developed a strong aptitude for survival by defusing land mines. Later, as Director of the French Treasury during the early years of the Mitterrand presidency, he helped design the shift to a stable anti-inflationary policy stance in 1983. He served as chairman of the Paris Club of official creditors when the group negotiated the first delicate compromises with major debtors in Latin America and elsewhere to reschedule debts after the crisis of 1982 while restoring discipline in economic policies. He chaired the Monetary Committee of the European Economic Community when the European Monetary System was stabilizing its exchange rates more firmly on the deutsche mark, and he pushed hard for an expanding international role for the ECU (European currency unit). He then took the reins at the Banque de France in 1984 and oversaw the key stages in the liberalization of both monetary policy (replacement of quantitative credit controls with open market operations as the primary policy tool) and bank regulation (strengthening of capital requirements and reducing government intervention in bank lending).

If de Larosière was the IMF's "Gallic mastermind," Camdessus was its "Gallic charmer," and it was that charm that enabled him to apply a firmness of will that often surprised and confounded those who equated good nature with invertebracy. When he arrived at the IMF in 1987, he spoke English with what journalists liked to describe as an "Inspector Clouseau" accent and was more at home in Spanish, which he spoke as flawlessly as his native French. (A decade later, a more common description of his English was "lilting.")

Camdessus imposed discipline on a willing Executive Board, limiting the length of oral statements and urging Directors to avoid oral statements altogether by circulating written statements in advance. During a period of increasing demands on the Fund to consider funding requests and to review its policies and procedures, the Board was thus able to stabilize and eventually to reduce the time it spent in meetings.

To an even greater extent than his predecessor, Camdessus quickly came to be on first-name terms not only with most of the world's finance ministers, but also with many heads of state. When de Larosière went on a fishing holiday in Canada with colleagues after the Annual Meetings of IMF and World Bank governors in Toronto in 1982, it was widely viewed as a rare display of relaxation. When Russian Prime Minister Viktor Chernomyrdin persuaded Camdessus to hunt boar with him during a break in the negotiations for a stand-by arrangement in 1994, it was only the form of relaxation that occasioned surprise.

In contrast to de Larosière's background in the center-right Gaullist tradition of French politics, Camdessus—though politically neutral—was promoted by

Michel Camdessus, Managing Director January 1987–February 2000

François Mitterrand, the head of France's Socialist Party. His social concerns also were reflected in his deep and open commitment to religion as a guiding principle for his life. As a Roman Catholic as much as Managing Director, he often met with religious leaders, including Pope John Paul II, and vigorously advocated a role for the Fund in ameliorating global poverty and promoting "high-quality growth" in developing countries.

In view of the self-confident manner in which Camdessus pushed to strengthen the Fund's role in the world economy with little apparent concern for the opposition of officials in major countries, the world's financial press wrote him off in 1990 as unlikely to win a second term as Managing Director. He was written off again five years later as unlikely to win a third. That disparaging view, however, failed to take account of Camdessus's ability to know when to defer on points that were most important for creditor countries and when to insist on points that were critical for the institution. In January 1997, he became the first Managing Director to enter his eleventh year in the job. By the time Camdessus stepped down in February 2000, the membership had grown to 184 countries, and the assets under the Fund's control exceeded $400 billion, more than double the level when he first took office.

The differences in working styles and personal philosophies were reflected inevitably in the priorities and in the strengths and weaknesses that each Managing Director brought to the job. Nonetheless, on the most fundamental level, both men stressed the same view of the Fund as an institution that could help strengthen the world economy only by maintaining both its own financial strength and the rigor of its standards for economic policies. Consequently, the evolution of Fund surveillance, lending practices, and the strategy for resolving the international debt crisis of the 1980s all unfolded in more of a continuum than one might have expected. Such notable successes as the establishment of a major new endowment to finance low-interest loans to the world's poorest countries and the negotiation of global standards for macro and structural economic policies are directly attributable to initiatives by Camdessus, but they built directly on the achievements of his predecessor, de Larosière.

At the Precipice of the 1980s

The World Economy

The 1970s will long be remembered as a decade of poor economic performance and poor economics. Poor performance is the easier of the two to document: high inflation around the world, sagging productivity growth, rising unemployment, and wide domestic and international imbalances. That combination of ills even brought a new word, "stagflation," into the language. A charge of poor economic analysis and policymaking is inherently more controversial, but in this case many examples may be cited: attempts to live with and accommodate inflation, attempts to fine-tune aggregate demand to sustain economic growth, attempts to use nominal policy tools to achieve real goals, and faith in the power of general principles such as Keynesian or monetarist macroeconomics and purchasing power parity (PPP) in exchange rates.[6]

Four issues dominated the debates on international economic policy in the late 1970s: restoring economic growth to the rates that had prevailed before 1973, reducing price inflation, managing exchange rates for the major currencies in the context of a pronounced "overhang" of U.S. dollars in official portfolios, and financing the current account deficits of oil-importing developing countries.

Growth

For the industrial countries as a group, real output growth averaged 4¾ percent a year from 1960 through 1973 and then slowed to 2¾ percent a year for 1973–79. Was this slowdown cyclical, in which case it could be countered through expansionary fiscal or monetary policies; was it an inevitable slowdown from high postwar growth rates; or was it a structural shift in response to the first "oil shock"— the sharp rise in oil prices in 1973–74? The possible need for a sustained policy response to a long-term problem was recognized officially as early as November 1975, when the Ministerial Council of the Organization for Economic Cooperation and Development (OECD) initiated a study by an international group of experts—chaired by a former chairman of the U.S. President's Council of Economic Advisers, Paul McCracken—to recommend a strategy for achieving both full employment and price stability over the medium term.

The McCracken Report (1977) concluded that pre-1973 growth rates were both desirable and achievable and that countries should adopt cautiously expansionary policies until private sector growth began to accelerate on its own. The following year, the leaders of the major industrial countries agreed at their annual summit meeting in Bonn, Germany, that countries with relatively low inflation and strong external positions—notably Germany and Japan—should adopt more expansionary fiscal policies in the common interest of world growth. That strategy, which became known as the "locomotive" approach and which was supported by the Fund, served to spur inflation more than real growth and gave policy coordination a bad reputation that took years to overcome. The fundamental problem, however, was not any intrinsic weakness of the cooperative approach but rather that Germany's growth rate (then about 2½ percent) was already about as strong as the economy could support. Only later, when the structural break in potential output growth was more fully understood, would policy coordination bear less bitter fruit.

Inflation

Inflation in the 1970s was at its highest levels since just after World War II. When inflation finally peaked in 1980, consumer prices around the world rose by

---

[6]Macroeconomic thought in the 1970s was dominated by a synthesis of Keynesianism and monetarism in which either fiscal or monetary policy could be assigned to stabilize aggregate demand; see Leijonhuvud (1968) and Friedman (1970). For a prominent example of the relatively benign view of inflation in the 1970s, see Tobin (1972, 1987).

nearly 18 percent over the year before: 12½ percent in industrial countries and almost 29 percent in developing countries. A decade earlier, that problem would have been analyzed as a simple case of "too much money chasing too few goods"; in Milton Friedman's catchphrase, inflation was said to be "always and everywhere a monetary phenomenon."[7] After 1973, however, inflation seemed different, partly because it clearly had been aggravated by major structural shifts—the oil shock and the rapid depreciation of the U.S. dollar—and partly because it persisted through a decade of sluggish demand. This structural stagflation fostered many attempts to develop a more comprehensive model of inflation, but not with much success at producing a new consensus.[8] Direct controls on wage or price increases, or "incomes policies," seemed to work only weakly and only in countries with a high degree of social consensus. If the only effective weapon against inflation was a restrictive policy on aggregate demand, then prices could not be restrained without further sacrifices on an already sluggish real growth.

The final inflationary impulse of the 1970s was the second oil shock. In December 1978, a ministerial meeting of the Organization of Petroleum Exporting Countries (OPEC) agreed to raise export prices by 5 percent from an initial base of less than $13 a barrel, and the group projected a further rise of close to 10 percent during the coming year. An already tight oil market then tightened dramatically the next month when a general strike in Iran forced the pro-western Shah to flee the country. Despite efforts by the largest producer, Saudi Arabia, to maintain stable prices, OPEC ministers agreed in March 1979 to approve selective price increases for other member countries, a move that signaled the beginning of the end for the organization's remarkably successful six-year run of controlling world prices. Experts soon were predicting oil price increases of 30–100 percent from the 1978 levels.

Oil markets tightened further in April 1979 following the meltdown of the Three Mile Island nuclear reactor in the United States, sanctions by the Organization of Arab Petroleum Exporting Countries against Egypt in response to Egypt's rapprochement with Israel through the Camp David Accords, and reports of a precipitous decline in oil exports by the Soviet Union. OPEC ministers met again, in Geneva, in late June, and set a new benchmark price of about $20. Although that decision was generally viewed as decisive, OPEC was doing little more than recognizing and validating market realities. After the U.S. government banned oil imports from Iran in response to the takeover of the U.S. embassy and the holding of American hostages in Tehran in November 1979, after the Soviet Union further strained its own dwindling resources and disrupted conditions in the Middle East by invading Afghanistan in December, and after Iraq invaded Iran the following September, no official action could have prevented world oil prices from rising further. By the end of 1980, when prices finally began to subside, the average price of a barrel of oil in world trade had doubled again, to $40 (Figure 1.1).

---

[7]Friedman's 1963 Bombay lecture, which stresses the "always and everywhere" argument, is reprinted in Friedman (1968), pp. 21–39.

[8]See, for example, the papers in Monti (1976) and Hall (1982); and Bruno and Sachs (1985).

Figure 1.1. Petroleum and Gold Prices, 1971–90

US$ per barrel of oil   US$ per troy ounce of gold

(Petroleum, left scale)

(Gold, right scale)

Exchange Rates

Almost everyone favored a laissez-faire policy on key-currency exchange rates in the late 1970s, despite the evident imbalances and instability of the period. After some twenty-five years of pegging rates to the U.S. dollar and five with more flexibility, most economists and policymakers were convinced that floating between the dollar and other major currencies was the only viable approach for the future. The oil shock and the general economic slowdown had affected countries differently, and it was difficult to envisage how any system of fixed rates could have been managed so as to reflect those differences. From the end of 1972 to the end of 1978, the U.S. dollar depreciated by 36 percent against the Japanese yen and by 43 percent against the deutsche mark. Policy adjustments to prevent changes of that magnitude would have lain somewhere between wrenching and impossible. Even more fundamentally, economic theory was understood to suggest that floating exchange rates would adjust quickly toward equilibrium PPP levels and would follow the "fundamentals" as encapsulated in monetary models. That is, PPP theory and the monetary approach of which it was a part meant not only that stable equilibrium exchange rates existed, but also that market forces would keep actual exchange rates close to equilibrium in the absence of government intervention. Few policymakers ever completely lost their fear of relinquishing control to the private markets, but belief in the viability of floating exchange rates gradually took hold during the first several years of experience after 1973 (see Isard, 1978).

Figure 1.2. Current Account Balances, 1973, 1980, and 1987

Billions of dollars

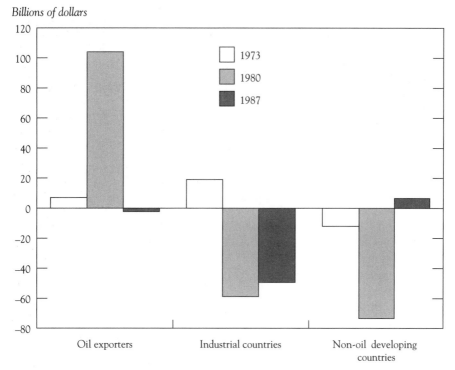

External Imbalances

The final thread in policy analyses of the time was the need to "recycle petrodollars." In addition to sapping growth and driving inflation, the rise in oil prices brought a major shift in external current account balances. From 1973 to 1980, the aggregate current account surplus of oil-exporting countries rose from $7 billion to $112 billion, the industrial countries as a group shifted from a $19 billion surplus to a deficit of $44 billion, and the non-oil developing countries saw their deficit explode from $12 billion to $80 billion (Figure 1.2).[9] Especially hard-hit were the many developing countries that had little or no access to international capital markets. Either they had to find some means of financing their deficits or they would have to cut back severely on imports and sharply curtail development plans and other essential spending. Multilateral official agencies including the IMF established special "oil facilities" to recycle surpluses to oil-importing countries, but the appropriate policy conditionality was lacking. The main intermediaries were the commercial banks that directly or indirectly were receiving large inflows of funds from the newly wealthy oil exporters. Faced with sluggish loan demand at

---

[9]Balances do not add to zero, owing to measurement errors and the exclusion of countries that were not members of the Fund in the 1970s (notably the USSR and the People's Republic of China).

home, many banks turned eagerly to the market for sovereign loans to developing countries as the means to invest their burgeoning liquid assets. From 1977 to 1980, net international bank lending ballooned from $68 billion to $160 billion, of which $49 billion went to non-oil developing countries. Only much too late did the realization set in that many of the recipients of those loans would be unable to service them, at least until they implemented difficult and time-consuming policy reforms.

The Fund

The period covered in this book begins at an arbitrary date—January 1979—that picks up the story of the IMF where Margaret Garritsen de Vries left off at the end of the last Fund History.[10] Since the seminal event for the evolution of the Fund in the 1980s—the Mexican debt crisis of 1982—was still some 43 months away, the early years may seem at first glance to form little more than a prologue. And in a real sense they were a prologue, because the shocks and policy shifts of 1979–81 set the stage for the financial reverberations of 1982. Prophetically, the very first gathering of the Fund's Executive Directors on returning from the holidays at the beginning of 1979 was for a meeting on Mexico. On January 3, the Executive Board approved the authorities' economic program for the coming year, which was to be supported by an extended lending arrangement that was entering its third and final year. It was an upbeat and congratulatory meeting, in which the Managing Director praised Mexico for its "excellent creditworthiness" and for keeping the fiscal deficit within manageable limits. Ariel Buira, the Alternate Executive Director for Mexico, predicted a flourishing future in which Mexico's economic growth would be fueled by revenues from petroleum exports and would no longer be constrained by the need to finance the balance of payments.[11] Only much later would the ironies of this routine meeting become apparent.

Surveillance

The dominant focus of the Fund's energies in 1979 was on surveillance over the exchange rate policies of member countries. After the United States formally terminated the convertibility of the U.S. dollar into gold in August 1971 and brought the Bretton Woods par value system to an end, the Fund's governors set out to devise a system of stable exchange rates without that gravitational center. The Group of Ten (G-10) industrial countries, which had become the predominant international policymaking group in the 1960s, initially took the lead by agreeing on a new set of fixed exchange rates against the dollar at a celebrated meeting at the Smithsonian Institution in Washington (December 1971). That agreement lasted little more than a year and collapsed with a bang in March 1973 when selling pres-

---

[10]The main theme of de Vries (1985) was the negotiation of the Second Amendment to the Articles of Agreement, which took effect in 1978.

[11]Minutes of EBM/79/1 (January 3, 1979), pp. 7 and 19 (Buira) and 20 (Managing Director).

sure on the dollar forced European countries to close foreign exchange markets for several days and then reopen with floating rates. Once it was apparent that the initial devaluation of the dollar had been insufficient and that policies among the G-10 were too divergent to sustain fixed rates, a more globally representative committee was formed to design a system that would be more flexible while—it was hoped—restoring stability.

The ministerial-level Committee of Twenty (C-20), on which nearly all Fund members were represented directly or indirectly, met periodically in 1972–74 and produced a report recommending that the par value system of exchange rates be restored. The new system, however, was to have "more symmetrical" adjustment of parities, and express allowance was to be made for the adoption of floating rates "in particular situations, subject to Fund authorization, surveillance, and review" (de Vries, 1985, Vol. 3, pp. 169–70). A successor was then formed to the C-20, with the same membership of 20 finance ministers from around the world. This Interim Committee failed to agree on a plan to restore the par value system but did agree (at a January 1976 meeting in Kingston, Jamaica) on a comprehensive set of amendments to the Fund's Articles of Agreement. The Second Amendment, which took effect in April 1978, eliminated the monetary role of gold, accepted that member countries could adopt whatever exchange arrangements they chose (except pegging to gold, and subject to Fund approval for certain restrictions), and authorized the Fund to exercise "firm surveillance" over the exchange rate policies of member countries.[12]

As discussed in more detail in Chapter 2 of this History, the mechanics for surveillance were already in place long before 1978, in the form of the annual consultations that the Fund held with most of its member countries. Article IV of the Articles of Agreement, which was completely rewritten for the Second Amendment, strengthened the mandate for those consultations by specifying principles both for the conduct of exchange rate policies and for the oversight role of the Fund. The task for the institution was to give content to those principles and to the meaning of the deliberately vague phrase, "firm surveillance."

Lending

A second field of focus was the expansion of lending to developing countries. Although it was not evident at the time, the demand for Fund resources by industrial countries was drawing to a close. Private capital markets were playing an ever-increasing role in financing international payments, especially for the most developed economies. Moreover, the end of the Bretton Woods system was providing scope for exchange rates to absorb much of the shock when economic events affected countries or regions differently. Those developments had limitations. Two

---

[12]For the full set of amendments, with explanatory commentary, see de Vries (1985), Vol. 3, pp. 317–76. The original Articles of Agreement as drafted at Bretton Woods (in 1944) are in Horsefield (1969), Vol. 3, pp. 185–214. The Articles after the First Amendment (1969) are in de Vries (1976), Vol. 2, pp. 97–157. The Articles after the Second Amendment are in de Vries (1985), Vol. 3, pp. 379–446.

Figure 1.3. IMF Lending, 1950–89

Billions of SDRs

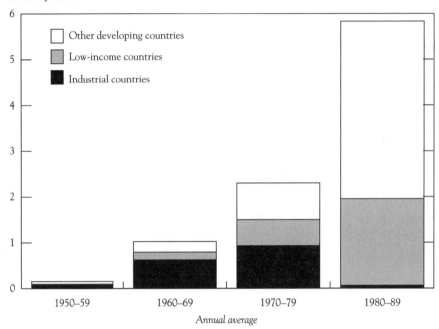

Annual average

major countries—the United Kingdom and Italy—borrowed heavily from the Fund in the mid-1970s, contingency plans were made for a lending arrangement with the United States when the dollar came under speculative pressure in 1978, and smaller industrial countries continued to borrow from the Fund until 1982.[13] It was by no means obvious in the late 1970s that industrial countries no longer needed the Fund's financial resources.

What was obvious was that the *world* needed the Fund's resources as much as ever. Virtually simultaneously with the decline in demand from countries with ready access to private capital markets, demand from less developed countries rose sharply (Figure 1.3 and Figure 1.4). A combination of adversities—a slowdown in growth in the industrial countries that were the principal markets for the world's exports, worsening terms of trade for exporters of primary commodities, and the failure of many developing countries to adjust promptly to disturbances—heightened the financing needs of countries in Asia, Africa, the Mediterranean region, and Latin America. Many developing countries that borrowed heavily from commercial lenders in the 1970s came to the Fund after 1982 when commercial financing suddenly dried up in the wake of the international debt crisis. More broadly, the poorer countries that lacked access to private capital markets increasingly turned to the Fund as well as to other multilateral agencies for help in the

---

[13]In addition, several industrial countries drew on their reserve tranche balances in the 1980s. The last such drawing occurred in 1987.

Figure 1.4. IMF Financing Arrangements in Effect, 1953–90

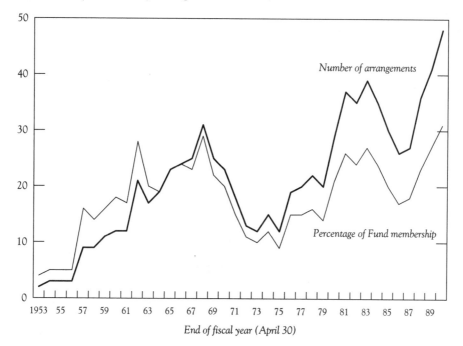

End of fiscal year (April 30)

1970s and even more so in the 1980s. Consequently, the portion of Fund resources being drawn by low-income countries rose in the 1970s and by even more in the 1980s.

The combination of abandoning the monetary role of gold and increasing lending to low-income countries led the Fund to begin selling or distributing a third of its massive stock of gold in 1976. Those gold sales, half of which financed the establishment of a Trust Fund to make highly concessional low-interest loans to impoverished countries, were being completed in 1979 and 1980 just as a speculative fever was driving the market price of gold to ridiculous heights (more than $800 an ounce for a few days in January 1980, compared with average prices of less than $200 in 1978 and less than $400 in 1982; see Figure 1.1). Overall, the sale of gold generated profits of $4.6 billion, an unexpectedly large sum that eventually provided the resources not only for the Trust Fund but for its 1986 successor, the Structural Adjustment Facility (SAF).

A further consequence of the shift in demand for the Fund's resources was an increased complexity in the procedures and financing for Fund lending. That development was reflected at the end of the 1970s in a moderate expansion of the special "facilities" or lending windows available to member countries. The Compensatory Financing Facility (CFF) was liberalized to allow for larger credits in a wider range of circumstances, the Extended Fund Facility (EFF) was liberalized to allow for longer maturities, and the Supplementary Financing Facility (SFF) came into effect in February 1979 to provide additional money for stand-by and EFF arrangements. Acronymic propagation, however, was far from over as the Fund prepared for the 1980s.[14]

The SDR

The IMF's most important acronym, and its most inscrutable, is the SDR. Created in 1969 through the First Amendment of the Articles, the Fund's Special Drawing Rights were often described at the time as "paper gold." Neither paper nor gold, the SDR is (among other functions) both the Fund's own unit of account and an unconditional line of credit to participating countries.[15] Originally defined as the gold equivalent to one U.S. dollar and intended to supplement dollars in official international reserves, the value of the SDR was redefined in 1974 as a basket of 16 internationally traded currencies and in 1981 as a basket of the 5 that were in the widest usage for international payments.[16] The Second Amendment asserted that the SDR was to become "the principal reserve asset in the international monetary system" (Article VIII), and it obliged member countries to collaborate with the Fund to fulfill that objective (Article XXIII). Although neither the goal nor the obligation was ever taken as seriously as that language seems to suggest, the SDR did take on a substantial role in the life of the Fund.

The importance of the SDR as a reserve asset was on the rise at the end of the 1970s. The initial allocations of SDRs in 1970–72 had put SDR 9.3 billion at the disposal of 112 participating countries, an amount that constituted 8½ percent of the world's nongold international reserves. Political disputes over the role of the SDR in a world of floating exchange rates precluded new allocations during the next several years, and the share of SDRs in reserves dropped below 4 percent. But allocations resumed in 1979, and by the time they concluded in January 1981, the stock of outstanding SDRs amounted to SDR 21.4 billion (worth approximately $27 billion), or 6½ percent of world reserves.

The usefulness of the SDR was also growing beyond the Fund's own accounts, as the unpredictability of the value of the U.S. dollar forced international holders to look for more stable alternatives. Several public and private organizations adopted the SDR as their own unit of account, as many as 15 countries pegged the values of their own currencies to the SDR, and markets were beginning to develop for loans, bonds, and bank deposits denominated in SDRs. The Fund encouraged that interest and nourished it through several moves to strengthen the liquidity and transparency of the asset. In 1979, management revived an earlier proposal for a "substitution account" to replace dollars with SDRs in official reserves, and for a

---

[14]The IMF's *Annual Report* for 1999 included a list of 21 abbreviations and acronyms for the institution's operations, 16 of them new since 1979.

[15]With remarkable devotion to acronymizing, the Fund adopted a formal decision in 1983—establishing Rule B-6 of the Fund's Rules and Regulations—that the term "SDR" (or "SDRs," as appropriate) was equivalent to "special drawing right(s)" and was to become standard usage in all Fund documentation. Decision No. 7481-(83/112), adopted July 26, 1983.

[16]In 1999, the number of currencies in the basket was reduced to four when the French franc and the deutsche mark were replaced by the newly created euro. The other three currencies are the U.S. dollar, the Japanese yen, and the pound sterling.

time the Interim Committee appeared likely to approve it. It was, however briefly, a golden age for the SDR.

Evolution and Revolution in the 1980s

The World Economy

The 1980s brought more economic success than the 1970s, especially through the stabilization of prices. Although global output growth continued the declining trend that began in the 1970s, a gradual improvement in policymaking laid the groundwork for the noninflationary growth that many countries would enjoy in the 1990s. Major parts of the world economy, however, suffered some of the most severe economic stresses of the century.[17]

End of Inflation

The greatest economic success of the 1980s was the taming of inflation in industrial countries. The second oil shock may have aggravated the problem, but it also finally galvanized policymakers in oil-importing countries into taking effective action against inflation. The centerpiece and the symbol of the new regime was the announcement in October 1979 of a new system for controlling monetary policy in the United States. Henceforth, the Federal Reserve System, instead of using short-term interest rates as a policy lever (which opened it to political pressure to prevent rates from rising), would focus more directly on the quantitative control of monetary growth through the supply of bank reserves and would use that power to break the expectation of continuing inflation. Although the growth rate of the basic money stock in the United States fell only slightly— from 8¼ percent in 1978 to 6½ percent in 1981—the shift in strategy had a dramatic effect on interest rates. Short-term rates doubled over those three years, and both long- and short-term rates increased sharply in nominal and real terms (Figure 1.5). The Federal Reserve's resolve effectively broke the psychology by which anticipations had been driving up prices. With a brief lag, consumer price inflation fell precipitately: from 13¼ percent in 1979 to less than 4 percent in 1982. Similar declines followed shortly thereafter in the other major industrial countries, and by 1983 inflation was essentially finished as a major *international* policy problem (Figure 1.6).[18]

The end of inflation was not an unmixed blessing, for two reasons. It did not bring stability in all markets, and it led to a sharp, though temporary, drop in output and employment.

---

[17]For an overview of the 1980s and the 1990s that emphasizes the evolution of the international financial system, see Solomon (1999a).

[18]As is clear from Figure 1.6, *world* inflation did not subside in the 1980s, owing to increases in developing countries. The aggregate data for that group are dominated by a few large countries with chronically high inflation in that period: notably, Argentina, Brazil, Nicaragua, Peru, Uganda, and Zaïre.

Figure 1.5. U.S. Interest Rates, 1972–90

Percent

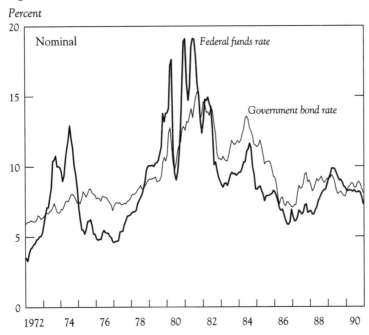

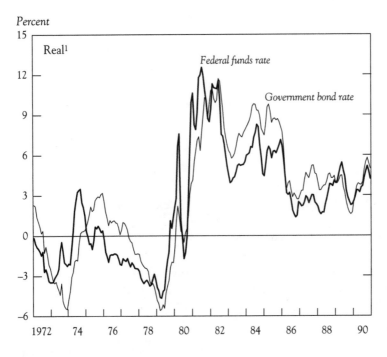

[1]Real rate equals nominal rate minus CPI inflation over next 12 months.

Figure 1.6. World Output Growth and Inflation, 1971–95

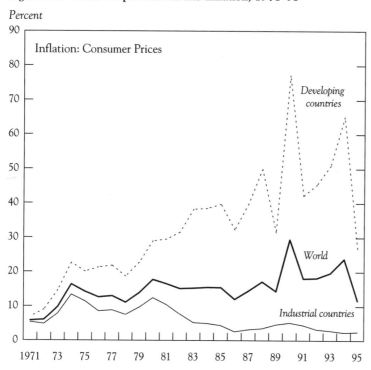

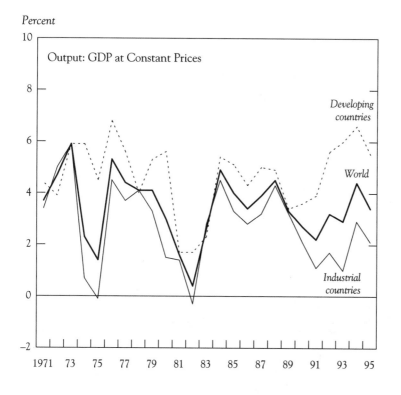

In the mid-1980s, markets collapsed for many primary commodities, causing what could reasonably be called the most severe decline in commodity prices in recorded history and severely aggravating economic declines in developing countries.[19] For low-income countries and multilateral development institutions, the worldwide depression in commodity markets was the single most devastating economic event of the decade.

From a global perspective, the single most important decline was in the price of oil (Figure 1.1). While this reversal of fortunes was welcomed in many parts of the world and contributed importantly to sustaining economic growth and stable price levels throughout the 1980s, it also disrupted the development plans and investment programs of exporting countries from Saudi Arabia to Indonesia to Mexico and Venezuela.

As a further illustration of the effects of weak market conditions, consider the case of coffee. World coffee prices were relatively stable in the first half of the 1980s, as the quota system administered by the International Coffee Organization (ICO) functioned fairly smoothly. Prices then surged briefly in 1985–86 following a drought in Brazil (the world's largest producer), and the ICO temporarily suspended its quotas. After the Brazilian crop recovered, the ICO had difficulty restoring the previous calm, and competition among suppliers pushed prices well below early-1980s levels for nearly a decade. When the quota system collapsed in July 1989, prices plummeted to less than half the 1980–85 average and to less than one-third the peak levels of 1986. Not until 1994 would a semblance of normalcy be restored.

From 1987 to 1993, developing countries that depended on coffee for their livelihood and in some cases for their economic survival faced some of the most difficult policy choices in their history. Those most affected included, in addition to Brazil, several other Latin American countries (most notably Colombia), much of East and Central Africa (notably Burundi, Kenya, Madagascar, Rwanda, Tanzania, and Uganda), and a scattering of Asian countries (notably Indonesia). From the Fund's perspective, the challenge posed by this long-term collapse was to find some means of promoting major structural reforms in these countries and of encouraging large-scale financial support from other creditors. Without reform and support, the traditional medicine of macroeconomic adjustment would ultimately fail and would lead only to further impoverishment.

The process of wringing out inflationary pressures also brought on a deep global recession in the early 1980s. Every region of the world except Asia experienced

---

[19]Evaluation of the timing and extent of the decline is sensitive to the choice of index, currency denomination, and comparator. The IMF's price index for nonfuel primary commodities declined by 27 percent from 1984 to 1987 when measured in SDRs and by 27 percent from 1980 to 1986 when measured in U.S. dollars. Relative to prices of manufactured goods, the index declined by 32 percent from 1984 to 1987. See IMF Commodities Division (1990), p. 26. Relative declines of similar magnitude occurred in the early 1930s, after both of the World Wars, and in the second half of the 1970s; all of those declines, however, were reactions to preceding major booms in commodity prices. Based on the long-run index (1870–1988) developed in Boughton (1991), the relative price of commodities reached its lowest all-time level in 1987.

marked declines in the growth of output, and the majority of the world's countries recorded one or more years of negative growth. Neither the causes nor the symptoms of the cyclical downturn were unusual, except that the primacy of inflation reduction as a policy goal made the adjustment more wrenching than in previous postwar episodes. What marked this experience most clearly was a series of commitments in some of the larger countries not to respond to the downturn with countercyclical policies. For the first time since the 1930s, the prevailing official response to recession was to eschew responsibility for economic growth and employment in order to focus on the goal of stabilizing prices. That response began in Japan, under Prime Minister Masayoshi Ohira in 1978–80, and continued (with varying degrees of commitment) after a series of political shifts in the United Kingdom (the election of Margaret Thatcher in 1979), the United States (Ronald Reagan in 1980), and Germany (Helmut Kohl in 1982). Even in France, where President François Mitterrand and Prime Minister Pierre Mauroy attempted from 1981 to 1983 to engineer a unilateral economic expansion, countercyclical policy was soon abandoned.[20]

New Classical Revolution

The shift in macroeconomic policymaking that ended global inflation was prompted by several interrelated developments in the mainstream of economic thought. Those developments together constituted a "new classical" revolution in economics. The essence of this revolution was the proposition that macroeconomic performance replicates the behavior of an immortal "representative agent" with perfect foresight of all relevant data and constrained only by budgets and technology. (For an exposition and critique, see Hahn and Solow, 1995.) From that article of faith flow four properties of macroeconomic policy that came to be widely accepted both by professional economists and policymakers in the 1980s.

First, "nominal instruments" (policy actions that directly alter the nominal values of macroeconomic variables such as interest rates or monetary aggregates) do not have predictable or stable effects on "real targets" such as unemployment or the growth rate of output. Attempting to target a below-equilibrium unemployment or real interest rate will drive up inflation with no permanent effect on the targeted variable. Second, for policymakers to try to target real variables dilutes and distorts economic incentives in labor markets. If employers and workers believe that wage increases will be validated by monetary expansion sufficient to prevent a rise in unemployment, then the equilibrium rate of wage increase will rise. Third, steady policies—implemented if necessary through fixed rules rather than through discretionary decisions by policymakers—over a period of several years (the "medium term") will provide a more stable environment for private sector activity than will policies that must be reversed over short periods. Fourth, those steady policies should aim primarily to provide a "nominal anchor" for expectations and market behavior.

---

[20]Solomon (1999b) gives a good overview of these shifts in political philosophy.

William Dale, Deputy Managing Director March 1974–June 1984

In the early 1980s, these propositions became associated with a variety of fad-dish theories, each of which was motivated by a distrust of discretionary macro-economic policy and employed extreme assumptions to argue that monetary or fis-cal policy or both would have negligible or pernicious effects on real target variables even in the short run.[21] The most prominent such fad was the "new sup-ply side" (or, to its detractors, "voodoo") economics, and its most notorious excess, the "Laffer curve." According to that school of thought, a combination of liberal-ization of markets and reduction of the size of governments would enable private sector activity to expand rapidly to fill the vacuum left by contractionary demand-management policies. As a related proposition, some supply-side economists pos-tulated that changes in tax rates might affect the fiscal deficit, but shifts between tax and deficit financing would have no effect on the real economy; that postulate was known as "Ricardian equivalence."[22]

A second fad was a simplified form of monetarism based on a belief that infla-tion was linked solely to the rate of monetary growth rather than to the relation-ship between the overall stance of macroeconomic policy and a possibly shifting potential rate of real growth in output. A third was a revived interest in the gold standard as a means of eliminating discretionary monetary policy.[23] By the end of the decade, however, the influence of these extremes had largely faded away.

The new classical revolution brought a second success in policymaking in the 1980s, in addition to the reduction in inflation: the introduction of structural pol-icy changes in both industrial and developing countries that emphasized the pro-motion of private sector activity and the opening of markets. Owing largely to re-ductions in trade barriers and to reforms encouraging and helping enterprises to compete in world markets, international trade grew at nearly twice the rate of out-put growth throughout the second half of the decade (7 percent a year, versus 3¾ percent). At the final gathering of the Fund's governors in the 1980s—in Wash-ington in September 1989—the importance of open trade and the success of lib-eralizing structural reforms were extolled not only in the welcoming address by

---

[21]Smithin (1990) analyzes the fads in economic policymaking in the 1980s. The central fail-ure in such models was the extension of theoretical long-run neutrality to the empirical horizons over which relevant policy effects occurred.

[22]For the extreme case for policymaking according to the new supply-side school, see Wanniski (1983). Canto, Joines, and Laffer (1983) provide a detailed theoretical background for the supply-side view of how fiscal policy affects economic activity. For a balanced critique, see Feld-stein (1986). The appellation "new" is from Feldstein, and "voodoo economics" was coined by George Bush when he was running against Ronald Reagan for the Republican nomination for U.S. president in 1980. The "Laffer curve" is based on the proposition that total tax revenue is a hyperbolic function of the tax rate; above the revenue-maximizing point, a reduction in the tax rate will raise revenues. Most empirical analyses suggested that in most countries, tax rates in the 1980s were well below that point and that cutting tax rates would reduce revenues. For a review, see Mirowski (1982). Ricardian equivalence also requires acceptance of a strong set of assump-tions or hypotheses, notably that households base saving decisions on an infinite horizon rather than on individual life expectancies. For a critical review of that proposition, see Tobin (1980).

[23]For the fringe effort to reestablish a form of gold standard in the 1980s, see Lehrman and Paul (1982), Mundell (1983), and Kojima (1990); Cooper (1982) provides a systematic rebuttal.

U.S. President George Bush but also in the speeches of finance ministers from such diverse developing countries as Angola, Nicaragua, Poland, and Vietnam.

These structural reforms—which Camdessus called a silent revolution and which responded to what John Williamson (1990) termed the "Washington Consensus"— did not come without controversy. State ownership, control, and guidance had always played major roles in development strategies, and it was not obvious that those roles could be reduced without exposing developing economies to instability, impoverishment of the less successful sectors, and domination by more established economies and multinational corporations.[24] At the 1989 Annual Meetings, dissenting voices on the global strategy were heard from (among others) the Governors for Afghanistan, Peru, and Romania. The Washington Consensus nonetheless had become the prevailing paradigm for the late 1980s and early 1990s.

The Rising Sun

A third major development, and one of the defining characteristics of the global economy of the 1980s, was the emergence of Pacific Asia as an economic power. Japan, the second largest economy in the world since 1968 and by far the largest in Asia, began liberalizing and opening the economy around 1980, including allowing foreign residents to buy Japanese securities more easily.[25] By 1985, when the United States embarked on a policy of multilateral policy cooperation, it turned first to Japan to work out bilateral agreements before bringing its more traditional European financial partners into the discussions. In 1989, when the Prime Minister of Australia, Robert Hawke, proposed establishing Asia-Pacific Economic Cooperation (APEC) as a forum for countries along the western rim of the Pacific Ocean, the U.S. government asked to be included so as not to be left out of the creation of one of the world's largest trading zones.

Japan participated in several large loans to the Fund, beginning with the oil facilities in the mid-1970s. In 1986, Japan's status as a major creditor was solidified when the government lent SDR 3 billion ($3.6 billion) to the Fund to help finance the "enlarged access" policy.[26] The Ninth General Review of Quotas, which began in 1987, would bring a rise in Japan's quota and voting power in the Fund to a tie with Germany in the number two spot (from number five, where it had been since 1971).

The rise of Asian economic strength was not confined to Japan. Korea transformed itself from a perennial debtor with an underdeveloped economy into a sur-

---

[24]Raúl Prebisch was perhaps the most eloquent exponent of this view. For a retrospective introduction to his argument, see Prebisch (1984).

[25]Virtually destroyed during World War II, the Japanese economy was well on the way to recovery by the time Japan joined the IMF in 1952. In 1964, the government made the yen a convertible currency, accepted the liberalization requirements of the Fund's Article VIII, and joined the OECD. Four years later, gross domestic product (GDP) in Japan surpassed that of West Germany, making the value of Japanese output higher than that of any other country except the United States.

[26]As an original member of the G-10, Japan had participated in the General Arrangements to Borrow (GAB) since 1962.

Richard Erb, Deputy Managing Director June 1984–August 1994

plus country with high growth rates and rapid modernization. Both Taiwan Province of China (whose authorities represented China in the Fund until 1980, under the name of the Republic of China) and the People's Republic of China (which assumed the seat at that time) recorded remarkable growth throughout the decade. Indonesia, Malaysia, the Philippines, Singapore, and Thailand all had far healthier economies at the end of the 1980s than at the beginning, both in absolute terms and relative to the rest of the developing world. Over the decade, developing countries in Asia averaged growth in output in excess of 7 percent a year, compared with less than 4 percent for all developing countries. Growth averaged 8 percent in Korea and more than 9 percent in China. The rigidities and economic weaknesses that would contribute to the crisis to this region in 1997 were well out of sight.

Financial Imbalances and Crises

These achievements—low inflation in industrial countries, structural reforms in many countries around the world, and strong economic growth in Asia—suggest that it was not the worst of times, but it was also far from the best. The decade also witnessed a worsening of economic imbalances, of which three were particularly troubling.

First, fiscal deficits widened throughout the world, reflecting the operation of automatic stabilizers, an infatuation in some countries with the extreme forms of supply-side economics mentioned above, and the practical need to maintain economic activity in the face of monetary restriction and adverse economic shocks. The combination of fiscal expansion and the reversal of earlier monetary excesses resulted in a sharp rise in real long-term interest rates—from about 1 percent in the late 1970s to an estimated 6 percent in 1983—and a global weakness in saving and investment rates. In industrial countries, net national saving rates fell by half from 1973 to 1983. That drop contributed to the reduced flow of capital into developing countries in the early 1980s, which was compounded by declining rates of domestic saving there as well (Aghevli and others, 1990).

Industrial countries began to correct their fiscal excesses in the second half of the 1980s, thereby laying the groundwork for more sustained and virtually noninflationary growth in the 1990s. The correction, however, also brought a marked slowdown in growth that became a widespread recession by the end of the decade, in many developing as well as industrial countries.[27]

Second, an international debt crisis erupted in 1982 as one developing country after another was forced to retrench from the excessive borrowing levels of the late 1970s. A combination of damaging external shocks—high world interest rates, adverse shifts in the terms of trade, and weak demand in industrial countries—and unsustainable economic policies at home destroyed the ability of many developing

---

[27]For an analysis of the effects of industrial country growth on developing countries, see Goldstein and Khan (1982). Real GNP growth in industrial countries fell from a peak of 4.5 percent in 1988 to 1.3 percent in 1991. Growth in real per capita GDP in developing countries fell from a peak of 2.2 percent in 1988 to –0.6 percent in 1990.

countries to service their external debts. Debtors then had to choose between defaulting on their debts or attempting to adjust policies by enough to reduce their external deficits to a financeable level. Most countries chose the latter approach, and efforts to form a united front (a "debtors' cartel") to force creditors to accept a reduction in the present value of debt-service payments never advanced beyond general expressions of desire. The debt crisis affected developing countries around the world: those that had borrowed mainly from commercial banks and those that relied primarily on support from official creditors. A few heavily indebted countries, notably in Asia, escaped the crisis through rapid adjustment that emphasized orienting production toward exports, but many more found that degree of adjustment to be beyond their reach.

The effects of the debt crisis were contained in the early 1980s through a "case-by-case" strategy in which external financial support was provided to countries willing to adjust their economic policies. That strategy succeeded in preventing a series of defaults on sovereign debts, but it did not lead to an early resumption of normal relations between debtors and creditors. A driving assumption in the development of the strategy, much debated in the subsequent literature, was that such defaults could have led to multiple bankruptcies of major commercial banks and possibly to a collapse of the international banking system. The debt strategy also succeeded in greatly reducing the payments deficits of many developing countries, but it did so more by forcing a reduction in imports than by fostering growth in exports.

By 1985, a consensus was forming among officials in creditor countries that new approaches were needed for a more favorable and more sustainable solution to the crisis. The focus of the debt strategy during the next few years was to encourage indebted countries to undertake growth-oriented structural reforms, financed largely by longer-term loans from the World Bank and regional development banks, and to encourage commercial banks to resume net lending to countries undertaking such reforms. That effort failed to generate either long-term growth or even much long-term financing, and by 1988 almost all of the countries hit by a debt crisis several years earlier were still struggling to escape from it. For much of the developing world, the 1980s were to be a "lost decade" for economic growth.

The denouement of the debt strategy arrived when the realization took hold that a high-growth equilibrium could be attained only through debt reduction. The debt-relief approach had two prongs: one aimed at the low-income countries that owed most of their external debt to creditor governments, and the other aimed at the middle-income countries that were heavily indebted to commercial banks.

The major industrial countries agreed in 1988 to reduce the present value of external debts of certain low-income countries through the Paris Club. The "Toronto terms" for official debt relief, named for the location of the summit meeting at which the agreement was reached, were gradually improved over the next several years to become the "London" terms in 1991 and the "Naples" terms in 1994. Each succeeding agreement provided incrementally greater concessionality for relief on bilateral official debts, but the problem was seemingly impervious. Finally, the limited effect of even the Naples terms on the sustainability of the aggregate debt service of the most severely indebted and poorest countries induced creditors in 1996 to support a joint proposal by the IMF and the World Bank for multilateral (not just bilateral) debt reduction. (See Boote and Thugge, 1998.) As that program—the "Heavily Indebted Poor Countries," or HIPC, initiative—began to operate in the late 1990s, and notwithstanding its limitations, the first real signs emerged that the debt crisis of low-income countries might ultimately be solvable.

The second prong was the "Brady Plan," introduced by the U.S. authorities in 1989. The Brady Plan offered a menu of options to heavily indebted middle-income countries to replace existing bank loans with bonds on more favorable terms and to help them buy back part of their outstanding debts at the prevailing market discounts. As with the relief plans for low-income countries, debtors had to qualify to participate by agreeing to implement more sustainable macroeconomic policies and structural reforms. In the next six years (to mid-1995), debt reduction schemes reduced the present value of the debts of 21 developing countries to commercial banks by more than $75 billion, at an official cost of $25 billion (Dunaway and others, 1995, pp. 6–7). Aided greatly by a serendipitous and massive decline in world interest rates, the Brady Plan thus provided substantial relief to qualifying countries and brought an end to the debt crisis as an international threat.

The third troubling development of the decade was a persistence of structural rigidities that contributed to economic stagnation and high rates of unemployment in Europe and to the decline in economic fortunes in some developing countries.

Differences in job creation statistics between the United States and western Europe were startling in the 1980s: more than 18 percent growth in total employment in the United States, against less than 4 percent in Europe. Although the political rhetoric of the time attributed much of the U.S. employment growth to the supply-side policies of the Reagan administration, that performance was part of a longer-term trend, fueled and lubricated by labor mobility, strong capital markets, and a generally light-handed approach to the regulation of markets. Those factors were less evident in Europe, where social cohesion, stability, and equality were the more prevalent political ideals (with, of course, marked variations between countries and over time). During the 1980s, in most western European countries the lowest-income groups received about twice as large a portion of total income as in the United States (see Atkinson, 1996). Even if that egalitarian outcome came at the expense of job creation, it was a price that many Europeans seemed prepared to pay as long as the overall standard of living was on the rise. In the difficult economic environment of the 1980s, however, it left European countries without the means to adjust to declines in traditional employment sectors. By the late 1980s, the absence of new employment opportunities and the persistence of unemployment at double-digit levels (dubbed "Eurosclerosis") forced a reexamination of the trade-offs between distributive and aggregative economic goals. Structural reforms aimed at liberalizing and strengthening market forces became an increasingly central topic in annual consultations with the Fund.

In many developing countries, the shift toward privatization and liberalization that began in the late 1980s was less a natural response to shifting economic philosophy than a forced response to desperate economic circumstances. Heavy government involvement in—and direction of—the economy had led to poor choices on capital investment, disastrously high concentrations of income, degradation of the natural environment, and financial ruin. Pervasive corruption became evident in several cases such as the Philippines under Ferdinand Marcos, Haiti under Jean-Claude Duvalier, and Zaïre under Mobutu Sese Seko; and it was also a problem in many other countries where it was still masked. As new governments came into power, they naturally sought new means of improving economic performance, and many of them joined the silent revolution.

A major financial consequence of these various difficulties was that a large number of developing countries were unable—and a few were simply unwilling—to continue to service their external debts. From 1980 to 1983, that problem was concentrated primarily in syndicated loans from commercial banks, which were the most expensive, the shortest in maturity, and the most amenable to renegotiation. By 1984, prolonged and wide-scale overdue payments had spread to official creditors, including the Fund. That problem turned out to be far less tractable than initially thought. Its solution would require the belated development of a coordinated effort on the part of the indebted countries, the Fund, and donor countries that would stretch through the 1990s. From the beginning, structural reform in economic policymaking would play a critical role.

International Monetary System

The system of floating exchange rates established in the vacuum of 1973 was put to a severe test from 1978 to 1985. Major currencies fluctuated massively and with seeming disregard for underlying economic conditions.

Unstable Exchange Rates

Faced with a collapse in confidence in the dollar, the U.S. authorities were forced into action in the fall of 1978. On November 1, President Jimmy Carter announced that the United States was mobilizing more than $20 billion to defend the currency's value in foreign exchange markets. Together with an earlier moderate tightening of fiscal policy, an expected tightening of monetary policy, and tighter enforcement of national standards on wage and price increases, the announcement of large-scale intervention finally ended the long downward slide and initiated a hesitant recovery. Over the next year and a half, the dollar appreciated by more than 40 percent against the yen, 12 percent against the deutsche mark, and just over 10 percent in effective terms. The gains, however, were short-lived, and by the fall of 1980, the effective exchange rate was not much above its level before the rescue.

The reasons for the dollar's backsliding in 1980 were much debated. U.S. monetary policy had been tightened, but its effects were obscured by the intermittent

Figure 1.7. Real Effective Exchange Rates, 1975–89

Index (1975 = 100)

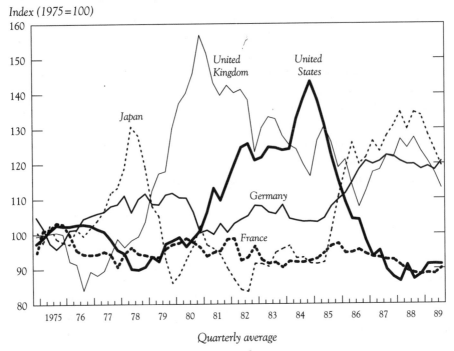

Quarterly average

application of credit controls.[28] Short-term interest rates fell by more than 7 percentage points in four months while controls were in effect, and confidence weakened. In the last quarter of the year, however, both interest rates and the exchange rate again reversed course. Then in March 1981, the newly elected administration of President Ronald Reagan announced that it would no longer intervene in exchange markets except *in extremis*: in effect, that it was returning to the laissez-faire policies of the period before the crisis of November 1978. Interest differentials and market sentiment were already favoring the dollar, and the realization that no official action would be taken only added to the upward pressure. The dollar appreciated without a major interruption for more than 4½ years. From September 1980 to March 1985, the dollar appreciated by 20 percent against the yen, 85 percent against the deutsche mark, and 54 percent in effective terms (Figure 1.7).[29]

---

[28]For detailed descriptions of the confusing course of U.S. monetary policy in 1980, see Greider (1987), Chapter 6; and Mussa (1994) and the associated discussion.

[29]Throughout the floating-rate period, major changes in the effective exchange rate of the U.S. dollar, as measured by the IMF, were approximately equal in nominal and real terms. This empirical regularity, which is unique among the major currencies, implies that increases in unit labor costs, measured in a common currency, were similar in the United States and collectively in its major trading partners. The reasons for the strength and persistence of that relationship are unclear. For the methodology used at the IMF to compute nominal and real effective exchange rates, see Zanello and Desruelle (1997). Also see Chapter 2, footnote 82, p. 107.

Other major currencies did not respond passively and identically to the wide swings in the value of the dollar. The pound sterling strengthened against the dollar throughout 1979 and 1980 in response to a combination of a tightening of monetary policy under Prime Minister Margaret Thatcher and the exploitation of Britain's North Sea oil fields as an important new source of export revenues (see Buiter and Miller, 1981). In a little over four years starting in 1977, the pound appreciated by one-third in nominal effective terms and by an astonishing (and unprecedented for a reserve currency) 87 percent in real effective terms (see Figure 1.7). The yen also appreciated in nominal effective terms during the period of the dollar's major appreciation, but because Japan's inflation was low, the real effective rate was stable.[30] The deutsche mark and the French franc were roughly stable in real effective terms, as a result of the relative stability of intra-European exchange rates.

Fluctuations among the major currencies created an incentive for investors and governments to diversify their foreign exchange portfolios, but the effects were less than dramatic. Since World War II, the U.S. dollar had been the dominant reserve currency, and that position was eroded only gradually as a result of inflation, instability of currency values, the strengthening of other national economies, and the economic integration of Europe. During the 1980s, the dollar's reported share in foreign exchange reserves dropped from about 70 percent to 60 percent. Most international bank loans (between 65 and 80 percent) were denominated in dollars, with only a slight downward trend. Only in external bond issues did the dollar's share decline sharply, from about two-thirds to one-third. The deutsche mark was the second most important reserve currency, and a few others were held in small amounts: principally ECUs and Japanese yen.[31]

Prevailing models of the determination of exchange rates were unable to account for the major swings in rates among the key reserve currencies in the early 1980s.[32] Nonetheless, it was generally accepted that the primary reason for the wide swings in exchange rates was that some major countries (notably the United

---

[30]The strength of the yen relative to the deutsche mark and other European currencies in the first half of the 1980s is attributable to the same causes as the strength of the dollar: the combination of a tight monetary policy and a less tight fiscal stance. As a result, interest rates fell by much less in Japan than elsewhere, and the currency appreciated against most major currencies other than the dollar.

[31]Data on the currency composition of official reserves are of poor quality because of marked differences in reporting practices. For a summary table showing the dollar figures reported here, see de Boissieu (1996), p. 132. Detailed tables may be found in the IMF *Annual Report*.

[32]The most widely accepted model at the time was the Dornbusch-Frankel "overshooting" model, which postulated an equilibrium based on PPP and an adjustment process based on a "rational" expectation that the actual rate would regress toward that level. A tightening of monetary policy in one country would initially raise the real interest rate relative to those in other countries, which in turn would bring a temporary appreciation of the real exchange rate. The extent of appreciation would be such as to create an expectation of a rate of depreciation equal to the interest differential, so that the expected rate of return on financial assets would be the same in all currencies. Early empirical tests of that model seemed favorable, but later tests showed that it had very weak explanatory power and implausible parameter estimates. See Meese and Rogoff (1983) and Boughton (1984, 1987, 1988).

States and the United Kingdom) were adopting restrictive monetary policies while maintaining expansionary fiscal policies, whereas others (notably Germany) had rather the opposite stance. The contrast produced relatively high real interest rates in the former group, which led to a continuing flow (not a sudden and massive shift, as predicted by the simple models of the 1970s) of funds into dollar- and pound-denominated assets. To explain this phenomenon, economists had to develop models that allowed for "preferred habitats" by different classes of investors and that incorporated the structure (not just the overall stance) of macroeconomic policies. Assessing the magnitude and timing of these effects was a tall order, and it was not clear how much of the observed changes in exchange rates were due to hard-to-measure but rational shifts in preferences and expectations, rather than to herd instincts and bandwagon effects. Only if the big swings were rationally based could it be said that the floating rate system was contributing to the health of the world economy.

Models that allowed for less complete substitution between financial markets in different currencies (and different countries) fared a little better than earlier perfect-substitution models, but the improvements were not enough to produce a new consensus on how exchange rates were determined. The 1980s therefore became a decade of agnosticism on exchange rates, as the notion that exchange rates followed a random walk and were subject to rational or irrational "bubbles" became prevalent.[33] When the U.S. dollar continued to appreciate at the end of 1984 and beginning of 1985 even after interest rate differentials and policy stances suggested that it should go the other way, the very idea of an exchange rate equilibrium grounded in relative economic conditions seemed to be in doubt.

External Imbalances

Globally, external current account imbalances diminished during the 1980s. Declining oil prices and rising imports erased the aggregate surplus of oil-exporting countries, while contractionary policies adopted in response to the debt crisis wiped out the aggregate deficit of non-oil developing countries (see Figure 1.2). Despite these trends, external imbalances became pronounced in the large industrial countries, for the same reasons that their exchange rates gyrated so greatly.

---

[33]This terminology was developed and became part of the economist's toolkit in the 1980s. A rational bubble occurs in the context of a model in which expectations are formed consistently with the model's predictions ("rational expectations"). If the current value of a variable such as the exchange rate depends on rational expectations of its future level, it can take on values that differ persistently from those that would otherwise be determined by the "fundamental" determinants in the model. By back-formation, a bubble that occurs because of herding behavior or other factors unrelated either to fundamentals or to rational expectations may be characterized as an irrational bubble. The seminal article on testing for rational bubbles, by Robert P. Flood and Peter M. Garber, was published in the *Journal of Political Economy* in 1980 and was collected with related papers in Flood and Garber (1994). Tests for the existence of rational bubbles in exchange rates were hampered by the empirical weakness of models of the fundamental determinants; see Meese (1986).

From 1981, when most of the largest countries had small current account positions, imbalances accumulated rapidly until 1987. In that year, the United States had a deficit of $166 billion (3½ percent of GDP), while Japan and Germany had surpluses of $87 billion (3½ percent) and $46 billion (4¼ percent), respectively. Opinions differed, however, on whether this phenomenon was a problem.

To some theorists and policymakers, a current account imbalance was a benign reflection of different time preferences between countries: nations that saved more than they invested had external surpluses, and conversely. The view that current account deficits were bad only if they reflected government rather than private sector deficits became popular for a time. After the British Chancellor of the Exchequer, Nigel Lawson, espoused that linkage in his speech at the 1988 Annual Meetings of IMF and World Bank governors in Berlin, it became known as the "Lawson Doctrine."[34]

Others argued that current account imbalances had the potential to reduce economic welfare regardless of their origins (Frenkel, Goldstein, and Masson, 1991, Chapter III). If households became more myopic and reduced their saving rates, then government action to raise its own saving (usually by reducing the fiscal deficit) would be an appropriate policy response. If a country developed a current account surplus because of a decline in the rate of domestic capital investment, then a fiscal stimulus (either as a tax cut to reduce the cost of investing or as investment spending by the government) might be called for.

The predominant view among policymakers in the 1980s was that current account imbalances were an important source of concern. Apprehensions in developing countries were heightened by the difficulty of financing large deficits after the onset of the international debt crisis in 1982. Misgivings in industrial countries were heightened by political pressures from industries that were having difficulty competing in world markets. If the alternative to external balance was an intensification of protection against import competition through tariff and other trade barriers, the choice was clear: large imbalances must be avoided. That political concern sometimes turned the spotlight on bilateral trade imbalances rather than the overall surplus or deficit. The most notable example was the trade surplus that Japan recorded vis-à-vis the United States. Measured in U.S. dollars, the bilateral surplus rose steadily from 1980 to 1987, when it amounted to $57 billion. Although the portion of the total U.S. trade deficit accounted for by the deficit against Japan fell slightly during that interval (from 41 percent to 36 percent), and although the rise in both the overall gap and the bilateral deficit were due primarily to expansionary fiscal policies in the United States, political discussions were

---

[34]See IMF, *Summary Proceedings*, 1988, pp. 78–85, and Lawson (1992), pp. 854–59. The Fund staff conducted a number of research studies during the 1980s on the questions of whether private sector deficits tended to be self-correcting and whether undesirable deficits were confined to those of the public sector; see Bayoumi (1990) and references therein, and Frenkel, Goldstein, and Masson (1991). W. Max Corden (1986, 1987), then a Senior Advisor in the Research Department, questioned the use of current account balances as a target for international economic policy, and he later embraced the Lawson Doctrine (Corden, 1994, Chapter 6).

driven by the highly visible bilateral imbalance and were leading to increasingly insistent calls for protection against Japanese imports.[35]

Policy Coordination

These problems created pressure for greater stability, which led first to a spate of studies on the possibility of restoring a degree of fixity to exchange rates and then to a major effort to promote cooperation in formulating macroeconomic policies in the large industrial countries. Although few argued seriously for restoration of a system of fixed exchange rates (aside from a fringe movement to reestablish some form of gold standard), and most economists and policymakers accepted that official attempts to hold rates within a limited range were likely to fail, a minority view developed in support of what came to be known as "target zones." In official circles, the leading exponents were in the French government, continuing a long tradition of French advocacy for official control and stability in exchange markets. By 1985, industrial countries as a group had rejected target zones as a policy option, but outside economists—notably at the Institute for International Economics (IIE) in Washington—continued to refine the analysis of how target zones might work. Staff studies at the IMF, particularly after Jacob A. Frenkel became Economic Counselor and Director of Research in 1986, were mostly skeptical of target zones as a practical option for the key currencies.[36]

Reaching with more muted ambition, the major industrial countries (originally the five largest but later expanded to the Group of Seven) forged a series of modest and only partially successful agreements in the second half of the decade aimed both at stabilizing exchange rates and reducing current account imbalances. This policy cooperation exercise began with coordinated intervention in exchange markets in February 1985 aimed at reversing the appreciation of the U.S. dollar. It was solidified in September 1985 with the "Plaza" agreement to push for further dollar depreciation and in December 1986 by the "Baker-Miyazawa" agreement that enabled the Bank of Japan to cut interest rates without fear of a destabilizing reaction in exchange markets. It culminated in the "Louvre" accord of February 1987, when the major countries agreed to stabilize exchange rates "around current levels" with the explicit objective of avoiding the reemergence of large external imbalances. By 1989, however, the objectives of stabilizing exchange rates and reducing imbalances were less easily reconciled, and cooperation in policymaking became less well focused.

In a more permanent move toward stability and cooperation, the European Monetary System (EMS) was founded in March 1979. The EMS was preceded by the European Payments Union (1950–58), which reestablished currency convertibility and multilateral trading relationships among European countries after the

---

[35]From 1980 to 1987, U.S. trade with Japan grew more rapidly than with other countries, and imports grew much more rapidly than exports. Merchandise exports to Japan rose by 33 percent, compared with 9 percent to all other countries. Imports from Japan, however, rose by 171 percent, while imports from all other countries rose by 49 percent.

[36]For a comprehensive statement of the IIE case for target zones, see Miller and Williamson (1987). For an overview of the more skeptical view that prevailed at the Fund in that period, see Frenkel and Goldstein (1996).

devastation of World War II; the European Monetary Agreement (1958–72), which effected convertibility and established a fund for financing temporary imbalances; and the European Monetary Cooperation Fund (from 1973), which administered short-term credit facilities in support of common margins around central values for intra-European exchange rates. The agreement on margins—known initially as the "snake in the tunnel" when it was established in 1972 and then just as the "snake" when the "tunnel" of dollar-based margins broke apart in March 1973—succeeded only intermittently at stabilizing intra-European exchange rates.[37] Since European countries had a wide range of experience on price stability and economic growth, they also had a wide range of interest rates in both nominal and real terms. The EMS therefore faced an uphill battle to establish credibility for its similar but more comprehensive exchange rate mechanism (ERM).

In its first several years, the EMS underwent a series of exchange rate realignments that made it function very much like a "crawling peg." The deutsche mark was both the largest and the strongest currency in the arrangement. The other currencies were occasionally devalued against the mark, which became the de facto anchor for the system. In 1987, however, the EMS was firmed up by the "Basel-Nyborg" agreement into a more stable system in which policy convergence was given greater prominence and realignments were to be avoided.

Open Capital Markets

These various efforts to reestablish a measure of stability were made against the backdrop of rapidly expanding international capital markets. Cross-border bank loans outstanding nearly tripled during the 1980s, from $1.1 trillion to $3.0 trillion. The stock of international bond issues grew even more rapidly, from $380 billion to $1.3 trillion. Both of those rates of increase were up sharply from the preceding several years (Figure 1.8).

By the 1980s, policymakers had come to accept and even to embrace the growth in internationally open capital markets. When this growth began in earnest, with the advent of the eurodollar market in the 1960s, much of the discussion of its implications concerned how to regulate and control it. The existence of unregulated offshore markets for bank deposits and loans in competition with regulated onshore markets threatened to weaken national monetary control and raised fears of unfettered inflation. By the late 1970s, empirical and theoretical research had demonstrated conclusively that the inflationary consequences of euromarket growth were negligible, because monetary authorities in the main industrial countries retained the ability to control domestic money creation (see, for example, Mayer, 1982). Moreover, internationally active banks had played an invaluable

---

[37]This picturesque terminology derived from the appearance of a graph plotting the values over time of European currencies against the dollar. The tight margins of fluctuations allowed within the group produced a sinuous joint movement within the wider band (the tunnel) allowed under the Fund's par value system. For a history of the snake in the context of world political and economic events in the 1970s, see Solomon (1982). For a history of monetary integration in Europe, see Ungerer (1997).

Figure 1.8. International Financing, 1974–90

Trillions of U.S. dollars

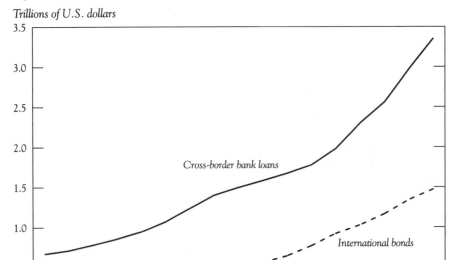

Source: Bank for International Settlements, *Annual Reports*.

role in financing the deficits of oil-importing countries after 1973. Consequently, in the late 1970s and throughout the 1980s, capital controls were loosened and dismantled throughout western Europe, North America, and Japan. Developing countries—many of them hesitantly and reluctantly—followed suit, and the pattern spread gradually as the decade progressed (Quirk, Evans, and others, 1995).

Growth and liberalization of capital markets contributed to the integration and interdependence of the world economy in the 1980s. The clearest benefit of that development was the strengthening of international trade as an engine of growth, as described above. The potential cost, which became abundantly clear in the second half of the 1990s, was that a financial crisis in one country was now more likely to affect other markets—and to affect them more quickly. One manifestation of that danger was the speed with which the international debt crisis spread around the world in 1981–83. A second came in the global stock market crash of October 1987. Moderate declines in equity prices in New York on October 16 and 17 were followed immediately by a similar softening in markets throughout Europe and Asia, and the record one-day decline of 22 percent in New York on October 20 then triggered a global sell-off in equities.[38] In the most vulnerable markets, the collapse of

---

[38]For a statistical analysis of international transmissions during the crash, see Bennett and Kelleher (1988).

equity values was prolonged and had serious consequences for economic activity. In Mexico, for example, the stock market lost 75 percent of its value in a sustained decline over six weeks. Some markets in the Asia-Pacific region, including Australia, Hong Kong, Singapore, and Malaysia, also suffered quite large percentage losses. As an international phenomenon, the stock market crash of 1987 was a brief storm, but if it was easily weathered, part of the credit must go to regulations introduced in the wake of the crash (see Allen and others, 1989, Chapter 5).

The Fund

As the Fund began to face the external challenges of the 1980s, it was also confronting some serious internal weaknesses. The surge in lending to developing countries at the end of the 1970s had come at the expense of maintaining the quality of adjustment programs and of the Fund's financial portfolio. The failure of the effort to establish a substitution account had weakened the potential for the SDR to play a central role in the international monetary system and deprived de Larosière of the centerpiece of a strategy for strengthening the institution. The waning of demand for the Fund's resources by industrial countries, together with the very limited consensus on whether and how to stabilize exchange rates, left the Fund struggling to define a clear role for its core function, surveillance. If the Fund was to remain the world's premier monetary institution, it would have to nurse its roots back to health or redefine its role. As the decade progressed, it did enough of both to dominate the global economic stage more than ever before.

The activities of the Fund, described in detail in the chapters that follow, had three primary dimensions in the 1980s: surveillance over the international monetary system and the "exchange rate policies" of member countries, development and management of the strategy for resolving the international debt crisis, and restoring and strengthening the quality of Fund lending and conditionality.

Surveillance

Surveillance was hampered from the outset by a lack of clearly defined objectives or standards. Before the Fund could assess the appropriateness of a country's exchange rate policies, it had to judge the correct level of the real exchange rate, and it had to have at least an implicit model linking that level to macroeconomic policies and to the behavior of the nominal exchange rate. Much of the evolution of the practice of surveillance by Fund staff in the 1980s was concerned with refining those assessments, both in the Article IV consultations and through periodic reports on the World Economic Outlook. More substantive improvements were to await the 1990s, when the international community became more willing to adopt a broad code of conduct for macroeconomic and structural policies.

At the same time, the Fund tried to develop effective procedures to make its surveillance both even-handed and "firm," but those two goals were hard to reconcile. Wielding a club was not always compatible with being part of a club. If surveillance was to be applied even-handedly to all member countries—to those with floating rates as firmly as to those with fixed rates, to countries with strong external balances as firmly as to those that were heavily in debt, and to large countries as firmly as to small ones—then it risked becoming pro forma and routine. Time and again, blame for the failure of the Fund to foresee and forestall economic crises was leveled at the genteel and diplomatic coziness of surveillance routines.

The Fund tried to mitigate this difficulty by developing procedures for identifying potential problem cases and holding special, ad hoc, reviews in addition to the regular annual consultations. The Executive Board, however, was reluctant to establish procedures that would cast a shadow over a member's economic policies, especially when the member was not seeking to borrow from the Fund. Two special consultations were held during the 1980s (with Sweden in 1982 and Korea in 1987), but that procedure was not flexible enough to be of general value, and it fell into disuse. An effort beginning in 1984 to give an "enhanced" operational value to surveillance by allowing countries in specified circumstances to release consultation reports to commercial creditors was marginally more successful but also was not widely applied.

Another factor that weakened the effectiveness of the consultation process was that gaps in the timing of some consultations made it difficult to maintain current knowledge about conditions in countries with emerging financial problems. In the early 1980s, that problem was most critical in Mexico: the Executive Board did not hold a review of the Mexican economy from March 1980 until July 1982, just a few weeks before the debt crisis hit. The frequency of consultations was subsequently increased, but improving effective continuity remained a goal until well into the 1990s.

Debt Strategy

The international debt crisis that erupted in 1982 catapulted the Fund into a vortex, and the ensuing efforts to contain the crisis greatly increased the Fund's role in the international monetary system. Arguably, the debt crisis was a greater catalyst for change—and certainly was a greater catalyst for growth—in the Fund than was the shift to floating exchange rates a decade earlier. That the 1980s marked the Fund's "coming of age," as asserted at the outset of this chapter, was due in large measure to the role that the institution played in developing and carrying out the debt strategy after 1982.

Before 1982, the IMF did not have a central role as a manager of international financial crises. The Fund lent sizable sums to the four countries involved in the 1956 Suez crisis—the first major wave of lending by the institution—and it extended credits to countries affected by subsequent shocks such as the collapse of the Gold Pool in 1968, the turmoil in G-10 currencies in the early 1970s, and the oil shocks of the 1970s. The character of that lending, however, differed only marginally from the multitude of credits extended to member countries in quieter times (Boughton, 2000). When Mexico moved to the brink of default in August 1982, the Fund was quickly drawn into the crisis in new ways. Other official lenders, including government agencies and the Federal Reserve in the United States and the Bank for International Settlements (BIS) in Switzerland, moved quickly to provide short-term financing to forestall default, but it became apparent that a lasting solution required centralized coordination of creditors.

The Fund stepped into that breach by insisting that it would provide financial support for debtors' adjustment programs only after receiving assurances from other creditors, especially commercial banks, that they would increase their own lending exposure to the indebted countries. This "concerted lending" tactic, which brought the Fund into a close ad hoc working relationship both with commercial banks and with U.S. government officials, became the cornerstone of the debt strategy for the next several years. Although the tactic ceased to work in the latter part of the decade, the presence of the Fund remained as the centerpiece of the strategy. The debt strategy evolved gradually through the 1985 Baker Plan (growing out of debt), experimentation by the Fund and other creditors with a menu of debt-relieving operations in 1987–88, and the decisive 1989 Brady Plan for debt reduction. That evolution broadened participation in ways that gave the World Bank, regional development banks, and bilateral official creditors a greater role but did not diminish that of the Fund.

Quality of Fund Lending

In addition to the development of the practice of surveillance and of techniques for resolving the debt crisis, the shift in composition in demand for Fund resources in the late 1970s and early 1980s posed challenges for the Fund that took all of the decade and more to resolve.

The traditional view of the Fund was similar to that of a bank for countries: a provider of short-term, self-liquidating loans to tide central banks over temporary disturbances to the balance of international payments. The Fund began to move away from that "monetary character" in 1976 by establishing the EFF, which provided Fund resources on longer maturities to countries with more deeply seated economic problems.[39] The average maturity of the Fund's regular stand-by arrangements lengthened as well, and more countries became prolonged users of Fund resources. By the early 1980s the Fund began to reexamine its lending policies in light of the continually worsening economic plight in many of its borrowing countries.

Several proposed financing arrangements provoked concerns among the Fund's Executive Directors in the late 1970s and early 1980s. Part III of this History recounts the debates over whether conditionality was sufficiently strong in proposed multiyear arrangements for Sierra Leone in 1979, Grenada in 1981, and India in 1981. The extended arrangement for India, which was the largest financial com-

---

[39]The Trust Fund, which was also established in 1976 and which also made longer-term loans, was funded and maintained independently from the Fund's general resources. The terminology stressing the Fund's "monetary character" originated with the Dutch central bank; see Duisenberg and Szász (1991).

mitment made by the Fund up to that time, was questioned by some senior staff as well as by Executive Directors, who wondered whether India really had a need to call on the Fund for balance of payments financing and whether the Fund's conditions for lending the money were sufficiently strong. Was conditionality meaningful and effective if it merely required a country to do what it planned to do anyway? These controversies had little effect on the flow of financing to the countries in question, but they were emblematic of a deepening sense of doubt—both inside and outside the Fund—about the overall quality of the Fund's portfolio of financial claims.

The customary conditions placed on Fund lending, which stressed the need for sound and sustainable macroeconomic policies, were certainly not misplaced. The need for macroeconomic adjustment was in fact as great as ever. Macroeconomic adjustment alone, however, was insufficient to cure the structural maladies that prevailed in many of the Fund's newer borrowers. Throughout the 1980s, the Fund experimented with ways to supplement its calls for monetary restraint and fiscal integrity with demands for structural reform, and ways to integrate those reforms more fully into the design of Fund-supported adjustment programs. Although that process took hold only partially and only rather late in the decade, it did eventually succeed in encouraging and helping many countries to liberalize their economic policies.

Before the silent revolution in policymaking took root, some countries—as noted above—became so heavily indebted to the Fund and other external creditors that they either would not or could not continue to service all of their debts on time. Quite apart from the defaults and threats of default that characterized the international debt crisis, several countries fell seriously behind in meeting their obligations to the Fund. In 1984, for the first time in its history, the Fund found itself facing a crisis of arrears. By the end of the decade, more than 10 percent of the Fund's claims would be on countries with protracted arrears to the institution. Developing a strategy for reducing and eventually eliminating those arrears absorbed an increasing portion of the energies of management and staff.

Institutional Change

The single greatest problem faced by the Fund in the 1980s was to garner the financial resources to meet the demand for its services. Three times—in 1980, 1983, and 1990—member countries were asked to approve increases in quotas, which are the basic source of permanent financing for the Fund. In addition, the Fund undertook on several occasions to borrow from surplus countries (though pointedly *not* from private credit markets) to supplement its resources temporarily. The pivotal development here came in 1981, when Saudi Arabia agreed to lend the Fund SDR 8 billion ($9 billion) for six years. When quotas were not raised in line with demand for Fund credits, the Fund used this borrowed money to stretch its resources by agreeing to approve credit arrangements that were larger in relation to quotas than had previously seemed prudent. In combination with the arrears problem, these developments pushed the Fund's balance sheet and income flows into a precarious position, especially in the second half of the decade. The quota increase that was approved in 1990 (and which took effect in 1992), along with development of a more effective arrears strategy and the resolution of the debt crisis, restored some order to the picture. The experience, however, also restored and strengthened the Fund's caution and its resolve to maintain its monetary character and its ability to preserve its resources for the continued use of countries in need.

As originally conceived, the Fund had a single focus to its lending: financing the overall balance of payments. Since 1963, however, it has sought to provide credits to member countries for specialized purposes related to the causes of payments problems or to the problems of certain groups of countries (particularly developing countries). The 1963 CFF was followed by the Buffer Stock Financing Facility of 1969, the "oil facilities" of 1974 and 1975, and the EFF and the Trust Fund of 1976. In addition, the Fund occasionally lent quick-disbursing funds for emergency disaster relief. Although the oil facilities and the Trust Fund were phased out in the early 1980s, the Fund still had a variety of specialized lending windows in effect (Table 1.1).

The inability of many low-income countries to service debts on market terms in the 1980s led to efforts to renew and expand the Fund's low-interest (concessional) lending. That activity had begun with the 1976 Trust Fund but had gone dormant once the Trust Fund became fully committed in 1981. Concessional lending to low-income countries resumed in 1986 with the establishment of the SAF and was expanded through the establishment of the Enhanced SAF (ESAF) the following year. The ESAF eventually became one of the Fund's great success stories, as the institution channeled billions of dollars at low cost and for long maturities to many of the world's poorest countries and served as a catalyst for much larger sums from other official creditors. Nonetheless, and even though ESAF money was completely separate from the Fund's general resources, the Fund came under quite a bit of criticism: for departing from its monetary character, for imposing strict adjustment conditionality on countries in need of increased economic growth, and especially for intruding into the traditional realm of the World Bank, which had a much clearer mandate to make longer-term loans on concessional terms.

In addition to coping with rising demand for financing against a background of limited resources, the Fund faced some subtle but profound changes in its membership. With the People's Republic of China represented in the Fund beginning in 1980, Hungary joining in 1982, and Poland rejoining in 1986, the Fund had a greater concentration of centrally planned and socialist economies to look after than at any other time in its history. The short-term consequences of the inclusion of Hungary and Poland were largely confined to those countries, neighboring countries in Europe, and the staff who were working with them. The consequences of the inclusion of mainland China were greater, owing to the size and global economic importance of the country and the fact that it had a seat on the Executive Board. The Fund worked closely with the Chinese authorities throughout the 1980s, as both sought to promote the opening up of the Chinese economy and its integration into the world economic system.

Table 1.1. Fund Financial Facilities, 1979–89

Reserve tranche	Available to each member country, subject only to a representation of a balance of payments need. Reserve tranche drawings are not subject to interest charges and need not be repaid.
First credit tranche	Drawings are subject to Fund approval and are conditional on the member cooperating with the Fund to resolve its balance of payments problems.
Emergency disaster relief	Similar to first credit tranche drawings but available in additional amounts. Designed to help countries cope with natural disasters.
Upper credit tranche stand-by arrangements	Drawings are phased over a specified period, subject to quantitative performance criteria and periodic reviews by the Fund.
Extended Fund Facility (EFF)	Similar to ordinary stand-by arrangements except that amounts are generally larger and are made available for longer periods; used for countries with longer-term structural problems.
Compensatory Financing Facility (CFF)	Designed to compensate countries for the economic effects of a temporary shortfall in export earnings or (beginning in 1981) a temporary increase in the cost of importing cereals. Subject to conditionality similar to that for a drawing under the first credit tranche, and to a finding that the problem arose for reasons beyond the authorities' control. Funds could be drawn immediately upon approval.
Compensatory and Contingency Financing Facility (CCFF)	Replaced the CFF in 1988; purpose and terms similar but with the addition of a mechanism to help countries maintain adjustment programs in the face of unanticipated adverse shocks.
Buffer Stock Financing Facility	Helped finance countries' contributions to certain international agreements to maintain buffer stocks of primary commodities.
Trust Fund	A concessional facility financed by profits from the sale of a portion of the Fund's stock of gold. The Trust Fund offered longer-term low-interest loans to low-income countries from 1976 to 1981.
Structural Adjustment Facility (SAF)	A concessional facility established in 1986 as a successor to the Trust Fund, financed primarily from repayments of Trust Fund loans.
Enhanced Structural Adjustment Facility (ESAF)	The successor to the SAF; financed partly from reflows from SAF loans but primarily from loans and grants to the ESAF Trust.

At the Brink of the 1990s

The World Economy

At the close of the decade, a strong record of several years of steady economic growth in industrial countries seemed to be coming to an end. In 1989, the only industrial country with negative growth was New Zealand, which was just beginning a radical new approach to monetary policy in an effort to rid the country of persistent inflationary pressures.[40] But Canada joined the list in 1990, followed by the United States, the United Kingdom, and four others in 1991. Part of the decline was a classical business cycle, as the long upswing from 1983 to 1989 produced an accumulation of sectoral imbalances. That ongoing process was aggravated in 1990 by the economic uncertainties that followed the invasion of Kuwait by Iraq. In contrast to the last widespread recession, however, this time the major countries had room to adjust monetary and fiscal policies, thanks to the absence of any serious threat from inflation. World interest rates fell quickly, and the recession of 1990–91 passed without a global decline in output.

Growth in developing countries was also beginning to slow at the end of the 1980s, in every region except Asia. African economies were still weighted down by weak markets for their commodity exports, and in many cases by ineffective economic policies and other domestic ills. Some of the larger Latin American countries, notably Argentina, Brazil, and Peru, were still stumbling under the hyperinflationary weight of the failed policies of the 1980s. Even before the crisis in Kuwait in 1990, growth in the Middle East was already slowing because of the continuing weakness in international oil prices. On the positive side, more and more countries were laying the preconditions for sustained growth by joining the silent revolution toward more stable and market-oriented economic policies. That movement was already pervasive in east Asia and was beginning to prevail in Latin America, including in the countries just mentioned. Even in sub-Saharan Africa, which had the highest preponderance of state-dominated policies in the late 1980s, the list of countries with reasonably successful policies was clearly lengthening.[41]

Overshadowing these developments was the most significant political shift in the postwar era: the beginning of the end for the Soviet empire and for communism as an international force. While the Soviet government in Moscow was preoccupied with its own economic troubles and with a growing number of

---

[40]The essence of the New Zealand policy innovation of 1989, which followed a gradual move toward economic liberalism and inflation reduction starting in 1984, was a contractual commitment by the governor of the Reserve Bank (Donald T. Brash) to keep the inflation rate within a narrow range (then 0–2 percent) and to free monetary policy from output and employment goals. Despite an initial three years of slight declines in output, the New Zealand approach became a model for central bank independence and contributed to strong growth beginning in 1993. For an official overview, see Spencer and others (1992); for an insider's analysis, see Archer (1997); and for a critical outside view, see Kelsey (1997).

[41]The road to economic success in Africa was still bumpier than elsewhere, and only a few of that continent's 50 countries achieved lasting progress. The May 1990 *World Economic Outlook* cited Ghana, Madagascar, and Uganda as countries where "a significant recovery in economic activity is now underway following fundamental macroeconomic and structural policy reforms," and it also praised Côte d'Ivoire, Nigeria, and Zambia for policy improvements (pp. 12 and 49). Policies in Ghana, Madagascar, and Nigeria were again cited favorably in May 1991, but in that year the other countries mentioned in this context were Kenya, Togo, and Tunisia (p. 14).

ethnic and regional conflicts in several Republics, the dictatorships that controlled its European satellites began to crumble in 1989. In that year and the next, Czechoslovakia, Romania, Poland, Hungary, and Bulgaria held multiparty elections for new governments and brought such already legendary figures as Václav Havel and Lech Wałęsa to power.[42] Massive demonstrations in East Germany (the German Democratic Republic) and an unstoppable emigration of its citizens through a newly open Hungary forced the downfall of the government of Erich Honecker in October 1989, brought down the Berlin Wall in November, and made possible the reunification of Germany less than a year later. The political consequences of these emancipations occurred swiftly. The economic consequences would take longer, as these and other socialist states gradually rejoined the world economic system in the 1990s, but they ultimately would be no less profound.

While eastern Europe was clawing free politically, western Europe was rumbling along toward economic unification. Under the terms of the Single European Act of 1987, the European Union was taking steps to establish the free movement of goods, capital, and labor by the end of 1992. Overcoming initial skepticism about the 1992 timetable, European leaders reached a further agreement in 1989 to end all capital controls within a year. Under the terms of the Basel-Nyborg Agreement of 1987, the European Monetary System was solidifying its commitment to maintaining stable exchange rates and strengthening policy coordination. This process would be severely tested in 1992–93 by speculative attacks against several currencies, but that crisis would turn out to be only a temporary setback to the drive for complete monetary unification.

The Fund

More than ever before, the Fund was at the heart of the international monetary system at the end of the 1980s. Its membership was nearly universal, except for the crumbling sphere of Soviet influence. Its surveillance over member countries' exchange rate and macroeconomic policies, though not yet as effective as it might have been, was universally accepted as an essential element in the system. Demand for its loans and other credits was high and rising: 22 countries were implementing adjustment programs supported by Fund stand-by or extended arrangements, and 29 low-income countries had programs supported by the SAF or the ESAF. Altogether, nearly half of all members (73 out of 152) had outstanding financial obligations to the Fund. To meet the demand without new borrowing by the Fund, a consensus was forming that quotas should be increased substantially and soon. When the debt crisis had erupted in 1982, the Fund's role in defining and organizing the strategy had emerged out of a void. As that crisis ended in 1989, there could be little doubt that the Fund would play a central role in managing the next one.

---

[42]Havel, a well-known dissident playwright and political prisoner, was elected president of Czechoslovakia in 1989. Wałęsa, a leader of the Solidarity movement since 1980, was elected president of Poland in 1990.

How well did the struggles of the 1980s prepare the Fund for the next decade? Future historians will have the luxury and the burden of viewing the period through what Barbara Tuchman called a "distant mirror," and they will thereby gain a perspective that is not available to the post–Bretton Woods generation. At the turn of this century, five implications of the 1980s seem to emerge clearly.

First, successful surveillance and conditionality require partnership. The Fund must understand the political and cultural constraints that are pressing down on a country's economy, and the country must understand the economic realities (macro and distributive) that limit the compass for political action. The mantra for local endorsement or "ownership" of adjustment programs captures only half of this requirement. Unless each side comprehends and even empathizes with the other, the process will fail: the Fund's policy advice will be ignored, and its conditions for lending will not be implemented. The more deeply ingrained the problem, especially when arrears to the Fund are accumulating, the more essential is the need for alliance.

Second, effective surveillance over exchange rate policies does not require a "system" of the Bretton Woods type, but it does require general agreement on the goals of those policies and on the role of the exchange rate in economic policy. Fund surveillance was hampered in the 1980s by a lack of such agreement. With a wide diversity of regimes being tried, ranging from exchange rates still pegged to the value of the U.S. dollar to those floating independently with little or no official intervention, policy advice could only be experimental and would often appear inconsistent. What was needed was a clearly articulated judgment on the circumstances when a country should peg to gain stability and when it should float to maintain international competitiveness. More generally, in dealing with economic systems that ranged from central planning to free and open markets and from pervasive state intervention to an absence of adequate regulation, Fund surveillance aimed to accommodate whatever system prevailed in each country. With neither an internationally accepted policy strategy nor an effective code of good practices on national economic structures, the Fund had to rely on its ability to persuade each country to make marginal improvements within a dizzying variety of regimes. The limitations and frustrations of that experience stimulated professional debate on economic policies in the 1990s and gradually strengthened the resolve of the international community to develop and accept a code of national economic conduct.

Third, private capital markets alone cannot generally achieve a satisfactory and stable response to an international financial crisis. Holders of sovereign debts and other cross-border claims are multifarious, are spread across many countries and regulatory systems, and have diverse interests in the outcome. That lesson was manifest in the 1980s when commercial banks holding large amounts of low-quality sovereign debt attempted to cease rolling over their loans and were able to coordinate agreements with debtors only after the Fund and other official creditors took charge of the process. In such conditions, which may involve severe overreactions to bad economic news, a multilateral arbiter can play a positive and even an essential role in arranging market-friendly solutions. Those solutions, however, require that creditors can be organized for concerted lending or orderly debt reduction. Optimism on that score was reasonably high at the end of the 1980s but deteriorated as capital markets grew more complex in the 1990s.

Fourth, the Fund, as a specialized monetary institution, cannot solve the world's economic problems alone. The reliance of many low-income countries on short- and medium-term financing from the Fund in the early 1980s and the attempt by many middle-income developing countries to rely on macroeconomic policy reforms in the mid-1980s exposed weaknesses in the coordination of multilateral assistance. Efforts by the Fund, the World Bank, and other agencies to collaborate more fully in the second half of the decade were only partially successful. That effort did, however, help prepare the institutions for the much greater level of coordination that would be needed in the 1990s, when countries in transition from central planning would have to make comprehensive structural and macroeconomic reforms in a very short period of time.

Fifth, the effectiveness of the Fund's financial assistance depends on the recipient countries committing to implement both macro and structural economic reforms. Throughout the 1980s, the Fund circumscribed its own scope for action by limiting explicit conditionality to macroeconomic policies and avoiding interference with policies that could be construed as politically rather than economically motivated. The initial successes of countries that liberalized policies on their own—the silent revolution—drew the Fund out of that reluctance in ways that would enable it to play a more active role in promoting structural reform in the 1990s.

Whether this last lesson—that macro and structural reforms go hand in hand—fully applies in general or was merely a circumstance of the 1980s cannot yet be judged. All of the countries with substantial debt problems in the 1980s had readily identifiable macro and structural imbalances that required major corrections. In the following decade, many countries were forced to reconsider the scope and speed of economic liberalization and focus instead on more mundane structural issues such as the regulation and soundness of financial systems. Moreover, nothing in the experience of the 1980s prepared countries or institutions for a financial crisis when macro policies were reasonable ex ante. The scale and breadth of the flow of capital into developing countries with fledgling financial markets after 1990 raised the possibility of a new type of financial crisis—and a first glimpse into the 21st century—in which the solutions of the 1980s could be no more than a platform from which to jump into the void.

The international flow of capital in the 1990s was a product of the confluence of three great events of the late 1980s: the successful conclusion of the debt strategy for middle-income developing countries, the silent revolution in policymaking, and an acceleration in the globalization of capital markets. As positive as those developments must be in the long run, it should not have been surprising that they had destabilizing effects in the short run. The oil and dollar shocks of the 1970s flowed inexorably from the policies and problems of the 1960s, exploded into new crises that required fresh solutions, and ultimately forced policymakers to adopt more open policies. The debt shock of the 1980s was merely the next wave in this course of economic history.

Appendix: Chronology, 1979–89

Date	World Events	Activities of the Fund
1979		
January	World petroleum prices begin sharp rise following the overthrow of the Shah of Iran by forces loyal to the Ayatollah Khomeini. Vietnamese forces overthrow the regime of Pol Pot in Cambodia (then known as Democratic Kampuchea) and rename the country the People's Republic of Kampuchea. The United States extends full diplomatic recognition to the People's Republic of China.	Third Basic Period of SDR allocations begins with the first allocation of SDRs since 1972 supplementary surveillance procedure introduced.
February		Supplementary Financing Facility (SFF) becomes effective, as the Fund borrows SDR 7.8 billion from 14 official creditors to supplement resources from quotas.
March	Margaret Thatcher elected Prime Minister of the United Kingdom, replacing James Callaghan; pound sterling begins major period of appreciation in response to monetary restriction and rising oil production. European Monetary System (EMS) is formed; the ECU is created as a common currency unit in the European Community (EC).	Major review of conditionality results in greater flexibility and concern for circumstances of individual countries. Interim Committee asks Executive Board to consider establishing a substitution account for converting foreign exchange reserves into SDRs.
April	Tokyo Round of multilateral trade negotiations concluded.	
June	Second oil shock initiated at OPEC ministerial meeting. Idi Amin Dada overthrown as Head of State in Uganda.	
August		Liberalization of the Compensatory Financing Facility (CFF) to provide for larger loans to countries facing temporary declines in merchandise exports.

Appendix *(continued)*

Date	World Events	Activities of the Fund
September	First of 11 realignments of EMS parities in which one or more currencies will be devalued relative to the deutsche mark. Sixth Summit of Non-Aligned Nations, in Havana, calls for "global negotiations" to give the UN General Assembly control over the IMF. Jean-Bédel Bokassa overthrown as Head of State in the Central African Republic.	
October	U.S. Federal Reserve adopts new operating procedures designed to get tighter control over monetary growth. President of Korea, General Park Chung-Hee, assassinated.	Interim Committee, meeting in Belgrade, urges industrial countries to pursue vigorous anti-inflationary policies; asks Executive Board to develop specific proposals for a substitution account.
November		Financing to Jamaica under the Extended Fund Facility (EFF) and the CFF brings Fund's holdings of Jamaican dollars to 462 percent of quota, a record for any country up to this time.
December	Soviet Union invades Afghanistan.	Liberalization of the EFF to allow countries to repay loans in ten years instead of eight.
1980		
January	Price of gold peaks at more than $850 an ounce.	
March	Robert G. Mugabe elected Prime Minister of Rhodesia, which is renamed Zimbabwe.	
April		People's Republic of China assumes China's seat. Kuwait accepts participation in the SDR Department; from this date, all Fund members are participants. Meeting in Hamburg, the Interim Committee decides not to establish a substitution account.

Appendix *(continued)*

Date	World Events	Activities of the Fund
May	Yugoslav President Josip Broz Tito dies.	Final sale of Fund gold under program that began in 1976; 24 million ounces had been sold for a total of $4.6 billion, leaving the Fund holding 103 million ounces.
		First publication of the *World Economic Outlook*.
June	Issuance of the "Arusha Initiative" by a conference in Tanzania, calling for major reforms in the Fund.	
September	Beginning of war between Iran and Iraq, which will continue for the rest of the decade.	Zimbabwe, newly independent, becomes the 141st member of the Fund.
November		Quotas under Seventh Review become effective, raising total quotas by just over 50 percent.
December		Subsidy account established for the SFF to reduce charges to low-income countries.
1981		
January	Ronald Reagan assumes office as President of the United States, replacing Jimmy Carter; proposes major tax cuts.	Final SDR allocation under Third Basic Period; SDR converted to five-currency basket.
	Greece joins the European Communities.	
March		Enlarged Access policy introduced; permits longer adjustment programs and increased access to Fund resources, and formalizes relationship between use of ordinary resources and use of borrowed funds.
April		Trust Fund lending program completed; assets transferred to the SFF subsidy account.
		Reconstitution requirement on SDR holdings abrogated.

Appendix *(continued)*

Date	World Events	Activities of the Fund
May	François Mitterrand elected President of France, replacing Valéry Giscard d'Estaing.	Saudi Arabia's quota is approximately doubled, and the Fund establishes SDR 8 billion borrowing arrangement with the Saudi Arabian Monetary Agency (SAMA) to finance the Enlarged Access policy.
		Cereals-imports facility established within the CFF.
		SDR interest rate set equal to combined market interest rate, ending the practice of setting it below market rates.
August		Borrowing arrangement agreed with BIS and central banks of industrial countries.
October	North-South summit meeting in Cancún, Mexico.	
November		Hungary and Poland apply for membership.
		EFF arrangement approved for India; at SDR 5 billion, the largest loan commitment in Fund history until 1995.
December	Declaration of martial law in Poland.	Membership discussions with Poland suspended.
	Formation of Preferential Trade Area for Eastern and Southern African States (forerunner of Common Market for Eastern and Southern Africa).	First SFF subsidy payments are made, to 21 low-income countries.
1982		
April	Three-month war begins between the United Kingdom and Argentina.	
May		Hungary joins IMF, begins negotiations for a stand-by arrangement.
June		Summit conference of the leaders of the Group of Seven (G-7) industrial countries at Versailles establishes a multilateral surveillance process with informal participation by the IMF Managing Director.

Appendix (*continued*)

Date	World Events	Activities of the Fund
July	Penn Square Bank fails in the United States, raising fears of similar problems in other major U.S. banks.	
	U.S. Federal Reserve shifts away from the restrictive policies that had contributed to record-high levels of real interest rates.	
August	Mexico unable to meet principal payments on bank debt; emergency rescue package assembled.	
	Liquidation of Banco Ambrosiano in Italy, owing to massive losses by its Luxembourg and offshore subsidiaries, raises concerns about stability of eurocurrency markets.	
September		Annual Meetings in Toronto; initial surveillance meeting between the Managing Director and the G-5 finance ministers.
October	Helmut Kohl elected Chancellor of Germany, replacing Helmut Schmidt.	
	Sweden devalues by 16 percent against a basket of currencies, triggering concerns in neighboring countries.	
December	Miguel de la Madrid inaugurated as President of Mexico.	EFF arrangement approved for Mexico, for SDR 3.4 billion; conditional on $5 billion new money package from banks.
		Supplementary surveillance procedure applied to the Swedish devaluation.
1983		
January		General Arrangements to Borrow (GAB) expanded.
		Stand-by and CFF loan approved for Argentina, for SDR 2 billion.
February		EFF arrangement approved for Brazil, for SDR 4.2 billion.
		Interim Committee approves quota increases, completing the Eighth General Review.

Appendix (*continued*)

Date	World Events	Activities of the Fund
March	French government shifts policy from expansion to stabilization.	Information Notice System introduced for large changes in real effective exchange rates.
June	G-7 summit at Williamsburg commissions a G-10 report on the international monetary system.	Jacques de Larosière begins a second five-year term as Managing Director.
July		Fund holdings of Jamaican dollars reach a record 653 percent of quota.
August		Oil Facility terminated.
September		Conditionality requirements are tightened for CFF loans.
October	United States invades Grenada after the government is overthrown in a coup.	
November		Quotas under Eighth General Review become effective.
December	Raúl Alfonsín elected President of Argentina, ending seven years of military rule.	
1984 April		Switzerland joins the GAB.
June	Bolivia suspends payments on external bank debt. Latin American leaders meet in Cartagena, Colombia, and set a strategy for resolving debt crisis without defaulting.	Richard D. Erb becomes the Fund's fifth Deputy Managing Director, succeeding William B. Dale.
July		Enhanced surveillance applied for first time, through decision to release staff report on Mexico to commercial bank creditors in order to promote agreement on multiyear rescheduling of debt.
September	Brian Mulroney elected Prime Minister of Canada. ECU currency basket revised, and Greek drachma added to it.	

Appendix *(continued)*

Date	World Events	Activities of the Fund
1985		
January	Brazil holds its first democratic election for President since 1964.	Vietnam becomes first country to be declared ineligible to use Fund resources owing to arrears.
February	Effective U.S. dollar exchange rate peaks, culminating a five-year appreciation.	
March	Mikhail S. Gorbachev becomes Head of State of the Soviet Union.	
	José Sarney assumes office as President of Brazil.	
April	Paris Club completes first MYRA, for Ecuador.	Fund records first annual budget deficit since 1977, owing to rise in arrears.
July	Alan García assumes office as President of Peru and announces debt-service limits that will result in arrears to the Fund and other creditors.	
September	Saudi Arabia abandons role as swing producer in OPEC, starts major oil price decline in motion.	
	G-5 meeting at Plaza Hotel.	
October	Baker-Miyazawa accord on interest rate policy.	Annual Meetings in Seoul; Baker Plan introduced; G-10 and G-24 reports submitted to Interim Committee.
December	Gramm-Rudman-Hollings deficit reduction act passed by U.S. Congress.	
1986		
January	Spain and Portugal join the EC.	
	Yoweri Museveni becomes President of Uganda.	
February	Corazon Aquino elected President of the Philippines, ending more than two decades of rule by Ferdinand Marcos.	
	Jean-Claude Duvalier overthrown as President of Haiti.	
	Single European Act signed; sets December 31, 1992 as deadline for economic integration of Europe.	

Appendix *(continued)*

Date	World Events	Activities of the Fund
March		Structural Adjustment Facility (SAF) established.
April	Major reactor accident at Chernobyl nuclear power plant in Ukraine.	
May	G-7 summit in Tokyo marks commitment to policy cooperation; President Mitterrand proposes debt concessions for poorest countries.	
June		Poland becomes 151st member.
September	Uruguay Round of trade negotiations launched at Punta del Este. U.S. federal government finishes fiscal year with record budget deficit of $238 billion.	Formal procedures adopted for conduct of enhanced surveillance.
1987 January	Paris Club of official creditors agrees to consider rescheduling requests for countries with SAF loans, rather than requiring a stand-by arrangement. Last EMS realignment of the decade.	Michel Camdessus becomes the Fund's seventh Managing Director, following the resignation of Jacques de Larosière.
February	Louvre Accord issued by six of the G-7 countries.	
May	Citibank sets aside $3 billion as a provision against potential losses on loans to developing countries.	
June	G-7 summit in Venice formalizes Fund role in assisting the policy coordination process.	
July	Single European Act takes effect, leading to economic integration in the EC by the end of 1992.	Access limits raised for SAF loans. Work begins on Ninth General Review of quotas.
August	Argentina signs the first restructuring agreement with commercial banks that incorporates the expanded menu approach.	
September	Basel-Nyborg Agreement strengthens the EMS and leads to greater currency stability in Europe.	
October	Global stock market crash.	

Appendix (*continued*)

Date	World Events	Activities of the Fund
November	Latin American leaders meet in Acapulco, Mexico; issue declaration on cooperative debt strategy.	
December		Enhanced Structural Adjustment Facility (ESAF) established.
1988		
January	United States and Canada sign Free Trade Agreement, to take effect in January 1989.	
June	G-7 summit in Toronto endorses debt-concession proposals ("Toronto terms").	
	EC agrees to lift all capital controls by July 1990.	
July	G-10 governors endorse Cooke Committee recommendations on capital standards for banks.	
August		CFF replaced by an expanded facility, the Compensatory and Contingency Financing Facility (CCFF).
September		Last repayment to the Buffer Stock Financing Facility, by Côte d'Ivoire.
October	Punta del Este declaration on debt strategy by seven heads of state in Latin America. Paris Club, implementing the Toronto Terms, introduces expanded menu of policies for debt relief to poorest countries. In the restoration of democracy in Chile, General Augusto Pinochet loses a plebiscite and is required to relinquish the presidency by 1990.	Interim Committee, meeting in Berlin, endorses debt reduction as part of menu approach; also endorses the "intensified collaborative approach" for dealing with arrears.
December	Benazir Bhutto becomes Prime Minister of Pakistan. Carlos Salinas inaugurated as President of Mexico.	

Appendix *(continued)*

Date	World Events	Activities of the Fund
1989		
February	General Alfredo Stroessner overthrown as President of Paraguay.	
	Soviet Union completes its withdrawal of troops from Afghanistan.	
March		U.S. Treasury Secretary Nicholas Brady proposes debt reduction scheme; Camdessus notes negative effects from large debt stocks in address to IBD annual meeting.
		Administered account established for Japanese contributions in support of the collaborative approach to settling arrears.
April	Polish government concludes "Round Table" talks, legalizes Solidarity, and agrees to hold free elections.	
May		Executive Board adopts guidelines on supporting debt reduction schemes. First Brady Plan programs completed, with Costa Rica, the Philippines, and Mexico; 25 percent (30 percent for Mexico) of purchases to be set aside for debt reduction.
June	EC summit meeting in Madrid receives report of the Delors Committee, recommending steps leading to full monetary union for member countries.	
	Spain joins the Exchange Rate Mechanism of the EMS.	
	Solidarity wins elections in Poland, leading to a non-Communist government headed by Tadeusz Mazowiecki.	
	Crackdown against prodemocracy demonstrations in Tiananmen Square, Beijing.	

Appendix *(concluded)*

Date	World Events	Activities of the Fund
September	ECU currency basket revised, and Spanish peseta and Portuguese escudo added to it.	Angola becomes the 152nd member of the Fund; all countries in Africa are now members of the Fund except Namibia, which will join in 1990.
	Vietnam withdraws from Cambodia.	
November	Berlin Wall dismantled, effectively ending the Cold War.	
	Inaugural ministerial meeting of the 12-nation Asia-Pacific Economic Cooperation (APEC).	
December	Overthrow of Nicolae Ceauşescu as Head of State in Romania.	
	Election of Václav Havel as President of Czechoslovakia, concluding the "Velvet Revolution."	
	U.S. troops invade Panama.	

References

Aghevli, Bijan B., James M. Boughton, Peter Montiel, Delano Villanueva, and Geoffrey Woglom, 1990, *The Role of National Saving in the World Economy: Recent Trends and Prospects*, IMF Occasional Paper No. 67 (Washington: International Monetary Fund).

Allen, Mark, and others, 1989, *International Capital Markets: Developments and Prospects* (Washington: International Monetary Fund).

Archer, David J., 1997, "The New Zealand Approach to Rules and Discretion in Monetary Policy," *Journal of Monetary Economics*, Vol. 39 (June), pp. 3–15.

Atkinson, A.B., 1996, "Income Distribution in Europe and the United States," *Oxford Review of Economic Policy*, Vol. 12 (spring), pp. 15–28.

Bayoumi, Tamim, 1990, "Saving-Investment Correlations: Immobile Capital, Government Policy, or Endogenous Behavior?" *Staff Papers*, International Monetary Fund, Vol. 37 (June), pp. 360–87.

Bennett, Paul, and Jeanette Kelleher, 1988, "The International Transmission of Stock Price Disruption in October 1987," *Quarterly Review*, Federal Reserve Bank of New York, Vol. 13 (summer), pp. 17–33.

Boote, Anthony R., and Kamau Thugge, 1998, *Debt Relief for Low-Income Countries: The HIPC Initiative*, IMF Pamphlet Series, No. 51 (Washington: International Monetary Fund).

Boughton, James M., 1984, "Exchange Rate Movements and Adjustment in Financial Markets: Quarterly Estimates for Major Currencies," *Staff Papers*, International Monetary Fund, Vol. 31 (September), pp. 445–68.

———, 1987, "Tests of the Performance of Reduced-Form Exchange Rate Models," *Journal of International Economics*, Vol. 23 (August), pp. 41–56.

———, 1988, *The Monetary Approach to Exchange Rates: What Now Remains?* Essays in International Finance, No. 171 (Princeton, New Jersey: International Finance Section, Department of Economics, Princeton University).

————, 1991, "Commodity and Manufactures Prices in the Long Run," IMF Working Paper 91/47 (Washington: International Monetary Fund).

————, 2000, "From Suez to Tequila: The IMF as Crisis Manager," *Economic Journal*, Vol. 110 (January), pp. 273–91.

Bruno, Michael, and Jeffrey D. Sachs, 1985, *The Economics of Worldwide Stagflation* (Cambridge, Massachusetts: Harvard University Press).

Buiter, Willem, and Marcus Miller, 1981, "Monetary Policy and International Competitiveness," *Oxford Economic Papers*, Vol. 33 (July), pp. 143–75.

Canto, Victor A., Douglas H. Joines, and Arthur B. Laffer, 1983, *Foundations of Supply-Side Economics: Theory and Evidence* (New York: Academic Press).

Cooper, Richard N., 1982, "The Gold Standard: Historical Facts and Future Prospects," *Brookings Papers on Economic Activity: 1*, Brookings Institution, pp. 1–56.

Corden, W. Max, 1986, "Fiscal Policies, Current Accounts and Real Exchange Rates: In Search of a Logic of International Policy Coordination," *Weltwirtschaftliches Archiv*, Vol. 122, No. 3, pp. 423–38.

————, 1987, "How Valid is International Keynesianism?" IMF Working Paper 87/56 (Washington: International Monetary Fund).

————, 1994, *Economic Policy, Exchange Rates, and the International System* (Chicago: University of Chicago Press).

de Boissieu, Christian, 1996, "Stability in a Multiple Reserve Asset System," in *The Future of the SDR in Light of Changes in the International Financial System: Proceedings of a Seminar Held in Washington, D.C., March 18–19, 1996*, ed. by Michael Mussa, James M. Boughton, and Peter Isard (Washington: International Monetary Fund), pp. 122–44.

de Vries, Margaret Garritsen, 1976, *The International Monetary Fund, 1966–1971: The System Under Stress*, Vol. 1: *Narrative*; Vol. 2: *Documents* (Washington: International Monetary Fund).

————, 1985, *The International Monetary Fund, 1972–1978: Cooperation on Trial*, Vols. 1 and 2: *Narrative and Analysis*; Vol. 3: *Documents* (Washington: International Monetary Fund).

Duisenberg, W.F., and A. Szász, 1991, "The Monetary Character of the IMF," in *International Financial Policy: Essays in Honor of Jacques J. Polak*, ed. by Jacob A. Frenkel and Morris Goldstein (Washington: International Monetary Fund and De Nederlandsche Bank), pp. 254–66.

Dunaway, Steven, and others, 1995, *Private Market Financing for Developing Countries*, World Economic and Financial Surveys (Washington: International Monetary Fund, March).

Feldstein, Martin, 1986, "Supply Side Economics: Old Truths and New Claims," *American Economic Review: Papers and Proceedings*, Vol. 76 (May), pp. 26–30.

Flood, Robert P., and Peter M. Garber, 1994, *Speculative Bubbles, Speculative Attacks, and Policy Switching* (Cambridge, Massachusetts: MIT Press).

Frenkel, Jacob A., and Morris Goldstein, 1996, "Macroeconomic Policy Implications of Currency Zones," in *Functioning of the International Monetary System*, ed. by Jacob A. Frenkel and Morris Goldstein (Washington: International Monetary Fund), pp. 420–65.

————, and Paul R. Masson, 1991, *Characteristics of a Successful Exchange Rate System*, IMF Occasional Paper No. 82 (Washington: International Monetary Fund).

Friedman, Milton, 1968, *Dollars and Deficits: Inflation, Monetary Policy, and the Balance of Payments* (Englewood Cliffs, New Jersey: Prentice-Hall).

————, 1970, "A Theoretical Framework for Monetary Analysis," *Journal of Political Economy*, Vol. 78 (March/April), pp. 193–238. Reprinted in *Milton Friedman's Monetary Framework: A Debate with His Critics*, ed. by Robert J. Gordon (Chicago and London: University of Chicago Press, 1974), pp. 1–62.

Goldstein, Morris, and Mohsin S. Khan, 1982, *Effects of Slowdown in Industrial Countries on Growth in Non-Oil Developing Countries*, IMF Occasional Paper No. 12 (Washington: International Monetary Fund).

Greider, William, 1987, *Secrets of the Temple: How the Federal Reserve Runs the Country* (New York: Simon and Schuster).

Hahn, Frank, and Robert Solow, 1995, *A Critical Essay on Modern Macroeconomic Theory* (Cambridge, Massachusetts: MIT Press).

Hall, Robert Ernest, 1982, *Inflation: Causes and Effects* (Chicago: University of Chicago Press).

Horsefield, J. Keith, ed., 1969, *The International Monetary Fund, 1945–1965: Twenty Years of International Monetary Cooperation*, Vol. 1: *Chronicle*, by J. Keith Horsefield; Vol. 2: *Analysis*, by Margaret G. de Vries and J. Keith Horsefield with the collaboration of Joseph Gold, Mary H. Gumbart, Gertrud Lovasy, and Emil G. Spitzer; Vol. 3: *Documents* (Washington: International Monetary Fund).

International Monetary Fund, *Summary Proceedings* (Washington: IMF, various issues).

———, 1990, *World Economic Outlook: A Survey by the Staff of the International Monetary Fund*, World Economic and Financial Surveys (Washington).

International Monetary Fund, Commodities Division, Research Department, 1990, *Primary Commodities: Market Developments and Outlook*, World Economic and Financial Surveys (Washington).

Isard, Peter, 1978, *Exchange-Rate Determination: A Survey of Popular Views and Recent Models*, Studies in International Finance, No. 42 (Princeton, New Jersey: International Finance Section, Department of Economics, Princeton University).

James, Harold, 1996, *International Monetary Cooperation Since Bretton Woods* (New York: Oxford University Press; Washington: International Monetary Fund).

Kelsey, Jane, 1997, *The New Zealand Experiment: A World Model for Structural Adjustment?* (Auckland: Auckland University Press).

Kojima, Kiyoshi, 1990, "Proposal for a Multiple Key Currency Gold-Exchange Standard," *Journal of Asian Economics*, Vol. 1 (spring), pp. 19–33.

Krueger, Anne O., 1993, *Political Economy of Policy Reform in Developing Countries* (Cambridge, Massachusetts: MIT Press).

Lavín, Joaquín I., 1987, *Chile, Revolución Silenciosa* (Santiago, Chile: Zig-Zag). Also available in English translation by Clara Iriberry and Elena Soloduchim, *Chile, A Quiet Revolution* (Santiago, Chile: Zig-Zag, 1988).

Lawson, Nigel, 1992, *The View from No. 11: Memoirs of a Tory Radical* (London: Bantam Press).

Lehrman, Lewis E., and Ron Paul, 1982, *The Case for Gold: A Minority Report of the U.S. Gold Commission* (Washington: Cato Institute).

Leijonhuvud, Axel, 1968, *On Keynesian Economics and the Economics of Keynes: A Study in Monetary Theory* (New York: Oxford University Press).

Mayer, H.W., 1982, "International Banking Flows and Their Implications for Domestic Monetary Policy," in *Recent Developments in the Economic Analysis of the Euro-Markets*, by the BIS (Basel: Bank for International Settlements), pp. 41–83.

McCracken, Paul, and others, 1977, *Towards Full Employment and Price Stability: A Report to the OECD by a Group of Independent Experts* (Paris: OECD).

McGuire, Martin C., and Mancur Olson, Jr., 1996, "The Economics of Autocracy and Majority Rule: The Invisible Hand and the Use of Force," *Journal of Economic Literature*, Vol. 34 (March), pp. 72–96.

Meese, Richard A., 1986, "Testing for Bubbles in Exchange Markets: A Case of Sparkling Rates?" *Journal of Political Economy*, Vol. 94 (April), pp. 345–73.

———, and Kenneth Rogoff, 1983, "Empirical Exchange Rate Models of the Seventies: Do They Fit Out of Sample?" *Journal of International Economics*, Vol. 14 (February), pp. 3–24.

Miller, Marcus H., and John Williamson, 1987, *Targets and Indicators: A Blueprint for the International Coordination of Economic Policy* (Washington: Institute for International Economics).

Mirowski, Philip, 1982, "What's Wrong with the Laffer Curve?" *Journal of Economic Issues*, Vol. 16 (September), pp. 815–28.

Monti, Mario, ed., 1976, *The New Inflation and Monetary Policy* (London; New York: Macmillan).

Mundell, Robert A., 1983, "Rally 'Round the Gold Standard," *Barron's* (March 14), pp. 8–9 and 34–35.

Mussa, Michael, 1994, "U.S. Monetary Policy in the 1980s," in *American Economic Policy in the 1980s*, ed. By Martin Feldstein (Chicago: University of Chicago Press), pp. 81–145.

Myrdal, Gunnar, 1968, *Asian Drama: An Inquiry into the Poverty of Nations* (New York: Twentieth Century Fund).

Prebisch, Raúl, 1984, "Five Stages in My Thinking on Development," in *Pioneers in Development*, ed. by Gerald M. Meier and Dudley Seers (New York; published for the World Bank: Oxford University Press), pp. 175–91.

Quirk, Peter J., Owen Evans, and others, 1995, *Capital Account Convertibility: Review of Experience and Implications for IMF Policies*, IMF Occasional Paper No. 131 (Washington: International Monetary Fund).

Rodrik, Dani, 1996, "Understanding Economic Policy Reform," *Journal of Economic Literature*, Vol. 34 (March), pp. 9–41.

Smithin, John N., 1990, *Macroeconomics After Thatcher and Reagan: The Conservative Policy Revolution in Retrospect* (Brookfield, Vermont: Edward Elgar).

Solomon, Robert, 1982, *The International Monetary System, 1945–1981* (New York: Harper and Row).

———, 1999a, *Money on the Move: The Revolution in International Finance Since 1980* (Princeton, New Jersey: Princeton University Press).

———, 1999b, *The Transformation of the World Economy* (New York: St. Martin's Press, 2nd ed.).

Sparks, Samantha, 1988, "Camdessus' Quiet Revolution," *South*, Vol. 95 (September), pp. 20–21.

Spencer, Grant, and others, 1992, *Monetary Policy and the New Zealand Financial System* (Wellington, New Zealand: Reserve Bank of New Zealand, 3rd ed.).

Tobin, James, 1972, "Inflation and Unemployment," *American Economic Review*, Vol. 62 (March), pp. 1–18.

———, 1980, *Asset Accumulation and Economic Activity: Reflections on Contemporary Economic Theory* (Oxford: Basil Blackwell).

———, 1987, "Inflation Control as Social Priority," conference paper presented in October 1976, in *Policies for Prosperity: Essays in a Keynesian Mode*, ed. by P.M. Jackson (Cambridge, Massachusetts: MIT Press), pp. 340–47.

Ungerer, Horst, 1997, *A Concise History of European Monetary Integration: From EPU to EMU* (Westport, Connecticut: Quorum Books).

Wanniski, Jude, 1983, *The Way the World Works* (New York: Simon and Schuster, rev. and updated ed.).

Williamson, John, ed., 1990, *Latin American Adjustment: How Much Has Happened?* (Washington: Institute for International Economics).

Williamson, John, and Stephan Haggard, 1994, "The Political Conditions for Economic Reform," in *The Political Economy of Policy Reform*, ed. by John Williamson (Washington: Institute for International Economics), pp. 527–96.

World Bank, 1991, *The Challenge of Development*, World Development Report (Oxford: Oxford University Press).

Zanello, Alessandro, and Dominique Desruelle, 1997, "A Primer on the IMF's Information Notice System," IMF Working Paper 97/71 (Washington: International Monetary Fund).

I

Revolutions in the International Monetary System

2

On the Map:
Making Surveillance Work

Surveillance, a central pillar of IMF activities and responsibilities in the modern era, is not an easy concept to grasp. Jacob A. Frenkel, a former Economic Counsellor at the Fund, has called it "a terrible word [that] . . . gives the impression of a policeman chasing criminals [or] . . . that somebody is looking after somebody, typically in a patronizing way." Surveillance, in his view, "should give way to concepts of cooperation, partnership, and consultation; of bringing on board the rest of the world's considerations." (Boughton and Lateef, 1995, pp. 238–39.) In practice, surveillance has encapsulated all of the above notions, but at its best it has been motivated by and has itself promoted a spirit of international cooperation.[1]

Surveillance was a latecomer to the Fund's lexicon. The first official use of the term came in the final report of the Committee of Twenty, issued in June 1974: "Fund consultation and surveillance regarding the adjustment process will take place at two levels, the Executive Board and the Council. . . ."[2] Four years later, the concept was enshrined in the Second Amendment to the Fund's Articles of Agreement: ". . . the Fund shall exercise firm surveillance over the exchange rate policies of members, and shall adopt specific principles for the guidance of all members with respect to those policies" (Article IV, Section 3(b); for the full text of the Article, see the Appendix to this chapter). Surveillance thus was to comprise both consultations with each member country on exchange rate and macroeconomic policies and analysis of the functioning of the international

---

[1]For a political science perspective on the nature of Fund surveillance, see Pauly (1997). Pauly explains the self-interest of states in submitting to surveillance by analyzing the process as an inherently ambiguous but still substantive means for states to cope with the conflict between the political ideal of national sovereignty and the economic ideal of global integration.

[2]"Final Report and Outline of Reform of the Committee of Twenty"; de Vries (1985), Vol. 3, pp. 165–96. The quoted passage is from paragraph 5 of the report, p. 168. The Committee of Twenty was the committee of IMF governors established in 1972 to negotiate reforms in the international monetary system. The Council mentioned in this passage was not established, and the role envisaged for that body was played by the Interim Committee. The term "surveillance" had long been used informally and internally at the Fund to describe the (largely futile) effort to assert a significant role for the institution in previewing proposals to change par values under the Bretton Woods system. James (1995), which provides a general history of the development of surveillance at the Fund, cites a 1964 report by the Group of Ten as the "first use of the term in discussions about the international economy" (p. 767).

monetary system and of the policy requirements for achieving a stable system of exchange rates.

It is clear from the record of the deliberations on the Second Amendment in the mid-1970s that the Fund's governors did not agree on the precise meaning of "firm surveillance" and even that the phrase was introduced as a substitute for agreement on a more precise reform of the exchange rate system. Those (notably U.S. officials) who sought a flexible system in which exchange rates could adjust freely in response to market forces saw surveillance as a means of discouraging countries from manipulating exchange rates in opposition to market pressures. Those (notably French officials) who sought greater stability in exchange rates saw it as a means of encouraging countries to adopt economic policies that would ensure such stability. Both sides recognized that the principles and procedures of surveillance would have to be worked out gradually through experience.[3]

The original purpose of surveillance was to ensure that each member country complied with its new obligations after the Second Amendment. Those obligations included notably "to collaborate with the Fund and with other members in order to assure orderly exchange arrangements and to promote a stable system of exchange rates" (Article IV, Section 1). Later, additional objectives for surveillance would be identified, and by the late 1990s the Fund was being asked to use surveillance to identify economies where financial crises might occur and to report to the membership and to the general public on the soundness of each economy and of each country's economic policies. In the 1980s, public dissemination of the findings from Article IV consultations was not generally seen as desirable, because of concerns that it could compromise the forthrightness and effectiveness of the confidential discussions.

Until the Jamaica accords of January 1976, when the Interim Committee agreed on the text of the amended Articles, the goal of the discussions on surveillance was to define a new way of stabilizing exchange rates without the central anchors of gold and a stable U.S. dollar.[4] After that effort failed, the goal became to implement Fund surveillance in a firm and effective manner so as to ensure that exchange rates would reflect underlying or "fundamental" economic conditions. Few if any countries, however, were prepared to be subjected to surveillance in that

---

[3]The basic reference on the negotiations is de Vries (1985), Parts Two (on the Committee of Twenty) and Eight (on the amendments to the Articles). Also see Chapter 4, pp. 190–91, below; James (1996), Chapters 9 and 10; and the papers by Boughton and James in *Comité pour l'Histoire Économique et Financière* (1998).

[4]This point was stated most clearly in the final report of the Committee of Twenty (June 1974): "The main features of the international monetary reform will include . . . better functioning of the exchange rate mechanism, with the exchange regime based on stable but adjustable par values and with floating rates recognized as providing a useful technique *in particular situations*" (emphasis added). The Jamaica communiqué (January 1976) tacitly acknowledged that floating would play a more pervasive role, and it concluded that stability would derive from underlying conditions, not from the form of the system: "The new system [of exchange arrangements] recognizes an *objective* of stability and relates it to achievement of greater underlying stability in economic and financial factors" (emphasis again added). See de Vries (1985), Vol. 3, pp. 167 and 227, respectively.

strong sense. The 1980s therefore became a decade of experimentation, in which the staff and management of the Fund constantly probed and prodded to see how far they could go in persuading countries to respond positively to Fund analysis and advice.

This chapter recounts the various efforts by the Fund in the period through 1989 to put some flesh on the bones of Article IV. It was not an easy task either to develop the right advice or to reach effective agreements, and the efforts often were not successful. Although the limitations to surveillance were easy to identify, the solutions frequently required political commitments that—usually for very good reasons—countries were not prepared to make. By the mid-1990s, partly because of the success of the "silent revolution" and partly because of the galvanizing influence of the 1994–95 financial crisis in Mexico, the world's economic policymakers were more prepared to subject themselves to a code of conduct and to quantifiable standards. The adoption of a series of "declarations" on desirable policy standards by the Interim Committee in 1993–96, the gradual opening up of surveillance conclusions to public scrutiny, the acceptance by many countries from all regions of the world to a Fund-established standard for the dissemination of economic data, the intensification of the Executive Board's direct scrutiny of countries' exchange rate policies: all made Fund surveillance a more effective process.

The backbone of surveillance after the Second Amendment was to be a regular cycle of consultations with each member country. The Fund was already holding consultations with members, originally (starting in 1952) under authority of Article XIV, the article that enabled members to maintain certain exchange restrictions temporarily, provided that they agreed to consult regularly with the Fund "as to their further retention." For the first decade, annual consultations were held only with members still operating under the transitional provisions. Starting in 1961, the Fund also held regular consultations with countries that were not under Article XIV, but on a strictly voluntary basis and with no formal conclusions by the Executive Board.[5] The intent of the new Article IV adopted in 1978 was to formalize, extend, and strengthen that process and to aim it at the goal of stabilizing the exchange rate system. (For more on exchange restrictions and Article XIV, see the section in this chapter on Reducing Exchange Restrictions.)

Although the Fund was not given any special powers to enforce its policy advice to nonborrowing countries, it did have a measure of influence in the international community. If surveillance was to have any substance, the Fund would have to develop that influence: through the power of persuasion (Fund management and staff to country authorities), through peer pressure (country to country in the forum of the Fund), and through publicity (Fund to the public). The relative merit

---

[5]The Executive Board enacted a decision on June 1, 1960, providing for voluntary consultations with countries that had accepted the obligations of Article VIII. The first such consultation was held in August 1961, with the United Kingdom. See Horsefield (1969), Vol. 1, pp. 479–82; Vol. 2, pp. 246–48; and Vol. 3, pp. 260–61.

of each of these channels was always the subject of much debate. Was publicity appropriate, or would it conflict with and even nullify the benefits of persuasion and peer pressure? Did surveillance mean that the IMF was expected to be a financial Interpol, seeking out and punishing errant behavior, or should its role be more that of a faithful confidant of those entrusted with implementing macroeconomic policies around the world? Even among IMF staff, those questions did not yield uniform answers.[6]

Aside from the general problem of how to make surveillance consultations effective, an important concern for the Fund in designing a strategy for surveillance was to make it evenhanded for all member countries: large and small, surplus and deficit, floaters and peggers. That last dimension was especially troublesome. After the collapse of the par value exchange rate system in the early 1970s, countries around the world adopted a wide variety of exchange arrangements. What defined the system, of course, was the decision of the largest countries—the United States, Japan, and Germany—to let their exchange rates float vis-à-vis one another. For those countries, the implicit primary task of Fund surveillance was to evaluate whether their macroeconomic policies were unstable or unsustainable to the point that they might detract from the stability of the exchange rate system. Many smaller countries chose to peg their exchange rates to a single currency or to a currency basket, or to manage exchange rate policy so as to maintain a degree of stability vis-à-vis a currency or basket. For that group of countries, the implicit task of surveillance was to determine whether macroeconomic and exchange rate policies were consistent. Since this latter task was more well defined, a major challenge was to ensure that the "floaters" were also held up to appropriate standards of conduct.

A further complication in the conduct of surveillance was the lack of an agreed objective for exchange rate policy that could apply to a broad range of countries. During the 1980s, the debate often was framed as follows: Was the exchange rate to be an instrument for external adjustment, a nominal anchor for financial stability, or a real anchor for maintaining international competitiveness? Both inside the Fund and more widely, views on how best to define and rank such goals varied between countries and over time. Although a degree of eclecticism and flexibility was no doubt necessary, the absence of an objective model or framework inevitably led to arbitrary judgments and prolonged disputes.

These issues are the subject of the present chapter. The first section examines the attempts made to strengthen the principles of surveillance during the first decade of experience under the Second Amendment. The second section takes a closer look at the issues that complicated the Fund's task of assessing countries' exchange rate policies. The chapter concludes with a review of the evolution of the practice of surveillance, including the use of special consultations in response to specific problems.

---

[6]For a general discussion of these issues, see the papers in Boughton and Lateef (1995), Chapter 11.

Implementing Article IV: The Principles of Surveillance

As soon as the language for the new Article IV had been accepted *ad referendum* at the January 1976 meeting of the Interim Committee in Jamaica, the Fund's Executive Board set out to devise a set of principles and procedures for implementing surveillance. After much debate, a formal decision was adopted on April 29, 1977.[7] But because the differences in view that had made the amendment itself difficult to pass had not disappeared after Jamaica, the language in the implementing decision was scarcely more concrete than the language in the Articles. The core of the decision was a set of five "principles" for identifying cases that "might indicate the need for discussion with a member," aside from the scheduled consultations. The first indicator was "protracted large-scale and one-way intervention in exchange markets." Countries were expected to intervene when necessary to counter disorderly market conditions, but not to the point where they might be seen as avoiding a needed exchange rate adjustment. The second, third, and fourth indicators related to excessive external borrowing or lending, exchange restrictions or incentives, or the adoption of domestic economic policies "that provide abnormal encouragement or discouragement to capital flows," provided that such actions were undertaken "for balance of payments purposes." And the fifth indicator was a portmanteau: "behavior of the exchange rate that appears unrelated to fundamentals."

All these principles or indicators eventually gave the Fund headaches. Protracted one-way intervention was neither controversial as an indicator nor especially difficult to identify, but its impact was decidedly asymmetric because it did not apply to the large industrial countries or other countries with floating rates. The limiting phrase "for balance of payments purposes" provided a virtually ironclad defense against any criticism, since economic policies could always be justified on domestic grounds. For example, although Executive Directors often criticized the policy strategy that produced large current account surpluses for Japan, the Japanese authorities consistently defended the practice. In their view, the strategy was dictated by a domestic need for large current net national saving to prepare for the decline that would inevitably follow the expected rise in the average age of the Japanese population in the 21st century. (See Chapter 3.) Moreover, it was very difficult to detect when capital flows were "abnormal." That judgment, which is equivalent to determining whether the current account surplus or deficit is abnormal, required making arbitrary assumptions and thus was useful more for analytical than for practical surveillance purposes.

The indicator that applied most directly to the large industrial countries was the last one: exchange rate movements unrelated to "fundamentals." That criterion was difficult to assess, because the idea of "fundamentals" was so elastic. For example, when a shift in the U.S. policy mix toward fiscal expansion and monetary

---

[7]The approved principles and procedures are reproduced in the Appendix to this chapter. For a review of the debate in 1977, see de Vries (1985), pp. 837–49.

contraction led to a sharp appreciation in the U.S. dollar in the first half of the 1980s, the appreciation could be judged inconsistent with fundamental underlying conditions only by first judging that this mix of policies was inconsistent with the fundamentals. U.S. officials argued (again, see Chapter 3) that their policy stance was an appropriate and necessary response to the inflationary pressures of the preceding years. Nonetheless, the Fund was able to base surveillance in that case on the argument that lax fiscal policy was unsustainable and thus could not be treated as an underlying fundamental condition.

The Executive Directors who adopted the 1977 surveillance decision recognized that these principles were quite weak and might have to be changed eventually once enough experience had been gained to produce a consensus on a means of improving them. Accordingly, they included a provision that the principles should be reviewed at least biennially. But the problems that made the original principles difficult to apply also made it difficult to reach agreement on strengthening them. In the first three reviews (1980, 1982, and 1984),[8] no formal proposals were made to amend the principles. By 1986, however, the recognition was growing that the principles were out of sync both with economic realities and with the evolving practice of Fund surveillance.

In 1986 and again in 1987, the staff—in an effort spearheaded by Andrew Crockett, Deputy Director of the Research Department—suggested that the principles should be changed, on several grounds. First, the distinction between policy actions taken "for balance of payments purposes" and those taken for domestic purposes was neither meaningful nor helpful. Second, the causes of fluctuations in exchange rates had turned out to be quite different from what had been thought in the 1970s. Although price stability had been largely restored, exchange rates had continued to show wide and persistent fluctuations, mainly because countries had adopted divergent mixes of monetary and fiscal policies. Third, the role of official intervention in affecting exchange rates had turned out to be much smaller than expected. Consequently, the staff concluded that the "current principles for the guidance of members' exchange rate policies do not, by themselves, provide sufficient guidance to generate medium-term exchange rate stability."[9]

The conclusion that the surveillance principles were flawed was an easy one to reach, but agreement on a revised list remained elusive. The staff offered several suggestions for either giving the Fund a more specific role in overseeing exchange rate policies or significantly extending the meaning of "exchange rate policies" beyond the narrow concept embodied in the 1977 decision. First, the Fund could encourage countries to establish target or reference zones for their exchange rates. Second, the Fund could encourage countries to set limits on shifts in the mix of

---

[8]The 1977 decision did not specify an initial date from which the biennial review cycle would ensue. In January 1979 the Managing Director suggested, and the Executive Board agreed, that the cycle should begin with the date on which the Second Amendment became effective: April 1, 1978. The first review was therefore to be concluded by April 1, 1980. "Revised Text of Decision," EBD/79/18, Rev. 1 (January 22, 1979).

[9]"Surveillance Over Exchange Rate Policies—Biennial Review of 1977 Document," SM/86/3 (January 10, 1986), p. 15.

monetary and fiscal policies so as to foster sustainability of exchange rates. Third, the Fund could ask members to set medium-term targets—or at least to make projections—for key economic variables and to discuss developments in those variables in consultations with the Fund.

When the Executive Board first discussed these suggestions in February 1986, Directors expressed considerable interest but limited enthusiasm. The one proposal that drew widespread support was the one that made the smallest departure from existing practice: strengthening the use of quantitative indicators as the basis for surveillance discussions. Support for that proposal—as discussed in more depth below—continued to build over the next year and was enshrined in the Interim Committee communiqué of April 1987 (Para. 3):

> Committee members considered that actual policies should be looked at against an evolution of economic variables that could be considered desirable and sustainable. They encouraged the Executive Board to examine the ways in which the existing principles and procedures of Fund surveillance could be updated to incorporate the use of indicators. . . .

In response, the Board took the unusual step of scheduling a special review of the principles of surveillance in July 1987, several months before the regular biennial review. When the time came for a concrete decision, however, support for change suddenly evaporated. The Fund was already cautiously expanding the use of quantitative indicators in surveillance, and Directors took the quite practical view that it could continue to do so without amending the surveillance principles. Thus the one real opportunity to strengthen the principles was allowed to pass.[10]

The source of the Board's reluctance to amend the surveillance principles was clear. Both the Articles of Agreement and the 1977 surveillance decision were crafted so as not to impose obligations on member countries to conduct domestic macroeconomic policies in a particular way, other than the general obligation to cooperate with the Fund in the conduct of surveillance. Specifically, Article IV of the Articles of Agreement distinguishes between "exchange rate policies" in a narrow sense and the broader set of economic policies that affect exchange rates. The article enjoins the Fund to practice "firm surveillance" over the narrower range of international policies (section 3(b) of the article) and to "oversee" the effects of the broader range of policies on the international monetary system (section 3(a)). The principles listed in the 1977 decision apply only to the narrow concept, which accounts for the language that circumscribes coverage to policies undertaken "for

---

[10]See the minutes of EBM/87/105–106 (July 22, 1987) and EBM/87/107 (July 23, 1987). The only amendments to the original Board decision in the 1980s concerned procedures rather than principles. For the first decade of surveillance, the Board agreed to review the implementation of surveillance annually and the principles biennially. At the conclusion of the 1988 review, it was agreed that henceforth both aspects would be reviewed only biennially. "Amendment and Review of Document Entitled 'Surveillance Over Exchange Rate Policies' Attached to Decision No. 5392-(77/63), Adopted April 29, 1977, As Amended," SM/88/39, Sup. 2 (April 20, 1988). The principles were later amended, in April 1995, with the addition of a sixth criterion for assessing potential problems related to "unsustainable [international] flows of private capital" (see *Annual Report 1995*, p. 202). Also see footnote 58, p. 95.

balance of payments purposes." Applying that distinction is inherently illogical and has little practical effect "in the field," because the dominant influence on exchange rates is domestic macroeconomic policy, but to modify it would substantially expand the scope of the Fund's authority.

At the July 1987 discussion, the U.S. Director, Charles H. Dallara, asked rhetorically, "Can anyone imagine a U.S. Article IV consultation that does not cover fiscal policy?"[11] Although the Fund certainly did offer strenuous and often effective advice on fiscal policy through those consultations, the unspoken corollary was (and remains), "Can anyone imagine the IMF dictating fiscal policy to the United States?"

Assessing Exchange Rate Levels and Policies

The central difficulty in conducting surveillance over countries' exchange rate policies is the absence of a generally accepted goal or standard for those policies. There is no generally accepted economic model that determines whether it is better for a country to float, fix, or manage its exchange rate or how to relate exchange rate policy unambiguously to one or more of several macroeconomic goals. This lacuna in the conduct of surveillance was manifest in three major issues during the 1980s. Was it feasible or desirable for the Fund to treat countries evenhandedly despite the presence of a wide variety of exchange arrangements? Was floating inherently preferable to fixing the exchange rate? What, if anything, should be the role of the exchange rate as a policy instrument or indicator?

Variety in Exchange Arrangements

The par value system of exchange rates that was established at Bretton Woods in 1944 sought to establish uniformity as well as stability in exchange arrangements. Stripped of its complexities, that system had two basic elements: the United States established the value of the U.S. dollar in terms of gold, and all other member countries established par values for their exchange rates in terms of the dollar. In stark contrast, the replacement system that was established in Jamaica in 1976 acknowledged that the monetary role of gold had ended, that the U.S. dollar could no longer serve as the sole reserve currency, and that countries should be free to adopt whatever exchange regime was best suited to their own circumstances. Nonetheless, the most popular regime by far—the choice of 38 of the Fund's 146 member countries in 1982—was still pegging to the U.S. dollar (see Figure 2.1). An additional 56 countries pegged to other currencies or to a currency basket, while only 10 countries were classified as having independently floating rates. The remainder were classified as having varying degrees of flexibility.[12] The

---

[11]Minutes of EBM/87/105 (July 22, 1987), p. 25.

[12]Prior to 1982, the Fund's classification scheme was less detailed and did not distinguish between independent floating and various intermediate schemes. When the first data were published in *International Financial Statistics* in 1979, 42 countries had pegged their currencies to the

Figure 2.1. Exchange Rate Arrangements, 1982 and 1989

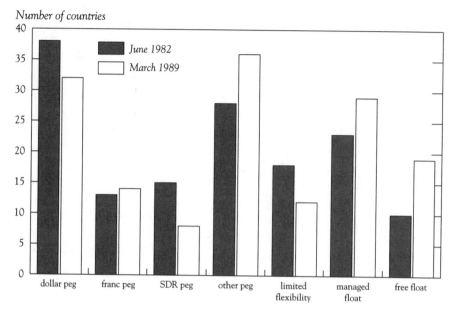

rest of the decade saw some move toward greater flexibility, but the general pattern persisted.

A consequence of this diversity was the difficulty of applying the principles of surveillance evenhandedly to all member countries. If a country that pegged its exchange rate decided to devalue its currency, it was required to notify the Fund and was subject to scrutiny. If a country with a floating rate allowed market forces to depreciate its currency without interference, no notification was required and no scrutiny would follow except in the normal cycle of Article IV consultations. The basis for this distinction was the expectation that market forces would push a currency toward equilibrium, whereas official action could constitute manipulation for a competitive advantage. When experience proved that currencies could float far off track without any official intervention, the wisdom of treating these situations differently was naturally called into question. Year after year, Executive Directors and other officials representing countries with managed exchange rates complained about what they perceived as deferential treatment to countries with floating rates. Jón Sigurdsson (Iceland) put the point succinctly in 1982:

U.S. dollar, and 52 countries had adopted other pegging arrangements. The data in Figure 2.1 are derived from tables for a single date each year: June 30 through 1987, and March 31 thereafter. See the Fund's Annual Reports for summary tables of arrangements in effect for each of those years, and the *Annual Report on Exchange Arrangements and Exchange Restrictions* for detailed descriptions for each member country. For a review of trends in exchange rate arrangements in the 1980s, see Quirk and others (1987), Chapter 2. Throughout the 1980s, one member country—Cambodia—did not notify the Fund of its exchange arrangements (see Chapter 19).

> The Board must be careful not to weight its surveillance procedures against a member that takes a precise step in one direction at one time [i.e., a devaluation], compared with another member that accomplishes an adjustment of the same—or greater—magnitude by means of gradual changes over time—be these administered or brought about through so-called free floating.[13]

The staff and management broadly accepted that argument and tried to alleviate the asymmetry by strengthening surveillance over countries with floating rates—such as the proposals discussed in the preceding section. The limited success of that effort was attributable in part to its inherent difficulty and in part to the size and economic power of the countries with floating rates at that time.

A special challenge arose in dealing with regional exchange rate arrangements such as those in Europe, Africa, and the Caribbean.[14] Several European countries established the European common margins arrangements (commonly known as the "snake") in 1972, which was modified and extended in March 1979 to form the "exchange rate mechanism" (ERM) of the European Monetary System (EMS). That mechanism required frequent exchange rate adjustments, especially during the first several years while the seven participating countries gradually brought their macroeconomic policies into closer alignment. (See Ungerer, Evans, and Nyberg, 1983.) In Africa, two groups of countries in the central and western regions maintained a common currency firmly linked to the French franc. Known collectively as the CFA franc zone, those countries eschewed exchange rate policy in favor of trying to discipline monetary and fiscal policies in line with those prevailing in France (see Chapter 13, p. 579). In the Caribbean region, eight countries adopted a common currency, the Eastern Caribbean dollar, which was pegged to the U.S. dollar. However, in contrast to the CFA franc zone's relationship to France, the Caribbean currency arrangement was not supported by the United States.

In conducting surveillance in these and similar cases, the Fund found itself holding separate discussions with each participating country while trying to develop a comprehensive analysis of the policy requirements for maintaining stability in the context of the multicountry constraints. The anomaly was that although the raison d'être for surveillance was the oversight of exchange rate policies, the Fund did not have a mandate to discuss those policies at the regional level at which decisions were taken and implemented.[15]

---

[13]Minutes of EBM/82/135 (October 13, 1982), p. 11.

[14]For the Fund's views on regional trading arrangements, see Chapter 20.

[15]An exception was initially made for the Belgo-Luxembourg Economic Union. Because the Luxembourg franc was tied to the Belgian franc through a currency union, Luxembourg subordinated its monetary and exchange rate policy to its much larger partner, Belgium. Furthermore, Luxembourg consistently maintained sound fiscal policies and avoided external imbalances and therefore had little need for surveillance in the traditional sense. Through 1982, the Fund accordingly adopted a minimalist but effectively regional approach. The staff conducting the Belgian consultations would spend a day in Luxembourg and would include a brief report on the Luxembourg economy in the Belgian report. The Board would then discuss the two economies simultaneously. In October 1982, Jacques J. Polak (Executive Director for the Netherlands; formerly head of the Fund's Research Department) suggested that it would be helpful to have a separate consultation for Luxembourg, so that the Fund could regularly review and learn from the

This complication is illustrated most clearly by the Fund's relationships with the member countries of the EMS. As discussed in Chapter 20, European countries had aimed since the late 1940s to avoid becoming too dependent on the Fund and to develop their own institutions that both reflected and promoted the high degree of intra-European economic interdependency. The EMS was a continuation of a series of institutions established in that spirit. The role of the Fund vis-à-vis the EMS was therefore more analytical and reactive than operational and would not be regarded as constituting regional surveillance. This limitation became of even greater operational significance at the end of the 1990s, when the inauguration of the euro as a regional European currency and of the European Central Bank (ECB) as a regional monetary authority forced the Fund to reexamine the nature of surveillance in such cases.

Several key senior staff and many non-European Executive Directors initially reacted skeptically and warily when the formation of the EMS was first announced in 1978.[16] However, the Managing Director, Jacques de Larosière, reacted more positively and emphasized the importance of establishing good working relations with what he believed would be a major force for stability in international economic relations.[17]

"well-managed" Luxembourg economy; minutes of EBM/82/133 (October 8, 1982), p. 15. (Polak was also aware that elevating the status of the consultations with Luxembourg would help soothe feelings in the wake of the February 1982 unilateral decision by Belgium, without consulting Luxembourg officials, to devalue the Belgian—and therefore the Luxembourg—franc.) Separate consultations were held from then on.

[16]Jacques Polak, then Economic Counsellor and Director of Research, argued in July 1978 that "the danger lies . . . in an arrangement which brings about a much tighter pegging of rates than divergences in domestic policies will permit. . . . [T]he Fund might quickly find itself involved with several" EMS participants. The Director of the European Department, L. Alan Whittome, suggested to the Managing Director a few days later that it was "very obvious that as a minimum we are going to be faced with formidable difficulties in the fields of exchange rate surveillance and conditional lending." When the Executive Board first discussed the embryonic system in December 1978, Byanti Kharmawan (Indonesia) recalled that "in the past the Fund had found it difficult to persuade some European countries to follow its advice," and he warned that "the problem would probably be exacerbated when individual participants were backed up by the powerful EMS bloc." In contrast, the Director of the Exchange and Trade Relations Department, Ernest Sturc, argued in September that "the scheme should be welcomed." Memorandums to the Managing Director from Polak (July 27, 1978), Whittome (August 4, 1978), and Sturc (September 7, 1978); and minutes of IS/78/13 (December 21, 1978), p. 21. All in IMF/CF (S 1817.1 "European Monetary System, 1978"). Also see Polak (1980), which discusses the importance of developing cooperative arrangements under which EMS members would be expected to make use of Fund as well as European resources in case of balance of payments difficulties.

[17]James (1996), p. 303, attributes the Managing Director's enthusiasm to personal persuasion by the President of the European Commission, Roy Jenkins, at a meeting in mid-December 1978. As early as September, however, de Larosière informed European leaders that "the Fund was ready to welcome wholeheartedly an arrangement which would contribute to international monetary stability," as long as the system was flexible and did not isolate its members from the Fund or the world economy. Memorandum for Files by R.G. Ware (Personal Assistant to the Managing Director), September 13, 1978, on the Managing Director's trip to Europe, September 8–12; in IMF/RD Managing Director file "BIS—Basle, September 1978" (Accession 84/21, Box 4, Section 168). Also see minutes of IS/78/13 (December 21, 1978), p. 22.

The Executive Board regularly reviewed the exchange rate policies of EMS members in the framework of Article IV consultations with individual countries, but that forum was obviously limited in scope. The EMS also was a regular topic in the World Economic Outlook (WEO) exercise. On several occasions from 1979 on, the staff prepared analyses for the Executive Board on the operation of the system, notably at times of major realignments.[18] On only two occasions, however—in April 1983 and in February 1989—did the Board meet to discuss the situation. The first instance was motivated by an exchange crisis that centered on a speculative attack on the French franc and culminated in the seventh realignment of EMS currency parities in four years (and the first to involve all eight[19] participating currencies). The Board, like the staff, viewed the realignment positively but expressed caution that the system would remain subject to strains and possibly to crises until its members achieved a higher degree of policy coordination. The second Board discussion was motivated by the increasing momentum toward full economic integration of the European Community (EC) that was manifest in 1989. Directors again agreed with the staff in painting a broadly positive picture: in the first decade of operation, the EMS had succeeded in creating a "zone of monetary stability" in Europe and had begun to show real progress in converging toward sustainable economic policies and performance.[20] A decade later, the Fund would respond even more positively to the introduction of the euro and the ECB and would move more aggressively to accommodate the practice of surveillance to the new realities.

In dealing with currency unions such as the CFA franc zone in Africa or the Eastern Caribbean dollar area, the Fund followed a broadly laissez-faire path in the 1980s. At the beginning of the decade, several Executive Directors from industrial countries prodded the staff into analyzing the viability of these arrangements, especially those of the franc zone. The resulting study, which was directed by Rattan J. Bhatia (Deputy Director of the African Department), drew generally benign conclusions. Specifically, the constraint against using the exchange rate as a policy instrument was judged as not having prevented countries from undertaking timely and effective adjustment when required, relative to nonparticipants facing

---

[18]Five of those studies were published in the Fund's series of Occasional Papers: Ungerer, Evans, and Nyberg (1983); Ungerer and others (1986); Guitián, Russo, and Tullio (1988); Folkerts-Landau and Mathieson (1989); and Ungerer and others (1990).

[19]The number refers to the currencies for which central rates were established, regardless of the degree of commitment to maintain them. At the time, 10 countries were members of the EMS, but only eight participated in the exchange arrangements, and 2 of those (Belgium and Luxembourg) maintained their own currency union. Thus there were, in effect, only seven independent currencies that were fully in the system. A notional central rate was assigned to the pound sterling, but the United Kingdom did not commit to maintain its exchange rates within fixed margins until October 1990. Greece joined the EMS in January 1981, but without a central rate, as did Spain and Portugal five years later. Spain began participating in the exchange arrangements in June 1989.

[20]See "European Monetary System—Realignment of Exchange Rates," SM/83/57 (April 1, 1983) and minutes of EBM/83/61 (April 15, 1983); and "The European Monetary System in the Context of the Integration of European Financial Markets," SM/89/3 (January 6, 1989) and minutes of EBM/89/9–10 (February 1, 1989).

similar circumstances. Directors who had called for the study expressed disappointment in it, but the Board as a whole did not take a position and did not consider the matter further at a regional level until 1990.[21]

In conducting Article IV consultations with members of currency unions, the staff usually chose not to call their participation into question, even when some members were experiencing much more severe economic problems than others. (In practice, this issue did not arise with regard to the Caribbean group.) If circumstances required external adjustment, the staff normally advised changes in monetary, fiscal, or other domestic policies aimed at strengthening international competitiveness. The major exception in the 1980s concerned Côte d'Ivoire, the largest country in the CFA franc zone. In concluding the 1987 consultations, the Executive Board expressed fears that Côte d'Ivoire's adjustment problem was so severe that it could not be tackled properly through restrictive domestic policies alone. Several Directors argued that "consideration of an exchange rate adjustment should not be precluded."[22] It would take several more years, but that urging finally took root when the CFA members jointly devalued the franc in January 1994.

A related complexity arose in dealing with countries that had no national currency and therefore no exchange rate policy. In the 1980s, only a few small countries chose that option. Panama used the U.S. dollar as its principal currency, Liberia used the U.S. dollar in the first part of the decade until the authorities lost control of the economy, and Kiribati (which joined the Fund in 1986) used the Australian dollar. That type of regime is an extreme variant of pegging, with the important additional constraint that the stock of domestic currency is limited by the country's net receipts of foreign exchange. Fiscal policy becomes the main macroeconomic instrument, but it is partially constrained because of the absence of monetary financing.

In conducting surveillance with these countries, the Fund took the view that as long as fiscal policies were sustainable, it would not question the choice of currency regime. As it happened, Kiribati's policies were unproblematic, Panama's policies were sound until a political upheaval occurred in 1987, and Liberia's political and fiscal weaknesses were abundantly evident throughout the decade. Through the Article IV consultations, the Fund urged Liberia both to strengthen its fiscal position and to adopt a more realistic currency and exchange regime.[23]

---

[21]See "Currency Unions," SM/82/183 (August 31, 1982), and minutes of Executive Board Seminar 83/1 (May 4, 1983). Directors who expressed disappointment that the study had not been more critical included notably Michael Casey (Alternate—Ireland), Richard D. Erb (United States), Tom de Vries (Alternate—Netherlands), and Peter Kohnert (Temporary Alternate—Germany). Also see Bhatia (1985), which is based in part on that study, and McLenaghan, Nsouli, and Riechel (1982), which was prepared as a form of technical assistance for the countries in the franc zone and did not occasion a discussion by the Executive Board. For the subsequent study, see "A Review of the CFA Franc Arrangements," SM/90/136 (July 9, 1990), and minutes of Executive Board Seminar 90/6 (November 5, 1990).

[22]Minutes of EBM/87/172 (December 15, 1987), p. 33. Also see the review of Fund lending to Côte d'Ivoire in Chapter 13.

[23]See, for example, the Chairman's summing up of the 1986 consultation; minutes of EBM/86/156 (September 15, 1986), pp. 15–16.

Liberia and Panama eventually fell into arrears to the Fund, but in the latter case the absence of a national currency was never an issue (see Chapter 16).

Assessments of the International Monetary System

From the earliest days after the collapse of the Bretton Woods par value system in 1973, the staff of the IMF sought a strategy for stabilizing exchange rates within a floating-rate framework. That search, however, was more fruitful on the theoretical than on the empirical level. Largely because the precise measurement of equilibrium exchange rates for the major countries was elusive, surveillance over the international monetary system remained based primarily on broad assessments of whether rates were over- or undervalued.

In 1974 the staff proposed a set of "guidelines" to the Executive Board under which countries would have been encouraged to intervene in exchange markets to stabilize rates within a "normal zone" agreed with the Fund. That proposal was watered down during the final negotiations, and the guidelines adopted in June 1974 called for the Fund to determine "medium-term norms" for effective exchange rates, defined as the rates that are expected to equilibrate the "underlying" balance of payments, and to encourage countries with floating rates to take actions as needed to keep their rates within reasonable bounds around the norm. Even that version, however, generated concerns among officials of countries adopting floating rates. The Board was never able to agree on a plan for implementing the guidelines, and the strategy embodied in the 1977 surveillance decision effectively abandoned the concept of quantified norms for floating rates.[24]

By the end of the 1970s, the conventional wisdom at the Fund was that the floating-rate system was working reasonably well, though it might work a little better if countries could adopt policies that were better aimed at preventing misalignments.[25] The initial wariness about the potential dangers of floating never really receded, and the dollar crisis of November 1978 served as a stark reminder. Nonetheless, once that crisis was passed, the Fund's concerns were muted for a couple of years.

The view began to change markedly in the spring of 1981, when exchange rates among the key currencies appeared to be moving in ways contrary to expectation and away from levels that the Fund staff and management considered appropriate.[26]

---

[24]The staff proposals and the 1974 guidelines are described in de Vries (1985), Vol. 1, pp. 297–302, and Vol. 3, pp. 487–91. The "underlying balance of payments" was defined as the "overall balance in the absence of cyclical and other short-term factors affecting the balance of payments" (ibid., p. 490).

[25]"Over the last decade, exchange rate movements have contributed to required adjustments in the current account, but this contribution was subject to a number of limitations. . . . The appropriate use of exchange rate policies to help in correcting excessive payments imbalances differs according to the prevailing world economic situation and the circumstances of the country concerned." *Annual Report 1980*, p. 50. For an early and influential expression of acceptance of the necessity of living with floating rates, see Emminger (1977).

[26]The debate over how closely the major currencies should be controlled related primarily to the U.S. dollar, the Japanese yen, and the deutsche mark. Except for the Canadian dollar and at times the pound sterling, the currencies of the other G-10 countries were all managed to some degree within the framework of the EMS.

As monetary and fiscal policies shifted in divergent directions in several of the largest countries, exchange rates were much more strongly under the influence of financial forces than of the balance of trade. De Larosière soon became convinced that the system that he had once helped design was no longer working. At a meeting of the Surveillance Committee (see below, pp. 103) in March 1981, he lamented to his senior advisors that over the previous year "almost everything had been going wrong with exchange rates." The next day, he asked the Research Department to prepare a thorough study on the behavior of exchange rates for the key currencies:

> Until late last year it seemed defensible to assert that the behaviour of exchange rates under the floating regime had been relatively satisfactory, leaving aside two currencies—sterling and the yen. It may still be true that the underlying trend in the major currencies has contributed to the adjustment process. Nevertheless the magnitude and speed of the swings in key exchange rates in recent months must raise a number of questions.[27]

The staff shared the view that there were "a number of questions," but they were less convinced that any useful answers were waiting to be discovered. Even if—as seemed increasingly likely—market activity could not be relied upon to push exchange rates toward equilibrium, could official intervention guided by economic analysis and measurement produce a better outcome?

On a practical level, the first question to be tackled was how to define equilibrium. The prevailing view in the economics profession was that an equilibrium exchange rate was one that established purchasing power parity (PPP); i.e., one that equilibrated prices of traded goods between countries. But to many of those in the Fund who were attempting to estimate empirical relationships among the key currencies, the influence of PPP on exchange rates appeared to be quite weak. Financial variables such as interest rate differentials (driven by differences in the mix of macroeconomic policies) were more important than PPP in the short run, and the structural determinants of the balance of payments were more important in the long run.[28] In addition, the PPP approach could yield a wide range of estimates for equilibrium exchange rates, depending on which index one used to compare price levels.[29]

---

[27]Memorandum from the Managing Director to William C. Hood, Economic Counsellor and Director of Research (March 20, 1981); IMF CF (S 490). The "going wrong" quotation is from a March 19, 1981, file memorandum by C. Maxwell Watson (Personal Assistant to the Managing Director); ibid.

[28]For reviews of the empirical and theoretical limitations of PPP-based models, see Isard (1987) and Boughton (1988).

[29]In 1986, when the U.S. dollar was retreating from a severe overvaluation, two seminars presented by prominent academic economists at the Fund's Research Department illustrated the extent of this problem. John Bilson, of the University of Chicago, concluded on the basis of a PPP model using consumer prices that the dollar was already undervalued relative to the Japanese yen; his estimate of the equilibrium rate was around 240 yen per dollar, compared with the then-prevailing rate of 180. A few weeks later, Paul Krugman, of the Massachusetts Institute of Technology, presented estimates based on the prices of manufactured goods that the equilibrium rate was "below 140," and therefore that the ongoing depreciation of the dollar had "a considerable way to go."

As noted above, the 1974 "guidelines for the management of floating exchange rates" had referred to the "underlying" balance of payments as the criterion for equilibrium, by which was meant the external balance that would emerge after cyclical and other short-term forces stabilized and worked their way through the economy. By the 1980s, it was becoming ever clearer that the underlying-balance approach was empirically more meaningful than PPP as a basis for evaluation.

The Fund's underlying-balance approach was set out in a staff paper that was discussed by the Executive Board at a seminar in January 1984 and was later published as an Occasional Paper (Artus and Knight, 1984).[30] That study concluded that estimating "sustainable" or equilibrium exchange rates was inherently difficult and that the proposed methodology could "only be expected to yield an approximate range for the sustainable exchange rate of each member country, rather than a precise level."[31] Although the calculations discussed by Artus and Knight did yield such estimates, the paper did not include them, either as points or ranges. Besides their caution about appearing to be too precise, the staff were quite sensitive to the notion that if their estimates became known, they could influence short-term pressures on the actual pattern of rates in the markets.

In spite of its caution, the Artus-Knight study marked a peak in the staff's confidence about estimating equilibrium exchange rates for the major countries. The view expressed there was that "the Fund *must* reach judgments about the appropriateness of the exchange rates of all of its members [i.e., including the large countries with floating rates] in a consistent manner, while watching for possible conflicts among those members" (p. 30; emphasis added). Almost simultaneously, however, Goldstein (1984) argued for an even more cautious approach in evaluating the functioning of floating rates among the major currencies. He concluded that floating might exacerbate "inflation differentials" but that it had enabled these countries to adjust to the massive macroeconomic shocks of the 1970s,

---

[30]The analysis in that study was an extension of the technique that had been pioneered by the staff in conjunction with the preparations for the Smithsonian meeting of the G-10 countries in December 1971, at which agreement was reached on a new set of exchange rate parities after the United States ended convertibility of the dollar into gold (see Chapter 5, under "Multilateral Exchange Rate Model"). Although conceptually linked to the "underlying balance of payments" mentioned in the 1974 guidelines, its empirical application was related to the current account rather than the overall balance of payments. That is, the equilibrium real effective exchange rate was defined as the rate that would make a country's underlying current account balance equal to its normal or sustainable net capital flow. The underlying-balance approach is also closely related to the portfolio-balance approach to explaining movements in real exchange rates, as pioneered by Fund staff economists Pentti Kouri and Michael Porter in the early 1970s (see Kouri and Porter, 1974).

[31]Occasionally the staff attitude became even more ambivalent, to the point of implying that one could reasonably make judgments about whether exchange rates were under- or overvalued even though one did not have a quantified view about what the right range of rates might be. For example, at the Executive Board seminar on the Artus-Knight study, William C. Hood (Economic Counsellor and Director of Research) summarized the view of both the staff and a number of Executive Directors as being "that it was easier to make a judgment about the direction in which an exchange rate in disequilibrium should move than to judge the appropriate level for an exchange rate." Minutes of Executive Board Seminar 84/2 (January 30, 1984), p. 24.

which had made it especially difficult to detect what the equilibrium levels were. "Indeed, in such an environment managed floating may well have been the *only* system that could have functioned continuously" (p. 45; original emphasis). That judgment received widespread support from Executive Directors when they discussed both the Artus-Knight and Goldstein papers in the January 1984 seminar.[32]

Internally, for a few years after those studies appeared, the Research Department regularly produced estimates of equilibrium rates, which were circulated solely for the information of management. Over the next few years, the staff became increasingly skeptical of the value of these estimates, and by 1987 the practice was quietly abandoned for the time being. (It came into vogue again in the second half of the 1990s.) Separately, beginning about 1987 (shortly after Jacob Frenkel became Economic Counsellor and Director of Research), the Research Department conducted several evaluations of proposals for "target zones" or other partial moves back toward greater fixity of rates among the key currencies.[33] Those evaluations yielded generally negative conclusions. In Frenkel's view (see his 1996 paper), the major countries had an unavoidable need to pursue independent monetary and fiscal policies, which made fixing or targeting exchange rates impracticable.

The Executive Board also got involved in the analysis of exchange rate developments in 1987. When the U.S. dollar suddenly started dropping in value in January, the Executive Directors for India and Italy (Arjun Sengupta and Salvatore Zecchini) called for a discussion of the situation by the Board. Zecchini observed that when major currencies started moving sharply, "it was embarrassing to have to say [to outsiders] that the Fund did not have an opinion on the subject."[34] Although some other Directors and the staff expressed concerns that the Fund might be drawn into reacting to short-term fluctuations that were inherently unpredictable, the Board agreed to begin holding informal discussions of market developments on a roughly quarterly schedule. Those discussions then became an increasingly important analytical tool in the Fund's surveillance of the functioning of the international monetary system.[35]

A persistent question about floating rates was whether volatility (as opposed to sustained misalignment) of exchange rates was a problem that should concern the Fund. Short-run volatility among the key currencies was a highly visible phenomenon in the early 1980s, and it was frequently raised as a policy issue by Executive

---

[32]See minutes of Executive Board Seminar 84/1–2 (January 30, 1984).

[33]Those proposals arose out of studies commissioned by both the G-10 industrial countries and the Group of Twenty-Four (G-24) developing countries in 1985, buttressed by the advocacy of a group of economists at the Washington-based Institute for International Economics. See Chapter 4 and Frenkel and Goldstein (1986).

[34]See minutes of EBM/87/8 (January 14, 1987), p. 48.

[35]See minutes of EBM/87/8 and 87/9 (January 14, 1987). From 1987 through 1992, the Board's discussions were in informal session under the heading of "Exchange Rates—Recent Developments" or simply "Exchange Rate Developments" and were normally confined to the currencies of Group of Seven (G-7) industrial countries. Beginning in 1993, the breadth of the discussion was widened, and the sessions were retitled "World Economic and Market Developments."

Directors during Article IV consultations with the major countries and in discussions on the world economic outlook. Few on the staff, however, were convinced that it was a serious problem, and for the most part the debate in the Fund concentrated on longer-term issues.[36]

Policy Role of the Exchange Rate

As noted above (p. 74), a general complication in the conduct of surveillance in the 1980s was the absence of a universally agreed objective for exchange rate policy. The Fund frequently advised countries in this period to adjust their nominal exchange rates to a level consistent with the country's price level relative to prices in other countries, so as to promote a sustainable external payments balance. Unfortunately, that principle often conflicted with other objectives that were important to the country's authorities.

Perhaps the most frequently proffered advice to countries—almost a symbol of the role of the Fund in some parts of the world—was to devalue the currency to compensate for an excess of domestic over world price inflation and thereby to restore the international competitiveness of the country's export industries. To try to keep the rate of domestic inflation from rising by enough to wipe out the gain in competitiveness or to destabilize economic activity, devaluation advice was always coupled with advice to exercise greater discipline over monetary and fiscal policies. The Fund also occasionally recommended devaluation to countries that had no inflation problem but that had developed troublesome current account deficits owing to external forces, such as a collapse in the world market for the country's principal exports. The key to success in those cases was to *retain* control over financial policies following a needed devaluation, which inevitably would bring losses in real incomes to a large part of the working population.

The converse also applied, but it came into play much less often. If a country had relatively low inflation and a fixed exchange rate, or undertook a devaluation without a prior loss in competitiveness, it could gain a competitive advantage over other countries. To forestall a series of competing devaluations (or other types of what are generally known as "beggar thy neighbor" policies),[37] the Fund might advise the country to revalue its exchange rate upward. Such cases, although a driving concern at Bretton Woods in 1944, occurred only rarely in the post–Bretton Woods era. On a few occasions, the Fund conveyed concerns that key currencies such as the U.S. dollar or the Japanese yen were undervalued (see Chapter 3), and

---

[36] For a succinct statement of the Fund position on exchange rate volatility, see *Annual Report 1982*, pp. 42–45. Staff studies on the subject included notably IMF Research Department (1984)—which was authored by Crockett—and Gotur (1985). Most empirical studies of industrial countries (surveyed in those papers) concurred that short-term volatility had only small real effects. Exceptionally, Kenen and Rodrik (1986) found more significance. Studies of the effects of volatility on trade in developing countries, however, typically found more sizable effects. See, for example, Caballero and Corbo (1989) and Grobar (1993).

[37]The term is attributable to Joan Robinson, whose original phrasing (see Robinson, 1937) was "beggar my neighbor."

in a very few cases the Fund investigated complaints that smaller countries might be deliberately undervaluing their currencies (see the discussions below on Sweden and Korea). Those exceptions aside, the Fund's preferred term for its advocacy—"exchange rate flexibility"—became in effect a euphemism for devaluation and maintenance of a competitive rate.[38]

Countries that resisted using the exchange rate as an instrument for adjustment usually did so for one or more of several reasons, only one of which was clearly bad. The obviously bad reason was that the exchange rate serves political as well as economic ends. Politicians all over the world and all over the political spectrum have equated a "strong" exchange rate (i.e., an overvalued currency) with a strong economy. That confusion—which in the early 1980s afflicted the Reagan administration in the United States just as much as the López-Portillo government in Mexico—has prevented many a government from acting rationally in the face of a deteriorating ability to compete in world markets.

A second and more legitimate reason for resistance was concern over the contractionary effects of large exchange rate changes on business solvency, the government's fiscal position, and consumer demand. Firms that rely heavily on external borrowing or on imported inputs are likely to suffer from devaluation and might not be able to absorb the cost. In many countries, the government also benefits fiscally from a strong currency and may be vulnerable to the increased costs resulting from devaluation. As businesses, consumers, and the government all retrench in the face of rising costs of imports and external debt service, economic activity might contract severely. In theory, these negative factors could be more than offset by the benefits to export sectors, but in practice the stimulus to exports might be slow to materialize or even virtually nonexistent.

Third, a substantial margin of error always surrounds measurements of the equilibrium level of the exchange rate. As noted above, the rate that equilibrates price levels between countries (the PPP rate) might vary substantially depending on the choice of price index or base period, and the PPP rate might be quite different from the rate that would equilibrate the balance of payments. It therefore was always easy for recalcitrant policymakers to insist—not without justification—either that the current rate was within acceptable bounds or that neither they nor the Fund had a better rate to suggest than the one produced by the market (again see the discussion below on Sweden).

A fourth reason, which took on increasing importance during the 1980s, was that many countries found it useful to treat the exchange rate as a "nominal anchor" for expected prices. A widespread difficulty with the use of the exchange rate as an instrument of adjustment is that devaluation can help perpetuate the inflation for which it is trying to compensate. Devaluation or depreciation directly raises the prices of imported goods and services, and businesses and workers are bound to try to bid up prices and wages in an effort to compensate. If a government

---

[38]For an inside review of the Fund's advice on exchange rate policy to developing countries in the mid-1980s, and for a pro-floating and pro-adjustment perspective, see Quirk and others (1987).

has experienced trouble stabilizing prices because of a limited ability to control monetary, fiscal, and incomes policies, then fixing the exchange rate may provide a viable alternative, albeit only if the strategy succeeds in breaking the inflationary psychology and enabling stable macro policies. Devaluation would threaten the credibility of an economic strategy based on an exchange rate anchor, and stable "exit strategies" for introducing a different anchoring regime have proved difficult to manage.[39]

Finally, countries resisted adjusting the exchange rate because they valued a fixed rate as a means of stimulating trade within a region. Because the empirical assessment of whether a particular group of countries is an optimum or natural area for a common currency or a set of fixed exchange rates is inherently slippery, disputes are bound to arise and persist. This type of debate was especially important in the Fund's relationships with European countries in the 1980s. Although the Fund staff and management generally acknowledged the value of fixed exchange rates for stimulating trade, they also were mindful of the dangers of adhering to fixed rates in the face of major divergences in economic policies or differences in economic conditions.

The Fund's approach to evaluating exchange rate policies evolved during the first decade of experience with Article IV surveillance, with a broad trend toward a greater sympathy with the stabilizing and trade-promoting virtues of fixed exchange rates.[40] That trend, however, was often obscured by differences in emphasis between countries and between regions. It is perhaps more easily discerned in the Fund's advice to countries that were using (or were seeking to use) Fund resources than in surveillance-only discussions, since explicit advice was seldom given on the exchange rate in the latter context. Moreover, the Fund often took quite different attitudes on exchange rate policy for developing and industrial countries. That dichotomy principally reflected the much greater importance of private financial markets in industrial countries during the 1980s. Where exchange rates were influenced as much by financial as by trade considerations, the assessment of equilibrium became more difficult, the ability of the authorities to control rates became more limited, and the risk increased that the Fund might destabilize market behavior if its criticism of a country's rate became publicized. In many developing countries, in contrast, both trade and finance were more controlled, and the main issue was not whether, but toward what end, the authorities were going to aim exchange rate policy.

While the Fund was shifting in the mid-1980s to a more skeptical view on targeting exchange rates in industrial countries, it was also developing a more balanced view on how developing countries should manage their exchange rate poli-

---

[39]Edwards (1998) examines two case studies—Chile in 1982 and Mexico in 1994—when the failure of the exchange rate anchor to reduce inflation contributed to the onset of a financial crisis. Eichengreen and others (1998) and Eichengreen (1999) discuss the difficulties of devising viable exit strategies.

[40]For a longer-term review of this evolution, see Polak (1995).

cies. Up to that time, the Fund had almost universally recommended devaluation to countries that were having trouble remaining competitive in international markets (see Chapter 13 and Johnson and others, 1985). As the limitations of that strategy became increasingly apparent, the staff's initial response was to encourage developing countries to adopt floating exchange rates. A staff study prepared in 1986–87 (Quirk and others, 1987) concluded that the 15 developing countries that had adopted floating rate regimes in the preceding few years were generally experiencing satisfactory results. However, the study (which was not discussed by the Executive Board) cautioned that successful floating required a sound institutional structure and the maintenance of sound macroeconomic policies and might not be universally applicable. As it happened, the popularity of floating was beginning to wane a bit around the same time as the study appeared. By 1989, only 12 developing countries still maintained independently floating rates.[41]

When the floating-rate option also appeared to be of limited applicability, the Fund shifted somewhat to a more eclectic approach that at least paid lip service to the values of exchange rate stability in developing countries. A Research Department review (Aghevli, Khan, and Montiel, 1991) concluded that what mattered most for economic performance was for countries to establish discipline and credibility in the conduct of fiscal and monetary policies. If they could do so while letting the exchange rate float, fine; otherwise, fixing the exchange rate could be a means toward that end. (Also see Aghevli and Montiel, 1996.) Nonetheless, a separate review prepared at the same time in the Exchange and Trade Relations Department (ETR) revealed that in Article IV consultations concluded in 1987 or 1988, the staff had reported favorably on exchange rate policies two-thirds of the time when the rate was "flexible" and just one-third of the time when the rate was fixed.[42]

One positive influence on staff thinking about the stabilizing role of exchange rate policy, as Polak (1991, 1995) has stressed, was the example of the EMS. After 11 realignments in the system's first 8 years, European leaders committed themselves in September 1987 to a set of reforms (known as the Basel-Nyborg agreement) aimed both at bringing about greater discipline and convergence in domestic policies and at strengthening institutional arrangements so as to reduce the need for exchange rate adjustments (see Ungerer and others, 1990, pp. 8–9). By the end of the decade, it appeared that the strategy was working: neither policy differences nor inflation differentials had vanished, but Europe was undergoing a gradual convergence toward low inflation and strong economic growth without the disruption of periodic currency

---

[41]The 1990s brought a resurgence of floating. In March 1995, the Fund classified 36 developing countries as having independently floating rates, along with 11 industrial countries and 12 countries in transition from central planning. To some extent, though, this resurgence was more apparent than real. The increase included many countries that managed their exchange rates without specifying a target value.

[42]"Review of Exchange Rate Policy Assessments in Recent Article IV Consultations," SM/90/200 (October 18, 1990), Tables 2 and 4.

crises.[43] Similarly, the largest industrial countries achieved a measure of exchange rate stability through the policy coordination exercise that culminated in the Louvre accord of February 1987 (see Chapter 4). In both cases, such stability was widely viewed as a contributor to improved economic performance. Set against those observations, however, was the rapidly deteriorating performance in some of the larger countries participating in the CFA franc zone in western and central Africa. As the world economy lurched toward the 1990s, about all that could be said with confidence about exchange rate policy was that no single model would work for all countries or even for a few countries in all circumstances.

Establishing Effective Procedures

The new Article IV that was agreed upon in 1976 required the Fund to "oversee the compliance of each member [country] with its obligations" to "assure orderly exchange arrangements and to promote a stable system of exchange rates." The procedures for doing so were left to be worked out by the Executive Board, which responded by setting out five general practices in its basic 1977 decision:
1. Members are required to notify the Fund of any changes in their exchange arrangements, such as changes in pegs, intervention policies, etc.
2. Periodic (normally annual) consultations are to be held under the provisions of Article IV.
3. The Board is to periodically review "broad developments in exchange rates," principally in the context of the WEO.
4. The Managing Director is to maintain close contacts with members regarding exchange arrangements and policies.
5. The Managing Director may initiate special consultation discussions with members under specified conditions.

The 1977 decision also specified that these procedures were to be reviewed annually in the light of experience. In contrast to the difficulty of trying to update the principles, the Board did periodically fine-tune its procedures throughout the 1980s. There were five branches to those efforts: attempts to strengthen the conduct of Article IV consultations, attempts to set standards for countries to live up to, attempts to assess performance of individual countries in a broader context, attempts to give greater publicity to the Fund's findings, and attempts to focus attention on the most serious problem cases.[44]

---

[43]For an example of the Fund's positive reaction, see the *World Economic Outlook* (IMF, 1990), pp. 43–44.

[44]In addition to the changes discussed here, the Fund introduced procedures for "enhanced surveillance" in 1985 (see Chapters 9 and 10). That practice was developed as a means of supporting countries' efforts to obtain or maintain loans from other creditors in cases where the countries preferred not to enter into a stand-by arrangement with the Fund or to use Fund resources.

Conduct of Article IV Consultations

On the surface, the Fund conducted consultations under the new Article IV in much the same manner as the old Article VIII or XIV consultations. A "mission" team of (usually) four or five economists, normally headed by someone with the rank of Division Chief or above (generally higher for the largest countries), would spend around two weeks in the country's capital city. During that time, the team would meet daily with senior officials from the finance ministry, the central bank, and other government agencies; and occasionally (especially after the mid-1980s) with representatives of "civil society," such as employers and labor unions. Prior to the mission, the team would prepare by drafting a detailed list of questions to be sent ahead of time to the authorities, by updating the database as much as possible, and by conducting research on specific issues. Missions would typically conclude in a meeting with the minister of finance and other senior officials, at which the staff would present its assessment of the country's policies and economic outlook. Returning to headquarters, the mission chief would immediately submit a confidential "back-to-office" report to the Managing Director. The mission team would then prepare two documents for circulation to the Executive Board: a staff report, summarizing the main policy issues, reviewing the work of the mission, and concluding with the staff assessment; and a background paper on "recent economic developments" (called the RED). The Board would then hold a formal meeting to conclude the consultation, no later than three months after the return of the mission except in exceptional circumstances.

The one real procedural innovation after the Second Amendment was that the Board meeting was to end with a formal "summing up" by the Managing Director of the views expressed by Executive Directors, which would then be sent to the authorities.[45] Previously, Board meetings on Article XIV consultations concluded with a formal decision that included a brief summary of the consensus view of Directors on the country's policies and performance. Article VIII consultations, being voluntary, did not require any formal conclusions, although occasionally the Managing Director did undertake to summarize the discussion to convey the Fund's views to the authorities.[46] The innovation of the formal summing up, which was unique to the Fund, turned out to have more than just procedural importance:

---

[45]The text of the original proposal for the summing up, which was approved by the Executive Board on March 20, 1978, is reproduced in the Appendix to this chapter.

[46]A good example occurred in July 1977, while the United Kingdom was implementing an adjustment program supported by a Fund stand-by arrangement. The Managing Director, H. Johannes Witteveen, closed the Board discussion of the Article VIII consultation by complimenting the authorities for what they had achieved so far but urging further action to contain inflation, which he suggested was "a precondition for the resumption of a more satisfactory growth pattern." He concluded by observing that the U.K. experience "showed how difficult it was for an economy that had strayed far from the path of balanced growth to return to it," and by calling for "patience and perseverance." (See minutes of EBM/77/103 (July 15, 1977), p. 12.) Although these remarks reflected views expressed by Executive Directors, they were made informally and personally by the Managing Director in his capacity as Chairman of the Executive Board.

it enabled the Fund as an institution to draw conclusions about a country's policies without having to negotiate and take a legal decision.[47] The summing up included references to positions taken by individual or groups of Executive Directors, and it did not necessarily even refer to a majority or predominant view. In most cases, however, it expressed clear conclusions on behalf of the international community and sent a clear message to the authorities as to the effects of their policies on the rest of the world. By the 1990s, the summing up also served as the basis for the Fund's public reports on surveillance discussions.

The challenge for the Fund was to focus the consultation process as clearly as possible on the economic policy issues that were most relevant to the international community. The central issue was always the same: are the country's macroeconomic policies oriented toward sustainable growth and consistent with its exchange rate policy?—or, if the exchange rate policy was one of laissez-faire: are macroeconomic policies sustainable and consistent with a stable system of exchange rates? With that question in mind, staff reports reviewed the policy stance and the overall performance of the economy, assessed the outlook for both, and offered recommendations for how policies might be improved. Paradoxically, owing to the sensitivity of the exchange rate as a topic for discussion—more specifically, the fear that an assessment that the exchange rate was overvalued might cause a run on the currency if it became publicly known—staff reports rarely discussed the sustainability of exchange rate policy directly. Instead, the staff discussed whether monetary and fiscal policies were consistent with exchange rate policy. If overly expansionary policies had made the exchange rate overvalued, the option of devaluing might be implied but was seldom stated openly.

Over time, structural economic issues—which had always been included in Article IV consultations—took on increasing importance in staff reports. Part of the impetus came from a growing recognition of the widespread need for structural reform to combat chronically high unemployment and sluggish growth, in industrial as well as developing countries. Further stimulus came from the Fund's growing involvement with centrally planned or state-controlled economies: new members or representatives such as the People's Republics of Angola, China, Hungary, Mozambique, and Poland; and older members such as Romania and

---

[47]The role of the summing up and the procedures for conveying Executive Directors' views to the authorities were agreed upon during the first Article IV consultation with a major industrial country: at the Executive Board meeting on the United Kingdom in July 1978 (see Chapter 3). At that time, Joseph Gold (General Counsel) explained that the summing up had the same legal effect as a formal Board decision, although its language was more flexible. On procedures, the Board agreed that the Secretary (rather than the Managing Director) would formally send the summing up to the authorities of the country concerned. (See minutes of EBM/78/102 (July 6, 1978).) It was understood that Executive Directors would normally also send it to the authorities of other member countries as part of their normal reports on Fund activities. Although the Board did not approve each summing up by taking a formal Decision, Executive Directors implicitly approved the text by not asking for a discussion of it when it was circulated internally. (See "Establishment of Document Series for Summings Up Concerning Surveillance," SUR/83/1 (July 19, 1983).)

Yugoslavia.[48] The staff recognized that exchange rate policy had only an indirect influence on the balance of payments in planned economies, because of the high degree of state control over both domestic prices and the quantities of traded goods. Surveillance over planned economies, in this view, therefore required surveillance over the macroeconomic implications of the country's economic plan, in addition to the usual indicators of economic policies and performance.

When the Executive Board discussed the matter in a June 1982 seminar, Tse Chun Chang (China) argued for a more fundamental rethinking of surveillance in dealing with planned economies. Unless the Fund dispensed altogether with the notion of profit maximization as a "decisive factor in the allocation of resources" and recognized the importance of national goals regarding equality of income distribution and the avoidance of both inflation and unemployment, it could not hope to understand the reluctance of these countries to adopt measures that promote economic efficiency but that also threaten these essential goals. Jacques Polak (whose constituency included both Romania and Yugoslavia) noted the "almost inevitable" ambivalence of the staff's views, which aimed to be evenhanded while encouraging countries to adopt more market-oriented regimes. Most important, he noted that whereas "the Fund did have a model for the market economies, there was no equivalent theory of the economic functioning of centrally planned economies." The view was pervasive that the Fund's (and the economic profession's) knowledge about the workings of planned economies was weak, and Polak's call for an "ad hoc" and "modest" approach to the task was widely endorsed around the table.[49]

The international debt crisis of 1982 provided a second impetus for the Fund to devote more attention to structural issues; in this case, through the use of medium-term (i.e., longer than the Fund's usual 18- to 24-month forecast horizon) scenarios for heavily indebted countries. At an April 1983 meeting on Fund policies in dealing with the debt crisis, the Board directed the staff to begin collecting more detailed debt statistics, to provide technical assistance to countries on the collection and compilation of debt data, to do more analyses of the global debt outlook, and to produce scenarios on the medium-term outlook for external debt in regular Article IV consultations.[50] In a particularly clear example, the 1985 staff report on Chile included a table projecting (correctly) that Chile's total external debt-

---

[48]China was represented in the Fund by the People's Republic from April 1980. The Hungarian People's Republic joined in May 1982, the People's Republic of Mozambique in September 1984, the Polish People's Republic in June 1986, and the People's Republic of Angola in September 1989. The Socialist Federal Republic of Yugoslavia was an original member of the Fund until the country ceased to exist in December 1992. The Socialist Republic of Romania joined in December 1972. For further information, see Chapter 19.

[49]Minutes of Seminars 82/3 and 82/4 (June 25, 1982), pp. 4 (Zhang) and 10–11 (Polak). Modesty may have prevented Polak from pointing out that he had played a seminal role in the development of the Fund's model of market economies. For a review of that development and Polak's role in it, see Chapter 13, p. 559, and Frenkel, Goldstein, and Khan (1991).

[50]Minutes of EBM/83/58 (April 6, 1983), pp. 33–35. The detailed staff proposal for preparing medium-term debt scenarios is in "Fund Policies and External Debt Servicing Problems," SM/83/45 (March 8, 1983), pp. 15–19.

service payments would steadily decline as a percentage of export receipts from nearly 50 percent in 1984 to just 26 percent by 1990.[51] Once the staff began developing the policy implications of those scenarios—which quickly became a standard feature of discussions with heavily indebted countries—it was inevitably drawn into analyses of structural problems affecting the levels of domestic saving and investment.

A third impetus came from the growing concern over the widespread resort to protectionist trade policies. Trade liberalization was the task of the General Agreement on Tariffs and Trade (GATT) and thus was not really the Fund's turf. In practice, though, it was often difficult to separate exchange rate policies from trade policies, since countries could always substitute between them to gain competitive advantage. When exchange rates began to display persistent swings and misalignments in the early 1980s, both industrial and developing countries reacted by raising a wide variety of tariffs and other barriers to trade. To monitor and discourage such practices, the Executive Board used the occasion of the 1983 review of surveillance to direct the staff to devote more attention to trade policies in Article IV reports.[52] Tables of major trade restrictions and discussions of changes in them then became a regular feature of staff reports. For example, the staff report for the 1984 consultation with France included a section describing France's use of trade restrictions to protect employment opportunities in certain sectors, and the RED included a detailed appendix on the subject. After explaining the authorities' position on the issue, the staff report concluded that "there remained considerable scope in France—as elsewhere—to dismantle trade restrictions of whatever type and coverage."[53]

Beyond those changes that related specifically to the content of Article IV consultations, the Fund's concerns and appetite for information continually expanded throughout the 1980s. In 1984, as World Bank lending became increasingly complementary to the Fund's, summaries of countries' relations with the Bank began appearing in Article IV reports. Discussions of the adequacy of countries' statistical data also took on more prominence around that time. And in the second half of the decade, staff reports or background papers increasingly included analyses of issues such as the extent of poverty and other issues arising from disparities in the distribution of income; structural distortions arising from controls on labor, goods, and financial markets; and the environmental impacts of macroeconomic policies. Overall, the Board welcomed those innovations but also (with a degree of inconsistency) insisted that emphasis and focus be kept on exchange rate policies and the balance of payments.

---

[51]"Chile—Staff Report for the 1985 Article IV Consultation and Request for an Extended Arrangement," EBS/85/122, Sup. 1 (July 12, 1985), pp. 10 and 22.

[52]Minutes of EBM/83/54–55 (March 28, 1983). Trade policies were regularly reviewed in the WEO exercise, beginning in 1978. Also see Chapter 20, on relations between the Fund and the GATT.

[53]"France—Staff Report for the 1984 Article IV Consultation," SM/84/109 (May 15, 1984), p. 19. The RED discussion is "France—Recent Economic Developments," SM/84/123 (May 29, 1984), Appendix II.

Figure 2.2. Coverage of Article IV Consultations, 1978–89

Percent of membership

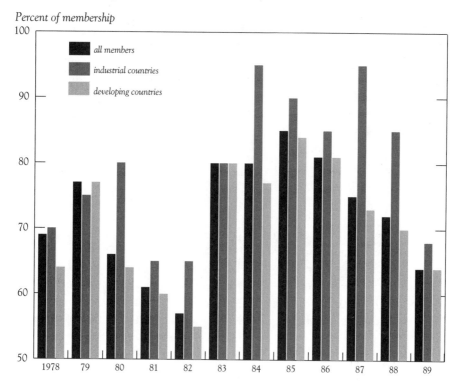

Frequency of Consultations

Although the goal of the Fund was to hold consultations annually with every member, this was not realistic. There was not enough time in the year for the Executive Board to review and discuss developments in every member country, and there were not enough staff to hold the consultations and write the reports. Moreover, circumstances such as elections, parliamentary budget cycles, civil unrest or war, and natural disasters often conspired to prevent discussions from taking place as scheduled. And finally, in numerous cases, authorities put off the Fund's efforts to hold consultations in order to prevent an embarrassing airing of the state of the country's economy. Nonetheless, over the first 12 years of surveillance, the Fund managed to complete consultations for an average of 72 percent of the membership each year (Figure 2.2).

The low point in the evolution of surveillance came in the early 1980s, when many countries had ready access to commercial bank loans and saw little need for frequent contacts with the IMF. After an initial flourish in 1978–79, the frequency of consultations dropped sharply: in 1982, meetings were held with barely over half the Fund's 146 member countries. There was a general problem of lack of continuity, in that the Fund was out of date in its awareness of economic developments in a large portion of its member countries. Even more seriously, the backlogged cases included some countries where major debt-servicing difficulties were developing. When the Executive Board met to discuss the Mexican economy in June 1982, it was doing so for the first time in 27 months (for the background, see Chapter 7, pp. 282–86). E. Walter Robichek (Director of the Western Hemisphere Department) had raised a warning to management in October 1981 that the Fund should undertake a more intensive monitoring—more often than annual consultations—with the three largest countries in Latin America (Brazil, Mexico, and Argentina), owing to their international importance and potential for macroeconomic imbalances.[54] Not until after the debt crisis hit in August 1982 was the Fund galvanized into action.

One person who was most disturbed by the gaps that had crept into the surveillance procedures was de Larosière. If the Fund could ensure that it would have regular contacts with and fruitful oversight of most of the membership on at least an annual basis, then in his judgment, the Fund would be much less likely to get caught off guard as it had been when the debt crisis struck. For the 1983 review of surveillance procedures, the staff prepared recommendations for improving the scheduling of consultations: adhering more strictly to the criteria for specifying annual consultations, setting an outer limit of 24 months between consultations for all members, setting dates at the conclusion of each consultation by which the next one should be held, and tightening the circumstances under which delays would be accepted.

The only real issue was that last point. Countries had frequently asked for delays on the grounds that they were revising policies or preparing budgets or getting ready for elections. As the staff paper for the 1983 surveillance review noted, a "strong case can be made that it is precisely at such times that Article IV consultations can be most constructive . . . particularly in countries that are experiencing a serious deterioration in their situation. Not infrequently, the member eventually has had to seek use of Fund resources on an emergency basis without the benefit of a recent consultation." Several Directors were no more enthusiastic about the idea than if they had been told they should go to the dentist more regularly rather than waiting until their toothache became intense, but no serious objections were raised.[55]

As is evident from Figure 2.2, the new guidelines made a big difference. Annual coverage rose from 57 percent in 1982 to 80 percent or more in each of the next four years.[56] Most important, the number of countries with which no

---

[54]Memorandum from Walter Robichek to William C. Hood, for circulation to the Surveillance Committee (October 9, 1981); in IMF/RD Managing Director file "Correspondence and Memoranda—1981" (Accession 87/27, Box 11, Section 535).

[55]"Annual Review of the Implementation of Surveillance," SM/83/43 (March 1, 1983), p. 17, and minutes of EBM/83/54–55 (March 28, 1983).

[56]Notwithstanding the pressures on the work program of the staff and the Executive Board, the Fund also accommodated the desire of the authorities in the Netherlands to have separate consultations for the Netherlands Antilles. Although a territory within the Kingdom of the Netherlands and not an independent member of the Fund, the Antilles maintained its own currency and its own exchange rate policy (the currency, the Netherlands Antillean guilder, was pegged to the U.S. dollar). The Fund began holding consultations with the Antilles under Article VIII in 1969 and under Article IV in 1978. When Aruba (formerly part of the Antilles) became a separate territory within the Kingdom in 1986, the Fund began holding Article IV consultations with it also.

consultation had been held for two years or more dropped from a peak of 19 in 1982 to 4 in 1984. By that time, the problem of surveillance being avoided at countries' requests had been almost eliminated.[57]

By 1986, the improved regularity of consultations was causing the balance of concerns to shift back to the burdens on the Fund's resources, especially on the time of Executive Directors and the staff. As it happened, in the mid-1980s demands on the Fund were high enough that regular consultation cycles longer than a year could be specified for only a limited set of countries without weakening the effectiveness of surveillance. A large and growing number of countries had stand-by or other borrowing arrangements with the Fund, and many also maintained exchange restrictions that were temporarily approved by the Fund in accordance with Article XIV of the Articles of Agreement. That group had to be kept on an annual cycle whatever their macroeconomic situation, because Article XIV requires countries to consult annually with the Fund on the retention of restrictions, with a view toward their eventual elimination (see below, p. 120).[58]

To reduce time spent on routine consultations, Hans Lundström (Executive Director from Sweden) suggested in July 1986 that the Fund establish a "bicyclic" consultation procedure under which the staff would hold discussions with the authorities every year, but without a concluding Board meeting in the odd years. Staff in area departments and in ETR generally responded favorably to this prospect, but de Larosière declared himself to be "rather reserved." Nonetheless, he judged that this was essentially a matter for the Board to decide, especially

---

[57]"Surveillance Over Exchange Rate Policies—Annual Review—Background Material," SM/86/4, Sup. 1 (January 28, 1986), p. 3 and Table 1. Three of the four backlogged cases resulted from security problems. The Fund had had no contacts with a succession of revolutionary and outlaw governments of Democratic Kampuchea (Cambodia) since October 1973. Consultations with Iraq and the Islamic Republic of Iran were suspended because the two countries were at war. Only in the fourth case, Cape Verde, was the delay attributable to reluctance of the government to receive a mission from the Fund.

[58]The legal constraint is explained in "Periodicity and Form of Article XIV Consultations," SM/87/30 (February 4, 1987). In March 1987, the Executive Board approved a technical amendment to the 1977 decision, by which the Fund could revert to the practice of holding separate consultations under Article XIV in cases where the Article IV consultation cycle was longer than one year. See the minutes of EBM/87/38–39 (March 4, 1987); "Periodicity and Form of Article XIV Consultations—Amendment of Document Entitled 'Surveillance Over Exchange Rate Policies' Attached to Decision No. 5392-(77/63), Adopted April 29, 1977," SM/87/30, Sup. 1 (March 30, 1987); and Decision No. 8564-(87/59), adopted April 1, 1987 (reproduced in the Appendix to this chapter). The following year, a procedure was introduced whereby the Board could indicate the completion of an Article XIV consultation on a lapse-of-time basis, based on a brief report by the staff. See "Annual Review of the Implementation of Surveillance," SM/87/29 (February 4, 1987), pp. 24–25. That procedure was first invoked for Libya in December 1988 and was used twice in 1989 (for Trinidad and Tobago and for Malta). On Libya, see Decision 9054-(89/1), adopted December 30, 1988, on the basis of the staff paper, "Socialist People's Libyan Arab Jamahiriya—Staff Report for the 1988 Article XIV Consultation," SM/88/281 (December 27, 1988).

since it had a large potential impact on the Board's own workload, and he instructed the staff to prepare a specific proposal.[59]

The Board approved Lundström's bicycle plan in general terms in March 1987 and, with some technical modifications, implemented it beginning that summer.[60] With this new procedure, 12-month cycles were to be retained for the 20 largest countries, for 4 others deemed to be "regionally important," for all countries with Fund-supported programs in place or under discussion (58 countries, initially), and for another 5 countries that had requested to be on an annual cycle. For 14 countries that did not fit into any of the categories requiring annual cycles, the staff proposed 18- or 24-month intervals. That left approximately 50 countries that were potentially eligible for the bicycle. In about half those cases, however, the staff responsible for conducting consultations with the country expressed concerns about the sustainability of the country's balance of payments or external debt-servicing capability, or about the country's maintenance of severe restrictions on international trade or payments. Twelve-month cycles were recommended for those cases, and the bicycle was proposed for just 25 countries.

In view of all the constraints imposed, it is perhaps not surprising that the bicycle was a failure. As long as only 25 countries were affected, and only half of those would be scheduled for an interim consultation in any given year, not much scope existed for reducing anyone's workload. Only 3 consultations were concluded on an interim basis in 1987, 11 in 1988 (the first full year of experience), and 15 in 1989. The pace never did pick up significantly, and the procedure was abandoned just a few years later, in 1993.

A reader of this account would be excused for dismissing the story of the bicycle as of little interest or importance, but it does contain a lesson about the culture of the Fund in the 1980s. No matter what gloss might have been applied, the countries on the bicycle were perceived to be less important for the institution. Is it

---

[59]Memorandums from Hans Lundström to Alexandre Kafka (Brazil), Dean of the Executive Board (July 10, 1986); and from C. David Finch (Director of ETR) to the Acting Managing Director (August 18, 1986), with pencilled comments from the Managing Director (September 8); both in IMF/CF (S 420.3, "Article IV Consultations (Second Amendment) 1982–1986").

[60]Ironically for a technical proposal aimed at streamlining Board procedures, Executive Directors spent nearly 2½ days of formal meetings over a period of four months hammering out an agreement. A large part of the difficulty was deciding whether the Board should have any involvement in the interim consultations. In the end, it was decided that interim staff reports would be sent to Executive Directors for information only, so that the Board would have no responsibility. The alternatives were to have the Board (substantively) approve the report on a lapse-of-time basis or (procedurally) approve the completion of the interim consultation on that basis. See "Annual Review of the Implementation of Surveillance," SM/87/29 (February 4, 1987); minutes of EBM/87/38–39 (March 4, 1987); "Consultation Procedures—Initiation of the Bicyclic Procedure and Proposed Changes in Cycles for Article IV Consultations," SM/87/117 (May 20, 1987), Sup. 1 (June 5, 1987), and Sup. 2 (June 24, 1987); minutes of EBM/87/84–85 (June 8, 1987); "Article IV Consultations—Options for Simplified Interim Procedures," SM/87/139 (June 23, 1987); and minutes of EBM/87/100 (July 8, 1987). The procedure was modified in February 1991 to give Executive Directors a lapse-of-time opportunity to request a Board discussion of an interim report.

then surprising that there was a general reluctance on all sides to put countries on it? What official would want to acknowledge that his or her country was unimportant, and what staff member would want to acknowledge that he or she was working on an unimportant country?

Setting Performance Standards

The most glaring gap in the design of Fund surveillance was that no agreed standard existed by which to judge a country's performance. The staff could evaluate the internal consistency of a country's policies and (especially in the WEO exercise) the consistency of policies among countries. But the Fund was on slippery ground when it tried to form judgments about whether policies or performance overall were up to par, simply because par had never been defined. From the beginning, several attempts were made to alleviate this problem by establishing general criteria to make surveillance as concrete as the Fund's financial programming exercises for borrowing countries.

The first effort to establish a standard of performance began at the Annual Meetings in Belgrade, in October 1979. The governor in the Fund for the United States, Treasury Secretary G. William Miller, proposed that the IMF should be able to challenge a country with a persistent balance of payments problem to devise a plan for reducing it, regardless of whether the country needed the financial resources of the Fund. Under this proposal for "greater symmetry" in surveillance, "any nation with an exceptionally large payments imbalance—deficit or surplus—must submit for IMF [i.e., Executive Board] review an analysis showing how it proposes to deal with that imbalance." (IMF, *Summary Proceedings*, 1979, p. 116) Miller's deputy for international affairs, Anthony Solomon, and the U.S. Executive Director, Sam Y. Cross, then pressed their colleagues from other countries in the Group of Five (G-5) to endorse the idea, without initial success.

With the urging of de Larosière, the U.S. initiative was included in a set of staff proposals in the first biennial review of the implementation of surveillance.[61] The staff envisaged that the Managing Director would be responsible for deciding whether a particular surplus or deficit was "large," based on staff analyses and preliminary confidential discussions with the country's authorities. The proposal was, however, put forward with some trepidation, because the staff who were involved (principally from ETR) were not convinced of its practicality. The difficulty, as they saw it, was that large imbalances were not necessarily undesirable. Notably, at the time (end-1979), external surpluses were concentrated in the major oil-exporting countries; given the price of oil, the challenge was not so much to reduce those surpluses as to ensure the orderly financing of the corresponding deficits in oil-importing countries. If those surpluses were excluded, then implementing

---

[61]"Review of the Implementation of the Fund's Surveillance Over Members' Exchange Rate Policies," SM/79/292 (December 21, 1979), pp. 7–8.

the U.S. proposal would detract from, rather than enhance, the symmetry of Fund surveillance.[62]

The Executive Board showed quite a bit of interest in the idea, but Directors raised several questions about how it would work in practice. Were countries to be required to submit a quantified official statement of policy intentions, equivalent to the Letter of Intent required of countries borrowing from the Fund? If so, the willingness of countries to cooperate with the Fund might be compromised. Was the imbalance to be measured by the current account or by the overall balance of payments? Directors representing countries with ready access to international capital markets preferred the latter, and conversely. Was "large" to be defined in terms of the national economy or world trade? Directors representing smaller countries were naturally prepared to insist on a test of international significance. Were surplus and deficit countries to be treated equally? If not, it was not clear what the proposal added to current practice.[63]

A modified and more specific proposal was submitted to the Board a few months later. In this version, the Managing Director would be called upon to form a preliminary judgment whether a country had an external imbalance that was "large" in relation to the national economy, in the sense that it reflected underlying macroeconomic problems. Considerable discretion was to be given to the Managing Director in determining how the Fund should respond to such an assessment. Although the staff and management expected this modification to allay many of the concerns that Executive Directors had raised in February, it had the opposite effect. Led by Joaquín Muns (Spain) and Byanti Kharmawan (Indonesia), Directors representing most developing and some smaller industrial countries objected that the proposal would impose "onerous" burdens and would attempt to replace "persuasion" with "prescription" as the foundation of surveillance. Mahsoun B. Jalal (Saudi Arabia) cautioned his colleagues by quoting an Arab proverb: "If you want to be obeyed, ask for the possible and not for the impossible." Although a clear majority favored accepting the proposal, de Larosière was more impressed by the intensity of the opposition than by the numerical superiority of the support and therefore declined to approve it: "it is not desirable to have twelve Executive Directors overrule nine on a matter of this nature; for the success of the surveillance process depends completely on sustaining confidence and trust in relations."[64] The proposal was never revived.

A second major effort to establish general performance standards was made in the context of discussions of "quantitative indicators" for surveillance, starting in 1985. The idea of using a standard set of uniform, quantitative, and objective in-

---

[62]C. David Finch, "Review of Surveillance: Aide Memoire," memorandum to the Managing Director (February 5, 1980), in IMF/CF (S 490 "Surveillance Over Exchange Rate Policies, June 1978–December 1980").

[63]Minutes of EBM/80/19–20 (February 6, 1980).

[64]Chairman's summing up, minutes of EBM/80/89 (June 11, 1980), p. 32. The "onerous" quotation is from Muns, p. 3, and "prescriptions" is from Kharmawan, p. 18. The quotation from Jalal is on p. 24.

dicators to assess the economic performance of countries was not a new idea in the mid-1980s. It had been an elusive goal ever since the collapse of the par value exchange rate system in the early 1970s. In November 1972, the U.S. deputies to the Committee of Twenty, Paul A. Volcker and J. Dewey Daane, proposed that countries should be required to undertake adjustment whenever their reserve balances moved outside predefined boundaries. Subsequent discussion of that proposal focused in part on whether the set of "objective indicators" should be broadened beyond reserve levels to include the fundamental determinants of reserve adequacy. When it became clear that defining an acceptable reserve target was an extremely complicated and controversial task, the whole effort was abandoned (see de Vries, 1985, pp. 165–76). The general idea of using a broad set of objective indicators as an analytical tool was revived by the Fund staff in 1985 as a means of strengthening the role of the Fund in the G-5 multilateral surveillance exercise (see Chapter 4). In 1986, the use of uniform indicators in the WEO was enhanced along similar lines (Chapter 5).

A parallel effort was made to find a role that objective indicators might play in strengthening the process of Article IV consultations with member countries. In February 1986, as part of a push for setting what eventually were called "monitoring zones" as the basis for assessing macroeconomic performance, Charles Dallara (United States) asked the staff "to explore the feasibility of . . . notional ranges for the outcome in such policy areas as growth, employment, inflation, and the external current account." Dallara suggested that "any substantial deviations from the notional range of outcomes in a country in any one of those policy areas could be a basis for considering the need to hold discussions with the member."[65] That idea was discussed further in a series of Board meetings in 1986 and the first months of 1987, by which time it appeared that a consensus was building in favor of rewriting the basic surveillance decision or at least supplementing it with a new decision covering the role of objective indicators.

Accordingly, in June 1987, the staff offered some specific proposals for giving objective indicators a central role in Article IV surveillance. Instead of continuing to be guided by criteria that had not been helpful, such as whether countries were pursuing, "for balance of payments purposes, . . . monetary and other domestic financial policies that provide abnormal encouragement or discouragement to [international] capital flows," Fund surveillance would be based in part on an evaluation of specific indicators. Under this proposal, the Fund would establish a set of indicators for a country's policies and macroeconomic performance and would determine a range of "desirable and sustainable" values for each indicator. A significant divergence of actual developments from that reference path would trigger consideration of whether special discussions with the country were warranted. To formalize such an approach, the staff suggested that the 1977 surveillance decision be amended by replacing the original five criteria for assessing the "need for discussion with" a member country by a single reference to the signaling role of an

---

[65]Minutes of EBM/86/30 (February 19, 1986), pp. 46–47.

agreed set of indicators, and by adding an obligation for members to furnish data on the indicators to the Fund. The Executive Board, however, was almost unanimous in its reluctance to introduce new formal procedures without first gaining experience through informal experimentation.[66] The proposal for monitoring zones thus got caught in a catch-22: no single country wanted to volunteer to be the subject of more intense scrutiny and pressure, while the Board as a whole was unwilling to jump into uncharted waters. No one was able to find an intermediate path, and this proposal also died.

Closely related to the quantitative indicators idea was the dream that the Fund could agree on a qualitative *global* strategy for assessing the policies and performance of member countries. In 1979, U.S. Treasury Secretary Miller suggested that "one possibility" for "bolder action" to strengthen surveillance "would be for the Fund to assess the performance of individual countries against an agreed global strategy for growth, adjustment, and price stability" (IMF, *Summary Proceedings*, 1979, p. 116). The staff paper for the first biennial surveillance review included a more modest version of the proposal, in which the seven largest industrial countries would each give the Fund a quantified policy strategy. The Fund would then assess the global implications of the implied aggregate strategy in the WEO and would assess actual performance against the implied standard in Article IV consultations. The time, however, was not yet ripe for even that level of commitment, and in February 1980 the Board—notwithstanding Cross's support—expressed considerable doubts whether the goal was practical.[67]

On a rather more mundane level, the Board did agree in 1980 that in principle it would be helpful to bunch the consultations with the G-7 countries as close together as possible, so that those countries could be considered in relation to one another and discussed in a consistent manner. If all of the major countries could be asked to discuss their economic outlook and their intended policy course at the same time, then perhaps something akin to a global strategy might emerge spontaneously. Unfortunately, neither the staff nor the Executive Board had the resources to take all seven countries in one bite. Instead, three countries were to be bunched before the spring WEO and the other four before the fall round. Brief staff visits were to be made to the countries in the latter group to obtain current data and policy intentions prior to the spring WEO. That general strategy was followed throughout the 1980s.

The requirements for agreeing on a global strategy were discussed further during the 1982 biennial review. The U.S. Executive Director, then Richard D. Erb, took a dimmer view than his predecessor, noting that "the Fund clearly did not possess" either the requisite analytical framework or the political power to impose

---

[66]See "The Use of Indicators in Surveillance—Review of the 1977 Decision on Surveillance Over Exchange Rate Policies," EBS/87/136 (June 24, 1987), pp. 7–11, and the Chairman's summing up in the minutes of EBM/87/107 (July 23, 1987), p. 6.

[67]See "Review of the Implementation of the Fund's Surveillance Over Members' Exchange Rate Policies," SM/79/292 (December 21, 1979), pp. 8–9; and the minutes of EBM/80/19–20 (February 6, 1980).

it on sovereign countries even if it had one. Notably, neither within the staff nor among Executive Directors was there a general agreement or understanding on the role of the exchange rate as a policy instrument or on the effectiveness of different exchange rate regimes. Without such agreement, there could be no global strategy.[68]

After 1982, the global strategy lay dormant for about a decade before being revived in the early 1990s in the context of the silent revolution. By that time, the proposed strategy was no longer confined to the appropriate conduct of exchange rate policy, but was broadened to cover the whole panoply of policies affecting macroeconomic stability and economic liberalization. The Interim Committee endorsed a general strategy in 1993 and then adopted a more comprehensive strategy at its meeting in Madrid in October 1994, in what became known as the Madrid Declaration (see *Annual Report 1995*, pp. 207–8).

Publicity

How much publicity should be given to the Fund's consultations with member countries? This has always been a delicate question, on which opinions shifted very gradually during the 1980s and then more dramatically several years later.

When the Fund began conducting surveillance under Article IV in 1978, the secrecy of the process was taken for granted (see de Vries, 1985, p. 850). The Fund would be asking the authorities of member countries to provide sensitive information about how they were conducting exchange rate policies, the staff were expected to prepare candid assessments of the consistency and sustainability of those policies, and both the staff reports and the summing up of the Executive Board discussion would be circulated on a timely basis to all member governments. To make those documents available to a wider audience, it was judged, could create economic and political problems for the authorities and could compromise their willingness to be forthright. Even when the Board decided in 1980 to add a section on surveillance to its Annual Report, it did so on the proviso that "there should be no publication of information on individual countries."[69]

With experience came a trickle of minor exceptions.[70] By the early 1980s, a scattering of countries began releasing the staff's preliminary appraisal to the press shortly after the conclusion of discussions with the staff mission. (Although the staff report was a document of the Fund, the preliminary appraisal delivered to the authorities at the conclusion of the mission was the property of the member country.) Beginning in 1984, countries under "enhanced surveillance" (see Chapters 9 and 10) were permitted to release the staff report to their private sector creditors,

---

[68]See the minutes of EBM/82/31–32 (March 17, 1982) and the Chairman's summing up in the attachment to "Review of the Document 'Surveillance Over Exchange Rate Policies' and Annual Review of the Implementaton of Surveillance," EBD/82/89 (April 13, 1982), p. 1.

[69]Chairman's summing up, minutes of EBM/80/20 (February 6, 1980), p. 40.

[70]A related issue, discussed in Chapter 5, was whether to publish the WEO documents. Publication was approved in 1980.

on a strictly confidential basis. (Since it was in the banks' own interest to keep the information to themselves, the confidentiality rule was generally obeyed.) Beginning in 1986, the Fund's *Annual Report* included a summary of the conclusions of the consultations with each of the G-7 countries, based on the summing up of the Board discussion. In 1988, the Fund began publishing—only for those countries that agreed—the indexes of nominal and real effective exchange rates that were the focus of surveillance discussions on exchange rate policy.

The basic principle of confidentiality of the staff report was not seriously questioned in the 1980s, but the background (RED) papers were occasionally treated more liberally. In a few cases, background studies for an RED would be circulated as Working Papers and published under the author's name as independent research papers. An early example was a study of the impact of North Sea oil on the U.K. economy, which was prepared as part of the 1980 consultation with the United Kingdom and later published in *Staff Papers* (Bond and Knöbl, 1982).[71] In 1989, the Fund broke precedent by publishing a revised version of the RED for the 1988 consultation with Germany (Lipschitz and others, 1989). These tentative steps culminated in a decision in 1994 to publish REDs and other background papers on a more regular basis, unless the authorities of a country objected.[72]

Handling Problem Cases

A central dilemma—perhaps *the* central dilemma—in devising effective procedures for surveillance was how to reconcile the need for evenhandedness with the desirability of devoting as much attention as possible to countries with serious economic problems and to countries whose policies have major impacts on their neighbors or on the world economy. How could surveillance be effective if the Fund treated all countries the same?

The Fund received a mandate to focus especially on problem cases, very shortly after the Second Amendment to the Articles came into force. At the end of April 1978, the Interim Committee responded to concerns about exchange rate misalignments, especially the collapse of the U.S. dollar, by noting "with approval . . . that particular attention will be focused on those cases in which there are ques-

---

[71]A summary of the main findings of the study was included in the RED: "United Kingdom—Recent Economic Developments," SM/81/30 (February 5, 1981), Appendix I.

[72]See *Annual Report 1995*, p. 39. In 1992, the Fund began publishing REDs for the new member countries that had been part of the former Soviet Union or were in transition from central planning, under the series heading of *Economic Reviews*. On an exceptional basis in the early 1990s, papers derived from consultations with Germany and the United States were published as Lipschitz and McDonald (1990) and Horiguchi and others (1992), respectively. In addition, the coverage of policy issues from consultations in the *Annual Report* was greatly expanded, from 3 pages on 7 countries in 1986 to 60 pages on 40 countries in 1997. The Fund then began issuing "Press Information Notices" (PINs; later redubbed "Public Information Notices") on many consultations, derived primarily from the summing up. Those notices were published separately, and the extended treatment in the *Annual Report* was dropped.

tions about whether the exchange rate policies of members are consistent with the agreed exchange rate principles."[73] Immediately afterward, Managing Director Johannes Witteveen established a secret internal Surveillance Committee (chaired by the Managing Director and including the Deputy Managing Director and the Directors of the area departments, ETR, and Research) to identify and discuss problem countries. The Surveillance Committee first met on June 1, 1978 (the only meeting chaired by Witteveen, who was succeeded as Managing Director by de Larosière later that month). Thereafter, it met two to four times a year throughout most of de Larosière's tenure at the Fund.

Jacques Polak—supported by most other participants including the Managing Director—argued forcefully at the early meetings of the Surveillance Committee, and in associated memorandums, that the Fund—and the Managing Director in particular—should take an active role in identifying and discussing with member countries cases where exchange rate movements were causing problems. But the Committee struggled with the question of how best to carry out this type of surveillance: through supplemental or ad hoc consultations, or merely through regularly scheduled but especially intensive Article IV consultations?

During its first couple of years, the Surveillance Committee identified several problem cases, mostly related to developing and small industrial countries. This led to some intensification of discussions of the exchange rate in the regular consultations, but not to much more. Perhaps the most notable effect was the handling of Denmark and Belgium, both of which were singled out by the Surveillance Committee in March 1980 as countries with an overvalued exchange rate. Besides having the staff raise the matter with the authorities during the scheduled Article IV consultations, de Larosière approved the idea of going public by mentioning the Fund's concerns in the WEO—which was to be published for the first time that spring. Although the language was typically circumspect, the evaluation of the exchange rate was unusually blunt:

> Prominent among [countries with severe adjustment problems] are *Belgium* and *Denmark*. . . . In both of these countries, there have been sizable increases in interest rates and other restrictive monetary measures designed to support the exchange rate, but in recent months intervention in the exchange markets has been required nonetheless (*WEO*, May 1980, p. 51).

Otherwise, the problem cases identified by the Surveillance Committee were usually handled routinely. Over time, the committee turned its attention ever more to the economies of the major industrial countries, and it became primarily a means of coordinating the analysis of the European, Asian, and Western Hemisphere Departments on those countries. By 1986, it had outlived its usefulness, and for a time it ceased to meet. (A new Surveillance Committee was formed in the 1990s, as part of a broad effort to strengthen surveillance.)

---

[73]Interim Committee communiqué, April 30, 1978, para. 4; in de Vries (1985), Vol. 3, p. 236. For background, see de Vries (1985), pp. 854–57.

1977 Decision on Ad Hoc Consultations

What the Interim Committee endorsed in the communiqué quoted above was a provision in the Executive Board's 1977 surveillance decision for ad hoc consultations at the initiative of the Managing Director. In addition to the scheduled consultations that were to be held with every member country, the 1977 decision enabled the Managing Director to initiate a confidential discussion with a country, and report on it to the Board, if he "considers that a member's exchange rate policies may not be in accord with the exchange rate principles" of Article IV.[74] In practice, despite the care that went into drafting that language and the explicit endorsement it received from the Interim Committee, this specific procedure was never invoked.

The staff and the Managing Director were eager to hold ad hoc consultations, to test and demonstrate the effectiveness of Fund surveillance. After discussions of several possible cases during the summer of 1978, they decided to try to tackle a small country first. At the beginning of September 1978, a newly elected government in Iceland announced that it was devaluing the exchange rate by 15 percent as an emergency measure. The Fund staff immediately prepared a paper on the background to the devaluation, which was placed on the agenda of the Executive Board for September 8 with the intention that the Board would decide whether to hold a formal consultation on the matter. The staff did not dispute the need for the devaluation, but they felt that the need for tighter financial policies and other supporting measures should be taken up by the Fund at an early date.[75]

When the meeting opened, the Executive Director speaking for Iceland, Frede Hollensen (Denmark), objected strenuously. Hollensen did not object in principle to the idea of the Fund discussing the devaluation of the Icelandic króna, but he argued that it was neither proper nor acceptable for the Fund to pick on Iceland while it effectively ignored the similarly large fluctuations in currency values of the major countries with floating rates. C. David Finch (Deputy Director, ETR) responded for the staff that the circumstances in this case were unique in the period since the Second Amendment had come into force. Although it was true that the Japanese yen and the U.S. dollar had shown substantial movement in the past few months, and both countries had implemented policy actions to affect the exchange rate, those developments were viewed by the staff as having occurred within the framework of an unchanged exchange rate policy. The Fund had dealt with other significant discrete changes in rates (by Jamaica, Peru, Ghana, and Nepal) through normally scheduled consultations with the member country. The Board, however, was not

---

[74]The Fund also had in place a procedure, initiated in 1970 and formalized in 1973, for conducting special consultations with member countries as background for the WEO. See de Vries (1985), pp. 276–79.

[75]Iceland's exchange crisis followed from a severe loss of international competitiveness for the main export industry, fishing. Exchange markets were closed on August 28, and the government that took office on September 1 informed the Fund on September 4 that it would reopen the markets on September 6 at the new exchange rate. "Iceland—Exchange System," EBS/78/501 (September 7, 1978).

convinced. Not a single Director spoke in favor of holding a substantive discussion of the Iceland case, and the matter was dropped from further consideration.[76]

A few months later, in response to an emergency package of policies announced by the U.S. authorities to reverse the rapid depreciation of the dollar, the Fund held a special consultation with the United States (see Chapter 3). In that case, the staff decided not to invoke the 1977 ad hoc procedure, and the consultation was treated instead as a "special consultation"—the first of its kind—under the general authority of the new Article IV.[77] In summing up that experience, the Managing Director noted that

> this was the first occasion on which the Board has undertaken special surveillance of the exchange rate and of the underlying policies of a major member country. This has been carried out with the active cooperation of the United States. This kind of surveillance should always be conducted whenever situations develop in major countries that have an important bearing on the economies of other countries.[78]

1979 Decision on Supplemental Consultations

In January 1979, the Executive Board formalized that approach by adopting a separate "supplemental surveillance procedure" instructing the Managing Director to initiate an ad hoc consultation with a member whenever he "considers that a modification in a member's exchange arrangements or exchange rate policies or the behavior of the exchange rate of its currency may be important or may have important effects on other members, whatever the member's exchange arrangements may be." An unusual feature of that decision was the accompanying statement by the Managing Director explaining its context, which was to be considered as having the same legal effect as if it had been part of the decision.[79] That statement (reproduced in the Appendix to this chapter) made it clear that "lack of movement" in an exchange rate could trigger such a discussion just as well as movement, if the level of the rate had become inappropriate to a country's circumstances. Further, the statement noted that the phrasing of the decision covered both importance to the member (which would be relevant for small countries) and importance to other members (which would be relevant for larger countries).

The 1979 decision on supplemental consultations was thus intended to ensure evenhandedness and to remove the stigma associated with the 1977 decision. Although it was explicitly framed as a "supplement" to the 1977 decision (which remained on the books), it effectively superseded it. Under the new procedure, the Managing Director was not required to submit a formal report on a discussion to the Executive Board, but he "may report to the Executive Board or informally ad-

---

[76]Minutes of EBM/78/136 (September 8, 1978).

[77]Later, the question of whether a supplemental consultation should be held with the United States (under the 1979 decision discussed below) was considered by the staff and management on several occasions, always without result.

[78]Minutes of EBM/78/198 (December 13, 1978), p. 20.

[79]On the role of the Managing Director's statement, see the minutes of EBM/79/13 (January 22, 1979), especially the statement by the General Counsel, Joseph Gold.

vise the Executive Directors," and a formal report and discussion might follow from such informal soundings.

The new procedure did not turn out to be much easier to apply than its unfortunate predecessor. During its first year, it produced only two hesitant actions. First, in January the government of South Africa announced that it was abandoning the practice of fixing the exchange rate on a daily basis, that it intended to move toward a unified exchange regime, and that henceforth it would let the market determine the rate subject to intervention by the central bank. In response, a staff team visited South Africa in February to discuss the implications with the authorities. The mission concluded that the policy shift was appropriate and welcome. A report on the matter was circulated to Executive Directors in April, but no one felt that a Board meeting was needed.[80] Second, in May the exchange value of the Japanese yen began to weaken markedly. Ernest Sturc (Director of ETR) suggested to the Managing Director that he initiate a supplemental consultation with Japan. De Larosière flew to Tokyo to meet with the Finance Minister and the Governor of the Bank of Japan, but no further action was taken for several months. When the yen weakened further in March 1980, the Surveillance Committee recommended a supplemental consultation. A staff visit was held, but again no Board discussion followed (see Chapter 3).

By then it was clear that the only way the Fund could hope to have special consultations become an effective part of surveillance was to make them less special and more routine. For the Board's 1980 review of surveillance, the staff proposed that supplemental consultations be employed with some regularity in cases where problems might exist or even be latent. That proposal was endorsed in principle, but Executive Directors again expressed concerns about the negative connotations that might be attached to such consultations. The Managing Director tried to reassure them by stressing that there should be "no formality" and "no stigma."[81] In practice, although the 1979 procedure was officially neutral, it did not escape being seen as stigmatic, and it was invoked only rarely. Several times throughout the 1980s, the Managing Director initiated informal discussions with members outside the usual cycle of Article IV consultations, but only twice did those talks lead to formal special consultations: with Sweden in 1982 and with Korea in 1987. Those cases are discussed below.

Information Notice System

Since the staff was reluctant to initiate special consultations after the 1978 rebuff on Iceland, the procedure could be used only when one country or a group of countries brought a complaint against another. What was needed was a more regular means of reporting potential problem cases to the Board, so that Directors could indicate in a more neutral framework whether they wished to hold a discussion on a country. During the supplemental consultation with Sweden in Decem-

---

[80]See "South Africa—Exchange System," EBS/79/220 (April 16, 1979).
[81]Minutes of EBM/80/20 (February 6, 1980), p. 41.

ber 1982, Polak suggested that the staff should develop a regular and quantitative procedure for initiating Board discussions of significant changes in exchange rate policies. That led to the establishment of the Information Notice System the following year.

The heart of the Information Notice System was a detailed database on real effective exchange rates that the staff had developed over a period of years.[82] By 1983, the data covered all but about 30 of the Fund's 146 member countries.[83] For countries with substantial exports of manufactured goods, effective changes were calculated using weights that reflected the country's overall competitiveness, rather than just its bilateral trading relationships as in most earlier estimates.[84] For the larger industrial countries, comparisons were based on unit labor costs, which the staff viewed as the most reliable measure of underlying costs. For developing and smaller industrial countries, where cost data were more limited, consumer price indexes were used instead. By plotting these data over enough years, one could get a prima facie indication of whether a country had been gaining or losing international competitiveness for its exports.

The Achilles' heel of the system was the lack of an unambiguous measure of the right level of competitiveness: of a clear way to judge whether a change in the index was moving the country toward, away from, or along an appropriate path. When working in detail on a single country, the staff usually looked for a period in the not-too-distant past when the country's balance of payments was in a comfortable position. A substantial appreciation of the real effective exchange rate since then would be considered a signal of a possible problem.[85] That methodology was too unwieldy for a system to be applied uniformly to the whole membership, so the Fund had to devise a rather arbitrary substitute. Since the point of the exercise was to help determine whether a special discussion should be held between the normally scheduled consultations, the obvious solution was to focus on large changes (in either direction) since the last time the Executive Board had discussed the country's economy.

The Executive Board agreed to establish the Information Notice System during the annual review of surveillance in March 1983. At de Larosière's suggestion, it

---

[82]Economists use the term "real exchange rate" in two distinct senses, reflecting the type of interaction that is being stressed (see Kenen, 1985, pp. 636–37): the real exchange rate is either the ratio of traded to untraded goods prices, or the product of the nominal exchange rate and the ratio of domestic to foreign prices. By either measure, a rise (appreciation) in the real exchange rate signals a loss of international competitiveness. The latter measure is the one commonly used at the IMF, both in policy discussions and in publications such as the *World Economic Outlook* and *International Financial Statistics*.

[83]The main limitation was that a number of countries did not compute monthly or even quarterly price indexes. In 1986, the system was made virtually universal by interpolating price data where necessary.

[84]The methodology was derived from the Fund's Multilateral Exchange Rate Model (MERM), which is discussed in Chapter 5. For details, see Zanello and Desruelle (1997).

[85]For a brief review of the issues, see Artus and Knight (1984), pp. 6–8. For a later detailed review of the difficulties of assessing the equilibrium behavior of exchange rates, see MacDonald (1995).

was agreed that the threshold for issuing a notice to the Board should be a 10 percent change in the real effective exchange rate since the last Board discussion (or over the previous 12 months, if the Board had not held a discussion in that time span). There was no particular rationale for that number, except that it was expected to produce a manageable number of notices. To round out the procedure, the Board also agreed to a suggestion from Polak that the staff prepare a quarterly report showing longer-run changes in the indexes for all countries.[86]

Like every other attempt to focus surveillance effectively on problem cases, the Information Notice System was a failure. During seven years starting in 1983, the staff issued 152 separate notices of large changes in real effective exchange rates (excluding notices issued as part of a more general staff report), covering 67 different countries. Not one of those notices ever led to a special Board discussion, and the whole system of individual country notices was disbanded at the conclusion of the 1990 biennial review of surveillance procedures.

Because the staff remained reluctant to flag specific problem cases, the country notices typically just reported the change and summarized the country's macroeconomic situation without drawing conclusions on whether the reported change might be good or bad. The arbitrary base period (normally the date of the last Board discussion of the country) added to the difficulty of interpretation. Furthermore, an unexpected complication arose. As it happened, the frequency of large changes was affected heavily by the behavior of the key reserve currencies, which occasionally led to a large number of irrelevant notices being issued. For example, 41 separate Information Notice System notices were issued in 1986—mostly for small countries— owing largely to the sharp depreciation of the U.S. dollar rather than to the country's own policies or economic conditions. In fact, it turned out to be more difficult for large countries to be the subject of a notice, partly because of the greater frequency of consultations but also because of the greater diversity of their trading relationships. (A small effective depreciation of the dollar might well cause a much larger effective depreciation of a small-country currency pegged to it.)[87]

Supplemental Consultations

The Fund held only two supplemental consultations under Article IV during the 11 years covered in this History, and none in the following decade. In each case, the Fund reached a cautious compromise and conveyed a muted criticism to the member country. For all its limitations, the process had an important strength, in that the Fund served as an objective referee in disputes between countries and diffused what had been quite heated political pressures. This cooling-off procedure helped economic policies to evolve gradually in the right direction.

---

[86]Minutes of EBM/83/54–55 (March 28, 1983).

[87]Over the seven years of the full-fledged Information Notice System, three separate notices were issued on the U.S. dollar (in 1985, 1986, and 1988), two on the pound sterling (in 1985 and 1987), one on Japan (in 1990), and none on the other G-10 countries. The largest number of notices (eight) was for the Nicaraguan córdoba, which was linked to the U.S. dollar.

Sweden

The first supplemental consultation was in response to a 16 percent devaluation of the Swedish krona in October 1982. Most observers agreed that a devaluation was needed, but the staff judged that the size was much larger than warranted.

Sweden, in contrast to many other countries with relatively high inflation, did not fear devaluation. Swedish officials especially recalled the benefits of the devaluation of the krona by just over 30 percent against the U.S. dollar in 1949, at a time when Swedish exports had become seriously overpriced in world markets.[88] During the global currency turmoil of 1971–73, the krona generally appreciated slightly against the dollar but depreciated against other European currencies, after which the government decided to try to stabilize the currency by fixing the exchange rate within the narrow margins of the European "snake" arrangements. That experiment, however, lasted just four years, until Sweden's first non-Socialist government since 1932 bailed out of the snake with a 10 percent effective devaluation in August 1977.[89] The krona then was pegged to a basket of 15 currencies that was weighted by trade shares except that the U.S. dollar was assigned a higher weight. Thus when the Fund began conducting "firm surveillance" in 1979, the krona was temporarily at a comfortable level. The underlying position, however, was troubled by a continuing inconsistency between the stable exchange rate and the high rate of Swedish inflation.[90]

Sweden's economic difficulties accumulated again to the boiling point by the beginning of 1981. The coalition government barely weathered an exchange crisis without a devaluation in January by tightening both fiscal and monetary policies, but the coalition fell apart a few months later in the midst of rising unemployment and other strains on the economy. A Fund mission—headed by Hans O. Schmitt, Senior Advisor in the European Department—arrived in Stockholm in late August to conduct the regular Article IV consultation. Schmitt advised the authorities that they would have difficulty reversing the 8 percent loss that Sweden had undergone in international competitiveness since 1973 without a "significant devaluation" or a large cut in social security contributions or in other compensation to employees: cuts that would have been anathema (and probably politically fatal) to the government.

---

[88]For the Fund staff's analysis of the 1949 devaluation (at which time Sweden was not yet a member of the Fund), see Rolf Evenson, "Note on Sweden's New Exchange Rate," Staff Memorandum No. 399, October 12, 1949; IMF/CF (C/Sweden/430, "Exchange Rates"). The devaluation against the dollar was by the same percentage as that of the pound sterling and a number of other currencies shortly beforehand, so the effective devaluation would have been much smaller. Nonetheless, it was cited as a prototype by the architect of the 1982 devaluation; see Feldt (1991), p. 59.

[89]Exchange rate changes beginning in the 1970s are measured in effective terms and thus are not commensurate with the 1949 devaluation. This brief summary also omits numerous smaller exchange rate adjustments.

[90]For the six years through 1982, consumer prices in Sweden rose at an average annual rate of 10½ percent, and in total by about 20 percent relative to the average for all industrial countries.

Figure 2.3. Sweden: Effective Exchange Rate, 1970–82

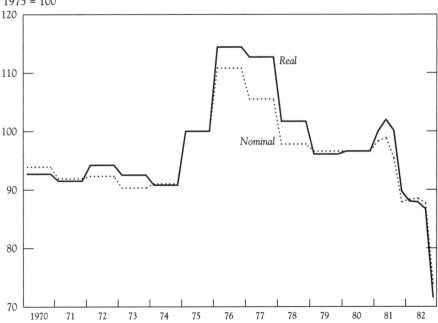

1975 = 100

Schmitt's advice on behalf of the IMF was very much in line with the views of the authorities. Ten days later, on September 14, 1981, the central bank (the Riksbank) devalued the krona by 10 percent against the basket, the first devaluation since the peg was established four years earlier.[91] Both the staff and the Executive Board judged this devaluation to be an appropriate response to circumstances, noted that it should fully offset the fall in competitiveness of the previous eight years (Figure 2.3),[92] and urged the authorities to implement supporting domestic measures aimed at restructuring the economy.[93]

Parliamentary elections in September 1982 returned the Social Democrats to power, led by Prime Minister Olof Palme.[94] During the three-week transition after

---

[91]At that time, the Riksbank had legal responsibility for exchange rate policy. The governor and the governing board were chosen by parliament, and the bank's policies were expected to be consistent with those of the government. In most cases (including this one), the initiative for a change in the rate was taken by the governor.

[92]The "real exchange rate" in Figure 2.3 is an index of unit labor costs relative to partner countries, adjusted for changes in exchange rates. Fourteen partner countries are included, weighted by importance for competitiveness; the weights reflect both bilateral trade and indirect competition, as in the MERM. This was the primary index used by the Fund staff at the time.

[93]The staff conclusions are in "Sweden—Staff Report for the 1981 Article IV Consultation," SM/81/201 (October 27, 1981), p. 11. For the Chairman's summing up of the Executive Board meeting, see the minutes of EBM/81/144 (November 18, 1981), pp. 15–16.

[94]Palme had been prime minister from 1969 to 1976, the last in a continuous succession of Social Democrats who had governed Sweden for 44 years.

the elections, Palme's Minister of Finance, Kjell-Olof Feldt, devised a plan to devalue the krona by 20 percent against the basket. He persuaded a reluctant central bank governor (Lars Wohlin) to go along with the plan, but he then ran into a buzzsaw of opposition from abroad.

The morning before the new government was to take office, on October 7, all of the other Nordic finance ministers and central bank governors (i.e., those from Denmark, Finland, and Norway) met secretly with Feldt at Arlanda Airport just outside Stockholm. Their reaction to the proposal was uniformly and strongly negative, but Feldt argued that it was necessary to strengthen the competitiveness of Swedish industry. The only alternative, in his view, would be a ruinous increase in domestic interest rates.[95] To regain credibility and stabilize the rate after the devaluation, Feldt was considering tying the krona to the deutsche mark. When he informed the president of the Deutsche Bundesbank, Karl-Otto Pöhl, of his intentions later in the day, Pöhl also reacted quite negatively on the grounds that Sweden's macroeconomic policies were not consistent with those of Germany. Pöhl managed to dissuade Feldt from the linkage to the deutsche mark but could not convince him to keep the devaluation within single digits. Finally, near midnight in Stockholm, Feldt reached de Larosière by telephone. The Managing Director also tried unsuccessfully to convince Feldt to reduce the magnitude of the devaluation and to back it up with a sharp increase in interest rates.

The only effect of all of this criticism on October 7 was to persuade the new government to reduce slightly the size of the planned devaluation. The next day, Palme took office and promptly announced a 16 percent devaluation against the basket.[96]

Even before the devaluation, Schmitt's staff team had concluded that the most that could be justified by lost international competitiveness was a devaluation of 4 to 5 percent. That technical finding coincided with political judgments across Europe, which made a confrontation in the Fund all but inevitable. When Jón Sigurdsson (Iceland), the Executive Director speaking for Sweden, informed the Board of the authorities' action that same day, Gerhard Laske (Germany) immediately asked for the matter to be placed on the Board's agenda. Laske was supported by Christopher Taylor (Alternate—United Kingdom), who suggested that a supplemental consultation might be the appropriate vehicle, and by all of the other European Directors and Dallara. Despite Sigurdsson's plea on behalf of Sweden to wait for more information to be made available, a preliminary discussion on procedures was scheduled to be held the following week.[97]

---

[95]Feldt (1991), pp. 57–77, describes this meeting and other elements of the preparations for devaluation. Additional information here is from background interviews and internal IMF memorandums. For what was known in the Fund at the time, see the memorandum from L. Alan Whittome to the Managing Director (October 12, 1982), in IMF/RD Managing Director file "Sweden, 1982" (Accession 85/33, Box 2, Section 376); also see the statement by Gerhard Laske at EBM/82/133 (October 8, 1982), p. 37.

[96]The exchange regime involved maintaining the value of the krona against an index, which was defined at 100 for the period from August 1977 to September 1981. The 1981 devaluation raised the index to 111, and the 1982 devaluation set it at 132.

[97]Minutes of EBM/82/133 (October 8, 1982).

On October 13, the Board took up the formal question of whether to hold a special consultation and, if so, under what authority: the 1979 "supplemental surveillance procedure" or the more stigmatic 1977 decision. Sigurdsson again issued a strong protest, not only because he believed the devaluation to be warranted but because it appeared that the Fund was singling Sweden out for undue scrutiny. Several other Directors, however, suggested that the devaluation was unjustified and was aimed at gaining Sweden an unfair competitive advantage over its trading partners; in effect, that it was a "beggar my neighbor" policy that could lead to a dangerous spiral of competitive devaluations. Sigurdsson himself was awkwardly placed by the situation, as he also represented two of the countries that were most adversely affected and were pushing the Fund to act: Denmark and Norway. His two-part intervention, arguing against and then for intervention by the Fund, was regarded around the table as a remarkable tour de force, but the second half must have been the more persuasive: the Board agreed to hold a special consultation under authority of the 1979 decision.[98]

The Swedish authorities clearly would have preferred that there be no special consultation, but it did present them with an opportunity. Given that several of their main trading partners were upset enough to be contemplating retaliatory or offsetting measures, cooperation with the Fund might help deflect criticism and forestall retaliation.[99] Schmitt and three other staff economists spent a week meeting with officials in Stockholm in early November, at the end of which they reiterated the gist of the conclusions that they had reached earlier. They agreed that Sweden faced a "structural" current account deficit (i.e., one that was too large to have resulted from business-cycle factors alone) and that a devaluation was an appropriate means of reducing it. "However, in the view of the staff, a devaluation of a lesser amount than that undertaken should have been ample to serve the purpose, especially given the devaluation of last year."[100] Although the staff team estimated that a devaluation of no more than 5 percent would have restored sustainability to the external accounts, they decided not to go too far out on a limb and instead cited a range of 5–10 percent—still well below the actual figure of 16 percent—as justifiable.

A critical issue for the Fund was the relationship between the exchange rate and the whole range of Sweden's other economic policies. If "other obstacles to competition from abroad," such as export credit subsidies, were eliminated, then "the possible adverse effects on other countries [could] be mitigated," the staff report

---

[98]The formal decision read, "The Executive Board, acting under Article IV and Decision No. 6026-(79/13), adopted January 22, 1979, invited the Managing Director to conduct special consultations with Sweden." Decision No. 7225-(82/135), adopted October 13, 1982; minutes of EBM/82/135 (October 13, 1982), p. 29.

[99]Finland devalued the markka by 10 percent in effective terms in two steps, immediately before and after the Swedish action. Norway had already devalued the krone by around 6 percent in August and September and took no action at this time. Denmark did not change its exchange rate.

[100]"Sweden—Staff Report for the 1982 Special Consultation Under Article IV with Sweden," EBS/82/222 (December 3, 1982), p. 11.

concluded.[101] Since the authorities seemed willing to take such action, Schmitt suggested to the minister of finance, Kjell-Olof Feldt, that he write a letter to the Managing Director detailing a strategy to carry out specific supporting measures. Feldt eventually agreed to do so, on the condition that it be a personal letter. The Managing Director could (and did) quote from the letter at the Board meeting, but could not circulate it; otherwise, it might be interpreted as equivalent to a Letter of Intent and exploited by opposition parties.

The Board met in restricted session on December 22 to conclude the special consultation and found in favor of the staff view: "it was considered that, on the whole, the size of the . . . devaluation was not justified by the underlying competitive devaluation and that a lesser move would have been appropriate."[102] It was an uneasy meeting. Several Directors were uncomfortable with the whole idea of the Fund making judgments about appropriate exchange rate adjustments, since so much uncertainty was involved. Since no one was prepared to argue against the legitimacy of devaluation as a policy tool for countries with large external deficits, Directors found themselves arguing more from instinct than from evidence. And there was a general discomfort with the circumstances that made it easier for the Fund to deal with discrete exchange rate adjustments than with the misalignment of floating rates, especially since this lack of symmetry served in some measure to give the major countries a free ride. Even so, at the end of the day, most of those involved felt that the conclusion was the right one and that the Fund had played a helpful role both in defusing a volatile situation by serving as an objective referee and in defining the right course for further policy action by Sweden.

Korea

The other special consultation during the 1980s was held with Korea in 1987. As in the Swedish case, the story of this conflict begins with an economic crisis of several years earlier. Korea had experienced rapid development in the 1960s and early 1970s, reflecting the implementation of policies promoting exports, including principally exchange rate and tax policies.[103] Drawings from the Fund's oil facility and the Compensatory Financing Facility (CFF), plus remittances from Koreans who were helping develop the economies of the Middle East states, helped Korea weather the first oil shock in 1973–74. But the industrial policies that had been so successful up to that point led to structural strains and a resurgence of inflation in 1977 and 1978 through overexpansion in petrochemicals and other sectors. These policy errors were aggravated severely in 1979–80 by a series of unrelated exogenous developments: the rapid rise in world oil prices, a severe winter that sharply reduced the rice harvest, and the assassination of President Park Chung Hee in October 1979.

---

[101]Ibid.

[102]Chairman's summing up, minutes of EBM/82/166 (December 22, 1982), p. 3.

[103]For a review of Korea's adjustment experience through 1984, see Aghevli and Márquez-Ruarte (1985). SaKong (1993) provides an overview of Korean experience with economic development, including relations with the IMF. The structural changes in the Korean economy in the 1980s are examined in Corbo and Suh (1992).

Figure 2.4. Korea: Growth, Inflation, and IMF Credits, 1971–90

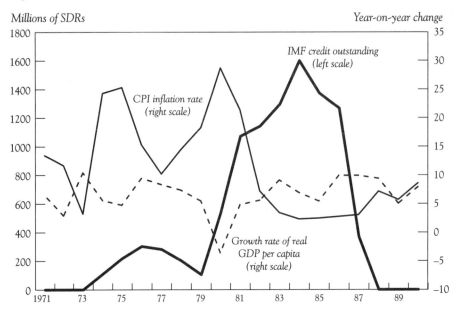

In response to this burgeoning crisis, the Korean authorities initiated a major adjustment program in 1980. The major elements of the program were a large devaluation (17 percent against the U.S. dollar in January 1980), adoption of a more flexible exchange rate regime,[104] a tightening of financial policies, and upward adjustments in domestic energy prices. The Fund supported this program by lending Korea a total of just over SDR 1 billion ($1.3 billion) in 1980–81, under two stand-by arrangements plus compensatory financing for a temporary shortfall in export receipts (Figure 2.4).[105]

By the time the second of these stand-by arrangements expired in 1982, the economy was on the rebound and Korea was regaining some of the international competitiveness that had been lost through inflation. Over the next two years, the exchange rate continued to depreciate sharply against the U.S. dollar. The dollar, however, was quite strong, and most currencies were falling relative to it in 1983–84. The Korean won dropped more than most in 1983 and thus depreciated in effective terms as well, but that trend was reversed in 1984. Overall, from 1981 through 1984, neither the nominal nor the real exchange rate showed much trend (Figure 2.5).

---

[104]Until January 1980, the Korean won was pegged to the U.S. dollar and was devalued occasionally to offset the inflation differential. Following the devaluation, the authorities managed the exchange rate to maintain competitiveness relative to a basket of currencies.

[105]The first arrangement provided for a loan in eight instalments of SDR 80 million each over two years, beginning in March 1980. The arrangement was enlarged in February 1981 by canceling the initial agreement and replacing it with a 12-month stand-by arrangement with four instalments of SDR 144 million each. The latter arrangement was fully utilized. Korea also borrowed SDR 160 million in July 1980 under the CFF.

Figure 2.5. Korea: Exchange Rates, 1979–89

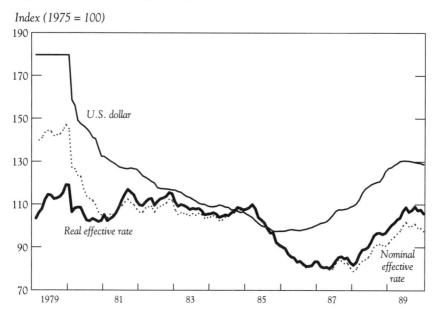

Index (1975 = 100)

In 1985, when the last of Korea's 16 stand-by arrangements was being negotiated and Seoul was preparing to host the Bank-Fund Annual Meetings, the government was aiming to eliminate the current account deficit by 1987: a remarkable turnaround from the beginning of the decade, when the deficit had exceeded 8 percent of GDP (Figure 2.6). In the event, the target was easily surpassed, and by 1987 Korea recorded a substantial external surplus. This apparently unexpected strengthening reflected both the depreciation of the dollar throughout 1985 and 1986 and more aggressive management of the won exchange rate. By letting the won depreciate slightly against the dollar, the Korean authorities obtained a very substantial overall gain in international competitiveness, as shown in Figure 2.5.

Meanwhile, the U.S. government was becoming increasingly sensitive to bilateral trade imbalances, which were concentrated in Asia.[106] The U.S. Treasury initiated talks with Korean officials during the summer of 1986, but those talks proved fruitless, as the two sides viewed the situation in radically different terms.

The 1986 debate involved three major issues. First, should Korea take advantage of the strengthening external balance to stimulate domestic growth? Second, should the authorities take early action to reduce the current account surplus by allowing the exchange rate to appreciate? Third, should the country liberalize its trade and finance regimes to promote more balanced international relationships over the longer run? The first issue was never elevated to a central role, because both the Korean government and the Fund sensed that Korea was already growing

---

[106]Concentrated, but not exclusively so. The four largest bilateral surpluses with the United States in 1985 were those of Japan, Germany, Taiwan Province of China, and Korea.

Figure 2.6. Korea: Current Account Balance and External Debt, 1970–89

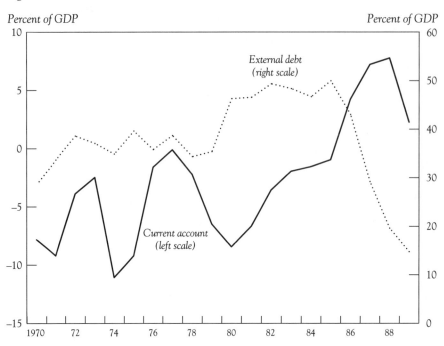

Percent of GDP

Percent of GDP

about as rapidly (10 percent a year in real per capita terms; see Figure 2.4) as could be sustained without producing structural imbalances. The memory of the excesses of 1976–78 was still fresh. The other two issues, exchange rate and liberalization policies, were more contentious and became the subject of arduous negotiations between the Korean and U.S. governments—negotiations that the IMF later helped to arbitrate. Curiously, neither issue had been the focus of previous consultations, for either the Fund or the U.S. authorities. As late as July 1985, Dallara was praising Korea's "impressive adjustment efforts" and supporting the Korean position that "high priority had to be given to strengthening the external account."[107] In the following year, however, U.S. officials began to pressure Korea to liberalize several key sectors in U.S.-Korean bilateral trade, such as beef, cigarettes, and intellectual property. This pressure resulted in little immediate policy change, forestalled at least partly because of forthcoming parliamentary elections.

The underlying question was whether the stock of external debt was a real constraint on economic policy. Korea had begun 1986 as the world's fourth largest international debtor, behind only Brazil, Mexico, and Argentina. During the parliamentary election campaign of 1985, the government had been strongly criticized by the opposition for allowing foreign debt to accumulate to that extent. The ruling Democratic Justice Party argued successfully that the debt had enabled Korea to develop its infrastructure and its export capacity, and that Korea had the ability

---

[107]Minutes of EBM/85/105 (July 12, 1985), p. 17.

not only to service its debt but also to reduce it through the surpluses that productive growth would ultimately bring. Now that a current account surplus was a real possibility, the government acknowledged a responsibility to achieve it and to reduce the stock of debt as rapidly as possible.

Not even the most visionary foresaw the extent and persistence of the shift in Korea's external fortunes, once the improvement was under way. The country's internal changes were reinforced by the collapse in world oil prices, the drop in international interest rates, and the rapid depreciation of the U.S. dollar (forces that became known in Korea as the "three lows"). Consequently, the current account was balanced by mid-1986, showed a surplus of $4.6 billion for the year as a whole, and would rise further to nearly $10 billion in 1987 and $14 billion in 1988. These surpluses enabled Korea to repay nearly $16 billion of its initial stock of $47 billion in foreign debt by the end of 1988, and simultaneously to raise its external assets by $12.7 billion.[108]

The swing to surplus quickly brought forth complaints from the United States, where the authorities were more impressed by the current surpluses—especially the bilateral trade surplus—than by the existing stock of external debt. In their view, the rate of return on capital investment in Korea was high enough to justify maintaining a high debt level. In August 1986, bilateral talks were held between officials of the U.S. Treasury and State Department on the one side, and the Korean finance and foreign ministries on the other. The U.S. officials insisted that the won should be allowed to appreciate against the U.S. dollar by at least 15 percent to be consistent with underlying economic conditions and with the shifts in other exchange rates (mainly the appreciation of the Japanese yen and the Taiwan dollar) that were then under way. When the Korean authorities refused, the Assistant Secretary of the U.S. Treasury, David C. Mulford, offered to go to Seoul to pursue these discussions. The Koreans discouraged him from doing so, fearing that such a visit would be publicized and would make the negotiations that much more difficult. So, over the next several months, discussions on both the exchange rate and the pace of trade liberalization took place in various other arenas: between Treasury Secretary James Baker and Finance Minister In-Yong Chung at meetings in Washington and at the Asian Development Bank in Manila, and between treasury or finance ministry officials and the other country's ambassador. Commerce Secretary Malcolm Baldrige also met with officials in Seoul for bilateral trade talks in April 1987.

During this period of intense behind-the-scene discussions, the IMF staff working on Korea—headed by Hubert Neiss, Deputy Director of the Asian Department—took the position that the emerging external surplus implied that some appreciation of the won would be appropriate. This view was communicated to the Korean authorities on several occasions by the Managing Director. Nevertheless,

---

[108]The decline in the foreign debt was even greater in relation to the rapidly expanding level of output and exports. As shown in Figure 2.6, the ratio of debt to GDP fell from 50 percent at the end of 1985 to less than 15 percent at the end of 1989. The ratio of debt-service payments to export receipts fell from 27 percent in 1985 to 12 percent in 1989.

the staff avoided suggesting any particular level or pushing for an early decision, and both the Korean authorities and those on the U.S. side came to view the Fund as a neutral and potentially helpful intermediary.

External pressure on Korea was stepped up in February 1987, in the form of a paragraph in the communiqué issued by major industrial countries following the famous Louvre meeting in Paris (see Chapter 4), calling on the "newly industrial-ized developing economies [to] assume greater responsibility for preserving an open world trading system by reducing trade barriers and pursuing policies that allow their currencies to reflect more fully underlying economic fundamentals." Al-though internal discussions in Korea at this time were revealing serious considera-tion of allowing a more rapid appreciation of the won, the publicity associated with the Louvre communiqué created a political embarrassment for the government and made a smooth policy adjustment more difficult to achieve.[109]

In April 1987, Dallara approached the Managing Director, Michel Camdessus, to request that the Fund hold a supplemental consultation with Korea to discuss competitiveness issues. Because the supplemental consultation procedure had been applied only once before, there was an obvious danger that Korea would raise the same objections as Sweden had five years earlier. However, when Camdessus telephoned Finance Minister Chung, he found a welcome reception. So in early May, the Managing Director notified the Executive Board that he in-tended to initiate a supplemental consultation with Korea under the 1979 Board decision, "with the full concurrence of the Finance Minister of Korea." Although a number of Executive Directors later came to have second thoughts, no one ob-jected at this time.[110]

The consultation, headed by Neiss, was held in Seoul over a three-week period starting in mid-May. It was a delicate period for the authorities, as a burgeoning pro-democracy movement was attempting (successfully, as it happened) to force the government to hold the first direct presidential election in nearly three decades, and massive demonstrations were turning violent. The consultation, however, was unaffected by the ongoing political turmoil. Based on these meetings, the staff noted that the current account surplus was running well above the official target of $5 billion and concluded that further measures would be needed if the sur-plus was to be contained within that range. The mission recommended some ap-preciation of the exchange rate and a further liberalization of import and exchange controls.[111]

When the Executive Board met in restricted session on July 6, 1987, to discuss the staff report, a number of Executive Directors from developing or smaller in-dustrial countries expressed reservations about both the procedure and the staff recommendation on exchange rate policy. This was only the second application

---

[109]In the Korean view, trade liberalization in Korea required a reduction in U.S. protectionism as well. See SaKong (1988), pp. 14–15.

[110]Minutes of EBM/87/72 (May 8, 1987). For the "second thoughts," see the minutes of EBM/87/97–98 (July 6, 1987).

[111]"Korea—Staff Report for the Supplemental Consultation," EBS/87/134 (June 22, 1987).

of the supplemental surveillance procedure, the first application to a country with a current account surplus, and the first application to a developing country. Questions were raised about whether the Fund had been drawn inappropriately into a bilateral trade dispute, whether it was appropriate for a developing country with a large external debt to try to limit its current external surplus, and whether the supplemental procedure should not be applied first to countries whose policies had global or systemic implications. Broad agreement existed on the need for Korea to liberalize its trading system by reducing controls and opening its markets, but the United States drew little support for its contention that Korea should aim for a current account surplus smaller than $5 billion. Similarly, on the exchange rate, few Directors were prepared to go quite as far as the U.S. chair in calling for a "substantial and prompt reversal" of the won's recent depreciation. Even so, the widespread view on the Board, expressed especially by Directors from the large industrial countries, was that the staff was right in recommending some further appreciation of the Korean currency.[112] The Chairman's summing up on that issue was subjected to an unusual degree of negotiation, even after the meeting. In its final form (approved July 24), the crucial passage read as follows:

> A number of Directors, endorsing further market opening, expressed understanding for the authorities' caution with regard to the appreciation of the won, while not ruling out further action on that front. However, the weight of opinion among Directors was that additional exchange rate appreciation was called for and that exchange rate policy should be used more actively together with an accelerated pace of market opening.[113]

Subsequently, Korea did allow the won to appreciate in effective terms as well as against the dollar, but the current account surplus continued to grow for another year or so, as normally happens in response to exchange rate action. In October 1988, the U.S. administration issued a "Super 301" report to congress (U.S. Treasury, 1988) concluding that Korea was still manipulating the won for an unfair trade advantage.[114] By 1989, however, the Korean surplus was beginning to shrink, the authorities were carrying out further measures to liberalize trade, and the political dispute finally faded away.[115]

---

[112]Minutes of EBM/87/97–98 (July 6, 1987).

[113]The original version was circulated as "The Acting Chairman's Summing Up at the Conclusion of the Supplemental Consultation with Korea, Executive Board Meeting 87/98—July 6, 1987," SUR/87/64 on July 20, 1987. The revised version was discussed at EBM/87/109 (July 24) and was included in the minutes of EBM/87/98 (July 6), p. 10.

[114]The report was issued pursuant to the requirements of the Omnibus Trade and Competitiveness Act of 1988. Under the popularly named "Super 301" provisions of that Act (which modified and extended Section 301 of the Trade Act of 1974, covering unfair trading practices by other countries), the administration was mandated to take retaliatory actions against countries deemed to be manipulating exchange rates or otherwise pursuing policies aimed at gaining an unfair advantage over the United States in international trade. As a preliminary step, the treasury was required to submit periodic reports to congress identifying such countries.

[115]For a general review of these and subsequent developments, see Lindner (1992).

Reducing Exchange Restrictions

When the Articles of Agreement were drafted in 1944, currency convertibility was a goal that most countries were prepared to approach only gradually. The economic devastation from the Second World War, the long-term disruption of international trade, the pervasive application of exchange controls, and the presence of vast differences in economic power implied that convertibility should come at the end of a possibly lengthy period of recovery. That conclusion was embodied in Article XIV, which permitted countries to maintain existing restrictions on current account transactions so long as they did so with due regard to the "purposes of the Fund" and (after five years of operation by the Fund) agreed to consult with the Fund "as to their further retention." Countries that had been "occupied by the enemy" were also permitted to introduce new restrictions if necessary.[116] To ensure that restrictions were temporary, the Fund was authorized to "make representations" to a member that its restrictions should be abandoned.

Although the establishment of the Fund was expected to lead to generalized convertibility within a reasonable time, the transition extended long after the effects of the war had fully dissipated. Initially, most of the Fund's original members took advantage of the transitional provisions. Until the 1960s, only a scattering of countries in North and Central America committed themselves to the avoidance of current account restrictions.[117] Even by the end of 1967, when the First Amend-

---

[116]Occasionally, countries justified the imposition of exchange restrictions on national security grounds unrelated to commercial trade. The Fund acknowledged in 1952 that although it was "not a suitable forum for discussion of the political and military considerations leading to actions of this kind," it might need to make judgments on whether the imposition of restrictions was motivated solely by such considerations. Members imposing restrictions for security reasons were required to notify the Fund, which would then have 30 days in which to register an objection. See Decision No. 144-(52/51), in Horsefield (1969), Vol. 3, p. 257. During the period covered by this History, three major cases were brought before the Fund, all involving the United States. In the first case, the United States blocked assets of the Iranian government in 1979, in response to the takeover of the U.S. embassy in Tehran and the holding of American hostages there. In January 1986, Libya complained that U.S. sanctions against it—imposed in retaliation for what the United States regarded as Libyan backing of terrorist attacks at the Rome and Vienna airports the previous month—were not justified on security grounds. And in April 1988, the United States froze Panamanian assets in an effort to bring Panama's General Noriega to justice (see Chapter 16). In each case, the Executive Board declined to object to the restrictions. On Iran, see "Communication from Iran" EBS/79/620 (December 7, 1979) and Sups. 1–6 (various dates), and minutes of EBM/79/191 (December 27, 1979). On Libya, see "Communication from the Socialist People's Libyan Arab Jamahiriya," EBS/86/8 (January 15, 1986) and Sup. 1 (January 22, 1986); "Communication from the United States," EBS/86/9 (January 16, 1986); "Communication from Arab Monetary Fund," EBS/86/17 (January 23, 1986); "Notification by the United States of Restrictions Imposed for Security Reasons under Executive Board Decision No. 144 and Complaint by the Socialist People's Libyan Arab Jamahiriya under Rule H-2," EBS/86/21 (January 29, 1986); and minutes of EBM/86/17 (January 31, 1986). On Panama, see "Notification under Executive Board Decision No. 144-(52/51) of Restrictions Relating to Panama," EBD/88/126 (May 9, 1988).

[117]Of the 40 original members of the Fund, only the United States, El Salvador, Mexico, and Panama accepted Article VIII status in 1946. Through 1960, five countries followed suit: Guatemala (1947), Honduras (1950), Canada (1952), the Dominican Republic (1953), and Haiti (1953). Thus at the end of 1960, 9 of 69 members (13 percent) were Article VIII countries. The establishment of currency convertibility in Europe then contributed to a wave of acceptances in the 1960s.

Figure 2.7. Acceptance of Article VIII Status, 1946–97

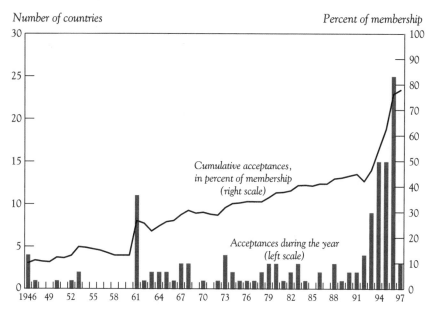

ment was being discussed by the Board, only 31 members (28 percent of the Fund's 110 members) had terminated their recourse to the transition by accepting the obligations of Article VIII (Figure 2.7).[118] Most nonoriginal members, including the large number of newly independent countries, were still claiming recourse to the transitional arrangements of Article XIV.

The Second Amendment (1978) implicitly recognized the generalized and extended recourse to transitional arrangements by dropping all references to the war and retitling Article XIV "transitional arrangements" instead of "transitional period." More substantively, it weakened the distinction between the status of countries accepting the full obligations of Article VIII and those having recourse to the provisions of Article XIV, in two ways. First, acceptance of Article VIII no longer affected the reserve status of a country's currency. Originally, Article VIII status was the criterion for determining whether a currency was defined as convertible and acceptable for use in Fund operations. That linkage was dropped. Second, as noted in the introduction to this chapter, the amendment provided for universal consultations between the Fund and its members, regardless of status. Previously, only countries that still maintained restrictions under the provisions of Article

---

[118]See de Vries (1976), Vol. 1, p. 571. The transitional arrangements specified in Article XIV relate only to members' acceptance of the obligations of Sections 2 ("avoidance of restrictions on current payments"), 3 ("avoidance of discriminatory currency practices"), and 4 ("convertibility of foreign-held balances") of Article VIII. All members accept the obligations of the other sections of Article VIII. For a complete list of dates (through April 1999) when members accepted the full obligations of Article VIII, see *Annual Report 1999*, pp. 162–63. For an analysis, see Galbis (1996).

XIV were required to consult, although the Fund held consultations with other members on a voluntary basis (see de Vries, 1985, pp. 726–29).

At the beginning of 1979, 47 member countries (34 percent) had accepted Article VIII status; of those, 17 were industrial countries. Of the 37 remaining original members of the Fund, 13 were still availing themselves of the transitional provisions of Article XIV.[119] The Fund adopted a passive attitude toward this division of the membership throughout the period; indeed, throughout its history until the 1990s. As Alan Whittome (Director of ETR) observed during the 1987 review of surveillance procedures, "the acceptance of the obligations of Article VIII had been a matter for the member, with the Executive Board approving the member's decision to change its status once it had been shown to have no restrictions. The Executive Board had not taken a strong position on the termination of the transitional arrangements of Article XIV, either in general or in specific cases."[120]

From 1979 through 1989, 19 additional members moved to Article VIII, bringing the total to 66 (43 percent) Of the new acceptors, four were industrial countries. When Spain accepted Article VIII status on July 15, 1986, all industrial members had moved to that column.[121] A large majority of developing countries, however, remained reluctant to do so.

At least three reasons may be adduced for governments to have been reluctant to let go of the transitional provisions of Article XIV, though none seems persuasive enough to explain the extent of the hesitance. First and most obviously, some countries simply wanted to keep using exchange restrictions. That desire, however, explains relatively little. Many countries that had already eliminated restrictions on current account transactions and that qualified for Article VIII status declined to make the switch. African countries participating in the CFA franc zone were notable examples.[122] Although acceptance of the obligations of Article VIII implies that the country has established convertibility for its currency, it does not automatically follow from convertibility.

Second, countries may have desired to keep open the option of readopting restrictions. Even though such action would be subject to Fund jurisdiction under Article VIII regardless of the member's status, some countries may have been reluctant to be seen as making a public commitment against adopting restrictions. Third—and probably accounting for most cases—countries may have been subject to inertia, not wanting to make a new commitment without some good reason for doing so. As Simmons (2000) has suggested, the most persuasive reason for a country to accept the commitments of Article VIII is to enhance the credibility of its

---

[119]Original members are defined officially as those that joined the Fund prior to the end of 1946. Of the 40 original members, 3 (Czechoslovakia, Poland, and Cuba) withdrew before the beginning of 1979.

[120]Minutes of EBM/87/39 (March 4, 1987), p. 45.

[121]Portugal accepted Article VIII status in September 1988, when it was still classified as a developing country. In the fall of 1989, Greece and Portugal were reclassified as industrial countries, raising the total in that category to 23. Greece accepted Article VIII status in July 1992.

[122]All 13 members of the CFA franc zone accepted the obligations of Article VIII on June 1, 1996.

economic policies. Only when openness to international finance became a wide-spread goal for developing countries in the 1990s would the value of Article VIII status become important for a large number of Fund members.

Not until 1993 did the Fund make a major effort to persuade members to accept the obligations of Article VIII, but when it did so, it met with marked success. By the end of 1999, 148 members had done so, bringing the total to 81 percent of the membership.

Appendix: Principles and Procedures of Surveillance

The Executive Board approved a set of principles and procedures for surveillance in 1977, in anticipation of the adoption of the amended Article IV of the Articles of Agreement the following year. Reproduced below are the new Article IV, the 1977 document, a description of the summing up procedure adopted in 1978, the decision introducing "ad hoc" consultations in 1979, and amendments to the 1977 decision that were adopted through 1989.

Article IV. Obligations Regarding Exchange Arrangements

Section 1. *General obligations of members*

Recognizing that the essential purpose of the international monetary system is to provide a framework that facilitates the exchange of goods, services, and capital among countries, and that sustains sound economic growth, and that a principal objective is the continuing development of the orderly underlying conditions that are necessary for financial and economic stability, each member undertakes to collaborate with the Fund and other members to assure orderly exchange arrangements and to promote a stable system of exchange rates. In particular, each member shall:

(i) endeavor to direct its economic and financial policies toward the objective of fostering orderly economic growth with reasonable price stability, with due regard to its circumstances;

(ii) seek to promote stability by fostering orderly underlying economic and financial conditions and a monetary system that does not tend to produce erratic disruptions;

(iii) avoid manipulating exchange rates or the international monetary system in order to prevent effective balance of payments adjustment or to gain an unfair competitive advantage over other members; and

(iv) follow exchange policies compatible with the undertakings under this Section.

Section 2. *General exchange arrangements*

(a) Each member shall notify the Fund, within thirty days after the date of the second amendment of this Agreement, of the exchange arrangements it intends to apply in fulfillment of its obligations under Section 1 of this Article, and shall notify the Fund promptly of any changes in its exchange arrangements.

(b) Under an international monetary system of the kind prevailing on January 1, 1976, exchange arrangements may include (i) the maintenance by a member of a value for its currency in terms of the special drawing right or another denominator, other than gold, selected by the member, or (ii) cooperative arrangements by which members maintain the value of their currencies in relation to the value of the currency or currencies of other members, or (iii) other exchange arrangements of a member's choice.

(c) To accord with the development of the international monetary system, the Fund, by an eighty-five percent majority of the total voting power, may make provision for general exchange arrangements without limiting the right of members to have exchange arrangements of their choice consistent with the purposes of the Fund and the obligations under Section 1 of this Article.

Section 3. *Surveillance over exchange arrangements*

(a) The Fund shall oversee the international monetary system in order to ensure its effective operation, and shall oversee the compliance of each member with its obligations under Section 1 of this Article.

(b) In order to fulfill its functions under (a) above, the Fund shall exercise firm surveillance over the exchange rate policies of members, and shall adopt specific principles for the guidance of all members with respect to those policies. Each member shall provide the Fund with the information necessary for such surveillance, and, when requested by the Fund, shall consult with it on the member's exchange rate policies. The principles adopted by the Fund shall be consistent with cooperative arrangements by which members maintain the value of their currencies in relation to the value of the currency or currencies of other members, as well as with other exchange arrangements of a member's choice consistent with the purposes of the Fund and Section 1 of this Article. These principles shall respect the domestic social and political policies of members, and in applying these principles the Fund shall pay due regard to the circumstances of members.

Section 4. *Par values*

The Fund may determine, by an eighty-five percent majority of the total voting power, that international economic conditions permit the introduction of a widespread system of exchange arrangements based on stable but adjustable par values. The Fund shall make the determination on the basis of the underlying stability of the world economy, and for this purpose shall take into account price movements and rates of expansion in the economies of members. The determination shall be made in light of the evolution of the international monetary system, with particular reference to sources of liquidity, and, in order to ensure the effective operation of a system of par values, to arrangements under which both members in surplus and members in deficit in their balances of payments take prompt, effective, and symmetrical action to achieve adjustment, as well as to arrangements for intervention and the treatment of imbalances. Upon making such determination, the Fund shall notify members that the provisions of Schedule C apply.

Section 5. *Separate currencies within a member's territories*

(a) Action by a member with respect to its currency under this Article shall be deemed to apply to the separate currencies of all territories in respect of which the member has accepted this Agreement under Article XXXI, Section 2(g) unless the member declares that its action relates either to the metropolitan currency alone, or only to one or more specified separate currencies, or to the metropolitan currency and one or more specified separate currencies.

(b) Action by the Fund under this Article shall be deemed to relate to all currencies of a member referred to in (a) above unless the Fund declares otherwise.

1977 Decision on Principles and Procedures

1. The Executive Board has discussed the implementation of Article IV of the proposed Second Amendment of the Articles of Agreement and has approved the attached document entitled "Surveillance over Exchange Rate Policies." The Fund shall act in accordance with this document when the Second Amendment becomes effective. In the period before that date the Fund shall continue to conduct consultations in accordance with present procedures and decisions.

2. The Fund shall review the document entitled "Surveillance over Exchange Rate Policies" at intervals of two years and at such other times as consideration of it is placed on the agenda of the Executive Board.

Decision No. 5392-(77/63), adopted April 29, 1977

Surveillance over Exchange Rate Polices

General Principles

Article IV, Section 3(a) provides that "The Fund shall oversee the international monetary system in order to ensure its effective operation, and shall oversee the compliance of each member with its obligations under Section 1 of this Article." Article IV, Section 3(b) provides that in order to fulfill its functions under 3(a), "the Fund shall exercise firm surveillance over the exchange rate policies of members, and shall adopt specific principles for the guidance of all members with respect to those policies." Article IV, Section 3(b) also provides that "The principles adopted by the Fund shall be consistent with cooperative arrangements by which members maintain the value of their currencies in relation to the value of the currency or currencies or other members, as well as with other exchange arrangements of a member's choice consistent with the purposes of the Fund and Section 1 of this Article. These principles shall respect the domestic social and political policies of members, and in applying these principles the Fund shall pay due regard to the circumstances of members." In addition, Article IV, Section 3(b) requires that "Each member shall provide the Fund with the information necessary for such surveillance, and, when requested by the Fund, shall consult with it on the member's exchange rate policies."

The principles and procedures set out below, which apply to all members whatever their exchange arrangements and whatever their balance of payments position, are adopted by the Fund in order to perform its functions under Section 3(b). They are not necessarily comprehensive and are subject to reconsideration in the light of experience. The do not deal directly with the Fund's responsibilities referred to in Section 3(a), although it is recognized that there is a close relationship between domestic and international economic policies. This relationship is emphasized in Article IV which includes the following provision: "Recognizing . . . that a principal objective [of the international monetary system] is the continuing development of the orderly underlying conditions that are necessary for financial and economic stability, each member undertakes to collaborate with the Fund and other members to assure orderly exchange arrangements and to promote a stable system of exchange rates."

Principles for the Guidance of Members' Exchange Rate Policies

A. A member shall avoid manipulating exchange rates or the international monetary system in order to prevent effective balance of payments adjustment or to gain an unfair competitive advantage over other members.

B. A member should intervene in the exchange market if necessary to counter disorderly conditions which may be characterized inter alia by disruptive short-term movements in the exchange value of its currency.

C. Members should take into account in their intervention policies the interests of other members, including those of the countries in whose currencies they intervene.

Principles of Fund Surveillance over Exchange Rate Policies

1. The surveillance of exchange rate policies shall be adapted to the needs of international adjustments as they develop. The functioning of the international adjustment process shall be kept under review by the Executive Board and Interim Committee and the assessment of its operation shall be taken into account in the implementation of the principles set forth below.

2. In its surveillance of the observance by members of the principles set forth above, the Fund shall consider the following developments as among those which might indicate the need for discussion with a member:

(i) protracted large-scale intervention in one direction in the exchange market;

(ii) an unsustainable level of official or quasi-official borrowing, or excessive and prolonged short-term official or quasi-official lending, for balance of payments purposes;

(iii) (a) the introduction, substantial intensification, or prolonged maintenance, for balance of payments purposes, of restrictions on, or incentives for, current transactions or payments or

(b) the introduction or substantial modification for balance of payments purposes of restrictions on, or incentives for the inflow or outflow of capital;

(iv) the pursuit, for balance of payments purposes, of monetary and other domestic financial policies that provide abnormal encouragement or discouragement to capital flows; and

(v) behavior of the exchange rate that appears to be unrelated to underlying economic and financial conditions including factors affecting competitiveness and long-term capital movements.

3. The Fund's appraisal of a member's exchange rate policies shall be based on an evaluation of the developments in the member's balance of payments against the background of its reserve position and its external indebtedness. This appraisal shall be made within the framework of a comprehensive analysis of the general economic situation and economic policy strategy of the member, and shall recognize that domestic as well as external policies can contribute to timely adjustment of the balance of payments. The appraisal shall take into account the extent to which the policies of the member, including its exchange rate policies, serve the objectives of the continuing development of the orderly underlying conditions that are necessary for financial stability, the promotion of sustained sound economic growth, and reasonable levels of employment.

Procedures for Surveillance

I. Each member shall notify the Fund in appropriate detail within thirty days after the Second Amendment becomes effective of the exchange arrangements it intends to apply in fulfillment of its obligations under Article IV, Section 1. Each member shall also notify the Fund promptly of any changes in its exchange arrangements.

II. Members shall consult with the Fund regularly under Article IV. The consultations under Article IV shall comprehend the regular consultations under Article VIII and XIV.

In principle such consultations shall take place annually, and shall include consideration of the observance by members of the principles set forth above as well as of a member's obligations under Article IV, Section 1. Not later than three months after the termination of discussions between the member and the staff, the Executive Board shall reach conclusions and thereby complete the consultation under Article IV.

III. Broad developments in exchange rates will be reviewed periodically by the Executive Board, inter alia in discussions of the international adjustments process within the framework of the World Economic Outlook. The Fund will continue to conduct special consultations in preparing for these discussions.

IV. The Managing Director shall maintain close contact with members in connection with their exchange arrangements and exchange policies, and will be prepared to discuss on the initiative of a member important changes that it contemplates in its exchange arrangements or its exchange rate policies.

V. If, in the interval between Article IV consultations, the Managing Director, taking into account any views that may have been expressed by other members, considers that a member's exchange rate policies may not be in accord with the exchange rate principles, he shall raise the matter informally and confidentially with the member, and shall conclude promptly whether there is a question of the observance of the principles. If he concludes that there is such a question, he shall initiate and conduct on a confidential basis a discussion with the member under Article IV, Section 3(*b*). As soon as possible after the completion of such a discussion, and in any event not later than four months after its initiation, the Managing Director shall report to the Executive Board on the results of the discussion. If, however, the Managing Director is satisfied that the principles are being observed, he shall informally advise all Executive Directors, and the staff shall report on the discussion in the context of the next Article IV consultation; but the Managing Director shall not place the matter on the agenda of the Executive Board unless the member requests that this procedure be followed.

VI. The Executive Directors shall review annually the general implementation of the Fund's surveillance over member's exchange rate policies.

1978 Agreement to Conclude Consultations with a "Summing Up"

(excerpted from "Consultation Practices and Procedures," SM/78/67; approved by Executive Directors at EBM/78/36, March 20, 1978)

. . . *III. Executive Board Action to Complete Consultations Under Article IV*

Executive Directors have expressed various views on the question of Executive Board action to conclude annual consultations under Article IV; however, the discussions (at EBM/77/47; 4/7/77) suggested general considerations to be taken into account in clarifying the operational meaning of Executive Board "conclusions", as required by paragraph II of the "Procedures for Surveillance". . . . Such considerations include: (1) the need for uniformity of treatment of members; (2) the recognition that while Executive Board consensus would be desirable, the procedures should be kept flexible so that dissenting views might also be brought to the attention of the authorities of the member concerned; and (3) the expectation that the appraisal in the Staff Reports on consultations under Article IV would focus on the issues involved in respect of members' situations and policies as they relate to the principles and obligations under Article IV as well as Articles VIII and XIV.

Uniformity of treatment of members, in this case, would be satisfied if the Executive Directors were to reach a "conclusion" on the basis of their discussion of the Staff Report on the consultations under Article IV with each member, and if that conclusion were to be an expression of the Executive Directors' views, in each instance, on the staff's appraisal of the member's circumstances and policies as set forth in its report on the consultations under Article IV. In many cases, it would be reasonable to expect that there would be a consensus among Executive Directors to the effect that they generally agreed with the staff's appraisal. However, the procedures should be kept flexible so that dissenting views could be recorded and also be brought to the attention of the authorities of the member concerned. Dissenting views of one or more individual Executive Directors regarding the staff appraisal could be included in the conclusion of the Executive Board.

It is suggested that the Executive Board conclusion take the form of a brief "summing up" by the Managing Director, in his capacity as Chairman of the Exective Board, at the end of the discussion by Executive Directors of the Staff Report on the annual consultation under Article IV. In many cases, this would consist of a short statement by the Managing Director to the effect that Executive Directors generally agreed with the views expressed in the staff appraisal contained in the report on the discussions, perhaps along the following lines:

> "My understanding is that Executive Directors have indicated widespread support for the views expressed in the staff appraisal contained in the report on the [year] consultation discussions with [member].
>
> [In addition my understanding is that Directors are willing to adopt a decision to be taken with respect to [the continued retention of restrictions under Article XIV] [exchange restrictions requiring approval under Article VIII]]."

Of course, if significantly different views had been expressed by Executive Directors, the Chairman's summing up would reflect such reservations. In the cases of relatively few members whose economic situations at the time were considered to be of special importance for the effective functioning of the international monetary system, the Chairman's statement would be somewhat longer and would highlight key points expressed by Directors. In most cases the Chairman would present his summing up of the Executive Board's conclusions directly following consideration of the report on the consultations. However, in some cases, including those mentioned immediately above, the Chairman could delay—until later in the day or the next Board meeting—the presentation of the conclusions so as to allow for the incorporation of differing views or key points expressed by Executive Directors.

Amendments to the 1977 Decision Adopted During 1979–89

A. *1979 Decision on Ad Hoc Consultations*

Managing Director's Statement following EMB/79/13,
(EBD/79/18, Rev. 1, January 22, 1979)

Surveillance: Ad Hoc Consultations

The discussion of the Executive Board on Friday, December 22, 1978 of the staff paper "Annual Review of Regular Consultations and Other Issues Related to Article IV" (SM/78/287, 12/11/78) at EBM/78/203 and EBM/78/204 (12/22/78) showed that there was broad agreement on all proposals except those made in Section III of the paper concerning supplemental surveillance procedures. On these procedures, while there was general acceptance of the judgmental approach described in the paper, there was widespread interest in flexible procedures for Executive Board reviews of developments involving the exchange rate policies of individual members between annual consultations. Executive Directors indicated a desire to have staff papers and Executive Board discussions not only when important modifications were made in the exchange policies of members, whatever their exchange arrangements, as proposed in the staff paper, but also when there were important movements of exchange rates even if there had been no modification of policies.

Some Executive Directors also showed an interest in having nonmovement of exchange rates as a possible basis for discussion when such nonmovement deserved examination as part of firm surveillance. To meet these desires, a draft revision of paragraph 3 of the proposed decision was circulated during the afternoon meeting, which took account of these views by adding "behavior of the exchange rate" as a possible basis for a special discussion by the Board. This language could justify discussion not only when there occurred what might be considered an important movement of the exchange rate but also when "behavior" in the form of lack of movement might be considered important because a change in underlying conditions had given, or could give, rise to a serious imbalance.

The proposed decision will authorize the Managing Director to judge whether the "behavior of the exchange rate" justified an ad hoc consultation with the member and, thereafter, a discussion by the Board, or the informal provision of information to Executive Directors.

In order to be properly selective, I would intend to take into account, in initiating the procedures, the importance of the effects on the member or other members of the member's exchange rate arrangements, exchange rate policies, or the behavior of the exchange rate of its currency.

I would also note that in view of the scope of the recent Executive Board discussion, I see no need to have a further discussion of procedural decisions before April 1, 1979, and paragraph 1 of the proposed decision has been revised accordingly.

Finally, there is the question of the review of the document "Surveillance Over Exchange Rate Policies," which is required to be held "at intervals of two years" in accordance with paragraph 2 of Executive Board Decision No. 5392-(77/63). It is not made explicit from what date the two years run, but it would seem clear that they should run from the date when the document became effective, i.e., April 1, 1978. I would propose therefore that it should be understood that the latest date for review would be April 1, 1980. A review can also be held, in accordance with the decision, "at such other times as consideration of it is placed on the agenda of the Executive Board." The discussion of the World Economic Outlook that Directors had on December 13 covered a number of important aspects of the working of the exchange rate system. Directors will no doubt want to return to these matters at a later date but in any case in the context of the 1979 Annual Report. In preparation for this, I have asked the staff to prepare a paper analyzing the opinions expressed by Directors and the issues involved, with a view to a further Board discussion around the middle of the year.

A draft decision taking account of the proposals described above is being circulated to Executive Directors (SM/78/287, Supplement 1) simultaneously with this statement.

In addition, some Executive Directors suggested at EBM/78/203 and EBM/78/204 that, since Executive Board decisions under Article VIII and Article XIV are confined to matters coming within the approval jurisdiction of the Fund, they fail to give due weight to members' adjustment policies and their efforts to reduce reliance on exchange restrictions.

Accordingly, I propose that when such decisions are taken in conjunction with an Article IV consultation, the first paragraph of decisions on consultations under Article VIII or Article XIV would be reworded appropriately, and the staff is preparing a brief paper for this purpose.

On the basis of the foregoing statement, the following decision was adopted by the Executive Board at Meeting 79/13, January 22, 1979:

1. *Review.* The Executive Board has reviewed the procedures relating to the Fund's surveillance over members' exchange rate policies. These procedures, and the procedures for regular consultations under Article IV, will be reviewed again by the Executive Board in December 1979. The Executive Board will review the document "Surveillance over Exchange Rate Policies" at an appropriate time not later than April 1, 1980, as provided for in paragraph 2 of Decision No. 5392-(77/63), adopted April 29, 1977.

2. *Annual consultations.* During the consultation year beginning January 1, 1979, annual consultations as stipulated under Procedure II in SM/77/81 shall be conducted under Article IV, which consultations shall comprehend the consultations under Article VIII and Article XIV, in accordance with the procedures approved by the Executive Board for 1978 consultations and the procedures set out in Section IV, *Article IV Consultations,* in SM/78/287.

3. *Supplemental surveillance procedure pursuant to EBD/79/18, Revision 1 (1/22/79).* Whenever the Managing Director considers that a modification in a member's exchange arrangements or exchange rate policies or the behavior of the exchange rate of its currency may be important or may have important effects on other members, whatever the member's exchange arrangements may be, he shall initiate informally and confidentially a discussion with the member before the next regular consultation under Article IV. If he considers after this prior discussion that the matter is of importance, he shall initiate and conduct an *ad hoc* consultation with the member and shall report to the Executive Board, or informally advise the Executive Directors, on the consultation as promptly as the circumstances permit after conclusion of the consultation. This procedure will supplement the proceedings in Executive Board Decision No. 5392-(77/63), adopted April 29, 1977.

Decision No. 6026-(79/13), adopted January 22, 1979

B. 1987 Decision to Allow for Separate Consultations under Article XIV

The second and third sentences of Paragraph II of Procedures for Surveillance contained in the document entitled "Surveillance over Exchange Rate Policies" attached to Decision No. 5392-(77/63), adopted April 29, 1977, shall be amended to read as follows:

"In principle, the consultations under Article IV shall comprehend the regular consultations under Articles VIII and XIV, and shall take place annually. They shall include consideration of the observance by members of the principles set forth above as well as of a member's obligations under Article IV, Section 1."

Decision No. 8564-(87/59), adopted April 1, 1987

C. 1988 Decision to Eliminate Annual Procedural Reviews

The first sentence of Paragraph VI of Procedures for Surveillance contained in the document entitled "Surveillance over Exchange Rate Policies" attached to Decision No. 5392-(77/63), adopted April 29, 1977, as amended, shall be amended to read as follows:

The Executive Board shall review the general implementation of the Fund's surveillance over members' exchange rate policies at intervals of two years and at such other times as consideration of it is placed on the agenda of the Executive Board.

Decision No. 8856-(88/64), adopted April 22, 1988

References

Aghevli, Bijan B., Mohsin S. Khan, and Peter J. Montiel, 1991, *Exchange Rate Policy in Developing Countries: Some Analytical Issues*, IMF Occasional Paper No. 78 (Washington: International Monetary Fund).

Aghevli, Bijan B., and Peter J. Montiel, 1996, "Exchange Rate Policies in Developing Countries," in *Functioning of the International Monetary System*, ed. by Jacob A. Frenkel and Morris Goldstein (Washington: International Monetary Fund), pp. 612–43.

Aghevli, Bijan B., and Jorge Márquez-Ruarte, 1985, *A Case of Successful Adjustment: Korea's Experience During 1980–84*, IMF Occasional Paper No. 39 (Washington: International Monetary Fund).

Artus, Jacques, and Malcolm D. Knight, 1984, *Issues in the Assessment of the Exchange Rates of Industrial Countries*, IMF Occasional Paper No. 29 (Washington: International Monetary Fund).

Bhatia, Rattan J., 1985, *The West African Monetary Union: An Analytical Review*, IMF Occasional Paper No. 35 (Washington: International Monetary Fund).

Bond, Marian E., and Adalbert Knöbl, 1982, "Some Implications of North Sea Oil for the U.K. Economy," *Staff Papers*, International Monetary Fund, Vol. 29 (September), pp. 363–97.

Boughton, James M., 1988, *The Monetary Approach to Exchange Rates: What Now Remains?* Essays in International Finance, No. 171 (Princeton, New Jersey: International Finance Section, Department of Economics, Princeton University).

———, and K. Sarwar Lateef, eds., 1995, *Fifty Years After Bretton Woods: The Future of the IMF and the World Bank* (Washington: International Monetary Fund and World Bank).

Caballero, Ricardo J., and Vittorio Corbo, 1989, "The Effect of Real Exchange Rate Uncertainty on Exports: Empirical Evidence," *World Bank Economic Review*, Vol. 3 (May), pp. 263–78.

Comité pour l'Histoire Économique et Financière (France, Ministry of the Economy, Finance and Industry), 1998, *La France et les Institutions de Bretton Woods, 1944–1994* (Paris: Imprimerie Nationale).

Corbo, Vittorio, and Sang-Mok Suh, 1992, *Structural Adjustment in a Newly Industrialized Country: The Korean Experience* (Baltimore, Maryland: Johns Hopkins University Press, published for the World Bank).

de Vries, Margaret Garritsen, 1976, *The International Monetary Fund, 1966–1971: The System Under Stress*, Vol. 1: *Narrative*; Vol. 2: *Documents* (Washington: International Monetary Fund).

———, 1985, *The International Monetary Fund, 1972–1978: Cooperation on Trial, Narrative and Anlysis*; Vol. 3: *Documents* (Washington: International Monetary Fund).

Edwards, Sebastian, 1998, "Two Crises: Inflationary Inertia and Credibility," *Economic Journal*, Vol. 108 (May), pp. 680–702.

Eichengreen, Barry, 1999, "Kicking the Habit: Moving from Pegged Rates to Greater Exchange Rate Flexibility," *Economic Journal*, Vol. 109 (March), pp. C1–C14.

———, and others, 1998, *Exit Strategies: Policy Options for Countries Seeking Greater Exchange Rate Flexibility*, IMF Occasional Paper No. 168 (Washington: International Monetary Fund).

Emminger, Otmar, 1977, "The Role of Monetary Coordination to Attain Exchange-Rate Stability," in *The New International Monetary System*, ed. by Robert A. Mundell and Jacques J. Polak (New York: Columbia University Press), pp. 3–24.

Feldt, Kjell-Olof, 1991, *Alla Dessa Dagar . . .* ["All Those Days . . ."; in Swedish] (Stockholm: Norstedts Förlag AB).

Folkerts-Landau, David, and Donald J. Mathieson, 1989, *The European Monetary System in the Context of the Integration of European Financial Markets*, IMF Occasional Paper No. 65 (Washington: International Monetary Fund).

Frenkel, Jacob A., 1996, "Should the International Monetary System Be Reformed?" Chapter 17 in *Functioning of the International Monetary System*, ed. by Jacob A. Frenkel and Morris Goldstein (Washington: International Monetary Fund), pp. 499–507.

———, and Morris Goldstein, 1986, "A Guide to Target Zones," *Staff Papers*, International Monetary Fund, Vol. 33 (December), pp. 633–73.

———, and Mohsin S. Khan, 1991, "Major Themes in the Writings of Jacques J. Polak," in *International Financial Policy: Essays in Honor of Jacques J. Polak*, ed. by Jacob A. Frenkel and Morris Goldstein (Washington: International Monetary Fund and De Nederlandsche Bank), pp. 3–57.

Galbis, Vicente, 1996, "Currency Convertibility and the Fund: Review and Prognosis," IMF Working Paper 96/39 (Washington: International Monetary Fund).

Goldstein, Morris, 1984, *The Exchange Rate System: Lessons of the Past and Options for the Future*, IMF Occasional Paper No. 30 (Washington: International Monetary Fund).

Gotur, Padma, 1985, "Effects of Exchange Rate Volatility on Trade: Some Further Evidence," *Staff Papers*, International Monetary Fund, Vol. 32 (September), pp. 475–512.

Grobar, Lisa Morris, 1993, "The Effect of Real Exchange Rate Uncertainty on LDC Manufactured Exports," *Journal of Development Economics*, Vol. 41 (August), pp. 367–76.

Guitián, Manuel, Massimo Russo, and Giuseppe Tullio, 1988, *Policy Coordination in the European Monetary System* (Washington: International Monetary Fund).

Horiguchi, Yusuke, and others, 1992, *The United States Economy: Performance and Issues* (Washington: International Monetary Fund).

Horsefield, J. Keith, ed., 1969, *The International Monetary Fund, 1945–1965: Twenty Years of International Monetary Cooperation*, Vol. 1: *Chronicle*, by J. Keith Horsefield; Vol. 2: *Analysis*, by Margaret G. de Vries and J. Keith Horsefield with the collaboration of Joseph Gold, Mary H. Gumbart, Gertrud Lovasy, and Emil G. Spitzer; Vol. 3: *Documents* (Washington: International Monetary Fund).

International Monetary Fund, 1979, *Summary Proceedings* (Washington: International Monetary Fund).

———, 1980 and 1990, *World Economic Outlook: A Survey by the Staff of the International Monetary Fund*, World Economic and Financial Surveys (Washington: International Monetary Fund, May).

———, Research Department, 1984, *Exchange Rate Volatility and World Trade*, Occasional Paper No. 28 (Washington: International Monetary Fund).

Isard, Peter, 1987, "Lessons from Empirical Models of Exchange Rates," *Staff Papers*, International Monetary Fund, Vol. 34 (March), pp. 1–28.

James, Harold, 1995, "The Historical Development of the Principle of Surveillance," *Staff Papers*, International Monetary Fund, Vol. 42 (December), pp. 762–91.

———, 1996, *International Monetary Cooperation Since Bretton Woods* (Oxford: Oxford University Press; Washington: International Monetary Fund).

Johnson, G.G., and others, 1985, *Formulation of Exchange Rate Policies in Adjustment Programs*, IMF Occasional Paper No. 36 (Washington: International Monetary Fund).

Kenen, Peter B., 1985, "Macroeconomic Theory and Policy: How the Closed Economy Was Opened," in *Handbook of International Economics,* Vol. II, ed. by Ronald W. Jones and Peter B. Kenen (Amsterdam: North-Holland), pp. 625–77.

———, and Dani Rodrik, 1986, "Measuring and Analyzing the Effects of Short-Term Volatility in Real Exchange Rates," *Review of Economics and Statistics,* Vol. 68 (May), pp. 311–15.

Kouri, Pentti, and Michael G. Porter, 1974, "International Capital Flows and Portfolio Equilibrium," *Journal of Political Economy,* Vol. 82 (May/June), pp. 443–67.

Lindner, Deborah J., 1992, "The Political Economy of the Won: U.S.-Korean Bilateral Negotiations on Exchange Rates," IFDP 434 (Washington: Board of Governors of the Federal Reserve System, International Finance Division).

Lipschitz, Leslie, and Donogh McDonald, 1990, *German Unification: Economic Issues,* IMF Occasional Paper No. 75 (Washington: International Monetary Fund).

Lipschitz, Leslie, Jeroen Kremers, Thomas Mayer, and Donogh McDonald, 1989, *The Federal Republic of Germany: Adjustment in a Surplus Country,* IMF Occasional Paper No. 64 (Washington: International Monetary Fund).

MacDonald, Ronald, 1995, "Long-Run Exchange Rate Modeling: A Survey of the Recent Evidence," *Staff Papers,* International Monetary Fund, Vol. 42 (September), pp. 437–89.

McLenaghan, John B., Saleh M. Nsouli, and Klaus-Walter Riechel, 1982, *Currency Convertibility in the Economic Community of West African States,* IMF Occasional Paper No. 13 (Washington: International Monetary Fund).

Pauly, Louis W., 1997, *Who Elected the Bankers? Surveillance and Control in the World Economy* (Ithaca: Cornell University Press).

Polak, Jacques J., 1980, "The EMF: External Relations," *Banca Nazionale del Lavoro Quarterly Review,* Vol. 134 (September), pp. 359–72.

———, 1991, *The Changing Nature of IMF Conditionality,* Essays in International Finance, No. 184 (Princeton, New Jersey: International Finance Section, Economics Department, Princeton University).

———, 1995, "Fifty Years of Exchange Rate Research and Policy at the International Monetary Fund," *Staff Papers,* International Monetary Fund, Vol. 42 (December), pp. 734–61.

Quirk, Peter J., Benedicte Vibe Christensen, Kyung-Mo Huh, and Toshihiko Sasaki, 1987, *Floating Exchange Rates in Developing Countries,* IMF Occasional Paper No. 53 (Washington: International Monetary Fund).

Robinson, Joan, 1937, "Beggar-My-Neighbour Remedies for Unemployment," in her *Essays on the Theory of Employment* (New York: Macmillan), pp. 210–28.

SaKong, Il, 1988, "The International Economic Position of Korea," in *Economic Relations Between the United States and Korea: Conflict or Cooperation?* ed. by Thomas O. Bayard and Soo-Gil Young (Washington: Institute for International Economics), pp. 7–17.

———, 1993, *Korea in the World Economy* (Washington: Institute for International Economics).

Simmons, Beth A., 2000, "The Legalization of International Monetary Affairs," *International Organization,* Vol. 54 (summer), pp. 573–602.

Ungerer, Horst, Owen Evans, and Peter Nyberg, 1983, *The European Monetary System: The Experience, 1979–82,* IMF Occasional Paper No. 19 (Washington: International Monetary Fund).

Ungerer, Horst, Owen Evans, Thomas Mayer, and Philip Young, 1986, *The European Monetary System: Recent Developments,* IMF Occasional Paper No. 48 (Washington: International Monetary Fund).

Ungerer, Horst, Jouko J. Hauvonen, Augusto Lopez-Claros, and Thomas Mayer, 1990, *The European Monetary System: Developments and Perspectives,* IMF Occasional Paper No. 73 (Washington: International Monetary Fund).

U.S. Department of the Treasury, 1988, *Report to the Congress on International Economic and Exchange Rate Policy: October 1988* (Washington: U.S. Treasury).

Zanello, Alessandro, and Dominique Desruelle, 1997, "A Primer on the IMF's Information Notice System," IMF Working Paper 97/71 (Washington: International Monetary Fund).

3

Seeking Symmetry: Article IV and the Largest Industrial Countries

> . . . WE, AS AN INSTITUTION, HAVE, I THINK, FAILED IN
> our task of industrial country surveillance. . . . we have to do a better job—if I may
> put it this way—of warning our authorities about the errors of their ways.
>
> Thomas C. Dawson, II
> U.S. Executive Director[1]

Nowhere is the difficulty of conducting surveillance more apparent than in the relations between the IMF and the major industrial countries. Effective oversight over the policies of the largest countries is obviously essential if surveillance is to be uniform and symmetric across the membership, but progress in achieving that goal has been slow and hesitant. The structure that evolved in the 1980s, though a bit jerry-built and complex, had three basic elements. First, the Fund conducted surveillance with[2] each country individually through the consultations required under Article IV of the Articles of Agreement and—both in the consultation itself and again in the World Economic Outlook exercise—proffered advice on the multilateral effects of each country's policies. Second, the major industrial countries held frequent meetings to discuss among themselves the policies that each country was pursuing, to convey any concerns about each other's policies, and to try to formulate joint policies on matters of mutual concern. Third, the Fund both participated in some of these multilateral meetings and, more generally, analyzed and evaluated the exercise for the membership at large.

The practice of bilateral surveillance with the five largest industrial countries is the subject of this chapter. The multilateral dimension (including the next two largest countries, Italy and Canada) is examined in Chapter 4. Broadly, this review

---

[1]Farewell remarks, EBM/93/123 (September 3, 1993).

[2]The phrase "surveillance with" is intended to express the idea that the Fund and the authorities of a country are jointly engaged in surveillance over the country's economic performance. Article IV enjoins the Fund to "exercise firm surveillance *over* the exchange rate policies of members," but it also obligates member countries "to collaborate *with* the Fund and other members to assure orderly exchange arrangements and to promote a stable system of exchange rates" (emphasis added). As used here, "surveillance with" stresses both the collaborative aspects of the process and the Fund's limited powers of enforcement.

suggests that the lack of symmetry in the effectiveness of surveillance (that is, the very limited influence over the policies of the largest countries) is attributable primarily to differences between countries in the demand for the Fund's advice, and not to differences in the effort devoted to the task by the Fund. In some instances discussed below, effectiveness was also limited by the staff's deference to the authorities and by its reluctance to question the existing course of economic policy. Overall, however, this review of bilateral surveillance showcases the Fund's continuous but evolving efforts to warn governments of "the errors of their ways."

Surveillance, as practiced by the IMF with the major industrial countries in the late 1970s and 1980s, had two principal goals. The first was to identify and discuss differences in interests and perspectives between the country (i.e., the authorities in charge) and the international community (i.e., the Fund's membership at large). Such differences typically arose from several sources:

- Conflicts in goals between countries; for example, with respect to their tolerance for inflation or unemployment or to the importance attached to external balance. Governments of large countries often assigned a lower priority to the implications of external imbalances than did their smaller trading partners.
- Conflicts in economic models between countries, for example with respect to the effects of fiscal or monetary policies on aggregate demand or supply. These differences in turn arose because of the differing credence given to Keynesian, neoclassical, or structural (supply-side) explanations of economic behavior.
- The possibility that exchange rate policy could be manipulated for domestic purposes, either to encourage depreciation to gain a competitive advantage or to encourage appreciation to fight inflation or foster an image of economic strength. In practice, however, manipulation is difficult to identify and was seldom a serious issue in the Fund's consultations with the major countries.

The second goal was for the Fund staff to examine economic developments and prospects objectively, abstracting as much as possible from political goals and constraints. The point about abstraction from politics is crucial for an understanding of the surveillance process. The staff were not necessarily better informed or more analytical than their counterparts across the table, but they were more likely to bring an objective viewpoint into the room. Owing to that difference, a comparison of staff and official analyses and forecasts often provided insights into the political constraints that inhibit effective economic policymaking.

From the beginning, Article IV consultations were conducted annually with each of the seven largest industrial countries. To the extent possible, these consultations were grouped in the periods before the semiannual World Economic Outlook (WEO) exercise. Thus, the Executive Board would usually discuss the United States, Germany, France, and Italy in July–August; and Japan, the United Kingdom, and Canada in January–March. To ensure that the WEO discussions were fully informed with the latest data, smaller staff visits were often held in the interval between consultations. The missions were headed by a senior officer of the relevant area department. In a few cases, as discussed below, the Managing Director joined the staff for the concluding meetings with the finance minister and other senior officials.

The preparation for and conduct of the annual consultations with the largest countries followed the same general procedures described in Chapter 2 for all member countries. The themes and objectives of each consultation were established in broad outline through a briefing paper, which was circulated and commented upon throughout the Fund and then cleared by management before the mission's departure for the country. In addition, the staff prepared for the mission by drafting a background paper that would later be revised and updated and then circulated under the heading of "Recent Economic Developments" (the RED) in the country being examined. The background paper assembled a detailed statistical base from published and internal sources, and often included research on topics of particular relevance to the forthcoming discussions. After the on-site discussions, the staff would return to headquarters to spend six to eight weeks preparing the staff report, the RED, and any special background or research papers required for circulation as supplements or annexes to the RED. The main staff report always included a brief summary of the major economic developments, an overview of the policy discussions, and a "staff appraisal" based primarily on the conclusions presented at the final meeting with the authorities.[3]

Within three months of the conclusion of the discussions with the authorities and about one month after circulation of the staff report, the Executive Board met and devoted all or most of a day (more, on rare occasions) to discussing the report. Two major themes dominated these discussions: exchange rate policies per se, and the conduct of macroeconomic policies. The first theme, however, was seldom of primary importance. As described below, the staff and the Executive Board occasionally examined the appropriateness of the authorities' exchange rate objectives (or, more often, the lack of objectives), and they frequently examined the appropriateness of official intervention practices. However, the exchange rate policies of the largest countries, which are inherently difficult to consider in isolation and apart from the actions of other major countries, were taken up more comprehensively in multilateral contexts: the WEO exercise, the Group of Seven (G-7) surveillance exercise, and general policy discussions. Even in those forums, exchange rate policies were treated as gingerly as those of smaller countries, owing to political sensitivities and concerns not to destabilize market activity.

Article IV discussions with the major countries therefore focused primarily on the conduct of fiscal and monetary policies, and in particular on the question of whether the country's policies were appropriate and sustainable over the medium term (generally meaning the course of three to five years). The difficulty with that approach was the lack of a real definition and of clear quantitative guidance for assessing appropriateness or sustainability. The goal was to assess simultaneously the country's internal and external balance, where internal balance refers to the

---

[3]Staff appraisals also took into account the responses of management and other staff to the mission's preliminary conclusions.

achievement of the maximum growth of output and the highest employment level consistent with (reasonable) price stability, and external balance refers variously to some combination of exchange rate stability and an appropriate and sustainable balance on current transactions in goods and services. Each of these concepts contains enough meat to serve as the basis for a serious discussion of the issues, but each also contains enough gristle to make the discussion difficult to digest.[4]

United States

A good place to begin this story is on November 1, 1978, seven months to the day after the amended Article IV came into effect. For most of that interval, the U.S. dollar had been depreciating against all of the other major currencies; in a year, the dollar had lost about 12 percent of its effective value. During the spring and summer of 1978, the U.S. monetary authorities attempted to counter the decline by tightening credit conditions by enough to raise short-term interest rates by about two percentage points, but that strategy produced little effect. The situation then became serious enough that the Fund's management and senior staff began exploring the possibility of an upper-tranche stand-by arrangement with the United States. Discussions to that effect were held in October between the Managing Director and the Secretary of the Treasury.[5] In late October, President Jimmy Carter announced new price and wage "standards," coupled with a tightening of fiscal policy. Those measures also failed to impress the exchange markets, and the downward spiral of the dollar was unabated.

Finally, on November 1, the Federal Reserve further tightened monetary policy, and the government announced a set of measures aimed directly at assuring the exchange markets that the dollar would be defended against further attack. These measures included a $7.5 billion increase in swap lines with the Deutsche Bundesbank, the Bank of Japan, and the Swiss National Bank;[6] plans to issue $10 billion in U.S. treasury securities denominated in foreign currencies; drawing down the U.S. reserve tranche in the Fund (SDR 2.3 billion, equivalent to $3 billion); and selling about half the country's holdings of SDRs, worth close to $2 billion. (Also see de Vries, 1985, pp. 858–66.) Mobilizing these resources in support of the dollar was described by the U.S. authorities as a "more vigorous" application of the existing policy of "intervening to counter disorderly conditions" in exchange mar-

---

[4]For a more detailed discussion of the issues and the difficulties, see Artus and Knight (1984) and Boughton (1989).

[5]Memorandum from the Managing Director to the U.S. Secretary of the Treasury (October 6, 1978); in IMF/CF (C/United States/820). Also see memorandum from the Deputy Managing Director to department heads (August 18, 1978); in IMF/RD Deputy Managing Director file "United States—1978" (Accession 82/22, Box 4, Section 139).

[6]A swap line is an agreement between central banks or national treasuries to permit either party to borrow the other's currency, up to the specified amount, for the purpose of reselling it in the foreign exchange market. It is, in effect, an overdraft facility to support official intervention.

kets,[7] but it was widely seen as a reversal of an attitude of indifference with respect to the level of the exchange rate.

The Managing Director responded to the U.S. announcement by calling for a "special consultation" under the new Article IV, the first such action with respect to a major country. In concluding the annual consultation, in July 1978, Executive Directors had judged that the depreciation and volatility of the dollar were attributable both to a failure to control U.S. inflation and to insufficient official intervention.[8] The Fund's goal now was to determine whether the new measures were an adequate response to those problems and to assess their consequences for the international monetary system. A staff team set out immediately to hold discussions with Treasury and Federal Reserve officials over the next few weeks, and a report was issued to Executive Directors on December 1.

The staff report unreservedly endorsed the U.S. effort to rescue the dollar. The "sharp depreciation of the U.S. dollar during October [had posed] a danger to the functioning of the international monetary system"; the November 1 policy package "was a welcome response in a situation in which exchange markets had become very disorderly and shifts in currency values were exaggerated in terms of both magnitude and speed." But the report also noted that solving the underlying inflation problem would require longer-term measures; the staff urged greater control of aggregate demand, notably through fiscal policy. The Executive Board, meeting two weeks later to discuss the report, supported those views and recommendations.[9]

The mission chief for that special consultation was the Deputy Director of the Western Hemisphere Department, Sterie T. Beza. Known universally as "Ted," Beza had participated in the U.S. consultations since 1969,[10] and had been leading those missions since 1973. He would continue to lead the U.S. consultations throughout the 1980s and right up to his retirement (as Counsellor, and Director of the Department) in 1994. His presence gave an unparalleled continuity to the discussions with the Fund's largest and predominant member country throughout the period of this History.

No more formal special consultations were held with the United States, but the handling of the 1978 episode set the tone for surveillance with this country over the next decade: the Fund, representing the interests of the international community, stressed the importance of implementing stable macroeconomic policies *and* of implementing exchange rate policies aimed at preventing misalignments. To illustrate further the application of Fund surveillance to the United States in the 1980s, two major themes will be examined here in some detail: the push by the Fund for greater fiscal discipline, and the treatment of exchange rate policy in re-

---

[7]"United States—Recent Economic Developments and Policy Actions," EBS/78/657 (December 1, 1978), p. 12.

[8]Minutes of EBM/78/106 (July 10, 1978), pp. 18–19.

[9]"United States—Recent Economic Developments and Policy Actions," EBS/78/657 (December 1, 1978), pp. 15 and 17; and minutes of EBM/78/197–198 (December 13, 1978).

[10]Consultations with the United States were held annually, beginning in 1962. For the background to the evolution of Fund consultations, see the introduction to Chapter 2.

sponse to the wide cycles in the value of the U.S. dollar. These debates show, sometimes almost painfully, how difficult surveillance can be when domestic political interests conflict with the economic interests of other countries.

Fiscal Deficit

The IMF took a remarkably strong and consistent stand in favor of fiscal moderation throughout the late 1970s and the 1980s, against the consistent and sometimes strong opposition of the U.S. authorities. Over time, the authorities gradually softened their own views, though the extent of the Fund's influence in that process is very difficult to judge and should not be exaggerated.[11]

As the United States struggled to recover from the 1974–75 recession, the fiscal deficit grew sharply, from less than $5 billion in 1974 to $75 billion (5 percent of GNP) two years later. By 1979, the Fund staff had identified deficit reduction as the key issue facing the U.S. government, and the issue remained at the top of the agenda throughout the 1980s. The Fund's focus, however, shifted during this period, as the perceived adverse effects of the deficit ranged from inflation to external imbalance to the crowding out of domestic investment and finally to the saddling of future generations with a mountain of debt. The authorities generally agreed that the deficit was a problem, but they consistently rejected the Fund's recommendations to take more aggressive action to reduce it; their reasoning also evolved markedly over time.

In the 1979 discussions, held just four months after the special consultation described above, the staff argued that cutting the fiscal deficit was a key requirement for reducing inflation, which was then running at about 13 percent a year, the highest rate experienced in the United States since the postwar release of pent-up demand pressures in 1947. Carter administration officials[12] agreed with the staff that deficit reduction was desirable, but they believed that they lacked the flexibility to take action before the next fiscal year. More fundamentally, they argued that inflation was largely a structural problem in the United States, and their strategy for reducing it was based primarily on supply-side measures such as deregulation of industry, simplification of government controls, and incomes policies.

Meeting in June 1979, the Executive Board was split almost evenly on this issue, between Directors who were satisfied that U.S. policy was on course and those

---

[11]Research for this chapter included interviews with senior officials from each country. (For a list, see the Preface.) Asked to recall an instance when a policy decision had been influenced by advice from the Fund, none of these officials admitted to being able to do so. To determine whether those negative responses reflected personal pride or a more general indifference to the surveillance process would require a much more detailed investigation than was possible here.

[12]The team of officials from the U.S. Treasury involved in the consultations was normally headed either by the Deputy Secretary (the number two official, after the Secretary) or, more commonly, the Under Secretary for International Monetary Affairs (directly below the Deputy Secretary on the organizational chart). Officials from other agencies, including the President's Council of Economic Advisers and the Office of Management and Budget, participated in some meetings. In addition to meeting with representatives of the administration, the Fund staff met regularly with officials from the independent Federal Reserve System.

who thought that more fiscal restriction was warranted. The summing up concluded, "Directors agreed that demand policy had a central role to play in the anti-inflationary strategy, and that *as a minimum* there needed to be firm adherence to the present stance of moderate demand restraint" (emphasis added).[13]

By 1980, finding the right course for U.S. fiscal policy had become even more difficult, as the economy had slipped into recession while inflation continued unabated. In part, this conjuncture was a coincidental result of the second oil shock, and in part it was an inevitable result of the Federal Reserve's October 1979 shift toward much stricter control over monetary growth; but it also showed that the potential for stagflation was greater than had seemed possible. Despite the recession, the staff argued against using either fiscal or monetary policy for countercyclical purposes and urged the authorities to stick to an anti-inflationary policy. This advice—which reflected a growing consensus among economists against attempting to "fine tune" macroeconomic policies—was in line with Carter administration and Federal Reserve thinking, and it generated little controversy when discussed by the Executive Board.[14]

The landscape changed dramatically in 1981, as the new administration of President Ronald Reagan proposed a bold strategy to stimulate output by cutting personal income tax rates and to stimulate investment by introducing an accelerated-recovery system for depreciating capital expenditures. Although similar proposals had previously been billed as stimulants to demand (notably in the Kennedy administration of the early 1960s), they now were repackaged as supply-side measures with the additional claim that the direct revenue losses to the government would be more than compensated by the effect of induced economic growth on revenues and on welfare and other spending programs (see Chapter 1, pp. 32–33). On that optimistic basis, President Reagan set a goal of balancing the federal budget by fiscal year (FY) 1984.[15]

The staff report rejected the administration's rosy growth projections and concluded that "relatively large fiscal deficits . . . are in the offing for the period ahead."[16] Executive Directors as well as the staff found the reasoning behind the U.S. shift toward fiscal expansion to be puzzling, and in July the unusual step was taken of inviting the newly appointed Under Secretary of the U.S. Treasury for International Monetary Affairs, Beryl Sprinkel, for a lunch with Executive Directors at the Fund. On that occasion, Sprinkel played down the significance of the deficit and asserted that monetary restraint would produce expectations of stable prices and so would lower interest rates, whatever the fiscal position. Neither the staff nor the Board accepted this line of reasoning: as Jacques J. Polak (Netherlands) noted,

---

[13]Minutes of EBM/79/93 (June 18, 1979), p. 22.

[14]See "United States—Staff Report for the 1980 Article IV Consultation," SM/80/144 (June 17, 1980) and the minutes of EBM/80/103–104 (July 11, 1980).

[15]Since 1977, the fiscal year for the federal government in the United States has ended on September 30. The goal of balancing the budget in four years was incorporated in President Reagan's initial budget, as submitted to the U.S. Congress in February 1981.

[16]"United States—Staff Report for the 1981 Article IV Consultation," SM/81/157 (7/14/81), p. 18.

the proposition could not possibly hold except in the very long run.[17] The stage was thus set for a clash of economic models that would dominate the discussions throughout the rest of the decade.

The case for supply-side economics was cogently argued by the U.S. Executive Director, Richard D. Erb, at the Board meeting that concluded the 1981 consultation. Erb rejected the staff's mainstream view that inflation reduction required "restraints on effective demand"; in the U.S. administration's view, that approach would discourage investment and limit growth. Instead, he argued that tax cuts aimed at stimulating investment were needed. Nonetheless, he averred, "I can assure you that the United States is determined to reduce the budget deficit and takes the goal of a balanced budget by 1984 very seriously." The Board, however, rebuffed this argument, and the summing up of the meeting noted that it was the "general view" of Directors that U.S. fiscal policy was too loose and would continue to produce large deficits and high real interest rates.[18]

In October 1981, trying to move beyond stalemate on this critical issue, the Managing Director, Jacques de Larosière, sent the U.S. Treasury a note via Erb, asking for a further exchange of views (in effect, an informal supplemental consultation, though without a meeting of the Executive Board) on the need for additional fiscal restraint, including "strengthening revenue." In response, at a series of meetings held around the beginning of December, Sprinkel argued that inflation control was a monetary problem that was essentially independent from fiscal actions. He also informed the Managing Director that the administration did not intend to introduce any revenue-raising measures until after spending had been effectively reduced.[19]

By the time of the 1982 consultation, the Reagan administration was backing away from promises to balance the budget by 1984, owing to recession, high interest rates, and the difficulty of cutting spending. The staff report (issued in July) again called for greater fiscal restraint, in spite of the recession, which had become the worst U.S. downturn since before World War II.[20] A few weeks later, as the Mexican debt crisis was approaching the bursting point, the Managing Director met with the Secretary of the U.S. Treasury, Donald T. Regan, both to discuss that crisis and to express his "very deep concern" about the growing U.S. fiscal deficit.[21] That concern was echoed at the Executive Board meeting that concluded the consultation, which was also notable for the strength of the view that counter cyclical policy no longer had any place in the strategy. The recession in the U.S. economy was attributed to the adverse effects of inflation rather than to a weakening of de-

---

[17]Minutes of EBM/81/110 (July 31, 1981), p. 9.

[18]Minutes of EBM/81/111 (August 3, 1981), p. 15.

[19]File memorandums by Beza (December 2 and 8, 1981); in IMF/RD Western Hemisphere Department file, "United States—1981" (Accession 84/70, Box 2, Section 74).

[20]"United States—Staff Report for the 1982 Article IV Consultation," SM/82/141 (July 16, 1982), pp. 1–2 and 16.

[21]File memorandum (August 12, 1982) by William B. Dale (Deputy Managing Director); in IMF/RD Deputy Managing Director file "United States—1982" (Accession 88/285, Box 5, Section 250).

mand, and the Board recommended steady policies as the cure for both inflation and recession.[22] The size and growth of the fiscal deficit were viewed as having severely limited the authorities' room for maneuver, and the Keynesian policies that were the most visible legacy of the Fund's most famous founding father were apparently orphaned and disowned. (See, however, the recounting below of the treatment of fiscal policy in the consultations with Japan.)

In 1983, the U.S. administration's viewpoint again shifted slightly. Tax increases were still rejected, but no longer because tax cuts were supposed to produce revenue increases via the Laffer curve. The argument now was that a tax increase would encourage the U.S. Congress to approve commensurately higher spending and therefore would do little to reduce the deficit. The staff rejoined that the deficit could not be reduced by enough through spending cuts alone and argued that the problem would have to be tackled comprehensively.[23] At the Executive Board meeting, Erb agreed with the staff that the deficit was having adverse effects, including appreciation of the dollar and a weakening current account position, but he was not able to offer any new initiatives to reduce it.[24]

By 1984, the Fund surveillance process was beginning to have an impact on the domestic debate in the United States, as critics of administration policy cited the Fund's views to buttress their arguments. For example, Senator William Proxmire of Wisconsin, questioning Assistant Treasury Secretary David C. Mulford during a Senate committee hearing on Argentina, cited a speech by the Managing Director noting the importance of reducing the federal deficit. Proxmire then asked Mulford whether he agreed that the deficit was the number one obstacle to a healthy world economy. Mulford replied that it was an issue, but that "up until now" it had not had an evident negative effect. Later in the hearing, Anthony Solomon, the President of the Federal Reserve Bank of New York, supported the Fund's view that reducing the deficit was important.[25]

The split between the U.S. administration and the Federal Reserve on this issue was noted by the Fund staff during the 1984 consultation. Sensing that the administration's indifference to the deficit was not widely shared even among U.S. officials, the staff drew a more specific and stronger conclusion than before, that "priority needs to be given to a large and rapid cutback of the federal deficit."[26]

---

[22]The Managing Director summarized this argument as follows: "Most Directors agreed that sustained growth of output and employment would require a lasting reduction of inflation, and they cautioned against a shift to expansionary policies, a shift that would likely cause a setback in the fight against inflation." Minutes of EBM/82/108 (August 16, 1982), p. 29.

[23]"United States—Staff Report for the 1983 Article IV Consultation," SM/83/135 (June 20, 1983), pp. 13 and 21.

[24]Minutes of EBM/83/106 (July 20, 1983), p. 5.

[25]Testimony before the Subcommittee on International Finance and Monetary Policy of the Committee on Banking, Housing, and Urban Affairs, United States Senate (S. Hrg. 98-782, *The Argentinean Debt*; hearings on "Details and Implications of U.S. Government Involvement in both the Argentinean and the Larger Latin American Debt Crises"), May 3, 1984; pp. 40 (Mulford) and 63 (Solomon).

[26]"United States—Staff Report for the 1984 Article IV Consultation," SM/84/162 (July 6, 1984), p. 21.

Perhaps also sensing its isolation on this major issue, the administration began to display what many in the Fund interpreted as an antipathy toward the whole consultation process.

By the time of the Executive Board meeting, on August 3, 1984, the U.S. administration's apparent attitude was producing a palpable frustration and disillusionment of Directors whose economies were being adversely affected by the persistence of the U.S. deficit.[27] The French Executive Director, Bruno de Maulde, led the attack on the United States, expressing his "intense frustration . . . because the U.S. administration appeared to pay no attention to the recommendations of the Board." He concluded that surveillance with the United States had become a "mockery, and consequently that the United States lacked credibility in propounding the idea that the exercise of surveillance by the Fund was the cornerstone of the smooth functioning of the international monetary system."

De Maulde's position, though a rare display of intemperance in these meetings, was supported by several other chairs. For example, R.N. Malhotra (India) observed that "unless the major economies of the world were prepared to play by the rules of the game, he did not see how the surveillance function of the Fund could be effectively discharged." Mary Bush, then the Acting Executive Director for the United States, reportedly remained stoic throughout this discussion, without even taking notes. When it was over, she responded only with a brief assertion that U.S. officials did pay attention to "constructive criticism from abroad" and that they did value the surveillance process. More substantively, however, Bush's opening statement at the meeting revealed a hardening attitude by the Reagan administration against pressures to reduce the deficit: "the weight of evidence," she argued, "suggests that there is no relationship between U.S. fiscal deficits and real interest rates" and that the deficit was not "inhibiting capital formation."

The American arguments on this point were soundly rejected and even mocked around the table. Gerhard Laske (Germany) concluded that the U.S. "authorities' arguments, which questioned the validity of the causal relationship between fiscal deficits and interest rates, were an interesting confirmation of his suspicion that it was permissible in economics to make the argument fit the desired theoretical proof." As the meeting progressed, Polak was concerned enough about the widening gulf between the United States and the rest of the world that he called for a supplemental consultation discussion to take place within six months.[28]

In December 1984, the Managing Director followed up on Polak's suggestion by meeting again with Secretary Regan. The administration, just reelected, was in the midst of preparing the budget for the next fiscal year, and the Managing Director

---

[27]The Managing Director's summing up of the discussion emphasized that the concern was that the surveillance process was being subverted, not just that there was a disagreement over policies: "Several Executive Directors were concerned that the recommendations of the Executive Board, which were part of the surveillance process and its effectiveness, did not seem to be reflected in U.S. economic policy in the fiscal area."

[28]On the last three paragraphs, see minutes of EBM/84/120 (August 3, 1984), pp. 9–10 (Bush), 13 (de Maulde), and 35 (Laske); and EBM/84/121 (same date), pp. 5 (Polak), 14 (Malhotra), 28 (Bush), and 30 (summing up).

again took the occasion to make the case for strong action. He conveyed to Regan the Fund's view that the current account deficit was unsustainable and that it should be reduced in an orderly fashion through fiscal action; the alternative, he argued, would be a disruptive depreciation of the dollar that would be difficult to control.[29]

The U.S. position began to shift in 1985, following a shuffling of key personnel in which James A. Baker III replaced Regan as Secretary of the Treasury and Richard G. Darman took over as Deputy Secretary.[30] That spring, however, witnessed a last and most difficult manifestation of the strains that had developed between the U.S. administration and the international community.

In response to the U.S. arguments during the 1984 consultation that there was no relationship between the fiscal deficit and real interest rates, the Research Department in the Fund had undertaken an extensive study of the issue as part of the regular WEO exercise. The results of the study were circulated to the Executive Board in March 1985 as part of the standard documentation for the WEO (under the modest heading of "Supplementary Note 7," belying its length of 140 single-spaced pages: a paper that covered all of the major channels by which shifts in fiscal policy might affect both the domestic and international economies and that included five detailed appendixes on empirical tests). The paper concluded, on the basis of an extensive examination of the empirical literature, that the conventional wisdom was correct: a cut in the U.S. fiscal deficit, whether from spending cuts or tax increases, would be expected to lead to a predictable decline in real interest rates.[31]

When the WEO was published in April, Executive Directors were surprised, and several expressed disappointment, to discover that Supplementary Note 7 had not been included. Nigel Wicks (United Kingdom) and Bruno de Maulde (France), after determining that the deletion had been made at the request of the U.S. authorities, called for an exceptional discussion in the Board, which was held on May 3.[32] Most speakers at the meeting supported their call for publication; they and the Managing Director noted that it could be published separately as an Occasional Paper or as an article in the IMF's academic journal, *Staff Papers*. But Bush—supported by four other Directors—was adamant, claiming that the study was "an outgrowth" of the U.S. consultation, objecting to publication on the

---

[29]Based on the Managing Director's draft notes for the meeting; in his file, "EXR 1985–1986" (IMF/RD, Accession 88/18, Box 6, Section 485).

[30]At the Treasury, Darman replaced Richard T. McNamar as Deputy Secretary, but he also assumed many of the international responsibilities formerly taken on by the former Under Secretary, Beryl Sprinkel; see footnote 12, p, 140.

[31]The essential point demonstrated in the paper was that most of the studies purporting to show weak or absent effects had failed to control adequately for the sources of the shift in the deficit, so that they treated changes arising endogenously from the business cycle as if they were similar to changes arising from direct policy actions. "World Economic Outlook: Supplementary Note 7—Domestic and International Effects of the U.S. Fiscal Position," SM/85/76 (March 11, 1985); the conclusion is stated on p. 36.

[32]Memorandum to the Managing Director (May 1, 1985); in IMF/RD (Historian's files).

grounds that it dealt with "a sensitive policy issue," and asserting that the United States would nonetheless have been willing to see it published if other Directors had supported a recent U.S. request for giving greater publicity to consultation reports. Publication was thus blocked, despite a further plea from the Managing Director for reconsideration.[33]

Relations improved markedly after that episode, but the fiscal deficit continued to be a major source of dispute between the Fund and its largest member country. At the conclusion of the 1985 consultation discussions in late June, the Managing Director met with both Baker and the Chairman of the Federal Reserve System, Paul A. Volcker, to discuss the Fund's main policy recommendations and to stress again the importance of taking wide-ranging measures to reduce the deficit. This appears to have been the first time since 1971 that the U.S. consultation had concluded with a ministerial-level meeting, which then became standard practice. In welcoming this development, Polak hoped that it would "help steer U.S. economic policy toward a less ominous course."[34]

The ominousness of that course was not easy to determine. Far from being balanced by FY 1984 as originally targeted by the president four years earlier, the fiscal deficit had risen from 2¾ percent of GNP in FY 1981 to 6½ percent in FY 1983 before dropping back to 5¼ percent. In the judgment of the Fund staff and the Managing Director, even if the deficit had peaked in relation to output, it remained extraordinarily high and was still the main policy problem facing the United States. Furthermore, the administration continued to insist that no causal link existed between high deficits and high real interest rates, and that debt and tax financing were essentially equivalent ("Ricardian equivalence"; see Chapter 1), a view that the staff "could not accept."[35] At the Executive Board meeting in early August 1985, the United States remained isolated in its expressed indifference to the consequences of the deficit, as Directors "unequivocally" agreed that deficit reduction should be the top priority for the U.S. administration.[36]

Between the 1985 and 1986 consultations, the U.S. Congress passed the Gramm-Rudman-Hollings (generally known more simply as Gramm-Rudman) legislation, mandating a gradual reduction in the fiscal deficit until it was balanced in FY 1991. The actual deficit, however, rose in FY 1986, owing to rising military spending and the passage of additional tax cuts. The administration nonetheless projected that its FY 1987 budget would be consistent with the Gramm-Rudman target, and it presented a plan to balance the budget by FY 1991.

---

[33]Minutes of EBM/85/69 (May 3, 1985). Also see memorandum from Kafka to the Managing Director (May 2, 1985); in IMF/CF, "WEO, Fund Reviews—March 21, 1985–December 1985" (S 321).

[34]Minutes of EBM/85/121, p. 9. As Director of the Research Department, Polak had been the mission chief for several U.S. consultations in the 1960s and early 1970s. He thus had first-hand experience of the significance of the willingness of the Secretary of the Treasury to meet with the mission.

[35]"United States—Staff Report for the 1985 Article IV Consultation," SM/85/199 (July 8, 1985), p. 12. The staff also examined this issue in Appendix I of the WEO document cited in footnote 31, above.

[36]Chairman's summing up, minutes of EBM/85/121 (August 5, 1985), p. 29.

In the consultation discussions in the spring of 1986, the staff argued that the FY 1987 budget would not meet the target, because it was predicated on an unrealistically optimistic growth forecast. They also noted that to balance the budget by FY 1991 would require up to $150 billion in additional spending cuts that had not yet been identified.[37] When the Managing Director met with Secretary Baker on June 24 to conclude the discussions, he again stressed that revenue measures would have to be taken: measures that, as Baker reminded him, the president opposed on a deep philosophical level.[38]

At the 1986 Board meeting on the United States, the usual differences of view on fiscal issues persisted (focusing now on the optimistic growth forecasts that the administration obviously was adopting only to meet the Gramm-Rudman targets ex ante).[39] Even so, the tension that had characterized the previous two meetings was now gone. As the Managing Director summarized the meeting, "Directors warmly commended the U.S. authorities for the open and thorough dialogue that had marked the 1986 consultation discussions . . . [and] welcomed the significant improvements in policy formulation and performance since the last consultation."[40]

Although the Gramm-Rudman law had little if any discernible impact on the deficit, it did serve to make the surveillance process more transparent and objective. Beginning in 1986, the staff made its own medium-term projections of the deficit, based on the assumption that current policies would continue and on what the staff regarded as a more realistic forecast of GNP growth. As shown in Figure 3.1, each year the U.S. administration presented a deficit-reduction plan that closely paralleled the Gramm-Rudman path;[41] each year the staff countered with a projection showing that unless further policy measures were specified and carried out and unless the administration's optimistic assumptions for economic growth were realized, the deficit would not fall significantly at all; and the outcome turned out to be consistently worse even than the staff projections.

In the 1987 consultations, treasury officials shared the staff's disappointment and acknowledged that Gramm-Rudman had led to an increased reliance on what commentators were calling "smoke and mirrors": accounting gimmicks and temporary actions such as asset sales.[42] To conclude the discussions, the new Manag-

---

[37]"United States—Staff Report for the 1986 Article IV Consultation," SM/86/167 (July 7, 1986), pp. 7–13.

[38]Background note sent to Secretary Baker in advance of the meeting, and minutes of the meeting; in IMF/RD Western Hemisphere Department file "United States: 1987 Article IV Consultation" (Accession 1996-0012, Box 4, Section 408).

[39]The legislation required the administration to submit a budget with a deficit no higher than the specified ceiling, based on the administration's economic assumptions; no ceiling was imposed on the outcome. If economic growth fell short of the assumptions, then the deficit would exceed the target for that fiscal year, and the ex ante reduction required in the following year would be that much larger.

[40]Minutes of EBM/86/132 (August 6, 1986), p. 59.

[41]By 1988, the Gramm-Rudman legislation had been amended so as to postpone the day of reckoning to FY 1993 and to raise the intervening ceilings commensurately.

[42]"United States—Staff Report for the 1987 Article IV Consultation," SM/87/179 (July 23, 1987), p. 11.

Figure 3.1. United States: Projections of the Fiscal Deficit
(*In billions of U.S. dollars*)

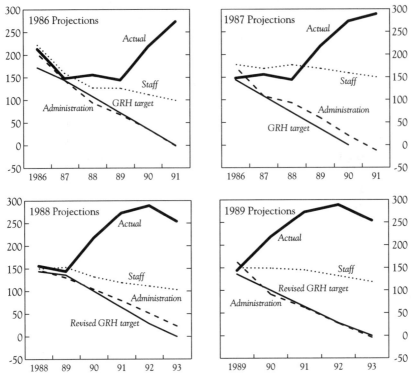

Note: GRH target = Gramm-Rudman-Hollings target.

ing Director, Michel Camdessus, met with Baker on June 3 and took up where his predecessor had left off in calling for tough additional measures to meet the Gramm-Rudman targets.

In 1988, the staff gave another turn of the screw to their perennial call for fiscal discipline by raising concerns over the prospect that the social security trust fund would shift into deficit after the year 2010. The staff report argued that the U.S. administration should prepare now to avoid major financial strains in the next century, and it even took the position—rejected as unrealistic by the administration—that the non–social security portion of the budget should be balanced and that the social security budget should show a surplus sufficient to fund the anticipated post-2010 deficits. In other words, in the staff's view, balancing the budget was not enough; the unified budget should show a substantial surplus. Executive Directors were more cautious on this score, but the Board did note that fiscal adjustment should be "front-loaded" and that the Gramm-Rudman targets "should be regarded as a minimal requirement."[43]

---

[43]Chairman's summing up; minutes of EBM/88/131 (August 29, 1988), p. 11.

Figure 3.2. U.S. Effective Exchange Rate, 1975–90

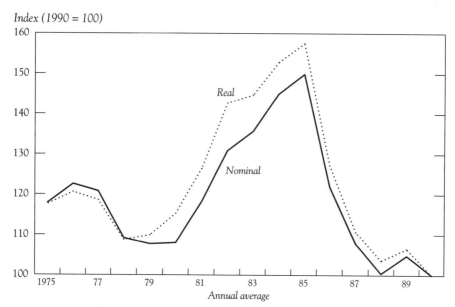

Index (1990 = 100)

The final consultation of the decade found these same themes still being debated. By this time, several Directors were getting concerned that the staff might be overstating the case by calling for a substantial fiscal surplus at a time when getting the deficit under control would be a major achievement. What brought everyone together was agreement that the Gramm-Rudman legislation had perverted the budget process in the United States and that a lasting solution would require a new and more serious approach in the years to come.

Exchange Rate Policy

A second overriding theme in the U.S. consultations during the 1980s was the desirability of stabilizing the exchange rate of the dollar.[44] From the low point in November 1978 that triggered the events described at the beginning of this section, the dollar strengthened through 1979 and then weakened in 1980 before beginning a four-year sustained appreciation against all other major currencies (Figure 3.2). Although the appreciation was substantially reversed in 1985 and 1986, concerns continued to be raised about the appropriateness of the level and about

---

[44]See Destler and Henning (1989), Frankel (1994), and Henning (1994), Chapter 6, for overviews of U.S. exchange rate policy in the 1980s. For the sake of exposition, the phrase "the exchange rate of the dollar" is used here to refer to the general tendency regarding exchange rates between the U.S. dollar and other major currencies. During the major 1980–87 cycle of the dollar, rates against the major European currencies and the Japanese yen tended to move in the same direction most of the time, and the nominal and real changes in the effective (weighted-average) rates tended to be quite similar.

whether more systemic measures should be taken to stabilize the rate. Nonetheless, differences between the U.S. authorities and the Fund were surprisingly mild, especially compared with the debates that raged over the fiscal policies that had largely produced the major swings in the dollar's exchange value.

Shortly before the 1981 consultations, Beryl Sprinkel announced that the United States would no longer intervene in foreign exchange markets except "when necessary to counter conditions of disorder in the market" (Sprinkel, 1981, p. 18). Although this position was nominally the same as that of the preceding administration, Sprinkel made it clear that it was an almost total pullback from the activist intervention policy of 1979–80 (see above, p. 139).[45] The staff report on the consultation discussions supported this position: "It is readily apparent that a substantial degree of exchange rate flexibility needs to be maintained in present circumstances . . . and the staff agrees with the U.S. authorities that the information obtained from exchange markets should be used as a guide to [domestic] policy."[46]

The Executive Directors from Germany and Japan attacked the nonintervention policy at the Board meeting at the end of July. In Gerhard Laske's view, "the notion of 'disorderly markets' should . . . not be interpreted too narrowly. . . . Experience has shown that markets are frequently motivated by unrealistic expectations, and that in such circumstances intervention in close coordination with the authorities of the [other] major countries is not out of place."[47] Speaking for the staff, however, C. David Finch (Director of the Exchange and Trade Relations Department, ETR) justified the staff support of nonintervention on three grounds: judging the equilibrium level of the exchange rate was hard, intervention often failed to work because it was not backed up by appropriate domestic policies, and in any event the U.S. administration's intention to pursue stable domestic policies might well suffice to stabilize the dollar. The Chairman's summing up of the discussion noted the concerns expressed by "some Directors," but it avoided drawing a general conclusion on behalf of the Board.[48]

By 1982, the appreciation of the dollar was beginning to be the focus of attention, but the staff continued to accept the U.S. administration's laissez-faire policy. In the staff's view, the appreciation—which was not yet generating a current account deficit—resulted partly from anticipated lower inflation and partly from safe-haven effects. At the Executive Board meeting, Jacques Polak characterized

---

[45]As reported in U.S. Council of Economic Advisers (1982), p. 190, the U.S. authorities sold $2.6 billion (net) in foreign exchange to support the value of the dollar from September 1977 to March 1978 and purchased $2.1 billion net over the next six months. Then, in the space of 28 months after the announcement of the dollar support package in November 1978, they purchased $11.9 billion net. The shift in strategy in 1981 was seen as a reaction to that large net purchase, which was viewed by the new administration as of "massive proportions by historical U.S. standards (although not by the more activist standards of many foreign governments)." The Council report (p. 173) clarified the meaning of the policy shift by adding "severe" before "disorder" in describing conditions that might be countered by intervention.

[46]"United States—Staff Report for the 1981 Article IV Consultation," SM/81/157 (July 14, 1981), p. 19.

[47]Minutes of EBM/81/109 (7/31/81), p. 19.

[48]Minutes of EBM/81/111 (August 3, 1981), pp. 9 (Finch) and 16 (summing up).

the official view as "the market can do no wrong." He rejected that view, criticized the staff for accepting it, and asked that the staff be more explicit in assessing the level of the exchange rate.[49] The summing up of the meeting was again cautious about drawing a general conclusion, except to note that "Directors were encouraged by the decision of the major industrial countries to conduct a study of the effects of intervention . . . to clarify some of the difficult issues. . . ."[50]

The staff position on U.S. exchange rate policy shifted in 1983, as the dollar's unabated appreciation began to look less benign. As one argument for deficit reduction, the staff report suggested that fiscal contraction would be "conducive to an orderly correction in the exchange value of the U.S. dollar." The staff also urged the authorities to participate in coordinated intervention, but only to counter "disorderly market conditions," not to try to influence the level.[51] Similarly, the summing up of the meeting reflected the growing consensus "that participation by the United States in coordinated intervention with other countries could, under appropriate circumstances, serve a useful purpose."[52] U.S. treasury officials, however, believed that the rising value of the dollar reflected a growing worldwide confidence in the strength of the U.S. economy, and that any feasible level of intervention would be swamped by the vastly larger resources of the financial markets.

The following year, the staff raised the specter of nonsustainability of the current account deficit that had now emerged. It could not be financed over the medium term, the report concluded, without either higher interest rates or a dollar depreciation. Executive Directors generally agreed with that assessment, but the U.S. authorities expressed indifference to the problem.[53] The discussion on this issue at the Board meeting was nonetheless muted, as the staff acknowledged that empirical models (including their own) provided no convincing explanation for why the dollar was continuing to appreciate.[54]

---

[49]Minutes of EBM/82/107 (August 16, 1982), p. 15.

[50]Minutes of EBM/82/108 (August 16, 1982), p. 30. The G-7 intervention study led to the 1983 Jurgensen Report (see Chapter 4, p. 197), which concluded that official intervention can have beneficial effects in the short run but that longer-run stability hinges on more fundamental policies.

[51]The U.S. authorities did intervene on three occasions in 1983, coordinated with Germany and Japan, but this practice remained exceptional. See Dominguez and Frankel (1993). The staff appraisal is in "United States—Staff Report for the 1983 Article IV Consultation," SM/83/135 (June 20, 1983), pp. 21–22. Intervention in 1983 is described in "United States—Staff Report for the 1984 Article IV Consultation," SM/84/162 (July 6, 1984), p. 17.

[52]Minutes of EBM/83/107 (July 20, 1983), p. 25.

[53]See "United States—Staff Report for the 1984 Article IV Consultation," SM/84/162 (July 6, 1984), and the minutes of EBM/84/120–121 (August 3, 1984).

[54]The then-prevailing empirical model for the expected path of the exchange rate hypothesized that the rate would move away from the long-run equilibrium level only in response to unanticipated changes in relative conditions such as interest rate differentials (see Chapter 1, section on "unstable exchange rates"). By mid-1984, these "fundamentals" were moving against the dollar and theoretically should have brought on a depreciation. Although portfolio balance models with more realistic and flexible expectations mechanisms, such as Boughton (1984), generated predictions consistent with a continued appreciation of the dollar at least through the third quarter of 1984, those models had little impact on the internal debate at the time.

By the time of the 1985 consultation, the dollar was beginning to depreciate, at least partly because of a return to more active and coordinated official intervention. Although the Executive Board meeting was held just six weeks before the Plaza meeting (see Chapter 4)—at a time when the Group of Five (G-5) countries were already planning a major initiative to ensure that the depreciation would be sustained—no serious concerns about the dollar were expressed, except indirectly through the continuing call for fiscal deficit reduction.[55]

The cautious and tentative approach to exchange rate policy continued through 1986, as the analysis of the persistent external deficit of the United States was hampered by the lack of a clear theoretical and empirical model of the relationship between exchange rates and current account positions. A staff study for the WEO prepared around that time (Boughton and others, 1986) argued that because these two variables were both endogenous, a depreciation might or might not be accompanied by a strengthening of the current account position. Nonetheless, the 1986 staff report, issued in early July, concluded that "a further downward adjustment in the value of the dollar may well be needed in order to achieve a sustainable current account position."[56]

In February 1987, officials from the major industrial countries, gathered at the Louvre in Paris, agreed that exchange rates between the dollar and other key currencies were at appropriate levels and that they would aim to maintain those rates (see Chapter 4). Within a few months, however, doubts were being raised by outside analysts about the appropriateness of the Louvre-agreed exchange rates. In that view, a further depreciation was needed to keep the improvement in the U.S. current account balance from stalling.[57] The staff report on the 1987 U.S. consultations supported both the Louvre process and the outcome, despite some skepticism by the staff as to whether the current account deficit could be reduced sufficiently without further depreciation. The report concluded that the U.S. authorities were correct in arguing that "in present circumstances a further substantial depreciation of the dollar could be counterproductive as it could retard the correction of external imbalances by depressing economic growth abroad."[58]

At the Executive Board meeting concluding the consultations in August, all the other industrial countries urged the U.S. authorities to maintain the pattern of exchange rates established at the Louvre. Guenter Grosche, in a statement that was notable because Germany had not been the biggest supporter of the Louvre process, declared that his authorities were "deeply satisfied" with the accord and the resulting pattern of exchange rates. Directors from developing countries, however, were more worried; although in principle exchange rates could be stabilized by coordinating interest rates at low levels, in practice they were being stabilized

---

[55]Minutes of EBM/85/120–121 (August 5, 1985).

[56]"United States—Staff Report for the 1986 Article IV Consultation," SM/86/167 (July 7, 1986), p. 27.

[57]Martin Feldstein and Paul Krugman were leading proponents of this view; see Feldstein (1988) and Krugman (1988).

[58]"United States—Staff Report for the 1987 Article IV Consultation," SM/87/179 (July 23, 1987), p. 19; on the staff's skepticism, see pp. 24–25.

by keeping rates high. Alvaro Donoso (Chile) pointed out that the Federal Reserve was tightening U.S. monetary policy to keep the dollar from depreciating, and the consequent high level of interest rates was depressing world growth. He, Arjun K. Sengupta (India), and others accordingly called for a further depreciation of the dollar against other key currencies.[59]

During the 1988 consultation, the U.S. authorities signaled a further shift in their policy regarding official intervention, stating that the Louvre experience had shown "that in suitable circumstances it could be more helpful than they had previously thought."[60] Furthermore, attitudes had shifted all around toward more sympathy for allowing the dollar to depreciate, partly because the exchange rate had appreciated in recent months in response to the government's inability to reduce the fiscal deficit sufficiently, and partly because the dangers identified in 1987 appeared more serious now. The summing up for the Executive Board meeting in late August concluded, with subtle asymmetry, that it would be undesirable to see a "further appreciation" or a "sharp depreciation" (implying that either the continuation of the present rate or an orderly depreciation would be acceptable outcomes).[61]

Finally, in 1989, while there was little overt discussion of the exchange rate, the related issue concerned whether the United States or "the surplus countries" should bear the primary burden of adjustment. The U.S. position was that those countries (a euphemism for Germany and Japan, in particular) should take measures to stimulate their economies in the interest of reducing global payments imbalances and strengthening world growth. At the Executive Board meeting, most Directors were critical of that view and argued (along with the staff) that deficit reduction in the United States was still the top priority.

Special Studies

Although macroeconomic and exchange rate policies were the natural focus of all of the consultation discussions in the 1980s, international interest in structural issues affecting the U.S. economy was also widespread. Accordingly, the staff devoted substantial and increasing effort to special studies undertaken as part of the consultation process. The number of studies circulated as background papers for the staff report on the United States more than doubled, from 8 in 1979 to 17 a decade later. The 1989 collection, which totaled 350 single-spaced pages, covered topics ranging from macroeconomic issues such as the outlook for the current account balance and the operation of the Gramm-Rudman legislation to microeconomic issues such as the crisis in the savings and loan industry and the performance of the U.S. health care industry.[62] Although many of the special studies were

---

[59]See minutes of EBM/87/124 (August 28, 1987), pp. 39 (Grosche) and 51–52 (Donoso); and EBM/87/125, pp. 3–4 (Sengupta).

[60]"United States—Staff Report for the 1988 Article IV Consultation," SM/88/160 (July 26, 1988), p. 14.

[61]Minutes of EBM/88/131 (August 29, 1988), p. 12.

[62]"United States—Recent Economic Developments," SM/89/176, Sups. 1 and 2 (August 18, 1989).

compilations of existing technical and factual material, many others were innovative theoretical and empirical analyses. Several staff studies were published separately as individual articles, and a selected collection was later published by the Fund.[63]

Japan

The IMF's consultations with Japan—the world's second-largest economy—were framed by strong expressions of admiration and support for the authorities' conduct of growth-oriented and financially stable policies. The staff report for the 1982 consultations, for example, paid "high tribute . . . to the skill and success that are evident in the management of the economy."[64] The 1985 report paid similar homage and commended "the willingness of the Japanese authorities to take account of views expressed in international fora."[65] Two years later, when the Managing Director met with the minister of finance to conclude the 1987 consultation discussions, his main recommendation was that the authorities should continue on their present course. Nonetheless, the French Executive Director in 1985, Bruno de Maulde, may have best captured the spirit of the Fund's position in stating that "Japan's performance and economic policies deserve admiration, but they also create an enormous problem for the rest of the world."[66] The challenge for the Fund in conducting surveillance with Japan throughout the 1980s was to strike the right balance between tribute and tribulation.

During the second round of major oil price increases, in 1979–80, Japan experienced two years of current account deficits; but as the 1980s unfolded, Japan became the world's largest creditor country, partly by conserving on fuel imports but more importantly through a remarkable growth in manufactured exports.[67] As Japan's major trading partners, especially in North America and western Europe, became increasingly edgy about the effects of imports from Japan on their economies, a key issue in the annual consultations became the extent to which the Fund should encourage the authorities to stimulate the economy to moderate the external imbalance. Related to this issue were concerns over Japan's slowness to open its trade and financial systems fully.

---

[63]See the papers in Horiguchi and others (1992), such as the studies by Krister Andersson on the effects of tax policy on housing investment, by Charles Adams and David Coe on measurement of potential output and the natural rate of unemployment, by Sharmini Coorey on the determinants of real interest rates, and by Ellen Nedde on modeling the external current account. Beginning in 1995, the Fund began publishing background papers in full and as a matter of course.

[64]"Japan—Staff Report for the 1982 Article IV Consultation," SM/83/36 (February 18, 1983), p. 23.

[65]"Japan—Staff Report for the 1985 Article IV Consultation," SM/86/24 (February 10, 1986), p. 29.

[66]Minutes of EBM/85/33 (March 4, 1985), p. 29.

[67]Japan had one of the highest national saving rates in the world at that time, but the saving rate did not increase during the 1980s and thus did not contribute to the shift toward external surplus. See Aghevli and others (1990).

The mission chief for the first few years of Article IV consultations with Japan was W. John R. Woodley (Deputy Director of the Asian Department), who retired in 1980. Tun Thin (Director of the Department) took over for the mission of November 1980, after which the consultations were headed by his Deputy, Prabhakar R. Narvekar. Narvekar succeeded Tun Thin as Director in 1986 and continued to lead the missions to Tokyo until his retirement from the staff in 1991. On the Japanese side, the discussion team was normally headed by the Vice Minister of Finance for International Affairs and by the Governor of the Bank of Japan. In December 1987, the Managing Director (Camdessus) and his Economic Counsellor (Jacob A. Frenkel) joined the mission in its closing days for meetings with the minister of finance (Noboru Takeshita) and the governor (Satoshi Sumita). That was the first such high-level visit in the context of the Article IV consultations with Japan, but—in contrast to the U.S. discussions—it did not become standard practice.[68]

Fiscal Policy

Throughout much of the period of this History, the IMF staff and the Japanese authorities took markedly different views on how fiscal policy should be conducted. They did learn from each other, and they gradually moved toward more central positions. Even so, the debates over Japanese fiscal policy in the late 1970s and 1980s would resurface in similar form after the financial crisis of the late 1990s.

By 1979 Japan had accumulated a substantial stock of public sector debt from the large fiscal (and external) deficits experienced throughout the 1970s. In view of the economic growth that Japan had achieved by that time, the authorities' top priority was to establish a greater degree of fiscal discipline. Accordingly, the government made a commitment in 1980 to reduce borrowing gradually and attain a zero deficit for current (i.e., noninvestment) spending by FY 1985 (ending March 31, 1985).

The staff agreed with the general goal of reducing the fiscal deficit. Nevertheless, they believed that it was being pursued too vigorously (i.e., that the authorities were trying to get there too fast) and with insufficient flexibility (i.e., that there was also a need for occasional recourse to expansion to counter weakness in domestic demand). Part of the basis for this argument was the belief that reducing the U.S. fiscal deficit was a much higher priority objective, from any perspective. If both countries attempted to balance their budgets simultaneously, world economic demand would contract dramatically. Moreover, if Japan acted aggressively to reduce its deficit while the U.S. government failed to control its own budget, the current account balances of Japan and the United States would become un-

---

[68]An additional purpose of the Managing Director's participation was to reach agreement on Japan's contribution to the Enhanced Structural Adjustment Facility; see Chapter 14. Apart from the U.S. consultations, this appears to have been the only instance in the 1980s in which the Managing Director participated in an Article IV consultation with the authorities.

sustainably large. In addition, the staff regarded Japan's fiscal deficit (6 percent of GNP in 1979) as sustainable as long as it was gradually reduced, since it was offset by a very high rate of household saving.[69]

On at least two occasions in the first quarter of 1979, Japanese officials—including the Vice Minister of Finance, Takehiro Sagami, and the governor of the Bank of Japan, Teiichiro Morinaga—visited the Fund to meet with the Managing Director. On both occasions, and again on a visit to Tokyo in early May, de Larosière suggested to them that they could be more open to the idea of fiscal stimulus. Taking a line similar to the one then being pushed to Japan by the U.S. government, he noted that a strong effort to balance the budget was likely to lead to slow growth and a persistent current account surplus, both of which would be difficult to sustain. The Japanese authorities were troubled by this criticism, but the differences in view were soon overshadowed by the sharp rise in oil prices that began around the middle of the year. Faced with a potentially large depressing effect on output, the authorities then had little choice but to allow the expansionary fiscal policy to continue.[70]

When Woodley's mission arrived in Tokyo in November 1979, the fiscal expansion was taking hold, and the authorities were preparing to pull back sharply. The staff supported that general policy, but they urged the authorities to be prepared again to take countercyclical action if necessary. At the Executive Board meeting that concluded the consultation, most Directors who addressed the fiscal issue sided with the staff, except for Robert J. Whitelaw (Australia), who criticized the staff position and urged the authorities to aim for a rapid restoration of fiscal discipline.[71]

A comparison of the Fund's advice on fiscal policy to the United States and to Japan at the end of the 1970s reveals an interesting contrast and suggests a lack of analytical consistency. Both countries were trying to reduce their fiscal deficits, and both were trying to establish and adhere to a medium-term goal and to reduce the use of tax and spending policies for countercyclical stabilization. In discussions with the United States, the Fund strongly endorsed those goals and pushed the authorities to pursue them more vigorously. For Japan, the Fund's advice was tilted more toward moderation and flexibility. On the question of how aggressively to pursue deficit reduction, the contrast reflected a judgment that the U.S. fiscal problem was far more severe than Japan's, both from a global vantage point and in relation to the aggregate level of national saving. The contrast in advice on the use of fiscal policy for countercyclical purposes is more difficult to explain, especially since the Japanese economy had shown a much greater intrinsic resilience in the face of negative shocks than had the United States. It may be noted, however, that

---

[69]Statement by Woodley at EBM/80/26 (February 20, 1980), p. 7.

[70]See memorandum from Woodley to management (January 15, 1979) and file memorandum by Woodley (March 12); in IMF/RD Asian Department Immediate Office file "Japan Correspondence, January–June 1979" (Accession 82/37, Box 3, Section 139). Additional information is from background interviews with participants.

[71]Minutes of EBM/80/25 (February 20, 1980), pp. 22–23.

the wisdom of fiscal stabilization was being hotly debated throughout the economics profession at the time, and both views were well within the broad mainstream of the day.

In 1980, the Japanese economy did weaken as expected, though output growth was still high by international standards (3½ percent, down from 5½ percent in 1979), as a sharp growth in real exports compensated for the withdrawal of fiscal stimulus. The staff continued to urge the authorities to be prepared to ease up on fiscal restraint if necessary for countercyclical purposes. At the Executive Board meeting in February 1981, Tun Thin made a twofold case. First, if output growth did weaken further, fiscal stimulus could be introduced without sacrificing the medium-term goal, by "front-loading" planned investment expenditures. Second, fiscal discipline was less of a priority in Japan than in other countries because of the high level of private sector saving. What mattered was the overall saving rate, not that of any particular sector.[72] The Japanese authorities did not strongly dispute the first point, but—as noted by their Executive Director, Teruo Hirao—they did not accept that high private saving justified high public dissaving.[73]

By late 1981, when the next consultation discussions took place, the staff was more convinced than ever that the authorities were being too optimistic about output growth and that they should be prepared to ease up on fiscal adjustment if necessary. Their case was now a little stronger, as growth had weakened during the year (see Figure 3.3), so Narvekar (who had taken over from Tun Thin in heading this mission) suggested that the authorities delay their timetable for eliminating deficit-financing bonds by 1985. More generally, the staff called for Japan to strengthen domestic investment, so as not to have to curtail national saving as the means of reducing the external surplus. At the Executive Board meeting, in February 1982, the Managing Director lent his voice to this theme, arguing that fiscal expansion was the right policy for domestic reasons (with high overall saving, Japan need not worry about "crowding out" private investment) as well as international (since it would raise interest rates and thereby strengthen the yen). Although most Executive Directors broadly agreed with that line of reasoning, Richard Erb (speaking for the United States) leaned more toward the Japanese position.[74]

---

[72]Minutes of EBM/81/20 (February 11, 1981), p. 35.

[73]Minutes of EBM/81/21 (February 11, 1981), p. 5.

[74]Minutes of EBM/82/18 (February 17, 1982), pp. 4 (Narvekar) and 18 (Erb). The summing up of the discussion (pp. 19–20) sought to reflect carefully the balance of opinion on the Board as well as the sensitivities of the national authorities:

While Directors were sympathetic to the effort to curtail the budget deficit in the medium term, many Directors wondered whether this objective would be appropriate if the expected autonomous recovery of domestic demand did not occur and if further relaxation of monetary conditions continued to be constrained by high interest rates abroad. Most Directors, thus, advocated some shift in the mix of monetary and fiscal policies, but a number of Directors added that the feasibility of such a shift would depend in part on the implementation of a more appropriate policy mix in other countries. The view was also expressed in the Board that it would be appropriate to maintain the firm commitment to a rapid reduction of the budget deficit as a medium-term objective.

Figure 3.3. Japan: Actual and Projected GNP Growth, 1981–90
(Fiscal years ending March 31)

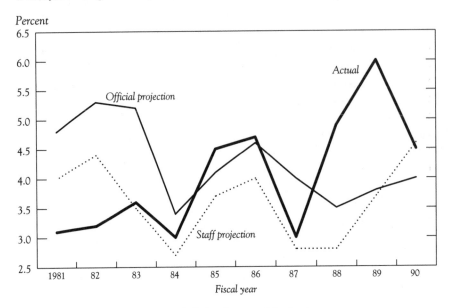

Note: Forecasts were made 3–4 months before the start of the fiscal year.

The landscape shifted just as the 1982 consultations were getting under way in Tokyo, when Yasuhiro Nakasone succeeded Zenko Suzuki as prime minister. Before that, fiscal policy had been eased following (though not necessarily in response to) the Fund's recommendations, but Nakasone shifted quickly to what the staff report called a "striking" austerity program. The goal of balancing the current budget by the mid-1980s was, however, dropped, as the earlier optimism in the official forecasts was replaced by a new realism.[75] The staff welcomed that development and again called for continued flexibility. They got European support at the Executive Board (from Gerhard Laske of Germany, Jacques Polak of the Netherlands, John Tvedt of Norway, and others), while the two North American Directors (Erb plus George W.K. Pickering, Temporary Alternate from Canada) continued to warn of the dangers of deviating from longer-term goals. Tse Chun Chang (China) worried that the staff was erring by, in effect, advising countries to adopt the U.S. policy mix (loose fiscal and tight monetary policy); he called for a more multilateral approach to surveillance that would take international interactions more heavily into account.[76]

---

[75]See Figure 3.3, noting that the forecast made at the time of the 1982 consultation was for FY 1984, the fiscal year starting a few months after the discussions.

[76]Minutes of EBM/83/48 and 49 (March 18, 1983).

Staff and official views came closer together in 1983. The authorities acknowledged that balancing the current budget by 1985 was no longer a realistic goal, and they set a new target, which the staff readily supported: to balance the current budget by FY 1991 (a goal that they did meet). On the Fund side, Narvekar acknowledged that the staff had "gained a better understanding" of the authorities' perspective on fiscal policy, though they continued to believe that the optimum strategy was to approach the medium-term goal flexibly. Most Executive Directors, however, continued to call explicitly for a more expansionary fiscal policy.[77]

The theoretical dimension of the debate over fiscal policy was made more explicit in 1984, as the staff drew a clear causal linkage from fiscal tightening to the ongoing rise in the current account surplus. The authorities rejected that argument, asserting that the national accounts identity had no causal implications and that a relaxation of fiscal policy would mainly crowd out private sector investment.[78] In the authorities' view, the external surplus resulted from "stable or falling commodity prices, rapid growth in the United States, and the strength of the dollar."[79] At the Executive Board meeting in March 1985, the United States—which at the time was still pointedly rejecting the Fund's advice regarding its own fiscal policy (see above, especially pp. 144–46)—continued to side with Japan on this issue. The dilemma felt by many other Executive Directors in discussing this issue was well captured by the remark by Bruno de Maulde, made at this meeting and quoted above on p. 154; no matter how much one admired Japan's economic performance and policies, the problem remained of how to get to a stable pattern of global output and demand.

The debate continued along similar lines in 1986, as the staff concluded that the appreciation of the yen was likely to depress output growth and that the case for fiscal expansion was therefore stronger than ever. The following year, the government did implement a fiscal stimulus package to counter the effects of the appreciation, and both the staff and the Executive Board welcomed the shift in policy priorities. Subsequently (in the final consultation of the decade, in February 1989), the staff broadly endorsed the conduct of fiscal policy in Japan. Not everyone on the Executive Board was completely comfortable in accepting what was still a very high rate of national saving. Dai Qianding (China), for example, wondered "whether a reduction in personal income . . . tax rates would increase the in-

---

[77]Minutes of EBM/84/33, pp. 14 (Narvekar) and 20–21 (summing up).

[78]By definition, a decline in the fiscal deficit must be matched by an increase in the excess of private saving over private domestic investment, by a strengthening of the external current account balance, or by some combination of the two. The staff position was based on the idea (supported by most macroeconomic models) that, for an economy operating near its capacity, net private saving will be relatively unaffected and the bulk of the adjustment will fall on the external balance. The authorities' argument that the offsetting changes would fall mainly on domestic saving and investment was based primarily on the idea that the effects of deficit reduction could vary substantially, depending on the specific policy actions that brought it about.

[79]"Japan—Staff Report for the 1984 Article IV Consultation," SM/85/33 (January 31, 1985), p. 10.

clination to consume" in Japan. Overall, though, the decade ended with a strong endorsement from the international community.[80]

Exchange Rate Policy

The behavior of the yen and the need for policy changes aimed at influencing the exchange rate were central topics for discussion in the Article IV consultations with Japan, especially during the first few years of Fund surveillance.

At the time of the 1979 consultation, the yen had been depreciating against other major currencies for about a year, partly in reflection of the recovery in the dollar after the 1978 crisis but also because Japan was pursuing a policy mix based on using easy money and credit conditions to offset the contractionary effects of fiscal adjustment. That combination was causing interest rates in Japan to fall while they were rising in the United States. In addition, the yen was being negatively affected by rising oil prices, since Japan was more heavily dependent on imported oil than the other leading industrial countries. Both Fund staff and the authorities saw the weakness of the yen as a problem, but they differed in their assessments of the causes.

Analyzing the relationship between a country's policies and its exchange rate contains an inherent ambiguity, because the rate reflects conditions in other countries as well. In 1979 and early 1980, the recovery of the U.S. dollar from the historic lows of October 1978 was the major story in the exchange markets. From the Fund's perspective, however, the key point was that the dollar was gaining far more against the yen than against European currencies. The yen dropped in value from 176 per dollar at the end of October 1978 to an average of 252 in April 1980, or by 43 percent. In contrast, the deutsche mark weakened by just 8 percent over the same period, and the pound sterling *strengthened* by 5 percent.

With that perspective in mind, the staff set out to assess the appropriateness of the Japanese policy regime, taking U.S. policy as given. Not only was the answer not obvious, it also was not clear that this was the right way to frame the question. In the WEO exercise, the staff could examine the policies of the major countries jointly, but that multilateral approach was not feasible in the Article IV consultations. Given that constraint, the staff report for 1979 concluded that "a stronger yen" would be appropriate and implied that the authorities should either engineer a rise in domestic interest rates or discourage (perhaps through official intervention) market speculation against the yen.[81] The Executive Board

---

[80]The 1986 debate is discussed in "Japan—Staff Report for the 1986 Article IV Consultation," SM/87/33 (February 6, 1987), esp. pp. 24–26. For the staff endorsement of the 1987 stimulus, see "Japan—Staff Report for the 1987 Article IV Consultation," SM/88/44 (February 18, 1988), p. 19. The 1989 report is "Japan—Staff Report for the 1989 Article IV Consultation," SM/89/75 (April 26, 1989), and the quote from Dai is from the minutes of EBM/89/70 (June 7, 1989), p. 57.

[81]"Japan—Staff Report for the 1979 Article IV Consultation," SM/79/295 (December 28, 1979), pp. 16–17.

focused particularly on the latter aspect and attributed the problem to the market, not to the mix of policies in Japan. As the Managing Director summarized the discussion in February 1980, "The view was expressed by many Executive Directors that the market had probably gone too far now in depreciating the yen."[82]

Two weeks after that Board meeting, the Japanese authorities announced a package of liberalization measures and an intensification of official intervention (coordinated with the U.S., German, and Swiss monetary authorities) aimed at supporting the yen, which was still hovering around the level of 250 per dollar. The mid-March announcement by the U.S. authorities of additional measures to control inflation then produced a temporary strengthening of the dollar that put substantial additional pressure on the Japanese authorities to prevent a commensurate weakening of the yen. Within days, the Bank of Japan raised both its discount rate and bank reserve requirements, and the government announced a fiscal tightening and other anti-inflationary measures.

Meanwhile, the Fund's informal Surveillance Committee (see Chapter 2) recommended on March 6 that the Fund undertake a special ad hoc consultation with Japan to discuss policies related to the exchange rate. The Managing Director agreed, and while the policy tightening was taking place on both sides of the Pacific, he approved a proposal to initiate a consultation aimed at encouraging Japan to take additional measures to push the yen into the range of 220–230 yen per dollar.[83] The Japanese authorities, however, agreed only to an informal staff visit, which was led by John Woodley in mid-May.

By the time Woodley arrived in Tokyo, the dollar's general appreciation was being reversed and the yen had strengthened to around 230, the weak end of the range at which the Fund had been aiming. De Larosière, however, instructed Woodley to push for a "further strengthening" beyond that level; without additional measures, the Managing Director was convinced, Japan's external deficit would rapidly vanish and turn into a surplus that other major countries would not readily accept.[84]

Woodley met with general agreement by the authorities that a strengthening beyond 230 would be desirable, and he concluded that a formal special consultation was unnecessary. Nonetheless, and despite an appreciation to 220 by the end of May, the Managing Director expressed to the Executive Director his concern that the authorities were continuing to intervene in large amounts and suggested that further strengthening was still needed. Though no formal discussion of the

---

[82]Minutes of EBM/80/26 (February 20, 1980), p. 13.

[83]Memorandum from Woodley to the Managing Director (March 18, 1980) in IMF/CF (C/Japan/810 "Mission, Woodley and Otani, May 1980").

[84]The May 5 briefing paper, approved by management the following day, included the phrase, "further strengthening beyond the current rate of ¥240 appears consistent with the medium-term underlying trends" (p. 8). On May 9, following a meeting with the Managing Director, Tun Thin cabled Woodley (at his stopover in Honolulu): "Terms of reference . . . remain valid if 230 is substituted for 240 on line 3, page 8."

matter was to be held by the Board, de Larosière informed Executive Directors on June 11, 1980, that informal discussions had taken place and that he found the results to be "encouraging."[85] That statement concluded the matter for the time being.

Throughout the next two years, the Fund staff and management continued to express concerns quietly over the weakness of the yen. While the authorities also would have liked to see an appreciation, they were reluctant either to set a target for the yen or to redirect monetary or fiscal policies toward influencing the exchange rate. These differences in view were particularly acute during the 1982 consultations, held in Tokyo around the end of November. For most of the year, the yen had been weakening sharply against the ascendant U.S. dollar, bottoming out around 280 yen per dollar in early November. Although the rate recovered strongly over the next few months, the staff report, reviewing developments in Japan, concluded that the renewed weakening of the yen had been "the most troubling development during 1982."[86]

The Japanese authorities, who had spent some $8 billion in 1982 defending the yen against downward pressures, agreed that the weak yen was a problem, but again they differed with the staff assessment on the root causes. They had taken several measures to enhance the attractiveness of the yen as an asset and liberalize the market for capital inflows; but it did not make sense, in their view, to loosen fiscal policy or tighten monetary policy to counteract the exchange rate effects of a similar shift in the policy mix in the United States. Nor did they believe that official intervention could be expected to have a stronger influence on exchange markets until the United States was ready to join in a coordinated effort. When Hirao presented these arguments at the Executive Board meeting in March 1983, he was supported by several other Directors, notably Heinrich G. Schneider (Alternate—Austria) on the need for coordinated intervention and by Chang on the dangers of implicitly expecting other countries to adopt the U.S. policy mix in order to stabilize exchange rates. The sense of the meeting was that a stronger yen would be beneficial but it was up to the markets rather than the policymakers to bring it about.[87]

After 1982, the level of the exchange rate effectively ceased to be a major issue between the authorities and the Fund for the rest of the decade. The yen remained weak against the dollar through 1983 and 1984, but it then began to appreciate against the other major currencies and in effective terms. After the Plaza meeting of the G-5 in September 1985, the yen's appreciation accelerated, and it continued to strengthen even after the Louvre agreement in February 1987. Throughout that period, both the staff and the Executive Board generally accepted that Japan's macroeconomic policies were consistent with an orderly appreciation of the currency.

---

[85]Minutes of EBM/80/89 (June 11, 1980), p. 3.

[86]"Japan—Staff Report for the 1982 Article IV Consultation," SM/83/36 (February 18, 1983), p. 6.

[87]Minutes of EBM/83/48 (March 18, 1983), pp. 8 (Hirao), 12 (Schneider), and 15 (Chang); and EBM/83/49, p. 4 (summing up).

Figure 3.4. Japan: Actual and Projected Current Account Balances, 1981–90
(Fiscal years ending March 31)

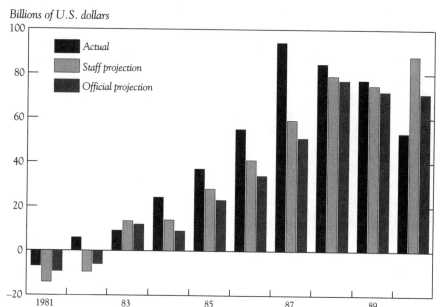

Note: Forecasts were made 3–4 months before the start of the fiscal year.

Monetary policy was eased in 1986 (notably after the Baker-Miyazawa agreement)[88] and remained "relaxed" through 1989, as the mounting evidence of asset price inflation (land and equities) was offset by stable consumer prices. Throughout this period, which came to be known as that of the "bubble economy" in Japan, the Fund supported the policy stance and failed to foresee the emerging imbalances. As the decade ended, inflation began to creep up and the yen began to weaken again, but the staff regarded those problems as minor: inflation in Japan was not "a matter of concern" in 1989, and therefore "no compelling reason" could be found to tighten monetary policy.[89]

Liberalization of Trade and Finance

A third major issue in the consultations with Japan, especially in the early 1980s, concerned the pace of liberalization of international trade and finance. Until the late 1970s, Japan maintained high barriers, both against many imports and against

---

[88]On the Plaza and Louvre accords, as well as the Baker-Miyazawa agreement, see Chapter 4.
[89]"Japan—Staff Report for the 1979 Article IV Consultation," SM/79/295 (December 28, 1979), pp. 13 and 17; and "Japan—Staff Report for the 1989 Article IV Consultation," SM/89/75 (April 26, 1989), p. 20 ("no compelling reason"); statement by Narvekar at EBM/89/71 (June 7, 1989), p. 3 ("matter of concern").

capital flows. Through a series of legislative and regulatory actions, Japan gradually lowered those barriers, but the extent and importance of the remaining restrictions were a source of continuing friction with the international community.

The focus of the discussions on trade was the effect of restrictions on the external current account imbalance, which shifted from deficit to surplus in 1982, reached a peak of $94 billion in FY 1987, and remained large throughout the rest of the decade. In projecting the external balance (see Figure 3.4), few significant differences arose between the staff and the authorities. Both forecasts missed the initial shift to surplus, both underpredicted the extent of the growth in the surplus from 1984 through 1987, and both failed to foresee the sharp drop that occurred in 1990. In most years, however, the direction of change and the general order of magnitude of the problem were clearly understood and agreed upon.

Throughout the decade, the position of staff and management was to commend the steps toward liberalization taken each year, to call attention to remaining problems while pointing out the ambiguities and uncertainties in assessing the picture, and generally to deal gingerly with this politically explosive subject. The Fund did, however, consistently object to reliance on restrictions rather than price and income adjustments for moderating trade imbalances. Notably, when the Fund began leaning on Japan in 1979 to allow the yen to appreciate to prevent a disruptively rapid growth in exports, the authorities responded that they expected "voluntary self-restraint" by exporters to prevent too rapid a buildup. The staff criticized that approach. Two years later, after Japan introduced (in May 1981) a formal system of voluntary export restraints on automobile exports to the United States, the staff expressed their "regrets" that the authorities were relying on such measures rather than tackling the underlying imbalance between saving and investment.[90]

From 1982 onward, the staff's consultation reports welcomed the measures that were being taken to liberalize imports but called for bolder actions to be taken to reduce administrative hurdles and open the distribution system. That issue was on the table for several years, especially during the discussions by the Executive Board. In the view of many Directors, the issue was not so much the existence of formal regulations as it was the perception of an invisible barrier against foreign penetration of Japanese markets. In March 1985, for example, the Japanese Executive Director, Hirotake Fujino, claimed that "the Japanese [goods] market has now become one of the most open markets among industrial countries"; to which Nigel Wicks (the United Kingdom) responded that "Japan's close-knit industrial structure inhibited imports." The Executive Board, noting that "access to the Japanese market remained difficult" and was producing "protectionist sentiment against Japan's exports," "urged the authorities to act resolutely to reduce remaining import restrictions and to open markets to imports."[91]

---

[90]"Japan—Staff Report for the 1979 Article IV Consultation," SM/79/295 (December 28, 1979), pp. 13 and 17; and "Japan—Staff Report for the 1981 Article IV Consultation," SM/82/13 (January 18, 1982), p. 19.

[91]Minutes of EBM/85/33 (March 4, 1985), pp. 16 (Wicks) and 11 (Fujino); and EBM/85/34, p. 20 (summing up).

Germany

Germany's[92] macroeconomic policies came under fire in 1978, as world leaders sought a means of escaping stagflation and getting their economies back onto a path of sustainable growth. In Germany, the growth of domestic demand had been unusually slow for a year or more, principally because of an unintended contractionary impulse from fiscal actions.[93] Output, instead of growing at the 4–5 percent rate that the government had targeted a year earlier, had grown "only" by 2½ percent. When analysts would look back at that growth rate a decade or two later, it would look like a reasonably successful outcome and about all that one could have hoped to sustain under the circumstances. In 1978, however, it looked like a serious shortfall from the potential inherent in the German economy.

The primary forum for trying to remedy the situation was the summit meeting of the G-7 heads of state and government, which fortuitously was held in Bonn on July 16–17, 1978. Chancellor Helmut Schmidt was under heavy pressure from his peers in the G-7 who wanted Germany to be a "locomotive" for the world economy, and he was eager to get a deal in which the United States would promise to take measures to curb its massive consumption of petroleum. At the summit, Schmidt agreed to quickly implement a stimulus package equivalent to 1 percent of GNP. Less than two weeks later, the German parliament enacted the package, including additional domestic spending, tax cuts, and—in a gesture of solidarity with other oil-importing economies—financing for programs to help poorer countries develop renewable energy sources.[94]

Two months before the Bonn summit, a staff team headed by the Director of the European Department, L. Alan Whittome, tackled these same issues with the authorities in the 1978 Article IV consultations in Bonn and Frankfurt.[95] Whittome and his team viewed Germany's slow growth rate as "of concern both from a domestic and an international point of view." Their report noted that the government had begun 1978 aiming to achieve a growth rate of 3½ percent (already scaled down from earlier projections), but neither the staff nor the authorities now thought that the goal was achievable. Unemployment was holding steady around 4 percent, while inflation was falling to around 3 percent, but in the staff view, the sizeable gap between actual and potential output was not being closed. Most wor-

---

[92]All references to Germany are to the Federal Republic of Germany, which was vernacularly known as West Germany during the period of this History. The German Democratic Republic (East Germany), which was not a member of the IMF, merged with the Federal Republic in October 1990.

[93]The contraction resulted from a combination of factors that had not been fully anticipated. States (länder) and municipalities curtailed spending to control their deficits, environmental objections delayed federal investment projects, and tax revenues were higher than had been projected. Consequently, the general government deficit fell from 3½ percent of GNP in 1976 to 2½ percent in 1977.

[94]For the background to the Bonn summit, see Putnam and Henning (1989) and Putnam and Bayne (1987), Chapter 4.

[95]For a broad summary of the 1978 consultation, see de Vries (1985), p. 916.

ryingly, "there appeared to be a protracted weakness of business investment," implying that the slowdown was not likely to end soon and that stimulus was needed for long-term growth as well as cyclical recovery.[96]

On the other side of the table, the authorities saw matters differently. In their view, the initial output gap was not that large, the potential growth rate was not that high, unemployment was almost entirely structural or frictional, and fiscal stimulus would not promote—and could well discourage—investment. The minister of finance, Hans Matthöffer, expressed strong skepticism about the rationale for changing the course of fiscal policy, but other officials—including Hans Tietmeyer, then Head of the Division of General Economic Policy in the Ministry of Economics—indicated that the government had not yet formulated a common position on the issue.[97]

The Fund staff was unconvinced by the authorities' arguments, and the report concluded that policies should be redirected:

> The staff would hope that fiscal and monetary policies designed to secure sustainable increases in domestic demand and in GNP—for the time being somewhat in excess of the growth of potential GNP—would, in conjunction with appropriate exchange rate policies, lead to a further contribution from Germany in the form of a significantly smaller current account surplus. . . . The danger of renewed pressure on prices . . . need [not] be a constraint on policy in the near future.[98]

By the time the Executive Board met at the end of July to discuss the staff report, the G-7 summit had already resolved the issue. It was understood, however, that the German authorities were less than enthusiastic about their own stimulus package and had implemented it only because of international pressure.[99] The Executive Director for Germany, Eckard Pieske, devoted most of his remarks to an explanation of why fiscal stimulus was unlikely to benefit the economy. Furthermore, the other G-7 countries presented less than a united front on the issue. Denis Samuel-Lajeunesse (Alternate—France) suggested that the German economy was already extremely well managed and concluded that the authorities were right to question what had become known as the "locomotive theory." William S. Ryrie (United Kingdom) noted that the international interest did not really concern the growth rate of output in Germany, but only the size of its current account surplus.[100] Over-

---

[96]"Federal Republic of Germany—Staff Report for the 1978 Article IV Consultation," SM/78/180 (July 5, 1978), pp. 4 and 16.

[97]Minutes of meetings held on May 17 and 18, 1978, in IMF/CF (C/Germany/420.3, "Article IV Consultations—1978, Minutes of Meetings").

[98]"Federal Republic of Germany—Staff Report for the 1978 Article IV Consultation," SM/78/180 (July 5, 1978), p. 17. Whittome later explained that the phrase "for the time being" meant two to three years; minutes of EBM/78/120 (July 28, 1978), p. 16. The reference to "appropriate exchange rate policies" meant that the deutsche mark should be allowed to appreciate.

[99]This conclusion applies only to the financial authorities dealing directly with the Fund. Chancellor Schmidt had been reelected in 1976 on a pro-growth platform and appears to have been personally more enthusiastic than his economic advisors. See Putnam and Bayne (1987), pp. 79–82.

[100]Minutes of EBM/78/120 (July 28, 1978), pp. 25–26 (Samuel-Lajeunesse) and 28 (Ryrie).

all, however, the Board concluded that the post-summit stimulus package was a minimum requirement for growth that might well turn out to be inadequate.

For the next ten years, the consultations with Germany were handled by senior officials just below the Director of the European Department. Brian E. Rose (Deputy Director) headed the 1979–82 and 1985–87 missions, after which he retired from the staff. The 1983 and 1984 missions were led by Hans O. Schmitt (Senior Advisor), and Manuel Guitián (Deputy Director) headed the 1988 mission. In 1989 the Director of the Department—by then it was Massimo Russo—again led the annual consultation mission. On the German side, the level of representation also varied. In that critical 1978 consultation, both the minister of finance (Matthöffer) and the president of the Deutsche Bundesbank (Otmar Emminger) met with the mission team. For the next two years, Emminger and then his successor, Karl Otto Pöhl, continued to participate, but the minister did not. There followed a drought of five years (through 1985), after which the finance minister and Bundesbank president began again to receive the Fund missions regularly.

Richesse Oblige: The Burdens of Economic Power

The Fund staff's analysis of German macroeconomic policies underwent both cyclical and more sustained evolution from 1979 through 1989. The cyclical fluctuations—essentially between recommending fiscal stimulus and endorsing the status quo—reflected both the actual business cycle and shifts in view about how much growth could reasonably be expected under prevailing circumstances. In addition, staff priorities trended away from cyclical concerns and toward the requirements for longer-term growth. Throughout this period and into the 1990s, the dominant underlying theme for the discussions between Germany and the Fund was the same as it had been in 1978: the responsibilities of surplus countries to contribute to the global adjustment process. As de Larosière put it in concluding the 1978 discussion by the Executive Board: Germany, "with its low rate of inflation and its strong balance of payments, is especially well placed to make a strong contribution to the recovery of the world economy and the alleviation of the balance of payments problems of other countries."[101]

The 1979 consultation took place just two months after the establishment of the European Monetary System (EMS), which heightened Germany's obligations to maintain fixed exchange rates with the other participating countries.[102] However, the factor that most affected the discussions was that the economy was growing with unanticipated robustness, and it was already apparent that the "locomotive" package had been ill-advised: the seeds of renewed growth had already been planted, and with a little patience the desired recovery would have occurred with no further feeding. Nonetheless, and despite this surprise growth, the current ac-

---

[101]Minutes of EBM/78/122 (July 31, 1978), p. 4.

[102]For simplicity of exposition, references here to the EMS generally refer to the currencies participating in the exchange rate mechanism (ERM) of the EMS. See the discussion of the system in Chapter 2.

count surplus was also larger than anticipated. Accordingly, the staff could focus on the requirements for moderating the surplus as the central policy issue.

The staff held that the external surplus could be kept under control if the authorities (1) remained ready to implement countercyclical fiscal policies if domestic demand appeared to be weakening, and (2) stopped intervening against the tendency for the mark to appreciate against the U.S. dollar. In practice, the German economy was better able to absorb the consequences of an appreciating currency than were some other members of the EMS, so occasionally realigning EMS rates would be better than trying to depress the value of the mark artificially.

The authorities, in contrast, believed that the main task of macroeconomic policy was to prevent inflationary pressures from arising, not to push for stronger growth. They also argued that it was important to maintain stability within the EMS, which was still a young and fragile mechanism. Throughout the first five months of 1979, the authorities had engaged in "massive" intervention vis-à-vis the dollar. They disclaimed having a specific target for the rate against the dollar, but their intervention policy suggested that they viewed the degree of market pressures as "disorderly."

The Executive Board was sharply divided in 1979 on the question of whether further stimulus was desirable. The U.S. chair (represented by Donald E. Syvrud—Alternate) put the case for growth in terms of the global effects of the second oil shock: "As we start a new round of major OPEC surpluses," Syvrud concluded, "there are only a limited number of countries that are in a position to accept a share of the burden. In this regard, few countries are better placed than Germany." On the other side, Masanao Matsunaga (Japan) empathized more with the Germans' desire for stable prices. He "fully endorsed" the recent tightening of German macroeconomic policies and concluded that there was "no case at the moment for additional stimulus from the fiscal front."[103]

By 1980, the staff had come around more closely to the views of the German authorities. Since the last consultation was completed, the economy had grown strongly, inflation had accelerated, and the current account had shifted into deficit. Consequently, the staff acknowledged that the authorities' earlier concerns about overheating had been "fully justified by events although some of them, such as the large increase in the price of oil in 1979, could not have been foreseen at the time." The main issue on the table now was whether the time was ripe to ease up. The staff report essentially endorsed existing policies and concluded that there was "no need for any drastic change in the direction of monetary and fiscal policy."[104] At the Executive Board meeting, although some chairs still would have preferred somewhat more expansionary policies, the controversy had largely died down.[105]

Staff views shifted further in 1981. Although the economy had weakened again, this time the mission chief (Brian Rose) did not attempt to persuade the authori-

---

[103]Minutes of EBM/79/135 (August 2, 1979), pp. 11 (Syvrud) and 14 (Matsunaga).

[104]"Federal Republic of Germany—Staff Report for the 1980 Article IV Consultation," SM/80/163 (July 3, 1980), pp. 3 ("fully justified") and 15 ("no need for change").

[105]Minutes of EBM/80/108–109 (July 23, 1980).

ties to use macroeconomic policies for countercyclical purposes. Instead, the staff report focused on the need for structural adjustment aimed at strengthening the economy's potential for growth and job creation. Most of the measures identified by the staff were similar to those already identified by the authorities as necessary or desirable and were as much macroeconomic as structural: further energy conservation, "cautious financial policies" that would discourage high wage demands, and maintenance of a competitive exchange rate (for which the staff judged the prevailing level to be about right).

A nuance of dispute nonetheless remained over the focus of macroeconomic policies. While acknowledging that the 1978–80 overheating of the German economy had demonstrated the "failure of the locomotive theory," Rose argued at the Board meeting that the avoidance of excessive slack in economic activity was still important. Directors generally agreed that the immediate priority was to restrain domestic demand, though not everyone was prepared to endorse the degree of restriction implicit in the current policy stance.[106]

Between the 1981 and 1982 consultations, the question of whether to ease up on fiscal restraint to combat the recession became a major issue in the German political debate. In October 1981, as the appreciation of the U.S. dollar began to impose inflationary pressures on Europe, Germany agreed to a 5½ percent upward revaluation of the deutsche mark within the EMS, a move that reinforced the position of the mark as the dominant currency in Europe (Figure 3.5). That move forestalled the importation of inflation, but it also weakened the demand for German exports and thus helped prolong the recession into 1982. Chancellor Schmidt and his Social Democratic Party then advocated tilting fiscal policy toward expansion, but they were opposed by some other parties in the ruling coalition (notably by the Free Democrats led by the Economics Minister, Otto Lambsdorff) as well as by the opposition coalition headed by Helmut Kohl.[107]

In the midst of this debate, the German authorities asked the Fund to hold a "special consultation" on fiscal policy, in conjunction with the normally scheduled staff visit for the WEO exercise, in January 1982. By asking for such a review, it appears that the advocates of stability and restraint were hoping that the staff had come far enough around from the locomotive days that the Fund would lend its intellectual prestige to their side. In the event, that is precisely what happened. Whittome, who led the mission, obtained the support of the Managing Director for a recommendation of continued restraint. Then, at the concluding session, with the authorities represented by a team headed by Klemens Wesselcock (Director of the International Affairs Department in the Ministry of Finance), Whittome argued that "What is now required is an effort to restore public confidence in the ability of the authorities to control the budget and to

---

[106]Minutes of EBM/81/113 (August 5, 1981). The quotation is from p. 38.

[107]Lambsdorff, who shifted to support for a tax cut (but not a spending increase) later in 1982, retained his position as Economics Minister under Kohl.

Figure 3.5. Germany: Exchange Rates, 1976–89

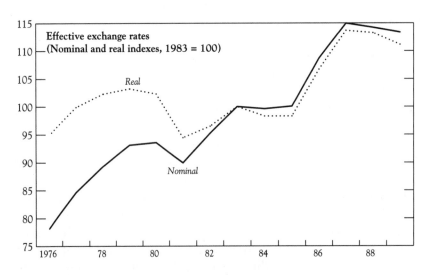

Source: IMF, *IFS*.

maintain a course of policy that promises a satisfactory rate of growth in the medium term. . . ."[108]

This cautious approach toward fiscal policy was repeated in the staff report on the regular 1982 consultations, held in May. That report focused more on ex-

---

[108]Concluding statement presented on January 16, 1982. Also see memorandums from Whittome to the Managing Director dated December 31, 1981 (with annotations by the Managing Director in response) and January 19, 1982. All in IMF/RD Managing Director file "Germany 1981" (Accession 83/89, Box 1, Section 378).

change rate policy, and in particular on the tendency for the EMS member countries to wait until crises developed in exchange markets before realigning rates. (The sixth realignment in less than three years, in which the central parity of the mark was revalued by 4¼ percent, took place on June 14: after the discussions but before the issuance of the staff report.) Consistent with the general support of policies of restraint, the report advised Germany to resist further depreciation of the mark against the U.S. dollar; until U.S. interest rates came down from their extraordinarily high levels, the authorities would have little choice but to keep their own rates higher than they would like. On this issue at least, the staff turned out to be *plus royalist que le roi.* As Gerhard Laske pointed out at the Executive Board meeting in mid-August—responding to a request for further tightening from the U.S. Director, Richard Erb—his authorities' ability to push interest rates up to calm the exchange markets was limited by the need to sustain demand in the face of still-weakening economic activity.[109]

In an election that hinged on the government's perceived inability to rein in the fiscal deficit (which had risen from 2½ percent of GNP in 1978 to 3¾ percent in 1981), Kohl's more conservative coalition, led by the Christian Democratic Union, defeated Schmidt in October 1982. Five months later, the deutsche mark was again revalued, rising by 5½ percent against all other currencies in the EMS. Even so, because of the continuing rise of the U.S. dollar and an easing of monetary conditions in Germany, the mark depreciated by 6½ percent against the dollar during the first half of 1983, and its real effective value showed virtually no change (see Figure 3.5). By the time the 1983 consultations took place, a modest economic recovery was under way in Germany, led by an unexpected rise in consumer spending.

The 1983 consultation (headed by Hans Schmitt) tilted back slightly toward recommending an easier fiscal policy. The new wrinkle on this occasion was an effort to place that recommendation firmly within a broader policy of fiscal consolidation. The staff report welcomed "the present policy of expenditure restraint," noting that it was aimed at freeing up resources for the private sector. "The positive effects of expenditure cuts," however, "may . . . be delayed, unless the authorities are prepared to shift their emphasis from reductions in the deficit to reductions in taxes that will raise private spending by raising disposable incomes."[110] In other words (as Schmitt explained the matter to the Executive Board), the spending cuts that had already been made had, in the staff view, created room in the budget for a cut in taxes aimed at "crowding in" private spending directly rather than indirectly through interest rate cuts. That view was shared by several Executive Directors who were skeptical that the incipient recovery could be sustained

---

[109]The Board meeting took place on Wednesday, August 18, 1982, just five days after the initial eruption of the debt crisis in Mexico. In Laske's view, that development, far more than events in Europe, was currently controlling the exchange markets. Minutes of EBM/82/110 (August 18, 1982), pp. 4 (Erb) and 6 (Laske).

[110]"Federal Republic of Germany—Staff Report for the 1983 Article IV Consultation," SM/83/153 (July 5, 1983), p. 16.

without some new stimulus, while others felt that German policies in 1983 were pitched about right.[111]

The 1984 report saw no immediate problem in the stance of fiscal policy. The deficit had been reduced from 4 percent to 2 percent of GNP, largely by cutting expenditure from 50 percent of GNP to 48 percent. Despite this withdrawal of direct stimulus, output growth had recovered to 2¾ percent in 1983 before dropping off in the first few months of 1984. Reviewing these developments, the staff attributed the improved performance of the German economy to a combination of factors: a strong private sector, growing confidence from the reduced deficit, shifts in the structure of spending toward boosting investment, and an easing of monetary conditions.[112]

On the negative side, the staff for the first time emphasized the theme that would take on increasing importance over the next several years: the resumption of economic growth had not brought any job creation in its wake. Indeed, no net job creation had been recorded for a decade, despite a fair record of output growth. The culprit, Schmitt argued, was "excessive labor costs," including not only wages but also social security, employee subsidies, generous paid leave, and other benefits. While widespread agreement existed both in Germany and elsewhere that these costs were a serious issue, the political reality was that there was little immediate prospect of seeing any real reforms.[113]

The emphasis on structural labor market reforms did not completely replace the more traditional view of fiscal policy as a means of sustaining aggregate demand. Economic growth continued at a modest rate in the months between the 1984 and 1985 consultations, but that growth derived more from exports than from domestic demand. Moreover, the prognosis in 1985 was that this situation would continue and would further enlarge the surplus in the current account. When the authorities argued that demand stimulus would do little to alter that outlook, the staff (led by Brian Rose) disagreed cautiously and concluded as follows:

> From an international perspective, it is essential that the major industrial countries achieve the maximum rate of growth that is sustainable over the medium term and is consistent with strict control of inflation. In the medium run, . . . a rate of growth sufficient to lower unemployment will depend upon a strengthening of domestic demand. . . . These considerations should not suggest that the appropriate policy response to the present situation is a *pronounced* shift to more stimulatory short-term demand management. . . . But changes in taxation can resolve the dilemma by raising disposable incomes without increasing labor costs.[114]

---

[111]Minutes of EBM/83/114 (July 29, 1983). Schmitt's views are stated on pp. 44–46.

[112]"Federal Republic of Germany—Staff Report for the 1984 Article IV Consultation," SM/84/142 (June 22, 1984); and remarks by Schmitt at EBM/84/113 (July 20, 1984), p. 4.

[113]Minutes of EBM/84/113 (July 20, 1984), p. 5; emphasis added. Also see "Federal Republic of Germany—Staff Report for the 1984 Article IV Consultation," SM/84/142 (June 22, 1984), pp. 15–17.

[114]"Federal Republic of Germany—Staff Report for the 1985 Article IV Consultation," SM/85/194 (July 5, 1985), pp. 17–19.

This highly nuanced statement attempted to carve out a tenable foothold between Keynesian and neoclassical or supply-side extremes. Tax cuts, in this view, would properly stimulate demand and would produce maximum benefit if they were structured to shift part of the burden of taxation away from labor costs.

Germany was being pressured along similar lines in multilateral meetings in 1985. The G-7 summit meeting had come around again to Bonn, for the first time since the debacle of 1978. This time the Economic Declaration stressed the importance of addressing structural rigidities, including those in Germany, and played down the role of demand management. Similarly, the G-5 ministerial meeting at the Plaza Hotel in September 1985 produced a communiqué (see Funabashi, 1988, pp. 264–65) in which Germany asserted its desire to generate a "steady economic recovery based increasingly on internally generated growth," while indicating its intention to aim policies at fiscal consolidation rather than stimulus, at removing "rigidities inhibiting the efficient functioning of markets," and at promoting "a stable environment" for domestic economic activity. The public defense of that approach, of course, reflected the presence of quiet diplomatic suggestions for a more active policy stance (Funabashi, 1988, esp. p. 41).

Partly in response to international pressures, the German parliament agreed in June 1985 to reduce taxes in two stages—in January 1986 and again two years later—by a total that was approximately equivalent to 1 percent of GNP. At the time, neither the government nor the staff regarded this reduction as a substantial stimulus, because it was designed merely to offset the effects of "fiscal drag" since the last major change in tax rates, in 1981.[115] Eventually, however, the staff recognized it as a shift in policy emphasis, "from reducing the deficit to reducing the tax burden."[116]

In 1986, the Fund staff and the authorities substantially agreed. The economy was doing well, and what few problems existed were mostly expected to be alleviated without any shift in policy. The staff suggested that the tax cut scheduled for January 1988 could be brought forward, as unemployment was sitting stubbornly around 8 percent of the labor force (Figure 3.6) and the economy was "still capable of accommodating a further growth of demand." Overall, however, the staff endorsed the existing macroeconomic policy stance and focused more on the requirements for achieving a sustained reduction in the persistent and growing current account surplus (Figure 3.7). To that end, the 1986 report concluded that "much more must be done to try to loosen constraints on supply, in particular by breaking down rigidities in the labor market." The suggestion was unexception-

---

[115]Because the progressive brackets for tax rates were fixed in nominal terms, the average tax rate rose automatically along with nominal incomes. This phenomenon was known variously as "fiscal drag" or "bracket creep." Only through a periodic lowering of the nominal brackets could tax policy be kept neutral in its effects on aggregate demand.

[116]For the initial interpretation, see "Federal Republic of Germany—Staff Report for the 1985 Article IV Consultation," SM/85/194 (July 5, 1985), p. 8. For the quoted later view, and for the conclusion that the action had been taken partly in response to international pressures, see "Federal Republic of Germany—Staff Report for the 1988 Article IV Consultation," SM/88/136 (June 24, 1988), p. 7.

Figure 3.6. Germany: GNP Growth and Unemployment, 1978–89
(In percent, and percent of labor force, respectively)

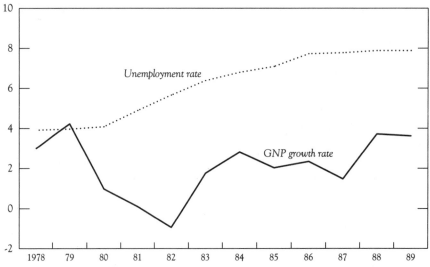

Source: *World Economic Outlook.*

able, and the only objection raised by the authorities was that "political sensitivities" made those rigidities difficult to supple.[117]

In January 1987, Kohl was reelected chancellor, following an election campaign in which he pointed to his government's success in reducing both government spending (from 50 percent of GNP to 47 percent) and the fiscal deficit (from 3¾ percent of GNP to 1¼ percent). A month later, to carry out a commitment made at the February 22 meeting of major industrial countries at the Louvre, the government agreed to grant tax relief amounting approximately to 2 percent of GNP over the period 1988–90. When Rose and his team arrived in Bonn at the end of April to conduct the 1987 consultation discussions, both output and domestic demand were growing reasonably well, and prices were essentially stable. The major strain was that the current account surplus had ballooned in 1986 to more than 4½ percent of GNP.

To buttress the argument that stimulus was needed to reduce the external surplus, the staff team presented the authorities with a detailed set of medium-term "scenarios" generated by econometric macro models estimated by the staff.[118] The

---

[117]"Federal Republic of Germany—Staff Report for the 1986 Article IV Consultation," SM/86/160 (July 2, 1986), pp. 2 and 21; and statement by Guenter Grosche at EBM/86/127 (August 1, 1986), p. 14.

[118]For a summary, see "Federal Republic of Germany—Staff Report for the 1987 Article IV Consultation," SM/87/144 (June 26, 1987), p. 14. The models and the detailed simulation results are in Appendixes I through IV of "Federal Republic of Germany—Recent Economic Developments," SM/87/156 (July 10, 1987), pp. 103–144.

Figure 3.7. Germany: Current Account Balance, 1978–89

Percent of GNP

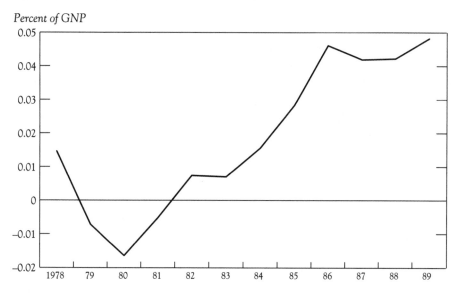

Source: IMF, *IFS*.

baseline scenario, with no change from current policies, suggested that by 1991 the current account surplus would fall gradually but would still be around 2 percent of GNP by 1991. Because the fiscal deficit was small enough in view of the high level of private saving in Germany, the staff report concluded that there was room for some fiscal easing and that, over the medium term, fiscal policy should be aimed more at sustaining demand and less at containing the deficit. Moreover, "little progress" had been made in reducing labor market rigidities.[119]

German economic growth slowed again in 1988, unemployment remained near 8 percent, and the current account surplus held stubbornly above 4 percent of GNP. All of that contributed to a general "uneasiness," a feeling "that there was something that Germany could do but was not doing to help international adjustment."[120] The Fund staff had now come around to the view (shared by the authorities) that the growth "problem" in Germany was almost entirely structural in nature, and the 1988 report on this issue was innovative in two respects.[121] First, as a supplement to the usual macroeconomic forecasts and scenarios, the report

---

[119]"Federal Republic of Germany—Staff Report for the 1987 Article IV Consultation," SM/87/144 (June 26, 1987), pp. 11 (labor market rigidities) and 16–18 (fiscal policy).

[120]Statement by the mission chief, Manuel Guitián; minutes of EBM/88/112 (July 22, 1988), p. 3.

[121]In addition to the problem of rigidities, the 1988 staff report called attention to Germany's relatively low rate of population growth. Although aggregate GNP had grown relatively slowly during the 1980s, growth in GNP per capita had been near the average for the major industrial countries. "Federal Republic of Germany—Staff Report for the 1988 Article IV Consultation," SM/88/136 (June 24, 1988); on the issue of population growth, see p. 2 and Chart 1.

presented detailed structural simulations derived from a four-sector computable general-equilibrium (CGE) model.[122] Those simulations showed that reducing rigidities could significantly strengthen economic growth. Second, the report delved into the structural problems in much more detail than before. Specifically, it stressed the need for further progress in reducing subsidies (especially those that protected industries against foreign competition); for reducing nontariff barriers (especially in iron and steel, textiles, and clothing); for easing sectoral regulations that prevented the supply of goods from responding to shifting conditions; and for easing labor market regulations that raised overhead costs, limited flexibility in hiring and firing, and reduced wage differentials across sectors.

This advice met with two types of resistance. First, as the staff acknowledged, the German authorities viewed many of the specific recommendations as "somewhat remote from the realities of the German situation" (i.e., as politically unrealistic).[123] Second, at the Executive Board, several Directors—from a diverse group of countries, including Denmark, India, Indonesia, Italy, Mexico, and Tanzania—expressed skepticism that Germany's large current account surplus could be effectively reduced by structural reforms alone. In their view, some fiscal easing was also required. As recorded in the summing up of the meeting, those Directors "took issue with the [government's] decision to reduce the budget deficit at a time when . . . growth would be below potential."[124]

The 1989 mission stuck to the structural position even more firmly than before. Although output growth had accelerated since the previous consultation, the external surplus had remained at 4 percent of GNP. The staff mission (in which both Russo and Guitián participated) concluded that the medium-term outlook was for a larger stream of surpluses than had previously been projected, and it called for a very specific set of reforms aimed at stimulating productive investment. These reforms included moving away from price-support programs such as the Common Agricultural Policy of the European Communities; reducing subsidies to coal and other energy sources; reducing protection of iron, steel, and other heavy industries; reducing labor market rigidities; and concomitant changes in the tax system. Fiscal expansion, however, was seen as having only temporary benefits that would be ineffective in reducing the surplus.[125]

---

[122]The parameters of macroeconomic models such as the Fund's MULTIMOD are estimated primarily by econometric regressions on time-series data. Parameters for CGE models are derived primarily by reference to the structure of the economy and may be estimated by a variety of techniques external to the model, including cross-sectional studies, or may be assigned by the model-builder for consistency or stability. The German model, the simulations, and the analysis of structural issues were published in Lipschitz and others (1989). That publication of a study undertaken for an Article IV consultation—an innovation in itself—was hailed in the financial press as a symbol of "glasnost at the IMF"; see Norman (1989).

[123]"Federal Republic of Germany—Staff Report for the 1988 Article IV Consultation," SM/88/136 (June 24, 1988), p. 17.

[124]Minutes of EBM/88/111–112 (July 22, 1988); the quotation is from meeting 88/112, p. 8.

[125]"Federal Republic of Germany—Staff Report for the 1989 Article IV Consultation," SM/89/126 (June 27, 1989), pp. 15–23.

At the Board meeting in July, several Executive Directors took quite strong exception to the staff position. Charles S. Warner (Alternate—United States) averred that he was "rather disturbed by the overall theme" of the staff report. The Interim Committee, the G-7 leaders, and the Executive Board in its WEO discussions had all "agreed that all countries—surplus and deficit alike—share responsibility for reducing external imbalances," and he was concerned that the staff was not holding Germany up to that standard. Hélène Ploix (France) and Yusuf A. Nimatallah (Saudi Arabia) both noted the need to reduce "excess savings" in the German economy. And Gustavo García (Temporary Alternate—Venezuela) and Renato Filosa (Italy) focused directly on the need for a more "active" fiscal policy "directed to increase domestic demand." Reflecting those views, the Managing Director summed up the meeting by noting that "no major country could be exempted from contributing to the adjustment process." Many other Directors, however, accepted that Germany in 1989 had (as Japan's Koji Yamazaki phrased it) "little room for expansionary . . . policies" before inflationary pressures would reappear.[126] As the decade drew to a close and the sledgehammers drew close to the Berlin wall, the international community still had not formed a consensus on what advice to give to the world's third largest economy.

France

Article IV consultations with France were largely routine affairs during this first decade, except in the period of economic crisis in 1982–83. The words "commended" and "congratulated" reached cliché status in summing up the views of both the staff and Executive Directors, and references were made to the "skill and determination" of the authorities in implementing "courageous" reforms in economic policy. Criticisms centered on the panoply of structural rigidities that distorted economic incentives and kept both inflation and unemployment higher than the average for industrial countries. Those rigidities included the de facto full indexation of wages to past inflation (until 1982), reliance on quantitative credit ceilings to keep monetary growth under control (until 1985), exchange controls to limit speculative pressures on the French franc (1981–84), controls over labor market practices (until 1986), and resort to protectionist trade policies (until 1988).[127]

The French authorities generally welcomed the Fund's advice on these issues. Most of the missions in the 1980s were led by the Director of the European Department (Alan Whittome through 1987 and then Massimo Russo), who—from 1985 on—usually concluded his visit with meetings with the minister of finance, the governor of the Bank of France, and the director of the treasury.

---

[126]Minutes of EBM/89/96–97 (July 24, 1989). The quotations are from meetings 86/96, pp. 14 (Ploix), 86/19 (Yamazaki), 86/20–21 (Warner), and 86/44 (Filosa); and meetings 86/97, pp. 7 (García) and 86/19 (summing up).

[127]The dates indicate when the effects of the policies had diminished by enough to defuse the issue in the consultations.

In the initial Article IV consultation, in December 1978, the Fund welcomed France's decision to join the exchange arrangements of the EMS when it commenced the following March. The staff, however, was mindful that success was hardly assured. France had a troubled history in its attempts to participate in the European currency "snake" over the preceding six years,[128] but the staff decided that the strengthening of the balance of payments in 1978 "now makes participation in the EMS technically feasible for France."[129] Although the franc was devalued three times in EMS realignments over 18 months through March 1983 (by a total of more than 16 percent), the staff did not seriously question either the exchange rate policy or the stance of macroeconomic policy.

The economic crisis of 1982–83 was a defining moment in the early days of the presidency of François Mitterrand, who led the Socialist Party to victory over the Gaullists of his predecessor, Valéry Giscard d'Estaing, in May 1981. Mitterrand swept aside the gradualist policies under which Giscard and Prime Minister Raymond Barre had attempted to restrict demand and liberalize the economy in order to reduce inflation while promoting investment. The new regime aimed instead to reduce France's extremely high unemployment rate (more than two million unemployed in 1982, or 8½ percent of the labor force) while avoiding an *acceleration* of inflation (close to 10 percent in 1982, compared with an average of 7½ in the G-7 and less than 6 in the EMS).

The staff initially took a wait-and-see attitude on the shift in policies. The mission that conducted the Article IV consultations in February 1982, led by Whittome, declared itself to be "sympathetic" to the government's goals, though it warned of "serious and unresolved questions" on how those goals were to be achieved. Even on the dramatic nationalization of several key industries and most of the banking system that was announced during the consultations, Whittome's report concluded that it was "too early to come to any judgment." Executive Directors focused more on the "serious risks" in the new strategy than on the opportunities for resolving the unemployment problem, but the tone of the Board meeting in May was still soft.[130]

By the time of the next consultation mission, in March 1983, the French franc had been devalued twice more, each time under heavy speculative selling pressure.

---

[128]France joined the snake when it was formed in March 1972, agreeing to maintain its exchange rate within margins of ±2¼ percent against the other participating currencies. However, when French inflation persisted at above-average levels, the authorities were forced to suspend the margins from January 1974 through July 1975 and again from March 1976 until the arrangements were replaced by the EMS in March 1979.

[129]"France—Staff Report for the 1978 Article IV Consultation," SM/79/35 (February 1, 1979), p. 14.

[130]"France—Staff Report for the 1982 Article IV Consultation," SM/82/63 (April 5, 1982), pp. 12–13; and the minutes of EBM/82/63–64. "Serious risks" is from the Chairman's summing up at meeting 82/64, p. 13. Jacques Polak (Netherlands) gave particular stress to the risks (meeting 82/63, pp. 13–16). In his view, French macroeconomic policy in 1982 "recalled the anticyclical policies applied in the industrial countries in the 1960s, policies that . . . had come to be acknowledged as not very effective in the short run and as counterproductive in the long run. . . . It seemed likely that in France, as in other countries, mastering inflation would prove to be the precondition for an effective reflationary policy."

The current account of the balance of payments had shifted into a substantial deficit, and the whole policy approach of the previous two years had clearly become unsustainable. The staff finally acknowledged that the policies of 1981–82 had been seriously misplaced and that substantial policy changes would be needed to overcome the "deeper weaknesses in the economy." The fiscal deficit should be cut, the nascent shift toward delinking wage increases from past inflation should be strengthened, quantitative ceilings on bank lending should be scrapped and interest rates allowed to rise, and so forth.

The Fund's advice to the French authorities was uncharacteristically belated. Two days into the mission, on March 25, the government announced a radical policy reversal that included deep cuts in spending, increases in public utility charges, a variety of tax increases, new exchange restrictions to protect the franc, and a cut in targeted money growth.[131] It was not exactly what the doctor had ordered—the exchange restrictions were unwelcome, and monetary restriction would still be engineered through credit ceilings—but it was an extraordinarily bold move in the right direction, especially by a government thought to be firmly in the traditional French socialist mold.[132]

When the Board met in June to conclude the consultation, the main lesson that it drew was not whether expansion or contraction of demand was the more prudent course for a country suffering from stagflation. The lesson was that in the modern global economy, no country could successfully pursue economic policies that were sharply at variance with those of its main trading partners. With the United States, Germany, the United Kingdom, and much of the rest of western Europe striving to restore price stability, France could not hope to restore high employment unless it first joined the club of low-inflation countries. That the French authorities now seemed determined to do so was "courageous," and the main task was to carry out the newly announced policies.[133] The unstated implication was that periodic devaluation of the exchange rate could not substitute for a convergence of domestic policies, because it would lead inevitably to new crises until the inflation gap was cut to a manageable level.

For the rest of the decade, the consultations raised few major issues. Despite a succession of shifts in government, French economic policies remained on the course

---

[131]Much of the package was designed by Finance Minister Jacques Delors and his deputy, Michel Camdessus, in mid-February, while they were stranded at the French consulate in New York trying to get home after the blizzard-bound meeting of the Interim Committee in Washington.

[132]The new exchange restrictions, which limited the acquisition of foreign currency by French residents for foreign travel, were under the jurisdiction of the Fund under the provisions of Article VIII. (France had accepted the obligations of Article VIII in 1961.) On May 17, the authorities informed the Fund that they intended to remove the restrictions by the end of the year. On that understanding, the Executive Board granted its approval of the restrictions until December 31, 1983, with only one Director—A.R.G. Prowse (Australia)—objecting. The controls were substantially eliminated on December 20. See "France—Exchange System," SM/83/69, Sup. 1 (5/23/83); and the minutes of EBM/83/81 (6/3/81), pp. 31, 38, and 39. The elimination of restrictions is described in "France—Exchange System," EBD/83/335 (December 27, 1983).

[133]Chairman's summing up, minutes of EBM/83/81 (June 3, 1983), p. 37.

set in 1983.[134] The last EMS realignment in which the franc was significantly devalued took place in April 1986, after which the French authorities made the strength of the currency a central pillar of their economic strategy (an approach that became known as the "hard currency" or "franc fort" policy). The Fund firmly endorsed that strategy, most clearly in the 1989 consultations, when the Executive Board praised "the primacy attached to maintaining the parity of the franc vis-à-vis the deutsche mark," which "constituted a strong anchor for the economy and a powerful device for conditioning domestic policies and the behavior of the private sector."[135] France's central role in the EMS and in the European economy had become not just "technically feasible," as it had been in 1979, but an undisputed reality.

United Kingdom

Of all the countries reviewed in this chapter, the United Kingdom was the one for which both the staff of the Fund and the Executive Board examined the exchange rate most openly and frankly. The exchange value of the pound sterling rose relentlessly throughout 1979 and 1980, in response to both the tightening of monetary policy by the fledgling government of Prime Minister Margaret Thatcher and the development of the North Sea oil fields at a time of sharply rising petroleum prices. Sterling then depreciated in spurts for the next five years and by the middle of the decade was subjected to occasional bouts of heavy selling pressure. It underwent a new, smaller cycle in the late 1980s (Figure 3.8).

When the Fund began holding consultations under Article IV in 1978, the United Kingdom had just borrowed SDR 2.25 billion (approximately $2.7 billion) under the stand-by arrangement of 1977.[136] That was the eleventh lending arrangement between the Fund and the United Kingdom, dating from the Suez crisis of 1956, but it would also be the last with the United Kingdom and one of the last with any industrial country. By the time the consultation mission arrived in London in May 1978—by happenstance, the first Article IV mission to a major industrial country—the economy was already on a path toward financial stability. Although the economy became "severely depressed" in 1980 and 1981 (in the words of the January 1982 staff report)[137] and inflation was all but intractable

---

[134]Mitterrand engineered a major cabinet reshuffle in July 1984 in which Prime Minister Pierre Mauroy resigned and was replaced by Laurent Fabius, and Pierre Bérégovoy replaced Jacques Delors as minister of finance. In March 1986, the Socialist Party lost control of parliament in general elections, after which Jacques Chirac became prime minister and named Eduard Balladur as minister with responsibility for finance. The Socialists regained power in June 1988 and returned the finance portfolio to Bérégovoy.

[135]Chairman's summing up, minutes of EBM/89/103 (July 28, 1989), p. 6.

[136]The approved amount of the arrangement—the largest in Fund history up to that time—was originally SDR 3.36 billion in January 1977, augmented to SDR 3.97 billion in June. The United Kingdom drew 1 billion in January and another 1.25 billion in three installments through August. For the full story, see de Vries (1985), Chapter 24; and James (1996), pp. 279–82.

[137]"United Kingdom—Staff Report for the 1981 Article IV Consultation," SM/82/19 (January 28, 1982), p. 1.

Figure 3.8. United Kingdom: Exchange Rates, 1979–89

1990 = 100

U.S. dollars per pound

throughout the decade, a succession of Fund missions under shifting leadership gave consistently good marks to the authorities for their handling of both macroeconomic and more structural policies.[138] During the 1980–82 recession, the staff consistently encouraged the government to persist with its "medium-term financial strategy"—which aimed to reduce both monetary growth rates and public sector deficits steadily over a period of years—despite the high and rising levels of unemployment. After real growth resumed and inflation remained disturbingly high, the staff regularly urged more "caution" (i.e., restriction) in fiscal policy to take the burden off monetary policy and interest rates, but the reports raised few other concerns about the stance of domestic financial policy. Toward the end of the decade, when the current account shifted into deficit, the staff accepted the authorities' argument that became known as the "Lawson doctrine": that the deficit was benign and would likely be self-correcting, because it resulted from a drop in private sector saving rather than government saving (see Chapter 1).

---

[138]The 1978 mission was led by Azizali Mohammed (Senior Advisor in the European Department). In 1979, David Finch (Deputy Director of ETR)—one of the chief negotiators of the 1977 stand-by arrangement—took over for one year. Then Hans Schmitt (Senior Advisor in the European Department) and Patrick de Fontenay (Deputy Director) took turns leading the missions from 1980 through 1986. Through that period, the Director of the European Department, Alan Whittome, avoided leading missions to the United Kingdom because of a general preference in the Fund for not having missions headed by a national of the country being reviewed. The 1987 and 1988 missions were led by Whittome's successor, Massimo Russo, and the 1989 mission was headed by Manuel Guitián (Deputy Director). In most years the mission chief—and occasionally other team members as well—met at the conclusion of the mission with the Chancellor of the Exchequer and the governor of the Bank of England.

With all this harmony on domestic policies, much of the focus of the consultations was on the exchange rate. The staff frequently took exception to the prevailing exchange rate policy, though it is difficult to discern a consistent philosophy or strategy on either side of the debate. In the 1978 consultation, the staff worried that the authorities were engaging in the sort of "protracted large-scale intervention in one direction" that the 1977 surveillance guidelines decried. In response to the tightening of financial policies under the stand-by arrangement with the Fund, the exchange rate had begun to strengthen in 1977; the Bank of England had then intervened heavily to limit the appreciation. At the Board meeting, the U.K. Executive Director, William Ryrie, complained that the staff seemed to be "interpreting Article IV as a gospel of free floating." The Managing Director, however, insisted that the staff's judgment was "very balanced," and most of the Board agreed.[139]

When the Conservative party assumed power under Prime Minister Thatcher, the government initially embraced the "gospel" and decided to let the exchange rate seek its own level. The 1979 staff report noted that the recent appreciation of sterling was "excessive by conventional standards" and was squeezing business profits. Even so, the staff accepted that the authorities had little choice if they hoped to get inflation under control after the "winter of discontent" that had disrupted economic activity in 1978 and had led to extraordinarily large wage settlements.[140] Some Executive Directors grumbled that the pendulum had swung too far, but the Board as a whole endorsed the new policy stance. A year later, the continuing appreciation of the currency had become a major economic problem for Britain, as by any standard the loss of international competitiveness was unprecedented among the large industrial countries. The staff again concluded that the very tight stance of monetary policy that had contributed to the problem was needed for domestic price and wage control.

By the time of the 1981 consultation, the U.K. economy was really being wrung out. The staff now concluded that it had become important not to let the appreciation go any further and if possible to let the currency fall a bit. In a subtle effort at asymmetry, the report concluded that economic stability would be threatened either by "an appreciation" of the exchange rate or by "too rapid a depreciation." The Executive Board was split on this issue, as several Directors argued that sterling was now "overvalued" and in need of "substantial depreciation."[141] At the same time, the staff began quietly suggesting that the United Kingdom might benefit by joining the exchange rate mechanism (ERM) of the EMS once the overvaluation was corrected. In part, that view reflected a belief that massive swings in

---

[139]Minutes of EBM/78/100 (July 5, 1978), p. 7 (Ryrie); and EBM/78/101, p. 9 (de Larosière).

[140]"United Kingdom—Staff Report for 1979 Article IV Consultation," SM/79/211 (August 9, 1979); the quotation is from p. 18.

[141]"United Kingdom—Staff Report for the 1981 Article IV Consultation," SM/82/19 (January 28, 1982), p. 17 (staff view); and the minutes of EBM/82/20 (February 19, 1982), remarks by Giovanni Lovato (Italy) on pp. 8–9 ("overvalued") and Teruo Hirao (Japan) on p. 25 (on the need for depreciation).

the exchange rate were severely damaging the economy; in part, that the British financial system was now so open and complex that something other than money growth was needed to measure the stance of monetary policy. Officially, the staff position was that the authorities should make more use of the exchange rate as an indicator. In context, that position implied that the exchange rate should be deliberately stabilized. Ryrie's feared "gospel of free floating" was no longer an option.

For the next few years, the staff continued to push gently for consideration of ERM participation as a means of stabilizing the exchange rate, while simultaneously calling for further depreciation. The authorities continued to resist the former but at least implicitly revealed a willingness to let sterling float gradually downward. They largely abandoned the attempt to target the growth rate of money, in favor of a monetary policy based on a variety of indicative targets that included both nominal income and the exchange rate. For about a year starting in March 1987, they experimented with a policy of "shadowing" the deutsche mark, as a sort of preview of what life might be like inside the ERM. As the U.K. Executive Director, Timothy P. Lankester, noted at the time, "the arguments against [ERM] membership are certainly not as strong as they had been in the past," owing to the depreciation that had already occurred and to the commitments toward stability that the United Kingdom had made as its part in the Louvre accord.[142] That experiment, however, ended badly, as the Bank of England was forced to provide excessive liquidity to keep the rate from appreciating.

From March 1988 until the United Kingdom finally joined the ERM in October 1990, the authorities let the rate appreciate and then depreciate again. When the latter phase began, the staff urged firm resistance, arguing that "a strong pound is an essential ingredient in the strategy to lower inflation."[143] No longer, however, did the staff push for ERM participation. The view now was that inflation had first to be brought down close to the level prevailing in Germany.[144]

To sum up, the consultations with the United Kingdom witnessed and encouraged a decade of bold but not wholly successful experiments in exchange rate policy. Because British economic policy was in poorly charted waters, inconsistencies and shifts in course should not be surprising and may have been inevitable—both for the authorities and for the Fund's advice. Whatever the successes and failures, the history of the process illustrates the difficulties of achieving macroeconomic and financial stability in a country where both had long been absent and of defining a clear policy strategy for the transition.

---

[142]Minutes of EBM/87/32 (February 24, 1987), p. 11.

[143]"United Kingdom—Staff Report for the 1989 Article IV Consultation," SM/90/33 (February 2, 1990), p. 23.

[144]The authorities were split on this issue. Both Lawson and his predecessor, Geoffrey Howe (by then the foreign minister), sought bitterly and unsuccessfully to convince Thatcher to anchor the pound in the ERM. Thatcher eventually replaced Howe with John Major, largely over this issue. When Lawson resigned a few months later, also over the ERM, Thatcher moved Major to the treasury. Ironically, these moves led to her downfall, as Major finally did persuade her to join the ERM and was promptly rewarded by the Conservative party with the prime ministership. For two sides of the story, see Lawson (1992), Chapters 73–77; and Thatcher (1993), Chapter 24.

References

Aghevli, Bijan B., James M. Boughton, Peter J. Montiel, Delano Villanueva, and Geoffrey Woglom, 1990, *The Role of National Saving in the World Economy*, IMF Occasional Paper No. 67 (Washington: International Monetary Fund).

Artus, Jacques, and Malcolm D. Knight, 1984, *Issues in the Assessment of the Exchange Rates of Industrial Countries*, IMF Occasional Paper No. 29 (Washington: International Monetary Fund).

Boughton, James M., 1984, "Exchange Rate Movements and Adjustment in Financial Markets: Quarterly Estimates for Major Currencies," *Staff Papers*, International Monetary Fund, Vol. 31 (September), pp. 445–68.

———, 1989, "Policy Assignment Strategies with Somewhat Flexible Exchange Rates," in *Blueprints for Exchange-Rate Management*, ed. by Marcus Miller, Barry Eichengreen, and Richard Portes (London: Academic Press), pp. 121–54.

———, Richard D. Haas, Paul R. Masson, and Charles Adams, 1986, "Effects of Exchange Rate Changes in Industrial Countries," in *Staff Studies for the World Economic Outlook* (Washington: International Monetary Fund, July).

de Vries, Margaret Garritsen, 1985, *The International Monetary Fund, 1972–1978: Cooperation on Trial*, Vols. 1 and 2: *Narrative and Analysis*, Vol. 3: *Documents* (Washington: International Monetary Fund).

Destler, I.M., and C. Randall Henning, 1989, *Dollar Politics: Exchange Rate Policymaking in the United States* (Washington: Institute for International Economics).

Dominguez, Kathryn M., and Jeffrey A. Frankel, 1993, *Does Foreign Exchange Intervention Work?* (Washington: Institute for International Economics).

Feldstein, Martin, 1988, "Rethinking International Economic Coordination," *Oxford Economic Papers*, Vol. 40 (June), pp. 205–19.

Frankel, Jeffrey A., 1994, "The Making of Exchange Rate Policy in the 1980s," in *American Economic Policy in the 1980s*, ed. by Martin Feldstein (Chicago, Illinois: University of Chicago Press, pp. 293–341).

Frenkel, Jacob A., Morris Goldstein, and Paul R. Masson, 1991, *Characteristics of a Successful Exchange Rate System*, IMF Occasional Paper No. 82 (Washington: International Monetary Fund).

Funabashi, Yoichi, 1988, *Managing the Dollar: From the Plaza to the Louvre* (Washington: Institute for International Economics).

Guitián, Manuel, 1988, "The European Monetary System: A Balance Between Rules and Discretion," Part I of *Policy Coordination in the European Monetary System*, by Manuel Guitián, Massimo Russo, and Giuseppe Tullio, IMF Occasional Paper No. 61 (Washington: International Monetary Fund), pp. 1–37.

Henning, C. Randall, 1994, *Currencies and Politics in the United States, Germany, and Japan* (Washington: Institute for International Economics).

Horiguchi, Yusuke, and others, 1992, *The United States Economy: Performance and Issues* (Washington: International Monetary Fund).

James, Harold, 1996, *International Monetary Cooperation since Bretton Woods* (Oxford: Oxford University Press; Washington: International Monetary Fund).

Krugman, Paul, 1988, "Louvre's Lesson: Let the Dollar Fall," *International Economy*, Vol. 1 (January/February), pp. 76–82.

Lawson, Nigel, 1992, *The View from No. 11: Memoirs of a Tory Radical* (London: Bantam Press).

Lipschitz, Leslie, Jeroen Kremers, Thomas Mayer, and Donogh McDonald, 1989, *The Federal Republic of Germany: Adjustment in a Surplus Country*, IMF Occasional Paper No. 64 (Washington: International Monetary Fund).

Norman, Peter, 1989, "Touch of Glasnost at the IMF," *Financial Times* (April 3), p. 25.

Putnam, Robert D., and Nicholas Bayne, 1987, *Hanging Together: Cooperation and Conflict in the Seven-Power Summits* (Cambridge, Massachusetts: Harvard University Press, rev. and enl. ed.).

Putnam, Robert D., and C. Randall Henning, 1989, "The Bonn Summit of 1978: A Case Study in Coordination," in *Can Nations Agree? Issues in International Economic Cooperation*, by Richard N. Cooper and others (Washington: Brookings Institution), pp. 12–140.

Sprinkel, Beryl W., 1981, "Statement of the Honorable Beryl W. Sprinkel, Under Secretary of the Treasury for Monetary Affairs, Before the Joint Economic Committee" (Washington: Department of the Treasury News, May 4).

Thatcher, Margaret, 1993, *The Downing Street Years* (New York: HarperCollins).

U.S. Council of Economic Advisers, 1982, "Annual Report," in *Economic Report of the President Transmitted to the Congress February 1982, Together with the Annual Report of the Council of Economic Advisers* (Washington: United States Government Printing Office).

4

Policy Cooperation: The Fund and the Group of Seven

The first purpose of the International Monetary Fund is to "promote international monetary cooperation through a permanent institution which provides the machinery for consultation and collaboration on international monetary problems."[1] Surveillance has therefore aimed not only to encourage governments to conduct policies so as to promote their own interests in isolation, taking the policies of other countries as given (as is typically done in Article IV consultations), but also to promote cooperative behavior that will lead to better outcomes for all. In carrying out the latter objective, the Fund has sometimes found itself both in competition and in collaboration with a variety of groups of countries that have come together regularly to deal with monetary problems from their own perspective.

The story of this chapter is how the Fund came to play a significant, if secondary, role when the major industrial countries tried to set up their own internal surveillance over monetary and exchange rate policies in the 1980s. This process had two unavoidable limitations. First, international coordination of economic policies is controversial, not always desirable, and extraordinarily difficult to achieve on a sustained (as opposed to crisis-driven) basis.[2] The major countries reached a series of helpful accords in the second half of the 1980s, but the formal surveillance and coordination exercise largely died out afterward. Second, the Fund participated only at the pleasure of the countries' officials and had no real standing to guide the process. The Fund did promote the strategy, in part by providing an analytical framework and an internationally consistent database. The Managing Director and other senior officials occasionally influenced the direction of the discussions, and they encouraged officials to extend and deepen their commitment to carry out sustainable and internationally consistent policies. For the Fund to play a more central role, or for policy coordination to achieve more lasting results, would have been an unrealistic goal.

Policy coordination in the 1980s emerged from a loose institutional structure developed by shifting coalitions of countries with similar economic interests. The history of industrial country "groups" began in 1961, when the 10 largest countries formed the "Group of Ten" (G-10) to organize and fund the General Arrange-

---

[1]Article I (i) of the Fund's Articles of Agreement.

[2]For an overview of the issues, see Blommestein (1991) and Cooper (1985). For a sympathetic insider analysis, see Dobson (1991), Chapter 2.

ments to Borrow (GAB).[3] That group was, and remains, officially connected with the Fund through the functioning of the GAB.[4] The smaller groups that emerged later, however, developed more independently of established international agencies. The finance ministers from the inner core of the largest industrial countries began meeting as the "Library Group" in 1973 and quickly became the G-5.[5] Meetings of that group typically were kept highly confidential and low-key, with no communiqués or other public announcements being issued until the mid-1980s. As an outgrowth, the heads of state or government of the seven largest industrial countries began holding annual, highly publicized, economic summit conferences in 1975.[6] From then on, the finance ministers of the G-7 countries met regularly, along with representatives of the heads of government (the "sherpas"), to prepare for the annual summit conferences, while those in the G-5 would meet separately—at least twice each year, in conjunction with the spring and fall Fund-Bank meetings—to discuss monetary issues.

Among the much larger and more diffuse circle of developing countries, the formation of small action or discussion groups was more difficult. At the original United Nations Conference on Trade and Development (UNCTAD), held in Geneva in March 1964, 77 developing countries decided to form the G-77, a loose coalition aimed at discussing issues of mutual interest on international trade policy. (Eventually, the membership of the G-77 exceeded 100 countries.) Then in November 1971, as a counterweight to the role that the G-10 was seeking to play in

---

[3]The G-10 originally comprised the United States, Japan, Germany, France, and the United Kingdom (which later would constitute the G-5); Italy and Canada (which, together with the G-5, would become known as the G-7); plus Belgium, the Netherlands, and Sweden. From 1964, Switzerland was affiliated with the G-10 through a related agreement with the Fund, and its role was formalized when it joined the GAB in 1984. On the changing role of the G-10 in the 1970s, see de Vries (1985), pp. 143–53.

[4]The G-10 countries also have a role within the Organization for Economic Cooperation and Development (OECD), as their membership is similar to that of Working Party 3 of the OECD's Economic Policy Committee; and within the Bank for International Settlements (BIS), where the central bank governors of the G-10 countries meet on a monthly basis. For the more recent history of the GAB, see Chapter 17.

[5]Prior to the second meeting of the Committee of Twenty in 1973, U.S. Treasury Secretary George Shultz invited his counterparts from Germany, France, and the United Kingdom to an informal gathering at the White House library on March 25 to discuss options for responding to the crisis in exchange markets. The group met again at the Annual Meetings in Nairobi that September. The finance minister from Japan was also invited, at Shultz's request, and the meeting was held at the residence of the Japanese ambassador to Kenya. From then on, that group of countries informally constituted the G-5. See Shultz (1993), pp. 147–48; and Volcker and Gyohten (1992), pp. 126 and 134.

[6]See Gold (1988) for the historical relationships between the G-5 and the IMF. As Gold notes, two of the heads of state at the first economic summit—Helmut Schmidt (Germany) and the host of the meeting, Valéry Giscard d'Estaing (France)—had previously participated in G-5 meetings while serving as finance ministers and "were eager to recreate those meetings, but at the highest level" (p. 107). The six original summit countries, represented at Rambouillet, France, in November 1975, comprised the G-5 plus Italy. Subsequent summits (starting with the meeting in Puerto Rico in June 1976) also included Canada, which thus rounded out what became known as the Group of Seven. Starting in 1977, the Commission of the European Communities also participated in the G-7 summit conferences.

guiding the discussions on the reform of the international monetary system, a smaller group of developing countries formed the Intergovernmental Group of Twenty-Four on International Monetary Affairs, or the G-24. (See map, Figure 4.1.) With a technical secretariat provided mainly by the United Nations, the G-24 played an increasingly important role in discussions of international financial issues.[7] Nonetheless, because of the diversity of interests among the member countries of the G-24 and because of the group's relatively weak economic power, its influence in the 1970s and 1980s was quite limited compared with any of the industrial country groups.[8]

From the beginning, the discussions at the G-7 summits dealt directly or indirectly with issues pertinent to the IMF. That pattern began with a bang at Rambouillet in 1975, when the summit ratified the Franco-American agreement on stabilizing the exchange rate system by amending the Fund's Articles of Agreement and mandating firm surveillance (de Vries, 1985, pp. 746–47). The 1976 summit, in San Juan, Puerto Rico, was more low-key and did not lead to any new initiatives. It did, however, obliquely endorse the Fund's new oil and extended financing facilities and the possibility of mobilizing the GAB if needed to support Fund loans to Italy or the United Kingdom. In 1977, at a time when the Fund was deepening its involvement in persuading countries to adopt more liberal trade policies, the summit in London "strongly endorsed" the expansion of IMF quotas and other resources, linked to conditional lending, as an important means of helping countries avoid taking refuge in protectionism.[9] And in 1978, shortly after the Fund had joined the push for a coordinated strategy to restore world economic growth, both in the World Economic Outlook (WEO) exercise and in Article IV consultations with the major countries, the Bonn summit endorsed the strategy and won the agreement of the German authorities to shift to a more expansionary fiscal policy.[10]

---

[7]The G-24 secretariat was headed from 1975 through 1990 by Sidney Dell, a senior official of the United Nations Development Programme (UNDP). Subsequently, Professor Gerald K. Helleiner of the University of Toronto became the Research Coordinator for the G-24, with funding from UNCTAD and a number of governments of industrial and developing countries. On occasion, the staff of the IMF assisted both the G-24 and the various industrial country groups with specific research projects. For an overview on the evolution and role of the G-24, see Mayobre (1999).

[8]Perhaps the most successful muscle-flexing by the G-24 occurred at the October 1994 meeting of the Interim Committee, when the developing country members of the Committee blocked an industrial country proposal for an allocation of SDRs to relatively new members of the Fund in order to gain leverage for a general allocation to all members.

[9]All of the communiqués through 1989, with some background documents, are compiled in Hajnal (1989). Those and later documents are also available through a website at the University of Toronto, www.g7.utoronto.ca. Hajnal (1999) gives an overview of the G-7 process and its documentation. For a critical analysis of the meaning of the communiqués, see von Furstenberg and Daniels (1992).

[10]The staff view that "there is now a need for greater emphasis on policies to stimulate economic growth" received "wide support" from Executive Directors in the WEO discussions of April 1978. See "World Economic Outlook—General Survey," ID/78/1 (April 3, 1978), p. 33; minutes of IS/78/6 (April 18, 1978), p. 11; and de Vries (1985), pp. 795–96. The Fund's position in the 1978 consultations with Germany is discussed above, in Chapter 3. The main forum for the initial development of the coordinated reflationary strategy was the OECD in Paris; see McCracken and others (1977).

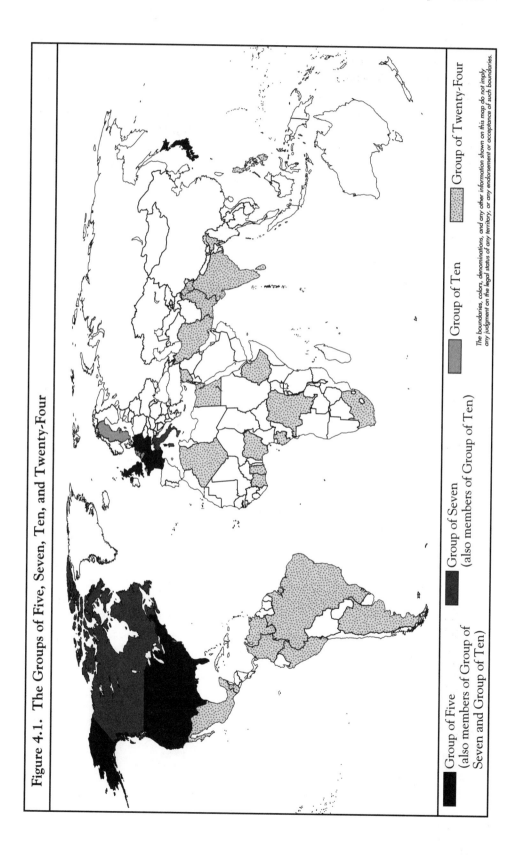

Figure 4.1. The Groups of Five, Seven, Ten, and Twenty-Four

The 1979 G-7 summit, held in Tokyo, dealt primarily with the large increases in petroleum prices that were then under way: an issue that was also the main focus of the WEO that year (see Chapter 5). The resulting policy shift toward control of inflation, which was manifest initially at the Annual Meetings in Belgrade in October 1979, was formally endorsed by the G-7 at the 1980 summit in Venice. The following year, in Ottawa, the G-7 leaders regretted the persistence of high real interest rates in the United States,[11] again striking an accord with positions taken by the Fund both in the consultations and in the WEO. Up to this point, the linkages between the Fund and the G-7 were both arm's length and coincidental, in the sense that the policy positions were for the most part independent responses to the same developments in the world economy. That relationship began to shift toward one of closer cooperation in 1982.

"In His Personal Capacity": 1982–84

In the spring of 1982, the functioning of the international monetary system was beginning to reemerge as a priority at international meetings. The tight financial policies that most industrial countries had been implementing for two years or more had succeeded in bringing down inflation rates, but the persistence of those policies had prolonged the weakness in output growth and had kept interest rates near record levels in real terms. The problem therefore was to plan the timing and extent of a monetary relaxation so as to rekindle growth without fanning the inflationary flames. Meanwhile, the U.S. dollar had been appreciating against most other key currencies for nearly two years, and concerns were mounting—especially in Europe—that the rapidity of this appreciation could cause inflationary pressures to be exported abroad rather than eliminated.

The central question in these circumstances was how best to ensure stability and continued growth of international trade and finance, along with a reasonable (noninflationary) growth of output. Views on these matters ranged widely, and within the G-7 the United States and France held diametrically opposed positions. The French view essentially was that exchange rate movements were a threat to growth and to economic stability and should be combated through coordinated official intervention in exchange markets. U.S. officials argued that intervention was ineffective and that stability could be achieved only if monetary policies were similar across countries.

This Franco-American debate was hardly new. A similar difference in view surfaced a decade earlier in the wake of the collapse of the par value exchange rate system, as the Committee of Twenty (the forerunner of the Fund's Interim Committee) attempted to forge a new structure to replace it. At that time, a compro-

---

[11]"Interest rates . . . are likely to remain high where fears of inflation remain strong. But we are fully aware that levels and movements of interest rates in one country can make stabilization policies more difficult in other countries by influencing their exchange rates and their economies." Declaration of the Ottawa Summit (July 21, 1981), para. 6; in Hajnal (1989), p. 105.

mise was reached through intense bilateral negotiations, the essence of which was that IMF surveillance would aim to ensure that member countries were fostering stable underlying economic and financial conditions and a "stable *system* of exchange rates" (emphasis added).[12] Although exchange rates would no longer be fixed, the intention and the hope on the French side had been that policy coordination would bring about stable rates and that surveillance would be sufficiently firm to prevent policies from diverging too greatly. By 1982, with the mix of U.S. policies shifting toward greater monetary restriction and fiscal expansion than other countries felt to be justified, that hope could no longer be sustained.

Versailles, 1982

The renewal of the debate came to a head at an April 1982 meeting of the deputies (or "sous-sherpas") who were preparing for the G-7 summit conference that was to be held at Versailles in June.[13] Michel Camdessus, the French deputy, wanted an agreement to stabilize exchange rates—especially among the three largest countries, the United States, Japan, and Germany[14]—through intervention. Beryl Sprinkel, the U.S. deputy, was adamantly opposed to that proposal and insisted that exchange rate stability could be achieved only through coordination of monetary policies. Although the other delegates at the meeting in Rambouillet, France (the historic site of the 1975 summit), tilted toward Camdessus in what became a "heated debate," Sprinkel effectively blocked agreement on intervention.[15]

On one level, the intervention debate was an exercise in semantics. The U.S. distrust of intervention was based in part on the logic that with monetary policy aiming to control the growth of the stock of money, intervention would have to be sterilized to keep monetary growth on target. This argument gave an apparent precision to the U.S. position that others may not have felt to be consistent with market practice. Everyone would have agreed that unsterilized intervention would have had greater and more lasting effects on exchange rates, but it was not so easy to agree on how practical this notion was. On a deeper economic level, the debate reflected different views about the efficiency of financial markets and about the importance of risk aversion by market participants. In the United States, most officials in the Reagan administration viewed markets as sufficiently efficient and

---

[12]The quotation is from the amended Article IV. See de Vries (1985), pp. 743–45, on the negotiations to draft the amendment. The main negotiations took place in the fall of 1975 between the U.S. representative, Edwin H. Yeo III, and the French representative, Jacques de Larosière. Also see Pauly (1992) for a discussion of the compromise.

[13]Except as noted, the discussion of this and other meetings of deputies and ministers is based on background interviews with participants.

[14]The French franc and (with wider margins) the Italian lira were already being stabilized against the deutsche mark through the exchange rate mechanism of the European Monetary System.

[15]The "heated debate" characterization has been used both by Putnam and Bayne (1987), p. 133, and by Volcker and Gyohten (1992), p. 353. For more on the U.S. stance against intervention, see the section in Chapter 3 on exchange rate policy in the United States, pp. 149–53.

risk-neutral that sterilized intervention would have only small and very temporary effects on exchange rates, while officials in most other countries at the time saw more scope to influence rates.[16] On a still deeper political level, the debate reflected disagreements about the importance of exchange rate stability (vital to Europe, secondary to the United States), the best strategy for coordinating economic policies (whether to force coordination as the required means to achieve exchange rate stability or to coordinate first and let exchange rates adjust accordingly), and even about the desirability of policy coordination.

The April 1982 deputies' meeting revealed strong differences on each of these levels that the G-7 clearly could not bridge in time for the Versailles summit. To keep from losing momentum and to provide some grist for the summit, Camdessus and Sprinkel agreed to meet separately and work out an acceptable compromise. That led to two proposals, both of which the other deputies reluctantly accepted. First, the summit would commission a study on experience with exchange market intervention, in the hope that it could provide guidance on resolving the Franco-American dispute. Second, in a move with the potential for much greater long-run significance, the deputies agreed to recommend that a multilateral surveillance exercise be developed within the G-7 and that it be conducted in cooperation with the IMF.

A broader issue also arose during these preparatory meetings for the Versailles summit. Whatever strategy evolved for strengthening the international monetary system, the G-7 was keen to play a major role in guiding it. In the 1960s, the G-10 had taken the lead role in developing a consensus among the industrial countries on major systemic issues. In the 1970s, this role had begun to be supplanted by both wider groups (notably the Committee of Twenty and its successor, the Interim Committee) and narrower ones such as the G-5 and the G-7.[17]

With finance ministers meeting often in these varying configurations, tension and confusion were bound to arise over the forum in which key issues of international finance were to be discussed. The largest countries argued that exchange rates and policy coordination were too sensitive to be discussed in a wide forum,

---

[16]Sterilized intervention in support of, say, the U.S. dollar against the deutsche mark is equivalent to an open market purchase by the Federal Reserve of a U.S. treasury bill and a simultaneous sale of a German mark-denominated treasury bill, to alter the currency composition but not the aggregate stock of securities held by the Federal Reserve. In a perfect risk-neutral market, such an exchange would be expected to leave interest rates unchanged in both countries and thus to have no effect on the exchange rate. If investors require a risk premium to hold securities denominated in a foreign currency, then the exchange rate would be expected to adjust in response to the shift in the currency composition of the outstanding stock of securities. See Boughton (1983) for a technical background on the accounting framework, and Edison (1993) and Dominguez and Frankel (1993) for reviews of empirical evidence (which largely rejects the risk-neutral, efficient-markets hypothesis but finds only weak support for the effectiveness of intervention as it has been practiced). Official views in the early 1980s are summarized (though not explicitly identified by country) in Jurgensen (1983).

[17]In addition to the summit meetings, G-7 officials met regularly as the informal "Bureau" of the Economic Policy Committee (EPC) at the OECD in Paris. At private dinners the evening before the semiannual meetings of the full EPC (in which all OECD member countries participated), the Bureau would review the agenda and prepare a preliminary assessment or summing up of the key policy issues.

but Italy and Canada were reluctant to be left out of the process. After some debate during the preparatory meetings for the Versailles summit, the benefits of the smaller group won out, but three limitations became clear. First, neither the G-5 nor the G-7 had a standing secretariat that could provide background information for multilateral discussions. The deputies and their separate staffs could continue to play that role, but only inefficiently. Second, some means had to be sought for reconciling major differences of view within the group. A decade earlier, the Franco-American debate over how to manage exchange rates was resolved through a bilateral compromise, but positions in 1982 appeared too polarized for that approach. Third, limiting the participants to the G-5 should not imply limiting the perspective of the discussion. Any major policy shifts by the G-5 would affect the rest of the world, and a broad view would therefore have to be taken.

Including the Managing Director of the IMF in the G-5 surveillance exercise would help alleviate each of these problems. The Managing Director could call upon the Fund staff for global information and analysis, he could interject a neutral and independent voice into the discussions, and he could represent the views of the rest of the world.[18] Because the Managing Director would not be precommitted to a particular view on the role of exchange market intervention, this form of surveillance might help bridge the gulf between the French and U.S. positions.[19] After the deputies accepted the Camdessus-Sprinkel proposal to invite the Managing Director to participate in G-5 discussions, the idea was endorsed by the G-5 finance ministers at a dinner meeting at the U.S. Embassy in Helsinki, Finland, just before the May meeting of the Interim Committee.

The formal endorsement of the IMF's role in the process came at the summit conference at Versailles, held on June 4–6, 1982. Attached to the summit communiqué was a "Statement on International Monetary Undertakings," the relevant passages of which were as follows:

1. We accept a joint responsibility to work for greater stability of the world monetary system. We recognize that this rests primarily on convergence of policies. . . .

2. We attach major importance to the role of the IMF as a monetary authority and we will give it our full support in its efforts to foster stability.

3. We are ready to strengthen our cooperation with the IMF in its work of surveillance; and to develop this on a multilateral basis taking into account particularly the currencies constituting the SDR.[20]

4. We rule out the use of our exchange rates to gain unfair competitive advantages.

---

[18]The G-5 reportedly considered the OECD before the IMF was chosen for this purpose. The Secretary General of the OECD also could call on a highly professional staff to produce an impartial analysis, and the OECD had specific expertise on policy issues affecting industrial countries. The global representation of the Fund was a factor in its favor.

[19]Though the Managing Director—Jacques de Larosière—was French, of course, it may be recalled (footnote 12, p. 191) that he had coresponsibility for the Compromise of 1975. He also had spent several years as the French deputy at G-5 meetings and was well known and respected by the group.

[20]The reference to the "currencies constituting the SDR" is a code for the Group of Five.

5. We are ready, if necessary, to use intervention in exchange rates to counter disorderly conditions, as provided for under Article IV of the IMF Articles of Agreement.

This statement was viewed by both U.S. and European officials as a partial victory. The wording was fully consistent with the U.S. position that stability depended on policy convergence and that intervention could play only a minimal role; but it was also fully consistent with the French view that exchange rate stability was important, that a mutual commitment to that goal was essential if it was to be achieved, and that countries should intervene in conditions of instability.[21] That it was possible to draft a series of apparently firm declarations that equally supported two diametrically opposed visions is a remarkable tribute to the obfuscating political skills of the sherpas and their deputies.[22] The Versailles summit did not resolve any major disagreements, but it did at least set in motion a process that seemed to have the potential for doing so.

De Larosière was, of course, quite ready to accept the invitation from the G-7 to participate in the G-5 ministerial meetings,[23] and he met with the G-5 deputies in early July to begin preparations. That invitation was extended and accepted on the explicit understanding that the Managing Director would be acting "in his personal capacity." His views would be informed both by the staff and the Executive Board, but he would not necessarily be expressing the official views of the Fund. This formulation served two purposes. First, it avoided a debate on the appropriateness of the Fund providing such services to a subset of its members without generalizing the offer to the membership as a whole or creating a formal mechanism for conducting regional surveillance. Second, it enabled the Managing Director to maintain both speed and confidentiality in his communications with the G-5. His positions would not be reviewed or approved by the Executive Board, and he would not be obligated to report formally to the Board on confidential meetings. It also had two drawbacks: it reduced, at least at the beginning, the political weight of de Larosière's presence at the meetings, and it precluded active participation by other Fund officials.

---

[21]French President François Mitterrand stated in a press conference following the issuance of the communiqué that "the mere fact of being able to examine interventions on the foreign exchange market, while there previously had been no question of it, is for me a source of satisfaction . . . it is not going as fast as I would like, but it is going much faster than others would wish it to." See Hajnal (1989), p. 199 (French original) and p. 220 (translation, from which the above was slightly modified).

[22]The U.S. official position on exchange market intervention (though not the practice of it) contained an element of ambiguity, or perhaps confusion. According to Jacques Attali, the French Sherpa at Versailles, when President Reagan was challenged during the summit by German Chancellor Helmut Schmitt to take charge of intervening to curb currency fluctuations and the rise of the dollar, Reagan replied, "We agree to intervene on the exchange market; that's settled." Later that day, however, Secretary Regan told reporters that he intended to do nothing to brake the rise of the dollar. See Attali (1993), p. 242 (French original). In practice, U.S. intervention remained virtually nil through 1984.

[23]The invitation was made by Camdessus on behalf of the G-7 countries, shortly after the Helsinki meetings in May.

Toronto, 1982

The Managing Director's role was low-key from the beginning. As it happened, the first G-5 ministerial following the Versailles summit was on September 3, 1982, in Toronto, where the ministers were gathered for the Annual Meetings. The surveillance issues that had seemed so important in the spring had been pushed onto the back burner, and the heat had shifted to the debt crisis and thereby to the increased urgency of the proposed quota increase. Nonetheless, de Larosière was invited to make a presentation to the G-5 on the world economic outlook and the policy requirements for convergence.[24]

The G-5 meeting began at 6:00 p.m. at the Harbour Castle Hotel, following the standard practice of the ministers getting together the evening before the Interim Committee meeting.[25] The first hour or so was devoted to the Managing Director's presentation and the ministers' reactions to it. On this seminal occasion, de Larosière stressed three themes: the policy requirements for convergence toward sustainable growth with low inflation (France being especially out of line); the problems stemming from an inadequate containment of government deficits (the United States being especially out of line); and the need to increase the flexibility of each economy (the European countries being especially out of line).[26] Although the meeting was explicitly designed as a surveillance exercise, the Managing Director deliberately avoided the question of whether exchange rates were misaligned. In doing so, he emphasized that, for the major countries, exchange rate alignment was a byproduct of macroeconomic policies and conditions, and that—at least at this time—what mattered most was getting the right medium-term orientation for those policies.

Much of the ensuing discussion centered on the question that de Larosière had not posed: whether the dollar was becoming overvalued and was likely to reinforce protectionist sentiment. De Larosière agreed with that widely held view—indeed, Regan and Sprinkel were the only ones in the room to express satisfaction with the dollar's rise—and noted the danger posed by the possibility that a too-strong dollar could worsen the U.S. external balance and bring a loss of market confidence. Establishing what would become the standard pattern for such meetings, the Managing Director then left. That is, he was invited only for the first agenda item, surveillance, and not for the ensuing discussion of specific policy options. Thus, while he was able to play a significant role in informing the ministers about the world economic outlook and the Fund's views on policy issues, he was not able to turn

---

[24]The G-5 finance ministers at the time of this meeting were Donald T. Regan (U.S. Treasury Secretary), Geoffrey Howe (U.K. Chancellor of the Exchequer), Michio Watanabe (Japan), Manfred Lahnstein (Germany), and Jacques Delors (France).

[25]Initially, the deputies had considered recommending that the surveillance meetings with the Managing Director be held on an ad hoc basis and be supplemental to the regular semiannual confidential G-5 ministerials. Following the summit conference, however, they decided that for the time being the discussion could be folded into the regular meetings.

[26]Managing Director's background note, in his file "G-10, Vol. I, February 1987–November 1988," in IMF/RD (Accession 88/285, Box 5, Section 250). The French and U.S. economic problems of the time are discussed in Chapter 3.

the occasion into a substantive surveillance exercise, as might have been possible had he been invited to participate throughout the meeting.

Standard practice in the IMF would have called for the Managing Director to report to the Executive Board on important meetings with outside groups such as the G-5 finance ministers. Because the G-5 wished to keep their meetings confidential, however, a formal report would have been impracticable. As noted above, the practice of having the Managing Director participate in his personal capacity had provided a way around this obligation. On the other hand, the Managing Director had no desire to bypass the Board, and he wanted to keep Executive Directors informed as best he could. With that objective in mind, he set up a pair of informal luncheons with groups of Directors in early October, during which he took the opportunity to brief them on his September 3 meeting and to indicate that further such engagements were likely. In this manner, although the Board was not called upon formally to approve the Managing Director's role, Directors were given an informal opportunity to react at an early stage.

The next G-5 ministerial meeting after the Toronto meetings was not seen as calling for a presentation by the Managing Director, although Fund-related topics were high on the agenda. The ministers met at a former royal palace in Kronberg, Germany, in December 1982, where they discussed the Brazilian debt crisis, the proposed quota increase, and a surprising and uncharacteristic proposal by U.S. Treasury Secretary Regan for an international conference on ways to reduce the instability in exchange rates.[27] On each topic, the objective was to develop a common position that could then be presented at wider gatherings. The discussions were therefore private and internal. Whatever input the ministers might have wished from the Managing Director on these issues would have to be sought in other forums or at a later date.

The first opportunity to continue the surveillance exercise came at the end of April 1983. This time the ministers were gathered in Washington on the evening before the Development Committee meeting. The format and the major issues were essentially unchanged from Toronto, with the Managing Director reporting on the world economic outlook and drawing attention to desired policy adjustments. Since the previous September, the main changes in the outlook were that the economic recovery in the United States had accelerated more rapidly than had been foreseen and that French fiscal policy had—just the month before—shifted sharply toward restraint. In these circumstances, the Managing Director emphasized three points: that continued monetary control was essential if inflation was to be held in check, that fiscal deficits had to be further reduced if investment was to recover, and that exchange rates needed to shift so as to "better reflect underlying economic conditions" if world trade and activity were to grow adequately. In particular, monetary growth in France should be further reduced, the United States needed to reduce its fiscal deficit, and—for exchange rate stability as well as for its

---

[27]Regan's proposal was floated to journalists a few days before the meeting. The goal that he reportedly wanted the proposed conference to achieve was "viscosity" of exchange rates. See the *New York Times*, December 7, 1982, p. A1.

own sake—the five countries together needed to converge toward policies that aimed similarly at achieving "sustained and noninflationary growth."

Williamsburg, 1983

As the next summit conference approached, very little progress had been made toward resolving the underlying differences in opinion regarding the costs of exchange rate fluctuations or the relative efficacy of exchange market intervention or policy coordination for reducing fluctuations. On April 29, 1983, the same day as the G-5 meeting described just above, the G-7 finance ministers held a preparatory meeting for the summit.[28] There they received the report on intervention that had been commissioned at Versailles and, after much debate among themselves that one participant later characterized as "group therapy" (Howe, 1994, p. 294), released the report to the public along with a covering statement. The report, which became known as the Jurgensen Report (after Philippe Jurgensen, the Deputy Director of the French Treasury who served as Chair of the Working Group), drew a carefully balanced conclusion (p. 17):

> . . . intervention had been an effective tool in . . . influencing the behaviour of the exchange rate in the short run. Effectiveness had been greater when intervention was unsterilized than when its monetary effects were offset. . . . sterilized intervention did not generally have a lasting effect, but . . . intervention in conjunction with domestic policy changes did have a more durable impact. At the same time, it was recognized that attempts to pursue exchange rate objectives which were inconsistent with the fundamentals through intervention alone tended to be counterproductive.

Nothing in the report suggested that the value of intervention was less than the mainstream of its advocates had suggested, but it did little to bridge the gulf between those advocates and the U.S. opposition. Consequently, the ministers' own statement acknowedged that gulf with unusual frankness ("Views have differed among us . . . and our practices . . . have differed widely") and then announced that they had reached agreement on the following:

A. The achievement of greater exchange rate stability, which does not imply rigidity, is a major objective and commitment of our countries.

B. The path to greater exchange rate stability must lie in the direction of compatible mixes of policies. . . .

C. In the formulation of our domestic economic and financial policies, our countries should have regard to the behavior of exchange rates. . . .

D. Under present circumstances, the role of intervention can only be limited. Intervention can be useful to counter disorderly market conditions and to reduce short-term volatility . . . while retaining our freedom to operate independently, [we] are willing to undertake coordinated intervention in instances where it is agreed that such intervention would be helpful.

---

[28]This meeting appears to have been the first in which the G-7 finance ministers met as a separate group rather than as the G-5 or as part of the full sherpa group planning the summit; see Garavoglia (1984), p. 34. It was, however, not a shift in structure, but rather an ad hoc event to release the intervention study commissioned by the summit countries.

The first three clauses were little more than a repetition of the Versailles communiqué, while the fourth was an attempt to resolve the debate over intervention. As the final sentence illustrates, however, with its curious reference to "retaining our freedom" (as if that had ever been in doubt), the ministers had in effect agreed to continue to disagree.

Shortly after the G-7 meeting, French President Mitterrand took up the stable-exchange-rate cause during a soirée at the Élysée palace for ministers of finance and foreign affairs attending the annual ministerial Council meeting of the OECD in Paris. After noting that the G-7 had agreed to act together when necessary to counter volatility in exchange rates, he concluded that "the time has come to think of a new Bretton Woods . . . organized . . . at the highest level, in the framework of the International Monetary Fund." Since Secretary Regan had made essentially the same suggestion five months earlier and reportedly expressed support for Mitterrand's proposal,[29] it was beginning to appear that the French and the Americans were moving closer together on the key issue of the need for an international monetary system founded on a new set of rules. Over the next few years, however, the U.S. position would continue to vacillate.

The language of the ministerial communiqué was repeated in abbreviated form in the communiqué issued at the conclusion of the Williamsburg summit, complete with the insistence that each country would retain its freedom in determining intervention policy (Hajnal, 1989, pp. 234–40). The summit conference, held in the historic reconstructed village of Williamsburg, Virginia, at the end of May 1983, reaffirmed the procedural innovations introduced at Versailles a year earlier and promised that the "consultation process" would be "enhanced to promote convergence of economic performance . . . and greater stability of exchange rates." As for a "new Bretton Woods"? The leaders asked the finance ministers, "in consultation with the Managing Director of the IMF, to define the conditions for improving the international monetary system and to consider the part *which might, in due course,* be played in this process by a high-level international monetary conference" (emphasis added). The fire that Secretary Regan had lit in December and whose flames President Mitterrand had stoked in May had not exactly been snuffed out, but the embers were now untended at the back of the hearth.[30]

---

[29]Attali (1993), p. 449, quotes from a May 18 letter from Regan to Mitterrand declaring his support. Four days earlier, however, Regan was described by *The Times* of London (May 14, 1983, p. 11) as having "poured cold water over" Mitterrand's call for a "Bretton Woods No. 2."

[30]Similar suggestions emanated from both within and without the G-7. Japanese officials expressed interest at that time in strengthening the system so as to limit exchange rate volatility, though no specific scheme was endorsed as official government policy. In May 1983 (in a speech in Toronto before the Financial Analysts' Federation), Toyoo Gyohten—the Japanese delegate on the Jurgensen committee and later the Finance Deputy at G-5 and G-7 meetings—advanced a proposal for a joint intervention account to be established by three or more of the largest countries and to be managed so as to apply pressure for policy convergence. In September 1983, the G-24 ministers issued a communiqué calling for "the convening of an international monetary conference" as a step in securing "a thorough-going reform of the international monetary and financial system" aimed at, inter alia, stabilizing exchange rates (paragraph 21); *IMF Survey* (October 10, 1983), p. 299.

The Managing Director's third meeting with the G-5 ministers came at Blair House on September 24, 1983, in the margins of the Annual Meetings in Washington. The IMF staff's preparations for these G-5 events had now developed into a regular production effort. An ad hoc interdepartmental working group had been formed to draft a paper on economic developments and policy options, which would be circulated to participants ahead of the meeting and would serve as a background note for the Managing Director's remarks. In addition, the staff would prepare an extensive set of tables and charts on macroeconomic developments in each of the five countries. These tables and charts (vernacularly known as the "Versailles tables") included annual data for the past several years and IMF staff projections for the current and following year on output, prices, and a wide range of financial variables. Overall, the data were intended to be commensurate across countries, except for policy measures such as monetary aggregates and fiscal deficits, where the officials preferred to use national definitions.

The Versailles tables, along with the background paper, were circulated to the deputies three or four weeks ahead of each ministerial meeting to facilitate discussion and concentrate attention on key areas where convergence was lacking. Unfortunately, the right formula had not yet been found for reconciling the conflicting goals of comprehensiveness and conciseness. More than forty data series were included, forming an intimidating thicket of numbers from which the crucial kernel could scarcely be extracted. The circulated material thus was too diffuse to succeed fully in stimulating or focusing discussion of the Managing Director's remarks to the ministers. As before, at the September 1983 meeting the Managing Director presented his assessment of the economic situation facing these countries and emphasized that fiscal policies should be aimed at the crucial objective of lowering interest rates to bring about a revival of private sector activity. He then answered a number of questions, but as usual he was not invited to stay through the more substantive policy debates.[31]

Meanwhile, the summit directive to finance ministers to "define the conditions for improving the international monetary system" was taken up by the G-10 ministers and governors at their September 1983 meeting, at the request of their Chairman, Jacques Delors (France). Although the G-7 had undertaken the study of intervention policy the year before, the ministers did not wish to set up a more permanent bureaucracy in competition with the others to which they already belonged, and the G-10 was the natural choice for the task at hand. Following a discussion in which the Managing Director took part, the G-10 instructed their deputies, chaired by Lamberto Dini of the Bank of Italy,[32] to "identify the areas in which progressive improvements may be sought" and to report back to the minis-

---

[31]For an account of this meeting, see Lawson (1992), p. 515.

[32]Central bank governors play a more substantive role in the G-10 than in the G-5 or the G-7. At ministerial meetings in the two smaller groups, participation is generally limited to the finance minister, the minister's deputy, and the governor; preparation for the meetings is the responsibility of the ministers' deputies. In the G-10, the preparatory role is shared between the governors' and ministers' deputies. See also footnotes 5 and 6, p. 187.

ters and governors in the spring of 1984.[33] This instruction would lead to a thorough study by the deputies, including recommendations on how to strengthen the functioning of the system and the role that IMF surveillance might play in that regard. What remained to be seen was whether those recommendations would include substantive changes or be limited to window dressing.

London, 1984

Little was said about surveillance at the London summit in June 1984, and little progress was made that year toward strengthening the multilateral process. The G-10 deputies submitted a progress report to their ministers and governors in May 1984, but no agreement was in sight on the most contentious issues on the roles of intervention and other means of stabilizing exchange rates. The French deputies (Camdessus and Gabriel J.A. LeFort, deputy governor of the Banque de France) were pushing to include a favorable finding on some concrete means of inducing exchange rates toward consistency with economic conditions, preferably in the form of "target zones": commitments to try to keep exchange rates within specified ranges, through intervention and policy convergence (Williamson, 1985; Williamson and Miller, 1987). Some of the smaller countries in the group seemed open to the idea, but the other G-5 countries were opposed. The London summit communiqué (see Hajnal, 1989, pp. 258–65) took no position and merely asked that the project be continued.

The Managing Director met once with the G-5 ministers, at Blair House in Washington in April 1984, but he was not invited to the September meeting. By that time, the appreciation of the U.S. dollar had reached alarming levels with no end in sight, and the Reagan administration was coming under increasing pressure to relax its stance against intervention. Secretary Regan, as the host of the meeting, decided not to include the standard surveillance session with the Managing Director, and during the meeting he again rejected his peers' requests for coordinated intervention (Lawson, 1992, p. 530).

The Executive Board held its annual review of the implementation of surveillance for 1984 in March, and the role of surveillance with the G-7 countries was a key issue for discussion. The background staff paper noted the Managing Director's participation in the G-5 meetings and reported on the Managing Director's efforts to focus attention on domestic policy adjustments for convergence and stability over the medium term.[34] Directors agreed that policy convergence was important for stability and that to monitor convergence required examining the

---

[33]Communiqué of the ministerial meeting of the Group of Ten, Washington, September 24, 1983; in *IMF Survey*, Vol. 12, No. 19 (October 10, 1983), p. 294. The decision to assign the task to the G-10 deputies was taken earlier, through bilateral contacts between Delors and his peers. It was taken up informally by the deputies at a meeting on September 15 and then formalized by ministers on September 24.

[34]"Review of the Document 'Surveillance Over Exchange Rate Policies' and Annual Review of the Implementation of Surveillance," SM/84/44 (February 15), p. 17.

whole spectrum of macroeconomic policies in each country. Nigel Wicks (United Kingdom) noted that when fiscal and monetary policies were "tugging in opposite directions," assessing the level of the exchange rate was especially difficult. Wicks concluded that with the application of a range of surveillance tools, including "the Managing Director's various informal contacts," the Fund could play a role in "steering domestic policy developments in a desirable direction." The benefits of the Managing Director's role in the G-5 meetings were also acknowledged by Ghassem Salekhou (Iran). Other Directors, however, were more skeptical. E.I.M. Mtei (Tanzania) argued that "the Fund had not yet devised an effective mechanism for making surveillance over the exchange rates and other policies of the large industrial and other surplus countries effective." The national interests of the G-7 countries frequently diverged, and he found it unlikely that policy coordination could be achieved without clearly defined rules.

The U.S. Executive Director, Richard D. Erb, also raised fundamental concerns about the application of multilateral surveillance, in an intervention that clearly suggested the skepticism toward international coordination that pervaded the U.S. Treasury under Secretary Regan.[35] Erb called into question two frequently made arguments for using surveillance to promote policy convergence. First, he argued that what was needed was convergence of economic conditions toward sustainable growth with stable prices; the policy requirements for achieving that goal might differ substantially from one country to another. In contrast to the view often expressed by the staff and by other Directors, he saw little evidence that exchange rate instability could be explained by countries adopting different mixes of monetary and fiscal policy.[36] This argument implied that the shift in the mix of U.S. policies in the early 1980s toward slower monetary growth and larger fiscal deficits need not be considered inconsistent with the radically different strategies being pursued by Germany and Japan. Second, the difficulty the major countries had experienced in achieving convergent economic conditions did not, in the U.S. view, result from a failure to take full account of the implications of their policies for other countries. If countries were independently to pursue policies that were in their own long-term interests, the international ramifications would generally be positive. In this view, the problem was rather that countries found it difficult to implement the policies that were in their own long-term interests.

With the largest member country reluctant to engage in exchange market intervention and skeptical of the value of policy coordination, there was little that the other G-5 countries or the IMF could do to strengthen the multilateral surveillance process. In the event, however, 1984 would be the dark hour before the dawn of a more cooperative spirit.

---

[35]Minutes of EBM/84/40 (March 12, 1984), pp. 5–6 and 14.

[36]The staff view, as expressed in the background paper, was as follows: "Experience in recent years suggests that, at least for the major industrial countries, recourse to a domestic policy stance that fails to take account of the implications for other countries has often been a more serious problem than the implementation of policies designed to manipulate exchange rates or the international monetary system." See "Review of the Document 'Surveillance Over Exchange Rate Policies' and Annual Review of the Implementation of Surveillance," SM/84/44 (February 15), p. 15.

Cooperation and Coordination: 1985–87

Bonn, 1985

The atmosphere for multilateral surveillance improved dramatically in the early months of 1985, largely out of necessity, as the view took hold that exchange rates had to be stabilized. Currency speculation—unrelated to the requirements of international trade and even going well beyond what could reasonably be attributed to the financial effects of differences in the mix of macroeconomic policies—was now almost totally controlling movements in exchange rates and was preventing the normal conduct of international economic policy. In the parlance of the times, exchange rate movements were judged to be "unrelated to the fundamentals," disrupting trade and inflaming pressures for protectionist policies. For the five months through late February 1985, the deutsche mark depreciated against the U.S. dollar by nearly 15 percent, to a record level of 3.47 marks per dollar; the Japanese yen, by more than 7 percent, to 263 yen per dollar; and the pound sterling, by close to 20 percent, to an all-time low of $1.04 per pound.[37] This bubble would surely burst, but when and with what force was the question that was echoing around the globe.

Threatened with a potentially calamitous currency panic, the German finance minister, Gerhard Stoltenberg, asked for a January meeting of the G-5 ministers to try to get the group to shift to a more actively cooperative approach. Now that the presidential elections were over in the United States, the chances for action to reduce the U.S. fiscal deficit were improved. That possibility might induce markets to reinforce an official nudge to reduce the cost of the dollar. Regan agreed to call a meeting, which was fixed for January 17 at the U.S. Treasury in Washington.[38] For the first time since the previous April, the Managing Director was invited for part of the all-day meeting, to make a 30-minute presentation on the outlook and on the key surveillance issues and to answer questions. He again stressed the need for a correction in U.S. fiscal policy as the basic underlying requirement for lasting stability in exchange rates and economic conditions. Whatever thoughts the ministers might have had in reaction to this injunction, their immediate purpose lay more in examining the art of the possible-in-the-short-run: what could they do now to foster a realignment of exchange rates? For the moment, what was needed was not so much surveillance as a common will to act.

---

[37]The extent to which exchange rates respond to purely speculative forces rather than to information on—and rational expectations of—economic policies and conditions was, and still is, controversial, because the effect of such "fundamentals" is difficult to measure. By any standard, however, the currency movements experienced in the last quarter of 1984 and the first month or two of 1985 were extreme outliers. The Fund staff conducted econometric tests of the behavior of the real effective exchange rate of the dollar as a background study for the 1985 Article IV consultations with the United States. That study concluded that "a substantial portion of the real appreciation of the dollar, particularly in the second half of 1984, remains unexplained." See "United States—Recent Economic Developments," SM/85/209, Sup. 1 (July 22, 1985), Appendix IX.

[38]This meeting is described in Lawson (1992), pp. 473–75, and in Volcker and Gyohten (1992), p. 240. Additional information is from interviews with participants.

For four years, the will to act together had been blocked by a U.S. policy stance founded on independence and opposition to intervention. In January 1985, the European members of the G-5 presented a united front for coordinated action. The three delegations—led by Stoltenberg for Germany, Pierre Bérégovoy for France, and Nigel Lawson for the United Kingdom—breakfasted together on January 17 before going to the meeting with the United States and Japan (Lawson, 1992, p. 473). At the treasury, the U.S. team was still headed by Regan, but this would be his last G-5 meeting. That evening, Paul A. Volcker, Chairman of the Federal Reserve System, held a dinner for the participants at the Federal Reserve headquarters. James A. Baker III, President Reagan's chief of staff, attended as a special guest; Baker and Regan had just won the president's approval to swap jobs, so Regan was introducing his successor to his G-5 colleagues. At the very moment when the Europeans were most eager to persuade the United States to change its stance on international economic cooperation, the U.S. baton was being passed to a man who would soon gain a reputation as a mastermind of policy coordination.[39]

The January meeting produced a commitment "to work toward greater exchange market stability." The text of the communiqué did not go beyond the vague commitments made earlier in the G-7 summit communiqués, but the mere fact that the G-5 finance ministers were willing for the first time to issue a public joint statement on the subject was seen as a major step forward. The signal was thus given that the period of benign neglect was over. The immediate goal of the G-5 in mid-January was to stop the free fall of the pound sterling, not necessarily to reverse the course of the dollar. Nonetheless, the meeting set the stage for what would soon be large-scale coordinated exchange market intervention to halt the dollar's appreciation. The European central banks took the lead in that effort, starting shortly after the January 17 meeting, and the U.S. Federal Reserve jumped in within a few days. In less than two months and after some $10 billion in official intervention by the central banks of the G-7,[40] the direction of the dollar was finally reversed around the end of February.

By April 1985, with the dollar firmly in retreat from its unsustainable heights, attention could be turned again to the longer-run question of how best to prevent such extreme swings in exchange rates. The G-10 deputies were in the final stages of drafting their report on the functioning of the international monetary system, and attention had to turn to the question of how to assess and carry out the recommendations that might be forthcoming. One possibility was to resuscitate the Regan-Mitterrand strange-bedfellow proposal for a "new Bretton Woods" conference. First in the ministerial Council of the OECD and then in the Interim Com-

---

[39]Destler and Henning (1989), Chapter 3, explain Baker's willingness to work toward greater cooperation as motivated largely by domestic political pressures, driven by the adverse effects of the strong dollar on the U.S. business sector. De Larosière (1992) discusses the strengthening of the coordination process after Baker replaced Regan.

[40]Volcker, in Volcker and Gyohten (1992), p. 240, indicates that the Federal Reserve accounted for $660 million of a $10 billion total by early March, the biggest participant having been the Deutsche Bundesbank ($4.8 billion). For an account of day-to-day intervention, see Dominguez and Frankel (1993), pp. 11–13, 88–90, and 150–51.

mittee, Secretary Baker floated that idea. As he put it at the Interim Committee meeting on April 18, the United States was

> prepared to consider the possible value of hosting a high-level meeting of the major industrial countries, following the conclusion of the [G-10] studies, in order to review the various issues involved in transforming their findings into appropriate action. Such a meeting could provide further impetus to strengthening the international monetary system through the IMF, in particular through the upcoming review of the G-10 studies by the IMF's Interim Committee.[41]

Baker's call for a high-level conference was again supported by the G-24 ministers[42] but nonetheless drew little support within the Interim Committee. The proposal was not included in the communiqué, and both Nigel Lawson (United Kingdom) and Onno Ruding (Netherlands) tried to dissuade Baker from pursuing the idea.[43] The Bonn summit conference was held a few weeks afterward (May 2–4, 1985). That communiqué took note of the continuing work of the G-10 on ways to improve the functioning of the international monetary system, but it did not mention any follow-up strategy other than for the Interim Committee to discuss the forthcoming report. By June, when the G-10 ministers were to meet in Tokyo, Baker had apparently abandoned the plan for a general conference in favor of organizing a coordinated (though ad hoc) strategy to manage exchange rates within the G-5. Despite that shift, the G-24 ministers again called for a conference, proposing in October that reforms be considered by "a representative committee of Ministers from developing and industrial countries, which could perhaps take the form of a joint subcommittee of both the Interim and Development Committees."[44]

Inside the IMF in the first months of 1985, attention was directed at changes to the practice of surveillance with the large industrial countries that might help to promote stability within the existing system. A February 1985 staff paper prepared for the annual review of the implementation of surveillance floated the idea that a system of "objective indicators" might help to strengthen multilateral surveillance by focusing attention on the data that mattered most.[45] Although the list of

---

[41]Statements made at the Interim Committee Meetings, Washington, D.C., April 17–19, 1985; Master File in IMF/CF.

[42]G-24 communiqué (April 16, 1985), paragraph 69; in *IMF Survey* (April 29, 1985), p. 137. See also footnote 30, p. 198.

[43]Baker's proposal at the OECD ministerial, and the reactions of Lawson and Ruding, were reported to the Managing Director by the Fund's observer at the meeting. Cable to the Managing Director from Aldo Guetta (April 12, 1985); in IMF/RD Managing Director file "G-10 January–May 1985" (Accession 87/136, Box 4, Section 168). Lawson's reaction is also described in Lawson (1992), p. 533. At the Interim Committee meeting, Baker told Camdessus privately that he favored the idea of trying to keep exchange rates within reasonable bounds as long as countries were not publicly committed to defending specific ranges.

[44]G-24 Communiqué (October 5, 1985); in *IMF Survey* (October 28, 1985), p. 313.

[45]"Enhancing the Effectiveness of Surveillance: The 1985 Annual Review of the Implementation of Surveillance," SM/85/65 (February 22, 1985), pp. 29–30. The case for indicators as part of a process for coordinating macroeconomic policies may also be found in Crockett (1988). The concept of objective indicators as the basis for IMF surveillance originated in a November 1972 paper by Paul Volcker and J. Dewey Daane, prepared in their capacity as U.S. deputies to the

specific indicators was yet to be specified, the idea was similar to the way perform-ance criteria are used in Fund-supported adjustment programs, albeit without the *requirement* of a policy response. If, for example, a country would indicate that it wanted to see its money stock growing at a rate within a specified range, then movements outside that range could trigger discussions of the policy adjustments that would be needed to restore balance.

When the Executive Board conducted its surveillance review in late March 1985, Directors generally reacted favorably in principle but skeptically in practice to the systematic use of objective indicators. The U.S. and French positions were the bookends, as they often were when exchange rate stability was on the agenda. The French Director, Bruno de Maulde, strongly supported the proposal but ex-pressed concern that not enough emphasis was given by the staff to what in his view was the central role of the exchange rate itself as an indicator. At the other extreme, the U.S. Director, Charles H. Dallara, criticized the proposal as not be-ing "particularly feasible or realistic," since countries without need of Fund re-sources might also feel no need for Fund policy advice. In between, most Directors who addressed the issue regarded objective indicators as worth trying but as un-likely to produce any significant changes in the practice of Fund surveillance. Without a clear mandate, the Managing Director concluded "that, for the time be-ing at least, the use of such indicators in particular cases where they might be ap-propriate and acceptable would be limited to providing a basis for reviewing, in the course of an Article IV consultation, developments against the background of the conclusion of the previous one."[46]

Meanwhile, the G-10 report on the functioning of the international monetary system and a parallel report by the G-24 deputies[47] were being circulated and dis-cussed. The G-10 deputies met in Paris in April, in Basel in May, and in Tokyo in June to finalize their report. Although the French team kept battling to include support for target zones for exchange rates, they were continually defeated by an op-

---

Committee of Twenty and submitted to the Committee as an official U.S. proposal. For the back-ground and context, see de Vries (1985), pp. 165–69. The paper, reprinted in U.S. Council of Economic Advisers (1973), summarized the proposal as follows (p. 163):

> Without objective indicators there is a danger that needed actions [to reduce external imbal-ances] will not be taken. It is much better to get advance agreement in principle that when certain internationally agreed indicators, recognized as being objective, signal adjustment is needed, there will be a strong presumption that appropriate measures will be adopted—but recognizing there might be valid reasons for overriding the indicators in exceptional cases.

[46]Minutes of EBM/85/48 (March 22, 1985), pp. 16 (Dallara) and 31 (de Maulde); and EBM/85/49 (March 25), p. 10 (summing up).

[47]The G-10 and G-24 reports are reproduced, as Appendix I and II, respectively, in Crockett and Goldstein (1987). The G-24 report was commissioned by the Chairman of the G-24 ministers, Juan V. Sourrouille of Argentina, on May 28, 1985. He appointed Arjun Sengupta—Executive Director (India) in the Fund—to chair a working group to prepare a draft report by end-July, and in the interests of time he authorized the deputies to act on behalf of the ministers and transmit the report directly to the Interim Committee. The staff of the Fund provided infor-mal assistance to the G-24 for the preparation of this report. (The background to the G-10 re-port is discussed above, on pp. 199–200.)

position led by U.S. deputy David C. Mulford. The U.S. authorities opposed target zones because they believed that private financial markets should be left alone to determine the exchange rate. They were joined by German officials (especially from the Bundesbank) who were opposed to any proposal that would require intervention to supersede domestic monetary control as a guide for central bank policy.

The G-10 finance ministers and central bank governors, with the Managing Director participating, met in Tokyo on June 21 to discuss the report and release it for publication. Two months later (August 19–21), the G-24 deputies met at IMF headquarters in Washington, completed work on their report, and issued the approved text to the Interim Committee on behalf of their ministers. That report noted the importance of exchange rate stability for developing countries and took a more favorable stance toward the adoption of target zones. The Interim Committee agreed to hold a preliminary discussion of both reports at its October 1985 meeting in Seoul, Korea, after which it would ask the Executive Board to prepare a report so that ministers could try to come to some conclusions at the next meeting.

As the summer of 1985 drew to a close, a variety of efforts thus were under way to reform the international monetary system. At the same time, more ad hoc efforts were being made to deal with the immediate problem of exchange rate misalignment through coordination of policies. Ultimately the success of the short-term effort would draw attention away from the more structural proposals and would even be seen as obviating the need for systemic reforms.

Plaza, 1985

The coordination effort began in great secrecy in June 1985, which for a time precluded any role for the IMF. This part of the story is recounted here because it helped resolve the systemic issues that had been debated since Versailles and because it laid the foundations for a later strengthening of the Fund's role in multilateral surveillance.

Baker's G-5 deputy, Mulford,[48] initiated the process by meeting with his Japanese counterpart, Tomomitsu Oba, the day before the ministerial meetings opened in Tokyo. Mulford informed Oba that Baker intended to propose a G-5 program to induce a further depreciation of the U.S. dollar. Oba was immediately receptive to the idea—as was the finance minister, Noboru Takeshita, when Baker raised it with him a day or two later—recognizing that the prevailing exchange rates were making it ever more difficult to control their large and growing current account surplus. Nonetheless, the seed would have to grow in the dark for a while before being transplanted more openly. It was not on the agenda at the private G-5 meeting on June 20, nor at the announced G-10 meeting on the 21st, nor for Baker's bilateral talks with the other G-5 ministers. Furthermore, although de Larosière

---

[48]The deputy responsibilities under Secretary Baker were shared between Mulford (Assistant Secretary of the Treasury for International Affairs) and Richard G. Darman (Deputy Secretary). Mulford was the delegate to meetings of the G-5 deputies. See Funabashi (1988), pp. 145–47, for a discussion of the political ramifications.

was in Tokyo from the 19th for the G-10 meeting, he was not invited to participate in the G-5 meeting and was not informed of the Baker initiative.[49]

In August, following further discussions with Japanese officials, Baker telephoned each of the other G-5 ministers to seek their support for holding a special meeting to coordinate a realignment of exchange rates. He asked them not to inform their central bank governors until the planning was well under way and suggested that their deputies meet to develop a detailed plan. Because of the extreme sensitivity of the endeavor, however, the deputies did not initially meet in their usual joint format. Over the next few weeks, Mulford and Richard Darman met bilaterally with Oba, Hans Tietmeyer (Stoltenberg's deputy), Geoffrey Littler (Lawson's deputy), and Daniel Lebègue (Bérégovoy's deputy). In early September, Mulford and Tietmeyer flew to Heathrow Airport outside London, where they met secretly with Littler to draw up the outlines of a draft communiqué. Finally, on September 15, all five deputies spent a full day in London drafting a communiqué and a discussion paper for the ministerial meeting.[50]

By September 1985, the effective exchange rate for the U.S. dollar had depreciated by 8½ percent from its February peak, but it was still generally acknowledged to be well above the range considered to be compatible with desirable or sustainable current account balances. Moreover, the decline had stopped in late August and had shown an alarming reversal during the first half of September. The finance deputies, having all lived through the seemingly irresistible rise of the dollar just a few months before, needed little convincing that a concerted effort might be required to nudge exchange rates in the right direction. They therefore concluded that a 10–12 percent further depreciation of the dollar against each of the other G-5 currencies was to be encouraged through coordinated official exchange-market intervention and backed up by a commitment by each country to pursue appropriate monetary and fiscal policies.

The ministerial meeting was to be held at the Plaza Hotel in New York on Sunday, September 22, 1985. As the weekend approached, no one except those immediately involved knew that the meeting was being planned. Even most of the central bank governors were kept in the dark, as was the Managing Director.[51] On

---

[49]The bilateral U.S.-Japan talks are described in Funabashi (1988), p. 11. The importance of the Tokyo meetings in setting the stage for the Plaza meeting in September is discussed by Gyohten in Volcker and Gyohten (1992), p. 251. Additional information is from background interviews with participants.

[50]For published accounts, see Funabashi (1988), p. 13, and Volcker and Gyohten (1992), p. 244 (Volcker's account) and pp. 253–54 (Gyohten's).

[51]Baker informed Volcker in August and asked for (but did not get) an assurance that U.S. monetary policy would not be tightened to counteract the intended depreciation. From that point, Volcker was heavily involved in the planning. Camdessus, then governor of the Banque de France, was peripherally involved. President Reagan was not informed until a day or two before the meeting; see Volcker and Gyohten (1992), pp. 242–43. The president of the Bundesbank, Karl Otto Pöhl, also learned of the meeting just days before, when Tietmeyer telephoned him in San Francisco (where Pöhl was attending a conference). Pöhl was angered by the slight and was persuaded not to rebel only after a breakfast meeting with Volcker and Camdessus on Sunday. Camdessus informed an unhappy de Larosière on Saturday that the meeting was scheduled, and Volcker debriefed him over lunch on Monday. The U.S. and French delegates, respectively, informed their excluded counterparts from Canada and Italy during the weekend.

Saturday, the three European finance ministers from the G-5 were in Luxembourg with their colleagues from other EC countries at their regular informal monthly meeting. Saturday evening, around the same time as the press were being notified in New York that a meeting would be held the next day, they notified the others of what was about to take place. They then flew on the Concorde to New York on Sunday morning, arriving in time for the 11 a.m. meeting.

The Plaza meeting lasted most of the afternoon. At its closure, the ministers and central bank governors issued a lengthy communiqué concluding that "some further orderly appreciation of the main nondollar currencies against the dollar is desirable" and announcing that they stood "ready to cooperate more closely to encourage this when to do so would be helpful." The tortured prose in the first clause was necessary to avoid the psychologically troubling idea of encouraging a dollar depreciation. Volcker, in particular, was concerned about the possibility of a *disorderly* depreciation that might be difficult to control.[52] The shunning of the word "intervention" in the second clause was more curious, since all five countries were now clearly prepared to intervene in the foreign exchange markets to achieve this objective. Without necessarily downplaying that commitment, the vague wording served to draw attention to the additional commitments to cooperate in getting monetary, fiscal, and structural policies right.

To understand the way the international financial system evolved in the post-Plaza period, one must first understand what the Plaza accord did and did not do. The most concrete agreement to emerge from the meeting was a specific joint commitment to intervene to achieve a realignment of exchange rates. That agreement was not the beginning of the process; the five countries had informally carried out joint intervention several times in the preceding months (Dominguez and Frankel, 1993, pp. 11–13). Nor did it dramatically change the direction or even the magnitude of the trend movements in exchange rates, although it may have prevented the dollar's depreciation from stalling. It did not represent a change in the structure of the G-5 process (the ministers and governors had been meeting for years, and the first communiqué was issued after the Washington meeting in January 1985), nor in the relationship between the G-5 and the IMF in overseeing the system. It did not even generate specific commitments to coordinate monetary policies. What the Plaza accord did was establish a basis for major-country cooperation in which the roles of intervention and underlying domestic policy adjustments were clearly and properly delineated. Although many of the policy commitments of the Plaza eventually died on the vine, the seed was now planted in the sunshine. At least on paper, the Plaza accord finally resolved the decades-old Franco-American intervention-convergence debate by recognizing that policy convergence was necessary but not sufficient for exchange rate stability.

---

[52]"The possibility at some point that sentiment toward the dollar could change adversely, with sharp repercussions in the exchange rate in a downward direction, poses the greatest potential threat to the progress that we have made against inflation" (Volcker, 1985, p. 695). Volcker had witnessed at close hand the disorderly attack on the dollar's parity in the early 1970s, when he was Under Secretary of the U.S. Treasury for Monetary Affairs.

The Plaza accord also made possible a strengthening and deepening of the role of the IMF in the multilateral surveillance process. Since the Versailles summit three years earlier, the process had amounted to a half-dozen ministerial meetings at which the Managing Director had presented his views on economic conditions and macroeconomic policy options. At no time had de Larosière felt it to be appropriate to suggest "right" levels for exchange rates, although he had supported the view that the strength being shown by the U.S. dollar at the time was harmful and unsustainable. In part this reluctance reflected the inherent ambiguities in assessing the market levels of floating exchange rates; in part it reflected a desire to concentrate more on underlying domestic policies. The deeper problem, then, was that the format did not provide him an opportunity to question the ministers systematically regarding their policy intentions. If the surveillance process was to be effective, there would have to be feedback and follow-up.

The first chance to sharpen the pencil came soon after the Plaza, at the Annual Meetings in Seoul in early October. The G-5 ministers met with the Managing Director on the Saturday afternoon preceding the formal meetings, October 5, at the Hilton Hotel. Reminiscent of the first such gathering in Toronto three years earlier, the ministerial minds were engaged more on debt than on policy cooperation, this time because the Baker Plan (see Chapter 10) was about to be unveiled. Nonetheless, de Larosière took the opportunity provided by the post-Plaza cooperative spirit to go beyond the now-routine litany by posing specific questions. For example, how far was the U.S. Federal Reserve now prepared to go in directing monetary policy at the exchange rate? When and by how much did the German authorities intend to implement tax reductions in 1986? How might Japanese policies respond if the correction in the yen-dollar exchange rate were to be reversed? The object was not to interrogate or to attempt to pry answers loose, but to direct attention to key issues that could be pursued in more detail in the forthcoming Article IV consultations. The result was a more substantive and concrete exchange of views than had been possible before.

Tokyo, 1986

By the beginning of 1986, the primary concern for the major countries was that economic growth was slowing, especially in the United States. As the Managing Director had noted at the October 1985 G-5 ministerial meeting, growth in both Germany and Japan had been sustained by strong external demand. As U.S. growth slowed, prospects for those and other countries would weaken as well. The use of tax cuts or public spending to stimulate growth was effectively ruled out because of the poor state of public finances, so the burden was on monetary policy. Aggregate demand and the demand for petroleum in particular were weak enough that interest rates could be lowered without rekindling inflation, but could the cuts be coordinated so as not to disrupt the exchange rate stability that was finally being achieved?

Engineering a coordinated reduction in interest rates proved to be quite difficult, and that experience led to the next (and apparently final) effort to develop a more formal IMF-related structure for coordinating policies. The first serious move to put interest rate reduction on the G-5 agenda came at a ministerial meeting in London on January 18–19, 1986.[53] The surface problem in winning agreement on a coordinated reduction was the opposition of central bank governors, especially Volcker (see Volcker and Gyohten, 1992, p. 247). In addition, there was a structural problem in that the G-5 meetings were essentially meetings of finance ministers, not all of whom had authority to effect the changes in monetary policy that would in turn move interest rates. Although the central bank governors participated in the meetings, their deputies did not participate in the preparatory meetings where the agendas were fixed and the background papers and communiqués were drafted. This structure conveyed a measure of political authority and camaraderie to the meetings, but it also limited the scope for action. In France and the United Kingdom, the governors served under the finance minister and the chancellor, respectively. The other three governors, however, were more independent, would not generally have felt bound by ministerial agreements, and in any case might not have been able to convince their own governing boards to carry out an agreed policy.

A few weeks after the London G-5 meeting, Volcker and Karl Otto Pöhl (president of the Deutsche Bundesbank) met privately during the monthly meeting of the BIS governors in Basel, Switzerland, and agreed to propose interest rate reductions to their respective boards.[54] By this time, the pressure to act was becoming severe for both men. Volcker was facing an internal revolt in the Federal Reserve Board over his opposition to a unilateral cut in the U.S. discount rate, and the monthly discussions of U.S. and German policies among governors at the BIS were becoming pointed and heated. The bilateral agreement between Volcker and Pöhl enabled a round of interest rate cuts by all the G-5 central banks, starting on March 6, 1986.[55] That achievement, however, was an ad hoc event that did not represent a breakthrough in the G-5's ability to coordinate policies for the commonweal.

While the G-5 was thus stumbling along the path to recovery in the spring of 1986, its existence as the primary forum for multilateral surveillance was coming to an end. Italy, where resentment at being excluded had remained strong ever since the G-5 had taken the reins at Versailles in 1982, was insisting that the G-7 was the proper grouping for this purpose. The Bank of Italy, despite Italy's exclusion from the Plaza meeting, had participated fully in the ensuing intervention exercise.[56] By early

---

[53]For accounts of this meeting, see Funabashi (1988), pp. 43–44, and Lawson (1992), pp. 543–44.

[54]See Funabashi (1988), p. 47. Additional information from background interviews.

[55]Between the Volcker-Pöhl meeting and the announcement of the interest rate cuts, Volcker was very nearly forced into a unilateral reduction of U.S. rates. On February 24, four of the seven members of the Federal Reserve Board (dubbed the "Gang of Four") forced and won a vote over Volcker's opposition, to accept a cut in the discount rate from 7.5 percent to 7 percent. The four agreed to reverse the decision only after Volcker promised to seek the coordinated reduction that he had already negotiated in secret. See Volcker and Gyohten (1992), p. 274; and, for a contemporary news account, Kilborn (1986).

[56]According to Funabashi (1988), p. 20, the proposal from the G-5 deputies had been that Germany would be responsible for 25 percent of the intervention needed to bring about the desired realignment, with France carrying a 10 percent share. At the Plaza, however, the ministers and governors modified the plan to give the EMS countries a collective 35 percent share. Italy thus became involved as a member of the EMS. Earlier, Italy had participated in the coordinated intervention of February 1985 that had been initiated by the G-5 (see pp. 202–03, above).

1986, the prime minister, Bettino Craxi, was able to win President Reagan's support for the creation of a G-7 finance minister's group. Craxi had built up a measure of political capital with the United States by banning weapons sales to Libya in support of the U.S. trade embargo and by allowing NATO missiles to be based on Sicily. He also felt strongly enough about the matter to have a credible threat to withdraw altogether from the summit process if Italy continued to be excluded from the financial meetings.[57] Baker, alone among G-5 ministers, liked the idea of expanding to the full G-7, because it would link the ministerial meetings to the summit process and because it was likely to strengthen support for U.S. positions by bringing in Canada.[58] The G-5 ministers reluctantly approved the idea in April (subject to an informal agreement among themselves to continue to meet as the Five alongside the larger group), and the creation of the G-7 finance ministers was formally announced in the communiqué of the Tokyo summit conference in May.[59] Thus de Larosière's surveillance meeting with the G-5 ministers on April 8, 1986—the eighth such assembly in four years—was intended to be the last in this form.

Also around the beginning of 1986, both the IMF and the G-7 were developing responses to the reports of the G-10 and G-24 deputies on the functioning of the international monetary system. These responses would further strengthen the multilateral surveillance process, though without bringing about systemic reforms. Within the IMF, the Research Department prepared an evaluation of the two reports, which was discussed by the Executive Board on February 12.[60] As summarized in the staff study, the deputies' reports had identified three weaknesses in the existing system of floating exchange rates among the major currencies. First, exchange rates showed a high degree of short-term volatility. This factor was largely discounted by the Fund staff as a problem affecting the large industrial countries, since most of the economics literature showed that the real costs of short-term volatility were minor. The study recognized, however, that volatility might be a more serious concern for smaller enterprises and for developing countries with less access to international capital markets. Second, and of more general importance, exchange rates were subject to large and persistent misalignments, even though the extent of those misalignments could not be accurately gauged. Third, the absence of a real system had contributed to a lack of discipline and coordination in macroeconomic policies.

---

[57]See Lawson (1992), p. 543 for one account of the pressure that was applied.

[58]Baker later noted in his memoirs that he "took special pride" in the move (Baker, 1995, p. 604). Most participants, however, concurred with Geoffrey Howe that the expansion caused the group to lose "its secrecy and its intimacy (and quite a bit of its effectiveness)" (Howe, 1994, p. 266). Dobson (1991, p. 45) cites an additional cost: the occasional need for interpretors as the increase in the number of participants made it less likely that everyone would be able to work comfortably in English.

[59]"The Heads of State or Government . . . request the Group of Five finance ministers to include Canada and Italy in their meetings whenever the management or improvement of the international monetary system and related economic policy measures are to be discussed and dealt with . . ." (Hajnal, 1989, p. 313).

[60]See Morris Goldstein, "The System of Floating Exchange Rates: Review and Assessment," Chapter I in Crockett and Goldstein (1987). The internal version of the paper was "Review and Assessment of the System of Floating Exchange Rates," SM/86/5 (January 10, 1986).

The G-10 and G-24 reports had broadly agreed on the desirability of greater stability of exchange rates but had recommended different approaches to achieve that goal. The G-24 report concluded (Crockett and Goldstein, 1987, Appendix II, para. 66) that "target zones for the exchange rates of major currencies could help achieve the objective of exchange rate stability and a sustainable pattern of payments balances." In contrast, the G-10 report (op. cit., paras. 31–32) concluded that, although *some* participating deputies believed that "credible commitments to target zones would contribute to stabilizing market expectations and would promote greater international policy consistency by reinforcing multilateral surveillance," the majority agreed "that the adoption of target zones is undesirable and in any case impractical in current circumstances." The G-10 deputies could agree only on marginal tinkering, such as asking (para. 51) that the IMF's *World Economic Outlook* (WEO) include a separate chapter "analyzing the international repercussions of national policies of Group of Ten countries and of their interaction in the determination of exchange rate developments and international adjustment."

In light of these conflicts, the IMF staff study concentrated on proposals for strengthening multilateral surveillance that could be carried out within the existing system. In particular, the staff revived its 1985 suggestion (see above, p. 204) for adoption of a system of "objective indicators" of economic policies and performance, which could be used both as the basis for a separate WEO chapter and as a means of focusing discussions with the major industrial countries (individually and jointly). The indicators could be grouped into measures of the stance of macroeconomic policies, of national economic performance, and of the linkages between the two. If agreement could be reached on a concise list of indicators, then surveillance could aim at discussing goals and reviewing the record on how well those goals had been met. If that approach proved to be useful, then target zones for exchange rates could emerge as a natural extension.

The Executive Board discussed the deputies' reports and the staff analysis on February 12, 1986.[61] Just the week before, the possibility of systemic reform had apparently been given a fresh boost through a surprise announcement in President Reagan's State of the Union address. After citing the crucial importance to the U.S. economy of "reliable exchange rates" and noting that the United States had "begun coordinating economic and monetary policy among our major trading partners," the President announced that he was "directing Treasury Secretary Jim Baker to determine if the nations of the world should convene to discuss the role and relationship of our currencies." Although once again nothing would come of the proposal (which had not been discussed previously within the G-7)—and this speech would turn out to be the last forum in which the idea of a new Bretton Woods would surface officially in the 1980s—it did help create a climate in which reform seemed possible.

The Executive Board meeting helped to clarify countries' views and to narrow some differences, though it did not reveal enough agreement to produce any immediate changes in the conduct of surveillance. The favorable attitude of the G-24 re-

---

[61]Minutes of EBM/86/25–26 (February 12, 1986).

garding target zones was explained by Yusuf A. Nimatallah of Saudi Arabia and by Pedro Pérez of Spain, who suggested that developing countries were adversely affected by exchange rate volatility to a much greater degree than were industrial countries that had ready access to sophisticated financial markets.[62] Without denying the importance of stability, however, Directors from G-10 countries emphasized policy coordination over systemic reforms as the best means to achieve it. Bernd Goos (Germany) regarded objective indicators as "mechanically imposed external constraints"; Hirotake Fujino (Japan) stressed the imprecision inherent in assessing equilibrium levels of exchange rates;[63] Jacques de Groote (Belgium) suggested that "target zones" should be replaced by the less precise but in his view more practical notion of "target directions"; and both Timothy P. Lankester (United Kingdom) and Marcel Massé (Canada) recalled that their own countries had found exchange rate flexibility to be a necessary part of their ability to absorb external shocks. Dallara—now representing the Baker Treasury and expressing more internationalist views than he had just a year earlier (see p. 205, above)—was alone among the G-10 representatives in making the case for a more systemic use of indicators. "Objectives relating to several key economic variables could help focus attention," he argued, and could "serve as an indication for policy action in particular areas and/or international consultation."

The next week, the Board again took up the indicators idea during the regular biennial review of the principles of surveillance. Members' positions on these issues had not changed, but this meeting provided an opportunity to examine specifically how the ideas in the deputies' reports might be taken on board in the conduct of surveillance. Dallara, making the opening intervention of the meeting, requested adoption of the G-10's suggestion for a separate chapter in the WEO, which could present and analyze a well-defined set of indicators for the major industrial countries. Although this recommendation was much weaker than other proposals for implementing a system of objective indicators—let alone target zones for exchange rates—it was nonetheless embraced by G-24 as well as G-10 executive directors as providing the Board a framework within which to discuss the international repercussions and interactions of the policies and objectives of the major countries.[64] In April, the general notion of formulating a set of objective indicators on which to base multilateral surveillance and the specific proposal of examining the indicators in the WEO exercise were formally endorsed by the Interim Committee (communiqué of April 10, 1986, paragraph 6).

---

[62]Empirical evidence tended to support that perception; see Chapter 2, footnote 33, p. 83.

[63]Speaking for the staff, Andrew Crockett suggested that it was reasonable to think in terms of a range of ±10 percent around an estimated equilibrium rate. Fujino, however, noted that empirical studies of the yen-dollar rate had put the equilibrium at levels ranging from 143 to 210 (compared with its then-current level of 185). The difference in view may be attributed to methodology. Estimates in the neighborhood of 210 were derived from calculations of purchasing power parity (Japan then being a high-price country for consumers), while those in the lower range were derived as the rates needed to establish equilibrium in external current account balances (Japan then being a low-cost country for producers).

[64]This characterization is given in the Chairman's summing up; minutes of EBM/86/30 (February 19, 1986), p. 49.

The United States also pushed the G-7 to adopt a system of objective indicators for its own work. Mulford saw the indicators approach to surveillance as a means of shifting the focus of G-5 meetings away from U.S. fiscal policy and toward a more general and balanced discussion of the requirements for medium-term stability. He first sold Baker on the idea, and then persuaded the other G-7 deputies that this was the most they could expect to agree on as a means of promoting stability and coordination. Following the surveillance meeting with de Larosière on April 8, 1986, the G-5 ministers approved the plan in principle. It was then formally endorsed at the Tokyo summit in early May:

> . . . the Heads of State or Government . . . With the representatives of the European Community:

> – Reaffirm the undertaking at the 1982 Versailles Summit to cooperate with the IMF in strengthening multilateral surveillance . . . and request that, in conducting such surveillance and in conjunction with the Managing Director of the IMF, their individual economic forecasts should be reviewed, taking into account indicators such as GNP growth rates, inflation rates, interest rates, unemployment rates, fiscal deficit ratios, current account and trade balances, monetary growth rates, reserves, and exchange rates; [and]

> – Invite the Finance Ministers and Central Bankers in conducting multilateral surveillance to make their best efforts to reach an understanding on appropriate remedial measures whenever there are significant deviations from the intended course; and recommend that remedial measures focus first and foremost on underlying policy fundamentals, while reaffirming the 1983 Williamsburg commitment to intervene in exchange markets when to do so would be helpful.[65]

On paper, this agreement on indicators was innocuous even by the standards of summit communiqués. In practice, however, it represented a step forward from the even more timid approach adopted just a few months earlier by the Executive Board, and it intensified collaboration between the IMF and the G-7. In effect, the Fund staff would become an informal secretariat responsible for preparing and analyzing the objective indicators on which multilateral surveillance was to be based. That function would extend the IMF's participation beyond the Managing Director's meetings with ministers to include staff participation in the deputies' preparatory work for those meetings. Since the most substantive decisions often were agreed upon initially by the deputies, involvement in those deliberations was potentially more valuable than the existing higher-level participation.

Shortly after the Tokyo summit, the G-5 deputies asked the Managing Director to offer suggestions on the role that the IMF might play in implementing the new indicators process. In early June, de Larosière circulated a proposal to the G-7 deputies[66] that called for Fund involvement in three of the four stages of the process:[67]

---

[65]See Hajnal (1989), p. 295.

[66]Several more months would elapse before the deputies from Canada and Italy would be fully integrated into the preparations for the surveillance meetings of finance ministers.

[67]"Note on the Use of Indicators in Surveillance Discussions of the Group of Five and Group of Seven" (June 11, 1986), in IMF/RD Managing Director file "Group of Seven" (Accession 88/285, Box 5, Section 250).

- to put national forecasts for key data on a comparable basis, including projecting variables not normally forecast by the authorities and ensuring that the assumptions underlying the forecasts were reasonably consistent;
- to identify and assess any remaining inconsistencies in the forecasts and ways in which the projections might be undesirable or unsustainable; and
- to suggest policy options for correcting inconsistencies and getting economic performance back on a sustainable path.

On the basis of that background work, the ministerial meetings could aim more clearly at making choices among the available policy options.

On a more technical level, the IMF also undertook to identify a concise but comprehensive set of indicators and to develop a clear framework for presenting them, both in the WEO and in the tables and charts prepared for ministerial meetings on surveillance. Meeting for this purpose in July 1986, the Executive Board cautiously agreed on a few basic circumscribing principles. First, it was agreed that if the indicators approach was to have any meaning at all, the chosen indicators would have to be "limited in number, quantifiable, timely, relatively easy to interpret, and comparable from country to country." Second, the development of such indicators should be viewed as an aid for a broadly based judgmental analysis, not as an end in itself. And third, the whole exercise would be useful only if the countries concerned displayed the political will to respond to it. That last requirement, of course, was understood to be a most difficult—and possibly insurmountable—hurdle.

The Board also broadly endorsed the staff's proposal that the requisite analytical framework be developed around national saving-investment balances. The intention of this proposal was to emphasize the linkages between domestic monetary and fiscal policies and external current account balances.[68] As the staff paper for the meeting put it (Crockett and Goldstein, 1987, p. 36),

> . . . if judgments are required concerning whether a given pattern of exchange rates is to be regarded as sustainable or desirable . . . [a] logical place to begin is by looking at the factors that influence the balance of domestic savings and investment (and therefore the net acquisition of foreign assets [i.e., the country's current account balance]. . . . Indicators that may be useful in this context include: (1) a measure of the overall fiscal position; (2) gross private savings flows; (3) gross private investment; and (4) real interest rates.

Although this description allowed fully for flexibility in application, it provided a framework for linking the "twin deficits" (fiscal and external) of the United States and the corresponding strong fiscal positions and external surpluses in Germany

---

[68]Modern theory linking current account balances to monetary and fiscal policies through the national saving-investment balances originated with Meade (1951). Bruno (1979) and Sachs (1981) developed influential analyses based on this approach, and Frenkel and Razin (1987) developed the model to its fullest and most rigorous extent. For the initial proposal to base the development of indicators in the Fund on the saving-investment approach, see "Objective Indicators," memorandum from James Boughton to Andrew Crockett (April 23, 1986), in IMF/RD Research Department Immediate Office file "Correspondence Originated by ADC, 1986 (Accession 89/263, Box 1, Section 49).

and Japan. The Executive Directors from the latter two countries, and a few others, expressed concern lest too strong a correlation be assumed between fiscal policy and external imbalances, and lest too much emphasis be given to external objectives in the implementation of fiscal policy. Nonetheless, the Board endorsed this saving-investment approach as a good way to focus on the main issue, which was keeping external imbalances from getting too large for too long.[69]

The G-5 deputies met once more over the summer to refine the approach that they intended to take, and then for the first time invited the Fund staff to participate in their next meeting, the third since the Tokyo summit and the one where the agenda would be prepared for the regular fall ministerial meeting on surveillance.[70] The deputies would be meeting in Paris on this occasion, at the secluded site of the Pré Catalan restaurant in the Bois de Boulogne. As with the Managing Director's participation in ministerial meetings, the IMF staff representative (Andrew Crockett, Deputy Director of the Research Department) was invited only for the first part of the meeting, after which the deputies were to turn to the task of drafting the ministerial communiqué.

This development of the indicators approach to surveillance in the second half of 1986 took place against the backdrop of a continuing slowdown in economic growth in the large industrial countries and, consequently, additional efforts within these countries to engineer further reductions in interest rates.[71] Following the cuts implemented in March, Volcker was prepared to push U.S. interest rates down further. However, he feared precipitating a flight out of dollars and therefore was reluctant to cut rates without some assurance that other central banks would follow suit. Throughout the summer, he and Baker tried without success to win such an agreement from their counterparts in Germany and Japan.[72] The German authorities resisted with particular firmness out of concern that further cuts in German interest rates would merely fuel price inflation.

---

[69]Minutes of EBM/86/114–15 (July 14, 1986). As noted in Chapter 5, the staff continued to develop and refine the empirical application of the saving-investment approach, and on two occasions in 1987 the Board further endorsed this line of analysis, both for the G-7 exercise and the WEO. See "Enhancing the Use of Indicators as a Tool for Surveillance," EBS/86/282 (December 18, 1986), "The Use of Indicators in Surveillance—Analytical Issues," EBS/87/135 (June 24, 1987), and the minutes of EBM/87/8–9 (January 14, 1987) and EBM/87/105–106 (July 22, 1987).

[70]The invitation for the Fund staff to participate in the deputies' meeting was conveyed by Mulford to de Larosière around the beginning of July, on behalf of the G-5 deputies. Memorandum to files by Andrew Crockett (July 7, 1986); in IMF/RD Research Department 1986 Chronological file (Accession 89/263, Box 2, Section 49).

[71]In retrospect, the slowdown in real GDP growth in the G-7 countries as a whole had been modest: from a peak of 4.7 percent in 1984 to 2.9 percent in 1986. Moreover, the slowdown was already being moderated by declining long-term interest rates: from 11.4 percent to 7.7 percent over those two years. The concern, however, was not misplaced, because the U.S. fiscal deficit had not yet been cut significantly; hovering around 4¾ percent of GDP, such an imbalance made a sustainable recovery all but impossible. It was to limit the resulting pressure on capital markets that attention was being directed to the use of monetary policies to reduce short-term interest rates.

[72]See Funabashi (1988), pp. 53, 156, and 168–69; and Volcker and Gyohten (1992), p. 264. In addition to the secret meetings described in those accounts, private discussions took place at the monthly central bank governors' meetings at the BIS in Basel, Switzerland.

Partly because of this frustration and partly because of the normal stress of international negotiations, the atmosphere had become quite tense. There was suspicion among the deputies as each jockeyed to promote his own country's policies and proposals, suspicion of the Fund by deputies who saw it as an interloper in the club, and suspicion between Fund staff battling over turf.[73] Nonetheless, the Pré Catalan meeting gave a strong beginning to the Fund's role in the indicators approach to surveillance. One of the more delicate issues to be decided was whether the basic indicator tables for ministers were to be based primarily on national or IMF forecasts. The use of national forecasts would give the deputies more control but would force them to waste time trying to reconcile and interpret what would inevitably be inconsistent, country-specific, numbers. After hearing Crockett explain how the IMF staff would make and present its projections, the deputies agreed to base their work on the Fund's numbers and assessments.

The principal ministerial surveillance meeting—still restricted to the G-5—was scheduled for Friday, September 26, 1986, preceding the Annual Meetings in Washington. Armed with the newly slimmed-down indicators tables and charts, de Larosière argued that current policies being pursued by the three largest countries were incompatible. To get to a stable equilibrium over the medium term, external current account imbalances would have to be attenuated, the U.S. fiscal deficit would have to be further reduced, and Germany and Japan would have to act to stimulate growth of private sector demand.

As usual, no policy decisions were taken at the G-5 meeting (nor at the G-7 meeting the next day), but the discussions provided a framework for the ongoing bilateral efforts to coordinate policy actions. On the same weekend as the G-5 meeting, Baker pressed both Stoltenberg and the newly installed Japanese finance minister, Kiichi Miyazawa, to take stimulatory measures. Separately, Volcker made a similar plea with Satoshi Sumita, governor of the Bank of Japan.[74] Stoltenberg felt that he could do little to influence the fiercely independent Bundesbank, and in any case he regarded the recent increases in German interest rates as too slight to worry about. At the end of October, however, Baker's diplomacy paid off in the form of a joint declaration with Miyazawa that the two of them had "reached agreement on cooperative action and understandings regarding a number of issues of mutual concern." On the Japanese side, the agreed actions included submission of a supplementary budget with additional expenditure, proposals to reduce income tax rates, and—most immediately—a cut in the discount rate by the Bank of Japan. On the U.S. side, the communiqué listed only a previously enacted tax reform and vague commitments to reduce the fiscal deficit, resist protectionist pressures, and promote economic growth. Though singularly unbalanced, this agreement represented, in

---

[73]Because three of the G-5 countries are European, the Fund task force established after the 1982 Versailles summit had been chaired by Alan Whittome, Director of the European Department. With the expansion of the Fund's role (including a closer linkage to the World Economic Outlook) and the extension of the coverage to the G-7, much of the background work was now the responsibility of the Research Department.

[74]See Funabashi (1988), pp. 54 and 158; and Lawson (1992), p. 552.

principle, a genuine breakthrough. Without waiting for Stoltenberg to come around, Baker and Miyazawa had found a formula by which policies could be adjusted in the direction that de Larosière had asked for in September, without the potentially disruptive effects of uncoordinated shifts in interest rates.

Louvre, 1987

Within a few weeks after the Baker-Miyazawa communiqué, the G-5 was preparing for a ministerial meeting that—for all of its limits—would turn out to be the apogee of the policy cooperation process in the 1980s. Like the Plaza meeting that preceded it by 17 months to the day, the Louvre accord on exchange rates was planned and executed outside the aegis of the IMF, though it would be carried forward with the institution's support and cooperation. Stoltenberg, Baker, and their deputies met in Kiel, Germany, in November 1986 for the initial discussions of how to consolidate the progress in restoring a measure of stability in exchange markets. In light of the Baker-Miyazawa agreement, Stoltenberg had little choice but to bring Germany into the process, or he would risk seeing the deutsche mark appreciate against both the dollar and the yen and thus also risk losing the momentum of European recovery. From November 1986 through January 1987, Tietmeyer met on several occasions with other G-5 deputies, especially with Darman, and agreed with them to try to establish some limits on exchange-rate movements and to agree on the required policy adjustments to achieve that objective.

The IMF staff became peripherally involved when the deputies next met as a group, at the Dolder Grand Hotel in Zurich, on January 29, 1987. Crockett represented the Fund (for the second time) and participated through the afternoon as the deputies analyzed the indicators and how they fit into the economic outlook. After four hours of discussion, he was then asked to leave the meeting around 5 p.m., and the deputies continued their meeting through the evening and again over breakfast the next morning. Only among themselves did the deputies discuss policies to stabilize exchange rates.

Though the IMF staff was excluded from the deputies' planning for the meeting at the Louvre, the Managing Director was involved serendipitously by the exchange of jobs between de Larosière and Camdessus. (De Larosière left the Managing Director's post in January 1987 and became governor of the Banque de France on February 16. Camdessus was the governor as the planning for the Louvre conference began and became Managing Director in mid-January.) Officially, Camdessus's role as Managing Director at the G-5 ministerial meeting on February 21 was the same as the role previously played by de Larosière. On a personal level, he was more deeply and directly involved in the G-5 process, as he had been from his days as the French deputy at Versailles and thereafter (1982–84), through his time as governor (1984–87), which included the Plaza.

For the Louvre conference, Camdessus submitted a note that dealt more openly with exchange rates than had been customary. His message asserted frankly that the exchange rate movements that had already occurred had reversed much of the previous misalignment and had contributed to a narrowing of current account imbalances;

that slow growth in industrial countries had now become a major problem that was hurting developing countries as well; and that the solution to the problem lay partly in slowing the pace of fiscal consolidation in some countries, especially Germany and Japan, and partly in structural reforms such as deregulation and privatization.[75]

The finance ministers, their deputies, and the central bank governors of the G-5 met at the Finance Ministry offices in the Palais du Louvre at 3 p.m. Saturday (February 21, 1987) for the now-customary surveillance discussion with the Managing Director. In his oral presentation to the ministers, Camdessus amplified the points made in his position paper by arguing that the risks of recession and protectionism now outweighed the risks of rekindling inflation, and that the success of the debt strategy required a resumption of sustainable growth in the major industrial countries. Following that kickoff session, the G-5 participants (without official IMF representation, but with de Larosière serving as what one participant has called "the ghost of the IMF") met for several more hours through dinner ("while all the participants were quite busy cutting their meat and sipping their wine")[76] to decide how to get better stability. Finally, they agreed not only that the then-current level of exchange rates was about right, but also that they should consult with one another if the dollar-yen or dollar-mark rates were to move beyond specified limits.[77]

Beyond the commitment to consult, what was agreed among the participants at the Louvre is in dispute. Some interpreted the meeting as establishing a system of target or reference zones for exchange rates, while others insisted that the ranges were only indicative. As an interesting twist on the systemic debates of the 1970s and early 1980s, the U.S. delegates, Baker and Volcker, were now teamed with the French side, Balladur and de Larosière, in arguing for close and comprehensive control through a combination of exchange market intervention and underlying policy actions. The Japanese and especially the German delegates resisted firm agreements and later interpreted the accords as nonbinding and flexible.[78] The British were in a delicate spot because the chancellor, Nigel Lawson, was on record as being much more hawkish for exchange rate stability than was his prime minister, Margaret Thatcher. The U.K. delegation went along with the ranges for the other currencies but insisted that no range be set for the pound sterling.[79]

---

[75]Memorandum from the Managing Director to G-7 Executive Directors (February 19, 1987); in IMF/RD Deputy Managing Director file "G-5" (Accession 91/455, Box 4, Section 489).

[76]Gyohten, in Volcker and Gyohten (1992), p. 268.

[77]Two midpoints were specified: 1.825 deutsche marks per dollar, and 153.5 yen per dollar. There was to be an allowed inner range of ±2.5 percent for each rate, and an outer range of ±5 percent. See Funabashi (1988), pp. 183–87; Lawson (1992), pp. 554–55; and Volcker and Gyohten (1992), pp. 267–68 and 282–83. This use of a soft inner and a hard outer range echoed the 1972 Volcker-Daane proposal for reserve indicators (see footnote 45, p. 204).

[78]The Bundesbank was particularly adamant in its insistence that no binding commitments had been made. Pöhl (1987) characterized the accord as a "commitment by the U.S. to cooperate in efforts to stabilize the dollar against the yen and the deutsche mark. . . ."

[79]At the time, the United Kingdom was a member of the EMS but did not participate in the system's exchange rate mechanism. The pound was floating relative to all of the other G-5 currencies. A separate range for the French franc would have been redundant, as it was already linked to the mark via the narrow (2.5 percent) band of the EMS.

These substantive differences in view within the G-5 were overshadowed at the time by a public turf battle waged on Sunday by the Italian delegation. Just over a year had passed since the original agreement to invite Canada and Italy to join the surveillance process, and the insistence of the G-5 on holding substantive councils before each G-7 meeting was becoming more and more irritating and embarrassing to Italy. The Italian delegation to the Louvre attempted to secure a compromise under which all seven countries would be invited to the working dinner on Saturday as well as to the concluding meetings on Sunday, but that strategy failed when the Canadian team indicated a willingness to remain on the sidelines. After dinner Saturday evening, Balladur and de Larosière visited Giovanni Goria, the Italian Minister of the Treasury, at his suite at the Hotel Meurice, just three blocks down the rue de Rivoli. They briefed him on the day's developments and tried but failed to persuade him to participate on Sunday.[80] The Italian delegation returned to Rome the next morning without visiting the Louvre, and when the February 22 communiqué was released—following a 9:30 a.m. meeting of all other delegations, including Camdessus on behalf of the IMF—it was issued on behalf of the other six members of the G-7.

The immediate effect of this stormy episode was to clear the air after several long months during which the G-5 had attempted to preserve the intimacy (and thereby, in the view of most of them, the effectiveness) of their club despite the formal acceptance of the wider membership. The G-5 met once or twice more at the ministerial level in the course of 1987, after which Canada and Italy became more fully involved.[81] By that time, however, the whole process had begun to bog down. What had started in the 1970s as private gatherings of four or five people had now evolved into closely watched conferences involving more than twenty active participants, numerous aides restlessly prowling the corridors outside, and packs of journalists in search of a good quotation. The process could still provide a useful forum for multilateral surveillance, but (regardless of whether five or seven countries were involved) it had also become a symbol of the pitfalls inherent in any attempt to establish a mechanism for international policy coordination.

Life After the Louvre: 1987–89

Two days after the Louvre meeting, Camdessus reported to Directors his impressions of the event. He stopped short of stating that the Group had entered into a secret agreement to stabilize exchange rates, but he spoke warmly of the enhanced commitment to coordinate policies so as to keep exchange rates around

---

[80]As it happened, the persuasion effort was hopeless because Goria had already received firm instructions from Rome not to accept this compromise.

[81]As noted by both Funabashi (1988, pp. 206–207) and Lawson (1992, p. 555), the G-5 met at the ministerial level in April 1987 to realign the target rate for the dollar-yen exchange rate. The Managing Director was not invited to that meeting, but he did participate in the G-7 meeting the next day. The G-5 deputies met at least once later that year, but in subsequent meetings Italy and Canada became full participants at all levels.

current levels. Arjun Sengupta (India) pressed unsuccessfully for a staff study on whether G-7 exchange rates really were "broadly consistent with underlying economic fundamentals," as claimed in the Louvre communiqué, but the general reaction was more supportive.[82]

Whatever its shortcomings, the Louvre meeting marked the extent of maturation of the multilateral surveillance process and of the Fund's supporting role. Although three more summits and a half dozen ministerial meetings were held before the end of the 1980s, the process underwent little additional deepening.[83] From the surveillance perspective, the most important remaining summit was held in Venice, just four months after the Louvre. The Venice communiqué not only endorsed the Louvre agreement to keep exchange rates near current levels. It went further by distancing the G-7 from reliance on changes in exchange rates as an instrument for adjustment: "Exchange rate changes alone will not solve the problem of correcting [external] imbalances while sustaining growth." Surplus countries, the leaders concluded, needed to "strengthen domestic demand," while countries with external deficits needed to reduce fiscal deficits. Of more direct relevance to the Fund, the communiqué also suggested that the indicators process could be strengthened considerably. It called for the G-7 to develop a "mutually consistent" set of "medium-term objectives and projections" and for the periodic assessment of economic performance based on indicators "in cooperation with the Managing Director of the IMF" (paras. 5, 11, and 12; see Hajnal, 1989, pp. 333 and 335–36).

The Venice initiative led to an increase in scope and detail in the indicators tables prepared by the staff as background for the G-7 meetings. It also seems to have emboldened Camdessus, who soon made a much more direct pitch for exchange rate action than he ever had before. At a Washington meeting of the G-7 in September 1987, he told the finance ministers and central bank governors that the current levels of exchange rates (which were still close to the levels approved at the Louvre or in Washington two months later) were not appropriate, based on current macroeconomic policies. Even if policies were adjusted in the appropriate direction (more saving in the United States and more stimulus in Germany and Japan), exchange rate movements would still be needed. At the end of the meeting, however, the G-7 reaffirmed its support for the already agreed levels.

The complacency of the G-7 was shaken but not shattered by the stock market crash of October 1987. For four days before the crash, Baker sharply and openly criticized the German authorities (in effect, the Bundesbank) for raising interest rates, which he viewed as a violation of the spirit of the Louvre and other G-7 agreements. One never knows what causes a sudden shift in asset prices, but the combination of Germany's actions and Baker's remarks must have contributed sig-

---

[82]Minutes of EBM/87/31 (February 24, 1987), pp. 1–5.

[83]Saccomanni (1988) argued that the process failed to mature because it lacked institutional structure. He proposed creation of a major-country "multilateral surveillance council," to be chaired by the Managing Director, as a way to perpetuate the process. Dobson (1991), Chapter 6, offered a comprehensive set of proposals for strengthening the process, including a stronger institutional role for the Managing Director and the Fund.

nificantly to the severity of the decline.[84] The crash then triggered a flurry of un-scheduled G-7 activity, including informal meetings between finance ministers and Camdessus at which the Managing Director urged everyone to continue to support the U.S. effort to reduce its fiscal deficit, not least because of the contribution that it would make to the stability of exchange markets.[85] The deputies met two or three times over the next several weeks to organize a ministerial meeting in December. Jacob A. Frenkel (Economic Counselor and Director of Research) participated in the final planning session, in Paris on December 9, and before that he and Crockett met individually with deputies in Tokyo, Bonn, and London. Throughout this period, however, Baker was preoccupied with trying to get the U.S. Congress to approve the government budget for fiscal year 1988 and end a stalemate that temporarily shut down much of the federal government. So the G-7 did not meet, but—uniquely—they issued a communiqué anyway, just before Christmas and immediately after congress finally approved the U.S. budget. This statement again confirmed the continuation of the Louvre strategy and warned especially against a depreciation of the dollar:

> . . . either excessive fluctuation of exchange rates, a further decline of the dollar, or a rise in the dollar to an extent that becomes destabilizing to the adjustment process, could be counterproductive by damaging growth prospects in the world economy.[86]

This carefully crafted asymmetry was repeated word for word in the next G-7 communiqué, issued after the April 1988 ministerial meeting, and again in the communiqué of the Toronto summit meeting two months later. Throughout those six months, the dollar appreciated strongly against the mark and more moderately against the yen, as the G-7 resisted pressure from the Fund and most independent analysts for exchange rate adjustments in the opposite direction.

On a more analytical note, the Fund and the G-7 continued to refine the indicators process. Beyond the expansion of the medium-term performance indicators after the Venice summit, consideration was given to two other innovations.

First, at the April 1987 meeting of the Interim Committee, Baker asked the Fund to develop a consistent set of "structural" indicators. What he particularly had in mind was a means of measuring rigidity in national labor markets. U.S. officials be-

---

[84]Baker's initial criticism was made at a White House press briefing on Thursday, October 15. On Friday, the Dow-Jones Industrial Average—which already had been declining gradually—fell sharply, by 108 points (4.6 percent). Baker repeated his criticism throughout the weekend, and on Monday the stock average fell by 508 points (22.6 percent). After Baker met with Stoltenberg and Pöhl over lunch in Frankfurt that same day, and the three issued a reconciliatory statement to the press, the controversy quieted down. Perhaps coincidentally, stock markets quickly began to recover. Camdessus later told the G-7 ministers that their public disagreements over interest rate policy had not only contributed to the crash but had threatened the credibility of the policy coordination process. See "G-7 Speaking Notes," memorandum from Frenkel to the Managing Director (March 29, 1989); in IMF/RD Managing Director file "G5/G7, January–June 1989" (Accession 1990-0079, Box 2, Section A).

[85]Report by the Managing Director at EBM/87/156 (November 17, 1987).

[86]Statement circulated to Executive Directors as "Statement of the Group of Seven," EBD/87/338 (December 23, 1987).

lieved, no doubt correctly, that European labor markets were much less flexible than those in North America and that this rigidity went far toward explaining the relatively weak job growth in Europe throughout the 1980s. If so, this structural gap could help explain the persistence of external imbalances within the G-7. The Fund staff prepared a report on the problem and concluded that rigidities in labor and other markets could not readily be compared between countries because of the great variety of experiences in this regard. Structural policies were discussed by the Executive Board in January 1989, and the staff papers were subsequently published (Bayoumi and others, 1989; Feldman and others, 1989; Wattleworth and Woglom, 1989), but the idea of developing an operational set of structural indicators quietly died.[87]

Second, there was the curious case of the commodity price indicators. In October 1987, the Interim Committee urged the Fund to refine the indicators further, and both Baker and Lawson made specific proposals in their Annual Meetings speeches for the use of an index of global primary commodity prices as an indicator of overall price movements. This idea—adding an indicator of commodity prices to a table of economic data—may seem trivial, but it was introduced to overcome a serious limitation of the G-7 surveillance exercise. Now that the process was focused primarily on maintaining a given pattern of exchange rates—a goal that required a measure of coordination of monetary policies—the participating countries risked losing control of the price level. Any set of exchange rates could be made consistent with any price level and any rate of inflation. Furthermore, none of the G-7 countries was a clear choice to serve as a numeraire for the system. German officials were reluctant to let the largest country take the lead, because the United States had a higher inflation rate than Germany was prepared to accept, and U.S. officials were unwilling to subjugate their own policies to any other country.

The fact that the U.S. and U.K. ministers made similar proposals simultaneously reflected the close working relationship between them, but the two proposals reflected subtle differences in rationale. Lawson stressed the potential for commodity prices to serve as a nominal anchor and to help "ensure that there is no inflationary (or for that matter deflationary) bias for the group [of major industrial countries] as a whole." Baker suggested a less directly operational role and noted only that commodity prices could serve as a leading indicator of more general price developments ("an early warning signal of potential price trends").[88] Baker nonetheless created a furor in the press and among analysts by specifically mentioning only one commodity: gold. To many, it seemed as if the U.S. government was testing the waters to see if the stuff of so much legend, discarded from the world's monetary systems no more than a decade earlier, could now be resurrected. In retrospect, however, it became clear that gold was included primarily to excite domestic political passions.[89]

---

[87]The Board discussion was at EBM/89/3–4 (January 13, 1989).

[88]IMF, 1987, pp. 92 (Lawson) and 108 (Baker). A few weeks later, Pöhl publicly endorsed the modest "early-warning" version and rejected the stronger "anchoring" version; see Pöhl (1987).

[89]For a sympathetic press report, see Fossedal (1989). Frankel (1994, p. 321) suggests that Baker included gold in his proposal to "outflank" U.S. Representative Jack Kemp, who was running for president on a platform that included returning the United States to a gold standard.

Again the staff duly set to work to study the problem.[90] The report, which was discussed by the Executive Board in January 1988, concluded that commodity prices could serve usefully as a supplementary leading indicator of major shifts in inflationary pressures. The report, however, threw cold water on the notion that stability in commodity prices would lead predictably to overall price stability. It thus found favorably for Baker's modest proposal but was less positive concerning Lawson's more ambitious goal. Executive Directors, for the most part, were more skeptical but were receptive to the suggestion that commodity prices should be featured more prominently in the World Economic Outlook.[91]

Separately, the staff assisted the G-7 in developing a pair of new indices of commodity prices "including gold" (with and without oil) specifically for the policy coordination exercise, with prices measured in SDRs. As it happened, the weight on gold was small enough and gold prices were highly enough correlated with other commodity prices that changes in the price of gold never had a substantive impact on the behavior of these indexes. The addition of the indexes to the surveillance process was considered important enough to be mentioned in the communiqué of the Toronto summit, held in June 1988. The G-7 then began regularly looking at commodity prices at their semiannual meetings, but the indices never were elevated to a central role.

References

Attali, Jacques, 1993, *Verbatim, Tome 1: Chronique des Années 1981–1986* (Paris: Fayard).

Baker, James A., III, and others, 1995, *The Politics of Diplomacy: Revolution, War and Peace 1989–1992* (New York: Penguin Putnam).

Bayoumi, Tamim, Robert Alan Feldman, Michael Wattleworth, and Geoffrey Woglom, 1989, "Structural Reform and Macroeconomic Adjustment in Industrial Countries," *Staff Studies for the World Economic Outlook* (Washington: International Monetary Fund), pp. 13–64.

Blommestein, H.J., ed., 1991, *The Reality of International Economic Policy Coordination* (Amsterdam: North-Holland).

Boughton, James M., 1983, "Conditions for an Active Exchange Rate Policy with a Predetermined Monetary Target," *Staff Papers*, International Monetary Fund, Vol. 30 (September), pp. 461–90.

———, and Willam H. Branson, 1990, "The Use of Commodity Prices to Forecast Inflation," *Staff Studies for the World Economic Outlook* (Washington: International Monetary Fund), pp. 1–18.

———, 1991, "Commodity Prices as a Leading Indicator of Inflation," in *Leading Economic Indicators: New Approaches and Forecasting Records*, ed. by Kajal Lahiri and Geoffrey H. Moore (Cambridge: Cambridge University Press), pp. 305–38.

---

[90]The present author had primary responsibility for the report on commodity prices. The technical analysis, prepared jointly with Professor William H. Branson of Princeton University, was published in a series of papers; see especially Boughton and Branson (1990, 1991).

[91]"Commodity Price Baskets as Possible Indicators of Future Price Developments" SM/87/291 (December 11, 1987), and the minutes of EBM/88/4 (January 11, 1988) and EBM/88/7 (January 15, 1988).

Bruno, Michael, 1979, "Stabilization and Stagflation in a Semi-Industrialized Economy," in *International Economic Policy: Theory and Evidence*, ed. by Rudiger Dornbusch and Jacob A. Frenkel (Baltimore: Johns Hopkins University Press), pp. 270–89.

Cooper, Richard N., 1985, "Economic Interdependence and Coordination of Economic Policies," in *Handbook of International Economics*, Vol. 2, ed. by Ronald W. Jones and Peter B. Kenen (Amsterdam: North-Holland), pp. 1195–1234.

Crockett, Andrew, 1988, "Strengthening International Economic Cooperation: The Role of Indicators in Multilateral Surveillance," in *The Quest for National and Global Economic Stability: In Honor of Hendrikus Johannes Witteveen*, ed. by Wietze Eizenga, E. Frans Limburg, and Jacques J. Polak (Boston: Kluwer Academic Publishers), pp. 1–16.

———, and Morris Goldstein, 1987, *Strengthening the International Monetary System: Exchange Rates, Surveillance, and Objective Indicators*, IMF Occasional Paper No. 50 (Washington: International Monetary Fund).

De Larosière, Jacques, 1992, "Comments on the Papers Presented in Perugia on the 'Outlook of the International Monetary System'" (unpublished; Perugia, Italy, July 10).

Destler, I.M., and C. Randall Henning, 1989, *Dollar Politics: Exchange Rate Policymaking in the United States* (Washington: Institute for International Economics).

de Vries, Margaret Garritsen, 1985, *The International Monetary Fund, 1972–1978: Cooperation on Trial*, Vols. 1 and 2: *Narrative and Analysis*; Vol. 3: *Documents* (Washington: International Monetary Fund).

Dobson, Wendy, 1991, *Economic Policy Coordination: Requiem or Prologue?* (Washington: Institute for International Economics).

Dominguez, Kathryn M., and Jeffrey A. Frankel, 1993, *Does Foreign Exchange Intervention Work?* (Washington: Institute for International Economics).

Edison, Hali J., 1993, "The Effectiveness of Central-Bank Intervention: A Survey of the Literature After 1982," Special Papers in International Economics, No. 18 (Princeton, New Jersey: International Finance Section, Department of Economics, Princeton University).

Feldman, Robert Alan, Ernesto Hernández-Catá, Flemming Larsen, and Michael Wattleworth, 1989, "The Role of Structural Policies in Industrial Countries," *Staff Studies for the World Economic Outlook* (Washington: International Monetary Fund) pp. 1–12.

Fossedal, Gregory A., 1989, "Payoffs From the (Other) Baker Plan," *Wall Street Journal*, April 6, p. A18.

Frankel, Jeffrey A., 1994, "The Making of Exchange Rate Policy in the 1980s," in *American Economic Policy in the 1980s*, ed. by Martin Feldstein (Chicago: University of Chicago Press), pp. 293–341.

Frenkel, Jacob A., and Assaf Razin, 1987, *Fiscal Policies and the World Economy: An Intertemporal Approach* (Cambridge, Massachusetts: MIT Press).

Funabashi, Yoichi, 1988, *Managing the Dollar: From the Plaza to the Louvre* (Washington: Institute for International Economics).

Garavoglia, Guido, 1984, "From Rambouillet to Williamsburg," in *Economic Summits and Western Decision-Making*, ed. by Cesar Merlini (London: Croom Helm), pp. 1–42.

Gold, Joseph, 1988, "The Group of Five in International Monetary Arrangements," in *Contemporary Problems of International Law: Essays in Honour of Georg Schwarzenberger on His Eightieth Birthday*, ed. by Bin Cheng and E.D. Brown (London: Stevens & Sons Limited), pp. 86–115.

Gotur, Padma, 1985, "Effects of Exchange Rate Volatility on Trade," *Staff Papers*, International Monetary Fund, Vol. 32 (September), pp. 475–512.

Hajnal, Peter I., ed., 1989, *The Seven-Power Summit: Documents from the Summits of Industrialized Countries, 1975–1989* (Millwood, New York: Kraus International Publications).

Hajnal, Peter I., 1999, *The G7/G8 System: Evolution, Role and Documentation* (Aldershot, United Kingdom: Ashgate).

Howe, Geoffrey, 1994, *Conflict of Loyalty* (New York: St. Martin's Press).

Jurgensen, Philippe (Chairman), 1983, "Report of the Working Group on Exchange Market Intervention" [Working Group on Exchange Market Intervention established at the Versailles Summit of the Heads of State and Government, June 4, 5, and 6, 1982] (March).

Kilborn, Peter T., 1986, "Volcker's Power Ebbing, Some Economists Say," *New York Times* (March 21), pp. D1, D8.

Lawson, Nigel, 1992, *The View from No. 11: Memoirs of a Tory Radical* (London: Bantam Press).

Mayobre, Eduardo, 1999, *G-24: The Developing Countries in the International Financial System* (Boulder, Colorado: Lynne Rienner Publishers).

McCracken, Paul, and others, 1977, *Towards Full Employment and Price Stability: A Report to the OECD by a Group of Independent Experts* (Paris: OECD).

Meade, James E., 1951, *The Theory of International Economic Policy*, Vol. 1: *The Balance of Payments*, (London: Oxford University Press).

Pauly, Louis W., 1992, "The Political Foundations of Multilateral Economic Surveillance," *International Journal*, Vol. 47 (spring), pp. 293–327.

Pöhl, Karl Otto, 1987, "Cooperation—A Keystone for the Stability of the International Monetary System," First Arthur Burns Memorial Lecture, at the American Council on Germany, November 2, New York.

Putnam, Robert D. and Nicholas Bayne, 1987, *Hanging Together: Cooperation and Conflict in the Seven-Power Summits* (Cambridge, Massachusetts: Harvard University Press, rev. and enl. ed.).

Research Department of the IMF, 1984, *Exchange Rate Volatility and World Trade*, IMF Occasional Paper No. 28 (Washington: International Monetary Fund).

Saccomanni, Fabrizio, 1988, "On Multilateral Surveillance," in *The Political Economy of International Co-operation*, ed. by Paolo Guerrieri and Pier Carlo Padoan (London: Croom Helm), pp. 58–86.

Sachs, Jeffrey D., 1981, "The Current Account and Macroeconomic Adjustment in the 1970s," *Brookings Papers on Economic Activity: 1*, pp. 201–68.

Shultz, George P., 1993, *Turmoil and Triumph: My Years as Secretary of State* (New York: Simon and Schuster).

U.S. Council of Economic Advisers, 1973, "Annual Report," in *Economic Report of the President, Transmitted to the Congress January 1973, together with the Annual Report of the Council of Economic Advisers* (Washington: United States Government Printing Office).

Volcker, Paul A., 1985, "Statement Before the Subcommittee on Domestic Economic Policy of the Committee on Banking, Finance and Urban Affairs, U.S. House of Representatives" (July 17).

———, and Toyoo Gyohten, 1992, *Changing Fortunes: The World's Money and the Threat to American Leadership* (New York: Times Books).

von Furstenberg, George M., and Joseph P. Daniels, 1992, *Economic Summit Declarations, 1975–1989: Examining the Written Record of International Cooperation*, Studies in International Finance, No. 72 (Princeton, New Jersey: International Finance Section, Department of Economics, Princeton University).

Wattleworth, Michael, and Geoffrey Woglom, 1989, "Indicators of Structural Policies and Performance," *Staff Studies for the World Economic Outlook* (Washington: International Monetary Fund).

Williamson, John, 1985, *The Exchange Rate System*, Policy Analyses in International Economics: No. 5 (Washington: Institute for International Economics, 2nd ed.).

———, and Marcus H. Miller, 1987, *Targets and Indicators: A Blueprint for the International Coordination of Economic Policy*, Policy Analyses in International Economics, No. 22 (Washington: Institute for International Economics).

5

Keeping Score: The World Economic Outlook

During the 1980s, the IMF developed its World Economic Outlook (WEO) into the polestar of its analytical work and of its communication with the public at large. It became the principal means for the Fund to conduct oversight over the international financial system and an important vehicle for providing information to governments struggling to cope with complex global economic relationships. Through it, the Fund aimed to strengthen bilateral surveillance by making policy recommendations more consistent and more reflective of the international context.

Throughout the 1970s, preparation and discussion of the WEO had been primarily an internal exercise at the Fund. As the period covered by this History began in January 1979, the staff prepared a 33-page general-survey paper, plus three background papers, for internal circulation and for a one-day discussion by the Executive Board in informal session. By the spring of 1989, the WEO operation had expanded to comprise two main papers, nine supplementary papers on a wide range of topics, and a statistical appendix, totaling more than 250 pages. The Executive Board then devoted two days in formal session to discussing the Outlook. At the time of the Interim Committee meeting—at which the WEO was a major agenda item—the key findings were announced through press conferences held by senior Fund officials, and a slightly edited version was subsequently published. The comprehensiveness and the analytical and empirical rigor of the exercise grew commensurately, as did the media and other attention that it received around the world.

This chapter covers three quite different but related strands of the history of the WEO. The first is the story of how the exercise itself evolved from the 1970s to the 1980s: in particular, how and why the "medium-term scenarios" became even more important than the short-term forecasts. Second comes the story of the economics of the WEO: What views has the Fund expressed in its analyses of the world economy, and what theories have led to those views? Third, there is a history of the development of empirical models at the Fund and of their application to the WEO exercise, which is based in part on Boughton (2000). The chapter concludes with a brief review of assessments of the forecasting record.

Evolution of the WEO Exercise

The WEO originated with a staff paper prepared as a background document for informal discussion by the Executive Board in June 1969. The Organization for

Economic Cooperation and Development (OECD) in Paris had been producing and publishing its *Economic Outlook* for industrial countries semiannually since 1967, but no official agency was doing an overall forecast of world economic conditions.[1] At the outset, the Fund staff merely reported the OECD secretariat's forecasts and offered its own interpretation of the policy implications for both industrial and developing countries.[2] In January 1971, the Executive Board began holding regular "informal" discussions of the WEO, based on increasingly detailed papers that included the staff's own projections for aggregated groups of developing countries.[3] It then quickly became apparent that, notwithstanding the good working relationship between the IMF and the OECD, the Fund staff would have to do its own forecast for the industrial countries if it wanted to produce timely and consistent forecasts for the world economy.

The production of the WEO was, from the beginning, the responsibility of the Research Department. The first director of the project—in effect the managing editor of the Outlook—was Charles F. Schwartz, who initiated the idea in 1969, built it into a major project, and ran the exercise until he retired from the Fund in 1983. Largely in recognition of his success in building the WEO into a major product for the Fund, Schwartz was promoted in 1979 to Associate Director of Research and Director of Adjustment Studies (with the rank of Department Director). On Schwartz's retirement, the editorship passed to Andrew D. Crockett (Deputy Director), who returned to Research from the Middle Eastern Department for this purpose. Crockett managed the WEO through 1988, after which he left the Fund.[4] Ernesto Hernández-Catá (Deputy Director) then took over through 1991.

---

[1]Other international organizations had long produced periodic papers on world economic conditions, dating back to the League of Nations' "World Economic Survey," published annually from 1932 to 1944. The United Nations began producing annual reports on global economic developments around 1948, and the World Bank introduced its *World Development Report* in 1978. In addition, the IMF *Annual Report*—which is a report of the Executive Board rather than the staff—has always included a review of world economic conditions. The focus of each of these reports was to analyze current developments, rather than to make projections. For a detailed description of the evolution of the WEO through 1978, see de Vries (1985), Chapter 40, pp. 785–97.

[2]"World Economic Outlook," document (no series designation given) 69/71 (June 26, 1969). The paper was discussed at Executive Board Informal Session No. 69/5 (June 30, 1969).

[3]"World Economic Outlook," ID/71/1 (January 12, 1971); discussed at IS/71/1 (February 1, 1971) and IS/71/2–3 (February 3, 1971). The staff, as well as a number of Executive Directors, wanted to promote a more open and frank discussion of the outlook than was possible in the regular consultations with individual countries. The staff therefore proposed in January 1971 that a new series of documents be established, to be called "Informal Documents," which would be given much more limited circulation than other staff papers. Similarly, the Board would meet in informal session, which enabled Executive Directors to discuss the staff papers without necessarily committing their national authorities to a position on the issues. The Secretary of the Fund would then prepare a "journal" recording the minutes of the meeting, which also would be given a more restricted circulation.

[4]Crockett began his career at the Bank of England. He returned there in 1988 as Executive Director, and he formally resigned from the Fund in 1989. In 1994, he was tapped to succeed Alexandre Lamfalussy as Managing Director of the Bank for International Settlements (BIS).

The impulse that first impelled the WEO into prominence was the oil price shock of 1973–74. The committee of Fund governors known as the Committee of Twenty had been meeting regularly for about a year to discuss proposals for reforming the international monetary system. When the committee met in Rome in January 1974, it widened its focus "by reviewing . . . the large rise in oil prices and the implications for the world economy."[5] At the initiative of the Managing Director, H. Johannes Witteveen, that review was based largely on the WEO papers, which were circulated to ministers for the first time.[6]

When the Committee of Twenty reincarnated itself as the Interim Committee (see Chapter 20), it began its first regular session by discussing "the world economic outlook and against this background the international adjustment process." The communiqué noted concerns about "the present recessionary conditions" caused by the oil shock and urged "that antirecessionary policies be pursued while continuing to combat inflation . . ." (de Vries, 1985, Vol. III, p. 218). That discussion of economic conditions and the implications for the conduct of macroeconomic policies became a standard and prominent feature of all subsequent Interim Committee meetings.

By the late 1970s—owing in large measure to the support given to the WEO by Witteveen and his successor, Jacques de Larosière—the WEO exercise had developed into a major Fund-wide forecasting project, complemented by analysis of key trends and policy developments. The exercise was conducted at least semiannually in the late winter and summer, and the conclusions of the informal Executive Board meetings were circulated as background papers for the Interim Committee meetings that followed soon afterward.

Publication

Another major boost to the role of the WEO was the decision to begin publishing the Outlook in 1980. Initially, the exercise was conceived for the staff to provide background information to member countries confidentially. As the importance of the Interim Committee as a forum for discussing the outlook grew, so did the interest from the media and the public. When a senior official (apparently the Managing Director) leaked a summary of the WEO to the press during the Interim Committee meeting in Mexico City in April 1978, the resulting coverage showed the desirability of making the projections and policy analysis available more widely. Two years later, de Larosière sensed that the mood had shifted enough

---

[5]Communiqué of the Committee of Twenty, January 18, 1974; in de Vries (1985), Vol. 3, p. 199.

[6]Minutes of IS/74/1 (January 7, 1974), p. 3; and IS/74/2 (same day), p. 20. The staff papers were "World Economic Outlook—General Survey," ID/73/4 and "World Economic Outlook—Background Information," ID/73/5 (both December 21, 1973). Owing to the length and complexity of the staff papers, the Managing Director also decided to submit a short "personal paper" as an executive summary for ministers; "External Policies in the Current Situation," C/XX/Doc/74/3 (January 11, 1974). That paper became the prototype for the later practice of submitting to the Interim Committee a statement by the Managing Director based on the summing up of the discussion of the main policy issues by the Executive Board.

that he could propose to the Executive Board that the paper be published. With no serious opposition, the proposal readily passed.[7]

The first published WEO appeared the following month, in May 1980.[8] That timing was intended to avoid conflicting with the *Annual Report* of the Executive Board, which was to be published in September, but it temporarily raised hackles at the OECD, where the twenty-seventh *Economic Outlook* was to be published in July.[9] Four years later, the Executive Board somewhat reluctantly[10] agreed to publish a second set of papers in the autumn, around the same time as the *Annual Report*.[11] The papers for the fall cycle—produced by the staff during July and August each year, discussed by the Executive Board in early September, and considered by the Interim Committee at the time of the Annual Meetings—were less extensive and comprehensive than the spring papers and were treated by the staff more as an updating than as a complete forecasting exercise. Nonetheless, by 1984 public interest warranted expanding to a semiannual publication schedule.[12] Two years

---

[7]The proposal to publish the WEO as a staff paper was initiated by the U.S. Executive Director, Sam Y. Cross, in a November 1979 note to Directors from other large industrial countries. The Executive Board first considered the matter in February 1980, but failed to reach agreement. See minutes of EBM/80/19–20 (February 6, 1980); Cross's proposal is on p. 8 of meeting 80/19. A draft of his initial note is in IMF/RD Managing Director file, "Exchange Rates—Surveillance by the Fund—Vol. III" (Accession 87/27, Box 9, Section 535). When de Larosière proposed publication in April 1980, a few Directors expressed concern that the WEO papers might include data on their countries that the authorities did not wish to have published. To obtain unanimous consent for the proposal, the Managing Director agreed to a request from José Gabriel-Peña (Alternate—Dominican Republic) and Silvio E. Conrado (Temporary Alternate—Nicaragua) that Executive Directors be given the opportunity to delete "any statement or data referring to their own countries" prior to publication. That practice was gradually diminished during the 1980s. See "Review of the Implementation of the Fund's Surveillance Over Members' Exchange Rate Policies," SM/79/292 (December 21, 1979); and minutes of EBM/80/71 (April 14, 1980), pp. 19–21, and EBM/80/74 (April 16), pp. 4–5.

[8]The full title of each WEO publication is *World Economic Outlook: A Survey by the Staff of the International Monetary Fund*, except for the autumn updates of 1984 through 1988. Those five were published as *World Economic Outlook: Revised Projections by the Staff of the International Monetary Fund*. The May 1980 and May 1985 papers were published as individual documents, not part of any other series. From 1981 through 1984, the WEO was published as part of the series of Occasional Papers. Beginning in 1986, a new series of World Economic and Financial Studies was established, comprising the WEO, related staff papers, and reports on capital market developments. Regardless of form, these publications are all cited here as *WEO* (date). Unless otherwise noted, quotations from the published papers are unchanged from the drafts circulated internally for discussion by the Executive Board.

[9]The Fund's WEO staff was no less irritated over conflicts in timing when the World Bank began publishing its own *Global Economic Prospects* in 1991.

[10]The reluctance was not only due to the timing conflict with the Board's *Annual Report*; it also reflected concerns about a perceived bias toward optimism in the medium-term scenarios in the fall 1984 papers. The latter issue is discussed below (p. 260).

[11]See the minutes of EBM/84/137–38 (September 7, 1984).

[12]The terms "spring" and "fall" are used loosely here to describe the timing of the semiannual schedule, in consonance with traditional terminology in the Fund. The idea of publishing the fall papers was first broached in a December 2, 1983, memorandum from Schwartz to the Managing Director, which argued that a greater frequency of publication would promote public awareness of the Fund's work in this area, especially in Europe where the OECD's *Economic Outlook* was still much better known (in IMF/CF, S 321 "World Development Outlook—Fund Review (*Tours d'Horizon*) September 1983–March 1984).

later, the Fund published the first collection of *Staff Studies for the World Economic Outlook*: research studies undertaken for the WEO exercise.[13]

This ever-expanding publication program should not obscure the continuing delicacy of the exercise. From the first discussions of publication, tension arose between the staff and the Executive Board regarding the balance between forthrightness and sensitivity to members' political concerns. Not infrequently, policy criticisms that were pointed in the papers presented to the Board became blunted or rounded in the published documents. Occasionally, chapters or even whole papers were deleted before publication.

Perhaps the clearest illustration of this balancing act is the handling of the detailed medium-term scenarios produced by the staff beginning in 1986 (see below, pp. 236–37). In the internal papers, these scenarios included projections through 1991 for key macroeconomic variables for each of the seven major industrial countries (the G-7), and an aggregate for the seven countries as a group. In the published papers, only the aggregate projections were included. On each occasion, a few Executive Directors objected to the inclusion of projections for the individual countries, with the strongest objections coming from the Executive Director for Japan.[14]

The Japanese concern about publication of the detailed scenarios arose partly out of a conviction that for the Fund to publish criticisms of a member country's policies could engender adverse reactions in financial markets and compromise the willingness of governments to engage in a frank discussion with the staff over confidential policy issues. That concern was shared by many other Executive Directors. A more specific Japanese concern was that the WEO reflected the Fund's view that the planned pace of fiscal consolidation in Japan was too rapid. The medium-term scenarios in the 1980s suggested that the planned reduction in the Japanese fiscal deficit was likely to leave Japan with a large current account surplus at least into the early 1990s. That projection added to the already widespread criticism of Japanese policies from the United States and other industrial countries. More fundamentally, the Japanese objected to the economic rationale for that scenario. In their view, the staff were being too mechanical in concluding that a reduction in the fiscal deficit would prevent the external surplus from falling.[15] The planned medium-term fiscal adjustment in Japan—which would alter the composition as well as the level of spending and revenue—was intended to spur private-

---

[13]A volume of *Staff Studies for the World Economic Outlook* was published each year from 1986 through 1990, and occasionally thereafter. Most volumes included four or five separate studies, which were either technical studies related to economic modeling or reviews of specific policy issues.

[14]See, for example, the interventions by Hirotake Fujino at EBM/86/152 (September 10, 1986), pp. 33–35; and by Koji Yamazaki at EBM/87/134, p. 56, EBM/88/48 (March 25, 1988), pp. 12–15, and EBM/88/50 (March 28, 1988), pp. 9–10.

[15]In standard national income accounting, a country's external current account surplus must equal the difference between net saving by the private sector (i.e., the excess of saving over investment) and the general government deficit. If there is no change in net private saving, a reduction in the government deficit would cause an offsetting increase in the external surplus. The essence of the debate was whether private investment would rise by enough to absorb a large portion of the increased saving by the government.

sector investment by enough to lower the fiscal deficit and the current account surplus simultaneously, but the Fund staff estimated smaller such effects than did the authorities. That conclusion was simply too controversial to publish.

Medium-Term Scenarios

As early as the mid-1970s, it became clear to the staff—and particularly to Schwartz—that the WEO had the potential to become much more than a forecasting exercise. To play an important role in the Fund, it would have to focus as much on the policy options available to member governments as on the staff's views on how the world economy might evolve. Out of that simple notion grew the idea of emphasizing "scenarios": conditional medium-term projections, the character of which evolved substantially during the 1980s. Throughout the period, the scenarios were a key to the success of the WEO in focusing the discussions on major policy issues. Rather than emphasizing short-term forecasts—in which cyclical and high-frequency fluctuations necessarily dominate—the WEO gave primary emphasis to medium-term considerations, notably the policy requirements for generating sustainable, noninflationary growth and for consistency between countries. As the fall 1984 paper summarized the point, the medium-term scenarios "should be viewed not so much as a forecast of what will happen, but as an indication of the policy challenges that will need to be faced if a satisfactory outcome is to be achieved."[16]

Initially, the WEO scenarios were stylized presentations of how the pattern of current account balances among industrial countries might evolve over a period of about three years under various assumptions. For two years starting in April 1978, the staff presented a "recommended" or "desirable" scenario based on the assumption that the major industrial countries would adopt the policies necessary to jointly achieve moderate, noninflationary growth. In that scenario, the large external imbalances observed in 1978 (notably a large current account surplus in Japan and a large deficit in the United States) were projected to be substantially reduced over the medium term.[17] This desirable outcome, however, was judged by the staff as "unlikely to come about without significant adaptations of policy in a number of countries."[18] But the alternative scenarios, rather than projecting the

---

[16]"World Economic Outlook—General Survey," EBS/84/177 (August 16, 1984), p. 40.

[17]The length of the "medium term" was not defined precisely in that comparative-statics exercise, but it was understood to be around three years. The methodology involved allowing lagged effects that either were already "in the pipeline" or were introduced by the assumed changes in growth rates to have their full effect on current account balances. Thus the medium term was the period over which equilibrium would be achieved in the absence of new shocks to the economy. For an exposition of the methodology, see Artus and Knight (1984), Chapter 4.

[18]The characterization of the scenario as "recommended" is from "World Economic Outlook—General Survey," ID/79/1 (February 9, 1979), p. 24; and as "desirable," from "World Economic Outlook—General Survey," ID/78/1 (April 3, 1978), p. 37. The "unlikely to come about" judgment was made in "World Economic Outlook—Background Developments," ID/79/2 (February 13, 1979), p. 33. When the scenario was first presented a year earlier, the staff commented only that the desirable outcome "would represent a very significant shift in strategy," notably through a "more expansionary stance" of fiscal policy in the surplus countries, without commenting on

consequences of specific deviations in policy from the assumed path, merely showed the effects of different assumptions about economic growth in the major countries. Notably, if the U.S. economy were to grow more rapidly, and Japan more slowly, then the desirable outcome would be less likely to be achieved.

This general approach was continued in the spring 1980 cycle.[19] Two important changes were introduced in the fall of 1980. First, the "medium term" was linked to a specific date (1985–86), implying that the projections could be interpreted as dynamic simulations rather than comparative statics. In this low-key manner, the staff made its first numeric projections for a date beyond the usual short-term forecast horizon. Second, the projections included the aggregate current account balance of developing countries and thereby extended the scenarios beyond the industrial countries for the first time.

The background for these first true medium-term scenarios was that the United States, Japan, Germany, and the United Kingdom were all embarked on an anti-inflation strategy to combat the effects of the second oil shock and (in the United States and the United Kingdom) the cumulative excesses of the late 1970s. Much of the public and internal discussion of economic policy was focused on the question of whether this reaction was excessive. Both the United States and the United Kingdom had slipped into recession with sharply rising unemployment, while Japan and Germany had developed large external surpluses. The major oil-exporting countries were registering large external surpluses, and the non-oil developing countries were facing dangerously large deficits. Was it therefore time for the major industrial countries to ease up on their policies of restraint?

To tackle that question, the staff produced a six-paragraph summary of how the world economy might evolve over the next five to six years, (1) with a continuation of existing policies in industrial countries, (2) with more expansionary policies until inflation resumed, followed by a policy reversal, and (3) with expansionary policies maintained even after inflation resumed. The staff's judgment, which Executive Directors endorsed when they discussed the paper in September, was that countries should continue with contractionary policies to restore a reasonable balance to the global pattern of current account balances while continuing to rein in inflation. Allowing inflation to heat up again would lead to a deeper and more prolonged downturn than the one then in progress, and failing to tighten policies after inflation heated up would only aggravate the eventual downturn.[20] Thus the first global scenarios, although in retrospect appearing

---

the likelihood of that shift taking place. See "World Economic Outlook—General Survey," ID/78/1 (April 3, 1978), pp. 38 and 41. The sharpening of the tone followed widespread criticism from Executive Directors and others that the staff was being too complacent.

[19]The General Survey paper prepared for discussion by the Executive Board in April 1980 included an updating of the 1979 scenarios. See "World Economic Outlook—General Survey," ID/80/2 (March 31, 1980), p. 11 and Tables 8 and 9. That section was not included in the WEO that was published in May.

[20]The scenarios are in "World Economic Outlook—General Survey," ID/80/7 (August 22, 1980), pp. 20–23. For the Board's reactions, see the minutes of EBM/80/141 (September 12, 1980), pp. 18 and 20.

rather primitive and unquantified, served—for better or worse—to bolster confidence in the use of contractionary demand-management policies to combat inflationary pressures.

Three further innovations were introduced in the spring of 1981: the global medium-term scenarios were more fully quantified, were disaggregated for several analytical groups of developing countries, and were included in the published WEO.[21] The staff presented two tables with projections for 1985 under two scenarios. The baseline scenario A was based on several specified assumptions, including a continuation of restrictive demand management policies in industrial countries and the implementation of "adjustment policies" in developing countries. A key conclusion of that exercise was that the aggregate current account deficit of the non-oil developing countries would nearly double between 1980 and 1985, from $77 billion to $140 billion, but would remain manageable in relation to those countries' exports (rising only from 15.3 percent to 18 percent). Debt-service ratios were projected to rise slightly for developing countries that exported mainly manufactured goods, to rise sharply for low-income countries, and to rise moderately for "other net oil importers."

The staff's 1981 projections of the 1985 debt burdens of developing countries are of particular interest because they foreshadow the problems that led, a year later, to a nearly global debt crisis. In the text as published in June 1981, the staff described the medium-term debt prospects of low- and middle-income oil importers as "worrisome" and "disturbing"; "in the absence of adjustment measures, [many of these countries] would soon find themselves unable to finance their deficits." The latter message was made more explicit in the version of the paper discussed by Executive Directors in April. That paper noted that the staff had prepared a scenario in which the non-oil developing countries did not carry out adjustment policies to reduce the buildup of external debt, but that such a scenario had not been quantified because it "produced financing implications that were completely infeasible."[22]

The WEO scenarios were expanded slightly further in the fall of 1981. In addition to the baseline and more pessimistic scenarios, a "favorable" Scenario C was now presented. This seemingly innocuous extension was a response to the new-found optimism among many policymakers under the influence of the "new" supply-side economists (see Chapter 1). The "favorable" scenario assumed that inflationary expectations would fall rapidly, and real growth would rise rapidly, in response to a cut in government expenditure. But the staff argued that such a favorable development was "unlikely," and the paper cautioned that if governments

---

[21]WEO (June 1981), pp. 13–16 and Tables 31 and 32. The published version was somewhat abbreviated; in particular, it included only the baseline scenario "A." In addition, the figures in the tables were revised slightly between March and June. See "World Economic Outlook—General Survey," ID/81/1 (April 6, 1981), pp. 22–29 and Tables 14 and 15.

[22]WEO (June 1981), pp. 16 and 17; and "World Economic Outlook—General Survey," ID/81/1 (April 6, 1981), p. 23. This cautionary message was not always clearly conveyed. For a broader discussion of the Fund's precrisis views on external debt, see Chapter 6.

relied on the rosy scenario, they could be led into relaxing policies prematurely and falling inadvertently into the "pessimistic" Scenario B.[23]

The spring 1985 WEO marked the next major expansion of the medium-term scenarios, to the point that a separate paper was devoted to describing them. For the first time, the staff presented a fully articulated set of medium-term projections for the world economy, rather than just focusing on external positions. That is, rather than assuming rates of growth and inflation and deriving current account positions, the staff now made assumptions regarding fiscal, monetary, and other policies, and on that basis derived projections for growth, inflation, unemployment rates, interest and exchange rates, and of course current account balances. In view of the flagging debt strategy, the paper included detailed scenarios showing how various groups of developing countries would fare, notably as to the debt burdens that they would face, under different assumptions about conditions and policies in industrial countries. As before, the baseline scenario was flanked by illustrative scenarios with better and worse outcomes, but now the basis for the exercise was the specification of better and worse policies in both industrial and developing countries (see WEO, April 1985, Chapter III).

From that point on, the scenarios became an ever more detailed exercise and an ever more central feature of the WEO. In the fall of 1985, the staff left the basic scenario unchanged from the spring, on the grounds that the world economy had progressed more or less as expected, but three "sensitivity analysis" scenarios were added to deal with certain "uncertainties" that had intensified as a result of the fall in world oil prices and the depreciation of the U.S. dollar. One scenario examined the consequences of a further 20 percent fall in oil prices; a second dealt with a 20 percent depreciation of the dollar against other major currencies; and the third looked at the global effects of a sharp slowdown in industrial country growth. From this analysis, the staff concluded that the capital-importing developing countries (i.e., all developing countries except eight Middle Eastern oil exporters) would be little affected as a group by a further decline in oil prices, would benefit substantially from a further dollar depreciation, and would suffer a substantial loss in income from a slowdown in the industrial world.

A further impetus for developing the medium-term scenarios came when both the Group of Ten (G-10) industrial countries and the Group of 24 (G-24) developing countries issued reports in 1985 calling on the Fund to strengthen its surveillance over the policies of the major industrial countries by more clearly explaining the consequences of pursuing unchanged policies and by specifying and evaluating options for policy adjustments.[24] In response, the staff significantly expanded the scope of the scenarios in the spring 1986 exercise. For the first time,

---

[23]"World Economic Outlook—General Survey," ID/81/8 (August 24, 1981), pp. 22–32 and Tables 10–12. An updated version of Scenario C was included in WEO (April 1982), pp. 19–24. The developing country scenarios were further updated and revised in the publication of May 1983, pp. 15 and 19–20 and Tables 36–38, but the industrial country scenarios were not updated until 1985.

[24]The reports were reprinted as Appendixes to Crockett and Goldstein (1987). For more on those reports, see Chapter 4.

the staff made quantitative projections for each of the next four years, rather than just for a single medium-term period, for key macroeconomic variables for the United States, Japan, and Europe, as well as aggregate figures for industrial countries. These projections were produced under several different sets of assumptions, an exercise that earlier would have been impossibly complex to complete in the limited time available. On this occasion, the Fund staff called on the staff of the U.S. Federal Reserve Board, the OECD, and the Philadelphia-based Project LINK to provide econometric model simulations based on a common set of assumptions about economic policies and conditions. Those simulations were then combined, and extended to cover the implications for developing countries in more detail, using the newly developed MINIMOD system (see below, pp. 256–57). In essence, the exercise showed that an easing of fiscal or monetary policy could mitigate the short-term decline in output that was otherwise projected to occur, but at some risk of a rekindling of inflation.[25]

As the staff's econometric modeling capabilities strengthened in the second half of the 1980s, the medium-term projections became increasingly more quantitative and subject to consistency checks, and the "alternative" scenarios became correspondingly more detailed and more focused on specific policy options. For example, in August 1987, in an exercise that had important implications for the success of the Louvre accord (see Chapter 4), the scenarios suggested that maintaining fixed exchange rates might make reduction of the large external imbalances of the largest countries quite difficult. A few months later, after the October 1987 crisis in equity markets, the staff for the first time since 1979 undertook to prepare a "mini-WEO": a special review of the outlook in the light of the "plunge" (as the staff called it) in stock prices.[26]

Objective Indicators

In April 1986, the Interim Committee examined several proposals for strengthening the international monetary system that had emerged from the 1985 reports of the Deputies of the G-10 and G-24 countries. Although no very concrete agreement could be reached on reforming the system, the Committee did agree that the medium-term scenarios in the WEO should be further quantified by incorporating a consistent set of objective indicators for at least the major industrial countries.

> [T]he Committee asked the Executive Board to consider ways in which its regular reviews of the world economic situation could be further adapted to improve the scope

---

[25]"World Economic Outlook—Policy Interactions in Industrial Countries," SM/86/46 (February 28, 1986), pp. 10–18.

[26]The term "plunge" is from "World Economic Outlook—Preliminary Assessment of Prospects and Policy Issues," EBS/88/1 (January 6, 1988), p. 1; it was also employed by Frenkel at EBM/88/6 (January 13, 1988), p. 21. The staff analyses of the Louvre accords and the October 1987 stock market crash are discussed further below (pp. 249–50). The 1979 interim WEO was conducted in response to the large increase in oil prices that year (see pp. 245).

for discussing external imbalances, exchange rate developments, and policy interactions among members. An approach worth exploring further was the formulation of a set of objective indicators related to policy actions and economic performance, having regard to a medium-term framework. Such indicators might help to identify a need for discussion of countries' policies.[27]

The indicators were introduced in the fall 1986 round, in the form of two tables and supporting text. The first table projected real output growth and inflation for the period 1988–91 (as an average over the four years) and current account balances for the terminal year, 1991. In the paper circulated for discussion by the Executive Board, these projections (or "quantified assumptions," as the staff called them to stress how limited the exercise was intended to be) were given for each G-7 country and for industrial countries as a whole (but not for developing countries). The version published in October 1986 included only the aggregate projections. The second table gave 1991 projections for the major components of the national saving-investment relationship: general government deficits, the "savings surplus" (i.e., the excess over investment) of the private sector, and the current account balance.[28] From that table, one could see the implications for external imbalances from the projected course of fiscal policies. Incompatibilities between countries in the stance of policies, it was hoped, would become that much clearer to assess.[29] With that extension of the indicators, combined with the development of the staff's own econometric models, the quantification of medium-term scenarios for industrial countries was essentially complete.[30]

Key Policy Issues in the WEO

The 1980s brought dramatic changes in thinking about how macroeconomic policy works. The difficulty of explaining the inflationary stagnation ("stagfla-

---

[27]Interim Committee Communiqué (April 10, 1986), para. 6. The development of quantitative indicators for the WEO scenarios paralleled the indicators exercise that the G-7 countries conducted themselves with the support of the Fund (see Chapter 4), but the indicators and the underlying data were not necessarily the same for the two purposes.

[28]"World Economic Outlook—Developments, Prospects, and Policy Issues," EBS/86/196 (August 20, 1986), Tables 2 and 4. The (truncated) published tables first appeared in WEO (October 1986), pp. 17 and 21.

[29]See footnote 15, p. 231, on the saving-investment identity. The analytical implications were developed further by the staff in the course of 1986–87, and the Executive Board discussed and generally endorsed the continuation of the approach at meetings in January and July 1987. See "Enhancing the Use of Indicators as a Tool for Surveillance," EBS/86/282 (December 18, 1986), "The Use of Indicators in Surveillance—Analytical Issues," EBS/87/135 (June 24, 1987), and the minutes of EBM/87/8–9 (January 14, 1987) and EBM/87/105–106 (July 22, 1987).

[30]Starting in 1987, the staff examined the possibility of adding indicators of structural policies such as the degree of liberalization in goods, factor, and financial markets, but that effort was eventually abandoned on the grounds that such indicators could not be made quantitative and internationally commensurate to the same degree as the basic macroeconomic indicators. See Chapter 4, pp. 222–24. The Executive Board decision not to adopt a system of structural indicators was taken at EBM/89/4 (January 13, 1989).

tion") of the late 1970s with classical or Keynesian or monetarist models left a vacuum that was filled in part by a series of short-lived fads such as distorted forms of supply-side economics, some extreme forms of monetarism, and the revival of "gold bugs" who advocated a return to the gold standard (see Chapter 1, pp. 27). As those movements inevitably faded away,[31] the vacuum was filled by a neoclassical revolution that brought a greater discipline to policy analysis and shifted attention away from the business cycle toward longer-term growth and stability. IMF surveillance encountered all these movements, and the staff's analysis of policy options both helped to shape the debate (at least internally) and evolved in important ways as a result.

Fiscal and Monetary Policies

WEO discussions always included an extended discussion of economic conditions and policies in the large industrial countries, especially for the United States, Japan, and Germany. To a large extent, that discussion overlapped with the annual Article IV discussions with those individual countries, described in Chapter 3. The WEO, however, gave the Executive Board a chance to discuss interactions among countries much more explicitly and consistently. Throughout the 1980s, the overarching issue in those discussions was the nature of the effects of fiscal and monetary policies.

At the risk of oversimplifying a complex theoretical debate, one could say that until the late 1970s, the WEO had a distinctly Keynesian tone. That tone reflected a general optimism about the ability of governments to regulate the degree of stimulus to the economy so as to maximize growth without unduly contributing to inflationary pressures. This view was expressed most clearly in the spring of 1978, when many industrial countries were struggling to find some means of restoring economic growth while simultaneously getting inflation back under control.[32] "There is now a need for greater emphasis on policies to stimulate economic growth," the staff concluded then. Moreover, "the risks of exacerbating inflation

---

[31]Jacques J. Polak (Executive Director for the Netherlands) predicted the demise in these terms, during a May 1982 Board discussion on France: "The world is witnessing a succession of experiments in major countries, such as extreme monetarism in Britain, 'Reaganomics' in the United States, and reflation in France. While those experiments might bring some new wisdom in economic policy, more probably they ultimately will tend to confirm most of the conventional wisdom at very considerable cost to themselves and to the rest of the world." Minutes of EBM/82/63 (May 3, 1982), p. 13.

[32]Perhaps the best-known statement of the prevailing official view of macroeconomic policy of that time is the OECD's McCracken Report (see Chapter 1). That report, issued in 1977, concluded that although the major countries faced a "narrow path" toward the objective of full employment with stable prices, "a relatively *active* demand management policy may be needed, involving a succession of injections of purchasing power over a period of months or even years, while at the same time standing ready to begin withdrawing stimulus as soon as endogenous forces gather momentum." McCracken and others (1977), p. 190; the italics and the mangled syntax are in the original.

[33]"World Economic Outlook—General Survey," ID/78/1 (April 3, 1978), pp. 33 and 34.

would be minimal if the policies of expansion were cautious and well designed."[33] By the time the 1970s ended, however, caution and good policy design were clearly elusive goals, and the structural underpinning of the post-1973 stagnation was better understood. The tone of subsequent WEO recommendations on macroeconomic policies became decidedly less activist.

In the early 1980s, the goal of macroeconomic policy throughout the industrialized world was to restrain the conduct of fiscal and monetary policies to bring inflation down gradually without incurring excessive costs through lost growth in output and employment. Most governments were more successful during this period at slowing monetary growth than they were at reducing fiscal deficits. At the IMF, it was relatively easy for the staff and Executive Directors to agree that more aggressive fiscal restraint was required, but devising a recommended course for monetary policy was rather more difficult. What was the right balance between fiscal and monetary restraint in these circumstances?

The Executive Board's discussion of the WEO in May 1981 included substantial debate about the appropriate "mix" of monetary and fiscal policies in the major industrial countries. The discussion was a little confused, because the phrase "the mix of monetary and fiscal policies" was not clearly defined. Logically, it would mean a shift in the degree of relative restraint, with no change in the overall degree of demand restraint. Specifically, because of the economic imbalances then prevailing, it would mean a recommendation to exercise greater constraint on fiscal policy to permit a correspondingly easier monetary policy (i.e., a higher rate of monetary growth). To many, however, it meant that fiscal restraint would permit only a lowering of interest rates through the exercise of greater overall demand restraint with unchanged monetary targets. That is, "changing the mix" was being used as a euphemism for a tighter anti-inflationary policy. Directors fell back on vague terms such as the "overuse of" or "excessive reliance on" monetary policy, but without specifying what the right monetary policy should be in case of greater fiscal restraint.[34]

By the spring of 1982, the discussion was more explicit, and it became clear that by a shift in the "mix," most Executive Directors meant overall tightening. As the Managing Director summarized Directors' views: "Because of the sensitivity of private market participants to the inflationary effects of monetary growth, a shift toward monetary expansion probably would cause the inflation rate to ratchet to a higher level. . . . A more decisive commitment to budgetary restraint and smaller

---

[34]Minutes of EBM/81/71–74 (May 1 and May 4, 1981). In mainstream macroeconomics, the growth rate of nominal income is determined by the combined stance of fiscal and monetary policy, subject to any shifts in private sector behavior. The stance of monetary policy is conventionally measured by the growth rate of the stock of money (or, more precisely, by the growth rate of the "monetary base": currency plus bank reserves); the fiscal stance, by a combination of government spending and tax policy. A cut in government spending, with no change in monetary growth, would tend to reduce income growth and inflation, but the extent of that effect would be blunted by the tendency for interest rates to fall in such circumstances. The moderating influence of falling interest rates is usually described as an easing of monetary conditions, not as an easing of monetary policy.

fiscal deficits would reduce market uncertainty as to the longer-run commitment of the authorities to programs of financial restraint, and thus accelerate the decline in inflationary expectations."[35]

This view of the effects of macroeconomic policies represented a significant departure from the mainstream economics of the 1960s and 1970s. In the conventional textbook model, a combination of fiscal tightening and monetary easing would leave aggregate demand initially unchanged but would stimulate growth over time by lowering real interest rates. The model implied by the summary just quoted differs in two ways. First, the stimulus to real growth from this shift in the mix would be thwarted by a resurgence of inflationary expectations, which were assumed to be determined by monetary growth and structural factors rather than by overall demand pressures. That assumption was widely accepted at the time because of the very high rates of inflation and monetary growth that had prevailed in the late 1970s. Second, the usual negative consequences of fiscal contraction on output would be offset by a supply-side stimulus arising from the expectation of a more stable and sustainable macroeconomic environment. Therefore, the recommended policy advice was to leave monetary targets unchanged while tightening control over ("consolidating") fiscal policy. Neither of these propositions had been verified empirically, and no doubt few would have claimed that they held universally. Rather, they were a reaction to the large imbalances of the time. Nonetheless, the confusion over this issue lingered throughout the rest of the decade, long after inflation and monetary pressures had subsided.

A more general question was whether monetary and fiscal policies should be used for countercyclical stabilization or applied steadily toward longer-term goals. As discussed in Chapter 3, the staff in the field did not always adhere to a party line on this question; they attempted to adapt their advice to the circumstances of the country at hand. The WEO, in contrast, took a consistent stand from 1980 on, against the activism of the 1970s and in favor of a consistent policy stance over the medium term. From 1980 through 1983, the argument was that progress toward price stability was still uneven and uncertain and required further persistence. By 1984, when inflation had been markedly and widely reduced in the major industrial countries, the staff had developed a clear and deeper view. As expressed in the General Survey paper for the spring 1984 WEO discussion:

> . . . continued adherence to the strategy of restoring and maintaining financial stability in the major industrial countries will provide the best framework for sustainable economic growth in the medium term. It is true that the reduction of fiscal deficits

---

[35]Minutes of EBM/82/54 (April 22, 1982), p. 18. De Larosière stated his views on this subject even more clearly during the March 1984 WEO discussion, in responding to a comment by Polak that "references to a change in the policy mix were often unclear" and should be avoided. "The reference to the policy mix in the staff paper," de Larosière replied, "had been meant to suggest that monetary policy in the United States should remain essentially unchanged while fiscal policy should be more restrained than hitherto; and the hope was that an appropriately restrictive monetary policy, together with a more restrained fiscal policy, would loosen monetary conditions somewhat." Minutes of EBM/84/50 (April 2, 1984), p. 9.

required by this process involves a withdrawal of stimulus. The staff believes, however, that such an influence would be offset in due course by the effects of lower interest rates and improved confidence on the investment climate.[36]

Most Executive Directors supported this view, but some took exception to it. For example, John Tvedt (Norway) noted that Japan and Germany had inflation "firmly under control" and "could usefully stimulate their economies without any inflationary consequences." Luke Leonard (Alternate—Ireland) and Mohamed Finaish (Libya) took a similar view. E.I.M. Mtei (Alternate—Tanzania) accepted that fiscal control was necessary but suggested that "monetary policy should be assigned a more active role to provide the necessary stimulus for the recovery. . . ." Jacques de Groote (Belgium) reasoned that medium-term restraint and inflation control were not sufficient to generate a recovery. If they were, then Germany and Japan would already have seen more robust growth. He attributed the recovery in the United States and the United Kingdom to the adoption of more flexible demand management than in Germany and Japan, and in particular to a "strong expansionary fiscal impulse" in 1983.[37] Not only was fiscal stimulus through "reduction of the tax burden" appropriate in countries where inflation had been brought under control (i.e., Japan and Germany); the "structural transformation" that they needed to remove market rigidities required "more buoyant economic activity." The prevailing view in the boardroom, however, was that if Japan and Germany would just persevere with restraint, recovery would come in due course.[38]

Throughout the 1980s, the WEO papers stuck to an advocacy of medium-term stability in macroeconomic policies, though without pushing that view to an extreme. The closest that the staff came again to advocating an active demand-management policy was in 1987, when Japan and Germany were being pressured by other countries to ease up on the restraint of aggregate demand. As Crockett explained the staff's support of that view to the Executive Board, the "medium-term assessment had tended to be qualified by the judgment that the speed with which progress was made toward that medium-term objective could be modified in the light of economic conditions prevailing at a given time. Based on the current belief that there would be a substantial withdrawal of fiscal stimulus in the United States, the occasion might be presenting itself for other countries to modify the pace of fiscal consolidation accordingly." That view was initially greeted with considerable skepticism on the Board, but six months later, it won endorsement: "There was widespread agreement [among Executive Directors in September 1987]

---

[36]"World Economic Outlook—General Survey," EBS/84/33 (March 2, 1984), p. 47.

[37]Table A-8 in the staff paper (Table 8 in WEO, April 1984) showed a fiscal impulse equal to 1.6 percent of GNP in the United States in 1983, and 2.4 percent in the United Kingdom; in contrast, the fiscal impulses for Japan and Germany were –0.4 percent and –0.1 percent, respectively.

[38]Minutes of EBM/84/48 (March 30, 1984), pp. 11 (Finaish), 28–30 (de Groote), and 36 (Leonard); EBM/84/49 (March 30, 1984), pp. 8 (Tvedt) and 17 (Mtei); and EBM/84/50 (April 2, 1984), p. 13 (Chairman's summing up).

[39]Minutes of EBM/87/48 (March 17, 1987), p. 5 (Crockett); and EBM/87/136 (September 14, 1987), p. 17 (Chairman's summing up).

that Germany and Japan need to aim for a rate of growth of domestic demand that is faster than the underlying growth in their productive potential."[39]

Perhaps the most interesting, and certainly the most important, example of the staff's attempt to steer a moderate medium-term course was the WEO analysis of the effects of the Gramm-Rudman-Hollings (or, as it was commonly known, Gramm-Rudman) legislation in the United States. That legislation, enacted in December 1985, mandated a schedule for eliminating the U.S. fiscal deficit (then running at approximately 5 percent of GNP) by fiscal year 1991.[40] The first WEO papers prepared after the start of Gramm-Rudman presented three scenarios on how the world economy might evolve through 1991. The baseline scenario assumed partial implementation of the law, with the deficit declining only to 2½ percent of GNP by the time the law decreed it should be reduced to zero. That scenario reflected a judgment by the staff that the Gramm-Rudman target was not just too ambitious politically, as was obvious, but excessively contractionary and thus economically unrealistic as well. In the alternative scenario with full implementation, U.S. and global economic growth were both shown to be significantly reduced during the first four years (1986–89), so that the level of output would remain below the baseline until well into the 1990s. The staff also discussed a second alternative, with no deficit reduction at all. Under that scenario, U.S. debt was shown to grow relentlessly relative to GNP, and the staff concluded that such a scenario would be disastrously unsustainable.[41] Reduction of the U.S. fiscal deficit was therefore essential but would best be pursued moderately over a period of years.

The staff's treatment of the Gramm-Rudman targets drew fire from several Executive Directors, led by the U.S. Director, Charles H. Dallara. While acknowledging that it was always appropriate for the staff to express a "healthy degree of skepticism" about policy implementation, Dallara argued that the staff's analysis appeared to be "too mechanically Keynesian," meaning that it made insufficient allowance for favorable shifts in expectations and other supply-side benefits.[42] Aggressive deficit reduction, he argued, would reap its rewards rapidly. That argument was endorsed by several other chairs, including those of Japan, Germany, the United Kingdom, Australia, and Saudi Arabia; the Directors from Belgium, Canada, and India sided broadly with the staff view.[43] In the event, these competing views of the world were never tested, because the U.S. deficit remained high

---

[40]The analysis of the Gramm-Rudman legislation in the context of the Article IV consultations with the United States is discussed in Chapter 3.

[41]The baseline scenario was presented in "The World Economy to 1991—General Survey," EBS/86/42 (February 28, 1986). The alternatives were presented in "World Economic Outlook— Policy Interactions in Industrial Countries," SM/86/46 (February 28, 1986).

[42]In fact, the model (MINIMOD) on which the zero-deficit scenario was largely based did incorporate endogenous, model-consistent expectations as well as other extensions of the conventional Keynesian model (see below, pp. 256–57). Those effects, however, dominated the effects on aggregate demand only after a lag of a few years, as was true in virtually all of the major econometric models then in use.

[43]Minutes of EBM/86/51 (March 24, 1986), pp. 5–12.

throughout the 1986–91 period, and the Gramm-Rudman legislation was eventually abandoned.

Inflation Control

At the end of the 1970s, by far the dominant economic problem in the world was inflation. Throughout the late 1970s and early 1980s, the Fund's Executive Directors generally treated inflation in the major industrial countries as a structural as well as a monetary problem, while the staff treated it more as the result of lax monetary policy. For example, the spring 1979 WEO paper included an analysis of overall monetary growth in the large industrial countries, which showed that a broadly defined aggregate money stock for the G-10 countries had grown by about 10 percent a year since 1975; the paper concluded that the primary method available for cutting inflation was to reduce that growth rate. That approach was criticized at the Executive Board meeting by Bernard J. Drabble (Canada), Lamberto Dini (Italy), and others. Drabble argued that in 1979 the United States was the only major country experiencing pressure from excess demand and that inflation elsewhere was the result of cost-push pressures. Dini stressed the importance of institutional factors that were left out of the staff analysis, and he questioned the attempt to gauge monetary pressures by aggregating money stocks across countries.[44]

If inflation was partly structural in its origins, then a case could be made for structural policies to control it. One leading candidate in the discussions of the 1970s and 1980s was "incomes" policy: direct limits on the rate of growth of wages and/or prices. Overall, the staff was skeptical of incomes policies, but with some prodding by Executive Directors and the Managing Director, the staff gradually adopted a more eclectic stance.[45] That process began in January 1980, when the staff paper for the WEO discussion noted that the recent tightening of monetary policies in several industrial countries was driving up interest rates and slowing output growth, and invited Executive Directors to discuss options for alleviating those pressures. The Board, with the "full agreement" of the Managing Director, responded that incomes policies could help.[46] A few months later, in the next WEO survey, the staff grudgingly gave its first qualified endorsement: "Incomes policies can sometimes help in solving the inflation problem while cushioning the impact of restrictive monetary policy on real activity" (*WEO*, May 1980, p. 7).

The soul-searching over incomes policies was far from academic. In 1981, five of the G-7 industrial countries were actively implementing incomes policies, and many policymakers in those countries had concluded that the strong ideo-

---

[44]Minutes of IS/79/1 (February 23, 1979), p. 21 (Drabble); IS/79/2 (same date), pp. 14–16 (Dini).

[45]J. Marcus Fleming, Deputy Director of Research under Jacques Polak (1964–76), favored the careful and limited application of incomes policies as an adjunct to stable monetary policy; see Fleming (1959). After his early death in 1976, the influence of his views on this matter apparently waned.

[46]See "World Economic Outlook—The Current Picture," ID/80/1 (January 3, 1980), pp. 14–15 and 25; and the Chairman's summing up, minutes of EBM/80/11 (January 17, 1980), p. 5.

logical opposition of the governments in the other two—the United States under President Reagan and the United Kingdom under Prime Minister Thatcher—was forcing an unnecessary reliance on monetary restraint and thus unduly driving up world interest rates. The undercurrent of the discussion was an attempt to bring the influence of the Fund to bear on the two holdouts. The staff paper for the spring 1981 discussion contributed to the debate by including a favorable analysis of several successful cases. The paper supported the idea of the "more flexible forms of incomes policies . . . in which efforts are made to relate the growth of real wages to the average economy-wide gain in productivity corrected for changes in the terms of trade" (WEO, June 1981, pp. 9–10). Much of the Executive Board, of course, endorsed that view, and Directors expressed particular admiration for the Japanese structural approach to inflation control. In concluding the discussion, de Larosière made a personal plea for the Fund to rise above the controversy of the subject: "I know incomes policies are not always popular, but some understanding in this field is necessary if we are to tackle the problem. . . ."[47]

Whatever the WEO may have contributed to an "understanding in this field," it did little to resolve the policy debate. Two years later, during the February 1983 WEO discussion by the Board, several Executive Directors complained that the staff paper had said little about incomes policies. Schwartz responded that the staff had—on this and earlier occasions—favorably characterized informal incomes policies such as those in effect in Germany, Japan, Canada, France, and Italy. He concluded, however, that the staff saw no point in trying to push the United States and the United Kingdom into adopting policies that they clearly opposed.[48]

By that time, inflation was beginning to recede as a major policy issue. The average inflation rate of consumer prices for the G-7 countries had been reduced from a peak of 12 percent in 1980 to just 4½ percent in 1983. The decline in the United States was even greater: from 13½ percent to just over 3 percent. Nonetheless, memories of the inflationary mess of the 1970s were still vivid enough that few were prepared to declare victory. The U.S. authorities occasionally professed to be pursuing a target of zero inflation, which struck many observers as excessively ambitious. The U.S. Executive Director, Richard D. Erb, put it slightly more guardedly: "price stability . . . was something quite close to a zero rate of inflation, perhaps in the range of 1–2 percent." In that context, a number of Executive Directors asked the staff to develop a view on the optimal inflation rate. Schwartz gave a cautious reply that preserved the Fund's credentials as a hawk on inflation while distancing the staff from an extreme view: "a low positive rate might be acceptable," he averred, but the optimal rate would be hard to assess and would not be uniform for all countries. In any case, he concluded, most

---

[47]Minutes of EBM/81/74 (May 4, 1981), p. 11 (Chairman's summing up). On the Japanese model, see the statement by Teruo Hirao, EBM/81/73 (May 4, 1981), pp. 13–17.

[48]Minutes of EBM/83/24 (February 2, 1983), p. 8.

[49]Minutes of EBM/83/23 (January 31, 1983), p. 4 (Erb); and EBM/83/24 (February 2, 1983), pp. 9–10 (Schwartz).

countries were still far enough from zero inflation that the question was essentially moot.[49]

Price of Oil

Of special importance for any discussion of inflation in the 1970s or 1980s was the price of oil in world trade. In the wake of the second major round of oil price increases, in 1978–79, the questions of how independent an influence the oil shock was for inflation and output growth and of how countries should adapt to the new circumstances were key issues in the WEO discussions.

When the Executive Board met on June 27, 1979, to discuss the WEO, the oil market and the world economy were at a critical juncture. On that same day, the oil ministers of OPEC were gathered in Geneva, in a meeting that would lead to a major jump in the price of oil. Measured in U.S. dollars, the official price of a barrel of Saudi Arabian light crude had already risen from $12.70 at the end of 1978 to $14.55 in April 1979. It would now be raised to $18.00, and the average export price for the major oil-exporting countries would soon be some 60 percent above the end-1978 level.[50] Also on that same day, the heads of state and government of the G-7 countries were assembled in Tokyo, in a summit meeting devoted predominantly to dealing with the growing pressures in the oil market.[51] In normal times, the WEO would not have been on the agenda for another two months, but a crisis was at hand. For the second time in seven months, the Fund was holding a special, ad hoc surveillance meeting on the WEO.[52]

The basic conclusion reached by Executive Directors in June 1979 was that the world economic situation was worse than when the first oil shock had hit in 1973, because inflation was higher, economic growth was weaker, oil output was "less elastic," and the oil-importing developing countries were financially weaker because of their heavy post-1973 borrowing. Consequently, the "industrial countries should pursue a coordinated demand strategy," in which the countries with "relatively strong external positions" should expand to "counteract the deflationary impact of the oil price increases. . . ."[53] In essence, the Board was reaffirming the "locomotive" strategy that had debuted to mixed reviews at the Bonn summit the year before.[54]

At the next regularly scheduled WEO discussion, in September 1979, the ongoing rise in oil prices was again the main agenda item, and the central issue was still the need for a global adjustment strategy for coping with it. The staff paper set

---

[50]At the Geneva meeting, OPEC ministers agreed that the official "marker" price for Saudi Arabian oil would be raised to $18, but other OPEC members could raise their own prices to as much as $23.50.

[51]For a review of the Tokyo summit discussions on energy, see Putnam and Bayne (1987), pp. 110–18.

[52]The previous ad hoc meeting, precipitated by the dollar crisis of October–November 1978, had been held on December 13 and 19, 1978.

[53]Chairman's summing up, minutes of IS/79/6 (June 29, 1979), pp. 24–25.

[54]For the development of the locomotive strategy and for other reactions to it in the Fund, see the section on Germany in Chapter 3.

out in some detail the consequences of the oil shock: a marked slowdown in industrial country growth, mainly owing to the onset of a recession in the United States; a consequent slowdown in growth of world trade; "a virtually worldwide acceleration in inflation"; substantial shifts in current account balances among the industrial countries (strengthening in the United States, weakening elsewhere: changes that would, serendipitously, foster external adjustment); and a large increase in current account deficits for oil-importing developing countries and other producers of primary commodities. The paper then noted that this last development raised the possibility that greater recourse to official—especially multilateral—financing would be required, but also that recycling of the oil exporters' surpluses by commercial banks would be crucial. Consequently, as the Managing Director noted in summing up the Board meeting, "increased cooperation between multilateral organizations and commercial banks would be useful."[55] That theme would take on increasing importance over the next several years, especially after the debt crisis hit Latin America in 1982.

The Fund's support for coordinated action in response to the oil shock was recorded in subsequent WEO discussions as well. For example, in January 1980, the Managing Director paid homage to the "significant role" played by "coordinated policy actions" in reducing the current account imbalances that had built up among the major countries. Officials from the major oil-exporting countries sounded a similar theme, but they also complained that they were being unfairly singled out as being responsible for the poor state of the world economy.[56] In their view, the oil-importing industrial countries also were to blame, for excess demand in general and excessive consumption of oil in particular. They pointed out that the standard WEO analysis, by limiting the forecast horizon to one or two years, caught the negative macroeconomic effects of a rise in oil prices but missed the offsetting benefits to global demand and output as the exporters' surpluses began to be recycled.[57] Subsequent staff papers typically took a slightly softer tone in dealing with the subject.

---

[55]"World Economic Outlook—General Survey," ID/79/7 (August 30, 1979), pp. 1–3; and minutes of IS/79/8 (September 12, 1979), p. 21.

[56]In December 1979, the Fund adopted a basic scheme for classifying countries in which oil trade played a dominant role. The staff at that time had proposed a tripartite scheme that would have divided the world into industrial, major oil-exporting, and non-oil developing countries. (This classification would replace the earlier practice of classifying countries as industrial, developing, or in an intermediate group called "more developed primary producing countries.") Following an extended discussion in which some oil exporters objected both to being singled out and to the apparent implication that they were not developing countries, the Executive Board decided that there should be two broad groups—industrial and developing—with the latter divided into oil-exporting and non-oil. See "Classification of Countries," SM/79/275 (November 28, 1979), and minutes of EBM/79/185–186 (December 17). That scheme was retained until January 1985, when the oil/non-oil distinction was relegated to a subsidiary status. See "Classification of Countries," SM/85/8 (January 3, 1985), and minutes of EBM/85/10 (January 23, 1985).

[57]The latter point was made most explicitly in an April 1980 letter to the Managing Director from the Minister of Finance of Kuwait, Abdul Rahman Salim Al-Ateeqy; in IMF/CF, S 321 "World Development Outlook—Fund Review (*Tours d'Horizon*), April 1980–August 1980.

The more fundamental issue concerned the extent to which the burgeoning current account deficits of the oil-importing countries (industrial and developing) should be financed, and the extent to which the authorities should be urged to restrict the growth of demand in order to reduce the deficits to more easily manageable levels. In the WEO discussion of May 1981, Ariel Buira (Mexico) laid out the case for financing over adjustment. The oil-importing countries, he argued, had overreacted to the emergence of large current account deficits, which were a normal by-product of the rise in oil prices that had occurred since 1973. By trying to reduce those deficits sharply, they risked producing a global contraction. That view, however, did not prevail. Overall, the Board by that time was gravely concerned about the "frightening" prospects for external deficits in the oil-importing developing countries, which were "probably not financeable."[58] As the 1980s began to unfold, the only choice was between a sharp downward adjustment in demand and a leap from crisis to crisis.

International Monetary System

The controversy that more than any other could be characterized as a battle for the heart and soul of the IMF was the debate over fixed versus floating exchange rates. As with other economic issues, this debate took place on two levels: in the field, especially in the policy recommendations given to countries requesting to borrow from the Fund, and at headquarters, especially in research and policy papers. The international monetary system of the time was usually described as a system of floating rates, in contrast to the pre-1973 system of adjustable pegs, but the reality was an eclectic jumble that had arisen more from historical accident, previously valid relationships, and inertia than from any rational political economy.

From 1982 to 1989, countries with independently floating rates ranged from 8 to 19, while about 90 countries pegged their currencies to a single reserve currency or to a currency basket. The rest of the world managed their currencies under more or less flexible arrangements (see Chapter 2). Within the G-7, the currencies of the three largest countries (the United States, Japan, and Germany) and the Canadian dollar floated relative to one another; two currencies (the French franc and the Italian lira) were linked to the deutsche mark through the Exchange Rate Mechanism (ERM) of the European Monetary System (EMS); and the pound sterling (which was not in the ERM though the United Kingdom was a member of the EMS) was managed with varying degrees of flexibility. Neither the economics profession at large nor the Fund staff had developed any real consensus on whether countries overall should edge closer to fixity or to flexibility.

The WEO papers and discussions seldom tackled this question directly. Rather, the emphasis was on defining the domestic macroeconomic policies that would be best suited to bringing about sustained (noninflationary) growth and thereby a stable or sustainable pattern of exchange rates for the major reserve currencies. As a

---

[58]Minutes of EBM/81/72 (May 1, 1981), p. 4 (Buira); and EBM/81/74 (May 4, 1981), p. 13 (Chairman's summing up). For a further discussion, see Chapter 6.

general proposition, the staff position evolved moderately during the 1980s, from one favoring laissez-faire on exchange rates to one that gave more prominence to the desirability of stabilizing rates.

In the spring of 1981, as the U.S. dollar, the Japanese yen, and the pound sterling were all appreciating strongly relative to other major currencies, the WEO staff paper concluded that exchange rate movements over the past year had "in some cases been excessive."[59] Nonetheless, it also concluded that the "first priority for monetary policy must be to counter inflationary pressures, and that a certain degree of short-term fluctuation in exchange rates has to be accepted." Executive Directors broadly agreed with that assessment.[60] Three years later, however, concerns about short-term volatility of exchange rates had given way to more serious anxieties about large and sustained misalignments—especially the continuing appreciation of the dollar. Still, the Managing Director noted at the conclusion of the April 1984 Executive Board meeting on the WEO:

> Directors did not in general suggest direct action to influence the pattern of exchange rates. They felt that an improvement in the U.S. fiscal position, coupled with a firm monetary policy, would facilitate a reduction of interest differentials between the United States and other countries, and that this would in turn lead to a gradual decline in the dollar and restoration of a more sustainable pattern of exchange rates and current account balances.[61]

In other words, bringing exchange rates back to a more sustainable pattern was important, but through policy adjustments rather than through direct intervention.

The controversy over the stability of the international monetary system climaxed in the spring of 1985, shortly after the major industrial countries had finally undertaken to engineer a reversal of the appreciation of the dollar through coordinated intervention in the foreign exchange markets. The staff produced a record amount of documentation for the Executive Board, comprising three main papers on the outlook and the main policy issues, the usual statistical appendix, and no less than 11 supplementary papers: in all, more than 550 single-spaced pages of text and tables. In response, the Board spent a record amount of time—two very long days and part of a third—discussing the outlook, much of which was directed at the question of whether the unstable values of the key reserve currencies were creating major problems for the world economy.

The central question at that time was whether the U.S. dollar was headed for a "hard landing." The strong dollar of the early 1980s had been associated with a growing current account deficit for the United States. The predominant creditor

---

[59]The characterization of exchange rate changes as having been "excessive" derived from the view that rates tended to "overshoot" the changes that were needed to restore equilibrium following a disturbance. Specifically, the staff paper argued that market participants seemed to have overreacted to the emergence of current account deficits in continental European countries and therefore to have excessively driven up the relative values of the dollar, the yen, and the pound. "World Economic Outlook—Situation of the Industrial Countries," ID/81/2 (April 15, 1981), pp. 23–26.

[60]Chairman's summing up, EBM/81/74 (May 4, 1981), p. 13.

[61]Chairman's summing up, EBM/84/50 (April 2, 1984), p. 15.

nation of the world just a few years earlier, the United States was now by some measures already becoming a net debtor. Once the dollar started tumbling from the heights, would it return to a normal and sustainable level, or would it overshoot and become seriously undervalued?[62] The WEO did not take a clear-cut position on this crucial issue, but the staff did raise a warning flag. Although the fundamental attractiveness to investors of the U.S. economy was strong in that inflation was low and investment returns were high, it was hard to see where the large continuing net inflows of funds to the United States would come from without large shifts in exchange rates, interest rates, or other prices.[63] On the whole, Executive Directors were more inclined than the staff to take these concerns seriously, and the Board concluded in April 1985 that "the vulnerability attached to the present and projected external positions was . . . one of the important challenges to policymakers in the industrial countries and to the Fund." Directors called for "carefully coordinated . . . policy measures that would facilitate a smooth convergence to a more sustainable pattern of exchange rates."[64] That call, however, did not extend to a specific recommendation for greater fixity in exchange rates or other changes in the functioning of the system.

The general position of the Fund on this issue underwent little further change in the second half of the decade. In March 1987, the Board convened to discuss the outlook just three weeks after the meeting at the Louvre at which major industrial countries announced their agreement "to cooperate closely to foster stability of exchange rates around current levels."[65] The staff took a neutral view on the wisdom of trying to keep the dollar from depreciating further in 1987, partly because of the ambiguity about whether the shifts that had already occurred would continue to pull down the U.S. external deficit, and partly because the staff generally viewed exchange rate changes as neither necessary nor sufficient for shifts in current account balances.[66] The medium-term scenarios for the spring 1987 exercise did show that the projected decline in the U.S. fiscal deficit was unlikely by itself to bring about a substantial reduction in the current account deficit. However, both the staff and the Executive Board were divided on the question of whether a shift in relative monetary conditions (lower interest rates in the United States, higher rates in Europe) aimed at further realigning exchange rates would lead to a more sustainable pattern of international trade. The Managing Director summarized the matter as follows:

---

[62]For an exposition of the "hard landing" scenario, see Marris (1985).

[63]See the staff statements at EBM/85/53 (April 3, 1985), pp. 12–13 and 17–18.

[64]Chairman's summing up, EBM/85/55 (April 5, 1985), p. 7.

[65]Communiqué of the ministers of finance and central bank governors of six major industrial countries (February 22, 1987), para. 10; reproduced in Funabashi (1988), pp. 277–80.

[66]The latter argument derives from the fact that the exchange rate and the current account balance are both endogenous variables that respond to a variety of disturbances such as monetary and fiscal policies and shifts in market perceptions. The theoretical arguments and empirical evidence were set out in a background paper for the spring 1986 WEO: Boughton and others (1986). A theoretical model and the implications for the international monetary system were discussed in Boughton (1989 and 1991).

... most Directors viewed the recent Louvre agreement as a major step toward a more viable payments pattern in the medium term. . . . While noting that further [exchange] rate movements might at some time be necessary, they felt that stability in rates was important at the present time. . . . Several speakers, however, noted that there was little sign so far of any narrowing in the payments imbalances, and little evidence in the staff's projections that a significant narrowing would take place in the medium term. Under the circumstances, these Directors questioned whether the Louvre agreement would be sufficient to prevent the reemergence of exchange market pressures.[67]

Several months later, in the wake of the stock market crash in October 1987, exchange market pressures did reemerge: in three months, the U.S. dollar depreciated by about 15 percent against both the mark and the yen. The staff—in a WEO paper prepared especially to analyze the effects of the market turmoil—concluded that it would be a mistake for the major countries to try to adhere rigorously to the original Louvre agreement: "cooperation on exchange rate matters should focus on underlying policies, rather than a particular pattern of rates."[68] At the Board meeting in January 1988, most Directors took a stance tilted more toward actively trying to prevent further depreciation of the dollar.[69]

By the end of the 1980s, exchange rates seemed to have stabilized reasonably well, but the external imbalances that had plagued the major countries for several years were still very evident. Whether rates shifted further or not was no longer considered very important, as long as they did not return to the volatility and gross misalignments that had characterized the first half of the decade. What mattered to the Fund was that the United States should finally get its fiscal deficit under control, that the "surplus countries . . . promote adequate growth of domestic demand in excess of output growth," and that industrial countries generally should adopt much more flexible structural policies, especially regarding labor markets. If those goals could be achieved, then the world economy could easily adapt to the prevailing pattern of exchange rates.[70]

---

[67]Chairman's summing up, at EBM/87/48 (March 17, 1987), p. 19.

[68]"World Economic Outlook—Preliminary Assessment of Prospects and Policy Issues," EBS/88/1 (January 6, 1988), p. 21.

[69]The Managing Director summed up part of the discussion as follows: "There was a widespread feeling that, by the end of 1987, the dollar had fallen enough and that a further decline would be counterproductive. Most Directors holding this view . . . felt that monetary policy could have a role in defending the desired pattern of exchange rates." Minutes of EBM/88/6 (January 13, 1988), p. 28.

[70]Chairman's summing up, at EBM/89/119 (September 8, 1989), p. 18.

[71]In addition to the issues summarized here, a wide range of other structural policy issues was examined occasionally. From 1978 on, for example, the WEO regularly reviewed the growing tendency of both industrial and developing countries to implement protectionist trade policies; that issue is covered in Chapter 2. Other structural policies are covered in Chapter 2 (on the general surveillance implications), Chapter 4 (on the implications for the use of indicators, as noted in footnote 30 of this chapter, p. 237), and Chapter 13 (on conditionality issues).

Structural Rigidities

Beginning around 1986, structural policies played an increasingly central role in the WEO.[71] One driving force behind this shift in emphasis was a conviction that structural rigidities in many countries had adversely affected the efficiency of markets—labor markets in particular—and had distorted estimates of the rate of growth of potential output. This problem was especially acute in the industrial countries of Europe, where the unemployment rate had risen from 5½ percent in 1978 and 1979 to 11 percent in 1984 and 1985. The staff argued, in a series of papers beginning with the spring 1986 WEO exercise, that excessive labor costs—associated in part with restrictive and protective labor laws and with high taxation of labor—accounted for a large portion of this problem.[72] As long as such policies persisted, potential output would be depressed and efforts to raise employment through stimulus to aggregate demand would result primarily in higher inflation. These propositions, which would have been controversial a few years earlier, were readily accepted by Executive Directors—including those representing European countries[73]—and gradually became central to the staff analysis both in the WEO and in Article IV consultations.[74] This evolution continued and became increasingly central for the Fund in the 1990s.

Forecasting Process

A key feature of the WEO exercise has always been the generation of forecasts that are conditional on standard assumptions. That is, the WEO forecasts are not necessarily the staff's best judgment of what will happen; they are the best judgment of what would happen subject to certain assumptions. The standard "technical" assumptions for the short-term forecasts (i.e., forecasts for the remainder of the current year plus the following one) were that exchange rates among industrial countries would remain fixed in nominal terms, that oil prices would remain fixed in terms of U.S. dollars, and that current economic policies would continue. The definition of current policies was interpreted to allow for changes that had been announced, regardless of whether they had yet been implemented. (See, for example, WEO, October 1985, p. 1.) Overall, the short-term forecasts incorporated enough flexibility that they could be interpreted as if they were unconditional. Similar assumptions underpinned the medium-term scenarios, except that exchange rates and key prices were fixed in real rather than nominal terms beyond the end of the short-term forecast horizon. In this context, the constraints were more fundamental.

---

[72]See Adams, Fenton, and Larsen (1987), Feldman and others (1989), and Bayoumi and others (1989). For the evolution of modeling of potential output at the Fund, see De Masi (1997).

[73]See, for example, the comments by Guenter Grosche (Germany) at EBM/86/49 (March 21, 1986), p. 6; and by Hélène Ploix (France) at EBM/86/50 (same date) p. 21.

[74]See in particular the discussion of the Article IV consultations with Germany, in Chapter 4.

The specification of policy assumptions for the medium-term scenarios became especially difficult when current policies were thought to be unrealistic and unsustainable. The projections often became less and less believable as the forecast horizon lengthened, and the staff was forced either to hedge the forecasts or to derive complex explanations. This problem first became acute in 1984, when the strength of the U.S. dollar was clearly unsustainable. It cropped up again around 1987, when the prevailing policy stance in the United States implied a growth in the stock of U.S. debt that was inconsistent with the maintenance of unchanged real exchange rates.

Crockett solved the inconsistency problem beginning with the fall 1986 WEO—and even made a virtue of it—by emphasizing the "tensions" in the unrealistic scenarios. As the spring 1987 paper phrased it, "Circumstances may arise, of course, in which current policies appear to be either unsustainable or inconsistent with the underlying exchange rate assumption. In such cases, the analysis focuses on the alternative ways in which incompatibilities might manifest themselves, or be reconciled" (*WEO*, April 1987, p. 11). This approach acknowledges explicitly that the projections are overidentified. Too many variables are treated as exogenous; in reality, policies will have to be adjusted if the authorities hope to keep the exchange rate stable. By focusing on the "tensions" in the overly constrained scenarios, the staff could discuss the requirements for a responsible policy stance without having to predict either policy changes or exchange rates.

The "indicators" tables in the spring 1987 WEO paper for the Executive Board suggested that from 1986 to 1991, the U.S. general government deficit would be reduced by 1.8 percent of GNP under the assumption of partial implementation of the Gramm-Rudman deficit targets. The counterparts of that deficit reduction were shown as a rise in gross private investment of 1.4 percent of GNP and a fall in the current account deficit by 0.4 percent of GNP (with no change in the private saving rate).[75] The text pointed out that this scenario involved tensions, in that a strengthening of investment by that size seemed unlikely—whether on the basis of economic theory, econometric evidence, or historical perspective—while a larger reduction in the external deficit would seem to require a real depreciation in the dollar (which was inconsistent with the technical assumptions underlying the scenario).[76]

Another anomaly in the scenarios was that they excluded the possibility of recession. The reasoning was that since the timing of the business cycle could not be predicted with any confidence beyond the next 18 months or so, the only reasonable strategy for a medium-term scenario was to project the course of the economy without cyclical disturbances. If the initial conditions were weak enough that a re-

---

[75]The 1991 projections were not included in the published WEO. See p. 242, above, on the staff treatment of the Gramm-Rudman targets; and footnote 15, p. 231, on the relationships linking investment and the current account to fiscal policy.

[76]"World Economic Outlook—Prospects and Issues," EBS/87/39 (February 24, 1987), Tables 2 and 3, and pp. 27–36.

[77]The most nearly explicit acknowledgment of bias was in the fall 1985 WEO, for which the staff decided to leave the baseline medium-term scenario unchanged from the spring but to stress the increase that had occurred in "downside risks." That strategy resulted in part from concerns

cession *sometime* in the next few years was all but inevitable, then the projections contained an inherent bias.

The bias in the medium-term scenarios was recognized implicitly in the staff analysis of the "downside risks."[77] Typically, the staff would describe a baseline scenario that showed moderate growth and was benign in its implications, and then separately would describe the various risks that might prevent such an outcome from materializing. In such cases, the baseline was primarily a reference point for discussing the policy requirements for achieving a good outcome. For example, the March 1988 paper on the medium-term scenarios noted that "the baseline case assumes that the large external imbalances among the industrial countries do not give rise to either interest rate or exchange rate pressures, on one hand, or to increased protectionism in the industrial countries, on the other. . . . The realism of this assumption is a key element in the sustainability of current policies . . . [and] there are very real downside risks."[78] Those risks were then analyzed through the presentation of alternative scenarios.

The process by which these forecasts were produced was, for much of the 1980s, a cumbersome and unwieldy routine that was necessary to get a globally consistent outcome but that imposed severe strains on the staff's limited resources. The Research Department, which had overall responsibility for the exercise, would initiate the forecasting round by circulating questionnaires to the area departments. Those questionnaires specified the main assumptions that were to underpin the forecasts (oil and other primary commodity prices, key-currency exchange rates, etc.) and asked the desk economists to provide initial projections for their countries on that basis. (Only the larger countries were included in this exercise. Small countries were assumed to follow the patterns of their larger neighbors or trading partners.) These first-round forecasts were produced by whatever economic theories, methodology, models, and data the desks believed to be relevant and appropriate for the country concerned. Some forecasts were derived primarily from official national projections, some were derived in part from models estimated and maintained by the area departments, and some were largely judgmental. The Research Department staff would then feed the results into the central WEO database for processing by (mainframe) computer and would carefully analyze the global and regional outcome for consistency and credibility. The results would then be returned to the area departments for further review and revision. Normally, several iterations would be required to produce a consistent forecast for the world economy, and over time this iterative interaction between the country desks

---

that to lower the medium-term growth projections might inappropriately "sound alarms" to the public. See statement by William C. Hood (Economic Counsellor and Director of Research) at EBM/85/144 (September 16, 1985), p. 35. It should be emphasized that the question of bias in the way the medium-term scenarios were constructed and presented is independent from the question of whether the short-term forecasts might have been biased. That issue is discussed below, in the section on evaluation, pp. 260–61.

[78]"World Economic Outlook—Medium-Term Scenarios," SM/88/52 (March 4, 1988), p. 4.

and the WEO staff became a year-round disciplinary influence on the Fund's forecasts and analysis.

The forecasting process gradually became more streamlined and efficient toward the end of the decade, partly because of the increased availability of computer technology and the successful development of multinational econometric models in the Research Department.[79] The latter development is examined in the next section.

Modeling the World Economy

The debate over the appropriate balance between individual judgment and the output of econometric models in macroeconomic forecasting has always been contentious. Even in the heyday of the large models of national economies in the 1960s, most successful forecasters used the models more for evaluating internal consistency than for making baseline projections.[80] During the 1970s, the preeminence of large-scale econometric models for macroeconomic forecasting was challenged by several developments, including a return to simpler, smaller, and more transparent models and the development of more sophisticated techniques for analyzing time-series data. After Robert E. Lucas, Jr., of the University of Chicago published an influential article (Lucas, 1976) that set out what became known as the "Lucas critique," the use of models for forecasting fell for a while into almost total disrepute. Lucas—who was awarded the 1995 Nobel Prize in Economics for his contributions in this and related fields—argued that models were estimated on the basis of reactions by households and businesses to observed government policies. If those policies had been different, then people would have behaved differently. Consequently, one could not use an econometrically estimated model to predict the effects of policy changes. Not until the mid-1980s would econometric modeling techniques advance to the point where forecasters could comfortably conclude that they had taken adequate account of the Lucas critique, principally by allowing expectations to be determined by and consistent with the structure of the model.

---

[79]Aside from the technological advancements, the forecast process improved in response to the need to reduce the amount of staff time devoted to it. In 1986, as the strains on the staff were reaching the breaking point and some area departments were close to open rebellion, the Fund hired a consulting firm to review the process and to prepare a detailed proposal for streamlining and automating it. Many of the firm's recommendations were implemented over the next few years, but the forecasting exercise was not fully automated until the early 1990s.

[80]Clive Granger (1980) summarized model-based forecasting experience as follows: ". . . the forecasts produced by the model are not necessarily the forecasts issued by the model's constructors. If a forecast . . . seems strange or out of line with . . . the econometrician's own judgment, then it will probably be altered to look more reasonable. This application of 'tender loving care' has been shown to result in improved forecasts . . ." (p. 119). For history and evaluation of policy analysis with econometric models, see Bodkin and others (1991) and (specifically in a multi-country setting) Bryant and others (1988).

Multilateral Exchange Rate Model

While these theoretical debates continued, the staff at the Fund slowly built up its modeling expertise. The first model to play a significant role in the WEO exercise was the Multilateral Exchange Rate Model (MERM).[81] The idea for the MERM, which was developed by Paul Armington in the late 1960s (Armington, 1969), was to derive equilibrium relationships between exchange rates and trade balances by reference to highly disaggregated production functions. The model provided a working framework for the preparations for the December 1971 ministerial meeting of the G-10 (the Smithsonian meeting) at which a new set of par values for the major industrial countries was to be negotiated. The staff's estimates of the pattern of rates that would equilibrate current account balances were a major input into the negotiations, and the par values that emerged from the political negotiations were quite close to the MERM solutions.[82] Although the agreed par values soon turned out to be unsustainable (the whole par value system collapsed just 15 months later), the problem was only partly with the initial pattern and was seriously aggravated by the lack of stabilization and coordination of macroeconomic policies afterward.

The MERM was formalized first by Artus and Rhomberg (1973) and later by Artus and McGuirk (1981). It was a purely static but highly disaggregated system of relationships that explicitly recognized the multilateral dimension of the external adjustment process: a country's "effective" exchange rate could be derived as a weighted average of bilateral weights, not by the traditional arithmetic based on the value of bilateral trade with each country, but by estimating the elasticity of trade in specific categories of goods to changes in exchange rates and by taking into account indirect competition between countries.[83] The MERM could be solved either for the pattern of exchange rates that would bring about a desired set of current account balances (as for the 1971 Smithsonian discussions) or for the current account balances that would result from an assumed set of exchange rates. It was in this latter mode that the MERM played a key role in quantifying the WEO forecasts in the 1970s and early 1980s.[84]

---

[81]Earlier partial-equilibrium empirical models were developed by Jacques Polak and others in the Research Department as early as the late 1940s; see notably Polak (1953), as well as Frenkel, Goldstein, and Khan (1991). In addition, throughout the late 1970s and 1980s, the WEO forecasting process made use of a basic computer model (known as the "WEO facility") to derive the global implications and to test the consistency of the forecasts generated by the country desks in area departments.

[82]For a review of the 1971 negotiations and the role of the staff's calculations, see de Vries (1976), Chapter 26; and James (1996), pp. 222–23.

[83]If two countries both sell the same good, or competing goods, to a third country, a change in either country's exchange rate vis-à-vis the third will affect the competitiveness of the other. That effect was captured by the MERM but not by models based on bilateral trade.

[84]The use of the MERM for computing equilibrium exchange rates in the 1970s after the collapse of the par value system is described in de Vries (1985), pp. 125–26. Its role in the WEO of that era and in the computation of effective exchange rates are described in de Vries (1985), pp. 790 and 810, respectively.

By the early 1980s, the comparative-static nature of the MERM had rendered it obsolete for most WEO purposes. As discussed above (pp. 235–36), the static medium-term scenarios were replaced by dynamic year-by-year projections starting in 1986. The MERM was still useful for computing the weights in effective exchange rates, but the WEO forecasting process had evolved enough that a more dynamic and more general equilibrium model was needed. For this limited purpose, however, the cost of keeping the MERM up-to-date became prohibitive, and it was eventually phased out before the end of the decade.[85]

World Trade Model

The second general empirical model developed at the Fund was the World Trade Model (WTM), which was introduced in the late 1970s as a complement to the MERM (see Deppler and Ripley, 1978). The WTM was a global, partial-equilibrium model designed to estimate the effects on international trade from changes in domestic economic activity. Like the MERM, it focused primarily on the larger industrial countries, but it did include more dynamic adjustment.[86] The model was used by the Research Department to check the area departments' forecasts for consistency and to start the iterative process by which a global economic forecast was to be produced. However, these initial trade forecasts were never accorded much credibility by the area departments and therefore had little real influence. The WTM was updated and expanded (see Spencer, 1984), but its basic limitations—the absence of expectations or a role for international capital flows, limited dynamic adjustment, and minimal feedback from international trade to domestic activity—remained. It played less and less of a role in the WEO process over time and—like the MERM—was phased out completely by the end of the 1980s.

MINIMOD

The real breakthrough in the evolution of modeling at the Fund came with the development of MINIMOD in 1986. The year before, the staff had produced an innovative simulation study of the medium-term implications of U.S. fiscal policy (see Chapter 3). Because the Fund still lacked a fully specified general-equilibrium

---

[85]The MERM computations were based on detailed input-output tables that ideally should have been updated every few years. By the mid-1980s, the principal consumers of the effective exchange rate data were the Bank of England and the Fund's own database for *International Financial Statistics*.

[86]The model comprised blocks of equations for 14 individual industrial countries, plus four blocks for groups of countries: developed countries producing mainly primary commodities, major oil-exporting countries, other developing countries, and centrally planned economies (including nonmember countries).

[87]Project LINK was established at the University of Pennsylvania in 1968, as an interlinked system of separate models of national economies. For a history of LINK and other early contributions to global economic modeling, see Hickman (1991).

model of the world economy, the staff examined simulations by several other groups—notably, the OECD, the U.S. Federal Reserve Board, Project LINK, and the Japan Economic Planning Agency—using their own multicountry models.[87] That study demonstrated the existence of a "Keynesian" consensus on how fiscal policy affects the economy, but the staff authors also stressed that these conventional simulation studies ignored the possibility that policy effects could be negated by endogenous shifts in expectations (that is, they did not take account of the Lucas critique). As a first step toward accounting for endogenous shifts in expectations, the staff study also reported the results of a comparison of policy effects with and without "rational" (i.e., model-consistent) formation of expectations about the economy.[88] That analysis showed that while policy effects were smaller when agents displayed perfect foresight, most of the qualitative conclusions of the more conventional models still applied.

Apart from the intrinsic interest of the analysis of how policy works, the 1985 study of U.S. fiscal policy illustrated both the potential value of econometric analysis of macroeconomic policies and the need for an in-house model of the world economy.[89] The following year, for the spring 1986 WEO, the Research Department asked the Federal Reserve Board, the OECD, and Project LINK to run special simulations with their models, using a common set of assumptions. The simulation results were then averaged and assessed by the Fund staff, and the results were used as the basic input for a set of medium-term scenarios, as described above (p. 236).

Clearly the practice of asking other organizations to run simulations with their own econometric models and then distilling the information through a derivative model at the Fund could not be a lasting solution to the need for timely policy analysis. As an intermediate step toward a fully homegrown product, the staff derived a scaled-down version of the Federal Reserve's Multi-Country Model (MCM). The Fund version, dubbed MINIMOD, not only had far fewer equations to be solved and thus was more manageable; it also incorporated endogenous, forward-looking, model-consistent, expectations and thus was relatively immune from the Lucas critique.[90] Relationships such as saving and investment functions

---

[88]The study, by Paul R. Masson and Adrian Blundell-Wignall, made use of a simplified version of the OECD's INTERLINK model, called "Minilink." It was first presented at a conference in Perugia, Italy, in 1984, and was published as Masson and Blundell-Wignall (1985). Both authors were on the OECD staff when they conducted the study. Masson moved to the Fund's Research Department in July 1984; when he developed the models discussed here, he was a Senior Economist in the External Adjustment Division.

[89]At Crockett's initiative, the Research Department conducted a thorough study during the second half of 1985 of the potential costs and benefits of developing a model or system of models in the Fund. The report, prepared by a working party chaired by Anthony Lanyi (Assistant Director of the Research Department), foreshadowed many of the characteristics of the MINIMOD approach. "Report of the Working Party on the Use of Models in Projections and Analysis," Research Department (December 6, 1985); in IMF/RD (Historian's files).

[90]See Haas and Masson (1986) and Masson (1987). The model could be solved either with or without endogenous expectations, but once the staff became convinced that the fully consistent solution gave the more realistic and credible forecasts, the partial version was largely abandoned.

depended in part on agents' expectations of future changes in interest rates, inflation, and exchange rates; and those expectations were formulated to be consistent with the long-run solution of the model (i.e., agents, on average, were assumed to forecast the eventual outcome of any policy or other exogenous action correctly).

MULTIMOD

The final step, a direct outgrowth of the MINIMOD project, was the development of MULTIMOD. Once the principle of generating alternative scenarios by running simulations with a global model was established and accepted, the Research Department staff set about estimating its own model. By the time of the spring 1988 WEO, MULTIMOD was ready for its debut. The new model (Masson and others, 1988) differed from its predecessor in several respects. It was much larger (a total of 308 equations covering seven countries or groups of countries, compared with a total of 67 equations for the United States and the "rest of the world" as a single bloc in MINIMOD);[91] the parameters were estimated by the staff using the Fund's own WEO database, rather than being borrowed from other models; and the role of endogenous and model-consistent expectations was more extensive. Like MINIMOD, it was used by the staff to generate the *alternative* scenarios: the baseline projections were still based on the judgment of the country desks, and the model generated the deviations from the baseline in response to specified policy changes or other shocks.

When the Executive Board met to discuss the WEO in March 1988, the MULTIMOD projections immediately became the star of the show. The staff paper on the medium-term outlook now included, besides the baseline, 11 alternative scenarios predicated on specific shifts in policies or other conditions. Three scenarios detailed how the "tensions" in the baseline scenario might be manifested if the major countries did not change their policies in time. There might be another stock market crash like that of October 1987, there might be severe deflation, or there might be a run on the U.S. dollar. The next five scenarios explained the types of policy changes that could avoid these dire consequences: improved structural policies in Europe, more fiscal consolidation in the United States, increased domestic investment and import penetration in Japan, or combinations of the above. The remaining exercises examined other possible policy actions, such as increased financing for the heavily indebted developing countries and increased protectionist

---

[91]MULTIMOD was later extended to include a larger number of individual countries and greater disaggregation of the groups; the nonindustrial world, however, remained highly aggregated. See Masson, Symansky, and Meredith (1990) and Laxton and others (1998).

[92]The "reference" scenario was described in the main "Prospects and Policy Issues" paper for the Board discussion, "World Economic Outlook—Prospects and Policy Issues," EBS/88/44 (March 3, 1988). The alternative scenarios were summarized in that paper and were set out in detail in "World Economic Outlook—Medium-Term Scenarios," SM/88/52 (March 4, 1988). The scenarios were discussed by the Executive Board at EBM/88/48–50 (March 25 and 28, 1988).

[93]For an independent (World Bank staff) evaluation of the analytical and forecasting properties of MULTIMOD, see Jamshidi (1989).

measures in industrial countries. These simulations—presented in detailed tables covering projections for each year from 1988 through 1992, with accompanying analysis—provided a much more concrete foundation for the Board discussion than had ever before been possible.[92] This type of exercise thus became the standard for the years to come.[93]

Developing Country Models

Empirical modeling of the economies of developing countries has always lagged well behind the analysis of industrial countries, owing to the much more rudimentary data and the much greater number of countries. The Fund staff began by constructing several partial- and general-equilibrium models of developing countries in the 1970s and 1980s. Two circumstances combined to spur this activity: Fund lending shifted heavily toward the developing world, which raised the demand by the Executive Board for detailed quantitative analysis of those economies, and the quantity and quality of data improved enough to support the estimation of at least rudimentary empirical models. Several early studies, such as Khan (1974) on Venezuela and Otani and Park (1976) on Korea, focused on the linkages between monetary policy and economic activity and inflation. By the beginning of the 1980s, more comprehensive macroeconomic models were appearing, such as the representative-country model published by Mohsin S. Khan and Malcolm D. Knight in 1981. Simultaneously with the empirical studies, Fund staff were conducting basic theoretical research on the structure of developing economies and the differences between modeling industrial and developing countries. That work culminated in a series of papers in the early 1990s by Nadeem U. Haque, Peter J. Montiel, and others.[94]

For the WEO scenarios, the Research Department developed two separate models of the developing world in the late 1980s. One, the developing country module of MULTIMOD, was used to project the implications of the industrial country scenarios for developing countries taken together. The other, LDCMOD, was used to disaggregate the projections so that the implications could be studied for both geographic and analytical groups of countries.[95] LDCMOD, which was designed by a team of economists in the Current Studies Division of the Research Department,[96] comprised some two dozen behavioral equations plus about 60 identities for close to 100 individual countries. Because of data limitations and the sheer size of the project, the structure and econometric sophistication of LDCMOD were far more rudimentary than those of MULTIMOD. The LDCMOD sim-

---

[94]Those papers, the 1981 Khan-Knight study, and others are collected in Khan, Montiel, and Haque (1991).

[95]Analytical categories included countries grouped by level of per capita income, type of principal exports, or degree of external indebtedness.

[96]See Adams and Adams (1989) and Kumar, Samiei, and Bassett (1993); the name LDCMOD was introduced in the latter paper. The project was initiated under the direction of Michael C. Deppler (Assistant Director in the Research Department and head of the Current Studies Division), who was also the senior author of the earlier World Trade Model.

ulations took the industrial country output from MULTIMOD as exogenous inputs; in principle, the LDCMOD simulations could have been fed back into MULTIMOD and so on through an iterative interaction to produce a globally consistent set of projections. The MULTIMOD team, however, preferred to iterate with their own highly aggregated developing country blocs (which, like the rest of the model, incorporated forward-looking, model-consistent expectations) to produce an *internally* consistent outcome. This procedure was obviously inelegant, but it had a certain practicality that enabled it to endure well into the 1990s.

Evaluation

How useful were the WEO forecasts in the 1980s? Answering that question is far more complicated than just comparing the forecasts with actual outcomes, because of the constraints in the forecast process. If countries' policies changed (as they inevitably did) in the interim, then the outcome would differ from the forecast even if the forecast was perfect on its own terms. Over a long enough period, however, such apparent errors should even out, and the forecasts should be unbiased. The two key questions, then, are whether a persistent bias has been evident—either in the observed forecast errors or in the qualitative approach taken by the staff—and whether the forecasts have been statistically efficient: that is, whether they have added significantly to the information that one could get simply by looking systematically at the historical time-series data without reference to an economic model.

In the policy discussions at the Fund, the question of bias arose primarily for the medium-term scenarios. As discussed earlier in this chapter, the staff acknowledged that the medium-term reference scenarios contained an inherent optimism in that they ruled out both recessions and exchange rate changes. That optimism was tempered by the construction of alternative scenarios that illustrated how the tensions in the baseline might be resolved, but the staff still ran into frequent criticism that it was viewing the world with rose-colored glasses. Even the alternative scenarios necessarily assumed that countries borrowing from the Fund would successfully carry out the economic programs on which stand-by arrangements were conditional. Since in practice many Fund-supported adjustment programs were not successfully completed, the potential for serious imbalances and crises was inherently greater than recognized in the scenarios.[97] Executive Directors often complained that the staff was failing to recognize the dire consequences that lay ahead like economic land mines. In September 1984, R.N. Malhotra (India) was skeptical that developing countries would enjoy falling debt and debt-service ratios over the medium term, as projected in the baseline scenario. Alexandre Kafka (Brazil) protested at a 1986 Board meeting on the WEO that the staff was being too optimistic about the willingness of creditors to finance the deficits of the heavily in-

---

[97]For a discussion of this point by the staff, see the minutes of EBM/88/144 (September 9, 1988), p. 7.

debted developing countries. Such optimism, he argued, was "dangerous," because it could lead to "policy inaction."

Occasionally, the question of bias arose in the discussion of the short-term forecasts. In February 1979, Executive Directors complained that the staff seemed to be overestimating likely growth in the industrial countries while underestimating the inflation problem. At the time, the OECD's *Economic Outlook* was projecting 3 percent growth in 1979–80 for the industrial countries as a whole, whereas the WEO was projecting 3.7 percent. Executive Directors, on the whole, concluded that the OECD forecast was more realistic.[98] (The outturn, incidentally, was 3.5 percent.) That type of dispute, however, was uncommon.

Two assessments of the track record drew mixed conclusions. In 1988, Professor Michael Artis of the University of Manchester (England) completed a detailed evaluation of WEO forecasts for the Fund. He concluded that the forecasts of economic growth had been biased toward optimism in the 1970s but not in the 1980s, that in general the forecasts were statistically efficient, and that overall the Fund had done no better or worse than national or other international forecasters during the 1970s and 1980s (Artis, 1988, pp. 1–3). Four years later, José M. Barrionuevo, of the Research Department at the Fund, concluded (Barrionuevo, 1992) that although the WEO forecasts were not biased in the 1980s, they were less accurate than forecasts made with simple time-series methods.[99]

Considering the size and complexity of the task, most observers would probably conclude that the WEO became a major success story for the IMF in the 1980s. As a complement to the Article IV consultations with member countries, the WEO provided the Fund with a means of analyzing economic interactions and the requirements for consistency of policies among countries. Publication of the staff forecasts and analysis helped to strip away a veil and to generate constructive criticism of both the process and the conclusions. By the end of the decade, the WEO exercise had largely matured in the detail, intellectual rigor, and transparency of its short-term forecasts, medium-term scenarios, and macroeconomic analysis.

References

Adams, Charles, and Claire Hughes Adams, 1989, "A Scenario and Forecast Adjustment Model for Developing Countries," in *Staff Studies for the World Economic Outlook* (Washington: International Monetary Fund, August), pp. 98–125.

Adams, Charles, Paul R. Fenton, and Flemming Larsen, 1987, "Potential Output in Major Industrial Countries," in *Staff Studies for the World Economic Outlook* (Washington: International Monetary Fund), pp. 1–38.

Armington, Paul S., 1969, "A Theory of Demand for Products Distinguished by Place of Production," *Staff Papers*, International Monetary Fund, Vol. 16 (March), pp. 159–76.

---

[98]Concluding remarks by the Chairman; minutes of IS/79/2 (February 23, 1979), pp. 42–43.

[99]For an informal but independent analysis, see Worswick (1983). Artis (1996) updated and extended his earlier study and drew similar conclusions.

Artis, Michael J., 1988, "How Accurate Is the World Economic Outlook? A Post Mortem on Short-Term Forecasting at the International Monetary Fund" in *Staff Studies for the World Economic Outlook* (Washington: International Monetary Fund, July), pp. 1–49.

———, 1996, "How Accurate Are the IMF's Short-Term Forecasts? Another Examination of the World Economic Outlook," IMF Working Paper 96/89 (Washington: International Monetary Fund).

Artus, Jacques R., and Malcolm D. Knight, 1984, *Issues in the Assessment of the Exchange Rates of Industrial Countries*, IMF Occasional Paper No. 29 (Washington: International Monetary Fund).

Artus, Jacques R., and Anne Kenny McGuirk, 1981, "A Revised Version of the Multilateral Exchange Rate Model," *Staff Papers*, International Monetary Fund, Vol. 28 (June), pp. 275–309.

Artus, Jacques R., and Rudolf R. Rhomberg, 1973, "A Multilateral Exchange Rate Model," *Staff Papers*, International Monetary Fund, Vol. 20 (November), pp. 591–611.

Barrionuevo, José M., 1992, "A Simple Forecasting Accuracy Criterion under Rational Expectations: Evidence from the World Economic Outlook and Time Series Models," IMF Working Paper 92/48 (Washington: International Monetary Fund).

Bayoumi, Tamim, Robert Alan Feldman, Michael Wattleworth, and Geoffrey Woglom, 1989, "Structural Reform and Macroeconomic Adjustment in Industrial Countries," in *Staff Studies for the World Economic Outlook* (Washington: International Monetary Fund), pp. 13–64.

Bodkin, Ronald G., Lawrence Robert Klein, and Kanta Marwah, eds., 1991, *A History of Macroeconometric Model-Building* (Aldershot, England: Edward Elgar).

Boughton, James M., 1989, "Policy Assignment Strategies with Somewhat Flexible Exchange Rates," in *Blueprints for Exchange Rate Management*, ed. by Marcus Miller, Barry Eichengreen, and Richard Portes (London: Academic Press). Reprinted as "Policy Assignment with Somewhat Flexible Exchange Rates," in *Functioning of the International Monetary System*, ed. by Jacob A. Frenkel and Morris Goldstein (Washington: International Monetary Fund, April 1996), pp. 466–98.

———, 1991, "The Role of Policy Assignment and Cooperation in Intermediate Exchange Rate Regimes," in *The Reality of International Economic Policy Coordination*, ed. by Hans J. Blommestein (Amsterdam: North-Holland).

———, 2000, "Modeling the World Economic Outlook at the IMF: A Historical Review," Chapter 4 in *Empirical Models and Policy Making*, ed. by Frank den Butter and Mary S. Morgan (New York: Routledge).

———, Richard D. Haas, Paul R. Masson, and Charles Adams, 1986, "Effects of Exchange Rate Changes in Industrial Countries," *Staff Studies for the World Economic Outlook* (Washington: International Monetary Fund), pp. 115–49.

Bruno, Michael, and Jeffrey Sachs, 1985, *Economics of Worldwide Stagflation* (Cambridge, Massachusetts: Harvard University Press).

Bryant, Ralph C., Dale W. Henderson, Gerald Holtham, Peter Hooper, and Steven A. Symansky, eds., 1988, *Empirical Macroeconomics for Interdependent Economies* (Washington: Brookings Institution).

Crockett, Andrew, and Morris Goldstein, 1987, *Strengthening the International Monetary System: Exchange Rates, Surveillance, and Objective Indicators*, IMF Occasional Paper No. 50 (Washington: International Monetary Fund).

De Masi, Paula R., 1997, "IMF Estimates of Potential Output: Theory and Practice," IMF Working Paper 97/177 (Washington: International Monetary Fund).

de Vries, Margaret Garritsen, 1976, *The International Monetary Fund, 1966–1971: The System Under Stress*, Vol. 1: *Narrative*; Vol. 2: *Documents* (Washington: International Monetary Fund).

————, 1985, *The International Monetary Fund, 1972–1978: Cooperation on Trial*, Vols. 1 and 2: *Narrative and Analysis;* Vol. 3: *Documents* (Washington: International Monetary Fund).

Deppler, Michael C., and Duncan M. Ripley, 1978, "The World Trade Model: Merchandise Trade," *Staff Papers*, International Monetary Fund, Vol. 25 (March), pp. 147–206.

Feldman, Robert Alan, Ernesto Hernández-Catá, Flemming Larsen, and Michael Wattleworth, 1989, "The Role of Structural Policies in Industrial Countries," in *Staff Studies for the World Economic Outlook* (Washington: International Monetary Fund), pp. 1–12.

Fleming, J. Marcus, 1959, "The Bearing of Noncompetitive Market Conditions on the Problem of Inflation," *Oxford Economic Papers* (New Series), Vol. 11 (February), pp. 36–62. Reprinted in *Essays on Economic Policy*, by J. Marcus Fleming (New York: Columbia Press, 1978).

Frenkel, Jacob A., Morris Goldstein, and Mohsin Khan, 1991, "Major Themes in the Writings of Jacques J. Polak," in *International Economic Policy: Essays in Honor of Jacques J. Polak*, ed. by Jacob A. Frenkel and Morris Goldstein (Washington: International Monetary Fund), pp. 3–39.

Friedman, Milton, 1968, *Dollars and Deficits: Inflation, Monetary Policy and the Balance of Payments* (Englewood Cliffs, New Jersey: Prentice-Hall).

Funabashi, Yoichi, 1988, *Managing the Dollar: From the Plaza to the Louvre* (Washington: Institute for International Economics).

Granger, C.W.J., 1980, *Forecasting in Business and Economics* (New York: Academic Press).

Haas, Richard D., and Paul R. Masson, 1986, "MINIMOD: Specification and Simulation Results," *Staff Papers*, International Monetary Fund, Vol. 33 (December), pp. 722–67.

Hall, Robert E., ed., 1982, *Inflation: Causes and Effects* (Chicago: University of Chicago Press).

Hickman, Bert G., 1991, "Project LINK and Multi-Country Modelling," in *A History of Macro-econometric Model-Building*, ed. by Ronald G. Bodkin, Lawrence R. Klein, and Kanta Marwah (Aldershot, England: Edward Elgar), pp. 482–506.

James, Harold, 1996, *International Monetary Cooperation since Bretton Woods* (Oxford: Oxford University Press).

Jamshidi, Ahmad, 1989, "Evaluating Global Macroeconomic Models: A Case Study of MULTI-MOD," World Bank Policy, Planning, and Research Working Paper, WPS 298 (Washington: World Bank, December).

Khan, Mohsin S., 1974, "Experiments with a Monetary Model for the Venezuelan Economy," *Staff Papers*, International Monetary Fund, Vol. 21 (July), pp. 389–413.

————, and Malcolm Knight, 1991, "Stabilization Programs in Developing Countries: A Formal Framework," in *Macroeconomic Models for Adjustment in Developing Countries*, ed. by Mohsin Khan, Peter J. Montiel, and Nadeem U. Haque (Washington: International Monetary Fund), pp. 38–85.

Khan, Mohsin, Peter J. Montiel, and Nadeem U. Haque, eds., 1991, *Macroeconomic Models for Adjustment in Developing Countries* (Washington: International Monetary Fund).

Kumar, Manmohan S., Hossein Samiei, and Sheila Bassett, 1993, "An Extended Scenario and Forecast Adjustment Model for Developing Countries," *Staff Studies for the World Economic Outlook* (Washington: International Monetary Fund), December, pp. 47–75.

Laxton, Douglas, Peter Isard, Hamid Faruqee, Eswar Prasad, and Bart Turtelboom, 1998, *MULTIMOD Mark III: The Core Dynamic and Steady-State Models*, IMF Occasional Paper No. 164 (Washington: International Monetary Fund).

Lucas, Robert E., Jr., 1976, "Econometric Policy Evaluation: A Critique," in *The Phillips Curve and Labor Markets*, ed. by Karl Brunner and Alan H. Meltzer, Carnegie-Rochester Conference Series on Public Policy, Vol. 1 (Amsterdam: North-Holland), pp. 19–46.

Marris, Stephen, 1985, *Deficits and the Dollar: The World Economy at Risk* (Washington: Institute for International Economics).

Masson, Paul R., 1987, "The Dynamics of a Two-Country Minimodel under Rational Expectations," *Annales d'Economie et de Statistique*, Institut National de la Statistique et des Etudes Economiques, Vol. 6/7 (April/September), pp. 37–69.

―――, and Adrian Blundell-Wignall, 1985, "Fiscal Policy and the Exchange Rate in the Big Seven: Transmission of U.S. Government Spending Shocks," *European Economic Review*, Vol. 28 (June/July), pp. 11–42.

Masson, Paul R., Steven Symansky, Richard Haas, and Michael Dooley, 1988, "MULTIMOD: A Multi-Region Econometric Model," *Staff Studies for the World Economic Outlook* (Washington: International Monetary Fund), pp. 50–104.

Masson, Paul R., Steven Symansky, and Guy Meredith, 1990, *MULTIMOD Mark II: A Revised and Extended Model*, IMF Occasional Paper No. 71 (Washington: International Monetary Fund).

McCracken, Paul, and others, 1977, *Towards Full Employment and Price Stability: A Report to the OECD by a Group of Independent Experts* (Paris: OECD).

Monti, Mario, ed., 1976, The "New Inflation," and Monetary Policy: Proceedings of a Conference Organized by the Banca Commerziale Italiana and the Department of Economics of the Università Bocconi in Milan (London: Macmillan).

Otani, Ichiro, and Yung Chul Park, 1976, "A Monetary Model of the Korean Economy," *Staff Papers*, International Monetary Fund, Vol. 23 (March), pp. 164–99.

Polak, Jacques J., 1953, *An International Economic System* (Chicago, Illinois: University of Chicago Press).

Putnam, Robert D., and Nicholas Bayne, 1987, *Hanging Together: Cooperation and Conflict in the Seven-Power Summits* (Cambridge, Massachusetts: Harvard University Press, rev. and enl. ed.).

Quirk, Peter J., Martin G. Gilman, Kyung Mo Huh, Pisit Leeahtam, and Joslin M. Landell-Mills, 1989, *Developments in International Exchange and Trade Systems*, World Economic and Financial Surveys (Washington: International Monetary Fund).

Spencer, Grant H., 1984, "The World Trade Model: Revised Estimates," *Staff Papers*, International Monetary Fund, Vol. 31 (September), pp. 469–98.

Worswick, G.D.N., 1983, "The IMF's World Economic Outlook: A Critique; Report to the Group of Twenty-Four" (UNDP/UNCTAD Project INT/81/046, UNCTAD/MFD/TA/24).

II

Revolutions in Managing International Debt

6

Crisis and Strategy

A CERTAIN POINT COMES WHEN A COUNTRY SUFFERING from a prolonged deficit, and which has failed to adopt policies that can reassure its foreign creditors, runs into a financial crunch. . . . Today we are seeing a worrying number of countries stumbling in this direction. We are all conscious of the risks that this opens up: the consequences that a major default by one or more of the larger countries would have for the system as a whole.

Jacques de Larosière[1]
January 14, 1982

It was seven months before the threat of major defaults would become not only a reality but the major preoccupation of the IMF for the rest of the decade. The speaker at the lectern was the Managing Director of the IMF. Gathered around the room were the chief executive and other senior officers of many of the largest banks in the United States.

Since November 1981, the Managing Director had been planning to address the major U.S. banks on the subject of lending to developing countries, but the theme of his remarks shifted as the time for the meeting approached. Initially, de Larosière envisaged the speech as a defense of the Fund's role in promoting economic adjustment in the developing world. He had been criticized earlier for allegedly relaxing conditionality on loans to poor countries, and he wanted to set the record straight. As 1981 drew to a close, those concerns had largely dispelled and had been replaced by worries about the vast cloud of foreign debts that had already brought storms to parts of eastern and southern Europe and that was inexorably—but still almost invisibly—threatening Latin America. For years the major industrial countries and the international financial institutions had been encouraging bankers to assist the fuel-importing developing countries to cope with the rising price of oil by onlending the deposits of the oil-exporting countries. The time for this recycling was now over.

---

[1]"Assuring International Financial Stability: The Role of the Financial Institutions," remarks by the Managing Director to U.S. bankers at a private function in New York, January 14, 1982. Unpublished final draft as prepared for delivery (December 22, 1981), p. 5; in IMF/RD Managing Director file "Bankers—1/14/82 (Drafts)" (Accession 86/34, Box 2, Section 208).

De Larosière did not want to go public with what might be seen as an alarmist speech, but he wanted to get the message across to the main international lenders. He invited the heads of the leading money-center banks to a private dinner at the River Club in Manhattan. As it happened, getting from Washington to New York took rather more effort than expected. Both cities, and the whole megalopolis that connects them, were buried in deep snow, and all of Washington was in shock and mourning. The day before, as the storm began to cripple the city, Air Florida flight 90 to Tampa had crashed on takeoff from National Airport, killing 78 people; a half hour later, in the ensuing confusion as the Washington bureaucracy was sent home early to escape the accumulating snow, the derailment of a Metro train beneath the downtown streets had killed another three people. The tragedy could have provided an excuse for the Managing Director to cancel the speech. He was under pressure from some members of the Executive Board who felt that the Fund was becoming too cozy with the commercial banks, but he chose to go ahead. This brief trip was his first real opportunity to set out a vision and a strategy for dealing with unsustainable sovereign debts.

At the River Club, an exclusive enclave tucked into the foot of Manhattan's 52nd Street and overlooking the East River, the Managing Director made three principal points in his remarks to the assembled bankers. First, the large increase in IMF lending to developing countries in 1980–81 had been primarily through high-conditionality programs that were aimed at promoting adjustment to sustainable policies (in contrast to the lending after the first oil shock, 1973–74, when the low-conditionality oil facility had been the main lending vehicle). Second, Fund resources could make no more than a "modest contribution" to financing the deficits of developing countries, and the Fund had "no intention of seeking to supplant the traditional sources of private and governmental financing flows to deficit countries." Third, he concluded by urging commercial banks to prevent borrowing countries from using the availability of bank financing to "postpone adjustment policies," but nonetheless to "maintain, or even increase, exposure levels when a country is seeking to deal with its economic problems" through adoption of appropriate adjustment programs.[2]

Be moderate but keep lending, and depend on the IMF to insist on adequate policies as a condition for its own lending. It was a simple and persuasive message, and it became the basis for the case-by-case strategy that would prevent the debt crisis from leading to widespread defaults or a collapse of sovereign lending in the 1980s.

Overview

The Crisis

By conventional reckoning, the developing country debt crisis began on Friday, August 20, 1982, when the Mexican finance minister informed bankers assembled

---

[2]Op. cit., pp. 8 and 15–16.

in New York that he could not repay the loan principal that was coming due on Monday. The study that follows places the eruption of the Mexican exigency a week earlier, when the Mexican authorities notified officials in Washington—including the Fund—that without an immediate rescue they would have no choice but to default. The organization of that rescue in the course of one frenetic weekend was unprecedented in its complexity and speed, but it was only the opening sprint in what would become an exhausting marathon of negotiations lasting through the end of the decade and beyond.

Mexico was not the beginning of the story. The first rumbles of the international debt crisis of the 1980s were heard in March 1981, when the government of Poland informed its bank creditors that it could not meet its obligations. Although that announcement generated scarcely a ripple of interest in the financial press at the time, it precipitated an international emergency: a number of western Europe's largest commercial banks were heavily exposed with loans to Poland; if they had failed to agree on rescheduling terms, European governments would have seen no choice but to rescue them. Also, Poland's problems were international because they squashed the ability of neighboring countries such as Romania, Hungary, and Yugoslavia to roll over or expand their own bank loans. Those countries had their own policy failures and shortcomings, and it is impossible to know whether they could have muddled through in the absence of the problems in Poland, but it is clear that Poland pushed them more quickly over the precipice.

But the story did not begin in Warsaw, either. The origins of the debt crisis of the 1980s may be traced back to and through the lurching efforts of the world's governments to cope with the economic instabilities of the 1970s. This story is familiar, even if arguments persist about how much space to give to each cause: the severance of the dollar-gold linkage in 1971, the shift to floating exchange rates in 1973, the first oil shock in 1973–74, the ensuing slowdown in the mid-1970s, and the inflationary binge of the late 1970s that culminated in the second oil shock of 1979–80 and that was halted by a monetary contraction in the United States (the "Volcker shock") that brought a sharp rise in world interest rates and a sustained appreciation of the dollar. By the late 1970s, developing countries were able to borrow freely in the rapidly growing international private credit markets, at low interest rates that were—for a while—negative in real terms. Money-center banks had received large deposits from oil-exporting countries, and they saw the oil-importing developing countries as a prime market for increased lending. Not surprisingly, many of those countries took advantage of the situation, and external debt continued to rise both absolutely and in relation to output (Figure 6.1). In too many cases, borrowers misapplied these loans to low-return investment projects or to current consumption. When interest rates soared in 1980–81, too many borrowers were too slow to adjust. Warning signals from the IMF and other agencies were too muted and too late and would likely have been ignored in any case.

As shown in the introduction to this chapter, the Fund was not oblivious to the dangers of excessive borrowing. The type of admonition given to banks by

Figure 6.1. External Debt of Heavily Indebted Countries, 1973–89

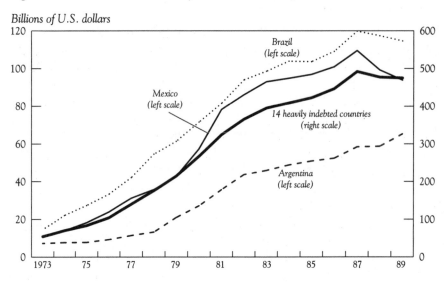

Billions of U.S. dollars

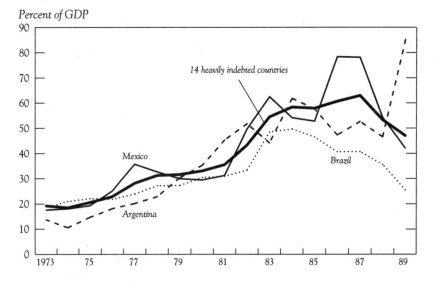

Percent of GDP

Source: World Bank, *World Development Indicators*.

de Larosière in January 1982 was merely one in a long series. As early as October 1977, de Larosière's predecessor as Managing Director, H. Johannes Witteveen, warned a meeting of the heads of the agencies of the United Nations that

> a number of developing countries . . . had over-accelerated their economies and were, as a result, borrowing up to 12 percent of their national income. Such a rate of borrowing was unsustainable, and urgent adjustments were called for in order to avert

major debt-servicing difficulties which would have serious repercussions on the entire international financial system.[3]

In January and March 1980, the Executive Board held discussions of the recycling process and concluded that while commercial borrowing by the oil-importing developing countries was essential, "borrowing will need to go hand in hand with adjustment" and therefore the Fund should play a "greatly increased" role in the recycling process.[4] A year later, the Managing Director noted at the conclusion of the Executive Board's discussion of the World Economic Outlook that the outlook for the oil-importing developing countries was "frightening," and that the projected current account deficits of those countries were "probably not financible under current assumptions about the evolution of [official development assistance]. . . . This concern struck a note of gravity, urgency, and insistence, . . . more strongly expressed than it ever had been up to now."[5]

The cautionary message, delivered occasionally by the Fund and usually in private, was offset by the more prevailing and openly expressed view that debt accumulation was, within reason, beneficial and even a key element in the solution to the problems of the 1970s. Published staff studies noted the potential problems that could arise in the most heavily indebted countries, but they argued more generally that the growing indebtedness of developing countries was essential for their growth and development, was an appropriate means of "recycling" the surpluses of the major oil-exporting countries (known at the time as "petro-dollars") to fuel-importing countries, and had the side benefit of helping governments "graduate" from dependence on official credits and gain access to loans on commercial terms.[6] No one in the Fund, of course, knew whether a crisis was coming, when it might come, or which countries would be most affected. Positive signals blurred the picture, and in any case the culture of the Fund did not encourage the sounding of alarms.

---

[3]Provisional summary record of the first meeting, Administrative Committee on Coordination, United Nations (31 October, 1977), p. 11.

[4]Chairman's summing up, minutes of EBM/80/11 (January 17, 1980), p. 5. The more extended discussion of the same topic held in March 1980 drew similar conclusions; see minutes of EBM/80/50–51 (March 19, 1980).

[5]Chairman's summing up, minutes of EBM/81/74 (May 4, 1981), p. 13.

[6]See, for example, the *World Economic Outlook* for May 1980, pp. 34–38, and Nowzad and Williams (1981). The latter study (p. 11) summarized the situation as follows: "In sum, the overall debt situation during the 1970s adapted itself to the sizable strains introduced in the international payments system. . . . Though some countries experienced difficulties, a generalized debt management problem was avoided, and in the aggregate the outlook for the immediate future does not give cause for alarm." Even after the fact, the Fund resisted officially recognizing that a crisis had occurred. The 1983 *Annual Report* referred obliquely to "debt servicing difficulties" and summarized the situation of the non-oil developing countries in similarly delicate language: "Confronted with much more cautious attitudes on the part of international lenders, these countries have had to adopt policies that give their creditors grounds for confidence in their capacity to bring their external obligations and resources into better alignment" (p. 1). Also see Edwards (1995), pp. 18–21, on the general failure to foresee the 1982 debt crisis.

Commercial banks as a group found the positive message to be more appealing than the negative. Many bankers later would complain—with some justification—that they had been misled by the calls for recycling and had been blindsided by the Volcker shock. Whatever importance those factors might have had, the fundamental point is that sovereign lending to developing countries was a highly profitable activity, but the risks were inadequately assessed by lenders.[7] Walter Wriston's well-known defense of sovereign lending (as chairman of Citibank), that a "country does not go bankrupt," was only the most quotable example of the prevailing view at the beginning of the 1980s.[8] After the crisis developed, the banks established their own agencies—notably the Institute of International Finance, in Washington, and the Japan Center for Finance, in Tokyo—in part to strengthen their ability to assess country risks.

Because the origins were global or widespread, so were the effects. The problems of Eastern Europe in 1981 did not lead to those of Latin America in 1982; those were just two manifestations of the shifting tectonic plates. Similarly, although it is often said that the problem in Mexico quickly "spread" throughout Latin America—and it would later be said that the 1997 crisis in Thailand spread throughout Asia—it is difficult to separate contagion (a decrease in the willingness of banks to lend to one country because of the debt-servicing problems of another country) from synchronicity (the tendency for global forces to induce similar reactions more or less simultaneously). Argentina, Brazil, Chile, Ecuador, Peru, Uruguay, and other countries across Latin America encountered debt crises in 1982 or 1983, and they all turned to the IMF for help. Those individual cases fed on one another, and the timing of the outbreak in a number of countries was no doubt accelerated by the eruption of crises elsewhere. Nonetheless—as the case studies discussed in the following chapters will show—all of the affected countries had been pursuing policies that were unsustainable in the global economic envi-

---

[7]Kindleberger (1978) presaged this failure: "When riding a tiger, or holding a bear by the tail, it seems rational—but may not be—to hang on. The model is apposite today, as the world banking community contemplates its large volume of loans to developing countries and to the Socialist bloc" (p. 3). Three years later, in 1981, the Group of Thirty sponsored a survey of 52 leading international banks to assess their attitudes toward lending to developing countries. A large majority of respondents (71 percent, against a 7 percent negative response) predicted that "bad debt experience and loan write-offs" would be more favorable on international than on domestic loans "over the next four to five years," and a similar majority thought that "a generalized debt problem affecting developing countries" was not likely to emerge. Mendelsohn (1981), pp. 26–27 and 20, respectively.

[8]Wriston's point was that the debt-servicing problems of developing countries in 1982 did not necessarily constitute a crisis, and that to resolve those problems required a combination of policy adjustment and financing arrangements rather than a writing off of the debt. The quotation is from Wriston (1982); for a further explanation of his views on sovereign lending, see Wriston (1986). For a review of the difficulties that banks experienced in analyzing country risks in that period, see Rimmer de Vries (1984). Also see Guenther (1984), which attributes the heavy bank lending to Mexico in 1981 to the banks' "long-standing relationship with borrowers" there.

ronment of the 1980s, and no country's crisis could be said to have resulted in any essential way from someone else's straits.[9]

Outside of Eastern Europe and Latin America, the evidence for a global cause looked different.

Many countries in Africa faced an even greater economic catastrophe in the 1980s, in which excess debt was merely one more trauma. The debts of most sub-Saharan African countries were primarily from official rather than commercial creditors, and the underlying problems were structural more than financial. Even where the banks had lent heavily in the 1970s, such as to Sudan, the resolution of those commercial debts was a minor problem in relation to civil war, the collapse of export markets, and the inability of the government to address the pervasive rigidities and imbalances in the domestic economy.

In contrast, most developing Asian countries largely escaped the debt crisis of the 1980s; partly because they faced less daunting circumstances, partly because they implemented more effective economic policies, and partly because political corruption and capital flight were less rampant (or at least less obvious).[10] Korea was the fourth-largest debtor in the world at the beginning of the decade, but the government undertook timely and effective adjustment and reform. Korea was able to service its debt without resort to rescheduling, and by 1987 was beginning to pay it off. Indonesia had faced its own debt problems a decade earlier and would face even more serious problems in the late 1990s. On this occasion, however, when the price of its petroleum exports began to fall in 1981, the government cut back quickly enough on investment projects to avoid recourse to rescheduling or even to the use of IMF credits. Low-income countries such as India, Pakistan, and China drew on the Fund to support ambitious development and reform plans, but their bank debts were relatively small and were never a major issue for most of them. An exception was the Philippines, where the government's slide into corruption and isolation deprived the country of the means to manage its large debts to foreign banks.

---

[9]For an historical perspective on the limited role of contagion in the spread of financial crises, see Bordo and Schwartz (1999). On the 1982 crisis, Stallings (1983) analyzed conditions in each country and concluded that the debt crises in Argentina and Chile resulted primarily from poor domestic policies. In contrast, although Mexico and to a lesser extent Brazil also suffered from poor policies, adverse external shocks played a larger role in these two countries. Only in the case of Brazil did she find that contagion—reluctance by banks to lend to any country in the region—was a major factor. The following chapters of the present study draw less favorable conclusions about policies in Brazil in that period.

[10]Although the measurement of capital flight is difficult and controversial, the Fund viewed it as an important component of the debt-management problem facing many developing countries in the 1980s. A 1987 internal staff paper defined capital flight as "the acquisition or retention of a claim on nonresidents that is motivated by the owner's concern that the value of his asset would be subject to discrete losses if his claim continued to be held domestically." Discussing the paper, Executive Directors noted that motivation could not be tested directly and that assessment of capital flight was therefore inherently ambiguous; nonetheless, they agreed that the Fund should collect information on capital flight, advise member countries on how to cope with it, and take it into account in designing Fund-supported adjustment programs. "Capital Flight—Concepts, Measurement, and Issues," SM/87/24 (January 23, 1987), p. 4; and the Secretary's précis (March 4, 1987) of Executive Board Seminar 87/1 (February 20, 1987).

Table 6.1. Commercial Debt Crises, 1981–89

Stage	Country and Year	Fund Involvement
I. Onset, 1981–82	Poland, 1981	None (nonmember)
	Yugoslavia, 1981	Stand-by arrangement (SBA)
	Costa Rica, 1981	Extended arrangement (EFF)
	Hungary, 1982	SBA
	Morocco, 1982	SBA
	Romania, 1982	SBA
II. Concerted Lending, 1982–86	Mexico, 1982	EFF, concerted lending (CL)
	Argentina, 1982	SBA, CL
	Brazil, 1982	EFF, CL
	Chile, 1983	SBA, CL
	Uruguay, 1983	SBA, CL
	Ecuador, 1983	SBA, CL
	Philippines, 1983–84	SBA
	Côte d'Ivoire, 1984	SBA, CL
	Peru, 1984	SBA
III. MYRAs and Enhanced Surveillance, 1984–85	Mexico, 1984	Support for multiyear rescheduling agreement (MYRA)
	Jamaica, 1984	SBA
	Venezuela, 1984	MYRA, enhanced surveillance (ES)
	Ecuador, 1984	SBA, MYRA
	Argentina, 1984–85	SBA, CL
IV. Experimentation, 1985–88	Chile, 1985	EFF, CL, support for debt-equity swaps
	Colombia, 1985	Seal of approval
	Bolivia, 1985	SBA, allowance of commercial arrears, support for debt buybacks
	Yugoslavia, 1985–86	MYRA, ES
	Uruguay, 1986	ES
	Mexico, 1986	SBA, CL
	Argentina, 1986	SBA, CL
	Costa Rica, 1986–87	SBA, allowance of commercial arrears
	Brazil, 1987–88	SBA
V. Debt Relief, 1989	Costa Rica, 1989	Brady-plan SBA
	Philippines, 1989	Brady-plan EFF
	Mexico, 1989	Brady-plan EFF
	Venezuela, 1989	Brady-plan EFF
	Argentina, 1989	SBA

The international debt crisis lasted from 1981 until 1989. It encompassed at least 30 distinct episodes involving nearly 20 countries around the world (Table 6.1). That it could not be quickly resolved was a product of two forces. First, for a number of countries, servicing the debt was only a symptom of a deeper problem of economic mismanagement; to bring about the needed reforms took a "silent revolution" in attitudes that did not gain strength until late in the decade. Second, for the most heavily indebted countries, no feasible reform program could suffice to break the country out of the maelstrom, restore normal economic growth, and restore the government's access to credit markets; some direct relief from the debt burden was also needed. Both elements of the solution were understood and were in place by 1989. A full resolution of the debt problems of developing countries would take years more, but the international crisis had become part of history.

Strategy

The strategy of the IMF and of the major creditor countries for managing the debt crisis evolved in stages, as illustrated in Table 6.1 and summarized below. The one constant throughout was that the central role for the Fund was to negotiate adjustment programs for countries and to support those programs with financing to cover a (usually small) portion of the external deficit. As the initial strains moved across Eastern Europe in 1981 and the first half of 1982, the Fund became increasingly involved in that manner, though without any noticeable shift in its role or its methods. From that perspective, at least, Mexico was a watershed. In working with Mexico in 1982, the management of the Fund realized that the situation called for major changes in relations between the institution and other creditors, notably commercial banks.

Traditional relations between the IMF and commercial banks may be characterized as an arm's-length mutual dependency. The Fund typically relied on the banks to provide an appropriate level of financing for the country, while the banks relied on the Fund to negotiate an appropriate set of supporting economic policies, but it was rare for either one to pressure the other. Starting with Zaïre in 1976, Fund staff members occasionally participated in meetings between a country's authorities and commercial banks. In 1978, in preparation for an extended arrangement with Jamaica, the Fund sought and obtained informal financing commitments from bank creditors.[11] The next year, when bank creditors reacted to deteriorating conditions in Sudan by trying to withdraw as rapidly as possible, the staff intervened to persuade them that the country's adjustment program deserved continuing support. Although the banks gave no firm assurances that they would maintain exposure, the staff felt confident that they would do so if the government could get current in servicing its debts. Accordingly, the Fund made the elimination of some $1 billion in arrears to commercial banks a precondition for the continuation of the arrangement beyond the first year.[12] These cases, however, remained exceptional. More typical was the case of Turkey, in which the Fund approved an unusually large stand-by arrangement in 1980 in the hope that the combination of a strong adjustment program and substantial commitments from official creditors as well as the Fund would persuade the banks to increase their own lending.[13]

---

[11]Minutes of EBM/78/86 (June 9, 1978), pp. 5–6. Drawings by Jamaica in the first year of the extended arrangement were phased to coincide with a schedule of anticipated bank loans that had been agreed upon through informal contacts between bank representatives and Fund staff; the bank loans were conditional on the provision of Fund financing, and in effect the Fund financing depended on the continued participation by the banks.

[12]"Sudan—Use of Fund Resources—Extended Fund Facility," EBS/79/250 (April 26, 1979); and minutes of EBM/79/71 (May 4, 1979), pp. 15–16.

[13]Jacques de Groote, the Executive Director representing Turkey at the Executive Board meeting on June 18, put it this way: "The influence of the Fund should not be limited to those cases where the Fund's decision to delay or suspend its financial assistance elicits from the banks a corresponding reaction. Banks should respond in a positive way when the Fund expresses its confidence in a country's recovery program and gives them a clear signal." When the Board met five

A central feature of the debt strategy that was developed in 1982 was an intensification of relationships between the Fund and the commercial banks. Because banks were now unwilling to lend to the most heavily indebted countries unless forced to do so, either out of self-preservation or in response to outside pressure, the Fund began requiring firm commitments as a precondition for Fund financing. Although the official policy was that this practice would be limited to exceptional cases, for a while it became almost routine for Latin America, starting in 1983.[14]

Three key assumptions underlay this strategy. First, the Fund staff and management viewed the problem as a threat to both debtors and creditors. They viewed the economic prospects of most of the indebted countries, especially the major economies in Latin America, to be strong enough that once the adverse shocks of the 1970s and early 1980s had been absorbed and adjustment policies had begun to work, those countries would be able to restore sustainable growth and service their debts. The Fund also viewed the international financial system as sound; if the initial threat could be averted, the money-center banks would be able to restore their balance sheets and would resume lending to developing countries voluntarily.

Second, the Fund judged that the problem could be solved only by cooperation between debtors and creditors. A unilateral default on payments would inevitably follow from a breakdown of negotiations and would have far worse consequences for both parties than would a negotiated settlement. That view was a strongly held article of faith at the Fund, and it was believed almost as strongly by many officials in the indebted countries.[15] It was challenged, not only by developing country advocates for unilateral action but also by some historians of earlier debt crises who noted that defaults had only temporarily stopped the inflow of capital.[16]

What persuaded the Fund in 1982 that the risk of default was a serious threat to the financial system was that the situation was fundamentally different from all ear-

---

months later to review the program, de Groote acknowledged with disappointment that the banks were continuing to withdraw support from Turkey. Minutes of EBM/80/92 (June 18, 1980), p. 8; and EBM/80/163 (November 7, 1980), p. 3. For a detailed survey of relations between the IMF and commercial banks through 1982, see "Payments Difficulties Involving Debt to Commercial Banks," SM/83/47 (March 9, 1983). For the background to the debt crisis in Turkey, see the papers in Aricanli and Rodrik (1990), especially Chapters 2 and 10.

[14]Remarking on the value of this practice in its first application, to Mexico, the Managing Director noted that "the Fund would have been happy to act in the same way a few years previously in a case like that of Turkey" (see footnote 13, above); minutes of EBM/82/168 (December 23, 1982).

[15]Jesús Silva Herzog, the Mexican finance minister from 1982 to 1986, wrestled with the idea of default throughout his term but always rejected it. Whether as warning or inspiration, a dominant feature of his office decor was an oil portrait of Benito Juárez, the great Mexican president whose moratorium on servicing foreign debts in 1861 led to invasion by France and the installation of the Emperor Maximilian in 1863.

[16]In a 1986 paper, Jeffrey Sachs (an occasional advisor to Latin American governments) argued that indebted countries would have been better off repudiating their debts in the early 1980s, as they had in the 1930s, except for the intervention of creditor governments and the IMF: "Countries that might happily break with the commercial banks are loath to break with the rest of the international system" (Sachs, 1986, p. 411). Eichengreen and Portes (1989) documented the relatively benign effects of defaults on bonds in the 1930s, but they warned against inferring that defaults would have led smoothly back to normal market access in the 1980s. For a thorough discussion, see the papers in Eichengreen and Lindert (1989).

lier debt crises. Those of the nineteenth and early twentieth centuries had been characterized predominantly by defaults on bonds held by individual investors, rather than by threats of default on syndicated bank loans. Losses—possibly exceeding the value of a bank's capital—to the leading international banks could have generated cascading losses and failures throughout the financial system. This new situation thus carried a systemic risk that had not previously been a central issue.

The third main assumption was that resolving the problem required coordinated and centralized action. In the words of one banker, it required a "conductor, in the electrical sense of the word, to bring the parties to agreement" (Leslie, 1983). The banks had a collective interest in negotiating a solution, but they could not be relied upon to coordinate their own response because of diverging interests: between banks in different countries, between competing banks within a country, and between large banks and small. Even though it would have been easier for creditors to organize themselves than in the days of bond financing, the difficulties still dominated.[17] The creditor countries also had a collective interest, but it was more efficient for a multilateral agency to assume responsibility than to coordinate on an ad hoc basis. While there was no specific mandate that made it more natural for the IMF to play that role than, say, the World Bank, the Fund demonstrated an ability to step in quickly and forcefully when the indebted countries requested its assistance.

Although the systemic crisis gradually subsided after 1983, the debt-servicing difficulties of many developing countries continued to mount. By 1985, IMF credit outstanding to many of the most heavily indebted countries was reaching its peak (Figure 6.2), reflecting the normal cycle of Fund lending. At the same time, more and more attention was being paid to the longer-term requirements for normalcy. Fund-supported adjustment programs began to include more structural elements and were aimed more at generating real economic growth, the multilateral development banks began to play a more active role in the indebted countries, and the banks became more willing to reschedule debts on longer terms. The period from 1985 to 1987 is appropriately characterized as one when the restoration of sustainable growth became viewed as the primary means by which developing countries could reduce the burden of servicing external debt.

The "growing out of debt" strategy failed. By 1987, most of the creditor banks had reduced their exposure to problem countries to a point where cohesive coordinated agreements among hundreds of banks could no longer be achieved. Banks then became more willing to wait for a better outcome, and approval of a program by the Fund became merely the starting point rather than the catalyst for an agreement with bank creditors. The restoration of economic growth remained an elusive goal, while the overhanging stock of debt continued to grow. The resulting stalemate between debtors and creditors forced the Fund to reexamine its opposi-

---

[17]See Dawson (1990) for an account of efforts by bondholders to organize themselves in the wake of the Latin American debt crisis of the 1820s. Jorgensen and Sachs (1989) examine the role of bondholders in the crises of the 1930s. Piñón-Farah (1996) discusses the limited experience with restructuring sovereign bonds in the 1980s: only three countries—Costa Rica in 1985, Nigeria in 1988, and Guatemala in 1989—succeeded in exchanging old for new bonds.

Figure 6.2. Fund Credit Outstanding to Heavily Indebted Countries, 1973–89

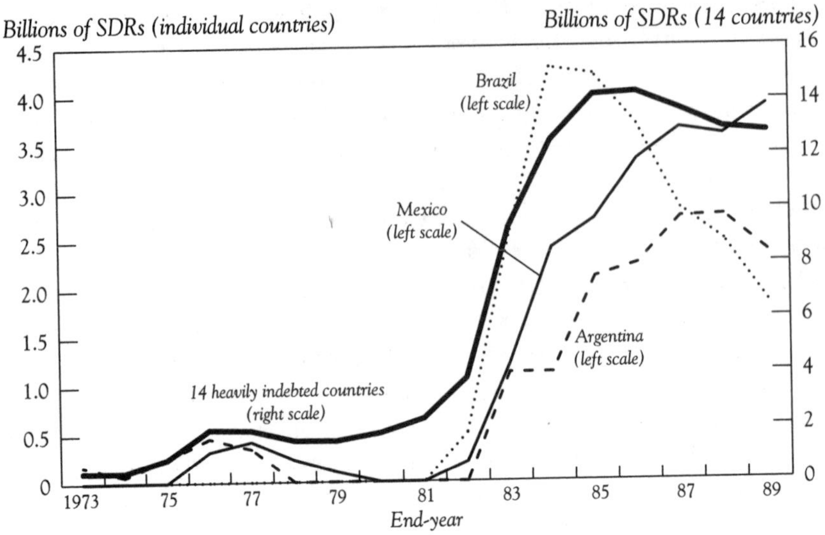
Billions of SDRs (individual countries)
Billions of SDRs (14 countries)
4.5
4.0
3.5
3.0
2.5
2.0
1.5
1.0
0.5
0
16
14
12
10
8
6
4
2
0
Brazil
(left scale)
Mexico
(left scale)
Argentina
(left scale)
14 heavily indebted countries
(right scale)
1973
75
77
79
81
83
85
87
89
End-year

tion to lending to countries that had not settled their arrears to commercial creditors, forced major creditor countries to reexamine their opposition to debt relief, and opened the way to the final phase of the debt strategy.

In May 1989, the IMF adopted new policies that allowed countries to use Fund resources to finance operations such as repurchases of their own debt at discounted prices (buybacks) and the establishment of escrow accounts to guarantee future interest payments in exchange for cuts in interest rates. That strengthening of the strategy, which fortuitously coincided with a marked improvement in the external economic environment facing many of the indebted countries, brought an end to the international crisis.

Managing the Debt Crisis: A Summary of Part II

Chapter 7 examines the central event of the initial period: Mexico in 1982. It begins by recounting the web of earlier policy mistakes and adverse shocks that prevented Mexico from avoiding a crisis in 1982, and the limited ability of the Fund to monitor, predict, or forestall the calamity as it unfolded. It then examines how the initial rescue package was assembled in August, analyzes the difficult and lengthy negotiations on the adjustment program that were successfully concluded in November, and reviews the initiatives that ensured that the banks would help finance the program. The Fund's approval of an extended arrangement in December and the banks' approval of a complex package of rescheduling and new lending three months later marked the end of an extraordinary effort to avert a possibly systemic collapse.

Chapters 8 through 11 examine the four broad stages in which the debt strategy evolved. Starting in 1982, the Fund organized "concerted lending" arrangements for several countries while they implemented adjustment programs grounded primarily in traditional macroeconomic policy corrections. The first two years of that strategy are reviewed in Chapter 8. The next two years, when creditors began searching for ways to extend the strategy beyond the short-term financial involvement of the IMF, are the subject of Chapter 9. By 1985, it was becoming clear that a resumption of longer-term growth in the most heavily indebted countries would require further innovations and a broader strategy. Chapter 10 examines the shift toward growth-oriented adjustment. The final stage came when creditors devised a strategy for debt reduction, as described in Chapter 11. Readers whose main interest is in one or more of the three largest affected countries will find a continuous history in the pertinent sections of each successive chapter. For Mexico, the story begins in Chapter 7 and continues in Chapters 9–11; for Argentina and Brazil, it is found in Chapters 8–11.

Chapter 8 looks at several related cases. First, it steps back in time to examine how three Eastern European countries—Poland, Romania, and Hungary—got into trouble in 1981–82 and how each case was handled. Each successive case involved the Fund a little more closely. The chapter then looks closely at the Fund's crisis management in Argentina, Brazil, and Chile. Each one faced a serious debt problem, but each had unique elements in both its origins and its implications. By the time programs were arranged for these countries in 1983, the Fund's case-by-case approach, as it came to be known, was firmly established.

Chapter 9 carries the story forward through to 1985 by examining how the programs with the three largest Latin American countries were handled. Sooner or later, the adjustment programs of Mexico, Brazil, and Argentina all ran aground. The chapter concludes by taking a broader look at how the overall strategy evolved during this period and why it could no longer be sustained without a major overhaul.

Chapter 10 takes up the second main phase of the strategy, which was dominated by the Baker plan to strengthen the growth prospects of indebted countries. After reviewing the development of that plan and other strategic innovations, this chapter picks up the stories of the major Latin American countries where they had been left off in Chapter 9. Each of the three, at some point in 1986 or 1987, showed promise of escaping the overhanging burden of debt, only to relapse into even deeper economic difficulties.

The effort to resolve the crisis through debt relief is the subject of Chapter 11. The keystone of the strengthened strategy was the Brady Plan of 1989, but the strategy gradually shifted from 1987 on. Chapter 11 summarizes the intellectual and bureaucratic battles on debt relief and then describes two cases—Bolivia and Mexico—where the Fund showed flexibility in supporting the efforts of the countries to negotiate reductions in their debts. After reviewing the development of the Brady Plan, the chapter examines the four Fund-supported debt-relief cases implemented in 1989: Costa Rica, the Philippines, Mexico, and Venezuela. The final section of Chapter 11 picks up once again the stories of Argentina and Brazil, both of which implemented Fund-supported programs in this period, though they were still a long way from qualifying for debt relief under the Brady Plan.

Part II concludes with an analytical retrospective on the role of the Fund in managing the debt crisis of the 1980s. Chapter 12 poses a series of questions about the assumptions and choices made by the institution from 1982 through 1989 and attempts to draw a few lessons for the future.

References

Aricanli, Tosun, and Dani Rodrik, 1990, *The Political Economy of Turkey: Debt, Adjustment and Sustainability* (Basingstoke, England: Macmillan).

Bordo, Michael D., and Anna J. Schwartz, 1999, "Under What Circumstances, Past and Present, Have International Rescues of Countries in Financial Distress Been Successful?" *Journal of International Money and Finance*, Vol. 18 (August), pp. 683–708.

Dawson, Frank Griffith, 1990, *The First Latin American Debt Crisis: The City of London and the 1822–25 Loan Bubble* (New Haven, Connecticut: Yale University Press).

de Vries, Rimmer, 1984, "How Much Debt Should LDCs Incur?" in *International Capital Movements, Debt and Monetary System*, ed. by Wolframs Engels, Armin Gutowski, and Henry C. Wallich (Mainz, Germany: V. Hase and Koehler Verlag), pp. 397–416.

Edwards, Sebastian, 1995, *Crisis and Reform in Latin America: From Despair to Hope* (New York: Oxford University Press for the World Bank).

Eichengreen, Barry, and Peter H. Lindert, eds., 1989, *The International Debt Crisis in Historical Perspective* (Cambridge, Massachusetts: MIT Press).

Eichengreen, Barry, and Richard Portes, 1989, "Settling Defaults in the Era of Bond Finance," *World Bank Economic Review*, Vol. 3 (May), pp. 211–39.

Guenther, Jack D., 1984, "The Role of Commercial Banks in the Adjustment Process," in *Adjustment, Conditionality, and International Financing*, ed. by Joaquín Muns (Washington: International Monetary Fund), pp. 184–205.

Jorgensen, Erika, and Jeffrey Sachs, 1989, "Default and Renegotiation of Latin American Foreign Bonds in the Interwar Period," Chapter 3 in *The International Debt Crisis in Historical Perspective*, ed. by Barry Eichengreen and Peter H. Lindert (Cambridge, Massachusetts: MIT Press), pp. 48–85.

Kindleberger, Charles P., 1978, *Manias, Panics, and Crashes: A History of Financial Crises* (New York: Basic Books).

Leslie, Peter, 1983, "Techniques of Rescheduling: The Latest Lessons," *Banker*, Vol. 133 (April), pp. 23–30.

Mendelsohn, M.S., ed., 1981, *The Outlook for International Bank Lending: A Survey of Opinion Among Leading International Bankers* (New York: Group of Thirty).

Nowzad, Bahram, and Richard C. Williams, 1981, *External Indebtedness of Developing Countries*, IMF Occasional Paper No. 3 (Washington: International Monetary Fund).

Piñón-Farah, Marco A., 1996, "Private Bond Restructurings: Lessons for the Case of Sovereign Debtors," IMF Working Paper 96/11 (Washington: International Monetary Fund).

Sachs, Jeffrey, 1986, "Managing the LDC Debt Crisis," *Brookings Papers on Economic Activity: 2* (Washington: Brookings Institution), pp. 397–431.

Stallings, Barbara, 1983, "Latin American Debt: What Kind of Crisis," *SAIS Review*, Vol. 3, No. 2, pp. 27–39.

Wriston, Walter B., 1982, "Banking Against Disaster," *New York Times* (September 14), p. A27.

———, 1986, *Risk and Other Four Letter Words* (New York: Harper and Row).

7

The Mexican Crisis:
No Mountain Too High?

As a prelude to the overall review of the debt crisis and the debt strategy in later chapters, this chapter takes an in-depth look at the handling of the crisis in Mexico. Although Mexico was not the first indebted economy to erupt, nor the largest, nor the one with the most serious economic or financial problems, the 1982 Mexican crisis was the one that alerted the IMF and the world to the possibility of a systemic collapse: a crisis that could spread to many other countries and threaten the stability of the international financial system. Moreover, the Fund's response to Mexico in 1982 introduced important innovations in the speed of negotiations, the role of structural elements in the policy adjustment program, the assembling of official financing packages, and—most important—relations between the Fund and private sector creditors. This story also illustrates the always complex relationships between the Fund and its major creditor members. A successful resolution of Mexico's financial difficulties was economically and politically crucial for the United States, but the extent of Mexican indebtedness put the solution out of the bilateral reach of the U.S. authorities. The challenge for the Fund was to balance the interests of all of the affected countries, whether debtor or creditor, in circumstances that were critically important to its largest member and principal creditor.

In the middle of August, the pace of work at the IMF normally loses some of its usual freneticism. The Executive Board takes an informal recess while Executive Directors, the Managing Director, and a good portion of the staff go on annual holidays. In 1982, however, the dog days had come early, as the Annual Meetings had been moved forward by a few weeks to accommodate an Islamic holiday.[1] To prepare for the meetings, which were to be in Toronto, Ontario (Canada), the first week in September, the Managing Director (Jacques de Larosière) had returned from a brief holiday in time to chair a full schedule of Board meetings starting August 9. When the telephone rang on August 12, much of the staff was in place, but no one could have suspected that life in the Fund was about to become more frenzied and intense than at any time since U.S. President Richard Nixon had suspended convertibility of the dollar on another August evening 11 years before.

---

[1]See the discussion at EBM/81/144 (November 18, 1981). The holy day Eid-ul-adja, the date of which is governed by the lunar calendar, fell on September 28, 1982.

Smoldering Embers, 1979–81

There was ample reason to fear a crisis in Mexico, but also ample reason to calm one's fears. The government, first under President Luis Echeverría and later under his successor, José López-Portillo, had been borrowing large amounts in foreign currencies (mostly U.S. dollars) from commercial markets since the early 1970s. From 1973 to 1981, the external debt of the public sector in Mexico had grown at an average annual rate of more than 30 percent, from $4 billion to $43 billion. The mountain was high, and the path steep, but a challenge is not necessarily an obstacle. Was this borrowing a problem, or was it part of a sustainable strategy for economic growth?

Mexico in the early 1980s was no longer the agricultural economy that it had been just a few years before: it had become a power in the international oil market at a time when the price of oil was at an all-time high and was widely projected to rise still further. Consequently, the government's ability to service its debt was now growing at such a rate that the portion of export receipts absorbed by debt service had fallen from a peak of 68 percent in 1979 to 36 percent in 1981. Output had been growing by 8½ percent a year for the past three years, and in spite of the government's adherence to a fixed exchange rate when inflation was running at more than 25 percent a year, the current account deficit appeared financeable, averaging about 4½ percent of GDP.[2]

The Mexican authorities clearly viewed prospects as rosy and as unblemished by the large stock of debt.[3] From 1979 on, once the magnitude of Mexico's oil reserves had become known, government officials regarded the country's growth prospects as no longer subject in practice to a balance of payments constraint. Ariel Buira, then Alternate Executive Director for Mexico in the IMF, noted with satisfaction in January 1979 that

> the resources arising from the oil exports will allow Mexico to overcome the two constraints that in the last two decades had limited its growth rate to around 6½ per cent to 7 per cent per annum. As the rate of domestic savings rises substantially, and the foreign exchange bottleneck disappears, the ceiling which in the past these factors imposed on the rate of growth of the economy will be removed.[4]

Borrowing against future oil revenues to finance investments in productive physical capital was not just good politics, it was sound economics—if the future revenues were secure, and if the investments were productive.

The ability of the IMF staff to sort through the thicket of information and forecasts was hampered in 1980 and 1981 by gaps in what should have been regular surveillance discussions with the authorities. In 1977–79, following an exchange

---

[2]"Mexico—Recent Economic Developments," SM/83/86 (May 17, 1983), pp. 4 (output and prices), 57 (current account), and 69 (debt service).

[3]The official view did not go unchallenged within the government, but the optimists prevailed. See Kapur, Lewis, and Webb (1997, pp. 602–3) for an account of a battle in 1981 between the ministries of planning (bullish on borrowing) and finance (bearish), which the planning officials won.

[4]Minutes of EBM/79/1 (January 3, 1979), p. 7.

crisis during the 1976 presidential election year, Mexico had implemented a Fund-supported adjustment program under the Extended Fund Facility (EFF). Although the program was certainly successful,[5] it was followed by a period when the authorities did not appear eager to pursue close relations with the Fund. An Article IV consultation mission, led by Walter Robichek (Director of the Western Hemisphere Department), concluded that notwithstanding the success of the program, Mexico needed to make further adjustments; in particular, public sector spending was rising excessively (at a rate exceeding 30 percent a year over the previous three years), pushing up inflation without making more than a "dent" in the unemployment problem. The Executive Board, in concluding the consultation in March 1980, agreed with these concerns but "commended the authorities for their success in reactivating the economy."[6] Nonetheless, two years would elapse before the government would again agree to host a Fund mission.[7]

The external environment began to sour in the first half of 1981, as a sharp increase in short-term interest rates in the United States and other major countries was followed by a softening of demand for oil and the beginning of what would become a disastrous downward slide in the price of Mexico's principal export. The national oil company, Pemex, and the Ministry of National Properties and Industrial Development (SEPAFIN) attempted for a time to avoid cutting export prices in line with the market, apparently on the belief that the comparatively high quality of Mexican oil would ensure a continued market.[8] Instead, Mexico's share of a shrinking market declined, the volume of oil exports for the year was more than 25 percent below projection, and public sector external borrowing jumped to a record $18.3 billion.[9]

Even more ominous than the amount of borrowing in 1981 was its maturity profile. More than half of the new debt was in short-term credits, as the lending banks were beginning to show reluctance to make longer-term commitments; a particularly large hump in repayments now loomed in August 1982. In the meantime, Mexican residents began to accelerate the shift in bank deposits out of the country; by the end of the year, private sector claims on foreign banks totaled an estimated $10 billion.[10] By November 1981, as a Fund mission finally prepared to go to Mexico City for discussions under Article IV, it was clear that all of the preconditions for an economic crisis were present.

---

[5]SDR 518 million (140 percent of quota, and approximately $600 million) was originally made available under the three-year program, later augmented by SDR 100 million. Only one drawing was made, however, for SDR 100 million in February 1977. Owing in part to the adjustment program and in part to the development of oil reserves, Mexico was then able to meet its external financing requirements through commercial banks. For further descriptions and analysis of the program, see de Vries (1985), pp. 377–80, and Guitián and Lindgren (1978).

[6]"Mexico—Staff Report for the 1979 Article IV Consultation," SM/80/24 (January 24, 1980), p. 17, and minutes of EBM/80/34 (March 3, 1980), p. 29.

[7]An informal staff visit, without a report being issued to the Executive Board, took place in July 1980.

[8]For accounts of this episode and its consequences, see Kraft (1984), pp. 34–35; Zedillo (1985), p. 313; and Bailey and Cohen (1987), p. 53.

[9]"Mexico—Staff Report for the 1982 Article IV Consultation," SM/82/121 (June 25, 1982), p. 10.
[10]Ibid.

Mounting Concerns: The 1981–82 Consultations

The 1981 consultations were not easy to complete, partly owing to the long interval since the previous meetings, and partly because the government was still preparing the 1982 budget when the mission arrived. After two weeks in Mexico City, the team returned to Washington and reported that it would be necessary to go back in January after the budget had been approved by congress. This they did, but the grounds for pessimism were not diminishing. The mission concluded that the prospects for fiscal adjustment were limited, the outlook for economic activity was poor, the exchange rate (which was fixed against the U.S. dollar) was inconsistent with a price level that was inflating more rapidly all the time, and debt service was likely to rise sharply. A presidential election would be held in July 1982, and not until a new administration took office in December were tough actions likely to be taken.

The mission report, however, did not go to the Executive Board right away, because a series of developments caused it to be updated several times. On February 17, 1982, the Mexican authorities announced that the central bank was temporarily withdrawing from the foreign exchange markets and would let the peso find its own level; within a week, the value of the peso in relation to the dollar had fallen by more than 40 percent (Figure 7.1). At the same time, to support the central bank's reentry into the market to stabilize the peso, Mexico drew down its reserve tranche at the Fund: the first use of Fund resources by Mexico in five years.

In mid-March, two senior officials were dispatched to Washington to explain to the Fund staff the measures that were being taken to control the economy. No sooner did they arrive than they were recalled to Mexico for what turned out to be a major shake-up in the leadership. The two officials were among the best that Mexico had yet produced: Jesús Silva Herzog was now to become finance minister (Secretary of Finance), a post that he would hold through more than four years of extraordinary pressure and that would make him one of the most renowned and respected officials in the developing world; and Miguel Mancera was to become governor (Director General) of the central bank (Banco de Mexico, or Bank of Mexico), a post that he would hold—with one interruption, discussed below—until 1997, and through which he would oversee Mexico's struggle to return to financial normalcy. But they began their day in the sun blinded by a fait accompli that marked a serious setback to the adjustment program: the day after their appointments, the government announced the authorization of large wage awards, averaging about 20 percent, which wiped out much of the benefit of February's devaluation and made an acceleration of inflation all but inevitable.

In April 1982, as worries over inflation deepened, capital flight escalated and the financial position of both the public and private sectors continued to deteriorate. Mexico's largest conglomerate, the Alfa Industrial Group, defaulted on the principal payments due on $2.3 billion in debts to foreign banks, in part because of the pressure on its balance sheet from the February devaluation.[11] A stabilization pro-

---

[11]"The Debt Burden on Alfa of Mexico," *New York Times*, May 10, 1982, pp. D1, D5.

Figure 7.1. Mexico: Exchange Rate, 1976–82

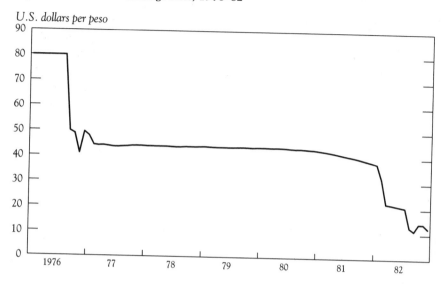

U.S. dollars per peso

gram—drawn up at the insistence of Silva Herzog—was announced on April 20, promising that the fiscal deficit would be reduced by 3 percent of GDP over the remainder of the year through expenditure control and revenue enhancements, but the specific measures to be taken were left open.[12] Meanwhile, official reserves were sliding precipitously, and at the end of the month the Bank of Mexico drew $800 million overnight on its swap line with the U.S. Federal Reserve to meet its month-end liquidity requirements. Within days, the IMF sent its team back to Mexico City to follow up on the consultation discussions that had apparently been concluded in January, and both Silva Herzog and Mancera flew secretly to Washington to explain developments directly to the Managing Director.[13] At this stage, the Fund's main concern was over the inconsistency between the policy of trying to keep the peso from depreciating against the dollar and the policy of propping up aggregate demand through wage increases and other expenditures that could be financed only through inflation. The Managing Director and the staff knew that the books could be balanced only through continued recourse to external borrowing, but no one could foresee how rapidly the availability of such funds would shrivel up.

---

[12]"Mexico—Economic Adjustment Program for 1982," EBD/82/99 (April 26, 1982).

[13]Silva Herzog made regular, though highly secret, visits to Washington throughout the period between his appointment in March 1982 and the onset of the crisis in August. On each such visit, he met with officials from the IMF, the World Bank, the U.S. Treasury, and the Federal Reserve. Paul A. Volcker (then Federal Reserve chairman) recalled that the standard advice to the minister was for Mexico to apply for a Fund program and reform the domestic economy, but that the advice was routinely rejected on the grounds that any such action would have to await the inauguration of a new president. See Volcker and Gyohten (1992), p. 199. As discussed below (p. 289), although the Federal Reserve allowed Mexico to make end-month overnight drawings against its swap lines throughout the second quarter of 1982 for window-dressing purposes, no longer-term drawings were allowed until Mexico agreed to seek a Fund arrangement in early August.

A final version of the staff report on Mexico was prepared in the first part of June. The government by this time was making plans for further spending cuts, but neither the authorities nor the Fund staff was under any illusion that the planned cuts would be sufficient to restore even a semblance of balance to reserves without additional measures. Either the exchange rate would have to be allowed to depreciate further or tough domestic measures would have to be taken. In an election year neither option seemed politically viable. At the end of June, a syndicate of commercial banks agreed to lend an additional $2.5 billion to the Mexican government, bringing the total of international bank loans to $9.6 billion for the first half of the year.

Attitudes began to shift in July 1982, as the commercial banks displayed increasing reluctance to lend to Mexico: spreads over the standard London interbank offer rate (LIBOR) were widening, and syndicates were taking longer to form.[14] Although export volumes were growing reasonably well in spite of the second "dip" in the U.S. recession, revenues were still disappointing because of the continuing slump in oil prices. The only signs of brightness on the horizon were that the Federal Reserve was easing up on U.S. monetary policy enough to bring interest rates down a little (by about 1 percentage point on three-month U.S. treasury bills from April to July)[15] and that Mexican elections on July 4 had produced a president-elect who seemed committed to financial stability. Miguel de la Madrid, however, would not assume office for another five months, and neither a major economic contraction nor a program with the IMF would be the finale that López-Portillo hoped to have for his presidency.

Caught between the obvious need to take further action and the desire to avoid a Fund program, the Mexican authorities explored the possibility of gaining some form of public approbation from the IMF that would enable them to improve their access to bank loans. On July 8, just before leaving on vacation, the Managing Director gave the staff team the go-ahead to explore with the authorities the idea of negotiating a policy program independently of any request to draw on Fund resources. If the proposed policy actions were strong enough to justify Fund financial support but could in fact be supported by bank loans instead, so much the better. The Fund, however, could not in any circumstances give its seal of approval to a weaker program just because its own money would not be put at stake.[16]

---

[14]Edwards (1986) documents the sudden rise in interest rate spreads and notes that it is "somewhat puzzling" (p. 583) that it did not occur months earlier.

[15]This episode has been the subject of much controversy. Kraft (1984, p. 8) and Lissakers (1991, pp. 205–206) attribute the easing in part to concerns over the effects that high interest rates were having on the cost of servicing Mexico's floating-rate external debt; but contemporaneous accounts generally give the dominant weight to domestic considerations. Volcker (in Volcker and Gyohten, 1992, pp. 179–180, and in interviews with the author) has argued that the easing in policy was unrelated to Latin America and could not have affected it very much in any case. It may also be noted that neither Volcker nor Anthony Solomon—the two most internationalist members of the Federal Open Market Committee—was the driving force behind the shift.

[16]Memorandum for files by Nigel Carter (Personal Assistant to the Managing Director), July 12, 1982; in IMF/RD Western Hemisphere Department file "Mexico—General Correspondence July–November 1982" (Accession 87/19, Box 2, Section 94). This proposal—developed at a meeting between de Larosière and Robichek—was the prototype for what would become known by 1984 as "enhanced surveillance" (see Chapter 9).

Figure 7.2. Mexico: Fiscal Deficit and External Debt, 1971–82

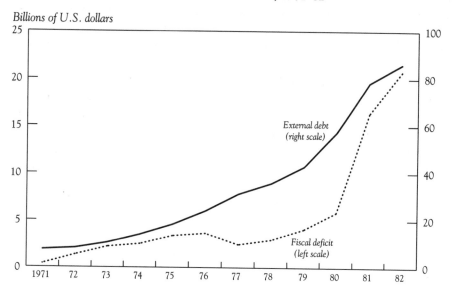

Billions of U.S. dollars

Sources: IMF, *IFS*; and World Bank, *World Development Indicators*.

On July 16, 1982, the Executive Board met to conclude the Article IV consultations: the first Board meeting on Mexico since March 1980. The gap in consultations prompted quite a little grumbling, reflecting concerns over the effectiveness of surveillance. Those concerns would become more acute later, when the full scope of the crisis could be viewed with hindsight; for the moment, the complaints came primarily from Christopher Taylor (Alternate—United Kingdom) and Douglas I.S. Shaw (Temporary Alternate—Canada), both of whom argued that major developing countries should be given as much and as frequent attention as the major industrial countries.

More generally, several Directors were worried about the buildup of external debt (Figure 7.2). Costa P. Caranicas (Alternate—Greece) noted that Mexico had the world's largest external debt and that the staff was projecting what he termed a "staggering" magnitude of new borrowing during 1982. International banks were becoming uneasy about the situation, and if they should withdraw from additional financing, Mexico could be forced to undertake a harsh adjustment. Tom de Vries (Netherlands) noted that the staff report had not expressed a clear view on whether the debt position was sustainable. The promised cut in the fiscal deficit —from nearly 15 percent of GDP to less than 12 percent within eight months— was substantial and yet insufficient. No doubt having reflected on the similar problems that his own country had faced after experiencing a major expansion of natural gas exports in the 1970s, de Vries observed that while in general it was perfectly sensible to finance capital investment by external borrowing, such a policy would appreciate the exchange rate and thus squeeze the country's traditional export sectors. Taylor added that much of the more recent borrowing carried very short maturities; a rephasing of the maturity structure, in his view, would have to be given a high priority.[17]

Notwithstanding these expressions of concern over the buildup of external debt, none of the discussion on July 16 suggested that a debt crisis was imminent.[18] Mexico's Executive Director, Ariel Buira, observed that the country had a good external credit rating and that he expected banks to continue to support the government's financing requirements. In sum, everyone involved knew that Mexico faced major financial difficulties that required a serious commitment to reduce the fiscal deficit and thereby sharply diminish reliance on external borrowing. Everyone knew that such a commitment could not become credible at least until de la Madrid assumed the presidency in December. But this knowledge was covered by an assumption—or a hope—that commercial financing would continue to be available until the necessary policy adjustments could be made.

The Board's complacency in July reflected the muted nature of the staff's warnings. For more than two years, the staff had been expressing concerns over the debt buildup by Mexico, albeit obliquely and without portending a *debt* crisis per se. In the January 1980 report on the 1979 consultations, the staff warned that "official external borrowing on the scale now being envisaged" could "lead to a level of domestic spending incompatible with the intended deceleration in the rate of domestic inflation." In November 1981, the mission concluded that borrowing had been used to support domestic consumption and had led to a widening of the current account balance; and that in "light of the above a major reorientation of public sector financial policies is needed." Finally, the June 1982 report noted that the "willingness of foreign lenders to extend credits to Mexico undoubtedly will depend on whether progress is being made toward a lower and more sustainable public sector financing requirement." As these passages indicate, the staff's emphasis was always on the need for policy adjustment as a prerequisite for financial stability. Projecting whether and when commercial lenders might decide to withdraw if adjustment fell short was outside the scope of the reports.[19]

---

[17]Minutes of EBM/82/100 (July 16, 1982), pp. 7 (de Vries), 11–12 (Caranicas), and 15 (Taylor).

[18]The July 16 meeting was chaired by the Deputy Managing Director, William B. Dale, because de Larosière was in Europe, where he had attended the monthly meeting of BIS governors in Basel, Switzerland. Several of the central bankers present in Basel reportedly expressed concerns about the ability of banks to survive defaults in Eastern Europe or Latin America. The sense of that discussion was reported to Dale on July 15, but the report did not specifically mention Mexico. Minutes of EBM/82/103 (August 9, 1982), p. 3; cable from Aldo Guetta (Director of the Paris Office) to the Acting Managing Director (July 15, 1982), in IMF/CF (I 300 "Bank for International Settlements 1979–1982").

[19]See "Mexico—Staff Report for the 1979 Article IV Consultation," SM/80/24 (January 24, 1980), p. 18; staff translation of the final statement presented to the authorities during the 1982 Article IV consultation discussions (November 27, 1981), p. 2 (attached to a December 2, 1981 memorandum from Beza to management, in IMF/RD Western Hemisphere Department file "Mexico, January 1981–December 1981" (Accession 84/70, Box 2, Section 74); and "Mexico—Staff Report for the 1982 Article IV Consultation," SM/82/121 (June 25, 1982), p. 18. Throughout the period leading up to the crisis, the staff and management of the World Bank were generally more optimistic about Mexico's prospects than the Fund; see Urzúa (1997), pp. 73–75.

Was it reasonable to expect banks to keep lending, when Mexico's financial imbalances were so evident? Certainly it was in the banks' collective interest to roll over the principal on existing loans, although the degree to which it was in their interest to make additional loans would have been more controversial. What was more difficult to foresee and was largely overlooked at the time was that the riskiness of loans to Mexico had become great enough that each individual bank had an interest in demanding repayment now, as long as it could do so ahead of any general stampede. This conflict between the individual and the collective interest was by this time a quietly but rapidly burning wick. An explosion was already inevitable.

The Crisis Erupts: August 1982

One week after the July Board meeting, Silva Herzog, once again in Washington, informed William Dale, then Acting Managing Director, that the financial situation was continuing to worsen and asked that the IMF send a mission to Mexico at once. No mention was made of a possible financial arrangement with the Fund. The minister was primarily interested in consulting closely on proposed policy adjustments, perhaps with an eye toward the sort of monitoring arrangement that had been discussed a few weeks earlier. But by the time Sterie T. Beza (Deputy Director, Western Hemisphere Department) and his team arrived in Mexico City at the beginning of August, the authorities, on instructions from President López-Portillo, were prepared to begin negotiations for a three-year arrangement under the EFF.

Discussions began on a hectic pace that was greatly accelerated in comparison with the Fund's usual practice and that prefigured the intense and telescoped negotiations that followed the Mexican and Asian financial crises in the 1990s. Beza's mission spent one week in Mexico City, gathering the detailed information that would be needed for the negotiations soon to follow. The authorities, aware of how quickly their ability to manage the debt portfolio was unraveling, hoped to complete work with the staff and win preliminary approval from the Fund's management by the end of August, and Beza was prepared to do everything possible to meet what must surely have seemed to be an impossible deadline.

Even before the week was out, two emergency measures had to be taken. On August 4, the Bank of Mexico drew $700 million on its swap line with the Federal Reserve; in contrast to the overnight drawings that had been made in the preceding months, this drawing carried a three-month maturity. Then, on August 5, a dual exchange market was introduced in an effort to isolate speculative capital flows within a market in which the exchange rate would float freely. This grudging and partial recognition of the ongoing fall in the market value of the peso (see Figure 7.1) could do no more than briefly delay the collapse of the policy regime. It might temporarily stem capital flight, but it would do nothing to revive and may even have helped to kill the already comatose financing from commercial lenders abroad.

Beza formally reported back to management on Monday, August 9, and was given the green light to prepare rapidly for a negotiating mission that would start the following Monday, August 16. If agreement could be reached on a comprehensive set of policies to control public expenditure, Mexico—which had no outstanding drawings from the Fund other than the reserve tranche purchase mentioned above—would qualify for maximum access under the EFF, which over three years would total SDR 3.6 billion, or the equivalent of 450 percent of Mexico's Fund quota. In addition, Mexican officials had requested authorization to draw the equivalent of 100 percent of their quota (SDR 800 million) under the Compensatory Financing Facility (CFF). Though a smaller amount, that money could be made available immediately upon approval by the Executive Board, perhaps as early as October.

Even this ambitious plan proved to be too slow to cope with the events that ensued that very week. On Wednesday, August 11, Silva Herzog concluded that Mexico could no longer contain the problem by negotiating only with commercial creditors. His principal debt negotiator, José Angel Gurría Treviño, informed him that banks were refusing to roll over the principal payments that were due next Monday, and the Bank of Mexico did not have sufficient reserves to meet them. If Mexico defaulted on those payments, the lending banks would be subjected to heavy pressure from regulators (who could require them to write down the value of their loan portfolio, not just to Mexico but to other countries as well), depositors, and shareholders. Mexico faced a simple choice: default or obtain outside assistance. Because the amounts involved were large enough to threaten the stability of the financial systems of the major creditor countries, there was a good chance of getting help.

On Thursday, August 12, Silva Herzog decided on several actions that would have to be carried out before the weekend. First, he ordered the exchange markets closed. Banks were authorized to purchase foreign exchange from the Bank of Mexico at a fixed rate (69.5 pesos per U.S. dollar) that was less favorable than the prevailing market rate (around 75), and dollar-denominated deposits were to be payable only in pesos, with balances converted at the official rate. Second, he had a letter sent to creditors informing them that Mexico was unable to pay the principal that would become due on Monday. Third, he telephoned de Larosière, Federal Reserve Chairman Paul Volcker,[20] and U.S. Treasury Secretary Donald Regan, and informed them of the actions he was taking. Fourth, accompanied by Gurría, Mancera, and other officials, he flew to Washington to make the case in person.[21]

Containing the Crisis: The First Weekend

It was Friday the 13th, but it was a pleasant sunny morning as Silva Herzog and his team went to the IMF for a nine o'clock meeting with de Larosière and the

---

[20]The Federal Reserve staff, at least, seems to have anticipated the crisis to some extent. As recounted in Volcker and Gyohten (1992), p. 200, Volcker had been alerted by his office on Monday that Mexico was imminently going to be unable to meet its payments to banks, a call that prompted him to return prematurely to Washington from a fishing holiday in Wyoming just before the crisis broke.

[21]See Kraft (1984), p. 2, for a description of Silva Herzog's initial actions.

Fund's Mexican team in the Managing Director's office.[22] De Larosière told them that the Fund was prepared to help them as much as possible, but first Mexico would have to find a way to avoid defaulting on its debts. Only if the government stayed current on its interest payments and reached agreement with its creditors regarding the scheduling of principal payments could the Fund be expected to have the requisite support for a substantial financial arrangement. More fundamentally, solving the problem would require adopting a severe adjustment program. The Managing Director suggested that the program would have to be designed by the Mexican authorities themselves and would have to meet their own political as well as economic requirements; the transition in the presidency would complicate matters, as the program would have to be endorsed by both the outgoing and the incoming administrations.

Silva Herzog assured the Managing Director that he had the authority to speak for both leaders and that President-Elect de la Madrid would name a representative to participate fully in the negotiations.[23] This assurance was in fact a bit of bluster: the current president was far from convinced that Mexico should undertake the commitments that such a program would entail, and there would be substantial opposition in the cabinet. All the more important, then, that the program be homegrown and not be seen as imposed from outside.

While the Fund staff continued to prepare for the previously scheduled negotiating mission, Silva Herzog spent the rest of that Friday and the weekend lining up U.S. official support for emergency funding. As has been documented elsewhere, that effort was nearly toppled by U.S. officials who insisted that Mexico should pay a high price for the rescue. To some extent, that position was motivated by a desire to design the deal so as to promote unrelated domestic or foreign policy objectives.[24] In addition, the U.S. administration's position was driven both by the need to win the approval of the U.S. Congress and by an innate Bagehot-like con-

---

[22]If Silva Herzog read his horoscope in the *Washington Post* that morning, he would have learned that "Your bargaining position is stronger than might be apparent on surface. . . . Your financial potential can be more fully exploited today." De Larosière was told to "Be prepared for revisions, rewrites. You are capable of building on a more solid structure. Individual who shares interests might 'lecture' you."

[23]Notwithstanding the interregnum, the Mexican negotiating team exemplified the country's unusual tradition of continuity in government under the ruling Partido Revolucionario Institucional (PRI). Silva Herzog had been appointed by López-Portillo in part because he was a close associate of incoming President de la Madrid; he later became ambassador to Spain and then to the United States under the two presidents who succeeded de la Madrid. The chief representative appointed by de la Madrid in the fall of 1982 was the head of his transition team, a Harvard-trained economist named Carlos Salinas de Gortari. Salinas became Minister of Budget and Planning in the new administration and in 1988 was elected to succeed de la Madrid as president. His assistant in the 1982 negotiations was Pedro Aspe Armella, with a Ph.D. from MIT. Aspe eventually became Secretary (Minister) of Planning under de la Madrid and Secretary of Finance under Salinas.

[24]See Kraft (1984), Bailey and Cohen (1987), and Leeds and Thompson (1987). The three books tell a generally consistent story, but they do not always agree on the details. The account here is based primarily on interviews with Mexican and U.S. officials who participated in the meetings.

viction that assistance to countries in economic difficulty had to be expensive to be effective.[25]

A key element in the package was an agreement that the United States would make an advance payment for imports of Mexican oil for its strategic reserve stockpile. In a meeting on Friday that occasionally became tumultuous and that lasted through much of the night, the U.S. negotiators offered terms that the Mexican representatives felt were far too expensive: in return for an immediate $1 billion payment, Mexico would agree to deliver oil later with a much higher market value, a gap that yielded an implicit interest rate of around 18 percent (which Paul Volcker would later describe as "egregiously high");[26] and would pay an up-front $100 million fee. At lunchtime on Sunday, with the U.S. treasury still insisting on these terms, Silva Herzog telephoned López-Portillo from the Mexican embassy for instructions and was told that if he could not get better terms, he had to reject the offer. The president saw the two countries as mutually dependent on resolving the crisis, and if the United States did not see the need for flexibility, then "Rome" would burn.

At this stage, Silva Herzog saw little choice but to call off the negotiations, return home, and order the Mexican banks closed as of Monday morning. Before he could leave, however, he received a telephone call at the embassy from the Deputy Secretary of the U.S. Treasury, Richard T. (Tim) McNamar. McNamar had managed to reach Secretary Regan, who was playing golf with President Reagan, and had persuaded him that insistence on the existing terms would cause negotiations to collapse and thereby pose an immediate threat to the international financial system. Regan authorized him to negotiate more flexible terms, and McNamar now persuaded Silva Herzog to stay for one more meeting. Having been meeting not only with the Mexican authorities but with officials from several U.S. agencies almost nonstop since Friday afternoon, and having had almost no sleep, McNamar no longer trusted himself to lead the negotiations. Volcker took over for the final discussions and negotiated a halving of the up-front fee and a reduction in the interest rate. Though the cost was still high, these adjustments were enough to win an agreement. Mexico would receive $1 billion from the U.S. Energy Department[27] on August 24, and—most important from the Mexicans' perspective—the possibility of completing other parts of the package on more favorable terms would be kept alive.

Two other arrangements with the United States were settled before Silva Herzog left for home Sunday night. First, the Commodity Credit Corporation (an agency of the Department of Agriculture) provided slightly more than $1 billion in guarantees for credits for food imports.[28] Second, the U.S. Treasury drew on the

---

[25]Walter Bagehot's classic 1873 treatise, *Lombard Street*, is generally credited as the origin of the doctrine that a central bank, acting as lender of last resort in a currency crisis, should lend freely to banks but only at a penalty rate.

[26]Volcker and Gyohten (1992), p. 201.

[27]To add to the unprecedented complexity of the package, since the Energy Department did not have an appropriation of funds large enough to provide this payment, the money was actually provided by the Defense Department in a transaction coordinated by the Treasury.

[28]See U.S. Department of Agriculture, Press Release 1014–82 (August 20, 1982) and FAS Report PR-158–82 (September 17, 1982). These guarantees covered loans by the U.S. private sector (primarily commercial banks) to Mexican importers of U.S. food products (mainly maize).

Table 7.1. Financial Assistance to Mexico, August–December 1982

Source	Type	Date	Amount (Millions of U.S. dollars)[a]
United States			
Federal Reserve swap lines	90-day credit	August 4	700
	BIS-linked, short-term	August 28	325
Strategic petroleum reserve	advance payment for imports	August 24	1,000
Department of Agriculture	credit guarantees	August 15	1,000
Treasury (Exchange Stabilization Fund)	line of credit:	August 15	
	commitment		1,000
	drawn	(repaid August 24)	(825)
	BIS-linked credit	August 28	600
Bank for International Settlements[b]	short-term credit	August 28	925
Other bilateral (France, Israel, Spain)	swap lines	August	550
IMF	first credit tranche (immediate)	December 23	220
	extended arrangement (three-year commitment)		3,750
	initial drawing		(110)
World Bank			
Inter-American Development Bank			
Commercial banks	medium-term concerted lending	December 23	5,000

[a]IMF assistance denominated in SDRs; amounts converted to dollars at market exchange rate.
[b]Non-U.S. G-10 central banks, plus those of Switzerland and Spain.

Exchange Stabilization Fund to establish a new temporary currency swap line for $1 billion. Mexico immediately withdrew $825 million on the swap line, which was repaid on August 24 using the proceeds from the advance oil payment.[29]

The immediately available resources from the United States (see Table 7.1) would enable the Mexican government to meet the interest payments due to banks and other commercial creditors on Monday, but bigger money would be needed soon if default was to be averted before Fund resources could be made available. After hearing Silva Herzog's story on Friday morning, at a ten o'clock meeting at the Federal Reserve headquarters a few blocks south of the IMF, Volcker got on the telephone to try to arrange an emergency meeting of the Deputies of the Group of Ten (G-10) central bank governors, under the aegis of the Bank for International Settlements (BIS) in Basel, Switzerland. This being mid-August, his task was not easy. He reached Fritz Leutwiler, President of the BIS, and asked him if the BIS could lend $1.5 billion to Mexico. Leutwiler was prepared to listen to the case, and

---

[29]*Federal Reserve Bulletin* (December 1982), p. 742.

he immediately called his senior staff back from vacations so that a meeting could be held on Monday. Volcker called Gordon Richardson, governor of the Bank of England; Richardson was on holiday, but he returned to work straightaway, and from that moment he would play the leading role in organizing European support for the rescue package. London was the major center for coordinating European bank loans to Latin America, and British banks had the highest exposure in Europe. Richardson instinctively recognized the magnitude of the crisis and the importance of global cooperation, and in any event the Bank of England could not have helped but play this role.

Volcker and Leutwiler both tried to telephone Haruo Mayekawa, governor of the Bank of Japan. He also was on holiday, but when his deputy, Takeshi Ohta, relayed the message to him, he returned at once to Tokyo and then flew to Basel. Japanese banks had the second highest exposure to Mexico after those in the United States. Both the Bank of Tokyo and the Industrial Bank of Japan would be threatened by a Mexican default, and the Bank of Japan was perhaps even more sensitive than the U.S. Federal Reserve to the possible systemic effects of a major portfolio writedown.

Between phone calls that Friday, Volcker found time to have a second meeting (over lunch) with Silva Herzog[30] and to meet twice with de Larosière. Though perhaps not a troika one would normally have thought to harness together, these three men would now meet and talk almost constantly over the next several months and together would assume the leadership of this most extraordinary rescue effort.

Bridge Loan from the BIS

As soon as the meetings with U.S. officials were concluded Sunday afternoon, Silva Herzog (who, himself, would have to return to Mexico City to direct the negotiations with the IMF) asked two of his associates—Ariel Buira and Alfredo Phillips (Mancera's international deputy at the Bank of Mexico)—to catch a plane that evening to Basel for meetings at the BIS. Neither man had anticipated having to go abroad so suddenly, but within two hours they managed to gather together a change of clothing, buy plane tickets, and catch the overnight flight from Dulles Airport to Paris.

The BIS credit package was a key element in the effort to provide enough emergency financing to the Mexican government to cover the period until IMF resources would become available. Arranging this package was complicated, because it was outside the usual business practice of the BIS. In normal times, BIS loans are made in secrecy to central banks, using funds on deposit from central banks, for the purpose of short-term reserve management. What was now being contemplated was for the BIS to coordinate a loan by a group of central banks to the Bank of

---

[30]Volcker later wrote that he and Silva Herzog had lunch at the Fed so frequently that year that Silva Herzog "indelibly" associated him with the lemon meringue pie that he (Volcker) always had for dessert; see Volcker and Gyohten (1992), p. 199.

Mexico; publicity would be an integral part of the operation, as the loan was intended not only to provide resources but to demonstrate an international commitment to helping Mexico work its way out of the crisis. The only real precedent for such concerted central bank action was the series of loans to Hungary that had been arranged earlier in the year (Chapter 8).[31] That lone precedent now proved to be extremely useful, as the lessons that had been learned in the spring could be applied directly to this new case, thereby enabling the BIS to act with an alacrity that was indispensable in the crisis at hand.

The first step toward arranging such a loan was to determine a basis for sharing the loan among the participating central banks. The work in Basel therefore began with a technical meeting of the BIS staff with the staff of the G-10 central banks, primarily to estimate the level of loan exposure to Mexico by commercial banks in each country. The available data were poor. Some countries had quite up-to-date estimates, while others lagged by several months. More fundamentally, allowance had to be made for the distortions produced by the use of foreign branches for making international loans; for example, if the New York branch of a Tokyo bank lent to Mexico, balance of payments data would treat it as a U.S. bank loan, but the underlying exposure should be allocated to Japan.

Once the background work was completed, the central bank deputies (i.e., the principal alternates to the governors of the participating central banks) met with the BIS management and the Mexican representatives on Wednesday, August 18, to determine the feasibility and appropriate terms of the requested loan. The G-10 central banks were all represented, along with the Swiss National Bank. (The Bank of Spain was also invited and would join in the lending operation, but they were unable to recall their staff from vacation in time to participate in the initial meetings.)

Volcker had suggested a loan of $1.5 billion, and his deputy at the meeting, Henry Wallich, indicated that the Federal Reserve and the U.S. Treasury Department were prepared to finance half of that amount. The starting point for the discussion thus was a request for $750 million from the BIS, backed by the other participating central banks. That amount was quickly raised from the G-10, and when the Bank of Spain offered an additional $175 million, the total was raised $1.85 billion ($925 million each from the United States and the BIS), which became the final agreed figure.[32]

---

[31]In 1977, the BIS had given similar publicity to a concerted loan to the Bank of England. That loan, however, was a medium-term credit designed to support a gradual and orderly reduction in the use of the pound sterling as a reserve currency. It was approved in January 1977, one week after the United Kingdom's request for an IMF stand-by arrangement was approved by the Executive Board; though conditional on compliance with the Fund program, the BIS loan served to complement the stand-by financing, not to provide a bridge to it. See de Vries (1985), pp. 475–76; and the 1976–77 *Annual Report* of the BIS, p. 144.

[32]Of the U.S. portion, $600 million would come from the Treasury's Exchange Stabilization Fund, and $325 million from a special swap line established by the Federal Reserve. These arrangements were formally linked to the BIS loan through cross-payment clauses, which provided that all payments would be shared equally between the United States and the BIS. During this same period, other short-term official financing was being made available separately, including swap lines with France, Israel, and Spain.

From the beginning, it was understood that a condition for the BIS loan was that Mexico should be actively negotiating with the Fund for an EFF arrangement. The two loans (from the United States and the BIS) would each be disbursed in three tranches, assuming that negotiations with the IMF were completed according to the anticipated schedule: the first immediately upon final agreement between the Banco de Mexico and the BIS together with the Federal Reserve, a second in mid-November, and a third in mid-December.[33] As the IMF's resources came on board, the BIS would get its money back; the $1.85 billion would not be in addition to the EFF money, but it would bring it forward (see Table 7.1).

Another condition to be resolved concerned the collateralization of the loan. In its usual short-term lending, the BIS accepts a central bank's gold reserves as collateral, but the Bank of Mexico's gold reserves amounted to less than half the size of the proposed loan. What Mexico did have was oil reserves, and the Deputies agreed that the revenues from future sales of oil could be pledged to secure the loan. A joint BIS–Federal Reserve mission then went to Mexico City to quickly negotiate the details of that pledge, and the first tranche of the loan was disbursed and publicly announced on August 28.[34]

First Agreement with the Commercial Banks

While the BIS was arranging this bridging operation and the IMF team was in Mexico City gathering information for the program negotiations, the commercial bank creditors were also scrambling to coordinate a response to the crisis. Mexico had made the payments due on August 16, but a protracted and coordinated effort would be required to ensure that the principal outstanding would be maintained and even raised so that Mexico could continue to meet interest payments as they came due. There were more than 500 banks with substantial loans to the Mexican government. Although many of these banks had small amounts outstanding, the sum of the small amounts was substantial enough to be of major concern to Mexico and the larger creditors, as well as to bank regulators and to the IMF. No plan could be successful unless it kept the small banks in the game.

During the initial crisis weekend in Washington, Silva Herzog had telephoned as many of the major bank chairmen as he could reach from his room at the Watergate Hotel. From those calls emerged the idea of holding a meeting with creditors as soon as possible. On Tuesday, August 17, he sent out more than 100 telexes to Mexico's main private and official creditors, and to the IMF, inviting them to a meeting in New York on Friday the 20th, to discuss Mexico's credit requirements and its plans for adjusting policies. The meeting would be at the Federal Reserve Bank of New York, hosted by the Bank's president, Anthony Solomon.

---

[33]1982–83 *Annual Report* of the BIS, p. 165.

[34]The principal negotiating parties were Remi Grós, Manager of the Banking Department at the BIS; F.-E. Klein, Legal Advisor at the BIS; Michael Bradfield, General Counsel at the Board of Governors of the Federal Reserve System; and Mancera. The loan agreement was formally approved by the governors of the BIS at a meeting in Toronto on September 5.

A large meeting was needed in order to inform and involve as many banks as possible, but it was already clear that a smaller group would need to take charge of relations with Mexico. Solomon therefore also arranged a small working dinner for Thursday evening at the Federal Reserve Bank. Buira and Phillips flew into New York from Switzerland, where they had been representing Mexico at the BIS meetings. Silva Herzog came up from Mexico. Volcker, his international deputy, Edwin M. Truman, and McNamar came up from Washington. All of those present were worried that the large and diverse group of banks that would be represented the next day would find it difficult to act decisively on the Mexican request. To deal with that concern, the group devised what would become the standard modus operandi for the debt strategy of the 1980s, in which the banks would establish a small coordinating committee, comprising senior officials from the largest creditors.

Early the next morning, August 20, at a meeting between Silva Herzog and the chairmen of four major New York banks—Walter Wriston of Citibank, Willard Butcher of Chase Manhattan, John McGillicuddy of Manufacturers Hanover, and Donald Platten of Chemical Bank—the idea of a coordinating committee was agreed upon. Over breakfast, Silva Herzog stressed that Mexico believed that it could stay current on its interest payments and that it would do everything possible to do so, but that he had to ask the banks to roll over the principal, of which perhaps another $1 billion would be coming due within a week. He asked for an extension of maturities of one or two years, but the bankers balked; Wriston, in particular, argued that the problem would appear unmanageable if payments were delayed for that long. The group agreed in principle to postpone principal payments for 90 days.

That same Friday morning, representatives of 115 commercial banks gathered at ten o'clock in the auditorium at the New York Fed. The IMF was represented by Robichek and by Manuel Guitián (Senior Advisor in the Exchange and Trade Relations Department). Silva Herzog explained the general adjustment measures that Mexico was prepared to take, and he related the assistance that had been assembled from official creditors. The government would stay current on its outstanding bonds, trade credits, and officially guaranteed export credits, and he did not expect to have to request a rescheduling of official bilateral credits from the Paris Club. Mexico expected support from the Fund, but Silva Herzog also needed help from the banks. He asked for a "purely temporary" 90-day rollover of principal on banks loans, and he promised that all banks would be treated uniformly.

Silva Herzog's candor, and his willingness to work with the banks in a cooperative spirit, had a salubrious effect. Many of the bankers may have come to the meeting prepared for a confrontation, and all must have been looking primarily for a way to get their money out as fast as possible. Now most of them saw that the problem could be contained if they all cooperated, even if that meant *increasing* their exposure in the short run. Much work would remain before new loan agreements could be drafted and signed, and the smaller banks knew that it was in their interests not to participate, as long as the large banks were prepared to raise their own exposure. Nonetheless, the meeting ended with a general oral commitment to try to work out the requested rollover.

That same morning, 14 of the largest bank creditors, based in 8 different countries on 3 continents, adopted the proposal that had been devised over breakfast, to establish an advisory committee to negotiate new loan agreements *ad referendum* on behalf of all banks holding syndicated loans to the country, organize participation in financing those agreements, and serve as liaison with the country and with official agencies including the Fund.[35] Although officially there were three co-chairs of the committee, the driving force was William Rhodes, a senior vice president of Citibank. Rhodes was relatively unknown outside his own turf at the time, but he had rushed back to New York from his Canadian vacation when the crisis hit, had taken charge of the process, and would stay at the helm for more than a decade—not just on Mexico, but on the other major Latin American debtors as well.

As noted in the introduction to this chapter, it had been common practice for bankers to visit the IMF to talk about general economic developments in countries where they were lending, but lending decisions by banks and financial arrangements with the Fund had always been strictly independent. Indeed, for several years the staff of the IMF had been concerned about the tendency of many countries to borrow too freely from the banks, taking advantage of the lendable funds accumulating in international banks in the aftermath of the sharp increases in oil prices (the so-called petrodollars) and of interest rates that were generally negative in real terms. A standard performance criterion in financial programs was a limit on foreign borrowing, including borrowing from banks.

These relationships would now change, as both sides recognized the extent of their interdependence in finding a solution to the debt crisis that had engulfed them. The banks needed the Fund's expertise in country analysis and the Fund's leverage in dealing with borrowing countries; the Fund needed the banks' resources to help cover the borrowers' financing requirements, and it needed the banks' cooperation if a systemic financial crisis was to be avoided.[36] Borrowing countries were seeking help both from banks and from the Fund, and effective communication between the two was in their interest as well, as long as the essential confidentiality and mutual trust on which the Fund's relations with member countries depends could be preserved.

In August 1982, it was still unusual (though by no means unprecedented) that Robichek and Guitián would not just attend the large meeting with 115 bankers, but also participate in the committee meeting that followed it. As the strategy

---

[35]These committees did not have formal names, and they were variously known as "steering," "coordinating," or "advisory" committees. The term "Advisory Committee" is used here for the sake of consistency. The number of banks in the Mexican committee later dropped from 14 to 13, when the one Mexican bank on the committee, the Banco Nacional de Mexico, was nationalized on September 1, 1982. For more detail on the nature of the committees, see Lomax (1986), Chapter 6.

[36]Also see Chapter 6, pp. 275–76. For a thorough discussion of the weakness of country risk analysis by commercial banks in the period leading up to the debt crisis, see Lissakers (1991), pp. 94–110. For a banker's view of the need for a strengthened role for the Fund, see de Vries and Porzecanski (1983).

evolved over the next few years, however, Fund staff would participate in many meetings of the bank committees, bankers would become frequent visitors to Fund headquarters, and the Fund would play a very active role in solidifying bank participation in loan agreements.[37]

Negotiating the Program: August–November 1982

First Mission

Silva Herzog returned to Mexico that weekend, and throughout the following week—the last week of August—he and Mancera engaged in intensive negotiations with Beza over the policy adjustments on which the use of Fund resources would be made contingent. Both sides were largely in agreement on the nature of the required adjustment, but they started out far apart in assessing the magnitude that could reasonably be expected. Most significantly, while everybody knew that the authorities had to find a way to cut expenditures by enough to reduce the fiscal deficit sharply from its then-current rate of about 15 percent of GDP, the Fund staff insisted that a 1983 deficit of much more than 6 percent of GDP could not be financed, while the authorities insisted that the deficit could not be reduced much below 10 percent of GDP by 1983 without having ruinous effects on the economy. Each side understood that both of these arguments were correct and that a compromise had to be reached quickly.

As August drew to a close, the negotiators decided that a retreat from the heat and pressure of Mexico City might help create the right atmosphere for reaching agreement on a draft Letter of Intent for the proposed program. Accordingly, Silva Herzog took Mancera on his motorcycle to the coastal resort of Oaxtepec, and Beza and his team drove over more conventionally by automobile. Over the weekend, the two sides hammered out a compromise, the essential feature of which was allowance for more external financing than the IMF team had thought was reasonable to expect. Up to that point, the negotiating position of the IMF staff had been that commercial banks could not be expected to significantly raise their exposure to Mexico. Relaxing that assumption would enable the government to finance a larger fiscal deficit without resorting to inflationary domestic finance. The agreement reached in principle at Oaxtepec was that the program would be predicated on an assumed $5 billion in external finance, of which $3.5 billion would have to come from commercial lenders. That program would still require cutting the fiscal deficit at least to a ceiling of 8 percent of GDP.[38]

---

[37]In the case at hand, a team of bankers—the Economic Subcommittee of the banks' Advisory Committee—was in Mexico City throughout the late-August Fund mission, gathering much of the same information as the IMF, but they were unable to meet with Beza or his staff team.

[38]Draft memorandum from Beza to the Managing Director, dated September 3, 1982, and conveyed in that form to the Managing Director in Toronto the following day; in IMF/RD Managing Director file "Annual Meeting—1982 (Briefs)" (Accession 84/21, Box 1, Section 168).

Driving back to Mexico City at the end of the weekend, everyone knew it would be a tough job selling the program to the banks, to President-Elect de la Madrid, and especially to outgoing President López-Portillo. The president had often staked his own reputation on maintaining the parity of the peso. He who devalues the currency devalues himself, he had famously said; he would defend the peso like a dog. For the moment, however, it looked as if López-Portillo might have finally recognized the inevitability of the economic forces that he faced. None of the negotiators could have known that their efforts would be undermined by mid-week. On Monday and Tuesday, Buira drafted a Letter of Intent based on the Oaxtepec understandings and gave it to Silva Herzog. The Secretary then told Buira that there had been no reason to hurry, because everything was going to change tomorrow.

At two o'clock Wednesday afternoon, September 1, the members of the IMF team were working on their reactions to the draft Letter. In the background they could hear López-Portillo on television, delivering his annual State of the Union (*Informe*) address. As the president delivered the early part of the speech, there was no hint of any major policy shift. The telephone then rang; it was their department head, Walter Robichek, calling from Toronto, where preparations for the IMF–World Bank Annual Meetings were under way. An advance copy of the *Informe* had been leaked to reporters and other participants there, and Robichek could scarcely believe what he was reading: the president was nationalizing the banks, introducing exchange controls, and blaming foreign creditors—including the IMF—for the country's economic crisis. Minutes after Robichek relayed this information, the team heard the president delivering the same message on television. The draft Letter of Intent lay still-born on the table.

The Mexican negotiating team was now in disarray. Mancera—who was on record as a strong opponent of exchange controls—was dismissed as central bank governor and replaced by Carlos Tello, an opponent of the policy reforms to which both sides had so nearly agreed. When Buira went back to his office at the Bank of Mexico after the president's speech, he found his way barred by army troops who had surrounded the building. Silva Herzog offered to resign, feeling that he lacked political support for the policies he knew were needed, but López-Portillo rejected his request. Beza, too, was ready to give up and go home, but when Silva Herzog told him he was not resigning and asked him to keep negotiating, he agreed to stay for another two days to assess the new situation.

Toronto

On Friday, Silva Herzog and Beza flew together to Toronto while the rest of the mission returned to Washington. Mexico, of course, was on the minds of virtually all of the thousands of bankers, bureaucrats, and politicians who were converging on Toronto from around the world that first weekend in September, and for the next week the focus of attention would be on this financial and convention center on the northern shore of Lake Ontario. The first task for de Larosière and Beza was to deflect Tim McNamar's frenzied insistence—at a midnight meeting that same Friday night—that the Fund should agree to lend money to Mexico immediately. McNamar feared that without quick and decisive action, a wave of defaults by several developing countries would destroy the banking system and throw the world economy into depression. De Larosière took a more temperate view, if only because he knew that the Fund could not lend to Mexico until an economic program had been negotiated and a complete financial package had been secured.[39]

Negotiations resumed at 8:15 Sunday morning, as de Larosière, Beza, and other IMF staff met at the Sheraton Center with Silva Herzog, Gurría, and Phillips to discuss how to respond to the political setback. Silva Herzog acknowledged the problem, but he emphasized that he did not want to abandon ship and that he wanted to move the process forward as best they could. He was authorized by the president to reach agreement with the Fund and to report back as soon as possible. De Larosière responded that the Fund was willing to act quickly, but the Mexican authorities needed a strategy, and there had to be agreement on a solid program. Drafting a new Letter of Intent during the Toronto meetings was probably not feasible, but perhaps they could agree on some general principles and prepare an aide-mémoire that Silva Herzog could take back to the president. The critical issue, all agreed, was the need for a commitment to reduce the fiscal deficit in 1983. Other issues such as the newly imposed exchange controls were only symptoms of the underlying fiscal problem.[40]

Conditions became only more chaotic as the week progressed. While the Fund staff and the Mexican authorities worked on the aide-mémoire in Toronto, a highly artificial exchange regime was being implemented in Mexico. Two separate fixed exchange rates went into effect on Monday morning, both of which entailed substantial subsidies that would place additional pressure on the fiscal budget, accelerate capital flight, and push transactions into the burgeoning parallel market near the U.S. border. By the end of the day, the extent and impact of the flight were as clear in Toronto as in Tijuana; that night, around 2 o'clock, Volcker telephoned Wriston to ensure that the CHIPS system for clearing cross-border interbank settlements would be protected in the event of a default on interbank claims.

By the next morning—Tuesday, September 7—there was indeed a panic in the interbank market. International banks were refusing to roll over lines of credit to Mexican banks. Unless calm could somehow be restored, the Mexican banks would have no choice but to default, and the whole interbank market could collapse overnight with incalculable consequences for financial markets. Throughout this Black Tuesday, Volcker, Leutwiler, Sam Y. Cross of the Federal Reserve Bank of New York, and Brian Quinn of the Bank of England all worked the telephones to persuade banks to maintain the level of interbank credits. A substantial portion of the BIS loan that had just been approved was parceled out to repay portions of

---

[39]This constraint on the Fund's capacity to respond to a crisis became increasingly unsettling in the 1990s. For a comparison of the response to Mexico in 1982 with the responses to Mexico in 1995 and Korea in 1997, see Boughton (2000).

[40]File minute on the meeting; in IMF/RD Western Hemisphere Department file "Mexico—General Correspondence (July–November 1982)" (Accession 87/19, Box 2, Section 94).

the outstanding claims, and the banks—knowing they could not get paid that day in any case—agreed to preserve the rest. By nightfall, the banking system had squeaked by without a default—and without a systemic collapse.

Early Wednesday morning, September 8, the aide-mémoire was approved by de Larosière and delivered to Silva Herzog. Avoiding specific numbers or other program details, it specified, inter alia, that the public sector deficit should be cut by more than half in proportion to GDP in 1983; that subsidies should be reduced; that wage policy should be consistent with a reduction in inflation; that interest rates should be allowed to rise by enough to encourage residents to keep their savings in domestic banks; and that exchange rate policy should help restore international competitiveness. Within that structure, it was hoped there would be room for the authorities to design a program that they could sell both at home and abroad.

Silva Herzog, weighed down by enormous pressure from all sides, was beginning to feel seriously ill. He telephoned his wife in Mexico City, hoping for a quiet respite before a late-morning meeting with U.S. officials, only to discover that Tello had just announced a new set of exchange controls and other measures that were completely at odds with the program that Silva Herzog was going to have to prepare. If the president was allowing the Bank of Mexico to shift policy in that direction while asking him to negotiate on his behalf in the opposite direction, what credibility could he, Silva Herzog, have?

With little hope left, Silva Herzog went to his meeting with the U.S. team. Everyone involved from Washington was there: Volcker and Truman from the Federal Reserve; and Regan, Beryl Sprinkel (Under Secretary for Monetary Affairs), and McNamar from the Treasury. To whom should we be talking, they wanted to know; did he still represent the president? All that Silva Herzog could tell them was that there was no viable alternative to assuming that he did. He was going home tomorrow, he would give López-Portillo an ultimatum, and if he failed, he would resign. The declaration was dramatic, all the more because of Silva Herzog's obvious exhaustion and dejection. Regan urged him not to resign, as would others in the course of the next two days. It was a critical moment for Mexico and for the international financial system, and Silva Herzog's resignation would have left a huge vacuum in the circle of power and influence.

The Toronto meetings wound down on Thursday with no real resolution of the Mexican crisis. Then on Friday there came a false dawn that temporarily calmed the financial markets. In the second stage of the drawn-out transition that characterizes the Mexican presidency, the election of de la Madrid was confirmed by congress. Perhaps more important for the short term, Silva Herzog announced that he would stay on as Secretary of Finance. He had met with López-Portillo on returning to Mexico City, and he believed that he had convinced the president that unless they reached agreements soon with both the banks and the IMF, Mexico would be unable to import even basic foods before the end of his term in office. De Larosière by this time had gone fishing with friends in a remote region in Ontario, but he had asked Silva Herzog to call him there as soon as he knew whether the negotiations could resume. For the moment, it seemed possible to relax.

Uncertainty reigns in Mexico after the government nationalizes private banks

Conclusion of Negotiations

Silva Herzog's illness proved to be serious. He was taken to the hospital the next day to be operated on for appendicitis and would be out of action for most of the rest of the month. Meanwhile, the IMF negotiating team returned to Mexico City on September 23 to try once again to get agreement on a program that could be supported by Fund resources. Unfortunately, the falseness of the dawn was now revealed in that the more radical forces, led by Tello, continued to block efforts to cut the deficit and rationalize the foreign exchange regime. Throughout the first half of October, rumors surfaced that a Letter of Intent was on the verge of being signed. In reality, Silva Herzog—now back at work—was still caught between the two camps and lacked political support for an effective program. Negotiations broke down once again, and both sides agreed to shift the scene back to Washington.

On October 22, Silva Herzog and his negotiating team arrived in Washington for two days of meetings with U.S. and Fund officials. The breakdown in negotiations was creating multiple problems for them, because the second tranche of the BIS loan was dependent on satisfactory progress vis-à-vis the Fund program. The Managing Director was still pushing for a 1983 fiscal deficit target of no more than 8 percent of GDP, and the authorities were still searching for a way to avoid that big a reduction in the first year. Other items on the agenda included the Fund's insistence on prior actions such as a rise in the heavily subsidized price of gasoline, on a commitment to undertake structural measures such as elimination of the dual exchange rate system, on establishment of a timetable for eliminating payments arrears, and on acceptance of the program by both the outgoing and the incoming administration; and the authorities' request for front-loading of the funds that would be available under the program.[41]

The Washington meetings produced no major breakthroughs, though they did reveal enough common ground and enough flexibility to warrant resumption of negotiations in the field. Silva Herzog reportedly attempted to persuade both Volcker and Rhodes to apply pressure on the Fund to ease up on their demands, but without success.[42] He met with de Larosière and his staff, twice in formal meetings and twice over lunch. On the surface, he went home empty-handed, but the meetings had persuaded the Fund to be a bit more optimistic about other external financing that might be available in 1983. When Beza boarded a plane for Mexico City at Dulles Airport a few days later, he was authorized to negotiate on the assumption that Mexico would get $2 billion in official credits in 1983, plus $5 billion in new medium-term credits from commercial banks. If that much financing could actually be put on the table—and that was a big "if"—then the fiscal demands on the Mexican government could indeed be relaxed.

---

[41]The request was to draw the equivalent of 450 percent of quota over three years, which would normally be made available in roughly even quarterly installments; that is, 150 percent of quota a year, as long as the performance criteria were met or were explicitly waived by the Executive Board. There was scope, however, for making a larger proportion available in the first year or two if the case was determined to be exceptional.

[42]Kraft (1984), p. 45.

The improved outlook for external financing was partially offset by the need to drop the request for a CFF drawing equal to Mexico's quota. As noted above (p. 290), this amount—SDR 800 million, or approximately $880 million—could have been made available immediately upon approval by the Executive Board in December. The difficulty was that the CFF request would have been justified on the grounds that export revenues had been depressed by the decline in oil prices. If Mexico drew on that basis, other oil-exporting countries would also have been eligible, and the Fund's liquidity position could have been severely squeezed. At an informal meeting between Executive Directors and the Managing Director on August 23, Mohamed Finaish, the Executive Director for Libya, had indicated that oil exporters would indeed plan to make such requests.[43] Consequently, Mexico eventually dropped its own request and the issue was dropped.[44] By November, therefore, Mexico was requesting only the EFF arrangement, to be phased over three years.

While the mission was in Mexico, de Larosière turned his attention to ensuring that the external financing would be there when it was needed. He was not worried about the official portion, but how could the Fund be sure that the commercial banks, especially the large number of smaller banks who had lent to Mexico, would not use the availability of official resources to try to get their own money out? The standard arrangement, under which the program would simply project the likely availability of external financing and treat that amount as an assumption underlying the program, would not work in this case. De Larosière therefore became convinced by the end of October that a more active policy of bringing the banks into the process was required.

During the first week in November, de Larosière consulted with Volcker, Solomon, and Richardson, among others, about the possibility of his meeting with bankers to impress upon them the necessity of their providing the requisite support for Mexico. As a result of these discussions, de Larosière invited representatives of 17 major banks to meet with him in the boardroom of the Federal Reserve Bank of New York on November 16.[45] To stress the importance of participation by non-American banks, Richardson separately invited a small group of mostly European and Japanese bankers to meet privately with de Larosière at the Bank of England the following week.

The program finally was falling into place. On November 8, Beza telephoned the Managing Director from Mexico to tell him that he had reached agreement with both administrations and the central bank on the draft Letter of Intent and

---

[43]File minute on the meeting, in IMF/RD Managing Director file "Mexico—1982" (Accession 85/231, Box 6, file 3, Section 177).

[44]The issue of under what circumstances a country could draw on the CFF to compensate for a decline in oil export revenues continued to plague the Executive Board throughout the 1980s. See Chapter 15.

[45]Because the meeting would deal with Argentina as well as Mexico, the invitees included all banks that were represented on the Advisory Committees for either country. Of these, seven were U.S. banks; Canada, France, Germany, and Switzerland were each represented by two banks; and Japan and the United Kingdom by one each.

that a technical Memorandum of Agreement was being finalized. Two days later, Silva Herzog and Tello signed the Letter and—in what was then an unusual move, intended to demonstrate the country's commitment to the program—released it to the press.[46] As the key compromise, the fiscal deficit was to be reduced (from the latest estimate for 1982, 16½ percent) to 8½ percent of GDP in 1983. Now full attention could be turned to securing a commitment from the banks.

Commitment from Commercial Banks: November–December 1982

On November 9, de Larosière addressed the fourth annual International Monetary Conference—a gathering of the leading international bankers—in Philadelphia. Using the occasion to alert banks to the role they would be asked to play in resolving the crisis, he emphasized the need for closer cooperation. "Avenues for collaboration between the Fund and the banks are being actively considered . . . the banks will have to maintain adequate net financing flows for those countries that have adopted strong adjustment measures . . . *all* of the banks must be involved . . ." (emphasis in the original text). With this speech, the Managing Director was dropping a fairly broad hint of the need for concerted lending, but the audience seems to have interpreted it more as a call for cooperation and a promise of IMF involvement. As the *Washington Post* noted the next day, participants at the conference had been discussing the desirability of the IMF "cofinancing" bank loans to developing countries; the reference by de Larosière to "collaboration" was thus seen as a possible endorsement of that approach, under which the banks would have been firmly in the driver's seat.[47]

Advisory Committee

Then came the key meeting with the major banks in New York, at 4:30 Tuesday afternoon, November 16.[48] De Larosière began his presentation by outlining the policy mistakes that had brought Mexico to the brink: sharp increases in public sector spending over several years, financed in large measure by foreign commercial borrowing. These policies were to be reversed in conjunction with the EFF program to which the Fund and the authorities had just agreed, but that program could not succeed without the full cooperation of the banks. He then came to the bottom line. In 1983, Mexico was expected to have a current account deficit of

---

[46]The Letter of Intent and the detailed Technical Memorandum of Understanding were published in full in the newsmagazine *Proceso*. For a report in the Mexican press welcoming the agreement, see the stories and editorials in *Excelsior*, November 11, 1982.

[47]Article by Hobart Rowen, *Washington Post*, November 10, 1982, p. D9.

[48]The following summary is based on de Larosière's speaking notes for the meeting, plus a file memorandum dated November 18, 1982, by Irwin D. Sandberg of the Federal Reserve Bank of New York; in IMF/RD Managing Director file "Mexico—1982" (Accession 85/231, Box 9, Section 177).

$4¼ billion, inclusive of some $10 billion in interest payments due to commercial banks on public sector debt alone. To this deficit would be added $2½ billion in required repayments on short-term official loans, notably those arranged in August by the BIS. Furthermore, official reserves would need to be rebuilt; that added another $1½ billion as the minimum increase that would permit normal functioning of the financial system, for a total financing requirement estimated at $8¼ billion.

The IMF was prepared to provide the maximum financing allowable under the rules of access: $1.3 billion in 1983, with equivalent amounts to be provided in 1984 and 1985. That would leave a gap of $7 billion to be financed by others. Of that, only $2 billion was expected to come from official bilateral sources, principally as credits for export cover.[49] The banks, therefore, would have to raise their exposure to Mexico by $5 billion, or the program would not add up. Finally, de Larosière dropped the bombshell: the $5 billion increase in bank exposure in 1983 was so crucial to the program that he could not take the EFF to the Executive Board until he had agreement from the banks to provide that amount. The required reduction in the fiscal deficit—by 8 percent of GDP in one year—was unprecedented; nothing more could be expected, and there was simply no choice.

De Larosière concluded his presentation by asking for a written commitment for $5 billion in "new money" for 1983, and additional commitments on three other points. First, the banks were asked to continue to roll over existing short-term credits. Second, they would need to reach agreement with the Mexican authorities on a rescheduling of intermediate and long-term debt. Third, they would need to "clean up" $1½ billion in private sector interest arrears that would be outstanding by the end of 1982. Executive Board consideration of the EFF was tentatively scheduled for December 23, but if written commitments were not in hand by December 15, the meeting would have to be postponed.

The pressure put on the banks by the Managing Director was unprecedented, and it sent shock waves through the banking community. When the shock was absorbed, however, it became clear that cooperation was in everyone's interest. The fundamental advantage to the banks as a group was that the package would enable them to get a net reflow of dollars from Mexico. As de Larosière had indicated, the Mexican public sector would owe about $10 billion in interest payments during 1983. Without a fully financed adjustment program, the chances were virtually nil that Mexico would be able to make those payments. De Larosière's arithmetic implied that Mexico would pay approximately $5 billion in interest to banks in 1983, while the remainder would be rolled over into new principle. Thus, by raising exposure by $5 billion, the banks would receive a similar amount in net reflows that they otherwise could not get. Furthermore, if the Managing Director had been prepared to follow standard practice and take the program to the Board without any prior commitment regarding private financing, the Advisory Committee would have had a far tougher job—perhaps an impossible task—raising the $5 billion be-

---

[49]On a net basis, taking into account the repayment of short-term credits mentioned earlier, this projection implied that official bilateral exposure would decline by about $550 million in 1983.

cause of the free-rider problem they would have faced. Each individual bank that was small enough not to threaten the agreement by itself had an interest in trying to get its money back as rapidly as possible. Only if those banks could be convinced that withdrawal was impossible could the cost to each bank in terms of increased exposure be kept to a reasonable level.

In the discussion that followed de Larosière's presentation, Rhodes and other bankers expressed three main concerns about the Managing Director's demands. First, they felt that the authorities could do more to solve the problem of private sector arrears to banks. In some cases, companies that could afford to meet their interest payments were being blocked by regulations prohibiting them from using foreign exchange for that purpose. Furthermore, much of the private sector debt was held by small banks whose participation in a new-money package would be contingent on a solution being found to this problem. If there was any significant attrition by small banks, the required increase in exposure by the remainder would be that much larger; if the burden could not be spread evenly across all creditor banks, securing a commitment by the remainder would be far more difficult. De Larosière recognized the dilemma, and although he was reluctant to put the IMF in the middle of the effort to settle private sector arrears, he promised to speak to the Mexican officials about it.

A second concern of the banks was what they perceived as the unequal burden between official and private creditors. Even assuming that official creditors did raise their exposure through $2 billion in export credits in 1983, their net exposure would decline, since they would be getting $2½ billion in repayments, as mentioned above (p. 307). Allowing for Fund drawings and the relatively small amounts expected from multilateral development banks, official credits would rise by about $1 billion, compared with $5 billion from commercial banks. Or, as Rhodes put it at the meeting, it looked as if the main effect of the EFF arrangement was to enable Mexico to repay its official creditors.

Third, banks were concerned about the attitude of the regulatory agencies: would they be penalized for increasing the outstanding balances of such risky loans? Solomon responded on behalf of the Federal Reserve, saying that loans made in support of a Fund-supported adjustment program would not be subjected to regulatory criticism. That same evening, Paul Volcker would be addressing bankers at the annual meeting of the New England Council (in a speech whose timing had been carefully coordinated with de Larosière's presentation) and would make this same point.[50] These assurances set the tone for similar responses by regulators in Europe and Japan in the weeks to come.

---

[50]"From the standpoint of the banks themselves, such restructuring and the provision of some additional credit, alongside and dependent upon agreed IMF programs, will in some instances be the most effective and prudent means available to enhance the creditworthiness of borrowing countries and thus protect their own interests. In such cases, where new loans facilitate the adjustment process and enable a country to strengthen its economy and service its international debt in an orderly manner, new credits should not be subject to supervisory criticism." Volcker (1982), p. 17.

Other Creditor Banks

Following the New York meeting, the Advisory Committee agreed to roll over Mexico's short-term principal payments for another 90 days. There were, however, more than 500 other creditor banks whose participation in concerted lending had to be secured before the Fund program could be approved, and only four weeks remained before the deadline. On Monday, November 21, de Larosière flew to London for a meeting and dinner the following day at the Bank of England.[51] Richardson had invited the bankers whose prestige and influence would be essential. It was a small group of bank chairmen, but with a global reach: Jeremy Morse of Lloyd's, Wilfried Guth of Deutsche Bank, Jean-Yves Haberer of Paribas, Franz Lutolf of Swiss Bank, Yusuke Kashiwagi of the Bank of Tokyo, and Lewis Preston of Morgan Guaranty.[52] Richardson, de Larosière, and Leutwiler made up the official contingent.[53]

The major issue for the major banks at this stage was how to structure the package so as to obtain participation by the maximum number of smaller banks. De Larosière's initial plan was to ask each creditor bank to increase its exposure to Mexico by 9 percent; this target would leave enough of a margin that even if a number of smaller banks declined, the $5 billion target could still be attained. If there was too much attrition, the large banks would have to make up the difference. Throughout the evening in London, the bankers impressed upon the Managing Director that they could not be expected to cover such deficiencies. The arithmetic was plain, and if the small banks knew they were expendable, they would certainly flee.

One conclusion that emerged from the London gathering was an understanding of the need for an active involvement by national regulatory authorities. As noted above, Volcker and Solomon had clarified the position of the Federal Reserve on November 16: sovereign lending that helped fill a country's financing gap in conjunction with an IMF program would not be considered problem loans. Although certainly helpful, this passive approach—even if shared by all of the G-10 central banks—would not be sufficient. The bankers therefore requested the assistance of the IMF in persuading national authorities to actively encourage banks in their territories to participate fully.

On November 23, Rhodes called de Larosière (who was in transit from London to Geneva to address a ministerial meeting of the GATT) requesting to meet with him on Mexico, along with the other two cochairmen of the Advisory Committee, as soon as possible on his return to Washington. De Larosière agreed, and a meeting was held in his office on November 30, the evening before de la Madrid's

---

[51]Based on the Managing Director's travel file, in IMF/RD (Accession 86/34, Box 16, Section 208), plus interviews with several participants.

[52]Kashiwagi, Lutolf, and Preston had also been at the November 16 meeting in New York.

[53]A rare feature of this gathering was the absence of Paul Volcker. Volcker's involvement in the development of the debt strategy was so pervasive in 1982 that a decade later, several participants at the Bank of England dinner mistakenly recalled to the author that Volcker had been there as well.

inauguration as president. There were two interrelated issues to be settled: how much banks could reasonably be asked to raise their exposure via the new-money package, and how close they would have to get to the $5 billion requirement before the Managing Director could safely propose approval of the program to the Executive Board. On the first question, although de Larosière preferred the safety margin that a 9 percent increase would provide, he was persuaded that a lower figure—though not so low as the 5 percent increase suggested by Rhodes—would be necessary to bring enough pressure on reluctant creditors. The group thus settled on the obvious compromise, 7 percent. At that rate, more than 500 banks would have to participate: only the very smallest creditors could be let off the hook.[54]

The second issue—the cutoff point for going forward—was equally risky. A late-December deadline was essential if Mexico's financing needs were to be met, but it posed a dilemma. The bank agreement could not be signed and delivered until the entire $5 billion had been pledged, and it would almost certainly be impossible to reach that figure in less than a month. De Larosière therefore devised the idea of setting a threshold on the basis of which one could be reasonably confident that the full amount would be reached within a matter of weeks. He proposed the idea to the bankers and suggested that 95 percent would constitute what he called a "critical mass."[55] The banks obviously liked the idea but wanted a much lower figure, on the order of 70 percent. Eventually they settled on 90 percent, and de Larosière agreed to propose acceptance of the EFF if the banks could get signed agreements totaling $4.5 billion by December 23.[56]

With this agreement between the Advisory Committee and the Managing Director on the financing required to support the Fund program, and the new administration installed in Mexico, the next requirement was a detailed agreement on the financing proposal between the Advisory Committee and the Mexican authorities. To that end, Gurría flew to New York on December 1, where he spent the next week negotiating specific terms. Four days later, Silva Herzog and Mancera[57] flew to Washington to meet with de Larosière and then on to New York, where the agreement with the major banks was finalized on December 8. The terms were harsh for Mexico and highly profitable for the banks, but that was a

---

[54]The establishment of a cutoff point, below which banks whose exposure was less than an agreed minimum absolute level would be excused from participating in a "new money" or concerted loan, became known as the *de minimis* principle.

[55]The term "critical mass" quickly became an accepted part of the lexicon of the debt strategy, with the specific meaning of a level of commitments from bank creditors that would provide reasonable assurance that the full amount of a syndicated loan would be forthcoming within a few weeks or months. Previously, de Larosière had used the phrase in other contexts. For example, in the January 1982 speech cited at the beginning of Chapter 6, he used "critical mass" to describe the "quantum of resources the *Fund* must be able to offer to members, when a program justifies it, to make its conditional financing an attractive proposition and to help unlock access by such members to other sources of external finance." (Op. cit., p. 7; emphasis added.)

[56]Statement by the Managing Director at EBM/82/167 (December 23, 1982), p. 4; and background interviews.

[57]On December 1, President de la Madrid had retained Silva Herzog as Secretary of Finance and had rehired Mancera as Director General of the Bank of Mexico.

price the Mexican government was willing to pay to extricate itself without a default.[58]

To complete the bank agreement required the participation of some 500 additional banks, and only two weeks remained before the Executive Board was to consider the EFF request. During those two weeks, all of the major participants worked virtually nonstop to persuade as many banks as possible to agree to raise their exposure by 7 percent.[59] De Larosière and Dale undertook to keep the authorities of the major creditor countries (the G-10, Switzerland, Spain, and several Middle Eastern countries) informed and to develop with them a uniform position that the concerted lending agreement would be treated favorably for regulatory purposes. The national authorities in turn undertook to persuade banks or at least to inform them of the favorable light in which the agreement was seen. In the end, the total on December 23 fell slightly short of the arbitrarily defined critical mass, with $4.32 billion in signed pledges, but enough other agreements were in the pipeline that de Larosière decided to proceed.

Role of the Fund

As detailed below, over the next few months the program would be approved and the bank loan agreement would be completed. Before leaving this subject, however, one should ask: What did the IMF achieve by insisting on the concerted-lending package, and at what cost? The case for this dramatic innovation rests on the argument that the package was in the interests of both Mexico and her bank creditors but that it nonetheless could not have been achieved—or could have been achieved only at a higher cost—in the absence of outside intervention. The first part of this case is straightforward; the second is more complex.

Because Mexico lacked the foreign exchange to meet its current external debt obligations, a rescheduling or similar agreement with creditor banks was necessary to prevent default. Avoiding default was in Mexico's interest because it preserved both trade and financial flows. It was in the banks' interest because default—compared with the position following an agreement—would have raised the current book value of outstanding credits (including unpaid interest) and lowered the expected return on them.[60] It was also in the interest of creditor countries, especially the United

---

[58]The concerted-lending agreement was contracted at a spread of 2⅛ percent over LIBOR or similar rates, plus substantial fees. Rowen (1983) calculated—using estimates made by Karin Lissakers of the Carnegie Endowment for International Peace—that the rescheduling and concerted-lending agreements together would cost Mexico some $800 million in fees and increased spreads; he quoted Lissakers as regarding the terms as "outrageous." In a speech on March 7, 1983, just after the bank deal was finalized, Martin Feldstein, chairman of the U.S. Council of Economic Advisers, noted that the banks were charging "substantial risk premiums," a practice that he predicted would be "self-defeating" because it would raise the "risk of non-payment" (Feldstein, 1983, p. 6). Although Feldstein did not mention it, the U.S. government had also exacted a high price for the official credits extended in August 1982 (see above, pp. 291–92).

[59]The base date for calculating exposure had been set as August 23, 1982.

States, for whom a bilateral bailout would have been economically and politically risky and, in the absence of policy improvements in Mexico, probably quite fruitless. A coordinated multilateral solution was obviously superior but appeared to be out of reach without the involvement of an established international financial institution.

The primary explanation for the difficulty in reaching a globally optimal solution without outside intervention is that there was a sharp split in interests *within* the banking community. Figure 7.3 illustrates the key role played by small banks in the Mexican agreement.[61] While the 25 largest creditors would provide for just over $2 billion of the $5 billion required by raising their exposure by the specified 7 percent, the next $2 billion would take another 75 banks, and the final $1 billion would require pulling in more than 400 additional banks. Furthermore, as a general rule, the banks with smaller exposure (and thus smaller required commitments) were not just smaller banks; they also had smaller exposure relative to their own size and thus would have been better positioned to cut their losses and run if the prospects of program success were judged to be poor.[62] One goal of the concerted-lending package was to raise the stakes for those small banks by making success depend on their participation. Every bank with significant exposure would face a linkage between its decision to participate and the likelihood of program success; the free-rider problem[63] was thereby greatly diminished.[64]

The two alternatives to officially sponsored concerted lending (other than default) would have been sanctions against nonparticipating banks or voluntary rescheduling agreements with a limited number of large banks. Any bank whose credits to Mexico were small enough not to affect the viability of the package would have an interest not to participate, unless some form of sanction could be imposed. Because contractual obligations required debtors to treat all creditors alike, a default on payments to nonparticipating banks would have made it impos-

---

[60]This statement appears to presume that the only alternative is a complete default, but the comparison of expected returns holds true even if allowance is made for a commensurate partial default. From a static financial perspective, there is no practical distinction between a partial default and concerted lending: in each case, creditors are forced to accept a rise in exposure. If, however, concerted lending in conjunction with a program of policy adjustment succeeds in raising the borrower's ability to pay, then it also raises the expected rate of return on outstanding credits. Nor does the conclusion depend on the red-herring argument that the country be illiquid but not insolvent. Given the uncertainty surrounding the valuation of future output and foreign exchange revenues, neither concept is empirically relevant for this problem. The only required assumptions are that the country be unable (not just unwilling) to meet its current debt-servicing obligations and that policy adjustment be facilitated by the avoidance of default. See Arora (1993) for a review of the literature on these issues, and Chapter 12, below, for further discussion.

[61]Data are from the credit agreement between Mexico and the commercial banks, dated March 3, 1983; in IMF/RD Western Hemisphere Department file "Mexico—Credit Arrangements with Citibank, 1983" (Accession 85/231, Box 9, Section 177).

[62]See Sachs and Huizinga (1987) for an analysis of 1986 data on exposure to developing countries by size of bank.

[63]See Sachs (1984), Krugman (1985), and Caskey (1989) for discussions of the conditions under which the presence of large numbers of small creditors can inhibit market agreements.

[64]Of the 526 banks participating in the loan agreement, 28 made commitments of less than $100,000 (implying initial exposure of less than approximately $1.4 million).

Figure 7.3. Distribution of the 1983 Concerted Lending Agreement for Mexico
(*Top 100 creditor banks*)

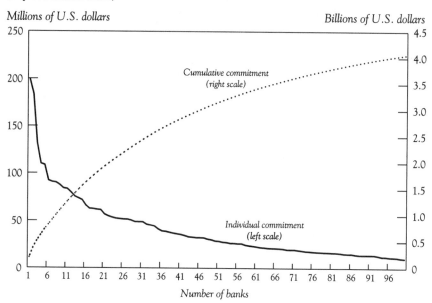

sible for national regulatory authorities or the Fund to support the package. The large banks could have threatened to exclude dissidents from future syndications, but in the competitive environment of the early 1980s such threats would have lacked weight.[65] Sanctions therefore would have had to come from the official sector, and there is no reason to think official sanctions would have been preferable in any way to the zero-margin concerted-lending package concept that was used instead.

The other alternative, under which only those banks whose exposure was too large to be withdrawn would have rescheduled their loans, would have required those banks to raise their exposure by a much larger percentage than in the concerted-lending package. Not only would that approach have induced considerable brinkmanship as banks at every level tried to leave the larger banks holding the bag; the resulting exposure levels would have made it far more difficult for regulatory agencies to treat the new loans as "performing."

Though concerted lending may have been necessary in the Mexican case, it did not come without cost. The banks had entangled themselves in the debt crisis over a number of years by failing to adequately analyze country credit risks and by failing to recognize the more general risks associated with sovereign lending. Encour-

---

[65]For discussions of relations between large and small banks in sovereign lending, and the problems associated with sanctions on holdouts, see Lipson (1985) and Fernandez and Kaaret (1992). For a review of the literature on the problems associated with heterogeneous commercial lenders, see Eaton and Fernandez (1995). Lissakers (1991) describes banking practices with regard to sovereign lending in the 1970s and 1980s.

aged by regulatory agencies and national authorities to "recycle" resources from surplus to deficit countries in the developing world, many banks had responded excessively and incautiously. Now, to help avoid a default, the IMF was providing assurances to the banks that the borrower's economic policies were being adjusted in ways that, inter alia, would improve the prospects that the banks could be repaid.[66] If the IMF were to put itself in a position whereby such assurances could become a *general* requirement for bank lending to developing countries, the institution's independence and neutrality could be threatened and the banks would face a serious moral hazard problem. Furthermore, if the programs failed to resolve the debt crisis within a reasonable time, the return to voluntary lending could be unduly delayed. Although the Fund recognized and discussed these dangers, it was unable to avoid them while responding to the initial crisis. For the moment, longer-run concerns were pushed to the back burner.[67]

Approval of the EFF Program: December 1982

On December 23, the Executive Board unanimously approved Mexico's request for an extended arrangement under the EFF totaling SDR 3,410.6 million ($3.75 billion).[68] Little of the discussion by the Board indicated reservations about the program. Jacques de Groote (Belgium) expressed concern that key elements of the program were insufficiently spelled out, and he concluded that what was before the Board "was not a program so much as a list of intentions."[69] Although he was prepared to approve the requested drawings, he (and other Directors) cautioned that frequent reviews would be required to ensure that intentions with regard to the level of fiscal borrowing and wage moderation were made concrete over the coming months. A number of Directors also indicated skepticism regarding the program's underlying assumption that oil prices would not fall further in 1983; without such an outcome, the required fiscal adjustment could not be realized. More generally, however, there was a very broad recognition by Directors that Mexico was committing itself to as much fiscal and wage adjustment as could reasonably be expected and that the Fund's support of that effort was both appropriate and essential to the success of the program.

---

[66]For example, the Managing Director's cable to the Advisory Committee on December 1, 1982, concluded that "the program should make possible a lowering of pressures on prices while at the same time permitting a reduction in the reliance on external financing, making provision for a reasonable volume of credit to the private sector, and ensuring a rebuilding of foreign reserves"; IMF/CF (C/Mexico/150.1 "Fund Relations with Commercial Banks, 1982–1983").

[67]For the limitations that were soon put on the procedure, see the discussion of the 1983 Uruguay program, in Chapter 9 (pp. 408–09).

[68]Mexico's quota at the time was SDR 802.5 million, and the Fund's holdings of pesos amounted to 100 percent of quota (i.e., there were no outstanding drawings other than the reserve tranche). On this date, the Board also approved an immediate purchase of the first credit tranche, SDR 200.625 million; that purchase plus the full amount of the EFF arrangement would have brought total drawings (other than the reserve tranche) to 450 percent of quota.

[69]Minutes of EBM/82/168 (December 23, 1982), p. 4.

The Board meeting was also an occasion for Directors to reflect on the more general issues raised by the Mexican situation. Directors generally supported the Managing Director's initiatives vis-à-vis commercial banks, though with the caveat that these procedures should be considered as exceptional and should not be generalized. Some concerns were expressed that the World Bank had not been involved in the assessment of Mexico's plans. In particular, it was standard practice for proposed EFF arrangements to include an assessment by the Bank of the country's public investment plans (see Chapter 15). That practice had not been followed in this case, because Mexico had been trying to "graduate" from Bank financing, and the Bank had not been actively involved while the program was being put together. The staff assured Directors that the authorities intended to ask the Bank to review their investment plans as soon as the new administration was established. Finally, a number of Directors questioned whether Fund surveillance had been adequately pursued in this case. Had the two-year gap in consultations made it more difficult for the staff to assess developments in Mexico, and could the crisis have been foreseen under better procedures? As Bruno de Maulde (France) phrased it, the "so-called surveillance process had obviously failed to produce adequate warnings,"[70] and the Board would have to take up the problem again in the context of a general review of surveillance (on which, see Chapter 2).

Completing the Package: January–March 1983

Approval of the EFF arrangement was not the end of the process: financing of the bank package had to be completed, official support had to be secured, and Mexico had to implement the policy program.

On December 23, 1982 (when the EFF arrangement was approved), just over $4.3 billion (86 percent of the required $5 billion) in new money from commercial banks had been pledged. Neither the banks' Advisory Committee nor the Mexican negotiators felt confident that they could bring in the remainder without help from governments and regulators, so they turned to the IMF for help. For the next two months, both de Larosière and Dale worked hard to ensure that the authorities in all creditor countries were helping to bring in as much bank financing as was needed. Maintaining the principle of uniform treatment was a critical element: if the banks in one country or region believed that they would end up shouldering more than their share of the load, they would likely pull out and bring down the house of cards.

The banks' reluctance to pledge new money was geographically widespread, with major difficulties evident in France, Japan, Switzerland, and the United Kingdom, and in U.S. banks outside the principal money markets. The position of the Japanese banks was especially sensitive in this regard. The Japanese banking sector—with its strong presence in the New York market—had the second largest

---

[70]Minutes of EBM/82/167 (December 23, 1982), p. 12.

exposure to Mexico, in dollar terms and in number of banks, after the United States. By mid-January, very little had been pledged from Japan, and the management of the IMF became convinced that the $5 billion total could not be reached unless they could turn that situation around. Cables and telephone calls to the Ministry of Finance and the Bank of Japan were cordially received but seemed to have had little effect.

The stalemate was effectively broken during the Interim Committee meeting in Washington in February 1983. In the margins of that meeting, the Mexican authorities met with the IMF staff and a number of senior bankers from Japan. The bankers were in a delicate position, because they were being increasingly criticized at home and could not necessarily count on the support of their own boards of directors for any concessions they might make in Washington. The once-profitable loans they had made to Mexico had turned sour, and it was not obvious at the time that patience would be the winning strategy. In New York, Washington, and Mexico City, the Japanese position was widely misunderstood. There never was any serious risk that the Japanese banks would refuse to participate, once other banks were also willing to commit. Agreements to that effect apparently had been reached between the principal bankers and the Japanese authorities at a very early stage. The main concern in Tokyo was that they had to be sure they would not be left holding the bag: that *all* banks, including the small U.S. and European banks, would be sharing the risk. They feared that if the Japanese banks, with their huge exposure, committed too early, the free riders would be back in the saddle. By the time of the Interim Committee meeting, the efforts of the IMF staff and the Mexican authorities to ensure wide participation had paid off enough that the Japanese bankers could take home some reasonably firm assurances. Much work remained, but at least everyone now understood how to get the job done.

For much of the rest of February, Gurría—accompanied by bankers from the Advisory Committee—circumnavigated the globe to line up reluctant banks and official creditors, especially in the Middle East and Japan. On the 24th, having enough confidence that the $5 billion package would soon be completed, the Committee banks extended Mexico a loan of $434 million to serve as a bridge. Three days later, with all but a handful of small banks uncommitted, they set the signing ceremony for March 3 in New York. Not until March 15, however, would the magic figure of $5 billion finally be reached, as the last 7 of 526 creditor banks signed on.[71]

Meanwhile, the IMF conducted the first review of the adjustment program, with a mission starting on March 7, headed by Joaquín Pujol (Chief of the Mexico/Latin Caribbean Division, Western Hemisphere Department). One concern of the mission team was that oil prices had slipped further since the program had been devised. They determined, however, that the fiscal effect of that slippage on export receipts had been more than offset by the effects on outlays from a 2 percentage

---

[71]An unknown number of other small creditor banks never did sign on, but a few of the large banks made additional commitments to make up the difference.

point drop in interest rates. The mission also met with their counterparts from the World Bank, who were in Mexico City reviewing the investment program that the Bank was supporting. Overall, the situation seemed well in hand in March of 1983: the program was on track, and the initial phase of the debt crisis had passed.

References

Arora, Vivek B., 1993, "Sovereign Debt: A Survey of Some Theoretical and Policy Issues," IMF Working Paper 93/56 (Washington: International Monetary Fund).

Bailey, Norman A., and Richard Cohen, 1987, *The Mexican Time Bomb,* A Twentieth Century Fund Paper (New York: Priority Press).

Bank for International Settlements, *Annual Report* (Basel: BIS, various issues).

Boughton, James M., 2000, "From Suez to Tequila: The IMF as Crisis Manager," *Economic Journal,* Vol. 110 (January), pp. 273–91.

Caskey, John P., 1989, "IMF and Concerted Lending in Latin American Debt Restructurings: A Formal Analysis," *Journal of International Money and Finance,* Vol. 8 (March), pp. 105–20.

de Vries, Margaret Garritsen, 1985, *The International Monetary Fund 1972–1978: Cooperation on Trial,* Vols. 1 and 2: *Narrative and Analysis;* Vol. 3: *Documents* (Washington: International Monetary Fund).

de Vries, Rimmer, and Arturo C. Porzecanski, 1983, "Comments, Chapter 1–3," in *IMF Conditionality,* ed. by John Williamson (Washington: Institute for International Economics), pp. 63–71.

Eaton, Jonathan, and Raquel Fernandez, 1995, "Sovereign Debt," Chapter 39 in *Handbook of International Economics,* Vol. 3, ed. by Gene M. Grossman and Kenneth Rogoff (Amsterdam: Elsevier), pp. 2031–77.

Edwards, Sebastian, 1986, "The Pricing of Bonds and Bank Loans in International Markets: An Empirical Analysis of Developing Countries' Foreign Borrowing," *European Economic Review,* Vol. 30 (June), pp. 565–89.

Feldstein, Martin, 1983, "Coping with the International Debt Problem," remarks to the International Management and Development Institute, Washington, March 7.

Fernandez, Raquel, and David Kaaret, 1992, "Bank Heterogeneity, Reputation and Debt Renegotiation," *International Economic Review,* Vol. 33 (February), pp. 61–78.

Guitián, Manuel, and Carl-Johan Lindgren, 1978, "Mexico's Adjustment Program Shows Success in Reducing Inflation Rate, Payments Deficit," *IMF Survey,* Vol. 7 (April 17), pp. 119–21.

Kapur, Devesh, John P. Lewis, and Richard Webb, eds., 1997, *The World Bank: Its First Half Century,* Vol. 1: *History* (Washington: Brookings Institution).

Kraft, Joseph, 1984, *The Mexican Rescue* (New York: Group of Thirty).

Krugman, Paul, 1985, "International Debt Strategies in an Uncertain World," Chapter 3 in *International Debt and the Developing Countries,* ed. by Gordon W. Smith and John T. Cuddington (Washington: World Bank), pp. 79–100.

Leeds, Roger S., and Gale Thompson, 1987, *The 1982 Mexican Debt Negotiations: Response to a Financial Crisis* (Washington: Johns Hopkins University, School of Advanced International Studies, Foreign Policy Institute).

Lipson, Charles, 1985, "Bankers' Dilemmas: Private Cooperation in Rescheduling Sovereign Debts," *World Politics* Vol. 38 (October), pp. 200–25.

Lissakers, Karin, 1991, *Banks, Borrowers, and the Establishment: A Revisionist Account of the International Debt Crisis* (New York: Basic Books).

Lomax, David F., 1986, *The Developing Country Debt Crisis* (New York: St. Martin's Press).

Rowen, Hobart, 1983, "Banks Charging $800 Million for Help to Mexico," *Washington Post,* March 20, pp. G1, G13.

Sachs, Jeffrey D., 1984, *New Approaches to the Latin American Debt Crisis*, Essays in International Finance, No. 174 (Princeton, New Jersey: Princeton University, Department of Economics, International Finance Section).

————, and Harry Huizinga, 1987, "U.S. Commercial Banks and the Developing-Country Debt Crisis," *Brookings Papers on Economic Activity: 2,* Brookings Institution, pp. 555–601.

Urzúa, Carlos M., 1997, "Five Decades of Relations Between the World Bank and Mexico," in *The World Bank: Its First Half Century,* Vol. 2: *Perspectives,* ed. by Devesh Kapur, John P. Lewis, and Richard Webb (Washington: Brookings Institution).

Volcker, Paul A., 1982, "Sustainable Recovery: Setting the Stage," text of a speech delivered to the Fifty-Eighth Annual Meeting of the New England Council; Boston, Massachusetts, November 16.

————, and Toyoo Gyohten, 1992, *Changing Fortunes: The World's Money and the Threat to American Leadership* (New York: Times Books).

Zedillo Ponce de León, Ernesto, 1985, "The Mexican External Debt: The Last Decade," Chapter 11 in *Politics and Economics of External Debt Crisis: The Latin American Experience,* ed. by Miguel S. Wionczek (Boulder, Colorado: Westview Press), pp. 294–324.

8

The Crisis Erupts

The global debt crisis of 1982–83 was the product of massive shocks to the world economy and serious misjudgments in the conduct of economic policy. A series of external shocks from mid-1979 to mid-1982, resulting essentially from policy inconsistencies and conflicts in industrial countries, made a large number of developing countries exceptionally vulnerable around the same time. The cumulative effect of long-standing policy errors in the affected countries then turned that vulnerability into a widespread financial crisis: first in Eastern Europe, then in Latin America, and finally in the rest of the developing world.[1]

The external shocks are all well known and can be briefly summarized. The first was the 1979–80 "oil shock," which more than doubled the real price of oil for the oil-importing developing countries.[2] For those countries as a group, the net cost of imported oil rose from 15 percent of exports in 1978 to nearly 23 percent two years later. Much of that increased cost could be covered in the short term only through increased recourse to external borrowing from commercial creditors. The second disturbance, close on the heels of the first, was the "Volcker shock." As the newly appointed Federal Reserve Chairman, Paul A. Volcker, set out to reverse the inflationary excesses of the preceding years, U.S. short-term interest rates (on which a large portion of external debt contracts were based) rose from 9½ percent in August 1979 to more than 16 percent in May 1981. Not until July 1982 did rates on U.S. treasury bills again drop below 12 percent.[3] The consequent sharp rise in real interest rates paid by oil-importing developing countries raised the cost of servicing ex-

---

[1]The debt crisis in sub-Saharan Africa was fundamentally different from that in most other areas because the affected countries were poorer, faced more deep-seated structural problems, and were much more dependent on official rather than commercial credits. See Chapter 14.

[2]The "real price" for a given country is the price of imported oil deflated by the index of the country's export prices. Except as noted, the calculations reported in this paragraph are based on Boughton (1984).

[3]The swing in interest rates, which is shown in Chapter 1, Figure 1.5, was much more severe in real terms, owing to the intervening drop in inflation. U.S. consumer prices rose by more than 13 percent in 1979, making the ex post real short-term interest rate negative. By 1982, inflation had dropped below 4 percent, while treasury bill yields remained above 10½ percent. If interest rates are deflated by the export prices received by oil-importing developing countries, the swing would be still larger. On that basis, Goldsbrough and Zaidi (1986) estimated that for capital-importing developing countries, the real interest rate averaged –5.3 percent for 1978–80 and +17.8 percent for 1981–82.

ternal debts by an estimated 7–8 percent of export earnings between 1979 and 1982. Third, the widespread recession in industrial countries in 1981–82 severely weakened the markets for developing country exports and thereby reduced debtors' ability to generate enough foreign exchange to service their debts.[4] Finally, the effective appreciation of the U.S. dollar by 25 percent from 1980 to 1982 added further to debt-service burdens, since developing countries' liquid liabilities were larger and more concentrated in dollars than were their liquid financial assets.

These external shocks were aggravated by a variety of policy errors in developing countries. Oil-exporting countries, notably Mexico, overestimated the sustainability of high oil prices around the beginning of the decade and found themselves in trouble when prices retreated in 1981–82. Social pressures in many countries led to wage increases that the government could not afford and could accommodate only by losing control of the supply of money. Efforts to use a fixed exchange rate as an anchor to stabilize prices often led to serious losses of international competitiveness as inflation proved to be ineradicable. Attempts to promote economic development by protecting and subsidizing uneconomic enterprises had ruinous effects. As these and other mistakes accumulated, time and again the first crisis to surface was an inability to service external debts.

Prelude: Crisis in Eastern Europe

The first area where the simmering debt crisis bubbled to the surface was the Soviet bloc in Eastern Europe. Several countries in that region embarked on large-scale industrialization drives in the 1970s, only to find that their economies were unable to compete with the more established and far more dynamic western powers. They borrowed heavily from commercial banks in western Europe and elsewhere, and they counted on the Soviet Union to be both a source of fuel and raw materials and a primary market for their output. But by the time the revenues from the projects failed to materialize at the beginning of the 1980s, the Soviet economy was also on the ropes, pummeled by falling oil prices and the war in Afghanistan as well as by its own internal economic ossification. Across the region, countries turned to the West for help.

Poland

The first signs of trouble came from Poland, which was not a member of the IMF but was already engaged in preliminary and quiet membership talks with the staff (Chapter 19). At the end of 1980, Poland had over $25 billion in external debts in convertible currencies, the bulk of which was owed to western governments and to some 500 foreign commercial banks. Adding to the dangers of a possible default

---

[4]GNP growth in industrial countries averaged 3 percent a year for 1973–80 and 0.5 percent for 1981–82. The volume of industrial country imports from developing countries rose at an average annual rate of 0.2 percent for the earlier period and fell at a rate of 8.6 percent for 1981–82. See Goldsbrough and Zaidi (1986), Tables 47 and 49.

of that magnitude were uncertainties about the size and distribution of the debts. A significant but unknown portion of Poland's bank debt was either explicitly or implicitly guaranteed by western governments, and no one could be sure of how the burden of a default would be shared between the public and private sectors or among countries.[5]

In the first months of 1981, the government of Poland found that it lacked the foreign exchange to service all of its debts, and in early March it approached both official and bank creditors to request reschedulings. Official creditors responded promptly through the Paris Club and agreed in April to defer some $2.2 billion in principal payments due in 1981. The banks—forced to innovate to deal with a problem country that was not a member of the IMF—responded by establishing a "multinational task force" of 20 lead banks, which was a less formal prototype of what would later be known as advisory or steering committees.[6] Default would have been a serious blow to some western banks, particularly those in the Federal Republic of Germany (which had the highest aggregate exposure) and Austria (where some of the larger banks also were heavily exposed).

Negotiations took more than a year to complete, during which Poland experienced a political upheaval that climaxed in December 1981 with a declaration of martial law that forestalled an imminent takeover by the Soviet army and suppressed the budding push for democracy spearheaded by Lech Wałęsa's Solidarity movement. This political setback made IMF membership an impossible goal for the moment, but it only moderately delayed negotiations with private creditors. In April 1982, a rescheduling agreement was signed with the banks. Thus the first threat of an international debt crisis was transcended without the involvement of formal multilateral institutions.

For the other two centrally planned economies that fell into a serious payments predicament in 1981—Romania and Hungary—the Fund played an active role. (Yugoslavia also encountered difficulties in this period, but its real crisis came somewhat later and is covered in Chapter 13.)

Romania

Throughout the 1970s, Romania's President, Nicolae Ceaușescu, used the IMF as an element of a strategy to distance his regime from the foreign policy goals of

---

[5]For a review of Poland's debt crisis from a bank creditor's perspective, see Eichler (1986). Eichler estimated that less than a third of Poland's debts at that time were owed to private banks; contemporaneous estimates, including those by the Fund staff, had suggested a much higher bank portion. Part of the uncertainty arose from German government guarantees on credits that were nominally extended by German banks. Contemporaneous press reports indicated that between 40 and 50 percent of $6 billion in outstanding credits from German banks to Poland in 1981 carried government guarantees. For the four German banks with the largest exposure, total claims were estimated at $1.4 billion, of which $442 million (31 percent) was thought to be guaranteed. See Tagliabue (1982) and Spindler (1984). Staff estimates are summarized in "Payments Difficulties Involving Debt to Commercial Banks," SM/83/47 (March 9, 1983), pp. 106–8.

[6]For a contemporaneous commentary on the difficulties posed for the banks by Poland's non-membership in the Fund, see Brainard (1981).

the Soviet Union. In 1972, after five years of quiet diplomacy and technical talks, Romania became the first country since 1955 to be a member of both the Soviet-bloc Council for Mutual Economic Assistance (CMEA) and the IMF (see Chapter 19). The following year, when Ceaușescu traveled to Washington for a state visit with U.S. President Richard M. Nixon, he made a point of also meeting with the Managing Director of the Fund, H. Johannes Witteveen. Over a four-year period starting in 1975, while Romania was engaged in a large-scale industrialization drive, the Fund entered into two stand-by arrangements with the country and made additional resources available through the Compensatory Financing Facility (CFF) to cover flood- and earthquake-related export shortfalls. By the end of 1980, Romania's indebtedness to the Fund amounted to SDR 257 million (70 percent of quota, or approximately $330 million).

The Romanian economy was in a fragile state by that time. The investment that had supported industrialization by bringing in foreign capital goods had also weakened the external current account during a period when the rising cost of oil imports and a series of natural disasters had left no room for excesses. The authorities therefore turned again to the Fund for assistance early in 1981, and a three-year stand-by arrangement was negotiated by May. The Executive Board was skeptical of the request, because the authorities would need both major policy changes and full cooperation from creditors to meet the performance criteria. At the very least, it was felt that the authorities should have requested an arrangement under the Extended Fund Facility (EFF), which would have allowed them to stretch out repayments over a much longer period. In addition, the U.K. chair (represented by John F. Williams, Temporary Alternate) argued that Romania was unlikely to be able to roll over its large stock of short-term debts and questioned the staff's judgment that the $9½ billion in outstanding convertible-currency debt was "manageable." Nonetheless, the arrangement—for SDR 1.1 billion (300 percent of quota, or $1.3 billion)—was unanimously approved.[7]

The Fund's confidence in the Ceaușescu government was misplaced, and matters deteriorated rapidly in the second half of 1981. Part of Romania's trouble was homegrown, notably in the form of abuses of international payments mechanisms and interbank credit lines by Romanian banks. To those troubles was now added the self-fulfilling fear of contagion from the crisis in Poland. Foreign banks were quietly but increasingly withdrawing deposits from Romania and canceling inter-

---

[7]See "Romania—Request for Stand-By Arrangement," EBS/81/111 (June 1, 1981), and minutes of EBM/81/91 (June 15, 1981), p. 13. Outside analysts were also skeptical. The week after the Fund approved the stand-by arrangement, Wharton EFA (a major U.S. commercial forecasting firm) concluded that "Romania is an excellent candidate to be the next 'Poland' in Eastern Europe. . . . the recent IMF decisions need to be explained." Those analyses, which turned out to be fairly close to the mark, were discounted internally at the time because they were based on a much more limited database than that available to the staff and because the staff believed that the full extent of the authorities' stated intentions to reform economic policies was not known outside of official circles. See "Romania," memorandum from L. Alan Whittome (Director of the European Department) to the Managing Director (July 15, 1981), and attachments; in IMF/CF (C/Romania/1760 "Stand-by Arrangements 1973–1981").

bank credit lines. Refusals to roll over maturing loans led to arrears rather than re-payments. By the end of 1981, Romania had accumulated more than $1 billion in arrears to foreign banks, had totally lost access to new credits, and was therefore out of compliance with the terms of the stand-by arrangement with the Fund. Al-though the staff met on various occasions with major bank creditors in the fall of 1981 to explain the nature and extent of the measures the authorities were taking to strengthen their finances, they gradually came to accept the banks' doubts about Romania's commitment to reform. The Fund refused to waive the terms of the stand-by, and it allowed no drawings during the first year of the program other than the one made at the time of initial approval.[8]

Romania began negotiating with a consortium of nine lead banks from six west-ern countries in January 1982, with the Fund staff participating as observers.[9] By April, as those talks continued, arrears to banks were approaching $3 billion, in-cluding arrears on interest as well as principal payments. Even so, the Fund staff expected the government to reach a rescheduling agreement with the lead banks in time to resume the stand-by arrangement in June, a hope that was soon dashed. In June, the staff backed off and proposed instead that the arrangement be resumed with only a token (SDR 10 million) drawing and that more substantive drawings be deferred until the arrears were settled in some fashion.[10]

The "token drawing" proposal was unprecedented, and it drew quite a bit of fire in the Executive Board meeting on June 21. The Board was, on the whole, im-pressed by Romania's perseverance in implementing its adjustment program, and a number of Directors (though holding a minority of the votes) proposed that a full scheduled drawing (SDR 76 million rather than 10 million) be allowed. The Man-aging Director, Jacques de Larosière, insisted on sticking with the staff proposal as a matter of "prudence," though he did note that this unique decision should not become general policy.[11]

Part of the explanation for the Executive Board's optimism on Romania was that official creditors had signaled a willingness to reschedule debts as soon as the Fund arrangement was resumed; a July meeting of the Paris Club had been scheduled for

---

[8]Under the original terms of the arrangement, Romania was to be entitled to purchase SDR 140 million immediately and SDR 76 million in November 1981, February 1982, and May 1982. Only the first drawing was made. The abuses by Romanian banks (allegedly including kit-ing of checks), as understood by western banks, were reported to Fund management in Septem-ber. See "Romania—Foreign Debt Position" (September 15, 1981), memorandum to Brian Rose (Deputy Director of the European Department) from the mission chief, Geoffrey Tyler, with cover memo from Rose to the Managing Director; in IMF/CF (C/Romania/1760 "Stand-by Arrangements 1973–1981").

[9]Altogether, Romania had outstanding debts to some 300 western banks at this time, plus loans from a few banks in Moscow and the Middle East. The latter two groups did not participate in the negotiations, waiting instead to reach a settlement on comparable terms.

[10]Compare "Romania—Staff Report for the 1982 Article IV Consultation and Review of Stand-By Arrangement," EBS/82/73 (April 29, 1982) with "Additional Information," EBS/82/73, Sup. 1 (June 14, 1982). Additional information is from the staff statement at EBM/82/85 (June 21, 1982), pp. 3–4.

[11]Minutes of EBM/82/85–86 (June 21, 1982). Beginning in 1983, the Fund developed a policy of approving arrangements "in principle" to deal with situations such as this. See Chapter 9.

that purpose.[12] That part of the package was successfully concluded in late July, but negotiations with bank creditors continued for several more months. Romania and the banks finally signed a rescheduling agreement in December 1982, ending this phase of the crisis and permitting a resumption of the stand-by arrangement.

Following the resolution of this crisis, the Romanian economy deteriorated further, and Ceauşescu's policies eventually lurched into a totally new direction. Around 1986, after difficulties arose in repaying the Fund and other creditors, the government began appropriating an increasingly disproportionate share of domestic output, even of basic foodstuffs, to export for foreign exchange. In a disastrous overreaction to the strains of 1981, part of those revenues were then used to repay foreign debts early and as rapidly as possible. As hardships and domestic unrest grew, Romania ceased providing basic data to the Fund in 1987 and repeatedly postponed the scheduled Article IV consultation. The economy, the political instability, and the international isolation of Romania continued to worsen until the overthrow of Ceauşescu in November 1989.

Hungary

Hungary developed a stronger and more open economy than its neighbors in the 1970s, and it became known as the crown jewel of the CMEA. That success, however, did not shield the country as the debt crisis spread across Eastern Europe. On the contrary, Hungary's economic growth had been nurtured by foreign borrowing, and those debts became unbearably costly to service as the 1970s faded into the 1980s.

Hungary's crisis began in the first quarter of 1982, while the government's application for membership in the IMF was still in process (see Chapter 19). The previous year had been hard, as export receipts fell in response to the deterioration in the world economy even as world interest rates were still rising. For two years, banks had been shortening the maturities at which they were willing to lend to heavily indebted countries, and Hungary—like so many other countries in similar circumstances—had failed to curb its appetite as the bill of fare had become ever richer. With over $10 billion in external debt, much of it short-term, Hungary faced a tightening squeeze between falling resources and rising debt-service costs. When the debts of first Poland and then Romania began to hemorrhage, the stain naturally ran toward Budapest. Bank creditors all tried to pull out at once, and by March 1982, Hungary was virtually devoid of foreign exchange.

Up to this point, the story had a familiar resonance. Where Hungary departed from the earlier cases was in the authorities' efforts to staunch the capital outflows by turning first to the Bank for International Settlements (BIS) in Basel, Switzerland. Hungary had participated actively in the BIS for decades, and since the 1950s

---

[12]The Board meeting on Romania was originally scheduled for June 14, 1982, but it was postponed by a week while the management of the Fund obtained assurances from Paris Club creditors that the outcome was likely to be positive. On June 11, the Managing Director indicated to the Board that such assurance was a necessary condition for reactivating the Fund arrangement. Minutes of EBM/82/81 (June 11, 1982), p. 3.

had normally been represented there by Janos Fekete, who in 1982 was the First Deputy President of the National Bank of Hungary. Fekete went to see Fritz Leutwiler, the newly elected president of the BIS, with a request for an innovative approach. Hungary did not have the foreign exchange or gold to put up as collateral for a conventional loan from the BIS, but perhaps an alternative could be found.[13] Would the BIS be willing to arrange for a bridge loan *from its member central banks* to help Hungary meet its payments obligations until it could join the IMF and get a stand-by arrangement?

Poland had sought a similar arrangement from the BIS the year before, but that request had not been enthusiastically received and had been dropped when Poland's reform momentum was brutally halted in December. Hungary's situation, however, was far more favorable. Leutwiler picked up the telephone and called de Larosière in Washington. When the Managing Director assured him that he fully expected Hungary to qualify for IMF credits within a few months, Leutwiler decided to support Fekete's request, and he set out to get the support of his fellow BIS governors and other major central banks. Within a few weeks, he was able to complete the deal, and the BIS made two syndicated loans to Hungary in March and May 1982, for $100 million and $110 million, respectively. Though small in relation to the demands on Hungary's meager reserves (and less than the $500 million for which Fekete had asked), the announcement of the loans had a calming effect on the financial markets.

The BIS bridge loans enabled Hungary to avoid defaulting on its bank loans while the authorities completed the IMF membership process (in May) and began negotiations for a stand-by arrangement. A further $300 million in short-term credits was provided by the BIS in September, and with that amount in hand Hungary was able to clear its outstanding arrears in time for the Executive Board to approve the use of the Fund's resources in December.[14] The Hungarian crisis was thereby put to rest, in part through coordinated international action that set a precedent that would turn out to be crucial for success when the debt crisis soon spread to Latin America.

In Concert: Crisis in Latin America

Mexico

As told in Chapter 7, the core of the debt crisis was in Mexico. Eastern Europe had been threatened, and that crisis had in turn endangered the solvency of major

---

[13]In earlier years, Hungary could have counted on the Soviet Union to lend it the gold for collateral, but part of the squeeze that Hungary now faced was a withdrawal of that type of support.

[14]The BIS loans are described in the BIS *Annual Report* for 1982–83, pp. 164–65; additional information used here is from background interviews. On December 8, 1982, the Executive Board of the IMF approved a 13-month stand-by arrangement for SDR 475 million (127 percent of quota, or $520 million), plus a drawing of SDR 72 million ($80 million) under the CFF to compensate for a shortfall in export earnings. Note that the three BIS loans were short-term credits; the amounts cannot be added together to derive total bridge financing to the Fund arrangement, because the first two loans expired between September and December.

Talk to the IMF, by Dan Wasserman

European banks; but it neither openly erupted nor posed an immediate direct threat to the functioning of the international financial system. When Mexico announced in August 1982 that it could neither roll over nor repay principal on its bank loans, it alerted the world that the crisis was spreading and growing and that the system itself was now at risk. The major U.S. and Japanese banks were threatened for the first time, and the European banks faced large new risks on top of those that still lingered from their eastern borders. The resources that the creditor countries had so far brought to bear could not begin to cope.

The Mexican crisis placed the IMF squarely at the center of the emerging debt strategy. From August 1982 through the rest of the decade, Mexico would be the crucible where the strategy would be developed and tested.[15] As the problems became manifest in other countries throughout the developing world, that strategy would be applied and modified in case after case. The remainder of this chapter examines three major cases in Latin America: Argentina, Brazil, and Chile.[16] The three stories have much in common—unsustainable external borrowing and a shortage of discipline in domestic economic policy—but also some important differences. Because of Brazil's economic strength and Chile's tradition of good policies, the Fund tried to avoid resorting to concerted lending to close their financing gaps. The failure of that effort showed just how deep and protracted the debt crisis was likely to become.

Argentina

The Managing Director had much on his mind at the Annual Meetings in Toronto. Managing the effects of the Mexican crisis was by itself a full-time job, but the rest of the world economy could not be ignored. On Tuesday morning, September 7, de Larosière would be called upon to attend the plenary sessions of the meetings of the Boards of Governors starting at 10:00, and at about 11:00 would deliver a major address. Before that, however, he had a series of meetings with the governors of several countries, including one with Dr. Jorge Wehbe, the minister of economy from Argentina, at 8:40 a.m. In a chain of threatened economies across Latin America, the Argentine link was about to break.

The story of Argentina's debt crisis had opened just before Christmas in 1978, some 2½ years after the military had wrested power from Isabel Perón. Adolfo Diz, the very able president of the central bank, had implemented financial reforms, negotiated a stand-by arrangement with the Fund, and generated enough credibility with foreign commercial banks that the country never had to draw on that line of credit.[17] This

---

[15]See Gold (1988) for a general history of the importance of Mexico to the development of IMF policies.

[16]For a more general overview on Fund-supported programs in the heavily indebted countries in this period, see Chapter 9.

[17]The stand-by arrangement was approved on September 16, 1977, for SDR 159.5 million (36 percent of quota). At the time, the Fund's holdings of Argentine pesos amounted to just over 200 percent of quota, reflecting earlier drawings on stand-by arrangements, the Oil Facility, and the CFF. The 1977 arrangement expired one year later, by which time the Fund's holdings of pesos were down to 75 percent of quota.

victory, however, was incomplete. In 1978, Argentina had a surplus in its external current account and in its overall balance of payments, but the domestic economy was in a shambles: output was falling while consumer price inflation raced along at about 175 percent a year. On December 20, the minister of economy, José Martínez de Hoz, announced a new set of policies designed to gradually weaken the inflationary psychology of the country and stimulate investment and output.

The basic elements of the Martínez de Hoz plan were to control and preannounce the rates of currency depreciation, wage increases, and growth of the domestic monetary base; gradually reduce import tariffs over five years; and strengthen the central government's finances by restraining spending and suspending central bank lending to the government.[18] The element that got the most attention and that gave the plan its popular name was the crawling peg for the exchange rate, for which the government issued printed tables—*tablitas*—in advance.[19] Inflation did fall under the *tablita*—to 160 percent in 1979 and 100 percent in 1980—but it remained well above the fixed rate of depreciation. Gradually but inevitably, Argentine exporters suffered a disastrous loss of international competitiveness. By 1980, the balance of payments was back in deficit, output (after a brief spurt of growth in 1979) was again stagnant, capital investment was plummeting, and the country was becoming dangerously dependent on continual borrowing from foreign banks.

In October 1980, the military junta named General Roberto Eduardo Viola to replace President Jorge Rafael Videla the following March. During this interregnum, exchange rate policy was administered erratically, speculation of a major devaluation became widespread, and maintaining the *tablita* became impossible. A 10 percent devaluation on February 2, 1981, did little to calm the markets and may even have accelerated the collapse of the exchange regime. When Viola took office at the end of March, his new economy minister, Lorenzo Sigaut, immediately announced a further devaluation of 23 percent but otherwise attempted to preserve the preannounced crawling peg. When speculation continued against the peso, Viola's team resorted more and more to exchange and other controls and failed utterly to manage the government's finances or to extinguish the inflation that the deficit was fueling. By late summer, when an IMF team (led by Christian Brachet, Chief of the River Plate Division in the Western Hemisphere Department) arrived in Buenos Aires to conduct the Article IV consultation, the economy was seriously destabilized.

Brachet's report warned of the dangers to the economy if measures were not taken to reduce the fiscal deficit and control monetary growth.[20] A few days after the mission's return to Washington, the Managing Director reinforced this message

---

[18]For a general analysis of economic policy under Martinez de Hoz, see Calvo (1986).

[19]Chile had adopted a similar crawling-peg policy from 1976 to 1979, and it later came into common use in several Latin American countries that were attempting to get inflation under control. The term *tablita*, however, originated in Argentina as a description of the "little tables" that listed the evolution of controlled prices.

[20]"Argentina—Staff Report for the 1981 Article IV Consultation," SM/81/233 (December 2, 1981), pp. 16–18

Figure 8.1. Argentina: Fiscal Deficit and External Debt, 1973–83

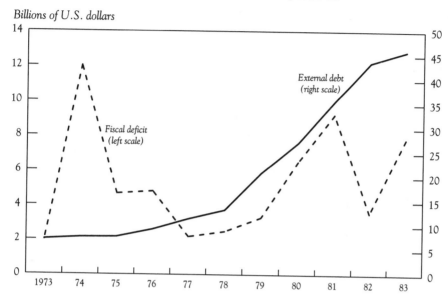

Billions of U.S. dollars

Sources: IMF, *IFS*; and World Bank, *World Development Indicators*.

in a meeting with Sigaut at the 1981 Annual Meetings. Sigaut expressed confidence that a rebound in economic activity would soon strengthen tax revenues enough to resolve the fiscal imbalance, but de Larosière cautioned him that this supply-side effect was no more likely to succeed in Argentina than it was in the United States.[21] Three months later, with no further progress toward stabilization being evident, an ailing Viola was overthrown in a coup, and a new economic team—led by Dr. Roberto T. Alemann—was brought in to restore order.

Alemann confronted an escalating external debt, which had already tripled in three years (Figure 8.1). He moved quickly to restore competitiveness by floating the exchange rate and to reduce the fiscal deficit by freezing public sector wages and cutting support to unprofitable public sector enterprises: both of which would help to ameliorate the rampaging borrowing from international banks. Brachet and his team returned to Buenos Aires in January 1982 to complete the Article IV consultations that the Executive Board was scheduled to discuss in mid-March. Although the team was worried that the military government was deeply divided in its support for Alemann's policies, they were impressed by the minister's own resolve, and the consultations were concluded without difficulty.[22]

---

[21]The exchange was noted in the departmental file memorandum of September 28, 1981, on the bilateral meeting; in IMF/RD Western Hemisphere Department file "Argentina Correspondence—I, January 1979–October 1982" (Accession 88/151, Box 1, Section 531).

[22]See "Argentina—Staff Report for the 1981 Article IV Consultation," SM/81/233 (December 2, 1981) and Sup. 1 (February 25, 1982), and minutes of EBM/82/29–30 (March 12 and 15, 1982).

Alemann was largely isolated from the junta's strategic planning, and he spent the last few days of March 1982 participating in the annual meetings of the Inter-American Development Bank (IDB) in Cartagena, Colombia. It appears he was completely surprised to learn on April 2 that Argentina had launched a military effort to occupy the islands in the southern Atlantic that the British called the Falklands but the Argentines knew as the Malvinas. Within days, the United Kingdom and Argentina had frozen each other's financial assets, and the European Community had banned all imports from Argentina; and by the end of April, the United States had banned arms sales to Argentina and had ceased providing trade support through the Export-Import Bank and the Commodity Credit Corporation. Servicing the external debt became all but impossible in these circumstances, as the banks only reluctantly agreed to roll over existing credits. The debt crisis had come to Latin America.

Throughout the war, Alemann did as much as could be expected to conduct business as usual. At the Interim Committee meeting in Helsinki on May 12, he assured both de Larosière (in a private meeting) and the Committee that he was determined to persevere with the adjustment policies that he had initiated before the invasion.[23] Nonetheless, by the time peace was restored in June, Argentina had accumulated more than $2 billion in external arrears and had no prospect of resuming normal financial relations with its bank creditors in the near future.

In July 1982, the army took effective control of Argentina, named General Reynaldo Benito Antonio Bignone to serve as president, and announced a commitment to hold elections for a civilian government by March 1984. Bignone brought in a new economic team headed by Economy Minister José María Dagnino Pastore, but little was done to restore order to economic policy. On July 6, just four days after Pastore's appointment, the peso was devalued (Figure 8.2) and the exchange market was split into commercial and financial segments. This effort to protect commercial transactions largely failed, however, as a parallel market arose with huge discounts (about 60,000 pesos per U.S. dollar, compared with 20,000 in the commercial market and under 40,000 in the financial market), and price and wage inflation accelerated. Brachet's team returned to Buenos Aires a week later and concluded that economic conditions were deteriorating and that these policies were doing little to improve them.[24]

---

[23]The Interim Committee meeting in Helsinki provided a prototypical demonstration of the separation of economics from politics that—though inevitably imperfect—gives life to the IMF's efforts to serve a varied and often fractious membership. Alemann and Sir Geoffrey Howe, the United Kingdom's Chancellor of the Exchequer, were both members of the 22-person Committee, and a confrontation between them would not have been surprising. Alemann spoke first at the afternoon session, avoided all references to the war, and gave what seemed to Howe to be even a Thatcherite commentary on the need for financial discipline and economic reform. Howe responded in kind with a speech that pointedly ignored the hostilities altogether. Afterward, the two ministers met and exchanged pleasantries, and the occasion passed without incident. ICMS/Meeting 18 (5/13/82), second session (3:00 p.m.), pp. 1 and 4–6. For Howe's published account, see Howe (1994), p. 268.

[24]Stiles (1987) erroneously reported (p. 62) that this mission was asked to discuss the possibility of a stand-by arrangement but drew negative conclusions. In fact, the authorities did not raise the question of a financial arrangement until several weeks later, as discussed below.

Figure 8.2. Argentina: Exchange Rate, 1976–82

U.S. dollars per million pesos; log scale

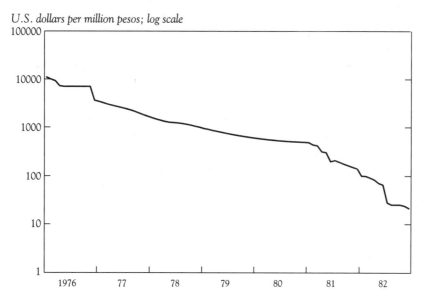

Note: Scale is in terms of the currency in effect from 1977 to 1983.

From an economic perspective, Argentina's fundamental problem was an inability to reduce the fiscal deficit. From the political perspective of the authorities, however, restoring fiscal discipline was a secondary issue. In the absence of access to foreign bank loans, only a draconian adjustment program could have resolved the domestic and external imbalances. With the military split, no government could have generated the political support for such measures. The authorities therefore focused much of their efforts on stanching the bleeding of bank credits. That effort, which would have been difficult in any case because of the lack of economic stability, was complicated further by Argentina's prohibition against making payments to British banks.[25]

The syndication agreements under which the banks had lent to Argentina gave any bank that was not paid its share the right to force a default against the entire loan. Facing this very real possibility and fearing the systemic consequences, senior officials of the Bank of England worked quietly with their counterparts in Argentina throughout the months following the war to keep everyone in the game. (The regular meetings of the BIS in Basel provided a convenient forum for such contacts.) A solution was finally negotiated at the Annual Meetings in Toronto, with assistance from Richard T. McNamar (Deputy Secretary of the U.S. Treasury). For their part, the Argentine authorities arranged to bypass the agent for the

---

[25]On May 18, in the midst of the war, Law 22591 was enacted, prohibiting business payments to residents (including banks) of the United Kingdom.

bank syndicate and instead pay—through their own agent—the individual banks other than the British. The receiving banks would then pay the British banks, as they were required to do under the sharing clauses of the syndication agreements. For several months, until normal financial relations were restored between Argentina and the United Kingdom, this string-and-bandages procedure held together, and a default was avoided.

When banks suddenly stopped lending to Mexico in August, Pastore realized that he would not have the luxury of time to deal with the deeper economic problems. After less than two months in office, he—along with the central bank president, Domingo Cavallo—abruptly resigned on August 24. The new team, headed by Wehbe, immediately decided to approach the IMF for financial assistance. First in Washington and then at the Annual Meetings in Toronto, Wehbe met with the Fund staff—including principally Walter Robichek, the Director of the Western Hemisphere Department—to discuss the feasibility of an arrangement. Robichek was receptive to the idea, but he expressed concern about whether there was enough political support in Argentina for implementing an effective adjustment program, especially in view of the elections that would be held around the end of 1983: Was it realistic to expect firm action during the run-up to the elections, and could the elected government be counted upon to continue with the required reforms? These concerns led Robichek to recommend against an extended arrangement (which would have required a three-year policy commitment) in favor of a 15-month stand-by arrangement.

These, then, were the circumstances that Wehbe faced as he met with de Larosière at the Toronto Sheraton early that Tuesday morning in September. The question of discrimination against British banks was crucial from the Fund's perspective, because Executive Board approval of an arrangement would have been impossible without a prior resolution of this problem. Wehbe was able to assure the Managing Director that they were working through indirect channels to ensure equitable treatment (as described above). The more substantive issue was whether Wehbe would be able to generate enough support among the military leaders to implement the program. For the moment, what mattered was that he was prepared to try. De Larosière agreed to send a mission in September to conduct the annual Article IV consultations and to begin negotiations on a program that could be supported by a stand-by arrangement for SDR 1.5 billion.

By the end of September, the Argentines were negotiating on several fronts. They were negotiating with the IMF team (led by Brachet, with Robichek taking over the negotiations after mid-October) on the terms of the proposed program; with the politicians who were likely to form a new government after the elections, for their implicit support for the program; with the leading bank creditors for a $1.1 billion bridge loan; and with the BIS for a $750 million bridge loan.[26] The BIS de-

---

[26]None of the large heavily indebted countries in Latin America requested a rescheduling of official bilateral obligations, through the Paris Club or other creditor group, in 1982. The first to do so was Mexico, in June 1983. Argentina had relatively few such debts at the time and did not seek a Paris Club deal until 1985.

murred for the time being (apparently owing to a disagreement over collateral), but agreement in principle was reached with both the Fund and the banks before the end of October.[27] At that point, the authorities felt ready to relax the controls on the foreign exchange market. The commercial rate was devalued by 13½ percent and partially unified with the financial rate, and it would then be depreciated regularly in line with domestic inflation to maintain competitiveness.

On the surface, Argentina was firmly on the path to recovery. Underneath, the footing was much less secure. The authorities had made a general commitment to control the main macroeconomic aggregates, but they had not yet fully specified the policy changes that would achieve those results. Not only were some of the spending cuts and revenue measures to reduce the fiscal deficit not yet defined, but also the readiness of the authorities to raise interest rates by enough to make domestic assets competitive and stop capital flight remained in doubt. This latter uncertainty reflected a difference in view that was (and is) common in negotiations between the IMF and developing countries: starting from a position where interest rates are sharply negative in real terms, how far and how fast *must* rates be raised to reverse the outflow of financial capital, and how much *can* rates be raised without undercutting real investment demand? For the time being, this debate was left to simmer.[28]

Furthermore, the program that the staff had negotiated assumed only that the commercial banks would continue to roll over existing medium- and long-term loans. By implication, all interest due on those loans would be paid when due. Except for the temporary effect of the bridge loan, the banks' exposure would not rise, and the additional financing would come entirely from the Fund and other official creditors. To restore more balance into these financing arrangements and to provide for a margin in the event that the still-unspecified policy measures turned out to be weaker than envisaged, the Managing Director insisted that the program be modified to include a $1.5 billion (roughly 7 percent) increase in bank exposure.

Julio Gonzáles del Solar, the president of the central bank, came to Washington in the second week of November 1982, and he and his staff worked intensely for several days to hammer out the details of the Letter of Intent with both the IMF staff and the Managing Director. Then on November 16, de Larosière flew to New York to meet with the bank creditors: the same dramatic meeting that confronted the Mexican crisis, as described above in Chapter 7. As with the Mexican EFF arrangement, the Managing Director made clear to the banks that he could not propose approval of the stand-by arrangement to the Executive Board until he received written assurances from the banks that they would grant an additional term loan (the so-called new-money loan, which in effect would refinance a substantial portion of the interest due on existing credits).

---

[27]The Fund discussions are described in the staff report, "Argentina—Staff Report for the 1982 IV Consultation and Request for Stand-By Arrangement," EBS/83/8 (January 10, 1983).

[28]This issue resurfaced often in the financial crises of the 1990s, especially in Korea at the end of 1997, and became a focal point for many critics of the Fund's crisis management.

Following the November 16 meeting, the main creditor banks organized themselves into an Advisory Committee—headed, as was the Mexico committee, by Citibank's William Rhodes—to negotiate the terms of the requested bridge and term loans. In addition to the financial terms, the banks were also concerned about the macroeconomic program negotiated by the Fund. During the next few weeks, Fund staff met on several occasions with the Committee or their representatives to explain the program, but they did not participate in the negotiations between the Committee and the authorities. By December 10, agreement was reached with the Committee, and on December 31, the Argentine authorities and the banks signed the contracts for both loans.

The Letter of Intent and Memorandum of Understanding, which formalized the request for the stand-by arrangement and the government's policy commitments, were submitted to the Managing Director on January 7, 1983, along with a more detailed memorandum on specific policy measures that had been taken or were being contemplated.[29] The proposed program was fairly standard and incorporated limits on the balance of payments deficit, the borrowing requirement of the nonfinancial public sector, and the growth of the net domestic assets of the central bank. The formulation of these limits, however, was unusually detailed and complex, owing to the need to account for inflation and to translate Argentina's domestic accounting structure into an internationally acceptable format.[30] Nonetheless, by the January 7 signing, the substance of the issue had been largely resolved.

The Executive Board met on January 24, 1983, to consider Argentina's request for the SDR 1.5 billion stand-by arrangement and a CFF drawing of SDR 520.1 million to cover a temporary loss of export receipts. Directors raised a number of issues regarding the proposed program. Jacques de Groote (Belgium), for example, expressed frankly what several of his colleagues phrased more delicately, that the planned adjustment effort "could impose such a heavy burden on the government as to exclude the possibility of complete observance." He also was bothered by the slow pace at which Argentina was eliminating the discriminatory practices against British residents, and he suggested that all restrictions be eliminated before the first scheduled performance review (May 1983), rather than by end-year, as proposed. Finally, de Groote questioned whether the temporary shortfall in export receipts that constituted the basis for the requested CFF drawing was really the result of circumstances beyond the control of the member (as required by the CFF decision) rather than "the events of 1982" (the war) over which they did have some control.[31]

---

[29]"Argentina—Stand-By Arrangement," EBS/83/8, Sup.1 (January 25, 1983), Attachment and Annexes I and II.

[30]This issue, for which no single approach is unambiguously preferred, is similar to the debate over the use of the "operational deficit" as a program criterion in Brazil (Chapter 9). The Argentine accounts treated the estimated inflation component of interest payments (i.e., the effects of interest rates being higher than they would have been in the absence of inflation) as amortization rather than financing. The actual deficit therefore was much higher than the recorded deficit, the gap between the two became progressively larger over time, and the calculation of the actual deficit had to be spelled out in detail.

[31]Minutes of EBM/83/17 (January 24, 1983), pp. 9–10.

The question of the authorities' resolve to implement the program could not very well be settled in January; the staff team reiterated its conviction that a serious adjustment effort would be undertaken, and the Board fully accepted that judgment. The question of the elimination of discriminatory practices was likewise deferred, on the basis of the assurance of Mario Teijeiro (Alternate—Argentina) that the "authorities will make their best efforts to ensure that all exchange arrangements that are in effect beyond the May review, including any restrictions that may temporarily remain, will be completely nondiscriminatory in both character and operation."[32]

Approval of the request for a drawing under the CFF required that the shortfall in export receipts be "largely" outside the control of the member, but that requirement was interpreted to treat political disturbances as if they were unavoidable (see Chapter 15). In judging the Argentine request, the staff position had been that macroeconomic policies had shifted in the right direction under Alemann after December 1981 but had been blown off course by "the hostilities in the South Atlantic." Therefore, as long as the war could be considered for this purpose as being outside the authorities' control, the request should be approved. Directors generally accepted this interpretation, and both the stand-by arrangement and the CFF drawing were approved without dissent.

For the next few months, the program was implemented with reasonable success. The BIS, led by the United States, granted a short-term stand-by credit in late January to serve as a bridge to the scheduled May drawing under the Fund arrangement, but the Argentine authorities—who wished to preserve control over their collateral—were able to avoid drawing on it. The Fund staff became nervous in March when Wehbe announced an intensification of price controls, fearing that this policy would deal with the symptoms rather than the root causes of inflation. Eduardo Wiesner (Director of the Western Hemisphere Department) then undertook a special mission in April to review the situation but concluded that fundamental progress was also being made. The scheduled May review mission, under Brachet, found that the program was on track, except for the assumption by the public sector of a substantial portion of private sector debts to foreign banks.[33] That practice required a modification of the performance criteria under the stand-by arrangement, which the Executive Board granted on a lapse-of-time basis in late May.[34]

---

[32]Minutes of EBM/83/17 (January 24, 1983), p. 7.

[33]During parts of 1981 and 1982, the Central Bank of Argentina granted exchange rate guarantees on $9.2 billion in bank loans to the private sector. By the time these loans began to mature in late 1982, the peso had depreciated heavily and the central bank lacked the foreign exchange to cover the guarantees. Consequently, the government offered to exchange the private sector loans for its own dollar-denominated securities on terms to be negotiated with the foreign creditors. The associated restrictions on the purchase of foreign exchange to repay the private sector debts were subject to approval by the Fund as a condition for the continuation of the stand-by arrangement.

[34]Minutes of EBM/83/76 (May 27, 1983), pp. 30–31. See also "Argentina—Modification of Performance Criteria Under Stand-By Arrangement and Approval of Certain Exchange Measures," EBS/83/97 (May 18, 1983).

At the end of May 1983, Argentina made its scheduled drawing under the stand-by arrangement, for just under SDR 300 million. Two days later, the government introduced a new "peso argentino" worth 10,000 of the badly devalued old pesos. Reform and optimism were in the "good air" of Buenos Aires, and the chill winter wind could not yet be felt.

Brazil

The debt crisis came a little later to Brazil than to either Argentina or Mexico, but its effects would ultimately be no less severe. Brazil had borrowed substantial amounts from foreign commercial banks through much of the 1960s and 1970s to finance economic development and had generated one of the highest sustained growth rates in the world. Notwithstanding the adverse consequences of the two oil shocks of the 1970s (by 1981, oil accounted for more than half of all of Brazil's imports), the growth in output and exports came reasonably close to keeping up with the growth in external debt through most of that difficult decade. By 1980, foreign bankers had begun showing some reluctance to raise their exposure in Brazil, and official foreign exchange reserves had fallen by some $3 billion. That year, and again in 1981, the Fund staff raised questions during the annual Article IV consultation regarding the adequacy of the fiscal retrenchment in the face of a deteriorating global environment and steadily rising external debt (Figure 8.3).[35] Most ominously, inflation was becoming ingrained, averaging more than 90 percent a year for 1980–81, more than double the rate of the preceding two years. In view of Brazil's pervasive wage indexation, stabilizing prices would become progressively more difficult over time. Nonetheless, the economy was strong overall, and there was no reason to think the situation was unmanageable.

Through the first seven months of 1982, Brazil was able to borrow from the banks as much as was needed to maintain reserves (albeit at somewhat higher spreads), even though the level of output had stagnated while inflation continued to mount. Twice in that period, a small staff team led by Horst Struckmeyer (Chief of the Atlantic Division, Western Hemisphere Department) visited Brazil to hold a mini-consultation on what increasingly appeared to be a shaky financial situation. The conclusions were upbeat in February, reflecting the effects of the adjustment measures implemented in 1980–81; but in early July, as the second mission was preparing to leave for Brazil, a weakening of the adjustment effort in the face of persistent stagflation led the Deputy Managing Director, William B. Dale, to comment on the briefing paper that the outlook was "beginning to look ominous again."[36]

The Mexican crisis in August 1982 brought a sudden end to business as usual in Brazil—through the remainder of the decade and into the 1990s. Almost immedi-

---

[35]The relevant staff reports are "Brazil—Staff Report for the 1980 Article IV Consultation," SM/80/141 (June 17, 1980), based on consultation discussions in Brazil in March–April 1980; and "Brazil—Staff Report for the 1981 Article IV Consultation," SM/81/205 (October 28, 1981), based on discussions in August–September 1981.

[36]Note on the cover memorandum to the briefing paper (July 12, 1982), in IMF/CF (C/Brazil/810 "Mission—Struckmeyer and Staff, July 1982").

Figure 8.3. Brazil: Fiscal Deficit and External Debt, 1970–83

Billions of U.S. dollars

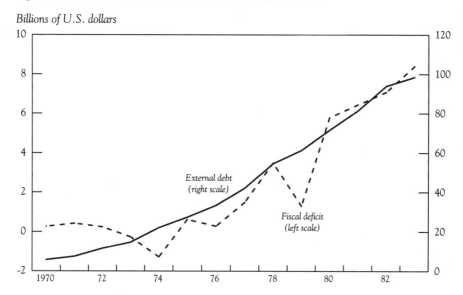

Sources: IMF, *IFS*; and World Bank, *World Development Indicators*.

ately, additional bank loans, without which the public sector debt could not be serviced, became impossible to get. Foreign exchange reserves totaled less than $6 billion and less than the debt-service payments that would come due by the end of the year. It must be said that the link with the crisis in Mexico does not imply that Mexico's problems caused those in Brazil. The fundamental causes were the Brazilian economy's dependence on a global economy that was no longer strong enough to generate the growth rate to which the country had become accustomed, and a serious domestic imbalance manifested in a persistently high inflation rate. The effect initially was "only" a financial crisis, but the authorities then allowed themselves to be lulled into believing that they could ride it out without implementing major policy adjustments.

For three months after the crisis erupted, policy in Brazil was frozen in place by the approach of the first nationwide congressional elections since the military had taken over in 1964. The bank creditors, however, had no patience for this political timetable. Some, including Lloyds Bank—the largest creditor outside the United States—were telling the authorities that they were prepared to consider additional credit, but only after a Fund-supported program was in place. Others, including Citibank—the largest creditor—were threatening to pull out altogether. To try to ward off a ruinous fight by banks to withdraw ahead of the competition, Anthony Solomon—president of the Federal Reserve Bank of New York—convened a small private meeting at his apartment on Park Avenue in Manhattan. The most heavily involved U.S. bankers were there, including Lewis Preston from Morgan Guaranty (along with his top Brazil hand, Tony Gebauer) and Walter Wriston from Citibank (with Rhodes). Paul Volcker was there, Beryl Sprinkel represented the U.S. Treasury, and de Larosière represented the IMF. Wriston made it clear at the outset that he saw Brazil as a poor credit risk and that his intention was to gradually withdraw credits until Citibank was completely out. The Federal Reserve officials argued, however, that the situation was too delicate for precipitous action: if Citibank started reducing its credit lines, everyone else would follow suit, no one would get his money out, and the stability of the banking system would be threatened. Wriston was not convinced that the problem was too big for the banks to handle by themselves, but he eventually agreed to participate in an advisory group to try to stabilize financial flows to Brazil. For the moment at least, the systemic crisis was averted.

Elections were held in Brazil on November 15, 1982, after which the economic team—which retained power—moved quickly to formulate an adjustment program that could command the necessary support from the Fund and from their commercial bank creditors. Carlos Langoni, the president of the central bank, went immediately to New York to secure a bridge loan from the committee banks[37] and then to Washington to request financial assistance from the IMF. In his initial meeting with the Managing Director and the Fund staff, everyone agreed on the main obstacle to adjustment: Brazil had a pervasive system of wage indexation that could be modified only with the concurrence of the congress, and the likelihood of any significant reduction in the inflation rate or improvement in international cost competitiveness was extremely remote before the spring of 1983 at the earliest.[38] In the meantime, the government would have to get its fiscal deficit under control by some means other than cutting wages or devaluing the exchange rate.[39]

A mission headed by Struckmeyer was sent to Brazil at the end of November to conduct the Article IV consultation for 1982, negotiate the terms of an EFF arrangement, and collect data related to Brazil's request to make drawings under the CFF and buffer stock facility. In contrast to the protracted negotiations with Mexico and Argentina—both of which faced more difficult economic straits than those of Brazil—all of the basic elements of the program were agreed upon in the course of this one mission: reductions in subsidies and increases in taxes designed to reduce the public sector borrowing requirement from nearly 14 percent of GDP in 1982 to less than 8 percent in 1983; reduced growth in net domestic assets of the monetary authorities; increases in domestic interest rates; reductions in the indexation of wages; and a continuation of the frequent "mini-devaluations" of the cruzeiro so as to more than offset domestic inflation and thereby strengthen international competitiveness.[40]

---

[37]That effort is described in Lampert (1986), p. 161.

[38]The meeting was described in memorandums prepared by participants, in IMF/RD Managing Director file "Brazil 1983" (Accession 89/46, Box 2, Section 224).

[39]In the context of Brazil's persistent inflation, the cruzeiro was depreciated on a regular basis, in small steps known as "mini-devaluations." What was at issue was the prospect of a "maxi-devaluation," which at that time was judged by both the Fund and the Brazilian authorities to be unfeasible owing to the expectation that any resulting cost reductions would be offset by mandated wage increases.

[40]"Brazil—Staff Report for the 1982 Article IV Consultation, Request for Extended Arrangement, and Use of Fund Resources—First Credit Tranche," EBS/83/33 (2/11/83), Appendix IV.

While the authorities in Brasilia were negotiating with the IMF staff, officials from the central bank were negotiating with the commercial bank committee to arrange a short-term loan for $2.4 billion and a medium-term "new money" loan. By early December, most of the major bank creditors from North America, the United Kingdom, and France were on board, but a number of banks in other regions—notably Germany, Japan, and the Middle East—were reluctant to join in. The New York bankers who were assembling the package were eager for the IMF to make an appeal to their recalcitrant competitors, similar to the appeal that de Larosière had made in November on behalf of Argentina and Mexico (as described in Chapter 7 and earlier in this chapter). For the moment, however, the Managing Director was hesitant to do so, partly because the outcome of the negotiations in Brazil was still uncertain and partly because he did not wish to resort to concerted lending if a package could be completed on a voluntary basis.[41]

In addition to financing from the IMF and the commercial banks, Brazil was seeking help from bilateral official creditors. Secretly, in October and November, the U.S. Treasury had already advanced nearly $1¼ billion in short-term credits to Brazil from the Exchange Stabilization Fund. In mid-December they provided another $250 million.[42] The United States also took the lead in pushing for a $1.2 billion bridge loan through the BIS.[43] Nonetheless, until Brazil could conclude its negotiations with the Fund, the crisis atmosphere continued to worsen. When the finance ministers and central bank governors of the five largest industrial countries met on December 8 in Kronberg, Germany (see Chapter 4, p. 196), they found themselves forced to spend much of their time trying to contain the crisis in Brazil. Then on December 13, as the IMF mission in Brasilia was wrapping up its work, de Larosière cabled Günther Schleiminger, the Managing Director of the BIS, indicating that he would soon be recommending approval of Fund financial support for the Brazilian adjustment program and requesting that the BIS approve a short-term loan as a bridge to those credits. After intense negotiations at Basel among the participating central banks, the BIS loan was approved and disbursed before the end of the year.[44]

By December 20, 1982, Brazil had won tentative approval for a Fund-supported program and had obtained substantial support from other official creditors. What remained was the bank package. On that date, de Larosière, accompanied by Alexandre Kafka, the Executive Director who had represented Brazil on the Board since 1966, met with the Brazilian authorities over lunch in New York. The Brazilian team was led by Antonio Delfim Netto, the planning minister and the effective head of the economic team; Ernane Galvêas, the finance minister; and Lan-

---

[41]The dangers of relying on concerted lending are discussed in Chapter 7, pp. 313–14, and Chapter 9, pp. 406–8.

[42]The loans were kept secret until December 1, at which time they were announced with the fanfare of U.S. President Ronald W. Reagan's state visit to Brasilia.

[43] The BIS loan was augmented in January 1983 to $1.45 billion, with the participation of additional central banks. That was the figure reported in the BIS *Annual Report*.

[44]See de Larosière's cable dated December 13, 1982 in IMF/CF (C/Brazil/1710 "Exchange Transactions, 1967–1983"). The BIS loan is described in "Payments Difficulties Involving Debt to Commercial Banks," SM/83/47, p. 60.

goni. At 2:30 that afternoon, they all went to the Plaza Hotel to meet with 100 or more bankers from the 50 or so largest creditor banks. This would be the key meeting: the official credits were important, but they paled in comparison with the money that Brazil had to get from or reschedule with the commercial banks.

The Managing Director's role at the Plaza that afternoon was simply to explain the Brazilian program to the assembled bankers and to indicate that he was satisfied that the program was viable and was likely to be approved by the Executive Board within a matter of weeks. The requested bank financing was indispensable to the program, but de Larosière still did not insist, as he had the month before for Argentina and Mexico, that the banks make a firm written commitment as a precondition for his taking the arrangement to the Executive Board for approval. He would give it more time, to see if it could go through without being forced. If not, he still had the doomsday ultimatum in reserve.

For 1983, Brazil faced a total financing gap of $12.7 billion, of which the IMF would cover $2.5 billion (approximately $1.6 billion from the first year of the EFF arrangement, and most of the rest from the CFF for temporary export shortfalls). Another $2 billion would come from governments, suppliers, and other multilateral institutions; $1.5 billion from anticipated foreign direct investment; and $1 billion from miscellaneous sources. That left $5.7 billion, or nearly half the total, to come from the commercial banks. Part of that subtotal was already committed through the short-term loans arranged a few weeks earlier, but the big-ticket remainder was the request that Delfim and his colleagues now put to the banks for a "new money" syndicated loan of $4.4 billion: much bigger than the Argentine loan, and nearly as large as Mexico's.

The banks reacted to the request in a rather chaotic way. From a systemic perspective, Brazil was "too big to fail," and all of Brazil's major creditors now sensed that there was no exit from their existing commitments in the immediate future. Nonetheless, surely every banker in the room would have preferred to cut and run; not only were they seeing their credit lines to weak Latin American economies rising dangerously as a result of the two earlier cases, but also the three-month delay in carrying out policy changes in Brazil had made many of them skeptical of the authorities' ability to deliver an effective adjustment program. Furthermore, the proposed financial package was extraordinarily complex. The $4.4 billion, which became known as Project 1, was only the beginning: equally important was the need to reschedule and maintain the level of all outstanding credits. Project 2 was to reschedule the principal on a large number of medium- to long-term loans, Project 3 involved rolling over trade credits and other short-term obligations, and Project 4—which turned out to be the most difficult of all—required persuading hundreds of banks to maintain overnight interbank credit lines. It would take nearly a month (to January 17) before the banks could organize an Advisory Committee for the four projects, and several months more before they would have the reins firmly in hand.

On January 6, Galvêas and Langoni signed a Letter of Intent, formally requesting IMF support for the adjustment program that had been negotiated with Struckmeyer's team the month before. To the Brazilian authorities, the key commitment was to raise the trade surplus from less than $1 billion in 1982 to $6 billion in 1983, a goal that they intended to achieve through a combination of spending cuts (mainly reductions in subsidies) and revenue measures (notably an acceleration of the schedule for collecting income taxes, and indexing payments to inflation). To the Fund staff and to de Larosière, of equal importance was a commitment to reduce the inflation rate from 100 percent at the end of 1982 to 70 percent in 1983 and to 40 percent in 1984.[45] Without stable prices, they reasoned, the trade surplus could not be sustained. Delfim and his team did not at all disagree with the conclusion that inflation ought to be reduced, but they saw that goal as secondary to stopping the hemorrhaging of their foreign exchange reserves, and they doubted that it was possible to solve both problems in 1983.

That year, Brazil already was experiencing what would later come to be called "inertial" inflation, driven less by excess demand pressures than by structural pressures marked by inconsistent demands on the distribution of income.[46] The choice, as the authorities saw it, was either to passively accommodate the existing inflation rate through monetary expansion or to aggravate the economic downturn through severe increases in interest rates. Since they did not believe that a squeeze on aggregate demand would succeed in reducing inflation in these circumstances, the choice seemed clear. To the IMF staff, the trade-off could be improved to the extent that wage indexation could be reduced. Real wages had to be cut in order to strengthen international competitiveness and to reduce inflation, and real wages could not be reduced until indexation was curtailed. The authorities were reluctant to act very decisively on indexation, partly because they sensed that the distributional battle would simply erupt on another front[47] and partly because they knew that congress would resist.

By late January, these divergent views on the structure of the inflation problem were leading the authorities to distance themselves from the program that they had just signed and that had not yet even been considered by the Executive Board. In telephone discussions with the staff, they proposed a weakening of the agreed changes in wage policy and a corresponding relaxation of the ceiling on domestic credit expansion. Informed that these proposals would permit real wages to rise further, de Larosière issued a warning via Kafka. But when Delfim and Galvêas insisted that they could not achieve the broader policy goals without accommodating these wage pressures, the Managing Director decided to retreat on the wage issue for the time being.

A few weeks later, on February 21, 1983, the Brazilians made a bold bid to strengthen their external finances but in the process threw the program totally off

---

[45]"Brazil—Staff Report for the 1982 Article IV Consultation, Request for Extended Arrangement, and Use of Fund Resources—First Credit Tranche," EBS/83/33 (2/11/83), pp. 8 (inflation) and 23 (trade surplus).

[46]The theory of inertial inflation is an offshoot of "structuralist" or "supply-driven" theories. For a treatment of the Brazilian case and the development of structuralist theories in Latin America, see Bresser Pereira and Nakano (1987). For an alternative view that stresses the role of fiscal excesses and downplays the importance of indexation, see Cardoso (1991).

[47]Bresser Pereira and Nakano (1991) later would articulate this concern, noting for example that indexation of bonds helped prevent or at least delay dollarization in Brazil, by offering a measure of protection to those who kept their assets in local currency (p. 43).

Figure 8.4. Brazil: Exchange Rate, 1976–82

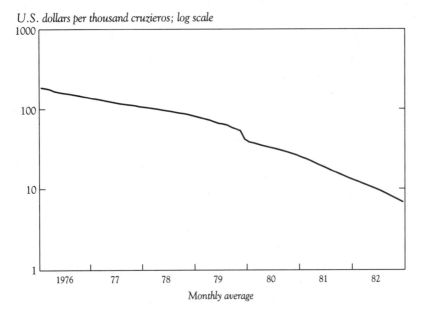

U.S. dollars per thousand cruzieros; log scale

Monthly average

course. Delfim and Galvêas had both concluded that the program was insufficient in that the exchange rate was too highly valued to promote a strengthening of the trade balance. Accordingly, without any warning to the IMF, they devalued the cruzeiro by 23 percent (Figure 8.4). Far more commonly, of course, it would have been the Fund pushing a reluctant government to take the politically risky but economically necessary course of devaluing to correct an overvalued exchange rate. In this case, however, the Fund's view was that depreciation should be limited to the initial rate of crawl to avoid an upsurge in inflationary pressures, and that the overvaluation should therefore be reduced by a more direct control over wage increases. Nonetheless, the Fund decided after the fact to support the decision, primarily because the authorities expressed a determination not to modify the wage indexation formulas. If inflation was higher than previously projected, the fixed formulas would not permit nominal wages to rise commensurately; hence real wages would decline and thus would act as an automatic stabilizer.[48] A revised Letter of Intent was quite hurriedly drafted and approved, and the program went forward to the Executive Board as planned.

---

[48]The predevaluation program envisaged that the average real wage rate would rise by 2 to 5 percent in 1983, but the real wage *bill* was expected to be reduced through a combination of staffing cuts and tighter control over promotions and productivity-related increases. The revised program envisaged that the real wage rate would decline by 2½ percent. See "Brazil—Staff Report for the 1982 Article IV Consultation, Request for Extended Arrangement, and Use of Fund Resources—First Credit Tranche," EBS/83/33 (February 11, 1983), pp. 11–13; statement by the Managing Director at EBM/83/40 (February 28, 1983), p. 18; and memorandum from the Secretary to Executive Directors, "Brazil—Extended Fund Facility" (February 25, 1983), in IMF/CF (C/Brazil/1791 "Extended Fund Facility, 1982–March 1983").

Meanwhile, the commercial bank creditors were busy assembling the financing for the four projects that the Brazilian authorities had requested at the Plaza Hotel just before Christmas. The new-money package (Project 1) was fully funded with relatively little difficulty, as were the rescheduling and trade-credit rollover commitments (Projects 2 and 3); Project 3 was actually oversubscribed by more than $1 billion by the end of February. Unfortunately, much of that effort was in vain because of the failure of Project 4. Many of the same banks who were making these other commitments were compensating by reducing their short-term credit lines. Of the $9.2 billion outstanding in overnight and other very short-term credits in June 1982, less than $6 billion remained at the beginning of February 1983.[49] The creditor banks argued that they had to retain flexibility and control over these lines, which were never intended to be a permanent source of funds, but that attitude created enormous problems all through the late months of 1982 and the first half of 1983. Problems for the Brazilian government, which had on-lent much of the money at longer maturities; problems for the adjustment program agreed with the Fund, which relied on a total financing figure from the banks; and problems for the banking system, because the Brazilian banks that were losing credit were often unable to cover their overnight commitments. Night after night, the solvency of the interbank clearing system (CHIPS) was in danger, but the committee bankers always managed, by working the phones ("dialing for dollars," in the mordant phrase of the day), to raise the money to cover each day's losses.

As the date of the Executive Board meeting (February 28) approached, the banks' portion of the financing for the program was still in doubt, and the Fund's management applied increasing pressure on reluctant banks to make the needed commitments. On February 8, Dale met with representatives of 50 creditor banks[50] in New York to stress the importance of their support. Two days later, on the evening following the Interim Committee meeting in Washington, de Larosière met in his office at the IMF with the Brazilian authorities and the governors from creditor (G-10) countries. He indicated that he was satisfied with the program and the authorities' commitment to implement it; but he was deeply concerned about the lack of firm financing commitments, and he needed their help. Finally, on February 25, four days after the devaluation and three days before the Board meeting, the Managing Director for the first time made an explicit threat to the banks, similar to his earlier action on Argentina and Mexico, that he would not recommend approval of the EFF arrangement for Brazil without a firm assurance that all four bank projects would be fully financed. The Fund's effort to distinguish the strategy for Brazil from the treatment of Mexico and Argentina had finally collapsed.

---

[49]Statement by the Deputy Managing Director at EBM/83/40 (2/28/83), p. 18.

[50]An unusual aspect of the banks' management of Brazilian debt was that there were two committees functioning in 1983: the standard Advisory Committee, comprising 13 banks, and a coordinating committee of some 50 banks. This structure was necessitated by the sheer size and complexity of the banks' exposure in Brazil.

By Monday, when the Executive Board gathered to consider Brazil's request for nearly SDR 5 billion ($5.4 billion) in financing over three years,[51] the Managing Director was able to assert his confidence that the program was viable and would be fully financed. Questions raised by Executive Directors tended to be technical rather than sweeping, and no one objected to the approval of the arrangement. Dale, who had spent many hours in contact with the banks to complete the package, explained to the Board that because of the slippages in Project 4, there was a financing gap estimated at $1–1.5 billion. The banks, however, had indicated informally that if this amount could not be raised in the interbank market, they would consider augmenting the amount of the new-money project. This was not a very firm commitment, but it reflected the reality that the banks could not offer a guarantee on the availability of short-term credit lines if those lines were to function properly as a highly liquid asset.

Unfortunately, the Fund's confidence in the banks was misplaced. Money market lines were still being withdrawn, and by the week after the Board meeting, the central bank of Brazil was frantically and unsuccessfully trying to get additional bridging loans from the U.S. Treasury and the BIS to make up for the shortfalls in Project 4. In mid-April, a major new effort was launched to stop the bleeding of the money markets, starting with a meeting in London of bankers, the Brazilian authorities, and observers from the Bank of England and the Federal Reserve. The goal now was not just to hold the line on Project 4, but to raise an additional $1.5 billion in money-market credits (from the $7.5 billion then still outstanding). That effort culminated on May 9, when the Advisory Committee banks met in New York and agreed on a slightly higher total, $9.4 billion, which finally concluded Project 4.

Although the banks seemed to have come through at last, the Brazilian authorities had not. By May 1983, just three months into the program, both domestic credit growth and the fiscal deficit were well above the targeted ceilings, and it was clear that inflation would not be reined in without additional policy actions. The drawing that Brazil could otherwise have made at the end of May (SDR 374 million) would now be denied by the Fund.

What had gone wrong? Without question, the authorities had undertaken a serious and substantial adjustment effort, after the disastrous delay in the fall of 1982. The trade surplus in the first half of 1983 was above target, and—aside from the effect of inflation on the government's domestic interest payments—the fiscal accounts had also strengthened.[52] To some extent, the program targets may have been misconceived in the first place, owing to the very poor quality of the data and to the quite different conceptions of the problems and the underlying economic

---

[51]The EFF arrangement was for SDR 4,239.375 million over three years (1983–85). In addition, Brazil requested to draw its first credit tranche (SDR 249.375 million) and to make a purchase under the CFF for SDR 466.25 million, for total scheduled drawings of SDR 4,955 million. At the time, the SDR was worth approximately $1.09.

[52]The effect of inflation on the fiscal deficit in Brazil and the adjustments that were eventually made to the fiscal performance criteria are discussed in Chapter 9.

model held by the Fund staff and the authorities. To some extent, the implementation of the program was weakened by the authorities' conviction that inflation could not (indeed, should not) be sharply reduced in the short term. And to some extent, the management of the Fund overestimated the ability of the committee banks to deliver. Even with the strongest adjustment effort, the program very likely would have gone off track owing to delays in obtaining the promised financial support from the banks. Mistakes had come from all sides, and now a fresh start would be needed in the second half of the year.

Chile

The debt crisis that hit Chile in 1983 differed in important respects from those that hit Mexico, Brazil, and Argentina. Viewed from the perspective of the end of the 1990s, this case is especially illuminating because it introduced some facets that became more generally evident in the Asian crisis of 1997–98. First, it occurred despite what appeared to be sustainable fiscal and monetary policies. Second, macroeconomic strains were compounded by a weak banking system and overly cozy relationships between banks and nonfinancial corporations. To restore international confidence, the government had to find an affordable way to prevent the collapse of the domestic financial system. Third, the crisis became very difficult to contain because of a heavy reliance on borrowing in foreign currencies. Fourth, the onset of financial strains was preceded by a period of large capital inflows that the authorities attempted to manage through selective controls.

Ten years of free-market reforms and economic success did not spare Chile from the debt crisis, but it did speed its recovery. For the last five months of 1982, Chile negotiated almost nonstop with the IMF to arrange an adjustment program and financial assistance that could get the country out of a slump that was threatening to destroy much of its banking system. The debt burden, however, was too heavy to shuck off in that little time, and the system finally collapsed in January 1983. How did Chile, without the dirigiste regimes that had ossified the economies of Mexico, Argentina, and Brazil, and without even suffering the contagion effects that had prevented many developing countries from rolling over maturing bank loans, end up in the same dinghy on the same sea?

The reform of the Chilean economy into a model of the marketplace had begun nearly a decade earlier with the most illiberal of political events: the violent overthrow of the democratically elected government of Dr. Salvador Allende in a coup led by General Augusto Pinochet on September 11, 1973. In one demonstration of the orthogonality of political freedom and economic progress, Allende's government had severely weakened the economy. Increased government spending could not be financed, protection from imports had created production bottlenecks, overvaluation of the currency had depleted foreign exchange reserves, and the economy had been sucked into a stagflationary eddy. Then, in a second, no happier, demonstration, the dictatorship that supplanted Allende used its powers to open the economy and to give market economics as free a rein as Latin America had ever seen.[53]

Well before Pinochet came to power, liberal free-market economics was taking root in Chile. The "Chicago boys" who took over the economy in the mid-1970s were not imported. They were Chileans who had learned their trade from notable Chicago-school economists, partly at the University of Chicago and partly at the Catholic University in Santiago. Across a broad part of the political spectrum, a consensus was developing that Chile could develop best by opening up the economy both internally and externally.[54]

After a brief transitional period in 1973–74 when reforms were handled by the military (under Pinochet's first minister of finance, Lorenzo Gotuzzo), the economic program was turned over to the civilian Chicago boys, beginning with Jorge Cauas, who continued and accelerated the reforms.[55] Cauas, and his successor, Sergio de Castro, implemented fiscal as well as structural reforms that kept the deficit low while generating real output growth that averaged nearly 7½ percent from 1975 to 1979. On the negative side, inflation—owing to the inertial effects from wage adjustments—remained high despite a sharp rise in unemployment, and skyrocketing imports widened the trade and current account deficits.[56]

During the initial reform phase, the IMF provided financial assistance through three different channels (Figure 8.5). A one-year stand-by arrangement was approved in January 1974, and the full SDR 79 million (50 percent of Chile's quota, or about $95 million) was drawn that year, along with a CFF purchase to cover temporary export shortfalls and a drawing on the oil facility to help with the effects of the first oil shock (approximately 25 percent of quota on each facility). A second stand-by arrangement in 1975 was largely unused, but Chile did make three further drawings on the oil facility in 1975–76 and one on the CFF in June 1976, for total net purchases over those 2½ years equivalent to SDR 382 million (242 percent of quota, or a little less than $450 million). From that point on, however, Chile had ready access to private capital markets and had no further need of official credits.[57] Virtually all of Chile's obligations to the Fund were repaid by the end of 1982.

---

[53]It must be emphasized that the point is not that political repression is either a necessary or a sufficient condition for economic reform in developing countries. The point is rather that political and economic liberalism are independent phenomena, both logically and empirically (see Chapter 1, footnote 4, p. 3).

[54]For histories and analyses of the role of the Chicago school of economic thought in Chilean politics and policy, see Barber (1995), Silva (1991), and Valdés (1995).

[55]Cauas studied at Columbia University in New York, not Chicago, but he was widely considered to be part of the same intellectual tradition.

[56]Economic developments in Chile during the 1970s are summarized in Hoelscher (1981). Corbo and Solimano (1991) provide a longer-term overview, as do Edwards and Edwards (1991).

[57]In addition, by 1977, political support for the Pinochet regime had begun to wither in the major industrial countries. The shift was especially pronounced in the United States, where the administration of President Jimmy Carter was elevating human rights to a central criterion in foreign policy and where the assassination of Allende's former minister of defense, Orlando Letelier, on the streets of Washington, D.C., in September 1976 had galvanized the opposition to Pinochet. Without U.S. support, approval of multilateral credits would have been difficult at best.

Figure 8.5. IMF Credit to Chile, 1973–89

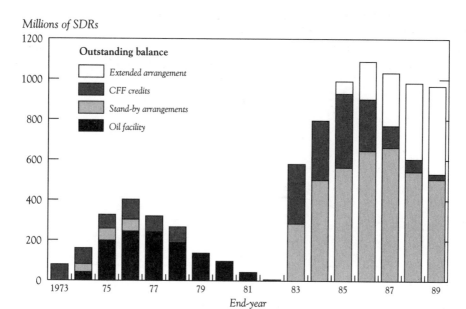

In 1978, Chile began to amass a large external debt to foreign commercial banks (Figure 8.6). Reflecting the privatization of state enterprises and a speculative boom fueled by the liberalization of domestic markets, most of this debt was owed by the private sector. In 1979–80, this borrowing was a natural byproduct of (and contributor to) economic growth, but in the next two years it was aggravated by a drop in world copper prices (Chile's principal export) and a severe recession in the domestic economy. From end-1978 to end-1981, the external debt of the private sector more than doubled, from $5.9 billion to $12.6 billion.

While these imbalances were still embryonic, the IMF monitored the situation primarily through routine annual surveillance consultations. As one such mission was preparing to go to Santiago around the middle of 1979, de Castro announced on June 29 that the crawling-peg exchange rate policy was being scrapped in favor of a firm peg against the U.S. dollar (Figure 8.7). The intent was to establish a nominal anchor for expectations and thus to put an end to the inertial force of inflation. Because the authorities had already made significant progress toward reducing inflation from the very high levels of a few years earlier (from 600 percent in 1973 to 30 percent in 1978), and because the shift was supported by a tightening of fiscal policy, both the staff and the Executive Board generally applauded the decision to tackle the problem head-on.[58] The strategy failed. Wage increases, by

---

[58]The staff report on the consultations described the decision to peg the exchange rate as a "bold step" aimed at bringing inflation into line with U.S. experience, "an expectation that does not seem unreasonable. . . ." See "Chile—Staff Report for the 1979 Article IV Consultation," SM/79/243 (September 18, 1979), p. 16. Specifically (as indicated in the mission's back-to-office

Figure 8.6. Chile: Fiscal Deficit and External Debt, 1970–83

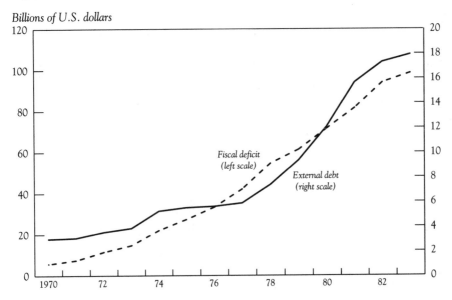

Billions of U.S. dollars

Sources: IMF, *IFS*; and World Bank, *World Development Indicators*.

law, were required to equal or exceed past inflation, so both actual and expected inflation came down only very slowly. The effect therefore was a steady rise of domestic costs relative to those abroad, and a gradual and ultimately severe loss of international competitiveness.[59] For the next three years, the need to restore the viability of exchange rate policy would be one of the central issues facing Chile and the IMF.

As costs rose, the current account deficit widened further, but the authorities treated it with what they thought was benign neglect. Their view was a precursor of what would later come to be known as the "Lawson doctrine," that a current account deficit was not a problem for macroeconomic policy as long as it resulted

---

report to management), the expectation was that by late 1979, inflation in Chile would fall from a rate of about 30 percent a year to about half that rate. See memorandum from Beza to the Managing Director (August 28, 1979), in IMF/RD Managing Director file "Western Hemisphere" (Accession 87/27, Box 15, Section 535). At the time, U.S. inflation was not much below 15 percent. At the Executive Board meeting concluding the consultations on November 16, 1979, the Managing Director summed up the discussion as follows: "Directors drew attention to the marked reduction in the rate of inflation from the high level reached during the mid-seventies. . . . [F]iscal and monetary management appeared to be consistent with the achievement of the deceleration of inflation that was being sought, and it was noted that the new exchange rate policy seemed to be appropriately geared to this objective." Minutes of EBM/79/176 (November 16, 1979), p. 23.

[59]The inflation gap was further exacerbated by the success of the U.S. authorities in reducing that country's inflation rate, beginning in the fourth quarter of 1979.

Figure 8.7. Chile: Exchange Rate, 1976–83

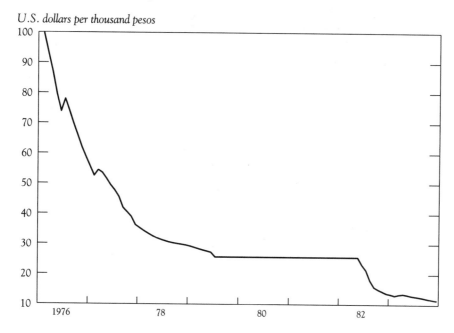

U.S. dollars per thousand pesos

from the actions of the private sector.[60] The Fund staff did not dispute the logic of this view, but they were less convinced than the authorities that government borrowing was under control. The Director of the Western Hemisphere Department, Walter Robichek, warned Chile of impending debt difficulties in a speech in Santiago in January 1980. What mattered, he argued, was not the current account deficit—which was still manageable at that time—but the level of public sector borrowing from private international creditors, in relation to various indicators. By that measure, he placed Chile in a group of potential problem countries in the region.[61]

An additional problem with applying the Lawson doctrine to Chile was that a growing portion of the financing of the deficit was not conducted at "arm's length," owing to the close ownership and management linkages between banks and enter-

---

[60]In a meeting with the Managing Director during the 1981 Annual Meetings, as recorded by the Fund staff, "the Chilean representatives replied that they were not [concerned about the current account deficit], because this deficit reflected exclusively the saving/investment gap of the private sector. This gap was by definition self-adjusting. . . ." See minutes of the meeting, in staff file, "Chile, August 1980 to March 1982, L.M. Koenig" in IMF/RD Western Hemisphere Department files (Accession 84/96, Box 5, Section 76). Nigel Lawson—Chancellor of the Exchequer in the United Kingdom, 1983–89—enunciated the doctrine in a speech at the Annual Meetings in 1988; see Chapter 1, p. 37.

[61]Speech by E. Walter Robichek, in IMF/RD Managing Director file, "'Some Reflections About External Public Debt Management,' Central Bank of Chile Seminar, January 21–22, 1980" (Accession 84/151, Box 3, Section 374). The other countries identified in the speech as possible problems were Bolivia, Brazil, Ecuador, Mexico, Panama, Peru, and Venezuela.

prises. In December 1979, the Fund responded to a request by the central bank for a technical assistance mission to review the functioning of the Chilean financial system. While praising the rapid transformation of the system into a dynamic private sector, the mission (headed by Vicente Galbis, Senior Economist in the Central Banking Service) also warned about the dangers of inadequate regulation over the interlocking directorates that had taken over both the banks and many nonfinancial enterprises. It would be necessary, the mission concluded, to correct the "emerging pattern of abuses" in order to limit the risk of bank failures and to protect depositors.[62] Other than these warnings, the sanguine view was generally endorsed by the Fund, and no other serious concerns were expressed about the deteriorating outlook until well into 1982.[63]

Toward the end of 1981, a severe recession set in, responding to weakness in copper prices, a reversal of the domestic investment boom under the pressure of high world interest rates and the overvalued exchange rate, and very high domestic real interest rates aimed at stemming the acceleration of capital flight. By the end of that year, growth had halted, the unemployment rate had risen to 13½ percent, and the current account deficit for the year had approached 15 percent of GDP. Notwithstanding the slowdown in both growth and inflation, interest rates had continued to rise and reached annual rates of 63 percent for loans. Commercial banks were badly overextended with loans that were increasingly difficult for the borrowers to service, and the central bank was being increasingly forced to provide emergency credits to prevent banks from failing.

In April 1982, Koenig and her staff team arrived in Santiago just as the economic strategy of the government was beginning to unravel. The first week of discussions was fairly routine, but on April 22 Pinochet announced a cabinet shuffle aimed in part at resuscitating the economy and restoring confidence in the peso. The Chicago boys would remain in charge, but with their most prominent member—Finance Minister de Castro—replaced by a close associate, Sergio de

---

[62]The lack of adequate regulation is discussed on p. 5 of the report, which was submitted to the authorities in draft form in May 1980 and in final form in October. The quoted phrase is from the debriefing memo to the Managing Director (December 28, 1979). Both documents are in the files of the Monetary and Exchange Affairs Department, IMF/RD Monetary and Exchange Affairs Department file "Chile: Financial Sector Survey" (Accession 83/62, Section FC59/FR).

[63]There was no full Article IV consultation in 1981, but a staff team headed by Linda M. Koenig (Assistant Director, Western Hemisphere Department) visited Santiago in March to review developments since the August 1980 mission and drew generally positive conclusions. In addition to reviewing exchange rate policy with the authorities, the staff visited several private companies that produced goods for export or in competition with imports. The managers of those firms reported that the hard-currency policy had resulted in some loss of profits, but they all viewed the policy positively and regarded it as both viable and necessary for inflation control. Memorandum of March 24, 1981, from Koenig to the Managing Director; in IMF/RD Western Hemisphere Department file, "Chile—January–December 1981" (Accession 84/70, Box 1, Section 74). Also see Hoelscher (1981), for a statement of the Fund's optimism at that time. Harberger (1985) explains the positive effects of the fixed exchange rate in this period as resulting from the stabilization of prices and the consequent rise in production. Edwards (1985) focuses more on the capital inflows that followed the exchange rate peg, and he documents the deterioration that set in around mid-1981.

la Cuadra. The intention of the new team was to keep the exchange rate fixed at 39 pesos per U.S. dollar, as it had been for nearly three years, and the IMF staff again responded favorably (though only after a difficult internal debate).[64] The new authorities recognized, however, that they had to quell the mounting speculation of an impending devaluation and to take action to protect the economy against the high and still-rising cost of international bank loans and the ongoing rapid loss of foreign exchange reserves. Toward the end of the mission, therefore, they approached Koenig to express interest in a CFF drawing related to the depressed level of world copper prices, and possibly a stand-by arrangement as well.

Less than a month later, the mission team returned to Chile to complete the Article IV discussions and to negotiate a program in support of the requested stand-by arrangement. The authorities proposed, and the staff agreed, to base the program on the assumption that the exchange rate would remain fixed at its current level. Pinochet had committed himself publicly to maintain the fixed exchange rate, and the cabinet was eager to make the promise good if at all possible. The cost imbalance that was causing the external disequilibrium would thus have to be eliminated through a cut in nominal wages.

On June 4, 1982, the mission concluded its work in Santiago, and by the following Thursday, June 10, the agreed Letter of Intent for the program was on the Managing Director's desk for his approval. Meanwhile, however, the cabinet in Chile was finding itself unable to agree on the proposed wage cut, without which—as they clearly understood—the exchange rate could not be maintained. By the weekend, they gave up: the wage cut was politically unfeasible, and devaluation was inevitable.

On Sunday evening, June 13, Minister of Economy Luis Francisco Danus announced that the peso would be immediately devalued to 46 pesos a dollar, and that it would then be depreciated at a fixed pace vis-à-vis a basket of the currencies of the G-5 countries. The next day, the government declared an end to the formal indexation of wages and announced a new round of privatization of state enterprises. At the same time, de la Cuadra telephoned the IMF to offer to come to Washington to renegotiate the stand-by arrangement on the basis of the new package of policies.

This sudden policy shift generated some additional intense debate within the IMF staff. With hindsight, the new regime was clearly more realistic than the old, but it was not clear that the exchange rate was now on a sustainable path. Despite some misgivings, the Washington meetings of the Chilean authorities (led by de la Cuadra and Miguel Kast, the president of the central bank) with the staff and with the Managing Director generated agreement on a new Letter of Intent by the beginning of July. A staff report was issued to Executive Directors on July 26, and a Board meeting was scheduled for August 23. This schedule, however, would

---

[64]See p. 5 of memorandum from Koenig to the Managing Director (May 5, 1982); in IMF/RD Western Hemisphere Department file "Chile, January 1982–December 1982" (Accession 85/19, Box 1, Section 393).

soon be run over by the continuing turbulence in financial markets and by the inability of the authorities to formulate a sustainable policy strategy.

The crawling peg of the Chilean peso collapsed on August 5, 1982, just 52 days
after its initiation and just 8 days before Mexico's revelation that it could no longer
service its foreign debts. Faced with plummeting foreign exchange reserves, unemployment rising to 20 percent, and a run on domestic bank deposits, the authorities were forced to allow the exchange rate to float. At the Fund, it was obvious
that the Board meeting could not go forward on August 23 as planned, and a new
mission—headed by Jan van Houten (Chief of the Pacific Division of the Western
Hemisphere Department)—was sent immediately to Santiago to assess the
situation.

The continuation of currency depreciation, which coincided with a crumbling
of demand for domestic output, put unbearable pressure on the already weak
Chilean banking system. Domestic firms had undertaken loan commitments denominated in U.S. dollars when the exchange rate was pegged at 39 pesos to the
dollar. By August, they were paying well over 50 pesos per dollar to service those
debts, and by September the cost would rise above 60. Many firms were unable to
service their debts to domestic banks, which in turn could service their debts to
foreign banks only by borrowing still more dollars. The government provided some
help by agreeing in August to establish a preferential exchange rate to subsidize the
servicing of existing obligations, but the authorities—and the IMF staff—were
concerned that further subsidies would seriously weaken fiscal stability and could
create expectations of a massive bailout. In the wake of the Mexican crisis, how
much longer would the banks be willing to lend to Chile, knowing that the dollars
were needed just to service the already outstanding loans?

The August mission resulted in agreement that the economic program to support the requested stand-by arrangement would have to be renegotiated for a second time, and the authorities requested that a mission be scheduled for that purpose after the Annual Meetings in Toronto. But Chile's turbulence was only just
beginning. On August 27, Pinochet once again replaced his cabinet; de la Cuadra's
five-month tenure as finance minister was ended, and he was replaced a few days
later by Rolf Lüders (also Chicago-trained). Lüders immediately headed for
Toronto, where he met with de Larosière during the Annual Meetings, explained
his intentions for stabilizing and reviving the economy, and won agreement for a
late-September negotiating mission.

Van Houten and his team arrived in Santiago on September 27, 1982, to resume
negotiations, where they found the authorities to be struggling to regain control
over the exchange rate following a depreciation of some 30 percent since the rate
had been allowed to float the month before.[65] On September 29, Lüders intro-

---

[65]For a detailed account of exchange rate developments during this period, see Meller (1992),
pp. 41–45. Meller infers from data on changes in foreign exchange reserves that the float was less
clean than was claimed by the authorities, especially in September. He cites rather larger percentage values for the depreciation of the peso, because he calculates the changes in local currency terms rather than in terms of dollars.

duced yet another deeply flawed policy regime, this time in the form of a real-exchange-rate rule. That is, the exchange rate would henceforth be controlled to depreciate daily according to the difference between the domestic CPI inflation rate and an assumed rate for foreign inflation, so as to keep the real exchange rate roughly constant.[66] The preferential exchange rate was to be continued for a few months, but—with the urging of the IMF staff, who observed that this constituted a multiple currency practice subject to Fund jurisdiction—the authorities agreed to terminate it by the end of the year.

When the mission finished its work on October 11, the authorities and the staff had agreed on a revised Letter of Intent. The Managing Director approved the program the following week, and a meeting of the Executive Board was scheduled for December 17. This schedule, like its predecessors, would again turn out to be overly ambitious. This time the fatal flaw was the government's decision to continue subsidizing the servicing of foreign debts, although a decision to terminate the subsidy might well have made debt servicing impossibly expensive for many companies and thus precipitated an even worse crisis.

Remarkably, notwithstanding the refusal of international banks to roll over credits to Mexico, Argentina, or Brazil, Chile was able (albeit not without difficulty) to persuade most banks to maintain lines of credit throughout the second half of 1982. Maintaining these lines, however, was not enough to enable firms to stay current without a subsidy.[67] Meanwhile, the only way the government could balance its books while subsidizing the preferential exchange rate was to expand domestic credit through the central bank. By the end of November, it was clear that the programmed ceiling on domestic credit expansion could not be met, and the staff informed the Managing Director that the program would be off track even before it was approved. De Larosière had no choice but to postpone the Board meeting to January 10, 1983, to give the authorities in Santiago time to get monetary growth back under control.[68]

During December 1982, the authorities made some progress in calming the markets and limiting their reserve losses. In mid-December, Carlos Cáceres, the president of the central bank, went to Washington to explain to de Larosière and the staff the measures they were taking to reduce credit expansion, and to get agreement on the degree of progress that would be needed for the Managing Director to recommend approval of the program to the Executive Board. On the basis of these assurances, the Executive Board met on Monday, January 10, 1983, and

---

[66]For a general discussion of the Fund's advocacy and critique of such rules, see Chapter 13, p. 573.

[67]Despite the prevailing free-market philosophy, the government supported the private sector in numerous ways, including serving as agent in debt negotiations with foreign creditors. See Ffrench-Davis (1991) for a discussion.

[68]The three-week delay would avoid the necessity of permitting the first drawing under the stand-by arrangement to take place in December, when the credit ceiling would not be met. If the program were approved in January, the end-year excess would not constitute a violation of the agreement, and—as long as the path of credit growth was on target by January—the authorities would have three months (until end-March) to regain control of the level.

approved a 24-month stand-by arrangement in the amount of SDR 500 million (154 percent of Chile's quota; $550 million) and a CFF drawing for SDR 295 million (91 percent of quota, or $325 million). The CFF drawing plus SDR 122 million under the stand-by arrangement would be available immediately, and the rest would be phased in the usual manner, subject to Chile's observance of the program criteria.[69]

Three days after the Board meeting, the debt crisis came to Chile. The authorities had been keeping the banking system barely afloat, hoping that the IMF's approval of the program would quickly restore confidence enough to stem capital flight and attract additional bank loans from abroad. With an earlier start on policy reform, the strategy might have worked, but the cumulative effect of eight months of ineffective backfilling could not be made up overnight. On January 13, Cáceres informed van Houten by telephone that they were declaring a bank holiday on the 14th, liquidating three major banks, and intervening in the operations of five others. The program was dead, and economic and financial recovery would require a major overhaul in government policies.[70]

One priority for the authorities after January 13 was to open a dialogue with the commercial bank creditors. Neither the private nor the public sector had the resources to service, much less to repay, the bank loans that were coming due. The government nonetheless undertook to guarantee the liabilities of the problem banks and to remain current on all public sector interest payments. Initially, the authorities announced that the government-owned Banco del Estado would assume the debts of the five banks in which they had intervened (up to a specified limit), but not those of the other three that they had closed. That policy contributed to a panic among foreign creditors, and in late January the guarantee was extended to the liabilities of the closed banks as well.

The foreign bank creditors recognized the difficulty, but they also realized that they had badly overestimated Chile's capacity to implement sound economic policies. Most of their loans were to the private sector, and they had been implicitly assuming that the authorities either would keep economic performance strong enough to enable the private banks to meet the payments or would bail out the problem debtors (as they had to some extent, through the preferential exchange rate). Analysis of "country risk" had not been a priority for the international banks. It was now, but the realization had come too late for a smooth recovery. The banks had no choice but to reschedule, and at the end of January they agreed to roll over the principal on their loans for 90 days while negotiating a more permanent settlement.

The other priority, which also foreshadowed crisis management of the following decade, was to obtain the assistance of the IMF and the World Bank in stanching the outflow of capital. Since most of the debts to foreign bank creditors were owed by private firms, many of which were in serious financial difficulties, the govern-

---

[69]Minutes of EBM/83/8 (January 10, 1983).

[70]For a detailed analysis of the crisis, see Larrain (1989). For an overview of the role of banks in the crisis, see Rojas-Suárez and Weisbrod (1995), Chapter III (and see references therein for further details).

ment gave some thought in January to guaranteeing all such debts. The Fund strongly discouraged them from that approach, and they quickly abandoned it. Instead, the Fund offered to help determine which firms were able to pay and which were not, so as to ensure that defaults could be contained and not generalized; and to renegotiate the program so as to ensure that the adjustment effort was sufficient to restore viability to the economy.

Van Houten took another staff mission to Santiago in late January and confirmed that the whole program would have to be renegotiated in light of the banking crisis. Meeting the end-March criteria for the next drawing under the stand-by arrangement was completely unrealistic (the ceiling on domestic credit expansion was already exceeded), and there was no real possibility of getting back on track without a much greater effort to strengthen the government's fiscal position. On January 27, Lüders and Cáceres met in Washington with de Larosière, who conveyed that message to them, along with his desire to help them reshape economic policy. From there, the officials went to New York for an initial meeting with the newly formed Advisory Committee of the commercial banks (chaired by Manufacturers' Hanover Trust).

Progress at this stage was agonizingly slow, because Chile was caught in a sequencing dilemma: without new money from the banks, the external financing gap could not be closed, and therefore there could be no Fund-supported adjustment program; but without a program, the banks were unwilling to commit themselves to an agreement. The Fund could have tried to impose a concerted-lending solution similar to those already in place for Mexico and Argentina, but—as with Brazil at the same time—both the Managing Director and the authorities preferred to try first for a market-based solution. In this instance, the strategy met with greater success.

Pinochet once again lost patience with his economic team, and on February 14 he replaced Lüders with Cáceres as finance minister. By the end of February, Cáceres had met with the IMF staff in Santiago and with the banks' Advisory Committee in New York. In March, van Houten led a new negotiating mission to Chile, though with a new mandate. Rather than attempting to resuscitate the stand-by arrangement immediately, the Fund staff were to negotiate a "shadow program" that would enable the government to convince the banks that their policies deserved financial support.

The mission completed its work on March 20, and on the 22nd Cáceres announced an emergency economic program. The key measures included an accelerated depreciation rate for the currency (while retaining the basic elements of the real-exchange-rate rule),[71] a rescheduling of the bank debts of private enterprises, a tightening of foreign exchange controls, and several fiscal measures including a

---

[71]Previously, the daily rate of depreciation had been based on the inflation rate of the CPI for the previous month, less 1 percent a month. That adjustment, which was intended to approximate the rate of foreign (i.e., U.S.) inflation, was eliminated as of March 23. U.S. inflation had averaged 11.7 percent a year for 1979–81 but had dropped to 6.2 percent in 1982 and would fall further to 3.2 percent in 1983. The policy shift (raising the depreciation rate by 1 percent a month) thus was from overcorrecting to undercorrecting for U.S. inflation.

temporary surcharge on import tariffs. The goal of this package was to revive economic growth and the financial system and to get the economy in line with the original targets of the adjustment program by end-September: an ambitious goal, but no more than was needed to restore confidence. From March to September, reserves would be lower and net domestic assets would be higher than programmed, reflecting the lower level of available financing.

Shortly after the emergency program was announced, the authorities reached agreement in principle with the banks' Advisory Committee on a package for the remainder of 1983. That package was to include $1.3 billion in "new money" as well as a rescheduling of principal payments on medium- and long-term official debts. Private sector debts to foreign banks, however, were omitted from the agreement: they could be renegotiated individually, but no official guarantee was to be given. The banks also asked the Fund to grant a waiver so that the stand-by arrangement could be reactivated before end-September if Chile established a track record by sticking with the shadow program through June. The Fund staff expressed reservations about weakening the requirements for its loans, and the Managing Director agreed only to propose a waiver *after* the banks had completed their own agreement and had made their initial disbursement. In addition, over the next month, de Larosière, with the assistance of U.S. officials, quietly arranged for a bridge loan through the BIS to prevent Chile's reserve levels from falling to an uncomfortably low level during this initial adjustment phase. He and the staff also met frequently with the principal bankers on the Advisory Committee to help explain the details of the shadow program and the necessity for the level of financing that was being asked. Some of the banks were balking at signing an agreement without a guarantee on corporate sector debts, but the Managing Director insisted to the banks that the authorities were right in refusing to bail out weak borrowers.

In July 1983, van Houten went once more to Santiago to review developments and found that Chile had met the fiscal and monetary targets set under the shadow program. Two days after he returned to Washington with this favorable report (the substance of which the Managing Director conveyed to the bank creditors), the banks agreed to sign the proposed loan agreement. Finally, on July 27, the Executive Board met to approve the waivers and to release both the delayed April drawing and the originally scheduled August drawing;[72] on July 28, the bank creditors formally signed their agreement. In just over six months, Chile had climbed from the depths of one of its greatest financial crises to the verge of financial stability. The next two years would show how precarious the footing was on that ledge, but Chile's initial debt crisis had been resolved.

References

Bank for International Settlements, 1983, *Annual Report, 1982–83* (Basel: BIS).

---

[72]Minutes of EBM/83/112 (July 27, 1983).

Barber, William J., 1995, "Chile con Chicago: A Review Essay," *Journal of Economic Literature*, Vol. 33 (December), pp. 1941–49.

Boughton, James M., 1984, "A Review of the External Positions of the Oil-Importing Developing Countries and Their Relationship to the World Oil Market," *Natural Resources Forum*, Vol. 8 (January), pp. 25–36.

Brainard, Lawrence J., 1981, "Polen und der Internationale Währungsfonds" ["Poland and the IMF"], *Neue Zürcher Zeitung* (March 26), p. 10.

Bresser Pereira, Luiz Carlos, and Yoshiaki Nakano, 1991, "Hyperinflation and Stabilization in Brazil: The First Collor Plan," in *Economic Problems of the 1990s: Europe, the Developing Countries, and the United States*, ed. by Paul Davidson and Jan Kregel (London: Edward Elgar).

———, 1987, *The Theory of Inertial Inflation: The Foundation of Economic Reform in Brazil and Argentina* (Boulder, Colorado: Lynne Rienner Publishers).

Calvo, Guillermo A., 1986, "Fractured Liberalism: Argentina Under Martinez de Hoz," *Economic Development and Cultural Change*, Vol. 34 (April), pp. 511–33.

Cardoso, Eliana, 1991, "From Inertia to Megainflation: Brazil in the 1980s," with Comments by Persio Arida and Juan Carlos de Pablo, in *Lessons of Economic Stabilization and Its Aftermath*, ed. by Michael Bruno and others (Cambridge, Massachusetts: MIT Press), pp. 143–89.

Corbo, Vittoria, and Andrés Solimano, 1991, "Chile's Experience with Stabilization Revisited," with Comments by Sebastian Edwards and Leonardo Leiderman, in *Lessons of Economic Stabilization and Its Aftermath*, ed. by Michael Bruno and others (Cambridge, Massachusetts: MIT Press), pp. 57–101.

Edwards, Sebastian, 1985, "Stabilization with Liberalization: An Evaluation of Ten Years of Chile's Experiment with Free-Market Policies, 1973–1983," *Economic Development and Cultural Change*, Vol. 33 (January), pp. 223–54.

———, and Alexandra Cox Edwards, 1991, *Monetarism and Liberalization: The Chilean Experiment, with a New Afterword* (Chicago, Illinois: University of Chicago Press).

Eichler, Gabriel, 1986, "The Debt Crisis: A Schematic View of Rescheduling in Eastern Europe," in *East European Economies: Slow Growth in the 1980's*, Vol. 2, *Foreign Trade and International Finance*, Selected Papers Submitted to the Joint Economic Committee, Congress of the United States, March 28, pp. 192–209.

Ffrench-Davis, Ricardo, 1991, "The Foreign Debt Crisis and Adjustment in Chile: 1976–86," in *Adjustment and Liberalization in the Third World*, ed. by H.W. Singer, Neelambar Hatti, and Rameshwar Tandon, New World Order Series, Vol. 12 (New Delhi: Indus), pp. 677–705.

Gold, Joseph, 1988, "Mexico and the Development of the Practice of the International Monetary Fund," *World Development*, Vol. 16, No. 10, pp. 1127–42.

Goldsbrough, David, and Iqbal Zaidi, 1986, "Transmission of Economic Influences from Industrial to Developing Countries," *Staff Studies for the World Economic Outlook* (IMF World Economic and Financial Surveys), pp. 150–95.

Harberger, Arnold C., 1985, "Observations on the Chilean Economy, 1973–1983," *Economic Development and Cultural Change*, Vol. 33 (April), pp. 451–62.

Hoelscher, David, 1981, "Chile's Economic Recovery Reflects a Merging of Both Demand- and Supply-Oriented Policies," *IMF Survey*, October 26, pp. 338–40.

Howe, Geoffrey, Sir, 1994, *Conflict of Loyalty* (New York: St. Martin's Press).

Lampert, Hope, 1986, *Behind Closed Doors: Wheeling and Dealing in the Banking World* (New York: Atheneum).

Larrain, Mauricio, 1989, "How the 1981–83 Chilean Banking Crisis Was Handled," World Bank Policy, Planning, and Research Working Paper No. WPS 300 (December).

Meller, Patricio, 1992, *Adjustment and Equity in Chile* (Paris: OECD).

Rojas-Suárez, Liliana, and Steven R. Weisbrod, 1995, *Financial Fragilities in Latin America: The 1980s and 1990s*, IMF Occasional Paper No. 132 (Washington: International Monetary Fund).

Silva, Patricio, 1991, "Technocrats and Politics in Chile: From the Chicago Boys to the CIEPLAN Monks," *Journal of Latin American Studies*, Vol. 23, Pt. 2 (May), pp. 385–410.

Spindler, J. Andrew, 1984, *The Politics of International Credit: Private Finance and Foreign Policy in Germany and Japan* (Washington: Brookings Institution).

Stiles, Kendall W., 1987, "Argentina's Bargaining with the IMF," *Journal of Interamerican Studies and World Affairs*, Vol. 29 (Fall), pp. 55–85.

Tagliabue, John, 1982, "Payments Reported by Poland," *New York Times* (January 13), pp. D1, D19.

Valdés, Juan Gabriel, 1995, *Pinochet's Economists: The Chicago School of Economics in Chile* (Cambridge: Cambridge University Press).

9

Containing the Crisis, 1983–85

W hen the debt crisis hit in 1982, the IMF worked alongside the authorities of major creditor and debtor countries, together with the leading commercial banks, to avert a possibly epic financial catastrophe. As recounted in the preceding chapters, the initial containment of the crisis was achieved through a combination of actions designed to prevent a collapse of the international banking system, assist countries in correcting macroeconomic policies to restore financial and economic viability, and thereby lay the foundation for sustainable economic growth and a restoration of normal financial relationships.

In a few cases, notably Chile, the crisis was thus largely passed. In others, however, the imbalances were so severe that several more years would be required to correct them. These cases included the three largest countries in Latin America: Mexico, Brazil, and Argentina. Until those three economies could recover, the debt crisis would continue to pose a systemic threat. This chapter details the struggles undertaken to keep that threat at bay during the first three years.

Mexico

Without doubt, Mexico was an early success case. By March 1983, the EFF-supported adjustment program was on track, the balance of payments was strengthening, and bank financing had been regularized through the signing of a concerted-lending agreement with over 500 banks (see Chapter 7). Barring further disasters, Finance Minister Jesus Silva Herzog and his team had bought enough time and had obtained enough outside support to bring the economy back from the brink. Also without doubt, however, this success was as fragile as glass. Ever more arduous negotiations would have to be completed before victory could be declared for the EFF arrangement and the Mexican economic recovery.

Rescheduling Official Credits

Once the bank package had been completed in March 1983, the next step was to secure similar financial relief from official creditors. Mexico did not want to formally request a rescheduling of official credits from the Paris Club, an avenue that heretofore had been crossed mainly by low-income countries that lacked access to commercial credits.[1] Having little alternative, however, the government requested that its official creditors consider a rescheduling confidentially, outside the formal auspices of the Paris Club, but otherwise in the usual manner. Accordingly, the creditor group met during June 20–23, 1983, at the OECD headquarters in Paris, under the chairmanship of Michel Camdessus (who also chaired the Paris Club). Mexico's chief debt negotiator, Angel Gurria, headed the official delegation, and several IMF staff—including Claudio Loser (Chief of the Stand-by Operations Division, Exchange and Trade Relations Department) and Joaquín Pujol (Chief of the Mexico/Latin Caribbean Division, Western Hemisphere Department)—participated in the meeting. The staff gave detailed explanations of the progress being made under the EFF arrangement, and the discussions covered a range of complex issues such as the treatment of officially guaranteed debts of the private sector. In the end, the 15 creditor countries agreed to reschedule approximately $1.2 billion in officially guaranteed private sector debts over a six-year period.[2] The main effect of this non–Paris Club deal, however, was not so much to strengthen Mexico's reserves as to lengthen the maturity of official credits, since it largely enabled Mexico to repay its bridge loan from the BIS (see Chapter 7) on time in August 1983.

Rescheduling Debts of the Private Sector

A simmering concern among Mexico's commercial bank creditors was the handling of private sector debts, a substantial portion of which was in arrears. Throughout the months of negotiations over the initial bank package, the banks and some official agencies had pressured the Mexican government to assume these debts. Supported by the Fund, Mexico had refused,[3] but it had compromised by introducing a program to cover private firms' foreign exchange losses. Known as the FICORCA scheme,[4] this program provided for firms to pay dollar-denominated commercial debts in pesos to the central bank. The creditor was required to reschedule the debts over several years, and the central bank would then guarantee to pay the creditor in dollars. Between March and November 1983, close to $12 billion in private sector debts were rescheduled under this program. The Fund staff initially were skeptical as to whether FICORCA was affordable without undermining the adjustment program,[5] but they eventually accepted it as a positive

---

[1]At the time, the only Latin American countries that had rescheduled debts through the Paris Club had been Chile in 1975, Peru in 1978, and Costa Rica in January 1983. For details, see Dillon and others (1985), Table 4. For background on the Paris Club and its relationship with the Fund, see Chapter 20.

[2]For further information, see Dillon and others (1985) and Kuhn and Guzman (1990).

[3]The assumption of private sector debts by the government would have counted toward the ceiling on official external debt under the EFF arrangement. Any large-scale assumption would have made it impossible to meet the program criterion.

[4]FICORCA is the acronym in Spanish for the "foreign exchange risk coverage trust fund."

[5]"Briefing for Mission to Mexico" (March 2, 1983), p. 6; in IMF/CF (C/Mexico/810 "Mission—Pujol and Staff, March 1983").

approach. FICORCA then became the prototype for similar schemes elsewhere, including in the aftermath to the Asian crisis of 1997–98.

Promoting Trade Liberalization

With the various financial arrangements in place, the Managing Director (Jacques de Larosière) turned his attention in mid-1983 to the longer-run issue of strengthening Mexico's international trade. The initial policy corrections had strengthened the trade balance by nearly $18 billion, but primarily through import compression. Exports (measured in dollars) had risen by 11 percent ($2 billion) from 1981 to 1983, while imports had fallen by two-thirds ($16 billion). To achieve better balance and longer-lasting relief, in August 1983 de Larosière proposed talks aimed at increasing Mexico's access to industrial country markets in exchange for trade liberalization by Mexico. Specifically, over lunch with Silva Herzog on August 29, he suggested that meetings be set up with officials from the major industrial countries during or shortly after the forthcoming Fund-Bank Annual Meetings, to discuss market access and the reduction of trade barriers. Silva Herzog quickly obtained the support of President de la Madrid for at least a general shift toward trade liberalization, and a Fund staff team visited Mexico City in September to press the initiative with trade officials. For the moment, those officials preferred to proceed deliberately, and primarily through quiet bilateral contacts. Nonetheless, de Larosière and Silva Herzog, with support from the World Bank, continued to make the case, and in 1986 Mexico acceded to membership in the GATT.[6]

1984 Adjustment Program

The second year of Mexico's adjustment program was negotiated in the course of two missions in the fall of 1983, headed by Pujol. Overall, the negotiations progressed smoothly. Differences in view regarding the fiscal stance and interest rate policy were largely technical and easily resolved. The Mexican authorities were confident that the requisite additional external financing could be obtained through a new rescheduling agreement with commercial bank creditors without the Fund having to impose concerted lending as a precondition for approval of the arrangement; they were, however, prepared to consent to such a precondition if the Managing Director deemed it necessary.[7] The bone of contention was wage

---

[6]On de Larosière's lunch meeting with Silva Herzog, see memorandum from C. David Finch (Director of the Exchange and Trade Relations Department) to the Managing Director (August 26, 1983), in IMF/RD Deputy Managing Director file "Mexico 1983 (2)—May–December" (Accession 85/99, Box 4, Section 229). On de la Madrid's initial support and on the September mission, see memorandum from Shailendra J. Anjaria (Chief of the Trade and Payments Division, Exchange and Trade Relations Department) to Finch (September 15, 1983), in IMF/CF (C/Mexico/810). On the World Bank's involvement, starting in 1984, see Urzúa (1997), pp. 79–81.

[7]Memorandum to management from Loser and Pujol (December 11, 1983), p. 2; in IMF/RD Deputy Managing Director file "Mexico 1983 (2)—May–December" (Accession 85/99, Box 4, Section 229).

policy. The authorities planned to raise the minimum wage by 30 percent around the beginning of 1983 and by another 10 percent in mid-1984. The staff concluded that the initial increase would be excessive and would risk fueling expectations of continuing inflation. That view was also conveyed to Silva Herzog and his team by the Managing Director, at a lunch that he hosted at the Fund in early December, while the staff mission was conducting technical negotiations in Mexico City. These warnings were in vain, however, as the authorities went ahead with the planned raise at the end of the year.

Notwithstanding the differences over wage policy, the Letter of Intent specifying the policy program for 1984 was agreed upon at the conclusion of the second staff mission on December 9, 1983. The staff report gave Mexico high marks, both for performance under the first year of the program and for the strength of the 1984 program. It expressed caution regarding the recent wage adjustment, which was viewed as leaving little margin for further increases; and about contingency funds in the budget, which, if mobilized, could destabilize fiscal policy. It also noted that Mexico should introduce additional measures to reduce trade and payments restrictions, and that the authorities would need the "continued cooperation of the international financial community" to be able to service its external debts.[8] These admonitions, however, did not detract from the Fund's strong support for Mexico's adjustment effort at the beginning of 1984.[9] The Executive Board met on March 2 and approved the continuation of the arrangement without difficulty.

1984 Commercial Bank Package

Financing Mexico's balance of payments deficit for 1984 required a further agreement with commercial bank creditors. Consideration of this second package began in earnest at a New York meeting of the Advisory Committee on December

---

[8]"Mexico—Extended Arrangement—Program for the Second Year," EBS/84/1, Sup. 1 (January 30, 1984).

[9]When the Eighth General Review of Quotas took effect at the end of November 1983, Mexico's quota rose from SDR 802.5 million to SDR 1,165.5 million. The annual access limit under the Enlarged Access Policy was reduced on January 6, 1984, from 150 percent of quota to 102 percent, with a provision that countries demonstrating both a serious balance of payments need and a strong adjustment program could be granted access up to 125 percent of quota. (For a discussion of the evolution of Fund policy on access limits, see Chapter 17.) That same day, Mexico requested that the EFF arrangement be augmented to reflect the quota increase. That is, rather than the planned four drawings totaling SDR 1.2 billion (150 percent of the old quota but just over 102 percent of the new), the authorities requested that they be allowed to draw 125 percent of the new quota (close to SDR 1.5 billion). The staff did not consider that the "need" test could be met, but they recognized that the measures to liberalize trade that the Fund was trying to persuade Mexico to implement could put pressure on reserves in the short run. After consulting with the Managing Director and informally with a number of Executive Directors, they therefore responded that if the balance of payments were to worsen, especially as a result of trade liberalization, augmentation could be considered at that time. See memorandum from Sterie T. Beza (Associate Director of the Western Hemisphere Department) to the Managing Director (January 18, 1984); in IMF/RD, Managing Director file "Mexico—January–August 1984" (Accession 85/231, Box 1, Section 177).

William R. Rhodes, Jesús Silva-Herzog, Jacques de Larosière, and José Angel Gurría on the occasion of debt restructuring agreement for Mexico, March 1985

12–13, 1983. Claudio Loser, attending the meeting for the IMF, described the proposed program and explained that the banks would have to provide additional financing of $4 billion to fund the balance of payments. That figure was met with some skepticism, because it allowed for both a substantial rise in imports and a partial restoration of foreign exchange reserves. Citibank's vice chairman, William Rhodes, asked the IMF not to make its approval of the program contingent on this level of bank financing. Doing without a bank agreement was clearly not feasible: the program had to be fully financed, imports had to rebound from the extremely depressed level of 1983, and trade could not take place without a reasonable level of working balances in foreign exchange. But when Loser reported back to de Larosière, the Managing Director agreed to be flexible regarding both the amount and the linkage to Fund approval. If the Advisory Committee would agree informally to put together a package of close to $4 billion, he would not necessarily make achievement of the "critical mass" a precondition in his presentation to the Executive Board.

On December 23, 1983, one year to the day after the Fund's approval of the initial EFF arrangement, de Larosière cabled the Advisory Committee that Mexico had met all of the performance criteria for 1983 by substantial margins, and asked for a $3.8 billion increase in bank exposure as support for the 1984 program. Within a week, the Committee had approved the request. This time around, the banks were able to coordinate the syndication effort largely on their own, and the $3.8 billion total was reached in late April with the participation of close to 500 banks.[10]

First Multiyear Rescheduling Agreement

Now that the adjustment process was under way, the Managing Director's focus could shift still more toward the long run. How could Mexico stay on course and generate sustained growth once imports had been restored to normal levels and the IMF's direct involvement through the EFF arrangement was over? At the same time, some of the key international bankers and officials of the U.S. Federal Reserve System were beginning to worry about how to move from crisis management through annual rescheduling agreements to a restoration of normal business relationships.

Around January 1984, Wilfried Guth, a member of the Governing Board of Deutsche Bank and of the Advisory Committee for Mexico, suggested to de Larosière that the time had come for a more medium-term approach to Mexico's financing needs. Large amortization "humps" would come due in 1985 and 1986, and early planning would be required if they were to be passed smoothly. Initially, the Managing Director felt that the EFF arrangement itself constituted a suffi-

---

[10]The number of participating banks was about 30 less than in the first package, owing mainly to mergers of U.S. banks. The $3.8 billion total was oversubscribed, and the difference was rebated pro rata.

ciently structured contribution from the Fund, especially as it was designed to allow for a resumption of imports while preserving the viability of the balance of payments. In March, Guth wrote to de Larosière with a more specific recommendation, that the banks be encouraged to arrange their financial support operations for two to three years at a time, rather than annually. Again, de Larosière was cautious in his response, feeling that the banks as a group might be reluctant to make financial commitments beyond the end of the Fund's involvement. Two weeks later, however, when Guth and Lewis Preston (Chairman of J.P. Morgan) called on the Managing Director to express exactly those concerns, de Larosière formulated the idea of devising a procedure under which the IMF would informally monitor the country's economic policies and performance in a way that could reassure creditor banks undertaking longer-term commitments. He introduced the idea in general terms at a private conference for central bankers at the Federal Reserve Bank of New York on May 7, 1984, and reported afterward that the idea seemed to be "gaining ground."[11] Meanwhile, both Paul Volcker (Chairman of the Board of Governors of the Federal Reserve System) and Edwin Truman (Director of the Federal Reserve Board's Division of International Finance) were meeting regularly with bank officials to promote the idea of medium-term commitments.

De Larosière's proposal for what would come to be known as a "multiyear rescheduling agreement" (MYRA) began to come to fruition in June 1984. Given the novelty of the idea and the controversies that were likely to arise, it would be necessary to lay the groundwork carefully. The International Monetary Conference that was sponsored annually by the American Bankers Association provided a convenient opportunity. Many of the world's leading commercial and central bankers regularly attended the event, and the Managing Director often gave a speech there; in 1984, it was to be held in Philadelphia, Pennsylvania, in early June. On May 28, after consulting with Rhodes, the Managing Director invited representatives of the Advisory Committee banks to a private late-afternoon meeting on June 4, at the ornate Union League Club in downtown Philadelphia, to discuss arrangements for Mexico.[12] The gathering was impressive: Volcker; the chairmen (or, in a few cases, their senior associates) of all 13 of the Committee banks; Fritz Leutwiler, the president of the Bank for International Settlements; and two of the IMF's top Mexican experts, Sterie T. Beza (Associate Director of the Western Hemisphere Department) and Claudio Loser. De Larosière's presentation to the group noted that in light of the "heavy amortization payments of the public sector due to banks over the period through 1990," it was "unrealistic to expect

---

[11]Memorandum for files by the Managing Director's office (May 1, 1984), in IMF/RD Managing Director Chronological file "January to December 1984" (Accession 88/274, Box 3, Section 269); speaking notes for the New York conference, in IMF/RD Managing Director file "New York, May 7, 1984" (Accession 85/231, Box 3, Section 177); and report to Executive Directors at EBM/84/74 (May 9, 1984), pp. 3–4. For a contemporary report on the conference, see Peter Norman and S. Karene Witcher, "Central Bankers' Meeting on World Debt Troubles European Finance Officials," *Wall Street Journal* (May 8, 1984), p. 39.

[12]Earlier in the afternoon, the Managing Director included a general proposal for multiyear agreements in his remarks to the full conference.

that they could be covered by syndications or other voluntary credits year by year." A multiyear approach would help to reduce uncertainty, provided that the country's house was in order:

> Of course, a proposal for a multiyear restructuring can be contemplated only in the case of a country that has brought adjustment to the point where there is a substantial degree of certainty about the outlook for the balance of payments in the medium term. The policies pursued by Mexico have produced such a prospect, and it is therefore in everyone's interest that Mexico's efforts be complemented by a change in its external debt profile in a way that would enhance stability.[13]

Following the Managing Director's presentation, Volcker also made a strong appeal for a MYRA for Mexico as an antidote to what he saw as a deteriorating debt strategy. Mexico's economic prospects were favorable, especially compared with the problem cases of Argentina and Brazil. Mexico was not expected to need large amounts of additional financing, but the banks' willingness to arrange a MYRA could serve as a positive example for other countries in the region that were more seriously bogged down. De Larosière then noted that the nature of the Fund's involvement after the conclusion of the current EFF was essentially to be decided by the Mexican authorities, and he suggested that the banks discuss possibilities with them. Options included a modest follow-up program, a shadow program, or some other monitoring arrangement.

The bankers present were initially divided as to whether the time was ripe for a multiyear agreement. Several of them feared that a MYRA for Mexico would encourage Argentina to ask for similar treatment, to which the Managing Director responded that it was important to be explicit that such an arrangement was a reward for good policies and performance. Walter Wriston (Chairman of Citibank), Guth, and several others supported the proposal, and the meeting in the end gave its blessing. Rhodes issued a press release the next day, indicating that the banks had agreed with the Mexican authorities to begin negotiations on a multiyear strategy for restoring normal financial relations. The MYRA approach was thus officially launched.[14]

Agreement in principle was only the first step in getting an actual rescheduling agreement in place. The next step was to determine the appropriate monitoring procedures for the Fund. That issue was taken up in a series of meetings in New York in mid-July 1984, involving principally Gurria for Mexico, Rhodes for the

---

[13]Speaking note for the meeting, as delivered; attached to a file memorandum on the meeting prepared by the Managing Director's office. In IMF/RD Managing Director file "Philadelphia Meeting, 1984" (Accession 85/231, Box 3, Section 177).

[14]Rhodes's announcement was widely reported in the press as a major breakthrough and as a tribute to the progress being made in restoring the Mexican economy to health. See, for example, *Excelsior* (Mexico City), June 6, 1984, p. 1; and *New York Times*, June 6, 1984, p. D1. Five days after the meeting between the Managing Director and the banks, the communiqué of the G-7 summit in London endorsed the use of MYRAs by indicating the leaders' willingness "in cases where debtor countries are themselves making successful adjustment efforts" to encourage the use of MYRAs for commercial debts and "where appropriate to negotiate similarly in respect of debts to governments and government agencies" (Hajnal, 1989, p. 262).

banks (followed by a meeting with the full Advisory Committee), and Beza for the IMF.[15] The Mexican authorities viewed the monitoring issue as highly sensitive, as they believed that it would not be appropriate for the Fund to play a larger formal surveillance role than in other countries that had concluded a financial arrangement, even if such a role might help to secure an agreement with the banks. Gurria therefore proposed that the IMF's activities be defined within the framework of the annual Article IV consultations, supplemented by interim technical missions if necessary. The Fund missions could review Mexico's financial program, so long as the program did not have to be negotiated with the Fund. Gurria was prepared to have the Fund supply the banks with reports on these consultations, as long as the reports focused specifically on the country's creditworthiness; but he did not want to submit to a contractual obligation from the banks for additional IMF surveillance, and he did not want a shadow program to be discussed by the Executive Board.

The banks, for their part, recognized the value of having the IMF monitor the economic policies of member countries. Although the Advisory Committee had an Economic Subcommittee (comprising staff economists from each committee bank) that advised the committee on economic conditions, there were legal and competitive reasons for not asking that group to evaluate adjustment programs. The Mexican authorities could communicate the details of their annual economic program directly to the banks, but only the IMF would be well placed to review and evaluate the program. The Fund would need to find an appropriate means of conducting such a review and communicating its findings to the banks.

Following these initial discussions, the Advisory Committee cabled the non-committee creditor banks that it was receptive to devising a multiyear strategy and intended to resume discussions in early August.[16] Meanwhile, the Managing Director and the staff began intense discussions over whether and how the Fund might support this process. The establishment of a MYRA was a matter to be decided purely between the creditor banks and the Mexican authorities, but the position of the Advisory Committee was that for an agreement to extend beyond the end of 1985 (when the EFF would expire), an IMF monitoring procedure would have to be in place. An informal commitment by the Fund to hold semiannual consultations and to allow the Mexican authorities to release the consultation staff reports to the banks would appear to satisfy both parties, but several of the Fund's senior staff members were worried that authorization to release consultation reports would set a precedent that many member countries would find troubling and that could compromise the Fund's role as a confidential advisor to governments. In any event, such authorization would require a decision by the Executive Board.

---

[15]Representatives of the monetary authorities of the major creditor countries, plus the World Bank and the Inter-American Development Bank, attended some of the meetings with the Advisory Committee. Memorandum for files (July 17, 1984) by Beza; in IMF/RD Managing Director file "Bank-Fund Collaboration, 1984" (Accession 85/231, Box 3, Section 177).

[16]Cable from the committee chairmen (July 20, 1984); in IMF/RD Managing Director file "Mexico, January–August 1984" (Accession 85/231, Box 1, Section 177).

Management would support a request from Mexico, but it could not be sure that the Board would go along.[17]

Fortunately, it was easy enough for all parties to postpone a final resolution of the procedural difficulties, because the EFF arrangement was on track and was scheduled to run through 1985. During the life of the program, a letter from the Managing Director to the banks certifying that Mexico continued to meet the program criteria and to remain eligible to draw on the arrangement would be all that the banks would need to activate the next tranche of the arrangement. On September 5, 1984, after consulting informally with Executive Directors, the Managing Director sent a cable to the Advisory Committee expressing his "strong support" for the proposed restructuring, which the Fund staff viewed as "appropriate for the circumstances of Mexico." Without mentioning the issues related to the release of consultation reports, the cable otherwise set forth the basic elements of what would come to be known as "enhanced surveillance":

> The Mexican authorities would make available at the beginning of each year their annual operative financial program. . . . [They] have also indicated their willingness to enhance their Article IV consultations with the International Monetary Fund. . . . In addition to the annual consultation . . . the Fund [would] conduct mid-year reviews of the performance of the Mexican economy. . . . [This proposal is] consistent with Fund policies on surveillance under Article IV and should facilitate assessment of economic performance in the period beyond the expiration of the extended arrangement at the end of 1985.[18]

That is, the IMF would not negotiate a program with the authorities, but both the staff and the Executive Board would review the program semiannually. In an as yet unspecified fashion, the conclusions of those reviews would be communicated to the creditor banks.

On September 8, 1984, after two months of negotiations during which the IMF staff had participated mainly by explaining the details of the adjustment program to the banks, the Advisory Committee and the Mexican government agreed in principle on the largest rescheduling yet: nearly $50 billion in public sector debts would be covered, comprising those that had been outstanding on August 22, 1982 and that were currently scheduled to mature from 1985 through 1990, plus the $5 billion syndicated loan of March 1983.[19] The maturity profile was both lengthened (from 8 to 14 years) and smoothed, interest rate spreads over the London interbank offered rate (LIBOR) were reduced from those of the earlier short-term packages (ranging from ⅞ to 1½ percent over LIBOR), and the whole atmosphere was much more positive.

---

[17]Except for countries under enhanced surveillance, the Executive Board did not agree to the release of consultation reports until 1999.

[18]"Mexico—Restructuring of External Debt," EBS/84/194 (September 10, 1984), pp. 1 and 5. The text in this document is dated September 8, but the cable was sent on September 5. For the cable, see IMF/RD Managing Director file "Mexico (1984)" (Accession 86/34, Box 29, Section 209).

[19]See Dillon and others (1985), p. 14 and Table 17.

Approximately half of the package was to be conditional on an IMF monitoring agreement after the end of the EFF arrangement. Specifically, the rescheduling of close to $24 billion in previously rescheduled debts now maturing from 1987 through 1990 was conditional upon the achievement of economic goals to be set by Mexico and monitored by the IMF on the basis of "enhanced" Article IV consultations starting in 1986, as described in the September 5 cable from the Managing Director. Such an arrangement could be implemented without any formal change in IMF procedures as long as no legal objection was raised to the release by Mexico of consultation reports that technically were the property of the Fund. Eventually, however, the Executive Board would have to approve specific procedures for the release of consultation reports to creditors (on which, see Chapter 10).

The 1985 Program: Storms Roll In

Even as Mexico's relations with its bank creditors were being put on a more solid footing, its ability to persist with strong adjustment policies in the face of ongoing economic difficulties and political pressures was becoming increasingly doubtful. The Article IV consultation that Loser conducted in May 1984 noted the strength of the adjustment effort but cautioned on two fronts. First, most of the improvement in the balance of payments was still coming from a compression of imports rather than stimulus to exports. That relationship was inimical to growth and therefore could not last indefinitely. Second, the exchange rate was becoming seriously overvalued as a result of a combination of large wage increases and a closely controlled rate of depreciation. International competitiveness was slipping away, and that situation could not last either.

Both the staff and management took the view that Mexico could maintain the crawling-peg exchange rate policy only by getting better control over wage increases. Even as the staff mission was still in Mexico City, the Managing Director met with the Mexican president, Miguel de la Madrid, at the Vista Hotel in Washington. De Larosière advised the president that unless the midyear increase in the minimum wage could be held to less than 10 percent, inflationary pressures were likely to again reach a destabilizing level. The president indicated that he shared that concern, but an increase that small was not feasible. In the president's view, the chief problem was the threat from the rising level of world interest rates, which could hurt developing countries both by raising the cost of servicing their debts and by choking off the recovery in world trade. The Managing Director, and later the staff, would convey these various concerns to the banks in the course of the summer, but the problems did not become manifest until the fall, after the authorities and the Advisory Committee had agreed on the terms of the MYRA.

The staff (again led by Pujol) began negotiating the third year of the program at the end of October 1984, but they immediately ran into trouble. The authorities acknowledged that they were not on course to meet the performance criteria for the end of 1984, yet they were devising a program for 1985 that would aggravate the problem and widen the gaps. On December 6, the central bank accelerated the rate of depreciation under the crawling peg, but the rate remained well below the inflation rate and the overvaluation of the exchange rate was becoming increasingly severe. Efforts to liberalize trade had bogged down, wage policy was lax, and fiscal adjustment had weakened. Two years of adjustment had left incomes depressed, the burden of servicing external debts was still harsh, elections for the House of Representatives and state governments were coming up in 1985, and fatigue was setting in. Pujol had no choice but to inform the authorities that the Fund could not accept the proposed policies as a basis for the 1985 program.[20]

In mid-December and again in mid-January, Mexican officials went to Washington to meet with officials in the Fund. Pujol then went back briefly to Mexico City in late January and again in February with a full negotiating team. At the end of that mission, in early March 1985, the pace of exchange rate depreciation was accelerated again, and the negotiations continued. After one more mission to Mexico and two more visits by officials to Washington (an extraordinary total of nine sets of meetings), a Letter of Intent was finally agreed upon in the third week of March. Within a few days, the commercial banks finally signed the MYRA that the Advisory Committee had negotiated six months earlier. For that occasion, de Larosière—who had declined many earlier invitations to attend such signing ceremonies—went to New York to be present at what was clearly a historic clearing of a hurdle on the way to resolving the Latin American debt crisis.[21]

By the time the Executive Board met on June 7, 1985, to review the program and approve the third year of drawings, the protraction of negotiations had already caused one scheduled drawing (February 1985) to be missed. If the three-year EFF arrangement was to be fully utilized, it would have to be extended through the first quarter of 1986. More seriously, Executive Directors raised numerous questions about the internal consistency of Mexico's exchange rate policy. Guillermo Ortiz (Alternate—Mexico) characterized policy as aiming to set the rate of depreciation consistently with the inflation target and not to accommodate inflation overruns; the large depreciations of 1982 had instilled heavy cost-push pressures through wage demands that had weakened competitiveness and placed further pressures on the exchange rate.[22] Other Directors noted that by raising the depreciation rate twice in the past year, the authorities had signaled a change in policy toward preserving competitiveness and that this shift may have added to the cost-push pressures. Jacques J. Polak (Netherlands) took note of the nine negotiating sessions over five months and concluded that, if the Fund were going to continue to point to Mexico as an example for other countries in the region to follow, it would have to ensure that a firmer policy stance was adopted. These and other concerns were strongly and freely expressed, but at the end of the day the continuation of the arrangement was approved.

From that point, matters deteriorated rapidly. Continuing exchange market pressures forced another devaluation of 17 percent on July 25, and on August 5 the

---

[20]Memorandum to management from Pujol (November 26, 1984); in IMF/RD Managing Director file "Mexico (1984)" (Accession 86/34, Box 29, Section 209).

[21]See *IMF Survey*, Vol. 14 (April 15, 1985), pp. 113ff.

[22]Minutes of EBM/85/91 (June 7, 1985), pp. 6 and 10.

"controlled" rate was placed on a managed float; by that time, the controlled rate was 22 percent below the rate in the parallel "free" market. In an effort to raise confidence, the authorities announced new spending cuts amounting to some 0.3 percent of GDP for the remainder of 1985, plus a new round of trade liberalization that would raise the portion of imports that was free of licensing requirements from 34 percent to more than 60 percent. These measures came too late, and when the world oil market began to soften markedly at the same time, they were also too little. When Pujol's team returned to Mexico City in mid-August for the next program review, they concluded that several program criteria were not being met: the fiscal deficit was too large, domestic credit growth was above target, and reserve growth was deficient. The program now had to be abandoned, and the drawing that was scheduled for the end of August was to be disallowed.

The timing could scarcely have been worse. Smack on the heels of these domestic policy slippages came a pair of the worst earthquakes in Mexican history. Measuring 8.1 on the Richter scale on September 19 and 7.5 the next day, these quakes killed thousands of people in and around Mexico City, severely damaged the area's infrastructure and economic capacity, and ultimately generated losses estimated at up to 3½ percent of annual GDP. Some $1 billion in principal was about to come due to foreign creditors, but Gurria feared that he and his colleagues in government would be lynched if they even proposed such a use of scarce resources in the midst of this calamity. He successfully negotiated a rollover of those credits, but the economic damage continued. The fear of complete collapse was palpable. When Mexico City officials announced the expropriation of damaged buildings that had to be condemned, investors accelerated the flight of capital in anticipation of widespread nationalization of property.

Press coverage following the earthquakes jumped on the IMF for cutting off funds to Mexico while the country was reeling from the earthquakes. Although those stories either ignored or played down the fact that the cutoff had preceded the earthquakes by several weeks and was not linked to them in any way, the adverse publicity complicated the task of figuring out how best to help Mexico recover.[23] Although reviving the EFF arrangement was out of the question under the circumstances, de Larosière immediately (on September 20) cabled President de la Madrid that the IMF was prepared to assess the possibility of providing emergency assistance. A week later, Silva Herzog went to the Fund to request such assistance and to convey the government's interest in working with the Fund in developing a viable program for 1986.[24] At the time, Executive Directors were getting ready to go to Korea for the Annual Meetings of the Boards of Governors and could not

---

[23]For example, the *Washington Post* front-page story on the earthquakes (September 20, 1985) was accompanied by a story on the cutoff of drawings (a story that in fact was then six weeks old but that had been largely ignored during August) under the headline, "IMF cuts off Mexico for failure to live up to agreements." To try to stem the adverse publicity, the IMF issued a correction in the form of a press release (PR/85/30, September 20, 1985).

[24]Speaking notes by de Larosière for an informal meeting of Executive Directors in Seoul, Korea (October 4, 1985); in IMF/RD Managing Director file "Annual Meetings, 1985—Mexico" (Accession 88/274, Box 9, Section 269).

immediately schedule a discussion on Mexico. As soon as the quorum had convened in Seoul, however, the Executive Board met in informal session and agreed to "look favorably" on a request for emergency assistance.[25] Two months later, on December 11, 1985, the authorities formally requested an emergency drawing of just over SDR 290 million, or $320 million (the equivalent of one credit tranche, the maximum normally allowed under Fund policies). On January 10, 1986, the Executive Board approved the request and made the funds immediately available.

Domestic wage pressures, election-year budget pressures, declining real incomes, falling prices for petroleum exports, earthquakes . . . the plagues came in waves in the fourth year of Mexico's debt crisis. As the first major phase of the debt strategy drew to a close, Mexico—the once and future epitome of the case-by-case adjustment strategy—was mired down with difficulties that seemed well beyond the capabilities of the IMF to resolve.

Brazil

The staff team working on Brazil had to start all over in June 1983, following the collapse of the EFF arrangement that had been approved just a few months earlier. As described in Chapter 8, there had been multiple failures by all concerned, and a promising start on adjustment had been lost. Now, a huge effort would be undertaken, and the Brazilian economy would be—for the moment—brought back under control.

Restoring the Program: 1983

Prospects were rather bleak when a review mission—headed by Eduardo Wiesner, Director of the Western Hemisphere Department—made a highly publicized visit to Brazil in June 1983 to begin renegotiating the EFF arrangement.[26] There were fiscal overruns, inflationary pressures were unabated, and external financing was limited; the trade balance was much improved, but the improvement had come largely by cutting back on imports. The biggest problem was that, whatever goodwill the government might have had to tighten its belt, it faced strong opposition in a badly divided congress. In the judgment of the Fund staff and management, the government would have to be very specific regarding policy measures to be taken as preconditions for resuming drawings under the EFF. Consequently, when Wiesner met with the top economic officials in Brasilia at the end of the

---

[25]See press release PR/85/32 (October 4, 1985). For a more general discussion of emergency assistance by the IMF, see Chapter 15.

[26]The public pressure on the mission was raised at the outset when Fritz Leutwiler, the president of the Bank for International Settlements, held a news conference in Basel, Switzerland, on the opening day of the mission, and signaled his confidence that the Fund would successfully negotiate a new program that would enable Brazil to repay the $400 million owed to the BIS. In Brazil, Wiesner held informal conferences with the Brazilian press as the mission progressed.

two-week mission—principally Antonio Delfim Netto, the minister of planning, and Ernane Galvêas, the minister of finance—he took the unusual step of insisting not just on a commitment to reduce inflation but on a specific commitment to change the rules governing indexation of wages. The Brazilians had misgivings about this requirement, and their long-standing and highly influential Executive Director, Alexandre Kafka, complained that this level of structural involvement in policymaking was unprecedented and inappropriate. The authorities nonetheless recognized that some such measure was needed to reduce inflation. Eventually, a compromise was struck, under which the indexation formula would not be made part of the formal conditionality on the program, but there would be an understanding that the Managing Director would not take the program to the Executive Board for approval until the indexation issue had been satisfactorily resolved.

Wiesner and the other senior officials on the team returned to Washington in late June to discuss options with management, while the technical staff remained in Brasilia (in part to avoid giving the impression to the voracious local press that negotiations might have broken down). They then returned in early July and achieved what appeared to be a breakthrough. On July 14, the government promulgated Decree 2045, limiting wage indexation to 80 percent of inflation. Congress would have 75 days to overturn the legislation, but such action was unprecedented and appeared unlikely. The Managing Director, however, had his doubts about the level of commitment; let us schedule the Board meeting, he suggested, but not until October, when the danger of a policy reversal would be greatly reduced. In the meantime, he suggested privately that the Fund station a resident representative in Brazil to monitor developments more closely. The authorities resisted that idea, fearing that it would be regarded as a sign of dependency by opposition parties, but they did agree to receive staff visits on a frequent basis to accomplish the monitoring objective.

When the staff team returned to Brazil in August 1983—led by Thomas Reichmann, Chief of the Atlantic Division in the Western Hemisphere Department—inflation was still accelerating and was carrying the fiscal deficit up with it. In the short run, this problem was essentially intractable, as it resulted from the interaction of unavoidable shocks (relative prices adjustments that were necessary for the adjustment program, plus the effect of bad weather on agricultural harvests) and a high degree of wage indexation. The staff and the authorities quickly reached agreement on a target of just over 150 percent inflation for 1983 (compared with the then prevailing rate of 160 percent) and a cut to 55 percent in 1984, but no one on either side had a great deal of confidence that either target could be reached. And if inflation remained out of control, whatever ceiling was set on government borrowing would run over as well.

In this environment, discussions began on the possibility of specifying the ceiling on the "operational" rather than the actual level of the deficit, where the operational balance was defined to exclude the effect of indexation for inflation on public sector debt service. This issue arose because most debt obligations in Brazil at that time were indexed to the rate of inflation. The overall public sector borrowing requirement (a ceiling on which would be the usual performance criterion in a

Fund-supported adjustment program) is equivalent to the total change in the stock of public sector debt outstanding. That total may be divided into two components: the change attributable to the difference between government outlays and revenues, and the change (called the "monetary correction") attributable to indexation (including the payment of interest other than the "real" component). The operational deficit is measured as the total minus this second component. Through the monetary correction, a rise in the inflation rate will generate a rise in the total fiscal deficit unless the government takes contractionary action, but it will leave the operational deficit unchanged. With rising inflation, targeting the total deficit would force the government into an offsetting fiscal contraction; targeting the operational deficit would permit a neutral fiscal policy. The latter strategy would leave inflation unchecked, but if inflation could not be controlled in any case, it at least would give the government a meaningful target that it could effectively control.

Proposals to target the operational deficit were made by several high-inflation countries in the 1980s, to which the Fund reacted skeptically. Like wage indexation, the operational deficit was seen as a way to accept and accommodate inflation, when what the country needed was greater price stability. Despite these reservations, the staff usually agreed eventually to include the operational deficit as a performance criterion, along with a more inclusive fiscal target. This acceptance was essentially a negotiating tactic, a way to get an agreement on the table. Programs ended up being overdetermined, since one fiscal instrument was aimed at multiple targets. Unless inflation subsided quickly, the total deficit was likely to be the binding constraint, and the adjusted measure would be irrelevant. In this seminal case, the matter was debated without resolution during the August mission, but the option of using the operational deficit remained open.[27]

While these negotiations were going on, the commercial bank creditors were also trying to regroup. By April 1983, the original committee had clearly failed to devise a strategy capable of securing the required degree of cooperation from the diverse and fractious hundreds of creditor banks, and the banks showed no signs of being able to coordinate a response. At that point, Gordon Richardson, governor of the Bank of England, came up with the idea of asking Bill Rhodes of Citibank to take control of the bank financing. Indeed, Rhodes would have been an obvious choice to anybody except that he was already carrying an enormous load as cochairman (effectively, chairman) of the Advisory Committees for Mexico, Argentina, and Uruguay. Richardson approached Paul Volcker with the suggestion; Volcker conveyed it to Rhodes's boss, Walter Wriston; and in early June, Wriston asked an eagerly receptive Rhodes to take up the gauntlet.

Rhodes organized a new Advisory Committee along lines similar to those that he had successfully managed in the other countries. This committee, which held

---

[27]In the 1983 program for Argentina, discussed in Chapter 8, the fiscal criterion was specified similarly to the operational deficit, but with the understanding that the target could be adjusted as the inflation rate changed. The Executive Board agreed in 1986 to consider the use of adjusted fiscal targets on a case-by-case basis (see Chapter 13). The 1986 and 1987 programs for Mexico, discussed in Chapter 10, contained multiple fiscal targets including the operational deficit.

its initial meeting in New York on June 15, 1983, would focus much more clearly than its predecessor on putting the total package together—on the forest, not the trees. Rhodes's principal deputy would be Guy Huntrods, an executive director of Lloyds Bank International in London and one of the most experienced and knowledgeable bankers on Brazil.[28] Realizing that the banks had to have much more thorough and more direct knowledge of economic conditions in Brazil, Rhodes appointed an economic subcommittee, chaired by Douglas Smee of the Bank of Montreal, and sent the members off to Brazil the next day to prepare a detailed report.

Rhodes also saw the importance of close cooperation with the IMF. Throughout July, it became increasingly evident that the authorities in Brazil were waiting to see if they could get a large enough extension of credit from the banks to enable them to bypass the Fund's conditionality and that Wiesner was thereby being hampered in his efforts to negotiate a resumption of the EFF arrangement. In mid-August, just as Delfim was preparing to go to Paris for a crucial meeting with the Managing Director, Rhodes and Huntrods made a hurried and secret trip to Brasilia to alert the officials that they could not go forward without first seeing agreement with the Fund. Three days later, Delfim and de Larosière reached a tentative and informal agreement on the program conditions.

Even with a strong policy adjustment in place, the financing gap for Brazil was enormous. For the 12 months that were being considered for the next year of the revived EFF, the staff team estimated $9 billion would be needed, in addition to the Fund's own resources. On August 31, de Larosière and a number of the key staff people working on Brazil went to New York to tell Rhodes and his committee colleagues that Brazil needed that amount in new money from the banks. Rhodes, however, convinced the Managing Director that the banks could not possibly get even close to that amount, and Smee sharply questioned the calculations underlying the estimated gap.[29] Undaunted, de Larosière adhered to the calculated gap but agreed to try to obtain as much as $3 billion in official financing if the banks could come up with the rest.

As the summer of 1983 drew to a close, everyone was still aiming toward winning Executive Board approval of the program in October, but neither domestic nor external support was yet in hand. On September 1, Carlos Langoni, the president of the central bank, resigned in protest over what he saw as the harshness of

---

[28]In 1965, Huntrods—then with the Bank of England—had helped set up the Central Bank of Brazil. Shortly thereafter, he spent two years at the IMF as the United Kingdom's Alternate Executive Director. When he moved to Lloyds in the mid-1970s, he quickly became their leading specialist on Latin American loans. When the debt crisis hit, he became actively involved in the work of the first Advisory Committee before becoming a cochairman (effectively, a deputy to Rhodes) along with Leighton Coleman of Morgan Guaranty Bank.

[29]The principal technical issue concerned the treatment of gold exports. The official Brazilian accounts treated the export of gold as a financing item regardless of whether it came from reserves or from domestic production. The IMF accepted this practice, though it inflated the financing gap. In addition, the gap had been calculated to allow for a $2 billion increase in official foreign exchange reserves. The Fund viewed that amount as a minimum rebuilding from a severely depleted level, while the banks naturally wanted a more modest adjustment.

the planned adjustment program. Huge demonstrations against the Fund were now being held in Brazil, including one in São Paulo on September 5 in which the Catholic Archbishop called on the 50,000 who were assembled before him to protest what he saw as the IMF's exploitation of Brazil. The government, however, had run out of reserves and had no choice but to adjust, with or without the assistance of the IMF. So on September 15, Delfim, Galvêas, and Langoni's successor, Affonso Pastore, agreed to a Letter of Intent setting out their policy program for the coming year.

Notwithstanding this agreement, the October approval deadline was by now too close to allow time for the financing of the $9 billion gap to be assembled. With the reluctant concurrence of the BIS, which had already been forced to roll over its $1.2 billion bridge loan to Brazil since the original due date at the end of June and which could not expect to be repaid until the EFF was reactivated,[30] the Executive Board meeting was pushed back to the second half of November. Even so, it was not at all clear whence the money would come. De Larosière hoped he could count on the banks for $6 billion, but he was making little headway in persuading official creditors to cough up the remaining $3 billion. To generate any momentum on that front, he would have to convince the banks to raise their share.

The Managing Director's opportunity to up the ante came at the Annual Meetings, since the major bank chairmen would all be coming to Washington anyway. On September 20, de Larosière sent invitations to the chairmen of all of the Committee banks to meet in the Executive Board room at the IMF on Monday, the 26th (the afternoon before the opening plenary session of the Annual Meetings). Virtually all accepted, as did Volcker, Leutwiler, and Tomomitsu Oba (vice-minister of finance in Japan). The Brazilian authorities were in town but were not invited to this meeting; nor were officials from other creditor countries, in order to keep the focus on the essential role of the banks in financing the program.

De Larosière opened the meeting with a statement indicating his endorsement of the policy measures that had already been taken and of the intentions set out in the September 15 Letter of Intent.[31] He then informed the bankers that allowing for the funds that the World Bank and the IMF could provide, there remained a fi-

---

[30]Brazil was the only country that failed to repay its loans from the BIS on time. In December 1982, the BIS agreed to lend Brazil $1.2 billion for three months, as a bridge to the EFF arrangement. That loan was augmented to $1.45 billion, then extended to the end of June, and subsequently extended to mid-July. From mid-July to mid-September, despite a personal intervention by the Managing Director at the July meeting of the BIS governors in Basel, there was no formal agreement to extend the due date. The BIS, however, informally agreed not to pursue the matter, pending a further progress report from the Managing Director. On September 13, the BIS agreed to extend the loan until the Fund approved the resumption of the EFF, after which the loan was repaid in full. For a summary of these developments, see the BIS Annual Reports of 1982/83, p. 165; and 1983/84, pp. 151–52.

[31]This account is based largely on interviews with participants. Attendance lists, speaking notes, and other documents are in IMF/RD Managing Director file "Brazil, September–November 1983" (Accession 86/34, Box 27, Section 209); and (Accession 85/33, Box 9, Section BD 375).

nancing gap for 1983–84 totaling $11.2 billion. The Paris Club was expected soon to grant some $2 billion in debt relief for that period, and he himself was "making every effort" to line up $2.5 billion in credits from other official sources. That left $6.7 billion that would have to come from increased exposure by commercial bank creditors. He concluded by noting that he could not ask the Executive Board to approve a program that was not adequately financed. To get a timely decision from the Board, he would need written assurances by November 14 that this amount would be forthcoming.

The Managing Director then left the room. He had earlier arranged for Walter Wriston to take over the meeting at this point, so that the bank chairmen could discuss among themselves how to respond. Initially, a number of objections were voiced, principally from those chairmen who had not been personally involved in the negotiations up to this point. Even most of those who were fully familiar with the case had come to the meeting expecting to be asked to raise their exposure only by $6 billion, not $6.7 billion. Eventually, however, the largest creditors—beginning with John F. McGillicuddy of Manufacturers Hanover Trust Company—spoke in favor of the request and turned the tide of the meeting. Eventually, they agreed to aim for $6.5 billion, a figure that would be close enough to the target but that provided no room at all for slippages. Nearly 800 other creditors would have to agree to go along before they could provide the needed assurances to the Fund, but at least they had made a start.

For the next several weeks, heroic efforts were made to put the financing package together. De Larosière formally requested the major creditor countries to make commitments for their part, and he and William B. Dale, the Deputy Managing Director, held numerous follow-up meetings. The Managing Director, Pastore, and Rhodes held a large meeting at the Fund for some 60 creditor banks on October 6, after which Pastore, Rhodes, and other key bankers flew around the world to line up support.

On October 20, 1983, just as Pastore was returning to Brazil after meeting with bank creditors in six countries in North America, Asia, the Middle East, and Europe, he learned that congress had just overturned Decree 2045, the wage bill of July 14. The linchpin of the adjustment program was gone, and the prospect of a collapse was suddenly very real. On October 26, a weaker version of indexation control (Decree 2065) was issued by the government, and Pastore went back to Washington to renegotiate the program. On November 2, he met with de Larosière, who agreed that the higher rate of wage indexation could be accepted if it was offset through tighter monetary control and additional fiscal measures. This agreement would then form the basis for a revised Letter of Intent. After congress formally approved Decree 2065 on November 9, Delfim and Pastore came one more time to Washington.

The Washington meetings focused specifically on the role of the operational fiscal deficit. As noted above, this measure of the fiscal balance had been suggested by the Brazilian authorities in August as a variable that they could control, regardless of unanticipated changes in the rate of inflation. The staff had resisted this suggestion, but they did acknowledge its usefulness for assessing the degree of fiscal adjustment. In the program set out in the September Letter of Intent, the performance criterion governing whether future drawings could be made was specified in the customary way, as a ceiling on the total deficit, while the operational deficit was introduced as part of the justification for waiving the overrun in the total deficit in 1983. Now it was given a new role: in addition to agreeing on a ceiling for the public sector borrowing requirement, the authorities committed themselves to taking specific measures to reach a floor on the operational surplus for 1984.[32] This revision was felicitous: it satisfied the authorities' desire to introduce the operational balance as a performance criterion while satisfying the desire of the staff and management of the Fund to introduce a realistic requirement to tighten fiscal policy. Delfim and Pastore returned to Brasilia, put the final touches on the revisions on November 14, and sent the Letter of Intent to the Managing Director.

This effort put the program back on track for the moment, but the financing was still not complete. The U.S. Treasury assured the Managing Director on November 7 that the United States would put up half of the required $2.5 billion in the form of additional credits from the Export-Import Bank, but little if any of the remainder was yet nailed down, and the banks' portion was coming together slowly. De Larosière decided to postpone the Executive Board meeting to the 22nd and to extend the banks' deadline by a week. During that week, the banks obtained commitments totaling $5.85 billion, or 90 percent of the agreed total, and the finance deputies from several G-10 countries gave vague assurances that appeared to put official financing within sight of the required total. It was a shaky foundation, but it was concrete enough that the risk from building the program on it was less than the risk—to the financial system as well as to Brazil—from a further delay.[33]

The Executive Board met in restricted session (at Kafka's request) on November 22, 1983, and approved the resumption of drawings by Brazil. A few Directors expressed concerns about the ability of the authorities to carry through on the intentions specified in the program, and even about the clarity of the information available on the current situation. As one Director put it, they "had only a kaleidoscopic impression of certain facts or policy measures subject to frequent change."[34] The shift in the staff's assessment of policies between September and

---

[32]The September 15 program is described in "Brazil—Staff Report for the Consultation Under Extended Arrangement, and Request for Waiver and Modification of Performance Criteria," EBS/83/227 (October 19, 1983). The November revision is in "Brazil, Supplementary Letter of Intent," EBS/83/227, Sup. 1 (November 15, 1983).

[33]In addition to the $6.5 billion loan (which, in effect, would cover a portion of the interest payments due on outstanding credits), the Advisory Committee was obtaining commitments for the other three "projects": rescheduling interest payments due in 1984, maintaining trade credit lines, and maintaining interbank lines. As of November 22, each of those projects was between 85 and 95 percent complete. See "Restricted Session—Brazil—Consultation Under Extended Arrangement—Request for Waiver and Modification of Performance Criteria; and Use of Fund Resources—Buffer Stock Financing Facility—International Sugar Agreement," EBAP/84/53 (March 20, 1984), pp. 1–2.

[34]"Restricted Session—Brazil—Consultation Under Extended Arrangement—Request for Waiver and Modification of Performance Criteria; and Use of Fund Resources—Buffer Stock Financing Facility—International Sugar Agreement," EBAP/84/53 (March 20, 1984), p. 13.

November, though necessitated by the weakening of the wage law and the subsequent offsetting tightening of fiscal policy, made the program a little hard to sell.

Notwithstanding these concerns, all Directors regarded approval of the program as vitally important for Brazil and for the Fund; the magnitude of the adjustment that the authorities were undertaking—especially by cutting government subsidies on many goods—was extraordinary and could be achieved only with the support of the Fund. Recognizing the importance of the frequent-monitoring arrangement that was being introduced for this program, Directors unanimously approved the resumption of the EFF arrangement and agreed to waive the performance criteria that had been missed earlier in the year.[35]

The next day, November 23, the Paris Club agreed to reschedule $2.7 billion of Brazilian debt obligations. The banks, however, began to lose momentum in obtaining the last $600 million of their loan syndication. Once again Delfim and Pastore, plus Huntrods and others from the bank committee, jetted around Europe and the Middle East trying to line up support, only to find that many bankers were still waiting to be sure that the official creditors put up the full value of their requirements. Not for another two months was the full $6.5 billion in hand; the bank loan was then formally signed at a dinner hosted by Delfim at the Pierre Hotel in New York.[36]

Success Slips Away: The Program in 1984

The November 1983 Letter of Intent contained several important provisions governing economic policies in 1984, with the primary intent of reducing the inflation rate. Interest rates were to be raised and other measures taken to restrict credit, so as to limit monetary growth to 50 percent for the year; several tax and spending measures were to be implemented so as to bring the government's operational budget into surplus by at least 0.3 percent of GDP; and the exchange rate against the U.S. dollar was to be depreciated by at least the rate of inflation so as to prevent any appreciation in real terms.[37] To monitor progress in meeting these goals, the IMF implemented the agreement reached in July 1983 (see above) to send a staff member to Brazil frequently (normally once each month) to collect information and hold informal discussions. Beginning in January 1984, Ana Maria Jul (Deputy Chief of the Atlantic Division) was given this assignment.

Reichmann's next review mission, which went to Brazil in the second half of February 1984, found a much-improved economy. Tax revenues were up, interest rates had been raised to more realistic levels, tighter control was being exercised

---

[35]At the end of November, Brazil drew SDR 1,122 million, plus SDR 64.7 million under the buffer stock facility ($1.2 billion and $68 million, respectively), raising its indebtedness to the Fund from 234 percent of quota to 353 percent. For details, see Chapter 15.

[36]Tracking the progress of the $2.5 billion in official credits is far more difficult. Through 1984, very little of that money materialized, but it is debatable as to how much of the shortfall was attributable to a shortage of supply rather than demand.

[37]"Brazil—Supplementary Letter of Intent," EBS/83/227, Sup. 1 (November 15, 1983).

over the monetary base, and the legislation of October 1983 was beginning to re-strain wage demands. Both the staff and the authorities were worried, however, that strict policies would become increasingly difficult to sustain in 1984. Around the end of the year, the electoral college would elect the first civilian president in more than 20 years, and pressures on government spending would inevitably rise as the election approached. A Letter of Intent reaffirming the program, subject to modifications necessitated by the delay in obtaining commercial bank credits, was quickly negotiated and signed by Delfim, Galvêas, and Pastore at the end of February.[38]

The Executive Board approved the 1984–85 program on May 9, 1984. Brazil had been out of compliance with the program at 1983, but only because of the delay in obtaining the $6.5 billion loan agreement from commercial banks.[39] With that loan in hand, the program was on track for the first quarter of 1984, and on that basis the Board granted a waiver for the earlier period. A more serious problem was that the effort to contain inflation was still hesitant and uncertain. Directors noted that getting inflation under control was now the top priority and the "major challenge" for economic policy in Brazil, and that to do so would require both tighter monetary control and a reorientation of indexation. With no change in indexation policy, the degree of demand restraint that would be needed to control inflation would produce unacceptably high costs in lost output and employment.[40] Mario Teijeiro (Alternate Executive Director—Argentina), for example, suggested predetermining the rate of exchange rate depreciation and setting wage and public sector pricing policies in advance, "consistent with a prospective decline in inflation."[41] Directors were nonetheless encouraged by the prospects for growth and external viability and readily approved the proposed program.

Through the summer of 1984, threats to the program continued to mount. On several occasions, de Larosière conveyed his concerns about the ongoing rise in inflation to Delfim, who replied that they were making strong efforts to control the problem. At the same time, the banks were complaining to de Larosière that the $2.5 billion in vague official commitments from creditor countries was not materializing, and some of his own staff members were expressing concerns to him that a planned rise in lending by the World Bank could add to government spending.[42] Press coverage, too, was harsh, not only in Rio but even in the northern hemisphere. The *New York Times* reported on August 12 that the "IMF-prescribed austerity measures" were forcing down living standards and not producing the "prom-

---

[38]The Letter of Intent was circulated in "Brazil—Second Year of Extended Arrangement," EBS/84/61 (March 19, 1984). Also see memorandum from Jul to the Managing Director (February 1, 1984); in IMF/RD Managing Director file "Brazil, January–February 1984" (Accession 85/231, Box 2, Section 177).

[39]"Brazil—Staff Report for the 1984 Article IV Consultation and Review Under Extended Arrangement," EBS/84/84 (April 11, 1984).

[40]Chairman's summing up; minutes of EBM/84/75 (May 9, 1984), p. 16.

[41]Minutes of EBM/84/74 (May 9, 1984), p. 14.

[42]Memorandum from C. David Finch (Director of the Exchange and Trade Relations Department) to the Managing Director (July 24, 1984); in IMF/RD Managing Director file "Brazil—1984, March–August" (Accession 85/231, Box 2, Section 177).

ised" recovery.[43] Even so, economic growth was higher than expected, as was the improvement in the current account balance.

This combination of outcomes—high inflation, high real growth, and a strengthening external picture—confounded the analysts. If price inflation—which was in excess of 200 percent a year—was due mainly to excessive demand pressures, notably the fiscal overruns (as the Fund generally believed), then the rising trade surplus had to be attributed to structural factors, and its magnitude was difficult to explain. If inflation was due primarily to structural factors, notably the indexation process (as the authorities and most Brazilian economists maintained), then the high growth rate had to be attributed to structural factors as well, and its magnitude was difficult to explain. If the truth was somewhere in the middle, as it surely was, then it was difficult to know how much of the trade improvement or the high growth could be sustained over time. This conundrum made the Brazilian situation unique, and it led to an extraordinary degree of uncertainty in the evaluation of the success of the adjustment program.

The Executive Board met next to consider the Brazilian program on November 9, 1984, again in restricted session in an effort by Kafka to minimize the possibility of leaks that could add to the political pressures that were already intense ahead of the January presidential election. The high inflation rate required the Board to grant another waiver, which it did, after an extended discussion of the problem. Polak observed that real wages, after dropping in 1983, had not risen in 1984; since not much more than that could be expected, any reduction in inflation had to result from better monetary control.[44]

The week after the Board meeting, which enabled Brazil to draw SDR 374 million (approximately the same in dollars) that month, Reichmann returned to Brazil to negotiate the terms of the program for 1985. This was to be Delfim's last opportunity to influence policy under the regime that was soon to be elected, and he took advantage of it by drafting a program aimed at continuing the gains already achieved on the trade balance and growth while reducing the inflation rate to a targeted 120 percent for 1985.[45]

Collapse: 1985

The Managing Director faced a very difficult situation as 1984 drew to a close. The outgoing government had agreed to an economic program that he and the staff had determined to be a sound basis for continuing Fund support. Was it now reasonable to expect the program to be implemented vigorously during the transition period and under the new government? In view of the implementation diffi-

---

[43]The next day, O Globo in Rio de Janeiro reported the story from the New York Times (p. 16), under the headline "New York Times culpa FMI pela crise brasiliera" ("New York Times blames the IMF for the Brazilian crisis").

[44]Minutes of EBM/84/163–164 (November 9, 1984).

[45]Letter of Intent, to de Larosière from Delfim, Galvêas, and Pastore (December 20, 1984), p. 4; circulated as "Brazil—Extended Arrangement," EBS/85/11 (January 15, 1985).

culties that were already apparent, de Larosière determined that the Fund would have to take a firm stand if it was to avoid undue risk. Commercial and official creditors would be meeting early in the year to decide whether and on what terms to grant additional credits or concessions to the Brazilian government, and they would expect a favorable recommendation from the Fund before proceeding. In March, the Executive Board was tentatively scheduled to consider whether to approve the next drawing under the EFF arrangement; that meeting also depended on a favorable recommendation from the Managing Director. The problem was to determine the preconditions for making such a recommendation.

The difficulty arose because parts of the program were succeeding remarkably well, while other elements were failing badly. For 1984, Brazil was estimated to have a trade surplus of $13 billion, a balanced current account, and a $7 billion surplus in the overall balance of payments—well in excess of the program's targets. This achievement, which resulted primarily from the devaluation of February 1983 but was also aided by the continued application of trade and exchange restrictions, was accomplished while real GDP was growing at a reasonably high rate (4 percent for the year). Government borrowing, however, was stuck at a rate of more than 20 percent of GDP—well above target, and a key contributor to the very high (220 percent for the year) and still rising rate of inflation.[46] In the Fund's view, as noted earlier, the gains in the external accounts simply could not be sustained without better control of the public finances and a better measure of monetary stability.

On January 15, 1985, the electoral college elected Tancredo Neves as the president of Brazil, to take office in two months. In the interim, liaison between the old and new governments on economic matters, including the program with the Fund, would be handled by the outgoing finance minister, Ernane Galvêas, and by the designated new finance minister, Francisco Neves Dornelles (nephew of the president-elect). As far as the program was concerned, the outgoing government was responsible for meeting the monthly targets through February, while the incoming officials were asked to endorse the continuation of policies beyond that date.

Although the election took place just two months after the Executive Board approved the continuation of the EFF arrangement, the program was already off track. Notably, the money supply, growth in which was to have been limited to 60 percent for the year 1985, was already some 20 percent above the interim target in December 1984. On February 1, President-Elect Neves met with President Reagan and other senior U.S. officials in Washington and was informed that Brazil would have to face the serious concerns being raised by the Fund. Against this

---

[46]The operational deficit was estimated at the time to have been approximately 2 percent of GDP and to have been consistent with the performance criterion under the extended arrangement. (The comparison was complicated by a definitional change made after the approval of the 1984 program, which called for a small surplus under the original definition.) The outturn was later revised to a deficit of 2¾ percent of GDP. The program targets for 1984 are given in "Brazil—Extended Arrangement," EBS/84/204 (September 28, 1984). The initial assessment of 1984 performance is in "Brazil—Staff Report for the 1985 Article IV Consultation," EBS/85/178 (July 31, 1985). For final figures, see "Brazil—Recent Economic Developments," EBS/87/184 (August 26, 1987).

background, Neves then sent Dornelles to inform the Managing Director that his government was prepared to implement the program vigorously once it took office, and to request the Fund's support in securing financing from other creditors in the meantime. If they had to wait even a few months to reschedule either official or commercial credits, keeping their finances together would be extremely difficult.

Dornelles met de Larosière on February 9 at his hotel in Paris, where the Managing Director was on a brief speaking tour. There were two issues on the table during this tête-à-tête. First, was the Neves government committed to implementing the program? That issue was readily resolved, as Dornelles indicated his own and Neves's support and their willingness to have a personal representative of the president-elect participate in forthcoming discussions with the Fund. Second, what prior actions would have to be taken before the Managing Director could convey a sense of confidence to the Executive Board and to outside creditors? In view of the existing disarray of the program, that issue was not so easily dismissed. After a two-hour discussion, it was agreed that the crucial question was whether Brazil could meet the program targets by the end of February. De Larosière would return to Washington over the weekend, and more detailed discussions would begin immediately on Monday, with a representative of Neves's participating. To get the program back on track in just three weeks would clearly take a minor miracle, but nothing less would do. Dornelles's mission had failed, and once again negotiations between Brazil and the IMF would have to start anew.

Part of the urgency of Dornelles's effort arose from the need to rapidly reach a MYRA with commercial bank creditors. When the Managing Director met with the Brazilian transition team at the Fund on February 11–12 after returning from Paris, the banks' Advisory Committee was on the verge of completing the deal. All that was lacking was a positive signal from the Fund. On the 12th, the three cochairs (Rhodes, Huntrods, and Coleman) spent the day at their attorneys' office putting the final touches on the draft agreement. Around 10 o'clock that evening, the phone rang, and de Larosière informed them that he could not yet give them the assurances of Fund support that they needed. The bankers then had no choice but to put the papers away and shelve the MYRA for what they thought would be a short delay but would turn out to be nearly a year's wait. The Managing Director emphasized, however, that Brazil had made remarkable progress in many areas, and he successfully urged the banks to continue to roll over existing credits while negotiations proceeded.

Brazil was having no better success in negotiations with official creditors. Less than $1 billion of the anticipated $2.5 billion in bilateral official credits had been made available in 1984, and there was little prospect of getting additional credits through that source in the coming year. Creditors never had been fully committed to following up on their vague initial promises, and the subsequent policy slippages had further weakened their interest in doing so. In January 1985, Brazil stopped paying interest on bilateral debts to official creditors and requested a rescheduling agreement through the Paris Club. That strategy also failed when the Paris Club responded in February 1985 by reaffirming its usual requirement that a stand-by arrangement with the IMF was a precondition for such a deal.

By March 1985, Brazil's prospects became even more clouded when the 75-year-old president-elect fell gravely ill and underwent emergency surgery the day before his scheduled inauguration. With Neves unable to assume the powers of the presidency, the vice-president-elect, José Sarney, became acting president on March 15; on April 21, Neves died and Sarney officially assumed the presidency. For the time being, he kept Neves's economic team intact, but he lacked Neves's political support, and everyone was now operating under extreme uncertainty.

In late May, Wiesner headed a mission to Brazil to conduct the annual Article IV consultations and to try to negotiate a new program. Those negotiations broke down, principally because of disagreements over the large extent of monetary financing of fiscal deficits, which the authorities saw as necessary and the staff saw as inflationary.[47] Nonetheless, the government introduced new fiscal controls in early July, and it appeared that the impasse might be breakable. On August 19, de Larosière and Dornelles met again in Paris, and the minister conveyed his support for the July policies. The question remained, however, as to how deep President Sarney's own support went and whether Dornelles could get approval for the required policies in the face of opposition from the planning minister, Joao Sayad. At least a hint of the answer to that question came just eight days after the de Larosière–Dornelles meeting, when Sarney abruptly fired Dornelles and replaced him with a far more radical finance minister, Dilson Domingos Funaro.

Funaro initially tried to maintain the existing policy stance and continue negotiating a resumption of the EFF arrangement with the Fund. In September, several government technicians visited the Fund headquarters to resume talks on the program. Those talks were inconclusive, and Funaro soon shifted to a more radical stance.[48] As he put it to the Interim Committee at its meeting in Seoul, Korea, on October 6,

> Brazil would honor its international commitments, but the government must also fulfill its responsibilities to its people. In the present circumstances, growth was an imperative dictated by the legitimate demands of the Brazilian population. . . . Any debt restructuring exercise would have to comply with that growth requirement.[49]

Funaro also met separately with de Larosière in Seoul, but the meeting was tense, as the two men were far apart in their conceptions of what policies were needed if Brazil was to regain financial stability. As 1985 drew to a close, there was little prospect of an early resumption of Brazil's access to Fund resources: access that Brazil needed, not so much for its own sake, but to regain the credibility that would unlock access to official and private creditors around the world.

---

[47]See memorandum from Reichmann to the Managing Director (June 18, 1985); in IMF/RD Managing Director file "Brazil—1985, Vol. II" (Accession 88/179, Box 7, Section 517). The level of consumer prices in Brazil more than tripled in 1985, and the rate of inflation had been on a rising trend for three years.

[48]Presgrave (1993), p. 184, discusses the turn in Funaro's attitude at that time.

[49]Minutes of ICMS/Meeting 25 (October 6, 1985), p. 8.

Argentina

Argentina had made a promising start in implementing its adjustment program in the first half of 1983 (see Chapter 8), but the effort would turn out to be difficult to sustain. Throughout the next three years, the staff and the authorities would struggle to keep the program from collapsing.

Stalemate with the Banks: June–November 1983

By mid-1983, although macroeconomic policies and conditions were reasonably well under control, the program was already in difficulty because of the dispute between Argentina and commercial banks regarding the treatment of payments to the United Kingdom (see Chapter 8, pp. 331–32). Since April 1982, Argentine law had prohibited financial transfers to British residents, including banks and corporations. Lloyds International was the largest single bank creditor to the Argentine government, and Guy Huntrods of Lloyds (see footnote 28, p. 375) was a cochairman of the banks' Advisory Committee, so maintaining a good working relationship with U.K. banks was a sine qua non for reaching any agreement. Furthermore, a commitment to eliminate discriminatory foreign exchange restrictions had to be reached by the end of July, as a performance criterion for future drawings under the stand-by arrangement with the Fund.[50] The government thus had to find a way around the strong domestic political pressure to maintain the restrictions.

In early June 1983, shortly after Argentina had drawn SDR 300 million ($320 million) from the IMF as the second installment of the stand-by arrangement, the authorities sought to deal with the restrictions problem quietly and administratively. Julio González del Solar, the president of the central bank, met secretly with Gordon Richardson, governor of the Bank of England, at the BIS governors' meeting in Basel, Switzerland, and assured him that they would find a way to pay British banks. That assurance helped reassure the Advisory Committee, and a tentative rescheduling agreement was reached in New York on June 23.[51] The next day, however, when González del Solar stopped in Washington on his way home, to meet with de Larosière at the Fund, the Managing Director reminded him that the Fund arrangement required Argentina to lift *all* discriminatory foreign exchange restrictions: those against commercial firms and individuals as well as those against banks. Two weeks later, González del Solar and Jorge Wehbe, the

---

[50] "Argentina—Staff Report for the 1982 Article IV Consultation and Request for Stand-By Arrangement" EBS/83/8 (January 10, 1983), p. 44.

[51] On the surface, British banks were covered, because the syndicated loan agreements not only required Argentina to pay all participating creditors proportionately, but also required the creditor banks to share any payments in the event that they were not made proportionately (see Chapter 8). The problem was that the British share was large enough that a refusal to repay U.K. banks would leave all creditors significantly short. In addition, a refusal to repay trade credits to British firms would indirectly affect those firms' banks.

minister of the economy, formally requested an extension until mid-August of the deadline for removing restrictions. The Managing Director agreed to this request; although the loan agreement with commercial banks was scheduled to be signed on August 12, the next scheduled drawing was not due to be made until the end of that month.

On Monday, August 8, the authorities cabled both the Fund and the Advisory Committee that they were now ending all discriminatory practices and that they intended to sign the bank agreement on the 12th as originally planned. When the committee bankers requested further information from the Fund, however, the staff informed them that the Argentine action was purely administrative; the discriminatory legislation remained on the books. The Committee then decided to postpone the signing.

That Thursday, the Acting Managing Director, William Dale, called an extraordinary meeting of the Executive Board for the following Monday, to discuss the single question of whether to grant a waiver for the end-August drawing on the basis of the assurances provided by the Argentine authorities. The use of Fund resources was dependent on the settlement of arrears with commercial banks, which required Argentina to sign agreements with the banks for both a $300 million bridging loan and the $1.5 billion medium-term loan that had originally been planned for April. If the Fund was satisfied that Argentina was no longer discriminating against another member country, then it appeared that the logjam could be broken.

At the August 15 meeting, the Executive Director for the United Kingdom, Nigel Wicks, noted that discrimination by one member country against another was "against the fundamental spirit of the Fund." Although the United Kingdom had imposed restrictions against Argentina during the war in the spring of 1982, it had since eliminated those restrictions and had repealed the enabling legislation. His authorities were concerned that the Argentine legislation remained in place, but they were prepared to wait to see if payments were nonetheless made promptly.[52] After further discussion, the Board agreed that the criterion should simply be whether discrimination was actually being practiced. Tenuous as this agreement was, it sufficed to enable Dale to assure the banks that Argentina would be eligible to draw as soon as it eliminated arrears or reached agreement with foreign commercial creditors on a means to settle them.

For the moment, it appeared that a crisis had been averted. Later that week, however, a staff team led by Christian Brachet (Assistant Director of the Western Hemisphere Department) went to Buenos Aires to conduct a more general review of compliance with the performance criteria of the stand-by arrangement. The mission found that the payments arrears were not the only problem: the authorities had lost control of wage policy and thereby of both their own budget and the country's international competitiveness, there were signs of excessive monetary growth, and a new multiple currency practice had been introduced in the form of

---

[52]Minutes of EBM/83/120 (August 15, 1983), p. 5.

a rebate on auto exports. Since the Executive Board had agreed only to waive the arrears test, the Fund now had no choice but to deny Argentina the drawing of SDR 300 million that had been scheduled for the end of August.

The miseries confronting the Argentine authorities continued to grow. On September 8, González del Solar called on the Managing Director to request a waiver for the missed performance criteria and was told that he would have to show more substantial progress first. When he returned to Buenos Aires, he was immediately jailed by a provincial judge on the grounds that by negotiating with foreign creditors he was violating an Argentine law prohibiting giving foreigners jurisdiction over public sector debt. Although he was released after only a few days, one of his first presents as a free man was a September 12 cable from the Advisory Committee (sent also to Wehbe and de Larosière) stating that they were not prepared to extend the repayment of the bridge loan (due September 15) or to sign the medium-term loan until the legislation enabling discrimination against U.K. banks was repealed.

There was little prospect of tightening macroeconomic policy in the fall of 1983, because the presidential election that would end nearly eight years of military rule was to be held at the end of October. A new government would take power in December, and only then could any progress toward stabilization begin. In the meantime, if no agreement could be reached with commercial banks, Argentina's arrears to commercial creditors would accumulate to a level that could pose a serious threat to the international banking system.

On October 14, de Larosière cabled Rhodes to say that the main reason for the delay in reactivating the program was the banks' refusal to sign an agreement with the authorities.[53] In his view, the banks were holding up the Fund, not the other way around. Three days later, he gave essentially the same message to Executive Directors in an informal meeting. Policies were off track and if not modified would prevent the authorities from meeting the performance criteria for the scheduled end-November drawing, but reaching a settlement with the banks was an essential first step toward getting back on track. Perhaps not surprisingly, the banks saw the matter differently: without a strengthening of policies, and without a more iron-clad assurance of nondiscrimination in repayments, they would be assuming undue risk in raising their exposure in Argentina.

On October 30, while the country was without a bank agreement and while its arrangement with the Fund was still suspended, Argentina elected Raúl Alfonsín to be its first civilian president since the coup that had overthrown Isabel Martínez de Perón in 1976. For the next month, the authorities concentrated efforts on securing a bank deal before the oft-extended bridge loan expired on November 30. At the last possible moment, after marathon negotiations had forced the banks to keep the interbank clearing system (CHIPS) open for a record 3½ hours beyond its normal closing hour to accommodate the massive settlements that fell due on that date, the bank loan was finally signed.

---

[53]IMF/CF (C/Argentina/150.1 "Fund Relations with Commercial Banks, 1975–1983").

Stalemate with the Fund: December 1983–June 1984

Alfonsín was inaugurated on December 10, 1983, and he appointed Bernardo Grinspun (minister of the economy) and Enrique García Vásquez (president of the central bank) to head his economic team. On the 21st, García Vásquez went to the IMF and declared to de Larosière that massive capital flight and dollarization of transactions in the last few months had left Argentina essentially a country without a currency.[54] What a few months ago had seemed to be primarily a political and diplomatic dilemma had overthrown the fragile stability of the country's finances to the point that a major reorientation of policies would be required to restore it. The Managing Director proposed starting negotiations for a longer-term program that could be supported by a financial arrangement under the EFF. The governor countered that speed was of the essence and that a new stand-by arrangement might be preferable, at least as an interim step. They agreed that a mission would go to Buenos Aires in February to begin negotiations, and that the terms of an arrangement could be settled by that time.

Grinspun could not wait two months to begin to restore financial stability. In early January, he went to New York to tell the Committee bankers that he was seeking a new financial arrangement with the Fund and to ask that they redouble their efforts to complete the syndication of the medium-term loan that had been agreed to some six weeks earlier. He then met with the Managing Director in Washington to convey directly his intent to reach an agreement both with the banks and the Fund. With nothing yet in place to demonstrate a commitment to stronger policies, however, this initial effort at persuasion was largely in vain. On January 23, the existing stand-by arrangement (on which SDR 900 million, roughly $915 million, had not been drawn) was formally canceled, clearing the way for a fresh start on a new program.[55]

The Fund mission, headed by Joaquín Ferrán (Senior Advisor in the Western Hemisphere Department) and later by Wiesner, arrived in Buenos Aires on February 6 for what would turn out to be an extraordinarily long and fruitless attempt to negotiate a program for 1984. Economic conditions had worsened dramatically in the run-up to the October election and had continued to deteriorate, the new authorities had not been able to design a consistent set of policies for 1984, and Grinspun appeared to have neither the inclination nor the political backing to correct the situation. After a wasted month, Wiesner returned to headquarters and reported to the Managing Director on the extent of the impasse, at a meeting that was also attended by senior U.S. officials. Real wages were still being raised in defiance of economic realities, he reported, interest rates were negative in real terms, inflation was eroding the competitiveness of the exchange rate, and the official ex-

---

[54]Memorandum for files, attached to memorandum from Beza to the Deputy Managing Director (January 5, 1984); in IMF/RD Managing Director file "Brazil—1984, January–February" (Accession 85/231, Box 2, Section 177).

[55]The cancellation of the stand-by arrangement was timed to save Argentina from having to pay a fee of some $50,000 for continuing a financial arrangement on which they were not expected to draw.

change rate was far from the rate that prevailed in the parallel market.[56] In short, it was a classic case of fiscal and monetary excess as the new government appeared to be trying to consolidate its political power before regaining control of the economy.

These economic mistakes were compounded by what nearly everyone concerned saw as an attempt by the government to cover up the extent of the problem and to negotiate as if the solution lay in the hands of foreign creditors rather than domestic policymakers. The day after the mission's return to Washington, Rhodes called Dale around midnight and asked him to come to New York the next morning to meet with him and a few of his colleagues on the Committee. Arriving in New York, Dale was told that the bankers were not being kept informed by the Argentine authorities and that consequently they were getting increasingly frustrated and angry. It was now clear that no progress could be made on financing until a much stronger adjustment program was agreed with the Fund and was put in place.

Alfonsín then made what appeared to be a positive move by sending the eminent (and octogenarian) Argentine economist Raúl Prebisch as his personal representative to meet with the Managing Director in Washington. Prebisch spent eight days at the Fund (March 23–31, 1984), talking extensively with the staff as well as management and generally trying to help calm the situation as best as he could.

While Prebisch was in Washington, Grinspun crossed the Río de la Plata from Buenos Aires to Punta del Este, Uruguay, for the annual meetings of the Inter-American Development Bank (IDB) on March 25–27. The IDB meetings provided a forum for the Argentine authorities to find a way to avoid a default if the banks refused to reschedule $500 million in interest payments that were coming due at the end of the month. To that end, the Mexican finance minister, Jesús Silva Herzog, proposed to his colleagues from Venezuela, Brazil, and Colombia that they jointly lend Argentina $300 million for up to three months. Both Mexico and Brazil faced serious debt problems of their own at the time, but Silva Herzog successfully argued that the greatest danger to the financial stability of the whole region was the risk of losing the good working relations that they had gained with international banks. All countries in Latin America thus had a stake in avoiding a collapse in the Argentine negotiations.

A critical element in putting together the four-country loan was establishing confidence that Argentina would soon succeed in negotiating a new financial arrangement with the Fund, a prospect that in fact was by no means certain. Although Wiesner participated in the IDB meetings on behalf of the Fund, and although negotiations with the Fund were then at a very preliminary stage, the loan agreement was predicated on the assumption that the $300 million would be repaid in June, following an anticipated resumption of IMF lending. U.S. treasury of-

---

[56]Memorandum from Beza to the Managing Director (March 21, 1984); in IMF/RD Managing Director file "Argentina, January–April 1984" (Accession 85/231, Box 2, Section 177).

ficials—notably Deputy Secretary Richard T. McNamar and Assistant Secretary David C. Mulford—also participated in the discussions leading to the four-country loan, and they agreed to arrange for the United States to lend Argentina another $300 million once Argentina signed a Letter of Intent, as a further bridge to the expected drawing on the Fund.

The Punta del Este meetings ended on March 27, which left just three days to work out the formalities of the lending agreements so that Argentina could make its interest payments on the 31st. Grinspun and Silva Herzog briefed Wiesner on the package as they all flew together to Buenos Aires on the 28th. Wiesner then telephoned the Managing Director, whose meetings with Prebisch were ongoing, to inform him that the lenders were asking for a positive progress report on the ne-gotiations as a precondition for completing the deal. With that motivation in mind, de Larosière and Prebisch set out to reach an accord on at least the outlines of a policy package before the deadline expired.

After a series of further discussions, Prebisch and other Argentine officials gath-ered in the Managing Director's office at 5:00 p.m. on March 30, along with Bra-chet and a few other Fund staff members. Mario Teijeiro, the Alternate Executive Director representing Argentina at the Fund, was present and was frequently on the telephone to the Finance Ministry in Buenos Aires to get instructions or sup-port. After five hours, they were on the verge of an agreement, until Teijeiro re-turned from a telephone call to say that Grinspun was insisting on policies that were substantially looser than those in the draft outline. The meeting then con-tinued until just after 11:30 at night, at which point de Larosière and Prebisch both felt able to sign a report that could be issued to creditors.

The Prebisch–de Larosière agreement included several key points. First, the fis-cal deficit was to be reduced from 18 percent of GDP in the last quarter of 1983 to 6 percent by the first quarter of 1985. Second, wage policy would be restructured so that adjustments would be based on prospective rather than past inflation. Third, interest rate policy would be tightened so as to maintain positive real interest rates; cuts in interest rates would be implemented only after a decline in inflation and in the fiscal deficit. Fourth, exchange rate policy would aim to strengthen competi-tiveness of exports sufficiently to achieve a balance of payments target that was con-sistent with external financing constraints. The specific policy measures that would be needed to meet these general goals were to be worked out in the course of con-tinuing discussions between the staff and the authorities.[57]

As of March 31, 1984, when the text of the agreement was released to the press, Argentina had managed to pull back from the very brink of default.[58] They had ob-tained $300 million from the four Latin American countries ($100 million each

---

[57]The "progress report" was circulated to Executive Directors via a memorandum from Teijeiro (April 17, 1984); in IMF/RD Managing Director file "Argentina, January–April 1984" (Acces-sion 85/231, Box 2, Section 177).

[58]U.S. Treasury Secretary Regan, describing the agreement to reporters on March 31, character-ized it as aimed at avoiding both a "crisis of government" in Argentina and an international bank-ing crisis; see the *New York Times*, April 1, 1984, pp. A1, A16. For a detailed account of the nego-tiations in Buenos Aires and in Washington, see *Clarín* (Buenos Aires), March 31, 1984, pp. 2–4.

from Mexico and Venezuela, plus $50 million each from Colombia and Brazil), at an interest rate of 1 percent over LIBOR. The 11 commercial banks represented on the Advisory Committee had kicked in a total of $100 million, at an even more favorable rate of ⅛ point over LIBOR.[59] Those sums, plus $100 million from Argentina's own foreign exchange reserves, were then used to pay the $500 million in interest due to the banks. Formally, the official and bank loans carried 30-day maturities, but everyone understood that the loans would be rolled over for up to two more months until the Fund arrangement was in place.

Negotiations between the authorities and the Fund continued in Washington throughout April but did not lead to any progress. During discussions held in the margins of the Interim Committee meetings, the authorities resisted a suggestion from the Fund staff for a devaluation aimed at stemming capital flight. In the view of the authorities, capital flight from Argentina reflected nothing more than uncertainty over the availability of external financing, not an inadequacy of the policy stance.[60] Later in the month, the authorities even proposed raising fiscal expenditures from 43 percent to 49 percent of GDP, raising questions about the seriousness of their negotiating stance.

Matters got even worse in May when Wiesner returned with a staff team to conduct the annual Article IV consultations in Buenos Aires. The Fund staff insisted that financial stability could be restored only by halting and then at least partially reversing the rise in public sector real wages that had been recorded since Alfonsín had assumed the presidency. Alfonsín, however, had publicly committed himself to increasing real wages by at least 6 percent through the year, and he was determined to keep that pledge. Grinspun informed the staff that he could agree with their technical analysis, but the course that they were insisting upon was politically unacceptable and could not be achieved. By the end of May, the commercial banks had agreed on financing terms, conditional only on a Fund-approved Letter of Intent, and official creditors had agreed to roll over their credits for another 30 days. The pressure on the Fund to approve a program was intense, but the negotiators were getting nowhere.

The bottom of this vortex was reached in June 1984. Grinspun and the planning minister, Juan Vital Sourrouille, having prepared a draft Letter of Intent that apparently had the blessing of Alfonsín, took the unusual gambit of going public with it and submitting it to the full cabinet for approval on June 9, before they had even submitted it to the Fund staff for consideration (which they did on June 11).[61] On

---

[59]The authorities obtained this low rate by granting a lien against an equivalent amount of their foreign exchange reserves held at the Federal Reserve Bank of New York, to be activated on June 30 unless a further agreement were reached or the loan were repaid. See the testimony by Anthony B. Solomon before the Subcommittee on International Finance and Monetary Policy of the U.S. Senate Committee on Banking, Housing, and Urban Affairs. S. Hrg. 98-782, hearings on "Details and Implications of U.S. Government Involvement in Both the Argentinean and the Larger Latin American Debt Crises," May 3, 1984.

[60]Memorandum from Beza to the Managing Director (April 25, 1984); in IMF/RD Managing Director file "Argentina, January–April 1984" (Accession 85/231, Box 2, Section 177).

[61]Report by the Managing Director at EBM/84/92 (June 13, 1994), pp. 7–8 .

the 12th, Argentina's ambassador to the United States, Lucio García del Solar, called on the Managing Director to explain the extremely charged and sensitive political environment then prevailing in Buenos Aires: Isabel Perón had made a temporary but tumultuous return from exile in Spain, and her Peronist party (the main political opposition to Alfonsín's Radical party) had mobilized an estimated two million workers in a general strike as a means of pressuring the government to get tougher in negotiations with the Fund. The government was severely constrained in what it could accomplish for the economy, but it needed the endorsement of the Fund to regularize its relationships with both private and official creditors. By the end of June, some $1.6 billion in principal and interest would be due, and Argentina could not pay without help from the Fund. Sympathetic though he may have been to the government's plight, to the Managing Director there was simply no question of the Fund giving a positive signal to creditors until a credible policy program was in place.

In the last week of June, Grinspun came again to Washington, in the hope of getting the Managing Director to overrule the staff and approve the draft Letter of Intent. Almost simultaneously, Alfonsín issued a statement in Buenos Aires reaffirming his commitment to increasing real wages by 6–8 percent for the year, thereby undermining his minister's mission. Nonetheless, both de Larosière and Rhodes found enough encouragement in Grinspun's explanations to warrant asking creditors to roll over existing credits for another month and thereby once again staving off the financial and political consequences of default.

Rebuilding Credibility: July–December 1984

The rebuilding process began tentatively in July 1984, when a technical mission, headed by Brian C. Stuart (Deputy Chief of the River Plate Division in the Western Hemisphere Department), visited Buenos Aires to discuss budgetary issues. Much of that mission's work focused on wage policy. The staff argued that stabilizing the budget was practically impossible as long as wages were indexed to past inflation. The authorities, like those in Brazil, insisted that indexation was a political issue, and they argued that the program should be developed around the main macroeconomic aggregates, principally the overall budgetary and external balances. When those talks made little progress, Grinspun decided to take his case directly to the Managing Director. On August 8, he arrived in Washington with a large contingent of other senior officials and plunged into three days of meetings at the Fund.[62] That effort also failed to produce agreement on a Letter of Intent, and as a result the commercial banks refused to roll over a $125 million loan that was due on the 15th, forcing the government to repay it.

Grinspun then virtually demanded that the staff return to Argentina to continue the negotiations. De Larosière agreed, and a mission was sent out in late Au-

---

[62]Memorandums to management from Stuart and Wiesner (July 27 and August 28, 1984, respectively); in IMF/RD Managing Director file "Argentina, July–August 1984" (Accession 85/231, Box 2, Section 177).

gust, headed by Ferrán. Inflation, the staff found, was continuing to worsen, but the authorities indicated their determination to tackle it through a combination of fiscal restraint, tighter credit, and further wage negotiations with labor and management groups.[63] As soon as the mission returned, the Executive Board met on September 4 to conclude the annual Article IV consultations. Tom de Vries (Alternate—Netherlands) considered that inflation—then in excess of 20 percent a month—was so high that the economy could be stabilized only through a major additional adjustment effort. Guenter Grosche (Germany) found it regrettable that the negotiations had been subjected to so much public debate that both the authorities and the Fund were being put under great pressure. Overall, however, the discussion was low-key, as most Directors were content to wait until the ongoing negotiations were concluded before passing judgment on the situation.[64]

Adding to the pressure on the Fund and the authorities, the commercial banks evidently were not inclined to extend maturity dates further in the absence of an agreed adjustment program. To generate some forward momentum, Grinspun decided to come to Washington early for the Annual Meetings and to make one more effort at finding a compromise. This time the effort succeeded: the Fund agreed to accept the continuation of wage indexation, in return for additional tightening of budgetary and monetary policies aimed at reducing the fiscal deficit from 11½ percent in 1983 to 5½ percent in 1985 and a commitment to adjust the exchange rate so as to achieve a substantial depreciation in real terms by the end of the year. A Letter of Intent was then signed on the opening day of the Annual Meetings, September 25.[65]

Almost immediately after returning home, Grinspun announced that wages would be increased by 14 percent a month for the final three months of the year, a commitment that the Fund staff concluded would make the achievement of the program's targets all but impossible. De Larosière sent Grinspun a cable to that effect,[66] as a result of which García Vásquez came back to Washington for further discussions. It was now the middle of October, and it was clear to de Larosière that the Fund had obtained all the adjustment that it could under the circumstances. Now the Fund either could go ahead with a weak—and weakly implemented—program, or it would leave Argentina without external financing and forced to default on its obligations.

For the rest of 1984, the Managing Director's efforts on Argentina were directed toward securing as much additional financing as he could. The condition of the program left no room for slippage on that front. Argentina, the staff calculated, would need $3.1 billion in external financing in 1985 to cover its balance of pay-

[63]Report by the staff at EBM/84/132/R-2 (September 4, 1984), p. 1.

[64]Minutes of EBM/84/132–133 (September 4, 1984).

[65]"Argentina—Request for Stand-By Arrangement," EBS/84/203 (September 26, 1984). The exchange rate commitment was an oral agreement and was not included in the Letter of Intent; see related memorandums in IMF/RD Managing Director file "Argentina—Vol. II" (Accession 88/274, Box 11, Section 269).

[66]Cable from the Managing Director (October 3, 1984); in IMF/CF (C/Argentina/1760 "Stand-by Arrangements, 1984–1985").

ments deficit; another $3.2 billion to clear arrears to commercial banks, suppliers and other commercial creditors, and official creditors; perhaps $0.5 billion to re-constitute foreign exchange reserves from their depleted level; and more than $1 billion to repay outstanding swap operations and bridge loans. That left a total of approximately $8 billion to be financed.[67]

That amount was too large to be financed by the Fund and the commercial banks alone; a substantial participation by creditor countries would also be needed. On October 22, however, Alfonsín and Grinspun, meeting with French officials in Paris, were told not to expect such an official package. In response, de Larosière set out to generate the necessary support himself.[68]

Following a series of bilateral meetings with officials of creditor countries, de Larosière called together the Executive Directors representing G-10 countries and asked for their help in assembling $1 billion in export cover guarantees to be avail-able in 1985. The United States, it appeared, would provide about one-fourth of that amount if the others would come up with the rest.[69] The Fund could provide close to $1.2 billion under a stand-by arrangement, but only if the Executive Board approved the arrangement before the end of the year, after which access limits were to be reduced.[70] Another $275 million could be made available through the CFF if a case could be made that Argentina had experienced a shortfall in export receipts owing to factors outside the authorities' control (a shaky proposition, since exports were by then already recovering). The World Bank and the IDB were dis-cussing loans that could total around $600 million in 1985, and a rescheduling of official credits through the Paris Club could be counted upon to bring in another $730 million. If all of those amounts materialized, there would remain a gap of about $4.2 billion that would have to be covered by commercial banks.[71]

---

[67]The figures are from a table (undated but apparently prepared by the staff around end-November 1984) in IMF/RD Managing Director file "Argentina, November 1984" (Accession 86/34, Box 29, Section 209).

[68]Memorandum from Wiesner to the Managing Director (October 25, 1984), with handwrit-ten response; in IMF/RD Managing Director file "Paris Club" (Accession 88/274, Box 7, Section 269).

[69]There were two logical difficulties with this approach to closing the financing gap. First, since official export cover would be provided in response to specific requests and would be evaluated by the agencies concerned on a case-by-case basis, governments could give only notional indications of amounts that might be made available up to specified ceilings. Second, increased availability of such guarantees could easily lead to increased imports and thus add commensurately to the gap that had to be filled. There was, however, no alternative source of funds available at the time.

[70]In 1984, member countries were permitted to draw up to 102 percent of their quota a year. In cases of exceptional balance of payments need and where an exceptionally strong adjustment pro-gram was being implemented, access could be granted up to 125 percent. On November 16, 1984, the Executive Board decided to reduce the limit to 95 percent, or 115 percent in exceptional cases. (See Chapter 17 for details.) Argentina's quota at the time was SDR 1,113 million (and approxi-mately the same in U.S. dollars), so the new limit would reduce Argentina's access by about $76 million. Though this reduction would have been small in relation to Argentina's total financing needs, it sufficed to make end-December an effective deadline for approving the arrangement.

[71]The figures are from a report by the Managing Director at EBM/84/172 (December 3, 1984), pp. 3–4.

The struggle to keep bank creditors on board revealed the first great rift in the concerted-lending strategy. Despite the banks' fatigue with the process, they had little choice but to approve a new-money loan once the stand-by arrangement was approved, but the magnitude of the gap they were being asked to fill was a problem. $4.2 billion would imply an increase in exposure to Argentina by about 15 percent, much larger than in most other cases. De Larosière therefore decided to take the case directly to the chairmen of the 11 Advisory Committee banks, and he arranged for a meeting at the Federal Reserve Bank of New York on November 26, 1984, with the top two Federal Reserve officials—Volcker and Anthony Solomon (president of the New York bank)—present. Also invited were A.W. Clausen and Antonio Ortíz Mena, the presidents of the World Bank and the IDB, respectively. Opening the meeting at 8:30 a.m., the Managing Director asked the banks if they could give him written assurances before Christmas that they could provide $4.4 billion in new financing for 1985—an amount that would close the gap without resort to the dubious call on the CFF. Without such assurances, he explained, he could not call a Board meeting to approve the stand-by arrangement, and any delay would bring the program under the new lower access limits.[72]

After a lengthy discussion of the adjustment program and its financing requirements, Sir Jeremy Morse, the Chairman of Lloyds Bank, called for a caucus of the bankers in the room. When they returned, they insisted that the requested amount was impossible, simply because they did not believe that they could sell it to the 300 or so other banks that would have to participate in the lending syndicate. There would be a significant dropout rate among smaller banks, and the package would fail. The only hope, in their view, was to keep the loan below $4 billion. Clausen and Ortíz Mena explained their institutions' lending plans and limitations, and de Larosière explained the difficulties with requesting compensatory financing through the Fund's CFF. The financing gap, he concluded, was $4.4 billion, and they could not escape that fact. After a second caucus around noon, the bankers agreed only to consider the matter further.

Over the next week, the bank committee held intensive meetings, including sessions with the Managing Director, at the end of which they agreed to a $4.2 billion loan, which they would propose to the banking community. For his part, de Larosière agreed to support the idea of a drawing under the CFF to close the gap. Thus, relative to the initial bargaining positions, the banks would commit an additional $600 million, while the Fund would contribute an additional $270 million.[73]

The Executive Board meeting to consider the program was tentatively scheduled for the very end of the halcyon days, December 28, a date that left only four weeks to secure a "critical mass" of commitments to ensure that the banks could come up with the promised $4.2 billion. As with earlier such packages, the goal

---

[72]Speaking notes and draft minutes ("Notes for the Managing Director's Statement on Argentina, November 26, 1984") in IMF/RD Western Hemisphere Department file "Argentina—General Correspondence, 1984" (Accession 89/35, Box 3, Section 236).

[73]Minutes of EBM/84/172 (December 3, 1984), pp. 3–4.

was to have 95 percent of the money committed by the date of the Board meeting. The Deputy Managing Director, Richard D. Erb, set off on December 8 on a round-the-world trip to meet with bankers in San Francisco, Tokyo, Bahrain, Zurich, Frankfurt, and Paris. De Larosière went to New York on the 13th to meet with bankers, together with García Vásquez. Other meetings involved the staff, Executive Directors, and senior Argentine officials. By the morning of December 28, as the Board meeting began on schedule, the Managing Director was able to report that 91 percent of the package was complete. Though this was slightly below target, it was sufficient to enable U.S. treasury officials to assure the Fund that they would provide a bridge loan until the loan was finally signed, and it was "an amount that, in the [bank Advisory] Committee Chairman's view, adequately demonstrated the international banking community's commitment to do its part in further assisting Argentina."[74]

Executive Directors expressed a number of concerns during the restricted session, but most speakers were nonetheless supportive of the program. The most dubious element of the package was the CFF drawing to which the Managing Director had agreed only in desperation. Jacques Polak (Netherlands) refused to support the requested CFF drawing, on three grounds. First, the shortfall in export receipts had resulted largely from an overvalued exchange rate and from high domestic consumption demand: factors that the authorities could have controlled. Second, although there were external contributing factors—weak demand in neighboring countries and protectionism by industrial countries—those factors were not temporary, as required by the terms of the facility. Third, if the latest available data had been used to calculate the shortfall, it would have been too small to warrant the drawing. Other Directors also expressed reservations, but none declined to support the request. In response, the staff acknowledged that exports were now recovering but insisted that the request did meet the CFF criteria under the procedures established by the Board. Furthermore, the external factors depressing exports were substantial and would prove to be temporary if the world economy grew in line with staff projections.[75]

A.R.G. Prowse (Australia) raised a technical objection to the way exchange rate policy had been formulated in the program. Rather than allowing the exchange rate to float, the authorities were targeting the real exchange rate: "the real appreciation of the recent past is to be reversed and thereafter the exchange rate is to be adjusted at least sufficiently to compensate for the difference between changes in domestic and international prices." Prowse was concerned that in view of the considerable degree of government intervention in the Argentine economy, including constraints on imports, this form of exchange rate policy might not be consistent with market forces. He would have preferred that the Fund encourage the authorities to float the rate. In response, the staff noted that it was customary for the Fund to encourage countries in similar circumstances to target the real ex-

---

[74]By the start of the afternoon session of the meeting, the total had risen to 92.8 percent. See minutes of EBM/84/190/R-1 (December 28, 1984), p. 1.

[75]Minutes of EBM/84/190–191 (December 28, 1984).

change rate, and the Managing Director added that the program as a whole deemphasized the pursuit of real rather than nominal targets.[76]

The Board approved the stand-by arrangement, but with somewhat less enthusiasm than was its custom. As the Managing Director noted in summing up the discussion, there was "no room for slippages and no margin for maneuver," while the declared policies "should be seen as a minimum . . . desired performance" and were in need of "more precise formulation." For the moment, Argentina would be eligible to make its first conditional drawing in more than a year and a half.[77]

The Austral Plan: 1985

In early January, the Fund began encouraging the authorities to strengthen the adjustment program, especially by more aggressively depreciating the exchange rate. Following a staff visit, the Managing Director cabled Grinspun that without a further real depreciation, exports were likely to fall well short of the program's requirements.[78] On the whole, however, optimism still prevailed that the existing program could be sustained. On January 16, the Paris Club, at the conclusion of a meeting at which Ferrán made a detailed presentation on the program and the Argentine economy, agreed to reschedule more than $2 billion in official credits, including some $1.3 billion that was then in arrears.

Matters deteriorated sharply a few weeks later, when Ferrán led a review mission to Buenos Aires and obtained more specific information that policies were no longer consistent with the program. Neither wage policy nor exchange rate policy was on course, and several performance criteria were not being met. Most critically, the government was attempting to control interest rates at artificially low levels, and rates were now highly negative in real terms. Severe tension arose between the staff and the authorities in the course of this mission and came to a head at a meeting on February 18. Ferrán set out the staff view that the only sustainable way to reduce real interest rates was first to implement tougher fiscal and monetary policies. In response, Grinspun insisted that interest rates could be maintained independently of the macroeconomic stance and that to raise either interest rates or public sector prices would aggravate inflationary pressures. These two positions

---

[76]"Argentina—Request for Stand-By Arrangement," EBS/84/251 (December 3, 1984), p. 35; and minutes of EBM/84/190/R-1 (December 28, 1984), pp. 38–39 (Prowse), and EBM/84/191/R-1 (same date), pp. 28–30 (Managing Director).

[77]Minutes of EBM/84/191/R-1 (December 28, 1984), p. 34. The last drawing under the 1983 stand-by arrangement had been made in May of that year. In December 1983, Argentina had drawn SDR 78 million against its reserve tranche following the quota increase obtained through the Eighth General Review. The decision taken on December 28, 1984, enabled Argentina to borrow SDR 236.5 million under the stand-by arrangement in January, and simultaneously to draw SDR 275 million under the CFF. The total amount available under the 15-month stand-by arrangement was SDR 1,419 million (127.5 percent of quota), which was equivalent to an annualized access rate of 102 percent. (All of these amounts were, at the time, approximately the same in dollars as in SDRs.)

[78]Cable from the Managing Director (January 23, 1985); in IMF/RD Managing Director File "Argentina—Vol. II" (Accession 88/274, Box 11, Section 269).

were so strongly held that negotiating a compromise became futile. Ferrán informed the authorities that he did not anticipate that the Fund would grant any waivers for the next scheduled drawing without a substantial tightening of policies—a tightening that Grinspun was insisting he could not make. The meeting was adjourned with a plan to meet again two days later but with no real hope on either side for meaningful negotiations.

Following the meeting, Grinspun and García Vásquez went to see Alfonsín to report that negotiations were at an impasse. The president had little choice: if the adjustment program was to succeed, he would need a new approach and new leadership. He dismissed both officials on the spot and replaced them with a team that presumably would be more open to change.[79]

The new minister of the economy, Juan Vital Sourrouille, requested that the Fund staff return to Buenos Aires as soon as possible to renegotiate the program. Unfortunately, when Ferrán and his team arrived on March 8, the two sides fell into disagreement over how seriously to interpret the fiscal overruns at the end of 1984. Negotiations never got started, and the mission was aborted after just four days.[80]

Alfonsín was scheduled to make a state visit to Washington starting March 18, and he seized the opportunity to try to mend fences with Argentina's creditors. He brought along his new economics team, led by Sourrouille. That team (including J.J. Alfredo Concepción, the new president of the central bank) met with the Fund staff, after which Alfonsín hosted a breakfast meeting with de Larosière and Erb at the Madison Hotel on March 20. Alfonsín desperately needed the support of the Fund for his policies; without it, he had learned, neither the U.S. government nor the commercial banks would provide financing. The Managing Director refused to consider a waiver for the fiscal overruns in the absence of strong prior actions to reduce the deficit, but he did agree to break precedent by issuing a statement of support to the banks merely on the understanding that Alfonsín would give his full support to negotiating a sustainable program for the rest of 1985. This meeting marked the beginning of an intense effort, not just to put the program back on track, but to develop a new and far more radical approach to economic stability in Argentina.[81]

Ferrán and his staff team returned to Buenos Aires on March 26 for three weeks of discussions, after which Sourrouille and his team came to Washington to present their policy proposals directly to the Managing Director and to the U.S. au-

---

[79]García Vásquez was retained by Alfonsín as a counselor, and in that capacity he participated in meetings with the IMF in the following months.

[80]See memorandum from Ferrán to the Managing Director (March 18, 1985), in IMF/RD Deputy Managing Director file "Argentina, 1985 (2)" (Accession 90/104, Box 6, Section 415).

[81]De Larosière reported on the various meetings to the Executive Board at the afternoon meeting on March 20; see the minutes of EBM/85/46, p. 3. Erb conveyed the Managing Director's support to the banks' Advisory Committee at the committee's meeting in New York the next day; and de Larosière sent a written message to bank creditors on the 22nd (in IMF/CF (C/Argentina/150.1 "Fund Relations with Commercial Banks, 1984–1985"), acknowledging the lapses in implementation but also noting the government's preparedness to move forward and concluding that the completion of the bank financing package was "of the utmost importance."

thorities. In an extraordinary meeting on April 15 in the Managing Director's office that began at 5:00 p.m. and lasted for four hours, Sourrouille sketched out for de Larosière, Volcker, and Mulford his intention of implementing a shock program in June.[82] In the meantime, he would decontrol prices and wages so that relative prices could seek equilibrium levels before a freeze was put in place. Volcker argued that the key to success would not be in the effectiveness of a price freeze, which in any case would have to be strictly temporary, but in whether the fiscal deficit could be financed outside the banking system. To make a financing plan credible, he suggested—and Sourrouille concurred—that the central bank be made more independent and prohibited from financing the government. The plan was yet only an outline, but both the Fund and the Americans were enthusiastic about it, and now it had momentum.

After that meeting, the authorities went to New York to try to persuade the bankers on the Advisory Committee to be patient while they continued to negotiate with the Fund. Argentina was not yet able to stay current on its interest payments to the banks, and a Fund agreement was essential before they could restore regular financial relations. Obviously, absolute secrecy would have to be maintained regarding the plans for implementing a shock program, so the authorities and the staff began an elaborate charade of negotiating a conventional gradual-adjustment program.[83] From late April through early June, almost continuous negotiations took place, alternately in Buenos Aires and Washington. Throughout that period, the technical staffs would meet regularly so as to appear to be hammering out details for gradually restoring stability, after which a small set of senior officials would meet secretly to discuss plans for the shock program.

On June 7, the Managing Director informed the Executive Board that the staff had reached a general agreement on a new (conventional) program. In addition, a group of official creditors, led by the United States and also including the BIS and three Latin American countries (Mexico, Brazil, and Venezuela) had agreed in principle to lend Argentina the funds needed to clear arrears to the commercial banks, thereby clearing the way for the Executive Board to consider a resumption of drawings under the stand-by arrangement.[84] On June 11, Sourrouille and Concepción signed the Letter of Intent. The next day, the U.S. Treasury issued a press release welcoming the agreement and announcing that a bridge loan was being negotiated for $450 million. To all appearances, the program originally approved by the Fund six months earlier was about to be revived.[85]

---

[82]On the context of this meeting, see Machinea (1990). Details are from background interviews.

[83]In mid-April, Sourrouille proposed that a conventional program built around a sharp fiscal adjustment be announced by Alfonsín at the beginning of May, conditional on the Fund's willingness to publicly support it; a wage-price freeze and monetary reform would then be announced in mid-June. When that schedule proved to be too ambitious, the alternative emerged of negotiating the conventional and shock programs simultaneously while keeping the latter as a closely held secret.

[84]Statement by the Managing Director at EBM/85/91 (June 7, 1985), p. 3.

[85]See Clarín (Buenos Aires), June 12, 1985, pp. 2–5; and June 13, pp. 2–3. On neither day was there any hint of consideration of a more drastic reorientation of policies.

The shock program, which was scheduled to be announced on Sunday, June 16, and to be put in place the next morning, was still a closely guarded secret. The few Fund staff who were involved in the planning were sent home on leave for the days leading up to the announcement to guard against inadvertent leaks, especially as the bank creditors with whom the staff were in regular contact were beginning to suspect that something unusual was afoot. In spite of the precautions, however, rumors surfaced in Buenos Aires a couple of days early, and the authorities were forced to announce what would become known as the Austral Plan on Friday instead of waiting for the weekend.

Because of the extreme secrecy that was required, the public perception of the Fund's role in the development of the Austral Plan was quite distorted. Press reports typically were predicated on the belief that the staff had naively negotiated a relatively weak program, only to be blindsided by the announcement of the shock program a few days later. One report even went so far as to quote an unnamed Executive Director resorting to "heavy irony" in a strong complaint to "the acutely embarrassed . . . de Larosière" (who, incidentally, was not even in town at the time) at the August 9 Board meeting where the program was approved. By that time, Executive Directors were all well aware of the background to the Plan, and no dissent was expressed.[86]

The centerpiece of the Austral Plan was a new currency, the austral, which was set equal to 1,000 pesos or US$1.25.[87] Prices were temporarily frozen, central bank financing of the fiscal deficit was to be ended, and the deficit for the second half of the year was to be limited to just 2½ percent of GDP. Most dramatically, in contrast to previous practice, contracts were to be deindexed. In practice, this policy could stick only if inflation fell close enough to zero that agents could have confidence in the value of nominal contracts.

Initially, the Austral Plan worked much as intended. Aided by the "Tanzi effect," real fiscal revenues surged temporarily once inflation subsided under the price freeze, and the fiscal deficit appeared to be on target.[88] Although the banks remained reluctant to sign a new agreement until more lasting and concrete measures were in place, the bridge loan from official creditors gave Argentina some respite.[89] The authorities signed a new Letter of Intent on July 22, and the Executive Board met on August 9 to embrace the new policies enthusiastically. As Erb (the Acting Chairman) summarized the meeting, "I believe it is fair to say, without creating a sense of unwarranted euphoria, that the spirit and the tone of the

---

[86]The report was in the *International Currency Review*, Vol. 17 (December 1985), p. 44; it was later cited by Stiles (1987, p. 77), who similarly misinterpreted the situation.

[87]This was the second currency reform in two years. One austral was equivalent to 10 million of the old pesos that had been in circulation before June 1983.

[88]The exposition of this effect was developed at the Fund by Vito Tanzi when he was a Division Chief in the Fiscal Affairs Department. The Tanzi effect predicts that in a country such as Argentina, a sudden drop in the inflation rate will raise the real value of tax collections because of substantial lags between the receipt of income and the payment of taxes. See Tanzi (1977, 1978).

[89]The bridge loan, provided by a group of 12 countries, was finalized in late June and totaled $483 million.

discussion today were quite different" from the last Board meeting the previous December. "All Executive Directors warmly welcomed the new economic program. . . . Directors have qualified the program as bold, courageous, and imaginative."[90] The Board's approval reactivated the stand-by arrangement, allowed Argentina immediately to draw the SDR 236.5 million ($245 million) that had originally been scheduled for May, and unlocked the negotiations with the banks, who signed the new-money loan in New York on August 26. A late-August review mission found the situation to be under control, enabling Argentina to draw a further SDR 236.5 million at the end of September.

This initial success did not last. Fiscal policy was kept formally on track but was undermined by a surge in off-budget spending. More important, monetary policy was loosened by the Central Bank through an explosion of rediscounting.[91] Inflation was greatly reduced from the first half of the year but was still running at 2–3 percent a month, a rate that was incompatible with the maintenance of deindexed contracts. Public sector workers demanded wage increases, and the freeze could not hold. Privatization plans were scrapped when announcements were met by protests and strikes. By November 1985, Argentina was in arrears to official creditors under the terms of the Paris Club agreement of January.

Congressional elections were held in Argentina on November 3, and the ruling Radical Party held control for Alfonsín. Shortly thereafter Ferrán led a mission to see if the program could be kept on track, but he returned discouraged. The government apparently had been waiting for the elections to be over before taking action to restore stability, but now they seemed to be confident that they could stay on the present course. Once again Argentina was out of compliance with its own program, and the scheduled December drawing would not take place.

Debt Strategy Through 1985

Case-by-Case Approach

The key phrase to describe the IMF's strategy for coping with the debt crisis of the 1980s is "case-by-case." That phrase became both a mantra and a cliché, but it also conveyed the essence and the core of the strategy: never was serious consideration given to imposing a uniform solution on the indebted countries or the financial markets. There was to be no restructuring of debts except through market-based negotiations, and the role of the IMF was to be limited to providing a relatively small portion of the indebted countries' financing needs, promoting the adjustment of economic policies so as to reduce those needs, and "catalyzing" the provision of additional financing by other creditors. To that extent, the strategy

---

[90]Minutes of EBM/85/125 (August 9, 1985), p. 8.

[91]Machinea (1990, pp. 33–38) discusses the problems with monetary control during this period. Also see Heymann (1991) for an overview of the Austral Plan and its aftermath.

Table 9.1. IMF Lending Arrangements with Heavily Indebted Middle-Income Countries, 1979–89[a]

(In millions of SDRs or percent of quota)

	Date	Type[b]	Length (Months)[c]	Amount Approved[d]	Percent of Quota	Amount Used	Peak Debt (percent)[e]
Latin America and the Caribbean							
Argentina	January 1983	SBA	15	1,500	187	601	260
	December 1984	SBA	17	1,419	127	1,183	
	July 1987	SBA	15	1,113	100	782	
	November 1989	SBA	18	1,104	99	506	
Bolivia	February 1980	SBA	12	66	148	53	
	June 1986	SBA	13	50	55	33	139
Brazil	March 1983	EFF	36	4,239	425	2,743	292
	August 1988	SBA	18	1,096	75	365	
Chile	January 1983	SBA	24	500	154	500	246
	August 1985	EFF	36	750	170	750	
	August 1988[f]	EFF	12	75	17	56	
	November 1989	SBA	12	64	15	64	
Colombia	None						0
Costa Rica	March 1980	SBA	24	61	98	16	
	June 1981	EFF	36	277	450	23	
	December 1982	SBA	12	92	150	92	272
	March 1985	SBA	13	54	64	34	
	October 1987	SBA	18	50	59	0	
Ecuador	July 1983	SBA	12	158	150	158	
	March 1985	SBA	12	106	70	106	268
	August 1986	SBA	12	75	50	15	
	January 1988	SBA	14	75	50	15	
	September 1989	SBA	18	110	73	39	
Jamaica	June 1978	EFF	36	200	270	25	
	April 1981	EFF	36	478[g]	431	403	553
	June 1984	SBA	12	64	44	64	
	July 1985	SBA	12	115	79	42	
	March 1987	SBA	15	85	58	85	
	September 1988	SBA	20	82	56	41	
Mexico	January 1977	EFF	36	518	140	0	
	January 1983	EFF	36	3,411	425	2,503	
	November 1986	SBA	18	1,400	120	1,400	335[h]
	May 1989	EFF	36	3,263[i]	280	3,263	
Peru	November 1977	SBA	26	90	55	10	
	September 1978	SBA	15	184	112	64	
	August 1979	SBA	18	285	174	248	
	June 1982	EFF	36	650	264	265	285
	April 1984	SBA	24	250	76	30	
Uruguay	March 1979	SBA	12	21	25	0	
	May 1980	SBA	12	21	25	0	
	July 1981	SBA	12	32	25	32	
	April 1983	SBA	24	378	300	151	
	September 1985	SBA	18	123	75	123	208
Venezuela	June 1989	EFF	36	3,703	270	1,852	55[j]

Table 9.1 *(concluded)*

	Date	Type[b]	Length (Months)[c]	Amount Approved[d]	Percent of Quota	Amount Used	Peak Debt (percent)[e]
Other regions							
Côte d'Ivoire	February 1981	EFF	36	485	425	447	517
	August 1984	SBA	9	83	50	62	
	June 1985	SBA	12	66	40	66	
	June 1986	SBA	24	100	60	24	
	February 1988	SBA	14	94	57	7	
	November 1989	SBA	18	176	106	147	
Morocco	October 1980	EFF	36	810	540	129	
	April 1982	SBA	12	281	125	281	
	September 1983	SBA	18	300	133	300	391
	September 1985	SBA	18	200	65	10	
	December 1986	SBA	15	230	75	230	
	August 1988	SBA	16	210	68	210	
Nigeria	January 1987	SBA	12	650	77	0	0
	February 1989	SBA	15	475	56	0	
The Philippines	April 1976	EFF	36	217	124	217	
	June 1979	SBA	6	105	50	91	
	February 1980	SBA	24	410	195	410	
	February 1983	SBA	12	315	100	100	320
	December 1984	SBA	18	615	140	403	
	October 1986	SBA	18	198	45	198	
	May 1989	EFF	36	661	150	236	
Yugoslavia	May 1979	SBA	12	69	17	69	
	June 1980	SBA	18	339	82	200	
	January 1981	SBA	36	1,662	400	1,662	481
	April 1984	SBA	13	370	60	370	
	May 1985	SBA	12	300	49	300	
	June 1988	SBA	12	306	50	122	

[a]Includes arrangements approved earlier that were still in effect in 1979.

[b]SBA = ordinary stand-by arrangement; EFF = extended arrangement.

[c]Initial length. Some arrangements were extended or canceled prior to expiration.

[d]Initial approved amount, except as noted below.

[e]Peak level of the Fund holdings of the member's currency in excess of quota, in percent of quota. Includes effects of other loans through special facilities from the General Resources Account. (Also see notes 8 and 10).

[f]Extension of the previous EFF arrangement.

[g]Approved initially for 236; augmented to 478 in June 1981.

[h]Obligations from the 1989 arrangement peaked in 1990 at 411 percent.

[i]Approved initially for 2,797; augmented to 3,263 in January 1990.

[j]Obligations from this arrangement peaked in 1991 at 166 percent.

would remain constant throughout the decade. What would change would be the focus of the adjustment effort (toward longer-term and more structural programs) and the tactics to keep the banks "in the game" (moving eventually away from concerted lending, toward broader menus for restructuring debts, and finally toward directly reducing the stock of debt).

The case-by-case approach did not mean that the Fund would provide assistance only to the better performers and leave others aside. Of the 17 middle-income developing countries that came to be recognized as "heavily indebted," all received assistance from the Fund in some form during the 1980s.[92] As is shown in Table 9.1, all but two drew on Fund resources at least once, and most had active stand-by arrangements for much of the 1980s. Of the two that did not use Fund financing, one (Colombia) had a "shadow program" monitored by the Fund (see below), and the other (Nigeria) had two stand-by arrangements on which the authorities chose not to draw.[93]

During the initial phase of the debt strategy (1982–85), in addition to the three major cases discussed above, the Fund engaged in lending arrangements with ten other heavily indebted countries. Without attempting to describe those arrangements in detail, it is worth noting a few key points.[94] First, these were all cases where the initial imbalances were large enough to constitute an economic crisis. Either the current account deficit was too large to be financed without extraordinary measures, or domestic economic activity was seriously depressed; often, both. When Chile, Peru, Uruguay, and Côte d'Ivoire sought the help of the IMF in this period, they were experiencing output declines of 10 to 20 percent. Chile and Côte d'Ivoire, as well as Costa Rica, Jamaica, and Morocco, faced current account deficits of more than 10 percent of GDP.

Second, in nearly every case, approval of the Fund arrangement was a precondition for financing agreements with commercial and official creditors.[95] On several occasions, however, especially by 1985, final agreements with banks took a year or more to conclude after the Fund arrangement was in place. Hence many of the negotiated programs were underfinanced, and the countries were forced either to intensify their policy adjustments or seek waivers and modifications to the original terms.

Third, during this period, adjustment was mostly confined to tightening monetary, fiscal, and wage policies, while attempting to maintain the exchange rate at a competitive level, often through devaluation. Other, more structural, reforms—liberalization of prices, privatization of state enterprises, simplification of regulations, etc.—which would later be seen as crucial to the restoration of growth, were not ignored but were not yet given the same emphasis.

---

[92]This grouping comprises the "Baker 15" countries (see Chapter 10), which were specified as heavily indebted in the *World Economic Outlook* classification from 1986 on, plus Costa Rica and Jamaica. The Fund, of course, also had financial arrangements with many of the less heavily indebted developing countries during this period.

[93]The Nigerian authorities indicated in the Letters of Intent for these arrangements that they did not intend to use the resources and were seeking only the Fund's endorsement of their structural adjustment program for the purpose of securing agreements with other creditors. "Nigeria—Stand-by Arrangement," EBS/86/246, Sup. 3 (December 17, 1986), pp. 14–15; and "Nigeria—Stand-by Arrangement," EBS/89/2, Sup. 1 (February 8, 1989), p. 7.

[94]The Chilean crisis was described in Chapter 8, and Costa Rica is examined below, in Chapter 11. The Philippines is discussed in the more general context of Fund conditionality in Chapter 13, while Peru is discussed in the context of the arrears problem, in Chapter 16.

[95]Commercial bank creditors, led by an Advisory Committee chaired by Chase Manhattan Bank, made an exception for Venezuela in 1983. Negotiations for a stand-by arrangement were not succeeding, as the staff concluded that adjustment was needed but was being delayed by impending presidential elections. Creditor banks nonetheless agreed to reschedule public sector debts falling due in both 1983 and 1984. No concerted lending was involved, so this agreement simply maintained the existing level of bank exposure.

Fourth, where the initial problems were severe, financing was delayed, and badly needed reforms were not undertaken, the Fund-supported programs usually failed. Of 25 arrangements approved with these countries in 1982–85, only 11 were fully utilized, and several of those required substantial modification before they were finished. The difficulties experienced in implementing programs in Mexico, Brazil, and Argentina have already been seen. Serious implementation problems were also encountered in programs with Côte d'Ivoire, Peru, the Philippines, and Uruguay, among others.

Fifth, notwithstanding the obstacles, almost all of these arrangements were repaid on time and in full. Peru developed protracted arrears, and later in the decade Argentina occasionally fell behind in payments for short periods. The others remained current, even as many of them went into arrears to other creditors. Abandoning the Fund was tantamount to giving up on regaining access to international financial markets. The debt strategy might not have been a complete success, but few of the indebted countries were prepared to turn their backs on it.

A primary goal of the debt strategy that emerged in the second half of 1982 was to reestablish normal financial relations between creditors and debtors, on the grounds that both groups would benefit and that a systemic crisis would thereby be averted. As the above brief review of the case-by-case approach suggests, the Fund's strategy to promote this objective was to assist countries in adjusting policies to a sustainable stance and to encourage commercial creditors to continue to provide enough financing until the indebted countries could get their economies back to a sustainable path.[96] The first half of that strategy involved little more than an intensification of the Fund's traditional role vis-à-vis member countries. The second half, in contrast, required a sharp break with the Fund's traditional arm's-length relations vis-à-vis private creditors. By 1985, a major preoccupation of the Fund was the search for a means of closing the strategy, of restoring normality so that the temporary surge in reliance on the Fund could be quickly ended.

Concerted Lending

Concerted lending agreements by commercial bank creditors played such a key role in the early years of the debt strategy, and the difficulty of continuing with these agreements played such a key role in forcing changes in the strategy later on, that it is worth a pause to review how they fit in with the overall structure.

Before the debt crisis hit in 1982, the standard practice in the Fund was to calculate a borrowing country's financing requirements: in part by determining how much the country could expect to borrow from commercial, as well as official, creditors; and in part by determining how much debt the country reasonably could take on without straining its ability to repay. Typically, one or more lead banks would have formed informal lending syndicates, and the banks' intentions were easily ascertained through informal contacts. (For notable exceptions, see Chapter

---

[96]For a summary of the Fund staff's view of the debt strategy, see "Implementation of the Debt Strategy—Current Issues," EBS/87/38 (February 20, 1987).

6, p. 275.) In problem cases, bank loans were often made conditional on the country entering into and complying with a stand-by arrangement with the Fund.[97] That strategy collapsed, at least for the most heavily indebted countries, with the Mexican crisis of August 1982.

As recounted in Chapter 7, Mexico's largest creditor banks agreed within a week of the blowup—with the tacit blessing of their national regulatory authorities—to organize an Advisory Committee to negotiate with the Mexican authorities on behalf of all of the banks in the various existing syndicates. A similar committee was formed for Argentina in November 1982, and a more complicated committee structure was attempted for Brazil a few months later (see Chapter 8). In forming these committees, the banks hoped to find a way to gradually reduce their loan exposure in each country without precipitating a default or a financial crisis. That goal, however, put the banks in direct conflict with the IMF: any additional lending by the Fund would be offset by greater withdrawals by the banks and would produce no benefit to the member country. Within the traditional structure of relationships, the only ways to avoid that result were for official creditors to provide still more financing (which would then be used indirectly to repay the banks) or for the country to refuse to repay its debts.

The turning point came at the November 1982 meeting in New York (see Chapter 7), at which the Managing Director informed the banks that the Fund would not approve Mexico's requests for an extended arrangement until the banks provided him with written assurances that they would increase their exposure by enough to cover a substantial fraction ($5 billion) of Mexico's scheduled interest payments for 1983. The threat was credible, because although the banks knew that the Fund had to help Mexico as best it could, they also knew that without the requested commitment from them, Fund lending would not help the country.

The concerted-lending process brought the Fund and the banks into a close working relationship. Fund staff occasionally attended the (usually monthly) meetings between the Advisory Committees and the authorities. Bankers often came to the Fund to review developments with the staff. After the banks set up their own monitoring organizations such as the Institute of International Finance (located just one block from the IMF headquarters in Washington), the staff regularly exchanged information with them. The Managing Director and the Deputy Managing Director spoke and met frequently with the chairs of the Committees and occasionally with other key bankers as well. Both staff and management met frequently with officials of the United States and other major creditor countries with regard to pending bank agreements.

As necessary as this coziness may have been, it gave rise to two problems. First, as an ironic twist to a policy aimed at ensuring that commercial banks would not withdraw support from countries in trouble, it gave the banks a virtual veto over the approval and financing of adjustment programs. With smaller countries where the banks' exposure did not threaten their solvency, and even in some larger coun-

---

[97]For a summary of pre-1982 relations with creditors, see "The Role of the Fund in Assisting Members with Commercial Banks and Official Creditors," EBS/85/173 (July 23, 1985), pp. 1–5.

tries where the banks had a strong interest in altering the outcome, they were able to use this power to force significant modifications to the program, often badly delaying approval and implementation.

This difficulty was illustrated in Chile in 1984. The stand-by arrangement that had been approved in January 1983 had gone off track twice in its first year, and negotiations were held in late 1983 and early 1984 on a program that could serve as the basis for resuming the arrangement. Negotiations were protracted, because the economy was sliding into recession, the Pinochet government was facing a rising tide of social unrest, a new team of economic officials was brought in through a cabinet shuffle at the beginning of April, and the new authorities were pushing for a greater easing of fiscal and monetary policies than the staff thought was warranted.[98] Meanwhile, the banks were insisting on the continued government subsidization of the servicing of private sector debts (see Chapter 8), without which they refused to sign an agreement covering official payments due in 1984. The staff were reluctant to approve that practice, which was being implemented through a preferential exchange rate and which raised the fiscal deficit substantially. The Fund was not prepared to approve an arrangement without a bank deal at hand, so it faced a Hobson's choice. Rather than testing the resolve of both the banks and the government, the staff agreed to allow a greater easing than it otherwise would have, and the Executive Board approved the continuation of the multiple currency practice and the resumption of drawings in May.[99]

The second problem was that concerted lending was seldom effective for smaller countries, where the banks had less of a stake in the outcome. This asymmetry complicated the Fund's efforts to treat all member countries evenhandedly. In a number of heavily indebted countries—including Costa Rica, Jamaica, and Yugoslavia—programs were negotiated in 1982–83 on the understanding that banks would contribute to the financing of the program through rescheduling agreements, but without a requirement that firm assurances be provided to the Fund.[100] In other cases, the Executive Board expressed grave doubts about generalizing the practice. At a meeting to review the debt strategy in April 1983, the Board endorsed the staff suggestion that the use of concerted lending should be limited to exceptional cases of debt-servicing difficulties:[101]

> In a relatively few circumstances of exceptional character where the difficulties encountered by major debtors have had broader implications for the orderly function-

---

[98]For the Chilean side of this story, see Escobar (1991), Chapter 11.

[99]See "Chile—Staff Report for the 1983 Article IV Consultation and Consultation Under Stand-By Arrangement," EBS/84/50 (March 9, 1984) and minutes of EBM/84/76 (May 14, 1984). The story had a happy ending. The bank agreement was finalized in June, and the government was able to get spending under control in the second half of the year. The stand-by arrangement was successfully concluded, and the final drawing was made in December.

[100]For a set of case studies, see "Payments Difficulties Involving Debt to Commercial Banks," SM/83/47 (March 9, 1983), Annex III.

[101]The staff position is in "Fund Policies and External Debt Servicing Problems," SM/83/45 (March 8, 1983), pp. 44–45. The Board meeting to discuss the paper was EBM/83/57–58 (April 6, 1983).

ing of the international financing system, the Fund management has taken the initiative, in concert with major creditors, in ensuring that before Fund resources could be committed, sufficient additional financial flows from both official and commercial sources were available. . . . In view of the exceptional nature of the initiatives, it would not be appropriate to formalize any general policy criteria concerning the precise role of the Fund in such situations. . . . [A] case-by-case approach . . . is suggested as the best course of action.

Concerns over the extent to which concerted lending was an appropriate adjunct to Fund lending arrangements came to a head when the Executive Board met on April 22, 1983, to consider a request for a stand-by arrangement with Uruguay. In response to a request from the authorities for Fund assistance in securing new bank loans to help close the projected financing gap, the Managing Director had asked for and had received assurances from bank creditors for a $240 million increase in exposure. Jacques Polak, supported by several other Directors, objected. Two weeks earlier, he had made a general plea for limiting the Fund's interference with private sector lending decisions. It was a mistake, he argued, to generalize the use of concerted lending to cases where good performance already made it in the banks' interests to lend to the country: "urging banks to extend credit . . . could not be a long-term activity of the Fund . . . [and] should remain limited to exceptional cases, and especially to those entailing risks to the international financial system. . . . In [my] view, the Fund has gone almost to the limit of what is proper. . . ."[102] Now he was ready to draw the line. Uruguay had a good record of conducting stable economic policies, and it had run into difficulty only because of adverse exchange rate movements and because of contagion from events in neighboring countries (Argentina and Brazil).[103] The banks, in this view, were using concerted lending as a "security blanket" and a substitute for their own business judgment. Uruguay, the banks, and the Fund would be better off in the long run if the banks were to reach a voluntary solution on their own. De Larosière responded that the approach was needed in this case, because the program could not succeed without exceptional financing from the banks. The Fund could not ask a small country to wait for the banks to come around voluntarily, while larger countries were receiving stronger assistance.[104]

---

[102]Minutes of EBM/83/57 (April 6, 1983), pp. 12–13.

[103]Uruguay at the time maintained a fixed exchange rate against the U.S. dollar. The combination of an appreciating dollar and devaluations by other Latin American countries had induced a sharp loss in international competitiveness. Some banks had then attempted to pull out of lending to Uruguay when they were forced to increase their exposure elsewhere in the region through concerted lending agreements. In addition, some of the largest creditor banks to Uruguay were located in neighboring countries and had also been cut off from access to international credits.

[104]The Fund staff later estimated that for the period 1983–86, the three largest heavily indebted countries (Brazil, Mexico, and Argentina) received $15 billion in net lending from international commercial banks. Over the same period, net lending to the 12 smaller heavily indebted middle-income developing countries (i.e., the rest of the "Baker 15") was negative (–$4 billion). Memorandum from L.A. Whittome (Director of the Exchange and Trade Relations Department) to the Managing Director (October 28, 1987); in IMF/RD Managing Director file "E.T.R.— July–December 1987" (Accession 89/72, Box 1, Section 164).

The Managing Director's view was accepted by the Board, and the use of concerted lending was endorsed for Uruguay.[105] The policy limiting it to exceptional circumstances remained in place, but no further attempt was made to delineate those circumstances.

Approval in Principle

In addition to concerted lending, a second element in the Fund's financing-assurances arsenal was to approve programs in principle but to withhold the provision of money until other financing agreements were in place. Frequently, the Fund found itself caught in a perverse Alphonse and Gaston routine in which each creditor insisted that the others make the first commitment. Waiting for the banks to secure a "critical mass" of commitments occasionally and with increasing regularity became counterproductive: the more the process was repeated, the more reluctant the banks were to participate; the absence of Fund approval made the critical mass even more difficult to obtain; and even once the critical mass (which might have covered anywhere from 85 to 95 percent of the required total) was in hand, the remaining commitments often took months to complete.

The tactic of approving a stand-by arrangement in principle began with Sudan, in January 1983.[106] In that case, the question was whether official creditors, acting through the Paris Club, would agree to provide an exceptional level of financing. The Fund was prepared to provide SDR 170 million ($187 million; 100 percent of quota) over 12 months, which left an estimated financing gap of $773 million. A Consultative Group meeting had generated some $300 million, and Saudi Arabia and Kuwait had promised to provide debt relief on terms comparable to those granted by the Paris Club. Sudan had accumulated substantial arrears to banks, but an agreement with banks was not expected and was not a precondition for program approval. The balance would therefore have to be covered by the Paris Club, which would not act until the Fund approved the country's adjustment program. Because the Fund could not be certain that official creditors would go along with the Sudanese request—Fund approval was a necessary condition, but it might not be sufficient—the Executive Board decided to approve the arrangement in principle, to become effective when "the Fund finds that satisfactory arrangements have been made for the reduction of Sudan's debt service obligations for 1983 to a level consistent with Sudan's program."[107] The Paris Club then agreed to provide the requested relief, and the Fund arrangement became effective in late February.

Over the next 18 months, the Board granted approval in principle for seven more stand-by arrangements (out of some 50 arrangements approved), usually to

---

[105]Minutes of EBM/83/65–66 (April 22, 1983).

[106]This case may be compared with the handling of Romania in June 1982 (see Chapter 8). When agreement with bank creditors was delayed in that case, the dormant stand-by arrangement was reactivated with a token drawing, and further drawings were left unscheduled pending settlement of arrears to banks.

[107]Minutes of EBM/83/21 (January 28, 1983), p. 35.

cope with similar uncertainties regarding official financing.[108] Only two of those—Ecuador and Côte d'Ivoire—involved commercial banks in a major way. In June 1983, negotiations between Ecuador and its bank creditors had been dragging on for months, and the Fund forced the issue by making its approval of a one-year stand-by arrangement conditional on the conclusion of those negotiations. The bank deal was completed as anticipated, and the arrangement went into effect in late July.[109] In May 1984, the Board approved in principle a one-year stand-by arrangement for Côte d'Ivoire, conditional both on financing arrangements and on policy actions being taken (increases in mass transit fares and water charges). Two days later, the Paris Club granted the expected debt relief, but the banks (through the London Club) reached agreement only in late July. The Fund arrangement became effective the following week.[110]

By that time, the Board was becoming concerned that the tactic was being used indiscriminately, without any clear governing principles. The staff were asked to develop recommendations, which the Board then approved in October 1984. Three main conditions were to be satisfied before the Fund would in future approve a program in principle rather than outright. First, the use of the procedure should be limited to exceptional cases, in which staff and management had been unable to obtain "reasonable assurances" from other creditors. That is, the traditional practice of acting on the basis of informal contacts between the staff and the Paris Club or bank advisory committees should continue to be the rule. Second, approval in principle should be used only to deal with financing problems. If prior policy actions were required (as in the Côte d'Ivoire case), they should be taken in advance of approval by the Fund (in principle or otherwise). Third, there should be a deadline on completion of external financing, normally 30 days. Otherwise, the effectiveness of the procedure in putting pressure on other creditors would be lost.

Those guidelines were generally adhered to, and approval in principle would be used in just eight cases over the next three years.[111] In most of those instances, the driving factor was the difficulty in getting to an agreement with commercial banks; relations with official creditors were no longer much of an issue. Overall, the practice was a success, perhaps largely because the 30-day deadline—which was applied in every case but one—was effective in putting negotiators on a short leash.[112]

---

[108]The use of approval in principle during this period is covered in "Approval in Principle of Fund Arrangements," SM/84/217 (September 25, 1984).

[109]Minutes of EBM/83/77 (June 1, 1983), and "Ecuador—Stand-By Arrangement," EBS/83/91, Sup. 2 (July 25, 1983).

[110]See minutes of EBM/84/70–71 (May 2, 1984) and "Ivory Coast—Stand-By Arrangement—Effective Date," EBS/84/81, Sup. 3 (July 31, 1984). The arrangement became effective through lapse-of-time approval on August 3, 1984.

[111]For a review, see "Financing Assurances in Fund-Supported Programs," EBS/87/266 (December 14, 1987).

[112]The exception was the approval in principle of the stand-by arrangement with Argentina in February 1987 (Chapter 10). No deadline was set, negotiations continued for five more months, and the arrangement became effective only in late July. That delay clearly contributed to the early demise of the program.

Enhanced Surveillance: Looking After MYRA

Another possible way around the stress of having to negotiate new agreements with various groups of creditors every year was to persuade them to make longer-term commitments. If that could be achieved, then all parties would gain: the country would know its financing possibilities for several years ahead, the Fund could enter into extended arrangements with confidence, and the banks would be freed from having to negotiate again and again under pressure. Even more important, multiyear agreements could be designed to reduce the magnitude of "humps" in amortization schedules that occasionally put severe pressure on heavily indebted countries.[113] It was not obvious, however, that the banks would see such a proposal as a net benefit. If they rescheduled debts that were to come due in three years' time, how could they know that the country would stick to its policy regime, and how could they know that other creditors would not pull out and leave them holding the bag?

The path through this thicket of concerns was found in the first half of 1984, in the form of the Managing Director's proposal for a multiyear rescheduling agreement (MYRA) for Mexico (see above, pp. 364–69). A critical factor in getting creditors to accept that proposal was the willingness of the Fund to closely monitor economic developments after the Fund-supported program had been completed, and the willingness of the country to provide the Fund's assessments to its creditors. In essence, creditors—especially commercial banks—wanted the Fund to evaluate credit risks for them, or at least to provide the information on which they could readily evaluate the risks themselves. The challenge for the Fund was to develop a means of satisfying creditors enough to meet members' financing needs, while staying within and not weakening the institution's mandated role as advisor and financier to its members.

This issue arose in three cases during the first several months in which banks were negotiating MYRAs with developing countries. In the seminal Mexican case, the country had an active extended arrangement with the Fund, which was scheduled to expire at the end of 1985. The hope and expectation of all parties was that after that date, Mexico would no longer need financial assistance from the IMF. To help Mexico secure a MYRA from commercial bank creditors under which loan maturities would be extended out to 1994, the Fund agreed to "enhance" the consultation process after 1985 by holding semiannual rather than annual consultations. There was an understanding between Mexico and the banks that the authorities would make the consultation reports available in some fashion, but the means of doing so was left vague. In the event, this plan was never activated, because conditions worsened enough that Mexico faced a continuing need for Fund resources throughout the period covered by the MYRA.

---

[113]The Fund acknowledged this difficulty internally in December 1983, when the Managing Director summed up an Executive Board seminar on debt issues by recognizing "the problems of the 'bunching' of debt that are looming [and that] cast doubts on the viability of financial packages. . . ." The solution to that problem, he concluded, was "more consistent, more comprehensive, and more forward-looking treatment" in rescheduling exercises. Minutes of Executive Board Seminar 83/3 (December 12, 1983), p. 32.

In December 1984, the commercial banks' Advisory Committee for Ecuador approved in principle a MYRA on terms similar to those for Mexico. Ecuador was in the midst of negotiating a stand-by arrangement with the Fund (a 12-month stand-by arrangement for SDR 105.5 million—and approximately the same in dollars—equivalent to 70 percent of Ecuador's quota). To ensure that the Fund would continue to monitor the economy of Ecuador after the expected end of that arrangement, the banks made the rescheduling of loans maturing in 1986 contingent on approval of a follow-up stand-by arrangement for that year, and they made the rescheduling of 1987–89 maturities contingent on the implementation of enhanced surveillance by the Fund. As with Mexico, however, the procedure was not activated, because Ecuador continued to draw on Fund resources into the early 1990s.[114]

The only country for which enhanced surveillance was activated in this period was Venezuela.[115] As a major oil-exporting country, Venezuela had never had recourse to Fund resources, and in 1984 it had a substantial creditor position in the Fund.[116] Following the decline in oil prices in the early 1980s, Venezuela experienced both a worsening of its current account deficit and substantial capital flight. The consequent loss in foreign exchange reserves made it difficult to service foreign bank loans, and in 1983–84 the authorities managed to reschedule bank debts coming due in those years despite the Fund's reluctance to agree to an adjustment program or financial assistance (see footnote 94, p. 404). In September 1984, bank creditors agreed in principle to reschedule loans maturing through 1988, with new maturities extending to 1997, conditional on (inter alia) the Fund conducting enhanced surveillance through that date. The Executive Board—meeting to conclude the annual Article IV consultation with Venezuela—accepted the authorities' request for enhanced surveillance on May 30, 1985, thus in effect commencing the practice. The authorities, however, did not release the staff report to creditors, because they had not yet completed negotiations with the banks on the terms of the proposed MYRA.

Some six months later, on December 13, 1985, the Executive Board met to consider what had now become the semiannual consultation report on Venezuela. Although the balance of payments outlook was "relatively favorable" and negotiations with commercial bank creditors were nearly completed, the staff report suggested that the adjustment of policies—though moving in the right direction—should be accelerated and strengthened. The staff called for a more restrictive stance on macroeconomic policy and for a more rapid pace of deregulation and other structural measures. Executive Directors concurred with the staff view on

---

[114]When the Executive Board met in March 1985, to consider the request for a stand-by arrangement, some Directors (notably the Directors for Germany and the United Kingdom) were concerned that the staff or management might have made a commitment to the commercial banks regarding future financing or enhanced surveillance. The staff responded that no such commitments had been made. See minutes of EBM/85/39 (March 11, 1985). Ecuador successfully implemented the policy program that underlay the 1985–86 stand-by arrangement, and it made all of the scheduled drawings. Ecuador then had four more stand-by arrangements spanning the next six years.

[115]For a chronology of enhanced surveillance with Venezuela, see "Review of Enhanced Surveillance," EBS/88/247 (December 2, 1988), p. 30.

[116]In September 1984, the Fund's holdings of Venezuelan bolívares amounted to just 64 percent of Venezuela's quota.

macroeconomic policy, and they expressed even stronger concerns about what they perceived as a reliance by Venezuela on demand stimulus rather than structural reform as a means of restoring output growth. In the course of the Board meeting, Charles H. Dallara (United States) suggested that it might be appropriate for the next staff report issued to creditors to include a proposed timetable for the implementation of structural reforms, but that suggestion was resisted both by the staff and other Directors. Overall, this first case of enhanced surveillance had begun reasonably well, albeit with some caution being expressed.[117]

One other case related to enhanced surveillance came up in 1985: Colombia. Colombia had not drawn on Fund resources since the completion of a long series of stand-by arrangements in 1974,[118] and—like its neighbor to the east—it was determined to avoid going to the Fund when it ran into difficulties in the 1980s. After initially attempting to counter the effects of worsening external conditions through expansionary monetary and fiscal policies, the authorities shifted gears in the second half of 1984. To establish credibility with commercial bank creditors, they then sought the informal support of the Fund. After an exchange of letters between President Belisario Betancur and de Larosière, a visit to the Fund by Betancur in early April, and informal consultations by the Managing Director with Executive Directors and with the U.S. authorities, the stage was set for an unprecedented agreement.

Colombia was asking the Fund (1) to certify that its adjustment program was strong enough to qualify for Fund financial support if requested, (2) to monitor and evaluate progress exactly as if a stand-by arrangement were in place, and (3) to authorize the government to release both the staff report and the Managing Director's evaluation (based on the consultation discussion held by the Executive Board) to its creditors.[119] In other words, the authorities wanted to have the Fund's—the Executive Board's and not just the staff's—"seal of approval" without the stigma that might be associated with a formal stand-by arrangement. The request thus gave the Fund a role that was less than under a stand-by arrangement but greater than under enhanced surveillance.

The Executive Board approved Colombia's request on July 26, 1985, despite the fact that most Directors expressed some degree of reservation about it.[120] Almost

---

[117]"Venezuela—Staff Report for the 1985 Article IV Consultation," SM/85/308 (November 15, 1985); and minutes of EBM/85/180–181 (December 13, 1985). Dallara's suggestion is on pp. 32–34 of meeting 85/180; further discussion is on pp. 15–19 of meeting 85/181. For later developments in this case, see Chapter 10.

[118]From 1957 through 1974, Colombia had 15 stand-by arrangements with the Fund. See de Vries (1985), pp. 362 and 427.

[119]"Colombia—Staff Report for the 1985 Article IV Consultation," EBS/85/149 (June 12, 1985), pp. 32–33.

[120]See minutes of EBM/85/114 (July 26, 1985). Some Executive Directors earlier expressed frustration at being presented with what they believed was a fait accompli. In that view, the Board should have established a general policy before the Managing Director undertook to bring a novel approach to them for approval. When those objections surfaced at a meeting on the work program in late May, de Larosière insisted that he had consulted fully with Executive Directors on an informal basis and that the only choice had been to proceed rapidly or not at all. Minutes of EBM/85/82 (May 29, 1985).

everyone would have preferred a standard request for a stand-by arrangement, accompanied by an indication that the authorities did not intend to use the money. They had little choice, however, because the banks had made the requested monitoring a condition for approval of the MYRA, and the Managing Director had already secured written assurances from the banks that they would provide more than $500 million in new credits to ensure that the Colombian program would be adequately financed. Several Directors indicated that they would not regard this case as a precedent if another member were to make a similar request.

Enhanced surveillance thus developed in an experimental and informal manner during its first year of existence. By the time the Venezuelan and Colombian requests came to the Board, it was already becoming clear that more requests would be coming in and that more formal criteria and procedures would have to be developed. That process and its consequences are examined in Chapter 10.

References

de Vries, Margaret Garritsen, 1985, *The International Monetary Fund, 1972–1978: Cooperation on Trial*, Vols. 1 and 2: *Narrative and Analysis*; Vol. 3: *Documents* (Washington: International Monetary Fund).

Dillon, K. Burke, G. Maxwell Watson, G. Russell Kincaid, and Chanpen Puckahtikom, 1985, *Recent Developments in External Debt Restructuring*, IMF Occasional Paper No. 40 (Washington: International Monetary Fund).

Escobar Cerda, Luis, 1991, *Mi Testimonio* (Santiago: Editorial VER).

Hajnal, Peter I., ed., 1989, *The Seven-Power Summit: Documents from the Summits of Industrialized Countries, 1975–1989* (Millwood, New York: Kraus International Publications).

Heymann, Daniel, 1991, "From Sharp Disinflation to Hyperinflation, Twice: The Argentine Experience, 1985–1989," with Comments by José Luis Machinea and Simón Teitel, in *Lessons of Economic Stabilization and Its Aftermath*, ed. by Michael Bruno and others (Cambridge, Massachusetts: MIT Press).

Kuhn, Michael G., with Jorge P. Guzman, 1990, *Multilateral Official Debt Rescheduling: Recent Experience*, IMF World Economic and Financial Surveys (November).

Machinea, José Luis, 1990, "Stabilization under Alfonsín's Government: A Frustrated Attempt," Document CEDES/42 (Buenos Aires: Centro de Estudios de Estado y Sociedad).

Presgrave de A. Faria, Hugo, 1993, "Brazil, 1985–1987: Pursuing Heterodoxy to a Moratorium," in *Dealing with Debt: International Financial Negotiations and Adjustment Bargaining*, ed. by Thomas J. Biersteker (Boulder, Colorado: Westview), pp. 133–52.

Stiles, Kendall W., 1987, "Argentina's Bargaining with the IMF," *Journal of Interamerican Studies and World Affairs*, Vol. 29 (fall), pp. 55–85.

Tanzi, Vito, 1977, "Inflation, Lags in Collection, and the Real Value of Tax Revenue," *Staff Papers*, International Monetary Fund, Vol. 24 (March), pp. 154–67.

———, 1978, "Inflation, Real Tax Revenue, and the Case for Inflationary Finance: Theory with an Application to Argentina," *Staff Papers*, International Monetary Fund, Vol. 25 (September), pp. 417–51.

Urzúa, Carlos M., 1997, "Five Decades of Relations between the World Bank and Mexico," in *The World Bank: Its First Half Century*, Vol. 2: *Perspectives*, ed. by Devesh Kapur, John P. Lewis, and Richard Webb (Washington: Brookings Institution), pp. 49–108.

10

Growth, the Elusive Goal: 1985–87

By 1985, the debt crisis was as major a problem as it had been in 1982, but it had changed greatly in character. Among all three of the principal players in the drama—the indebted countries, their commercial creditors, and the official creditors and multilateral institutions—there was an increasing realization that not even a full resolution of the initial financial crisis and successful implementation of traditional adjustment programs would produce a resumption of growth in the most heavily indebted countries. Furthermore, in some important respects, the initial financial crisis was already over and had been overtaken by longer-run problems.

The commercial banks at mid-decade were putting the systemic financial crisis behind them in several ways. First, the combination of concerted lending packages and adjustment programs had bought enough time for many banks (especially those outside the United States, in countries with relatively favorable tax and regulatory treatment) to set aside adequate liquid reserves as a provision against potential losses. By 1986, banks in continental European countries had provisions averaging more than 20 percent of the value of loans to developing countries experiencing debt-servicing difficulties. By the following year, even U.S. banks began to provision heavily.[1]

Second—notwithstanding the concerted lending arrangements, related reschedulings, and other commitments undertaken in conjunction with Fund-supported adjustment programs—bank creditors had begun to reduce their overall lending exposure to the heavily indebted developing countries. Net bank lending to those countries dropped sharply in 1985 and turned negative in 1986. By then the withdrawal was becoming widespread across developing countries.[2]

---

[1]See Watson and others (December 1986), pp. 66–67; and Watson and others (1988), pp. 63–64.

[2]IMF staff estimates made around the end of 1986 showed that for 1985, net lending was negative to 9 out of 28 covered countries; for the first nine months of 1986, negative figures were reported for 19 countries. In the aggregate, credits to the 28 countries rose by $9.7 billion in 1985 and fell by $6.8 billion over the next nine months. For the 15 countries classified as heavily indebted, negative net lending totaled $0.9 billion in 1985 and $4.4 billion in the first nine months of 1986. See "Implementation of the Debt Strategy—Current Issues," EBS/87/38 (February 20, 1987), p. 6. Later estimates showed essentially zero net lending to the 15 heavily indebted countries for the two years combined (slightly positive in 1985 and slightly negative in 1986); see Watson and others (1988).

Third, the banks had begun to develop a secondary market in sovereign debt instruments. It was still a small and fledgling market, with volatile prices reflecting a trading volume estimated at no more than $5 billion a year (Allen and others, 1990, pp. 37–38); but the existence of the market was beginning to provide the smaller banks with a means of escaping the vortex.

Fourth, banks in Europe and Japan had begun to benefit from currency movements. After three years of seemingly inexorable appreciation, the U.S. dollar had begun in March 1985 to depreciate against the Japanese yen and European currencies. Throughout 1985 and 1986, this depreciation reduced the local currency value of dollar-denominated loans on the balance sheets of banks outside the United States. Although such loans normally were matched by dollar-denominated liabilities, the portion of the portfolio deemed to be at risk thereby declined. For example, during 1986 total cross-border claims of Japanese banks increased by 58 percent in U.S. dollar terms, but only by 25 percent when measured in yen.[3]

These generally favorable developments had not as yet led to a significant resumption of voluntary (or "spontaneous," the preferred phrase of the day) lending to indebted developing countries, with the exception of a few countries that had successfully completed Fund-supported adjustment programs and had negotiated multiyear rescheduling agreements (MYRAs), such as Côte d'Ivoire, Ecuador, and Uruguay. Nonetheless, the indebted countries also had begun to wrest themselves from the initial financial crisis. Two points stand out.

First, three years of negotiations with creditors had led to a smoothing of amortization schedules and a lengthening of repayment periods. Especially for the countries that had successfully negotiated MYRAs, the prospects of a new crisis being brought on by the need to roll over large amounts of obligations all at once had been greatly reduced. Mexico, for example, had faced amortization payments averaging $9.6 billion a year for the period 1986–89; the MYRA reduced that figure to $1.1 billion.[4] Nonetheless, too many countries—including Mexico—still faced dangerously high ratios of debt-service obligations to export revenues.

Second, a number of the indebted countries had restored a measure of stability and confidence by implementing Fund-supported adjustment programs, but success was neither broad enough nor deep enough. Even in countries where financial stability was being restored, much or even most of the gain had been achieved through import compression rather than through growth in exports. Without export growth, output and employment were still depressed and stagnant. Social unrest, especially in the less successful countries, was rising, and efforts to organize debtors into a cartel to resist servicing debt on the originally contracted terms were continuing. From the vantage of the Fund and other official creditors in 1985, the most pressing task was to help countries reorient policies in a way that would produce the economic growth without which the initial gains could not be sustained.

---

[3]These figures include loans to industrial as well as developing countries. The dollar-denominated data are found in Watson and others (1988), p. 71.

[4]"Mexico—Recent Economic Developments," SM/85/148 (May 23, 1985), p. 62.

As the debt strategy pursued by the Fund and others shifted more heavily toward meeting longer-run development needs, a catalyst came in the form of the Baker Plan, introduced in October 1985. The Fund also began to examine more systematically the role that it could play once it was no longer financially supporting particular adjustment programs. This led to a formalization of the enhanced surveillance procedures that had first been applied with Mexico in 1984. More fundamentally, the focus of the Fund's policy advice began to shift toward the structural reforms that were now judged to be an essential underpinning for the restoration of sustainable growth.

The Baker Plan

Development of the Plan

When the Interim Committee convened in Seoul, Korea, on October 6, 1985, the U.S. Secretary of the Treasury, James A. Baker III, briefly sketched out a vision for reorienting the debt strategy. The problem, as he outlined it that Sunday morning, was threefold: the principal indebted countries were flagging in their adjustment efforts, official support by creditor countries and multilateral institutions was fragmented, and net lending by commercial banks was dropping. Consequently, the indebted countries were unable to reach their growth potential. To reverse these trends, he suggested a threefold response:

> First, principal debtor countries should adopt comprehensive macroeconomic and structural policies, which must be supported by the international financial community, to promote growth and balance of payments adjustment and to reduce inflation. Second, a continued central role for the IMF is called for, in conjunction with increased and more effective structural adjustment lending by the multilateral development banks in support of the adoption by principal debtors of market-oriented policies for growth. Third, private banks should increase their lending in support of comprehensive economic adjustment programs.

Baker had a more detailed set of proposals to offer, but he told his colleagues around the table that he would wait until his address to the plenary session of the Annual Meetings, two days later, to unveil the full plan.[5]

Baker's ministerial colleagues broadly agreed on the extent of the problem: the debt strategy had reached a critical stage. Chronic fatigue was setting in, and without new leadership, the crisis was only going to get worse. With hindsight, it is clear that the lending fatigue being displayed by bank creditors had at least two underlying causes. First, more and more of the smaller banks were becoming reluctant to participate in concerted lending syndicates. The tactic of treating all bank creditors equally, though it was thought to be a necessary element in the overall strat-

---

[5]Minutes of Interim Committee Meeting Number 25 (October 6, 1985), pp. 10–11. Notwithstanding Baker's intention to defer, the G-5 ministerial meeting had discussed the proposal at some length the day before.

egy, was seriously delaying the completion of financing arrangements. Alternatives to concerted lending would have to be sought, although few policymakers in the major creditor countries were yet ready to think in that direction. Second, even the larger banks were increasingly taking the view that they were being asked to shoulder too much of the burden relative to official creditors. That problem, which was the focus of official thinking in late 1985, could be tackled through a coordinated form of burden sharing among creditors.

In addition to the effects of lending fatigue, the debt strategy was being overwhelmed by adjustment fatigue in a number of indebted countries. With growth slowing in the industrial countries and stagnating in developing countries, and with the prices of many export commodities falling sharply, political leaders in the indebted countries were finding it more and more difficult to justify the need for trade surpluses and for paying large portions of export revenues in interest to foreign creditors.[6] Officials in creditor countries saw that they had to find a way to revitalize the strategy, not only because depression in developing countries would weaken growth globally, but also because it would lead inexorably toward a rebellion against the full servicing of external debts and could push the international financial system back into the abyss of 1982.[7]

Within the IMF, there was a growing realization that program design ideally ought to be broadened to include structural measures aimed at strengthening the basis for economic growth; but that realization was tempered by concerns that such measures lay outside the Fund's mandate and expertise and that the empirical linkages between structural reform and growth were not well established. Both inside and outside the Fund, the World Bank and the regional development banks were seen as being more suitably placed to provide the capital and the technical advice for promoting investment and growth.

For several months between the spring and fall meetings of the Interim Committee, U.S. officials in the Treasury and the Federal Reserve System worked to develop a comprehensive plan to deal with the identified problems. Treasury officials, particularly the Assistant Secretary for International Affairs, David C. Mulford, tried to develop an ambitious plan aimed at resolving the crisis, but they were unable to formulate a proposal that would win general agreement. By late summer, after consulting on several occasions with the Managing Director of the IMF, Jacques de Larosière, both the Treasury and the Federal Reserve settled on a more modest and practical approach that would emphasize the need for greater cohesiveness among the various groups of creditors and that would call for more involvement by

---

[6]Several of the heavily indebted countries were facing scheduled interest payments equal to more than one-third of the revenues from exports of goods and services. Argentina faced the highest burden, at more than 50 percent.

[7]One participant in developing the Baker Plan at the U.S. Treasury wrote later (Broad, 1987) that it was "primarily rhetoric . . . pasted together quickly in breakfast meetings" between Baker and Volcker and that it "was simply an attempt to steal the thunder from" Peru's unilateral decision (discussed below in Chapter 16) to limit external debt service to no more than 10 percent of its foreign exchange earnings. Also see Lissakers (1991), p. 229.

and coordination with the multilateral development banks.[8] No one expected the idea to be a panacea, but they did hope that it would reinvigorate the debt strategy and would convince the developing countries that official creditors were concerned about their problems.

This was the background when Baker walked to the lectern in the ballroom of the Hilton Hotel in Seoul on October 8, 1985, to deliver his first address at a plenary meeting of the governors of the Fund and the World Bank. In that speech, Baker called for a "Program for Sustained Growth," built on the three principles that he had outlined for the Interim Committee two days earlier. On the first point, he stressed the importance of building and liberalizing market institutions, strengthening the private sector, and promoting domestic saving and investment. Second, he called on the World Bank and the Inter-American Development Bank (IDB) to "increase their disbursements to principal debtors by roughly 50 percent from their current annual level of nearly $6 billion." Later, treasury officials explained that this figure related to a group of the 15 most heavily indebted developing countries, a group that henceforth would be widely referred to as the "Baker 15."[9] Third, Baker called on commercial banks to resume net lending to these heavily indebted countries: "Our assessment of the commitment required by the banks . . . would be net new lending in the range of $20 billion for the next three years."

The $20 billion "indicative target" for net bank lending had been suggested to Mulford by de Larosière during a casual meeting at the Managing Director's home in northwest Washington in the summer of 1985. Though Mulford initially viewed the number as surprisingly large, he became persuaded that it was realistic and decided to stick with it. If the goal could be achieved, it would raise the banks' lending exposure in the 15 countries by less than 3 percent, and it was roughly com-

---

[8]In Washington, Federal Reserve officials were particularly cognizant of the need to strengthen the role of the World Bank. Many of the elements of what would become the Baker plan were sketched out by the Federal Reserve Chairman, Paul A. Volcker, in a May 13, 1985, speech to the Bankers' Association for Foreign Trade, in Boca Raton, Florida. That speech noted that the debt strategy was moving into "'stage two'—the continuing, hard-slogging effort to maintain over years internal discipline, reasonable external balance, and adequate financing, while also finding ways to restore and maintain necessary growth." Volcker observed that the IMF would soon be seeing net repayments from the indebted countries, and he called for a strengthened role for the World Bank and a renewed commitment from commercial banks. On July 30, Volcker testified before a subcommittee of the U.S. House of Representatives that "all the heavily indebted countries in Latin America and elsewhere need to move from a situation of endemic financial crisis to another stage in development, looking toward what is necessary to sustain growth. As they do, the particular skills and resources of the World Bank become increasingly relevant. Heavy reliance on the shorter-term tools of the IMF should then be phased down and out." (U.S. House of Representatives, 1985, p. 21.) C. Fred Bergsten, Director of the Institute for International Economics, expressed similar views to the same subcommittee two weeks earlier (July 18, pp. 39–40).

[9]Only 10 of the 15 were Latin American members of the IDB (Argentina, Bolivia, Brazil, Chile, Colombia, Ecuador, Mexico, Peru, Uruguay, and Venezuela). The other five were Côte d'Ivoire, Morocco, Nigeria, the Philippines, and Yugoslavia. The deliberate decision not to include the list of countries in Baker's speech reflected in part the concern of the Fund that the debt strategy be comprehensive rather than exclusive. In practice (especially at the World Bank), the strategy generally encompassed two additional countries: Costa Rica and Jamaica.

mensurate with the commitment that was being suggested for the multilateral development banks ($27 billion in gross disbursements over the three-year period 1986–88).[10]

These proposals were pretty mild in relation to the magnitude of the problem, but Baker's speech generated substantial interest in Seoul and in the world financial press. Part of the interest came because most observers interpreted the speech as a call for official coordination of lending by commercial banks, which would have been a major departure from previous practice. And, in part, there was a widespread belief that the speech was a slap at the IMF, that Baker wanted the World Bank to guide the strategy from now on, rather than the Fund.[11] That Baker had taken pains to defuse that impression ("emphasizing growth does not mean deemphasizing the IMF") only added to the smell of blood in the hall. As one reporter put the question to de Larosière at the Managing Director's closing press conference in Seoul, "Who is actually going to be running the show from now on?"[12] De Larosière, however, viewed the Baker initiative as an opportunity for the Fund to get the strategy moving forward again.

Reactions

De Larosière stopped in Paris for some days on his way back from Seoul and used the occasion to discuss the Baker Plan with a number of prominent bankers.[13] Flying home to Washington on October 20, he drafted a background note for circulation to selected senior staff, describing the bankers' reactions and some possible responses by the Fund.[14]

Bankers generally agreed, according to de Larosière's assessment, that the cessation of net lending by banks to the heavily indebted countries was a problem that should be reversed but that could not be corrected by individual banks acting alone. Bankers were comfortable with the case-by-case strategy under which lending was encouraged principally for countries that had successfully negotiated ad-

[10]The $20 billion and $27 billion figures were not strictly commensurate. The former related to net lending (i.e., increase in exposure), while the latter referred to gross disbursements. Given the structure of multilateral development bank lending at the time, the Fund staff estimated that $27 billion in gross disbursements in 1986–88 would have implied about $17–18 billion in net lending.

[11]See, for example, the articles published in the *Financial Times* under the headlines, "The Watchdog Loses Some Teeth" (October 3, 1985) and "IMF Falls from Grace" (October 6).

[12]Transcript of the press conference (October 11, 1985), p. 3; in IMF/RD External Relations Department file "Annual Meetings—Press Matters 1985, Seoul, Korea" (Accession 88/16, Box 3, Section 490).

[13]See his report to Executive Directors, minutes of EBM/85/154 (October 21, 1985), p. 3.

[14]"Thoughts on how commercial banks can be involved in solving the financing problems of indebted countries," note drafted by de Larosière (October 21, 1985); in IMF/RD Research Department file "Baker Initiative, October 1985–September 1988" (Accession 89/129, Box 3, Section 276). This practice was rare and indicates the importance that de Larosière attached to the occasion. Normally, when a paper was required for a meeting, it was prepared by the staff, not the Managing Director.

justment programs with the Fund, and they supported the idea of the multilateral development banks being brought more fully into the picture. What they did not like was what many of them saw as a reluctance by the major creditor countries to provide bilateral financial support for the adjusting countries, or even to fully support the capital requirements of the World Bank or the IDB. In the view of many bankers, an essential condition for the success of the Baker Plan was for official export credits to be made more readily available and for the major shareholders to commit the resources that were needed if the development banks were to play their envisaged role.

The Managing Director saw the possibilities for a consensus in these reactions, but he also feared that splits within the banking community could make it difficult to develop a new direction for the debt strategy. Non-U.S. bankers were highly suspicious of any attempt to replace the concerted-lending syndicates by some arrangement that would exempt smaller banks from participating. The small banks were concentrated in the United States, and any such move was likely to redistribute risks toward Europe and Japan. Furthermore, well-provisioned banks, notably in Germany and Switzerland, were reluctant to make sizable new financial commitments, while the more weakly provisioned banks were reluctant to agree to less profitable terms in any new agreement. If the banks were to be persuaded to support the Baker Plan, there would have to be enough official commitment to overcome these obstacles.

The October 22 staff meeting to discuss de Larosière's note did not generate a new direction for the Fund's role in the debt strategy; nor was there much discussion of the possibility of reorienting program design toward structural reforms aimed at promoting growth.[15] Indeed, there was general agreement that the case-by-case strategy of trying to negotiate strong adjustment programs and commit enough Fund money to catalyze substantial financing from other official and private creditors should continue without major changes. The focus of the meeting was on how to ensure that commercial banks would provide the necessary financing to make the Baker initiative work. In addition to the need for support from creditor governments, a solution had to be found for the "small bank" problem. Although it was much too early to formulate an institutional view on the question, this meeting produced the first real consideration of supplementing the concerted-lending approach with a variety (in effect, a menu) of options that the multitude of smaller bank creditors might be more willing to accept: establishment of country-specific and officially supported trust funds, debt-equity swaps, exit bonds, and interest capitalization were all considered to be live options.

Further discussions over the next two weeks led the Managing Director to propose two specific changes in the strategy being applied by the Fund.[16] First, staff

---

[15]Memorandum for files prepared by Robert M.G. Brown (Personal Assistant to the Managing Director), October 30, 1985; in IMF/RD Research Department file "Baker Initiative, October 1985–September 1988" (Accession 89/129, Box 3, Section 276).

[16]Memorandum to heads of departments, November 7, 1985; in IMF/RD Research Department file "Baker Initiative, October 1985–September 1988" (Accession 89/129, Box 3, Section 276).

missions dealing with the heavily indebted countries were instructed to develop longer-term scenarios—through 1988 if possible—projecting policy intentions and likely financing flows and forecasting the expected performance of the economy. To clarify the financial flows, staff were asked to collaborate closely with their counterparts in the multilateral development banks. Second, the Fund's Research Department was asked to develop procedures to regularly monitor overall financial flows to developing countries, including the progress being made toward meeting Baker's indicative targets for additional lending by commercial and multilateral development banks. These were not dramatic changes, but they would help keep the Fund's work from being marginalized by the new emphasis on longer-run developments affecting the overall group of heavily indebted countries.

Up to this point, the Baker initiative had no official multilateral standing. It had not been formally discussed, much less approved, by the Interim Committee or by other groups of governors at the Annual Meetings.[17] To get the Fund on board, the Managing Director asked the staff to prepare a short paper summarizing the main features of the Baker initiative;[18] that paper could then be discussed by the Executive Board at its already scheduled annual review of international financial markets.

At that meeting, on November 13, 1985, which the Managing Director characterized as "historically important," the Executive Board gave its "very broad support" to the Baker initiative.[19] The U.S. Executive Director, Charles H. Dallara, opened the discussion by stressing that while the Baker initiative aimed at strengthening the role of the multilateral development banks in promoting structural reform, the Fund would continue to play a central role in providing both resources and policy advice and in catalyzing other financing. The U.S. authorities had concluded that a principal reason that banks were reluctant to lend to developing countries was that they doubted that some countries' adjustment efforts were adequate; a more comprehensive adjustment and reform strategy was needed to allay those concerns.[20]

After a long day of deliberation, the Managing Director's summing up of the Board meeting stressed six points regarding the Fund's detailed response to the Baker initiative.[21]

- First, the Fund should directly support growth-oriented adjustment. Fund-supported programs should include supply-oriented measures aimed at foster-

---

[17]Official support for the Baker Plan accumulated gradually in the weeks following the Seoul meeting. In mid-November, for example, Volcker explained the plan to his fellow central bank governors at their monthly meeting at the BIS in Basel, Switzerland. After the meeting, Karl Otto Pöhl, the president of the Deutsche Bundesbank, signaled his support and that of his colleagues. See "Des banques centrales approuvent le plan Baker" ["Central banks approve the Baker plan"], *Le Figaro* (November 13, 1985), p. 18.

[18]"International Capital Markets—Developments and Prospects, 1985—U.S. Treasury Initiative on Debt," SM/85/267, Sup. 1 (November 1, 1985).

[19]Minutes of EBM/85/166 (November 13, 1985), pp. 36 and 33.

[20]Minutes of EBM/85/165 (November 13, 1985), pp. 4–7.

[21]Minutes of EBM/85/166 (November 13, 1985), pp. 31–34.

ing domestic savings, restoring confidence in (i.e., credibility of) fiscal and monetary policies, and promoting investment. Thus, in contrast to the staff's reluctance to sail in uncharted waters, the Executive Board felt that this shift in direction was of primary importance.

- Second, the Fund should strengthen its collaboration with the World Bank and regional development banks, the institutions that would now have a crucial role to play in making the debt strategy work. There was, however, an undercurrent of doubt that this aspect of the strategy would bear fruit. As the Managing Director put it, "the willingness of industrial countries to increase the capital of these institutions . . . will be a test of the cooperation required under Secretary Baker's proposal."

- Third, the Fund should move—albeit cautiously—toward strengthening its role in encouraging commercial banks to provide new lending to the heavily indebted countries. During the Board's discussion, Directors had been sensitive to the need to preserve the commercial and market-oriented nature of bank lending. Attempting to force banks to lend, or providing incentives through government or other official guarantees, was seen as inappropriate. But Directors also had stressed that increased lending to countries making appropriate adjustment efforts was in the banks' own collective interest and should be encouraged and catalyzed wherever it was suitable to do so.

- Fourth, Directors were uneasy about endorsing, even implicitly, Baker's indicative list of 15 countries. Countries not on the list would also need concerted lending arrangements, and not all of the countries on the list would merit such financing.[22] More generally, it was important for the Fund to be evenhanded in its relations with member countries. The Baker 15 existed only as a list; it would become an analytical subgroup for the World Economic Outlook and other purposes, but it would have little practical significance for the work of the Fund.

- Fifth, the Board generally viewed Baker's $20 billion indicative target for new bank lending as a minimum requirement for financing the external deficits of the 15 countries. Directors (especially Guillermo Ortiz, Alternate—Mexico) had pointed out that this increase (less than 3 percent over initial exposure) would be negative in real terms and would still result in substantial net transfers from the indebted countries to bank creditors.[23] Nonetheless, to achieve this target would be a real accomplishment, since banks currently were doing no more than maintaining the existing level of exposure. With regard to how to encourage banks to cooperate, there had been some tentative discussion of the need for a broader menu approach as a means of preventing the basic concerted-lending approach from collapsing.

---

[22]The Managing Director's summing up noted that the list had been compiled "without regard to the degree to which any of these countries have progressed toward the regularization of their relations with commercial banks." Minutes of EBM/85/166 (November 13, 1985), p. 34.

[23]That is, net lending would be less than the scheduled interest payments due on the outstanding debt.

- Sixth, there was a recognition that the Baker initiative could not work without substantial support from the major creditor countries (in addition to financing for the multilateral development banks). In particular, creditor governments would have to implement supporting policies, including flexibility
in regulating financial institutions, providing adequate export cover (a potentially major source of financing that had not been mentioned at all in the
Baker initiative),[24] reducing protectionism, and (especially for the United
States) reducing fiscal deficits.

The November 13 meeting gave an official IMF stamp of approval to the Baker
Plan,[25] and on December 2 the Managing Director and the President of the World
Bank, A.W. Clausen, issued a joint press release expressing their "strong support"
for the initiative.[26] This unusual joint statement served to some extent to counteract the widespread speculation in the press (see above) that the Baker Plan
would result in a shift in power and influence from the west side of Washington's
19th Street (the Fund's headquarters) to the east side (the World Bank).

Implementation

Operationally, the main advantage to the Fund from the Baker Plan was that it
provided a systematic channel for catalyzing resources from other creditors at a
time when the Fund's own net financial contribution would inevitably be declining.[27] The Managing Director's number one priority therefore was to do whatever
he could to make sure that the financing from other creditors came as close as possible to the indicative targets. By December 1985, commercial bankers were generally expressing quite positive views of the plan, but that enthusiasm would not
necessarily be converted into cash for developing countries. On the contrary, the
primary basis for the banks' enthusiasm seemed to be that they expected (or
hoped) that it would lead to more money being provided by official creditors. For
example, representatives of 58 creditor banks met in Washington on October 28
to consider the implications of the Baker initiative, with IMF and World Bank staff
participating along with Mulford. At the end, the banks issued a press release stat-

---

[24]Export cover refers to guarantees provided by official agencies in creditor countries, covering
private (usually bank) loans to importers of goods from the guaranteeing country. The $20 bil-
lion indicative target for bank lending was understood to refer only to unguaranteed loans.

[25]The Interim Committee endorsed the plan at its April 1986 meeting. "The Committee welcomed the progress that is being achieved in strengthening the current debt strategy along the
lines proposed by the United States at the last Annual Meetings. . . . The Committee reaffirmed
the central role of the Fund . . ." (Communiqué, April 10, 1986, Paragraph 3).

[26]IMF Press Release No. 85/37 (December 2, 1985); in *IMF Survey*, Vol. 14 (December 9,
1985), p. 369.

[27]The anticipated decline in IMF net lending reflected both the scheduled repayments from
the large arrangements of the preceding years and the desirability of avoiding prolonged use of
Fund resources by individual member countries. As the *Annual Report 1986* summarized the situation (p. 43), the Fund's "financial support is not likely to be on the same scale as in the early
stages of the debt crisis; thus a somewhat greater emphasis has been given to the catalytic role of
Fund support."

ing that they "welcomed the idea of a coordinated approach involving, together with a renewed effort in the debtor countries and support from the industrialized countries' governments, an extended role for the international financial institutions."[28] Then on November 8, at a meeting in New York, members of the Committee of Advisory Banks told the Deputy Managing Director, Richard D. Erb, that they were asking for a guarantee from the World Bank on new lending that they were being asked to make to the Baker 15 countries. Erb warned them not to expect such a guarantee. In mid-December, groups of banks in the United States, the United Kingdom, Japan, Canada, and continental European countries issued a coordinated series of statements that generally expressed positive but qualified support.[29] On December 15, de Larosière and Clausen again issued a joint statement, to "welcome these positive and encouraging expressions of support for the debt initiative from the banking community."[30]

Clearly the bankers were confused during the first few months after Baker's speech. They believed that they were being asked to participate in a forced lending scheme that would be officially organized on noncommercial terms. They accepted that such a scheme could be preferable to the increasingly burdensome task of organizing massive concerted lending syndicates, but they insisted that the idea made sense only if their risks were to be covered in some fashion by official guarantees. Their coordinated but tentative expressions of support were predicated on the view that a detailed official plan was being developed to flesh out the Baker initiative.

The banks were not alone in believing that the Baker Plan was more sweeping in scope than it actually was. Unless the $20 billion that banks were being asked to lend to the Baker 15 was to be aggregated and coordinated in some fashion, then it was difficult to view the request as having any more substance than some form of moral suasion. At the November 13 Executive Board meeting, Jacques J. Polak (Netherlands) concluded that "the essence of Secretary Baker's plan was that the commercial banks would not set the conditions that would apply to their new credits under the plan." He envisaged that the Fund, in collaboration with the World Bank, would exercise responsibility for determining which countries qualified for

---

[28]Quoted in the *IMF Survey*, Vol. 14, No. 21 (November 11, 1985), p. 349, under the headline, "Banks Express Support for Debt Plan of U.S." The press release was issued by the Institute of International Finance (IIF), which organized the meeting of its member banks. The *Survey* article also quotes the IIF Managing Director, André de Lattre, as saying after the meeting that "no public commitment was being made at this time."

[29]Typical of these pronouncements was one issued on December 12 through the Bank of England on behalf of major British banks and clearing houses, stating that the signatories "confirm their willingness to play their part on a case-by-case basis, provided that all other parties, governmental, institutional, and banking, do the same." The message was released to the press and simultaneously sent to de Larosière and Clausen. For examples of the press coverage, see *The Guardian* (December 13, 1985), p. 23, on the Bank of England announcement; and *The Journal of Commerce* (same date), p. 5, on similar announcements by Japanese banks. Also see related cables in the Managing Director's file, "Baker Plan"; IMF/RD "Debt Initiative—The Baker Plan, December 1985" (Accession 88/285, Box 5, Section 250).

[30]IMF Press Release No. 85/41 (December 15, 1985); in *IMF Survey*, Vol. 15 (January 6, 1986), p. 3.

additional support.[31] In fact, neither the banks nor the U.S. authorities saw matters in that light.[32] The truth was that the plan was fabricated from much thinner cloth than most observers believed.

For four years now, from the first days of itching concerns over the possibility that a debt crisis might emerge (see the opening pages of Chapter 6), de Larosière had found it useful to meet informally with small groups of key bankers to discuss possible innovations in the debt strategy. In early December, he decided to hold such a meeting as soon as he returned from the Christmas holidays. It would be a small gathering, on January 6, 1986, at which he and Clausen could explain how they saw the implications of the Baker initiative and could get a clearer sense of the views and concerns of the key bankers.[33]

De Larosière opened the meeting by outlining the key issues as he saw them.[34] The Baker initiative was unquestionably the right approach to deal with the "disquieting factors" that were undermining the effectiveness of the debt strategy: the indebted countries had to resume economic growth, the World Bank was well placed to help them do so, and the commercial banks had to continue to help finance these countries' Fund-supported adjustment programs during this period of global slowdown and falling commodity prices. For their part, the bankers were mainly worried that the creditor governments would leave them stranded: What commitments were governments prepared to make, to correspond to the extra burden that the banks were being asked to carry? De Larosière was not in a position to answer that question. On a more positive note, there was common ground for all to agree that a greater focus on structural reforms in developing countries was essential; banks would be more willing to lend if the obstacles to private investment could be breached. Nonetheless, there was little reason to conclude from this gathering, however convivial it might have been, that a revival of bank lending to the heavily indebted countries was on the horizon.

The most salient operational question for the IMF raised by the Baker initiative was whether the design of Fund-supported adjustment programs could be broad-

---

[31]Minutes of EBM/85/165 (November 13, 1985), p. 9.

[32]In the days surrounding Baker's speech in Seoul, U.S. officials apparently did envisage a more concrete plan emerging, though they had not yet worked out any of its details. As soon as Baker returned to Washington from the Annual Meetings, he told the press that Volcker had suggested—and the U.S. administration was considering—that the major creditor banks form an "international superbank" to arrange loans to developing countries. The superbank would have replaced the existing informal bank syndicates and Advisory Committees, but the idea met with general skepticism and was quickly abandoned. See Jane Seaberry, "International 'Superbank' Proposed," *Washington Post*, October 11, 1985, pp. D1–D2.

[33]The dozen or so participants in this private meeting included the chief executive officers of several of the world's largest banks: Yusuke Kashiwagi (Bank of Tokyo), Franz Lutolf (Swiss Bank Corporation), Sir Jeremy Morse (Lloyds Bank), Lewis T. Preston (Morgan Guaranty Trust Co.), John Reed (Citibank), and Jacques Thierry (Banque Bruxelles-Lambert).

[34]This account is based in part on a January 8 file memorandum on the meeting, in IMF/RD Managing Director file "Debt Initiative—The Baker Plan, December 1985" (Accession 88/274, Box 8, Section 269); and in part on the report that the Managing Director made to the Executive Board on that same day (minutes of EBM/86/4, January 8, 1986, pp. 3–8).

ened to more directly promote economic growth. That question was taken up by the Executive Board in the first quarter of 1986, as part of the regular review of the guidelines for conditionality on financial arrangements. As described in Chapter 13, Directors were reluctant to push very hard in that direction. They approved of the fact that the staff was encouraging borrowing countries to adopt structural reforms aimed at liberalizing markets, increasing efficiency, and strengthening incentives to invest; but they were less comfortable with the idea of mandating the staff to more generally require countries to adopt such policies as a condition for drawing on Fund resources. They were concerned that many programs were failing because of an overemphasis on demand restraint over structural adjustment, but they generally accepted that the World Bank had both a clearer mandate and greater expertise on structural issues. Increased collaboration with the Bank, rather than an expansion of the Fund's role, was seen as the principal requirement for promoting growth in program countries.[35]

For the Fund, then, the Baker initiative amounted to a plan to closely monitor developments for a specific group of 15 heavily indebted countries, to pay greater attention to the requirements for restoring sustainable growth in those countries, and to collaborate more intensively with the World Bank, especially in dealing with that group of countries. Success would be judged, at least by outside observers, by whether the suggested financing flows were forthcoming and by whether the recipients of all of this attention actually saw a strengthening of real economic growth.

Effects

How well did the Baker Plan work? Did the commercial and multilateral development banks provide the level of financing that was envisaged, and did the targeted countries see a significant improvement in economic performance? These questions are more difficult to answer than they appear at first, owing to methodological and data problems, but the monitoring exercise carried out by the Fund staff over the three years that the plan was in place provides some strong clues.

The Research Department issued its first monitoring report to the Managing Director on February 14, 1986, three months after the Executive Board had given its approval to the plan. The staff then submitted reports every quarter through September 1988, aimed at shedding light on the questions posed above. The most straightforward question is whether the multilateral development banks provided their indicated share of financing: to a remarkable degree, they did. The initial monitoring report projected gross disbursements to the Baker 15 of about $24 billion for 1986–88, compared with the indicative target of $27 billion, which implied net lending of just over $15 billion. The projections also implied increases of about $2 billion a year over the previous level of lending in 1984–85, in both gross and net terms, compared with Baker's call for an extra $3 billion. The staff's final

---

[35]The Executive Board held another detailed review of the debt strategy on March 24–25, 1986. With respect to the implications of the Baker initiative, that discussion essentially confirmed the conclusions of the January meeting. Minutes of EBM/86/51–54 (March 24–25, 1986).

monitoring report, in September 1988, estimated that actual net lending for the three years totaled about $16½ billion, very close to the initial projection and the original U.S. proposal.[36] The fear that the multilateral development banks would not get enough support to do their job was largely unfounded.

The answer to the second question, whether the commercial banks increased their own lending commensurately, is much more controversial. From the very beginning, the staff's monitoring reports revealed that actual net lending by banks had been negative since the onset of the Baker Plan, and they projected no more than small increases through 1988 (in fact, over much of the period, the staff predicted no increase at all). The reports noted that the banks appeared to be skeptical about the level of official support that would be forthcoming and were reluctant to be left holding the bag. The last report indicated essentially zero net lending for 1986 through 1988, and the final outcome was estimated to have been significantly negative.[37] In contrast, one prominent outside study concluded that the banks' net lending to the Baker 15 totaled $13 billion for the three years through 1988: less than asked, but still considerable. The banks had indeed made substantial new commitments to a number of the heavily indebted countries, but they had reduced their exposure through other channels. Whether they had contributed to the financing of these countries' external payments deficits depended on how one valued those offsetting transactions.[38] In any event, by 1988 there was no question that the banks' willingness to provide new financing was essentially finished.

Perhaps most surprisingly, the Fund staff did reasonably well at forecasting total real growth for the Baker 15 countries as a group. The February 1986 report projected real GDP growth of 2½ percent for 1986–88 for the whole group, and

---

[36]By that time, the staff had stopped monitoring gross disbursements. After September 1988, the detailed monitoring of the Baker initiative stopped, because the 15 countries were no longer viewed as a centrally important grouping and because the focus of thinking was shifting toward more comprehensive solutions to the debt crisis. (Baker resigned as Secretary of the U.S. Treasury in August 1988 to become chairman of Vice President George Bush's campaign for the presidency.)

[37]The September 1988 internal monitoring report estimated net bank lending to the Baker 15 countries to have been –$1.3 billion for 1986 and +$1.6 billion for 1987, and it projected –$2.0 billion for 1988. (Preliminary data were then available only for the first quarter of 1988.) A year later, the *World Economic Outlook* for October 1989 (Table A42) estimated the outcome to have been –1.6, +2.3, and –15.3 for the three years, respectively. For a discussion of the statistical problems in estimating these flows, see the *World Economic Outlook* for April 1989, pp. 26–27.

[38]The $13 billion figure, which was cited (without specific attribution) by Rhodes (1992) in a defense of the banks' contribution, was from Cline (1989). Cline later (1995, p. 209) updated his estimate to +$18 billion. The primary difference between estimates made by the Fund staff and those made by some outside analysts, the U.S. treasury staff, and by the banks is that the latter looked at actual flows (and in some cases focused on gross lending in the form of new-money agreements), while the Fund staff looked at changes in stocks. Measuring by changes in stocks implicitly adjusted for flows that were offset by such diverse and otherwise incommensurate operations as swaps, write-downs, and buybacks. There is, however, no single, generally accepted measure of the banks' contribution. See Watson and others (February 1986), pp. 73–76, for the staff position; and Cline (1995), pp. 208–15, for an alternative view. The U.S. treasury staff's view was expressed in a letter from Mulford to de Larosière dated August 4, 1988 (in IMF/CF, S 1190 "Debt Renegotiation and Multilateral Aid, June 1988–November 1988"); that letter cited an estimate of $17 billion in net lending by banks since October 1985.

throughout the period the aggregate forecast ranged from that level to about 3 percent. The outcome was 2½ percent.[39] This degree of accuracy is surprising, not only because of the inherent difficulty in such an exercise, but also because the staff was frequently criticized at the time for being excessively optimistic about the growth prospects of the heavily indebted developing countries. At a 1988 Executive Board meeting on the World Economic Outlook, for example, Guillermo Ortiz (Mexico) argued that the staff projections were "overly optimistic, . . . encouraged the view that the problem will somehow sort itself out, and presented a perspective that is at odds with reality and also with economic analysis done elsewhere."[40]

A growth rate of 2½ percent was an improvement over the early 1980s (output declined from 1981 through 1983 and grew by just 2 percent in 1984), but it was well below the heady days of the 1970s when growth averaged nearly 6 percent a year (Figure 10.1). Furthermore, the highest growth years were 1985 (pre-Baker) and 1986, after which rates on average dropped off again. Whatever the Baker Plan might have achieved in laying the groundwork for growth, it did not by itself bring robust growth back to the heavily indebted countries.

Enhanced Surveillance

Another manifestation of the effort to use the Fund as a catalyst for external financing by other creditors was the development of "enhanced surveillance" procedures in 1985. As the reader will recall from Chapter 9, when commercial banks first assented to reschedule sovereign loans via MYRAs, they insisted that the Fund undertake to monitor developments more intensively than under the standard Article IV consultation cycle. If the country did not have a financial arrangement with the Fund, this procedure would provide a means for the authorities to provide the banks with the Fund staff's assessment of policies and economic conditions in the country on a frequent (semiannual) basis. In the second half of 1984, the existence of this option made it possible for the banks to approve MYRAs for Mexico and Ecuador and to approve in principle a MYRA for Venezuela.

The idea of enhanced surveillance was cautiously endorsed in the course of 1985 both by the Group of Ten (G-10) industrial countries and by the Group of Twenty-Four (G-24) developing countries. Creditors, however, were somewhat more enthusiastic than debtors. The report on the international monetary system that was issued by the deputies of the ministers of finance of the G-10 countries in June 1985 stated that "the Deputies encourage the IMF to continue to develop [enhanced surveillance] procedures on a case-by-case basis . . ." (para. 47). In re-

---

[39]WEO, October 1989, Table A5. The initial staff forecast was that growth would start slowly and then build up (the projected growth rates for 1986–88 were 1.8, 2.3, and 3.4 percent, respectively); the outcome was that growth was robust in 1986 and then tapered off (4.0, 2.6, and 1.1 percent). The data shown in Figure 10.1 are aggregated from later World Bank tables and exclude Yugoslavia, but the discrepancies are minor and do not affect the conclusions.

[40]Minutes of EBM/88/141 (September 7, 1988), p. 7.

Figure 10.1. Output Growth in Heavily Indebted Countries, 1971–89

Real U.S. dollars

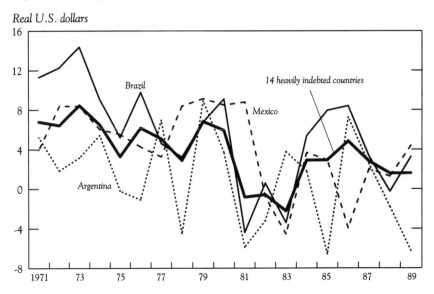

Source: World Bank, *World Development Indicators*.

sponse, the G-24 deputies argued that the case for enhanced surveillance rested on "creditor unwillingness to restore normal access to external financing despite significant adjustment efforts" by the indebted countries. Their report (para. 89) recognized that in these circumstances enhanced surveillance might be necessary for countries seeking a MYRA, and it endorsed its temporary and exceptional use as a means of securing "the early normalization of market relations between the member country and the international financial system."[41]

While these outside assessments were being made, the Fund staff produced its own evaluation of enhanced surveillance, calling for its use in exceptional circumstances and proposing a set of criteria for judging whether it was appropriate in a particular case. The Executive Board met to consider the proposals shortly after Directors returned from their annual mid-August recess.[42] Both the staff and the Board were concerned that the Fund could be drawn into becoming a credit-rating agency on sovereign debts for the banks. They also were concerned that if enhanced surveillance provided a viable alternative to stand-by arrangements as a means of restoring normal access to commercial credits, the Fund's influence and "condi-

---

[41]"The Functioning of the International Monetary System: A Report to the Ministers and Governors by the Group of Deputies," June 1985; and "The Functioning and Improvement of the International Monetary System: Report of the Deputies of the Group of 24," August 21, 1985; both reprinted in Crockett and Goldstein (1987).

[42]"The Role of the Fund in Assisting Members with Commercial Banks and Official Creditors," EBS/85/173 (7/23/85), pp. 15–18; and minutes of EBM/85/130 (August 30, 1985) and EBM/85/131–132 (September 4, 1985).

tionality" could be weakened. As Guenter Grosche (Executive Director for Germany) noted, the "Fund's ability to influence policies of members under enhanced surveillance was extremely limited."[43] Directors generally supported the idea of enhanced surveillance, but only as a temporary and strictly limited expedient.

On September 4, 1985, the Executive Board agreed on basic principles for conducting enhanced surveillance. First, the procedure would have to be requested by the member country. Members had no obligation to accept enhanced surveillance, and it was seen as important to recognize that the procedure was being introduced as a service to those members that wanted to undertake it.[44] Second, the member would have to have already achieved a good record of adjustment and must have developed "a fully articulated and quantified policy program." In other words, the Board had to be confident that the member was willing and able to carry out an adjustment program without the conditionality of a stand-by arrangement. Third, enhanced surveillance should be limited to cases where creditors have approved a MYRA and where the procedure therefore would promote improved market relations with creditors.[45]

"Enhanced surveillance" was an unfortunate choice of terminology, because it created resistance in some countries where the procedure was considered. It seemed to imply even more severe outside policing of the government's policies and a further weakening of economic sovereignty. Translation of the phrase into other languages occasionally worsened this connotation. Officials in Yugoslavia preferred the term "enhanced monitoring," and those in Brazil preferred the even more equivocal "enhanced contacts" (or, a decade later, "enhanced collaboration"). The Fund agreed to use these euphemisms when requested, and the choice of phrasing had no substantive effect on the arrangements.[46]

---

[43]The staff paper also stated this point succinctly: "Clearly, the Fund's leverage under enhanced surveillance is substantially less than in the implementation of Fund policies for the conditional use of Fund resources." See "The Role of the Fund in Assisting Members with Commercial Banks and Official Creditors," EBS/85/173 (July 23, 1985), p. 23; and minutes of EBM/85/130 (August 30, 1985), p. 36. The concern about "conditionality" was also noted in the Managing Director's summing up, at EBM/85/132 (September 4, 1985), p. 5.

[44]The legal basis for conducting enhanced surveillance as an extension of the standard Article IV consultation process was Article V, section 2(b), of the Fund's Articles of Agreement: "If requested, the Fund may decide to perform financial and technical services . . . that are consistent with the purposes of the Fund. . . . Services under this subsection shall not impose any obligation on a member without its consent." The legal position was stated by the Director of the Legal Department at EBM/85/131 (September 4, 1985), p. 6.

[45]See the Chairman's summing up of EBM/85/132 (September 4, 1985), in *Selected Decisions, Twenty-First Issue*, pp. 50–53. The summing up listed four criteria; the description here collapses the retrospective second and the prospective third into one. In February 1986, the Board clarified the terms on which members were permitted to release staff reports to creditors. Release was to be on the understanding that the reports were for no other purpose and were to be held confidentially. Decision No. 8222-(86/45), March 12, 1986; *op cit.*, pp. 49–50.

[46]See "Yugoslavia—Enhanced Surveillance—Note Prepared by the Staff for the Background Information of Executive Directors," EBS/85/171 (July 19, 1985), p. 5. "Enhanced contacts" was the brainchild of the Executive Director for Brazil, Alexandre Kafka, who coined it in 1986 to break an impasse in negotiations between de Larosière and the finance minister, Dilson Funaro.

Venezuela

In view of these doubts and strictures, it is not surprising that there were few applications of enhanced surveillance and that each of these posed its own problems. The seminal case of Venezuela (see Chapter 9) finally got fully under way after the banks signed the MYRA in February 1986, closing 17 months of negotiations. Five months later, creditors were given a staff report that detailed the staff's doubts about the adequacy of the authorities' policy stance following the sharp drop in the price of oil (Venezuela's principal export): fiscal and monetary policies were too lax, the exchange rate was overvalued and was sustained by a distortionary system of multiple rates, and structural reforms were badly needed.[47]

In discussing the staff report in late July 1986, Executive Directors endorsed the staff's views.[48] It was clear that if the banks had required Venezuela to have a Fund stand-by arrangement in place as a condition for the MYRA, a greater adjustment effort would have been required. The banks were nonetheless satisfied to accept the situation as long as the authorities stayed current in paying the interest that was due under the terms of the MYRA, and they were even prepared to renegotiate the MYRA in response to a further sharp drop in oil prices in the first half of 1986. And there the situation remained throughout the next two years, until the lack of adjustment finally induced a newly elected government (headed by President Carlos Andrés Pérez) to request an extended arrangement in February 1989 (Chapter 11).[49]

Yugoslavia

The second case of enhanced surveillance was also problematic. In August 1985, commercial bank creditors approved in principle a MYRA for Yugoslavia, under which enhanced surveillance was to become effective when the existing stand-by arrangement (the fifth consecutive such arrangement since 1979) expired in May of the following year. This time, the banks protected themselves to some extent by setting aside a portion of the debts to be covered later, conditional on a finding by creditors that Yugoslavia would be able to service the debts. The Fund reports that were expected to be provided under the enhanced surveillance procedure would be a major input for that decision.[50]

Although the Fund had earlier indicated a willingness to consider enhanced surveillance for Yugoslavia, the Managing Director was becoming increasingly reluctant to accept the proposal; the state of macroeconomic and structural policies

---

[47]"Venezuela—Staff Report for the 1986 Article IV Consultation," SM/86/152 (June 25, 1986); the staff appraisal is on pp. 24–26.

[48]Minutes of EBM/86/122 (July 25, 1986).

[49]For a chronology of enhanced surveillance with Venezuela, 1984–88, see "Review of Enhanced Surveillance," EBS/88/247 (December 2, 1988), p. 30.

[50]See "Yugoslavia—Enhanced Surveillance—Note Prepared by the Staff for the Background Information of Executive Directors," EBS/85/171 (July 19, 1985), to which the commercial banks' draft MYRA is attached.

was too far from what the Fund considered reasonable. At the end of May, he informed the visiting prime minister, Mrs. Milka Planinć, that a further strengthening of policies was needed before Yugoslavia would be ready for enhanced surveillance.[51] As discussions continued through the second half of the year, however, the authorities met the performance criteria under the stand-by arrangement. As the expiration of the arrangement drew nearer, the obstacles to moving ahead became less imposing. Finally, on February 12, 1986, Yugoslavia submitted a formal request to the Fund for enhanced surveillance (to be called "enhanced monitoring"), which the Executive Board approved a month later.[52]

Before the enhanced surveillance procedure was implemented for Yugoslavia, a complication arose when official creditors participating in the Paris Club asked to be included as well. When the Paris Club met in mid-April to consider Yugoslavia's request for a MYRA, it faced an exceptional situation. Official creditors normally required the indebted country to have an upper-tranche (i.e., high-conditionality) Fund arrangement in place before it would consider a rescheduling, but Yugoslavia's existing stand-by arrangement was in trouble and was about to expire.[53] Furthermore, despite the difficulties in stabilizing the economy, Yugoslavia's current account balance had shifted into surplus and the authorities were aiming to enter a period of solid debt reduction. New borrowings from the Fund were therefore ruled out. Creditor governments wanted to approve Yugoslavia's request for a multiyear rescheduling, and the Fund's intention to conduct enhanced surveillance provided a convenient basis for breaking precedent.

The implication of this development was that the Fund would have to be a bit more flexible in conducting enhanced surveillance for Yugoslavia, in order to meet the needs of official as well as commercial creditors. In particular, official creditors would—in the normal course of affairs—receive not only the staff report, but also the record of the discussion of the report by the Executive Board. Since this was the first case of enhanced surveillance in support of an agreement with official creditors, some Directors were concerned that the release of the Board's views to those creditors would necessarily trigger on/off decisions regarding the MYRA. That is, if Executive Directors agreed that the authorities had not met the goals of their program, official creditors might well use that information to not go ahead with the next installment of their rescheduling. The Fund in that case could find itself taking responsibility for decisions and actions over which it had little influence and no control, as it had in the special arrangement with Colombia a year earlier (Chapter 9).

---

[51]Memorandum for files (June 13, 1985) by Brian E. Rose (Deputy Director, European Department); in IMF/RD Managing Director file "1985—Yugoslavia I" (Accession 87/136, Box 3, Section 168). Also see memorandum of May 30, 1985, by L. Alan Whittome (Counsellor and Director, European Department); same file.

[52]The request was in a letter reproduced in "Yugoslavia—Staff Report for the 1985 Article IV Consultation and Review Under the Stand-By Arrangement," EBS/86/38 (February 19, 1986), pp. 36–37. The Executive Board considered the request at EBM/86/44–45 (March 12, 1986) and approved it via Decision No. 8221-(86/45), adopted March 12, 1986.

[53]The first four drawings had been made on time, but two waivers would be required from the Executive Board for the authorities to make the last scheduled drawing in mid-May.

The distinction that the staff emphasized in allaying these concerns was that under enhanced surveillance the member country did not undertake to meet specific quantitative performance criteria. The staff report would discuss the extent to which various goals had been reached, but it would emphasize whether the thrust of the program was being carried out, not whether each target had been met. Both within the Executive Board and among official creditors, opinions might well differ on the significance of departures from desired performance. Furthermore, once initiated, enhanced surveillance could continue regardless of whether the program was carried out as intended; there was no requirement for waivers in case of missed targets as there was for stand-by arrangements. There would thus be no automatic triggers implied either in the staff report or in the Board discussion. On the basis of that understanding, on May 12, 1986, the Board approved the extension of enhanced surveillance with Yugoslavia to cover official creditors acting through the Paris Club.[54]

The Fund's experience in implementing enhanced surveillance with Yugoslavia was not entirely happy. By the time the first consultation report was discussed, in August 1986, policies were already going off track. Economic policy in Yugoslavia was at a crossroads in the mid-1980s: the momentum was toward liberalization, but the inertia of the old "workers' self-management" system remained strong. At the Executive Board meeting on August 8, a number of Directors noted that they had approved the use of enhanced surveillance rather than insisting on a new stand-by arrangement in the belief that the authorities were committed to pushing ahead toward a market economy. Now, just a few months later, that commitment was in doubt.[55]

The Fund's confidence in the thrust of policies in Yugoslavia continued to deteriorate over the next year. In March 1987, the Executive Board (in consonance with the views of the staff) expressed even stronger reservations than before. Not only was the liberalization of the economy proceeding at a very slow pace; monetary and fiscal policies were lax, and inflation was accelerating. Directors were beginning to have second thoughts about continuing with enhanced surveillance ("a sense of some discouragement about the experience to date," as Dallara phrased it, was not uncommon), and some urged the Yugoslav authorities to apply once again for a stand-by arrangement.[56]

Following the Board meeting, the Yugoslav authorities quickly reformulated policies to strengthen the adjustment effort before the Paris Club met at the end of March. On March 30, the Federal Secretary for Finance (i.e., the finance minister), Svetozar Rikanović, presented the new measures to the Paris Club: notably, interest rates were being raised to levels that exceeded the inflation rate, and leg-

---

[54]Specifically, the Board authorized the Managing Director to release the summing up of the Board discussions, along with the staff reports, to the Chairman of the Paris Club. Whereas the reports released to commercial creditors would be purged of confidential information such as recaps of earlier consultation discussions, the Paris Club would receive the unexpurgated version. Minutes of EBM/86/80 (May 12, 1986), pp. 23–24.

[55]Minutes of EBM/86/134 (August 8, 1986).

[56]Minutes of EBM/87/44–45 (March 13, 1987). Dallara's remark is on p. 20 of EBM/87/44.

islation was being implemented to limit the growth in wages.[57] Official creditors demurred, responding that they would reconsider the request for a MYRA only after the Fund reevaluated Yugoslavia's policies on the basis of the minister's presentation.

When the Executive Board met again just three weeks later to resume the enhanced surveillance discussion on Yugoslavia, Directors were less than impressed. Most of what was announced on March 30 had already been known when the Board had met earlier, and what was new was still less than what Directors had already said was needed. The Board concluded that a further strengthening of policies would be needed before the authorities could expect to see a sufficient improvement in economic conditions.[58]

Other creditors were somewhat more upbeat. In May, the banks proceeded with the second tranche of their MYRA, and the next month the Paris Club followed suit. But the Executive Board remained adamant. The next time Directors met to consider the situation, on August 31, 1987, most of them were agreed that Yugoslavia could not get policies under control until they undertook a new conditional arrangement with the Fund. As the Managing Director summed up the discussion:

> Yugoslavia's record of adjustment under enhanced surveillance had been disappointing and this had adversely affected both Yugoslavia's credibility abroad and the needed flow of foreign financing. . . . Directors concluded that a firm stabilization program accompanied by supply-promoting measures was essential to get inflation under control and to pursue satisfactory rates of growth and that such a program should be elaborated and implemented in a close and formal relationship with the Fund.[59]

In short, enhanced surveillance had failed in this case: it had succeeded in catalyzing external financing on a multiyear basis, but at the cost of a serious delay in stabilizing the economy.

Before the end of 1987, the Fund's view prevailed with other creditors as well. By November, both the banks and the Paris Club informed the Yugoslav authorities that they would have to negotiate an upper-tranche arrangement with the Fund as a precondition for any further rescheduling. The authorities requested a stand-by arrangement in December, a program was successfully negotiated over the next four months, and in June 1988 the Executive Board approved a one-year arrangement for SDR 306 million (50 percent of quota, or just over $400 million).[60]

---

[57]For the first quarter of 1987, inflation had been running at an annualized rate of about 130 percent. On April 1, interest rates on term deposits of six months or more were raised from around 60 percent to more than 80 percent. On the basis of a partial price freeze that had been put in place on March 20, these interest rates were projected to be positive in real terms. "Yugoslavia—Consolidation of External Debt Vis-à-Vis Official Creditors," EBS/87/79 (April 13, 1987), pp. 6–15.

[58]Summing up of the discussion; minutes of EBM/87/62 (April 20, 1987), pp. 53–54.

[59]Summing up of the discussion; minutes of EBM/87/126, pp. 29–30.

[60]Minutes of EBM/88/88 (June 1, 1988).

Uruguay

The third and final application of enhanced surveillance in the 1980s was at least initially more successful. Uruguay was in the middle of an 18-month stand-by arrangement with the Fund when the banks approved a MYRA in July 1986. The bank agreement provided that reschedulings in 1987–89 were to be contingent on Uruguay either having a new stand-by arrangement with the Fund or being under enhanced surveillance. Uruguay successfully completed the Fund-supported program in March 1987, and the Executive Board approved the authorities' request for enhanced surveillance in July.[61] The Fund then conducted enhanced surveillance with Uruguay for the next two years. Through 1988, both the staff and Executive Directors gave a generally good report card to the authorities for the implementation of stable economic policies. By 1989, however, the authorities were losing the momentum of their adjustment effort, and fiscal policy was becoming increasingly lax. Enhanced surveillance was successfully completed, but the following year, the newly elected authorities requested a new stand-by arrangement.

Assessment

Judging only from the record of implementation in the 1980s, enhanced surveillance would have to be rated a failure: three cases were approved in the first five years of operation, and in at least the first two cases the process probably delayed and certainly did not prevent the need for more stringent and Fund-supported adjustment measures. There were, however, several other cases in which the option of having the Fund conduct enhanced surveillance in the future gave confidence to private or official creditors that were contemplating requests for multiyear reschedulings. In addition to the cases of Mexico and Ecuador that were discussed in Chapter 9, commercial bank creditors approved MYRAs with enhanced surveillance provisions for both the Dominican Republic and Côte d'Ivoire in 1986, and in several more countries in later years. With this broader perspective in mind, though no one would consider enhanced surveillance to have been an unqualified success, a case could be built for its continued use in dealing with the exceptional strains facing some of the world's most heavily indebted countries.[62]

---

[61]Minutes of EBM/87/110 (July 27, 1987).

[62]The Executive Board conducted three general reviews of enhanced surveillance in this period. In March 1987, the Board approved continuation of the procedure but suggested that some means should be found of terminating it in case of noncooperation by the authorities. In March 1988, no further changes were recommended. In February 1989, it had become clear that the Fund had no effective means of extricating itself from undertaking enhanced surveillance once the procedure had been initiated. The Board determined that the use of the procedure should be further restricted by applying the criterion of "a strong record of adjustment" more strictly. See the minutes of EBM/87/48–50 (March 17–18, 1987); EBM/88/53–55 (March 30–31, 1988); and EBM/89/12–13 (February 8, 1989).

Stand-By Arrangement with Mexico

Mexico was in crisis at the beginning of 1986. Fiscal policy had to be reined in substantially to cut public sector borrowing from the extraordinarily high level (about 10 percent of GDP) of 1985, and the adjustment would have to be made at a time when the economy was scarcely in shape to absorb another shock. As recounted in Chapter 9, the Fund lent just under SDR 300 million (approximately $330 million) in January 1986 under the natural disaster relief program to help Mexico rebuild after the earthquakes of the previous year. A few months later, the IBRD lent Mexico $400 million for the same purpose. Long-run growth prospects were brightening in response to the substantial measures being implemented to liberalize foreign trade; Mexico was now close to completing its accession to the GATT.[63] These and other efforts were, however, small in relation to the magnitude of the initial economic imbalances in Mexico, and they were completely swamped by the ongoing collapse in the world price of petroleum, Mexico's primary export.

Relations between Mexico and the IMF in 1986–87 revolved around two main problems. First, there was a major dispute over fiscal policy: how much adjustment was needed to contain inflationary pressures and reduce the external deficit, how much could the budget be reined in without unduly restraining economic growth, and how should the adjustment be measured and assessed? After several months of negotiations, a compromise was reached under which Mexico agreed to strengthen its adjustment effort, while the Fund agreed to include a contingency plan in case of an unanticipated decline in output and to use an inflation-adjusted measure of the fiscal balance as one measure of success. Second, commercial bank creditors—especially the smaller banks—were reluctant to help finance the Mexican program on the large scale that the Fund judged to be necessary. Overcoming that reluctance seriously delayed and complicated implementation of the program and nearly caused it to fail altogether.

Negotiating on a Treadmill: October 1985–June 1986

The IMF planned to send a staff team to Mexico City in October 1985 to begin negotiations on a possible stand-by arrangement. The Mexican authorities, however, preferred to come to Washington instead. Consequently, a number of Mexican officials, led by the minister of finance, Jesús Silva Herzog, made several visits to Washington between December 1985 and March 1986, meeting not only with the Fund staff but also with the Managing Director, U.S. officials, the management and staff of the World Bank and the IDB, and commercial bank creditors. The key issue during these meetings was fiscal policy. The government had proposed, and congress had approved, a budget for 1986 calling for a public sector borrowing requirement of about 4 percent of GDP. That target was down from the outturn of nearly 10 percent in 1985 and was sufficiently ambitious, but the Fund staff

---

[63]Mexico formally joined the GATT on August 26, 1986.

pointed out that the target for 1985 had also been about 5 percent. In the circumstances, the staff believed that credibility could be achieved only by taking substantial action early in the year. The authorities countered that the adjustment had to be gradual to avoid throwing the economy into an even more serious tailspin.

By mid-March, Mexico faced a mini-crisis in its external financing, in that a payment of $950 million in principal was due to foreign commercial bank creditors on March 21, and little progress had been made toward establishing the terms on which the banks would be prepared to roll it over. The banks' position was that they could not agree to an overall financing plan until the Fund approved and Mexico signed a Letter of Intent for a stand-by arrangement. After Mexico agreed to open full negotiations with the Fund, however, the banks agreed to the six-month rollover. Soon afterward, Joaquín Pujol (Assistant Director, Western Hemisphere Department) led two missions to Mexico City to negotiate terms for a stand-by arrangement.[64]

The outlook for the economy and for success in these talks was grim. From December 1985 to April 1986, while the government tried to implement tax and spending measures aimed at nearly halving the fiscal deficit, the decline in the export price of Mexico's oil reduced fiscal revenues by some 4 percent of GDP. Meanwhile, higher-than-anticipated inflation and depreciation raised the government's projected interest outlays for the year by 4½ percent of GDP. The government responded by making further cuts in the budget, but they were being beaten back on the treadmill. The deficit was going up, not down.

Pujol recommended that the authorities find a way to cut the deficit by another 5–6 percentage points of GDP. Otherwise, they would be unable to cover it without heavy recourse to inflationary finance. The authorities responded that the effects of inflation and depreciation on interest costs should be accommodated and thus excluded from the calculated financing requirement. Accordingly, they proposed to limit additional measures to 2½ percent of GDP, or just under half what the Fund was asking. In effect, the Mexican position was the same as that of Brazil since 1983: that the appropriate measure of fiscal policy was not the actual deficit, including inflationary effects on interest payments, but rather the operational budget, excluding those effects.

Pujol's missions having ended in an impasse, a team of Mexican officials went to Washington on May 21–23, 1986, to talk directly with the Managing Director. De Larosière did not budge, believing that Mexico had to undertake a major fiscal retrenchment if the government was to escape its dependence on external borrowing. The authorities indicated that they were prepared to open discussions with bank and other creditors with or without the Fund, but what little ability they might have had to do so was rapidly disappearing. Through April, Mexico had

---

[64]The decision to limit the request to a stand-by arrangement rather than a longer-term extended arrangement was dictated in part by the electoral cycle; a new government would take office in 1988. In addition, there was a general view at the time that the EFF was to be reserved for detailed structural programs; Mexico having just completed such a program in 1985, an ordinary stand-by arrangement was considered more appropriate.

maintained a measure of credibility in foreign exchange markets by keeping the exchange rate competitive and by pursuing a tight domestic credit policy. By May, however, worries about the fiscal deficit were inducing an acceleration of capital flight. On June 3, the central bank announced that it had lost $500 million in reserves during May, bringing the total loss for the first half of the year to more than $1.5 billion and leaving net reserves at a precarious level.[65] Mexico had to negotiate a solution quickly—or default.

Discussions between Mexico and the Fund continued nonstop through the first half of June, with de Larosière and Silva Herzog both actively involved and Volcker and Mulford serving as U.S. intermediaries. The sequence of events was complex, but it is worth examining in some detail in light of what followed.

By June 6, de Larosière agreed in principle with Silva Herzog that Mexico could use the operational deficit as one fiscal target, so long as the overall deficit was also targeted; the two sides, however, remained far apart on the issue of how large the fiscal adjustment should be. On June 9, Volcker traveled to Mexico City to meet with President Miguel de la Madrid, under an elaborate cloak of secrecy aimed at preventing reporters from spotting the extremely visible Chairman and generating speculation about the meaning of his visit at this delicate time.[66] Over breakfast that morning, he impressed upon the president the importance of reaching an agreement both with the Fund and the commercial banks, and he received what he interpreted as a positive and encouraging response. The next day, Silva Herzog phoned de Larosière to say he was encouraged by Volcker's visit, and he suggested that negotiations be quickly resumed.

Silva Herzog immediately sent a team of officials to Washington, but negotiations remained deadlocked over the ceiling on the fiscal deficit. When Silva Herzog telephoned de Larosière again on the evening of June 12, the Managing Director insisted that Mexico make a commitment to cut the deficit by 2½ percent in 1986 and another 2½ percent in 1987. Although that would leave the deficit larger than originally envisioned, it would require much larger program cuts to achieve, reflecting the adverse shocks that had already occurred. Silva Herzog replied that such measures would be impossible to undertake, and he offered to come to Washington himself the next day for face-to-face talks.

---

[65]Mexico's gross foreign exchange reserves totaled $7.3 billion at the end of 1984, $4.7 billion at the end of 1985, and less than $3.2 billion at end-June, 1986. For those three dates, net international reserves (including payments agreements but subtracting net liabilities to the IMF and to official creditors for swaps) amounted to $6.5 billion, $3.1 billion, and $1.2 billion, respectively. "Mexico—Staff Report for the 1986 Article IV Consultation and Request for Stand-By Arrangement," EBS/86/161, Sup. 1 (August 15, 1986), p. 11.

[66]At a height of 6 feet, 7 inches, Volcker proved difficult to hide, though he made part of the trip in a Mexican government plane and was housed at a private home instead of a hotel. His presence was soon discovered by the Mexican press (see *Uno Más Uno*, June 10, 1986, p. 3). In Washington, President Reagan inadvertently broke the secrecy by mentioning the trip *en passant* during a press conference on June 11. Years later, Volcker discussed the trip in Volcker and Gyohten (1992), p. 214–15. Additional information here is from background interviews and file memorandums.

De Larosière also was encouraged by the way events were unfolding. He and Silva Herzog knew and respected each other well, having struggled together for four years to put Mexico on a sustainable path. On the morning of the 13th, he reported to the Executive Board that the staff was in close contact with the authorities and that—although the political situation was "fluid"—discussions were "moving in a constructive way."[67] His optimism was premature. Silva Herzog had to postpone his trip to the Fund, which he now planned to make on June 17. In the meantime, de Larosière met on the 16th with U.S. Treasury Secretary James Baker, who applied pressure by reminding him that if the Fund did not show enough flexibility to reach an agreement with Mexico, the alternative would be a confrontation with creditors that could have repercussions on other countries in the region.

The stage was thus set for a likely agreement, but then the curtain fell. Silva Herzog, either because he was seen as too closely identified with Washington or because he was being outmaneuvered by others in the cabinet who saw him as an obstacle to their political ambitions, apparently had become isolated from the inner circle in the government.[68] On June 17, instead of coming to Washington to meet with de Larosière, Silva Herzog resigned. The president immediately named Gustavo Petricioli to replace him, and before the day was out de Larosière telephoned the new minister to "renew our acquaintance" and to suggest an early resumption of negotiations.

Approval "In Principle": July–September 1986

Petricioli headed north on June 27 for his first meeting as minister with the Managing Director. His message was straightforward: too much fiscal contraction would stifle economic growth, and without growth Mexico would be unable to meet its obligations to foreign creditors. He did not want an agreement to which he could not adhere. De Larosière responded that the current fiscal stance would aggravate inflation; the only way to resume and sustain growth was to undertake substantial structural reforms. An agreement was as distant as ever, but the two men agreed to meet again in two weeks, on July 11.

On July 7–8, the Managing Director attended the monthly meeting of the BIS governors in Basel, Switzerland, to make the case for a bridge loan to Mexico from the major central banks. He felt that the authorities were still very close to reaching an agreement with the Fund, and it would be essential for Mexico to have enough money up front to staunch the outflow of reserves in the interval before the Executive Board could meet to approve the loan. The Basel discussion, however, was preliminary, and no action was taken on the request.

---

[67]Minutes of EBM/86/96 (June 13, 1986), p. 3.

[68]In the 1980s, responsibility for the budget in Mexico was split between the secretary of finance and the secretary of budget and planning. Basically, the former (Silva Herzog) controlled revenues while the latter (the future president and eventual fugitive, Carlos Salinas) controlled spending.

Petricioli's message to the Managing Director at their second meeting, at the end of the afternoon of July 11, was distinctly pessimistic. Mexico was losing reserves so rapidly that it could not afford to continue negotiating. He understood that the Fund had to adhere to its conditions, but he had no more concessions to give. It would be better for him to go home with no agreement, even knowing that such a failure would force Mexico to default on its interest payments and impose exchange controls, than to go home with an agreement that would wreck economic growth and that would be seen as an external imposition of policies on the government. In fact, he had already made his airplane reservation for the next morning, and he showed his ticket to de Larosière as a demonstration of his resolve. Although Petricioli may have been bluffing, de Larosière was determined that these talks should not fail: they were critically important both for Mexico and for the Fund. He responded to the minister that the two sides were not that far apart, and he persuaded him to stay in Washington and to meet with him again the next morning (Saturday) to consider how they might break the impasse quickly.

The day before this meeting, Petricioli's technical advisors had tabled a new proposal to the Fund staff, to the effect that the government would agree to implement additional fiscal cuts if the price of oil were to fall below a benchmark level. Friday night, after consulting with a few of his senior staff, de Larosière decided to use that idea as the foundation for an innovative program. His meeting with Petricioli had convinced him that the government's fundamental concern was that additional fiscal action would reduce growth. The Fund staff, in contrast, based its recommendations on projections indicating that growth could be sustained better with some additional fiscal restraint. By 10:00 Saturday morning, when Petricioli and his team[69] returned to the Managing Director's office on the twelfth floor of the IMF, de Larosière had devised a plan to reconcile the two positions.

De Larosière's proposal was to introduce a growth contingency into the program. As he presented it on Saturday morning, the idea was that the authorities would agree up front to make an extra fiscal effort. If GDP growth were to fall below a benchmark level, then they could implement an additional public investment program, financed by additional loans from the Fund. If the Mexican growth forecast was correct, they would get the program they wanted. If the Fund forecast was correct, Mexico would implement the more austere budget suggested by the Fund staff. Petricioli agreed that this proposal could serve as the basis for continuing the negotiations.

Meetings between the staff and the Mexican technical team, and between the Managing Director and the finance minister, continued throughout Saturday and Sunday.[70] De Larosière—after consulting with Barber Conable, the president of

---

[69]Petricioli's strong group of advisors on this trip included the three men who would succeed him as finance minister over the coming decade: Pedro Aspe Armella (1988–94), Jaime Serra Puche (1994), and Guillermo Ortíz Martínez (1994–97).

[70]This account of the negotiations is based in part on the author's interviews with participants and on notes taken by the staff during the meetings, in IMF/RD Managing Director file "Mexico—Vol. IV" (Accession 88/274, Box 9, Section 269).

the World Bank—modified his proposal so as to shift the commitment to finance the contingent investment program from the Fund to the International Bank for Reconstruction and Development (IBRD) and the commercial banks. Meanwhile, the Mexican team insisted that in addition to the growth contingency, they needed to allow for the possibility of a further decline in the price of their oil exports. The Fund accepted that idea, with the modification that the mechanism be symmetric: the Fund would provide additional resources if the export price fell below $9 a barrel, and its commitment would be commensurately reduced if the price rose above $14. For its part, Mexico agreed to strengthen its measures to reduce the fiscal deficit, primarily by raising public sector prices enough to raise revenues by about 1 percent of GDP.

By Sunday evening, agreement had been reached on the substance of a program that Petricioli felt comfortable taking to President de la Madrid for approval and that de Larosière felt comfortable taking to the Executive Board for its approval. The economic program was to be supported by an 18-month stand-by arrangement for SDR 1.4 billion (120 percent of quota, or approximately $1.7 billion), including SDR 1 billion from borrowed resources made available under the enlarged access policy (see Chapter 17). If the oil-price contingency was fully utilized, another SDR 800 million would be made available. In less than a week, the president approved the program, and on July 22, Petricioli returned to Washington to sign the Letter of Intent. The main remaining difficulty was a rather large financing gap that would have to be filled by other official and commercial creditors.

The official financing would be large and complex, involving both short-term bridge financing from the United States and from G-10 central banks via the BIS, but it would not be out of line with previous practice since 1982. To make sure there would be no slippages, de Larosière took personal responsibility for lining up support. He met with Mulford and other U.S. officials on Thursday, July 17; a few days later, Secretary Baker publicly supported the program, and the treasury began quietly arranging for additional short-term financing including assistance from the Export-Import bank and similar agencies in other major creditor countries. The following week, de Larosière cabled the BIS governors, all of whom responded favorably to the request for a bridge loan; the BIS formally approved the loan in late August. On July 22, Conable announced the World Bank's intention to support the program with new loans. The Bank announcement, for a series of loans totaling some $1.4 billion, was especially important for the program, not only because it would provide medium-term support for investment and structural reforms, but because it constituted the second leg of the Baker strategy for three-legged support.[71]

To complete the official package, Mexico requested a rescheduling of outstanding obligations through the Paris Club. What complicated this process was the web

---

[71]Conable issued a press release on July 22, announcing that the Bank's Executive Directors would soon be considering three loans totaling $698 million, that additional loans totaling $700 million would be considered within a few months, and that the International Finance Corporation (IFC, a member of the World Bank Group) would also be lending to Mexico. The Board approved the initial request on July 29.

of interrelationships between various pieces of the official financing. The Paris Club required Fund approval for Mexico's program and maintenance of export cover by bilateral creditors. Those bilateral credits in turn depended on the Paris Club. The BIS bridge loan and the Fund stand-by arrangement depended on each other, and the BIS deal also depended on participation by private as well as central banks and the U.S. Treasury. Throughout August and early September, the Managing Director acted as an intermediary, keeping various creditors informed on the status of others' deliberations and intentions and making sure the package held together.

The third leg of the strategy—a rise in exposure by commercial creditors—was even more of a problem, both because many bankers were skeptical about Mexico's promises and because the amount of the financing that the Managing Director was about to request would have to be so large that there was a real risk that it would be rejected. On July 23, de Larosière and Petricioli flew together to New York for a pair of meetings with bank creditors: a general meeting and dinner at the Pierre Hotel that evening with some 80 bankers (attended as well by Conable) and a smaller session with the Advisory Committee the next day at the offices of Citibank's legal advisors. De Larosière explained to the bankers the complex financial package, including the oil and growth contingency mechanisms. While the latter would be financed largely by the World Bank, the oil-price contingency would have to be funded partly by the IMF and partly by the banks; de Larosière suggested that the banks make a contingent commitment of $1.6 billion, compared with the Fund's SDR 800 million commitment.[72] Apart from this contingency, he asked the banks to arrange a "new money" loan for $6 billion covering the rest of 1986 and 1987.

The Advisory Committee for the commercial banks sent its economic subcommittee to Mexico City in early August (following a briefing at the Fund) to review the economy and assess Mexico's financing needs. The authorities, meanwhile, were devising a complex financing proposal of their own, which included partial capitalization of interest payments, several options relating to different maturities, and indexing interest payments to oil prices. Detailed negotiations between the Committee and the authorities (led, as always, by Mexico's chief debt negotiator, Angel Gurría) did not begin until September, by which time there was no possibility of reaching an agreement—much less assembling a "critical mass" of commitments—before the scheduled meeting of the Executive Board on September 8.

On Thursday, September 4, William Rhodes, Citibank's vice chairman and head of the Advisory Committee, informed the Managing Director that the banks'

---

[72]This 2:1 ratio, as the Managing Director characterized it, became an accepted part of the ensuing negotiations, but the term initially was misleading because the two shares were denominated in different currencies (SDRs from the Fund and U.S. dollars from the banks). At prevailing exchange rates, the Fund's contingent exposure was approximately $940 million, and the effective ratio of commitments was therefore 1.7:1. The total contingent liability to Mexico under this mechanism, which would have come into play if the oil export price had fallen persistently below $9 a barrel, was intended to be $2.5 billion. In the final agreement, as explained below, these amounts were reduced, but the notional 2:1 ratio was essentially retained.

negotiations were going to take quite a bit longer. That evening, de Larosière telephoned several of the Fund's Executive Directors to seek their support for holding the Board meeting as scheduled but with the intention of taking the "exceptional" step of approving the stand-by arrangement "in principle," subject to provision of financing by the banks and Paris Club creditors.[73] He made a more formal report to the Board Friday morning, and without objection the meeting was left on the schedule for Monday.

The Board meeting on September 8 was tense. Several Executive Directors, including Jacques Polak (Netherlands), expressed serious reservations about Mexico's ability to service the additional debts that it was proposing to take on. In their view, the staff's medium-term scenarios were unduly optimistic. Directors also expressed doubts about the wisdom of including a target for the operational fiscal deficit, on the grounds that it could weaken the authorities' incentive to control inflation. For the most part, however, these objections were swept away by the fear that refusal to approve the arrangement would undermine the adjustment program, that without the program the Mexican economy would collapse, and that failure in Mexico would have global and systemic repercussions that the world could not afford. Polak, for example, noted "the crucial role of Mexico in the development of the international debt situation," and Michael Foot (Alternate, United Kingdom) stressed the "importance of its orderly adjustment to the international monetary system."[74]

Some Directors also questioned the appropriateness of the two contingency mechanisms in the program.[75] As a matter of principle, Polak would have preferred that the oil-price contingency be handled through the Compensatory Financing Facility (CFF) rather than as part of a stand-by arrangement. Those Directors representing developing countries, however, found the handling of the growth and oil-price contingencies to be a welcome sign of flexibility, and Charles Dallara (United States) and Hirotake Fujino (Japan) also supported the innovation. De Larosière defended the growth contingency by noting simply that it was designed to bridge the difference in view between the authorities and the staff on the effects of fiscal contraction: the authorities believed it would slow growth, while the staff believed "strongly" that it would promote the growth of the private sector. Introducing the contingency mechanism had persuaded the authorities to accept "what they had believed to be an excessively demanding fiscal component" of the program.[76] In any

---

[73]The practice of approving programs in principle, pending completion of agreements with other creditors, began with the 1983 stand-by arrangement with Sudan (see Chapter 16). For a general discussion of the practice between that case and that of Mexico in 1986, see Chapter 9; on the interaction between stand-by arrangements and purchases under the CFF when arrangements are approved in principle, see Chapter 15.

[74]See minutes of EBM/86/148–49 (September 8, 1986). The remarks by Polak and Foot are at meeting 86/148, pp. 23 and 24.

[75]The proper treatment of contingencies was under general discussion at the time, in the context of reviews of the design of Fund-supported programs. See Chapter 15.

[76]Minutes of EBM/86/149 (September 8, 1986), p. 34; also see the statement by Pujol on the growth contingency, p. 39.

case, concern over the growth contingency was no doubt muted by the fact that the Fund's involvement in it was largely technical rather than financial.[77]

One Director, Yusuf A. Nimatallah (Saudi Arabia), complained that the Managing Director had acted unilaterally during the negotiations and had not adequately consulted with the Board. In response, de Larosière expressed his concerns and asked the Board collectively whether there was a lack of confidence in his handling of the negotiations. Alexandre Kafka (Brazil), the Dean of the Board, spoke for his colleagues in expressing their "full confidence" in him, and the moment passed.[78]

In the end, only one Director—C.R. Rye (Australia)—abstained from approving the arrangement in principle. In Rye's view, Mexico's economic problems had arisen from fundamental policy errors that predated the earthquakes and other exogenous disturbances; real interest rates were negative, the real effective exchange rate had been allowed to appreciate, and growth in domestic credit was excessive. He doubted, therefore, that the proposed program was sufficient to correct the imbalances in the economy. Other Directors, including Dallara and Jacques de Groote (Belgium), shared the view that Mexico had failed to implement its previous program but were less pessimistic about the future.

Financing the Program: September–November 1986

The Executive Board approved the arrangement on the condition that the bank and Paris Club financing be in place by September 29.[79] That left just three weeks to complete the negotiations and obtain a critical mass of commitments. Few people other than the Managing Director seemed to believe it could be done, but de Larosière was determined to try. On September 11, he met with Ortiz and the minister of planning, Carlos Salinas. His message to them was that the Fund was refusing to give in to pressure from the banks to reduce the financing request below $6 billion, but Mexico would have to be flexible and realistic in discussing terms with the banks. He specifically asked that Mexico drop its insistence on capitalizing interest and linking interest payments to the price of oil, both of

---

[77]Under the final terms of the arrangement, the Fund assumed responsibility for certifying whether industrial production had fallen by more than a 1 percent annual rate in any period. If so, and if the growth facility—formally known as the "supplementary capital expenditure contingency mechanism"—were then activated by a request from the authorities, the performance criteria for the arrangement would be modified to allow the public sector borrowing requirement to rise by up to $500 million. The IBRD agreed that under these circumstances, it would seek to identify investment projects that would promote real growth. Such projects then would be cofinanced by the IBRD and the commercial bank creditors. "Mexico—Stand-By Arrangement," EBS/86/161, Sup. 6 (November 20, 1986), pp. 20–21.

[78]Minutes of EBM/86/148 (September 8, 1986), pp. 13–14.

[79]"The stand-by arrangement . . . shall become effective on the date on which the Fund finds that satisfactory arrangements have been made with respect to the financing of the estimated balance of payments deficits for the period of the stand-by arrangement, but provided that such finding shall be made not later than September 29, 1986." Executive Board Decision No. 8385-(86/149), adopted September 8, 1986.

which the banks were extremely reluctant to accept.[80] An interim deadline of September 19 had been set for concluding an agreement with the Advisory Committee, but that deadline could be met only if rapid progress was made on such issues.

The Paris Club agreed on September 15 to reschedule official credits, but the September 19 deadline for a committee agreement came and went without seeing much progress on that front. Negotiations between Mexico and its bank creditors were still deadlocked on the handling of the contingency mechanisms and other terms. At the end of the month, however, the expiration of the provisional Board approval of the stand-by arrangement provided an incentive for both sides to reach an accommodation. The Annual Meetings were being held in Washington, and on September 30 the chairmen of the Advisory Committee banks met with the Mexican negotiators at the Sheraton Hotel to try to unblock the agreement.[81] Volcker, Conable, and de Larosière also attended at least part of the meeting, which lasted for several hours. The World Bank helped the process along by offering to guarantee up to 50 percent of the banks' disbursements under the growth contingency, applied to the longer maturities.[82] Eventually, all that was preventing an accord was a disagreement over the interest rate to be charged. The Mexican government was refusing to pay more than ¾ of a percent over LIBOR, while some of the major banks were holding out for ⅞. At one point, it appeared that a compromise would be reached whereby part of the loan would be at one rate and the rest at the other, but the bankers could not agree among themselves as to how to split it. Finally, Volcker—clearly frustrated—found the winning formula by suggesting that they make the whole loan at ¹³⁄₁₆ over LIBOR: a solution that had escaped everyone simply because such a fraction had never been used before and seemed silly on its face.[83] (Oddly, in future bank deals, the use of sixteenths in computing spreads became a fairly common practice.)

After Rhodes informed de Larosière that the banks and the Mexican authorities had reached agreement in principle on the $6 billion package, the Managing Director called an Executive Board meeting for that evening (held, exceptionally, at 6:15 p.m., at the Sheraton). The decision taken on September 8 to approve the program contingent on bank financing had lapsed the day before. The banks now also had an agreement in principle, but the Fund had to give the Advisory Committee time to negotiate detailed terms and then to secure commitments from hundreds of creditor banks. In the meantime, Mexico would have some additional

---

[80]In fact, it was primarily the U.S. banks that were opposing the capitalization of interest. In many countries, bank creditors preferred that option to concerted lending.

[81]A separate meeting was held across town, at the National Geographic Building, at which a Mexican team headed by Ernesto Zedillo (an advisor to Petricioli and later president of Mexico) successfully negotiated terms for rescheduling private sector debts under the FICORCA scheme (on which, see Chapter 9, p. 360).

[82]"Mexico—Request for Stand-By Arrangement," EBS/86/161, Sup. 5 (October 29, 1986), pp. 11–12.

[83]For an account of this meeting, see Volcker and Gyohten (1992), p. 215. Additional information is from background interviews with participants and from IMF files.

financing available in the form of the bridge loan from the BIS.[84] De Larosière informed the Board that Rhodes believed the banks could obtain a critical mass of commitments by the end of October;[85] if they failed, then it would be difficult for the banks to disburse any money from the new loan before the end of December. He was not asking Directors to renew their provisional approval at this time, but he expected to be in a position to ask for final approval by October 31.[86]

The banks also had to agree on the details of their participation in the two contingency clauses, a process that took another precious ten days to complete and that further complicated and delayed final approval of the stand-by arrangement. The banks insisted that their participation be linked to that of the IBRD as well as the Fund. After some resistance, Mexico agreed. The banks also obtained agreement from the Fund that its participation in the oil-price contingency would be front-loaded, so that the 2:1 participation ratio would be reached only if the facility were fully utilized.[87] Erb reported to the Executive Board on October 10 that discussions on these and other points were continuing and were likely to require some modification to the program.[88] Agreement on terms was finally reached among the Mexican authorities, the Advisory Committee, and the management of the Fund and the Bank on October 16. That evening, the Managing Director cabled the Committee banks that he would need written assurances of their financing commitments (i.e., a critical mass of acceptances) by October 31 in order for the stand-by arrangement to proceed.

The second half of October was a virtually nonstop "road show" in which the Advisory Committee, the staff and management of the Fund and the IBRD, the central banks of creditor countries, and the Mexican authorities all tried to sell the loan package—which now had a potential total value of $7.7 billion—to reluctant bankers around the world.[89] Matters were not helped when the Mexican govern-

---

[84]The bridge loan totaled $1.6 billion: $400 million from the BIS, guaranteed by 11 central banks; $700 million from the U.S. Treasury and the central banks of Argentina, Brazil, Colombia, and Uruguay; and $500 million from a syndicate of 54 commercial banks. See BIS, *Annual Report*, 1986/87, p. 184.

[85]The magnitude of the critical mass was understood in this particular case to be "approximately 90 percent." Cable from de Larosière to the office of Shearman and Sterling, the principal attorneys for the Advisory Committee (November 21, 1986); in IMF/RD Managing Director file "Debt—1985" (Accession 88/179, Box 3, Section 517). The 90 percent level had been used in the original concerted lending package for Mexico in December 1982 (Chapter 7), but subsequently 95 percent had become more customary.

[86]Minutes of EBM/86/163 (September 30, 1986).

[87]Under the final terms of the agreement, the Fund agreed to cover the first $200 million shortfall in export receipts in the event of a decline in oil prices below the benchmark level. Beyond that, the participation ratio would be 3:1 up to a maximum of $1.2 billion from the banks and $600 million from the Fund. (In a further departure from standard practice, the Fund's commitment under this clause was made in dollars, not SDRs. The ratio thus had an outer limit of 2:1.) "Mexico—Stand-By Arrangement," EBS/86/161, Sup. 6 (November 20, 1986). See also footnote 72, p. 443.

[88]Minutes of EBM/86/168 (October 10, 1986).

[89]The basic concerted "new money" loan had been reduced to $5 billion, but it was supplemented by $1 billion in cofinancing with the IBRD, another $500 million in cofinancing with the IBRD of the growth contingency facility, and $1.2 billion in contingent financing linked to oil prices. On the terms of the agreement, see "Mexico—Request for Stand-By Arrangement," EBS/86/161, Sup. 5 (October 29, 1986).

ment announced that it was switching from semiannual to quarterly adjustments in the minimum wage and would thereby be granting workers an unscheduled increase immediately. With inflation already running over 100 percent a year, this seemingly technical policy change ran the risk of throwing the program off track before it was even approved. Skepticism about Mexico's economic prospects was rampant, and when the Executive Board met on October 31, less than 40 percent of the necessary commitments from banks had been obtained. Directors had no choice but to extend the deadline a second time, to November 19.[90]

November finally brought success. While Pujol led a mission to Mexico City to review progress under the still-pending program, the multipronged effort to win bank support continued. By November 19, when the Board next met to consider the requested arrangement, the critical 90 percent level of commitments was in hand. The stand-by arrangement was approved without dissent, enabling Mexico to borrow the first two SDR 225 million ($270 million) installments (the first of which had been originally anticipated for September).[91]

Keeping the Program on Track: December 1986–June 1987

Mexico's economic program began well despite the earlier hiccup with the minimum wage, but the government failed to maintain that initial success. In mid-December, Pujol informed the Board that Mexico was in compliance with the various program criteria "by ample margins."[92] However, when he returned to Mexico City in February 1987 to try to negotiate the program for that year, he realized that the fiscal effort was already being relaxed, and he had to postpone the negotiations. He went again in March and found an ever-worsening fiscal position. The question now was not whether Mexico was in compliance with the program; multiple criteria had not been met at the end of 1986. The question was whether it was reasonable to expect the authorities to comply, given that the criteria had been formulated on the assumption that bank financing would be available at an early date. As it happened, the last few percentage points of the bank package were taking a painfully long time to obtain, not least because of the fears generated by Brazil's declaring a moratorium on interest payments to banks in February 1987 (see below). Mexico was unable to draw on the bank loan until April 30, 1987, long after the bridge loan arranged by the BIS had expired.[93]

The March mission led to an agreement, and Petricioli sent a Letter of Intent for the 1987 program to the Managing Director (now Michel Camdessus) on April 7. In addition to setting quantitative targets for the original performance criteria

---

[90]Minutes of EBM/86/175 (October 31, 1985). November 19 was the date that the government was scheduled to present its budget for 1987 to the congress.

[91]Minutes of EBM/86/185 (November 19, 1986).

[92]Minutes of EBM/86/201 (December 17, 1986).

[93]The initial drawing amounted to $3.5 billion out of the $6 billion total. The $1.6 billion bridge loan (see footnote 84, p. 447) was repaid in February. "Mexico—Review Under Stand-By Arrangement and Program for 1987," EBS/87/103, Sup. 1 (May 12, 1987), p. 11.

for each quarter in 1987, the amended agreement added two new elements designed to monitor inflation more directly. First, a floor on the primary fiscal surplus (i.e., the overall balance minus interest payments on the public debt and thus the most directly controllable component) was added as a third measure of fiscal stringency, along with the overall deficit and the operational balance. Second, the authorities agreed that if inflation were to rise above the rate on which their program was based (an annual rate of 85 percent), they would negotiate new understandings on fiscal policy aimed at relieving inflationary pressures.[94]

The staff report reviewing the program, issued on May 12, implicitly acknowledged the effect of the delay in obtaining bank financing. It detailed the fiscal overruns that had occurred, but it recommended that the fiscal performance criteria for 1987 be relaxed relative to the government's own budget of December 1986, and that the Fund allow Mexico to draw SDR 400 million ($510 million) under the stand-by arrangement in June without regard to whether the end-March performance criteria were met. Three weeks later, just one day before the Board meeting, the staff was able to certify that—despite the fiscal problems—all of the newly established performance criteria had been met and that no waiver would be required at this time.[95]

When the Executive Board met in restricted session on June 3 to review Mexico's performance in implementing the economic program, the financing role of the banks was a key issue to be examined. Two weeks earlier, the strategy of depending on the banks for additional financing had been dealt an unexpected blow when Citibank announced on May 19 that it was adding $3 billion to its reserves as a provision against possible losses on its loans to developing countries. Citibank's action was by no means the first, but it was the largest and most dramatic provisioning by a U.S. bank. Competitors such as the Bank of America that had much weaker capitalization would be forced to respond in kind, and that would weaken their ability to participate in concerted efforts to maintain the level of financing for Mexico and other major debtors. Coming on the heels of the destructive delays in approving the Mexican bank package, this development made it highly likely that future financing arrangements of this genre would be even more difficult to secure.

At the Board meeting (in restricted session), following an opening statement by Ortiz, de Groote laid the blame for Mexico's weak implementation of the program squarely on the banks, who, in his view, had "shot themselves in the foot."[96] The banks' sluggish response had deprived the private sector of essential financing for investment and had thereby stifled economic growth. Consequently, the

---

[94]"Mexico—Review Under the Stand-By Arrangement and Program for 1987—Letter of Intent," EBS/87/103 (May 12, 1987).

[95]Under the terms of the stand-by arrangement, Mexico normally would have drawn SDR 200 million in February and another SDR 200 million in May. The various delays resulted in the two drawings both being made in June. "Mexico—Review Under Stand-By Arrangement and Program for 1987," EBS/87/103, Sup. 1 (May 12, 1987) and Sup. 2 (June 2). On fiscal conditionality, see Sup. 1, pp. 13 and 38.

[96]Minutes of EBM/87/81/R-1 (June 3, 1987), p. 7.

growth contingency clause had kicked in, and the banks now had to provide additional financing.[97] Ortiz argued that the fiscal austerity required by the Fund had also been a significant contributor to the decline in output. Although Mexico did not need additional bank financing for balance of payments purposes, it did need to finance major investment projects in order to restart economic growth. Consequently, he concluded, Mexico intended to activate the growth contingency mechanism.[98] Overall, the Board viewed Mexico's performance as satisfactory under difficult circumstances. The program targets for 1987 were approved, and Mexico was able to draw SDR 600 million over the next two months, bringing its total indebtedness to the Fund to nearly SDR 3.8 billion ($4.9 billion), or 324 percent of quota.

Crash and Recovery: July 1987–March 1988

The second half of 1987 brought a new crisis that required yet more innovative efforts to stabilize the Mexican economy.

For a year now, the Mexican stock market had been booming, in response to trade liberalization, reprivatization of banks, a program to "swap" external debts for domestic equity, and the general effects of the agreements reached with the Fund and other foreign creditors. In mid-August, Mexico and its bank creditors agreed to convert $9 billion of private sector debt to commercial banks into a loan to the public sector. That agreement covered debts that had previously been restructured under the FICORCA scheme. The difficulty was that the banks still preferred to get as much of their money back as they could right away rather than take on yet more exposure to the government. Substantial discounts were offered to borrowers as an incentive for them to prepay their loans before the restructuring was to go into effect in February 1998. Between $3.5 and $4 billion in face value was prepaid in this way at a cost of $2.7 billion. The Fund staff generally supported this process, as it was a relatively economical means of reducing external debt. By October, however, private sector borrowers were selling large volumes of assets to raise the cash to pay off their FICORCA debts, putting severe downward pressure on asset prices. When equity markets came under attack in major markets around the world on "Black Monday," October 19, the Mexican market went into an uncontrolled stall and crashed. In six weeks through mid-November, shares listed on the Mexi-

---

[97]This judgment was premature. Mexico ran into difficulties meeting some of the conditions for the bank loan, and the banks' commitment was reduced by the activation of the oil-price contingency when the export price rose above the projected range of $9–14 a barrel. In total, the banks disbursed $4.4 billion under the new-money loan in 1987, $600 million less than originally planned. The growth contingency mechanism was not activated until 1988. The shortfall in output, which normally would have activated the growth contingency process, is documented in "Mexico—Review Under Stand-By Arrangement and Program for 1987," EBS/87/103, Sup. 2 (June 2, 1987), p. 1. The effect of the two contingencies on bank financing in 1987 is described in "Mexico—Staff Report for the 1987 Article IV Consultation and Second Review Under Stand-By Arrangement," EBS/88/23 (February 4, 1988), p. 14n.

[98]Minutes of EBM/87/81/R-1 (June 3, 1987), pp. 31–32.

can stock market lost 75 percent of their market value—far in excess of the global declines.[99]

The bursting of the stock market bubble, coming at a time of growing concerns over inflation (now approaching 150 percent a year) and doubts about the sustainability of the economic program as the presidential election approached, precipitated a resumption of large-scale capital outflows from Mexico. As the crisis developed, a Fund mission—led by Claudio Loser, Assistant Director of the Western Hemisphere Department—went to Mexico City to review progress under the stand-by arrangement and to conduct the annual Article IV consultations.[100]

On November 18, while the mission was in progress, the peso came under strong enough pressure that the Bank of Mexico was forced to withdraw from supporting it in the "free" market.[101] Within a few days, the free-market exchange rate lost a third of its value against the U.S. dollar. Barring a dramatic shift in policies, the program and the stand-by arrangement would inevitably fall apart.

The dramatic shift came in mid-December with the announcement of a heterodox regime, the *Pacto de Solidaridad Económica* (known simply as the *Pacto*). The *Pacto*, developed independently of the discussions that had just been held with the Fund staff, had four key goals: immediately restore and then maintain international competitiveness, strengthen the fiscal balance over the coming year, further liberalize trade policy, and establish a permanent basis for maintaining a social consensus on wage policy. To achieve the first goal, the controlled exchange rate was devalued straightaway by 18 percent in a successful bid to wipe out the spread that had emerged between the controlled and free rates.

Second, the *Pacto* aimed to raise the primary fiscal surplus by 3 percent of GDP in 1988, through a combination of expenditure cuts and higher prices for energy products, utilities, etc. Third, trade liberalization would be promoted by a sharp reduction in tariffs and the virtual elimination of nontariff trade barriers such as requiring import permits. Fourth, wage policy would be controlled at the national level through periodic agreements to be made between the government and representatives of employers and labor unions on the basis of projected inflation (not on actual past inflation, as before). The Fund staff endorsed all elements of this package. The shift to forward-looking wage indexation was seen as a valuable contributor to the fight against inflation. The pegging of the exchange rate was ac-

---

[99]In the major industrial countries, major declines in equity prices were mostly confined to the few days around October 19 and ranged from 11 to 22 percent. See Allen and others (1989), pp. 62–65.

[100]Under the amended terms of the stand-by arrangement, Mexico could not make the next drawing (SDR 200 million, originally scheduled to be made in December 1987) until this review was completed and until understandings were reached on policies to bring inflation back to an annual rate of 85 percent or less. See paragraph 10 of the Technical Memorandum of Understanding, as amended on April 7, 1987; "Mexico—Review Under the Stand-By Arrangement and Program for 1987—Letter of Intent," EBS/87/103 (May 12, 1987), Attachment II, p. 7.

[101]Mexico had maintained a dual exchange market since August 5, 1985: a "controlled" market for most trade-related transactions and a "free" market for transactions not eligible for the controlled market. The controlled rate was determined by a managed float, and the authorities also intervened in the free market to keep the two rates close together. "Mexico—Modifications of Exchange and Trade System," EBS/85/188 (August 9, 1985).

cepted on the understanding that the authorities would switch to a real-rate rule (adjusting the nominal rate in line with inflation) within a few months.[102]

If the *Pacto* could be made to work, it was clearly both bold enough and comprehensive enough to put the economy back on a sustainable path.[103] Loser took his staff team back to Mexico City in January 1988 to review the situation. Although fiscal policy, as measured by the primary or operational fiscal balance, had been implemented in keeping with the program, the effect of inflation on interest rates had forced the overall public sector borrowing requirement above the programmed ceiling. Hence a waiver would be required before Mexico could be permitted to make the final drawings under the stand-by arrangement.[104] The mission concluded that the *Pacto* framework provided the potential for overcoming the problem and that the measures now being taken to implement it appeared to warrant granting the waiver.

At the end of February 1988, the government granted a small increase in the minimum wage and then implemented a freeze on prices and on the exchange rate. These measures ran the risk of reversing the progress on competitiveness, because the price freeze was certain to be less effective than the fixing of the exchange rate. It was nonetheless judged by the authorities (and accepted as such by the Fund staff and management) to be essential for getting inflation under control. Without it, targeting the real exchange rate raised the risk that the momentum of inflation would be unchecked.[105]

At the same time, Petricioli finally initiated a request to the Managing Director to activate the commercial banks' Growth Contingency Financing Facility. With policies in place to control inflation, the time was ripe to implement the intention expressed the previous June to stimulate growth through externally financed investment projects.

On March 10, 1988, the Executive Board endorsed the staff's appraisal that the Mexican economic program deserved the Fund's continuing support. On the basis of a waiver of the end-1987 requirements, it approved the final two tranches of the

---

[102]Memorandum from Sterie T. Beza (Director of the Western Hemisphere Department) to the Managing Director (December 18, 1987); in IMF/RD Managing Director file "Mexico, December 1987–December 1988" (Accession 89/131, Box 3, Section 282).

[103]For an analysis of the *Pacto* as the culmination of the evolution of economic policy in Mexico in the 1980s, see Rojas-Suárez (1992).

[104]One other program criterion had also been violated for reasons that were essentially beyond the control of the authorities: growth of net domestic assets of the monetary authorities was too high, having been inflated by the cash-flow requirements of firms prepaying FICORCA debts and by the need to compensate for continuing shortfalls in the availability of external financing to the public sector. See "Mexico—Staff Report for the 1987 Article IV Consultation and Second Review Under Stand-By Arrangement—Request for Waiver and Supplementary Information," EBS/88/23, Sup. 1 (March 7, 1988), p. 3.

[105]The weaknesses of targeting real exchange rates are discussed in Chapter 13, pp. 573. The staff view on this case is given in "Mexico—Staff Report for the 1987 Article IV Consultation and Second Review Under Stand-By Arrangement—Request for Waiver and Supplementary Information," EBS/88/23, Sup. 1 (March 7, 1988). Also see memorandum from Beza to the Managing Director (February 29, 1988); in IMF/RD Managing Director file "Mexico, December 1987–December 1988" (Accession 89/131, Box 3, Section 282).

stand-by arrangement.[106] Once again, although previous hopes had been dashed by events, the spring of 1988 was bringing a renewal of optimism for Mexico.

Brazil: From the Cruzado Plan to Default

The mid-1980s were a fallow period in financial relations between the Fund and Brazil, but the Fund continued to push for reform policies and to try to improve Brazil's relations with other creditors. The third year of the 1983–85 extended arrangement had not been activated, as a year of negotiations had failed to produce an agreement on an economic program. The arrangement expired in February 1986 with SDR 1.5 billion (just under $2 billion) of the original SDR 4.2 billion commitment unused. For the next year, the Brazilian government sought to avoid requesting new loans from the Fund while it tried to negotiate separate deals with other creditors. That effort partially succeeded, but it collapsed in February 1987 when Brazil unilaterally stopped paying interest on its bank debts.

Development of the Cruzado Plan: November 1985–February 1986

In the months following the 1985 Annual Meetings in Seoul, the minister of finance, Dilson Funaro, visited Washington twice to discuss Brazil's plans and needs with the Managing Director. In Seoul, de Larosière had stressed to Funaro the need for a major shift in policies as a precondition for restoring normal relations with creditors. On Sunday, November 24, Funaro and de Larosière lunched together at the Brazilian Embassy on Massachusetts Avenue, in a meeting that stretched through the whole afternoon.[107] Funaro's message was that by mid-week he would be announcing a new orientation to economic policy in Brazil; he did not want either financial assistance or enhanced surveillance from the Fund, but he did want the Managing Director to issue a statement of support to Brazil's commercial bank creditors. De Larosière was wary, because the policy shift was not comprehensive: it was narrowly focused on limiting the inflationary pressures arising from indexation and would do little to stabilize the public finances. Fiscal policy was still to be aimed primarily at maintaining strong economic growth (on the order of 7 percent for 1986) rather than raising the domestic saving rate. Without stronger policies and more direct support from the IMF, Brazil would have little hope of avoiding a new payments crisis.

Bank creditors also reacted with skepticism when the policy package was unveiled in Brasilia on November 27. The Advisory Committee met with Brazil's debt negotiators in New York on December 12 and 13, but the talks broke down

---

[106]Following the meeting, Mexico borrowed SDR 350 million ($480 million). The stand-by arrangement was thus fully utilized, and Mexico's obligations to the Fund totaled just under SDR 4 billion (335 percent of quota), the highest level reached up to this time.

[107]Memorandum for files by the Managing Director (November 25, 1985); in IMF/RD Managing Director file "Brazil, 1985—Vol. II" (Accession 88/179, Box 7, Section 517). The trip was intended to be kept secret, but the news that Funaro was traveling to Washington to meet with U.S. and IMF officials was carried on wire services beginning November 22.

without any sign of progress. Follow-up discussions were scheduled for mid-January, which prompted Funaro to make his second trip to Washington, on January 9, to seek a statement of support from the Managing Director. The situation was now a little cloudier, because the authorities were formulating an ambitious stabilization program for 1986, but they were not yet ready to specify the policy actions to achieve the program's goals. After hearing the staff's view that there were serious doubts about the government's ability to implement the program, de Larosière informed Funaro that he could give only a guarded endorsement to the banks. Funaro made the best he could of the matter by telling the press afterward merely that the Managing Director had agreed to issue a supporting statement.[108] De Larosière then conveyed the following statement to Rhodes (quoted in its entirety), in which the caveats are as plain as a bureaucracy can stand to make them:[109]

1. In early January 1986, I met with Mr. Funaro, Minister of Finance of Brazil, and Mr. [Fernão Carlos Botelho] Bracher, President of the central bank of Brazil.
2. The Minister of Finance outlined the economic policies of the Government of Brazil for 1986. The staff had earlier received the pertinent documentation.
3. Achievement of the objectives as set by the Brazilian authorities would strengthen the economic performance of the country, and would help to maintain the favorable external results of recent years.
4. However, fulfillment of these objectives would require implementation of strong measures in order to deal with the risks in the present economic situation.

On January 16, 1986, the Advisory Committee of commercial banks agreed to roll over existing credits to Brazil—totaling $16 billion in principal—until March 1987. That decision, on which the banks really had no choice under the circumstances, set the stage for the announcement of the new policy package at the end of February. The Cruzado Plan, as it became known, included several "heterodox" elements and minimized the more conventional—and essential—stabilization policies.[110] Brazil got a new currency, the cruzado, worth 1,000 of the old cruzeiros. Prices were temporarily frozen, but nominal wages were raised by an average of 15 percent. Wages then were to be fixed for a year unless prices rose by 20 percent in the meantime, in which case they would be automatically indexed. The exchange rate was fixed at the prevailing level; i.e., the crawling peg was suspended as part of the general effort to deindex the economy. Fiscal policy was essentially unchanged.

---

[108]The Brazilian press interpreted Funaro's statement as a prediction that the Fund would give the banks a "green light" for renegotiating Brazilian debt. See *O Globo* (Rio de Janeiro), January 12, 1986, p. 1.

[109]The message was initially conveyed (on January 13) only by telephone, in an effort to maintain strict confidentiality. The next day, however, the Dow-Jones news service carried a story on the report, which it characterized as a "qualified approval" by the Managing Director. Four weeks later, the text of the message was sent to the Advisory Committee by cable. Cable of February 7, 1986; in IMF/RD Western Hemisphere Department file "Brazil, January 1986–December 1986" (Accession 89/2, Box 1, Section 91).

[110]The Cruzado Plan is summarized in "Brazil—Financial Measures," EBD/86/57 (March 3, 1986). Edwards (1995, pp. 33–40) discusses its development and compares its heterodoxy to those of other plans introduced in Latin America in the late 1980s.

Stabilizing Without the Fund, March 1986–January 1987

For several months, the Cruzado Plan worked largely as intended. To succeed, inflation had to be brought down very quickly from the pre-Cruzado rate of about 250 percent a year and then had to be kept very near to international levels; otherwise, wage indexation would kick in, the exchange rate would soon become unsustainable, and the value of the cruzado would plummet. For March and April 1986, the price level was more or less unchanged, owing largely to the strict freeze on price increases. Over the same two months, the monetary base expanded by 36 percent; some portion of that was attributable to a remonetization of the economy following the currency reform, and it was easy for the authorities to overestimate the extent and sustainability of that phenomenon. In July, the government implemented some selected tax increases and cuts in government subsidies (dubbed the "Cruzadinho" plan by the press) in an effort to mop up some of the excess liquidity and strengthen the credibility of the program (see Faria, 1993, p. 187). Pressures from monetary growth began to build up, but it would now take a bit longer before the system would collapse.

Brazil's next goal was to normalize relations with official creditors, to whom they had been accumulating arrears for more than a year. In 1985, Brazil had been rebuffed by the Paris Club on the grounds that any rescheduling would first require Brazil to have a program agreed with the Fund. In March 1986, the authorities renewed their request for a rescheduling of official credits through the Paris Club, but they were told that they first needed at least to make progress toward a Fund-supported program and that they needed to take action to clear their arrears, neither of which Brazil was prepared to do. Faced with this impasse, Brazil shifted to a more conciliatory stance in May, promising to make payments aimed at limiting the rate of increase in arrears to official creditors as long as they could do so without reducing their own international reserves. This was not enough, however, and the standoff continued.

Once again Brazil found itself in need of an endorsement of its policies by the Fund, and once again Funaro decided to try to walk a narrow plank between asking for a financial arrangement and going it alone. Around the end of August, Thomas M. Reichmann (Chief of the Atlantic Division, Western Hemisphere Department) led a mission to conduct the annual Article IV consultations, which had been postponed several times during the spring and early summer. Although Reichmann concluded that both monetary and fiscal policies had to be tightened if the Cruzado Plan was to hold together, he also recognized that so far the plan was still working reasonably well. Publicly, President José Sarney was taking an anti-Fund, go-it-alone stance.[111] Behind the proscenium, however, he was more conciliatory. Notably, a few days after the mission was completed, the president— in Washington on a state visit and to address a joint session of the U.S. Congress—

---

[111]On September 4, he told a visiting reporter that the "IMF formulas for Brazil simply did not work. They led us into the most dramatic recession in our history. But we have addressed our problems with seriousness." *New York Times* (September 7, 1986), p. A10.

took the time to meet with the Managing Director. De Larosière conveyed the same message to the president that Reichmann had just delivered to his advisors: additional policy measures were needed. Sarney's response, which went well beyond previous promises, was that he was prepared to take the necessary measures even if it meant accepting an interruption in the strong economic growth that Brazil had experienced for a number of years.

By the time of the 1986 Annual Meetings of the Board of Governors, in early October, de Larosière was taking a more optimistic view of Brazil's prospects. At his scheduled press conference at the conclusion of the meetings, he described to reporters his "sympathy and admiration" for the "very courageous actions taken in Brazil." Then when the Paris Club next met, in the third week of October, delegates appeared to be looking for ways to help, even though they recognized that Brazil was still a long way from qualifying for an arrangement with the Fund. The tide was still out, but it was turning.

The question now was how to formulate the steps that would eventually normalize relations with creditors. On October 27, de Larosière met with Mulford and other officials at the U.S. Treasury. He suggested that both the authorities and the various creditors might be ready to accept a form of enhanced surveillance as a step in that direction. That is, the Fund staff would conduct more frequent consultations (perhaps semiannually), and he, as Managing Director, would issue reports to creditors assessing the progress of stabilization and reforms. This procedure—contrasted with the standard enhanced surveillance, under which the authorities would release the staff reports on semiannual consultations to creditors—would lend additional weight to the assessment but would stop short of giving creditors an official seal of approval from the Fund. Both de Larosière and Mulford were concerned about setting a precedent that would induce other heavily indebted countries to seek similar treatment, but they agreed nonetheless that the idea was worth trying for Brazil. Funaro still resisted accepting that much monitoring, but he relented after the Managing Director agreed to call the procedure "enhanced contacts."[112]

The next step was for Brazil to strengthen its policies. Following the congressional and gubernatorial elections of mid-November, the government announced a package of policy changes on November 21. These heterodox measures included reductions in government subsidies, controls on wages, the introduction of new financial instruments to promote saving, and the reintroduction of a daily adjustment in the exchange rate (suspended since the introduction of the Cruzado Plan in February) aimed at dampening speculation of a large devaluation. The Fund staff viewed these adjustments as making "an important contribution in correcting . . . imbalances" in the economy.[113]

The Executive Board met on December 10, 1986, to conclude the Article IV consultations, the first such review since August 1985.[114] Much of the discussion

---

[112]See footnote 46, p. 431.

[113]"Brazil—Staff Report for the 1986 Article IV Consultation," EBS/86/253, Sup. 1 (December 4, 1986), p. 9.

[114]The delay was necessitated by the timing of the elections in Brazil.

focused on the Cruzado Plan and its subsequent refinements, which Directors generally viewed quite positively. (Speaking for the United States, Dallara viewed it as having brought "historic, positive change" to Brazil.)[115] The groundwork was now in place for a positive report to creditors. That same day, de Larosière wrote to Jean-Claude Trichet, the chairman of the Paris Club, summarizing developments in Brazil and the Fund's reactions, and concluding: "I share the view that these developments, together with the Brazilian authorities' intention to enhance their contacts with the Fund, provide the basis and impetus for an early normalization of relations between Brazil and its creditors. A Paris Club agreement would be an essential step in that process."[116]

The battleground now shifted to Paris, where official creditors met on December 18. Brazil requested a rescheduling of its debts on terms that were far weaker than those that had ever been granted by the Paris Club up to this time. Not only would creditors have to pin their hopes on the effectiveness of "enhanced contacts" with the Fund rather than a financial arrangement with all of the standard conditions attached; Brazil also was asking that it not be required even to make current interest payments (as opposed to catching up on payments that were already in arrears) until July 1987. Even so, on the basis of the Managing Director's request, creditors agreed to consider the request at their next meeting.[117]

The rescheduling request was approved on January 21, 1987, at the conclusion of a Paris Club meeting of record length. Reichmann and K. Burke Dillon (Chief of the External Finance Division, Exchange and Trade Relations Department) led the delegation from the Fund.[118] The agreement broke precedent in three ways.[119] First, it was the first time in this decade that a rescheduling had been agreed upon in the absence of either an upper-tranche financial arrangement with the Fund or even a formal agreement for enhanced surveillance. Second, completion of the arrangement was linked in part to the successful completion of negotiations with commercial bank creditors. Though creditors agreed that this linkage was needed in this case, they were reluctant in general to expand the number of linkages in such agreements. Third, a substantial part of the debts to be rescheduled were set aside until July, and that portion of the deal was made conditional on the IMF Executive Board drawing positive conclusions from the upcoming Article IV consultation or agreeing on a financial arrangement. These terms obviously represented a very delicate balance between the desire to main-

---

[115]Minutes of EBM/86/193 (December 10, 1986), p. 25.

[116]Letter of December 10, 1986; in IMF/CF (S 1191 "Brazil—Debt Renegotiation and Multilateral Aid").

[117]Executive Directors were formally notified of the request on January 9, 1987; "Brazil—Request for Renegotiation of External Debt Owed to the Paris Club" (EBD/87/2).

[118]For a summary of the agreement, see Dillon and others (1988). For a detailed report, see "Brazil—Report on External Debt Renegotiation," EBS/87/32 (February 13, 1987).

[119]January 30, 1987, memorandum by Dillon and Peter M. Keller (Deputy Chief of the External Finance Division, Exchange and Trade Relations Department); in departmental file, "External Debt: Paris Club 1987"; in IMF/RD Exchange and Trade Relations Department file "Paris Club, 1987" (Room 4384, Section 6, Shelf 1, Bin 4).

tain forward momentum and an inescapable skepticism about the prospects for success.[120]

Moratorium: February–December 1987

On February 20, 1987, President Sarney shocked the world—and the Fund—by declaring a "moratorium" on the payment of interest on medium- and long-term loans from foreign banks. As explained in a cable sent the same day by Funaro to creditor banks, Brazil viewed the moratorium as justified because circumstances had made the outward transfer of resources incompatible with economic growth. As of that day, the Brazilian government would deposit all principal and interest due to foreign commercial banks in an escrow account at the central bank. Payments would continue to be made on short-term loans and trade credits.

Sarney's and Funaro's decision[121] to default was prompted by the continuing depletion of Brazil's foreign exchange reserves. Brazil, however, did still have the means to meet its interest payments for the next several months, assuming that policies could be strengthened at the same time. Gross reserves had fallen from approximately $9¼ billion at the end of 1985 to $5¼ billion at end-1986 and to about $4 billion by the time of the moratorium. At that level, reserves were just about equal to Brazil's projected financing requirements for the year. More fundamentally, the moratorium reflected the disarray in policymaking at the time. Fiscal policy had been far too lax throughout most of 1986, as essential actions were delayed until after the November elections. By the time the November package was introduced, the distorting effects of price controls had become severe, and inflationary pressures were becoming uncontainable. Restoration of exchange rate flexibility had given the coup de grace to price stability. Under the terms of the Cruzado Plan, wage indexation would resume once inflation was rekindled; inflation thus would be impossible to stop without further reforms. For the first quarter of 1987, inflation was already running at an annual rate of about 400 percent.

The moratorium and the accompanying collapse of stability in Brazil posed problems not only for Funaro and the bank creditors, but also for Camdessus, who had just taken over from de Larosière as Managing Director. The only way to keep the crisis with the banks from further contaminating relations with official creditors was to be sure that Brazil could meet the conditions for the second tranche of the Paris Club deal in July. An IMF mission would have to go to Brazil by April or early May, and—more important—new policies would have to be implemented before then. Funaro submitted a new financing plan to congress at the beginning of

---

[120]At one point in the meeting, negotiations reportedly almost collapsed when the Brazilian delegation relayed a message from Funaro calling the creditors' proposals "an insult and equal to a declaration of war" and threatening to suspend all payments at once if the terms were not relaxed. Memorandum by Reichmann (January 23, 1987); in IMF/RD Western Hemisphere file "Brazil, 1987" (Accession 89/14, Box 1, Section 550).

[121]The moratorium was not universally supported by senior economic officials in Brazil. Notably, João Sayad, the minister of planning since March 1985, and Fernão Bracher, president of the central bank since August 1985, both resigned in protest.

April, and shortly thereafter he went to Washington to meet with Camdessus, but the Managing Director made it clear that much stronger and more specific actions would be needed to resolve the crisis.

Sarney finally realized that he would need to make a clean break with the past, and at the end of April he replaced Funaro as finance minister with Luiz Carlos Bresser Pereira, a professor of economics at the Getúlio Vargas Foundation and an official in the state government in São Paulo. Bresser Pereira, moving quickly to attempt to restore order, called his staff together and told them he wanted to implement a conventional macroeconomic stabilization program: a Fund-type adjustment program, though for the moment without involving the Fund. To make it work quickly enough, he would once again temporarily freeze prices and wages, but this time he would make sure that the supporting macroeconomic policies were put in place at the same time. By stabilizing the economy first, he reasoned, he could then get on favorable terms with the banks and other creditors, and only then would he go to the Fund for financial assistance.

An IMF Article IV mission had already been scheduled to take place in the middle of May, and that provided Bresser Pereira with an opportunity to sound out the staff on the Fund's views. This initial meeting with Reichmann, however, was awkward because Bresser Pereira did not feel that he could yet inform the staff that he intended to implement a shock program. Reichmann—like Bresser Pereira—saw an economy that was in free fall, and the gradual adjustment that Bresser Pereira outlined for him did not look adequate. After a week of talks, they agreed to break off for a few weeks and to resume once the new policies had been announced. Meanwhile, Bresser Pereira's sketchy plans were also failing to impress the banks. The day Reichmann left Brazil for Washington, Citibank made its dramatic announcement that it was setting aside some $3 billion to cover possible losses on loans to developing countries (see above, p. 449).

The Bresser Plan, introduced on June 12, 1987, called for a 90-day freeze on wage or price increases, backed up by a tightening of monetary policy, a small fiscal correction (mainly adjustments in public sector prices), and a devaluation of the exchange rate.[122] It was only a start, but the plan appeared to have an internal consistency that had been missing from the Cruzado Plan. When Reichmann and his team returned to Brazil later that month to finish work on the Article IV consultations, they were able to draw reasonably positive conclusions.

The next step, in Bresser Pereira's mind, was to convince the bank creditors that Brazil both needed and deserved more relief from its debt burden. He was prepared to let the Paris Club agreement lapse and to put off seeking an arrangement with the Fund. Official creditors eventually would come around, and he regarded the Fund and the World Bank as little more than "delegates" or "arms" of the U.S. government (Bresser Pereira, 1999, pp. 15–16). In mid-July, Bresser Pereira made his first trip to Washington as finance minister. He met with both Camdessus and Conable, but his real focus was on getting debt relief from commercial banks.

---

[122]For details and background, see Bresser Pereira (1999).

Camdessus and others told him that the idea was premature. The banks could not grant significant debt relief until the various national authorities were ready to support it, which at this point they were not. Camdessus urged him instead to work toward a stand-by arrangement, but Bresser Pereira was not interested.[123] A few days later, Bresser Pereira went to New York to meet with the chairmen of the major creditor banks, whom he asked for a major new-money loan at zero interest. The banks, not surprisingly, were not interested in that offer. Instead, they also urged the minister to concentrate on first reaching an agreement on policies with the Fund.[124]

The Executive Board met on September 9 to conclude the 1987 Article IV consultations. Everyone now agreed that policies were on the right track; the authorities were "praised . . . for having moved promptly since late April 1987" (i.e., since Bresser Pereira had become minister) to deal with the "very difficult economic situation." The difficulty was that some means had yet to be found to normalize relations with the banks, or the external deficit could not be properly financed. "Several" Directors concluded that a stand-by arrangement should be pursued, as in their view such an arrangement was a precondition for a bank agreement, but "a few" others thought that "shadow programs or enhanced contacts might be considered an alternative."[125] Following the meeting, Camdessus sent his summing up to Trichet for information. The summing up could not confirm that orderly arrangements were in place to finance Brazil's 1987 balance of payments deficit, so it did not meet the requirements of the January 1987 agreement of the Paris Club. Arrears to official as well as private creditors would therefore continue, and the Brazilian authorities would have to negotiate with the banks on their own.

To settle his affairs with bank creditors, Bresser Pereira would have to come up with a convincing adjustment program and demonstrate flexibility in negotiations. Accordingly, he asked the Fund to send a mission to discuss the possibility of a program to be supported by Fund resources. Camdessus was not convinced that Brazil was ready for a financial arrangement. The operational fiscal deficit was projected to be about 5 percent of GDP for 1987, the staff estimated that it would have to be brought down to about 2 percent in 1988 for it to be adequately financed, and there was no indication at this time that policies could be changed sharply enough to achieve that result. The staff's instructions for the mission (in the second half of November) were therefore merely to assess the situation and establish a dialogue.[126]

Negotiations also proceeded with the banks throughout October, and in November Bresser Pereira signed an "interim agreement" with a subset of the creditor banks, aimed at gradually settling Brazil's still-accumulating arrears. Brazil owed foreign banks some $1.5 billion in interest for the fourth quarter of 1987. Under the agreement, Brazil would pay one-third of that amount from its reserves, and the

---

[123]For more on the development of Bresser Pereira's views on debt relief, see Chapter 11.

[124]The meeting with bankers was reported in the *New York Times* (July 27, 1987), pp. D1 and D2.

[125]"The Chairman's Summing Up at the Conclusion of the 1987 Article IV Consultation with Brazil, Executive Board Meeting 87/133—September 9, 1987," SUR/87/98, 9/17/87.

[126]Memorandum from Reichmann to management (November 9, 1987), with handwritten response; in IMF/RD Managing Director file "Brazil, 1987–1988" (Accession 89/118, Box 1, Section 511).

participating banks would lend Brazil the remainder, so that current interest payments could be made in full. The agreement also set a target date of mid-January, 1988, for settling with the Advisory Committee on terms for a full medium-term financing plan that would then become effective by June 1988. The coverage of that plan would include the $3 billion in interest that was still in arrears from the first three quarters of 1987.

Relations both with the Fund and with the banks thus were beginning to improve, but to maintain this new momentum, policies—especially control over the public finances—would have to be strengthened. That task was the Achilles' heel of the strategy. To reduce the operational deficit by 2–3 percentage points of GDP for 1988, Bresser Pereira proposed implementing a package of substantial spending cuts and tax increases, but the proposal was strongly resisted by others in the cabinet and by much of the business community in Brazil. President Sarney, whose political power and influence were still weak, rejected much of the package, leaving only token fiscal adjustments. Bresser Pereira, knowing that the rejection meant that Brazil could not hope to gain an accord with either the IMF or its bank creditors in 1988, resigned from office in mid-December.[127] For Brazil, another major opportunity to regain economic stability had been lost.

Argentina: After the Austral Plan

Argentina was in trouble at the beginning of 1986. The stabilization program known as the Austral Plan was failing: well designed on paper, it was simply too ambitious in its goals for the Alfonsin government to sustain it for more than a few months. The new currency introduced in June 1985, the austral, was pegged to the U.S. dollar, an arrangement that could be sustained only if inflation in Argentina was quickly reduced to the level of U.S. inflation. In the event, inflation was substantially reduced from the extremely high pre-Austral levels, but by nowhere near enough. By late in the year, Argentine prices were still rising by 2–3 percent a *month*, while those in the United States were rising by about 3 percent a *year*. Before the November elections, the government lacked the political power either to stabilize wages or to take needed fiscal actions (notably privatization of job-creating but money-losing state enterprises); after winning the elections, the government lacked the political will. Consequently, as noted in Chapter 9, the Fund staff's review of the program in December 1985 ended in failure, and Argentina was not able to make the stand-by drawing that had been scheduled for that month.

The parallels between the macroeconomic difficulties facing Argentina and those just described for Brazil were numerous. Perhaps the most fundamental similarity, from which all the others sprung, was that both countries were struggling

---

[127]Some accounts of this episode interpret it differently. For example, Pang (1989), p. 138, concludes that Bresser Pereira was fired by Sarney for his failure to successfully negotiate a settlement with the Fund and the banks. That interpretation, however, conflicts with the factual record of the state of those negotiations at the time.

new democracies in which the baton of economic control had very recently been passed from the military (March 1985 in Brazil, December 1983 in Argentina). Political support for economic stability and reform was weak, and reform advocates faced substantial populist pressures both from the electorate and within the government. Both fledgling governments had already failed to implement the economic programs that had been drawn up by their predecessors in the wake of the initial debt crisis, and consequently their financing from the Fund had been withdrawn. Brazil's EFF arrangement was dormant throughout 1985 and expired in early 1986 with about one-third of the original commitment unused. Argentina's stand-by arrangement failed around the middle of 1983 and expired with less than half of the money drawn.

Argentina, like Brazil, faced seemingly uncontrollable inflationary pressures in the mid-1980s, and in neither case was the government able to stabilize the economy. In Brazil, consumer prices in 1985 were more than three times their 1984 level, and in February 1986 alone rose by 12½ percent (an annual rate of more than 300 percent); in Argentina, 1985 prices averaged nearly eight times the level of the year before and by midyear were rising at an annual rate of more than 2,300 percent. In both countries, inflation was perpetuated by a pervasive indexation of wages and other prices, but fiscal imbalances were at the heart of the problem. As discussed above and in Chapter 9, Brazil had a persistently high public sector borrowing requirement (PSBR) (27½ percent of GDP for 1985); even taking out the effect of inflation, the operational balance was persistently in deficit (4¼ percent of GDP in 1985). The elected Argentine government inherited a public sector deficit of 18 percent of GDP for 1983; they reduced it sharply, to 13 percent in 1984 and 5½ percent in 1985, but that level was still too high to be comfortably financed. And of course in both countries, the fiscal problem was severely exacerbated by an overhang of external debt: Brazil owed $105 billion (46 percent of GDP) to foreign creditors at the end of 1985, while Argentina owed $48 billion (75 percent of GDP).

The gist of the policy response was also similar, but with a major difference. Argentina's Austral Plan, like Brazil's Cruzado Plan that came a few months later, was a heterodox package whose essence was to stop inflation suddenly through deindexation and the introduction of a new currency. The crucial difference was that, in contrast to Brazil's attempt to implement the Cruzado Plan and its subsequent refinements without financial assistance (or conditionality) from the Fund, Argentina maintained a more active dialogue with the Fund throughout the period.

Promises and Waivers: January–June 1986

In January and February 1986, Argentine officials went to Washington to negotiate a resumption of the stand-by arrangement with the Fund. These talks led to an agreement by the government to implement fiscal reforms aimed at reducing the budget deficit from 5½ percent in 1985 to less than 3 percent in 1986. On February 20, a Letter of Intent setting out policy commitments for the first half of 1986 was signed by the minister of economy, Juan Vital Sourrouille, and the president

"Good afternoon. In which office of this ministry does Mr. Jacques de Larosière work?"
by Landrú

of the central bank, J.J. Alfredo Concepción.[128] They also agreed to state their intention to seek a new stand-by arrangement following the expiration of the current one. On that basis, the Managing Director agreed to recommend to the Executive Board that the stand-by arrangement be extended through May 1986, with drawings in March and May.[129]

The Executive Board met on March 10 to consider the Argentine request. There was a general feeling that policies were on the right track, that the program for 1986 was adequate, and that the time to push for stronger adjustment would come when the staff negotiated the anticipated stand-by arrangement for 1987. Without dissent, the Board approved the proposed modifications in the existing arrangement.[130]

A month later, in mid-April, Joaquín Ferrán, Senior Advisor in the Western Hemisphere Department, took a staff team to Buenos Aires to determine whether Argentina had met the criteria for the May drawing and to begin negotiations for a new stand-by arrangement. The news was bad. At least three program criteria had not been met at the end of the first quarter: the net domestic assets of the central bank, the public sector deficit, and the level of arrears to foreign creditors were all above the agreed ceilings. The budget deficit was at a rate of about 5 percent of GDP, and the monthly inflation rate had more than doubled, to about 4½ percent.[131] The mission spent more than a month evaluating the problems and trying to persuade the authorities to take immediate measures to get the program back on target. For their part, the authorities were doubly concerned: if they could not reach an agreement, they not only would lose the SDR 236.5 million loan from the Fund ($270 million), but also could lose a $600 million installment that was due to be made at the end of June under the concerted bank loan signed the previous August. Nonetheless, Sourrouille was unwilling to bend to the Fund's demands, and when Ferrán returned to Washington in mid-May he recommended against granting a waiver in the absence of strong prior actions by the government.

The Executive Board agreed in late May to extend the stand-by arrangement by another month while the staff conducted further negotiations in Washington and Buenos Aires.[132] (The technical discussions took place in Washington, while

---

[128]"Argentina—Staff Report for the 1985 Article IV Consultation and Review of Stand-By Arrangement," EBS/86/39, February 21, 1986.

[129]The arrangement approved in January 1985 had called for six drawings of SDR 236.5 million, for a total of SDR 1,419 million, with the last drawing scheduled for March 1986 (approximately $240 million and $1.44 billion, respectively, at average 1985 exchange rates). The second drawing, scheduled for March 1985, was not allowed until August, after the Austral Plan was in place. The third drawing then took place in September, which still left the program three months behind schedule. When no drawing was allowed in December, the program was six months behind. The intention now was to approve a drawing for March 1986, reschedule one of the two missed drawings for May, and cancel the other by reducing the total size of the arrangement to SDR 1,182.5 million (approximately $1.36 billion at March 1986 exchange rates).

[130]Minutes of EBM/86/43 (March 10, 1986).

[131]For a detailed description of the difficulties in meeting program criteria, see "Argentina—Request for Waiver Under Stand-By Arrangement," EBS/86/131 (June 18, 1986).

[132]"Argentina—Stand-By Arrangement—Extension of Period," EBS/86/39, Sup. 1 (May 29, 1986); and Executive Board Decision No. 8297-(86/91), adopted May 29, 1986.

Sterie T. Beza, Associate Director of the Western Hemisphere Department, met with senior officials in Buenos Aires.) The Managing Director also joined the effort, telephoning Sourrouille to let him know that he fully concurred with the staff that further measures had to be taken before he could recommend a waiver to the Board. Sourrouille then sent one of his principal deputies, José Luis Machinea, to Washington to talk directly with de Larosière. None of this activity had much immediate effect on Argentine policies, but the authorities did at least agree to reduce their arrears to official creditors and to seek a rescheduling of official debts through the Paris Club, and they set out their general intention to tighten policies in the second half of 1986.[133] Despite the staff's obvious skepticism about the authorities' ability to carry out their intentions, they recommended a waiver principally out of concern that otherwise the banks would refuse to reschedule Argentina's debts.[134] De Larosière finally agreed on June 14 to recommend approval of the final drawing under the stand-by arrangement, and he scheduled a meeting of the Executive Board for the following week.

The Board met on June 23 in the midst of intense interest from the press, both in Argentina and in Washington. Without the approval of the Fund, journalists understood that Argentina could scarcely avoid defaulting on its loans from foreign banks.[135] The impact of Citibank's large-scale and quite recent provisioning against its loans to developing countries (see p. 449, above) was still very much on everyone's mind, and Argentina was thus seen as a key test case for the debt strategy and for the continued solvency of major international banks. Although several Executive Directors expressed concerns, reservations, and even, in one case, "trepidation" (Marcel Massé—Canada), no one was prepared to oppose this one final drawing on the existing arrangement.[136] The waiver was unanimously approved, and Argentina then drew down the SDR 236.5 million. Argentina's obligations to the Fund now stood just under SDR 2.5 billion (224 percent of quota and approximately $2.9 billion), their highest level to date.

A New Stand-By Arrangement "In Principle": September 1986–February 1987

Discussions between Argentina and the Fund resumed in September. By this time, fiscal and monetary policies were slipping further out of control, even in re-

---

[133]"Argentina—Request for Waiver Under Stand-By Arrangement," EBS/86/131 (June 18, 1986), Attachment II.

[134]The staff report concluded in hedged tones that "implementation of these policies ... would make an important contribution toward bringing the adjustment program back on track. . . . In these circumstances, it is proposed that the nonobservance of performance criteria ... be waived, in order to permit the final purchase. . . . This purchase also would be of significance to the financial relations between Argentina and the commercial banks on which the continuing normalization of Argentina's external situation depends." "Argentina—Request for Waiver Under Stand-By Arrangement," EBS/86/131 (June 18, 1986), p. 13.

[135]See, for example, *Clarín* (Buenos Aires), June 24, 1986, p. 14.

[136]Minutes of EBM/86/101–102 (June 23, 1986). The quotation is from meeting 86/102, p. 4.

lation to the scaled-down effort applied in June. Preliminary talks in Washington and Buenos Aires revealed deep differences in view as to what was needed. The staff team, now headed by Brian C. Stuart (Deputy Chief of the River Plate Division in the Western Hemisphere Department), concluded that Argentina could not reduce either its stubbornly high inflation rate or its unsustainably high current account deficit without a renewed tightening of policies. The Argentine officials believed that their adjustment effort was sufficient and that greater flexibility was called for, from the Fund and from other creditors. In particular, they wanted any arrangement with the Fund to include contingency clauses similar to those granted to Mexico (see above, pp. 441–42) and to provide as much access to Fund resources, in relation to quota, as had been allowed for Mexico. The Fund considered the Mexican arrangement to have been exceptional, and it was not ready to formulate a general policy on the use of contingency mechanisms in stand-by arrangements. Starting in late October, Stuart spent a full month in Buenos Aires trying to reconcile these views, without success.

Negotiations continued in Washington through much of December and early January. A first breakthrough occurred on Christmas Eve, when Machinea called Erb from Buenos Aires to say that Argentina was prepared to accept the Fund's request for a lower target for the current account deficit and to offer to come immediately to Washington to draft a Letter of Intent.[137] A second and final breakthrough came on Saturday morning, January 10, when the negotiating team in Washington agreed to reduce their inflation target. Finally, on January 12, 1987, Sourrouille and Machinea (who was now president of the central bank, having replaced Concepción) signed a Letter of Intent setting out policies for 1987 and requesting a 15-month stand-by arrangement for SDR 1,113 million (100 percent of quota, equivalent to some $1.4 billion).[138]

Agreement on macroeconomic policies was to be only the beginning of a lengthy process to bring the Fund arrangement to fruition. Although de Larosière informed the Executive Board on January 13 (at his penultimate meeting with the Board before the chairmanship passed to Camdessus) that the staff and the authorities had agreed on a program, he was not yet ready to set a date for the Board to consider the proposed arrangement.[139] Argentina had not even begun negotiations with commercial bank creditors on a financing agreement for 1987, and the recent experiences of other developing countries (notably Mexico, Nigeria, and the Philippines) indicated that those negotiations were likely to be even more prolonged and difficult than in the past. The staff estimated that, even with maximum access to Fund credits, Argentina would face a financing gap of more than $3 billion for 1987, of which close to $2 billion would have to be filled by a concerted-lending deal with

---

[137]It is important to note that by this time, negotiations were focused on targets for economic conditions (e.g., inflation or the external deficit) rather than policies that were more directly under the authorities' control (notably the fiscal deficit, which was the real culprit). As Machinea (1990, p. 58) later observed, the authorities "felt helpless to reduce the fiscal deficit" because of the depressed state of the economy and the strength of the political opposition.

[138]"Argentina—Request for Stand-By Arrangement," EBS/87/5 (January 13, 1987).

[139]Minutes of EBM/87/7 (January 13, 1987).

bank creditors.[140] Even if negotiations began immediately, disbursements from the banks were unlikely to start before September.[141] Argentina also needed to reach an accord with official creditors through the Paris Club, and that process was being delayed by Argentina's reluctance to finalize bilateral agreements that were still outstanding under the Paris Club rescheduling of January 1985.

In the first part of February 1987, Camdessus consulted on several occasions with Executive Directors on how the Fund might proceed. Meanwhile, Argentina took the necessary actions to unlock discussions with the Paris Club, and negotiations between the authorities and the banks' Advisory Committee began on February 12 (in New York, at a meeting in which Erb made a presentation both on the program and on Argentina's financing needs). Those developments, of course, would lead nowhere without a positive signal from the Fund. Accordingly, Camdessus decided to seek approval of the program "in principle," as had been done a few months earlier for Mexico (see above, pp. 443–45).

The Executive Board met on February 18 to consider Argentina's request for a stand-by arrangement, along with a separate request for a drawing under the CFF to compensate for a temporary shortfall in export receipts. The management proposal was to approve both requests in principle, to become effective after a critical mass of bank financing had been committed (provided that Argentina was in compliance with the program at that time). Most Directors were cautiously optimistic about the adjustment program, notwithstanding their concern about Argentina's record of slippages in implementing earlier programs. As was often the case in this period, the strongest expression of concern came from Rye (see pp. 445, 465), in whose view this was a particularly "high-risk" program for the Fund to support.[142] Nonetheless, no Director abstained from approving the arrangement in principle.

A more widespread concern surfaced over the handling of two aspects of the approval process. First, several Directors objected to the proposal to delay final approval of the CFF financing until the critical mass was secured. François Gianviti, Director of the Legal Department, reminded Directors that the 1983 guidelines for the CFF (see Chapter 15) required the member to be cooperating with the Fund

---

[140]Although the expected balance of payments deficit for 1987 was only $1.7 billion, Argentina also needed $2.4 billion to service existing debts to official creditors and to replenish its reserves, plus $0.5 billion to clear outstanding arrears. The gross financing requirement was therefore about $4.6 billion. A Fund arrangement could cover $1.4 billion, a Paris Club deal would reduce financing needs by another $1.1 billion, and about $0.2 billion could come in the form of bilateral official export credits. Those calculations left a residual of some $1.9 billion to be covered by commercial bank creditors.

[141]In addition to the general problem that banks were becoming increasingly reluctant to participate in concerted lending packages, delays were expected to arise because of the length of the "tail" in the distribution of outstanding exposure to Argentina by bank creditors. Participation by the 150 largest creditors would secure a critical mass of commitments covering 95 percent of the required amount, but it would take another 120 banks to get to 99 percent and that many again to cover the final 1 percent. Memorandum from Maxwell Watson to the Managing Director (February 18, 1987); in IMF/RD Managing Director file "Argentina, January to March 1987" (Accession 88/274, Box 2, Section 269).

[142]Minutes of EBM/87/29 (February 18, 1987), p. 3.

for a drawing of this nature, and that the relevant test of cooperation in this case was that a financing arrangement be in place. Seven of the 22 Directors nonetheless preferred to grant the CFF drawing immediately and opposed the decision to approve it only in principle.[143] Second, a number of Directors were uncomfortable with the unprecedented request to make the in-principle approval of indefinite duration; normal practice would have been to require financing to be in place within 30 days. In view of the limited progress that had been made so far in Argentina's negotiations with banks' creditors, setting a 30-day limit in this case would have been tantamount to denying approval altogether and could effectively have undone the positive signal that the Board was attempting to send. Camdessus agreed, however, to bring the matter back quickly to the Board so that a reasonable date could then be set.

The follow-up meeting was set for February 26. On the 25th, Sourrouille surprised everyone by announcing a temporary wage-price freeze and a set of related fiscal actions. The fiscal adjustment, however, was relatively weak, so that these measures actually worsened the inconsistency between macroeconomic and incomes policies. The new package would soon lead to a worsening of price pressures, but that problem was not immediately evident.[144] At the beginning of the Board meeting, Ernesto V. Feldman (Alternate—Argentina) briefed his fellow Directors on the development, suggesting that it was not a shift in the policy regime, but rather an effort to bring expectations in line with the government's intentions. Inflation had been accelerating since the beginning of the year, not because of a loosening of policies but because people did not believe that the program would succeed in stabilizing prices. The staff, who had had no advance notice, were unable to draw a judgment on whether this new package was consistent with the existing program, but Directors were generally prepared to wait and see.

Most of the discussion on February 26 focused on the application of the "in-principle" procedure to the CFF. The Managing Director's proposal was to make the CFF drawing available to Argentina by July 15, regardless of the status of the financing package for the stand-by arrangement, "provided that Argentina continues to cooperate with the Fund." This amendment would provide an additional incentive for the authorities to adhere to the program over the next several months, even if difficulties in the negotiations with banks made it unlikely that the stand-by arrangement were to be activated. The problem was how to define whether the member country would be cooperating with the Fund if the stand-by arrangement were not activated by that date. The Managing Director suggested that he could inform creditors that the test of cooperation would be satisfied if (1) the criteria of the stand-by arrangement were met, regardless of whether the

---

[143]Minutes of EBM/87/28–29 (February 18, 1987); Gianviti's explanation is on pp. 25–26 of meeting 87/29. The seven objecting Directors, holding a total of 24.5 percent of the voting power on the Board, were Alhaimus (Alternate—Iraq), de Groote (Belgium), Feldman (Alternate—Argentina), Nimatallah (Saudi Arabia), Ortiz (Mexico), Salekhou (Iran), and Sengupta (India).

[144]See Machinea (1990), pp. 61–62, which concludes: "It is quite clear now that this freeze was a mistake."

arrangement was effective; (2) the economy was performing as expected, even if a waiver would have been required; or (3) the member was "actively negotiating with the Fund . . . on a revised or new stand-by arrangement." A few Directors objected to this last suggestion, on the grounds that it was too open-ended, but most Directors either liked the proposal or preferred to wait until the forthcoming CFF review to discuss it. The level of enthusiasm for the process was minimal, but the proposal was accepted so that attention could be focused squarely on the task of finding the money to finance the Argentine deficit for the year ahead.[145]

Financing the Program: March–August 1987

Normally, as soon as the Fund approved a stand-by arrangement with a member country, the member could expect to receive favorable consideration for a rescheduling of official bilateral credits through the Paris Club. In this case, that process was still being delayed, not only because the Fund was not yet providing any financing to Argentina, but because the process of clearing arrears under the previous Paris Club agreement was still ongoing. To get some official financing in place, Camdessus asked the main creditor countries to provide a $500 million bridge loan through the BIS. The United States took the lead in assembling the participation of 11 other industrial countries (and contributed just under half of the total). That deal was completed in early March, but not without difficulty. It was exceptional in that the loan was secured by the resources that the Fund had just committed in principle to Argentina.[146]

Argentine officials, led by the chief debt negotiator, Mario Brodersohn, met almost nonstop with representatives of the banks' Advisory Committee over a two-month period starting in mid-February 1987. Stuart also met with the bankers on several occasions, providing independent information on policies and economic conditions in Argentina. Negotiations nearly broke down entirely around the end of March, but by mid-April the deal was ready to be signed. The banks agreed to reschedule some $30 billion in loans and to assemble the new-money loan for $1.95 billion that had been requested by the Fund. Part of the difficulty was that the deal being negotiated was unusually complex and contained a number of innovative features designed to ameliorate Argentina's debt burden (discussed below, in Chapter 11). Another difficulty was that whenever one indebted country succeeded in negotiating terms that were more favorable than those granted previ-

---

[145]Minutes of EBM/87/33 (February 26, 1987), p. 9; and Executive Board Decision No. 8535-(87/33).

[146]Specifically, the government instructed the Fund to pay any sums that Argentina would be eligible to draw under the stand-by arrangement or the CFF into an escrow account at the Federal Reserve Bank of New York until the bridge loan had been fully repaid. Such instructions had been issued on a number of occasions starting in the late 1970s, but until this instance, the practice had been applied only to bridge loans from commercial banks, not official creditors. The terms of the escrow agreement are specified in a March 5, 1987, cable from the central bank to the Federal Reserve Bank of New York; in IMF/RD Managing Director file "Argentina, January to March 1987" (Accession 88/274, Box 2, Section 269).

ously to other countries, those terms would become the expected norms by in-debted countries around the world. The fact that Mexico had persuaded its bank creditors in September 1986 to price its new-money loan at $^{13}/_{16}$ of a percent over LIBOR, rather than at $^7/_8$ (see above, p. 446), emboldened Argentina to press for similar terms; the banks felt it necessary to resist, if only to avoid having to fight similar battles elsewhere. The compromise solution priced the new-money loan at a spread of $^7/_8$ and the rescheduling at $^{13}/_{16}$.[147]

The Advisory Committee estimated in mid-April that they could produce a critical mass (95 percent) by the end of May. With help from Eduardo Wiesner (Director of the Western Hemisphere Department) and Desmond Lachman (Chief of the River Plate Division), Committee bankers and Argentine officials went on a global "road show" through much of May, trying to secure the participation of hundreds of small to medium-sized banks throughout Europe, North America, the Middle East, and Asia. Lachman also participated in the May meeting of the Paris Club, at which official creditors agreed to reschedule Argentina's outstanding ob-ligations on favorable terms. Set against these positive developments, however, were early signs that Argentina was once again failing to stick with its economic program. Lachman went directly from the road show and the Paris Club meeting to Buenos Aires, where a staff team had just spent ten days reviewing the latest economic statistics. Monetary policy had slipped, and inflation was running well above program targets. Fiscal policy also was off target and would have to be tight-ened if the targets were to be met. The source of the problem was obvious and fa-miliar: parliamentary elections were to be held in September, and until then the authorities' room for maneuver was limited.

Because of these difficulties, progress came slowly; but it did come. On June 19, Rhodes (who was chairing the Argentine Advisory Committee, along with those for Mexico and Brazil) informed Erb that 92 percent of the concerted lending package was now committed, and he expected to complete the deal sometime in July.[148] Discussions continued between the staff and the authorities, and a new Let-ter of Intent—spelling out a number of actions aimed at raising fiscal revenues and implementing structural reforms—was signed in Washington on July 8.[149] On pa-per, at least, all of the required conditions for the stand-by arrangement were in place: official financing, bank financing, and a viable economic program. When the Executive Board considered (in restricted session) the proposal to implement the arrangement (Argentina's twelfth) on July 23, Directors expressed widespread disappointment with the many policy slippages that had occurred since they had approved the program in principle back in February, but they felt that they once

---

[147]For a detailed description of the deal, see "Argentina—Recent Economic Developments," SM/87/162 (July 15, 1987), pp. 102–5.

[148]By July 9, commitments covered 99 percent of the total. The agreement was finalized at a ceremony in New York on August 20, which Camdessus attended on behalf of the Fund.

[149]Lachman's mission concluded its work in Buenos Aires on June 3. Subsequently, Sourrouille and Machinea went to Washington to hold talks with the Managing Director and conclude the negotiations. Those talks ended in success in early July. "Argentina—Letter on Economic Pol-icy," EBS/87/155 (July 8, 1987).

again had to give the authorities the benefit of the doubt. The SDR 1.1 billion ($1.4 billion) arrangement was unanimously approved.[150]

Collapse of the Program, August 1987–March 1988

As the time of the parliamentary elections approached, Alfonsín found himself heavily criticized for caving in to the demands of foreign creditors. The Peronist (Justicialista) Party, with a platform of unilaterally halting the servicing of external debt, gained enough seats in the September 6 election that Alfonsín's Radical Civic Union lost its majority in parliament. When Sourrouille and Machinea arrived in Washington a few weeks later for the Annual Meetings, Argentina seemed more likely than ever before to join with other major Latin American indebted countries in resisting pressure from the banks to pay large amounts in interest or from the IMF to adjust policies further.

In spite of these difficulties, the authorities showed a willingness to try to keep their economic program on track and to keep the stand-by arrangement with the Fund alive. The task would not be easy. It was only two months since the arrangement had been activated in July, but the program's quantitative targets were already being breached, in some cases by wide margins. Both the staff and the Managing Director stressed to the authorities at the Annual Meetings that Argentina would not be eligible to make the next drawing under the arrangement (scheduled to be made on October 20) without some tightening of the policy stance.[151] Several officials stayed on in Washington after the Meetings to negotiate a set of program commitments for 1988, and on October 14, the government announced a new package of revenue measures and policy reforms that the staff judged to be adequate to restore viability to the program. Two days later, the U.S. Treasury issued a press release announcing plans for a new $500 million multilateral bridge loan, in anticipation of an early resumption of Fund lending under the stand-by arrangement.[152] After the remaining details were worked out, on November 12 Camdessus approved the program for submission to the Executive Board.

Executive Directors were being asked, for the sixth time in 4½ years, to approve a drawing for Argentina under a stand-by arrangement after the original criteria had not been fulfilled.[153] In each case, Directors had shown a sensitivity both to the political difficulties that prevented the government from undertaking more effective adjustment and to the dangers of forcing Argentina into a default on its external debt. (The elected government at this time was enduring frequent army rebellions and coup attempts.) Each case, however, brought into sharper focus the

---

[150]Minutes of EBM/87/107/R-2 (July 23, 1987).

[151]See "Argentina—Amendment of Stand-By Arrangement," EBS/87/234 (November 16, 1987).

[152]As had been done in February, this loan was to be secured by a pledge against future drawings on the Fund arrangement.

[153]Under the stand-by arrangements approved in January 1983, January 1985, and July 1987, Argentina made a total of 10 drawings. Three were made upon the initial approval of the arrangement; the other seven (of which this was the sixth) required either a waiver or a new Letter of Intent that modified the original commitments.

contrast between promise and performance. In this instance, the uncertainty was compounded by the absence of a firm assurance on financing. Rather than requiring a fixed increase in lending exposure from bank creditors (with a critical mass of commitments) prior to the Board's approval—a commitment that was simply unachievable at the time—the Fund was merely noting that future drawings would require a review by the Board. If the banks failed to sign an agreement with Argentina, then the program would be underfinanced, and the Fund would have to decide at that time whether to suspend the arrangement or grant yet another waiver. On December 2, 1987, Directors finally began to rebel a bit.

Most Directors, especially those from creditor countries, agreed that the government's program was inadequate and was unlikely to be fully implemented,[154] and that the balance of payments deficit for 1988 could not be financed; but they also feared that to disallow the request would bring severe financial consequences to Argentina, to other indebted countries, and to the international financial system. Perhaps Guenter Grosche (Germany) best represented the view of the Board in concluding that he was supporting the request "with considerable reservations, and only because Argentina is an exceptional case." Once again, Rye was among the strongest critics, complaining that the program had "been patched beyond recognition," contained "unacceptable risks," and would set "an extremely dangerous precedent." Along with two other Directors (T.P. Lankester of the United Kingdom, and G.A. Posthumus of the Netherlands), Rye abstained from approving the request.

Two Directors—Jorgen Ovi (Denmark) and Posthumus—attempted to steer the Board onto a middle course by suggesting that extra conditions be placed on future drawings under the arrangement (i.e., from February 1988 on), but the staff objected that such conditions would decrease the already precarious likelihood that the commercial banks would be willing to approve their part of the required financing.[155] Other Directors expressed concerns that the Fund's hands were being tied by the practice of closely linking Fund approval to the bank packages, but no one had any practical alternative to offer. At the end of the day, the request was approved.[156]

---

[154]The October 14 package of fiscal actions was still awaiting approval by the parliament, in which Alfonsín's party no longer controlled a majority.

[155]Under the terms of the existing agreements with bank creditors, Argentina's failure to draw the full scheduled amount of Fund resources would make the previously rescheduled payments immediately due. Ovi's proposal was to make the second drawing under the arrangement conditional on adoption of the authorities' proposed fiscal package; Posthumus's variation was to propose that a portion of the initial drawing be withheld until a track record of fiscal adjustment had been established.

[156]The Executive Board decision waived the conditions on the drawing originally scheduled for October 1987, approved conditions governing the four remaining drawings scheduled to be made through August 1988, and permitted a drawing under the CFF to compensate for a temporary shortfall of export receipts. The next drawing was scheduled for December 20 and was conditional on compliance with the newly established quantitative performance criteria for October 31. The three 1988 drawings were made conditional on the successful completion of an additional review by the Board. Minutes of EBM/87/163/R-1 (December 2, 1987) and EBM/87/164/R-1 (same date). References to individual Directors in this and the preceding paragraphs are from meeting 87/163, pp. 14 (Grosche), 15–18 (Rye), 20 (Ovi), and 39 (Posthumus). The modifications to the stand-by arrangement are described in Decision No. 8739-(87/164), adopted December 2, 1987.

Directors' fears were not in vain, and slippage was not long in coming. The review mission that had been scheduled to go to Buenos Aires immediately after the Board meeting was delayed by difficulties in getting the October budget revisions through parliament. The package was finally approved in early January, but only after it had been watered down to satisfy opposition demands. By the time Lachman's team arrived, the government was projecting a fiscal deficit for 1988 equivalent to at least 4¼ percent of GDP, compared with the 2 percent ceiling under the program signed two months earlier.[157] While the mission continued with its work, Sourrouille and Machinea went to Washington to ask the Managing Director to consider letting them raise the ceiling, but Camdessus held his ground, insisting that Argentina could not finance a deficit of that magnitude. In late January, when Beza went to Buenos Aires to deliver the same message, not only did the authorities reject the suggestion that they tighten policies; they also skipped a payment due to the Fund on January 26, thus going into arrears to the Fund for the first time. The mission ended in an impasse.

In an attempt to resolve these differences, Camdessus and Alfonsín met tête-à-tête in secrecy in Madrid, Spain, at the beginning of February.[158] Camdessus promised the president that he would help him make the case for debt relief, on condition that Argentina adopted a tough adjustment program that the Fund could support. On that basis, Alfonsín indicated that he could accept a lower target for the fiscal deficit.[159] The details would still have to be worked out, but the two leaders appeared to have found a winning formula.

Sourrouille and Machinea went again to Washington in mid-February 1988 to negotiate the terms for restoring the financial program. Argentina had cleared its arrears to the Fund, and the U.S. government was putting together plans to provide an additional $500 million in short-term financing for Argentina as a bridge to anticipated drawings from the Fund.[160] The authorities were prepared to make a commitment to the Fund to reduce the deficit to 2 percent of GDP for 1988 and to balance the budget in 1989, but they preferred not to put those targets in a formal Letter of Intent that inevitably would be subjected to public scrutiny at home.

---

[157]The rapid deterioration of economic conditions in Argentina at that time gave rise to an unusual circumstance: although the performance criteria governing the December 20 drawing under the stand-by arrangement applied to data as of end-October and had been set retroactively by the Executive Board on December 2 (on the basis of a Letter of Intent that had been finalized and signed on November 12), those criteria were not met, and the drawing was delayed. The decision to set the criteria retroactively was questioned at EBM/87/163/R-1 (December 2, 1987), pp. 45–46, by Angelo G.A. Faria (Temporary Alternate—Kenya). The basis for this unusual practice was explained by the staff in the afternoon session of the meeting (EBM/87/164/R-1, pp. 1–3).

[158]Camdessus had met with Alfonsín on earlier occasions, while he was chairman of the Paris Club. Those meetings were usually in Buenos Aires and were always held in secrecy, to avoid complicating ongoing negotiations with creditors. On this occasion, Alfonsín was in Spain on a state visit, and Camdessus made a side trip from a stopover in Paris.

[159]Polak (1994), p. 33, describes this as "a meeting in which Alfonsín had received the impression that Argentina might obtain substantial debt relief." Polak's account is based on a private conversation with Alfonsín in 1992.

[160]This amount was made available in the form of a swap facility with the U.S. Treasury.

Camdessus responded positively to these signals, and after a week of further negotiations, agreement was reached on a revised Letter of Intent with a 1988 deficit target of 2.7 percent of GDP.[161]

Obviously, Executive Directors could not be expected to be much happier with the new proposal than they were in December. If one focused on what had actually been achieved, as opposed to what was being promised, Argentina was no closer either to balancing the budget or to reaching an agreement with its commercial creditors. The staff now estimated that the external financing gap could be closed only if the banks agreed to increase their exposure by about $1.75 billion in 1988, on top of the $700 million to which they were already committed under the existing agreement. A deal of that magnitude, given the state of economic conditions and policies in Argentina, would take several months at best to complete. Nonetheless, both the adjustment program and the financial arrangement were important enough for Argentina that the Managing Director was prepared to argue that pushing ahead was the best course "for Argentina, the Fund, and the cooperative debt strategy."[162]

Meeting on March 18, Directors made a rare show of resistance and insisted that the terms of the stand-by arrangement be strengthened before they would approve it. This resistance was all the more remarkable, in that Feldman announced early in the meeting—without alluding specifically to the Camdessus-Alfonsín agreement—that "additional measures [were] being developed to limit the deficit [for 1988] to 2.0 percent of GDP to set the basis for achieving equilibrium [i.e., a zero deficit] next year." In view of the frequent and substantial slippages in implementing programs throughout the 1980s, it was not easy to establish credibility for a promise of that dramatic an improvement.

Ovi initially requested that the proposed decision be modified to require that appropriate financing be in place before any more drawings be allowed. Ovi's proposal was supported by Rye, who indicated that he would abstain unless the amendment was accepted; by Charles Enoch (Alternate—United Kingdom), who indicated that he would prefer even stronger assurances; and by Posthumus. At that point, however, Feldman intervened to state that his authorities could not accept such an amendment, and Camdessus noted that—with only two months to go before the next drawing would be due—it was unlikely that any bank financing would be ready in time. Camdessus therefore proposed that the amendment be amended to require only that "satisfactory progress" be made by May on financing and on eliminating arrears to commercial and bilateral official creditors. Objecting on behalf of the United States, Dallara argued that the Fund's normal practice was to require financing assurances only at the time of initial approval, not at a midterm review; to which the Managing Director replied that the Argentine situation was "without precedent owing to the magnitude of the possible gap that could emerge over the next few months." Several other Directors made strong

---

[161]"Argentina—Letter on Economic Policy," EBS/88/41 (February 24, 1988).

[162] Minutes of EBM/88/40/R-2 (March 18, 1988), p. 1.

statements of reservation, but the Ovi-Camdessus amendment was accepted and the revised program was approved without objection.[163]

The program, unfortunately, was dead on arrival. At the end of March, Argentina began missing interest payments on its foreign bank loans, effectively halting what little progress had been made in negotiating a settlement. Shortly afterward, new slippages in implementing fiscal policy became apparent. Under the circumstances, Camdessus no longer felt that he could take the case for debt relief to creditors. In view of the strong opposition by the U.S. authorities to any form of officially sanctioned debt relief (as discussed in the next chapter), it seems highly unlikely that the Managing Director could have delivered on his promise even if Argentina had stayed the course on fiscal policy. Be that as it may, by June (when the next Fund mission went to Buenos Aires and by which time the scheduled May drawing had not been made), it was clear that the deficit for 1988 could not be kept below 5 percent of GDP. Further discussions (even to complete the annual Article IV consultations) were put on hold, and the Argentine stand-by arrangement lapsed into history.

References

Allen, Mark, and others, 1989, *International Capital Markets: Developments and Prospects* (Washington: International Monetary Fund, April).

———, 1990, *International Capital Markets: Developments and Prospects* (Washington: International Monetary Fund).

Bank for International Settlements, 1987, *Annual Report 1986/1987* (Basel, BIS).

Bresser Pereira, Luiz Carlos, 1999, "A Turning Point in the Debt Crisis and the Bank: A Brazilian Memoir," *Revista de Economia Política*, Vol. 19 (April–June), pp. 103–30.

Broad, Robin, 1987, "How About a Real Solution to Third World Debt," *New York Times* (September 28), p. A25.

Cline, William R., 1989, "The Baker Plan and Brady Reformulation: An Evaluation," in *Dealing with the Debt Crisis*, ed. by Ishrat Husain and Ishac Diwan (Washington: World Bank).

———, 1995, *International Debt Reexamined* (Washington: Institute for International Economics).

Crockett, Andrew, and Morris Goldstein, 1987, *Strengthening the International Monetary System: Exchange Rates, Surveillance, and Objective Indicators*, IMF Occasional Paper No. 50 (Washington: International Monetary Fund).

---

[163]Rye was particularly forceful: "I challenge the staff to recall one previous arrangement where so much effort has been expended, and so much has been conceded, to keep a foundering program afloat." The Board's approval allowed one drawing (for SDR 165.5 million, equivalent to approximately $225 million and 15 percent of Argentina's quota, originally scheduled for December 1987) to take place immediately under the stand-by arrangement, reduced the total size of the arrangement by that same amount by canceling the drawing originally scheduled for February 1988, and allowed a drawing of SDR 233.15 million ($320 million and 21 percent of quota) under the CFF. At this stage two future stand-by drawings (also for SDR 165.5 million) remained scheduled, for May and August 1988. Minutes of EBM/88/40/R-2 (March 18, 1988) and EBM/88/41/R-1 (same date). References to individual speakers are from meeting 88/40, pp. 2 (Feldman), 24 (Rye), 47 (Camdessus), and 47–48 (Dallara). Approval was in Decision Nos. 8820- and 8821-(88/41), adopted March 18, 1988.

Dillon, K. Burke, and Luis Duran-Downing, with Miranda Xafa, 1988, *Officially Supported Export Credits: Developments and Prospects*, World Economic and Financial Surveys (Washington: International Monetary Fund, February).

Edwards, Sebastian, 1995, *Crisis and Reform in Latin America: From Despair to Hope* (Oxford: Oxford University Press for the World Bank).

Faria, Hugo Presgrave de A., 1993, "Brazil, 1985–1987: Pursuing Heterodoxy to a Moratorium," in *Dealing with Debt: International Financial Negotiations and Adjustment Bargaining*, ed. by Thomas J. Biersteker (Boulder, Colorado: Westview Press), pp. 133–52.

Lissakers, Karin, 1991, *Banks, Borrowers, and the Establishment: A Revisionist Account of the International Debt Crisis* (New York: Basic Books).

Machinea, José Luis, 1990, "Stabilization under Alfonsín's Government: A Frustrated Attempt," Document CEDES/42 (Buenos Aires: Centro de Estudios de Estado y Sociedad).

Pang, Eul-Soo, 1989, "Debt, Adjustment, and Democratic Cacophony in Brazil," in *Debt and Democracy in Latin America*, ed. by Barbara Stallings and Robert Kaufman (Boulder, Colorado: Westview Press), pp. 127–42.

Polak, Jacques J., 1994, *The World Bank and the IMF: A Changing Relationship* (Washington: Brookings Institution).

Rhodes, William R., 1992, "Third-World Debt: The Disaster that Didn't Happen," *The Economist*, September 12, pp. 21–23.

Rojas-Suárez, Liliana, 1992, "An Analysis of the Linkages of Macroeconomic Policies in Mexico," in *Mexico: The Strategy to Achieve Sustained Economic Growth*, IMF Occasional Paper No. 99, ed. by Claudio Loser and Eliot Kalter (Washington: IMF), pp. 14–26.

U.S. House of Representatives, 1985, "Role of Multilateral Development Institutions in Global Economy," Hearings before the Subcommittee on International Development Institutions and Finance of the Committee on Banking, Finance, and Urban Affairs, July 18 and 30.

Vo476lcker, Paul A., and Toyoo Gyohten, 1992, *Changing Fortunes: The World's Money and the Threat to American Leadership* (New York: Times Books).

Watson, Maxwell, Donald Mathieson, Russell Kincaid, and Eliot Kalter, 1986, *International Capital Markets: Developments and Prospects*, IMF Occasional Paper No. 43 (Washington: International Monetary Fund, February).

Watson, Maxwell, Russell Kincaid, Caroline Atkinson, Eliot Kalter, and David Folkerts-Landau, 1986, *International Capital Markets: Developments and Prospects*, World Economic and Financial Surveys (Washington: International Monetary Fund, December).

Watson, Maxwell, Donald Mathieson, Russell Kincaid, David Folkerts-Landau, Klaus Regling, and Caroline Atkinson, 1988, *International Capital Markets: Developments and Prospects*, World Economic and Financial Surveys (Washington: International Monetary Fund, January).

11

Debt Denouement, 1987–89

For five years after the debt crisis hit in 1982, the IMF's strategy was to help countries adjust policies and obtain enough new financing so that they could stabilize and strengthen their economies and eventually be able to service their debts on normal market terms. Normal terms in that context meant the terms on which the debt had been contracted, regardless of changes in circumstances and without allowance for arrears unless authorized through an agreement with creditors. This "financing assurances" policy came under increasing fire as time passed without a resolution of the crisis.

The policy of requiring financing assurances was formalized by the Executive Board in April 1983. (For the full text of this and of the 1980 policy that it modified, see the Appendix to this chapter.) That policy stated that, as a condition for approving a credit arrangement, "the Executive Board would need sufficient safeguards to ensure that the Fund's resources would be used to support a viable and financeable adjustment program." To that end, stand-by arrangements would include "review clauses . . . linked, if necessary, to the satisfactory outcome of discussions on balance of payments financing from other sources."[1] In other words, if bank creditors refused to reschedule the country's debts, the Fund would normally suspend access to its own money.

Before adoption of that policy, the strategy had been based primarily on plans, rather than results. Until 1980, the Fund had insisted that a country's policies should provide for the elimination of any external payments arrears during the period of a stand-by arrangement. From 1980 to 1983, Fund policy acknowledged that in some cases the avoidance of additional arrears would be a more feasible goal.[2] With that mandate for flexibility, the method of determining whether a proposed adjustment program would be adequately financed varied substantially from

---

[1]Also see "Fund Policies and External Debt Servicing Problems," SM/83/45 (March 8, 1983), pp. 24–26, and the minutes of EBM/83/58 (April 6, 1983).

[2]The 1980 modification (see the Appendix) stated that, "depending on the member's circumstances and the length of the program, it might not be feasible in the early stages of the program to go beyond an understanding that the member would try to avoid any further increase in outstanding arrears." That understanding implied that the requirement of eliminating arrears would not necessarily apply to one-year programs. In practice, most arrangements approved in the early 1980s called for only a partial reduction of external arrears during the first year.

case to case, reflecting the diversity of circumstances facing countries and of bank practices regarding rescheduling. Several cases in the early 1980s stretched the informal financing assurances policy, though without formally accepting the continuation of an ex ante financing gap. For example, the 1981–84 stand-by arrangement with Romania, discussed in Chapter 8, was resumed in June 1982 while arrears to both official and private creditors persisted, but the Fund allowed only a token purchase until the anticipated agreements with creditors were in place. The 1980 stand-by arrangement with Turkey (see Chapter 6) was approved, and the 1983 stand-by arrangement with Sudan (Chapters 9 and 16) was activated, when official creditors agreed to cover the financing gap, even though no agreement had been reached with commercial banks. Even later, the initial drawing under the 1985 stand-by arrangement with Yugoslavia (Chapter 13) was allowed while negotiations were continuing with bank creditors, on the grounds that those negotiations were proceeding smoothly.

By 1987, many observers were convinced that the debt strategy had to be more forcefully separated from the interests of commercial banks. The most heavily indebted countries might never be able to shed their burden without substantial relief from the contractual obligations that they had undertaken in the carefree days before 1982. Moreover, most banks had already dodged the threat of bankruptcy, the risk of a systemic collapse was long past, and bank creditors no longer had a clear incentive to increase their exposure to developing countries. That view, however, was rejected by some prominent analysts, and it ran into substantial political opposition in some creditor countries. At the IMF, as in the economics profession and the political establishment, both sides of the argument were fiercely debated while the debt-relief proponents gradually gained the upper hand. This process culminated in 1989 when the U.S. government swung its weight from one side of the debate to the other. From that point on, the Fund regularly supported the adjustment programs of countries that were negotiating relief from debt or debt-service obligations, and on several occasions provided direct financial support for debt relief.

Toward Debt Relief: Turning the Titanic

The need for relief from debt-service obligations had, to some extent, been recognized from the beginning. Several of the heavily indebted countries lacked the foreign exchange to repay the principal on loans coming due, and rescheduling postponed that difficulty for months or years at a time. Some lacked the reserves to pay interest as well, and concerted lending enabled them to borrow enough to cover a substantial part of it. The introduction of multiyear rescheduling agreements (MYRAs) in 1984 provided a mechanism for the further smoothing and delaying of amortization schedules. Through all of this stopgap activity, however, the discounted present value of the contractual stream of future payments remained essentially undiminished. Eventually, economies would have to grow by enough to produce the required cash, or governments would have to default. As the years ticked by, it became increasingly obvious that, for the most heavily indebted, the burden of foreign claims on future export receipts was an insurmountable barrier to new foreign investment and even to the retention of domestic savings. Without true debt relief (reduction of the discounted present value), growth was impossible.

Latin American governments regularly made the case for negotiated debt relief throughout the early 1980s, with little success. From 1984 to 1987, they attempted to take joint action either to persuade creditors to soften their stance or, if necessary, to reduce or suspend payments unilaterally. That process started with the Quito Declaration of January 13, 1984, in which the heads of state or their representatives of 26 Latin American and Caribbean countries rejected suggestions that they declare a moratorium on servicing external debts but stated that debt service should be subordinated to the goal of development. The declaration called for creditors to negotiate formulas aimed at limiting debt service in relation to export earnings.[3] Five months later, when the ministers of finance and of foreign affairs of 11 Latin American countries met at Cartagena, Colombia, the prospects for joint action (or, as the financial press liked to call it, formation of a "debtors' cartel") seemed to be growing.[4] On June 22, 1984, the ministers issued a communique known as the "Cartagena Consensus," which reaffirmed their determination to meet their debt obligations but also concluded that the debt crisis was a political crisis and that solutions to it were the coresponsibility of debtors and creditors.[5]

The Cartagena group continued to meet periodically, but the "consensus" did not run very deep. Some of the key countries, such as Mexico and Chile, preferred to negotiate on their own. Others, such as Peru during the administration of Alan Garcia and Brazil during the administration of José Sarney, decided to take unilateral action on their own—with disastrous consequences.[6] By the middle of 1987, the drive for concerted action had stalled, bogged down by the difficulty of finding a strategy on which a critical mass of indebted countries could agree.[7]

Farther north, several plans were advanced as early as 1983 for official action by creditor countries to relieve countries from the burden of foreign debt. The major

---

[3]For the full text, see the *CEPAL Review* (United Nations, Economic Commission for Latin America), No. 22 (April 1984), pp. 39–51. For the list of participants, a summary, and related stories, see the *UN Chronicle*, Vol. 21, No. 3 (March 1984), pp. 13–17.

[4]The term "debtors' cartel" was introduced very early after the crisis hit Latin America, long before the Cartagena conference. For example, the *New York Times* of December 6, 1982 (p. D9), described the "fear among bankers in New York and London . . . that [Latin American] countries might organize a 'debtors' cartel' and unilaterally declare a moratorium on all their debt servicing."

[5]For a summary, see *IMF Survey* (July 2, 1984), pp. 201–2.

[6]The Brazil moratorium is discussed in Chapter 10. The case of Peru, which led to arrears to the Fund as well as to other creditors, is covered in Chapter 16.

[7]The last major effort to establish a unified bargaining position came in the fall of 1987, when Sarney persuaded his counterparts in Mexico and Argentina to ask their finance ministers to develop a plan. The ministers met in September, in the margins of the IMF Annual Meetings, and aimed to produce an agreement at the time of a summit meeting of eight Latin American presidents in Acapulco, Mexico, in November. The idea died, however, when Mexico pulled out. For a review, see Bresser Pereira (1999), esp. pp. 20, 26, and 37. For a political analysis of the failure to establish a cartel, see Kugler (1987).

international banks were receptive to such ideas in principle, but little progress was made toward developing an operational proposal or an equitable approach to burden sharing.[8] By 1986, the momentum for such proposals began to build, albeit still slowly and predominantly in the United States.[9] Bill Bradley, a prominent member of the U.S. Senate, concluded in 1986 that the debt crisis had cost U.S. firms at least a million jobs, and he proposed the establishment of a $42 billion fund to reduce the outstanding stocks of sovereign debts of developing countries. Over the next two years, Peter Kenen of Princeton University, Jeffrey D. Sachs of Harvard University, investment banker Felix Rohatyn, U.S. Representative John LaFalce, James D. Robinson III of American Express, and others advanced schemes to forgive debt through creation of an official fund. A number of the proposals suggested that the IMF be asked to manage such a facility.[10]

Curiously, *official* support for a relief plan then was still concentrated in Europe and Japan. In the United States, Paul A. Volcker, the Chairman of the Federal Reserve System until mid-1987, was strongly opposed, primarily because he believed that countries would be more likely to regain normal market access to foreign credits if they could meet their contractual payments. James A. Baker III, Secretary of the U.S. Treasury until mid-1988, was just as strongly opposed, mainly because of concerns about the political consequences of granting debt relief to foreign countries and not to domestic borrowers. The Japanese government, however, developed a proposal—the Miyazawa Plan—in the spring of 1988, which attempted to sidestep the delicate issue of forgiving principal by restricting debt relief to reductions in interest rates.[11] That proposal was tabled at the summit meeting of the

---

[8]For an early debt-relief proposal from the banking community, see Zombanakis (1983). The potential role of debt relief was a major agenda item at the annual International Monetary Conference sponsored by the American Bankers Association, held in Brussels in May 1983; for a summary, see Hummer (1983). In an April 1984 meeting of the Executive Board on the World Economic Outlook, Jacques J. Polak (Netherlands) noted that indebted countries were exposed to "cyclical risks" because their debt-service payments were invariant with respect to fluctuations in their export earnings. He argued therefore that it "might be useful to think of a country's debt service as a function of its exports, or perhaps of the external conditions under which it could reasonably hope to achieve the best possible export performance." That suggestion, which was not very far from the call of the Cartagena group for export-based limits on debt service, was supported by Jacques de Groote (Belgium) but apparently had no further impact on thinking in the Fund. Minutes of EBM/84/50 (April 2, 1984), pp. 12–13.

[9]In addition, and with more success, support was growing for debt relief for low-income countries with heavy debts that were primarily to official creditors on concessional terms. See Chapter 14.

[10]See Corden (1989) and Williamson (1988). The Fund also was prominently featured in the 1983 Zombanakis proposal. The 1989 plan of Lawrence Klein and Angelos Angelopoulos proposed reorganizing the World Bank to manage debt relief.

[11]Kiichi Miyazawa was the minister of finance; the principal author of the plan was Makoto Utsumi, Director-General of the International Finance Bureau in the Ministry of Finance. Specifically, the plan called for securing a portion of a country's debt by setting up a reserve fund financed partly from the country's own reserves and partly from money set aside from a medium-term Fund loan. Participating countries could buy back all or part of the unsecured portion of the debt. Bank creditors would be asked to forgive interest due on the unsecured portion for a fixed period and to reschedule principal.

Group of Seven (G-7) countries at Toronto in June 1988, and again in September at the Interim Committee meeting in Berlin. The Miyazawa Plan was not endorsed, but it did contribute to the growing consensus for some form of debt relief.[12]

At the IMF, an intense intellectual debate began in 1987, after Jacob A. Frenkel became Director of Research and L. Alan Whittome became Director of the Exchange and Trade Relations Department (ETR). Staff views were divided between those who believed that debt relief would primarily benefit creditors and would delay the restoration of normal creditor-debtor relations (a view associated with but not universally held in ETR), and those who concluded that the existence of a large stock of debt with a heavily discounted market value was an insuperable barrier to normalcy. Even among the latter, few believed that the Fund could move much beyond its standard practices until a more general political consensus developed in creditor countries.[13] Nonetheless, when Jacques de Larosière—the architect and the godfather of concerted lending—retired as Managing Director in January 1987, he forecast the demise of the prevailing strategy in his farewell address to the Executive Board:

> But we may be entering a phase in which the banks may have to make more options available. Perhaps because they are strengthening their positions, the commercial banks have adopted a somewhat more diversified attitude toward new money packages. This reality of the marketplace may well have to be taken into account by the banks to ensure the success of future financing packages and the maintenance of solidarity among the financial community.[14]

---

[12]To the debtor, reduction of the stock of principal outstanding (forgiveness, or as Lissakers (1991, p. 234) put it, the "dread f-word") and reduction of the interest rate are essentially equivalent operations: either approach reduces the discounted present value of the outstanding obligations. To the creditor, however, these options might have quite different costs, owing to regulatory or tax policies. By limiting relief to interest payments, the Miyazawa Plan was attractive to Japanese banks but was too limited in scope to generate broad support in other countries. The other major official debt-relief plan tabled in 1988—the Mitterrand plan, which led to the adoption of "Toronto terms" for official debt forgiveness—was restricted to low-income countries and to official rather than commercial credits; see Chapter 14.

[13]The earliest staff paper arguing that debt overhang was a major problem was Dooley (1986). The reluctance of the staff to take a general position on debt relief in the early days of the debate is reflected in the following rather tortuous passage from the April 1986 World Economic Outlook: "Some arguments have been put forward for financial arrangements that would ease both current and future burdens for debtor countries. Whatever the benefits and drawbacks of such an approach, a strong case can be made for the appropriateness of private creditors responding to the financing needs of adjustment programs that, if successful, would result in more adequate debt-servicing capacity in the future" (p. 101). Also see footnote 36, p. 490. Throughout 1986, the staff for the most part avoided the issue of debt reduction while concentrating on analyzing the factors that would be needed to enable countries to grow out of their debt problem via the Baker strategy. Even in 1988, much of the staff analysis on debt relief was leading to ambiguous conclusions. See, for example, Corden (1988), which examines conditions under which debt relief would not promote investment; and Dooley (1988), which examines conditions under which buyback and debt-equity swap schemes would not benefit debtors.

[14]Minutes of EBM/87/9 (January 14, 1987), p. 34.

From then on, the Fund began to distance itself from the concerted-lending approach by endorsing the development of a "menu" that would give bank creditors the option of exiting from the relationship by swapping loans for equities or negotiable bonds. The Deputy Managing Director, Richard D. Erb, suggested in February 1987 that exit bonds "could . . . be viewed as a more general means of dealing with the debt overhang" (Corbo, Goldstein, and Khan, 1987, p. 498). In April, the Interim Committee "welcomed the exploration of a wider range of procedures and financing techniques by commercial bank creditors as appropriate, such as debt-equity swaps, exit bonds, and greater securitization with a view to expediting the mobilization of financial support for indebted countries."[15] Meanwhile, as more and more banks strengthened their capital base and were able to set aside large provisions to cover possible losses on sovereign loans, they became increasingly resistant to calls to participate in exposure-raising concerted-lending agreements and increasingly willing to participate in the exit strategies of the menu approach.

The menu approach led naturally to the inclusion of options for debt relief. Gradually in the course of 1987 and 1988, as the Fund implicitly or explicitly accepted and supported debt reduction operations in dealing with Bolivia, Costa Rica, and Mexico (as discussed below), those options became increasingly viable. The new Managing Director, Michel Camdessus, quietly but increasingly encouraged the relief option during that period. In a speech to the Institute of International Finance in May 1987, he called for "a wider range of financing options . . . carefully designed so as to guard against an unintended reduction of resources available to the debtor country." To the Interim Committee that fall, he suggested that "such options as securitization and interest capitalization might prove helpful."[16] The following May, in a speech at a Caracas seminar organized by the Aspen Institute, he endorsed the "additions to the menu of options that in effect work to reduce the existing stock of debt, while countries simultaneously pursue a return to more normal debtor-creditor relations." As examples, he cited the innovations that had recently been launched in Bolivia, Chile, and Mexico.[17] Those cautious feelers were, however, firmly rooted in an adherence to the basic strategy.[18]

---

[15] Communiqué, para. 5 (April 10, 1987).

[16]Summary Record, Interim Committee, Informal Plenary Session (September 27, 1987), p. 1.

[17]"Managing the Debt Problem—Next Steps," remarks by Michel Camdessus before the Institute of International Finance, Washington (May 22, 1987), p. 5; and his remarks to the seminar on "Latin America in the World Economy," organized by the Aspen Institute Italia and SELA, Caracas (May 2, 1988), p. 8. Bolivia is discussed in the next section. Chile was an innovator in the exchange of debt obligations for equity shares ("debt-equity swaps"). Mexico's debt-conversion agreement with Morgan Guaranty Bank was also innovative (see below, p. 490–91).

[18]At a speech to the Second Committee of the United Nations General Assembly in October 1987, Camdessus noted that governors at the Annual Meetings had "expressed dissatisfaction with the implementation of the debt strategy," but "there remained a broad and strong consensus that the basic principles underlying the strategy continue to be valid." *IMF Survey* (November 2, 1987), p. 321. In November, the staff circulated a paper for Executive Board discussion, warning that commercial bank recalcitrance "had the potential to jeopardize the implementation of a country's adjustment program" and suggesting that the Fund could decide to lend into commercial

In February 1988, Camdessus circulated a confidential note to a few senior staff, suggesting that the Fund should try to assist the securitization of discount bonds, perhaps by providing guarantees. Simultaneously, he led a concerted but ultimately unsuccessful effort to interest senior U.S. officials in the plan. Although this specific proposal was not pursued further, a staff paper was issued later that month calling for the Fund "in certain cases, as in Bolivia," to "play a role in facilitating the 'sharing of the discount' on outstanding debt through buybacks or analogous transactions." That idea, however, failed to win consensus support when it was taken up by the Executive Board at the end of March.[19]

To generate some momentum for new ideas on debt relief, an informal, interdepartmental committee was established within the Fund in June 1988, known simply as the "Debt Group." Its primary task was to review the various proposals and ideas being generated inside and outside the Fund and to exchange information on countries where innovative approaches were being tried, with an eye toward developing a new institutional view on debt relief. (After the Brady Plan was announced, a higher-level group was constituted under the chairmanship of the Managing Director; the new group became the "Senior Debt Group," and the original—chaired by C. Maxwell Watson, Advisor in the Exchange and Trade Relations Department—became the "Junior Debt Group.") This work was considered to be so sensitive that few other staff members even knew of the group's existence at that time. As early as July 1988, the group developed the argument that the Bolivian buyback scheme could serve as a useful model for a number of other countries, so long as the Fund had a proper appreciation of the risks.[20]

Finally, in September 1988, when the Interim Committee met in Berlin, ministers were ready to endorse the general idea of expanding the menu approach in a way that could encompass debt relief (see below, p. 491–92). Although five more months would elapse before the cornerstone was set in place in the form of the Brady plan, the momentum was already unstoppable.

---

arrears in "exceptional cases." In February 1988, the Board reaffirmed the existing strategy and concluded that any relaxation should be applied "only in very limited circumstances." See "Financing Assurances in Fund-Supported Programs," EBS/87/266 (December 14, 1987), pp. 1 and 14; and minutes of EBM/88/17 (February 5, 1988), pp. 9–10. The staff also considered but did not formally pursue the idea of using the Fund's powers under Article VIII to approve exchange restrictions for countries attempting to negotiate settlements with recalcitrant banks, which might have provided a measure of protection against lawsuits.

[19]"Management of the Debt Situation—Developments, Issues, and the Role of the Fund," EBS/88/55 (March 9, 1988), p. 8; and minutes of EBM/88/5 (March 31, 1988).

[20]Memorandum to the Deputy Managing Director from the Debt Group, July 19, 1988; in IMF/RD Deputy Managing Director file "Debt Schemes, 1988–May 1989" (Attachment III to Debt Group's Review of Activities of January 31, 1989; Accession 91/455, Box 4, Section 489). The 1988 Debt Group was an outgrowth of an interdepartmental working party on debt restructurings that was established in 1984. See memorandum and report from C. David Finch (Director of ETR) to the Managing Director (April 27, 1984); in IMF/RD Managing Director file "Debt Negotiations (Documents)," (Accession 86/34, Box 5, Section 208).

Pre-Brady Debt Relief: Two Case Studies

In a few cases in 1987 and 1988, the Fund supported the efforts of debtors and creditors to put an end to years of painful and costly negotiations by arranging for partial relief from existing debt-service obligations. Two cases stood out: Bolivia in 1986–87 and Mexico in 1987–88.

Bolivia

Bolivia, like so many other countries in Latin America, faced a debt crisis in 1982. This case, however, differed in important respects from the others and did not involve the Fund until some three years later.

Hyperinflation and Collapse: 1981–85

Bolivia's economy weathered much of the 1970s reasonably well. The government of General Hugo Banzer, which took over through a coup in 1971, enjoyed favorable terms of trade, allowed foreign direct investment to flourish, and had ready access to external financing from commercial creditors.[21] After Banzer was ousted in 1978, political chaos ensued at the same time as external economic conditions were deteriorating. A stabilization program was launched in 1980, supported by a stand-by arrangement with the Fund. That program went off track, and the Fund arrangement was canceled without the final drawing having been made. Bolivia nonetheless reached an agreement with its commercial bank creditors in April 1981 on the understanding that a new Fund arrangement was imminent. The Fund staff, however, concluded that none in a parade of Bolivian governments had the ability to implement an adjustment program, and no agreement was reached.[22] The military finally relinquished power to a democratically elected government in October 1982, but the new regime, led by President Hernán Siles Suazo, still lacked the political base to implement an effective program. The Siles government soon went into arrears on the debt that had been rescheduled the year before, after which it had essentially no access to external financing. Throughout Siles's tenure, which lasted until August 1985, the government attempted to maintain public sector spending well beyond its limited and fading ability to generate internal revenue. The inevitable result was a sharp rise in inflation, from just under 300 percent a year in 1982 to more than 2,000 percent in 1984 and to a hyperinflationary 23,500 percent for the last 12 months before a successor government—led by President Victor Paz Estenssoro—could introduce a

---

[21]For a history of Bolivia's political and economic fortunes in the 1970s and 1980s, see Morales and Sachs (1990).

[22]Bolivia did continue to use Fund resources: SDR 0.14 million as a final borrowing from the Trust Fund in March 1981 (bringing Bolivia's total borrowings from the Trust Fund to SDR 36.2 million, or $45 million); SDR 24.5 million ($27 million) through the Buffer Stock Financing Facility in June 1982, to finance stocks accumulated under the International Tin Agreement; and SDR 17.9 million ($20 million) under the Compensatory Financing Facility in January 1983, to compensate for a temporary shortfall in export receipts.

new policy regime on August 29, 1985. By that point, the economy was in a total shambles. In just three years, GDP per capita had fallen from $570 to $470; merchandise exports had fallen by 20 percent in dollar terms; and even with no new foreign borrowing, external debt of the public sector had risen from 39 percent of GDP to 133 percent. For more than a year, Bolivia had made no interest payments on its debts to commercial banks. The new government would have its hands full in trying to restore stability and credibility, not to mention growth.

Financing Stabilization with Arrears: 1985–86

The Paz government turned immediately to the IMF for assistance. On September 26, 1985, a mission headed by Hans Flickenschild (Deputy Division Chief of the Pacific Division, Western Hemisphere Department) arrived in La Paz to make an initial assessment of the New Economic Policy announced on August 29. Without question, the turnaround in policy was extremely ambitious and—if the government could deliver on its promises and resist domestic political opposition—appropriately designed to deal with the immense distortions and weaknesses in the economy.[23] The exchange rate had been allowed to float and become unified with the black-market rate. The huge subsidies implicit in most public sector prices (such as very low petroleum prices) had been largely eliminated. Reforms aimed at broadening the tax base were being implemented. Although the Fund mission believed that additional fiscal measures would have to be taken if the program was to succeed in stabilizing the economy, it concluded that there was a sufficient basis to open negotiations for the use of Fund resources.[24]

In late November, Flickenschild's team returned to La Paz to negotiate a program. Their instructions were unusual: the Managing Director was prepared to treat Bolivia as a special case, especially with regard to the handling of its external debt. Of Bolivia's nearly $4 billion in medium- and long-term external public sector debt, some $700 million was principal on loans from commercial banks. Much of that was in arrears, and overdue interest on bank loans added more than $200 million to the total amount due.[25] From the Fund's perspective, it would be important for Bolivia to reach an agreement with commercial banks on these debts to help the country regain credibility and restore normal trading relationships. The usual strategy for doing so, however, in which the banks would be expected to participate in a new concerted lending package and reschedule existing debts, did not make sense in this case. Bolivia—the poorest country in South America—could afford neither to take on new external debt on commercial terms nor to make more than a goodwill gesture in paying interest on its already outstanding commercial

---

[23]Morales and Sachs (1990), Chapter 7, provides a detailed review of the various measures taken.

[24]Bolivia stayed current on its obligations to the Fund throughout the crisis period and reduced its total indebtedness from a peak of SDR 94 million (139 percent of quota; $103 million) in January 1983 to SDR 74 million (56 percent of its increased quota; $76 million) in September 1985.

[25]"Bolivia—Recent Economic Developments," SM/86/290 (December 2, 1986), Tables 51 and 52. The authorities did not at that time have comprehensive data on short-term debts outstanding.

obligations. Whatever arrangement Bolivia reached with the Fund, the commercial banks would have no choice but to grant very generous debt relief in some form. Accordingly, de Larosière asked the staff to develop alternative scenarios based on the assumption that such debt relief would be forthcoming.[26]

In view of the comprehensiveness and strength of the August 29 policy package, negotiation of the performance criteria for the proposed stand-by arrangement was relatively straightforward. The mission's main concern was to ensure that political pressures did not undermine implementation of the government program. Confidence was bolstered during the mission when the authorities reacted to a series of shocks—including a sharp drop in world tin prices, one of the country's principal exports—by allowing the exchange rate to depreciate by about one-third. Opposition political parties called a general strike in protest, but the government held its ground and declared a temporary "state of siege" to maintain control of the economy.

Assessing Bolivia's financing requirements was more difficult. To have any hope of restoring economic growth, Bolivia had to raise the level of its imports before it could expect to raise exports. To do so, it would need additional financing well beyond what could be provided by the Fund. The scenario developed by Flickenschild in December 1985 assumed a rise of about $50 million in imports in 1986 (8 percent over the previous year); no change in exports; and full capitalization of more than $1 billion in arrears to banks and bilateral official creditors, offset marginally by payment of about $100 million in current interest to those creditors, of which some $60 million would go to commercial banks.

That last number became the principal point of contention. It was small in relation to the total arrears to the banks, but it was large in relation to Bolivia's pent-up demand for imports. Moreover, while the staff saw its proposal as a reasonable manifestation of the Managing Director's call for flexibility and bank creditors saw it as an unreasonable concession to the debtor, Bolivia and many outside observers saw it as an unrealistic demand on a desperately impoverished country. At this time, Harvard Professor Jeffrey D. Sachs was serving as an economic advisor to the Paz government, and he advised the authorities against accepting the Fund's recommendation to resume paying interest to the banks. The Bolivian negotiating team, led by Minister of Planning and Coordination Guillermo Bedregal,[27] pro-

---

[26]The clearest statement of de Larosière's initial position on debt relief for Bolivia is in the form of his handwritten response to the briefing paper for the mission, made on November 17, 1985. There he asked the mission to estimate how the economy would be affected "if debt relief were to be *very* generous and cover a *bold* stretch out of interest payments, and if new money were to be granted by the [World Bank, the International Development Agency], and the banks in an active way"; and he concluded that, "given the *extreme* characteristics of the case (virtual collapse of the export sector, breakdown of the administrative apparatus, existence of massive arrears—all factors that the commercial banks have taken account of in writing off or provisioning their claims on the country) we need *more* than the classical remedies." (The emphasis is in the original.) The scenarios developed by the staff did not include concerted lending from the banks, on the grounds that such an assumption was unrealistic.

[27]President Paz Estenssoro also met twice with the IMF staff team during this mission.

posed cutting the figure by close to half, and the issue was not resolved by the end of the mission.[28]

The staff returned to La Paz in late February 1986 to try to conclude negotiations, by which time economic conditions had seriously deteriorated. Export prices were badly depressed, agricultural harvests were being wrecked by heavy rainfalls, and the government—under increasing political pressure to abandon its commitment to stable wages—had begun intervening and introducing controls to prop up the peso in the foreign exchange market. Flickenschild cautioned the government against losing momentum in liberalizing the economy, and he again advised them to resume paying interest to commercial creditors as a means to get a favorable rescheduling agreement. With Sachs now playing a more active role in the negotiations, the authorities—led by a new planning minister, Gonzalo Sanchez de Lozado—strongly resisted that suggestion, and the issue was once again left unresolved. The mission did, however, succeed by mid-March in negotiating all but a few loose ends for an adjustment program to be supported by a 12-month stand-by arrangement with the Fund. That preliminary agreement also would open the door for Bolivia to seek debt relief from official creditors through the Paris Club.[29]

After two visits by Bolivian officials to the Fund to clarify the remaining technical issues, the Letter of Intent for the Fund arrangement was signed at the end of May 1986. In the meantime, the Bolivian authorities continued to meet with U.S. officials and with commercial bank creditors, without getting much official encouragement or making much progress toward an agreement. The Fund had now reached a crossroads. The proposed program had to be financed in some form by the commercial banks: either through a rescheduling agreement or through the accumulation of arrears. To this point, as described in the introduction to this chapter, Fund policy had been not to accept the accumulation of arrears to external creditors as a means of financing a program. If it adhered to that stance in this case, there would be no program at least until Bolivia caved in to the demand that it resume paying interest to the banks.

In spite of the potential for setting a troublesome precedent, the decision not to wait for an accord with bank creditors was never seriously questioned within the Fund.[30] Bolivia was a low-income country struggling to emerge from economic and

---

[28]The figure of $60 million assumed payment of current interest on the outstanding principal at a fixed rate of 7 percent. Bolivia's proposal was to pay interest at 4 percent. The LIBOR rate on three-month U.S. dollar deposits in December 1985 was 8.1 percent.

[29]In addition to the treatment of external arrears, exchange rate policy was a key policy issue. Sachs advised the government to peg the exchange rate to the U.S. dollar as an anchor for price expectations, while the Fund staff argued that a fixed-rate regime would be impractical since Bolivia lacked the reserves to back it up. Eventually, Bolivia officially floated the peso but stepped up the level of intervention in order to stabilize the rate. Under the terms of the stand-by arrangement, credit policy was tight enough to stabilize the exchange rate, and the strategy succeeded.

[30]It must be stressed that the lack of objection arose entirely because of the extreme circumstances facing the Bolivian authorities, which made the issue of precedence essentially moot. An interesting comparison may be made with Chile, where delays in negotiations with the banks had delayed the Fund's work as well (see Chapter 9).

financial chaos, and it had formulated a strong adjustment program. It was the first program to come before the Board for a country that was included under the umbrella of the October 1985 Baker initiative, and it was understood that Bolivia would soon be coming back to the Fund for support under the just-implemented Structural Adjustment Facility (SAF). To decline such a program was simply not a viable option. In the end, the staff merely *assumed* that some cash payments would resume in the second half of 1986 and that Bolivia would on that basis reach an agreement with its bank creditors. That strategy was communicated to the banks, who raised no objections to it.[31]

The stand-by arrangement was approved by the Executive Board on June 19, 1986. Remarkably, for a case in which the Board was departing from normal practice, no one on the Board questioned the proposal to approve a program that was being financed in large measure through the accumulation of arrears to banks. Directors all agreed that Bolivia had no alternative, and the issue of precedent never arose.[32]

Through the second half of 1986, Bolivia implemented the adjustment program, met all of the performance criteria for the stand-by arrangement except for the ceiling on external arrears, and drew the funds that were available. In December, the Fund made additional resources available through the SAF and the Compensatory Financing Facility (CFF), and for the year as a whole became the largest single source of external financing for the country.[33]

Buying Back the Debt: 1987–88

Toward the end of 1986, Bolivia made a bold move to reach a negotiated settlement with its bank creditors, by proposing to buy back a portion of its debt at a heavily discounted price. The Advisory Committee, chaired by Ulrich Merten of the Bank of America, responded favorably on the condition that the buyback be financed entirely by contributions from donor governments, not by Bolivia's own resources. The Fund staff and management also responded positively and urged the authorities to determine the buyback price through an auction rather than through a predetermined fixed price. Neither the authorities nor Sachs (their principal outside advisor on the economics of the deal) were receptive to the auction proposal, and that idea was soon dropped. The Advisory Committee approved the buyback

---

[31]See "Bolivia—Request for Stand-By Arrangement," EBS/86/120 (June 2, 1986), p. 29. The Advisory Committee met on June 9, and then cabled the authorities that it was prepared to cooperate with them in resuming negotiations after the anticipated Fund approval of the program.

[32]Minutes of EBM/86/98 (June 19, 1986). Bolivia's contractual debt-service obligations for 1986 exceeded the country's total expected earnings from exports of goods and services.

[33]Bolivia made three drawings under the stand-by arrangement, totaling SDR 32.7 million; drew SDR 64.1 million through the CFF to compensate for a shortfall in export receipts following declines in the world prices of the two major export commodities, natural gas and tin; and borrowed SDR 18.1 million from the SAF. Total disbursements to Bolivia in 1986 thus amounted to SDR 114.9 million (127 percent of quota and approximately $156 million). Other major multilateral support came from the World Bank and its soft-loan affiliate, the International Development Association (IDA); the Inter-American Development Bank (IDB); and regional funds.

proposal in March 1987, along with a general plan for the conversion of debts into equities. For the next few months the committee set out to line up the required unanimous consent of the 120 or so other creditor banks, while Bolivian officials concentrated on securing official contributions.

The Fund became more deeply involved in the buyback scheme at the request of the Advisory Committee, when some of the noncommittee creditors insisted that the Fund be brought in as a condition for their approval. The problem was that some of the donor countries were insisting on anonymity, while the banks were insisting on proof that all of the funds used for the buybacks were external donations. The Fund therefore agreed to serve as an intermediary: to receive the donations in a trustee account, administer the account, and make payments to the Advisory Committee at Bolivia's request.[34]

Meanwhile, economic conditions were beginning to deteriorate again. Fiscal and monetary policies were loosened in a vain effort to counter a deepening recession. Export receipts were severely threatened by a dispute with Argentina over the price of Bolivia's natural gas (which then accounted for more than half of Bolivia's exports). And when Bolivia attempted to reorganize the central bank to make it more efficient and accountable, the effort went awry and left the government unable to provide the data that the Fund needed to determine whether the country was still in compliance with the terms of the stand-by arrangement. The arrangement expired in July with the last two scheduled drawings unmade.

Notwithstanding these difficulties, the staff believed that Bolivia's economic prospects were reasonably bright. The general thrust of policies was reasonable, and inflation—which had been the highest in the world just two years earlier— was well under 1 percent a month. In July 1987 Flickenschild negotiated a medium-term program to be supported by a three-year Extended Fund Facility (EFF) arrangement, but that tentative agreement turned out to be premature. By the fall, it appeared that Bolivia's prospects were too cloudy, and in any event Bolivia could ill-afford additional debts on nonconcessional terms. On that basis, the staff decided to shelve the EFF plan and instead to wait until a program could be jointly negotiated with the World Bank for a program to be supported by the newly established Enhanced Structual Adjustment Facility (ESAF).

The buyback scheme was approved in final form by the banks in November 1987, shortly after the Fund completed the paperwork establishing the "voluntary contributions account" for Bolivia. Earlier in the year, Bolivian debt had been selling in a very thin secondary market for about 6 percent of its face value, but as it became clearer that the scheme would be implemented, the price began to rise. When Bolivia formally offered in January 1988 to buy back a portion of the debt,

---

[34]The Deputy Managing Director, Richard Erb, approved the proposal in principle in late June, 1987. A general description of the proposed account was circulated to Executive Directors in mid-August, and the establishment of the account was approved by the Executive Board (with only France dissenting) on October 21. See "Bolivia—Debt Buyback Arrangement," EBS/87/181 (August 19, 1987), "Bolivia—Establishment and Administration of Voluntary Contribution Account," EBD/87/251 (October 5), and minutes of EBM/87/147 (October 21).

it offered 11 cents on the dollar. That price held, and when the books were closed in March, Bolivia was able to purchase some $240 million of its outstanding $650 million in bank loans, using just over $26 million in cash that had been donated by European and Latin American countries.

Whether the buyback benefited Bolivia was much debated. Bulow and Rogoff (1988) observed that the scheme did not reduce the market value of Bolivia's outstanding debt (6 percent of the original face amount was approximately the same as 11 percent of the reduced amount), and they concluded that the full benefit of the donated cash had gone to the banks rather than to Bolivia. Critics of that view questioned whether the change in the market value of the debt was a good measure of the benefit to the country. Taking a broader view of the relevant costs and benefits of buyback schemes, Fund staff conducted several studies and generally derived more positive conclusions than those of Bulow and Rogoff.[35]

Mexico

In the halcyon days just after Christmas of 1987, the Mexican authorities completed negotiations for a path-breaking deal to relieve their debt to foreign banks. As discussed in the preceding chapter, the stand-by arrangement with the Fund was in difficulty because of policy slippages aggravated by the almost total collapse of the Mexican stock market. Negotiations were under way with the Fund staff for a renewed adjustment effort that could serve as the basis for a waiver of the end-year program criteria. That effort produced a major new policy regime in mid-December (the *Pacto*; see Chapter 10, above). Separately, Mexico was negotiating with the U.S. authorities and with Morgan Guaranty Bank to exchange part of its bank loans for bonds that would be partially guaranteed by the U.S. Treasury. When the deal was announced on December 29, it made headlines as a breakthrough from a general impasse between creditors and debtors on the handling of debt obligations.

The Mexico-Morgan deal worked as follows. The Mexican government extended an offer to the banks to exchange up to $20 billion in outstanding loans for negotiable bonds. The bonds would be sold to the banks at a discounted price to be determined by auction, but the principal would be guaranteed by the U.S. Treasury. To implement that guarantee, the treasury issued zero-coupon bonds with 20-year maturities, to be held in custody by the Federal Reserve Bank of New York.[36] Although the principal was only a small fraction of the total discounted present value of the bonds, the hope was that Mexico's impeccable record of paying interest on time throughout the debt crisis would make the bonds an attractive exit from the seemingly endless cycle of new-money packages.

The banks were given less than two months to respond to the offer, at the end of which fewer than 100 banks (out of some 500) exchanged $3.67 billion in loans

---

[35]See Cline (1995), pp. 187–93, for an introduction to the controversy, and Dooley (1989) for a staff analysis.

[36]See "Mexico—Recent Economic Developments," SM/88/47 (February 25, 1988), pp. 64–65.

for $2.56 billion in bonds. Both the amount and the discount (30 percent, compared with an expected 50 percent) were disappointingly small. Part of the problem was that some of the Advisory Committee banks (including the largest creditor, Citibank) resented the negotiation of the deal outside the established committee structure. Part of the problem was the absence of a guarantee on interest payments. Part of the problem was the reluctance by some banks to realize a loss on their loans, especially in countries where regulators were making relatively unfavorable rulings on how those losses should be reported.

Nonetheless, the Mexico-Morgan deal was a watershed for the debt strategy. It showed that there was a market for discount bonds, if they could be packaged and marketed attractively. It showed that creditors could cope with the wide range of circumstances facing individual banks if the menu was flexible enough. And it showed that creditor governments could generate substantial leverage by using guarantees to support debt-relief operations. On a very small scale and with tentative force, it contained many of the elements of the Brady Plan that was still more than a year away. As Alan Whittome noted a few weeks later, the "Mexico exchange open[ed the] door wider to encouraging some degree of forgiveness."[37]

The first opportunity that the Fund had to assess the plan was in March 1988, when the Executive Board completed the Article IV consultations with Mexico and reviewed performance under the stand-by arrangement. The staff view was that the debt conversion scheme would make a positive contribution toward resolving Mexico's debt problem by reinforcing cooperation with creditors and by bringing market signals into the process. At the Board meeting, several Directors expressed disappointment that the amounts of debt exchanged were small, but they nonetheless gave Mexico high marks for having made a positive innovation in the debt strategy.[38]

The Brady Plan

In August 1988, Baker resigned as Secretary of the U.S. Treasury in order to manage the campaign of George Bush for the presidency. He was replaced the following month by investment banker Nicholas F. Brady. Almost immediately after taking office, Brady found himself at the IMF Annual Meetings in Berlin, where reviving the debt strategy was a key item on the agenda of the Interim Committee. Camdessus opened the meeting by clearly stating the need for debt relief:

> ". . . we have to recognize that the burden of current and prospective debt service obligations places significant economic and political constraints on policy formulation. . . . techniques must be found, not just to provide additional finance, but also to

---

[37]Memorandum to the Managing Director (January 5, 1988); IMF/RD (Historian's files).

[38]"Mexico—Staff Report for the 1987 Article IV Consultation and Second Review Under Stand-By Arrangement," EBS/88/23 (February 4, 1988), p. 31; and minutes of EBM/88/36 (March 10, 1988).

lighten, in a mutually agreeable, market-based way, the relative burden of existing indebtedness."[39]

Pierre Beregevoy, the French minister of finance, noted that the G-7 finance ministers (who had met the day before) had been able to agree on implementing the "Toronto terms" for relieving the debt burdens of low-income countries but had not been able to deal with the problems facing middle-income developing countries. He and others alluded to the Mexico-Morgan deal as a model, but none of the assembled ministers was able to offer a concrete proposal for strengthening the debt strategy. At the conclusion of the meeting, the committee issued a communiqué stating (para. 4) that "the menu approach should be broadened further, including through voluntary market-based techniques which increase financial flows and which reduce the stock of debt without transferring risk from private lenders to official creditors." No one yet had any idea how that goal was to be achieved.

Cooking Up a Plan: November 1988–March 1989

Although Brady expressed skepticism at the Berlin meetings about officially funded debt-relief schemes, he soon gave his deputy, David C. Mulford, instructions to devise a new strategy to be introduced after the new administration took office in January 1989. Whether it was to be a debt-relief plan or a more aggressive promotion of the growth-oriented strategy introduced by Baker three years earlier was still to be worked out, but Mulford's goal was to convince the government and the Federal Reserve that the crisis could not be resolved without a radical new approach.

The basic plan was worked out within the circle of U.S. officials during the period between the November election (won by Bush) and the January inauguration, after which Mulford presented it to his G-7 counterparts. To hone the plan and make it acceptable to all involved parties, Mulford discussed it with Camdessus on several occasions and sought the advice of Fund staff. By February, all of the necessary support was in place, and Brady prepared to announce the plan a few weeks before the next Interim Committee meeting (scheduled for April 3) so that the committee could formally endorse it at that time. He had already agreed to address a Washington symposium on debt, sponsored by the Bretton Woods Committee and the Brookings Institution, on March 10. Camdessus—with whom the U.S. authorities had consulted on the role that the Fund would play in this new strategy—was also speaking on that occasion. It would provide the ideal setting.

As the date of Brady's speech approached, the need for a new debt strategy became critically and painfully urgent. The Venezuelan government, trying to effect adjustment policies so as to qualify for financial support from the IMF and other creditors, was confronted with violent protests that left hundreds of people dead (see the section on Venezuela, pp. 516–20). One of Latin America's wealthiest

---

[39]Record of discussion, ICMS Meeting 31 (September 25, 1988), p. 3.

economies and a country with a democratic tradition, Venezuela now was poised on the edge of a knife and could well collapse without decisive support from the United States and the IMF. As word of Brady's impending speech began to leak, the plan appeared to be a response to the riots in Caracas and was widely billed as a rescue for Venezuela.[40]

As Brady outlined the proposal over lunch at the U.S. State Department on March 10, the plan contained five new elements.[41] First, he suggested that commercial banks agree to a "general waiver of the sharing and negative pledge clauses for each performing debtor," to enable individual banks to "negotiate debt or debt service reduction operations." Without this element, which was inserted after some prodding from Fund staff, any small creditor bank could continue to block agreement, and negotiating flexible and innovative exit strategies would remain cumbersome and time-consuming. Second, the IMF and the World Bank should dedicate a portion of loans to qualified countries "to finance specific debt reduction plans." For the Fund, this proposal was to become known as the provision of "set-asides," primarily to help countries buy back their bank debts at a discount. Third, the Bretton Woods institutions should "offer new, additional financial support to collateralize a portion of interest payments for debt or debt service reduction transactions," a suggestion that would become known as "augmentation." Fourth, Brady signaled a shift in the U.S. position toward favoring an increase in Fund quotas, to support the provision of resources for the new debt strategy (see Chapter 17). Fifth, he called upon the IMF to reconsider the policy of requiring firm financing assurances to be in place. The banks and the country should negotiate the type of financing needed, and if arrears accumulated while those negotiations proceeded, the Fund should not let that problem prevent it from approving a financial arrangement.

That afternoon, at one of the conference's panel discussions, Camdessus welcomed Brady's initiative and noted that it deserved a "positive response from the international community." How positive that response would be was not yet clear, especially since some of the leading commercial bank creditors remained adamantly opposed to debt relief.[42]

---

[40]For example, a front-page story in the *New York Times* on March 9 began, "Prompted in part by the debt-related violence in Venezuela last week, the Bush Administration has decided to encourage bank creditors of third-world nations to reduce the value of the debt and therefore the countries' cost of making payments on it, officials say."

[41]For a report on the speech in the context of the conference, see the *IMF Survey* (March 20, 1989), pp. 90–92. For more detailed descriptions of the Brady Plan and its implementation, see Collyns and others (1992), Clark (1993), and Cline (1995).

[42]At the same meeting of the Bretton Woods Committee where Brady introduced his plan, Yusuke Kashiwagi (Chairman of the Bank of Tokyo) gave a speech arguing that the "resolution of the debt issue depends more than anything else on the strong will and efforts of the debtor countries themselves to come to grips with the structural adjustments and revitalization of their economies. . . . More debt reduction or debt relief will not solve the debt issue because the underlying issues . . . remain unaddressed" (manuscript).

Implementing the Plan: March–May 1989

The Executive Board was already scheduled to discuss the debt strategy the week following Brady's speech, so Directors had an early opportunity to react. Although there was broad support in principle for the U.S. initiative, there was a great deal of initial skepticism about the suggested innovations in the Fund's role. If the Fund were to set aside a portion of a loan to finance buyback operations, that money would not be available to the member to finance its adjustment program. If the Fund were to augment the loan, the risk to the Fund would be that much greater, and fewer resources would be available for other members. If the Fund were to abandon its traditional policy on requiring financing assurances (i.e., if it were to lend while the country accumulated arrears to other creditors), both the Fund and the member could face a backlash that would threaten and delay the restoration of normal market access.[43] This discussion was preliminary, but it suggested that revamping the strategy might not be easy.

The major difficulties were resolved two weeks later, at the regularly scheduled meeting of the ministers of finance and central bank governors of the G-7 countries (held in Washington, the day before the Interim Committee meeting). Both Germany (represented by Gerhard Stoltenberg) and the United Kingdom (Nigel Lawson) were opposed to some elements of the proposal, especially the burden and the risks that could be imposed on the use of IMF resources. To allay those concerns, the United States reportedly agreed to limit the proposal for additional use of Fund resources to the support of interest reduction. That is, any funds to be set aside for buybacks or other debt reduction operations were to be found within the normal access limits. With that amendment, the G-7 endorsed the plan, making its acceptance the next day by the Interim Committee all but inevitable.[44]

On April 3, the Interim Committee formally endorsed the Brady Plan. Ministers flatly rejected the arguments that had been made earlier against the Fund financing debt reduction operations through set-asides or other means, and the committee "requested the Executive Board to consider as a matter of urgency" the proposals that had been put forward (communiqué, para. 3). Stoltenberg cautioned that "the use of the Fund's resources—including the use of these resources in support of debt reduction operations—must be in conformity with its task as a monetary institution," and that the Fund's resources "must supplement, not substitute for, other sources of finance."[45] He concluded, however, that the Brady initiative (as modified) was consistent with those principles. In that context, the committee welcomed Japan's offer to provide parallel financing and noted the importance of

---

[43]Chairman's summing up; minutes of EBM/89/36 (March 17, 1989), pp. 31–33.

[44]For two insider accounts of the G-7 involvement, see Toyoo Gyohten's discussion in Volcker and Gyohten (1992), pp. 223–24; and Lawson (1992), pp. 860–63. (Lawson erroneously places the G-7 meeting on February 2, not April 2, but he correctly describes it as on the "eve" of the Interim Committee meeting.) Lawson credits the Japanese support for the Brady Plan to a quid pro quo in which the United States agreed to support Japan's bid for an ad hoc IMF quota increase.

[45]Record of discussion, ICMS Meeting 32 (April 3, 1989), pp. 48–49.

"close collaboration" between the Fund and the World Bank in implementing the strengthened debt strategy.

When the Executive Board returned to the issue on Friday, May 19, 1989,[46] the only real questions concerned the specifics of the Fund's involvement in four contentious areas: magnitude and treatment of additional access to Fund resources, the handling of set-asides, eligibility of countries for the plan, and modifications to the policy on financing assurances. But this would turn out to be one of the most complex, lengthy, and fractious meetings of the Executive Board during the whole period covered by this History, and the meeting was not concluded until Tuesday morning, May 23.[47] Essentially, Germany and the United Kingdom, backed to varying degrees by some other European countries, sought to limit the degree to which the Fund would modify its procedures and intensify its involvement in the debt strategy; the United States, backed to varying degrees by other industrial and most developing countries and by the Managing Director, sought to retain as much of the proposals for change as possible.

First, the most contentious area, the magnitude and treatment of additional access to Fund resources. The staff proposed that a Fund arrangement might be augmented by "up to 40 percent" of the member's quota to support the member in securing agreements for debt or debt-service reductions.[48] The United States preferred that the 40 percent figure be only an indicative norm and to retain the option of approving larger amounts in some cases. The United Kingdom had a strong preference for limiting the use of these additional resources for interest rather than principal reduction, as had been agreed in general terms by the G-7 and the Interim Committee. That is, the Fund would supply additional resources that would be set aside in an escrow account to serve as a guarantee to the banks in exchange for a reduction in the rate of interest on outstanding loans. Charles Enoch (Alternate—United Kingdom) argued that the ceiling on augmentation should be 25 percent rather than 40 and that in any case the augmented arrangement should not exceed the Fund's normal access limits. Bernd Goos (Alternate—Germany) supported that amendment and added that to qualify for augmentation, a country should be required to match the additional funds with its own resources.[49] Sup-

---

[46]To prepare for the complexity of the discussion, Executive Directors had a preliminary exchange of views in informal sessions on May 5 and 10.

[47]The Board met all day Friday for a *tour de table* in which Directors stated their positions and debated the key issues. At the end of the day, there were at least simple majorities on all of the disputed issues, but minority positions were still strongly held. The meeting resumed on Monday afternoon to reconsider the points where substantive differences remained and to try to establish a consensus. After some discussion, the Managing Director read out a draft summing up. That draft was discussed in detail and in some respects hotly disputed, and the meeting was adjourned in the evening, to be continued on Tuesday morning. After several amendments, the summing up was finally approved just before lunchtime on Tuesday, though still without a consensus on all points.

[48]"Fund Involvement in the Debt Strategy—Further Considerations," EBS/89/96 (May 12, 1989), p. 5.

[49]Enoch's statement is at EBM/89/58 (May 19, 1989), pp. 8–9; Goos's is at EBM/89/59 (same date), p. 12.

ported by a few other Directors, they argued long and hard for the limits and restrictions. Although they were in the minority, Camdessus felt that achieving a consensus on this point was extremely important.

A related issue on augmentation that arose during the meeting concerned the possible establishment of escrow accounts. The staff proposal was that once the member had reached or was about to reach an agreement with the banks, the Fund could consider making extra resources available to catalyze that agreement. Enoch suggested that any such funds be segregated and placed in an escrow account outside the control of the Fund (possibly at the Bank for International Settlements, the BIS). The funds would remain in the escrow account for the life of the Fund arrangement unless they were needed to meet the interest payments. Goos, supported by others including Jorgen Ovi (Denmark) and Renato Filosa (Italy), went further and proposed that the Fund should wait to disburse the funds until they were needed, and then release them only if the country was in compliance with the performance criteria for the Fund arrangement. That amendment worried the staff, which was convinced that the funds would be of no use to the member if not made available up front and that it was essential for the Fund to stay at arm's length from the negotiations between the member and the banks.

Several Directors concurred that if the use of escrow accounts were endorsed, the accounts should not be held at the Fund. They objected both to the possibility that the Fund, rather than the member country, would be guaranteeing the country's interest payments; and to the possibility that the Fund would be thereby drawn into the negotiations with the banks. In response, Camdessus argued very strongly that the Fund was the most well-suited institution to hold the escrow accounts, and he insisted that this option not be precluded.

On Tuesday, after several hours of debate, a compromise was reached on augmentation. First, 40 percent of quota was to be a ceiling, not a norm; to qualify, the member would have to show that the extra resources would be "decisive" in enabling agreements with creditors. Second, if the funds were not used "within an appropriate period," the member would be "expected" (though not required) to make early repayment.[50] Third, an arrangement, including augmentation, could exceed the normal access limits only if the Board agreed at the time of approval to invoke the "exceptional circumstances" clause. Fourth, the nature of any escrow accounts was to be determined later and was omitted altogether from the summing up of this meeting. For the text of the summing up, see the Appendix to this chapter.

The second contentious area for discussion was the handling of set-asides. The staff proposed that a portion, perhaps 25 percent, of qualifying Fund commitments be set aside to finance either debt reduction operations (i.e., principal-reducing operations such as buybacks of discounted debt) or reduction of debt service (e.g., negotiated reductions in interest rates). Brady's original proposal suggested limiting

---

[50]The distinction, which was introduced as an expedient, was explained in a statement by the General Counsel, François P. Gianviti; minutes of EBM/89/61 (May 23, 1989), pp. 9–10. To introduce a policy requiring the member to make an early repayment would have taken a higher and possibly unattainable majority of the voting power on the Board.

the use of set-asides to principal rather than interest reduction, but the distinction lacked a clear economic rationale. Several Directors, led by Hélène Ploix (France) and supported by the Managing Director, noted that since money was fungible once it had been disbursed, it was senseless to insist on this differentiation. Furthermore, the staff paper noted that it would be counterproductive to hinder the banks from developing financial instruments that combined debt and interest reduction.[51] The U.S. Executive Director, Charles H. Dallara, countered that the basis for the distinction was political rather than economic: to make the plan work would require a quota increase for the Fund, and the Bush administration believed that the only way it could persuade congress to go along was to demonstrate that the Brady Plan was capable of reducing the stock of bank loans to developing countries.[52] Separating the two elements was also important to those who wanted to restrict the use of additional resources to interest rate support (which would in most cases mean that the funds would not be used). The final wording of the agreement acknowledged those differing vantage points and yet restricted the set-asides to principal-reducing operations.

The third contentious topic was eligibility. The staff proposed that the Brady Plan apply primarily to countries whose foreign debts were selling at "a sufficiently deep discount" in the secondary market.[53] The logic behind this proposal was that setting aside Fund resources for buybacks or other debt reduction operations made sense only if the country could conduct the operation at a substantial discount; otherwise, there would be no leverage. Furthermore, the Fund's own liquidity position was tight, and any additional use of resources had to be limited to the most difficult cases.[54] Several Directors from developing countries (led by Alexandre Kafka of Brazil) objected, on two grounds: a moral hazard problem could arise if countries were told that they could gain access to the plan only if they could first show that their debts were being discounted by the market, and the proposal could unfairly punish countries that had already made progress or had made the sacrifices necessary to keep their debt selling at par.[55] The Managing Director maintained that the moral hazard problem was of no practical significance; any advantage to a country from devaluing its debt in the market to get access to set-asides would be overwhelmed by the disadvantages to its reputation and to the soundness of its finances. In the end, the proposal was formally dropped, but the wording of the fi-

---

[51]"Fund Involvement in the Debt Strategy—Further Considerations," EBS/89/96 (May 12, 1989), p. 4.

[52]Also see footnote 12, p. 481.

[53]"Fund Involvement in the Debt Strategy—Further Considerations," EBS/89/96 (May 12, 1989), p. 3.

[54]See "The Fund's Liquidity and Financing Needs—Update," EBS/89/100 (May 17, 1989), p. 7.

[55]Kafka's position was stated at EBM/89/58, p. 16. Some speakers also questioned whether the proposal might violate the "equal treatment" of members required by the Fund's Articles. The staff argued in response that the "deep discount" requirement was an example of a type of "balance of payments need." As long as any member facing that particular problem was eligible, then equal treatment was satisfied. See the statement by William E. Holder (Deputy General Counsel), at EBM/89/60, p. 3.

nal agreement implied that only countries with deeply discounted debt would be likely to qualify.

The fourth area of contention concerned modifications to the policy on financing assurances. The basic policy then in effect specified that the Fund would approve arrangements only when it had received firm assurances that the member's adjustment program would be fully financed. Accumulation of arrears did not count as financing, although—as discussed above—the Fund had allowed a few exceptions to that policy over the preceding three years. The staff now concluded that other creditors should no longer be allowed to determine whether an arrangement would be approved. They proposed that the policy be broadened to include toleration of arrears in some cases, while retaining critical-mass requirements and "approval in principle" as options.[56] Directors had no objection to the idea of accepting arrears to bank creditors (i.e., approving the program while negotiations were ongoing), but several of them (Enoch, Goos, Ovi, and others) did object to changing the policy vis-à-vis official creditors.[57] That view was accepted, and the final agreement was that "an accumulation of arrears to banks may have to be tolerated where negotiations continue and the country's financing situation does not allow them to be avoided. . . . The Fund's policy of nontoleration of arrears to official creditors remains unchanged."

It had, after all, not been easy, but the Brady Plan was adopted essentially intact, and the debt strategy was substantially expanded.

Debt Reduction Programs in the Fund

The Fund began implementing the new strategy immediately. Visibly, the institutional role was to negotiate and finance adjustment programs with qualified countries and to provide for augmentation of the arrangements in support of negotiated settlements with bank creditors. Less visibly but just as crucially for the success of the strategy, the staff responded to requests from debtors for technical assistance in preparing for negotiations with creditors. A key element of the Brady Plan was a menu of options for creditors to choose from, each of which was designed to have approximately the same discounted present value as the current price of the country's bank debt in the secondary market. Basing the menu on market prices was designed to reduce the scope for dragging out negotiations as each side sought to gain advantages, but it introduced new and technically complex elements into the process that were not immediately accepted by all parties. The

---

[56]"Fund Involvement in the Debt Strategy—Further Considerations," EBS/89/96 (May 12, 1989), p. 7–8.

[57]The staff recommendation, in part, was that the Fund "should be prepared to approve outright an arrangement with a member before agreement on a suitable financing package has been agreed with creditors in cases where negotiations with creditors proved to be prolonged, and where it was judged that such prompt Fund support was essential to the economic program. . . ." "The Fund's Policy on Financing Assurances," EBS/89/79 (April 20, 1989), p. 13.

Fund staff—especially Michael P. Dooley (Assistant Director of the Research Department), who had first developed the analytical structure for the menu approach, and Maxwell Watson, who chaired the Junior Debt Group—met frequently (often secretly and over the objections of the U.S. authorities) with officials of indebted countries to advise them on how to evaluate creditors' proposals for menu options. During 1989 alone, such assistance was given to Argentina, Brazil, Costa Rica, Mexico, the Philippines, and Venezuela.[58] Separately, the staff also met with bankers to help explain the authorities' position in the negotiations.

By mid-May, the staff reports for three possible financing cases—Costa Rica, the Philippines, and Mexico—had already been circulated and were waiting only for the approval of the guidelines. A fourth—Venezuela—was in the final drafting stages. Having finished its marathon debate on the morning of May 23, 1989, the Executive Board caught its collective breath over lunch and then went to work on the first two cases that same afternoon.

Costa Rica

The path that brought Costa Rica to the front of the queue for the Brady Plan was essentially the same path trod by so many other developing countries in the 1980s. What made this case stand out was the magnitude and the persistence of the deadlock between the indebted country and her commercial bank creditors.

The Crisis Develops: 1980–83

The journey began in a familiar place. Costa Rica developed severe macroeconomic imbalances in the early 1980s as the result of excess government spending, fueled by external borrowing contracted at interest rates that were initially negative in real terms and that became unbearably costly by 1980, and aggravated by a substantial deterioration in the terms of trade (by 20 percent from 1980 to 1982).[59] Costa Rica's initial response to the external shocks incorporated too little policy adjustment. The authorities negotiated a stand-by arrangement and then an EFF arrangement with the Fund in 1980 and 1981, respectively, but the programs were not well implemented and—notwithstanding the onset of a severe recession—failed to resolve the imbalances.[60]

---

[58]For a report on the seminal visit, see "Technical Assistance Visit to Mexico," memorandum from Guillermo Calvo (Senior Advisor in the Research Department), Dooley, and Watson to the Managing Director (June 6, 1989); IMF/RD Managing Director file "Mexico, January–October 1989" (Accession 91/455, Box 2, Section 446).

[59]For detailed discussions of the development and treatment of the Costa Rican crisis, see Castillo (1988) and Nelson (1990).

[60]Prior to the 1980 stand-by arrangement, Costa Rica's obligations to the Fund totaled SDR 35.4 million (86 percent of quota, or about $45 million), owing to loans under the oil facility and the CFF. The government made only one drawing under each program, plus one more CFF drawing in June 1981. When the EFF arrangement was canceled in December 1982, obligations totaled SDR 84.2 million (137 percent of quota, or $93 million).

The economic crisis became a debt crisis in July 1981, when the government suspended paying interest or principal on bank debts. That put the EFF arrangement on hold (though payments to the Fund and other multilateral institutions continued on schedule). A new government was elected in February 1982; soon after they took office in May, they sought a new stand-by arrangement with the Fund. Negotiations for that arrangement were prolonged, partly because the more general debt crisis exploded around Latin America at the same time, but principally because bank creditors were reluctant to approve a rescheduling for Costa Rica. Although the Fund's policy of requiring financing assurances was working effectively in situations where the banks' solvency would have been threatened by a failure to reach agreement, it was less effective where the banks' exposure was relatively small. In dealing with Costa Rica, whose external debt was less than 5 percent of Brazil's (though far larger in relation to GDP), the bank creditors decided to bargain hard.

In December 1982, shortly after the banks agreed to reschedule outstanding loans and settle arrears (on terms that were substantially more severe than those granted to the larger indebted countries), the EFF arrangement was canceled and replaced by an ordinary stand-by-arrangement. This time the program was fully implemented, the arrangement was fully utilized, and by the end of 1983 Costa Rica had made remarkable progress toward stabilization.[61] The difficulty—little appreciated at the time—was that the settlement had left the country with a debt-service burden that would absorb more than 50 percent of Costa Rica's total export revenues over the next several years and that would block the restoration of stable growth.

Standoff with Bank Creditors: 1985–87

Two years later, Costa Rica went again to the Fund for assistance in coping with its debts. A stand-by arrangement was negotiated in early 1985, but it went off track: first temporarily, because of delays in obtaining external financing from commercial banks and the World Bank, and then more seriously because of slippages in controlling monetary growth. The arrangement expired with two of the five scheduled purchases undrawn.[62]

---

[61]At the conclusion of the 1983 stand-by arrangement, Costa Rica's obligations totaled SDR 183.3 million (the all-time peak): 218 percent of the just-increased quota, or approximately $191 million.

[62]The arrangement, approved on March 13, 1985, was for SDR 54 million (64 percent of quota, or $52 million), to be drawn in five installments over 13 months. The text is in "Costa Rica—Stand-By Arrangement," EBS/85/31, Sup. 2 (March 14, 1985). Costa Rica drew SDR 14 million on approval and another SDR 10 million in April. In October 1985, the Executive Board granted a waiver for the failure to meet the test on reducing external arrears (Decision No. 8109-(85/155), adopted October 23, 1985). Costa Rica then drew down another SDR 10 million. No further drawings were made, and the arrangement expired on April 30, 1986, with an undrawn balance of SDR 20 million. Repayments of earlier obligations exceeded the drawings under this arrangement, and at end-April, Costa Rica's obligations to the Fund totaled SDR 165.7 million (197 percent of quota, or $195 million).

A new government, headed by the future recipient of the Nobel Peace Prize, Oscar Arias Sanchez, was elected in 1986 and immediately sought to negotiate a new stand-by arrangement with the Fund. That effort failed over differences in view regarding the appropriate pace of adjustment in fiscal policy, and in July Costa Rica again went into arrears to its commercial bank creditors. Although the Fund staff believed that the first priority was to strengthen the adjustment effort, they also concluded that the debt burden had become an independent problem that had to be resolved. As the staff report for the 1986 Article IV consultation put it, "even under the most optimistic scenario, there will be a continuous need for substantial debt relief in the years ahead."[63] Without debt relief, the economy could not achieve its growth potential; without growth, the country could not generate enough foreign exchange to service the foreign debt.

In September and October 1986, President Arias's finance minister, Fernando Naranjo Villalobos, met in New York with the banks' Advisory Committee (chaired, like that of Bolivia, by Merten) to propose a long-term solution to Costa Rica's vicious-circle debt problem. The proposal—radical for its day but judged by the Fund staff to be realistically based on the government's capacity to pay—called on the banks to reschedule debts over 25 years, with interest rates rising from 2½ percent initially to no more than 6 percent after seven years and with interest payments capped at no more than 1½ percent of GDP. As evidence of good faith, in October the government unilaterally began making partial interest payments to limit the accumulation of arrears.[64] The Advisory Committee, unwilling to set a precedent that could affect its ongoing negotiations with the larger countries in Latin America, rejected the proposal.

Simultaneously with the bank negotiations, Naranjo met several times with the Fund staff and management to try to get support for the government's economic program. On December 3, 1986, Arias joined the battle, coming to the Fund for a meeting with de Larosière.[65] The Managing Director continued to insist that stricter control of the budget deficit was needed before the Fund could agree to a stand-by arrangement.

After two more missions by the staff to Costa Rica, agreement was reached in April 1987 on the terms of an economic program that the Fund was prepared to support with a stand-by arrangement. Before the proposal could be presented to the Executive Board, however, the authorities would have to make substantive

---

[63]"Costa Rica—Staff Report for the 1986 Article IV Consultation," SM/86/241 (September 15, 1986), p. 14.

[64]At the time, Costa Rica's arrears to bank creditors amounted to about $33 million. The government began paying interest at the rate of $5 million a month, which was somewhat less than the amount coming due.

[65]This visit was part of a wider effort by Arias to get additional financial support to cover the spillover costs to Costa Rica from the civil war in neighboring Nicaragua. In late 1986, an estimated 250,000 Nicaraguan refugees were in Costa Rica, equivalent to 10 percent of the local population. The United States, which had been providing covert support to the insurgency in Nicaragua, was also providing official assistance to Costa Rica that amounted to nearly 5 percent of Costa Rica's GDP.

progress in their negotiations with the banks. Those negotiations had been going badly for months, and in the wake of the Brazilian moratorium on debt servicing (Chapter 10), they were going nowhere at all. Although no one could have predicted it at the time, the difficulties that were already evident were leading to a stalemate in the negotiations between Costa Rica and its bank creditors that would persist until 1989.

The banks' Advisory Committee had three main concerns. First, it wanted to avoid any deal that included innovative options or an unusual degree of concessionality, which could complicate its negotiations with Brazil and other heavily indebted countries. Second, the banks represented on the committee had different needs and perspectives, and they were having great difficulty agreeing among themselves on the best approach to take with regard to Costa Rica. Although an innovative approach seemed to be called for to cater to these differences, there was a danger that any new proposal could further complicate the process.[66]

The banks' third concern was that they were being asked to fill the lion's share of Costa Rica's financing gap. The Fund was proposing to accept a stand-by arrangement totaling SDR 50 million (59.5 percent of quota, or roughly $68 million), to be made available in six installments over 18 months. Even assuming full utilization of the arrangement, scheduled repayments to the Fund from earlier loans would exceed drawings during this period, so the Fund's exposure in Costa Rica was anticipated to decline by SDR 15 million before the arrangement expired. Small changes were projected for Paris Club creditors and the World Bank, while the banks were being asked to raise their exposure by $200 million (approximately a 10 percent increase) through the end of 1988. Throughout 1987 and into 1988, the Advisory Committee banks tried without success to convince the Fund to accept a larger arrangement that would at least result in a net cash flow to Costa Rica.[67] The Fund's position was that its role should be primarily to assist the government in obtaining longer-term financial assistance from other creditors by promoting adequate macroeconomic and structural policies, and that the requested bank financing was moderate and reasonable.

After the Managing Director (Camdessus) approved the Letter of Intent for the stand-by arrangement in April 1987, the government tried to resolve the impasse

---

[66]In May 1987, Citibank's decision to set aside $3 billion in reserves as a provision against losses on loans to developing countries gave it a greater ability to resist pressures to accept costly solutions for individual countries. Bank of America had a larger ratio of nonperforming loans and was less able to extricate itself through loan-loss provisioning. Both banks were members of the Advisory Committee.

[67]Costa Rica could have requested an additional SDR 55 million ($70 million) through the CFF to compensate for the depressed level of world prices for coffee (Costa Rica's principal export commodity). The Fund discouraged the authorities from making that request. While it would have facilitated an agreement with the Advisory Committee, the staff were concerned that the primary effect would have been to correspondingly reduce the amount that the country could have expected to obtain from the banks.

with the banks by proposing a menu of long-term financing options, including exit bonds and debt-equity swaps, as a means of coping with the diversity of needs and strategies among creditor banks. Arias came to the Fund for a second time, in June, but there was little that Camdessus could do other than to try to encourage the banks to be more forthcoming. In late July, the Advisory Committee informed Naranjo that it had decided to wait until October to resume discussions, apparently so as first to achieve some progress with Brazil. The minister then went to Washington to tell Sterie T. Beza, the Director of the Western Hemisphere Department, that as long as the Fund put off approving the stand-by arrangement, Costa Rica had no real hope of getting help from other official creditors. Beza did not believe that approving the arrangement "in principle" would make much difference. That procedure worked reasonably well in situations where negotiations with banks were nearly finalized, which was not the situation here. Naranjo asked if the Fund could approve the arrangement without waiting for the banks, by accepting the accumulation of external arrears. Beza responded that this would be a "major departure from present practices," but he agreed to take up the request with management.[68]

Camdessus took the view that the Fund could consider approving the program under these circumstances, but only with the concurrence of the Advisory Committee banks and other creditors. Throughout August 1987, both Beza and the Deputy Managing Director, Richard Erb, sounded out various private and official creditors, all of whom agreed on the desirability of showing flexibility in this particular case. A detailed strategy was then developed in September and finalized during the Annual Meetings at the end of that month. First, the government agreed with the Fund to tighten credit policies by enough to ensure that the program would stay on track. Second, the government agreed with the banks on an interim schedule of partial interest payments. Third, the banks—while refraining from formally accepting the accumulation of arrears—agreed to provide a general statement of support for the strategy. On that basis, the Managing Director approved presenting the proposed stand-by arrangement to the Executive Board and asking the Board to approve temporarily the continued accumulation of arrears:

> In the particular circumstances of this case, the staff recommends that the Executive Board approve the stand-by arrangement and the exchange restrictions evidenced by existing external payments arrears and by the external arrears that will remain pending rescheduling agreements until April 30, 1988, or the completion of the second

---

[68]The quotation is from a memorandum from Beza to the Managing Director (July 28, 1987), reporting on his meeting with Naranjo; in IMF/RD Managing Director file "Costa Rica, November 1986–December 1987" (Accession 88/14, Box 1, Section 550). As discussed in Chapter 10, the Fund had approved a stand-by arrangement with Bolivia in 1986, while Bolivia had outstanding arrears to bank creditors. The Costa Rica case was more complicated in that the government was using an exchange restriction, which was subject to IMF jurisdiction, to prevent the transfer of foreign exchange for the purpose of servicing bank debts. Moreover, Bolivia was regarded as an exceptional case because of its very low per capita income.

program review, whichever is earlier. This action would provide Costa Rica and the commercial banks with the time needed to make satisfactory progress toward the conclusion of a financing package. This package will be the subject of the second review of the program.[69]

The Executive Board meeting to consider the proposal was to be held on October 28, 1987. Shortly before the meeting, some Executive Directors objected informally to the proposal to approve the exchange restriction that was the basis for the accumulation of arrears to banks. The staff then decided to finesse the issue by withdrawing that element of the proposed decision. That amendment meant that the Fund would approve the loan but not the restriction. Costa Rica would be out of compliance with its obligations under Article VIII, section 2(a), but in the opinion of the Fund's legal counsel, approval of a stand-by arrangement neither required the member to be in compliance with that provision nor implied the Fund's approval of a restriction that conflicted with the Articles.[70] The Board accepted that interpretation, albeit reluctantly, and the stand-by arrangement was approved.[71]

Debt Relief: 1988–89

Unfortunately, Costa Rica was able neither to implement the 1988 economic program underlying the stand-by arrangement nor to negotiate an agreement with the banks. To keep monetary policy on track required either a tightening of the budget or a rise in domestic interest rates, and the government was unwilling to do either. The authorities decided not to request any drawings under the arrangement until they could establish a record of keeping the program on track. Although policies improved in the course of 1988 and departures from the program criteria were relatively minor, no drawings were ever made.[72]

The Advisory Committee met regularly throughout 1988 but was unable to resolve its internal differences. In May, the Bank of America proposed a complex scheme involving the issuance of zero-coupon bonds financed in part by a new-money loan, "rolling" interest-rate guarantees (i.e., establishment of a fund to

---

[69]"Costa Rica—Request for Stand-By Arrangement—Letter of Intent," EBS/87/91, Sup. 1 (October 16, 1987), p. 22.

[70]Minutes of EBM/87/150 (October 28, 1987), pp. 4–5.

[71]Several Executive Directors (notably Bernd Goos—Alternate, Germany; Filippo Di Mauro—Temporary Alternate, Italy; and Masahiro Sugita—Alternate, Japan) expressed misgivings about the procedure and noted that their preference would have been to approve the arrangement in principle, pending completion of the financing arrangements. None abstained from approving the proposed decision.

[72]The Fund's initial approval of the arrangement entitled Costa Rica to make the first scheduled drawing, but the authorities elected not to avail themselves of it. The next scheduled drawing was dependent on completion of a review. When a staff mission in January 1988 determined that the credit ceilings were not met, the authorities elected not to request a waiver. For a summary of the problems with the stand-by arrangement, see "Costa Rica—Staff Report for the 1989 Article IV Consultation and Request for Stand-By Arrangement," EBS/89/87 (May 3, 1989), pp. 3–5.

guarantee interest payments for four quarters ahead), concessional interest rates linked to economic performance, and with official support to be coordinated by the World Bank through a consultative group. That proposal was eventually shot down by other banks on the committee, and the World Bank declined to participate in it.[73] Meanwhile, the Fund staff (Dooley and Watson) began providing technical assistance to the authorities on how to arrange to buy back their bank loans at market-based discounts.

A partial breakthrough was finally achieved at the end of November, 1988, when the government and the Advisory Committee agreed on the outline for a two-stage approach to reducing Costa Rica's debt burden and settling arrears. In the first stage, Costa Rica would buy back a substantial portion of its bank loans from a subset of creditor banks that were willing to participate, at heavily discounted prices reflecting the prevailing prices in the secondary market. In the second stage, the full set of creditor banks would be asked to choose from among a menu of options to replace the existing loans with bonds or other financial instruments. That specific proposal failed to gain enough support from noncommittee banks, but it did generate the momentum that would carry negotiations to a successful conclusion within a few months.[74]

In February 1989, the government opened negotiations with the Fund on a program to be supported by a new stand-by arrangement. The staff mission to the Costa Rican capital, San José, failed to get an agreement, principally because of differences over the size of the fiscal deficit: the authorities wanted to set a target for the 1989 deficit that was approximately unchanged from the 1988 outturn (3½ percent of GDP), while the staff (led by Armando Linde, Chief of the Central American Division in the Western Hemisphere Department) argued that the deficit had to be reduced by at least ¾ of a percentage point. Naranjo went to Washington to make the case to the Managing Director, and after a telephone conference between Camdessus and Arias, a compromise was reached under which small additional fiscal cuts were accepted.[75]

The ink was barely dry on the Letter of Intent when Secretary Brady announced his support for an institutionalized debt-relief plan on March 10. Costa Rica and the Advisory Committee continued to negotiate over the next two months, but now both sides felt able to telescope the process into a single operation in which the debt buyback would be part of the general menu of exit options offered to par-

---

[73]See "Summary of negotiations with commercial banks" (undated), in IMF/RD Managing Director file "Costa Rica, January–May 1989" (Accession 91/454, Box 4, Section 446).

[74]The buyback scheme required each nonparticipating bank to waive its right to receive a proportional share of any payments, and a number of banks were unwilling to do so on the terms that were offered.

[75]The agreement met the Fund's request that the fiscal deficit be reduced by ¾ of 1 percent of GDP; but it did so by cutting budgeted spending by just ¼ of 1 percent of GDP and deriving the rest by reestimating projected losses by the central bank. The revisions are summarized in memorandums from Beza to the Managing Director, dated February 28 and March 13, 1989; in IMF/RD Managing Director file "Costa Rica, January–May 1989" (Accession 91/454, Box 4, Section 446).

ticipating banks. Agreement on terms was finalized in mid-May, setting the stage for the Fund to consider its own role in the process.

The proposed stand-by arrangement had much to recommend it when the Executive Board met to consider it in the afternoon of May 23, 1989. Not only had the government already demonstrated an ability to implement reasonable policy restraint under extraordinarily difficult circumstances; the country also clearly needed support from the Fund. Costa Rica's external debt to bilateral creditors was large, growing, and heavily in arrears, while obligations to the Fund were at their lowest level since 1981.[76] There were problems, however. One difficulty was that this first case brought forward under the Brady Plan fell short of the guidelines that the Fund had just promulgated that very morning. Because presidential elections would be held in less than a year, the staff had thought it prudent to limit the arrangement to a 12-month stand-by arrangement; the guidelines called for a medium-term program to be in place and supported by an EFF arrangement. The guidelines also called for the program to promote investment, in particular through the support of the Multilateral Investment Guarantee Agency (MIGA, part of the World Bank Group). Costa Rica was not yet a signatory to MIGA and it was still too early in the reform process to project a rise in investment. Nonetheless, as Dara McCormack (Alternate—Ireland) observed, it made no sense to penalize Costa Rica simply because it was a test case for the Brady Plan.[77]

A second problem was the same one that had plagued Costa Rica for five years: the persistence of arrears to the banks. The Brady Plan elements of the stand-by arrangement might help to eliminate those arrears: 25 percent of each scheduled drawing was to be set aside for debt reduction through buybacks or similar schemes, and—once a financing agreement was reached with the banks—Costa Rica had the right to request an augmentation of the arrangement by up to 40 percent of its quota (i.e., by SDR 33.64 million, or approximately $43 million), to support debt-relief operations. But those amounts were small relative to the level of arrears, and it was clear that Costa Rica did not have the means to eliminate arrears completely until it had negotiated concessional terms from the banks, obtained additional assistance from official creditors, and successfully implemented the adjustment program.[78] The staff argued that because the government had adopted a program to eliminate arrears gradually, the Fund should "tolerate" (but not "condone") the temporary continuation of arrears. The Managing Director recommended (for the second time in less than two years) that the Fund approve the exchange restriction under which Costa Rica was accumulating arrears, but (as before) several Executive Directors objected. The proposed decision was ap-

---

[76]At the end of April 1989, Costa Rica owed the Fund SDR 46.84 million (31 percent of quota, approximately $61 million).

[77]Minutes of EBM/89/62 (May 23, 1989), pp. 22–23.

[78]Costa Rica's arrears to the banks amounted to about $300 million. The stand-by arrangement totaled SDR 42 million ($53 million), so the maximum amount available under set-asides and augmentation was on the order of $56 million.

proved only after acceptance of an amendment eliminating the approval of the restriction.[79]

Of more general concern was the proposal to provide for augmentation of the arrangement at a future date. This proposal was without precedent, and several Directors suggested that the Board should avoid prejudging the issue until after the authorities had concluded their negotiations with the banks. In the course of the meeting, both Camdessus and Erb offered amendments that addressed those concerns, and a slightly watered-down version was passed.[80]

Three days after the Fund approved the arrangement, the Paris Club agreed to reschedule Costa Rica's bilateral official debts. Unfortunately, this official support did little to help accelerate an agreement with the banks, who continued to show little interest in compromising. Not only were the banks still fearful about setting a precedent for larger countries, but now many of them were worried about making a longer-term commitment while the Fund's commitment was limited to 12 months.

Naranjo met frequently with Merten and the Advisory Committee throughout the summer, while Linde's staff team worked with the authorities to try to keep the adjustment program—especially fiscal policy—on track. Neither effort had much success, and both became increasingly more difficult as the 1990 election neared. Only after political intervention at the highest level did the Advisory Committee agree to the outlines of an agreement—announced jointly in San José by Arias and U.S. President George Bush—at the end of October, 1989.[81] Meanwhile, owing to an excessive money-financed fiscal deficit (arguably an inevitable result of the delays in obtaining external financing from bank creditors), Costa Rica never did draw on the stand-by arrangement, which expired unused in May 1990.

Although the Fund was unable to provide any money to Costa Rica, the institution did help keep the negotiations on the details of the bank agreement from collapsing, first by having the staff advise both the authorities and the banks on the valuation and the consistency of various options and later by providing what

---

[79]The quotations are from "Costa Rica—Staff Report for the 1989 Article IV Consultation and Request for Stand-By Arrangement," EBS/89/87, Sup. 1 (May 19, 1989), pp. 2–3. The Executive Board Decision was No. 9154-(89/62), adopted May 23, 1989. For the context, see p. 500, above.

[80]After noting the authorities' intention to request the augmentation by 40 percent of quota, the amended decision read: "The Fund will be prepared to consider [such] *an* augmentation in the event that the arrangements for the financing of Costa Rica's program provide for appropriate debt service reduction and upon determination by the Fund that such arrangements are consistent with the [objectives of the program] *guidelines on Fund involvement in the debt strategy, approved at EBM/89/61 (5/23/89)*." The first amendment (deletions in square brackets; additions in italics) was suggested by Erb, to avoid prejudging the amount that might be considered. The second was offered by Camdessus to ensure that the Board would retain the right to consider whether the request was consistent with the Fund's general policy guidelines. Executive Board Decision No. 9155-(89/62); minutes of EBM/89/62 (May 23, 1989), pp. 46–49.

[81]The occasion was a two-day summit meeting of 16 elected heads of government from the Americas, called by Arias to celebrate a century of democracy in Costa Rica.

Erb characterized as a "highly qualified" letter of support to the banks.[82] Finally, on May 5, 1990, just three days before Arias's four years as president were also to expire, Costa Rica and the banks completed the agreement that would go a long way toward ending Costa Rica's decade of crisis. The banks agreed to make at least 60 percent of the $1.8 billion of outstanding medium-term debt (including $325 million in past-due interest) available for Costa Rica to repurchase at 16 cents on the dollar (approximately equal to the price in the secondary market). The remaining debt was to be converted into bearer bonds, a portion of which was to be included in a debt-equity conversion program; and terms on the bearer bonds were to be enhanced if Costa Rica's GDP reached a level 20 percent above the 1989 level. The bulk of the $225 million cost of the package was to be covered by official bilateral sources, most of which had been arranged by U.S. officials.[83] Thus the first case under the Brady Plan ultimately succeeded, with the Fund playing a purely catalytic role.

The Philippines

In many ways, the request by the Philippines for an extended arrangement under the guidelines of the Brady Plan was relatively straightforward. After more than a quarter century of prolonged use of Fund resources, the government that had been elected in 1986—headed by President Corazon Aquino—had finally established a track record of adjustment and adherence to programs. (For the history of the earlier period, see Chapter 13.) Most recently, economic performance had been satisfactory throughout the period of the stand-by arrangement of 1986–88, and that arrangement had been fully utilized. In March 1989, the authorities had signed a Letter of Intent requesting a three-year arrangement under the EFF and had indicated their intention to request that the special features of the Brady Plan be applied to it. The staff assessment was that the authorities' economic program

---

[82]The letter, sent on December 18, 1989, over Camdessus's signature, read in part: "Performance under the stand-by arrangement has been positive in many respects. . . . However, fiscal performance has fallen short of projections. . . . The finalization of the agreement [between the government and the banks], in the context of the implementation of sound economic policies, will be a necessary step toward attaining payments viability for Costa Rica. On the basis of policies that would assure performance in line with the medium-term economic path that had been established, the Fund would be in a position to contribute resources. . . ." In IMF/RD Managing Director file "Costa Rica, May 1989–December 1990" (Accession 91/454, Box 6, Section 446).

[83]Costa Rica put up $42 million from its own foreign exchange reserves. The remainder came from external grants from the United States, Canada, and the Netherlands ($43 million); a medium-term loan from Taiwan Province of China ($40 million); and short-term loans from Mexico, Venezuela, and an offshore affiliate of Costa Rica's National Bank ($100 million). The package is described in detail in "Costa Rica—Debt and Debt-Service Reduction and Refinancing Operations Contemplated Under the 1989 Financing Package," EBS/89/243 (December 27, 1989). The official financing arrangements are described in "Costa Rica—Staff Report for the 1990 Article IV Consultation, Request for a Stand-By Arrangement and External Contingency Financing, and Request for a Purchase Under the CCFF," EBS/91/40 (March 14, 1991), pp. 52–53.

fully qualified for the requested support.[84] When the Executive Board met to consider the request, immediately following the meeting on Costa Rica on May 23, the only question was whether the situation met the just-approved guidelines for the new debt strategy.

The difficulty was that the authorities had made little headway in negotiations with creditors during the two months since the Letter of Intent had been approved, partly because of long-standing differences over how much debt service the country could afford to pay, but also because creditors were reluctant to negotiate until the scope for Fund and World Bank assistance under the Brady Plan was clarified. Consequently, there was a very large ($1.7 billion) financing gap for 1989–90, which would have to be filled through the accumulation of arrears to the banks until an agreement could be reached. Moreover, there was as yet no rescheduling agreement with the Paris Club, and the guidelines emphasized that the Fund would not normally tolerate arrears to official creditors.

Charles Enoch, on behalf of the United Kingdom, objected to the proposal to approve the Philippines' request outright. He preferred instead to approve it in principle, pending further progress in negotiations with official and commercial creditors. He noted that the Philippines had sufficient foreign exchange reserves to fund the program over the next several months, and he concluded that there was no solid basis for going beyond the new guidelines. That view was supported by Directors from Germany, Italy, the Netherlands, and Finland. The majority of the Board, however, concluded that it was important to signal the Fund's support immediately and forcefully both to the Paris Club (which was meeting the following week to consider the Philippines' request for a rescheduling) and to the banks. With five Directors abstaining, the requested arrangement was approved in short order.[85]

The arrangement began well, as the authorities managed to adhere to most of the program targets throughout 1989 while continuing to negotiate with the banks. An agreement was reached in January 1990, under which the Philippines was able to buy back some $1.34 billion in bank loans at a 50 percent discount. The buyback was financed in part using SDR 94 million ($125 million) that had

---

[84]The staff report, "Philippines—Staff Report on Request for an Extended Arrangement and Possible Access to Contingency Financing Under the CCFF," EBS/89/59, Sup. 1, was circulated on May 1, 1989. On May 23, a supplement was circulated requesting the use of set-asides and noting the possibility that a request for augmentation might be forthcoming at a later date.

[85]Minutes of EBM/89/62 (May 23, 1989). The abstaining Directors held approximately 26 percent of the voting power on the Board. The three-year arrangement totaled SDR 661 million ($830 million, or 150 percent of quota). The Board also approved the provision of external contingency financing under the Compensatory and Contingency Financing Facility (CCFF), up to a ceiling of SDR 286 million, and it agreed to consider a request to augment the arrangement by up to 40 percent of quota (SDR 176 million) once an appropriate agreement had been reached with bank creditors. Of that SDR 1.1 billion in potential access, the Philippines borrowed just SDR 236 million, all before the end of 1989. The extended arrangement was canceled in February 1991.

been set aside from Fund drawings made in 1989.[86] Another $150 million was provided by the World Bank through its program under the Brady Plan. Although the economic program of the Philippines later went off track, in this case the Brady Plan had already led directly to a small but significant reduction in the country's debt burden.

Mexico

The third Brady deal came right on the heels of the first two, before the week was over. Three days after approving the Costa Rica and Philippines arrangements, the Executive Board met on Friday, May 26, 1989, to consider a much larger request: a three-year EFF arrangement and related financing for Mexico with a potential value of more than SDR 3.7 billion ($4.6 billion). In contrast to Costa Rica, Mexico had been a prolonged user of Fund resources since 1982 and now owed the Fund SDR 3.36 billion (288 percent of quota, or $4.2 billion). If Mexico were to make maximum use of the proposed arrangement, including the 40 percent augmentation for debt reduction provided by the new guidelines and assuming timely repayment of the existing loans, those obligations would rise to nearly SDR 4.7 billion (400 percent of quota, or $5.8 billion) by mid-1992. The Fund was about to make one of the largest loan commitments in its history.[87]

Coupling Reform with Relief: July 1988–April 1989

Mexico had established a reasonably good record of economic stability by 1989 but was still being buffeted by internal imbalances and external shocks. The 1986–88 stand-by arrangement, discussed in Chapter 10, had been fully utilized, after which the authorities' intention had been not to seek further financial assistance from the Fund but rather to arrange for enhanced surveillance as a means of encouraging support from other creditors. However, 1988 was a presidential election year: Carlos Salinas de Gortari was elected in July with just a hair over 50 percent of the vote, and the once-invincible *Partido Revolucionario Institucional* (PRI) would continue to rule but with a diminished and shaky political foundation. By the time Hurricane Gilbert hit the Yucatan

---

[86]The amount that was to have been set aside from the first drawing (in May 1989) was not disbursed, owing to the lack of progress in negotiations with banks. To support the January 1990 buyback operation, the Executive Board agreed in December 1989 to make that amount available, along with the amount scheduled for that month, and to front-load the set-asides that were to become available in June and December 1990. That decision enabled the authorities to use SDR 94.4 million of the SDR 165.2 million December drawing for this purpose. See "Philippines—Staff Report for the 1989 Article IV Consultation and Review, Waiver, and Modification of the Extended Arrangement," EBS/89/229 (December 1, 1989), pp. 1–3; and minutes of EBM/89/167 (December 20, 1989).

[87]The total potential lending commitment including the possible augmentation and the CCFF drawing had been exceeded in absolute size only by the extended arrangements with India in 1981 and Brazil in 1983.

peninsula in late September, inflation was accelerating, Mexican exporters were losing international competitiveness, and the central bank was rapidly losing the reserves without which it would soon be unable to keep paying interest on the external debt. In short, the government had lost whatever opportunity might have once existed to finance the external deficit without help from the Fund.

Discussions on the possibility of financial assistance began quietly just after the July 1988 elections, when the head of the central bank, Miguel Mancera, went to Washington to meet with the Managing Director. Mancera then arranged a quiet meeting between Camdessus and Salinas in Monterey, Mexico, so that the Managing Director could impress upon the incoming president the importance of strengthening economic policies. (As planning minister, Salinas had advocated much higher spending than the Fund had thought prudent.) Discussions continued at the Annual Meetings in Berlin, and shortly afterward Mexico requested a loan under the CCFF to compensate for a shortfall in petroleum exports and a rise in the cost of cereals imports (maize, sorghum, and wheat) in response to the effect of poor weather on domestic production.

In February 1989, after Salinas had been in office for two months and had implemented a new adjustment program (a modification of the *Pacto*, described in Chapter 10), he decided to seek an extended arrangement from the Fund. Salinas insisted, however, that any arrangement be part of a broader financial package that included substantial debt relief from bank creditors. When the staff team—led by Claudio Loser, Senior Advisor in the Western Hemisphere Department—arrived in Mexico City in mid-February, it was not at all clear how much support the Fund could offer with regard to debt relief, but the mission was cleared to discuss that option along with the terms of a three-year EFF arrangement. That mission did not conclude the negotiations, principally because the authorities had made little progress in securing external financing commitments.[88] The delay was just as well, because the mission ended just one week before Secretary Brady's March 10 speech changed all the assumptions and ground rules on debt relief.

The effect of all of this activity was that when the Brady Plan was launched, discussions were well advanced between Mexico and the Fund on exactly the type of program that the plan was aimed to support. At the end of March, when Mancera went to the Fund to conclude the negotiations, he found a whole new landscape. For the first time, the staff was prepared to acknowledge openly that the magnitude of the external debt was a major independent barrier to the resumption of economic growth: Mexico could no longer expect to get enough "new money" from the banks to reduce its debt-service obligations to a sustainable level, and unless it

---

[88]Memorandum from Loser to management (March 7, 1989); in IMF/RD Managing Director file "Mexico, January–October 30, 1989" (Accession 91/454, Box 2, Section 446). Negotiations over performance criteria were not difficult in this instance. As Jacques Polak observed, the staff "accepted the program essentially as presented" (Polak, 1991, p. 50).

could get to that level, the government could not expect to attract and retain the capital that was essential for growth.[89]

Up to this point, the IMF had only rarely considered exceptions to the practice of requiring that programs be fully financed prior to the release of the Fund's own resources. Those exceptions had been limited to the cases discussed above— Bolivia and Costa Rica—in which the country had substantial arrears to external creditors that could be cleared only gradually. Now that the Brady Plan was in place, it arguably was no longer necessary or even appropriate to wait for other creditors to agree to terms: banks were no longer being asked to increase their exposure, but rather were expected to reduce their claims according to a generally agreed plan that was to be financed in part by the arrangement with the Fund.[90]

The staff was reluctant to abandon the old strategy until it was clear that the banks would support the new one, but the Managing Director accepted that to do so was essential in this case. The critical meeting came on April 3, when Camdessus acceded to the arguments of Mancera and his deputy, Ariel Buira, that Mexico did not have the means to service its debts unless it received financial assistance before financial arrangements were fully in place. With that understanding, the authorities signed a Letter of Intent on April 11, and Camdessus agreed to schedule a meeting of the Executive Board for an early date after the approval of Brady Plan guidelines.

Mexico's Brady Deal: May–July 1989

When the Board met on May 26, 1989, negotiations between Mexico and the banks still had a long way to go. The finance minister, Pedro Aspe Armella, had started the ball rolling by meeting with bank creditors in New York in early April, and the Mexican negotiating team had subsequently presented the Advisory Committee with a menu of alternative debt reduction schemes that were estimated to be equivalent in risk-adjusted net present value but that were tailored to fit the regulatory and other diverse circumstances of individual banks. The committee had, however, expressed skepticism about the menu. Months would be required before enough proposals and counterproposals could be tabled and examined to bring the two sides together.

Directors were mostly satisfied with the program and the proposed financial arrangement. The Fund's resources were expected to be part of a broadly based

---

[89]The use of concerted lending from commercial banks, which less than seven years earlier had been introduced by Managing Director Jacques de Larosière as an emergency measure in the heat of the initial debt crisis, was now dismissed in the staff report as the "traditional new money approach." "Under the assumption that the external financing being sought would be obtained entirely through the traditional new money approach," the report noted, Mexico would see little if any improvement in its external balance or its growth rate. "Debt reduction operations would help avoid these adverse effects. . . ." "Mexico—Staff Report for the 1989 Article IV Consultation and Request for Extended Fund Arrangement," EBS/89/91 (May 9, 1989), pp. 15–17 and 32.

[90]In the Mexican case, the bank deal was also dependent on financing from a structural adjustment loan from the World Bank, loans from the IDB, and a rescheduling agreement with the Paris Club of official bilateral creditors.

package of official support, including substantial "parallel" financing from the Japanese government as a supplement to the usual resources from the Paris Club and multilateral development banks.[91] Several speakers were plainly worried, however, that negotiating an innovative and expensive deal with commercial banks could be a protracted process. Leonor Filardo (Venezuela), speaking on behalf of Mexico, suggested that perhaps the Fund staff should inject their presence more fully into the negotiations, but the Managing Director noted that this was not their proper function.[92] The staff was providing information to the banks regarding the Mexican economic program and was advising the authorities on the financial implications of various debt-reduction options, but it was not participating in the negotiations.

The only point of serious contention at the Board meeting was the handling of the new Brady elements: the proposal to set aside 30 percent of each drawing for debt reduction and to permit augmentation of the arrangement by 40 percent of quota (SDR 466 million, or $580 million) to help finance the pending bank agreement. The guidelines that had been approved three days earlier called for a 25 percent set-aside, not 30 percent. Although a few Directors groused a bit, the general feeling was that Mexico needed the money for this purpose and could be treated as a special case. The proposed augmentation produced more general consternation. The staff proposal was to note that Mexico intended to request augmentation by "up to" 40 percent of its quota, and that the Fund was "prepared to consider an augmentation" when the negotiations with bank creditors were completed. The Mexican authorities countered that proposal with a request that the Board immediately approve a 40 percent augmentation, to become effective upon completion of the bank package.[93] Approval of that request would not only have preceded the completion of an agreement with bank creditors; it also would have taken Mexico over the normal limit on access to Fund resources for the first year of the program.[94]

Mexico's goal in asking for approval at this stage was to impress upon the banks that sufficient money would be available for debt reduction once the banks agreed on terms, and the authorities justified the request on the basis of the strength of their adjustment program.[95] A number of Directors were reluctant, however (as they had been three days earlier when discussing Costa Rica), to commit the Fund ahead of the banks. It was the same problem that had plagued the debt strategy from the beginning: how to turn a vicious circle of reluctance into a virtuous cir-

---

[91]Mexico was not yet a signatory to MIGA, but it had formulated a medium-term investment program that would be supported in part by loans from the World Bank and the IDB.

[92]Minutes of EBM/89/64 (May 26, 1989), p. 47.

[93]Statement by Filardo at EBM/89/64 (May 26, 1989), pp. 15–16.

[94]The access limit in place at the time was 110 percent of quota a year, exclusive of any CCFF drawings. The basic EFF arrangement allowed for 80 percent access, so the augmentation would have raised it to 120 percent. To approve that level, the Executive Board would have to invoke the exceptional circumstances clause of the Fund's access policy. (See Chapter 17.)

[95]Mexico was not asking that the SDR 466 million be made available for immediate disbursement; only that the amount of the augmentation be approved up front. Statements by Filardo at EBM/89/64 (May 26, 1989), pp. 15–16 and 28.

cle of commitments. The Mexican request (approval of which required only a simple majority of votes cast) was supported by a substantial majority, but it lacked a clear consensus. Guenter Grosche (Germany) opposed it, as did most other European Directors with the exception of France; Frank Cassell (United Kingdom) stressed that his opposition was based on the principle of not precommitting before full information on the package was available, not because he had any doubts about the viability of the Mexican program.[96] Altogether, those who preferred to stick with the staff proposal represented about 37 percent of the total votes on the Board.

Not wanting to force a decision on the minority, the Managing Director proposed a typically cautious compromise. He noted that even those Directors who favored waiting agreed that the exceptional level of access would be justified if the debt reduction package was strong enough. On that basis, he suggested that the Board approve the staff's original proposal without the Mexican amendment and that the Board agree by consensus that the access limits would not impede the later approval of 40 percent augmentation. Filardo agreed to go along with that compromise, and it was approved without dissent.[97] The effect was that full augmentation could not take place until the Board had the opportunity to conduct a full review of the implementation and financing of the program.

Other official credits fell quickly into place once approval of the Fund arrangement was secured, and attention turned to the banks.[98] Just a few days after the Executive Board meeting, a high-level team of staff experts on financing options went to Mexico City to provide technical assistance to the authorities on developing a viable menu of debt reduction options (see above, p. 499–500). The following week, E. Gerald Corrigan (President of the Federal Reserve Bank of New York) hosted a meeting in Madrid at which Camdessus, Barber B. Conable (President of the World Bank), and Enrique V. Iglesias (President of the IDB) gave a pep talk to the banks on the Mexican adjustment program and the importance of bank support for the debt reduction strategy.[99] Negotiations continued at an intense level through June and much of July, with the Fund staff providing information and with senior U.S. Treasury and Federal Reserve officials intimately involved, goading the banks along and reminding them of the public policy implications of the agreement.

Finally, on July 23, 1989, the Mexican authorities and the Advisory Committee reached agreement: the first Brady deal to be completed. The term sheet covered

---

[96]Minutes of EBM/89/64–65 (May 26, 1989). Cassell's position is stated in meeting 89/65, pp. 11–13.

[97]Executive Board Decision No. 9162-(89/65), adopted May 26, 1989.

[98]The Paris Club agreed on May 30 to grant Mexico $2.5 billion in debt relief over a three-year period: $1.9 billion by reducing the principal outstanding and $0.6 billion by reducing the present value of scheduled interest payments. On June 13, the IBRD approved three Structural Adjustment Loans totaling $1.5 billion. Additional financing was provided during the year by the IDB and the Export-Import Bank of Japan.

[99]Citibank press release (June 7, 1989); in IMF/RD Managing Director file "Citibank" (Accession 92/194, Box 3, Section 333).

a menu of debt reduction options, each of which was designed to represent approximately a 55 percent discount from the face value of the covered debts (equivalent to the prevailing price of Mexican obligations in the secondary market). In addition to the option of rescheduling existing loans through a new-money facility, the menu permitted banks to replace their loans with 30-year bonds with fully collateralized principal, which could be issued either at par with the loans but with a lower interest rate or at a discount and with a market-oriented interest rate.[100]

From Crisis to Reform: 1989–93

The EFF arrangement and the Brady deal with the banks marked the beginning of the end of Mexico's debt crisis of the 1980s. When Camdessus and Salinas sat down to dinner together in Washington in early October of 1989, the adjustment program was on track, Mexico had made the first two drawings under the arrangement with no difficulty, and the mood of the evening was decidedly upbeat. Though there were a few slips in implementing policies in 1990 (requiring a waiver of some performance criteria),[101] the Mexican economy underwent a rapid transformation and stabilization throughout the period of the EFF arrangement. Inflation fell to single-digit levels, the public sector shifted into a sustained surplus position, net external debt fell by nearly half in relation to domestic output, and private capital began flowing eagerly into the country.[102] Mexico made all of the scheduled drawings under the arrangement, including the augmentation by 40 percent of quota, which was approved by the Executive Board in January 1990.[103]

A much more serious slip would come at the end of 1994, when a new financial crisis would once again place Mexico at the center of the world's attention and create a new and dramatic set of challenges for the IMF. But that is a story for another History.

Venezuela

From Creditor to Debtor: 1988–89

As 1988 drew to a close, the Fund had been conducting enhanced surveillance with Venezuela for 3½ years, in support of a MYRA between Venezuela and its commercial bank creditors. In the last few months, however, deteriorating eco-

---

[100]For a discussion of the agreement, see Wijnbergen (1991). The interest rate on both the new-money facility and the discount bonds was set at 13/16 of a point above LIBOR, the same odd spread that had been agreed upon after so much agony in September 1986 (see Chapter 10). For further details, see "Mexico's Financing Package," EBS/89/171 (August 23, 1989).

[101]See "Mexico—Waiver and Modification Under the Extended Arrangement," EBS/90/58 (March 26, 1990) and "Mexico—Extended Arrangement—Request for Waiver and Modification," Sup. 1 (April 5, 1990), and Executive Board Decision No. 9409-(90/60), April 18, 1990.

[102]See Loser and Kalter (1992) and the paper by Pedro Aspe Armella in Boughton and Lateef (1994), pp. 126–38.

[103]The arrangement was extended in May 1992 and augmented by an additional 40 percent of quota (SDR 466.2 million), but the authorities at that time expressed their intention not to make any additional drawings unless circumstances worsened materially; the arrangement expired in May 1993 with that amount undrawn.

nomic conditions and the cumulative effect of delayed adjustment (aggravated by the campaign for presidential elections that were scheduled for December) had brought a precipitous drop in foreign exchange reserves. Although the crisis was still incipient,[104] the trend—coupled with the country's massive financing needs for 1989 to cope with maturing commercial debts—would soon make it impossible for the government to continue avoiding drawing on Fund resources.[105] Throughout the 1988 electoral campaign, the leading candidate for the presidency, Carlos Andres Pérez, played a delicate verbal game of abusing the Fund as a vicious foreign power while suggesting that he nonetheless intended to use its resources to get the debt problem and the economy under control.[106]

Following Pérez's election on December 4, Venezuela drew the balance of its reserve tranche in the Fund (SDR 254 million, or $340 million) and requested to draw the first credit tranche (SDR 460 million, or $460 million) as well. A team of officials representing both the outgoing and incoming governments went to Washington in mid-January 1989 for discussions aimed at determining the basis for the requested drawing. Through these meetings, the staff learned that the new economic team was planning both a strong adjustment program and a major liberalization of the economy. The discussions therefore quickly moved beyond the requirements for the drawing of the first credit tranche, onto the financing requirements for Venezuela's longer-term program. A general plan was agreed, under which a stand-by arrangement would be negotiated soon after the first-tranche request was considered, to be followed by an extended arrangement once a track record had been established for policy stabilization and toward normalization of relations with bank creditors.[107]

At the end of January, on the weekend before Pérez's inauguration, Camdessus went to Davos, Switzerland, to participate in the annual World Economic Forum, but especially to meet with Pérez. In an hour-long meeting, Camdessus encouraged the president-elect to pursue the proposed program and assured him of his support. Two weeks later, Pérez announced a dramatic shift in economic policy in a televised speech on February 16: interest rate ceilings would be ended, the exchange rate would be unified and determined by market conditions, fuel prices would be doubled (from extremely low and highly subsidized levels), food subsidies would be reduced, and the tax base would be broadened as part of a general package of tax reforms.[108]

---

[104]Net reserves at end-1988 were the equivalent of about 5 months of imports, though much of that amount was illiquid or committed.

[105]Venezuela had never drawn on Fund resources other than to make purchases within its reserve tranche. There had been one stand-by arrangement, in 1960, but it had not been drawn upon; see Horsefield (1969), Vol. 2, pp. 413–14.

[106]Pérez, of the Accion Democratica party, had been president from 1974 to 1979, during the boom years of sharply rising oil revenues.

[107]The authorities also indicated a preference for requesting a drawing through the CFF to compensate for the decline in the world price of oil, but that idea was rejected by the Managing Director when it became clear that the Executive Board was unlikely to accept it without a battle. That issue is discussed in Chapter 15.

[108]For a historical perspective on Pérez's break with the traditional policy orientation in Venezuela, see Naím (1993).

No one expected that such a major turnaround could be achieved easily, but the violence of the public reaction to the announcement stunned the world and quickly led to tragedy. On February 27, the announcement of a rise in bus fares triggered massive riots and looting that left more than 300 people dead. Press reports, taking a view that the government did not discourage, widely blamed the IMF for "imposing" or "dictating" the measures that led to the violence. The Fund, signaling a shift in policy against being used as a scapegoat in such situations, responded with public denials. Notably, in a March 2 speech in Washington to the Institute of Foreign Affairs, the Managing Director stated that the Fund had "not dictated—nor can it ever dictate—measures to a sovereign country." In response to those remarks, Pérez wrote a letter to Camdessus, copies of which he sent to leaders of the major creditor countries, arguing that the "formulas" of the IMF "take no account at all of the . . . economic realities in the countries where they are implemented." The letter, which was to receive wide attention in the world press, concluded: "It is impossible to carry out the necessary and urgent measures to adjust our economy" as long as the major creditor countries "refuse to alter the framework within which we are obligated to pay the external debt."[109] Though Pérez could not have known it, the change that he was seeking in that "framework" was to be announced by Secretary Brady just six days later.

Rhetoric aside, negotiations between Venezuela and the Fund proceeded smoothly through this period of turmoil. Pérez's economic team was aiming to sharply reduce government controls, strengthen private sector activity, and promote the use of market signals. A key element, from the vantage of the Fund, was the replacement of a complex system of multiple exchange rates with a unified and market-determined rate. The government hoped thereby to rebuild reserves by inducing a substantial repatriation of private capital held abroad. Though there were many points of detail to negotiate, there were no fundamental disagreements. Agreement was reached on a Letter of Intent for the first-tranche purchase on February 28, well before Pérez's letter was sent.

When the Executive Board met on March 29, 1989, to consider Venezuela's request to use its first credit tranche, the main issue was the lack of financing assurances from other creditors. In particular, although the authorities had begun negotiations with the banks' Advisory Committee on rescheduling and concerted-lending agreements, those talks had a long way to go. The staff had begun exploring various options for a flexible approach as early as January and had determined (well before the Brady Plan was introduced) that the Fund should not let the banks hold the adjustment program hostage as a means of strengthening their bargaining position vis-à-vis the government. As with Bolivia and Costa Rica, the staff was prepared to recommend to the Board that the Fund tolerate arrears to commercial

---

[109]Pérez's March 4 letter and Camdessus's March 6 reply—which noted that the Fund was supporting the "indispensable" measures that had been decided upon by the Venezuelan government—were published in the *IMF Survey* (March 20, 1989), pp. 81f. For more on this episode and on the more general "scapegoat" issue, see Chapter 14.

creditors as long as the program was on track.[110] Several Directors from industrial countries (including the United States, Japan, and Germany) objected to that recommendation, regarding it as "premature" until the Board could examine the pending request for an extended arrangement. Filardo, speaking for Venezuela, rejoined that to deny approval would seriously weaken the authorities' negotiating position in the coming weeks. In the end, a compromise was reached under which the Fund agreed to tolerate arrears only until the expected date of approval of an upper-tranche arrangement.[111]

Adjustment and Relief: 1989–90

With the hurdle on the treatment of arrears behind them, the staff set out quickly to negotiate a more detailed Letter of Intent for a medium-term program that could be supported by a three-year arrangement under the EFF, with set-asides and augmentation for debt relief under the Brady Plan. A mission (led by R. Anthony Elson, Assistant Director of the Western Hemisphere Department) went to Caracas in mid-April to begin the process, and the Letter was finalized at follow-up meetings in Washington around the middle of May.

Again, the strength of the economic program was not a major issue; agreement was quickly reached. The question now was whether Venezuela was a viable candidate for debt relief under the Brady Plan. The commercial banks were balking, on the grounds that Venezuela was a relatively prosperous and resource-rich country. Whereas the first three Brady cases to come before the Board had per capita incomes in 1988 ranging from $630 (the Philippines) to $1,760 (Mexico), Venezuela's income level was far higher ($3,250). The staff argued, however, that the country's large debt burden meant that per capita income could no longer grow until the debt burden was reduced, and the burden could be reduced only through negotiated relief.[112]

At the Executive Board meeting to consider the EFF request on June 23, 1989, Cassell took up the case against debt relief for Venezuela. Venezuela's debt problem, he argued, was short term, and the country would gain more in the long run by seeking "new money" (concerted lending) and rescheduling rather than relief

---

[110]The draft decision, prepared in early March and circulated to Executive Directors on March 14, read in part, "Venezuela continues to retain exchange restrictions on payments and transfers for current international transactions as evidenced by arrears on certain debt service payments pending the negotiation of restructuring agreements with foreign commercial creditors. . . . The Fund notes the intention of the authorities to eliminate these restrictions . . . and grants approval for their retention until September 30, 1989." "Venezuela—Staff Report for the 1989 Article IV Consultation and Use of Fund Resources—First Credit Tranche Purchase," EBS/89/34, Sup. 1 (March 14, 1989), pp. 24–25.

[111]The draft decision quoted in the preceding footnote was amended by substituting July 5 for September 30 and adding the sentence, "The Fund will review this decision upon approval by the Fund of an upper credit tranche arrangement for Venezuela or on July 5, 1989, whichever is earlier." Decision No. 9112-(89/40), adopted March 29, 1989.

[112]"Venezuela—Staff Report on the Request for an Extended Arrangement," EBS/89/107, Sup. 1 (June 7, 1989), pp. 31–32 and 46–47. Long-term external debt service in 1988 was equivalent to 40 percent of GDP. The comparable figures for Mexico, the Philippines, and Costa Rica were 44, 28, and 20 percent, respectively.

through a Brady deal.[113] That view was supported by a few other speakers from industrial countries (notably Grosche, and E.A. Evans—Australia), but they noted that Venezuela had already embarked on a debt-relief course, so the point was largely moot.

The specific Brady Plan elements of the Venezuelan request were controversial but did not block approval by the Board. The staff proposal to invoke the exceptional circumstances clause and augment the arrangement by 40 percent of Venezuela's quota to support debt reduction was supported by a narrow majority, but Filardo nonetheless withdrew the request at the end of the meeting so as not to threaten the consensus. Directors agreed instead—as they had for Costa Rica and Mexico—that they would be prepared to consider a request for augmentation once negotiations were concluded with bank creditors. The Board then approved the arrangement—including 25 percent set-asides for debt-relief operations—making it the fourth and final Brady deal to be approved by the Fund in 1989. Venezuela was eligible to draw SDR 247 million (just over $300 million) immediately, and the full potential over the next three years (including the possible augmentation) was more than SDR 4.25 billion ($5.3 billion).[114]

The Board's confidence in Venezuela's policies and its concerns about the prospects for an early settlement with the banks were both well placed. To a remarkable degree, Pérez's government succeeded in implementing its economic program, at least for the first two years. For 1989, the overall public sector deficit was held to just 1¼ percent of GDP (compared with 9¼ percent in 1988 and a program target of 2¾ percent), and a surplus of 5½ percent of GDP was recorded for the current account (compared with a 1988 deficit of 10¼ percent and a program target deficit of 3¼ percent). But in July the banks rejected Venezuela's request for debt relief, on the grounds that Venezuela had the capacity to pay its debts in full.[115] An interim financing agreement was finally signed in September 1989, but the Brady deal was not completed until June 26, 1990, a full year into the extended arrangement. In the meantime, the Fund granted waivers for the authorities' inability to maintain the required level of international reserves, and Venezuela basically stayed on track with the arrangement through the middle of 1991.[116]

---

[113]Minutes of EBM/89/80 (June 23, 1989), p. 35.

[114]Enhanced surveillance was effectively suspended for Venezuela in March 1989, in that the authorities agreed not to send the staff report for the first-tranche purchase to the banks. (Fund policies prohibited circulation of reports that also evaluated a request to use Fund resources.) The authorities formally requested suspension of enhanced surveillance along with their request for the extended arrangement; that request was approved by the Board on June 23.

[115]According to Willard C. Butcher, the Chairman of Chase Manhattan Bank (the lead bank on the Advisory Committee), "The banks rejected the proposal because [Venezuela]'s request for debt reduction was excessive and not based on needs. . . . We think Venezuela has the resources to service its debts. . . ." July 25, 1989, letter to the *New York Times*, published on July 29, p. A24.

[116]Following the completion of the bank financing package, the Fund augmented the EFF arrangement in December 1990. At end-1990, Venezuela had drawn close to SDR 1.8 billion ($3 billion) under the arrangement and had an undrawn balance of SDR 2.1 billion ($2.6 billion). The program then went off track, and no further drawings were made.

Adjustment Without Relief: Argentina and Brazil

Not all of the Fund's efforts to help countries reduce their debt burdens in 1989 arose out of the Brady Plan. For two of the three largest debtors in Latin America, the only realistic goal for the Fund at that time was to maintain a dialogue and to try to promote a restoration of stable economic policies.

Argentina

Argentina had some early success in normalizing relations with commercial bank creditors. In particular, the August 1987 agreement between Argentina and its foreign bank creditors introduced several innovative options that prefigured the more formal menus that were adopted after the Brady Plan and that helped Argentina. These options included issuing relatively small claims under the new-money package in the form of bearer securities; substituting low-interest exit bonds (i.e., bonds not subject to future calls to participate in new-money agreements) for new-money claims; and the use of early-participation fees to encourage banks to commit at an early stage.[117] By 1989, however, when a more systematic and substantial effort might have been possible, the economy and government policy were mired down, and the authorities were unable to take advantage of the improved environment.

Plan Primavera: May–August 1988

Argentina's debt situation was becoming desperate in the early months of 1988. The 1987–88 stand-by arrangement with the Fund had been kept barely alive through waivers and amendments, and the United States was still providing short-term financing bilaterally,[118] but the banks had been less willing to compromise. When negotiations bogged down through the first quarter of 1988, Argentina quietly went into arrears to the banks and then for a time paid just enough interest to keep arrears from accumulating to 90 days (a trigger point, after which some creditor banks would have had to declare the loans to be nonperforming). The authorities were convinced that the first priority was to obtain relief from the debt burden, after which they could implement a stronger adjustment program; the Fund, however, saw stronger adjustment as a precondition for progress in debt negotiations. This difference in perspective had been papered over in the compromise that had temporarily reactivated the stand-by arrangement in March 1988 (see Chapter 10), but it had not been resolved.

In May 1988, President Raúl Alfonsín got personally involved in the public effort to obtain debt relief from the banks. In a major May 1 speech to congress, he

---

[117]For the background on the development of the 1987 agreement, see Chapter 10; for a summary of the agreement, see Watson and others (1988), p. 11.

[118]As described in Chapter 10, two multilateral bridge loans had been provided in 1987 by a group of creditor countries led by the United States; when additional financing was required in March 1988, the United States provided the full amount on its own.

rejected suggestions for unilateral action but called for creditors to negotiate relief through operations such as interest rate reductions, debt-equity conversions, and direct cancellation or reduction of the stock of outstanding debt. Then at the end of the month, he met with the Managing Director in Washington to see what help the Fund might provide. Camdessus, however, could offer only limited encouragement. Whatever debt relief might be obtainable was an issue to be settled between Argentina and the banks. As he had in the February meeting described in Chapter 10, Camdessus promised to support Argentina in that effort, but only after the government presented a credible and effective economic program. The president then went to New York, where he met with the heads of a number of the major creditor banks. A few days later, Camdessus met with several of those same bankers and painted a mixed but generally upbeat picture. Argentina and its creditors, he noted, faced two problems: the need for better economic policies and the need for additional external financing while those policies were being implemented. The first problem was a matter for the Fund, while the second required help from the banks, and he asked for cooperation from the banks as negotiations continued.[119]

Alfonsín was publicly taking a hard line on debt, but the basis for Camdessus's expression of support was that the government was also secretly developing a new policy program. The authorities knew they had to stabilize the economy through the next year: the year of the first presidential election since the one that ended military rule and brought Alfonsín to power in 1983. To make sure the program would generate international support, they consulted with the Fund throughout July, as the plan was being developed. Beza and Desmond Lachman (Chief of the River Plate Division) met with senior officials in Buenos Aires in mid-July, and a team of officials then visited the Fund for further talks. Although the staff repeatedly objected that the plan was lacking in specific proposals to rein in the fiscal deficit, the talks led to an agreement that once the new policies were announced, formal negotiations could begin on a new stand-by arrangement with the Fund.[120]

The Plan Primavera was unveiled on August 3, 1988, in anticipation of the coming spring in the southern hemisphere. Like the Austral Plan and its variants, the Plan Primavera was a heterodox package that aimed to break the momentum of inflationary expectations, but which included too little fiscal adjustment to produce lasting stability.[121] The exchange rate was devalued by 11.5 percent and was to be fixed against the dollar for two months; after that, both the rate of deprecia-

[119]Based on speaking notes prepared for the meeting; in IMF/RD Managing Director file "Argentina, 1988–1987" (Accession 89/118, Box 1, Section 511).

[120]The Fund staff had made a brief effort earlier in the year to persuade the authorities to develop a medium-term stabilization plan that could be supported by an extended arrangement with the IMF, but the government was unwilling to do so without the (unobtainable) support of the opposition Peronist party.

[121]The details of the Plan were circulated to Executive Directors on August 17; see "Argentina—Economic Policy Package of August 3, 1988," EBS/88/170. For a list of references and a brief discussion of how this plan fit into the evolution of economic policy in Argentina, see Kamin and Ericsson (1993), pp. 2–5. For a detailed "insider" account, see Machinea (1990), pp. 73–88.

tion and the rate of increase in controlled prices were to be fixed at 4 percent a month in a bid to prevent the plan from unraveling and to preserve the gain in international competitiveness from the devaluation.[122]

Sibling Rivalry: September 1988

The Plan Primavera produced a brief outpouring of optimism, but the Fund insisted on seeing firm policy implementation before it would resume lending. In August, Camdessus refused to yield to a direct appeal from Secretary Baker and other U.S. officials. Nonetheless, in early September, Lachman took a mission to Buenos Aires to try to negotiate a one-year stand-by arrangement. Although arrears to banks had reached $800 million by the end of August, negotiations with the Advisory Committee were progressing, and achievement of a preliminary agreement and a critical mass of commitments before Christmas seemed like a realistic goal. Arriving in Buenos Aires, however, the staff learned (as it had several times before) that fiscal policies were not being implemented as planned and that the deficit therefore could not be held under the anticipated ceiling without major new policy actions. For 1989, the government intended to set a target of about 3¾ percent of GDP for the deficit, a level that to Lachman appeared unsustainable.

The staff team returned to Washington on September 15, just a week before the center of Fund activity was to shift temporarily to Berlin, where the Annual Meetings were to be held at the end of the month. The goal of the staff and the Managing Director was now quite simple: to persuade the Argentine authorities that a renewed tightening of fiscal policy was a precondition for making any progress with the Fund or other creditors. That view, however, was not universally held, and a major rift was about to erupt that would significantly dilute the Fund's message.

Throughout 1988, a dispute had been brewing between those in the Fund and the World Bank who were independently negotiating with the Argentine authorities on the terms of pending loans.[123] The Fund's focus on fiscal control was sharply questioned by the Bank staff, who sided with the Argentine authorities in viewing the most urgent problem as being structural reform. In the Bank staff's view, being tough on the stance of fiscal policy made it too difficult for the authorities to implement the very reforms that the Bank was proposing to finance.

---

[122]The Austral Plan, as discussed in Chapter 10, had failed in large measure because the fixed exchange rate could not be sustained once domestic inflation rose above world levels.

[123]The differences in view were deep-seated and predated the open policy dispute by more than two years. In January 1986, while the Fund and the Bank were attempting to develop a coordinated response to the Baker plan, de Larosière expressed concerns to the Bank president, then Tom Clausen, that the Bank's draft country strategy paper on Argentina was taking a position on macroeconomic policies that was at variance with the views of the Fund. The Managing Director was reassured by the response, but later efforts by the staff to persuade the Bank to modify the tone of the paper were unsuccessful. See memorandum for files prepared by the Managing Director (January 23, 1986); in IMF/RD Research Department file "World Bank Collaboration, September 1983–February 1989" (Accession 89/129, Box 3, Section 276).

The Bank staff also argued that sufficient external financing was available to cover a somewhat larger fiscal deficit than the level on which the Fund was insisting. In the Fund staff's view, Argentina could not expect to control inflation or achieve a sustainable balance between domestic saving and investment without a more ambitious program to control expenditure and broaden the tax base. Intense political pressure from the U.S. authorities for the Fund and the Bank to lend—and lend quickly—did not help to resolve the matter.

Both staff positions were reasonable, but the resolution of the debate was further complicated by a conviction on both sides that they had to protect their turf in dealing with member countries. The two Bretton Woods institutions had periodically confirmed the general understanding that the IMF had primary responsibility for "policies related to balance of payments adjustment" and that it was essential to avoid giving conflicting advice to member countries; nonetheless, it was also understood that the "financial implications of economic development programs" were a matter of concern to both institutions.[124] Those understandings did not preclude the Bank from reaching agreements with a member country regarding the appropriate stance of macroeconomic policy to underpin a Bank loan, but it did imply that the Bank should fully take the Fund's views on such policies into account. In dealing with Argentina in 1988, the Fund staff believed that their counterparts across 19th Street were acting improperly in reaching an understanding with the government on policies that were at the very heart of the Fund's own negotiations. The Bank staff believed that such an agreement was essential to safeguard the Bank's own interests and the Bank's own relations with the member country. Camdessus and Barber Conable (President of the Bank) often discussed the need for coordination and cooperation on Argentina as the dispute developed, but with little effect.

By September 1988, the Bank staff had negotiated a "Letter of Development Policy," on the basis of which the Bank was to make a package of four loans totaling $1.25 billion.[125] Although that Letter included a statement of the authorities' intentions with respect to fiscal policy that was more expansionary than the policy on which the Fund staff was insisting as a condition for the stand-by arrangement, it was approved by Conable for submission to the Bank's Executive Board. After informing Camdessus, Conable then announced on September 25, in a press conference in Berlin, that he was proposing that the Bank go ahead with the loans. The announcement gave rise to a general impression that Argentina was prepared to bypass the Fund in developing its adjustment strategy, and it suggested that the Bank was prepared (on this occasion) to concede more to pressure from the United States than was the Fund. It also gave rise to concerns in some creditor countries and among bankers that indebted countries might try to play the two institutions

---

[124]The first quotation is from the Managing Director's summing up of a 1980 review of Fund-Bank relations; the second is from the original 1966 understanding on the subject. For a fuller discussion, see Chapter 20.

[125]One loan was related to trade policy; the other three were sectoral loans related to housing, banking, and electric power.

against each other in an effort to reduce conditionality on multilateral credits.[126] Whatever view one takes regarding the wisdom or appropriateness of Conable's decision,[127] it unquestionably complicated the Fund's effort to persuade Argentina to tighten fiscal policy and thereby delayed the negotiation of a stand-by agreement.

Hyperinflation: October 1988–July 1989

Following the meetings in Berlin, discussions with the Argentine authorities drifted for a few months without making much progress. A late-October staff visit concluded that the fiscal deficit was still worsening and was unlikely to be held below 4 percent of GDP for 1989. In November, the banks' Advisory Committee proposed terms for a package deal that would have covered the authorities' request for $3.5 billion in financing in 1989 through $2 billion in concerted lending, of which $500 million was to be guaranteed by the World Bank, plus $1.5 billion in exit bonds. Much remained to be negotiated, however, and the prospect of a guarantee from the World Bank was by no means certain. While those negotiations continued, Argentina still was not paying current interest on its existing bank loans.

The Plan Primavera collapsed in February 1989, just six months after its introduction. As the authorities had been unwilling to let interest rates rise sharply in this preelection period and had therefore been unable to hold price inflation to the specified rate of 4 percent a month, the fixed rate of depreciation had been insufficient to maintain international competitiveness or stabilize the level of official reserves. Now the government introduced a system of multiple exchange rates and allowed the rate for capital account transactions to float; that slowed down the reserve losses, but it also led to a reacceleration of inflation and a resumption of capital flight.

In the last three months before the May 1989 presidential election and the two months between the election and the inauguration of Alfonsín's successor, the Argentine economy slid rapidly toward total collapse.[128] Despite various efforts by the

---

[126]For typical press reports, see The Wall Street Journal (September 26, 1988), p. 3 ("a furious behind-the-scenes quarrel between the U.S. and . . . Camdessus"); and London's The Independent (September 26, 1988), p. 18 ("an unprecedented break with past practice"). The facts were that the U.S. authorities were lobbying hard behind the scenes for both institutions to approve the loans to Argentina and that the Fund's management specifically rejected that advice. The extent to which the Bank's approval resulted from U.S. pressure rather than from the Bank staff's undoubted conviction that the loans were appropriate is a difficult judgment.

[127]On October 27, the Executive Board of the World Bank approved the loans with three abstentions and one vote against. The opposition focused primarily on the potentially adverse effects on Fund-Bank relations. The process was supported by a $500 million bridge loan arranged through the BIS with backing or financing from ten central banks, the U.S. Treasury, and the Kreditanstalt für Wiederaufbau of the Federal Republic of Germany. (See the BIS Annual Report, 1988–89, pp. 198–99.) After the initial disbursement, Argentina's failure to meet the Bank's conditions prevented the completion of the loans. For other accounts of this episode, see Polak (1994), which is largely complementary to the one given here; and Kapur, Lewis, and Webb (1997), pp. 527–31, which presents a contrasting view from the Bank's perspective.

[128]The constitution provided that the new government would take office in December, seven months after the election. In June, a deal was struck under which Alfonsín agreed to resign in early July so that his successor could take early action to deal with the economic crisis.

authorities to regain control over the exchange rate, the austral depreciated from 20 per dollar in mid-April to 655 on July 10. By then, official intervention had stopped, owing to a lack of reserves; arrears to foreign banks had surpassed $5¼ billion; payments to the Fund had also gone back into short-term arrears;[129] and inflation had hit the astronomical level of nearly 200 percent a month. All that anyone could do in such circumstances was to wait for the new government to turn policies around.

First Steps Toward Renewal: July–November 1989

The May 1989 election would eventually bring historic change to economic policy in Argentina and confound the conventional wisdom. The main opposition candidate and the man who would win the election was Carlos Saúl Menem,[130] who, partly because he was the leader of the traditionally populist Peronist party, partly because of occasional campaign rhetoric advocating a hard line on external debt service, was not expected to become a leader of the "silent revolution" in Latin America. On taking office on July 8, Menem demonstrated that necessity is the mother of revolution as well as invention.[131]

Menem's first move was to announce a new shock program, not unlike the Austral or Primavera plans in its heterodoxy, but unlike them in also being orthodox and recognizing the need for fiscal discipline. The exchange rate was sharply devalued on July 9, and Menem announced a broad range of fiscal measures that included tax reforms, curtailing of subsidies, and extensive privatization of public sector enterprises. To promote credibility, Menem also proposed to give the central bank independence from having to finance the government.[132]

---

[129]Argentina had briefly fallen behind in its payments to the Fund in January and February 1988 (see Chapter 10), but then had stayed current for a year. The government next missed a payment to the Fund at the end of March 1989. A number of partial payments were made over the next several months, and the level of arrears generally fluctuated between 30 and 60 days overdue (less than the threshhold for triggering action by the Fund) before being cleared in the second half of the year.

[130]Under the Argentine constitution, Alfonsín was limited to one term in office. The Radical party was represented in the election by Eduardo Angeloz, who garnered 37 percent of the vote, compared with 47 percent for Menem. The constitution was later amended, and Menem successfully ran for reelection in May 1995.

[131]Fears of a confrontational approach were also fueled by Menem's decision during the transition to take on Harvard economist Jeffrey D. Sachs as an advisor. As noted in Chapter 10 (Bolivia) and below (Brazil), Sachs had previously advised Argentina's neighbors to insist on debt relief from commercial and official creditors. Sachs, however, had a deeper message: lowering debt-service outflows was a means of ensuring that the country would retain the benefits of fiscal adjustment. Since Argentina had already delayed paying interest on bank debts, Sachs's advice to Menem apparently focused primarily on the design of the adjustment program.

[132]"Argentina—Staff Report for the 1989 Article IV Consultation and Request for Stand-By Arrangement," EBS/89/199 (October 17, 1989), pp. 7–19. Just before the devaluation, the official exchange rate was 300 australes per dollar, and the rate in the parallel market was about 560. The devaluation set the official rate at 650; the parallel rate quickly moved to that level, and the spread between the two rates remained quite small for the next few months.

Menem invited the Fund to send a mission right away to conduct the annual Article IV consultations. When the staff team (led by Lachman) arrived in late July, they were informed that the government wanted to negotiate a new stand-by arrangement as soon as possible. This time, negotiations moved swiftly and smoothly. A follow-up mission in September, headed by Joaquín Ferrán (Deputy Director of the Western Hemisphere Department), produced a general agreement on terms, including a fiscal target of 1¼ percent of GDP for 1990 (compared with an expected outturn of 16 percent in 1989).[133] The authorities signed a Letter of Intent specifying their program goals in mid-October, submitted the supporting legislation to Congress the following week, resumed negotiations with the banks' Advisory Committee, and submitted a request to the Paris Club to reschedule official credits.

The Executive Board approved the request for Argentina's thirteenth stand-by arrangement (the fourth since 1982) on November 10, 1989. The staff report on the proposal stressed that while Argentina was making substantial strides, it had a long way yet to go.[134] There was as yet no possibility of considering debt relief under the Brady Plan. The authorities still had to normalize relations with the creditors to whom they had outstanding arrears, including the World Bank and other official creditors as well as the banks. If that effort proceeded as expected, then the Fund could expect to consider granting an extended arrangement with set-asides or augmentation for debt relief sometime in 1990. Despite the reservations expressed by several Executive Directors—lingering doubts engendered by six years of repeated program failures—there was no dissent from the approval of the new arrangement.[135]

That Board meeting concludes the history of relations between Argentina and the IMF in the 1980s. It ends, much like Richard Wagner's *Götterdämmerung*, with the promise that a new order will soon emerge from the destruction of the old. The new order, however, was not yet fully defined at the end of 1989. Like its predecessors, the 1989–91 stand-by arrangement quickly ran into a conflict between the need for even stronger adjustment and reform and the political realities at home. Not for another two years would Argentina finally find the will and the means to achieve financial stability.

Brazil

Seeking Debt Relief: July–December 1987

Brazil's effort to gain relief from its debt burden began in earnest in the middle of 1987. Shortly after implementing a temporary wage-price freeze in mid-June,

---

[133]"Argentina—Letter of Intent," EBS/89/194 (October 12, 1989), p. 2.

[134]"Argentina—Staff Report for the 1989 Article IV Consultation and Request for Stand-By Arrangement," EBS/89/199 (October 17, 1989). The arrangement totaled SDR 1,113 million (100 percent of quota and equivalent to $1.4 billion), to be disbursed in six installments through March 31, 1991.

[135]Minutes of EBM/89/145 (November 10, 1989).

the finance minister, Luiz Carlos Bresser Pereira, made his first official trip to Washington, with the goal of winning support for a proposal to capitalize up to 60 percent of the interest due on outstanding bank loans.[136] He met with Senator Bill Bradley, who told him that the banks were unlikely to accept the plan. He then had dinner with Camdessus, who told him that officials in creditor countries were not ready to support such a plan. But the next day, he met and spent several hours with Jeffrey Sachs, who told him that he could never get both economic growth and price stability without first obtaining substantial debt relief. Bresser Pereira went home more discouraged but also more determined.

Back in Brazil, Bresser Pereira—still determined to avoid seeking assistance from the Fund—decided to modify his proposal for debt relief by asking for a 50 percent discount on 20 percent of the debt rather than a capitalization of interest. U.S. Treasury Secretary James Baker then invited him to meet with him in Washington in early September to discuss the idea. At that meeting, Bresser Pereira thought that he had won Baker's support for a voluntary debt reduction scheme along the proposed lines and for delinking negotiations with the banks from those with the Fund. Baker, however, publicly denied that a deal had been struck, and the effort succeeded only in sowing ill will.[137]

The Brazilian authorities pushed ahead with their bid to obtain debt relief. In late September, just before the Annual Meetings, the negotiating team presented a detailed proposal to the Advisory Committee in New York. The proposal called for "securitization of a portion of the debt" owed to commercial banks and expressed interest in "a menu of alternatives," including the conversion of debt into equities. It proposed that interest payments be capped, with the ceiling no higher than LIBOR and linked to the country's "true payment capacity." It suggested issuing "debt conversion bonds" (essentially, exit bonds) that would not be subject to rescheduling or new-money requests because their terms would be linked to capacity to pay.[138] The negotiators asked that these proposals be deliberated independently of the status of Brazil's discussions with the Fund.

The banks rejected this last request, insisting that Brazil would have to show progress in negotiating a Fund program before any medium-term agreement could be completed. Nonetheless, the prospect of granting relief was kept alive enough that Bresser Pereira finally agreed to seek an arrangement with the Fund. That opening generated enough progress to get to an "interim agreement" in December 1987, under which Brazil would pay one-third of the current interest due for the fourth quarter and the rest would be financed by a group of creditor banks. Unfor-

---

[136]The following account is based partly on Bresser Pereira (1999) and partly on background interviews.

[137]Bresser Pereira (1999) blames David Mulford, Baker's deputy, for scuttling the agreement. In any event, it seems likely that the dispute arose from a misunderstanding and that Baker conveyed more sympathy than he really intended. For a contemporary report, see *New York Times* (September 9, 1987), p. D1.

[138]"Proposal with Respect to Certain Brazilian External Debt Held by Commercial Banks," (September 25, 1987), pp. 3–6; in IMF/RD Managing Director's files (Accession 89/14, Box 1, Section 550).

Número 8990

CORREIO BRAZILIENSE

ÓRGÃO DOS "DIÁRIOS ASSOCIADOS" LONDRES, 1808, HIPÓLITO JOSÉ DA COSTA. BRASÍLIA, 1960, ASSIS CHATEAUBRIAND

Brasília, segunda-feira, 23 de novembro de 1987

FMI chega para preparar o acordo

Bresser, com o apoio do PMDB, diz que o pacote não incluirá congelamento

JORGE CARDOSO

Oliveros, Rossi, Reichmann e Clifton: a missão do FMI espera uma pizza, exercitando a paciência que deverá ter para descobrir o déficit
GIVALDO BARBOSA

A missão do Fundo Monetário Internacional, que chegou ontem a Brasília, reúne-se hoje com o Banco Central para começar a levantar a situação da economia brasileira e preparar as bases para um futuro acordo com o País. "Já que vamos fazer um acordo no futuro, solicitei a vinda de uma missão precursora", — explicou o ministro da Fazenda, Luiz Carlos Bresser Pereira, ao desembarcar no aeroporto em companhia do presidente do PMDB, da Câmara e da Constituinte, Ulysses Guimarães. O chefe da missão do Fundo, Thomas Reichmann, confirmou que uma das suas preocupações é avaliar o tamanho do déficit público, que começará a ser cortado com o próximo pacote de

medidas econômicas destinado a conter a inflação. Antes do acordo com o Fundo, o Brasil pretende concluir o acerto da dívida externa com os bancos credores. "Somente depois disso é que formalizaremos as bases das negociações com o Fundo" — disse Bresser, que destes os rumores sobre sua saída do Governo ao procurar, e obter em São Paulo, o apoio de Ulysses. O ministro garantiu que o "plano de emergência" para segurar a inflação, a ser divulgado antes do fim do ano, não inclui um novo congelamento de preços. O pacote tem como principal objetivo aumentar a arrecadação fiscal, principalmente através de cortes nos gastos públicos, sem taxar o assalariado.   Página 7.

Headline news: IMF mission members Eric Clifton, Doris Ross, Thomas Reichman, and Gumersindo Oliveros featured on Brasilia newspaper's front page as "waiting for a pizza, exercising the same patience that they will need to discover the size of the deficit."

tunately—as recounted in Chapter 10—it was not enough to generate political support for fiscal reform in Brazil, and Bresser Pereira felt compelled to resign when he realized that he could not deliver an effective adjustment program.

Negotiating New Agreements: January–September 1988

The new year brought new momentum. Brazil's negotiators met with the Advisory Committee on the terms of a medium-term agreement throughout the first two months of 1988 and reached agreement—conditional on reaching understandings with other creditors, including the Fund—at the end of February. Then, after a series of technical discussions, the Fund sent a staff team out in May—led by Thomas Reichmann (Assistant Director for the Atlantic Division of the Western Hemisphere Department)—to negotiate a stand-by arrangement. The mission had a limited objective, aiming simply to maintain the momentum until more effective and sustainable adjustment could be implemented later. This strategy was governed by what Reichmann saw as a sequencing problem: inflation was running at such a high level (about 600 percent a year) that it could be stopped only by a shock program, but the operational fiscal deficit was so high (about 7 percent of GDP) that it had to be brought under control before a shock program could work. The goal of both the Fund staff and the new authorities in Brazil (led by Bresser Pereira's successor as finance minister, Mailson Ferreira da Nóbrega) was therefore to get a conventional adjustment program in place quickly, to buy time until a shock program could be implemented in 1989.

The strategy succeeded. In quick succession in June 1988, the authorities signed a Letter of Intent for a Fund-supported program, finalized the agreement with the banks' Advisory Committee for a medium-term package that included several of the innovative menu options that Brazil had requested a year earlier, and persuaded the Paris Club to consider rescheduling official credits. The Executive Board then approved the stand-by arrangement in principle on July 26, pending completion of the other financing arrangements. The Board meeting was a collective sigh of relief, as Directors welcomed the return of "the prodigal son," which they regarded as both "an important day in the history of the Fund" and "a cause for particular rejoicing."[139]

The rejoicing was not confined to Washington. Two days after the Fund approved the stand-by arrangement in principle, Paris Club creditors agreed to reschedule Brazil's obligations to them. Moreover, commercial bank creditors responded with unaccustomed alacrity, and the Advisory Committee rounded up the critical mass of commitments (covering 95 percent of the $5.2 billion loan) by August 18, 1988:

---

[139]Minutes of EBM/88/115/R-1 (July 26, 1988), pp. 36 (G.P.J. Hogeweg, Alternate—Netherlands), 41 (Jacques de Groote, Belgium), and 14 (Frank Cassell, United Kingdom), respectively. The arrangement was for SDR 1,096 million (75 percent of quota), or approximately $1.4 billion. It was to run through February 28, 1990, with six scheduled disbursements. The cutoff date for the arrangement to come into effect, conditional on a finding by the Fund "that satisfactory arrangements have been made for Brazil's foreign commercial bank financing," was September 9, 1988. Executive Board Decision No. 8927-(88/115), adopted July 26, 1988.

three weeks ahead of schedule. The stand-by arrangement then went into effect on August 23, enabling Brazil to immediately draw one-third of the total amount of the arrangement (SDR 365.3 million, or approximately $470 million).[140]

The Program Fails: October 1988–November 1989

By mid-November, Brazil applied part of the proceeds of the Fund, Paris Club, and commercial bank packages to clear all of its arrears to foreign creditors. Domestically, the government signed a social pact with labor and business groups, as the first stage of a plan to stabilize prices by de-indexing the economy. There was much to celebrate, but true stabilization was still years away. As it had been from the beginning, the debt crisis was, at its heart, a fiscal crisis. Without fiscal discipline, Brazil could do no more than delay the day when it once again would be unable to pay. On October 5, 1988, a new constitution was adopted, under which the obligation of the federal government to transfer revenues to the states was sharply increased. When Reichmann's team went to Brazil later that month to begin what would become a long effort to conduct the annual Article IV consultations and review progress under the stand-by arrangement, the devastating effects of the constitutional change were not yet clear. By the time the consultations were completed nearly a year later, the government's accounts were out of control.

The authorities tried to regain control over the economy in January 1989, through what became known (in an echo of Argentina's Plan Primavera) as the Summer Plan. The key elements of the program were the introduction of a new currency (the new cruzado, replacing the old one at an exchange of 1:1,000), a 14 percent devaluation against the U.S. dollar, a freeze on prices, and an end to automatic wage indexation. It also included some fiscal measures, but they were small in relation to what was required.[141] The Summer Plan failed to brake inflation, which nearly doubled from 934 percent in 1988 to 1,765 percent in 1989, and it failed to control the operational budget deficit, which rose from 4.8 percent of GDP in 1988 to 6.9 percent in 1989.[142]

Discussions between the Fund and the authorities continued throughout 1989, both in Brazil and in Washington. Although there was no shortage of goodwill on either side, all efforts to keep the program on track were doomed by the constraints on fiscal policy. The August 1988 drawing was the only one that Brazil would make on the stand-by arrangement—Brazil's only drawing, in fact, since the extended arrangement had collapsed nearly four years earlier.

---

[140]Executive Directors of the Fund were officially notified on August 19 that the critical mass of bank commitments had been obtained. They then approved the stand-by arrangement on a lapse-of-time basis, without further discussion. The bank package became effective on September 22. See "Brazil—Stand-By Arrangement—Effective Date," EBS/88/130, Sup. 3 (August 19, 1988), and Decision No. 8956-(88/126), adopted August 23, 1988.

[141]"Brazil—Staff Report for the 1988 Article IV Consultation," EBS/89/189 (September 27, 1989), p. 16.

[142]The inflation figures are for the consumer price index. Other general indexes showed similar rates of increase. See "Brazil—Recent Economic Developments," SM/91/201 (September 30, 1991), pp. 11 (inflation) and 20 (fiscal deficit).

At the end of October 1989, the Executive Board finally concluded the 1988 Article IV consultations, in a meeting that was dominated by what Cassell (who just 15 months earlier had spoken of Brazil as a source of "rejoicing") called "a sense of sadness." Everyone who spoke expressed concern about the failure to control the fiscal accounts or to stabilize prices. Some representatives of developing countries laid a good part of the blame on the difficult external environment, but most stressed that Brazil needed to come to grips with its internal political constraints. Brazil's Executive Director, Alexandre Kafka, noted that part of the explanation for the fiscal overruns originated in the effect of the impending presidential election on the budget; and part of it originated in the constraints imposed by the new constitution. Johann Prader (Alternate—Austria) observed that these constraints led to a "minimalist approach to adjustment . . . in which excessive damage to the economy was avoided rather than . . . one in which conditions were created for a durable solution to Brazil's financial imbalances." On the whole, the Board was hopeful that the elections would bring real change to Brazil. "The time for gradualism had clearly run out," as the Managing Director put it, but if the new government were to make a "fundamental attack on inflation," the 1990s would not have to be a repeat of the 1980s.[143]

Appendix: Fund Policy on Financing Assurances and Arrears

In 1970, the Fund formalized a policy that recognized that external payments arrears generally resulted from governmentally imposed exchange restrictions. That policy stated that Fund approval of such restrictions should be granted only if the authorities adopted a program aimed at eliminating them within a fixed period. It also provided that "Fund financial assistance to members having payments arrears should be granted on the basis of performance criteria or policies . . . [that] provide for the elimination of the payments arrears within the period of the stand-by arrangement." For the complete statement and decision, see de Vries (1985), Vol. 3, pp. 214–15. For background, see de Vries (1985), Vol. 1, pp. 591–93.

That policy was modified in 1980 by an agreement that, "depending on the member's circumstances and the length of the program, it might not be feasible in the early stages of the program to go beyond an understanding that the member would try to avoid any further increase in outstanding arrears." The new policy was as follows.

The Fund's policies on payments arrears are also concerned with their treatment in the context of stabilization programs supported by use of the Fund's resources. In these programs, member countries are expected to take steps to reduce and eventually eliminate payments arrears relating to capital transactions as well as to payments and transfers for current international transactions. In formulating policy guidelines in these programs, the staff will continue to be guided by the approach set forth in the Executive Board decision of 1970 . . . [cited above]. This approach will also be followed with respect to payments arrears arising from default. The technique chosen by a member to reduce outstanding arrears will reflect its institutional arrangements, as well as the magnitude of the arrears and the severity of the

---

[143]Minutes of EBM/89/137/R-1 (October 27, 1989). The quotations are from pp. 18 (Prader), 30 (Cassell), 55 (Kafka), and 56 (Camdessus).

balance of payments problem. When payments arrears are large in relation to a member's available foreign exchange resources, it may not be possible to aim at the elimination of the arrears within the program period. Special arrangements may be needed for the renegotiation of outstanding debt obligations when debt problems are particularly severe. Depending on the member's circumstances and the length of the program, it may not be possible, in the early stages of a program, to reach an understanding with the member that goes beyond requiring the avoidance of any further increase in arrears.[144]

Fund policy was modified further in April 1983 in light of the debt crisis. The Managing Director summed up the Executive Board's discussion of policies on "External Debt Servicing Problems" with the following remarks on financing assurances.

Executive Directors commented on the relationship between balance of payments assistance from non-Fund sources and the implementation of Fund-supported adjustment efforts by members experiencing debt-servicing difficulties.

First, Directors considered the way in which the Fund collaborates with official institutions in multilateral debt renegotiations to be generally satisfactory. Some of them had said that the various official creditors should receive similar, evenhanded treatment, if only to ensure continued cooperation among official creditors. Directors felt that any special elements that might be involved in the relationship between Fund-supported programs and the debt relief envisaged by the Paris Club, or other groups concerned with official multilateral debt renegotiations, should continue to be handled on a case-by-case basis.

It was evident that in the case of some countries, only the provision of further concessional aid could make the rescheduling exercise successful. In those circumstances, it would be the duty of the Fund to put the matter squarely before the members of the international community able to provide aid. The straightforward rescheduling of official debt might occasionally be inadequate; more might be required even if the provision of extended assistance were to complicate the renegotiations.

Directors recognized that the procedures for rescheduling commercial bank debt were not as well developed as those for official debt negotiations. Nonetheless, the Fund could play, and had played, a useful role in bringing about a successful outcome to discussions between a debtor country and the commercial bank groups involved. Since the summer of 1982, certain "exceptional" circumstances had arisen, in which the difficulties encountered by major debtors have had broader implications for the orderly functioning of the international monetary system. The Fund management—in concert with major creditors, central banks, the BIS, and governments—had taken the initiative in ensuring that before Fund resources could be committed, sufficient additional financial flows from governments, official sources, and commercial sources were available to support the adjustment efforts of the member concerned. Directors had endorsed that approach, although some of them had cautioned against the Fund as a matter of general policy interjecting itself too closely or too systematically into traditional commercial bank/client relationships. They had encouraged the Fund to maintain a generally neutral role. The consensus was that the Fund should proceed on a case-by-case basis in full consultation with all the parties involved, bearing in mind the need for evenhanded treatment between cases.

---

[144]This paragraph was taken from the concluding section of EBS/80/190 (August 27, 1980), except that the final sentence was amended by the Executive Board. It was accepted as a statement of Fund policy at EBM/80/154 (October 17, 1980) and was published in *Selected Decisions*.

Third, Executive Directors noted the inevitable degree of uncertainty regarding the amount and timing of external financing that could be made available during the period of an adjustment program supported by the Fund's resources. Such uncertainties should not necessarily prevent a member country wishing to enter into an arrangement with the Fund from doing so. But the Executive Board would need sufficient safeguards to ensure that the Fund's resources would be used to support a viable and financeable adjustment program. The best means of providing such safeguards—in the absence of any conclusion to the negotiations on non-Fund financing of a Fund-supported program—was considered to be the practice of introducing review clauses at an early stage of the program, linked, if necessary, to the satisfactory outcome of discussions on balance of payments financing from other sources. The staff would indicate in its reports what additional adjustment measures should be contemplated by the authorities if the amounts of external financing assumed by the staff did not materialize.[145]

Finally, in May 1989, the Board adopted a much more flexible policy in response to the Brady Plan. The full text of the summing up of that discussion is reproduced here.

The Chairman's Summing Up on Fund Involvement in the Debt Strategy
Executive Board Meeting 89/61, May 23, 1989

This has been an important discussion, following the guidance of the last meeting of the Interim Committee, with a view to laying the basis for broad guidelines for the Fund's role in the evolving debt strategy and, in particular, for Fund support for debt and debt service reduction. It is clearly the wish of this Board that the Fund discharge in full its central responsibilities in the debt strategy, but without interference in negotiations between debtors and creditors. We recognize that we are at an experimental phase in the debt strategy and will keep all aspects of developments under review as I will describe more specifically below.

In considering Fund support for debt and debt service reduction operations in conjunction with appropriate flows of new money, Directors emphasized the central importance of sustained implementation of policy reforms in debtor countries. They stressed that all parties in the debt strategy should continue to play their respective roles and, in particular, that official creditors should not substitute for private creditors. Fund support for debt reduction operations would be linked to medium-term adjustment programs with a strong element of structural reform, adopted in the context of stand-by or extended arrangements. Particular emphasis would be given to measures that would improve the climate for saving and investment in borrowing countries, and help reverse capital flight and attract private capital inflows and direct investment. Adherence to MIGA was seen by a number of Executive Directors as a useful step in the investment area. Utilization of debt-equity swaps, where compatible with a member's fiscal and monetary policy framework, has also been seen by a number of Directors as a particularly effective means of attracting a return of flight capital.

Executive Directors agreed that requests for Fund support of debt and debt service reduction operations would be considered on a case-by-case basis. Particular reference would be made to three elements—the strength of economic policies; the scope for voluntary, market-based debt reduction operations that would help the country regain access to credit markets and attain external viability with growth; and an assessment as appropriate that such operations represent an efficient use of scarce resources.

---

[145]Minutes of EBM/83/58 (April 6, 1983), pp. 36–37; published in *Annual Report 1983,* pp. 162–63.

Executive Directors strongly emphasized the importance of ensuring continued support for countries that have succeeded in maintaining market access and would not engage in officially supported debt reduction. The creditor community, including the Fund, will need to watch the situation of these countries carefully to ensure that they are not harmed by changing circumstances and that appropriate assistance continues to be forthcoming. This is an important area to which Directors have agreed to return before the Annual Meetings.

Directors stressed that it will be important to keep the Fund's liquidity position under close review. It is considered that the provisions for Fund support of debt and debt service reduction operations that have been discussed could be accommodated without an undue deterioration in the Fund's liquidity position in the near term. However, the implications of the Fund's support of debt and debt service reduction operations will need to be taken into account by Executive Directors in considering the factors bearing on the need for an increase in quotas under the Ninth General Review of Quotas. In particular, Fund support for debt reduction operations must not be allowed to reduce the Fund's ability to support members that are not engaging in such operations.

As regards the particular modalities of Fund support for debt and debt service reduction, Executive Directors agreed that in appropriate cases part of a member's access under an extended or stand-by arrangement could be set aside to finance such operations. The exact size of the set-aside would be determined on a case-by-case basis, but would involve a figure of around 25 percent of access determined on the basis of existing access policy. A number of Directors noted the importance of principal reduction in helping to ease the member's debt burden, and it was agreed that set-aside amounts should be used to support operations involving principal reduction, such as debt buy-backs or exchanges.

The availability of the set-aside amounts would generally be phased in line with program performance. Where warranted, some front-loading could be considered or purchases could be phased in accordance with the specific financing needs of the member's debt reduction program.

Directors agreed that there could be an initial release of Fund resources in support of debt reduction if the program was on track, if the Board was satisfied with the authorities' description of the debt reduction program, and on the understanding that debt reduction operations would be market based or, at market-related prices, involving substantial discounts. Initial purchases under the set-aside could be made available from the outset of an arrangement if these conditions were met. Otherwise, purchase rights would accumulate and be made available upon completion of a review by the Board of the debt reduction plan.

Executive Directors also agreed that in appropriate cases the Fund would be prepared to approve requests for additional resources of up to 40 percent of a member's quota,[146] where such support would be decisive in facilitating further cost-effective operations and catalyzing other resources, consistent with significant further progress toward external viability. The additional resources from the Fund are to be used for interest support in connection with debt reduction or debt service reduction operations. It was understood that the amount of additional resources to be provided would be determined on a case-by-case basis, in light in particular of the magnitude of the member's balance of payments need and the strength of its adjustment program as well as its own efforts to contribute resources, as feasible, in support of the operations. The limit for additional access is not to be regarded as a target. In considering a request for additional resources, the Executive Board would be presented with detailed information, as available, on the operations to be supported; the timing of actual

---

[146]This limit was reduced to 30 percent of a member's quota (see Buff/92/133).

disbursements to the member would need to be determined in light of the specific operations. Access pursuant to such requests would be additional to that determined under the existing guidelines for enlarged access, it being understood that the present policies on enlarged access will continue to apply, including the exceptional circumstances clause.

In the event a commitment by the Fund to provide additional access for the purposes specified were not used, the commitment would expire at the end of the arrangement period. The member would be expected to make early repurchases of amounts drawn under a commitment of additional access, to the extent that the amounts were not used within an appropriate period for the purposes described in the member's request.

Directors stressed the importance of ensuring that resources made available for debt and debt service reduction operations were used effectively. Directors agreed that there would be a need for periodic reviews to consider how debt reduction operations compare to the Board's initial expectations; if appropriate, the Board could in such reviews reconsider the modalities of the Fund's support for the member's debt reduction plan.

Executive Directors noted that the World Bank would likely be involved, along with the Fund, in supporting debt reduction operations when these are important elements in a country's financial and development strategy. In these cases, Directors stressed that it was important that the two institutions work together closely in securing effective debt reduction. This does not mean each institution must provide equal amounts in each case, as the amounts will need to be taken on a case-by-case basis. The managements of the two institutions are working closely on these matters and Executive Directors will be kept informed of the progress made in support of these operations on a continuing basis.

In discussing financing assurances, Executive Directors reaffirmed the basic objectives of the Fund's Policy—ensuring that the program is fully financed; that the financing is consistent with a return to viability and with the ability of the member to repay the Fund; that there is fair burden sharing; and that the program, if appropriately implemented and supported, would contribute to the maintenance or re-establishment of orderly relations between the member and its creditors.

Nevertheless, Directors agreed that there is a need for cautious adaptation of the Fund's policy in light of the changed financial environment and the possibility that in some cases significant time may be needed for banks and the member to agree on an appropriate financing package. In such circumstances, the Fund would on a case-by-case basis approve an arrangement outright before the conclusion of such negotiations, provided that prompt Fund support is judged essential for program implementation, that negotiations between the member and its bank creditors have begun, and that it can be expected that a financing package consistent with external viability will be agreed within a reasonable period of time. Management would continue to consult with Executive Directors at an early stage in such cases. Progress in the negotiations with bank creditors would be closely monitored, and any unforeseen development brought to the Board's attention. When circumstances warrant, the practice of seeking a critical mass, as well as the possibility of approving an arrangement in principle, would remain valid.

Directors stressed that in promoting orderly financial relations, every effort must be made to avoid arrears, which could not be condoned or anticipated by the Fund in the design of programs. Nevertheless, an accumulation of arrears to banks may have to be tolerated where negotiations continue and the country's financing situation does not allow them to be avoided. Directors emphasized that appropriate safeguards would need to be incorporated into the monitoring procedures of the Fund arrangement. The Fund's policy of nontoleration of arrears to official creditors remains unchanged. The debtor member would be expected to continue to treat creditors on a nondiscriminatory basis. Directors agreed that while negotiations with bank creditors were continuing, the situation would need to be monitored closely. Performance criteria would be quarterly. A review of progress in the negotiations would be scheduled at an appropriate time and, normally, before the second disbursement.

These essential points provide a clear, and clearly limited, basis for the Fund to proceed with initial country operations. We are at an early stage, but we must move forthrightly to begin implementation. It is understood that the Fund's policy, and the precise modalities for application of the policy, will evolve under the Board's guidance as individual cases come forward, or are reviewed, and in light of continuing staff studies. We will take stock of progress in connection with our discussion of the management of the debt situation before the Annual Meetings, and we will plan to review the overall experience in a year or earlier if the situation requires.

References

Bank for International Settlements, 1989, *Annual Report 1988/98* (Basel: BIS).

Boughton, James M., and K. Sarwar Lateef, eds., 1994, *Fifty Years After Bretton Woods: The Future of the IMF and the World Bank* (Washington: IMF and World Bank Group).

Bulow, Jeremy, and Kenneth Rogoff, 1988, "The Buyback Boondoggle," *Brookings Papers on Economic Activity: 2* (Washington: Brookings Institution), pp. 675–704.

Bresser Pereira, Luiz Carlos, 1999, "A Turning Point in the Debt Crisis and the Bank: A Brazilian Memoir," *Revista de Economia Politica*, Vol. 19 (April–June), pp. 103–30.

Castillo, Carlos Manuel, 1988, "The Costa Rican Experience with the International Debt Crisis," in *Development and External Debt in Latin America: Bases for a New Consensus*, ed. by Richard E. Feinberg and Ricardo Ffrench-Davis (Notre Dame, Indiana: University of Notre Dame Press), pp. 210–36.

Clark, John, 1993, "Debt Reduction and Market Reentry under the Brady Plan," *Quarterly Review*, Federal Reserve Bank of New York, Vol. 18 (winter), pp. 38–62.

Cline, William R., 1995, *International Debt Reexamined* (Washington: Institute for International Economics).

Collyns, Charles, and others, 1992, *Private Market Financing for Developing Countries*, World Economic and Financial Surveys (Washington: International Monetary Fund).

Corbo, Vittorio, Morris Goldstein, and Mohsin Khan, eds., 1987, *Growth-Oriented Adjustment Programs* (Washington: International Monetary Fund).

Corden, W. Max, 1988, "Debt Relief and Adjustment Incentives," *Staff Papers*, International Monetary Fund, Vol. 35 (December), pp. 628–43.

_____, 1989, "An International Debt Facility?" in *Analytical Issues in Debt*, ed. by Jacob A. Frenkel, Michael P. Dooley, and Peter Wickham, pp. 151–71.

de Vries, Margaret Garritsen, 1985, *The International Monetary Fund 1972–1978: Cooperation on Trial*, Vols. 1 and 2: *Narrative and Analysis;* Vol. 3: *Documents* (Washington: International Monetary Fund).

Dooley, Michael P., 1986, "An Analysis of the Debt Crisis," IMF Working Paper 86/14 (Washington: International Monetary Fund).

_____, 1988, "Buy-Backs and Market Valuation of External Debt," *Staff Papers*, International Monetary Fund, Vol. 35 (June), pp. 215–29.

_____, 1989, "Buy-Backs, Debt-Equity Swaps, Asset Exchanges, and Market Prices of External Debt," in *Analytical Issues in Debt*, ed. by Jacob A. Frenkel, Michael P. Dooley, and Peter Wickham, pp. 130–50.

Frenkel, Jacob A., Michael P. Dooley, and Peter Wickham, eds., 1989, *Analytical Issues in Debt* (Washington: International Monetary Fund).

Horsefield, J. Keith, ed., 1969, *The International Monetary Fund, 1945–1965: Twenty Years of International Monetary Cooperation*, Vol. 1: *Chronicle*, by J. Keith Horsefield; Vol. 2: *Analysis*, by Margaret G. de Vries and J. Keith Horsefield with the collaboration of Joseph Gold, Mary H. Gumbart, Gertrud Lovasy, and Emil G. Spitzer; Vol. 3: *Documents* (Washington: International Monetary Fund).

Hummer, William B., 1983, "A Report on the 1983 International Monetary Conference: Brussels, Belgium" (unpublished; Chicago, Illinois: Wayne Hummer & Co.).

Kamin, Steven B., and Neil R. Ericsson, 1993, "Dollarization in Argentina," International Finance Discussion Paper No. 460 (Washington: Board of Governors of the Federal Reserve System).

Kapur, Devesh, John P. Lewis, and Richard Webb, 1997, *The World Bank: Its First Half Century*, Vol. 1: *History* (Washington: Brookings Institution).

Klein, Lawrence R., and Angelos Th. Angelopoulos, 1989, *Third World Debt: Some Proposals for Action* (New York: Athens Printing Co.).

Kugler, Jacek, 1987, "The Politics of Foreign Debt in Latin America: A Study of the Debtors' Cartel," *International Interactions*, Vol. 13, No. 2, pp. 115–44.

Lawson, Nigel, 1992, *The View from No. 11: Memoirs of a Tory Radical* (London: Bantam Press).

Lissakers, Karin, 1991, *Banks, Borrowers, and the Establishment: A Revisionist Account of the International Debt Crisis* (New York: Basic Books).

Loser, Claudio, and Eliot Kalter, 1992, *Mexico: The Strategy to Achieve Sustained Economic Growth*, IMF Occasional Paper No. 99 (Washington: International Monetary Fund).

Machinea, José Luis, 1990, "Stabilization under Alfonsín's Government: A Frustrated Attempt," Documento CEDES/42 (Buenos Aires: Centro de Estudios de Estado y Sociedad).

Morales, Juan Antonio, and Jeffrey D. Sachs, 1990, "Bolivia's Economic Crisis," in *Developing Country Debt and Economic Performance*, Vol. 2: *Country Studies—Argentina, Bolivia, Brazil, Mexico*, ed. by Jeffrey D. Sachs (Chicago: University of Chicago Press), pp. 157–268.

Naím, Moisés, 1993, *Paper Tigers and Minotaurs: The Politics of Venezuela's Economic Reforms* (Washington: Carnegie Endowment for International Peace; distributed by the Brookings Institution).

Nelson, Joan M., 1990, "The Politics of Adjustment in Small Democracies: Costa Rica, the Dominican Republic, Jamaica," in *Economic Crisis and Policy Choice*, ed. by Joan M. Nelson (Princeton, New Jersey: Princeton University Press), pp. 169–213.

Polak, Jacques J., 1991, *The Changing Nature of IMF Conditionality*, Essays in International Finance, No. 184 (Princeton, New Jersey: International Finance Section, Department of Economics, Princeton University, December).

———, 1994, *The World Bank and the IMF: A Changing Relationship*, Brookings Occasional Papers (Washington: Brookings Institution). Reprinted in Vol. 2 of *The World Bank: Its First Half Century*, by Devesh Kapur, John P. Lewis, and Richard Webb (Washington: Brookings Institution, 1997).

Volcker, Paul A., and Toyoo Gyohten, 1992, *Changing Fortunes: The World's Money and the Threat to American Leadership* (New York: Times Books).

Watson, Maxwell, and others, 1988, *International Capital Markets: Developments and Prospects*, World Economic and Financial Surveys (Washington: International Monetary Fund,).

Wijnbergen, Sweder van, 1991, "Mexico and the Brady Plan," *Economic Policy*, Vol. 6 (April), pp. 13–42.

Williamson, John, 1988, *Voluntary Approaches to Debt Relief* (Washington: Institute for International Economics).

Zombanakis, Minos, 1983, "The International Debt Threat: A Way to Avoid a Crash," *The Economist* (April 30), pp. 11–15.

12

Case by Case:
A Retrospective on
the Debt Strategy

As the preceding chapters have shown, the IMF played a major role in managing the strategy for overcoming the debt crisis that engulfed Latin America in the 1980s, and in fostering a remarkable transformation in economies throughout the region. Although the value of the Fund's role was widely acknowledged, a number of criticisms became part of the conventional wisdom about the debt crisis. Some of these criticisms reflect a perception that the Fund tended to act on behalf of the interests of creditors and industrial countries more than those of the indebted developing countries; others, that the Fund was acting outside the traditional framework established at Bretton Woods; and some, that the technical analysis was limited or weak.[1] This chapter reviews the main criticisms.

Was the Debt Crisis One of Solvency and Not Liquidity?

When the crisis hit in 1982, the IMF and creditor governments sought to contain it through a "case-by-case" strategy aimed at providing enough additional financing to cover the time required for the indebted countries to implement adjustment programs and generate enough growth to restore normal financial relations. The additional financing, however, was mostly in the form of debt obligations: obligations which, as Cline (1983) was early to note, would be appropriate only if the debtor faced a liquidity rather than a solvency crisis. As Eichengreen and Kenen (1994) later summarized the implications, "In imprecise but helpful terms, an insolvent debtor must pursue a debt-reducing strategy, but an illiquid debtor should pursue a debt-raising strategy so as to make its interest payments and defend its creditworthiness."

The primary difficulty with this argument, as Eichengreen and Kenen acknowledged, is the ambiguity of the distinction between a liquidity shortage and insol-

---

[1]Left aside here is criticism concerning specific elements of program design in individual countries, or concerning any failure to foresee or forestall the initial onset of the crisis. Those issues are clearly important, and they are examined in earlier chapters. The emphasis in this overview chapter, which is based in part on Boughton (1994), is on systemic issues relating to the role that the IMF played in crisis management during this period.

vency.[2] If a country has enough real resources to generate the foreign exchange to service its debts but faces a temporary inability to convert resources into foreign exchange, then it faces a liquidity crisis; without sufficient real resources, it faces a solvency crisis. In that strict sense, none of the heavily indebted Latin American countries ever faced a solvency crisis in the 1980s.[3] Mexico—to take the most readily quantifiable example—had petroleum and natural gas reserves totaling some 72 billion barrels, valued at more than $2,000 billion in 1982, compared with outstanding external public sector debts totaling just over $60 billion. Merchandise exports (mostly by the public sector) totaled $21 billion, compared with scheduled debt-service payments (amortization plus interest) on external public sector debts of $16 billion.[4] Brazil's situation was more precarious: export receipts in 1982 amounted to $18 billion, compared with scheduled debt-service payments of more than $15 billion, and by end-year net international reserves were negative. Even in that case, however, the problem was not a shortage of real resources. It was rather that the degree of required adjustment in domestic expenditure or tax policy for the authorities to mobilize those resources was simply not feasible within the available time horizon.

Even if this criticism has been inaccurately formulated, its underlying premise is still valid. A more accurate—and more relevant—phrasing would be to charge that insufficient attention was paid to the political feasibility of the required

---

[2]A number of analysts avoided this pothole by jumping into even deeper ones. For example, Edwards (1989) contrasted what he regarded as the view of the Fund staff in 1983, that the crisis was "a temporary liquidity problem," with his own conclusion that it "has become a development problem" (p. 38). Meller (1994) contrasted a "temporary lack of liquidity" with "a critical problem of stock imbalance" (p. 4). A 1987 Fund staff paper distinguished between "liquidity problem countries" and "debt overhang cases"; "World Economic Outlook—Recent Economic Developments and Short-Term Prospects," SM/87/54 (February 25, 1987), p. 92. While such taxonomies are helpful for some purposes, they are not clear analytical distinctions. A liquidity shortage, far from being inconsistent with deeper and more fundamental problems, is often an indicator that such problems may be developing.

[3]A less strict approach to distinguishing between liquidity and solvency is to examine whether the country has actually mobilized the resources to service its debts, either through a general adjustment program to generate a sufficiently large trade surplus or through fiscal contraction sufficient to generate the required revenues directly. By a measure focusing on the trade surplus, Cohen (1985) concludes that most Latin American countries undertook sufficient adjustment to remain solvent in the first year or two of the debt crisis; the exception was Argentina, but only because capital flight had wiped out the benefit of the trade surplus. In a later and more detailed analysis, Cohen concluded that Brazil, Mexico, and Venezuela undertook sufficient adjustment in the early 1980s to be considered solvent by this criterion, while most other countries in his sample did not. See Cohen (1991), Chapter 6. More arbitrarily, one could attempt to assess whether the required adjustment would be feasible or practicable to undertake. For example, in March 1984, Alvaro Donoso—the Executive Director for Chile at the Fund—argued that "almost all" of the heavily indebted developing countries were solvent, in that they could stabilize or reduce their external debt in relation to GDP by generating moderate trade surpluses and thereby accepting moderate losses in domestic investment and output growth; minutes of EBM/84/49 (March 30, 1984), p. 14.

[4]Figures are contemporaneous IMF staff estimates derived from government data. Estimates for private sector debts are less reliable. Adding them in would raise both debt and debt service by about one-third.

adjustment or to the real economic costs of the increased indebtedness engendered by the additional financing that characterized the first few years of the debt crisis (see, for example, Dornbusch, 1993, pp. 53–55). To continue with the example of Mexico, imports in dollar terms fell by two-thirds from 1981 to 1983 and remained depressed through 1987, and real wages declined by a similar magnitude; meanwhile, the stock of external debt *rose* by more than a third. The magnitude of these changes and the effects that they had on Mexico's economic stability were far greater than anyone foresaw in 1982.

To some extent, lack of foresight on how much adjustment was required resulted from optimism in assessing the growth prospects of Latin American countries after the debt crisis. Throughout the region, the adjustment programs developed in 1982 and 1983 were predicated on forecasts of a rapid resumption of economic growth that would gradually bring down-debt service *ratios* to sustainable levels. In Mexico, the late-1982 staff projection for real GDP showed zero growth in 1983, 3 percent growth in 1984, and 6 percent in 1985. For Brazil, the program initially assumed a 3½ percent decline in real GDP in 1983, to be followed by growth of 2 percent in 1984 and 4 percent in 1985. Not surprisingly, output growth proved to be difficult to forecast in the prevailing crisis conditions. Perhaps more surprisingly, however, the forecasts *on average* were only modestly optimistic. At one extreme, in Mexico, three-year growth totaled 2 percent, compared with the initial projection of 9 percent. But in Brazil, growth totaled 10 percent through 1985, compared with a forecast 2 percent. For the whole region, the one-year-ahead forecasts published in the IMF's *World Economic Outlook* added up to just over 6 percent growth, and the outturn was closer to 4 percent.[5] Excluding Brazil, of course, the gap would have been wider.

The explanation for the slowness of growth to resume in some but not all heavily indebted countries after 1982 is complex and cannot be encapsulated in the liquidity-solvency dichotomy. First, a drop in real wages was essential to restore financial balance, but wage cuts also depressed aggregate demand. Hence, a few countries that resisted adjustment were able to maintain short-run growth better than those that took early action—but that growth was unsustainable without the needed adjustment.[6] Second, both the Fund staff and officials in indebted coun-

---

[5]The three-year forecasts described above were made only for countries requesting the use of IMF resources through the Extended Fund Facility. For other countries, forecasts were normally made only for 12 to 18 months ahead (or for the period of a requested stand-by arrangement). For Argentina, for example, in December 1982 the staff projected 4 percent growth for 1983. The outturn for that year was 3¾ percent, and growth faltered only after the end of the program period. For Chile's two-year stand-by arrangement, the staff projected 4 and 5 percent growth for 1983 and 1984, respectively. The outturn was ¾ of 1 percent for 1983, followed by almost 6½ percent growth the following year.

[6]Brazilian output essentially stopped growing after 1986, while growth resumed in Mexico. For 1983–86, the average annual growth rates for the two countries were 4½ percent and –½ of 1 percent, respectively. For 1987–92, growth averaged ¼ percent a year in Brazil and 3 percent in Mexico. (Subsequently, Mexico developed a new crisis, and Brazil implemented new reforms.) Also see Chapter 10, especially Figure 10.1.

tries were slow to recognize the breadth of structural reform that was necessary if macroeconomic stabilization was to be implemented without stunting growth. Not until the mid-1980s did market liberalization and reform become a full partner with stabilization. Third, and largely for these reasons, political resistance to effective adjustment was strong and prevented some countries from fully implementing the programs to which they had agreed. These factors were in principle foreseeable. If they were not fully incorporated in the projections, bias would result.[7]

In addition, however, important unforeseeable factors were at work. For one, protectionism, especially through nontariff barriers, reduced the markets for developing country exports and affected different markets in quite different ways.[8] Even more important, export market conditions varied across commodities: oil prices (important for Mexico) drifted downward throughout the first half of the 1980s and collapsed in 1985–86; coffee prices (important for Brazil) were reasonably strong in the early 1980s, skyrocketed in 1986 in response to a disastrous harvest, and then collapsed; copper prices (important for Chile) weakened at the beginning of the decade and rose sharply toward the end. On balance, commodity price declines weakened growth in Latin America during the critical adjustment period in the early 1980s. Correcting for that effect would explain part—but only part—of the bias.[9]

Did the IMF Serve the Interests of Banks and Not Its Member Countries?

Sachs (1989, p. 84) stated this argument clearly: "The basic strategy of the IMF and the creditor governments since 1982 . . . has been to ensure that the commercial banks receive their interest payments on time."[10] Dooley (1995, p. 10) concluded "that for a long time the strategy that was intended to force the banks to continue to lend while the debtor countries embarked on reform programs worked in the narrow interests of the banks." Lissakers (1991, pp. 201 and 206) characterized the IMF of the early 1980s as an "enforcer" for creditors that "let the banks exact harsh terms from already desperate borrowers on the grounds that this was the only way to keep smaller banks in the game."

The basis for this criticism is that the net effect of indebted countries reaching agreements with the Fund and the banks in the 1980s was to transfer resources from debtors to creditors. That is, the combination of the temporary reduction in debt-service payments under rescheduling agreements and the provision of "new

---

[7]IMF forecasts assume that programs that have been agreed upon will be implemented. The question is whether the projections made in the course of negotiating the program were realistic.

[8]See World Bank (1987), pp. 133–53.

[9]For an assessment of the effects of commodity price changes on output growth, see World Bank (1994), Chapter 2.

[10]Also see Sachs (1986) for elaboration.

money" through IMF-supported concerted lending was generally less than the originally scheduled debt service. Hence indebted countries still had to make net payments to banks and thus in a direct financial sense were worse off than if they had just defaulted.[11]

The underlying premise is that in the absence of concerted lending, the indebted countries would have had to default, after which the discounted value of the banks' assets would have been substantially lower. Moreover, because the exposure of a number of the major money-center banks to heavily indebted countries exceeded their capital, a series of defaults—but not a series of negotiated reschedulings—could have led to a collapse of the international banking system. Clearly the IMF played a key role in preventing that catastrophe. The right question, however, is not whether the Fund helped the banks. The question is whether it did so at the expense of, rather than to the mutual benefit of, the indebted countries.

The case for mutuality of interests rests directly on two arguments: that default would result in a loss of access to international capital markets, and that the value to indebted countries of maintaining access exceeds the real economic and political cost of the adjustment that is required if the country is to be able to service its debts. Both the requirements for and the value of capital market access have been extensively debated, without a clear resolution.[12] The Fund position, however, was based on the logically prior proposition that the required adjustment would be beneficial for its own sake, regardless of its ability to crowd in private foreign capital.

To understand the IMF position on this issue requires a perspective broader than that of a game-theoretic model of financial relations. From a macroeconomic perspective, maintaining debt service is one element of a strategy to prevent a slide into autarky. The heavily indebted countries in the early 1980s could not service their debts in the short term without obtaining external support, and they could not service them in the longer run without undertaking fundamental policy reforms. Even if these countries could have defaulted without rupturing future relations with creditors, the prevailing view in the Fund was that they would have been worse off in that case than if they had undertaken the required policy adjustment and stayed current on interest payments to creditors. The case for this proposition rests essentially on the value of the adjustment program, rather than on the expected penalties from default.

Alternatively, taking a financial perspective, it is instructive to focus on the size of the country's financing gap and the means of filling it in. Given external and domestic economic conditions, the magnitude of the adjustment in policies determines the size of the external deficit to be financed. Ex post, that deficit must be

---

[11]Some critics of the Fund have drawn the opposite conclusion, namely, that concerted lending worked against the banks' interests. Roland Vaubel, for example, has argued that Fund lending generally benefits bank creditors by improving debtors' creditworthiness. Through concerted lending, however, "the IMF extracts from the banks part of the gain that its lending confers to them" (Vaubel, 1991, pp. 217–18).

[12]Calvo (1989) develops a "theory of penalties" to explain the ambiguities. For a sympathetic view of default from a former World Bank vice president, see Knox (1990).

equal to the sum of multilateral, bilateral official, and private credits. The standard procedure for the IMF in dealing with most heavily indebted countries from late 1982 through early 1989 was to negotiate as much adjustment as was feasible, factor in as much official financing as was available, and insist that the lending exposure of the existing bank creditors increase by enough to fill in the remaining gap. This procedure was effective as long as the residual was substantially less than the scheduled interest payments due to banks during the period in question, and as long as the banks' initial exposure was large in relation to their capital base. Only if both conditions were met, as they were during the first three or four years after the crisis began in 1982, did the banks have a collective interest in playing the game and in not trying to use their leverage to exact highly favorable terms from desperate borrowers. Given the short-term constraints imposed by the feasibility of adjustment, the availability of official financing, and market conditions, the alternative strategy in those years would have been to fill the gap through the accumulation of arrears. As discussed in Chapter 11, the IMF rejected that strategy until late in the decade on the grounds that it would have endangered the international financial system and rendered the persistence of effective adjustment impossible.

Although economic theory does not suggest that default is necessarily an inferior option to negotiated settlements, the record on policy reform in Latin America suggests that it usually is. Countries that adopt unilateral policies on debt service seem likely to experience economic deterioration quickly, and countries that delay macroeconomic adjustment seem likely to become worse off after a spurt of short-term benefits. The first category would include Peru under Alan García and Brazil under José Sarney. The second category would include (for much of the 1980s) Argentina as well as Brazil. In contrast, successful postcrisis adjusters such as Chile, Mexico, and Bolivia at least laid the basis for more balanced growth over the longer run. The eventual realization of that growth will provide the surest test of the case-by-case strategy.

Did the IMF Recognize the Need for Debt Relief?

When the Brady Plan was introduced in March 1989, the IMF reacted quickly to support it and to play a key role in implementing it. For several years preceding that development, however, a variety of debt-relief proposals were floated by advocates including Bill Bradley, Henry Kaufman, Peter Kenen, James Robinson, and Felix Rohatyn; and the emergence of official support was reflected during 1988 in proposals such as the Mitterrand and Miyazawa plans. During that period, the IMF kept a low profile on the issue, and a general perception arose that the institution was opposed, or at best indifferent. As I.G. Patel later put it, "the Fund . . . was certainly too late in actively advocating debt relief—as indeed was the [World] Bank" (Patel, 1994, p. 12).

The official public stance of the Fund reflected its role as an intergovernmental institution: it could not get too far ahead of political leaders in the main creditor countries without generating a backlash. Nonetheless, as detailed in Chapter 11,

Camdessus and other senior Fund officials began urging creditor countries to develop debt reduction plans in 1987, and by early 1988 they were actively—but quietly—promoting specific proposals. A more aggressive public posture might have accelerated the process, or it might have been counterproductive. As an inherently conservative and multinational institution, the Fund judged the risk to be not worth taking. In any event, the case for generalized debt relief could not have gained credence until enough time had elapsed to allow both creditors and debtors to pass from crisis to quagmire: that is, until 1987 at the earliest. Citibank's decision in May 1987 to add $3 billion to its reserves as a provision against possible losses on sovereign loans was a major stepping stone, because it demonstrated that at least the stronger banks had reached the point where they could afford to absorb the losses that debt reduction would bring.

Related questions are whether the staff was a leader or a follower in the intellectual field, and whether the Fund was prepared to accept debt relief once the countries and the banks agreed on a deal. Staff members, of course, were not always of one mind on this issue. Concerns about encouraging unilateral debt repudiation or discouraging a return to voluntary bank lending, accompanied by doubts about the reliability of both coercive and market-based approaches, kept the bandwagon in the garage. Nonetheless, the staff position increasingly favored recognition of the need for debt relief once the initial systemic crisis began to fade, and several staff members—notably in the Research Department—contributed to the literature on how debt relief could be accomplished within a market framework. Michael P. Dooley was an early proponent. His string of studies on the issue began in 1985 with a paper arguing that the existence of a stock of bank debt selling at deeply discounted prices implied that a bank making a new loan to that borrower would face an immediate capital loss. Only by eliminating the debt overhang could the borrower expect to regain normal access to such credits.[13] At the beginning of 1987, the staff used a *World Economic Outlook* paper to take a clear stand in favor of debt relief for the most heavily indebted countries, identified collectively as "the debt overhang cases":

> For these countries, the lack of an appropriate international mechanism for writing down the book value of the debt to a level more reflective of its market value may be resulting in market failures: investment opportunities that would otherwise have been seized are being neglected because of the effect on the expected post-tax rates of return of the need to meet the outstanding debt-service claims of the public sector's existing creditors.[14]

---

[13]The paper was circulated informally in 1985 and then as an IMF Working Paper, Dooley (1986). A revised version was published much later as Dooley (1989). The publication lags no doubt reflected the controversy of the conclusions. For overviews of the staff contributions, see the collection of papers in Frenkel, Dooley, and Wickham (1989); and Dooley and others (1990).

[14]The quoted passage is from "World Economic Outlook—Recent Economic Developments and Short-Term Prospects," SM/87/54 (February 25, 1987), p. 92. Following an objection from Charles H. Dallara, the Executive Director for the United States, the references to "debt overhang cases" and "an appropriate international mechanism" were omitted from the published version of the paper (IMF, 1987, p. 84); see minutes of EBM/87/46 (March 16, 1987), p. 47.

Operationally, the Fund implicitly moved toward an acceptance of debt relief in the 1986 stand-by arrangement with Bolivia, in that the program was approved without a prior agreement between the country and its commercial creditors and on the assumption that interest obligations would be met only in small part. The buybacks that gave Bolivia its initial debt relief in 1987 were implemented while that program was active and were administered by the IMF through a contribution account. In October 1987, the Fund approved a stand-by arrangement with Costa Rica under which the accumulation of arrears to bank creditors was accepted as a form of financing the payments gap. Shortly thereafter, the December 1987 deal between Mexico and the Morgan Guaranty Bank, in which a portion of Mexico's bank debt was voluntarily replaced by collateralized bonds with a lower face value, was also undertaken with the implicit support of the Fund, with which Mexico had an active stand-by arrangement at the time. Hence, while the Fund displayed no less than its usual caution and played a largely contemporaneous rather than leading role, both its words and its actions in the 2½ years before the Brady Plan broadly supported the development of debt reduction plans.[15]

Was the Debt Strategy Consistent with the IMF's Mandate?

The view is often expressed that the IMF's role of overseeing the international monetary system and helping countries overcome short-term balance of payments problems is incompatible with—or at least orthogonal to—assisting and advising developing countries on longer-term structural problems. This general criticism was stated by the Bretton Woods Commission (1994, p. 6), which concluded that "in developing [countries] the IMF should focus on short-term macroeconomic stabilization." With specific respect to the debt crisis, Edwards (1989, p. 8) characterized the criticism as being that "the Fund has ceased to operate as a financial institution" and "is acting more and more as a development aid–granting agency." This line of criticism continued to gain adherents throughout the following decade, as the Fund became increasingly engaged in the pursuit of structural reforms.

What specifically did the IMF do in response to the debt crisis, and how did those activities relate to the Articles of Agreement and the Fund's previous work? In general, the Fund assisted countries in designing macroeconomic adjustment programs and supported those programs financially through stand-by and extended arrangements. The only relevant question in that regard is whether these loans were consistent with the Fund's mandate to provide temporary financing for balance of payments purposes. The creation of the Extended Fund Facility (EFF) in 1974 provided a mechanism for making the IMF's general resources available for longer periods than under ordinary stand-by arrangements. The EFF, which was de-

---

[15]A related question is whether the exceptional treatment of Bolivia and Costa Rica should have been generalized *before* the adoption of a formal plan for debt relief. That issue is covered in the above discussion of the "handmaiden" criticism.

signed to cover situations where a country's payments imbalance resulted from deep-seated structural problems, was activated for several Latin American countries in the 1980s, including Peru in 1982, Mexico and Brazil in 1983, Chile in 1985, and Mexico and Venezuela in 1989.

How temporary was this financing? A number of these countries became prolonged users of Fund resources as they dug out from the initial crisis, but only Peru fell into protracted arrears with the IMF.[16] Most Latin American borrowers gradually but punctually repaid their debts. Mexico's indebtedness peaked in 1990 at SDR 4.8 billion ($6.5 billion) and fell to SDR 2.6 billion ($3.8 billion) in January 1995, before Mexico undertook a new stand-by arrangement the following month. Argentina reduced its obligations from SDR 4 billion in 1988 to 1.6 billion in early 1992 (from $5.4 billion to $2.2 billion) before undertaking new drawings under the EFF. And Brazil reduced its indebtedness from a peak of SDR 4.3 billion ($4.4 billion) in 1984 to less than 100 million by end-1995. Maturity profiles were elongated in the 1980s, but they did not vitiate the requirement of temporariness.

The IMF did, however, introduce some important innovations in the course of managing the debt crisis.[17] First, it assumed a much more active role than heretofore in arranging the total financing packages for adjustment programs. As discussed in Chapter 11, the standard practice for the staff before the crisis was to estimate the financing that would be provided by other private and official creditors under normal conditions and with good policies in place. The Fund would then negotiate a program that would make such financing possible, and it would provide financing (within the established access limits) to close any remaining gap. For Mexico and Argentina in 1982, the initial working assumption had to be that the commercial bank creditors would make every effort to reduce their exposure as rapidly as possible, in which case (1) the access limits would be inadequate to finance the program and (2) IMF financing would do little more than to enable the country to service its dwindling bank debts.

The solution was to require concerted lending by the banks so as to stabilize their aggregate financing. That solution worked because it was in the collective interest of the banks but not in the individual interests of those who might otherwise become free riders. If the procedure had been generalized, it would have represented a major extension of the IMF's activities. In practice, however, it was used only in cases where the program could not otherwise have been financed. By the late 1980s, the debt strategy evolved away from concerted lending into a more general "menu" approach in which the role of the IMF was generally the traditional one of approving an adjustment program that could serve as the basis for the use of Fund resources and a catalyst for outside financing.

---

[16]Protracted arrears are obligations that are overdue by six months or more; Argentina occasionally had shorter-term (less than 60 days) overdue payments in the late 1980s. The Fund did, of course, face a significant problem with protracted arrears starting in the mid-1980s (see Chapter 16). The point is that the arrears problem did not result either from the debt strategy or from prolonged use of Fund resources.

[17]For a longer historical perspective on these innovations, see Boughton (2000).

The second major innovation was the development of procedures for monitoring adjustment programs that were *not* supported by IMF financing. Under the heading of "enhanced surveillance," the IMF in 1984 began authorizing the release to private creditors of staff reports that evaluated programs that were financed by creditors other than the Fund (Chapters 9 and 10). In most cases, the programs were undertaken in conjunction with multiyear rescheduling agreements (MYRAs) that extended beyond the conclusion of IMF financing. As with concerted lending, it quickly became apparent that the practice had merits but that it would be a mistake to generalize it. In particular, care had to be taken to ensure that private creditors did not come to think of the IMF only as a credit-rating agency, and that the institution's credibility would not be undermined by delinking policy advice from financial commitment. The practice therefore was limited primarily to cases in which the Fund had provided financing and maintained close contact with the authorities through the subsequent completion of the adjustment process. In addition, it was usually applied by making information and analysis available to private creditors without implying an official seal of approval. After 1989, there were few new cases of enhanced surveillance.

Finally, the practices of the IMF were extended in 1989 to provide for the application of IMF resources to support reduction of bank debt under the Brady Plan. Fund resources were lent to member countries but were earmarked for the repurchase of bank loans at prices approximating those prevailing in secondary markets. To ensure that benefits accrued to the borrower and not just to creditors, buybacks under this program initially were restricted to cases where banks were increasing their exposure; and, in selected cases, programs were approved and drawings were permitted before the borrowing country had reached agreement with commercial creditors to settle arrears. As the plan evolved, banks took advantage of an increasingly sophisticated menu of options for participating.

The temporary effect of these three innovations was to make bankers into something between bedfellows and hostages of the IMF: for several years starting in 1982, bankers working on Latin American loans had to maintain close and frequent contacts with IMF staff and management. By 1989, however, when the first Brady deals were being negotiated, the traditional arm's-length relations had been restored. At least for the 1980s, the Fund largely avoided the risks of moral hazard and bureaucratic overreach that could have ensued if crisis management had ossified into standard operating procedure.

Was There Enough Coordination with the World Bank?

The IMF and the World Bank have been criticized for dancing to different drums and for stepping on each other's toes. Feinberg and Bacha (1988) expressed the allegation of coordination failure as follows: "The Fund's financial reaction to the Latin American debt crisis was both swift and deep—but it was not lasting. [Meanwhile,] . . . Initially perceiving the debt crisis to be a temporary phenomenon, the World Bank sat back and watched the IMF take the lead" (pp. 377 and 383).

During the first phase of the crisis, the Bank played a relatively limited role while it concentrated instead on longer-run development problems, especially of lower middle-income countries.[18] The Bank made substantial adjustment loans to Brazil, but it lent less to Mexico and little to Argentina. In 1983–84, the IMF took the lead and extended net credit totaling approximately $9 billion to the 11 most heavily indebted Latin American countries, compared with a net flow of just over $3 billion from the World Bank. By 1985, the picture began to change: Brazil's and Mexico's Fund-supported adjustment programs faltered, and the Bank began to step up its lending throughout the region. Overall, net flows from the Bank were slightly larger in 1985 than those from the Fund (more than $1¾ billion, compared with $1½ billion).

One purpose of the Baker strategy, introduced in October 1985 at the Annual Fund-Bank Meetings in Seoul, Korea, was to promote investment and growth in the indebted countries by strengthening the role of the Bank group (Chapter 10). Secretary Baker called for the International Bank for Reconstruction and Development (IBRD) and the Inter-American Development Bank to increase their lending to the "principal debtor countries" and for other agencies in the World Bank group (International Finance Corporation and Multilateral Investment Guarantee Agency) to work toward attracting equity capital flows to those countries. This initiative significantly strengthened the Bank's role in the debt strategy: not only did its own lending rise sharply, but the example of IBRD disbursements to some extent supplemented IMF credits as a trigger for commercial bank rescheduling agreements. Over the next three years (1986–88), Bank lending to the 11 major Latin American borrowers totaled nearly $6½ billion, at a time when net credit from the IMF was just about $500 million, as the normal flow of repayments to the Fund nearly matched new lending.[19]

Neither before nor after the Baker plan was lack of coordination between the two Bretton Woods institutions a *systemic* problem. In the early 1980s, the Fund took the lead, and in the second half of the decade the Bank played a larger role. Total net flows from the two institutions were reasonably stable throughout. Rather than reflecting a coordination problem, this passing of the baton reflected the long-standing differences in mandate and priorities of the Fund and the Bank. Lack of coordination did sometimes reduce the effectiveness of each institution in dealing with individual countries. Moreover, both institutions did occasionally tread heavily and clumsily on each other's toes, most notably in 1988 when they differed in their assessment of the viability of Argentina's proposed fiscal reforms.

---

[18]Underwood (1989) provided a detailed analysis of the World Bank's response to the debt crisis. On the Bank's "graduation" policy for countries that have reached a sufficiently advanced stage of development, see its *Annual Report* for 1982, p. 35. On the more general background for the Bank's limited response to the debt crisis in 1983–84, see Miller (1986), pp. 181–91.

[19]The figures cited in the text are aggregated from flow data for the 11 countries: Argentina, Bolivia, Brazil, Chile, Colombia, Costa Rica, Ecuador, Mexico, Peru, Uruguay, and Venezuela. Broader groupings confirm that the major increase in Bank lending came in the period 1985–87. For example, the stock of IBRD loans outstanding to the severely indebted middle-income countries rose from $10.6 billion at the end of 1984 to $27.3 billion three years later. Over the same period, IBRD loans outstanding to Latin American and Caribbean countries rose from $12 billion to more than $30 billion. Source: IBRD, World Debt Tables.

While the IMF was still negotiating the terms for a stand-by arrangement to replace the one that was about to expire and was holding out for more substantial cuts in the budget deficit, the Bank weakened the Fund's bargaining position by announcing (at the Annual Meetings in Berlin) the approval of four loans (three sectoral loans plus one for trade policy) totaling $1¼ billion (Chapters 11 and 20). That embarrassing *contretemps* forced the institutions to develop somewhat more detailed understandings of their respective responsibilities. Though those understandings were still vague and did not remove the potential for overlap and conflict, the Argentine incident remained an aberration.

Was the Adjustment Strategy Appropriate for Latin America?

In an influential paper, John Williamson (1990) characterized the IMF's approach to adjustment programs as part of a "Washington consensus" founded on "prudent macroeconomic policies, outward orientation, and free-market capitalism." While supporting that general orientation, Williamson also noted that it implicitly dismisses "the ideas spawned by the development literature" (pp. 18–20). With respect to Latin America, he concluded that it "is not at all clear that the policy reforms currently sought by Washington adequately address all of the critical current problems" (p. 18). As examples, he cited the need for price controls as a component of inflation-reducing strategies, the need to allow for skepticism by entrepreneurs when projecting the ability of adjustment programs to generate new investment, and the need to allow for the likely persistence of capital flight following implementation of a stabilization program.[20]

No one would argue seriously against the view that the IMF has insisted that financial responsibility and stability require market-oriented policies, low fiscal deficits, and limits on the growth of domestic credit financed by the monetary authorities. The issue is whether these prescriptions were applied rigidly in cases where they were not strictly appropriate. In practice, the specific elements of adjustment programs vary greatly according to the circumstances facing each country, but the real issue is whether a different approach altogether might have been required in some cases. In Latin America, possible exceptions include the following, in addition to the specific examples cited by Williamson:

- Countries where the state plays a large role in promoting development, for example through the operation of state enterprises or by directing capital flows toward favored sectors, may not be susceptible to market-oriented stabilization policies;
- Countries where inflation arises primarily from structural or inertial forces may suffer especially high real costs from conventional stabilization programs;[21] and

---

[20]Also see Killick and others (1984).

[21]Bresser Pereira (1992, p. 10) noted that "inertial inflation theory had been fully developed in Latin America in the early 1980s, though it was virtually ignored by Washington and the IMF."

- Countries where confidence in the domestic currency or in domestic financial institutions is low may be destabilized by a dismantling of capital controls.

Without attempting to resolve such issues in this short summary, it seems clear that there are grounds for a debate here. Throughout Latin America, the adjustment programs supported by the IMF in the wake of the debt crisis were predicated on a model in which the development role of the state, inertial inflation, and the autonomous role of financial weakness played little part. Rather, the basis for IMF policy advice was that price stability is essential for growth and can be promoted effectively only through appropriate macroeconomic policies; that structural reforms should aim at reducing market distortions and giving full play to market incentives; and that capital controls are ineffective at best and are usually counterproductive. Furthermore, the last two elements of that approach received relatively little attention until about the middle of the 1980s, before which the Fund's policy advice focused rather more heavily on stabilization than on development-oriented structural reforms. The fact that—in some cases, especially in the early 1980s—negotiators on each side of the table were arguing on the basis of such different models was doubtless an important contributor to the failure of negotiations to produce programs that governments could "own" and could implement firmly in the face of domestic political opposition.

Following the intensive and extensive dialogues that took place between the IMF and the authorities of indebted countries in the 1980s, these debates were partially resolved. On the side of the Latin American countries, the silent revolution gradually weakened the belief in state-dominated economic development and in the need for capital controls.[22] Edwards (1995, Chapter 3) has argued that what emerged by the early 1990s was not an acceptance of a "Washington consensus" but rather the development of a "new Latin American consensus." For its part, the IMF showed an increasing degree of flexibility as the decade progressed. For example, program conditions (beginning with Brazil in 1984) acknowledged the role of inertial inflation through acceptance of the operational deficit as one measure of fiscal policy. In a few cases where the threat of external shocks made the success of a program especially risky (most notably in the EFF arrangement negotiated with Mexico in 1986), the Fund incorporated innovative contingency clauses in the program terms. More generally, the Fund endorsed and even helped design a wide range of heterodox programs, such as Argentina's 1985 Austral Plan. Nonetheless, much room remained for further dialogue and for research on the linkages between the literature on macroeconomic stabilization and on structural reform and development (see Corbo and others, 1987; and Khan and Montiel, 1989).

---

[22]For a general discussion of the evolution of thought on the developmental role of the state, see Krueger (1993).

Should the IMF Have Been Willing to Write Down Its Claims?

The Brady Plan provided for a coordinated approach to debt reduction in which commercial banks, bilateral official creditors, and international financial institutions (IFIs) would all play a role. The new role for the IMF was to allow borrowers to apply a portion of their drawings from the Fund to reduce their outstanding bank claims on the basis of market, rather than face, values. Subsequently, however, criticism arose because the debt owed to the IMF and other IFIs was spared from any rescheduling, much less writing down in value. Helleiner (1996) summarized the views of many in developing countries: "The possibilities and modalities for writing-down some IMF/Bank debt need to be discussed directly and openly rather than remaining unacceptable topics for discussion" (p. 7).

The IMF resisted suggestions that it write down or reschedule member countries' obligations, primarily on the grounds that to do so would be inconsistent with the institution's mandate to make its resources available on a temporary and conditional basis. Instead, countries with debt-servicing difficulties were encouraged to implement Fund-supported adjustment programs that could serve as the basis for rescheduling or debt relief agreements with private and official bilateral creditors. New credits from the Fund to already indebted countries served de facto to reschedule those countries' repayment obligations. The Fund's argument was that this process, which underpinned the debt strategy from the beginning, would be seriously compromised by any effort to weaken member countries' commitments to it.[23] (For a more general discussion of the Fund's policies on rescheduling, see Chapter 16.)

More fundamentally, this issue is largely irrelevant from a financial perspective. The post-Brady debt strategy recognized that countries could not extricate themselves from a depressed-growth path unless their debt overhang was eliminated and debt-service obligations were reduced to a sustainable level in relation to anticipated export receipts. Although there are nominally three tranches to external debt (obligations to private creditors, bilateral official creditors, and IFIs), practically speaking there are only two: private and official. Since official creditors already had numerous mechanisms for taking joint action in this field, including the Paris Club and the G-7 summit process, there is only a limited free-rider problem that would have required intervention by the IFIs.[24] Whether creditor governments choose to take the full "hit" on bilateral credits or allocate

---

[23]For a statement of Fund policy on rescheduling, see "Overdue Payments to the Fund—Experience and Procedures," EBS/84/46 (March 9, 1984), pp. 9–11.

[24]Not all creditor countries participate in the Paris Club, but in general no country is able to obtain better repayment terms than those agreed to in Paris. There is, however, a free-rider problem of a sort, in that some countries might be multilateral but not bilateral creditors to a heavily indebted country. As long as the IFIs do not write down their own claims, those countries would not share in the cost of debt reduction.

some portion of it to IFI credits has little financial or even political relevance to the debtor.[25]

What is relevant are the total size of the write-down on official credits and the IMF's role in supporting debt reduction. For the six years from the Bolivian buy-backs of 1987 through mid-1993, 11 Latin American countries with IMF-supported adjustment programs were granted rescheduling agreements through the Paris Club. Those agreements covered more than $35 billion in debts. With only a few exceptions (notably for Bolivia and Nicaragua), official bilateral debt cancellations were not applied to this region.[26] Private sector debt relief, supported both by official bilateral creditors and by the IMF and other IFIs, was much larger: over the same period, eight Latin American countries used a variety of operations to reduce their debt and debt-service obligations by $42 billion (on an initial stock of $104 billion), at a cost of just over $14 billion.[27] Given the political and economic constraints on public-sector debt reduction operations for middle-income countries, there is no basis for thinking that a more direct participation by the IMF would have been either necessary or sufficient for providing greater relief.

Conclusions

Even if much of the criticism of the IMF's role in Latin America was either mis-placed or exaggerated, it contains some essential lessons for successful crisis management in the future. Assessing what the IMF did wrong in managing the debt crisis of the 1980s, two points stand out. First, the initial forecasts of the likelihood of a resumption of sustained output growth—and thereby for meaningful reductions in debt-service ratios—were, with important exceptions, optimistic. The bias in these cases resulted only in part from unforeseeable external shocks posterior to the crisis. In part, it resulted because the growth forecasts did not allow for the political resistance that often prevented the government from implementing the adjustment programs that were needed before growth could be restored. Second, the importance of combining macroeconomic adjustment with structural reforms aimed at promoting sustainable development gained operational significance only gradually as the decade progressed. Both of these problems reflected the difficulty of developing a comprehensive approach to adjustment and growth: of synthesizing the macroeconomic and development aspects of political economy. That the-

---

[25]This conclusion obviously does not apply to those low-income countries whose external debt is concentrated in obligations to the IFIs, but that issue is not relevant to the present review. A more general caveat (with the opposite effect) is that the indebted countries as a group would actually be worse off if the IFIs rather than bilateral creditors wrote down their debts, because the consequent reduction in net IFI earnings would be borne in part by higher charges on borrowings (see Chapter 17).

[26]IMF lending to both Bolivia and Nicaragua was shifted from the General Resources Account to the concessional trust funds administered by the Fund (the SAF, for Bolivia in 1986; and the Enhanced Structural Adjustment Facility (ESAF), for Bolivia in 1988 and Nicaragua in 1994).

[27]See IMF (1993) and Kuhn and Gajdeczka (1994).

oretical and empirical shortcoming poses a challenge not only for the analysis of the Latin American debt crisis, but also for reforms aimed at strengthening the IMF's response to crises throughout the developing world.

References

Boughton, James M., 1994, "The IMF and the Latin American Debt Crisis: Seven Common Criticisms," IMF Paper on Policy Analysis and Assessment 94/23 (October).

———, 2000, "From Suez to Tequila: The IMF as Crisis Manager," *Economic Journal*, Vol. 110 (January), pp. 273–91.

Bresser Pereira, Luiz Carlos, 1992, "Off the Mark: The Misguided Policies of Washington Economists," *Harvard International Review* (fall), pp. 8–11.

Bretton Woods Commission, 1994, *Bretton Woods: Looking to the Future* (Washington: Bretton Woods Commission).

Calvo, Guillermo, 1989, "A Delicate Equilibrium: Debt Relief and Default Penalties in an International Context," in *Analytical Issues in Debt*, ed. by Jacob A. Frenkel, Michael P. Dooley, and Peter Wickham (Washington: International Monetary Fund), pp. 172–93.

Cline, William R., 1983, *International Debt and the Stability of the World Economy* (Washington: Institute for International Economics).

Cohen, Daniel, 1985, "How to Evaluate the Solvency of an Indebted Nation," *Economic Policy*, Vol. 1 (November), pp. 140–67.

———, 1991, *Private Lending to Sovereign States: A Theoretical Autopsy* (Cambridge, Massachusetts: MIT Press).

Corbo, Vittorio, Morris Goldstein, and Mohsin Khan, eds., 1987, *Growth-Oriented Adjustment Programs* (Washington: IMF and World Bank).

Dooley, Michael P., 1986, "An Analysis of the Debt Crisis," IMF Working Paper 86/14 (Washington: International Monetary Fund).

———, 1989, "Market Valuation of External Debt," in *Analytical Issues in Debt*, ed. by Jacob A. Frenkel, Michael P. Dooley, and Peter Wickham (Washington: International Monetary Fund), pp. 75–82.

———, 1995, "A Retrospective on the Debt Crisis," in *Understanding Interdependence*, ed. by Peter B. Kenen (Princeton, New Jersey: Princeton University Press), pp. 262–87.

———, David Folkerts-Landau, Richard D. Haas, Steven A. Symansky, and Ralph W. Tryon, 1990, *Debt Reduction and Economic Activity*, IMF Occasional Paper No. 68 (Washington: International Monetary Fund).

Dornbusch, Rudiger, 1993, *Stabilization, Debt, and Reform: Policy Analysis for Developing Countries* (New York: Hemel Hempstead, United Kingdom: Harvester Wheatsheaf).

Edwards, Sebastian, 1989, "The International Monetary Fund and the Developing Countries: A Critical Evaluation," *Carnegie-Rochester Conference Series on Public Policy*, Vol. 31 (autumn), pp. 7–68.

———, 1995, Crisis and Reform in Latin America: From Despair to Hope (New York: Oxford University Press for the World Bank).

Eichengreen, Barry, and Peter B. Kenen, 1994, "Managing the World Economy Under the Bretton Woods System: An Overview," in *Managing the World Economy: Fifty Years After Bretton Woods*, ed. by Peter B. Kenen (Washington: Institute for International Economics), pp. 3–57.

Feinberg, Richard E., and Edmar L. Bacha, 1988, "When Supply and Demand Don't Intersect: Latin America and the Bretton Woods Institutions in the 1980s," *Development and Change*, Vol. 19 (July), pp. 371–400.

Frenkel, Jacob A., Michael P. Dooley, and Peter Wickham, eds., 1989, *Analytical Issues in Debt* (Washington: International Monetary Fund).

Helleiner, Gerald K., ed., 1996, *The International Monetary and Financial System: Developing-Country Perspectives* (New York: St. Martin's Press).

International Monetary Fund, 1987, *World Economic Outlook: A Survey by the Staff of the International Monetary Fund*, World Economic and Financial Surveys (Washington: International Monetary Fund).

———, Policy Development and Review Dept, 1993, *Private Market Financing for Developing Countries* (Washington: International Monetary Fund).

Khan, Mohsin S., and Peter J. Montiel, 1989, "Growth-Oriented Adjustment Programs: A Conceptual Framework," *Staff Papers*, International Monetary Fund, Vol. 36 (June), pp. 279–306.

Killick, Tony, Graham Bird, Jennifer Sharpley, and Mary Sutton, 1984, "The IMF: Case for a Change in Emphasis," in *Adjustment Crisis in the Third World*, ed. by Richard E. Feinberg and Valeriana Kallab (New Brunswick, New Jersey: Transaction Books), pp. 59–81.

Knox, David, 1990, *Latin American Debt: Facing Facts* (Oxford: Oxford International Institute).

Krueger, Anne O., 1993, *Political Economy of Policy Reform in Developing Countries* (Cambridge, Massachusetts: MIT Press).

Kuhn, Michael G., and Przemyslaw Gajdeczka, 1994, *Official Financing for Developing Countries* (Washington: International Monetary Fund).

Lissakers, Karin, 1991, *Banks, Borrowers, and the Establishment: A Revisionist Account of the International Debt Crisis* (New York: Basic Books).

Meller, Patricio, 1994, "The Roles of International Financial Institutions: A Latin American Reassessment," in *The International Monetary and Financial System*, ed. by G.K. Helleiner (New York: St. Martin's Press), pp. 245–71.

Miller, Morris, 1986, *Coping Is Not Enough! The International Debt Crisis and the Roles of the World Bank and International Monetary Fund* (Homewood, Illinois: Dow Jones–Irwin).

Patel, I.G., 1994, "Global Economic Governance: Some Thoughts on Our Current Discontents," lecture delivered at the Asian Development Bank (February 28).

Sachs, Jeffrey, 1986, "Managing the LDC Debt Crisis," *Brookings Papers on Economic Activity: 2*, (Washington: Brookings Institution) pp. 397–431.

———, 1989, "The Debt Overhang of Developing Countries," in *Debt, Stabilization, and Development: Essays in Memory of Carlos Díaz-Alejandro*, ed. by Guillermo Calvo and others (Oxford: Basil Blackwell for World Institute for Development Economics Research), pp. 80–102.

Underwood, John, 1989, "The World Bank's Response to the Developing Country Debt Crisis," *Contemporary Policy Issues*, Vol. 7 (April), pp. 50–65.

Vaubel, Roland, 1991, "The Political Economy of the International Monetary Fund: A Public Choice Analysis," in *The Political Economy of International Organizations: A Public Choice Approach*, ed. by Roland Vaubel and Thomas D. Willett (Boulder, Colorado: Westview Press), pp. 204–44.

Williamson, John, 1990, "What Washington Means by Policy Reform," in *Latin American Adjustment: How Much Has Happened?* ed. by John Williamson (Washington: Institute for International Economics), pp. 5–24.

World Bank, 1987, *World Development Report* (Washington: World Bank).

———, 1994, *Global Economic Prospects and the Developing Countries* (Washington: World Bank).

III

Revolutions in
Structural Adjustment

13

Lending for Adjustment and Growth

The goal of conditionality on IMF credit arrangements is to promote a combination of internal and external economic balance in borrowing countries. In its lending practices, the Fund seeks "to help members to attain, over the medium term, a viable payments position in a context of reasonable price and exchange rate stability, a sustainable level and growth rate of economic activity, and a liberal system of multilateral payments" (Guitián, 1981, p. 3). This description is essentially similar to the accepted definition of overall macroeconomic equilibrium. John Williamson, for example, has defined an exchange rate as being in "fundamental equilibrium" when it "is expected to generate a current account surplus or deficit equal to the underlying capital flow over the cycle, given that the country is pursuing 'internal balance' as best it can and not restricting trade for balance of payments reasons" (Williamson, 1985, p. 14). Of all the complex relationships embodied in these descriptions, the most difficult to model and analyze is also the most important: the linkage between adjustment and economic growth.

The Fund did not always make its credits conditional on the conduct of economic policy.[1] The Fund's first credits, starting with a drawing by France in March 1947, were disbursed immediately and without further conditions, subject only to an agreed schedule of repayments. When the Fund began entering into stand-by arrangements in 1952, the typical arrangement was only for six months and included no policy conditions. The first example of a conditional arrangement came in February 1954, when the Executive Board approved a stand-by arrangement for Peru in which the authorities agreed not to draw if certain conditions were not met, notably if they changed their policy regarding intervention in the foreign exchange market. Two years later, an arrangement was approved in which Chile's right to draw was "phased"; that is, the country could draw up to specified amounts every 30 days for

---

[1]In addition to this summary and the earlier IMF Histories, sources on the evolution of Fund conditionality include Guitián (1981, 1995), Mohammed (1991), Polak (1991), and references therein. The general practice of Fund conditionality in the 1980s is analyzed in detail in IMF Assessment Project (1992). For an introduction, see Rajcoomar and others (1996), especially Chapter 3. For an external critique of conditionality, see Dell (1981). Also see Robichek (1984), which notes that it "is no secret that the argument [in favor of making IMF credits conditional] was settled under pressure from the U.S. Government, against the solid opposition of the rest of the Fund's membership" (p. 68).

the life of the arrangement. Most lending arrangements in that period, however, were still unconditional (Horsefield, 1969, Vol. 1, pp. 373–75 and 430–31).

In July 1957, a stand-by arrangement for Paraguay introduced the "performance clause," under which failure to satisfy certain "performance criteria" would result automatically in suspension of drawing rights. In this seminal case, three ceilings were specified: on domestic assets of the central bank and on both current and capital spending by the government.[2] By 1964, the practice of imposing performance criteria became virtually universal for arrangements that would extend a country's indebtedness beyond the first credit tranche.[3] To make the government's more general policy intentions as explicit and as comprehensive as possible, the authorities were required to submit a Letter of Intent to the Fund, which was appended to the text of the stand-by arrangement. That practice began with an arrangement for Peru in February 1958. Also in 1958 (starting with an arrangement for Brazil in June), the Fund began requiring the completion of periodic reviews before the later drawings could be made.

These various practices that evolved during the first two decades were formalized following a comprehensive review of Fund lending policies in 1968. That review established that performance clauses and phasing of drawings should be standard practice in all upper-tranche arrangements. It also reacted to the large number of performance criteria (as many as 15) that had crept into some programs by establishing the (slightly hedged) principle that the Fund should not attempt to micromanage a country's economic policies:

> Performance clauses will cover those performance criteria necessary to evaluate implementation of the program with a view to ensuring the achievement of its objectives, but no others. No general rule as to the number and content of performance criteria can be adopted in view of the diversity of problems and institutional arrangements of members. (Decision No. 2620-(68/141), November 1, 1968; reproduced in de Vries (1976), Vol. 2, pp. 197–98)

While the Executive Board was developing broad policies on Fund lending in the 1950s and 1960s, the staff was developing the theoretical and empirical underpinning for conditionality. As noted above, the seminal Paraguay program included constraints on both monetary policy (domestic credit expansion) and fiscal policy (current and capital spending). This shotgun approach, which was aimed at reducing domestic expenditure to a level commensurate with the value

---

[2]Paraguay succeeded in staying within the ceilings. The dubious honor of being the first country to be (temporarily) denied a scheduled drawing because it had failed to carry out the agreed policies goes to Bolivia, in September 1958 (Horsefield, 1969, Vol. 1, p. 433).

[3]From 1964 on, the only upper-tranche stand-by arrangement without a performance clause was for the United Kingdom in November 1967. Stand-by arrangements for 1964–67 are summarized in "Fund Policy with Respect to Use of Its Resources and Stand-by Arrangement," SM/68/128 (July 23, 1968). The last time that the Fund permitted an upper-tranche drawing without a stand-by arrangement and not linked to a specialized facility or emergency assistance was for Egypt in March 1968 (de Vries, 1976, Vol. 1, p. 319). Readers unfamiliar with the "tranche" policies of the Fund will find a brief introduction in the Preface to this History.

of national income, reflected two major theoretical developments to which the Fund staff made key contributions in the 1950s. The first contribution was the "absorption approach" expounded in early *Staff Papers* articles, notably Tsiang (1950) and Alexander (1952).[4] An implication of that approach was that excess domestic spending ("absorption"), whether fed directly by the government or indirectly by monetary expansion, would worsen the external current account balance. The second contribution was the monetary approach to the balance of payments, to which Jacques J. Polak (who succeeded Edward M. Bernstein as Director of Research in 1956) made a pivotal contribution by setting out a dynamic general equilibrium model in which the primary cause of a weak external balance is domestic credit expansion (Polak, 1957).[5] Empirical verification of the importance and reliability of the monetary approach required several years of research, but the Polak model quickly took root as the foundation of all financial programming in the Fund.

Although both the principles and the practice of Fund conditionality came under heavy criticism in the 1970s, the Fund essentially reconfirmed the 1968 guidelines after an extended review in 1978–79. Criticisms from actual or potential borrowers quite naturally focused on both the harshness and the extensiveness of the conditions, but the standardized application of the monetary approach also came under fire from those who favored flexibility or who wanted the Fund to pay greater attention to social concerns. Nonetheless, when the Executive Board approved new guidelines in March 1979, the main effect was to enshrine the concept that countries should not wait until their economic prospects became desperate before seeking assistance. In other words, the Fund should be a lender of *first*, not last resort. (See de Vries, 1985, Chapters 25 and 26.) The 1979 guidelines, which were confirmed again in the comprehensive review of 1988, are reproduced in the Appendix to this chapter.

The first section of this chapter examines the controversy that flared up in the early 1980s about whether the Fund was inappropriately weakening its conditionality. The second section covers several specific issues that were raised about con-

---

[4]For a review of the contributions of Fund staff to the theoretical development of balance of payments theory, see Blejer, Khan, and Masson (1995).

[5]The stock of money is endogenous in this model and reflects the effects of the balance of payments on the foreign assets of the banking system. For the development of the modern monetary approach outside and within the Fund, see Frenkel and Johnson (1976) and IMF (1977). Polak (1991), pp. 33–36, summarizes the application of the approach in Fund programs, and Polak (1998) reviews the evolution of the model over 40 years. The origins of the monetary approach date back at least two centuries, to an essay by David Hume:

> . . . suppose that all the money of Great Britain were multiplied fivefold in a night . . . ? Must not [the prices of] all labour and commodities rise to such an exorbitant height, that no neighbouring nations could afford to buy from us; while their commodities, on the other hand, became comparatively so cheap, that, in spite of all the laws which could be formed, they would be run in upon us, and our money flow out; till we fall to a level with foreigners, and lose that great superiority of riches, which had laid us under such disadvantages? (Hume [1752], p. 63)

ditionality and the design of Fund-supported adjustment programs and then reviews the evidence on the success of programs. The final section takes up the overarching issue, the relationship between Fund conditionality and economic growth.

How Much Conditionality?

Although the Fund began conditional lending to developing countries in the
late 1950s, this was hardly its principal financial activity. Conditionality moved to
center stage only in 1979, and the following years witnessed a prolonged and sometimes bitter debate about how extensive the Fund's conditions should be.

Most of the Fund's lending in the five years between the first and second oil
shocks was either to industrial countries or on terms that required little or no policy adjustment. For fiscal years 1975 through 1979, low-conditionality credits
through the first credit tranche, the oil facilities, the Compensatory Financing Facility (CFF), and the Buffer Stock Financing Facility totaled SDR 11.7 billion ($14
billion). Another SDR 5.1 billion ($6 billion) in funds were provided through un-
conditional reserve-tranche purchases, and SDR 1.3 billion ($1½ billion) through
the Trust Fund (either as loans or as distributed profits from the sale of part of the
Fund's stock of gold) and as grants to subsidize interest payments. These amounts
far exceeded the SDR 6.1 billion ($7¼ billion) in credits extended via regular and
extended upper-tranche stand-by arrangements, SDR 4 billion of which went to
two large industrial countries (Italy and the United Kingdom). Overall, only 25
percent of the Fund's disbursements in those years was subject to high conditionality (Table 13.1).

Not only was lending low in conditionality in that era; it also slowed in volume after the initial burst of activity in response to the first big increase in oil
prices. In calendar years 1974–76, gross disbursements from the General Resources Account averaged SDR 4.3 billion a year; in 1977–79, just 2.1 billion. By
the end of the decade, reflecting the normal cycle of flows from the Fund's short-
term lending, repayments of earlier credits exceeded new lending. Consequently,
at a time when Fund quotas were being raised sharply, total Fund credit outstanding fell from a peak of SDR 13.2 billion at the end of 1977 to 9.3 billion two
years later (Figure 13.1).

When the second oil shock hit in 1979, the Fund came under pressure from
both borrowers and creditors to play a more active role in helping the oil-importing developing countries cope. That pressure came to a head at the Annual Meetings of Fund and Bank governors in Belgrade, Yugoslavia, that October, where the
Fund was heavily criticized for standing on the sidelines while an increasing number of developing countries urgently needed external financing. Criticism from
creditors was as widespread as it was unexpected. The French finance minister,
René Monory, representing Giscard's center-right government, put the case
bluntly:

> . . . the possibilities of access to the Fund for countries in difficulty have been
> expanded: conditionality has been eased so as to take better account of the adjust-

Table 13.1. Conditionality of IMF Disbursements, 1975–89

(Fiscal years; in SDR millions)

	1975–79	1980–84	1985–89
I. General Department	22,867	38,231	21,644
A. Low (or no) conditionality	16,753	13,936	6,373
Reserve tranche drawings	5,082	4,264	1,353
First credit tranche drawings[a]	1,290	990	799
Oil facilities	6,902	0	0
Other special facilities[b]	3,479	8,682	4,221
B. Higher conditionality	6,114	24,295	15,271
Upper-tranche stand-by arrangements	5,565	13,400	11,157
EFF arrangements	549	10,895	3,240
SAF loans	0	0	874
II. Administered accounts	1,055	2,259	1,860
A. Trust Fund	970	2,022	0
B. Grants[c]	85	237	1,596
C. ESAF loans[d]	0	0	264
Total (General Department plus administered accounts)	23,922	40,490	23,504
Percent of total with high conditionality			
Total disbursements [(I.B + II.C)/total]	26	60	66
General Department credits only[e]	34	72	75

[a]Includes emergency assistance for natural disaster relief.
[b]Compensatory, contingency, and buffer stock financing.
[c]Subsidies for selected users of the oil facilities and the Supplementary Financing Facility.
[d]Includes SAF resources committed under ESAF arrangements.
[e]Excludes reserve tranche purchases.

ment problems peculiar to developing countries. . . . [The] IMF has sufficient resources today to double or triple the annual volume of its assistance. In the present situation, it therefore has the necessary resources to play a central role in financing developing countries' balance of payments deficits (IMF, *Summary Proceedings*, 1979, p. 62).

Monory's reference to conditionality having been eased appears to have been an allusion to the adoption of revised guidelines earlier in the year. Although on paper the 1979 guidelines made little substantive change, the fact that they were adopted in response to criticisms of the Fund's practices raised expectations in some quarters that conditionality would become simpler and less burdensome.

Even representatives of some quite conservative creditor governments urged the Fund to lend more without worrying too much about conditionality. Witness Geoffrey Howe, the U.K. Chancellor of the Exchequer:

Now that the rules governing conditionality have been liberalized, I hope that developing countries will find it acceptable to work closely with the Fund and exploit to the full the resources now available to help them overcome their problems (IMF, *Summary Proceedings*, 1979, p. 100).

This general viewpoint was given official sanction in the communiqué issued by the Interim Committee a few days earlier:

Figure 13.1. Availability and Use of Fund Resources, 1973–89

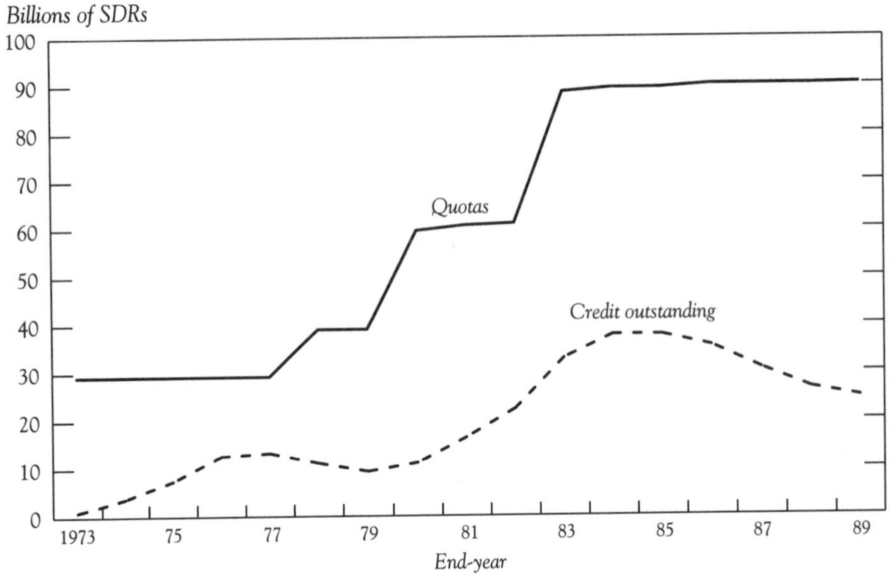

Billions of SDRs

The situation of the non-oil developing countries . . . underlined the need for a larger flow of external resources. . . . The Committee noted with satisfaction that . . . a number of developments [had] enhanced the Fund's ability to provide balance of payments assistance to its members. [paragraphs 2 and 4]

The communiqué cited several contributing developments, including the new conditionality guidelines, the liberalization of the CFF, the establishment of the Supplementary Financing Facility (SFF), and the impending creation of an interest subsidization mechanism.

It was standard practice in those days for the Managing Director to gather his senior staff together in the Executive Boardroom after each Annual Meeting, for a debriefing on the implications for the work program in the coming months.[6] The post-Belgrade meeting was long remembered by many participants as especially significant because the Managing Director, Jacques de Larosière, used it as the occasion to lay out the plight of the developing world—particularly of low-income countries—and to exhort the staff to respond positively to the calls for more lending. Although he also cautioned that more lending should not imply less conditionality, and although official policy of the Fund stressed that "adjustment and financing have to go hand in hand," the demand for heightened

---

[6]By the late 1980s, the increased size of the institution forced a choice between squeezing out division chiefs from these meetings or moving the meetings to a larger hall. The latter option won out, and the new forum was large enough that deputy chiefs and senior economists could also be included. Consequently, the debriefings lost much of their operational significance.

activity was widely interpreted as having the higher priority. It was not at all clear to many on the staff how lending could be increased without loosening conditions.

De Larosière subsequently stressed again to the staff that what he had in mind was conditional lending. When the Economic Counsellor, Jacques Polak, submitted a proposal a few weeks later for a "temporary intermediation facility" that would provide more or less automatic credits for deficit countries to replace an expected decline in the availability of bank lending, the Managing Director quickly quashed it: "What the world needs is, in my view, (1) conditionality and (2) appropriate conditions (because of the debt service problems), and not an Oil Facility No. 2." Nonetheless, de Larosière's greater stress in that period was on the importance of increasing the volume of lending. At a staff retreat in 1981, he recalled his earlier views: "So what I tried to do at the beginning of my stay here was to ask you to put the emphasis on showing the countries in which we were operating how the Fund could help. I remember telling a large staff committee: 'You have to be sellers.' I thought that it was important to try to persuade countries that there was something we could offer them." He went on to note the importance of conditionality and admitted that the two views seemed to conflict. His point, he concluded, was that "if an organization wishes to be effective, it must not turn people down before they start listening to its advice."[7]

What is clear is that Fund lending accelerated markedly, beginning in the second half of 1979, predominantly through a rise in conditional credits enabled by a policy of expanding members' access to Fund resources. (On enlarged access, see Chapter 17.) For the five fiscal years through April 1979, upper-tranche conditional lending averaged SDR 1.1 billion ($1¼ billion) a year; for the next five years, SDR 2.7 billion ($3¼ billion), as the Fund sought to play a major role in the process of "recycling petrodollars." As a portion of total disbursements, upper-tranche arrangements rose from 26 percent in the earlier period to 59 percent in fiscal years 1980–84 and to 66 percent in the second half of the decade (see Table 13.1). Was this surge in conditional lending achieved by easing up on the conditions?

John Williamson (1983, Chapter 24) examined the increase in lending to evaluate what he characterized as "hearsay evidence" (i.e., anecdotes told to him by Fund staff) that a "major loosening" in "the toughness of IMF conditionality . . . occurred after . . . Belgrade" (p. 641). Williamson was working with one hand tied behind his back, in that he did not have access to data on performance criteria in the Fund's lending agreements. His often-cited study therefore relied on two indirect indicators, neither of which provides unambiguous information. First, he

---

[7]Memorandum from Polak to the Managing Director (January 15, 1980), with handwritten response in the margin (January 16); in IMF CF (S 651); and opening remarks at the Seminar on Adjustment Policies, Annapolis, Maryland (July 16, 1981), pp. 2–3; in IMF/RD Managing Director file, "Use of Fund Resources/Conditionality (Memos), 1980–1981" (Accession 84/188 A–2 (15), Box 1, Section 343).

noted that an unusually large portion of the programs approved during the 18 months after the Belgrade meetings covered more than one year, which he regarded as implying a tolerance for more gradual adjustment and thus weaker conditionality. (An alternative interpretation would be that longer programs reflect more extensive adjustment, including structural reforms that take longer to carry out.)[8] Second, he calculated that this period was marked by a tendency for borrowing countries to experience exchange rate appreciation in real terms, which he interpreted as a weakening of the Fund's insistence on devaluation as a policy condition. (An alternative interpretation would be that economic conditions made it more difficult for countries to realize real gains in competitiveness.) On that basis, Williamson concluded that the "evidence seems to confirm that Fund conditionality was eased in mid-1979 (though before the Belgrade Annual Meetings) and retightened in mid-1981" (p. 646).

The case studies given below and in the next three chapters, as well as a large number of interviews with the staff who were involved, illustrate plainly that the Fund was eager to meet financing requests around 1979–81 and that conditionality was not as strong or as effective as it later became. To understand that development, one must take account of a crucial development not stressed by Williamson: the increase in lending to countries with deep-seated long-term structural problems, countries that needed to undertake major structural reforms to have any hope of graduating from dependence on continued official financing. Low-income countries, which until then had not been a major locus of Fund lending, were facing particularly desperate circumstances and were coming to the Fund for help in increasing numbers. In 1975–79, low-income countries borrowed an average of SDR 630 million a year from the Fund, 19 percent of the total. In the next five years, annual borrowings by this group quadrupled to SDR 2.5 billion, or 33 percent of the total (Figure 13.2). When the necessary reforms were not forthcoming, and when external economic conditions turned out worse than expected, a large portion of stand-by arrangements was suspended, many countries required repeated and prolonged access to Fund resources, and several went into arrears to the Fund and other external creditors. Whatever effect on the quality of the Fund's portfolio might have resulted from weak conditionality, the predominant factor was this shift in the nature of the demand for the Fund's resources. (The problem of arrears to the Fund is discussed in detail in Chapter 16.)

As Figure 13.1 illustrates, the surge in lending continued until 1984. By Williamson's indicators, however, conditionality effectively "retightened" after

---

[8]In setting out this issue for the Interim Committee in April 1980, de Larosière argued that "the structural problems faced by many countries may require that adjustment take place over a longer period than has been typical in the framework of our programs in the past. . . . Our putting forward increased resources for balance of payments financing would of course facilitate adjustment and stretch it over a realistic period." (For the full paragraph, see Appendix IV of Chapter 17.) The central question is whether the increase in lending served primarily to facilitate adjustment or to stretch it out.

Figure 13.2. Drawings from the IMF, 1973–89

Millions of SDRs

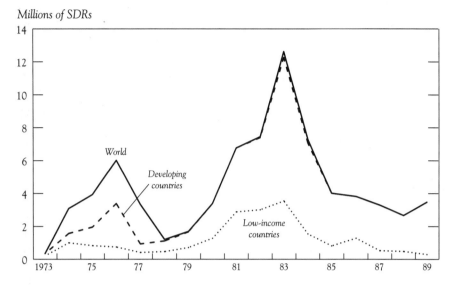

Source: IMF, *IFS*. Includes all drawings from the General Department except reserve tranche purchases. Low-income countries include the 47 developing countries classified as low-income in the 1989 WEO, plus 18 others that were eligible for ESAF loans.

mid-1981. That assessment, which is consistent with the evidence discussed below, is striking because the views expressed at that time in the main policy discussions about conditionality were still mixed. When the Interim Committee met in May 1981 in Libreville, Gabon, a few speakers (notably Howe, and Horst Schulmann, representing Germany) cautioned that the Fund should continue applying conditionality to its lending, but no one argued for a tightening.[9] At home and in the field, however, both staff and management were beginning to realize that they might have gone too far too fast in responding to calls for help.[10]

Much has been made of the fact that the Reagan administration, which took office in the United States in January 1981, viewed Fund conditionality as insufficient and pushed for it to be tightened. Criticizing a proposed stand-by arrangement for Grenada in May of that year, Donald Syvrud (Alternate—United

---

[9]Minutes of the Sixteenth Meeting of the Interim Committee (May 21, 1981), Second Session, pp. 37 (Howe) and 55 (Schulmann).

[10]An early indication of the retightening is a January 1981 memorandum from the Managing Director to department heads, noting the increased number, size, complexity, and political sensitivity of upper-tranche programs; and calling for special clearing procedures by his office whenever program negotiations were expected to involve "novel or difficult issues." See "Strengthened Procedures for Dealing with Country Program Issues" (January 14, 1981); IMF/RD Managing Director file "Extended Fund Facility, 1981–1983" (Accession 86/32, Box 3, Section 379).

States)[11] complained that "while Executive Directors talked a great deal about the need for adjustment and financing to go hand in hand, in practice he saw more and more financing and less and less adjustment."[12] The United States withheld support for that small arrangement (see Chapter 15), and later in the year made a more dramatic and more public flourish by abstaining from very large requests from India and Pakistan on similar grounds (Chapters 15 and 14, respectively).

Less well known is that Directors from industrial countries, especially from Europe, expressed similar concerns about what they viewed as weak programs almost as soon as the Fund began lending more frequently to low-income countries. A particularly dramatic example came just a month after Belgrade.

Sierra Leone

On the surface, Sierra Leone's 1979 request for a one-year stand-by arrangement for SDR 17 million ($22 million, or 55 percent of quota), plus a loan of SDR 10 million ($13 million) from the Trust Fund, was routine. The country faced a severe balance of payments problem that had resulted mainly from weak control over domestic spending over an extended period. The payments deficit now was exacerbated by the need for large capital outlays in anticipation of a major conference of the Organization of African Unity, which was to be held in Freetown in July 1980. Sierra Leone had some outstanding obligations to the Fund, primarily from drawings on the oil facility and the CFF, but they were not unusually large.[13] The only question was whether the authorities were prepared to adjust economic policies by enough to restore viability to their external accounts.

The prior record was not promising. In 1977, a stand-by arrangement was approved for Sierra Leone following negotiations in which the authorities successfully resisted the pleas of the Fund staff for a devaluation. (The currency, the leone, was pegged to the pound sterling at the time.) While that arrangement was in effect, the authorities failed to control government spending as planned, and they did not make the final scheduled drawing.[14] Fiscal overruns continued into 1978 while the authorities negotiated with the Fund staff on a new, larger, stand-by arrangement. Throughout 1978, the Fund again insisted on an up-front devaluation of the currency, partly because of doubts regarding the authorities' ability to carry out the large spending cuts that otherwise would be required to balance the

---

[11]Syvrud was appointed in 1979 as the Alternate for Sam Y. Cross. In May 1981, he was Acting Executive Director pending the appointment of Cross's replacement by the Reagan administration.

[12]Minutes of EBM/81/79 (May 11, 1981), p. 5.

[13]At the time of the request, Sierra Leone's obligations to the Fund amounted to 73 percent of quota (slightly below the mean for all countries with outstanding obligations), of which all but 8 percent of quota was from the CFF or the oil facility.

[14]The 1977 arrangement, which covered only the "enlarged" first credit tranche (36.25 percent of quota), called for three drawings spread over 12 months. The first two were made on schedule. Following a review that concluded that policies were unsustainable, the third drawing was not made.

external accounts, and partly because of a view that the authorities had to show a willingness to set out on a new policy course. Following a meeting in Washington between the President of the Republic, Siaka Stevens, and the Acting Managing Director, William B. Dale, the authorities agreed to devalue the leone by 5 percent at the end of October 1978, to change the peg from the pound sterling to the SDR, and to devalue by a further 15 percent over the next two months. The first two actions were taken immediately, but the authorities backed away from their commitment to devalue further, "for political and social reasons," and continued to focus on making selected cuts in government spending.[15]

Negotiations continued along these lines throughout the first half of 1979. As late as June, the Managing Director supported the view that any agreement had to include a further devaluation. Finally, however, after a July mission and a meeting with Stevens in Zurich failed to budge the authorities from their position, de Larosière went along with a suggestion from the mission chief (Rattan Bhatia, Senior Advisor in the African Department) that the Fund agree to accept the authorities' program.[16] Thus, for the second time in just over two years, the Fund's management approved Sierra Leone's request for a stand-by arrangement in which policy adjustment was to be effected through promised spending cuts without an initial devaluation, even though everyone in the Fund regarded the program as a risky and decidedly inferior solution to the country's economic problems.

When the Executive Board met to consider the request at the beginning of November (just a few weeks after the Belgrade Interim Committee meeting), some industrial country Directors chose the occasion to make a stand for stronger conditionality, and Sierra Leone's case was defended by several Directors from developing countries.[17] The meeting developed into a dramatic confrontation in which, as Byanti Kharmawan (Indonesia) noted, "principles were at stake."

Knowing that the arrangement would be criticized, the authorities had taken measures before the meeting to cut spending and credit growth, and they had agreed to schedule an early review—to be held in January 1980—of progress in carrying out the program. Several Directors, however, remained unimpressed. H. Onno Ruding (Netherlands) argued that "the proposed program did not meet the

---

[15]See the statement by the mission chief (Bhatia) at EBM/79/168 (November 2, 1979), pp. 3–6. The "political and social" quotation is from p. 3.

[16]In IMF/CF (C/Sierra Leone/810 "Mission, Bhatia and Staff, June–July 1979"), see memorandum from J.B. Zulu (Director of the African Department) to the Managing Director (June 22, 1979), with undated handwritten reply from the Managing Director; and memorandum from Bhatia to the Managing Director (July 12), with handwritten reply the same date. In IMF/RD African Department file "Sierra Leone, 1979" (Accession 82/13, Box 2, Section 211), see file memorandum by Bhatia (June 26).

[17]Also see Polak (1997), p. 496 and note 60, where this case is presented as a rare example of the Executive Board overruling the Managing Director; and Sampson (1981), p. 305. Polak incorrectly suggests that the Sierra Leone case may have been the only time that the Executive Board overruled a financing request from the Managing Director. Two instances occurred in 1981, involving a CFF rescheduling requested by Sudan and an extended arrangement requested by Grenada (see Chapter 15). Sampson incorrectly interprets the Board meeting as a debate over the specifics of conditionality.

standards normally applied to drawings in the higher credit tranches" and thus might encourage other countries to seek lenient terms. He also worried that the record suggested that the authorities "might not be able" to carry out their expressed policy intentions. On that basis, he asked that Sierra Leone not be allowed to draw beyond the first credit tranche until after the January review. This amendment would reduce the funds immediately available to the country only by SDR 2.1 million (from SDR 9 million to 6.9), but it would send a message that the Board was not prepared to approve upper-tranche arrangements without strong justification.

Ruding felt strongly enough about setting an example with this case that he had prepared for the Board meeting by lobbying many of his colleagues for support. As the meeting progressed, all of the Directors representing the Group of Seven (G-7) industrial countries supported his amendment. Akira Nagashima (Alternate—Japan) averred that he "was beginning to feel uneasy about the gradual shift toward easier conditionality, which might undermine the basic principles and the credibility of the Fund." Similarly, Costa P. Caranicas (Alternate—Greece), after detailing what he believed to be weak elements in the program, noted that this "case was not the first in which a weak or inadequate program had been brought to the Board for approval, and his chair [i.e., the constituency headed by Italy] in the past had voiced dissatisfaction with the trend, seen particularly in Trust Fund loan approvals."[18]

Other Directors, defending the proposed arrangement, pointed out that Ruding's amendment seemed inconsistent with the Fund's tranche policies, which limited the use of performance criteria to the upper credit tranches. Jacques de Groote (Belgium), for example, observed that if Sierra Leone was permitted only to draw on its first credit tranche, it would "seem a little odd" for the Fund to require the authorities to implement an adjustment program. Joaquín Muns (Spain) added that the amendment would represent a "fundamental departure from what had been negotiated with the country." And Samuel Nana-Sinkam (Cameroon) pointed out that requiring a country to meet preconditions was unprecedented for the Board before it could draw in the upper credit tranches.[19] De Larosière, who was chairing the meeting, also defended the strength of the authorities' program. Echoing the Fund's long-standing concerns about trying to adjust only through fiscal contraction without a devaluation, he warned that the proposed cuts could lead the Sierra Leonean economy "to the verge of very great difficulties. Indeed, the one weakness of the program might well be that it would be almost impossible for the authorities to adhere to it."

---

[18]For the quotations in these three paragraphs, see the minutes of EBM/79/168 (November 2, 1979), pp. 3 (Kharmawan), 10–12 (Ruding), 19 (Caranicas), and 28 (Nagashima).

[19]George Nicoletopoulos, Director of the Legal Department, confirmed that the Fund had not imposed preconditions in any case in the previous ten years (i.e., since the adoption of formal conditionality guidelines in 1968). See also the discussion below on the distinct practice of requiring "prior actions" (p. 605–06).

With eight chairs holding 53 percent of the voting power lined up against the original proposal and most others strongly opposed to Ruding's amendment, de Larosière sought to forge a consensus. He suggested that the Board could lower the amount to be made available immediately, but to keep it above the first credit tranche by at least a token amount. Ruding and Syvrud initially demurred, but after further discussion the Board unanimously accepted a specific compromise by Kharmawan to set the initial drawing at SDR 7.5 million.[20] It had been a long and often bitter debate over a small financial matter, but the outcome preserved all of the principles that had been raised. The stand-by arrangement would provide immediate access to upper-tranche credit; the Board's approval of an arrangement could not be presumed, especially when the conditionality was suspect; and yet the Fund was prepared to show flexibility in responding to a country's circumstances.

Whatever general effect this debate might or might not have had on the evolution of Fund conditionality, it did mark the beginning of a more positive period in economic policymaking in Sierra Leone. The adjustment program was successfully carried out and reviewed, and the full amount of the stand-by arrangement was drawn and later repaid on schedule.

Program Design Issues

The most comprehensive review of the design of Fund-supported programs undertaken in the 1980s came in response to a series of studies finding that a large portion of programs had failed. One of the most exhaustive studies, prepared by the staff around the beginning of 1987, examined results for 34 countries that had borrowed from the Fund under conditional arrangements in 1983.[21] From then through 1986, those countries had entered into a total of 71 stand-by or extended arrangements, many of which had gone off track. More often than not, these countries were not much closer to achieving "external viability" (broadly speaking, a sustainable balance of payments, achieved at a sustainable rate of economic growth) than they had been four years earlier, and their prospects for economic growth were bleak.[22]

---

[20]Minutes of EBM/79/169 (November 2, 1979), pp. 5–22. For the statements quoted in the preceding paragraph, see pp. 8–11.

[21]The sample covered all countries with stand-by or extended arrangements (i.e., longer-term arrangements under the Extended Fund Facility, or EFF) approved in 1983 except for Grenada, whose extended arrangement was canceled soon after approval. The EFF and the Grenadian case are discussed in Chapter 15.

[22]Only 7 of the 34 countries were judged to be "relatively close to achieving viability"; 21 others were thought to be in a position where they could achieve viability within five years, although some of those would need "major further shifts in policies." Of the seven "successful" cases, four (Korea, Mauritius, Portugal, and Turkey) had no further need of Fund resources in the next seven years; two (Bangladesh and Togo) drew only on the concessional structural adjustment facilities; only one (Uruguay, in 1990 and 1992) had a new stand-by arrangement. Of the six with the most deep-seated problems (Haiti, Liberia, Sudan, Uganda, Zaïre, and Zambia), all either were or soon would be in arrears to the Fund and would remain in serious difficulty for several years.

What had gone wrong? Almost everything imaginable. First, most borrowers had started off in dreadful circumstances, having taken on large external debts in the 1970s only to watch their markets and their terms of trade weaken while the interest rates on their debts soared. Many of these countries had also experienced droughts, floods, storms, or other natural disasters. Second, to a large extent, the mid-1980s brought an even more hostile external environment: very high real interest rates, an expensive U.S. dollar,[23] collapsing prices for export commodities, and sluggish market growth. Third, for the poorer countries that depended on concessional lending and other forms of aid, the declining willingness of many industrial countries to provide official assistance weakened these borrowers' ability to service debts and obtain essential imports. Fourth, many countries, especially those with weak governments, had difficulty carrying out their policy commitments.[24] The question for the Fund, however, was whether a fifth problem was also important: Were the adjustment programs poorly designed, and if so, was there an alternative paradigm that could be expected to raise the rate of success?

The staff had already prepared a preliminary report on this crucial question (published later as Research Department, 1987) and had concluded that the Fund's adjustment strategy was appropriate, partly because the basic monetary model was applicable to a wide range of circumstances and partly because the model was applied flexibly to take account of the specific circumstances facing each country. Executive Directors, however, were more skeptical and suggested that programs could be made more flexible, more structural, and more growth-oriented.[25]

Developing countries, represented by the Group of Twenty-Four (G-24), were especially critical, but in retrospect their recommendations for reform seem surprisingly mild. A Working Group of the Deputies of the G-24 prepared a report (Sengupta and others, 1987) that suggested two changes in Fund conditionality procedures.[26] First, the Fund should use ranges, not single points, for performance criteria, to give borrowers more flexibility in setting macroeconomic policies. For example, instead of requiring a country to keep the net domestic assets of the banking system below a specific ceiling, the country would be allowed a margin of error. Second, the Fund should allow drawings to continue when specific performance criteria were not satisfied, as long as the overall program objectives were being met. For example, excessive domestic credit creation might not disqualify a country from borrowing unless its current account deficit was also too large.

---

[23]The appreciation of the dollar against other key currencies in the mid-1980s adversely affected most developing countries because their debts were larger and more heavily concentrated in dollars than their financial claims.

[24]See "External Adjustments, Financing, and Growth—Issues in Conditionality," EBS/87/40 (February 25, 1987).

[25]"Theoretical Aspects of the Design of Fund-Supported Adjustment Programs," SM/86/162 (July 2, 1986); and minutes of Executive Board Seminar 86/11 (October 20, 1986).

[26]In addition to these specific suggestions, the report also endorsed the principle that the number of performance criteria should be kept to a minimum; see below, pp. 602–05. The report also dealt with broader issues, particularly the challenge of endogenizing growth in Fund programming, on which it offered more sweeping recommendations; see below, p. 612.

The U.S. authorities offered a similarly technical suggestion for reform. Treasury Secretary James A. Baker III, in his address to the 1987 Annual Meetings (IMF, *Summary Proceedings*, 1987, p. 111), proposed that the Fund use semiannual rather than quarterly intervals for performance criteria. Reasoning that macroeconomic deviations are inherently difficult to correct within a calendar quarter and that even to try can force a government or central bank to pursue a disruptively erratic policy course, Baker sought both to give borrowers more flexibility and to promote a steadier medium-term strategy.

The Executive Board discussed these "monitoring" proposals as part of a general review of conditionality in April 1988.[27] As in all discussions of Fund conditionality, most actual and potential borrowers lined up on one side and most creditors on the other, though the lines became a little ragged at times. On the question of whether to move to ranges rather than specific values for performance criteria, several Directors from both camps—including Hélène Ploix (France) and Alexandre Kafka (Brazil)—recognized that the issue was a red herring ("more apparent than real," in Ploix's phrase). If the staff judged that a given degree of restriction was needed, it would simply aim to set the ceiling lower if it had to allow for a margin of error.[28] Similarly, the proposal to waive small violations automatically drew little support; most Directors were satisfied that the Fund was already flexible enough in waiving minor breaches. The U.S. proposal for semiannual monitoring was embraced by Directors from developing countries and supported much more reluctantly by a few Directors representing industrial countries. Summing up the discussion, the Managing Director suggested that the idea could be tried experimentally in cases involving longer-term arrangements for countries with a well-established "track record" on policy implementation. In practice, however, few such cases were ever found.

Despite the nearly universal dissatisfaction with experience in the field, the Fund thus decided in 1988 not to make any radical departures in the design or monitoring of conditional adjustment programs. Far from being a reluctance to fix a system that was not broken, the conclusion instead was that the Fund was hemmed in by the need to balance several conflicting objectives. The Fund required a borrower to develop a program to restore external viability but encouraged it to do so in a way that would promote sustainable growth. The Fund wished to promote structural reforms while respecting the social and political choices of the country. The Fund tried to design programs that were politically feasible but that could be carried out quickly and strongly. The Fund tried to take account of the special circumstances facing each country while ensuring uniformity of treatment. The Fund sought to collaborate with the World Bank in recommending structural reforms while avoiding cross-conditionality. The Fund had to monitor the implementation of programs but tried to minimize interference with the authorities'

---

[27]Minutes of EBM/88/58–59 (April 6, 1988). The Chairman's summing up of the discussion was presented at EBM/88/60 (April 8, 1988).

[28]The proposal for ranges was originally made by the staff, in the background paper for the 1968 review of conditionality. The idea was abandoned at that time because it was thought to be unnecessarily complex.

management of the economy. Changing the guidelines or the procedures would do little to resolve these conflicts, all of which were cited by the Managing Director in his summing up of the 1988 review.

The Fund did devote considerable effort throughout the 1980s to examining specific technical features of conditionality, with an eye toward improving implementation and performance. The cumulative effect was not just to refine conditionality but to extend its reach. As Jacques Polak phrased it (with a modicum of exaggeration) in his 1991 essay, the "restraining provisions have not prevented the intensification of conditionality in every direction that the guidelines attempted to block" (p. 54). The remainder of this section reviews several of the main issues.

Exchange Rate Policy

Although a basic tenet of the Fund's approach on macroeconomic stabilization is that countries should aim to maintain a competitive exchange rate, that premise does not imply that overvaluation should necessarily be corrected by depreciation. If the real exchange rate (the country's price level relative to prices abroad, expressed in a common currency) is overvalued, it can be reduced either by depreciation or by price reductions. The Fund's long-standing emphasis on exchange rate depreciation was based on the empirical assessment that price reductions are difficult to achieve and sustain and are less likely to lead to a broadly based strengthening of economic efficiency and international competitiveness. Moreover, although the Fund often recommended floating exchange rates in the context of its surveillance activities (see Chapter 2, p. 86), that option was seldom viable in the context of conditionality. Countries seeking to borrow from the Fund often lacked the institutional soundness and macroeconomic policy strength that are required for exchange rate stability in a floating-rate regime.

During the first half of the 1980s, the great majority of countries borrowing from the Fund undertook to depreciate their exchange rates, most often shortly before beginning a stand-by arrangement. In 1985, the Exchange and Trade Relations Department (ETR: the department that was responsible for reviewing the Fund's policy advice to countries) prepared a review of the Fund's experience in recommending currency devaluation or depreciation as a condition for borrowing from the Fund (Johnson and others, 1985). The study revealed that in 1983, almost all countries that could adjust the exchange rate had done so as part of their Fund-supported adjustment programs.[29] Although the consequences of exchange rate adjustment were not easy to separate from other determinants of economic performance, a number of Executive Directors expressed concerns when the paper was discussed that it did not appear that depreciation had generally led to better outcomes.[30]

---

[29]Out of 35 cases reviewed, 25 had involved devaluation or managed depreciation. Eight of the exceptions were countries that were participating in currency unions or were using the U.S. dollar as the domestic currency. In the other two cases (Guatemala and Haiti), the Fund staff had concluded that the countries could undertake adjustment in domestic policies while keeping their currencies pegged to the dollar. See Johnson and others (1985), p. 13.

[30]See the minutes of EBM/84/174–175 (December 5, 1984).

Because the initial gains from depreciation often were frittered away through subsequent wage and price inflation, the staff frequently recommended that countries adopt what became known as a "real exchange rate rule." In that framework, the use of which peaked in the first half of the 1980s, the authorities would adjust the exchange rate continually or periodically during the program so as to keep compensating for any remaining differences in inflation.[31] That is, they would peg (or try to peg) the real rather than the nominal exchange rate. In a typical case, at the outset of a Fund-supported adjustment program, the authorities would announce a big enough devaluation to restore international competitiveness after an extended period of erosion resulting from a combination of loose monetary and fiscal policies and a fixed or inflexibly managed exchange rate. Following the devaluation and the adoption of more disciplined financial policies, the rate might still be pegged to a major currency such as the U.S. dollar, or to a currency basket, but the rate would be adjusted—possibly daily, perhaps monthly—to offset any excess of domestic over international inflation.[32]

In 1986, Charles Adams and Daniel Gros (both Economists in the Research Department) published a critique of the real-rate rule (Adams and Gros, 1986) that helped persuade at least some operations staff to have second thoughts about the efficacy of the practice. Their argument was that the adoption of such a rule may negate the effectiveness of monetary discipline for stabilizing the price level; in extreme cases, the authorities could completely lose control over inflation. Although the Fund recommended real-rate rules on the understanding that monetary restraint would eventually stabilize prices, Adams and Gros argued that capital inflows could be quite difficult to sterilize and could undermine monetary control. Experience soon validated that proposition in several cases. When Yugoslavia, attempting to operate a real-rate rule at a time when it was experiencing severe internal and external shocks, saw its inflation balloon and then explode, the realism of the Adams-Gros model became all too clear.[33] By the end of the 1980s, the Fund had greatly reduced its advocacy of real-rate rules.

Adjustment of economic policies away from an unsustainable course was often extremely difficult, regardless of how the exchange rate was managed. Although the choice of exchange regime was important, it was not a substitute for making hard choices in monetary, fiscal, and structural policies. This point may be illustrated by reviewing two cases of adjustment in the 1980s: Yugoslavia, where ag-

---

[31]Quirk and others (1987), pp. 16–17, lists 106 Fund-supported programs approved during 1983–86, nearly two-thirds of which included "frequent adjustment to the exchange rate under managed floating arrangements with the aim of maintaining or increasing competitiveness."

[32]See Johnson and others (1985), Table 3, for descriptions of eight cases implemented in 1983; and Quirk and others (1987), Table 2, for a list of 48 cases implemented in 1983 through 1986. A 1990 internal review listed 15 cases during 1988–89; see "Analytical Issues Relating to Fund Advice on Exchange Rate Policy," SM/90/198 (October 16, 1990).

[33]Overall, according to Quirk and others (1987), p. 31, more than 60 percent of countries that adopted real-rate rules in conjunction with Fund-supported programs in 1983–86 experienced an acceleration of inflation. For analyses of the problem, see the series of articles by Montiel and Ostry (1991, 1992, and 1993).

gressive depreciation eventually led to hyperinflation, and Côte d'Ivoire, where a reluctance to consider devaluation also eventually led to economic collapse.

Yugoslavia: Targeting the Real Exchange Rate

The prototypical real-rate rule, employed as part of a Fund-supported adjustment program, occurred in Yugoslavia beginning in 1980.[34] At the time, the Yugoslav economy was suffering from a combination of macroeconomic imbalances, a large and growing external deficit, and structural rigidities, which everyone understood would take at least several years to fix. The process of adjustment had begun tentatively in 1979, supported by financing from the Fund in the amount of the first credit tranche (SDR 69.25 million, or $95 million, fully drawn in June). A key element in the government's strategy—taken on its own initiative, not imposed by the Fund—was to reverse the deterioration in the trade balance by depreciating the exchange rate aggressively. Over the next year, the dinar was depreciated by 9 percent against the U.S. dollar and by 17 percent in effective (trade-weighted) terms. Allowing for Yugoslavia's relatively high inflation rate, however, the real effective exchange rate was estimated to have depreciated by just 5 percent. The death in May 1980 of President Josip Broz Tito, who had led Yugoslavia since liberation in 1945 and who was widely acknowledged to be the only real glue holding the fragile federation together, significantly raised the uncertainty about the future of the economy. Consequently, in June, the authorities announced a large additional devaluation, by 23 percent in terms of dollars.

An upper-tranche 18-month stand-by arrangement was approved by the Fund in June 1980 in support of this adjustment program,[35] and it was soon superseded by a larger and even longer-term deal: a three-year stand-by arrangement for 1981–83, under which the authorities would borrow another SDR 1,662 million ($1.9 billion, or 400 percent of quota).[36] With that arrangement, the emphasis shifted toward a more sustained effort to remedy the formidable structural weaknesses in the economy. The current account was already improving in response to

---

[34]All references to Yugoslavia are to the Socialist Federation of Yugoslavia, which was dissolved as a country in 1992. See Chapter 19.

[35]The June 1980 devaluation, announced the day after the Executive Board approved the stand-by arrangement, was not part of the program agreed between the staff and the authorities and was not expected by the staff. When, as a result, inflationary pressures intensified, the monetary and credit ceilings were soon breached. The Fund nonetheless welcomed the move. In December, the Board approved a waiver for the missed criteria, permitting Yugoslavia to make the second scheduled drawing under the terms of the arrangement.

[36]Prior to 1979, Yugoslavia (an original member of the Fund) had had five stand-by arrangements: three in the 1960s and two in the early 1970s. The authorities then drew on the oil facility in 1974–76, and by mid-1979 had a small level of outstanding obligations to the Fund (equivalent to about 40 percent of quota) resulting only from those purchases. Over the next year, the authorities drew the equivalent of 100 percent of their quota under the CFF, in addition to drawing on their reserve tranche and taking out the first-tranche arrangement. Under the June 1980 arrangement, the authorities borrowed SDR 200 million out of an approved total of SDR 339.33 million, bringing their outstanding obligations to just under SDR 600 million ($760 million; 143 percent of quota) at the end of 1980.

the depreciation strategy, but inflation was already rising for the same reason. The staff—led by mission chief Geoffrey Tyler, Assistant Director of the European Department—was perfectly aware of the inflation effect but regarded it as a controllable problem. As summarized in the January 1981 staff report:

> The least satisfactory area was prices. However, it is important to note that the acceleration in inflation [from 16 percent during 1978 to 24 percent in 1979 and 37 percent in 1980] reflected to a considerable extent deliberate and desirable policy actions such as the depreciation of the dinar and structural price increases, combined with the unexpected rapid increase in world prices of oil and other raw materials. There are grounds for hoping that not all such factors will be so adverse in 1981.[37]

The goal of the depreciation strategy, and of the whole adjustment program, was not just to eliminate the current account deficit but more importantly to strengthen exports by providing incentives for firms to shift production into competitive export activities. Depreciation therefore was accompanied by direct government actions to promote and finance investment in export industries and by a restructuring of administered pricing policies to encourage agricultural exports. To combat inflation, monetary and fiscal policies were to be tightened. Moreover, growth in aggregate demand was expected to weaken and, in any event, high inflation was a fact of life in the world economy in 1980. The government even partially dismantled price controls in a further effort to encourage the growth of market activity.

The 1981 stand-by arrangement was based on a commitment initiated by the authorities to "continue to aim at maintaining external competitiveness through any necessary adjustments in the exchange rate of the Yugoslav dinar in accordance with relative price and cost movements and the evolution of the current account."[38] During 1981, the exchange rate was depreciated by 23 percent in nominal effective terms, which almost exactly offset the estimated difference between domestic and partner-country inflation.[39] Retail price inflation in Yugoslavia, rather than decelerating to 25 percent or less as forecast by both the authorities and the staff, rose slightly to 39 percent.

Aside from a few slippages, the Yugoslav government carried out the agreed program through 1981 and 1982, but it did not succeed in resolving the underlying imbalances or in convincing international creditors that it was still a good credit risk in the less-friendly environment of the 1980s. By the second half of 1982, the reexamination of risks by bankers in the aftermath of the crises in Poland and Mexico simply dried up the provision of commercial loans to Yugoslavia. When

---

[37]"Yugoslavia—Request for Stand-by Arrangement," EBS/81/5 (January 16, 1981), p. 17.

[38]This language is from "Yugoslavia—Request for Stand-by Arrangement," EBS/81/5 (January 16, 1981), pp. 15 and 57. The Letter of Intent submitted by the authorities included only a more general statement: "Exchange rate policy will be implemented to ensure that the Yugoslav economy is competitive." Later staff papers omitted the vague reference to changes based on the evolution of the current account.

[39]In October 1982, the staff estimated that the real effective exchange rate had appreciated by 1 percent during 1981. See "Yugoslavia—Stand-by Arrangement—Review of Developments," EBS/82/181 (October 7, 1982), p. 17.

the Fund staff (now headed by Helen Junz, Senior Advisor in the European Department) arrived in Belgrade in November 1982 to negotiate terms for the third year of the stand-by arrangement, they knew that they would have to insist on toughening the program.

Inflation in Yugoslavia was aggravated by structural inconsistencies created by the government's attempt to decentralize decision making within a planned economy. In contrast to economies with central planning, firms had the right to set their own output prices; in contrast to market economies, those pricing decisions were not subject to hard budget constraints because firms normally could sell all of their output in the domestic market. An exogenous shock such as a depreciation would provide an excuse for workers to demand wage increases to compensate for the higher cost of imported goods. Firms would readily grant those demands and then would raise output prices commensurately, triggering a spiraling effect on wages and prices throughout the economy. The central bank would provide the credit that was needed to validate the resulting claims on national income.

To short-circuit the inflationary spiral, the Fund imposed ceilings on credit creation and encouraged the adoption of policies aimed at supporting productive investment while controlling wage increases. At the same time, the authorities were gradually liberalizing the trade and exchange system as part of an effort to position the economy for trading more and more with western markets rather than within the Soviet-centered region.[40] The process of liberalization frequently required price increases that aggravated the inflationary spiral and frustrated the effort to become more competitive. By 1982, the authorities were trying to dampen inflation by slowing the rate of currency depreciation, which of course was eroding the earlier gains in international competitiveness. For the 1983 program, the Fund imposed a very detailed rule for managing the exchange rate through a formal stabilization of the real effective exchange rate. It was not different in substance from the policy that the Yugoslavs themselves had begun in 1980, except that it took away the authorities' discretion to trade off competitiveness against price stability.[41]

A few Executive Directors expressed reservations when the program was reviewed by the Board in March 1983. Notably, Caranicas complained that it was not clear to him how a complete pass-through of depreciation into higher prices could be avoided, and Gerhard Laske (Germany) worried that excessive depreciation was simply covering up more fundamental deficiencies in the quality of the products that Yugoslavia was trying to sell in western markets. Overall, however, the Board welcomed the design of the adjustment program.[42]

---

[40]Yugoslavia, which conducted much more trade with the west than did other countries in central and eastern Europe, was an associate member of the Soviet-dominated Council for Mutual Economic Assistance (CMEA). See Chapter 19.

[41]"Yugoslavia—Staff Report for the 1982 Article IV Consultation and Review Under Stand-by Arrangement," EBS/83/46 (February 24, 1983), especially pp. 8, 24, 26, 45, and 49.

[42]Minutes of EBM/83/46–47 (March 11, 1983); for the cited remarks, see pp. 21 (Caranicas) and 25 (Laske) of meeting 83/46.

Figure 13.3. Yugoslavia: Nominal and Real Effective Exchange Rates and Inflation, 1980–90

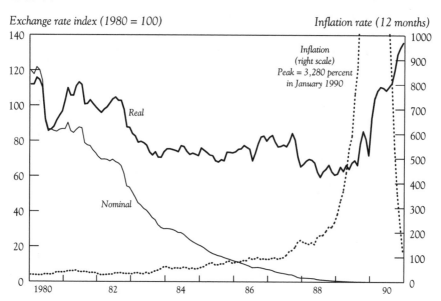

In the event, the Yugoslav authorities began anew to depreciate the dinar aggressively in 1983 and achieved a 25 percent drop in real effective terms during the year. That level then became the benchmark for subsequent programs and stand-by arrangements during the next five years.[43] On its own terms, the real exchange rate rule was spectacularly successful. Throughout the rest of the 1980s, international competitiveness as measured by the real effective exchange rate averaged about 25–30 percent better than it had been at the start of the adjustment process in 1980. The improvement eroded in 1986 and the first half of 1987, but another large devaluation in May 1987 more than offset that loss and brought a permanent strengthening (Figure 13.3). The current account deficit (excluding CMEA trade), which had been as large as 6 percent of national output in 1979, was eliminated by 1983, and a surplus equivalent to 4½ percent of output was recorded in 1988.

Throughout the 10 years that the real-rate rule was in effect, both the Yugoslav authorities and the Fund staff consistently underpredicted inflation. From an initial level of 16 percent in 1978 (well below the average for non-oil developing countries), retail price inflation in Yugoslavia rose to a plateau of 30–40 percent in the early 1980s, to 80–90 percent in the mid-1980s, and to more than 200 percent

---

[43]Following the 1981–83 stand-by arrangement, two 12-month arrangements were approved in 1984 and 1985. Yugoslavia then became the first country to have a formal "enhanced surveillance" relationship with the Fund, as described in Chapter 10. That relationship, in which the Fund staff continued to monitor progress in adjustment, was in effect for two years, until the Fund approved a new 12-month stand-by arrangement in June 1988.

by the time of the 1988 stand-by arrangement (Figure 13.3). Each year, inflation was forecast to fall; each year but one, it rose. When the country's already weak federal cohesion began to unravel completely in 1989, high inflation quickly exploded into hyperinflation. In the last four months of 1989, following Slovenia's announced intention to secede from the federation, prices were rising by 50 percent a *month*.

It would be too simplistic to blame Yugoslavia's inflation (especially the hyperinflation) on the application of a real exchange rate rule, but neither can the policy be absolved of blame.[44] If political cohesion had been stronger, if the government had given the central bank the authority and the means to control credit growth, if firms had been subject to hard budget constraints, if income policies had been applied more realistically and more consistently, and if financial liberalization had been coordinated with the development of an effective system of monetary control, then inflation certainly could have been better curtailed. Those conditions, however, were obviously not present, and the exchange rate policy interacted with an inefficient economic and political structure to produce hyperinflation.

Finally, in late 1989, the authorities and the Fund decided to try an entirely different strategy. Negotiations on a new economic program began in October (led by Jan van Houten, Assistant Director of the European Department, and initiated by a meeting in Washington between the Managing Director, Michel Camdessus, and the Prime Minister, Ante Marković), and on December 18, the government announced a comprehensive disinflation program. The dinar was replaced immediately by a new dinar at a ratio of 10,000:1, and the new currency was pegged to the deutsche mark. Wages and a wide range of prices were temporarily frozen, and residents were given the right to exchange dinars freely for foreign currency. Fiscal and monetary policies were both to be tightened sharply.

The Fund supported these policies in March 1990 by approving a new stand-by arrangement—Yugoslavia's last—for SDR 460 million ($600 million; 75 percent of quota) payable over 18 months. It was, however, too late for stabilization. Yugoslavia in 1990 and 1991 was paralyzed by conflicts between those (especially in Slovenia and Croatia) seeking autonomy and those seeking to retain central control. The authorities made only the initial drawing on the stand-by arrangement, and by the time it expired in 1992 the political federation had been dissolved by civil war. Even the major economic questions—how to stabilize prices and competitiveness and how to apportion responsibility for Yugoslavia's outstanding debts among five successor states—were overwhelmed by the immense human tragedies that engulfed the region.

Côte d'Ivoire: Adjusting Without the Exchange Rate

In contrast to the case of Yugoslavia, where choosing an exchange rate policy was a critical element in designing an effective adjustment program, Côte d'Ivoire

---

[44]Pleskovic and Sachs (1994, p. 196) infer that the exchange rate policy was imposed by the Fund and imply that it was the cause of the hyperinflation.

illustrates a situation in which exchange rate adjustment was rejected as a policy instrument until quite late in the game. This situation arose because Côte d'Ivoire participated in a currency union, the CFA franc zone, that enabled the country to enjoy the benefits of both a freely convertible currency and stable domestic prices. Only after exhausting all other adjustment options were the authorities willing to undertake the considerable risk of tampering with the exchange rate.[45]

As a member of the CFA franc zone, Côte d'Ivoire was effectively precluded from using the exchange rate as a policy instrument and had only limited ability to use monetary and fiscal tools. The CFA franc was pegged to the French franc at a fixed rate (50:1) throughout this period, and that parity could be changed only through the unanimous consent of the participating countries.[46] The rules of the system provided that France would guarantee the convertibility of the CFA franc by providing overdraft facilities with the French treasury, on condition that certain rules were observed. In particular, the stock of loans from the regional central bank (the BCEAO) to the government was not to exceed 20 percent of the government's fiscal revenues in the preceding year. Although this "20 percent rule" was designed to circumscribe the country's fiscal policy, it left open some loopholes by adopting a narrow definition of the government in which borrowing by public sector enterprises was not covered. In any case, fiscal policy was the main policy tool left for macroeconomic adjustment. Debit balances with the French treasury were subject to interest charges, and the central banks' charges on rediscounting of government obligations varied inversely with the government's deposit balance. While the overdraft and rediscounting system left some room to adjust monetary policy, it was intended only to prevent major inconsistencies between the regional exchange rate policy and each country's domestic credit conditions.

Côte d'Ivoire in the 1980s was the world's largest exporter of cocoa and the third largest exporter of coffee. Despite a diversification effort in the 1970s, the economy's fortunes remained highly dependent on the world markets for these two primary commodities. Following a coffee and cocoa boom of unprecedented scope in 1975–77, the government of Felix Houphouët-Boigny (the man who had led Côte d'Ivoire to independence in 1960 and had been its president ever since) undertook a massive program of capital investments. That strategy generated rapid growth but brought the country to a major financial crisis when commodity prices returned to normal levels in 1979 and 1980. At that point, Côte d'Ivoire—which

---

[45]For an analysis of the costs and benefits of participation in the CFA franc system, see Boughton (1993a, 1993b).

[46]The CFA franc zone comprises two distinct currency unions, each with its own currency and its own regional central bank: the West African Monetary Union, where the Central Bank of West African States (known by its French acronym, BCEAO) issues currency for Benin, Burkina Faso, Côte d'Ivoire, Mali, Niger, Senegal, and Togo; and a central African region where the Bank of Central African States (BEAC) issues a separate currency for Cameroon, the Central African Republic, Chad, Republic of Congo, Equatorial Guinea, and Gabon. Technically, the exchange rate of either currency could be modified independently of the other, but such action was never contemplated during the period reviewed here. For details on the history and operations of the system, see Boughton (1993a) and references therein.

had never before had a stand-by arrangement since joining the Fund in 1963—requested a three-year arrangement under the EFF.[47]

A staff team headed by Louis Goreux (Deputy Director of the African Department) quickly negotiated a program under which adjustment focused on cutbacks in several major categories of government spending, a redirection of public investment toward more efficient businesses, and a rationalization of government finances to bring parastatal enterprises under closer control. The Fund's Executive Directors agreed that the program was reasonable and ambitious, and only a few expressed reservations about the ability of the authorities to effect substantial adjustment without changing the exchange rate. The arrangement was readily approved in February 1981, giving Côte d'Ivoire a commitment totaling SDR 513 million ($625 million, or 450 percent of quota).[48]

Côte d'Ivoire adhered to the terms of the EFF arrangement remarkably well, especially considering how adverse global conditions were. Coffee and cocoa prices were still depressed but import prices were rising rapidly, so the terms of trade fell sharply in 1981 and did not recover until 1984. Export market growth was weak, owing to an unexpectedly severe recession in industrial countries. Even though the strengthening of the U.S. dollar against the franc improved Côte d'Ivoire's international competitiveness, it also substantially raised the local-currency cost of servicing the country's huge and rapidly growing external debt (which was largely denominated in dollars). A sustained increase in world interest rates further exacerbated the debt-service problem.

The authorities responded by cutting back capital investment plans even more drastically than originally planned, and they managed to keep the fiscal and monetary accounts close to the agreed limits throughout most of the three years that the program was in effect. Economic growth ground to a halt and then turned negative, and the current account deficit remained large, but both the authorities and the staff believed that the groundwork had been completed for a return to sustainable growth.[49]

Prospects for external viability were less bright. Côte d'Ivoire's current account deficit in 1983 amounted to 10 percent of GDP, largely because of the high cost of servicing the external debts contracted during the late-1970s boom years. Even under optimistic assumptions about trade, the deficit was projected to remain large for the next few years. Consequently, the authorities requested a new stand-by arrangement for 1984, which the Executive Board approved with the understand-

---

[47]Côte d'Ivoire (then known as the Republic of Ivory Coast) borrowed through the Oil Facility in 1974–76, through the CFF in 1976, and from the Trust Fund in 1978–81. Aside from the long-term concessional Trust Fund loans, all borrowings were completely repaid by 1979.

[48]"Côte D'Ivoire—Use of Fund Resources—Extended Fund Facility," EBS/81/34 (February 13, 1981); "Ivory Coast—Staff Report for the 1980 Article IV Consultation," SM/81/41 (February 17, 1981); and minutes of EBM/81/29 (February 27, 1981).

[49]Côte d'Ivoire made all scheduled drawings on the arrangement except for the very last one, which was disallowed owing to overruns on public sector borrowing in the second half of 1983. See "Ivory Coast—Staff Report for the 1983 Article IV Consultation and Request for Stand-by Arrangement," EBS/84/81 (April 6, 1984).

ing that the country was likely to need continual financial support from the Fund for the foreseeable future.[50] That forecast proved to be depressingly accurate. Côte d'Ivoire would have five more stand-by arrangements virtually back-to-back, lasting through 1992, at the end of which it would still need major policy adjustments and external financing before it could hope to reach equilibrium.[51]

For the next few years, occasional difficulties arose that prevented the full amount of the stand-by arrangements being drawn, but Côte d'Ivoire's overall record of adjustment continued to look strong through 1986. Indeed, when the 1986 stand-by arrangement was approved, Executive Directors from creditor countries praised Côte d'Ivoire's efforts as exemplary. The authorities were "continually designing and successfully implementing far-reaching structural policies" (Hélène Ploix—France); their "program had been very successful in 1985" (J. de Beaufort Wijnholds—Alternate, Netherlands); "performance . . . had been excellent and the authorities deserved to be particularly commended" (Bernd Goos—Alternate, Germany); and that record "had helped to restore the confidence of the international financial community" (Mary K. Bush—Alternate, United States).[52]

Throughout those first six years of adjustment, Côte d'Ivoire's exchange rate was not a significant policy issue. In effective terms, the rate was quite stable until the U.S. dollar started reversing its appreciation in March 1985 (Figure 13.4). Moreover, the tightening of monetary and fiscal policies in Côte d'Ivoire gradually reduced the domestic inflation rate to well below world levels, so that the real effective exchange rate depreciated by 28 percent from 1980 to 1985. From that point on, however, circumstances severely deteriorated. Coffee and other export prices declined again, foreign aid dried up, and the authorities ran out of ways to generate the resources to keep servicing the external debt. Consequently, Côte d'Ivoire's arrears to foreign creditors (official and private, but mostly to commercial banks) skyrocketed from just $21 million at the end of 1986 to nearly $1.8 billion at the end of 1989.[53]

When the authorities requested a new stand-by arrangement in 1987, the staff concluded that exchange rate policy was still broadly appropriate. By then, the exchange rate was appreciating in both nominal and real terms (Figure 13.4), but the

---

[50]During the discussion of Côte d'Ivoire's request for the 1984 arrangement, the Managing Director observed that the "prospect was for long-term balance of payments difficulties, with relatively little hope of regaining a viable balance of payments position in the short term; . . . the Fund would probably be called upon to assist Ivory Coast for a number of years to come . . . "; minutes of EBM/84/70 (May 2, 1984), pp. 37–38.

[51]The financial effect of the stand-by arrangements was to offset a portion of Côte d'Ivoire's repayments of the 1981–83 extended arrangement and thus to limit the decline in the Fund's exposure. From a peak of SDR 670 million ($675 million; 405 percent of quota) in August 1984, Côte d'Ivoire's outstanding obligations to the Fund declined gradually to approximately SDR 270 million ($335 million; 160 percent of quota) by the fall of 1989 and then remained around that level until they began to decline further in 1992.

[52]Minutes of EBM/86/101 (June 23, 1986), pp. 6 (Ploix), 9 (Wijnholds), 12 (Bush), and 14 (Goos).

[53]Converted to U.S. dollars from data in CFA francs in "Côte D'Ivoire—Review Under Stand-by Arrangement," EBS/90/209 (December 6, 1990), p. 21.

Figure 13.4. Côte d'Ivoire: Nominal and Real Effective Exchange Rates and Inflation, 1979–90

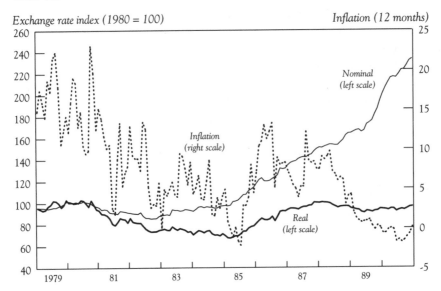

Exchange rate index (1980 = 100)

Inflation (12 months)

principal problem was the sharp drop in the terms of trade. Accordingly, the adjustment program incorporated "stringent domestic demand-management policies and increased efforts to improve productivity and reduce production costs." Moreover, participation in the currency union with neighboring countries and with France enabled Côte d'Ivoire to "maintain an open exchange and trade system" and to obtain "exceptional financing" (from France) to stay current on external payments obligations.[54]

In December 1987, the Fund's Executive Directors reacted skeptically to this optimistic assessment, and they directly examined Côte d'Ivoire's exchange rate policy for the first time. By then, this matter was becoming an international political issue, as some officials in the United States and other industrial countries had concluded that the tight link between the CFA and French francs was diverting trade away from their exporters and toward France.

The Board discussion was initiated by Charles Enoch (Alternate—United Kingdom), who expressed disappointment that the exchange rate had been largely ignored. Despite the difficulties, he argued, "the Board must recognize that it was being asked to approve a Fund-supported adjustment program that did not achieve balance of payments viability, while one instrument which could help in that regard—the exchange rate—had simply been set aside." Directors from the United States, Germany, Canada, and Australia also indicated their desire to see the authorities and the Fund take a fresh look at whether the level of the exchange rate

---

[54]"Côte d'Ivoire—Staff Report for the 1987 Article IV Consultation and Request for a Standby Arrangement," EBS/87/249 (November 30, 1987), pp. 17–18 and 30.

was still appropriate. C.R. Rye (Australia) went so far as to claim that there was "clear evidence that Côte d'Ivoire's exchange rate is substantially overvalued. . . . The Ivoirien authorities cannot seriously address their country's balance of payments weakness . . . without early action on the exchange rate." Although both the staff and the Directors speaking for Côte d'Ivoire (Corentino V. Santos, from Cape Verde) and France (Hélène Ploix) defended the status quo, the summing up of the discussion sent a clear signal to the authorities: "Although it was clear that difficult issues were raised by Côte d'Ivoire's membership in a currency union, several Directors thought that, given Côte d'Ivoire's prospective external environment, consideration of adjustments in currency relationships should not be precluded."[55]

The requested stand-by arrangement was approved in principle that day, and it took effect at the end of February 1988.[56] The adjustment program, however, immediately went off track, largely because the authorities—who believed that the disastrous decline in world prices for coffee and cocoa would be temporary—refused to cut the guaranteed prices paid to growers. When the decline continued, the price stabilization agency incurred enormous losses that put the country into a financial crisis.

From 1987 to the first half of 1989, Côte d'Ivoire's fiscal deficit rose from a nearly unmanageable 7 percent of GDP to a completely unfinanceable 16 percent. Nonetheless, a succession of Fund missions from December 1988 through April 1989 was told directly by President Houphouët-Boigny and other officials that the government did not see the need for further moves toward austerity. Then, on April 21, 1989, Houphouët-Boigny met tête-à-tête with Camdessus for some 2½ hours in Paris, at the end of which he agreed to put in place a major new adjustment program including substantial cuts in producer prices.[57] With that breakthrough, the authorities entered into detailed negotiations on a new adjustment program with a staff team headed by Christian A. François (Assistant Director in the African Department). Throughout these discussions, no serious consideration was given to a devaluation, and the new adjustment program was built around a 50 percent cut in prices paid to coffee and cocoa growers and a freeze on public sector wages.[58]

---

[55]Minutes of EBM/87/172 (December 15, 1987), pp. 14–15 (Enoch), 25 (Rye), and 33 (summing up).

[56]Final approval of both the stand-by arrangement and a drawing under the CFF was contingent upon a satisfactory conclusion to rescheduling and financing negotiations that were taking place between Côte d'Ivoire and external private and official creditors. On February 29, 1988, the Board gave its final approval, and Côte d'Ivoire then borrowed SDR 7 million ($10 million) under the stand-by arrangement (out of a total commitment of SDR 94 million—57 percent of quota—to be made available over 12 months) and SDR 83 million ($115 million) under the CFF to cover a temporary shortfall in export earnings.

[57]Minutes of EBM/89/43 (April 24, 1989), pp. 3–4; and memorandums in IMF/RD Managing Director file "Côte d'Ivoire, January–October 1989" (Accession 90/223, Box 2, Section 473).

[58]"Côte D'Ivoire—Staff Report for the 1989 Article IV Consultation and Request for Stand-by Arrangement," EBS/89/212 (November 2, 1989), pp. 15–27.

No sooner was the 1989 program agreed upon than conditions deteriorated even more. With the collapse of the marketing agreements and quotas of the International Coffee Organization in July, the price of Côte d'Ivoire's coffee exports dropped by a further 30 percent. Both the staff and the Managing Director recognized that the government could not be expected to tighten its domestic policies any more at this stage, and it was agreed to try to seek additional external financing commitments instead.

After a delay of several months while additional loans and grants were being arranged from the World Bank and from a group of official donors, the Executive Board approved a new 18-month stand-by arrangement in November 1989. Approval did not come without qualms, however. Thomas C. Dawson II (United States) worried that "social constraints to adjustment" would be "exacerbated" by reliance on "highly visible cuts in nominal incomes" of agricultural producers, especially when the relatively high incomes in the public sector were being protected from cuts. Overall, the Board was impressed by the government's new seriousness of purpose, but Directors were split as to whether the government could carry out draconian cuts in wages as an alternative to changing the exchange rate, and as to whether the planned adjustment would suffice to restore balance and eventually regenerate growth.[59]

External conditions continued to worsen, so François and his team returned to Abidjan in January 1990 to negotiate terms for tightening the program enough to keep it on track. This time the authorities relented and agreed to cut public sector wages as well. When news of the agreement leaked to the public, however, protests broke out and continued until the government deployed troops to restore order. To restore a semblance of order, the government was forced not only to roll back the wage cuts but to begin to open up what had always been a very closed political process. Houphouët-Boigny appointed Alassane Ouattara, the governor of the BCEAO (and former Director of the Fund's African Department; see Chapter 20), to head a special Interministerial Committee with powers to redesign the adjustment strategy. Ouattara's committee decided to continue to concentrate on fiscal tightening, but through measures to raise substantial new tax and other revenues rather than through wage cuts. On that basis, a modified program was negotiated, and in June 1990 the Executive Board approved the resumption of drawings under the stand-by arrangement.

The revised program held together well enough to carry Côte d'Ivoire through the remainder of that stand-by arrangement and then through one more, but it was not sufficient to free the country from the burden of its foreign debt. Without more aggressive action to improve competitiveness, the authorities had no hope of diversifying the economy by enough to eliminate its dependence on the vagaries of the world markets for a few primary commodities. When further efforts to enforce austerity failed in 1992 and 1993, the only remaining option was to devalue the currency. After intense negotiations among the several member states, the CFA

---

[59]Minutes of EBM/89/150–151 (November 20, 1989). Dawson's quoted remarks were made at meeting 89/151, pp. 7–8.

franc was devalued against the French franc in January 1994: the first change in the rate since 1948.[60]

Standards for Fiscal Policy

Starting in 1983, some countries with high domestic inflation rates began asking the Fund to use inflation-adjusted measures of the government's budgetary balance as the performance criterion for fiscal policy. The Fund agreed to add such measures to the criteria in credit arrangements for Argentina and Brazil that year (see Chapters 8 and 9, respectively) and for Mexico in 1986 (Chapter 10). Those agreements, however, were exceptions to the general practice of setting ceilings only on the overall deficit or on monetary financing of the deficit.

Though the debate on how to measure fiscal restraint was technical, the central issue was quite important. Part of government interest payments reflects an inflation premium and is not expected to have the same depressant effect on private sector saving as the "real" component. In economies with high inflation, the nominal deficit can seriously overstate the pressures on the economy resulting from fiscal expansion.[61] Moreover, if the rate of inflation was assumed to be beyond the authorities' control during the coming year (or over whatever period the performance criteria covered), then the actual budget deficit was also beyond their control, because changes in inflation would alter borrowing costs, tax revenues, and many types of expenditure. Adjusting the deficit to exclude the effects of inflation on interest costs would produce a performance criterion for which the authorities could be held more accountable. If, instead, reducing the rate of inflation was viewed as a key element in the effort to stabilize the economy and therefore as an essential goal of macroeconomic policy, then the actual deficit should be targeted. Setting targets for both variables enabled the Fund to avoid resolving the underlying debate unless the authorities managed to meet the operational target while missing the unadjusted ceiling. In that case, the Executive Board would have to decide whether to grant a waiver for the missed performance criterion.

The staff of the Fiscal Affairs Department prepared a study of this issue (published later as Tanzi, Blejer, and Teijeiro, 1987), which was discussed by Executive Directors in a seminar in June 1986: just when Mexico was pressing for flexibility on the fiscal constraint.[62] The staff view was that no single measure of the fiscal deficit was adequate by itself and that the two measures provided complementary information. At the seminar, the Mexican Director, Guillermo Ortiz, offered a detailed rationale for making the operational deficit a primary performance criterion. At the other end of the spectrum, Berndt Goos (Germany) argued that only the conventional unadjusted deficit could measure the required degree of fiscal

---

[60]For a Fund staff analysis of the 1994 devaluation, see Clément and others (1996).

[61]The range of possible effects of inflation on the government's accounts is more complex than this brief summary suggests. For a review, see Heller, Haas, and Mansur (1986).

[62]"Inflation and the Measurement of Fiscal Deficits," SM/86/53 (March 3, 1986).

adjustment. Reduction of inflation was critical to the success of an adjustment program, and in his view external viability could not be assured unless the overall budget deficit was reduced. Most Directors, however, agreed that the matter could not be resolved in favor of any single statistic and supported the Managing Director's conclusion that the Fund should experiment with different practices on a case-by-case basis.[63] In the field, however, the operational deficit never did take hold as a performance criterion except as a supplemental indicator in isolated high-inflation cases.

Fiscal standards were reviewed more generally in 1988. A central issue in that review was whether the conditionality guidelines should be extended (or interpreted more broadly) to make structural reforms—not just overall deficit reduction—a performance criterion or at least a benchmark for reviewing the progress of adjustment programs. The staff suggested some ways to incorporate qualitative structural benchmarks, for example by asking the authorities to specify detailed reform plans in the Letter of Intent. Donald C. Templeman (Temporary Alternate—United States) laid out the clearest argument for increasing the Fund's focus on fiscal reforms:

> Of course, it is not the Fund's business to tell a member country what role the public sector should play in its economy. However, the Fund does have a legitimate role in pointing out the different effects on the achievement of economic objectives that are likely to result from specific fiscal measures or from the failure to introduce such measures.

In rebuttal, A. Vasudevan (Temporary Alternate—India) argued that no matter how valuable fiscal reforms might be in particular circumstances, the general case was not empirically established and even analytically was "less than fully convincing." Moreover, "once an array of structural measures is allowed to creep into fiscal conditionality, there will be a tendency . . . to lengthen the program period . . . without a corresponding increase in access to Fund resources." After a full day of deliberation, the best that the Managing Director could suggest as a conclusion was that "we will have to proceed in a pragmatic way, looking at individual cases."[64] The result was a gradual increase in attention to the quality of government spending and revenue policies, though generally without explicit conditionality.[65]

External Debt Limits

An especially controversial performance criterion was the practice of limiting the overall amount of external debt that a country could undertake while operat-

---

[63]Minutes of Executive Board Seminar 86/7 (June 4, 1986).

[64]Minutes of EBM/88/81 (May 20, 1988), p. 5 (Templeman) and p. 23 (Vasudevan); and EBM/88/82 (same date), p. 21 (Managing Director's summing up). Also see "Fiscal Aspects of Fund-Supported Programs," SM/88/53 (February 29, 1988).

[65]For staff views on the structural aspects of fiscal conditionality, see Tanzi (1987), IMF Fiscal Affairs Department (1995), and Mackenzie, Orsmond, and Gerson (1997). In the 1990s, the Fund paid increasing attention to the distribution and quality of government spending.

ing under a Fund-supported program. Throughout the 1970s, the Fund expressed concerns that the ready availability of inexpensive and unconditional bank credits was inducing many developing countries to overborrow and to postpone needed adjustments of economic policies. Consequently, from 1973 through 1978, two-thirds of all upper-tranche arrangements (36 out of 54) included some form of limitation on external borrowing as a performance criterion.[66] The staff, had, however, found it difficult to establish general rules governing such limitations that would ensure both efficacy and uniformity of treatment.[67] Finally, a few months after the completion of the general rewriting of the conditionality guidelines, the staff proposed an additional, specific guideline covering the use of external debt limits. After lengthy debate on technical issues, the Board accepted the addition of performance criteria on debt ceilings "when the size and rate of growth of external indebtedness is a relevant factor in the design of adjustment programs."[68] That criterion turned out to apply to almost every case from then on.

From 1979 through 1982, external debt ceilings were included in more than 90 percent of upper-tranche arrangements. The policy was reviewed in April 1983 in light of the onset of the international debt crisis. That review found that in the great majority of cases (61 out of 68 upper-tranche arrangements), countries had stayed within the agreed debt ceilings. The staff concluded that experience with these ceilings had been positive and was now more important than ever. Executive Directors concurred and suggested that the coverage should be made even more inclusive (covering both short- and longer-term debts; see footnote 67).[69] From that point on, a ceiling on external debt was used in virtually all Fund-supported programs.

This insistence on limiting foreign borrowing provides a further illustration of the uneasy relationship between the Fund and private financial markets. Restoring and maintaining access for developing countries to credits from international banks was a major goal of the Fund's approach to adjustment and reform. That approach, however, forced the question of whether bilateral negotiations between the author-

---

[66]"External Debt Management Policies," SM/79/125 (May 11, 1979), Table 1, p. 14.

[67]The major issue related to efficacy concerned the types of debt to include under the ceiling. As finally adopted, the Fund's guideline excluded both very long-term debts (particularly debts with initial maturities of more than 12 years), which were assumed to be beneficial to development, and short-term debts (with maturities less than one year), most of which were trade credits. This maturity-based criterion, though arbitrary in its dating, was judged to be more practical than earlier, largely abandoned, efforts to distinguish debts directly by purpose. The guideline also specifically exempted concessional loans.

[68]For the text of the decision, see the Appendix to this chapter. The Executive Board met on July 6, 1979 (EBM/79/106–107) to consider the staff paper, "External Debt Management Policies," SM/79/125 (May 11, 1979). The Managing Director then prepared a summing up that set out the proposed guideline along with several paragraphs of interpretation in light of the July 6 discussion. That draft was discussed at EBM/79/121 (July 23, 1979). A final version ("Text of Revised Summing Up," EBD/79/183, Rev. 1; August 2, 1979) was accepted on a lapse-of-time basis on August 3.

[69]"Fund Policies and External Debt Servicing Problems," SM/83/45 (March 8, 1983); minutes of EBM/83/57–58 (April 6, 1983).

ities of developing countries and commercial bank creditors could be relied upon to regulate the provision of credit and prevent overborrowing. Once a country had access to credit on market terms, foreign borrowing could substitute for domestic credit creation and could finance excessive growth in domestic demand. The judgment of the Fund staff and management, supported by the Executive Board, was that the danger of market excess was very real in these circumstances.[70]

Structural Conditionality?

Throughout the 1980s, the Fund became increasingly concerned with structural policies. Chapter 2 recounted how the coverage of Article IV consultation reports gradually became more structural, in response to a growing political and academic interest in the supply side of the economy, the Fund's increasing involvement with planned economies, its role in dealing with the international debt crisis, and the need to counteract political pressures for protectionist trade policies. Those same forces, plus the development of structural adjustment lending by the World Bank after 1979, also led to periodic calls for the Fund to devise performance criteria for certain structural policies in addition to the standard criteria on macroeconomic policies. More fundamentally, the increase in the portion of Fund lending directed to countries with deep-seated structural problems meant that requests for credit arrangements could no longer be evaluated solely in terms of macroeconomic stability. The Fund's conditionality, however, was constrained by the 1979 guidelines, which stated that performance criteria "will normally be confined to (i) macroeconomic variables, and (ii) those necessary to implement specific provisions of the Articles or policies adopted under them." (See Guideline 9, in the Appendix to this chapter.)

In 1981, just as the arrival of the Reagan administration in the United States was giving a high profile to "supply-side economics," the Research Department prepared a background paper on the scope for structural reforms that was generally sympathetic to the notion that economic liberalization could significantly strengthen aggregate supply. Policies designed to reduce market distortions, enhance incentives for saving and investment, improve education and training programs, or stimulate technological innovation were singled out as potentially beneficial. In addition, exchange rate devaluation was examined as a beneficial supply-side policy in situations where an economy was in external disequilibrium, perhaps because of a sustained terms-of-trade loss or the cumulative effects of high domestic inflation.

Ariel Buira (Mexico) opened the Board meeting on this topic by launching a blistering attack on the staff approach as it applied to developing countries. Regarding the paper's argument that the economic role of the state should be limited, which he saw as a "nineteenth century liberal concept in which the state has . . .

---

[70]For a clear statement of Fund policy, see "The Use of Limits on External Debt in Fund Arrangements," EBS/88/51 (March 4, 1988).

no development responsibilities," he responded that his authorities "did not expect Fund guidance on this matter." Furthermore, assigning a central role in adjustment programs to price incentives was a matter of "ideology and fashion," not economics. Many developing countries were likely to reject the Fund's advice on structural reforms, not because of "special interest groups," as alleged in the staff paper, but because of fundamental differences in economic analysis. The essence, if not the tone, of Buira's arguments was echoed to a degree by Directors from other developing countries.[71] The silent revolution was still some years away.

Throughout the first half of the 1980s, the staff often encouraged countries to implement liberalizing structural reforms, though usually without formal conditionality linked to borrowing rights under a lending arrangement. In some cases, countries were required to eliminate restrictions or other incentive-distorting policies before entering into a stand-by or extended arrangement. In other cases, progress in carrying out reforms was monitored through periodic reviews during the life of the arrangement. For example, almost all arrangements approved in the aftermath of the 1979–80 increase in world oil prices required the borrowing country to price petroleum products domestically so as to cover fully the cost of importing or producing the oil. In a few isolated cases (notably in arrangements for Argentina, Sudan, and Yugoslavia), performance clauses related specifically to structural reforms on interest rate, pricing, and subsidization policies.[72] More generally, staff recommendations on ways to cut fiscal deficits became increasingly structural, with emphasis on matters such as broadening the tax base and strengthening the administration of expenditure restraints.

The 1986 conditionality review revealed a more sympathetic view toward structural reforms than had been evident a few years earlier. Buira's successor in the Mexican chair, Guillermo Ortiz, accepted that "the recent emphasis on structural policies is certainly well placed," and he cautioned only that the Fund should defer to the World Bank with regard to many structural issues and that structural concerns should not lead to a proliferation of performance criteria. At the end of the day, the Managing Director concluded that the staff should continue to explore avenues for monitoring structural progress outside the realm of formal performance criteria.[73]

The Fund edged closer to embracing structural conditionality in a 1987 review of monitoring techniques for structural reforms. As the Managing Director summarized the review:

---

[71]The staff paper was "Supply-Oriented Adjustment Policies," SM/81/78 (April 6, 1981), and the Board discussion was held at EBM/81/62 (April 20) and 63 (April 21). Buira's statement is in the minutes of meeting 81/62, pp. 13–19.

[72]"Program Design and Performance Criteria," EBS/86/211, Sup. 1 (September 11, 1986), pp. 15–16. For a review of the Fund's practice with regard to petroleum pricing, see memorandum from Vito Tanzi (Director, Fiscal Affairs Department) to the Managing Director (May 6, 1983), in IMF/RD Managing Director file "Extended Fund Facility, 1981–1983" (Accession 86/32, Box 3, Section 379).

[73]Minutes of EBM/86/190 (December 3, 1986), p. 20 (Ortiz); EBM/86/191 (same date), p. 51 (summing up).

> Most Directors supported the principle that conditionality should be attached to structural reform when the latter was seen as essential for the achievement of external viability—often but by no means always the case—and hence for safeguarding the revolving character of the Fund's resources.[74]

Consensus, however, was less comprehensive than this sentence suggests. In contrast to the Fund's conventional adjustment levers—monetary, fiscal, and exchange rate policies—there was no generally accepted model or paradigm linking specific structural policies either to macroeconomic performance or to external viability. The Board in effect was authorizing the staff to experiment further in trying to develop a general approach, but structural conditions would still have to be applied case by case.

Despite this gradual slide toward an increased Fund involvement in structural reforms, the Board consciously declined to take the extra step of extending formal conditionality to cover structural policies in any general way. For the 1988 review of the conditionality guidelines, the staff asked Executive Directors to consider whether cases in which structural reforms were essential for the success of an adjustment program should still be regarded as "exceptional," as stated in Guideline 9 (but apparently contradicted by the 1987 conclusion quoted above). Broadly speaking, Directors agreed that a strict interpretation of that guideline would be too narrow, but they preferred to let staff and management continue to experiment liberally and to "place more emphasis on structural reforms" rather than to tinker with the governing principle.[75]

South Africa: Structural Impediments to Growth

An especially delicate issue of structural reform arose when South Africa applied for a stand-by arrangement in 1982: the most controversial case the Fund had ever had to consider. It was not the first time that the Fund had approved a stand-by arrangement for South Africa, but it came at a time of increasing international outcry against the apartheid policies of the regime. From 1958 through 1976, the Fund approved four stand-by arrangements and one CFF drawing, without provoking any generalized political objections. Subsequently, events such as the 1976 Soweto uprisings and the 1977 murder of imprisoned resistance leader Stephen Biko led to a more widespread awareness of the implications of apartheid, the imposition by many countries of restrictions on economic and other contacts with South Africa, and a series of condemnations of the regime by the General Assembly of the United Nations. Consensus on tactics, however, was less than universal. Notably, although the United States imposed sanctions beginning in 1977, the Reagan administration shifted to a policy of "constructive engagement" upon taking office in 1981. Hence in 1982, most countries were officially opposed to the maintenance of

---

[74]Minutes of EBM/87/176 (December 18, 1987), p. 8.

[75]Minutes of EBM/88/60 (April 8, 1988), p. 6 (summing up). The handling of structural conditionality became a more urgent issue after 1997, as a result of the role of inadequate banking supervision and other structural deficiencies in the financial crisis in Asia.

normal relations with South Africa, but the United States and a few other industrial countries were resisting moves to isolate the country economically.[76]

South Africa joined the Fund in 1945 as an "original member." Although since 1974 it had been one of a handful of pariah states not represented on the Executive Board,[77] it retained full rights of membership. When the UN General Assembly implored the Fund to sever relations, the Fund's response was that it was prohibited by its Articles of Agreement from considering political or other noneconomic issues in its relations with its members.[78] The central question was whether apartheid was a relevant economic issue.

South Africa's balance of payments weakened considerably in 1981 and 1982, partly as a result of the retreat in the price of gold (the country's principal export) from the heights reached in 1979–80, but also because of weaknesses in the prices of several other exports (mostly other minerals). In February 1982, the authorities informed the staff that they wanted to use the impending Article IV consultations to discuss a possible stand-by arrangement or other use of Fund resources. Staff and management readily agreed that such a request would have to be considered apolitically, on the basis of equal treatment of all members. The Managing Director took the precaution of sounding out Executive Directors from the major industrial

---

[76]In the UN General Assembly, the United States, the United Kingdom, and Germany consistently voted against resolutions condemning relations between the Fund and South Africa. Most other industrial countries, and a few developing countries, joined them in some instances but more often abstained.

[77]In 1946–48, South Africa was a member of the constituency headed by the Netherlands. From 1948 (when the National Party took power) through 1974, it was in the constituency headed by Australia. For the next two decades, South Africa did not participate in the election of Executive Directors. At Board meetings dealing with South Africa, the government was normally represented by a Special Resident Representative. Throughout that time, consultations with the country and the negotiation of stand-by arrangements were handled by the Fund's European Department. Following the adoption of a nonracial constitution and the election of Nelson Mandela as president, South Africa joined the group of Anglophone African countries through the election of Executive Directors in 1996, and responsibility for dealings with the authorities was transferred to the Fund's African Department.

[78]As discussed in Chapter 20, the basic agreement defining relations between the Fund and the United Nations respects the independence of the Fund in all respects. It does, however, require the Fund to give "due consideration" to requests by the United Nations that items be placed on the agenda of the Board of Governors. In November 1981, the General Assembly adopted Resolution A/Res/36/52, stating that it "deeply deplores the persistent collaboration between the International Monetary Fund and South Africa in disregard of repeated resolutions to the contrary by the General Assembly and calls on the International Monetary Fund to put an end to such collaboration." The resolution also requested that relations between the Fund and South Africa be placed on the agenda of the Annual Meetings of the Board of Governors. The following month, the General Assembly adopted Resolution 36/172 D, calling on the IMF to cease lending to South Africa and to suspend it from membership. Both resolutions were circulated to and discussed by Executive Directors, and a formal reply was made to the United Nations. De Larosière, however, declined to place the matter on the Annual Meetings agenda, and no governor moved to do so. The UN resolutions were circulated internally at the Fund as attachments to "United Nations General Assembly—Thirty-Sixth Session," SM/82/15 (January 22, 1982) and "Resolution of the United Nations Assembly on Relations with South Africa," EBD/82/107 (April 30, 1982). The latter document also included a letter of response on behalf of the Fund.

countries and was assured of their support.[79] Even so, the staff mission (led by Adalbert Knöbl, Advisor in the European Department) reached an understanding with the authorities that, to avoid a possible political confrontation during the Annual Meetings in Toronto, no formal request would be submitted until the fall.[80]

Knöbl's team returned to South Africa in August 1982 to negotiate the terms of a stand-by arrangement and also to review the authorities' informal request for a CFF drawing to compensate for a shortfall in export earnings. Two aspects of these discussions turned out to be controversial. First, although the price of gold was then above $350 an ounce and rising, the staff decided to base the economic program for 1983 on an assumed price of $315 (the average price for June 1982). The purpose was to "safeguard the adjustment," to ensure that policies would be tightened by enough to restore external balance even if gold prices weakened again. This choice, however, appeared to overstate the case for the requested credits by making the balance of payments outlook worse. Although the existence of a "balance of payments need" for borrowing from the Fund could have been made even at the higher gold price,[81] the dubiety of this assumption would be cited by several Executive Directors as a possible reason for turning down the request.

The second controversy arose from the staff's judgment that structural policies were not relevant for evaluating a request for a 12-month stand-by arrangement. The staff report discussed the need for adjustment of monetary and fiscal policies but did not deal with the economic consequences of the country's labor market policies. One element of apartheid was a panoply of restrictions on the employment, movement, training, and education of nonwhite workers. Those restrictions obviously stunted the economy's growth prospects and had contributed to the weaknesses underlying the request to use Fund resources. In the staff view, however, improvements in labor policies would not affect economic performance until after the one-year life of the proposed arrangement, and it would therefore not be appropriate to require such adjustment in this case.[82]

Once the authorities announced publicly in early October that they were requesting the credits, a storm of protest erupted. The UN General Assembly passed another resolution, specifically asking the Fund to deny the request. Letters and ca-

---

[79]Memorandum from William B. Dale (Deputy Managing Director) to the Managing Director (February 18, 1982), with attachments; in IMF/RD Managing Director file "South Africa, 1982" (Accession 84/21, Box 5, Section 168).

[80]Memorandum for files (July 8, 1982) by Nigel Carter (Personal Assistant to the Managing Director); in IMF/RD Managing Director file "South Africa, 1982" (Accession 84/21, Box 5, Section 168).

[81]The CFF drawing was fully justified on the basis of shortfalls in receipts on goods other than gold, and the projected current account deficit for 1983 would still have been substantial with an assumed gold price of $350. See "South Africa—Request for Stand-by Arrangement," EBS/82/173 (October 4, 1982), p. 6, and minutes of EBM/82/141 (November 3, 1982), p. 3.

[82]The staff view on this point was stated most clearly by Whittome at EBM/82/141 (November 3, 1982), pp. 6–7. Also see "South Africa—Request for Stand-by Arrangement," EBS/82/173 (October 4, 1982).

bles from religious groups, political leaders, and others around the world carried a similar message. On October 29, four days before the Executive Board was scheduled to consider the proposal, de Larosière received a delegation from the United Nations' Special Committee on Apartheid. Two days later, he met with the UN Secretary General, Javier Pérez de Cuéllar, to explain the Fund's position. Through it all, he expressed determination not to be swayed by political considerations, no matter how fundamental they might be.[83]

Executive Directors from developing countries (known then as the "G-9") caucused on November 2 and agreed to request a postponement of the Board meeting. Several among them had just arrived at the Fund, having been elected in September for a term beginning November 1, and they wished for time to reflect. They knew that they lacked the votes to defeat the request by themselves, but if a vote could be put off even for a few days while they studied the documentation, the pressure on others was likely to rise. When the Board met the next morning, the G-9 spokesman, Mohamed Finaish (Libya), opened the discussion with a motion to postpone. Positions were quickly tallied, and no one outside the caucus supported the move. The nine chairs in favor of postponement held just 31 percent of the voting power, and the eight chairs opposed—all from industrial countries in the Group of Ten (G-10)—held 55 percent. (Four chairs were silent, and one was vacant on that day.)[84]

Next, the discussion turned to the substance of South Africa's program. Most speakers accepted that both the CFF drawing (SDR 636 million, the equivalent of $680 million, or 100 percent of quota) and the stand-by arrangement (for SDR 364 million; $390 million, 57 percent of quota, and sized so as to make a total of SDR 1 billion available) were justifiable on technical grounds, despite the controversies described above. Five Directors spoke out against the program, primarily on the grounds that structural reform should have been required.

The case that apartheid incorporated debilitating labor market policies was introduced by Yusuf A. Nimatallah (Saudi Arabia), who argued that "unless the labor supply bottlenecks are eliminated, South Africa will be unable to embark on a noninflationary growth path. Removing the rigidities in the labor market should be part of the adjustment program." He was joined in this line of attack by Finaish, A. S. Jayawardena (Alternate—Sri Lanka), Ghassem Salehkhou (Iran), and Tai Qianding (Alternate—China). Neither of the Directors from sub-Saharan Africa argued against the substance of the program, and neither voted against it. Having argued that the discussion should be postponed, both stated only that they were "reserving their positions" on whether the credits should be approved. With 14

---

[83]Minutes of EBM/82/140 (November 3, 1982), pp. 4–5.

[84]The Executive Director for Indonesia, Byanti Kharmawan, had died a few weeks earlier, and his successor was to take office on November 4. The Group of Nine Executive Directors from developing countries was formed as an informal caucus in November 1966, as a counterweight to the Group of Ten industrial countries in the negotiations on the creation of the SDR; see de Vries (1976), Vol. 1, p. 107.

chairs in favor, 5 opposed, and 2 in effect abstaining, the Fund approved the request.[85]

South Africa made the CFF drawing and the initial drawing on the stand-by arrangement, but the authorities did not seek to draw the remaining amounts under the arrangement. Gold and other mineral prices strengthened in 1983, and the tightening of monetary and fiscal policies contributed to a further improvement in the current account. When the Executive Board met in June 1983 to review the program, the issue was not whether the performance criteria had been met (they clearly had) but whether the lack of progress in eliminating structural impediments to growth warranted canceling the arrangement. This time, the staff report devoted an entire section to "labor market policies as a constraint on growth," and a background paper included a detailed appendix on actual labor market policies and practices. Those reports left no doubt that apartheid was having severe economic effects, both on the majority of the population that was directly affected and in the aggregate.[86]

At the Board meeting, six constituencies voted against the continuation of the stand-by arrangement (the five that had opposed the initial approval in November, plus the then-unrepresented group headed by Indonesia). Others, even while not opposing the decision to continue, now spoke out more clearly for the proposition that Fund lending should be linked to structural reform. On this occasion, the case was stated most eloquently by E.I.M. Mtei (Tanzania):

> The so-called job reservation regulations, which excluded certain race groups from some categories of employment, had impeded vertical mobility of labor, discouraged the acquisition of skills by certain race groups, distorted the occupational allocation of labor, and hindered optimal use of the labor force and proper functioning of the labor market. Impediments to horizontal or geographical mobility of labor also affected morale and hindered efficiency. All those factors led to high interregional and interrace group pay differentials and added to inflationary pressures. With excess supply of labor in some areas and shortages in others, the natural consequences were economic inefficiency and higher costs of production. In that regard, it was regrettable that there was no indication of any clear prospects of improvement in the educational system or of the abolition of those irrational regulations in the present employment policies and practices of South Africa.

At the time, the South African case demonstrated the Fund's commitment to political neutrality, even in the most egregious circumstances. More fundamentally, however, it forced the Fund to begin to reconsider its aloofness with regard to economic malpractices that derived from political or social mores. Throughout

---

[85]Minutes of EBM/82/140–141 (November 3, 1982). The quotation from Nimatallah is from meeting 82/140, p. 15. As a further indication of how far removed this case was from the Fund's usual apolitical environment, the normal secrecy of the Board's deliberations could not be maintained. The *Wall Street Journal* ran a story the next morning that included detailed information about the positions taken by individual Executive Directors. Eventually the entire text of the draft minutes of the meeting was in wide circulation among journalists, UN delegates, and others.

[86]"South Africa—Staff Report for the 1983 Article IV Consultation and Review Under the Stand-by Arrangement," EBS/83/100 (May 20, 1983), pp. 14–16, and "South Africa—Recent Economic Developments," SM/83/111 (June 3, 1983), Appendix.

the remaining decade of minority rule in South Africa, the Fund's policy advice focused with increasing intensity on the economic consequences of apartheid. As the authorities made no further requests to borrow, the question of imposing structural conditionality never arose again in this specific context. The incident was nonetheless a pivotal step in moving the Fund's policies in that direction.

East Africa: Balancing Stabilization and Reform

Many African economies in the 1970s and 1980s were managed by dominant central governments that exercised tight controls over most aspects of economic activity. When that system produced reasonable economic performance, as in Kenya, the Fund and other international creditors and donors tended to focus on the need for macroeconomic stability and not to push very hard for structural reforms. That complacency led to a "halo" effect in Washington and a "spoiled child" effect in Kenya that delayed progress and resulted in more manifest problems in the 1990s.[87] When economic policies were less successful, as in Tanzania, the Fund placed greater emphasis on the need for structural reforms as an adjunct to macroeconomic adjustment.[88]

Kenya

Kenya joined the Fund in 1964, less than two months after gaining independence from British rule. The new government of Jomo Kenyatta set out to control the economy through a complex set of parastatal enterprises and marketing boards, but it adopted a distinctly more capital-friendly and open economic environment than most of its neighbors. It inherited and then built on a relatively modern infrastructure, including one of the more advanced transportation systems in sub-Saharan Africa. By 1973, Kenya was able to present Nairobi as a showcase of African development when it hosted the Annual Meetings of Fund and Bank governors.

The Fund's financial assistance to Kenya began with SDR 108 million ($130 million; 224 percent of quota) in mostly low-conditionality credits in 1974–77,[89] followed by SDR 47 million ($60 million) in Trust Fund loans from 1977 to 1981. Kenya enjoyed good access to international capital markets on commercial terms, and the World Bank also was an active creditor. The Bank took an unusually "protective" attitude toward what it saw as one of the best governments in the region, and it showed little interest in pushing for policy reforms (Kapur and others, 1997, pp. 289–93).

The Fund's low-conditionality credits were followed by a series of three stand-by arrangements (1979 to 1982) for the successor government of Daniel arap Moi, on which conditionality was not very strong or effective. Notably, despite a persistent upward trend in the real effective exchange rate and a recognition that Kenya was thereby becoming uncompetitive in world markets, the Fund did not

---

[87]On the "halo" effect, see Kapur and others (1997), p. 761. The "spoiled child" effect was cited in interviews for this study by officials in Nairobi.

[88]For the story of the Fund's assistance to the third country in the East Africa region, Uganda, see Chapter 14.

[89]The only high-conditionality lending was an EFF arrangement approved in July 1975, on which just one drawing was made. See de Vries (1985), pp. 370–73, and Killick (1984).

insist on a devaluation as a condition for financial assistance until 1981.[90] Two devaluations that year improved matters only temporarily, were soon overtaken by overly expansionary monetary and fiscal policies, and did not restore viability to the balance of payments.[91] By late 1982, Kenya found itself with substantial outstanding debt obligations to the Fund and other creditors and an undiminished need for policy adjustment.

A serious effort to get macroeconomic policy under control began around the end of 1982, not long after the government survived an attempted coup by Air Force officers. At the urging of the Fund, Kenya adopted a policy of targeting (and gradually depreciating) the real effective exchange rate. The government also took a few tentative steps toward decontrolling prices, but without alleviating the major distortions in the price structure; and they began to rationalize both the tax system and the financing of parastatal enterprises.[92] Despite some major economic shocks (including a severe drought in 1984) and lack of progress in reforming parastatal enterprises or agricultural marketing, the gradualist strategy worked reasonably well for the next three years. In 1985, in the midst of a boom in world coffee prices, Kenya was able to wean itself temporarily from dependence on Fund financing.

No sooner had Kenya begun to experience strong performance than the authorities let policies slip. Excessive monetary growth and government borrowing in 1986, followed by a deterioration in the world coffee market in 1987, brought Kenya quickly back to the Fund for more help. In February 1988, the Executive Board approved a combination stand-by and SAF arrangement, under which Kenya could draw SDR 28 million ($38 million, or 20 percent of quota) immediately and a total of SDR 175 million ($235 million; 123 percent of quota) over three years. Policy conditions for this financing stressed the standard prescriptions for macroeconomic stability, while the overall adjustment program incorporated structural reforms as well. Monitoring of those reforms—development of the private sector, strengthening of parastatal enterprises, and improvements to agricultural marketing—was left largely to the World Bank,[93] but the Bank also was focused more on stabilization than on laying the groundwork for future growth.[94]

---

[90]A September 1979 staff study found that Kenya had lost between 8 and 15 percent in relative price competitiveness during the three years through the end of 1978. On the basis of that study and related staff analysis, the staff concluded that a devaluation should be a necessary condition for further use of Fund resources. Although the Managing Director supported that conclusion, the authorities successfully resisted it in the subsequent negotiations. The exchange rate study is attached to a December 19, 1979, memorandum from Zulu to the Managing Director; in IMF/CF (C/Kenya/810 "Mission, Stillson and Artus, September 1979"). The Managing Director's support is indicated in a handwritten note on the memorandum. For the program subsequently approved, see "Kenya—Request for Stand-by Arrangement," EBS/80/215 (September 30, 1980).

[91]See "Kenya—Request for Stand-by Arrangement," EBS/81/241 (December 10, 1981).

[92]"Kenya—Request for Stand-by Arrangement," EBS/83/41 (February 23, 1983).

[93]See "Staff Report for the 1987 Article IV Consultation and Request for Stand-by Arrangement and for Arrangements Under the Structural Adjustment Facility," EBS/88/2 (January 7, 1988), especially Appendix II.

[94]See the criticisms of Bank policy on Kenya advanced by Stanley Fischer (then the Bank's Chief Economist) in 1989, quoted in Kapur and others (1997), pp. 754–55.

By the time the Fund considered a request for an ESAF arrangement in 1989, Kenya still was showing little progress on structural reforms.[95] Although several Executive Directors lamented that fact, any concerns were easily outweighed by optimism on macroeconomic stability. The most detailed critique of Kenya's structural policies was offered by Mary Elizabeth Hansen (Temporary Alternate— United States), who noted that while Kenya had a "sound macroeconomic framework," the economy still lacked "efficiency and dynamism." She called attention specifically to the need for cuts in the size of the civil service, management reform in the parastatal enterprises, liberalization of import licensing requirements, and better management of the natural resources that underpinned the tourist industry. No Director, however, questioned the appropriateness of approving the requested loans.[96]

Conspicuously absent from the Fund's deliberations on Kenya in the 1980s was any mention of the official corruption that dominated discussions at times in the following decade. Four reasons may be advanced for the shift, although it is still too early to fully assess their importance. First, the effects of corruption on economic performance in Kenya did not become severe until later. Second, as Kenya's macroeconomic policies weakened, the devastating effects of weak structural elements—including corruption—became increasingly evident. Third, the international community (in both the northern and southern hemispheres) became less tolerant of corruption after the end of the Cold War, as assistance to questionable governments could no longer be justified on geopolitical grounds. Fourth, the Fund had not yet found a formula for dealing with corruption as a structural impediment without fear of compromising its political neutrality. Once these various barriers fell, the Fund would be in a position to insist on fundamental reforms in Kenya before resuming financial assistance.

Tanzania

In the background to the Fund's efforts to instigate structural economic reform in Tanzania was an impasse over conventional conditionality that erupted in

---

[95]Kenya's last drawings on the Fund's general resources came in the fourth quarter of 1988 under the 1988 stand-by arrangement and to compensate for export shortfalls under the terms of the CFF. By that time, the Fund was encouraging Kenya to shift its borrowing into the lower-cost and longer-term structural adjustment facilities. Staff and management tried unsuccessfully to dissuade the authorities from applying for the compensatory financing, but the authorities insisted on getting the additional money. From the end of 1987, just before the first SAF loan, to the end of 1994, Kenya's total indebtedness to the Fund did not change materially, but all of it was shifted from the General Resources Account to the SAF and ESAF. For the dispute on Kenya's October 1988 request for compensatory financing, see memorandums and cables in IMF/RD African Department file "Kenya—Correspondence, 1988" (Accession 91/31, Box 3, Section 576).

[96]Minutes of EBM/89/55 (May 15, 1989). For Hansen's remarks, see pp. 28–30.

[97]Tanzania gained its independence from the United Kingdom in 1961 and became a member of the IMF the following year. Tanzania was formed through the union of Tanganyika and Zanzibar in 1964. It made occasional low-conditionality drawings starting in 1974 and had a small stand-by arrangement in 1975 on which it did not draw. At the end of the decade, Tanzania owed SDR 85 million ($112 million; 155 percent of quota) to the Fund's General Department and SDR 30 million ($40 million) to the Trust Fund.

1979.[97] Earlier, the government of President Julius Nyerere obtained substantial external financial assistance from donor countries and from the World Bank, which it applied to a variety of large-scale infrastructure and other developmental projects (see Duncan, 1997). The collapse of the East African Community (EAC),[98] an extended drought, a successful but costly war to drive Idi Amin out of Uganda, and the 1979 increase in petroleum prices all contributed to a balance of payments crisis that induced Tanzania to seek a stand-by arrangement with the Fund.

Nyerere and much of his government in 1979 were prepared to make no more than minimal policy concessions to the Fund as conditions for getting access to the Fund's money, and they were strongly opposed to any linkage between Fund credits and structural reform. The finance minister, E.I.M. Mtei (later to serve as Executive Director at the Fund), was virtually alone in seeing the need for fundamental change, including a major devaluation of the exchange rate. When negotiations were scheduled to begin in October 1979, Mtei knew that he would have to battle to win the approval of the president, so he decided to impress him with the seriousness of the problem as soon as the Fund staff team (led by Bo Karlstroem, Assistant Director of the African Department) arrived in Dar es Salaam. Mtei, a few other officials, and Karlstroem all went to see Nyerere at his home on a Saturday afternoon, October 27. Unfortunately, the strategy backfired when the meeting went badly. After Karlstroem seemed to insist that the government would have to abandon much of its system of direct and quantitative economic controls, and he forecast a decline in foreign assistance (including bank loans) if the talks failed, Nyerere concluded that he could not negotiate under these conditions. He abruptly terminated the mission and told the staff team to leave the country. Mtei had no choice but to resign as minister, which effectively ended the prospects for a strong adjustment program for the time being.[99]

Nyerere, one of the most highly respected political leaders in Africa, soon went on the offensive against the IMF. In an address to the diplomatic community in Dar es Salaam on New Year's Day, 1980, he questioned the whole basis for the Fund's central role in the world economy:

> When did the IMF become an international Ministry of Finance? When did nations agree to surrender to it their powers of decision making? . . . It has an ideology of economic and social development which it is trying to impose on poor countries irrespective of [our] own clearly stated policies. And when we reject IMF conditions we hear the threatening whisper: "Without accepting our conditions you will not get our money, and you will get no other money."[100]

---

[98]The EAC was formed in 1967 by Kenya, Tanzania, and Uganda to promote trade and other economic relations within the region and to coordinate the development of infrastructure. It was doomed by a widening gulf of political and economic divergences between its members.

[99]See memorandums by Karlstroem (memorandum for files of October 27, 1979; memorandum to management of November 8; and draft note of November 20); in IMF/RD African Department file "TA16, Use of Fund Resources—EFF, October 1979 EAD" (Accession 84/53, Box 1, Section 100). Additional information here is from interviews with officials in Tanzania and with Fund staff.

[100]The speech was reproduced in *Development Dialogue*, 1980, No. 2, pp. 7–9; the quotation is from p. 8.

A few days later, he sent his ambassador in Washington to call on de Larosière, to convey his displeasure at what he saw as the "paternalistic and condescending" treatment he had received from the Fund staff. Commercial banks had cut off lending to Tanzania pending a successful conclusion of negotiations with the Fund, and Nyerere believed that the Fund had encouraged them to do so as a means of pressuring his government. Moreover, he had concluded that the Fund was part of a "western conspiracy" to force Tanzania to abandon its socialist principles in favor of capitalism, a move that he believed would lead to corruption, a widening maldistribution of income that would work to the disadvantage of ethnic Africans, and possibly even to mass starvation.[101]

De Larosière was not about to be dissuaded by this setback. Without either economic reform or Fund financing, Tanzania had no hope for recovery, and the Managing Director felt that the Fund carried a responsibility to help if it could. Moreover, the Annual Meetings in Belgrade, where the major industrial powers had pushed the Fund to increase lending to developing countries (see above, pp. 560–63), had only recently concluded. He quickly wrote to Nyerere to express his "deep concern" over the president's reaction to events, and he promised to do "everything in my power to prevent any threat to . . . good relations" between the Fund and Tanzania. Nyerere also was eager to get an agreement, and he responded positively to the Managing Director's letter and then gave his new team (led by Finance Minister Amir H. Jamal) the go-ahead to resume talks.[102] The Director of the African Department, Justin B. Zulu, then visited Dar es Salaam at the end of March to help ease the diplomatic tension.

A second staff team (led by Evangelos A. Calamitsis, Assistant Director of the African Department) went to Dar es Salaam in April 1980, with more flexible instructions to negotiate a program that would be acceptable to the authorities. Despite the presence of goodwill on both sides, however, the Fund and Tanzania were on a collision course. The government still believed that the Fund was trying to impose an entirely different economic system on the country, and the Fund's insistence on moving toward more rational pricing policies provided some justification for that fear.[103] The ensuing negotiations produced the devaluation that the Fund thought was necessary, but the supporting measures to get the government's budget deficit under control were left for later implementation.

---

[101]Memorandum for files by C. Max Watson (Personal Assistant to the Managing Director), January 7, 1980; in IMF/RD African Department file "TA16, Use of Fund Resources—EFF, October 1979 EAD" (Accession 84/53, Box 1, Section 100). The "western conspiracy" phrase is from the November 20 note cited in footnote 99.

[102]Letter from de Larosière to Nyerere (January 11, 1980); in IMF/RD African Department file "TA16, Use of Fund Resources—EFF, October 1979 EAD" (Accession 84/53, Box 1, Section 183). Letter from Nyerere to de Larosière (February 22, 1980); in IMF/RD African Department file "Tanzania—Correspondence, 1980" (Accession 83/45, Box 3, Section 183).

[103]The blueprint for developing the Tanzanian economy was the "Arusha Declaration" of January 1967, in which Nyerere outlined a strategy of state ownership and control of major industries, commerce, and finance, and of development through agriculture rather than industrialization. See TANU (1967) and Nyerere (1977).

As negotiations proceeded, Nyerere again denounced the Fund's conditions, leaked selected Fund documents to the international press, and publicly called for a special United Nations conference to develop alternative solutions.[104] That the government lacked commitment was obvious, but the staff agreed both to soften conditions somewhat and to raise the amount of credit being offered in order to reach an agreement. The Executive Board shrugged off the apparent risks and approved a stand-by arrangement (plus a CFF drawing to compensate for shortfalls in · export revenues) in September 1980.[105] That enabled Tanzania to draw SDR 40 million (73 percent of quota) in October, with the prospect of another SDR 140 million over the next 21 months if the conditions were met. Inevitably, the government failed to carry out the program, and only that initial drawing was allowed.

The next few years were among the most difficult in Tanzanian economic history.[106] Output in manufacturing fell sharply, overall output stagnated, prices rose rapidly, and shortages of basic and other goods pervaded economic life. While the government attributed the decline primarily to adverse external conditions, the Fund staff regarded the external environment as a secondary issue. The main problem, in the Fund's view, was a host of inappropriate macroeconomic and structural policies: controls that distorted the price structure, excessive monetary financing of fiscal deficits, heavy reliance on subsidies on consumer goods, inefficient management of parastatal enterprises, and overvaluation of the exchange rate. By 1984, the authorities—led by a new but highly experienced finance minister, C.D. Msuya[107]—were moving away from ideological confrontation, and they gradually began to make piecemeal reforms. Overall economic performance, however, remained extremely poor.[108]

The economic crisis in Tanzania worsened further around the beginning of 1985, when official donors (principally Nordic countries) began withdrawing financial support and telling the authorities that they would have to reach a new agreement with the Fund or face a more severe loss in bilateral assistance. With-

---

[104]The public forum for what became known as the "Arusha initiative" for a new international economic order was a conference in Arusha at the end of June 1980, sponsored by the Dag Hammarskjöld Foundation and other nongovernmental organizations. The communiqué was published in *Development Dialogue*, 1980, No. 2, pp. 10–23. Also see Sampson (1981), p. 301, and references therein; and (for an example of the effects of the leak of Fund documents) "Le F.M.I. embarrasse les autorités," by Paul Fabra, *Le Monde* (Paris), July 5.

[105]See memorandum to management (July 24, 1980) by Oumar B. Makalou (Deputy Director of the African Department) and Subimal Mookerjee (Deputy Director of ETR), in IMF/RD African Department file "Tanzania, 1980" (Accession 83/45, Box 3, Section 183; and minutes of EBM/80/142 (September 15, 1980).

[106]For retrospectives on the economic crisis in Tanzania and the break in relations with the IMF, see Biermann and Wagao (1986), Ndulu (1987), and Campbell and Stein (1992).

[107]Msuya held various cabinet positions throughout most of the 1970s and 1980s, including three years (1980–83) as prime minister.

[108]For overall reviews of these issues for the first half of the 1980s, see "Tanzania—Staff Report for the 1985 Article IV Consultation," SM/86/23 (February 7, 1986) and "Tanzania—Request for Stand-by Arrangement," EBS/86/183 (August 8, 1986).

out large aid inflows, Tanzania was no longer able to service its external debts, and the economy virtually collapsed. Basic goods disappeared from store shelves, and vehicles waited in long queues to buy scarce supplies of petrol. After nearly 25 years in power, Nyerere decided to forgo another five-year term as president. Shortly before announcing that decision, he authorized Msuya to resume negotiations with the Fund.

Negotiations dragged on throughout 1985 without much progress. Although Nyerere seems to have seriously wanted an agreement before he left office, he was unprepared to make the major concessions on liberalizing the economy that the Fund required. Once Nyerere relinquished his post, however, matters quickly improved. Although the top economic officials did not change, they were now less bound by the rigid socialist policies of the past twenty years. In response to their newfound flexibility, the Fund relaxed its own policies and gave Tanzania extra time to clear its arrears.[109]

The economic program for 1986–87, which was to be supported by a stand-by arrangement from the Fund, included a wide range of liberalizing reforms.[110] Those reforms would fundamentally alter the structure of the economy, including the financing and operations of government departments and parastatal enterprises, the setting of the exchange rate, the control of imports, and the marketing and pricing of agricultural output. On most of these issues, the World Bank took the lead in helping the authorities design appropriate policies. The Fund's main structural concern—its obsession, in the eyes of the authorities—was ensuring that the exchange rate was maintained at a level that would enable Tanzania to compete in the world economy. To that end, the authorities abandoned the politically contentious policy of periodically devaluing against a basket of currencies, and adopted a policy of frequently adjusting the rate to achieve a gradual depreciation in real effective terms. Nonetheless, while the quantitative performance criteria for the stand-by arrangement related mostly to the exchange rate and other conventional macroeconomic policies and conditions, adoption of the comprehensive program was the sine qua non for the whole arrangement.

Agreement on all of the key measures was reached by mid-year 1986, and in July Tanzania was able to obtain new funding from Sweden that enabled it to repay its arrears to the Fund. A month later, the Fund approved an 18-month stand-by arrangement, only the third such financing in Tanzania's 24 years of membership. Although the arrangement was for a modest 60 percent of quota (SDR 64 million, or $77 million), it unlocked the door for sizeable funding from other creditors and put an effective end to Tanzania's economic isolation.

Following this stand-by arrangement, the Fund provided financing to Tanzania exclusively through the less expensive and longer-term structural adjustment facilities: a structural adjustment facility (SAF) arrangement in 1987 and an enhanced

---

[109]In January 1986, on the same day that the Executive Board declared Liberia ineligible to use Fund resources (see Chapter 16), it declined to impose a similar sanction on Tanzania. See minutes of EBM/86/11 (January 24, 1986).

[110]"Tanzania—Request for Stand-by Arrangement," EBS/86/183 (August 8, 1986), Annex III.

structural adjustment facility (ESAF) arrangement in 1991. As conditions for those loans, the Fund became more actively involved in advising the authorities on structural reforms, including notably agricultural production incentives and marketing arrangements, banking reforms, and improvements in the operations of parastatal enterprises.[111] The most far-reaching changes, however, those that would imply unleashing the private sector, remained too controversial at that time.

Proliferation of Performance Criteria

As noted earlier, another guiding principle for conditionality is to impose no more conditions than are necessary to ensure the success of the program in restoring external viability. Nonetheless, in the years following the affirmation of that principle in 1979, the number of criteria jumped sharply (Figure 13.5). That fact generated criticism both from borrowers and academic economists, who argued that the Fund was meddling unnecessarily and inefficiently in the management of countries' economic affairs.[112] Inside the Fund, almost everyone expressed a desire to simplify the system, but the Executive Board was unable to agree on where or how to cut.

A core set of three performance criteria defines the Fund's approach to conditionality. At least since the late 1960s, most upper-tranche lending arrangements have included a monetary ceiling, on domestic credit creation by the banking system or the monetary authorities; a fiscal ceiling, on overall government borrowing or on borrowing from the banking system; and a prohibition against introducing or intensifying exchange or trade restrictions. The increase in the number of proscriptions that took place in the 1980s reflected two developments: the addition of new general criteria, and the proliferation of subceilings and other specific criteria in cases where the core standards were thought to be inappropriate or inadequate.

Two general additions were particularly important. One, discussed earlier, was a foreign borrowing ceiling, usually on official medium- and long-term external debt. The increased use of such ceilings in the 1980s often added two or more criteria, when the overall ceiling was supplemented by a subceiling on certain categories of debt or by a separate limit on short-term borrowing. Second, restrictions on accumulating arrears to external creditors became much more common. When a country asking to borrow from the Fund has outstanding arrears to other creditors, the arrangement usually requires a phased reduction and eventual elimination of those arrears; such cases became more common in the 1980s.[113] Moreover, the Fund began making preemptive strikes, prohibiting the introduction of arrears in cases

---

[111]See "Tanzania—Second Review Under the Stand-by Arrangement and Request for Arrangement Under the Structural Adjustment Facility," EBS/87/213 (October 8, 1987).

[112]See Sengupta and others (1987), paras. 57–63; and the paper by Tony Killick in Boughton and Lateef (1995), pp. 146–52.

[113]For the evolution of Fund practice regarding arrears to external creditors, see Chapter 11.

Figure 13.5 Performance Criteria, 1968–90

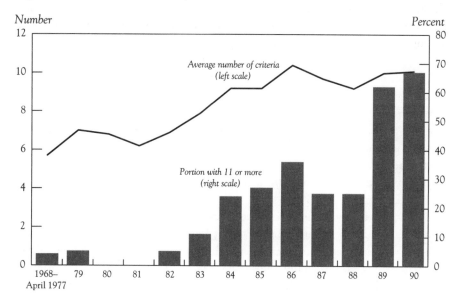

where no arrears existed but where a real danger was thought to be present.[114] Largely because of these two factors, all Fund arrangements beginning in 1983 included at least five performance criteria, whereas many earlier arrangements had fewer clauses.[115]

The larger and more controversial issue relates to the proliferation of subceilings and other criteria that derive from the circumstances in a particular country. A substantial minority of programs in the 1980s included "balance of payments tests," most often as a floor on the net foreign assets of the monetary authorities. That criterion was designed to prevent the authorities from running down reserves or running up short-term debts to defend an overvalued exchange rate. Alternatively, as described earlier in this chapter, many programs included "real exchange rate rules" requiring the authorities to adjust the nominal exchange rate in response to changes in the inflation rate. Since exchange rate policy was commonly an important concern in program design, criteria such as these often raised the total number of performance clauses to the high single digits without doing any violence to the injunction limiting criteria to the key macroeconomic indicators. In fact, by 1986 all upper-tranche arrangements contained at least eight performance clauses, and many contained several more than that.

---

[114]For several months in 1984–85, Fund arrangements also included a performance criterion prohibiting drawings while payments to the Fund were in arrears. Subsequently, that clause was replaced by a general condition governing arrangements with countries in arrears; see Executive Board Decision No. 7678-(84/62), adopted April 20, 1984; and No. 7908-(85/26), adopted February 20, 1985 (in the Appendix to Chapter 16). The Fund-arrears criterion is excluded from the 1984–85 data in Figure 13.5.

[115]See "Program Design and Performance Criteria," EBS/86/211, Sup. 1 (September 11, 1986).

If the Fund was vulnerable in the 1980s to a charge of micromanaging the economies of some borrowing countries, the issue related primarily to those cases with double-digit performance criteria. As a rule, where more than ten criteria were applied, the Fund staff had concluded that the standard macroeconomic statistics were inadequate measures of progress, usually because the country's policies included controls that distorted the signals from prices and from monetary and credit aggregates.[116] A few stand-by arrangements with as many as 15 criteria had been written as early as the 1960s. By the mid-1980s, the portion of programs in which micromanagement was judged (rightly or wrongly) to be necessary for the success of the adjustment program had ballooned. Through 1982, fewer than 5 percent of upper-tranche arrangements contained 11 or more performance clauses. That portion rose sharply throughout the 1980s until it became the rule rather than the exception (Figure 13.5).

Proliferation of very specific conditions took two forms. First, many programs for countries without a strong record of policy implementation included subsidiary as well as overall constraints, such as a ceiling on noninvestment public sector spending and a floor on fiscal revenues in addition to a ceiling on the fiscal deficit. Second, when the authorities themselves undertook to micromanage the national economy through central planning or extensive use of controls on market prices and activity, stand-by arrangements often incorporated constraints on several of the government's own policy levers.[117]

Yugoslavia provides a clear example of micromanagement in programs for a highly controlled economy. In April 1984, the IMF agreed to lend Yugoslavia up to SDR 370 million (approximately $390 million) on a stand-by basis over the next 12 months. In applying for the stand-by arrangement, the finance minister and the central bank governor submitted a 24-paragraph Letter of Intent specifying their economic policy program for the coming year. The letter was supplemented by nine detailed "technical notes" explaining exactly how the authorities intended to adjust public sector prices, control the exchange rate, ensure financial discipline in the financial sector, determine interest rates in the banking sector, limit the growth of the banks' domestic assets, control public sector revenues, limit bank lending to the public sector, limit borrowing from abroad, and strengthen the balance of payments. The stand-by arrangement approved by the Executive Board specified a list of some 15 performance criteria that would have to be met before each of the scheduled quarterly drawings could be made. For example, the Letter of Intent stated that the existing freeze on prices would be lifted by May 1, and it set out a plan for subsequently keeping certain public sector prices in line with

---

[116]Counting the number of performance criteria is somewhat arbitrary. If, for example, a stand-by arrangement requires the authorities to remove certain exchange restrictions and prohibits them from introducing new restrictions, the constraints could be written in one clause or two. The Fund's practices in this regard did fluctuate over time, and the late-1980s data in Figure 13.5 may not be strictly commensurate with the earlier figures, but the difficulty does not negate the fact of a sharp increase in the 1980s.

[117]See Chapter 2 for a discussion of the more general implications of the Fund's analysis of centrally planned economies.

market forces. The stand-by arrangement provided that "Yugoslavia will not make purchases . . . [d]uring any period in which . . . the intention regarding the price freeze . . . has not been carried out; or . . . the targets regarding prices of railway transportation [etc.] . . . have not been met."[118] In the event, Yugoslavia met most of the conditions, the Executive Board granted waivers for the exceptions, and the full amount of the arrangement was drawn.

The most comprehensive review of this issue took place in 1987. Directors from indebted countries generally attributed the "irritating" and "intimidating" proliferation of performance clauses to an "increasing aversion to risk" on the part of the Fund (in the phrase of Alexandre Kafka, the Director for Brazil) and on an "obsession" with quantitative precision (Ghassem Salekhou of Iran) rather than to an increasing complexity of problems the Fund was called upon to solve. Directors from creditor countries, however, were cautious about trying to reduce the complexities; some, such as Charles H. Dallara (United States), called for a broadening of the range of performance clauses to cover structural policies as well.[119] Given these divergent views, it is not surprising that no consensus was reached on changing the Fund's policies. Even so, the issue had been aired at the table, and the staff subsequently did manage to whittle down the number of performance clauses slightly.

Prior Actions

Yet another delicate balancing act arose with regard to whether the Fund should insist that borrowers take corrective actions *before* drawing on the Fund's resources. Requiring prior actions was considered punitive by some and merely prudent by others. Accordingly, the 1979 guidelines stipulated that a "member may be expected to adopt some corrective measures before a stand-by arrangement is approved by the Fund, but only if necessary to enable the member to adopt and carry out a program consistent with the Fund's provisions and policies" (Guideline 7). In practice, this guideline often meant that countries with a poor "track record" of policy implementation might be required to prove a new level of determination before management would agree to present the request to the Executive Board. It thus raised the specter of unequal treatment and was to be used as sparingly as possible.[120]

During the 1980s, the requirement of prior actions became common, especially in the form of exchange rate devaluations or other action to correct for an earlier loss of international competitiveness. Tax reforms and adjustments to administered prices also were frequent candidates for prior action. Since the management of the

---

[118]"Yugoslavia—Stand-by Arrangements," EBS/84/65, Sup. 1 (April 19, 1984).

[119]Minutes of EBM/87/70 (May 6, 1987), p. 6 (Kafka), p. 26 (Salekhou), and p. 41 (Dallara). The point about excessive conditionality being intimidating to potential borrowers was made by Janardana Reddy (Alternate—Fiji).

[120]Note the distinction between "prior actions" taken before Board approval and "preconditions" to be carried out after Board approval but before drawing on the arrangement. Avoidance of preconditions was one of the issues raised in the discussion of Sierra Leone described earlier in this chapter.

exchange rate usually was too sensitive an issue to be controlled through an explicit performance criterion, an initial devaluation often preceded Fund approval of an arrangement (either as a required prior action or as a preemptive move by the authorities). Commitments on subsequent actions in many cases were handled through a separate letter from the authorities seen only by the Fund's management and a few senior staff, not by the Executive Board.

The staff gradually abandoned the notion that the use of prior actions should be minimized. The background paper for the 1986 conditionality review argued that "the importance of prior actions in establishing the credibility of the member's program cannot be overstressed." Although that conclusion was challenged by several Executive Directors at the review (notably Finaish, Kafka, Julius Ismael of Indonesia, Samba Mawakani of Zaïre, and Salekhou), the Managing Director summed up the sense of the Board by saying that "most Directors stressed that prior actions were often critical to the success of programs." [121]

Allowing for Contingencies

Economies never evolve in quite the way that economists and politicians expect. Owing to misjudgments about the structure of the economy or to external shocks (or both), the Fund sometimes found that a country was failing to progress satisfactorily toward external viability even though it had met all of the specified performance criteria. Similarly, failure to meet the performance criteria in a stand-by arrangement did not necessarily mean that the economy was in poor shape.[122] In either case, the Fund had liberal recourse to waivers for and revisions in performance criteria.[123] Because of the uncertainties and potential delays associated

---

[121]"Program Design and Performance Criteria," EBS/86/211 (September 8, 1986), p. 7; minutes of EBM/86/190–91 (December 3, 1986); and Polak (1991), p. 13.

[122]In 1988, the staff reviewed 149 stand-by and extended arrangements approved during the preceding five years. In 25 percent of the cases, the performance criteria had been observed and the overall external objectives of the program had been met; in another 36 percent, neither category had been satisfied. Of the remainder, in 17 percent of the cases the authorities had met the performance criteria but had failed to meet their external goals, while in 21 percent the external goals had been met despite a breaching of some of the performance criteria. See "Conditionality," EBS/88/50 (March 2, 1988), Table 4, p. 28.

[123]When performance clauses were introduced in the late 1950s, the intention was that the country would have an automatic right to draw on the stand-by arrangement as long as it met the specified criteria. Post-approval program reviews were primarily to set criteria for the remaining part of the arrangement in situations where complete data were not available at the outset. As experience increasingly showed that the linkages between performance criteria (adhering to the agreed policies) and economic performance (achieving external viability in the sense described on p. 557) were not always firm, midterm reviews increasingly were used to reevaluate the proper settings for the performance criteria or to evaluate the need for waivers of the original requirements. As Polak (1991, p. 56) observes, this practice weakened the guarantee implicit in the initial agreements, but it did introduce a necessary degree of flexibility. Although no survey of the incidence of waivers was made at the time of the study mentioned in the preceding note, a 1987 review found that waivers or modifications in performance criteria were granted in about half of the programs approved during 1983–86; "Program Monitoring—Recent Experiences," EBS/87/48 (March 2, 1987), p. 14.

with having to request a waiver or modification, some borrowers began pressing for contingency provisions in the initial agreement.

The Fund was galvanized into action on this issue by the necessity of including contingency provisions in the 1986 stand-by arrangement with Mexico. As related in Chapter 10, the Managing Director broke a stalemate in the negotiations with Mexico by introducing two innovative contingency clauses: one that would allow the government to undertake additional investment spending (financed in part by loans from the World Bank) if output growth fell below a benchmark rate, and one that linked the amount of financing to the price of oil (an unexpected fall in the price of Mexico's exported oil would trigger additional credits from the Fund and the commercial banks, and a rise would trigger a reduction).[124] Even before the ink was dry, the Fund had to decide whether this type of provision should be made more generally available.

The staff prepared a paper in the fall of 1986 that set out the issues related to contingency provisions but avoided taking a position on whether their use should be generalized in the Fund. The paper particularly stressed the danger that relaxing conditionality in the event of adverse external developments could weaken the authorities' commitment to undertake adjustment at the very moment when the need for adjustment was greater than ever. Provision for automatic adjustment could, however, strengthen the initial agreement and increase the likelihood of its success (as had clearly happened with the Mexican arrangement).[125] Executive Directors, on the whole, were more impressed by the dangers than by the promises, and no action was taken: "Most Directors were not ready to consider any *generalized* use of such schemes *at this time* and emphasized the need to approach this matter *with caution and on a case-by-case basis*" (summing up; emphasis added).[126] Contingency mechanisms related to a borrower's growth rate were particularly discouraged, and most Directors felt that contingencies related to export prices should be examined again in the next scheduled review of the Compensatory Financing Facility (see Chapter 15). For the moment, the Managing Director had a limited mandate to experiment if necessary but not to push the boundaries any further.

---

[124]For several years prior to 1986, many Fund arrangements provided for automatic technical adjustments in cases where the quality of the data base was inadequate, and for more substantive adjustments in response to exogenous shifts in the availability of financing. The closest precedents for the type of automatic contingency adjustments included in the 1986 Mexican program are found in arrangements for Chile and South Africa. Chile's stand-by arrangements of 1968 and 1969, and the 1985 extended arrangement, included provisions for revising certain performance criteria in case of major changes in the price of copper. The 1982 stand-by arrangement for South Africa provided for revisions if the price of gold fell below a benchmark level.

[125]"Program Design and Performance Criteria—Automatic Adjustments in Response to Developments in Commodity Prices and Economic Growth," EBS/86/211, Sup. 2 (November 11, 1986); see Appendix I and II for the pre-1986 experience summarized in the preceding footnote.

[126]The Board discussion was at EBM/86/190–91 (December 3, 1986) and 192 (December 5); for the Managing Director's summing up on the role of contingency allowances and automatic adjustments, see the minutes of meeting 86/91, pp. 51–53. The quoted passage is found on p. 52.

Growth-Oriented Adjustment?

> The purposes of the International Monetary Fund are: . . .
>
> (ii) To facilitate the expansion and balanced growth of international trade, and to contribute thereby to the promotion and maintenance of high levels of employment and real income and to the development of the productive resources of all members as primary objectives of economic policy.
>
> *Articles of Agreement*, Article I

The single issue that dominated the conditionality debates more than any other was the relationship between adjustment and growth. So crucial was this linkage for economic success and political stability that partisans often resorted to demagoguery. On one side, it was argued that adjustment was synonymous with austerity and that austerity was the enemy of growth; on the other, that growth could not be sustained without effective adjustment. Both arguments, of course, were true, but neither was much help. An excessive current account deficit can be reduced either by stimulating exports (which will raise growth) or by compressing imports (which may depress growth). During an adjustment phase, import compression almost always precedes whatever stimulus may occur to exports, so that growth is likely to be weakened in the short run. Countries can sometimes sustain growth temporarily by ignoring the balance of payments constraint, but sooner or later—usually within a few years—they will have to confront the unpleasant calculus of the adjustment process.

Until the mid-1970s, the Fund's lending arrangements were always for a short enough period that conflicts between growth and adjustment did not arise. Extended arrangements, whether made through the EFF or categorized as longer-term stand-by arrangements, raised the problem of perseverance: What could the Fund do to ensure that borrowers could adhere to an adjustment program for three years or more and not be thrown off course by a severely depressed economy? The staff recognized this problem explicitly in a paper prepared for a 1978 review of conditionality:

> Purely deflationary policies . . . may . . . have a deleterious effect on investment and fail to encourage the required shift of resources to the external sector. In the absence of an improvement in . . . growth . . . political and social pressures will in the course of time cause a reversal of [adjustment] policies with the result that the task of eventual correction may become more formidable.[127]

The Executive Board discussion in February 1979 revealed a fundamental split in perception. Byanti Kharmawan argued that developing countries frequently got into economic difficulties because of factors outside their control, such as natural disasters or declines in the prices of their export commodities. Forcing countries to adopt contractionary macroeconomic policies at such times was likely to depress

---

[127]"Conditionality in the Upper Credit Tranches," SM/78/103 (April 19, 1978), p. 3.

their growth prospects further and to be counterproductive both for the borrowing country and for the preservation of the Fund's assets. Kharmawan concluded that the nature of conditionality should take account of and vary with the source of the country's problems. Eckard Pieske (Germany) and others threw cold water on that idea, responding that a country's obligation to bring its external accounts into balance did not depend on the origins of the problem.[128]

The staff, in any event, did not have a model for making adjustment more conducive to economic growth, and efforts to find one floundered quietly throughout the first half of the 1980s. In a debriefing after the Interim Committee meeting of February 1983, de Larosière asked the staff to use a "keen eye to single out only those elements of economic activity that really have to be restricted, in order to sustain as much real growth as possible." Because of the ongoing debt crisis, growth would be more difficult to achieve than in the past, and the Fund would have to be "more imaginative" and to get "involved in aspects of economic development that are more fundamentally political."[129] Without a specific blueprint, however, it was difficult to make much headway in that direction.

The Fund was galvanized into a more concerted effort after the 1985 Annual Meetings in Seoul, principally in response to U.S. Treasury Secretary James Baker's call for "growth-oriented adjustment."[130] As discussed in Chapter 10, the "Baker strategy" identified a set of heavily indebted countries and aimed to prod creditors into providing additional financing on terms that would enable those countries to maintain essential imports in the short run and to reorient adjustment toward export- and growth-stimulating activities. Part of the Fund's response was to undertake a thorough reexamination of whether the standard conditionality on Fund lending could be restructured to support this growth-oriented strategy. During the conditionality review held a few months later, Executive Directors stressed that "more thought and more work was called for on the . . . relationship between Fund programs and growth."[131]

For the 1986 conditionality review, the issues paper prepared by ETR argued that, despite the persistence of "public misperceptions," conventional adjustment programs were already well designed to promote sustainable growth over a medium-term period; the misperceptions were attributable to the fact that adjusting countries often experienced a temporary slowdown in growth from *unsustainable* levels. The paper concluded that although more effective structural adjust-

---

[128]Minutes of EBM/79/29 (February 16, 1979), pp. 3–5. This argument, however, cut in both directions. At the Board meeting on Sierra Leone several months later (see above, p. 566), Onno Ruding argued that the arrangement should be subjected to especially strong conditionality because the economy's problems were largely domestic in origin.

[129]Summary notes (prepared February 23, 1983) on the Managing Director's remarks of February 17, prepared in the Managing Director's office. In IMF/RD Managing Director file (Accession 85/33, Box 3, Section 376).

[130]Separately but simultaneously, the Fund increased its focus on growth in structural adjustment programs for low-income countries that were financed by the structural adjustment facilities (SAF and ESAF). See Chapter 14.

[131]Chairman's summing up, minutes of EBM/86/13 (January 27, 1986), p. 12.

ment measures could contribute further to the promotion of growth, the existing guidelines on conditionality—which permitted the imposition of conditions on microeconomic variables "only in exceptional cases"—provided sufficient scope for the design of growth-oriented programs.[132] "Widespread attention" had been paid to structural issues in the design of programs in the first half of the 1980s, although the staff acknowledged that "the reforms achieved were often of a stepwise, piecemeal character."[133]

After discussing the matter for two days, Executive Directors agreed on January 27 that the Fund should do more to promote the restoration of growth in the heavily indebted countries, but they also supported the staff's view that the guidelines on conditionality in Fund-supported programs should not be changed to support a more growth-oriented strategy.[134] In summing up the Board discussion, the Managing Director concluded:

> A number of Directors felt that the Fund should give higher priority to the supply-side, structural aspects of Fund programs . . . in close association with the World Bank. . . . However, several other Directors warned the Fund staff not to go too far in the formulation and follow-up of microeconomic policies. While a few Directors held the view that conditionality guideline 9 on performance criteria should be extended to cover microeconomic criteria in a more routine way, this view was not supported by the majority of the Board.[135]

This reexamination continued with a review paper prepared in the Research Department, which was discussed at an Executive Board seminar in October 1986. While again defending the Fund's macroeconomic orientation to conditionality, the Research Department paper laid out several policies that could be expected to raise a country's sustainable growth rate. Setting interest rates at realistic levels (positive in real terms) helps to prevent capital flight, strengthen the domestic financial system, and provide funds for domestic investment. Public sector investments should be aimed at those with the highest social rates of return. And relative prices, including exchange rates, should be set so as to reflect underlying market pressures. The Fund's neoclassical emphasis on liberalization and macro-

---

[132]"Issues in the Implementation of Conditionality: Improving Program Design and Dealing with Prolonged Use," EBS/85/265 (December 5, 1985), p. 11 (on the growth issue) and pp. 36–37 (on the guidelines for conditionality).

[133]"Aspects of Program Design—A Review of the Experience in the 1980s of Countries with Upper Credit Tranche Arrangements Approved in 1982," EBS/85/277 (December 17, 1985), p. 63.

[134]The prevailing view was that the guideline limiting the use of microeconomic variables as performance criteria to "exceptional cases" had not prevented the staff from introducing such variables where it was appropriate to do so, and that the practice should not be generalized any more than it already was. Luke Leonard (Alternate—Ireland) suggested that it would be better to amend the guideline to reflect the already fairly general practice, and J. de Beaufort Wijnholds (Alternate—Netherlands) suggested that if the Board wanted the staff to go further in this direction, then the guideline should be amended. Most other Directors spoke in favor of the status quo.

[135]Minutes of EBM/86/13 (January 27, 1986), p. 14.

economic stabilization should, the report argued, provide the economic strength needed to pursue these longer-run growth-oriented policies.[136]

The Executive Board seminar brought forth several suggestions for broadening the design of Fund-supported programs to promote economic growth more directly. E.I.M. Mtei observed that the basic monetary model describes static equilibria; to study the requirements for economic growth, one needs a dynamic model that takes account of the fact that activity-depressing effects often work much more quickly than those that stimulate longer-run growth. Finaish remarked that since the usual staff approach was to assume a growth rate and to examine its implications, the first step should be to endogenize the growth rate in the model. On more specific issues, Jacques Polak argued that more could be done to strengthen banking systems in developing countries, Guillermo Ortiz suggested that the Fund had to take account of the fact that excessive indebtedness depressed growth, and Charles Dallara noted the importance of taking account of the supply-side effects of macroeconomic instruments such as fiscal policy.[137]

The next step involved a public airing of the issues, which gave the staff an opportunity to obtain the views of leading academics and policymakers, and to try to develop a coordinated response with the World Bank. The two institutions held a joint symposium in February 1987, which generated a stimulating collection of papers (Corbo, Goldstein, and Khan, 1987) but no consensus on how the Fund might alter its adjustment strategy other than at the margins. Stanley Fischer suggested that the Fund could help alleviate the recessionary effects of adjustment by recognizing that inflation may worsen government deficits and by promoting productive public sector investment. He also cited devaluations supported by incomes policies and the "avoidance of excessively high interest rates" as potentially growth-inducing tactics (p. 172). More generally, Fischer endorsed the neoclassical strategy of economic liberalization and export promotion, as did many other speakers at the conference. Jeffrey Sachs, however, warned of the dangers of accepting a "facile orthodoxy" that equated "outward orientation with market liberalization." The latter, he argued, was a distraction that often conflicted with the primary need for macroeconomic stability (pp. 292–94). Moreover, Sachs argued that because "extremely unequal income distributions" increased the difficulty that governments faced in improving economic efficiency, adjustment programs should be designed to alleviate distributional problems (p. 323). Manuel Guitián, however, concluded that the Fund's mandate was to help countries restore external viability; if it did that job well, growth would follow as the natural complement (p. 69).[138]

---

[136]In the published version of the paper, Research Department (1987), see pp. 32–35. Also see above, p. 570.

[137]Minutes of Executive Board Seminar 86/10 (October 20, 1986), pp. 15–16 (Mtei), 21 (Polak), 31–32 (Finaish), 36–37 (Ortiz), and 40 (Dallara).

[138]Fischer was Professor of Economics at MIT at the time of the symposium. He later served as Chief Economist at the World Bank and as First Deputy Managing Director of the IMF. Sachs was Professor of Economics at Harvard. Guitián was Deputy Director of ETR.

Empirical tests of these propositions are difficult to devise, but the general complementarity of stabilization and growth was demonstrated most clearly by occasional attempts to deny or ignore it. At the time of the symposium, Peru was in the early stages of an experiment in which the government unilaterally ran up arrears to foreign creditors, ran down its foreign exchange reserves, allowed inflation to rise sharply, and ignored the consequent collapse in its international credit rating. The economy achieved an output growth rate averaging 9 percent a year for 1986 and 1987 but then ran out of steam. For the next two years, output fell by 9 and 13 percent, respectively. At the end of the decade, Peru's GDP was 5 percent lower in real terms than in 1985 and inflation was raging at an annual rate of 3,400 percent, a collapse that set the stage for a return to economic orthodoxy in the 1990s.[139] Such experiences unfortunately provided little guidance for strengthening the economies of countries that took the medicine needed to stabilize but still found growth elusive.

The 1987 G-24 Report (Sengupta and others, 1987; also see above, p. 570) sought to provide help for the latter group of countries by reorienting financial programming more directly toward raising growth rates. Specifically, the report suggested that the Fund should conduct "growth exercises" as a prelude to its financial program exercises. Developing countries typically faced two gaps, the report argued: a shortage of domestic saving to finance potentially profitable capital investment, and a shortage of foreign exchange (from export receipts and inflows of foreign capital) to finance essential imports (for basic consumption needs and capital investment). From those two gaps and a model linking investment to growth, one could in principle calculate the minimum level of external financing needed to sustain a targeted rate of economic growth. Together with the Fund's conventional approach linking domestic financial policies to the balance of payments, one could solve simultaneously for the policy and external-financing requirements for external viability and sustainable growth.[140]

The staff responded to the G-24 by producing two papers, one setting out a methodology for conducting "growth exercises" and the other analyzing more broadly the determinants of growth in developing countries.[141] Essentially, these papers took the basic growth-exercise proposal as a starting point, showed how it could be integrated with financial programming based on the conventional monetary model, and discussed the many theoretical and empirical extensions that

---

[139]The Peruvian economy is discussed more fully in relation to the country's arrears to the Fund, in Chapter 16. The Brazilian experience with rapid but short-lived growth was similar; see the sections on Brazil in Chapters 9–11, and the summary in Chapter 12.

[140]The two-gap growth model, derived from seminal work by Hollis Chenery and others in the 1960s (see Chenery and Strout, 1966), had long been in use at the World Bank. In the mid-1980s, Bank economists undertook to combine that model with the Fund's monetary approach to produce an operational framework for adjustment with growth; for an exposition, see Khan, Montiel, and Haque (1990). That synthesis provided the theoretical framework for the suggestions from the G-24 Deputies.

[141]"Issues in the Design of Growth Exercises," SM/87/267 (November 17, 1987), and "Financial Programming and Growth Exercises," SM/87/268 (same date).

might be needed to make the approach applicable to the real world. The staff agreed that growth depended in part on the availability of external financing, but the papers stressed that this relationship was complex and must be embedded in a much broader model in which the roles of structural policies and of potential shifts between capital and labor in production were fully incorporated. In that spirit, the Executive Board approved the growth exercise idea, in principle, in December 1987.[142]

A few months later, at the 1988 review of the conditionality guidelines, the Board considered anew whether the analysis of the adjustment-growth nexus had progressed to the point where it could be incorporated into the guidelines. The staff paper for the review stated frankly that the primary goal in designing adjustment programs was achieving balance of payments viability. Restoring growth was important for preventing "adjustment fatigue," but no consensus existed on how to direct conditionality toward that objective.[143] Nikos Kyriazidis (Alternate—Greece) rejected that conclusion and asked that "the objective of promoting orderly economic growth, as spelled out in Article IV, Section 1, should be explicitly incorporated into the guidelines." Dallara agreed and proposed that Guideline 9 be amended to state that "nonmacroeconomic" performance criteria are no longer to be limited to "exceptional cases." Dallara suggested several growth-enhancing structural policies that could be stressed in the design of conditionality: elimination of nonmarket pricing systems, measures to strengthen the financial system, improvements in tax and expenditure policies, and efficiency improvements in public enterprises.

The attack on growth-oriented conditionality was led by Directors from developing countries. Ortiz and Arjun Sengupta (India), among others, questioned the view that market liberalization and reduction of institutional constraints would necessarily improve efficiency or raise growth. Sengupta also pointed out that improving efficiency was not sufficient for raising growth in low-income countries, because "savings growth cannot take place without an increase in . . . incomes." Rather than more complex conditionality, what was needed in this view was more flexibility in program implementation. In the words of Mawakani Samba (Zaïre), the Fund should eschew "shock" programs and aim for "gradual adjustment that will preserve growth." If the period for programs were lengthened, borrowers would have the time to carry out their own structural reforms. Similarly, Ahmed Abdallah (Kenya) agreed that structural reforms were needed in many countries but ar-

---

[142]The endorsement was tentative, as the Managing Director's summing up of the meeting made clear: "Directors emphasized that Fund-supported programs should promote sustainable economic growth in a medium-term perspective. . . . [A] number of Directors felt that quantified 'growth exercises' would be a useful complement to the financial exercises in the design of Fund-supported adjustment programs. . . . Directors expressed concern about the uncertainty necessarily involved in this approach . . . although some speakers noted that uncertainty was also characteristic of the traditional financial programming approach. . . . Directors encouraged the staff to continue its efforts to examine and strengthen the analytical foundations of growth exercises." Minutes of EBM/87/174 (December 16, 1987), pp. 23–25.

[143]"Conditionality—A Survey of Current Issues," EBS/88/50 (March 2, 1988), pp. 9–10.

gued that it was the authorities' role, not the Fund's, to design and carry out institutional change.[144]

Despite a universal agreement that growth was a "primary objective of economic policy" and that adjustment would often fail if growth was too long in coming, all efforts to link adjustment to growth foundered on this simple dilemma. Lacking a well-established and validated model of economic growth, the Fund could not require structural reforms as a condition for its credits. Not until domestic political support would emerge for those reforms in their own right—not until the silent revolution could be won—would the dichotomy between growth and stability finally fade away.[145]

Evaluating the Success of Fund Programs

The experimentation of the 1980s confirmed the difficulty of designing and carrying out effective adjustment programs, but it did not by itself resolve the underlying questions posed at the beginning of this chapter: Was the basic model appropriate, and was the basic strategy successful? Unfortunately, the extensive literature that emerged to evaluate the success of Fund programs is as difficult to evaluate as its subject. An ideal study would compare each country's performance under an adjustment program with the performance it would have had without adjustment. Since that ideal was unattainable, each study tried to approximate it as well as possible given the limitations of data and techniques.

Mohsin Khan's 1990 review of this literature distinguished four branches.[146] First, several early studies compared the economic performance of countries before and after implementing Fund-supported adjustment programs. Those studies—which mostly covered programs before the 1980s—generally reached ambiguous conclusions. Whether such studies reveal weak effects from Fund conditionality or offsetting effects from other forces is, however, impossible to judge. Second, several other studies of programs from the 1970s and early 1980s compared economic performance of adjusting countries with a "control sample" of nonadjusting countries that are thought to have faced similar conditions. The most sophisticated example of this genre—Goldstein and Montiel (1986)—found no statistically significant effects on performance from adjustment programs.[147] Third, a few published

---

[144]Minutes of EBM/88/58 (April 6, 1988), pp. 5 (Mawakani), 25–26 (Kyriazidis), 31–35 (Dallara), and 40 (Abdallah); and EBM/88/59 (same date), pp. 4 (Ortiz) and 7 (Sengupta).

[145]In the first half of the 1990s, the staff continued to analyze relationships between adjustment and growth, primarily through detailed case studies. For two such multicountry studies, see Goldsbrough and others (1996) and Hadjimichael and others (1996).

[146]Khan (1990) includes a comprehensive list and detailed discussion of the studies alluded to in the text of this paragraph. Also see Haque and Khan (1998), Killick (1995), Polak (1991, pp. 41–45), and the papers in Williamson (1983).

[147]Selecting a control group with similar initial conditions is not easy. Santaella (1996) studied more than 100 Fund-supported programs in the period 1973–91 and found that on average, countries faced significantly worse conditions in the period preceding adoption of an adjustment program than in nonprogram periods.

studies by Fund staff have compared outcomes for selected macroeconomic variables with the targets specified in the lending arrangements. Those studies—though they reveal little about the effects of programs on overall economic performance—found that program targets were met or exceeded in between one-half and two-thirds of the cases. Fourth, econometric studies based on simulation of estimated macroeconomic models, notably by Khan and Knight (1981, 1985), found significant positive effects from the successful implementation of adjustment programs.

Some later studies derived more positive conclusions by isolating the effects of Fund-supported programs from the more general effects of adjustment. For example, Edwards and Santaella (1993) examined 48 devaluations by developing countries between 1948 and 1971 and concluded that devaluation was more likely to have beneficial real effects when undertaken in the context of a Fund-supported adjustment program. Bagci and Perraudin (1997) found beneficial program effects in a comparison of economic performance within countries between periods with and without Fund-supported programs in effect.

The staff also conducted detailed studies for internal review almost annually during this period, as mandated by Guideline 12 (see Appendix). On five occasions, the staff reviewed in detail the experience under all of the upper-tranche arrangements approved in a particular period; on three other occasions, the analysis pertained to selected arrangements of a particular type. In all cases, the straightforward objective was to examine the extent to which countries had carried out their programs and the extent to which they had succeeded in achieving their objectives. These internal studies did not break new methodological ground, but they benefited from more extensive data than was accessible to outside researchers. Broadly speaking, the internal studies confirm the picture that emerges from the published literature: successful adjustment and sustainable growth are elusive goals, largely but not entirely because of the difficulty of carrying out stringent programs over a long enough period. The following summary relates the major findings.[148]

The first internal study, which covered the 11 arrangements approved in 1977, uncovered a widespread implementation failure. Most of the fiscal ceilings, and about half of the credit ceilings, had been breached. In only three of seven multiyear arrangements had negotiations succeeded in reaching understandings for the second year. Most countries had nonetheless experienced the expected improvements in their balance of payments and in inflation, though not necessarily in economic growth. This study was completed in 1979, shortly after the conclusion of most of the covered arrangements. The authors therefore were not particularly concerned by the apparent failure of programs to restore growth, since the benefits for growth were thought to take longer to appear.[149]

---

[148]In addition to the unpublished studies summarized here, Schadler (1995) and Schadler and others (1995) present a comprehensive analysis of arrangements approved in 1988–92.

[149]"Adjustment Programs Supported by Upper Credit Tranche Stand-by Assignments, 1977," EBS/79/635 (December 26, 1979).

The next review looked at the 22 stand-by arrangements approved in 1978 and 1979.[150] The staff found that performance criteria had been met in about half of these cases and that macroeconomic performance generally had improved but often had fallen short of the objectives specified at the outset. Output growth in countries with Fund arrangements had remained below the average for all non-oil developing countries, but the initial gap had been partially closed.[151] Similar conclusions emerged from a 1982 review of 17 stand-by arrangements approved in 1980 and 12 extended arrangements approved in 1978–80. The biggest factor determining success or failure of these arrangements was judged to be the country's own commitment to carrying out the program, the factor that later became known by the buzzword "ownership." The paper acknowledged that more work was needed to ensure that programs were politically viable, especially in multiyear programs where adjustment fatigue was likely to be a problem.[152]

Next, a review of 27 arrangements approved in 1981 shifted attention away from whether performance criteria were met and toward whether more fundamental objectives (balance of payments viability and restoration of growth) were achieved. The broad assessment, however, was unchanged: success was mixed. Successful countries usually were those who had acted quickly, had sustained the adjustment process throughout the period of the arrangement, and had responded flexibly to changing circumstances so as to stay on target.[153]

The 1984 review offered a longer-run and more intensive analysis of a selected sample of large borrowers (the 25 countries to which the Fund made the largest cumulative commitments relative to quota during 1977–80). This study stressed the "key role of widening budget deficits" as a cause of the initial problems that led countries to borrow from the Fund, and the correspondingly important role of fiscal adjustment in reducing external deficits. With the longer lens of this study, it became clear that countries that undertook sustained fiscal retrenchment experienced, on average, a strengthening of economic growth within four years after the initiation of adjustment.[154]

The next study examined results for the 22 countries that had undertaken adjustment programs in 1982: the year of the international debt crisis. By 1985, six of those countries had successfully carried out their programs and appeared to be

---

[150]Two of the nominal total of 23 stand-by arrangements were combined for the study: the 1979 arrangement with Peru was treated as an augmentation of the 1978 arrangement rather than as a new program. The seven extended arrangements were excluded from the study on the grounds that they were still active and could not yet be evaluated.

[151]"Review of Upper Credit Tranche Stand-by Arrangements Approved in 1978–79 and Some Issues Related to Conditionality," EBS/81/152 (July 14, 1981).

[152]"Review of Recent Extended and Upper Credit Tranche Stand-by Arrangements," EBS/82/97 (June 9, 1982) and "Additional Information," Sup. 1 (June 10).

[153]"Review of Upper Credit Tranche Arrangement Approved in 1981 and of Some Issues Related to Conditionality," EBS/83/215 (October 4, 1983) and "Upper Credit Tranche Stand-by and Extended Arrangements Approved in 1981," EBS/83/216 (October 4, 1983)."

[154]"Experience with Adjustment Policies," EBS/84/228 (November 13, 1984); the quotation is from p. 50.

at or near a viable external payments position; the others all still had large and un-sustainable payments deficits. The reasons for failure to carry out programs to completion or for performance to rebound followed a now-familiar pattern. Most commonly, countries had been unable to implement either the large cuts in government spending or the large increases in tax revenues that so many of them needed. In addition, in several cases both the countries and the Fund had underestimated the amount of adjustment that was ultimately needed.[155] These findings were reinforced further by the 1987 review summarized at the outset of this section, which examined the experience of the record number of 34 countries that had entered into upper-tranche arrangements in 1983.

In 1989, the staff took a different approach and presented a detailed analysis of nine country studies (with a total of 40 Fund arrangements, 1976–87), representing a broad spectrum of developing countries.[156] This study identified several instances in which the specific conditionality appeared not to have been appropriate for the circumstances at hand. Explanations included initial underestimation of the country's economic problems, excessive optimism about the availability of external financing, willingness by the Fund to enter into arrangements in the face of inadequate policy commitments, laxity in the granting of waivers or modifications, and concern about the systemic implications of withholding financial support. For programs to be successful, the staff concluded, they had to center on strong adjustment of financial and exchange rate policies, backed up in many cases by major structural reforms. The problem, in short, was not with the basic model for designing adjustment programs; the problem was to be both firm and flexible in applying that model.

All of these surveys, of necessity, stopped short of answering the ultimate question of whether adjustment programs were designed as well as could be realistically expected. When countries failed to carry out policies that they had promised to implement, did they fail because they lacked will, wisdom, and courage, or because they had made unrealistic promises under duress? When the Fund failed to apply its own standards and allowed countries to borrow under poorly designed and weakly implemented programs, did it fail because it lacked will, wisdom, and courage, or because it recognized the political and social constraints on its borrowers and weighed the risks of lending against the risk of letting the country's economy sink even further? In a world of national governments and international organizations with limited vision and powers, is a success rate of between one-fourth and one-half in rescuing floundering economies alarming or simply realis-

---

[155]"Aspects of Program Design," EBS/85/277 (December 17, 1985).

[156]The sample included three African countries (Ghana, Morocco, and Zambia), two Asian (Bangladesh and the Philippines), two from Latin America (Chile and Mexico), and one each from Europe and the Middle East (Yugoslavia and Egypt). This selection was designed to include low-income countries eligible for concessional (SAF) loans as well as middle-income countries; borrowers from commercial as well as official sources; heavily and less indebted countries; and successful and less successful adjusters. All nine had undertaken at least three stand-by or extended arrangements with the Fund in the preceding decade.

tic?[157] Such questions underlie any empirical analysis, but they do not admit of unambiguous answers.

Prolonged Usage

One widespread consequence of the difficulty of implementing successful adjustment programs was that many countries became regular and prolonged users of Fund resources. Despite the Fund's goal of restoring external viability to borrowing countries, the number of prolonged users (as defined in the Fund) rose from 6 in 1980 to more than 30 in 1987 before dropping back (Figure 13.6). Notably, 5 countries—mostly with very low incomes—had lending arrangements in effect for at least part of each of the 11 years covered here, 1979–89. In West Africa, Senegal, Togo, and Zaïre each had 7 or more stand-by or extended arrangements in those years plus concessional loans from the Fund's structural adjustment facilities. And in the Caribbean, both Haiti and Jamaica had lending arrangements in effect throughout the period.

Although the reasons for countries being unable over long periods to extricate themselves from economic difficulties—and from the Fund—obviously vary from case to case, the underlying cause is nearly always a political paralysis that prevents rational economic policymaking. By the 1980s, some critics were charging that the Fund was fostering that paralysis by providing what amounted to insurance against bad economic outcomes. Roland Vaubel, a leading exponent of applying "public choice" analysis to international institutions, acknowledged that conditionality could reduce the "moral hazard" from the availability of credits to countries in trouble, but he complained that it was ineffective because it was applied only after the country was already in trouble.[158]

A close examination of actual cases suggests that the prevailing problem is usually a gap between the short-term horizons over which the authorities try to maximize their own utility and maintain power and the longer horizons over which social welfare is maximized. The empirical question is whether the authorities are forward-looking enough to take account of the expected costs of submitting to the policy constraints that accompany Fund credits. If conditionality is applied appropriately and is effective within the authorities' horizon, it should nullify the expected net short-run benefit from myopic policymaking. In many cases, that point has been reached only after long and bitter experience.

---

[157]The 1992 Wapenhans Report on World Bank lending found that although three-fourths of Bank-financed projects were earning satisfactory rates of return, nearly 40 percent of borrowing countries had "major problems" with at least 25 percent of their projects. The report noted that any measure of success or failure of a development institution was arbitrary, and that a very low failure rate could indicate that the Bank was "not taking risks in a high-risk business" (p. 3).

[158]See Vaubel (1991), especially pp. 230–35. Public choice theory attempts to explain the actions of public sector institutions by examining the incentives facing the principal agents (management, staff, major stakeholders). The moral hazard problem is that insurance must be coupled with adequate safeguards so that insured parties will have an incentive to prevent losses. Vaubel argued that the Fund could reduce moral hazard by refusing to lend to countries that had followed inappropriate policies, but the Fund was unlikely to do so because it would restrict lending and because the staff derives utility from lending.

Figure 13.6. Prolonged Users of Fund Resources, 1980–90

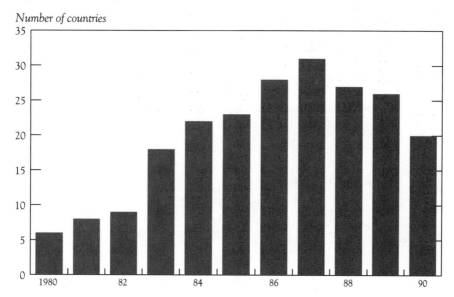

Number of countries

Note: A prolonged user is defined here as one with five or more annual programs in the preceding 10 years and with outstanding credit of at least 100 percent of quota in the year indicated.

As an illustration, consider the following story.

The Philippines

> The story of our debt restructuring is really the story of my life. A large part of my recent experience has involved the tension between the internationally oriented sectors of our economy, which directly benefit from the debt restructuring exercise, and the much larger domestically oriented sectors, which get constricted through the austerity measures and may not share the benefits to the same extent.
>
> Cesar E. A. Virata
> Prime Minister of the Philippines
> September 1985[159]

The Philippines had one of the longest outstanding debit positions in the Fund, having attempted to implement a total of 23 Fund-supported adjustment programs between 1962 and 1998 and having had outstanding obligations to the Fund continuously since 1968 (Figure 13.7).[160] The explanation for the country's seemingly perpetual need for extraordinary external financing and adjustment is complex and extends well beyond the boundaries of a history of the work of the IMF. As Prime Minister Virata's poignant statement suggests, this problem be-

---

[159]For the text of this speech, which was given in London, see IMF/RD Managing Director file "Philippines, Vol. VI" (Accession 87/136, Box 2, Section 168).

[160]Sudan and Pakistan have had outstanding drawings since 1965, but they have had fewer Fund-supported programs than the Philippines.

Figure 13.7. Philippines: IMF Borrowing and Outstanding Credit

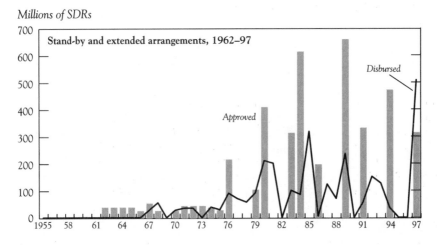

Millions of SDRs

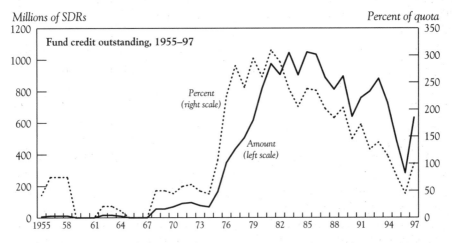

Millions of SDRs   *Percent of quota*

came a national obsession, a barrier that had to be breached before normalcy could be restored to economic affairs in the Philippines. The central part of this story developed from a domestic investment boom that began in earnest in 1979, through to a major financial crisis that peaked in the latter part of 1983, and on until a new government replaced the regime of President Ferdinand Marcos in 1986.

As this History opened in 1979, a three-year extended arrangement had been fully utilized, raising the country's obligations to the Fund from less than SDR 40 million ($45 million, or 25 percent of quota) in mid-1975 to just over SDR 500 million ($650 million, or 240 percent of quota) at end-1978.[161] That program was

---

[161]For the background on the development of the Philippines' economic difficulties and the 1976–78 extended arrangement, see de Vries (1985), pp. 373–77. The end-1978 figure for obligations to the Fund also includes some outstanding balances from the oil facilities and the CFF, plus SDR 64 million ($83 million) in Trust Fund loans.

considered to have been reasonably successful, although it had been necessary to modify its targets and although the country clearly remained a long way from shore as it struggled to reach external viability. The Philippines was riding the crest of the surge in growth in the Middle East, as remittances from workers in that region limited the weakening of the current account and, in 1978, produced a fiscal surplus. The sustainability of that wave, however, was subject to doubt and was soon to be tested.

When the Executive Board met in June 1979 to consider the Philippines' request for a new six-month stand-by arrangement (for SDR 105 million, equivalent to $135 million or 50 percent of quota), the dominant issue was the effect of adverse external shocks on the country's ability to restore equilibrium to the balance of payments.[162] The prices of two of the country's principal exports—sugar and copper—had fallen precipitously on world markets at a time when the price of imported oil was rising sharply. It was thus appropriate that the resources to be made available under the stand-by arrangement would be supplemented by a CFF drawing (for SDR 44 million) to help cover the shortfall in export earnings. With this support, the authorities were thought to have the means to solidify the achievements of the previous three years.

What was not foreseen at the June 1979 meeting were the depth and persistence of the Philippine economy's structural problems. There was no dissent from the view expressed by Richard Lang (Alternate—New Zealand, speaking for the Philippines) that the economy had the capacity to sustain the real growth rate of about 6 percent a year that it had reached under the extended arrangement of 1976–78. But that growth had been achieved through investments in export-oriented industries that would eventually prove to be inefficient, import-dependent, and uncompetitive. Moreover, much of the external financing for those investments had come from commercial banks. As with so many other developing countries, the cost of servicing this debt would soon become prohibitive, and the flow of new money would suddenly dry up in the second half of 1982 in the wake of the international debt crisis. In the Philippines, the burden of the debt was known to be dangerously high even in mid-1979, but the magnitude of the danger could not be foreseen.[163]

The 1979 program, like its predecessor, was viewed as a success even though the balance of payments continued to deteriorate and external commercial debt continued to accumulate. The culprits were identified to be the low price of sugar—which was on the rebound by the end of the year—and the high price of oil. In these circumstances, another and much larger stand-by arrangement (along with

---

[162]Minutes of EBM/79/88–89 (June 11, 1979). The statement by Richard Lang cited in the next paragraph is on p. 27.

[163]One technical difficulty that faced the Fund staff was that while most countries reported official debt service separately from that on private debt, the Philippines did not. The debt-service ratio was relatively high for the Philippines, but part of the difference could be attributed to this reporting practice. It was natural to conclude that the country was in no worse shape than others, but in the event the argument turned out to be a lullaby.

another CFF drawing) was a clear necessity, and the Executive Board met to consider the request at the end of February 1980. Several Directors expressed concerns.[164] To take a few examples: Gerhard Laske (Germany) was worried, as he had been the previous June, about the debt buildup; Donald Syvrud (Alternate—United States) was worried about the inflationary effects of low interest rates, which were negative in real terms; Bernard Drabble (Canada) was worried about the unusually high proposed use of the Fund's supplementary (borrowed) resources; and Onno Ruding (Netherlands) was worried about the long-term continuous use of Fund resources without a solution to the balance of payments problem. In no case, however, were these concerns major enough to warrant formally objecting to or abstaining from approving the program.

External developments did not improve over the next two years, and in 1981 the domestic money market nearly collapsed in the wake of a scandal that became known as the Dewey Dee affair (after the local financier who triggered it).[165] Nonetheless, the program remained essentially on track, with the continuing and crucial exception of the nagging lack of improvement in the balance of payments.[166] By 1982, however, doubts about the ability of the authorities to effect the necessary degree of adjustment in the face of continuing domestic and external difficulties began to dominate discussions at the Fund. When the Philippines informally requested a new stand-by arrangement that February, de Larosière concluded that stronger measures—especially for budgetary control—would be needed before a program could be approved.[167] The fiscal, current account, and external debt positions had become unsustainable, and the authorities' views on what measures could feasibly be undertaken were far apart from those of the Fund's management and staff.

An important element of the difference in perspective in 1982 concerned the evaluation of the uses to which external financing had been put since the late 1970s. As noted above, a major component of the growth realized in 1976–78 had been investment in new industries. Most of those investments—for government-guaranteed private sector projects—had subsequently soured. The objectives certainly were laudable. Textile production had been modernized, copper smelting and nickel production facilities had been developed, a tree-planting program had been undertaken to promote timber exports, and so forth. In the aggregate, however, these projects required substantial inflows of foreign capital and failed to generate returns sufficient to service the resulting debt. The reasons for the lack of profitability of these investments are diverse. Ex ante, they were viewed as good prospects not only at home but also by major commercial banks who bid aggres-

---

[164]Minutes of EBM/80/30–31 (February 27, 1980).

[165]See Broad (1988). The longer-term costs of the resulting financial crisis are analyzed in Nascimento (1990).

[166]The 1980–82 stand-by arrangement, in the amount of SDR 410 million ($525 million; 195 percent of quota) was fully drawn.

[167]The Managing Director's disapproval of the request was noted on February 28, 1982 as a response on the February 19 back-to-office report from the Article IV consultation mission; in IMF/RD Managing Director file "Philippines, 1982" (Accession 84/21, Box 3, Section 168).

sively to help finance them. Subsequently, both the Fund and the World Bank questioned the viability and efficiency of a number of projects, and the realization emerged that many investments had been intended to benefit individuals close to the government (the original "crony capitalism") rather than the economy at large.[168] In contrast, officials in Manila emphasized the role of adverse external developments, such as the effects on fuel costs from the 1979–80 rise in oil prices, and they argued that structural reforms could not be implemented without such investments.

Hampered by these divergent views, negotiations dragged on for several months in 1982 after the initial negotiating mission in April (led by Ranji Salgado, Assistant Director of the Asian Department). The Philippine team, led by Virata, met with the staff and often with the Managing Director, on several occasions and in different locations around the world during the spring and summer. Finally, around the end of August, when the flow of bank loans was suddenly drying up in the wake of the Mexican crisis (Chapter 7), the outlines of a solution were resolved via a controversial compromise under which the degree of required fiscal adjustment for 1983 was to be relaxed.[169] In October, Tun Thin, Director of the Asian Department, met with President Marcos in Manila and emphasized the necessity of the proposed fiscal measures. Before the end of November, agreement was reached on a draft Letter of Intent for a 12-month stand-by arrangement. Final approval was granted by the Executive Board in February 1983, for a 12-month stand-by arrangement in the amount of SDR 315 million ($410 million; 100 percent of quota).

Another factor hampering these negotiations was the effect of extraordinary publicity on the political dimension. As opposition to Marcos's rule intensified, the U.S. government entered into sensitive but well-publicized negotiations to renew its expiring leases on two large military bases in the Philippines. A Fund staff report that was critical of economic policies in the Philippines was leaked to an anti-Marcos group in April 1982. The resulting flurry of news stories (see, for example, Nations, 1982) raised the danger that any effort to find a workable compromise would be interpreted as a response to political pressures and would inhibit the return of private financing that was essential for the success of the program.

---

[168]See Broad (1988) and De Dios (1984) for analyses of the high-investment strategy that was initiated in 1979.

[169]This compromise was proposed to IMF management by the staff team working on the Philippines, following extensive negotiations with the authorities. Others on the staff objected, arguing that the only problem with greater adjustment was the government's unwillingness to act. The Managing Director indicated that he found the proposal "worrying," but he declined to overrule the staff recommendation. See memorandum to the Managing Director from Tun Thin, Director of the Asian Department, and Manuel Guitián, Senior Advisor in ETR (August 25, 1982), with August 27 annotation by the Managing Director; memorandum to Tun Thin from Alan A. Tait, Deputy Director of the Fiscal Affairs Department (August 26); and memorandum to Tait from Tun Thin and Guitián (August 27); in IMF/RD Managing Director file "Philippines, 1982" (Accession 84/21, Box 3, Section 168).

Money did begin to flow again from the major banks in the early months of 1983; a $300 million bank loan to the central bank was syndicated in January by Manufacturers Hanover Trust and Fuji Bank, and it was quickly oversubscribed. Unfortunately, a new set of problems soon stanched this flow. In June, Salgado took a mission to Manila to conduct the annual Article IV consultation and review the progress of the stand-by program. During the course of this mission, the staff became concerned about the accuracy of the central bank's records and of their consistency with the country's deteriorating external position.

Since about the beginning of 1983, Fund staff had been meeting occasionally with private bankers, at the request of the Philippine authorities, to share information and views on the country's prospects and financing requirements. By June, these bankers were reporting that the central bank was having difficulties meeting payments to them. Official data, meanwhile, showed that the central bank held foreign exchange reserves of about $2 billion. Confirming the likelihood of a discrepancy, the balance of payments deficit was now much larger than had been foreseen and suggested that official reserves must be falling sharply. Banks were withdrawing credit lines, and there seemed to be a serious risk of a financial crisis of major proportions.

In July 1983, Virata met with de Larosière in Washington and then flew to Paris to meet with the major official and private creditors and with Salgado. Pending the resolution of the technical issues raised by the June mission, these meetings produced agreement in principle for a successful review of the progress of the stand-by arrangement with the Fund. Then, in August, the Fund sent Anoop Singh (Division Chief in the Asian Department) to Manila, to investigate the apparent discrepancies more fully. As with the previous mission, he was confronted with numerous obstacles to measuring the extent of the problem, but he was able to determine that the central bank's reserves were substantially overstated. Against the backdrop of a rapid deterioration in the country's political stability—opposition leader Benigno S. Aquino, Jr. was assassinated upon his return from exile on August 21—a financial crisis now appeared inevitable, and continuing the program on its original terms was no longer possible.[170]

Intense negotiations over a revised program took place in Washington and in Manila from the latter part of September 1983 through early November, simultaneously with continued efforts to pinpoint the extent of the country's actual foreign exchange reserves and the source of the discrepancy.[171] Meanwhile, as the crisis began to unfold, the peso was devalued by 21 percent on October 5, and on October 14 Virata met with the commercial banks' Advisory Committee to pro-

---

[170]Of the original SDR 315 million available under the arrangement, the Philippines drew SDR 50 million ($54 million) in March 1983 and another SDR 50 million in May. No further drawings were allowed.

[171]In October, it was agreed that the IMF would assign a resident representative to Manila, for the first time in three years; in the interim, the office had been staffed by a consultant. From January 1984, a resident representative was stationed in the Philippines at least through 2000.

pose a "stand-still" on principal payments on bank loans. The banks, facing a Hobson's choice, readily agreed. A few days later, Virata met with U.S. Treasury Secretary Donald Regan, who reportedly indicated that the United States was prepared to provide short-term bridge financing once a new agreement was reached with the Fund.[172] On October 19, however, the Advisory Committee gleaned the full extent of the reserve discrepancy and concluded that the requirements for their participation in financing a new program would have to be even more strict than they had anticipated.

The overstatement of the central bank's reserves was eventually determined to have gone as high as $1 billion in mid-1983. For more than a year (apparently beginning in the aftermath of the Mexican crisis), as cash reserves dwindled, the central bank had made increasing use of time differences in global money markets—going from Singapore to Bahrain to London and on to New York—to cover payment obligations with very short-term borrowings. By mid-1983, this practice had been refined into one in which the source of the funds vanished altogether. For example, the central bank would wire a deposit to an overseas branch of the government-owned Philippine National Bank. The branch would redeposit the funds in the Manila home office, which would then complete the circle by depositing them at the central bank.

The details of this scandal became known through two formal investigations, first by an internal review ordered by the Monetary Board (the governing body of the central bank) and then by an outside auditing agency. The governor of the central bank, Jaime Laya, consequently resigned in January 1984 to pave the way for needed reforms, but in the meantime the country's and the IMF's efforts to assemble a credible economic program had suffered a severe setback. The Philippines ultimately would spend more than a year and a half without access to credits from either the Fund or the banks, and a full recovery from the debacle would take several years.

The appointment (on the specific advice of the Fund) of a strong new governor, Jose B. Fernandez (known universally as "Jobo"), breathed new life into the negotiations but did not produce any immediate breakthroughs. When the Executive Board met in June 1984 (in restricted session) to conclude the long-overdue Article IV consultations, Directors were more skeptical than ever of the sustainability of economic policies and of the credibility of the adjustment program. The Board concluded that four types of reform were needed: liberalization of exchange markets, tightening of monetary and fiscal policies, rehabilitation of public financial institutions, and stricter control over public sector investment decisions.[173] These conclusions would underpin a new round of program negotiations, which began less than two weeks later.

---

[172]The Fund's liquidity position at this time was unusually tight, owing to delays in obtaining approval of the Eighth General Review of Quotas (Chapter 17). Secretary Regan's support was reported to the Managing Director by Virata during a meeting at the Fund later the same day. See memorandum for files by P.R. Narvekar (October 18, 1983), in IMF/RD Managing Director file "Philippines, July to October 1983—Vol. II" (Accession 86/34, Box 28, Section 209).

[173]Summing up by the Managing Director; minutes of EBM/84/102 (June 29, 1984).

After two additional missions by the Fund team, now headed by Hubert Neiss (Deputy Director of the Asian Department), and extended visits by Virata and other leading officials to Washington in the period surrounding the Annual Meetings, agreement was reached on the terms of a new program, and a Letter of Intent was signed on October 31, 1984. By this time, new policies were already being carried out, including notably a liberalization of the exchange regime introduced in mid-October: the peso was allowed to float, resulting in a 10 percent depreciation, and monetary policy was tightened to stabilize the rate near this new level.[174] Given the high priority attached to reducing inflation, the principal monetary target in this program was a ceiling on growth in reserves of the banking system, rather than the usual ceiling on domestic credit expansion.[175] The authorities also provided understandings for limiting increases in public sector wages and for the elimination of external payments arrears by the end of 1985.

Perhaps more important than these macroeconomic measures were the structural reforms that the authorities planned to carry out as part of the program. These reforms, which were to be monitored by the prime minister's office, included tax measures such as replacing distortionary taxes on international trade with taxes on domestic economic activity; establishment of a framework to monitor the performance of nonfinancial public corporations; restrictions on lending by public financial institutions, and the termination of the practice by these institutions of guaranteeing foreign loans; and some decentralization of the highly monopolized sugar and coconut sectors. In addition, the Philippines sought technical assistance from the Fund with regard to the tax system and its administration. Although these structural reforms were not formal performance criteria for the stand-by arrangement, they were to be examined by the Fund staff as part of the regular program reviews. In that way, any major delays could trigger a postponement of drawings.[176]

---

[174]From 1970 until October 1984, policy aimed to maintain stability of the peso against the U.S. dollar. The effect of devaluations in October 1983 and June 1984 was limited by the concurrent appreciation of the dollar against other major currencies. See Houben (1997).

[175]The concern that determined this shift was that a ceiling on domestic credit expansion might lead to large and inflationary capital inflows. Polak (1991), p. 35, observes that the Fund agreed to rely on a reserve target for this program only after "much soul searching." For the staff assessment, see "Philippines—Request for Stand-by Arrangement," EBS/84/226 (November 5, 1984), pp. 25–27.

[176]The program approved in December 1984 incorporated performance criteria for end-December and for end-March 1985. Following a review, criteria were then to be set for the following two quarters. A second review should then have led to agreement on criteria for the next two quarters, and so forth. Because not all criteria were met in the initial two quarters, the first review was delayed by two months and performance criteria were then set for May, July, and September. Although all performance criteria for July were met, those for September were not (see below). The second review therefore was delayed until November 1985, at which time the July requirements were waived and new complete criteria were set only for end-December. (Some criteria for end-March 1986 were deferred until the third review.) In both reviews, the progress of the structural reforms was examined in detail.

The new stand-by arrangement, which was intended to last through the end of 1986, was approved by the Executive Board on December 14, 1984.[177] The following week the Paris Club approved a rescheduling agreement covering the same period, provided the Fund program was in place. Almost immediately, however, the program went off track, and completion of the third leg of the financial support for the program—a planned commercial bank rescheduling agreement—was put on hold.

On January 23, 1985, barely a month after the program was approved, de Larosière informed Virata by cable that he was "greatly concerned to learn of recent monetary and exchange rate developments which are at variance with the program and, unless reserved quickly, will irretrievably undermine achievement of the program's objectives."[178] Monetary policy had been eased, and that had caused a breaching of the program's ceiling on the growth of reserve money. In addition, most of the depreciation of the peso had been reversed, and the Managing Director questioned whether there might have been "administrative or other delays that are limiting the demand for foreign exchange."

Virata replied that these developments had resulted largely from unanticipated capital inflows, that only through lower interest rates could the economy revive, that a revival of demand would lead to increased production, and that higher production was essential both to stimulate export growth and to control inflation in the longer run. He then flew to Paris to meet with Singh and on to Washington to see de Larosière, seeking agreement on a revision of the program targets, which he regarded as being "so tight you could hear everything squeak" (interview, November 1992). Meanwhile, Governor Fernandez met with the Deputy Managing Director (Erb) and with Neiss at a conference in Kuala Lumpur, Malaysia, where he made a similar request. But although the Fund was prepared to discuss modifications, there was no real choice on the necessity of responding to the immediate problem. The Philippines therefore was not allowed to make the drawing that would have been scheduled for the first quarter of 1985. Neiss took another mission to Manila in March, but when the program criteria were violated again at the end of that month, the second-quarter drawing was disallowed as well.[179]

On the surface, the Philippines now faced a classic midadjustment dilemma as the authorities tried to get the program on track. To control inflation and maintain financial stability, controlling monetary growth was important; to stimulate economic growth, maintaining and even strengthening international competitiveness was important. However, as capital began to flow back into the country, both strategies were threatened. What distinguished this case from so many others was that it was not clear whether capital was really coming back—after all, inflation

---

[177]The arrangement totaled SDR 615 million ($605 million; 140 percent of quota), of which SDR 85 million was available immediately. As discussed below, the Philippines drew an additional SDR 106 million in July 1985 and SDR 212 million in December 1985. The arrangement was canceled in June 1986 with an undrawn balance of SDR 212 million.

[178]The cable is in IMF/CF (C/Philippines/1760 "Stand-by Arrangements, 1985").

[179]"Philippines—First Review Under Stand-by Arrangement," EBS/85/109 (May 1, 1985).

was still above 50 percent a year and there was still a great deal of political uncertainty and even turmoil—or whether—as suggested in the Managing Director's January cable—it was being discouraged from leaving. Structural reforms were under way, but implementation was slow and difficult to gauge.

When the Executive Board met to review the program on May 30, 1985, Directors were cognizant that the Fund's support was essential for the continued implementation and strengthening of structural reforms. The Fund (and the World Bank) had been pushing hard for months to convince the authorities to dismantle some of the most egregious monopolization and centralization of trade in export commodities, notably in the marketing of coconuts and sugar; substantive progress was finally evident. Reflecting a general commitment to reform, the authorities had agreed to a revised program in April. In mid-May the commercial banks had finally approved the rescheduling agreement. Apprehensively but without dissent, the Board approved the revised program.[180]

To underline the apprehensions that Directors had expressed about the success of the adjustment effort, the Managing Director took the unusual step of preparing a summary of the discussion to convey to the authorities.[181] This summary, as noted in de Larosière's covering letter to the prime minister, highlighted "the considerable emphasis placed by Directors on the need to persevere with tight monetary policies, to carry through with the implementation of structural reforms anticipated in the program, and to remove remaining rigidities in the foreign exchange market." He also noted the "broad consensus that these policies will create the basis for a sustained recovery over the medium term."[182]

What the program might have achieved over the medium term will never be known, because the Philippines was now heading toward presidential elections that would lead to far more substantial political and economic reforms. Meanwhile, the last eight months of the Fund's dealings with the Marcos regime were dominated by a mutual effort to keep the program patched together. The annual Article IV consultation mission, which was held in Manila in July 1985, revealed that the existing policy stance would not enable the authorities to meet the performance criteria for the remainder of the year. Although the criteria had been met for July, the second program review could not be completed in conjunction with the Executive Board's conclusion of the consultation in September. Consequently, the purchase scheduled for the third quarter was not allowed. Then another mission visited Manila in November, only to find that the fiscal deficit had overrun the ceiling in September; the fourth quarter drawing was also disallowed.[183] These circumstances set the stage for the final program under the *ancien régime*.

---

[180]Minutes of EBM/85/83 (May 30, 1985).

[181]As discussed in Chapter 2, Article IV consultations are always concluded by a "summing up" by the Chairman, which is then conveyed to the authorities as well as to other member countries. Program reviews, however, do not require a summing up, and normally none is prepared.

[182]Letter of June 13, 1985; IMF/CF (C/Philippines/1760 "Stand-by Arrangements, 1985").

[183]"Philippines—Second Review Under Stand-by Arrangement," EBS/85/261 (November 25, 1985).

Between the July 1985 mission and the November mission, the Philippine authorities had decided to implement several policy changes aimed at meeting the program targets. First, the excess fiscal deficit for 1985 would be reduced, principally by restricting transfers to government-owned financial institutions. Second, the tax system would be reformed to reduce reliance on taxes on foreign trade and exchange, in favor of a broadening of the domestic tax base. Third, the sugar and coconut sectors would be restructured according to a plan worked out with the World Bank, with the aim of promoting competition. Fourth, exchange rate policy would be actively pursued to promote competitiveness; in practice, this would imply intervening in exchange markets to ensure a moderate depreciation of the peso against the U.S. dollar. These actions, together with revised agreements on the quantitative performance criteria, would form the basis for a program that would enable the Philippines to make the two previously disallowed purchases in December 1985. That strategy was approved by the Executive Board on December 20, 1985, and the Philippines drew SDR 212 million ($235 million) a few days later.[184]

With the campaign for the presidency in full swing in January 1986, fiscal policy turned very expansionary. Like its 1984 predecessor, this final program was already headed for an early grave when the election was held on February 7, 1986. Mrs. Corazon Aquino won the election over Ferdinand Marcos, but Marcos declared himself the winner and scheduled a competing inauguration. Fortunately, this constitutional crisis lasted less than two weeks as military support for Marcos crumbled. A four-day "people power" revolution culminated in Marcos fleeing the country on February 25.

The shift in regime did not, of course, immediately solve the economic problems that had built up over more than two decades. It did, however, restore a sense of optimism in the country and a sense of goodwill in the international community. Within a few weeks, a staff team (led by Neiss) was back in Manila, and a new 18-month stand-by arrangement was quickly negotiated. That arrangement (for SDR 198 million, equivalent to $235 million or 45 percent of quota) was successfully completed and fully drawn. And in May 1989, the Philippines was one of the first countries to obtain debt relief through an EFF arrangement under the terms of the Brady Plan (see Chapter 11). Even then, however, the size of the debt problem remained too large to conquer in a few years, and the Philippines' continued dependence on new injections of credit from the Fund lasted into the late 1990s.

Appendix: Conditionality Guidelines

The Executive Board approved the following guidelines on the use of the Fund's resources in March 1979 (Decision No. 6056-(79/38), March 2, 1979). These guidelines remained in force throughout the period covered in this history.

---

[184]Minutes of EBM/85/183–184 (December 20, 1985).

Use of Fund's General Resources and Stand-By Arrangements

1. Members should be encouraged to adopt corrective measures, which could be supported by use of the Fund's general resources in accordance with the Fund's policies, at an early stage of their balance of payments difficulties or as a precaution against the emergence of such difficulties. The Article IV consultations are among the occasions on which the Fund would be able to discuss with members adjustment programs, including corrective measures, that would enable the Fund to approve a stand-by arrangement.

2. The normal period for a stand-by arrangement will be one year. If, however, a longer period is requested by a member and considered necessary by the Fund to enable the member to implement its adjustment program successfully, the stand-by arrangement may extend beyond the period of one year. This period in appropriate cases may extend up to but not beyond three years.

3. Stand-by arrangements are not international agreements and therefore language having a contractual connotation will be avoided in stand-by arrangements and letters of intent.

4. In helping members to devise adjustment programs, the Fund will pay due regard to the domestic social and political objectives, the economic priorities, and the circumstances of members, including the causes of their balance of payments problems.

5. Appropriate consultation clauses will be incorporated in all stand-by arrangements. Such clauses will include provision for consultation from time to time during the whole period in which the member has outstanding purchases in the upper credit tranches. This provision will apply whether the outstanding purchases were made under a stand-by arrangement or in other transactions in the upper credit tranches.

6. Phasing and performance clauses will be omitted in stand-by arrangements that do not go beyond the first credit tranche. They will be included in all other stand-by arrangements but these clauses will be applicable only to purchases beyond the first credit tranche.

7. The Managing Director will recommend that the Executive Board approve a member's request for the use of the Fund's general resources in the credit tranches when it is his judgment that the program is consistent with the Fund's provisions and policies and that it will be carried out. A member may be expected to adopt some corrective measures before a stand-by arrangement is approved by the Fund, but only if necessary to enable the member to adopt and carry out a program consistent with the Fund's provisions and policies. In these cases the Managing Director will keep Executive Directors informed in an appropriate manner of the progress of discussions with the member.

8. The Managing Director will ensure adequate coordination in the application of policies relating to the use of the Fund's general resources with a view to maintaining the nondiscriminatory treatment of members.

9. The number and content of performance criteria may vary because of the diversity of problems and institutional arrangements of members. Performance criteria will be limited to those that are necessary to evaluate implementation of the program with a view to ensuring the achievement of its objectives. Performance criteria will normally be confined to (i) macroeconomic variables, and (ii) those necessary to implement specific provisions of the Articles or policies adopted under them. Performance criteria may relate to other variables only in exceptional cases when they are essential for the effectiveness of the member's program because of their macroeconomic impact.

10. In programs extending beyond one year, or in circumstances where a member is unable to establish in advance one or more performance criteria for all or part of the program period, provision will be made for a review in order to reach the necessary understandings with the member for the remaining period. In addition, in those exceptional cases in which

an essential feature of a program cannot be formulated as a performance criterion at the beginning of a program year because of substantial uncertainties concerning major economic trends, provision will be made for a review by the Fund to evaluate the current macroeconomic policies of the member, and to reach new understandings if necessary. In these exceptional cases the Managing Director will inform Executive Directors in an appropriate manner of the subject matter of a review.

11. The staff will prepare an analysis and assessment of the performance under programs supported by use of the Fund's general resources in the credit tranches in connection with Article IV consultations and as appropriate in connection with further requests for use of the Fund's resources.

12. The staff will from time to time prepare, for review by the Executive Board, studies of programs supported by stand-by arrangements in order to evaluate and compare the appropriateness of the programs, the effectiveness of the policy instruments, the observance of the programs, and the results achieved. Such reviews will enable the Executive Board to determine when it may be appropriate to have the next comprehensive review of conditionality.

On August 3, 1979, the Executive Board approved the following text for a guideline on conditionality on external debt. [Decision No. 6230-(79/140)]

The Chairman's Summing Up on External Debt Management Policies

In the context of a general discussion of the issues relating to external debt management policies, the Executive Board considered the following guideline on the performance criteria with respect to foreign borrowing:

> When the size and the rate of growth of external indebtedness is a relevant factor in the design of an adjustment program, a performance criterion relating to official and officially guaranteed foreign borrowing will be included in upper credit tranche arrangements. The criterion will include foreign loans with maturities of over one year, with the upper limit being determined by conditions in world capital markets; in present conditions, the upper limit will include loans with maturities in the range of 10 to 12 years. The criterion will usually be formulated in terms of loans contracted or authorized. However, in appropriate cases, it may be formulated in terms of net disbursements or net changes in the stock of external official and officially guaranteed debt. Normally, the performance criterion will also include a subceiling on foreign loans with maturities of over one year and up to five years. Flexibility will be exercised to ensure that the use of the performance criterion will not discourage capital flows of a concessional nature by excluding from the coverage of performance criteria loans defined as concessional under DAC criteria, where sufficient data are available.

Adoption of this guideline will be subject to the understanding that the staff will be guided also by the following points:

1. The above guideline will be applied with a reasonable degree of flexibility while safeguarding the principle of uniformity of treatment among members. The external debt guideline should be interpreted in the light of the general guidelines on conditionality [reproduced above], especially guideline No. 4, which states:

> In helping members to devise adjustment programs, the Fund will pay due regard to the domestic social and political objectives, the economic priorities, and the circumstances of members, including the causes of their balance of payments problems.

Also, guideline No. 9 includes the following:

> The number and content of performance criteria may vary because of the diversity of problems and institutional arrangements of members. Performance criteria will be limited to those that are necessary to evaluate implementation of the program with a view to ensuring the achievement of its objectives.

Furthermore, guideline No. 8 states:

> The Managing Director will ensure adequate coordination in the application of policies relating to the use of the Fund's general resources with a view to maintaining the nondiscriminatory treatment of members.

2. While uniformity of treatment indicates a need for a common upper-maturity limit, this limit will be reviewed annually by the Executive Board at the time of its consideration of staff papers on conditions in international capital markets. In analyzing the amount and terms of new borrowing that would be appropriate—in the member's circumstances—over the medium term, the staff will take into account prospective developments in the member's external payments situation and the profile of its external indebtedness.

3. In formulating external debt criteria, the staff will be mindful of the need to ensure consistency between external debt management policies and domestic financial policies. Where external debt per se is not a matter for concern, but adjustment programs have as a main objective to reduce excess demand pressures and restore overall balance to the public sector finances, the credit ceiling for the public sector would cover both domestic and foreign financing of the overall public sector deficit.

4. Normally the performance criterion will relate to official and officially guaranteed foreign borrowing. The coverage will include official entities for which the government is financially responsible as well as private borrowing for which official guarantees have been extended and which, therefore, constitute a contingent liability of the government.

5. In cases where the member's external debt management policy covers private sector borrowing without official guarantee and there is an established regulatory machinery to control such borrowing, it will be proposed that the performance criterion on foreign borrowing should be adapted accordingly.

6. Normally, loans of less than one-year maturity will be excluded from the borrowing limitations. In exceptional circumstances where nontrade-related loans of less than one year of maturity become a source of difficulty, such loans will be included in the limitations. The Managing Director will inform Executive Directors in an appropriate manner of the reasons for including such loans in the limitation.

7. The last sentence of the guideline provides for excluding from the coverage of performance criteria those loans defined as concessional under DAC criteria. Available information on loans by multilateral development institutions indicates that all of the recent loans of the IBRD and the Inter-American Development Bank have been outside the 10- to 12-year limit and that most of the loans by the Asian and African regional development banks have also been outside the upper limit. In discussing with member countries the total amounts of permissible borrowing of less than 10 to 12 years' maturity, the staff would take into account possible lending of less than this maturity range by multilateral development institutions. In some cases, member countries utilize credits associated with concessional loans. The staff will take into account these developments in discussing the appropriate amount of borrowing.

References

Adams, Charles, and Daniel Gros, 1986, "The Consequences of Real Exchange Rate Rules for Inflation: Some Illustrative Examples," *Staff Papers*, International Monetary Fund, Vol. 33 (September), pp. 439–76.

Alexander, Sydney S., 1952, "Effects of a Devaluation on a Trade Balance," *Staff Papers*, International Monetary Fund, Vol. 2 (April), pp. 263–78.

Bagci, Pinar, and William Perraudin, 1997, "The Impact of IMF Programmes," Global Economic Institutions Working Paper No. 24 (London: Centre for Economic Policy Research, April).

Biermann, Werner, and Jumanne Wagao, 1986, "The Quest for Adjustment: Tanzania and the IMF, 1980–1986," *African Studies Review*, Vol. 29 (December), pp. 89–103.

Blejer, Mario I., Mohsin S. Khan, and Paul R. Masson, 1995, "Early Contributions of *Staff Papers* to International Economics," *Staff Papers*, International Monetary Fund, Vol. 42 (December), pp. 707–33.

Boughton, James M., 1993a, "The CFA Franc Zone: Currency Union and Monetary Standard," in *Financial and Monetary Integration*, a Special Issue of the *Greek Economic Review*, ed. by Anthony S. Courakis and George Tavlas, Vol. 15, No. 1 (autumn), pp. 267–312.

———, 1993b, "The Economics of the CFA Franc Zone," in *Policy Issues in the Operation of Currency Unions*, ed. by Paul R. Masson and Mark P. Taylor (Cambridge: Cambridge University Press).

———, and K. Sarwar Lateef, 1995, *Fifty Years After Bretton Woods: The Future of the IMF and the World Bank* (Washington: International Monetary Fund and World Bank Group).

Broad, Robin, 1988, *Unequal Alliance: The World Bank, the International Monetary Fund, and the Philippines* (Berkeley, California: University of California Press).

Campbell, Horace, and Howard Stein, eds., 1992, *Tanzania and the IMF: The Dynamics of Liberalization* (Boulder, Colorado: Westview Press).

Chenery, Hollis B., and Alan M. Strout, 1966, "Foreign Assistance and Economic Development," *American Economic Review*, Vol. 56 (September), pp. 679–733.

Clément, Jean A.P., with Johannes Mueller, Stéphane Cossé, and Jean Le Dem, 1996, *Aftermath of the CFA Franc Devaluation*, IMF Occasional Paper No. 138 (Washington: International Monetary Fund).

Corbo, Vittorio, Morris Goldstein, and Mohsin S. Khan, eds., 1987, *Growth-Oriented Adjustment Programs* (Washington: International Monetary Fund).

De Dios, Emmanuel S., ed., 1984, *An Analysis of the Philippine Economic Crisis* (Quezon City, Philippines: University of the Philippines Press).

de Vries, Margaret Garritsen, 1976, *The International Monetary Fund, 1966–1971: The System Under Stress*, Vol. 1: *Narrative*; Vol. 2: *Documents* (Washington: International Monetary Fund).

———, 1985, *The International Monetary Fund, 1972–1978: Cooperation on Trial*, Vol. 1: *Narrative*; Vol. 2: *Analysis*; Vol. 3: *Documents* (Washington: International Monetary Fund).

Dell, Sidney, 1981, *On Being Grandmotherly: The Evolution of IMF Conditionality*, Essays in International Finance, No. 144 (Princeton, New Jersey: International Finance Section, Department of Economics, Princeton University).

Duncan, Alex, 1997, "The World Bank as a Project Lender: Experience from Eastern Africa," in *The World Bank: Its First Half Century*, Vol. 2: *Perspectives*, ed. by Devesh Kapur, John P. Lewis, and Richard Webb (Washington: Brookings Institution), pp. 385–434.

Edwards, Sebastian, and Julio A. Santaella, 1993, "Devaluation Controversies in the Developing Countries: Lessons from the Bretton Woods Era," in *A Retrospective on the Bretton Woods System: Lessons for International Monetary Reform*, ed. by Michael D. Bordo and Barry Eichengreen (Chicago, Illinois: University of Chicago Press), pp. 405–55.

Frenkel, Jacob A., and Harry G. Johnson, 1976, *The Monetary Approach to the Balance of Payments* (Toronto: University of Toronto Press).

Goldsbrough, David, and others, 1996, *Reinvigorating Growth in Developing Countries: Lessons from Adjustment Policies in Eight Economies*, IMF Occasional Paper No. 139 (Washington: International Monetary Fund).

Goldstein, Morris, and Peter J. Montiel, 1986, "Evaluating Fund Stabilization Programs with Multicountry Data: Some Methodological Pitfalls," *Staff Papers*, International Monetary Fund, Vol. 33 (June), pp. 304–44.

Guitián, Manuel, 1981, *Fund Conditionality: Evolution of Principles and Practices*, IMF Pamphlet Series, No. 38 (Washington: International Monetary Fund).

——, 1995, "Conditionality: Past, Present, Future," *Staff Papers*, International Monetary Fund, Vol. 42 (December), pp. 792–835.

Hadjimichael, Michael T., Michael Nowak, Robert Sharer, and Amor Tahari, and others, 1996, *Adjustment for Growth: The African Experience*, IMF Occasional Paper No. 143 (Washington: International Monetary Fund).

Haque, Nadeem U., and Mohsin S. Khan, 1998, "Do IMF-Supported Programs Work? A Survey of the Cross-Country Empirical Evidence," IMF Working Paper 98/169 (Washington: International Monetary Fund).

Heller, Peter S., Richard D. Haas, and Ahsan S. Mansur, 1986, *A Review of the Fiscal Impulse Measure*, IMF Occasional Paper No. 44 (Washington: International Monetary Fund).

Horsefield, J. Keith, 1969, *The International Monetary Fund, 1945–1965*, Twenty Years of International Monetary Coperation, Vol. 1: *Chronicle* (Washington: International Monetary Fund).

Houben, Aerdt C.F.J., 1997, "Exchange Rate Policy and Monetary Strategy Options in the Philippines: The Search for Stability and Sustainability," IMF Paper on Policy Analysis and Assessment 97/4 (Washington, International Monetary Fund).

Hume, David, 1752, "Of the Balance of Trade," in his *Political Discourses*, reprinted in *David Hume: Writings on Economics*, ed. by Eugene Rotwein (Madison, Wisconsin: University of Wisconsin Press, 1970).

IMF Assessment Project, 1992, *IMF Conditionality 1980–1991: A White Paper* (Arlington, Virginia: Alexis de Toqueville Institution).

International Monetary Fund, 1977, *The Monetary Approach to the Balance of Payments* (Washington: International Monetary Fund).

——, *Summary Proceedings* (Washington: International Monetary Fund, various issues).

——, Fiscal Affairs Department, 1995, *Guidelines for Fiscal Adjustment*, IMF Pamphlet Series No. 49 (Washington: International Monetary Fund).

Johnson, G.G., and others, 1985, *Formulation of Exchange Rate Policies in Adjustment Programs*, IMF Occasional Paper No. 36 (Washington: International Monetary Fund).

Kapur, Devesh, John P. Lewis, and Richard Webb, 1997, *The World Bank: Its First Half Century*, Vol. 1: *History* (Washington: Brookings Institution).

Khan, Mohsin S., 1990, "The Macroeconomic Effects of Fund-Supported Adjustment Programs: An Empirical Assessment," *Staff Papers*, International Monetary Fund, Vol. 37 (June), pp. 195–231.

——, and Malcolm D. Knight, 1981, "Stabilization Programs in Developing Countries: A Formal Framework," *Staff Papers*, International Monetary Fund, Vol. 28 (March), pp. 1–53.

——, 1985, *Fund-Supported Adjustment Programs and Economic Growth*, IMF Occasional Paper No. 41 (Washington: International Monetary Fund).

Kahn, Mohsin, Peter Montiel, and Nadeem U. Haque, 1990, "Adjustment with Growth: Relating the Analytical Approaches of the IMF and the World Bank," *Journal of Development Economics*, Vol. 32, pp. 155–79.

Killick, Tony, 1984, "Kenya, 1975–81," in *The IMF and Stabilisation: Developing Country Experiences*, ed. by Tony Killick (London: Heinemann Educational Books).

———, 1995, *IMF Programmes in Developing Countries: Design and Impact* (London; New York: Routledge).

Mackenzie, G.A., David W.H. Orsmond, and Philip R. Gerson, 1977, *The Composition of Fiscal Adjustment and Growth: Lessons from Fiscal Reforms in Eight Economies*, IMF Occasional Paper No. 149 (Washington: International Monetary Fund).

Mohammed, Azizali F., 1991, "Recent Evolution of Fund Conditionality," in *International Financial Policy: Essays in Honor of Jacques J. Polak*, ed. by Jacob A. Frenkel and Morris Goldstein (Washington: International Monetary Fund and De Nederlandsche Bank), pp. 244–53.

Montiel, Peter J., and Jonathan D. Ostry, 1991, "Macroeconomic Implications of Real Exchange Rate Targeting in Developing Countries," *Staff Papers*, International Monetary Fund, Vol. 38 (December), pp. 872–900.

———, 1992, "Real Exchange Rate Targeting Under Capital Controls: Can Money Provide a Nominal Anchor?" *Staff Papers*, International Monetary Fund, Vol. 39 (March), pp. 58–78.

———, 1993, "Targeting the Real Exchange Rate in Developing Countries," *Finance and Development*, Vol. 30 (March), pp. 38–40.

Nascimento, Jean-Claude, 1990, "The Crisis in the Financial Sector and the Authorities' Reaction: The Case of the Philippines," IMF Working Paper 90/26 (Washington: International Monetary Fund).

Nations, Richard, 1982, "A Chiller for Manila," *Far Eastern Economic Review*, Vol. 116 (April 30), pp. 40–41.

Ndulu, Benno, 1987, "Stabilization and Adjustment Programs in Tanzania, 1978–1985," WIDER Country Study No. 17 (Helsinki: World Institute for Development Economics of the United Nations University).

Nyerere, Julius K., 1977, *The Arusha Declaration Ten Years After* (Dar es Salaam: Government Printer).

Pleskovic, Boris, and Jeffrey D. Sachs, 1994, "Political Independence and Economic Reform in Slovenia," in *The Transition in Eastern Europe*, Vol. 1 (Country Studies), ed. by Olivier Jean Blanchard, Kenneth A. Froot, and Jeffrey D. Sachs (Chicago, Illinois: University of Chicago Press), pp. 191–220.

Polak, Jacques J., 1957, "Monetary Analysis of Income Formation and Payments Problems," *Staff Papers*, International Monetary Fund, Vol. 6 (November), pp. 1–50. Reprinted in *The Monetary Approach to the Balance of Payments*, by the International Monetary Fund, 1977, pp. 15–64.

———, 1991, *The Changing Nature of IMF Conditionality*, Essays in International Finance, No. 184 (Princeton, New Jersey: International Finance Section, Department of Economics, Princeton University).

———, 1997, "The World Bank and the IMF: A Changing Relationship," in *The World Bank: Its First Half Century*, Vol. 2: *Perspectives*, ed. by Devesh Kapur, John P. Lewis, and Richard Webb (Washington: Brookings Institution), pp. 473–522.

———, 1998, "The IMF Monetary Model at Forty," *Economic Modelling*, Vol. 15 (July), pp. 395–410 .

Quirk, Peter J., Benedicte Vibe Christensen, Kyung-Mo Huh, and Toshihiko Sasaki, 1987, *Floating Exchange Rates in Developing Countries: Experience with Auction and Interbank Markets*, IMF Occasional Paper No. 53 (Washington: International Monetary Fund).

Rajcoomar, S., Michael Bell, and others, 1996, *Financial Programming and Policy: The Case of Sri Lanka* (Washington: International Monetary Fund).

Research Department, IMF, 1987, *Theoretical Aspects of the Design of Fund-Supported Adjustment Programs*, IMF Occasional Paper No. 55 (Washington: International Monetary Fund).

Robichek, E. Walter, 1984, "The IMF's Conditionality Re-Examined," in *Adjustment, Conditionality, and International Financing*, ed. by Joaquín Muns (Washington: International Monetary Fund).

Sampson, Anthony, 1981, *The Money Lenders: Bankers in a Dangerous World* (London: Hodder and Stoughton).

Santaella, Julio A., 1996, "Stylized Facts Before IMF-Supported Macroeconomic Adjustment," *Staff Papers*, International Monetary Fund, Vol. 43 (September), pp. 502–44.

Schadler, Susan, Franek Rozwadowski, Siddharth Tiwari, and David O. Robinson, 1993, *Economic Adjustment in Low-Income Countries: Experience Under the Enhanced Structural Adjustment Facility*, IMF Occasional Paper No. 106 (Washington: International Monetary Fund).

Schadler, Susan, ed., 1995, *IMF Conditionality: Experience Under Stand-By and Extended Arrangements, Part II: Background Papers*, IMF Occasional Paper No. 129 (Washington: International Monetary Fund).

———, and others, 1995, *IMF Conditionality: Experience Under Stand-By and Extended Arrangements, Part I: Key Issues and Findings*, IMF Occasional Paper No. 128 (Washington: International Monetary Fund).

Sengupta, Arjun, and others, 1987, *The Role of the IMF in Adjustment with Growth*, Report of a Working Group established by the Deputies of the Intergovernmental Group of Twenty-Four on International Monetary Affairs (Washington: International Monetary Fund).

TANU, 1967, *The Arusha Declaration and TANU's Policy on Socialism and Self-Reliance* (Dar es Salaam: TANU, Publicity Section).

Tanzi, Vito, 1987, "Fiscal Policy, Growth, and Stabilization Programs," *Finance and Development*, Vol. 24 (June), pp. 15–17.

———, Mario I. Blejer, and Mario O. Teijeiro, 1987, "Inflation and the Measurement of Fiscal Deficits," *Staff Papers*, International Monetary Fund, Vol. 34 (December), pp. 711–38.

Tsiang, S.C., 1950, "Balance of Payments and Domestic Flow of Income and Expenditures," *Staff Papers*, International Monetary Fund, Vol. 1 (September), pp. 254–88.

Vaubel, Roland, 1991, "The Political Economy of the International Monetary Fund: A Public Choice Analysis," in *The Political Economy of International Organizations: A Public Choice Approach*, ed. by Roland Vaubel and Thomas D. Willett (Boulder, Colorado: Westview Press), pp. 204–44.

Wapenhans, Wili, and others [World Bank Portfolio Management Task Force], 1992, *Effective Implementation: Key to Development Impact* (Washington: World Bank).

Williamson, John, ed., 1983, *IMF Conditionality* (Washington: Institute for International Economics).

Williamson, John, 1985, *The Exchange Rate System* (Washington: Institute for International Economics, 2nd ed.).

14

The IMF and the Poor: Soft Loans, Hard Adjustment

When H. Onno Ruding assumed the chair of the Interim Committee in the spring of 1985, one of his top priorities was to lower the barrier of formality that limited the ability of ministers to interact and to introduce and develop fresh ideas. For his first meeting, on April 17, he suggested that after the morning session, in which each member would make his traditional formal statement covering the main agenda items, the afternoon would be devoted to an informal exchange of views with restricted attendance. To give some structure and guidance to the discussion without restricting it to a set agenda, he asked Michael Wilson (finance minister of Canada) and V.P. Singh (finance minister of India) to outline a few key issues that members might address. In the morning session, Singh had raised the issue of the need to provide additional financing for low-income countries, stressing the role that an allocation of SDRs could play in that regard along with increases in official development assistance, Fund quotas, World Bank capital, and IDA (International Development Association) resources. In this less formal setting, he decided to toss another idea onto the table: over the next few years, the Fund would be receiving some SDR 3 billion in repayments from the Trust Fund loans made in the late 1970s. Why not plan now to rededicate those funds to the benefit of low-income countries, whose needs now were even much greater than they had been then? Why not reactivate the Trust Fund and establish an interest subsidy account to provide concessional assistance?[1]

Singh's proposal was eagerly embraced by his colleagues around the table, from industrial as well as developing countries. It avoided the legal and ideological pitfalls that blocked agreement on an SDR allocation, it directed resources where they were most needed, and it provided a means of assisting low-income countries without putting the Fund's general resources at risk. The communiqué for the meeting was redrafted accordingly, to call on the Executive Board to "consider the use of the resources that will be available following repayment of loans that have been made by the Trust Fund, to help forward the adjustment process by providing assistance to low-income developing countries," and asking the Managing Director to make a progress report to the Committee when it next met in October.

---

[1]Summary record of the informal session; in IMF/CF (G 142.42 "Interim Committee Meeting (24th), Washington, DC, April 17–19, 1985").

This initiative—unusual in that it arose spontaneously from the Interim Committee without prior staff input—led directly to the establishment of the Structural Adjustment Facility (SAF) in 1986 and indirectly to the creation of the much larger Enhanced Structural Adjustment Facility (ESAF) in 1987. It embodied two roles for the Fund that had emerged only in the preceding decade: lending on concessional terms and lending for structural adjustment.

The idea of a concessional or "soft loan" window for the IMF originated with the Oil Facility Subsidy Account in 1975, which was closely followed by the Trust Fund in 1976.[2] Both facilities were administered by the Fund as entities separate from the Fund's general resources.

The Subsidy Account was financed by contributions from 25 countries totaling SDR 160 million ($195 million), plus SDR 27 million ($33 million) in income from investing contributed funds until needed. Those funds were used to reduce the interest cost of borrowing from the 1975 Oil Facility by 5 percentage points for 25 countries deemed to be most severely affected by the sudden rise in oil prices. Over the life of the Oil Facility (through 1983), the account covered more than two-thirds of interest charges due from those countries.[3]

The Trust Fund, which was administered by the IMF as an entity separate from the institution's general resources, was financed by the sale of 25 million ounces (16 percent) of the Fund's stock of gold from 1976 through 1980. Of the $4.6 billion in profits from those sales (bolstered by the sharp rise in the price of gold during the life of the program),[4] $1.3 billion was distributed directly to eligible developing countries and the remaining $3.3 billion plus related income and some transfers (approximately SDR 3 billion) constituted the Trust Fund.[5] That money was lent to 55 low-income countries at an interest of ½ of 1 percent a year, with the principal to be repaid in installments beginning after 5½ years and ending after ten years. Since the initial loans were made in January 1977 and the last ones in February 1981 (Figure 14.1), significant reflows of cash into the Trust Fund began in July 1982 and were expected to conclude in February 1991.[6]

---

[2]For details, see de Vries (1985), pp. 351–55 (on the Subsidy Account) and Chapter 34 (on the Trust Fund).

[3]The initial eligibility list included 41 countries, but only 25 of those drew on the 1975 Oil Facility. When the Subsidy Account was terminated in 1983, the Fund distributed its remaining assets in the form of an additional subsidy of 33 basis points; see *Annual Report 1984*, p. 180.

[4]The first auction, in June 1976, yielded a price of $126 per fine ounce. If that price had continued, and if the exchange rate between the dollar and the SDR had remained constant, the auctions would have yielded total profits of $2 billion through May 1980, compared with the actual figure of $4.6 billion. The mean gold price for the four years of auctions was approximately $240, and the mean profit per ounce was about $200. (Aside from the Fund's expenses, profit in U.S. dollars equaled the difference between the sale price and the dollar equivalent of the official price, SDR 35.) At the most profitable auction, held at the height of the speculative boom in gold in January 1980, the Fund sold 444,000 ounces at an average price of $712.12.

[5]For a more detailed summary, see *Annual Report 1980*, pp. 85–89.

[6]At the end of fiscal year (FY) 1991, six countries had failed to repay Trust Fund loans on time, and SDR 158 million ($210 million) in principal remained outstanding. Seven years later, SDR 90 million ($120 million) lent to three countries was still outstanding.

Figure 14.1. IMF: Concessional Lending, 1977–89

Millions of SDRs

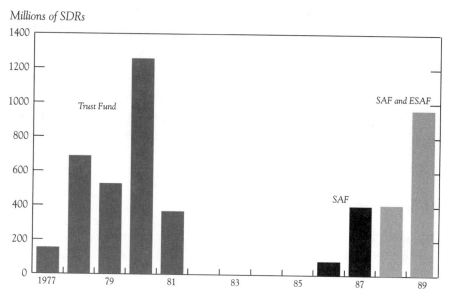

Loans from the Trust Fund were subject only to first-tranche conditionality. That is, an eligible member country was required to represent that it faced a balance of payments need for the loan and to demonstrate that it was making a reasonable effort to correct it. Performance criteria, as used in upper-tranche arrangements, did not apply. Consequently, nearly all countries that were eligible on the basis of having low per capita income borrowed their share of the available funds. By the time the Trust Fund was exhausted, however, the idea of making even concessional loans conditional on specific policy commitments was becoming more widely accepted.

When the Trust Fund was established, the IMF had recently established the Extended Fund Facility (EFF), to help countries carry out "comprehensive programs that include policies of the scope and character required to correct structural imbalances in production, trade, and prices."[7] Although EFF credits would have longer maturities and would make it easier for the Fund to provide substantial support to countries for three or more years in a row, the interest rate would be the same market-related rate charged on ordinary stand-by arrangements. For low-income countries, the intention was to make a blend of financing available, including conditional stand-by or extended arrangements at regular rates and low-conditionality loans at concessional rates.

This, then, was the situation at the beginning of the 1980s: part of the IMF's own lending was going to low-income countries, part was conditional on programs

---

[7]Executive Board Decision No. 4377-(74/114), September 13, 1974; in de Vries (1985), Vol. 3, pp. 503–06.

to implement structural reforms, and a separately administered account was providing loans on concessional and low-conditionality terms only to low-income countries. Partly because the SDR 3 billion in the Trust Fund had been completely disbursed, but also because of the growing reluctance to make low-conditionality loans (as discussed in Chapter 13), the soft-loan window was allowed to lapse in 1980. When discussions of ways to help the least developed countries rose again to the fore in the middle of the decade, an important consideration was whether and how to integrate concessional with conditional lending: how to make soft loans less soft while increasing their value to the countries that needed them most.[8]

Closing Down the Trust Fund

The Trust Fund was designed to be temporary. Low-income countries, many of them newly independent and most of them needing to import oil to fuel economic growth, faced a cruel economic environment in the 1970s. Eventually, they would be expected to compete on the global field, and the concessional loans from the Trust Fund would be one means of helping them reach that stage. By 1980, however, when the resources of the Trust Fund were nearly all committed, it was apparent that the environment was not improving and that the transition was going to take much longer and require a more sustained commitment from creditors and donors. Should the Trust Fund be extended and perhaps made permanent, or should a new approach be tried?

While this question was arising, two seemingly unrelated events altered the course of the debate. First, the IMF was grappling with the effects of extraordinarily high world interest rates. The Supplementary Financing Facility (SFF; 1979–81), like the earlier oil facilities, was financed with money borrowed by the Fund at market interest rates, and the interest charges on the Fund's corresponding credits were matched to the cost of borrowing. While that operation made credit more readily available, it also raised its cost, especially in the inflationary circumstances of the late 1970s. For example, in the second half of 1979, the rate of charge on credits financed by the SFF was just over 10 percent, compared with the Fund's standard rate of charge of 5¼ percent. Low-income countries could not afford to borrow at those rates, and even most middle-income countries were reluctant to do so. Consequently, the Fund began exploring ways

---

[8]The Compensatory Financing Facility (CFF) was conceived in 1963 as a low-conditionality means of lending primarily to developing countries (Chapter 15). In the course of discussions in 1987 on how to strengthen the utility of the CFF, Hélène Ploix (France) proposed that CFF credits to low-income countries be made on concessional terms by lengthening maturities and subsidizing interest charges; see minutes of EBM/87/36 (March 3, 1987), pp. 5–6. That proposal generated some support but not enough to bring it to fruition. The idea was dropped several months later as part of an effort to concentrate concessional resources on the ESAF, which (as discussed below) had more clearly defined conditionality.

to subsidize the interest charges on SFF-financed credits, as it had with the oil facilities.[9]

Second, the Fund's program of gold sales was coming to an end just as the market price of gold was soaring to unimagined heights. The institution still held the world's second largest stockpile of the precious metal (after the United States), and in January 1980 those 103 million ounces had a market value of more than $70 billion. The potential income from selling and reinvesting that stock, even if the market price fell sharply, could have brought enormous benefits to the poorest countries.

The Managing Director, Jacques de Larosière, proposed in December 1979 that the Fund consider selling up to an additional 9 million ounces of its holdings of gold and investing the proceeds in interest-bearing securities. The income would be used to subsidize the cost of using the SFF and possibly other Fund lending, and to strengthen the Fund's income position. An additional portion of the gold, perhaps as much as 32 million ounces, would be dedicated to supporting a proposed "substitution account," as described in Chapter 18.[10] The goal was to create a consensus for action by presenting these suggestions as a package that included something of benefit to everyone, but in the end it failed to generate much enthusiasm. After extensive consideration by the Executive Board and the Interim Committee in the first half of 1980, the Managing Director's plan to sell gold was quietly dropped.[11]

With gold sales likely to be ruled out, attention focused on the projected SDR 3.1 billion ($3.9 billion) in Trust Fund reflows (mostly principal repayments, plus a small amount of interest), which would begin trickling in during the second half of 1982 but would not peak until 1986.[12] The Fund had three options: renew the

---

[9]See "Final Texts of Letter of Transmittal and Joint Statement," EBD/79/187, Rev. 4 (August 10, 1979), and "Mechanisms to Reduce the Cost of Using the Supplementary Financing Facility," EBS/79/547 (September 5, 1979). Exploratory discussions with potential donors for SFF subsidies revealed what in retrospect was the first major drop-off in the willingness of some of the wealthiest states to provide budgetary support for low-income countries. The large budget deficits incurred by the United States, the United Kingdom, and other major countries engendered a shift in attitudes toward foreign aid that persisted long after the deficits had been brought under control. By the end of 1979, proposals for financing subsidies on Fund lending therefore focused primarily on options that would not require direct budgetary outlays.

[10]Minutes of EBM/80/5 (January 11, 1980), pp. 3–9. The statement was originally circulated as Buff 79/243 (December 21, 1979), for the January 11 meeting.

[11]A decision to sell gold from the Fund's holdings requires an 85 percent majority. No vote was taken on the proposal in the Executive Board, and it was not formally placed on the agenda of the Interim Committee, as proponents realized that it would not pass; see minutes of EBM/80/96 (June 23, 1980). U.S. support, which was essential, would have required legislative action to overcome a prohibition under U.S. law against using the Fund's gold for the benefit of a subset of the membership. As long as the U.S. authorities favored creation of the substitution account, it seemed possible to win their support by linking the two ideas in a package. That possibility waned as the year progressed. The next serious consideration of gold sales came only in the mid-1990s, as part of a plan to create a permanent fund for concessional lending.

[12]Some SDR 14 million ($18 million) in interest charges was already being paid each year, at an annual rate of 0.5 percent on outstanding balances. Principal payments were scheduled to begin in July 1982.

Trust Fund and channel repayments back into it for new concessional lending, convert outstanding loans into grants, or liquidate it and transfer reflows into the Fund's "Special Disbursement Account" (SDA).[13] Any one of those options could be structured to ensure that low-income countries would benefit, but the value of the benefit and the number of beneficiary countries could vary widely.

The option of converting old loans into grants was quickly dismissed, since it would have arbitrarily prevented new members from sharing in the benefits and would have raised moral hazard problems on future lending. Moreover, staff, management, and most Executive Directors preferred to replace the Trust Fund with some method that would give the Fund more control over how the money was used. Governors from developing countries, however, feared that the diversion of Trust Fund repayments to subsidize the SFF would dilute the resources available to the poor. In April 1980, the Group of Twenty-Four developing countries (G-24) issued a communiqué calling for the continuation and even augmentation of the Trust Fund and urging the completion of talks on finding other means of subsidizing the cost of SFF credits for low-income countries.[14]

Despite the official G-24 position, most Executive Directors from developing countries took the pragmatic view that no new funding was likely to be forthcoming for low-conditionality credits, so they might as well try to have the Trust Fund reflows put to the best possible use.[15] A compromise soon emerged in which subsidies for SFF credits would be limited to low-income countries (essentially to the same countries for whom the Trust Fund had been set up) and would be financed partly by Trust Fund reflows and partly by new contributions from creditor countries.

A specific plan was developed over the next few months and was approved by the Board in November. (For the text of the decisions, see *Annual Report 1981*, pp. 146–51.) The scheme had four main elements. First, the Trust Fund would be terminated as soon as practicable after the last loans were disbursed in February 1981. Second, the first SDR 750 million ($950 million) in reflows would be earmarked for a Subsidy Account, and the remainder would be transferred to the SDA. Third,

---

[13]The Second Amendment to the Articles of Agreement created the SDA as a separate account within the General Department, and the instrument establishing the Trust Fund provided that repayments of loans could be transferred to the SDA. Article V, Section 12(f), authorized the Executive Board (subject to qualified majorities) to transfer assets from the SDA to the General Resources Account (GRA) for general operations, to use the funds for the benefit of low-income countries, or to distribute the funds to developing countries that were members of the Fund as of August 1975. For the background on the creation of the SDA, see de Vries (1985), pp. 723–24, and Vol. 3, pp. 347–51.

[14]"The Ministers . . . noted the progress report on the supplementary financing facility and urged early completion of discussions on reducing the cost of borrowing under the facility . . . Ministers urged that the Trust Fund should be continued and its resources augmented." Paras. 10 and 13 of the G-24 communiqué; *IMF Survey*, Vol. 9 (May 5, 1980), p. 137.

[15]At the decisive Board meeting on this subject, in July 1980, only S.D. Deshmukh (India) and Semyano Kiingi (Alternate—Uganda) argued strongly for renewing the Trust Fund. Onno Ruding (Netherlands) reported the support of the Yugoslav authorities for the G-24 position, but the rest of his constituency favored placing the reflows in the SDA. See minutes of EBM/80/102 (July 9, 1980).

the Subsidy Account would be used to reduce the interest charge on Fund credits financed by the SFF by up to 3 percentage points (though not to a level below the Fund's regular rate of charge). Fourth, only low-income countries would be eligible for subsidies.

The most difficult issue in those discussions was the dividing line for eligibility. How poor would a country have to be to qualify for a subsidy? A few of the countries that had qualified for Trust Fund loans had grown rapidly in the late 1970s. Differences of view were expressed on whether they had grown by enough to be reasonably excluded from the subsidy scheme, but to include them would require raising the ceiling rather high and making the subsidies much more expensive. After much debate, an inelegant but practical solution emerged: the 69 countries that would have been eligible for a new Trust Fund on the same basis as the old one would qualify for a full subsidy covering up to 3 percentage points of interest, and 14 additional countries would qualify for subsidies at half of that rate.[16]

The SFF Subsidy Account did not enable the Fund to make concessional loans, as it had through the Trust Fund. All it did was reduce the cost of supplementary credit to the same level as for ordinary credits under the Fund's tranche policies. For the next four years, therefore, the Fund was temporarily without a soft-loan window, but it did pay subsidies to low-income countries that averaged SDR 56 million a year (1982–85) and eventually totaled just under SDR 450 million ($530 million).[17] Twelve countries, led by Saudi Arabia, provided SDR 62 million ($68 million) in donations and short-term loans to help pay for those subsidies, and the rest came from Trust Fund reflows and the income from investing those monies until subsidies were due to be paid (Table 14.1).[18]

Once the bulk of the Trust Fund repayments began to flow in, pressure began to mount for a new and more substantial means of helping low-income countries.

---

[16]Sixty-two low-income countries had been eligible for Trust Fund assistance. Eligible countries in the First Period (1977–78) were those that were members of the Fund in August 1975 and had annual incomes in 1973 of less than SDR 300 per capita (as estimated by the World Bank). Guatemala (which had a slightly higher 1973 income) and Papua New Guinea (which joined after the cutoff date) were added on an exceptional basis. For the Second Period (1978–81), the income ceiling was set at $520 per capita in 1975 (the same level that was then used by the World Bank to determine eligibility for borrowing from the Bank's concessional lending arm, the International Development Association or IDA); that change brought in Zambia but excluded Guatemala, Mauritius, and Paraguay. See de Vries (1985), pp. 670–71 and 682. By 1979, the eligible country with the highest per capita income was Jordan, at $1,180. Setting the cutoff at that level and including new members of the Fund would make 83 countries eligible for SFF subsidies. Alternatively, setting the cutoff at the inflation-adjusted equivalent of the 1975 level ($680 in 1979, the then-current ceiling for IDA assistance) would reduce the list to 69 countries. See "Supplementary Financing Subsidy Account—List of Beneficiaries and Related Matters," SM/80/239 (October 20, 1980).

[17]All subsidies were paid at the maximum allowable rates, either 3 or 1.5 percentage points.

[18]Through FY 1985, SDR 401 million in Trust Fund reflows was transferred from the SDA to the SFF Subsidy Account. Beginning in FY 1986, SDR 72 million in excess balances in the Subsidy Account was returned to the SDA. The bulk of the subsidy payments was completed by FY 1990. As of 1998, however, SDR 2.2 million in subsidies to two countries—Liberia and Sudan—was still pending settlement of those countries' arrears to the Fund (see Chapter 16).

Table 14.1. SFF Subsidy Account, 1982–98

(Millions of SDRs; fiscal years)

Transfers from SDA (net)		328.8
Investment income		62.1
Valuation gains (net)		0.5
Contributions		
Saudi Arabia	32.0	
France	9.3	
Netherlands	4.1	
Switzerland	2.4	
Sweden	2.2	
Australia	2.0	
Denmark	1.5	
Norway	1.4	
Finland	1.3	
Austria	1.2	
Total		57.4
Loans (1982–84)		
Belgium	4.4	
Luxembourg	0.2	
Total	4.6	
Total resources	448.7	
Subsidy payments	446.3	
Ending balance	2.4	

Source: *Annual Reports*, 1982–98.

Structural Adjustment Facility

The idea of creating a replacement for the defunct Trust Fund had widespread support in 1985, but several specific issues had to be resolved. Which countries would be eligible to borrow on concessional terms? What conditions would be imposed in exchange for loans? And what role (if any) should the World Bank play?

Initial Consideration, 1985

Following the April 1985 Interim Committee meeting described in the introduction to this chapter, the staff reacted quickly to ensure that maximum funds would be available to support concessional lending under the proposed facility. The projected reflows from the Trust Fund were expected to amount to about SDR 3 billion, but much of that money was yet to come in. Furthermore, the repayments that were already being made had been set aside to finance the SFF Subsidy Account. By this time, however, the SDR 400 million that had already been transferred was judged to be sufficient to cover all anticipated obligations of the SFF with subsidies being paid at maximum allowable rates. The staff therefore proposed, and the Executive Board approved, that transfers to the Subsidy Account be stopped and that all remaining reflows be deposited in the SDA and invested in short-term SDR-denominated securities, pending a further decision on their disposition.[19]

A major issue to be decided was how closely to adhere to the terms of the original Trust Fund. As a practical matter, a simple reactivation of the original Trust Fund was out of the question, because the termination decision had transferred the assets from the Trust Fund to the IMF under the SDA. The staff therefore decided to respond to the Interim Committee request by proposing to establish a new lending facility within the SDA. More substantively, the staff—notably C. David Finch (Counsellor and Director of the Exchange and Trade Relations (ETR) Department)—regarded the Trust Fund as having been seriously flawed, and felt that the new facility should be designed to remedy those defects. What followed was a major skirmish in the never-ending battle for the soul of the institution, the battle to

---

[19]See Decision No. 7989-(85/81) SBS (suspension of transfers) and 7990-(85/81) (investment policy), both approved on May 28, 1985; in *Annual Report 1985*, pp. 123–24.

strike the right balance between assistance and prudence. De Larosière maintained that the funds were clearly intended to be used for the benefit of low-income countries and that the economic circumstances that those countries faced had generally deteriorated since the time of the Trust Fund. He concluded that the initial staff paper should be symmetrically agnostic on the question of whether the terms imposed on the use of these resources should be loosened or tightened.[20]

The staff paper on the proposed facility was issued to Executive Directors in early August, as background for a Board meeting to be held the following month. Although the paper was clearly supportive of the Indian initiative, it laid out a vision of a facility that differed in key respects from the way the Trust Fund had worked: loans would be made on the same concessional terms, but they would be available to a smaller group of borrowers and on tighter conditions—though, in deference to the views expressed by de Larosière, less strict than those on upper-tranche stand-by arrangements.[21]

In reviewing the limitations of the Trust Fund, the staff paper argued that easy access to loans with low conditionality, combined with a general deterioration in the external environment that borrowers faced (falling terms of trade for exporters of primary commodities, rising world interest rates, etc.), had enabled financing to prevail over adjustment. Consequently, many countries were in worse straits at the end of the availability of Trust Fund loans than at the beginning. The paper also noted that the policy had been to review borrowers' economic progress only annually, as part of an overall deemphasis of conditionality. Countries had been asked to develop medium-term strategies, on the assumption that the global economy would improve over that term. This review process had been too limited to be effective.

The staff paper noted that although the expected reflows from Trust Fund loans were sizable, they would arrive only gradually. In the meantime, the staff felt that the small currently available resources should be carefully directed toward those countries with the "greatest [balance of payments] need and least access to alternative sources of finance." The problem was how to restrict the number of eligible countries so that each borrower could get enough financing to make a difference, without eliminating countries with a clear need for concessional assistance. For the moment, this problem was still awaiting a solution. The option proposed by the staff was to re-

---

[20]Memorandum from Finch to the Managing Director (June 17, 1985), in IMF/CF (S 1794 "Structural Adjustment Facility (SAF), April–December 1985"); and memorandum from Walter O. Habermeier (Treasurer), Finch, and James G. Evans, Jr. (Deputy General Counsel) to the Managing Director (same date), in IMF/RD Managing Director file "Special Drawing Account" (Accession 88/274, Box 1, Section 269).

[21]The 1980 termination decision provided that SDR 1.5 billion of the reflow was to be used similarly to the Trust Fund. Funds remaining after that use and the transfers to the SFF Subsidy Account were also to be used on those terms unless the Executive Board decided to dispose of them differently, as long as such alternative use was for the benefit of countries in difficult circumstances and taking account of per capita incomes. See "Use of Resources of the Special Disbursement Account Arising from Termination of the Trust Fund—Preliminary Considerations," EBS/85/183 (August 6, 1985). The complex voting requirements are described in the memorandum from Habermeier and others cited in the preceding note.

strict eligibility to what the World Bank called "IDA-only" countries, excluding the "blend" countries that had enough creditworthiness to qualify for assistance from the IBRD as well as IDA.[22] The mathematical appeal of the IDA-only option—and its political Achilles' heel—was that it would eliminate the two countries that were by far the largest potential users: China and India. Both were low-income countries with serious economic problems, but if allowance were made for their potential borrowings from the facility, the access limits would have to be cut by about half.

While the Fund was developing its response to Singh's initiative, the U.S. authorities were taking up another aspect of the matter. Treasury Secretary James A. Baker III was looking for ways to augment the role of the World Bank in development finance and to promote greater collaboration between the Bank and the IMF. By October, that venture would bear fruit in the form of the "Baker Plan" for strengthening the debt strategy (see Chapter 10). It began, however, in June, at a meeting of the finance ministers of the Group of Ten (G-10) countries in Tokyo. There, Baker supported the Indian initiative of dedicating the Trust Fund reflows to the benefit of low-income countries and added that the facility should be operated in collaboration with the World Bank to ensure that the structural elements of the adjustment that borrowers needed to undertake could be taken fully into account.[23]

These two interrelated ideas—promoting structural adjustment and bringing in the World Bank—were incorporated in the August staff paper, but to a lesser extent than proposed by the United States. The Fund, the paper noted, had expertise in some areas of structural policy—notably, exchange rate, monetary, fiscal, and pricing policies—but not in others, so it was natural that an overall program of structural adjustment should be worked out in conjunction with the World Bank. In addition, the Bank and other multilateral development banks should be expected to help finance countries' overall adjustment programs. In the staff version, however, the facility itself would be purely under Fund control.

The Executive Board met to consider these various facets of the proposal in September 1985, some three weeks before the Interim Committee was scheduled to convene in Seoul, Korea. This meeting was to be merely a preliminary exchange of views, but one issue, at least, had been largely resolved in the days leading up to it. The authorities in both China and India felt that their eligibility was an important issue of principle: they should not be singled out for less favorable treatment from other low-income countries simply because of their size. They recognized, however, that insistence on that position could severely restrict access to the facility by the 50–60 other low-income countries and leave no country with enough resources to alleviate its imbalances significantly.[24] Both countries there-

---

[22]"Use of Resources of the Special Disbursement Account Arising from Termination of the Trust Fund—Preliminary Considerations," EBS/85/183 (August 6, 1985), pp. 15–17.

[23]Baker's statement to the G-10 was summarized by the U.S. Executive Director, Charles Dallara, at EBM/85/141 (September 13, 1985), p. 35.

[24]For the same reason, the idea of applying only part of the Trust Fund reflows to this facility, a possibility envisaged in the 1980 termination decision, was not seriously considered in the 1985 deliberations.

fore agreed to voluntarily forgo drawing on the facility as long as they were deemed to be formally eligible. Arjun Sengupta (India) noted that since "some poor countries were in greater difficulties than others," his authorities could state that for the two- to three-year period until the facility could be reviewed by the Board, they would not draw on it. Zicun Zhang went somewhat further, stating that China's commitment not to use the facility was based on the authorities' assessment that China did not have, and did not expect to have, a protracted balance of payments need for such assistance.[25] With those two countries out, the eligible country with the largest potential access would be Pakistan, whose quota was less than one-fourth that of India or China.[26]

By this time, the United States had taken the lead in advocating the plan. The U.S. Executive Director, Charles H. Dallara, argued before the Board that the goal of the proposed facility should be to "promote structural adjustment and growth" and—in what he called a "bold step"—that "programs should be developed and negotiated jointly by the Fund, the Bank, and the member" country. He suggested that the member should commit to a two-year macroeconomic and structural economic program; that a joint mission from the two institutions should negotiate a program; that both Boards should consider it around the same time and approve funds under their separate jurisdictions; that there should be semiannual drawings based on targets that would be evaluated judgmentally; and that structural elements should cover a broad range of policies, not just those covered by the Fund's own expertise.[27]

Most of Dallara's points were endorsed in general terms by the Board for transmittal to the Interim Committee for further consideration. Some specific issues remained open, the most important of which was the question of the level of conditionality to be attached to loans made through the facility. The staff paper suggested that disbursements might be linked to performance criteria, similar to those of a conventional Fund stand-by arrangement; but it also suggested that an alternative might be to monitor programs under a looser arrangement involving program reviews but no quantitative performance criteria. E.I.M. Mtei (Tanzania), the lead speaker for the low-income countries, disagreed strongly with the view that the Trust Fund had been remiss in encouraging too easy access with too little conditionality, and he objected to the proposal for performance criteria:

> The structural nature of the imbalances and the depth and duration of the economic problems experienced by these countries, particularly in sub-Saharan Africa, limit the speed at which progress in adjustment can be achieved and therefore would require a longer framework than normally envisaged under Fund programs. Because the

---

[25]Minutes of EBM/85/142 (September 13, 1985), pp. 16 and 42.

[26]The four largest quotas among IDA-eligible countries (in SDR millions) were China (2,390.9), India (2,207.7), Pakistan (546.3), and Zaïre (291.0). The complete list of low-income countries at the time, with World Bank status, per capita income, and Fund quota, is given in "Use of Resources of the Special Disbursement Account Arising from Termination of the Trust Fund—Preliminary Considerations," EBS/85/183 (August 6, 1985), Table 2.

[27]Minutes of EBM/85/141 (September 13, 1985), pp. 36–39.

economies of these countries have already been trapped by the low level of demand
as a result of continued austerity measures over extended periods, additional demand
management conditionality of the type attached to Fund programs would be counterproductive. What is needed is structural adjustment programs developed within a
medium- and long-term framework stressing growth. . . .[28]

Mtei also expressed concern over the proposal for joint Fund-Bank negotiations, on the grounds that this practice could give rise to "cross-conditionality";
that is, to one institution withholding approval for a loan until the conditions of
the other institution were satisfied. More generally, he asked for assurances that
the plan really would raise the total flow of resources to low-income countries and
not just displace existing assistance. Without true "additionality," as this concern
came to be called, the facility could achieve little more than to raise the barrier of
conditionality.

Several other Directors raised questions about the U.S. proposal for joint negotiation of structural adjustment programs, which would have sharply altered the
normal working relationships between the Fund and the World Bank and could
have led to impossibly complex programs. As Yusuf A. Nimatallah (Saudi Arabia)
pointed out, the Fund would be negotiating on the basis of assessments of the
member's balance of payments need, while the Bank would be negotiating on the
basis of assessments of the requirements for medium-term structural adjustment.
Nimatallah, Sengupta, and Jacques J. Polak (Netherlands) all argued that it would
be preferable to think in terms of two parallel programs rather than one program
that would have to be jointly and "laboriously" (in Polak's term) negotiated.

The Managing Director's report to the Interim Committee, based on the discussion by the Executive Board, noted both the broad agreement on principles and
the need for further discussion on modalities. When the Interim Committee met
on October 6–7 in Seoul, the ministers did not attempt to resolve those issues.
Rather, they endorsed the areas of agreement and asked the Executive Board to
reach an accord on the unresolved issues before the next meeting of the Committee in April 1986. Significantly, despite a further appeal from Baker for a "bolder"
approach, the Seoul communiqué avoided the term "joint," noting only that "the
Fund should work in close collaboration with the World Bank, whilst avoiding
cross-conditionality." The communiqué also welcomed India's and China's offers—
reaffirmed by Singh and Liu Hongru (Deputy Governor of the People's Bank of
China) during the meeting[29]—to abstain from using the proposed facility, and it
noted the importance of ensuring additionality by stressing that the plan "should
not adversely affect" other concessional lending to low-income countries (*Annual
Report 1986*, pp. 106–08).

---

[28]Minutes of EBM/85/141 (September 13, 1985), p. 33.

[29]See notes made by the Managing Director during the meeting, in IMF/RD Managing Director file "Interim and Development Committees, October 1985, Seoul" (Accession 87/136, Box 3,
Section 168).

Establishment of the Facility, 1985–86

The U.S. authorities were not yet ready to abandon the "bold" approach under which the Fund and the Bank would negotiate programs jointly. For some two months after the meeting in Seoul, officials of the U.S. Treasury attempted to line up support for that approach from other major countries, with little success. By end-year, however, they abandoned the quest in favor of the more limited idea of having the Fund and the Bank, together with the authorities of the borrowing country, jointly develop a "policy framework" that would be consistent with but more specific on structural adjustment than the Fund's usual Article IV report and the Bank's country economic memorandum. The framework then would be considered more or less simultaneously by the two Executive Boards, after which each institution would negotiate a specific program based on its own criteria.[30]

Although the Interim Committee communiqué endorsed the use of IDA eligibility as the primary criterion for eligibility to draw on the proposed facility, Finch and his colleagues on the Fund staff continued to look for alternatives. Apart from the substantive question of which countries should be eligible, the issue of bureaucratic turf arose: relying on IDA eligibility implied that the World Bank, not the Fund, would have responsibility for deciding any future changes in the list of eligible countries. About a month after the meetings in Seoul, the staff and the Managing Director agreed that the Fund should propose a list of eligible countries that would be identical to the list of countries then eligible for IDA financing but that would not be formally or automatically linked to that list. If the IDA-eligible list changed, or if the Fund decided on its own to introduce a change, the Fund's Executive Board would retain full responsibility for changing the list of countries eligible to draw on the Fund facility. Executive Directors, however, wary of getting into debates over eligibility of individual countries, backed away slightly from that proposal and determined that "all low-income countries eligible for IDA resources that are in need of such resources and face protracted balance of payments problems" would be eligible initially to use the Fund's new facility.[31] With this wording, the Board retained its discretion to determine future eligibility independently of IDA.

The most important issue that remained unresolved after Seoul concerned conditionality. When the Executive Board met in February 1986 for its second substantive discussion of the proposed facility, it was presented with a staff proposal to require essentially the same level of conditionality as for an upper-tranche standby arrangement. The main difference would be that compliance would be monitored through semiannual "benchmarks" rather than quarterly performance criteria.[32] Mtei made one last attempt to dissuade his colleagues from that course, which he regarded as "a major departure . . . from the letter and spirit of the Trust

---

[30]The revised approach is described in a paper transmitted to the Managing Director by Dallara on January 6, 1986; in IMF/CF (S 1794 "Structural Adjustment Facility (SAF), April–December 1985").

[31]Chairman's summing up, minutes of EBM/86/24 (February 11, 1986), p. 40.

[32]"Use of Resources of the Special Disbursement Account," EBS/85/283 (December 17, 1985), pp. 16–18.

Fund." Inadequate and delayed financing, in his view, had been the principal cause of program failures in sub-Saharan Africa; accepting the staff proposals would only aggravate the problem. Dallara responded that the real problem was a lack of progress in policy adjustment and that the facility had to aim at overcoming that weakness. The majority view, which was thought to represent a compromise, was that quantified policy benchmarks could be required, as long as they were distinguished in some fashion from performance criteria.[33] In a formal sense, this procedure was equivalent to the relatively low-level first-tranche conditionality applied to Trust Fund loans, but it was also understood that in practice the Fund would expect borrowing countries to exceed that standard.

Although the Interim Committee had directed that the new facility should not give rise to cross-conditionality between the Fund and the World Bank, the Board had to decide what that meant. A broad interpretation, favored by Directors representing low-income countries, would be that the Fund should not hold up its own lending because of a disagreement with the Bank (or conversely). If the two institutions disagreed on how viable the country's proposed program was, then whichever one took the more favorable view should proceed with its loans. A stricter interpretation, favored by the staff and the Managing Director as well as by a majority of Directors, would be that once a lending arrangement was approved by both institutions, *disbursements* should not be held up simply because the other institution's conditions were not being met. This interpretation would strengthen Fund-Bank collaboration in the *design* of adjustment programs, even if the two staffs initially disagreed on the country's policy requirements. After de Larosière pointedly stated his strong opposition to any cross-conditionality resulting from adherence to this narrower definition, proponents of the wider view decided to back off.

Cross-conditionality continued, however, to be the most difficult issue. The World Bank was expected to provide a roughly equivalent amount of support, principally through IDA loans.[34] Although the U.S. authorities abandoned their proposal for jointly negotiated adjustment programs, they continued to push for as much collaboration as possible. Dallara's January 1986 proposal for a collaborative "policy framework" paper (see footnote 30, p. 649) specified that such a document should be "explicit in defining policy objectives, timetable and areas for priority attention" and should form "the basis for agreement on these issues and priorities between the Bank and the Fund." To many on the Fund staff, however, that proposal raised the danger that negotiations could get bogged down by the quite different working styles

---

[33]Minutes of EBM/86/23 (February 11, 1986), pp. 12–21; and the Chairman's summing up at EBM/86/24 (same date), p. 41.

[34]Loans from IDA at that time were interest-free, with longer maturities (50 years instead of 10) and grace periods (10 years instead of 5½) than the SAF; see *Annual Report* of the World Bank for 1986, p. 3. In December 1986, IDA resources were enlarged from $9.7 billion (in the IDA-7 period, 1985–87) to $12.4 billion (in the IDA-8 period, 1988–90), but maturities were reduced to 35–40 years. A minimum of $3 billion of that amount (roughly equivalent to SDR 2.5 billion) was expected to be lent "in conjunction with" the SAF. The role of IDA was outlined in "Proposals for Enhancing Assistance to Low-Income Countries Facing Exceptional Difficulties," EB/CW/DC/87/6 (August 19, 1987), pp. 8–9.

and requirements of the two institutions. Since developing countries generally shared that concern, the Managing Director crafted a compromise in February that supported a central role for what would become known as the Policy Framework Paper (PFP) while cautioning that the PFP "should not be overly precise," that the institutions' "respective mandates and expertise" should be preserved, and that "some flexibility must be maintained in the specific working of these arrangements."[35] How precise and how flexible would have to be judged after experience was gained.

One of the last issues to be decided was the name for the new facility. Even at the February 1986 meeting, after several months of discussion, people were still talking about "proposals to use the Trust Fund reflows" ("Trust Fund II," as one Director suggested) or the "use of resources in the Special Disbursement Account" (or "SDA Facility"). Shortly afterward, the staff came up with a phrase that stressed the linkage between these resources and the requirement that eligible countries adopt comprehensive adjustment programs: the Structural Adjustment Facility. That name caught on, and the SAF was formally created on March 26.[36]

Operations, 1986–89

The IDA criterion initially implied that 60 of the Fund's 149 member countries would be eligible to borrow from the SAF. That number rose to 62 by the following year, but with the voluntary withdrawal of China and India, the available funds had to be apportioned among the 60 smaller, low-income countries.[37]

To ensure that the facility would not run out of resources prematurely if all eligible countries borrowed from it, the Board agreed to set a low ceiling on loan size: 20 percent of the borrower's quota in the first year and 13.5 percent in each of the next two years, for a cumulative three-year access limit of just 47 percent.[38] In contrast, countries that had made full use of available Trust Fund loans in the 1970s had borrowed the equivalent of about 80 percent of their quota. But since interest rates on Trust Fund loans were so low, and since a portion of the reflow from those loans had been earmarked for other purposes, the total size of the SAF was smaller, even in absolute size, than the Trust Fund of a decade earlier. Relative to quotas, which had been enlarged in 1980 and again in 1983, it was even smaller. Access

---

[35]Chairman's summing up, minutes of EBM/86/24 (February 11, 1986), p. 42.

[36]The Executive Board of the World Bank expressed its approval of the proposal, conditional on an adequate expansion of IDA resources, at a meeting on March 17. For the Fund decisions, and the summing up of the March 26 meeting, see *Annual Report 1986*, pp. 92–99. A summary of the World Bank discussion was circulated in the Fund as "Special Disbursement Account—World Bank Board Discussion on the Trust Fund Proposal," EBS/86/53, Sup. 2 (March 20, 1986). The Fund decision to create the SAF was made at EBM/86/56 (March 26, 1986).

[37]Tonga had joined the Fund in September 1985 and had not yet been deemed IDA-eligible when the SAF was established six months later. In early 1987, both Tonga and Kiribati (which joined the Fund in June 1986) were declared by the Bank to be IDA-eligible and by the Fund to be SAF-eligible. For the initial list, see *Annual Report 1986*, p. 98.

[38]The aggregate quota of the 60 eligible countries (excluding China and India) was SDR 4.2 billion. Available resources during the first three years of operation were expected to total just under SDR 2 billion.

limits therefore had to be set much lower. To compound the problem, many of these countries faced balance of payments deficits that were much larger in relation to quota than they had been in the earlier period.

As it happened, these initial limits were overly conservative because a substantial number of eligible countries either did not apply to borrow or were unable to develop adequate adjustment programs. The first SAF loan, to Burundi, was not approved until August 1986, and by the time the Board first reviewed the facility, in June 1987, only 15 loans had been approved. Consequently, the access limit for the second year was raised to 30 percent of quota, making the cumulative limit 63.5 percent. Nonetheless, the facility remained "painfully" small (in de Larosière's words),[39] relative to the former Trust Fund, to the Fund's general resources, and to the financing needs of low-income countries.

Conditionality for SAF loans was applied similarly to the Fund's extended (EFF) arrangements, with a few key differences. As with EFF programs, countries were expected to formulate a medium-term policy framework, but here the PFP process required the World Bank to be involved. Although the SAF decision anticipated that the PFP would be drafted by the authorities with the help of the staff of the two Bretton Woods institutions, in practice PFPs were drafted initially by the staff and then refined with the help of the authorities. This practice was necessitated by a decision in April 1986 that a draft PFP should be made part of the pre-mission briefing papers submitted for approval by management.[40] The process worked as follows. After the country requested a SAF loan, the Fund staff would prepare, in collaboration with the Bank staff, a draft outline for a medium-term policy framework to be negotiated. That draft would be approved by the Fund management as the basis for a negotiating mission in which Bank staff would participate informally.[41] If the negotiations succeeded, the authorities would then submit to the Fund both a final PFP describing their policy intentions in general terms and a Letter of Intent that set out their specific policy commitments for the coming year. While agreement on the PFP was a requirement for loan approval, the Letter of Intent became the basis for conditional disbursements, just as it was for stand-by arrangements.

Once management approved the documents submitted by the authorities, the PFP was discussed first by the Bank's Executive Directors, sitting as a Committee of the Whole and "reviewing" but not formally "approving" the document.[42] The

---

[39]Speaking notes for remarks to the Development Committee (October 7, 1985); in IMF/RD Managing Director file "Interim and Development Committees, October 1985, Seoul" (Accession 87/136, Box 3, Section 168).

[40]Memorandum from Finch to the Managing Director (April 10, 1986), with handwritten agreement by de Larosière (April 13); in IMF/CF (S 1794 "Structural Adjustment Facility (SAF), April–December 1985").

[41]In practice, this arrangement meant that Bank staff would visit the country at the same time as the Fund mission and would participate in relevant meetings with the authorities but would not act under the direction of the Fund mission chief.

[42]The practice of sitting in committee was designed "to safeguard the fiction that the [Bank's] Board did not discuss countries' general economic programs" (Polak, 1995, p. 29). Polak goes on to note that PFPs did not have a central operational role in guiding the Bank's decisions on requests for IDA loans. PFPs thus became more associated with the Fund than the Bank.

Bank would then transmit the summing up of its discussion to the Fund. The Fund's Board thus would have four primary documents before it: the PFP, the Letter of Intent, the staff report, and the summary of the Bank's views. Upon approval by the Board, the Fund would disburse the first year's loan proceeds; in contrast to stand-by and extended arrangements, SAF loans were not paid in installments throughout the year.

These various distinctions might seem in retrospect to signify nothing more than technical hairsplitting, but they represented a carefully crafted compromise between those who viewed the SAF as a form of financial assistance administered by the Fund and those who saw it as an extension of the Fund's conditional lending. In the latter view—which was strongly held by staff and management—the policy requirements for a country to restore balance of payments viability were not diminished by the availability of SAF financing. Loan approval therefore was to be conditional on the specification of a detailed set of policy commitments, but the country was to be given a much greater benefit of the doubt on its willingness and ability to carry out those commitments than it would have been with a conventional upper-tranche arrangement.

The expectation that the SAF, like the Trust Fund that preceded it, would be a nearly universal source of finance for eligible countries was far from realized, largely because of the complexities of the PFP process and the World Bank's inevitable ambivalence toward it. On the one hand, because review of the PFP by the Bank's Executive Directors was not directly connected to the Bank's lending decisions, both the Board and the staff on that side of the street naturally viewed PFPs as more of a Fund document.[43] Not infrequently, Bank staff seemed less eager to sign off on a draft PFP quickly than were their counterparts in the Fund. On the other hand, the Bank's senior staff worried that the Fund was not applying conditionality as strictly to SAF borrowers as it did for stand-by arrangements, and the Bank was reluctant to approve its own Structural Adjustment Loans (SALs) to countries without a conventional stand-by arrangement. On that point, at least, many in the Fund were just as worried; without intra-year phasing of drawings and without formal performance criteria, the SAF was sailing in weakly charted seas.

For countries that succeeded in obtaining SAF loans, the money from the facility typically covered only a small part of their total financing needs. As with all Fund loans, it was hoped that the Fund's commitment would encourage (or "catalyze") other lenders to do the same. Most SAF-eligible countries, however, had little or no immediate hope for loans from commercial creditors. Nor could they afford loans on commercial terms, even if they had been offered. The goal, therefore, was to ensure that adequate financing was available from official creditors, especially bilateral aid from donor countries and debt rescheduling through the Paris Club. That goal, however, was difficult to pursue, because donor countries preferred to keep bilateral aid decisions separate from their dealings with the IMF. In

---

[43]For the Bank staff's assessment of the role of PFPs in the Bank, see "Policy Framework Papers—A First Review of Experience in the World Bank," EBS/88/65, Sup. 1 (March 23, 1988).

most countries, the government agencies that disbursed aid to low-income countries operated independently from the treasury, which dealt with the Fund, and any blurring of those roles could have subjected the SAF and even the Fund itself to greater political pressures.[44] To avoid that problem, the staff focused on trying to persuade donor countries to associate aid decisions in some way with "the PFP process."[45]

Whether the existence of the SAF or the PFP process ever affected bilateral aid, positively or negatively, is difficult to establish. What borrowing countries feared most was that donors, having agreed to support the SAF, would then abdicate their bilateral role. What the Fund aimed for was to make the process effective in promoting policy reform and thereby catalyze substantial additional bilateral financing. The outcome doubtless fell between apprehension and ambition, but a measure of success is evident. The U.S. Treasury used the SAF and the PFP process as levers to persuade congress to approve an enlargement of the U.S. contribution to IDA, from $2.3 billion in 1985–87 (IDA-7) to $2.9 billion in 1988–90 (IDA-8), and it seems likely that the aggregate size of IDA-8 would otherwise have been substantially smaller.[46] In January 1987, after a long battle, the Paris Club agreed to consider rescheduling requests from countries with SAF loans, rather than requiring a regular stand-by or extended arrangement.[47] That agreement offered expanded possibilities for heavily indebted countries to obtain relief from official creditors without first having to obtain more expensive financing from the Fund's general accounts. The Fund also made a concerted effort to persuade creditor countries to link bilateral assistance to the PFP process, but that effort had little success.

Despite the difficulties, the pace of SAF lending picked up somewhat in its second year of operation, before tapering off in deference to its "enhanced" successor, the ESAF (see below). Through 1995, after which all such lending was done through the successor facility, 37 of the 62 eligible countries borrowed a total of SDR 1.8 billion ($2½ billion) through the SAF. A substantial majority of those loans either were fully drawn by the borrower or were replaced by a larger ESAF loan. In 10 instances, the SAF loan program was abandoned before the second or third year, either because the required adjustment policies were no longer being carried out or because the borrower was overdue in payments to the Fund.

Initial fears that access to the SAF would be substantially smaller than under the Trust Fund were not borne out. Owing to the weeding-out effect of requiring a

---

[44]For a discussion, see "Structural Adjustment Facility (SAF)—Review of Experience," EBS/87/46 (February 27, 1987), pp. 41–42.

[45]In February 1988, the Fund and the Bank held a seminar for chief officers of aid agencies in donor countries, to explain how PFPs could help in aid decisions. Participants came from 19 donor countries, 7 multilateral agencies, and 3 borrowing countries. See "Policy Framework Paper (PFP)—Seminar on the PFP and Aid Coordination and Related Issues," EBS/88/65 (March 23, 1988).

[46]For IDA contributions, see the *Annual Reports* of the World Bank, 1985 and 1987.

[47]Actual practice began in June 1987, when the Paris Club agreed to reschedule debts of Mozambique and then Uganda, just a few days after the Fund approved SAF loans for those countries. See Keller (1988).

PFP and a Letter of Intent, countries that borrowed from the SAF ultimately could borrow nearly as much relative to quota as had been available under the Trust Fund. Having initially decided that eligible countries could borrow 20 percent in the first year and then having permitted loans of 30 percent in the second year, the Executive Board agreed in March 1989 on a 20 percent limit for the third year.[48] So as not to penalize countries that had qualified earliest, these access limits were applied retroactively, and almost all SAF loan commitments (31 of 38) were for 70 percent of the borrower's quota.[49]

Pakistan

As an illustration of how SAF loans worked in practice, consider the loan to Pakistan in December 1988—at SDR 382 million ($516 million), the largest loan made through this facility.[50] Pakistan had drawn on Fund resources frequently before, most notably through a series of seven stand-by arrangements during the two decades through 1978 and then through a three-year EFF arrangement approved in 1980 (the largest extended arrangement up to that time, although much larger loans were made later on). By 1988, Pakistan had repaid most of those credits and had outstanding obligations amounting to just 68 percent of quota (SDR 370 million, or $500 million) plus a small amount still due from its Trust Fund borrowings in the late 1970s (Figure 14.2). When Pakistan again sought assistance in 1988, the SAF provided a more flexible and less costly medium for Fund financing and conditionality.

Before the 1980s, the Fund's credits to Pakistan had been classic cases of balance of payments support, predicated on the government's commitment to adjust macroeconomic policies so as to stabilize the economy and to maintain a competitive and stable exchange regime. Pakistan maintained a fixed exchange rate between the rupee and the U.S. dollar throughout much of the turmoil of the 1970s, devaluing by 57 percent in 1972 to correct a major overvaluation and then revaluing by 10 percent the next year in the wake of the floating of the dollar against

---

[48]The staff first examined the possibility of raising access to 70 percent in the summer of 1988 but rejected that option out of concern that resources could become overcommitted. The Executive Board agreed to accept the staff recommendation, over the objections of 10 Directors. See "Structural Adjustment Facility—Third Year Access," EBS/88/129 (July 6, 1988) and minutes of EBM/88/118 (July 29, 1988); and "Structural Adjustment Facility (SAF) and Enhanced Structural Adjustment Facility (ESAF)—Review of Operations," EBS/89/35 (March 3, 1989), pp. 17–19, and minutes of EBM/89/40 (March 29, 1989).

[49]Of the seven smaller loans, five were at 63.5 percent of quota (the limit established in 1987) because they expired prior to the March 1989 increase. All five of those countries obtained ESAF loans, and after the final increase in SAF access went into effect, financing for the relevant portion of the ESAF commitment (6.5 percent of quota) was shifted from the ESAF Trust to the SDA. All other commitments through 1992 were for 70 percent of quota. After that date, the Fund approved just two one-year SAF loans, in conjunction with larger three-year ESAF commitments: to Sierra Leone in March 1994, for 35 percent of quota; and to Zambia in December 1995, for 50 percent.

[50]A loan for SDR 346.9 million was approved in December 1988; the amount was raised in March 1989. For another and much more detailed case study, on the SAF loan to the Gambia in September 1986, see Hadjimichael and others (1992).

Figure 14.2. Pakistan: Concessional Loans and Other Credit Outstanding, 1976–91

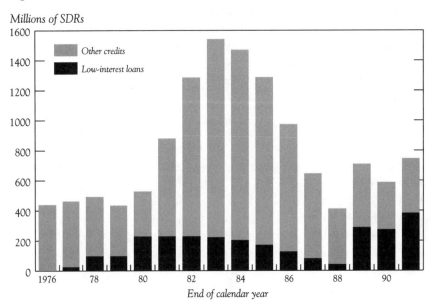

Millions of SDRs

other major currencies (that is, revaluing to keep the rupee's value roughly constant against major currencies other than the dollar). The exchange rate established in 1973 remained realistic for several years, aided by the weakness of the dollar in 1977 and 1978, but the recovery of the dollar in 1979 exposed the underlying weakness that had crept into the rupee over time.

When the authorities applied in 1980 for a three-year arrangement under the EFF, they initially fended off the staff's recommendation for a devaluation of the rupee by promising to cut the fiscal deficit, liberalize the external sector to promote exports and attract capital inflows, and undertake substantial restructuring of the economy to promote efficiency and mobilize savings.[51] They hoped to gain enough time for reforms to work by drawing heavily on the Fund; the EFF arrangement would provide close to SDR 1.3 billion (445 percent of quota, or $1.6 billion) over three years. Both the fiscal cuts and the restructuring, however, proved to be difficult to achieve, even after the United States committed itself to providing $3.2 billion in official assistance to Pakistan over a six-year period.[52] A year into the EFF

---

[51]From 1976 through 1979, the staff argued without success that the rupee should be devalued. In the spring of 1980, the staff accepted the authorities' confidence in their ability to correct macroeconomic imbalances through demand management without a devaluation. That agreement cleared the way for negotiations on an extended arrangement. Memorandum from A. Shakur Shaalan (Director of the Middle Eastern Department) to the Managing Director (April 30, 1980); in IMF/CF (C/Pakistan/810 "Mission, El Selehdar and Staff, May 1980").

[52]U.S. aid to Pakistan fell off in the late 1970s but was revived in recognition of Pakistan's strategic importance during the Soviet occupation of Afghanistan. U.S. support, however, remained tenuous, and the U.S. Executive Director (Richard D. Erb) abstained from approving the continuation of the EFF loan in December 1981.

arrangement, after both the staff and Executive Directors pressed for a devaluation and a more flexible policy, the authorities decided to shift course.[53] In January 1982, the government agreed to abandon the currency peg and to let the central bank begin managing the exchange rate against a basket of currencies. Under that regime, the rupee drifted gradually downward against the dollar by enough to strengthen international competitiveness a bit, and the arrangement held together for another year. By mid-1983, however, the staff concluded that both fiscal and monetary excesses had thrown the program off track, despite an overall strong record of policy implementation. The arrangement expired in November of that year with the final drawing unmade.[54]

For the next four years, the economy seemed to do reasonably well despite the persistence of fiscal stresses and structural rigidities and the country's dependence on the fortunes of a few agricultural crops (mainly cotton) in world markets. The exchange rate was managed so as to generate a depreciation of more than 30 percent in both nominal and real effective terms between early 1985 and the end of 1987, and the overall balance of payments was further strengthened by substantial foreign official assistance and by large inflows of workers' remittances. Real economic growth averaged about 7 percent a year for several years, and inflation fell by nearly half, to an annual rate of less than 5 percent by 1987. Nonetheless, the economy remained highly vulnerable to external shocks, owing largely to structural rigidities and a persistently high fiscal deficit.

The creation of the SAF in 1986, which coincided with a renewed weakening of Pakistan's fiscal balance and the end of large-scale official assistance from the United States, induced the government to contemplate taking on new borrowings from the Fund. For a July 1986 mission, the Fund and Bank staff prepared a draft PFP that sketched out a plan for policy adjustment and reform that could be supported by a SAF loan. The authorities, however, decided that the staff proposals were too draconian and that they would do better to forgo the loans for the time being.[55]

Some months later, as the outlook for the balance of payments failed to improve, the government again approached the Fund, to ask for a multiyear stand-by arrangement combined with a relatively small SAF loan. That plan would help to

---

[53]The staff's position was summarized in a memorandum from Shaalan to the Managing Director (September 28, 1981); in IMF/RD Managing Director File "Pakistan, 1981" (Accession 83/108, Box 2, Section 376).

[54]The EFF arrangement approved in November 1980 was replaced a year later by a new agreement that provided for the same total amount of credits but on slightly more favorable terms. The improvement was made possible by the increase in Pakistan's quota under the Eighth General Review, which raised the amount available from the Fund's own resources rather than from borrowings. Drawings proceeded somewhat more slowly than initially envisaged, owing to delays in negotiating specific conditions and occasionally because of the need for waivers of conditions. The final drawing was made in May 1983, and when the arrangement expired, SDR 189 million (15 percent of the agreed amount) remained unused.

[55]Memorandum from Said H. Hitti and S. Kanesa-Thasan (both Senior Advisors in the Middle Eastern Department) to the Managing Director (January 20, 1987); in IMF/RD Managing Director file "Pakistan, January–December 1987" (Accession 89/14, Box 7, Section 550).

preserve SAF resources for future loans to other countries, especially those in sub-Saharan Africa that had an even greater need for concessional financing. (Pakistan, in contrast to many SAF-eligible countries, was able to obtain loans from international commercial banks.) Throughout 1987, however, the gap between the staff's and the authorities' views on the need for major policy changes could not be breached, and the government dropped the idea for the time being.

When discussions resumed in the early months of 1988, the type of arrangement that might be offered became a major issue. The Fund's management had no difficulty accepting a proposal for a short stand-by arrangement, but whether Pakistan's policy intentions qualified for a longer-term loan aimed at supporting structural adjustment was less clear. Negotiations—led by Malcolm D. Knight (Division Chief in the Middle Eastern Department)—continued through the summer. Not until the time of the Annual Meetings (held in Berlin around the end of September) was the staff convinced that the authorities' plans for trade liberalization and fiscal reforms were comprehensive enough to resolve the structural imbalances in the economy. Even so, management was not prepared to recommend to the Board that the Fund make the large-scale and long-term commitment that an ESAF loan would have implied. After a sometimes stormy series of meetings in Berlin, agreement was reached on a plan to provide Pakistan with a pair of arrangements: SDR 273 million (50 percent of quota) of the Fund's general resources through a two-year stand-by arrangement, and SDR 347 million (63.5 percent of quota) over three years through the SAF.[56]

By that time, the country was in a political turmoil triggered by the death of President Mohammad Zia ul Haq in an airplane crash in August 1988. The Fund was now negotiating with an interim government, and elections were scheduled for November 16. Although the government would have liked the Executive Board to approve the loan request before it went to the polls, the Managing Director insisted that the Fund had to have a commitment from the newly elected leaders as well. On December 11, three weeks after Benazir Bhutto was elected prime minister, her newly formed government (in which the finance minister who had negotiated the final agreement, Mahbub ul Haq, retained his portfolio) assented to carry out the program. The Board meeting took place on December 28, and more than two months after the conclusion of negotiations, Executive Directors approved the loans without dissent.[57]

The strains on the Pakistan economy that had made it so difficult to reach agreement in the first place also made it difficult for the government to keep the program on track. Refugees from war-plagued Afghanistan continued to flow into

---

[56]See memorandums to management from Shaalan and Kanesa-Thasan (July 7, 1988) and from Knight (October 11, 1988); in IMF/RD Managing Director file "Pakistan, 1987–1988" (Accession 89/131, Box 3, Section 282). The World Bank provided a similar amount of assistance during the same period. Over the two years beginning in August 1988, the Bank approved four sectoral loans to Pakistan, for a total commitment of $784 million (SDR 580 million).

[57]See "Pakistan—Staff Report for the 1988 Article IV Consultation and Request for a Stand-by Arrangement and for Arrangements Under the Structural Adjustment Facility," EBS/88/250, Sup. 1 (December 27, 1988); and minutes of EBM/88/185 (December 28, 1988).

Pakistan; by the end of 1989, the total number of refugees was estimated to be around 3.8 million. The external terms of trade deteriorated markedly in 1989, and by the second half of 1990, the crisis brought on by Iraq's invasion of Kuwait brought a sharp drop in fiscal revenues. Nonetheless, although some disbursements under the stand-by arrangement were held back, the second year's installment of the SAF loan was approved on schedule and disbursed in December 1989. From then on, between 40 and 50 percent of Pakistan's outstanding obligations to the Fund were long-term, low-interest loans.

The Gulf War of 1991 aggravated Pakistan's economic problems and brought further disbursement delays. Only after additional policy adjustments were made was the SAF loan fully paid out: one year late, in December 1991. The lack of performance criteria and intra-year phasing caused some anxious moments along the way, but ultimately they did not prevent the Fund from maintaining a measure of conditionality in its loans to Pakistan while sharply reducing the country's debt-servicing costs.

Bangladesh

The second-largest SAF loan, after the one to Pakistan, went to Bangladesh in February 1987.[58] The main problems faced by the authorities were long-term and structural: severe overcrowding of the large population; a consequent near-total dependence on external funding for economic development; a very narrow base for output and especially exports, heavily dependent on the market for jute; and frequent natural disasters, notably floods and cyclones that often destroyed much of the country's vital agricultural output.

Bangladesh, despite its extreme poverty and this litany of recurring difficulties, had established a generally strong record of program implementation before applying for the SAF arrangement. Following the breakaway from Pakistan in 1971, Bangladesh (formerly East Pakistan) joined the IMF in August 1972 and pegged its currency (the taka) loosely to the British pound. Throughout the rest of the 1970s, the authorities had frequent recourse to Fund credits, though generally for modest amounts. Drawing on the Compensatory Financing Facility (CFF), the oil facilities, three stand-by arrangements (all successfully completed and fully drawn), and the Trust Fund, by the end of the decade Bangladesh raised its indebtedness to approximately SDR 170 million ($225 million, or 114 percent of quota) to the General Resources Account and SDR 90 million ($120 million, 60 percent of quota) to the Trust Fund (Figure 14.3). The Fund's assistance up to this point helped the country finance its balance of payments deficits, but it was not aimed directly at addressing the chronic underlying structural problems.

In December 1980, the Fund approved a three-year EFF arrangement for Bangladesh, aimed at helping the government to absorb the effects of the 1979–80 oil shock and other external problems, begin to deal with the distortions and struc-

---

[58]A slightly larger loan was approved for Zaïre a few months later, but it was not fully disbursed.

tural rigidities in the economy, and ultimately reduce the crushing level of poverty in the country. That arrangement ran into trouble, however, largely because of external conditions: a drop in the world market price of the principal export (jute) and an unexpected decline in foreign aid. To compound the problem, the president of Bangladesh, Ziaur Rahman (vernacularly known as Zia), was assassinated in May 1981, after which the government was effectively paralyzed and unable to take remedial action for several months. Credit growth quickly breached the programmed ceiling, the interim government was unable to get the economy back on track, and a new military government—headed by General Hussain Mohammed Ershad—took power in March 1982. In the midst of this turmoil, for the first and only time the Bangladeshi authorities had to abandon a Fund arrangement because of poor policy implementation.[59]

Bangladesh then obtained two more stand-by arrangements from the Fund: a small 5-month arrangement in 1983 and a larger 19-month arrangement beginning in December 1985. The 1983 arrangement was intended to serve as a bridge to a 12-month arrangement for 1983–84, but the authorities decided not to pursue that option. By mid-1983, conditions had improved markedly, if temporarily: policy adjustments had been stronger and more effective than the Fund staff had expected, weather had been favorable for crops, competitiveness had been improved by the appreciation of the U.S. dollar against sterling and other major currencies,[60] and foreign aid commitments had picked up again. Consequently, Bangladesh's balance of payments had improved by enough that the government could get by without the Fund's money, and the authorities were eager not to submit to the Fund's conditionality.

By 1985, conditions worsened again, primarily owing to a further collapse in the international jute market but also because of disastrous weather conditions (floods and cyclones) and a drop in demand for Bangladeshi and other foreign workers in the Middle East. Moreover, the World Bank and other official creditors were getting concerned about the risks of lending to a country without a macroeconomic stabilization program approved by the Fund. So Bangladesh again applied for a stand-by arrangement. Negotiations (led by Kadhim Al-Eyd, Assistant Director in the Asian Department) were long and difficult, especially concerning the need for greater flexibility in managing the exchange rate. Perhaps more than in most low-income countries, the Bangladeshi authorities felt that they held a strong hand in these negotiations, because they had a solid policy record, because at least some external creditors sympathized with their position on key policy issues, and because the amount of the proposed arrangement was not very large in relation to their

---

[59]The arrangement, as approved in December 1980, provided for SDR 800 million in loans over three years ($1.02 billion, or 350 percent of quota). Of that, SDR 220 million was disbursed through June 1981. After several months of unsuccessful negotiations on a new economic program, the government canceled the arrangement in June 1982.

[60]In 1979, the authorities began pegging the taka to a basket of currencies rather than to the pound sterling. Nonetheless, because of the importance of the bilateral exchange rate, especially for attracting the repatriation of earnings by Bangladesh nationals working in the United Kingdom, the rate frequently was adjusted so as to maintain stability against the pound.

overall financing needs.[61] A compromise program was finally agreed upon toward the end of the year, and the Executive Board approved the arrangement in December. Economic policy then was still on track, and the economy was doing better than anyone had expected just a few months earlier. Throughout this period, the Fund again focused primarily on macroeconomic stabilization, while the World Bank made several loans to Bangladesh aimed at financing essential imports and promoting structural reforms.

Soon after the 1985–87 arrangement was approved, the staff began discussions aimed at developing a medium-term policy framework that could be supported by a SAF loan. The authorities, however, were initially reluctant. From their vantage point, it appeared that they were being asked to develop a full-scale medium-term adjustment program equivalent to what the Fund would have required for an extended arrangement, but with only a small fraction of the resources that could have been provided through the EFF. Moreover, the medium-term framework would have to be approved by the World Bank even though the Bank was not then committed to providing any additional resources.[62] The authorities understood, of course, that a SAF loan would be on much more favorable (i.e., concessional) terms than a regular Fund arrangement, but they also believed that the nonfinancial constraints would largely offset that benefit.

The Fund's staff and management believed that the SAF was important for Bangladesh, because the economy needed much structural reform if it hoped to raise its growth rate, and because the country could not afford to take on more debt except on highly concessional terms. Negotiations continued through several months in 1986 until a tentative medium-term agreement was hammered out during the Annual Meetings in Washington between the Managing Director (de Larosière) and the finance minister, M. Syeduz-Zaman. A detailed PFP was then drafted jointly by Al-Eyd's team, the authorities in Dhaka, and the World Bank staff. The framework called for a wide range of structural reforms, including strengthened tax collection, a higher rate of "recovery" or repayment of government loans to businesses and farmers, enhanced incentives for both government and private enterprises, and liberalization of the trade and exchange systems. Many

---

[61]The main dispute concerned exchange rate policy. The Fund staff and management insisted that the exchange rate be managed so as to prevent any appreciation in real effective terms (i.e., that the authorities implement a "real exchange rate rule," as discussed in Chapter 2), and that certain restrictive and preferential practices be eliminated. The government was prepared to implement a real-rate rule but argued that it could not implement all of the Fund's suggestions without weakening incentives for capital investment and for the repatriation of earnings by Bangladeshi workers abroad. The small size of this and earlier stand-by arrangements reflected the view—which was held especially firmly by the Managing Director—that Bangladesh could not afford to take on large amounts of debt except on highly concessional terms. The arrangement approved in December 1985 provided for SDR 180 million in drawings over 19 months ($200 million, or 62.6 percent of quota).

[62]The World Bank was unable to commit IDA funds until the Eighth Replenishment was approved, and Bank officials were reluctant to make new IBRD commitments until disputes were resolved regarding a high rate of defaults on government loans to small farmers and businesses made in conjunction with the Bank's existing sectoral loans to Bangladesh.

of these reforms were structured specifically to minimize any adverse impacts on the poorest groups in the economy.[63] It was a strong and viable program aimed at moderately raising the annual growth rate (from 4 percent in 1983–86 to 5 percent starting in 1987), which the Executive Board enthusiastically approved in February 1987.[64]

The direct financial effect of the SAF loan was to provide a modest net inflow of cash during the three years in which the program was in effect, while restructuring Bangladesh's indebtedness toward low-interest loans (see Figure 14.3). Without this arrangement, the country would have had to make large net repayments to the Fund. When the loan was approved, Bangladesh was scheduled to make approximately SDR 365 million in payments on principal and interest through the end of 1989. The SAF loan covered SDR 201 million of that, another SDR 48 million was offset by forthcoming drawings on the existing stand-by arrangement, and a CFF credit for SDR 89 million was approved at the same time as the SAF loan.[65] After the country was hit by major floods both in 1987 and 1988, the Fund also offered SDR 72 million in emergency relief credits in November 1988. On balance, outstanding obligations rose in 1987 and then stabilized.

Unfortunately, the government, which came under increasing domestic political pressure,[66] did not carry out many of the planned structural measures. Tax collection was especially weak, and public sector investment fell in relation to output. Consequently, the growth rate slipped to 3 percent a year instead of rising to the targeted 5 percent rate. On the brighter side, the authorities did move to liberalize both imports and exchange transactions, and they contained inflation through prudent monetary policies. Foreign aid was stable, and the balance of payments improved. Although the macroeconomic program was broadly successful and the SAF loan was fully disbursed on time, when it was over the economy was not much better off than it had been at the beginning. Lasting improvements would have to wait, aided by a much larger injection of Fund support through the ESAF in the 1990s.[67]

---

[63]For example, the PFP noted the government's intention to better enable small farmers to restructure loans if necessary after bad harvests, to phase in the elimination of food subsidies gradually, and to use the revenues from the elimination of subsidies for social programs targeted directly at the poor. For a general assessment of Bangladesh's program for poverty alleviation, see Gotur (1991).

[64]"Bangladesh—Staff Report for the 1986 Article IV Consultation, Second Review Under the Stand-by Arrangement, and Request for Arrangements Under the Structural Adjustment Facility," EBS/87/7 (January 15, 1987), and minutes of EBM/87/23 (February 6, 1987). The poverty alleviation program mentioned in footnote 63 is described on pp. 44–45 of EBS/87/7.

[65]At the time of approval, the SAF loan commitment totaled just SDR 135.1 million, of which SDR 57.5 million was disbursed immediately. The subsequent general increases in SAF access limits ultimately made SDR 201.25 million available through April 1989.

[66]President Ershad held elections in October 1986, which he won, and he lifted martial law the next month. Opposition parties questioned the legitimacy of the elections, and public protests and strikes were held with increasing frequency and success throughout the next four years. Ershad resigned in December 1990.

[67]Bangladesh received SDR 345 million ($475 million) in ESAF loans from 1990 to 1993. By then, all of its outstanding obligations to the Fund were on concessional terms.

Figure 14.3. Bangladesh: Concessional Loans and Other Credit Outstanding, 1976–91

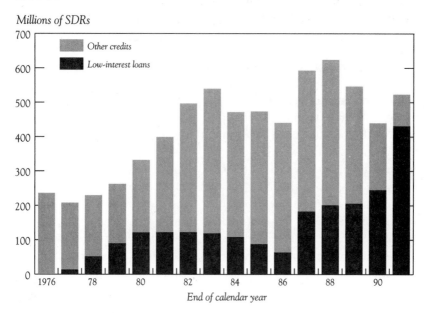

Millions of SDRs

End of calendar year

Enhanced Structural Adjustment Facility

Planning and Designing, 1987

Michel Camdessus's first meeting with the Interim Committee as Managing Director came in April 1987, three months after his arrival on the twelfth floor of the Fund's Washington headquarters. Much of his energy that winter had gone into the Fund's surveillance activities, especially in assessing the major industrial countries' Louvre accord and the efforts by U.S. officials to reduce the runaway fiscal deficit (Chapters 4 and 3, respectively). The time was coming, though, for what he would later call his "first major initiative as Managing Director," a drive to "enhance" or raise the resources that the Fund could put into concessional lending to low-income countries. His goal initially seemed hopeless to almost everyone, but not even he could have imagined how far the quest would carry him and how fundamental it ultimately would be to history's judgment of his years in office and of the Fund's ability to contribute to the alleviation of the world's worst poverty.

As discussed above, it was obvious from the beginning that the resources of the SAF were too small to have much of an effect unless they could be supplemented somehow. The strategy during the first year of the facility was to encourage donor countries to provide separate but related bilateral assistance to countries with SAF-supported adjustment programs.[68] After a year of trying, it was clear that this

---

[68]"Committee members stressed . . . that it would be desirable to enhance the catalytic role of the structural adjustment facility in mobilizing additional multilateral and bilateral concessional resources" (communiqué of September 29, 1986, para. 6; *Annual Report 1987*, pp. 110–11).

strategy was not working. As the Chairman of the Interim Committee, H. Onno Ruding (Netherlands), put it to his ministerial colleagues in April 1987, "the response . . . has been far from impressive."[69] No one yet had an alternative, however, so this time the communiqué merely repeated the call for bilateral aid, though without specifying whether the "necessary additional financial support" should be provided independently or through the Fund's facility.[70]

A few weeks later, in a mid-May meeting with Ruding in Paris, Camdessus informally raised the issue of asking donor countries to contribute additional resources to the SAF rather than just hoping that they would make parallel bilateral commitments. When Ruding encouraged him, the Managing Director was off and running.[71] Over the next two weeks, he met with heads of state, finance ministers, and other senior officials from each of the G-7 countries. At first, his goal was to get the ministers to approve the idea, but they went a step further: their bosses were looking for a way to move the debt-relief process forward at the forthcoming summit meeting in Venice, so why not include a proposal to augment the Fund's resources dedicated to the poorest countries? With especially strong backing from French President François Mitterrand and Canadian Prime Minister Brian Mulroney (both of whom met with Camdessus in Ottawa in late May), the lobbying effort quickly succeeded. Nearly at the last minute, a sentence was inserted into the Venice communiqué of June 10, 1987, stating that the Heads of State and Government of the G-7 countries "welcome the . . . proposal by the Managing Director of the IMF for a significant increase in the resources of the Structural Adjustment Facility over the three years from January 1, 1988. We urge a conclusion [of] discussions on these proposals within this year" (Hajnal, 1989, p. 342).

Meanwhile, on June 1, Camdessus further widened the appeal by writing to the Fund's governors for the G-10 countries and several other potential donors. For the first time, he mentioned a specific goal: tripling the resources of SAF, to SDR 9 billion, by raising contributions from official donors for a new trust fund to be administered by the IMF. On the same day, he brought the Executive Board into the picture for the first time by meeting with Directors from the G-10 countries plus Saudi Arabia.[72]

Camdessus was encouraged by the widespread support he was hearing, but he also knew that warm words did not make a victory. The next day he appointed a high-level staff team to undertake the massive job of designing a trust fund that the

---

[69]Draft speaking notes, as given to the Managing Director before the meeting; in IMF/RD Managing Director file "Interim Committee, 1987" (Accession 89/14, Box 4, Section 550).

[70]"Committee members noted the forthcoming review by the Executive Board of the structural adjustment facility and they expressed their hope that arrangements under the facility would serve to elicit from bilateral and multilateral donors the necessary additional financial support" (communiqué of April 10, 1987, para. 5; *Annual Report 1987*, p. 115).

[71]Letter from Ruding to Camdessus (June 29, 1987) and Camdessus's reply (July 16); in IMF/RD Exchange and Trade Relations Department file "SAF Correspondence, July 1987–" (RM4387, Section 4, Shelf 1, Bin 6).

[72]Memorandum for files by the Director of ETR, L. Alan Whittome (June 1, 1987); in IMF/RD Managing Director file "G-10 Meetings, June–July 1987" (Accession 89/46, Box 3, Section 224).

whole world could support, and the even more massive job of raising billions of SDRs to fund it.[73] Once the G-7 heads of state endorsed the proposal in Venice, the staff would have to move quickly, because the Managing Director was committed to having the new facility working by the end of the year.

Although the target of "tripling" SAF resources was a bit arbitrary,[74] neither the order of magnitude nor the sense of urgency about fulfilling it was by any means artificial. In mid-1987, the 34 SAF-eligible countries in Africa alone faced scheduled repayments to the Fund totaling SDR 5.3 billion through 1990, approximately triple the amounts that the Fund could extend to them through the SAF over the same period. It was crucial both for the Fund and for the indebted countries that those repayments be made. A few countries already were in arrears to the Fund, and if that problem snowballed, then bilateral aid would dry up just when the wisdom of the Fund remaining involved in sub-Saharan Africa would be increasingly called into question.[75] Without something close to a tripling of resources or an equivalent amount of other forms of aid, the economic plight of many very poor countries would be imperiled. It is no exaggeration to conclude that the economic future of Africa was at a critical juncture.[76]

Designing how the ESAF Trust (as it would be called) would dispense funds turned out to be a fairly straightforward operation, because little dissent developed to the notion that it should work similarly to the SAF in most respects. Notably, eligibility was to be the same (essentially, all countries that were eligible for loans from IDA were also to be eligible for loans from the enhanced SAF, although the Fund would determine the exact list). Both India and China, as they had a year earlier, indicated that they did not intend to draw on the facility, to allow greater access for the other 60 eligible countries. Access limits would depend on whether and how quickly resources could be tripled, but in principle, of course, they might also have been tripled. The key decision made by the Executive Board on that issue was to abandon the tactic embodied in both the Trust Fund and the SAF of granting, in effect, equal access to all borrowers. Instead, loans now would be made

---

[73]Report by the Managing Director at IS/87/3 (June 12, 1987), p. 6. The team comprised John T. Boorman (Deputy Director of the Exchange and Trade Relations Department), Thomas Leddy (Deputy Treasurer), and Reinhard H. Munzberg (Assistant General Counsel, Legal Department).

[74]Furthermore, the "triple" ratio was only a rough approximation. At the time, SAF resources were expected to reach a peak of SDR 2.7 billion by 1991; in the event, the peak was slightly smaller, because three countries wracked by civil wars (Liberia, Somalia, and Sudan) accumulated arrears to the Trust Fund totaling some SDR 120 million. Actual SAF loans outstanding peaked in 1993 at just under SDR 2 billion; by that time, as explained below, resources were being transferred to the ESAF Trust.

[75]At the time, more than two-thirds of all outstanding Fund lending arrangements were with sub-Saharan African countries.

[76]For comprehensive assessments of the economic plight of sub-Saharan Africa at that time, see Organization of African Unity (1986) and United Nations (1986). The UN report was cited by the Fund in December 1987 as an impetus for the creation of the ESAF (Press Release No. 87/44, December 29, 1987). The role of the SAF and the ESAF in contributing to the UN "Programme of Action for African Economic Recovery and Development" was assessed in United Nations (1987).

in amounts that reflected the circumstances of each country (financing needs and strength of adjustment program), within broad guidelines and limits (Section II, para. 2, of the Instrument establishing the ESAF Trust; *Annual Report 1988*, p. 121).

More contentious was the question of how strict and detailed conditionality should be on ESAF loans. Ahmed Abdallah (Kenya) argued in November 1987 against adding conditions beyond those already used with SAF loans. While agreeing that "there is no alternative to strong comprehensive adjustment," he suggested that "excessive conditionality will only be counterproductive." The staff and management, however, never doubted that weak conditionality had damaged the effectiveness of the SAF as a vehicle for structural reform, and they were determined to solve that problem with the ESAF. In any case, the issue was essentially moot, because the Fund could never have raised the necessary funds from donor countries without a guarantee of effective conditionality. So the Board agreed that ESAF loans would be disbursed semiannually (not annually, like SAF loans, but also not quarterly, like stand-by arrangements) and would be subject to performance criteria on both structural policies and macroeconomic data.[77] With this change, ESAF conditionality would differ only slightly from that on EFF arrangements.

As soon as general agreement was reached on these broad principles, the Board—spurred on by the Interim Committee in September—agreed on December 18, 1987, to create the ESAF Trust "to support programs [of low-income developing countries] to strengthen substantially and in a sustainable manner their balance of payments position and to foster growth" (Section I, para. 1, of the Instrument establishing the Trust; *Annual Report 1988*, p. 120).

Once the picture clarified on how much money would be available from donor countries, the Executive Board agreed in April 1988 on three other key provisions. First, the access limit was set at a cumulative 250 percent of quota over three years, with a provision that access could reach 350 percent in exceptional circumstances. Under prodding from several Directors from donor countries, the staff and the Managing Director agreed that "exceptional" would be strictly interpreted to mean "highly exceptional."[78] For most countries, actual access was expected to be well below even the lower ceiling, and loans were expected to average about 150 percent of quota (roughly 2½ times the SAF limit that was then in place). Second, the financial terms of ESAF loans were to be identical to those from the SAF: interest would be charged at 0.5 percent, loans would mature in ten years, and repayment was to begin after 5½ years. Third, the ESAF, like its predecessors, would be a temporary facility; November 1989—less than two years away—was set as the cutoff date for approval of loans.[79]

---

[77]For Abdallah's remarks, see the minutes of IS/87/7 (November 20, 1987), p. 11. For the agreement on conditionality, see the Chairman's summing up, at EBM/87/171 (December 15, 1987), pp. 7–10.

[78]Minutes of EBM/88/61 (April 20, 1988).

[79]In March 1989, the cutoff date was moved back to November 1990. Subsequent decisions extended its life until a successor trust was established in 1994.

Financing, 1987–88

The goal set by Camdessus was to raise SDR 6 billion ($8 billion) and to have enough of it in hand to allow the Fund to start lending early in 1988. Remarkably, although at least some of the senior staff involved regarded that target as the maximum that they could hope to attain and assumed that the final amount would be negotiated downward, the Managing Director's figure quickly became accepted by most creditor countries. Discussions focused on how to allocate the responsibility for contributing to it.

Raising the money required a great deal of political invention and a strong defense of the Fund's own interests. The primary difficulty was that the largest industrial country, the United States, initially was unwilling to contribute to the Trust and eventually made only a modest contribution (a grant of $140 million, or approximately SDR 107 million, pledged in November 1989 for disbursement over 12 years—the tenth largest among the 27 contributing countries and about 4 percent of total grant commitments of SDR 2.5 billion).[80] The U.S. position was not articulated on a lack of concern for low-income countries but rather on a decision to concentrate first on securing appropriations for the eighth replenishment of IDA. Even so, potential borrowers were distressed that the United States would be deaf to their appeals for help, and other creditors were dismayed at the prospect of asking their legislatures and parliaments for appropriations to a multilateral facility that would not be supported proportionally by others.

From the Fund's vantage, a serious complication was that with the United States on the sidelines, the staff was effectively precluded from using any sort of "burden-sharing" formula for determining appropriate amounts to request from each creditor. (For a time, the U.S. authorities argued for a formula based on the size of a country's current account surplus, but Japan and other surplus countries naturally rejected that idea out of hand.) The entire amount therefore would have to be raised through voluntary ad hoc contributions or through another means.

To avoid these complications, officials from several countries suggested financing the ESAF through the sale of part of the Fund's gold stock: the same technique used to finance the original Trust Fund in the late 1970s. In 1987, the staff estimated that selling roughly 20 percent of the Fund's remaining gold stock at the then-prevailing market price could generate the resources to fund the new facility.[81] That idea, though, was strongly opposed both by the U.S. authorities—

---

[80]A U.S. contribution of $150 million was proposed in the budget submitted by the outgoing administration of President Ronald Reagan. In November, the U.S. Congress approved an appropriation of $139,398,000, heavily backloaded; the first installment, paid in June 1990, was in the amount of $3 million. The United States made additional contributions to the ESAF in the 1990s.

[81]"Further Considerations on the Mobilization of Resources in Association with the Structural Adjustment Facility (SAF)," EBS/87/190 (September 2, 1987), p. 6. The IMF held 103 million ounces of gold, valued on its books at SDR 35 ($45) per ounce. The market price of gold at the time was about $440; if that price held up, each ounce would generate profits close to $400, and the sale of 20 million ounces would yield profits of just under $8 billion.

without whom it could not succeed[82]—and by the Managing Director—who viewed gold as the Fund's "crown jewels." In mid-July, to nip the idea before it could take firm roots, Camdessus rejected it unequivocally during an informal meeting with Executive Directors:

> The Fund's gold holdings are one of the institution's main sources of strength. . . . We must not reduce the Fund's capital base to solve a particular problem of the moment when in all likelihood the Fund will continue to face serious challenges in the years to come. Selling the Fund's gold holdings might well weaken the institution's ability to help its members, including—perhaps especially—the poorest countries.[83]

Although several Executive Directors argued that the Fund should consider selling enough gold to finance at least a substantial portion of ESAF lending—notably those from Germany, Japan, the United Kingdom, Belgium, and Brazil—the majority either were opposed altogether or were prepared only to consider quite small sales, possibly to cover the Trust's credit risks.[84]

Two other ideas were floated during the early stages of discussion. One would have had countries lend for this purpose to the Fund's General Resources Account. That scheme appealed particularly to the Japanese authorities as a means of coping with restrictions under Japanese law on lending to a separate Trust, and to several other potential contributors as a means of shifting the credit risk on ESAF loans from creditors to the Fund. It was, however, judged to be an ineffective alternative, because the Fund could not restrict its general lending to a subset of the membership. The second alternative (favored notably by the Belgian authorities) would have required an allocation of SDRs, after which donor countries would have lent their allocations back to the Fund for onlending to low-income countries.[85] That scheme faced drawbacks similar to those of the one just described, plus the difficulty of securing the 85 percent majority required for an SDR allocation. Both ideas therefore were abandoned in the fall of 1987.

Attention then turned toward finding ways to make investments in a Trust more liquid and especially more secure for creditors. In that regard, the key innovation was to establish a Reserve Account within the Trust to cover possible losses. Once the ESAF Trust was established, all income from SAF and Trust Fund loans

---

[82]Any decision to sell part of the Fund's holdings of gold would have required approval by 85 percent of the total voting power. U.S. support (essential for obtaining an 85 percent majority) for a proposal to sell gold for the benefit of a subset of the Fund's membership would have required the explicit approval of the U.S. Congress, which was considered extremely unlikely.

[83]Minutes of IS/87/4 (July 15, 1987), p. 4. This formulation left the door open in principle for the Fund to sell gold, retain ownership of the proceeds to preserve the value of the Fund's capital base, reinvest the money in interest-bearing assets, and use the income to support concessional lending. That proposal surfaced nearly a decade later, during the discussions on how to convert the ESAF into a permanent facility.

[84]Minutes of EBM/87/138 (September 15, 1987).

[85]On the first proposal, see "Further Considerations on the Mobilization of Resources in Association with the Structural Adjustment Facility (SAF)," EBS/87/190 (September 2, 1987), pp. 3–5. On the second, see Annex II to the minutes of EBM/87/138 (September 15, 1987), pp. 47–48.

and from SAF-related investments, all other funds in the SDA that were not otherwise committed, and all repayments of principal on SAF and Trust Fund loans were to be transferred into this new Reserve Account. Over a period of 15 years, the staff projected that the reserve would eventually amount to SDR 4.8 billion and would easily cover any reasonable estimate of possible losses on bad loans.[86] In addition, to cover any residual risk to creditors, the Fund undertook "to consider fully and in good faith all such initiatives as might be necessary to assure full and expeditious payment to lenders" (Decision No. 8759-(87/176) ESAF, adopted December 18, 1987; *Annual Report 1988*, p. 119). This provision was intended specifically to keep open the possibility of selling gold if the reserve and other possible measures were inadequate.[87] Neither staff nor management was particularly concerned about the extremely remote possibility of this clause ever being invoked. In their view, the first line of defense—the quality of the adjustment programs underpinning the loans—and the second line—the Reserve Account—were far more than adequate protection.

When the Trust was created in December 1987, after remarkably quick negotiations, staff and management were still working practically around the clock to raise enough money. To allow each creditor to find a means of contributing that was politically and technically feasible within the country's own constraints, the Fund was seeking contributions for two separate accounts within the ESAF Trust: a Loan Account for receiving loans (at concessional or near-market terms) for on-lending to eligible members; and a Subsidy Account for receiving grants and concessional loans for payment of interest subsidies to borrowers, to reduce the interest cost to 0.5 percent a year.[88] (Those two accounts, plus the Reserve Account, constituted the Trust.)

By far the largest contributor was Japan. Several months of discussion culminated in a December 1987 visit to Tokyo by the Managing Director (in conjunction with the annual Article IV consultation—see Chapter 3). Following that meeting, the government of Japan agreed to lend (through its Export-Import Bank) to the Fund (as Trustee) up to SDR 2.2 billion (just over $3 billion) and to provide an additional SDR 329 million ($465 million) in grants.[89] Not only did this contribution make the ESAF viable, it also marked the beginning of a heightened role for Japan in the IMF and in the provision of financial assistance to developing countries.

---

[86]"Enhanced Structural Adjustment Facility (SAF)—Proposed Financial Arrangements," EBS/87/228 (October 29, 1987), p. 5.

[87]Minutes of EBM/87/168 (December 11, 1987), p. 59.

[88]To make the wide variety of contributions commensurate, the staff computed a "grant-equivalent" value on below-market loans. For example, if a country agreed to make a loan to the Trust at 0.5 percent interest for a fixed period, the present value of the difference between the actual interest cost to the Trust and an estimate of what the Trust would have paid at market rates (assumed to be 6 percent) was treated as a grant.

[89]Japan also agreed to augment its loan by up to SDR 300 million if needed by the Fund to make full use of subsidy grants from other contributors. "Enhanced Structural Adjustment Facility (ESAF)—Proposed Borrowing Agreement with the Export-Import Bank of Japan," EBS/88/69 (March 28, 1988), and minutes of EBM/88/56 (April 4, 1988).

Table 14.2. ESAF Trust: Contribution Commitments
as of April 30, 1990

| Contributor | In SDR millions[a] | | U.S. dollar equivalent | |
	Subsidies[b]	Loans	Subsidies	Loans
Austria	42		55	
Belgium	84		109	
Canada	163	300	212	390
Denmark	45		59	
Finland	38		49	
France	380	800	495	1,041
Germany	130	700	169	911
Greece	25		33	
Iceland	2		3	
Italy	201	370	262	481
Japan	329	2,200	428	2,863
Korea	47	65	61	85
Luxembourg	5		7	
Malaysia	35		46	
Malta	1		1	
Netherlands	68		88	
Norway	27	90	35	117
Saudi Arabia	109	200	142	260
Singapore	24		31	
Spain	22	260	29	338
Sweden	121		157	
Switzerland	119	200	155	260
Turkey		35		46
United Kingdom	411		535	
United States	107		139	
Other (undisclosed or not final)	38	95	49	124
Total[c]	2,570	5,315	3,344	6,917
Adjustment[d]	−32		−42	
Net Contributions	2,538	5,315	3,303	6,917

Source: *Annual Report 1990*, p. 79.

[a]Some contributions were in local currency or U.S. dollars.

[b]Figures in italics are staff estimates of the grant-equivalent value of the contribution.

[c]Columns may not add to total, owing to rounding.

[d]Adjustment to reflect the high cost of one loan.

By the end of May 1988, when the Fund was ready to begin considering loan applications, the ESAF Trust had received at least tentative commitments from 24 countries, for a total of SDR 5.3 billion in loans plus grants or grant-equivalents of SDR 2 billion. Another half-billion in grant commitments came in during the next couple of years, by which time the Trust was essentially complete (Table 14.2).[90] Commitments came from all of the G-10 countries, several smaller industrial countries, two major middle-eastern oil exporters, and even some middle-income developing countries, several of which had recent and painful experience

---

[90]Data in Table 14.2 that are not shown in *Annual Report 1990* are from "Structural Adjustment Facility (SAF) and Enhanced Structural Adjustment Facility (ESAF)—Review of Operations," EBS/90/106 (June 12, 1990), p. 56.

Table 14.3. ESAF and SDA: Combined Balance Sheet for April 30, 1990
(In thousands)

	SDRs	Equivalent in U.S. Dollars
Assets	3,576,862	4,658,863
Investments	1,553,148	2,022,975
Loans	1,964,605	2,558,898
Receivables	59,109	76,989
Liabilities and Resources	3,576,862	4,658,863
Resources	2,920,623	3,804,112
Contributions to ESAF	203,890	265,567
Transfers from Trust Fund	2,363,040	3,077,860
Transfers from SFF Subsidy Account	63,945	83,288
Retained income	289,748	377,397
Borrowing	647,352	843,176
Accrued interest payable	8,630	11,241
Deferred Income	229	298
Other liabilities	28	36
Memorandum items:		
Additional commitments:		
Contributions (grant equivalent)	2,332,110	3,037,573
Borrowing	4,667,648	6,079,612
Potential assets	10,576,620	13,776,048

Source: *Annual Report, 1990*. Dollar amounts have been calculated at SDR 1 = $1.3025, the rate prevailing on April 30, 1990.

with their own external debt problems. After Japan, the second- and third-largest contributors were France and Germany, respectively.

Although many of these contributions were slated to be paid in over several years, the Fund was able to begin operations in 1988, using a combination of resources: contributions (18 percent of the total for the first two years), borrowings (57 percent), and transfers from the SDA (20 percent).[91] ESAF loans outstanding at the end of 1989 totaled SDR 416 million, and a further SDR 708 million was in hand and invested. As shown in Table 14.3, the combined resources of the ESAF Trust and the SDA at that time were still largely derived from the original Trust Fund and totaled some SDR 3.6 billion ($4.7 billion). Taking future ESAF commitments into account, however, total potential resources amounted to SDR 10.6 billion ($13.8 billion) by that time.[92] Preparations thus were largely complete for a continued flow of concessional lending and subsidies through the first half of the 1990s.

---

[91]The remaining 5 percent came mostly from income on investments. These percentages refer to the end of April 1990.

[92]Not all of these resources could be lent or disbursed as subsidies. As of April 1990, SDR 273 million was being held in the ESAF Reserve Account to guarantee repayments to lenders.

Figure 14.4. SAF and ESAF Loan Commitments, 1986–90

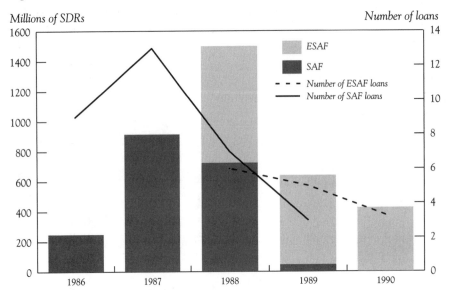

Operations, 1988–89

ESAF lending activity began with a loan to Malawi on July 15, 1988. Although only a handful of loans was to be approved each year, the new Trust quickly overtook the SAF as the Fund's main window for concessional loans (Figure 14.4).[93]

By this time, the Fund was ready to abandon the practice of providing parallel financing for low-income countries through both the Fund's general resources (at market interest rates) and its concessional lending facilities. While the original Trust Fund was operating in 1976–81, 71 percent of the countries that borrowed from it (39 out of 55) were also drawing on the Fund's general resources. During the first two years of SAF operations, before the establishment of the ESAF, two-thirds of the borrowing countries (18 of 27) also had stand-by or extended arrangements. In the second half of 1988, two of the four countries that borrowed from the SAF (Mali and Pakistan), but none of the ESAF borrowers, had active stand-by arrangements.[94] For loans approved after 1988, none did.

Most commonly, ESAF borrowers in those early years had recently completed adjustment programs under which they had drawn on the Fund's regular facilities. Of the 11 countries that borrowed from the ESAF through the end of 1989, all but one had either completed a stand-by arrangement in the year or so preceding the initial loan, or had abandoned the existing arrangement when the softer loan became

---

[93]For a detailed review of ESAF lending through 1992, see Schadler and others (1993).

[94]Malawi had entered into a relatively small stand-by arrangement (SDR 13 million, or 35 percent of quota) just a few months earlier and had drawn most of the approved amount (25 percent of quota) at once. Although the arrangement remained in effect until May 1989, Malawi did not draw on it again.

available.[95] A major effect of the new facility therefore was to enable low-income countries to replace expensive with highly concessional and more stable financing.[96]

Although the total amount of ESAF loans in 1988–89 was not large relative to the two earlier facilities (refer back to Figure 14.1), it was much more concentrated on a few countries, and loans were much larger relative to borrowers' quotas (Table 14.4). Compared with about 80 percent of quota or less for the 55 Trust Fund borrowers and 70 percent or less for the 32 SAF borrowers, these first 11 ESAF borrowers obtained commitments averaging just over 160 percent of quota. Reflecting the decision to vary countries' access depending on the extent of need and the strength of the adjustment program, loans ranged in size from a low of 116 percent of quota (to Madagascar) to a high of 180 percent (to Ghana and Uganda).

Ghana

One of the earliest ESAF loans was also the largest. At SDR 368.1 million ($500 million) and 180 percent of quota, the loan to Ghana in November 1988 was the largest commitment in the first two years of ESAF operations, in both absolute and percentage terms.

The Fund had been closely involved in assisting the Ghanaian authorities since 1982, when the military government of Flight Lieutenant Jerry John Rawlings appointed Dr. Kwesi Botchwey—who would become one of Africa's most highly respected monetary officials—as finance minister and began devising a long-overdue program of macroeconomic stabilization and structural reform.[97] In 1983–86,

---

[95]The sole exception was Uganda, which had last drawn on Fund resources in 1984.

[96]The interest rate charged on stand-by and extended arrangements in 1988 averaged close to 6 percent, compared with 0.5 percent on ESAF loans. For both EFF arrangements and ESAF loans, borrowers received principal over three years and repaid it over a period ending in 10 years, although ESAF borrowers received moneys slightly sooner and began repayments a year later. Overall, the expected discounted present value of interest and principal repayments was cut nearly in half by switching from the EFF to the ESAF. Since in most cases borrowers were switching out of ordinary stand-by arrangements rather than the EFF, they also benefited from longer maturities and grace periods and from a reduced need to negotiate policy conditions with the Fund.

[97]Ghana joined the Fund in September 1957, just six months after becoming the first independent state in sub-Saharan Africa (excluding South Africa). In February 1966, a military coup overthrew the government of Kwame Nkrumah and set out to implement economic reforms with the support of the Fund. In 1966–69, the Fund approved four consecutive one-year stand-by arrangements, most of which were fully utilized. The Fund also assisted Ghana in the late 1960s by helping arrange reschedulings of heavy external debts incurred by the Nkrumah government and by organizing meetings of official donors. From 1970 through mid-1983, Ghana made relatively little use of Fund resources and repaid virtually all of its obligations. By that time, however, the economy was suffering from multiple ills, including a bloated and inefficient bureaucracy, a depressed world market for the principal export (cocoa), a prolonged drought, and the repatriation of more than a million Ghanaians who were being forced out of Nigeria. The combined effect was severe enough that the World Bank reclassified Ghana from a middle-income to a low-income country. Overall, real per capita income fell by 30 percent from 1970 to 1982. For more background on Ghana's early relations with the Fund, see de Vries, 1976, Vol. 1, pp. 471–72 and 597–600, and James (1996), pp. 539–41. For an analysis of the post-1982 reforms and their effects, see Kapur and others (1991). Nowak and others (1996) gives a longer-run overview and references to the more detailed literature on the Ghanaian economy.

Table 14.4. Concessional Loans to Low-Income Countries, 1977–89

Country[a]	Facility	Date Approved[b]	Amount Approved		Amount Disbursed	
			Millions of SDRs[c]	Percent of quota[d]	Millions of SDRs[c,e]	Percent of quota[d]
Bangladesh	Trust Fund	1976, 1978	122.2	80.4	122.2	80.4
	SAF	1987	201.3	70.0	201.3	70.0
Benin	Trust Fund	1976, 1978	12.7	79.4	12.7	79.4
	SAF	1989	21.9	70.0	21.9	70.0
Bolivia	Trust Fund	1976, 1978	36.2	80.4	36.2	80.4
	SAF	1986	57.6	63.5	18.1	20.0
	ESAF	1988	136.1	150.0	136.1	150.0
Burkina Faso (Upper Volta)	Trust Fund	1976, 1978	12.7	79.4	12.7	79.4
Burundi	Trust Fund	1976, 1978	18.6	80.7	18.6	80.7
	SAF	1986	29.9	70.0	29.9	70.0
Cameroon	Trust Fund	1976, 1978	34.2	76.0	34.2	76.0
Central African Republic	Trust Fund	1976, 1978	12.7	79.4	12.7	79.4
	SAF	1987	21.3	70.0	15.2	50.0
Chad	Trust Fund	1976	5.4	33.7	5.4	33.7
	SAF	1987	21.4	70.0	21.4	70.0
China	Trust Fund	1978	309.5	56.3	309.5	56.3
Congo	Trust Fund	1976, 1978	12.7	74.7	12.7	74.7
Dominica	SAF	1986	2.8	70.0	2.8	70.0
Egypt	Trust Fund	1976, 1978	183.7	80.6	183.7	80.6
El Salvador	Trust Fund	1978	19.7	45.8	19.7	45.8
Equatorial Guinea	Trust Fund	1978	4.5	45.0	4.5	45.0
	SAF	1988	12.9	70.0	3.7	20.0
Ethiopia	Trust Fund	1976, 1978	26.4	73.3	26.4	73.3
Gambia, The	Trust Fund	1976, 1978	6.8	76.0	6.8	76.0
	SAF	1986	10.9	63.5	8.6	50.0
	ESAF	1988	20.5	120.0	20.5	120.0
Ghana	Trust Fund	1978	49.0	46.2	49.0	46.2
	SAF	1987	129.9	63.5	40.9	20.0
	ESAF	1988	368.1	180.0	368.1	180.0
Grenada	Trust Fund	1976, 1978	2.0	65.2	2.0	65.2
Guinea	Trust Fund	1976, 1978	23.5	78.2	23.5	78.2
	SAF	1987	40.5	70.0	29.0	50.0
Guinea Bissau	SAF	1987	5.3	70.0	3.8	50.0
Guyana	Trust Fund	1978	11.3	45.0	11.3	45.0
Haiti	Trust Fund	1976, 1978	18.6	80.7	18.6	80.7
	SAF	1986	30.9	70.0	8.8	20.0
Honduras	Trust Fund	1978	14.1	41.4	14.1	41.4
India	Trust Fund	1978	529.0	46.2	529.0	46.2
Ivory Coast	Trust Fund	1976, 1978	50.8	66.9	50.8	66.9
Kenya	Trust Fund	1976, 1978	46.9	68.0	46.9	68.0
	SAF	1988	99.4	70.0	28.4	20.0
	ESAF	1989	241.4	170.0	216.2	152.2

Table 14.4 (continued)

Country[a]	Facility	Date Approved[b]	Amount Approved Millions of SDRs[c]	Amount Approved Percent of quota[d]	Amount Disbursed Millions of SDRs[c,e]	Amount Disbursed Percent of quota[d]
Lao P.D.R.	Trust Fund	1976, 1978	12.7	79.4	12.7	79.4
	SAF	1989	20.5	70.0	20.5	70.0
Lesotho	Trust Fund	1976, 1978	4.9	69.8	4.9	69.8
	SAF	1988	10.6	70.0	10.6	70.0
Liberia	Trust Fund	1976, 1978	28.3	76.6	28.3	76.6
Madagascar	Trust Fund	1976, 1978	25.4	74.7	25.4	74.7
	SAF	1987	46.5	70.0	13.3	20.0
	ESAF	1989	76.9	115.8	51.3	77.2
Malawi	Trust Fund	1976, 1978	14.7	77.2	14.7	77.2
	ESAF	1988	55.8	150.0	55.8	150.0
Mali	Trust Fund	1976, 1978	21.5	79.6	21.5	79.6
	SAF	1988	35.6	70.0	25.4	50.0
Mauritania	Trust Fund	1976, 1978	12.7	74.7	12.7	74.7
	SAF	1986	23.7	70.0	17.0	50.0
	ESAF	1989	50.9	150.0	17.0	50.0
Mauritius	Trust Fund	1976	9.1	33.8	9.1	33.8
Morocco	Trust Fund	1976, 1978	110.4	73.6	110.4	73.6
Mozambique	SAF	1987	42.7	70.0	42.7	70.0
Myanmar (Burma)	Trust Fund	1976, 1978	58.6	80.3	58.6	80.3
Nepal	Trust Fund	1976, 1978	13.7	72.0	13.7	72.0
	SAF	1987	26.1	70.0	26.1	70.0
Niger	Trust Fund	1976, 1978	12.7	79.4	12.7	79.4
	SAF	1986	21.4	63.5	16.9	50.0
	ESAF	1988	50.6	150.0	23.6	70.0
Pakistan	Trust Fund	1976, 1978	229.7	80.6	229.7	80.6
	SAF	1988	382.4	70.0	273.2	50.0
Papua New Guinea	Trust Fund	1976, 1978	19.5	65.2	19.5	65.2
Philippines	Trust Fund	1976, 1978	151.5	72.1	151.5	72.1
Rwanda	Trust Fund	1978	10.7	46.5	10.7	46.5
São Tomé & Príncipe	SAF	1989	2.8	70.0	2.8	70.0
Senegal	Trust Fund	1976, 1978	33.2	79.1	33.2	79.1
	SAF	1986	54.0	63.5	42.6	50.0
	ESAF	1988	144.7	170.0	144.7	170.0
Sierra Leone	Trust Fund	1976, 1978	24.4	78.8	24.4	78.8
	SAF	1986	40.5	70.0	11.6	20.0
Somalia	Trust Fund	1978	10.7	46.5	10.7	46.5
	SAF	1987	30.9	70.0	8.8	20.0
Sri Lanka	Trust Fund	1976, 1978	95.8	80.5	95.8	80.5
	SAF	1988	156.2	70.0	156.2	70.0
Sudan	Trust Fund	1976, 1978	70.4	80.0	70.4	80.0
Swaziland	Trust Fund	1978	4.5	37.5	4.5	37.5
Tanzania	Trust Fund	1976, 1978	41.0	74.6	41.0	74.6
	SAF	1987	74.9	70.0	74.9	70.0

Table 14.4 *(concluded)*

Country[a]	Facility	Date Approved[b]	Amount Approved Millions of SDRs[c]	Amount Approved Percent of quota[d]	Amount Disbursed Millions of SDRs[c,e]	Amount Disbursed Percent of quota[d]
Thailand	Trust Fund	1976, 1978	131.0	72.3	131.0	72.3
Togo	Trust Fund	1976, 1978	14.7	77.2	14.7	77.2
	SAF	1988	26.9	70.0	7.7	20.0
	ESAF	1989	46.1	120.0	38.4	100.0
Uganda	Trust Fund	1978	22.5	45.0	22.5	45.0
	SAF	1987	69.7	70.0	49.8	50.0
	ESAF	1989	179.3	180.0	179.3	180.0
Vietnam	Trust Fund	1976, 1978	60.6	67.3	60.6	67.3
Western Samoa	Trust Fund	1976, 1978	2.0	65.2	2.0	65.2
Yemen, P.D.R.	Trust Fund	1976, 1978	28.3	69.1	28.3	69.1
Zaïre	Trust Fund	1976, 1978	110.4	72.7	110.4	72.7
	SAF	1987	203.7	70.0	145.5	50.0
Zambia	Trust Fund	1978	42.8	30.3	42.8	30.3
Totals:						
55 countries	Trust Fund	1976–78	2,991	63%	2,991	63%
32 countries	SAF	1987–89	1,955	69%	1,379	49%
11 countries	ESAF	1988–89	1,370	161%	1,251	147%

[a]Country names in parentheses were in effect at the time of the Trust Fund loan.

[b]For the Trust Fund, 1976 and 1978 indicate approval of loans for the First and Second Period, respectively.

[c]In some cases, ESAF loans were augmented after 1989.

[d]For the Trust Fund, the denominator is the quota at April 1980; for SAF and ESAF, April 1988.

[e]For SAF and ESAF, this is the total amount disbursed through the end of the arrangement, of the amounts approved through 1989.

Ghana obtained three stand-by arrangements and drew twice on the Compensatory Financing Facility (CFF). By October 1986, Ghana's indebtedness to the Fund (including to the Trust Fund) reached an all-time peak of some SDR 645 million ($780 million or 315 percent of quota; see Figure 14.5). The Fund also provided substantial technical assistance on various structural reforms, reestablished a resident office in Accra in 1985, and worked with United Nations Children's Fund (UNICEF) officials on issues related to the protection of impoverished groups from the brunt of the adjustment program.

The authorities' efforts brought substantial rewards. From 1983 to 1986, real output grew by more than 13 percent, the volume of exports grew by 35 percent, the annual inflation rate fell from well over 100 percent to 25 percent, and the fiscal deficit was virtually eliminated. Nonetheless, the Ghanaian economy was skirting the edge of a dangerous precipice, largely because nearly half of all export revenues were required to service debts to foreign creditors.

Essential though the Fund's support was in the mid-1980s, it added to Ghana's debt burden at a time when the government was struggling hard to keep its grip on the economic foothold that it had just attained. Not only was the debt to the Fund carrying a market rate of interest (then approximately 6 percent); it also had short

Figure 14.5. Ghana: Concessional Loans and Other Credit Outstanding, 1976–91

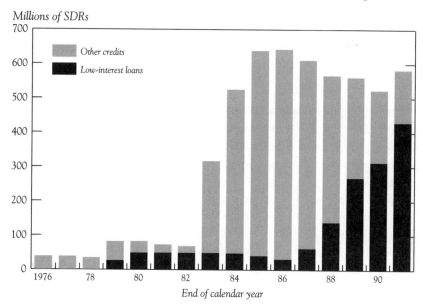

Millions of SDRs

End of calendar year

maturities and would have to be repaid almost entirely over the next few years. When Botchwey first requested an extended arrangement rather than another one-year stand-by arrangement in 1985, he stressed that all he wanted was to stretch out the maturity of Ghana's outstanding obligations to the Fund.[98]

The resumption of concessional lending by the Fund opened a new opportunity, but the small size of the SAF was initially a severe limitation. In the summer of 1987, while Ghana's eighth and final short-term stand-by arrangement was running its course, the authorities requested that the Fund provide a blend of longer-term support through the EFF (on nonconcessional terms) and the SAF (on concessional terms). The request raised difficult issues for the Fund. For one, the EFF was essentially moribund: no extended arrangement had been approved for the past two years, and many in the Fund believed that it no longer served a useful purpose (see Chapter 15). For another, management was wary of entering into a new large-scale and longer-term commitment—even through the SAF—in a region with little record of successful adjustment.

To assess prospects in Ghana, the first negotiating mission (in June 1987) included not only the regular mission chief, Evangelos A. Calamitsis (Senior Advisor in the African Department), but also the Department Director, Alassane D. Ouattara, and the Deputy Managing Director, Richard D. Erb. After meeting with Rawlings and other top officials, the team gave an upbeat assessment. In August, Botchwey went to Washington to meet with Camdessus and resolve the few remaining policy is-

---

[98]Letter from Botchwey to the Deputy Managing Director, Richard D. Erb (November 14, 1985); in IMF/CF (C/Ghana/1791 "Extended Fund Facility").

sues.[99] A month later, the authorities submitted a PFP (largely drafted by Fund and World Bank staff) that set out their policy intentions for the period through June 1990. The program was approved by the Bank in mid-October, and on November 6 the Fund approved a package of EFF credits and SAF loans totaling SDR 375 million ($505 million; 184 percent of quota). Although the 10-year maturity on these obligations would help reduce Ghana's near-term burden of debt servicing, two-thirds of the commitment (the EFF portion) was still relatively expensive money.[100]

Ghana carried out the agreed policy reforms, and economic performance remained good in 1988. Consequently, the staff soon began negotiations for an ESAF loan. Discussions on economic policies proceeded smoothly, and a new PFP—much of which was drafted in Accra by the authorities—was quickly finished.[101] Some wrangling still took place, however, over the size of the loan and whether it would replace or supplement the more expensive EFF arrangement that was already in place. Finally, at a meeting in Washington in late August, Botchwey persuaded Camdessus that Ghana had established a strong enough track record on both adjustment and reform to warrant unusually large access to ESAF funds. In November, the Board approved Ghana's request, and both of the 1987 loans—the extended arrangement and the SAF loan—were scrapped in favor of the slightly larger and much less expensive ESAF deal.[102]

The ESAF loan brought four main benefits to Ghana. First, it committed the Fund to maintain its loan exposure for several years and freed the authorities from having either to repay large sums or to negotiate a series of short-term arrangements. Second, it sharply reduced the interest cost of the country's external debt. Third, it enabled the government to carry on the process of structural economic reform that it had begun five years earlier. Fourth, it helped convince donor countries and multilateral agencies to increase their own support.

That fourth benefit, the catalytic effect on donors, though perhaps less direct and obvious than the others, was no less important. From 1978 through 1985, official development assistance to Ghana averaged about $160 million a year (around 5 percent of GDP). Aid then began to rise sharply, and for the five years

---

[99]See memorandums from Calamitsis (July 14, 1987) and Ouattara (August 25) to the Managing Director; in IMF/RD Deputy Managing Director file "Ghana, 1987" (Accession 93/151, Box 3, Section 397).

[100]The EFF arrangement provided for SDR 245 million (120 percent of quota) in credits over three years, drawable quarterly. The SAF loan was scheduled to provide SDR 130 million (63.5 percent) in three annual installments, of which SDR 41 million was available immediately. The scheduled credits were similar in magnitude to Ghana's scheduled repayments to the Fund on the 1983–86 stand-by arrangements, so the Fund's exposure now was projected to show little net change through 1990 (see Figure 14.5) instead of falling sharply.

[101]On the role of the authorities in drafting the 1987 and 1988 PFPs, see memorandums to management from Goodall E. Gondwe (Deputy Director of the African Department) and Boorman (April 27, 1988) and from Reinold H. van Til (Senior Economist in the African Department; May 20, 1988); in IMF/RD Deputy Managing Director file "Ghana, 1988" (Accession 94/026, Box 2, Section 518).

[102]At the time, a total of SDR 237 million remained undrawn on the 1987 loans and available for the remaining two years. The ESAF loan would provide SDR 272 million during those two years, plus SDR 96 million in the third year.

after the ESAF loan was approved (1989–93) averaged over $600 million a year (more than 10 percent of GDP).

One impetus for the increase in aid to Ghana was the government's development in 1988 of a package of measures known as PAMSCAD (Program to Mitigate the Social Costs of Adjustment; see Kapur and others, 1991). The objective of this program was to enhance the delivery of basic services to the poor, raise the productivity of lower-income workers, and enhance their employment opportunities. In support of PAMSCAD and the government's more general efforts to improve social policies, the Fund's assistance via the ESAF was designed not only to ensure the viability of macroeconomic policies, but also to support the establishment of a "Special Efficiency Fund" for the retraining, relocation, and redeployment of public employees displaced by the restructuring of the economy. PAMSCAD itself was financed externally, largely through support pledged from bilateral donors at an international conference convened by Ghana in Geneva in February 1988. The bulk of the aid increase, however, was a generalized and broadly based vote of confidence in the management of the Ghanaian economy, at a time when the aggregate level of aid to developing countries was stagnant in real terms.

Uganda

Uganda's drive for economic recovery and development began after the overthrow of the dictatorship of Idi Amin Dada by Tanzania in 1979. Political turmoil lasted for another two years, until former Prime Minister Milton Obote was elected president in December 1980. The new government quickly obtained a one-year stand-by arrangement from the Fund, for what was then the exceptionally large amount of SDR 112.5 million ($150 million; 225 percent of quota), to support an adjustment program that included a massive up-front devaluation of the exchange rate (from a badly overvalued 8.4 shillings a dollar to 96).[103] Over the next few years, supported by three consecutive 12-month stand-by arrangements from the Fund, IDA credits from the World Bank, and other external assistance, the government gradually strengthened the economy.

That initial adjustment phase took place against the backdrop of continuing brutal abuses of human rights, which provoked a renewal of civil war and threw the government's fragile economic strategy off course. The third and last stand-by arrangement was therefore abandoned in the spring of 1984, at which point Uganda's outstanding obligations to the Fund (including Trust Fund loans) amounted to SDR 374 million ($390 million, or 375 percent of quota; see Figure 14.6).[104] After that, a general deterioration set in until Yoweri Museveni became president in January 1986, following the military overthrow of Obote.

---

[103]The Fund lent about SDR 50 million (125 percent of quota) to Uganda during the first five years of Idi Amin's eight-year reign, starting in 1971. It then provided a small amount of assistance in 1980, in the form of a stand-by arrangement for SDR 12.5 million (25 percent of quota) and Trust Fund loans totaling SDR 22.4 million.

[104]The second arrangement, approved in August 1982, was also for SDR 112.5 million. Both loans were fully drawn. Under the third arrangement, approved in September 1983 for SDR 95 million, Uganda drew 65 million.

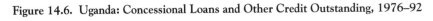

Figure 14.6. Uganda: Concessional Loans and Other Credit Outstanding, 1976–92

Millions of SDRs

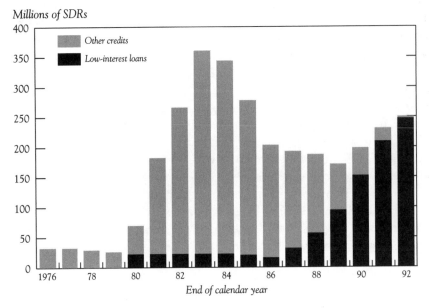

End of calendar year

Museveni inherited a fiscal policy that was in almost total disarray, as the government was unable either to collect adequate tax revenues or to control its spending. Moreover, Uganda faced sizable foreign debt repayment obligations at the same time that it had to rebuild a totally destroyed economy. With advice from a team of outside economists based in Canada, the new government quickly developed a plan for economic stabilization and reform that would retain many elements of the existing system of centralized planning and control and would only gradually phase out other elements.[105] At that stage, the overall policy strategy in Uganda was still far from the advice being offered by the Fund, which stressed the need for a much more comprehensive and rapid liberalization of markets. These internal stresses and problems were aggravated by a severe drop in international prices for coffee, Uganda's principal export commodity.

Uganda's economic and political problems were so severe in 1986 that it seemed obvious that no government could hope to solve them in a short time. When the Executive Board held its annual Article IV discussion on Uganda in July, Directors stressed the need to address a wide range of fiscal and other policy imbalances.[106]

---

[105]See Uganda Economic Study Team (1987), a report prepared under the auspices of the International Development Research Centre (IDRC) in Ottawa and presented to the Ugandan government in July 1986. The IDRC report itself recommended numerous liberalizing measures within an overall strategy that retained substantial governmental direction and control over economic activity.

[106]Minutes of EBM/86/111 (July 9, 1986).

But during the Annual Meetings in Washington, at the end of September, the finance minister, Ponsiano Mulema, strove to begin to change the world's perception. To that end, he invited Alassane Ouattara (Director of the African Department) to come to Kampala, meet with Museveni, and judge for himself whether Uganda qualified for a new round of international support. Although it was not yet apparent, Museveni was beginning to rethink his initial economic strategy and would eventually become one of the leading advocates of the silent revolution in Africa.[107]

Two months later, Ouattara met with Museveni and other officials in Kampala[108] and agreed to consider the government's request for a SAF loan, which he emphasized would be conditional on a commitment to reverse the three years of backsliding in economic policies. The staff then rapidly prepared a draft PFP, and a mission—headed by Jacques R. Artus (Assistant Director in the African Department)—returned to Kampala in March 1987 and reached tentative agreement with the authorities on a comprehensive adjustment program that would include a substantial depreciation of the exchange rate as part of a comprehensive monetary reform and liberalization of prices.[109]

Negotiating the SAF loan was complicated by the authorities' failure to stay current in their repayments to the Fund on earlier credits. By 1986, the government was running extremely low on foreign exchange reserves and was frequently a few weeks late in its payments to the Fund. These delays got worse in 1987–89 and occasionally resulted in the issuance of formal complaints for brief periods.[110] In April 1987, the Fund urged donor countries to provide new quick-disbursing aid to Uganda, while the staff hastily put together a plan to supplement the SAF loan with the Fund's general resources through the CFF. The authorities then managed to scrape together enough foreign exchange to pay off their arrears in May, just a

---

[107]Museveni quickly embraced price liberalization, and later embraced privatization and other measures to boost the private sector, as cornerstones of reform. See Museveni (1997), pp. 180–82.

[108]The visit began ominously, as Museveni sacked both Mulema and the governor of the central bank on the day that Ouattara and his colleagues arrived. The new team—C.W.C.B. Kiyonga as finance minister and Suleiman I. Kiggundu as governor—had little time to learn before facing the task of convincing the Fund to support the government's program.

[109]Throughout the 1980s, the Uganda shilling was pegged to the U.S. dollar and was periodically devalued to compensate for Uganda's extremely high rate of domestic inflation. As noted earlier, that process began with a devaluation from 8.4 to 96 shillings per dollar in preparation for the June 1981 stand-by arrangement with the Fund. By March 1987, the official rate was 1,400 per dollar, and the rate in the unofficial market was fluctuating between 12,000 and 16,000. The currency reform, which took effect on May 15, 1987, introduced the new shilling at a conversion rate of 100:1 and set the exchange rate at 60 per dollar (equivalent to 6,000 old shillings). The reform also sought to absorb excess liquidity in the economy by imposing a 30 percent conversion tax and by more strictly controlling credit afterwards.

[110]Fund regulations required the Managing Director to issue a notice to the Executive Board whenever a member country fell two months behind in making scheduled payments of interest, charges, or principal on Fund credits (see Chapter 16). Notices on Uganda's arrears were in effect from April to May 1987, for part of August 1988, and from January to February 1989.

few weeks before the Board was scheduled to consider the SAF and CFF loan requests.[111]

In February 1988, Artus returned to Kampala for a review mission and concluded that the economic program was off track, for familiar reasons: weak export markets (especially for coffee, which accounted for more than 90 percent of Uganda's export earnings), a failure to adjust the exchange rate by enough to compensate for high domestic inflation, and weak control of the fiscal accounts. Nonetheless, to compensate for the effects of the continuing decline in world coffee prices, the Board approved a CFF drawing for an additional SDR 25 million, without which Uganda would almost certainly have developed substantial new arrears in its payments to the Fund.

The problem now was how to get policies and the economy back on track before the Board was scheduled to consider whether to release the second year's installment of the SAF loan. President Museveni was actively involved, not only in policy formation, but also in the effort to keep the Fund's support. In meetings with Camdessus and U.S. officials in Washington and with Erb and the Fund staff in Kampala, Museveni made the case that Uganda not only deserved the Fund's approval: they also were ready to move up to the higher level of conditionality and funding of the ESAF. From the Fund's vantage, however, the case looked shaky. A May 1988 mission—led by Joseph G. Keyes (Advisor in the African Department)—successfully concluded negotiations for the second year's economic program, but Uganda still had to meet the targets for the current program and once again had to find a way to clear its arrears to the Fund. Erb reinforced the mission by going to Kampala himself and personally persuading Museveni that Uganda first had to establish a better track record with the SAF loan before tackling the ESAF. In fact, even for the staff to negotiate terms for continuing the SAF while the country was in arrears was stretching the Fund's normal practices, but Camdessus and Erb were both convinced that supporting Museveni's efforts was essential and would pay off eventually.

By the time ESAF negotiations began, in February 1989 (led now by Michael Edo, Division Chief in the African Department), Uganda's financial position was increasingly precarious. The money it was getting from the SAF and CFF loans was not even sufficient to cover the payments that were still due on earlier credits from the Fund, and it was not yet doing much to catalyze support from other creditors. Even the Paris Club was having difficulty reaching an agreement to reschedule Uganda's obligations to official creditors, owing to a long-simmering dispute between Uganda and Israel over obligations incurred before and during

---

[111]When the Managing Director issued the complaint at the end of April, Uganda's arrears to the Fund amounted to SDR 15 million, and another SDR 56 million was scheduled to be repaid by the end of the year. Although the SAF loan would provide SDR 20 million immediately, the next installment would not become available for another 12 months. By adding in a proposal for a CFF loan for SDR 25 million (to cover shortfalls in revenues from coffee exports), the Fund enabled Uganda to obtain enough short-term money from other creditors to settle its arrears. See "Uganda—Overdue Financial Obligations to the Fund—Report and Complaint Under Rule K-1," EBS/87/92 (April 29, 1987), p. 13.

Idi Amin's rule. Museveni was nonetheless encouraged by a personal promise from Camdessus that if the government could put together a strong enough program to stabilize and liberalize the economy, he would propose maximum ESAF access for Uganda. Edo thus found a much improved atmosphere: the authorities agreed to devalue the shilling by enough to regain international competitiveness, to give up trying to peg the exchange rate to the U.S. dollar and instead manage the rate flexibly against a basket of currencies, and to introduce fiscal reforms aimed at sharply reducing the government's deficit. And even before the mission left town, the authorities managed to pay off their arrears, this time for good.[112]

As the time approached for the Executive Board to consider Uganda's request for an ESAF loan commitment totaling just under SDR 180 million ($235 million; 180 percent of quota, the same level of access approved for Ghana the year before but more than for any other country), the question was whether the government had enough credibility to convince the world community that it could implement much stronger policies than it had in the past. Without stronger policies, everyone understood that Uganda would stay mired in an inflationary maelstrom, would fail to rebuild foreign exchange reserves to minimum requirements, and would soon slip back into arrears to the Fund. To help persuade wavering Directors, Finance Minister Kiyonga agreed to accept the initial disbursement of the loan in SDRs rather than foreign exchange and to maintain "significant balances in Uganda's SDR account in the Fund's SDR Department in order to facilitate timely payment of forthcoming Fund obligations."[113] Effectively, Uganda agreed to build up its reserves in the form of SDR holdings at the Fund as a guarantee that it would have the means to meet its obligations. While this commitment would reduce the cash that the government could tap directly to pay for imports, it was expected to help mobilize additional support from other creditors. With that capstone in place, the Board agreed to the ESAF loan request without dissent, on April 17, 1989.[114]

The ESAF loan marked the beginning of a period of economic transformation in Uganda. Within six months, despite the disastrous effects of the final collapse in international marketing agreements for coffee and a consequent sharp drop in export prices, policies were mostly on track. Flexible exchange rate policies strengthened and maintained international competitiveness, fiscal and monetary prudence brought inflation down gradually, external official grants and other assistance rose sharply, structural reforms brought a sustained rise in government revenues and stabilized the fiscal deficit, and market-oriented pricing and development policies stimulated growth and broadened both production and exports. Over the next seven years (1989–95), real output growth would average more

---

[112]Although Uganda still occasionally had some short-term delays in making payments, they did not again face the need for a formal complaint.

[113]"Uganda—Request for Arrangements Under the Enhanced Structural Adjustment Facility," EBS/89/62 (April 4, 1989), p.18.

[114]Minutes of EBM/89/42 (April 17, 1989).

than 6 percent a year, while inflation would fall from triple to single digits.[115] Credit for this remarkable turnaround goes of course to the authorities. The financial role of the SAF and ESAF loans was primarily catalytic rather than direct, as was the role of the IMF and World Bank staff in helping the authorities reform the direction of economic policy. Nonetheless, the reforms could not have been carried out without the rise in foreign assistance, that assistance could not have been mobilized without the prior support of the Fund for a medium-term and structurally oriented reform program, and Uganda could not have afforded to borrow the necessary amounts from the Fund without a highly concessional facility. The ESAF therefore was the linchpin for the reform process in Uganda.

Evaluating the ESAF

Despite its modest beginnings, the ESAF was destined to become a success story of assistance to desperately poor countries in an era when such success was elusive. Eventually, nearly 40 low-income countries not only would receive financial assistance from the Trust but also would have the opportunity to establish a track record of economic progress that would bring in bilateral assistance and in some cases private capital flows and direct investment. The question remains, however, whether the ESAF succeeded at the expense of other forms of official assistance, or whether ESAF money was truly additional to funds that would otherwise have been available. In a technical sense, ESAF contributions were no doubt partially additional. Most donor countries took pains to ensure that existing aid budgets were not cut to offset contributions to the new facility, although contributions to the World Bank's IDA probably suffered as a consequence. Whether the long-run effect of the ESAF was to displace or supplement IDA and other forms of official assistance is more difficult, if not impossible, to judge.

Overall, evidence for additionality is scant but not nonexistent. In nominal U.S. dollar terms, official development assistance (ODA) of industrial countries—of which ESAF contributions were a part—rose steadily after the establishment of the ESAF Trust: from $36.7 billion in 1986 to $59.2 billion in 1994. The roughly $4½ billion in grants and low-interest loans to the ESAF Trust by these countries was a significant portion of that increase. Relative to donor countries' GDP, however, ODA declined during those years from 0.35 percent to 0.30.[116] The IMF's structural adjustment facilities were created at a time of se-

---

[115]For an overview of Uganda's adjustment experience, see Sharer and McDonald (1996). On the contributing role of the SAF and ESAF loans, see Schadler and others (1993). On the broader African context of this experience, see Jones and Kiguel (1994).

[116]Data (except for ESAF contributions) are from the *Annual Report* (various years) of the OECD's Development Assistance Committee (DAC) and are aggregates for all DAC member countries. Also see OECD (1990), esp. Table III.2, which reports a small but steady increase in nominal-dollar net ODA flows to low-income countries starting in 1985.

vere political pressure against external assistance (especially, but by no means only, in the United States, where ODA was stagnant even in nominal terms over those eight years), and it may well be that without a multilateral and high-conditionality outlet, official aid would have registered an even steeper relative decline.

A stronger case for additionality emerges from the details, from examples of co-financing and other forms of "catalyzed" assistance. To jump-start that effort, a group of official donors representing 16 industrial countries plus the African Development Bank and the European Economic Community met in Paris in December 1987 at the request of the World Bank. That meeting produced pledges of an estimated $3 billion in additional grants and other concessional financing to "debt-distressed low-income African countries," to support the structural adjustment facilities of the Bank and the Fund. Over the next four or five years, Schadler and others (1993, pp. 29–31) estimated that 13 of 21 countries with ESAF-supported programs also received increases—in several cases, quite large increases—in official grants.[117] On average for all ESAF countries, grants rose from less than 23 percent of imports in the year before the country embarked on its adjustment path to nearly 28 percent during the life of the ESAF-supported program.

In view of the aggregate weakness in ODA, much ESAF-linked assistance may ultimately have been diverted from other applications or other countries. Even so, by focusing assistance on countries committed to economic reform, the creation of the ESAF almost certainly improved the effectiveness of ODA and may have helped stave off a truly ruinous backlash. It is natural to expect that political pressures against foreign aid would lead not only to a reduction in the overall amount of official assistance but also to a redirection toward countries with the best track records or the greatest potential for recovery and growth. Whatever the ESAF did to enhance that sort of redistribution would also have moderated the overall weakness in bilateral aid.

This view of the ESAF as a means of combating budgetary pressures against foreign assistance is supported further by its coincidence with the emergence of extrabudgetary debt-relief plans for low-income countries. Rather than budgeting new aid to those countries, much of which might be used to repay old debts, donors could achieve a similar outcome by forgiving all or part of the existing debts. Such schemes typically were linked to the Fund's approval of SAF or ESAF loans for the recipients.

Three major proposals for debt relief to low-income countries were made by senior officials in 1987 and 1988. Although none was accepted in its original form,

---

[117]An earlier internal study of the experience of SAF recipients drew a similar conclusion: 20 of 26 countries experienced an increase in bilateral aid during the first year of their SAF-supported programs. "Policy Orientation and Balance of Payments Assistance of Bilateral and Multilateral Aid Agencies—Status and Current Issues," SM/89/252 (November 30, 1989), pp. 6–7.

they led eventually to a considerable improvement in the opportunities available to qualifying countries.[118]

This effort began at the Development and Interim Committee meetings in April 1987, when the Chancellor of the Exchequer in the United Kingdom, Nigel Lawson, tabled a proposal. The Lawson plan built on an idea originally advanced by UNCTAD in 1978, calling on donor countries to convert all old aid loans to grants and to make all new aid as grants. Lawson proposed to give donors additional flexibility, in that the practice of rescheduling some existing debts would continue but on more generous terms. Neither of the ministerial committees, however, endorsed the proposal. The Development Committee limited its response to a general endorsement of increased concessional flows to low-income countries, while the Interim Committee urged creditor countries to provide debt relief bilaterally. For the moment, the enhancement of the SAF was a higher multilateral priority than debt relief.[119]

Paralleling these initiatives, discussions of debt relief were gaining steam at the Paris Club. Following the January 1987 decision to approve rescheduling requests for countries with SAF loans rather than stand-by arrangements (see above, p. 654), the Paris Club agreed in June to grant longer-term reschedulings on more liberal terms. As a group, however, official creditors were still unwilling to grant interest-rate concessions on rescheduled debts (Keller, 1988, p. 7).

Once the ESAF was up and running, the debt-relief effort intensified. In June 1988, French President François Mitterrand circulated a proposal to the other G-7 leaders, calling for a menu of three options: immediate cancellation of one-third of the debt of qualifying low-income countries, consolidation of all debts with a maturity of 25 years at market rates, or consolidation over 15 years at concessional

---

[118]For the poorest countries, including most but not all of the 34 SAF-eligible countries in Africa, the debt problem was largely one of obtaining and servicing official credits. However, several of the larger low-income countries, including Sudan and Zaïre, had obtained substantial bank credits in the 1970s that now had to be serviced at much higher interest rates. (The rise in interest payments between the late 1970s and the mid- to late 1980s was especially large in relation to export revenues. In nominal terms, rates on commercial credits, most of which were either floating or applied to short-term loans, rose sharply in the late 1970s in world markets and then remained high through most of the 1980s. When deflated by export prices that were severely depressed by the mid-1980s, that rise was greatly magnified.) Obtaining significant relief on those commercial debts was much more difficult. Even after a secondary market developed in which these credits traded at very deep discounts, the most relief that African countries could obtain from commercial banks (usually through the so-called London Club) was a rescheduling of principal, without the "new money" provisions granted to middle-income developing countries in other regions. In other words, the banks typically insisted on full payment of current interest.

[119]This conclusion was illustrated also by the Venice Summit of the G-7 countries. Although various European proposals for debt relief to low-income countries were discussed, the communiqué breathed life only into the ESAF (see above, p. 664). In December 1987, the European Economic Community followed up on the Venice discussions by enacting legislation to provide 60 million ECU ($78 million) in new aid, targeted at low-income countries that were so highly indebted that their ability to import essential goods was impaired. Notwithstanding that linkage, however, recipients were required to use the money directly for imports rather than for reducing debts.

rates. That proposal, along with the Lawson plan and a similar outline put forward by the Canadian government, was discussed at the G-7 summit meeting in Toronto. This time, with the impossibility of servicing external debt becoming increasingly apparent for an increasing number of countries, the G-7 reached a consensus on a plan very close to what Lawson and Mitterrand had proposed.[120] The precise menu of options for the "Toronto terms" was left for the Paris Club to work out, but the summit achieved the essential breakthrough: for the first time, a multilateral framework was in place for not just delaying payments but also reducing the present value of the official debt-service obligations of low-income countries. Once that principle was established and applied, then the extension and deepening of relief terms occurred naturally and almost inevitably in several stages in the 1990s (see Chapter 1, pp. 31–32).

Protecting the Poor[121]

> ... the fact that adjustment need not conflict with growth and protection of basic human needs does not mean that the latter automatically result from the former. ... The extent to which adjustment is compatible with growth and with an improvement in living standards depends in large part on what *form* that adjustment takes.
>
> Jacques de Larosière (1986)

> When I look at the many operations—one could say rescue operations—on behalf of countries in difficulties ... I can say that the essential missing element—despite the admirable efforts of the United Nations and its specialized agencies—is a sufficient regard for the short-term human costs involved during adjustment or transition to a market economy.
>
> Michel Camdessus (1992)

Even more than a failure to raise overall living standards through economic growth, a failure to confront and alleviate widespread human misery will eventually bankrupt any country's economic policies. As long as the Fund was dealing primarily with countries' short-run financing problems, the inevitability of this conflict interfered but little with the institution's work. As the number, size, and length of arrangements for developing countries increased in the late 1970s and early 1980s, the Fund was led—gradually but inexorably—into a much greater concern with structural issues in general, and with social aspects of adjustment in particular. While other agencies aimed more directly to alleviate poverty in the long run, the role of the IMF in this context became to provide support for adjustment programs that not only would make economic growth sustainable but also would mitigate the adverse effects of adjustment measures on the poor in the short run.

---

[120]For the communiqué of the Toronto summit, see Hajnal (1989), pp. 362–76. The framework for the Toronto terms is set out in paragraph 30. Also see Lawson (1992), pp. 739–44, for the background to Toronto from the British perspective.

[121]This section is based in part on Bernstein and Boughton (1993).

Those seeking to evaluate the social implications of adjustment programs face three basic challenges. The first is to identify the severely disadvantaged, those who would be least able to absorb the transitional costs of adjustment. The World Bank and other development agencies have produced and analyzed data on relative income distributions, "basic needs" requirements, and numbers of people living in "absolute poverty";[122] for the most part, the Fund has drawn on that statistical and analytical work rather than producing its own data. The second challenge is to assess the effects of conventional macroeconomic adjustment programs on the disadvantaged. The staff devoted considerable effort to that problem in the 1980s, but it was at least as problematic as the more general task of assessing the macroeconomic implications.

The third challenge is to find alternative strategies that could ameliorate the short-term effects on the poor without sacrificing the longer-run macroeconomic benefits. The staff prepared several papers in the 1980s on the social and distributional effects of Fund programs. Two general policy studies, originally prepared for discussions by the Executive Board in 1985 and 1988, were later published, one on the effects of Fund-supported adjustment programs on income distribution (IMF, 1986), and the other more specifically assessing the empirical effects of adjustment programs on low-income groups (Heller and others, 1988). A third study outlined social components of several Fund programs (Gupta and Nashashibi, 1990). The Fund's official position on the institution's role in dealing with poverty was summarized in two Development Committee pamphlets (1989, 1990). Those various papers reveal an effort by the Fund both to explain how conventional macroeconomic adjustment can benefit all groups in society and to refine its conditionality and advice so as improve the distributional effects of adjustment. What follows is an analysis of how and why the Fund's approach to dealing with poverty evolved through the 1980s.

Internal and External Influences

Political Pressures

As the Fund's lending shifted increasingly toward lower-income developing countries, those drawing on Fund resources faced increasingly daunting conditions: large fiscal and external deficits and debt, high unemployment often combined with chronic inflation, low growth aggravated by structural problems, and weak demand for exports exacerbated by protectionism. Especially when adjustment programs included cuts in spending on basic programs such as education, health, and social services in order to meet the required fiscal targets, generating domestic political support often became a formidable task.[123] Moreover, even allowing for

---

[122]See IBRD (1990), which provides a comprehensive review of the issues and of the World Bank's work on poverty.

[123]For an analysis of the political constraints on implementing structural adjustments under the EFF, see Haggard (1985).

overall gains in efficiency and economic growth from effective adjustment, the political challenge was often aggravated by the need to reconcile the interests of various domestic groups that could be adversely affected by the program.

If an adjustment program is designed without regard to its effects on the poor, its insensitivity may become the subject of protests, and it will be unlikely to command the broad support (either within the country or among potential creditors and donors) that is essential for sustained success. On the other hand, targeting the poor for protection may impose substantial short-term costs on other groups that are better off economically but that have greater political power. Often, ignoring the needs of the influential urban middle class could undermine the program just as greatly as ignoring the needs of the poor. This point has been a recurring theme in internal discussions at the IMF over the years, and it is a political reality that missions face in negotiations with program countries. Nonetheless, the management of the IMF came down squarely and clearly on one side of this debate. The Fund's growing emphasis on targeting the poor emerged from an explicit recognition that importance must be attached to equity and to the development of human resources if programs are to be viable in the long run.[124]

On several occasions in the late 1970s and 1980s, the political pressures from conventional adjustment programs based principally on macroeconomic measures erupted in violent protests. Often the IMF felt the brunt of the attack.[125] Jahangir Amuzegar, a former Executive Director (Iran), wrote in 1986 that "national strikes, riots, political upheavals, and social unrest in Argentina, Bolivia, Brazil, the Dominican Republic, Ecuador, Egypt, Haiti, Liberia, Peru, Sudan, and elsewhere have been attributed directly or indirectly to the implementation of austerity measures advocated by the IMF." As Amuzegar also noted, however, such protests were infrequent relative to the number of conditional lending arrangements undertaken by the Fund. For example, during the 1980s the Fund entered into 61 arrangements with 21 countries in Latin America and the Caribbean. Large-scale demonstrations against austerity measures occurred in fewer than ten of those cases. Perhaps the most systematic study undertaken of this phenomenon, Sidell (1988), concluded that no statistically significant link could be found between Fund conditions and political instability. Nonetheless, violent and even deadly protests arose often enough that the problem cannot be dismissed.

---

[124]As Managing Director, Camdessus also stressed the interdependence of poverty reduction and preservation of the natural environment. In a visit to Norway in late January 1989, he met with Prime Minister Gro Harlem Brundtland, other government officials, and a joint parliamentary committee, where he addressed concerns being raised about the impact of Fund programs on the environment. Camdessus suggested that poverty can lead to serious environmental degradation, and he concluded that by attempting to alleviate the one the Fund indirectly benefits the other. See minutes of EBM/89/9 (February 1, 1989), p. 3.

[125]See de Vries (1985), pp. 490–94, for a discussion of political criticism of Fund conditionality in the 1970s. Political pressure to impose conditionality based on the distributional effects of programs and the protection of basic needs also came occasionally from creditor countries. For a review of such pressures emanating from the U.S. Congress, see Gerster (1982).

In almost every case, the proximate cause of riots or other protests against Fund-related adjustment programs was an announcement by the authorities of cuts in subsidies for consumer goods, most often for basic foods. Such cuts were frequently recommended by the Fund because consumer subsidies were judged to be inefficient, costly, and only weakly targeted at the low-income groups they were supposed to benefit. Even when the Fund suggested replacing subsidies with more efficient programs aimed at protecting the poor, the prospect of large price increases for basic goods provided a trigger for violent reactions by those who stood to lose.

Protests over adjustment programs may be classified into three types: political opposition to government policies, social disturbances bolstering government opposition to Fund advice, and anger directed at the Fund as a scapegoat for actions the government knows it must take. The first type has been the most common and also the most troublesome, as it weakens a willing government's ability to stabilize the economy. Often cited as an example are the 1977 "bread riots" in Egypt. During the 1980s, similar cases arose in Morocco, the Dominican Republic, and Zambia.

Egypt

In January 1977, the government of President Anwar Sadat was in the midst of negotiations with the IMF over the terms of a possible stand-by arrangement. The staff had been pressing for a combination of exchange rate devaluation (through a unification of the official and parallel markets) and spending cuts, but the government had resisted making major adjustments to exchange rate policy. Since much of the central government budget was politically off-limits to cuts—including public sector employment, parastatal enterprises, and the military—the only way to resolve the budgetary crisis was to reduce outlays for subsidies of basic goods. The government finally agreed to make cuts that would have resulted in retail price increases approaching 50 percent for selected commodities (including flour, fuels, and cigarettes) that were important for low-income consumers.[126]

During the two days after the government announced its intention to raise prices (January 18–19), demonstrators protested in major cities throughout Egypt. At least 79 people (the official total) died in the ensuing tragic violence. Hundreds more were injured, and thousands were arrested. Although the riots were directed primarily at the government, press reports gave prominence to the connection

---

[126]To mitigate the impact on consumers, the staff accepted a proposal for the government to establish a temporary "price adjustment fund" that would permit certain prices to be raised more gradually. Goods to be covered by the fund would be selected on "social or other considerations" but not to protect "particular companies." See memorandum of December 23, 1976, to the Managing Director from John W. Gunter (Acting Director of the Middle Eastern Department); cable of December 27, 1976, to the governor of the central bank of Egypt from the Managing Director; and memorandum to the Managing Director from Hans W. Gerhard (Assistant Director of ETR); all in IMF/CF (C/Egypt/810 "Mission, Gunter and Staff, December 1976"). The quotations are from the attachment to the December 23 memorandum.

with the Fund negotiations.[127] The budget was withdrawn, the Fund helped the authorities devise a plan under which the subsidies could be reduced more gradually, and a stand-by arrangement incorporating the new budget was approved a few months later.[128]

Morocco

Morocco faced widespread rioting in June 1981 while trying to implement a program supported by an EFF arrangement. External shocks and structural weaknesses had prevented the government from carrying out reforms for some three years. The authorities entered into an extended arrangement from the Fund in October 1980, which was replaced by a larger arrangement in March 1981 to reflect the increase in Morocco's quota through the Seventh General Review (see Nsouli and others, 1995).

The 1981 adjustment program was fully implemented until opposition erupted on June 20, in riots in which at least 60 people were killed. The trigger for the riots was the government's announcement of sharp increases in food prices, mandated by the Fund's demand for reductions in subsidies on consumer goods. Although the authorities publicly accepted full responsibility for the decision to raise prices, enmity was directed as much at the Fund—which had helped "light the powder," as one press account put it—as at the government.[129] The program then quickly went off track, partly because the government was forced to roll back the price increases and partly because external conditions continued to worsen.

Dominican Republic

The Fund approved an EFF arrangement for the Dominican Republic in January 1983, but the program went off track before the end of the year. Negotiation of a program for 1984 was complicated by what the Fund staff saw as the need for a unification of the exchange rate and a large increase in controlled and subsidized prices, especially petroleum but also basic foodstuffs. The authorities were willing to implement a strong adjustment program but feared (correctly, as it turned out) that they lacked the necessary political support at home. In January 1984, President Salvador Jorge Blanco sent a personal letter to de Larosière, pleading that the program requested by the mission was "excessive and . . . could not be absorbed in the short period of one year, without provoking social shocks which would threaten the stability which it has cost the Dominican Republic so much effort and sacrifice to obtain and preserve."[130]

The staff was less sympathetic to this appeal than was the Managing Director, and negotiations remained deadlocked for another three months. President Jorge

---

[127]See, for example, *The Economist* of January 22, 1977, p. 59, and January 29, pp. 59–60; and Lippman (1989), pp. 114–21.

[128]See EBS/77/90 (April 1, 1977) and minutes of EBM/77/59 (April 20, 1977).

[129] ". . . ces financiers internationaux qui ont mit le feu aux poudres" (Andriamirado, 1981).

[130]Undated letter (in Spanish), delivered by hand to the Managing Director on January 13, 1984, and translated by Fund staff; in IMF/RD Managing Director file "Dominican Republic, 1984" (Accession 85/231, Box 4, Section 177).

Blanco then flew to Washington in early April to try to pry loose some assistance from the U.S. government and to make a personal appeal to de Larosière to ease up on the Fund's conditionality.[131] When his mission generated goodwill but no tangible results, he announced new policies that went partway toward meeting the Fund's requirements, but he warned publicly that high social costs could follow. Austerity was unavoidable, but without external aid the required sacrifices would be severe.

After extremist opposition groups organized protests, both the demonstrations and the response by the police and army got out of hand. An estimated 60 to 80 people were killed in riots that began the same day that the Fund mission returned to Santo Domingo to try to conclude negotiations.[132] The president then concluded that he had no choice but to back off from his commitment to raise oil prices. Negotiations between the Fund and the authorities continued for several months, after which the extended arrangement was canceled.[133]

Zambia

Zambia faced serious opposition disturbances in December 1986. The economy had been deteriorating throughout the year, a two-year stand-by arrangement approved by the Fund in February had quickly been derailed, and the government had gone into arrears to external creditors, including the Fund. The essence of the problem was that when export prices for copper declined sharply, the government weakened its adjustment effort to try to prop up incomes rather than intensifying it to compensate for lost revenues. Urged on by President Kenneth D. Kaunda, the authorities successfully negotiated a program for 1987 that the Fund was prepared to support as soon as arrears were cleared. A Consultative Group meeting was scheduled for mid-December to devise a means of financing the clearing of arrears. But when the government announced a doubling of prices for maize meal in early December, riots quickly spread throughout the country, in which at least 100 people died. The president rescinded the price increase, the Consultative Group meeting failed to generate much financial assistance, and the authorities went back to the bargaining table to look for alternative fiscal measures.[134] That effort failed, and Zambia remained in arrears to the Fund and other creditors for another nine years. (Also see Chapter 16, on Zambia's arrears problem, pp. 787–91.)

---

[131]See memorandum from Finch to the Managing Director (April 9, 1984); in IMF/RD Managing Director file "Dominican Republic, 1984" (Accession 85/231, Box 4, Section 177).

[132]On the linkages between the riots and the negotiations with the Fund, see articles in the *New York Times*, April 29, 1984, p. A14, and April 30, p. A9. On the effect of the riots on the negotiations, see memorandum from Sterie T. Beza (Associate Director of the Western Hemisphere Department) to management (May 11, 1984), in IMF/RD Western Hemisphere Department file "Dominican Republic, 1984" (Accession 87/16, Box 2, Section 61).

[133]In April 1985, the Fund approved a 12-month stand-by arrangement for SDR 78.5 million ($78 million or 70 percent of quota). The stand-by arrangement, which provided less than half the annual access of the canceled extended arrangement, was fully drawn.

[134]See memorandum from Ouattara and Kanesa-Thasan to the Managing Director (January 20, 1987), and memorandum for files by Keyes (April 28, 1987); in IMF/RD Managing Director file "Zambia, November 1985–August 1987, Vol. I" (Accession 89/164, Box 1, Section 263).

Sudan

The second type of social disturbance serves to bolster the position of authorities who are resisting Fund advice to stabilize the economy. One example occurred in Sudan in the early 1980s.

After Sudan first developed arrears to the Fund in September 1981 while trying to reactivate a stalled EFF arrangement, negotiations began on a program for 1982 that could be supported by a new stand-by arrangement. Initially, the government agreed to implement strong measures, and took prior actions that included a devaluation and a rise in petroleum prices. Creditors, however, retained doubts about the authorities' commitment to adjustment, especially after President Gaafar al-Nimeiri installed a new finance minister who appeared less than enthusiastic about reform. Discussions with the new minister led nowhere. The Fund, reacting both to Sudan's poor track record and to the need to convince creditors of the authorities' intentions, insisted that much of the adjustment be put in place up front.

Violent protests broke out in Khartoum at the beginning of 1982 when the government announced a partial implementation of the program (notably, a rise in the price of sugar). The government put down the disturbance but used it as a lever to convince individuals in the U.S. Congress and State Department to pressure the Fund to relax its demands. In February, the Executive Board approved the stand-by arrangement, under which Sudan made one drawing after it (temporarily) settled its arrears.

A third type of protest, in which the Fund itself is the principal target rather than the government, arises when the authorities agree to implement an adjustment program but publicly blame the Fund for imposing specific policy changes. Until the late 1980s, the Fund generally accepted that tactic as a necessary strategem to enable governments to implement unpopular policies. When management did protest, it usually did so only in private communications to the authorities. In May 1987, following the deadly outbreak of antigovernment rioting in Zambia described above, the Managing Director took a tentative step toward abandoning that passive attitude. President Kaunda had reacted to the riots by accusing the Fund of being a "killer" and of contributing to unemployment, malnutrition, and starvation in his country. After Kaunda's public statements continued in that vein for a few weeks, Camdessus wrote to him to deny the accusation, but he confined his remarks to the charge that the Fund was deliberately trying to harm Zambia's people or its economy. The Fund circulated copies of the letter to the wire services that had reported Kaunda's attack, but it took no further action.[135] Less than two years later, however, Camdessus was ready to respond more forcefully and publicly when the Fund was blamed for actions that led to rioting in Venezuela.

---

[135]See memorandums from Azizali Mohammed (Director of the External Relations Department) to the Managing Director (April 17 and May 4, 1987); memorandum from Charles Gardner (Deputy Director of the department) to the Managing Director (May 5); and cable from Camdessus to Kaunda (May 5); in IMF/RD Managing Director file, "Zambia, November 1985–August 1987, Vol. I" (Accession 89/164, Box 1, Section 263).

Venezuela

As recounted in Chapter 11, the riots in Venezuela in February 1989 were a clear example of the use of the Fund as a scapegoat. The newly elected president, Carlos Andres Pérez, had attacked the Fund in speeches throughout the campaign, but he nonetheless turned to the Fund for financial assistance as soon as he was in office. When he sent an open letter to the Managing Director linking the deadly riots to the "unjust terms" imposed by a global system in which the Fund stood at the "apex," Camdessus responded immediately with a personal and equally public rebuttal that signaled a new level of resistance by the Fund to being used as a scapegoat. "It is a prerogative of sovereign states to decide themselves what measures are required for recovery, however unpleasant those measures may be," he wrote. "And it does them honor if they take responsibility for policies in the eyes of their people, even in the most adverse circumstances" (*IMF Survey*, March 20, 1989, p. 82).

More generally, the Fund's position was always that the formulation of specific adjustment policies was an internal matter for the member country and could not be imposed by the Fund. There was a clear delineation of responsibilities, in which the role of the Fund was to provide technical advice and assistance to the authorities in developing an effective adjustment program that would avoid imposing undue costs on the most vulnerable groups, and to both provide and catalyze financing in support of such a program. Nonetheless, the Fund also had an interest in ensuring that the needs of the poor were adequately safeguarded in any adjustment program. The challenge was to reach that goal in situations where the authorities were either unwilling or politically unable to take adjustment measures in ways that would protect or offset the subsidies on which the poor rely in many developing countries.

External Criticism of the Focus on Macroeconomics

Literature on the social costs of adjustment burgeoned in the early 1980s, reflecting the growing importance of the subject as more countries faced the need to implement painful policy changes. Tony Killick's work at the Overseas Development Institute (1984) typifies academic critiques. He recognized both the Fund's insistence on prudent economic policy mandated by its Articles of Agreement and the domestic political constraints faced by governments assisted by the IMF. Though he noted that the specific impacts of an adjustment program could not be predicted or even determined afterward, he held that the Fund should realize that its recommendations might considerably increase inequalities. To enhance the institution's effectiveness, therefore, Killick urged Fund staff to consider the sociopolitical context of economic disequilibria and to explore the distributional effects of its programs. Similar criticisms were made in Helleiner (1987) and Helleiner and others (1991).

The World Bank launched a more fundamental critique of conventional adjustment paradigms in its *World Development Report* of 1984. The report noted that the emphasis given to increased taxation and higher interest rates in many pro-

grams could lead to a squeeze on the private sector and restrict long-term investment and growth. At the same time, reducing or eliminating subsidies for food, education, and health would decrease real income—worsening the plight of the
poorest—while damaging the country's growth potential. The Bank's analysis
questioned the foundations of the Fund's long-held view that orderly adjustment
necessarily benefited the poor in the long run, a view that Jacques Polak (1991)
characterized as a "trickle-down" approach that was no longer adequate.[136] A study
sponsored by UNICEF (Cornia, Jolly, and Stewart, 1987), similarly encouraged a
reorientation to more "people sensitive" adjustment programs.

Jeffrey Sachs (1989, pp. 116–18) also analyzed the distributional impacts of
Fund programs. He noted that many of the same critics who attack the effect of adjustment programs on income distribution would object as well to the Fund's meddling in countries' internal affairs. Yet he wrote that there are compelling reasons
for the IMF to pay more attention to the linkages between distribution and adjustment. The long-run viability of an adjustment program "may well depend on
an adequate distribution of income," because extreme income inequalities generate political pressures that make fiscal mismanagement much more likely. Many
governments, Sachs argued, may want to pursue adjustment programs that minimize the long-run costs of adjustment, and Fund staff should be able to design such
programs.

Internal Debate at the Fund

The Fund's traditional approach to conditionality included a focus on the importance of orderly and timely adjustment. This approach was derived implicitly
on the assumptions that a comprehensive adjustment program would protect the
interests of the most vulnerable in the short run, by preventing the inevitable
chaotic adjustment process arising from suppressed macroeconomic imbalances;
and in the long run would aid the poor, by fostering sustainable growth. The distribution of income, in this approach, is left primarily to the country concerned, to
be determined in the light of the country's political and social structure. In countries where the authorities recognized and were sensitive to the needs of the poor
and had the political ability to act positively, this approach allowed Fund-
supported adjustment programs to include income-supporting measures such as increases in producer prices and improvements in access to credit by the agricultural
sector. When conditions were less favorable, the interests of the poor often got
short shrift.

Although orderly adjustment is a prerequisite for sustainable growth, experience
with financial programming made it increasingly clear that the traditional approach was insufficient in cases where a country's long-term interests were sub-
sumed under shorter-term social hardship and political realities. The Fund's management therefore initiated and encouraged several internal studies, beginning in
the late 1970s, to focus attention more specifically on the protection of the inter-

---

[136]Broad (1988) offered a detailed criticism of what she viewed as the IMF's trickle-down approach in the Philippines in the mid-1970s.

ests of the poor. These studies comprised both evaluations of specific programs for individual low-income countries—which amply demonstrated the difficulties posed for program viability when the poor are unduly affected—and general studies of the links between program design and income distribution.

The first of the general studies was that of Omotunde Johnson and Joanne Salop, undertaken at the request of Managing Director H. Johannes Witteveen in 1977. Witteveen initially was concerned that proposals for lending strategies favoring projects that aimed to provide "basic needs" to the poorer segments of the population raised the risk of softening the loan portfolio, which would defeat the purpose of the adjustment program. Yet he also recognized the dangers of ignoring distributional issues, and he called on the Fund staff to study the problem more carefully.[137] Consequently, Johnson and Salop (1980) analyzed the effects of policies most commonly adopted in Fund-supported programs using a simple model of traded and nontraded goods. They concluded that stabilization programs "necessarily had distributional repercussions," but that the specific effects could be positive or negative and would depend on the structure of the economy.[138] In an economy where the export sector was large and marked by small-scale operators, as in Ghana, a devaluation might have egalitarian effects. In others, implications were not as favorable. In Bolivia, for example, much of the primary export (mineral products) was produced in public enterprises, whereas lower-income segments of the population produced mostly nontraded agricultural products and simple manufactures. The shift in internal terms of trade required by adjustment therefore would tend to disadvantage poorer groups in Bolivia. The study gained wide publicity and, though it contained no policy recommendations for the Fund, grew to be considered by academics as the Fund's response to the question.

A more theoretical internal study, Borpujari (1980), drew favorable attention from de Larosière.[139] Borpujari's work (see also his published 1985 paper) developed a framework for incorporating financial constraints into a model in which development depends essentially on an economy's ability to provide for the population's basic production and consumption needs. In this framework, conventional macroeconomic financial programming is appropriate only for economies where

---

[137]See memorandum from Ernest Sturc (Director of ETR) to the Managing Director (June 9, 1977); in IMF/CF (B/100 "Liaison and Exchange of Information"). On June 20, Witteveen responded, "It seems important for us to follow these [World Bank] studies closely. The IBRD seems to be on a risky and debatable course that could easily lead to some conflict with Fund policies. I wonder whether we should not do some research of our own in this field"; Historian's files, in IMF/RD.

[138]Blejer and Guerrero (1990) drew similar conclusions on the basis of an empirical study of the Philippines. More generally, Edwards (1989) studied 36 devaluation "episodes" in 23 developing countries and found no link to a worsening of income distributions; the evidence was "remarkably inconclusive" (p. 48).

[139]Memorandum from C. Max Watson (Personal Assistant to the Managing Director) to Borpujari (March 17, 1980); in IMF/RD Managing Director 1980 Chronological file (Accession 87/27, Box 20, Section 536).

development is not constrained by inflexibility in the supply of basic goods. In economies that are so constrained, an increased inflow of foreign exchange will strengthen development potential only if it is used to import investment goods or ease shortages of basic consumption goods. Although this model had little direct influence because it was seen as outside the mainstream of financial programming at the Fund, it did point the way toward modifying the traditional focus on macro-economic adjustment.

Some years later, the Fund's Fiscal Affairs Department undertook a more comprehensive study of the distributional effects of adjustment programs (IMF, 1986; also see Sisson, 1986). The authors surveyed fiscal economists for 78 IMF program missions to create a stylized, typical Fund-supported program. They compared this program with a synthetic counterfactual experience depicting what would have happened without a stabilization program, focusing on short-term effects. The paper concluded that there was no basis for believing that Fund-supported adjustment programs were more damaging to income distribution than were the practicable alternatives. But it did identify several policies that could have relatively beneficial distributional effects in the context of a comprehensive program. These included elimination of restrictive exchange practices, expansion of access to credit markets, broadening of the tax base, restructuring of indirect taxes, limiting expenditures on defense and "grandiose public works," and—in some circumstances—correction of an overvalued exchange rate.[140]

Developing and Implementing a Policy Framework

Operational Studies

The Executive Board discussed the effects of adjustment programs on income distribution in July 1985, using the Fiscal Affairs study described above as background. Two basic messages crystallized from this meeting.[141] First, Directors were reluctant to draw firm conclusions about the effects of traditional programs without specifying viable alternatives. As had already been apparent after the Johnson-Salop study, there was insufficient evidence to conclude that a typical program would have positive or negative effects on income distribution. To firm up the conclusions would require asking whether another adjustment program would have been as effective at promoting sustainable growth but with more favorable distributional effects. The second message was that, whatever conclusions might emerge from this and further research, the Board still felt that policies toward the distribution of income were essentially a domestic matter and should not be subjected to Fund conditionality. The Fund's role should be to assist member countries—only on request—to determine the likely effects of their adjustment policies, including distributional effects. To further that objective, more detailed staff research

---

[140]For a related study, see Kanbur (1987).

[141]Minutes of Executive Board Seminar 85/1–2 (July 19, 1985) and 85/3 (July 22).

would be warranted, as would a strengthening of cooperation in this field with development institutions such as the World Bank.

As a follow-up to the Executive Board meeting, the staff prepared case studies on seven countries: Chile, the Dominican Republic, Ghana, Kenya, the Philippines, Sri Lanka, and Thailand. The results were analyzed in Heller and others (1988).[142] The methodology underlying the case studies was eclectic; in some cases, the authors used a "before-after" approach while in others they drew comparisons with a reasonable alternative. The studies focused on the effects on poverty, reflecting a concern for those groups least capable of bearing the burden of adjustment. The review concluded that the effects of adjustment on poverty depended on the choice of policy instruments—the policy mix—and on the structure of domestic poverty. The cases suggested that supply-side policies and compensatory assistance could effectively mitigate the effects of demand restraint.

In 1988, the implications of these case studies were considered in several ways. First, the Executive Board reviewed the analysis and approved the development of additional expertise within the Fund both through continuing research and by calling on the experience of other UN agencies such as UNICEF, the International Labor Organization (ILO), the UN Development Program (UNDP), and the World Bank. Second, the subject was considered as part of the Board's major review of conditionality. That review reaffirmed the 1985 decision not to impose conditions on the use of Fund resources related to the distribution of income, but rather to assist members in evaluating distributional effects of policy changes. Third, the Development Committee urged both the Fund and the World Bank to intensify their efforts, working closely together, to help design adjustment programs and adopt, as needed, well-targeted compensatory measures.[143]

Following the operational discussions in the Executive Board and the recommendations of the Development Committee, interdepartmental groups met on several occasions to discuss work on poverty. Analysis of poverty issues as part of negotiations for Fund loans was gradually expanded, and in 1991 Camdessus directed the staff to expand the consideration of social costs to all Fund-supported programs.[144] Subsequently, he undertook to publicize the Fund's efforts, most notably in his annual addresses to the Economic and Social Council of the United

---

[142]The full case studies were circulated as "The Implications of Fund-Supported Adjustment Programs for Poverty Groups: Country Case Studies," DM/87/5 (December 23, 1987); summaries were published in the Appendix to Heller and others (1988).

[143]On the first two points, see minutes of Executive Board Seminar 88/2 (February 8, 1988), p. 55, and minutes of EBM/88/60 (April 8, 1988), pp. 3–7. For a summary of staff recommendations to the Development Committee, along with related papers by the World Bank staff and the Committee's conclusions, see Development Committee (1989, 1990).

[144]The Managing Director's directive on extending poverty analysis to all Fund-supported programs was made in a memorandum to department heads on March 8, 1991; Historian's files, in IMF/RD. Also see the "Chairman's Summing Up on Poverty Issues at Committee of the Whole for the Development Committee Meeting 88/4 (9/2/88)," (September 12, 1988); and a memorandum for files (March 13, 1989) by Vito Tanzi (Director of the Fiscal Affairs Department) on a meeting on poverty with the Managing Director on March 7, 1989. The latter two items are in IMF/RD Fiscal Affairs Department file "Poverty, Folder 2" (Accession 94/249, Box 1, Section 540).

Nations. Within the Fund, the Fiscal Affairs Department was designated to coordinate the institution's initiatives on poverty.

Besides the studies prepared for the Executive Board, the Fund held seminars on poverty for staff working on countries with adjustment programs, starting in 1988. Contributors, including Fund staff, experts from universities, and staff of other agencies, particularly UNICEF and the World Bank, examined conceptual and practical questions regarding poverty.[145] In one such meeting in 1990, presentations on social aspects of particular recent Fund-supported programs examined the incidence of domestic poverty and outlined known poverty effects. They related varied country experience with compensatory measures and presented models for the future study of poverty at the Fund. Several of the studies were subsequently circulated as IMF working papers.[146]

Coordination with Other Agencies

Various agencies of the United Nations conduct programs aimed at the alleviation of world poverty. Although the Fund's contacts with those agencies have been sporadic, a few efforts were made in the 1980s to coordinate the Fund's fledgling work on poverty with ongoing UN projects. In 1984, de Larosière asked the Executive Director of the ILO, Francis Blanchard, to help set up informal meetings between ILO and IMF staff to discuss means of ensuring that adjustment programs do not entail unnecessary social costs and do not sap economic development. Shortly afterward, the Managing Director also invited the Executive Director of UNICEF, James Grant, to meet with him and with Fund staff to try to strengthen the social content of adjustment programs. The resulting contacts led eventually to an initiative under which UNICEF would encourage governments of selected countries to redesign adjustment programs to include more measures targeted at the poor, and the IMF would assist governments in that effort.[147]

More generally, the IMF's empirical work on poverty drew on UN agencies' data bases, and many interagency staff meetings were held. During a seminar held at the Fund in October 1990, for example, representatives of the World Bank and 12 UN agencies met with Fund officials to discuss ways to enhance cooperation on social and sectoral aspects of adjustment. Seminar participants recognized the need for cooperation among agencies from the very beginning of the adjustment process and agreed to increase open communication and dialogue, and to share data and assessments. By the early 1990s, the exchange of information and analysis between the Fund staff and various UN agencies was becoming regularized.

---

[145]See memorandum (December 8, 1988) to the Managing Director from Tanzi on the initial poverty seminar, held November 29 through December 2, 1988; Historian's files, in IMF/RD.

[146]Ahmad (1991) on Jordan; Gotur (1991) on Bangladesh; Gulde (1991) on Sri Lanka; Hicks and Brekk (1991) on Malawi; Liuksila (1991) on Colombia; and Lopes and Sacerdoti (1991) on Mozambique.

[147]The initiative is summarized in a letter from Grant to de Larosière (June 14, 1984); in IMF/CF (I 128.5 "United Nations International Children's Emergency Fund"). See Jolly (1991) for more background. The position paper prepared by UNICEF for the initial meetings with the IMF in 1984 was published much later as Helleiner and others (1991).

Anti-IMF grafitti on the Brandenburg Gate, Berlin, 1988 Annual Meetings

Coordination with the World Bank on poverty alleviation also developed during the 1980s. Although much of the work of the two Bretton Woods institutions proceeded independently, Fund staff occasionally participated in World Bank missions on poverty in countries where the Fund was also actively engaged.[148] Much more systematic collaboration developed in the second half of the decade through the SAF and the ESAF, as described earlier in this chapter. The primary vehicle for collaboration under those facilities was the PFP, designed as a framework for medium-term programs of policy reform agreed among the country, the Bank, and the Fund. Most PFPs included a section on the social implications of the adjustment program, and some also included a discussion of mitigating measures and requirements for social safety nets. Such measures could be divided into four categories: targeted subsidies of essential goods; cash transfers to vulnerable groups; direct support for wages, producer prices, and targeted public works; and protection of education and health expenditures. During the first few years of experience, relatively few ESAF-supported programs contained specific social measures, but the practice became more common in the early 1990s (Schadler and others, 1993).[149]

---

[148]A published study by Blejer and Guerrero (1990) arose from a World Bank mission on poverty in the Philippines. Guerrero was the Bank's mission chief, and Blejer participated on behalf of the Fund.

[149]For a review of the early ESAF experience with social measures, see "Structural Adjustment Facility (SAF) and Enhanced Structural Adjustment Facility (ESAF)—Background Information," EBS/91/110 (July 8, 1991), pp. 29–32.

Perhaps the most well-publicized example of the use of the structural adjustment facilities to promote programs that protect the interests of the disadvantaged was the case of Ghana. As discussed above (pp. 673–79), the Ghanaian adjustment programs—supported by the Fund for four years starting in 1987—were initially implemented under the EFF and the SAF (1987–88), and later under the ESAF (1988–91). Throughout this period, the government sought to improve its social policy, especially beginning in 1988 with the implementation of PAMSCAD, with external support from the ESAF and from bilateral donors.

Overall, the dominant constraint on the Fund's work on poverty alleviation was not its mandate as a monetary institution, but its dependency on cooperation from the countries concerned. As Killick and Malik (1991, p. 613) noted, "The priorities of the government in power, rather than those of the IMF, are probably the principal determinant of the ways in which programmes impinge upon the poor." Because the poor are not the only group—and almost certainly are not the most politically powerful group—that could be affected adversely by the need for adjustment, governmental support for measures targeted at the poor was not always easy to secure.[150]

References

Ahmad, S. Ehtisham U., 1991, "Jordan: Restructuring Public Expenditure and Protecting the Poor," IMF Working Paper 91/82 (Washington: International Monetary Fund).

Amuzegar, Jahangir, 1986, "The IMF Under Fire," *Foreign Policy*, Vol. 64 (fall), pp. 98–119.

Andriamirado, Sennen, 1981, "Quand la 'vérité des prix' déclenche l'émeute," *Jeune Afrique* (July 1), pp. 10–11.

Bernstein, Boris, and James M. Boughton, 1993, "Adjusting to Development: The IMF and the Poor," IMF Paper on Policy Analysis and Assessment 93/4 (Washington: International Monetary Fund). (Reprinted in abbreviated form in *Finance & Development*, Vol. 31, September 1994, pp. 42–45.)

Blejer, Mario I., and Isabel Guerrero, 1990, "Impact of macroeconomic policies on income distribution: an empirical study of the Philippines," *Review of Economics and Statistics*, Vol. 72 (August), pp. 414–23.

Borpujari, Jitendra G., 1980, "Toward a Basic Needs Approach to Economic Development with Financial Stability," IMF Departmental Memorandum 80/16 (February 28).

———, 1985, "Savings Generation and Financial Programming in a Basic Need Constrained Developing Economy," in *Financing Problems of Developing Countries: Proceedings of a Conference held by the International Economic Association in Buenos Aires, Argentina*, ed. by Armin Gutowski, A.A. Arnaúdo, and Hans-Eckart Scharrer (New York: St. Martin's Press), pp. 59–82.

Broad, Robin, 1988, *Unequal Alliance: The World Bank, the International Monetary Fund, and the Philippines* (Berkeley, California: University of California Press).

Camdessus, Michel, 1992, International Monetary Fund Speeches (92/14), Address to the Economic and Social Council of the United Nations, New York, July.

---

[150]For an elaboration of the political dimensions of this problem, see Nelson (1989) and Graham (1992).

Cornia, Giavanni Andrea, Richard Jolly, and Frances Stewart, 1987, *Adjustment with a Human Face*, Vol. 1: *Protecting the Vulnerable and Promoting Growth* (New York: Oxford University Press).

de Larosière, Jacques, 1986, Address before the Economic and Social Council of the United Nations, Geneva, July.

Development Committee, 1989, "Strengthening Efforts to Reduce Poverty," Development Committee Pamphlet No. 19, prepared by the staffs of the World Bank and the International Monetary Fund for the Development Committee (Washington: Joint Ministerial Committee of the Boards of Governors of the World Bank and of the International Monetary Fund).

———, 1990, "Development Issues, Presentations to the 39th Meeting of the Development Committee," Development Committee Pamphlet No. 26 (Washington: Joint Ministerial Committee of the Boards of Governors of the World Bank and of the International Monetary Fund).

de Vries, Margaret Garritsen, 1976, *The International Monetary Fund, 1966–1971: The System Under Stress*, Vol. 1: *Narrative*; Vol. 2: *Documents* (Washington: International Monetary Fund).

———, 1985, *The International Monetary Fund, 1972–1978: Cooperation on Trial*, Vols. 1 and 2: *Narrative and Analysis*; Vol. 3: *Documents* (Washington: International Monetary Fund).

Edwards, Sebastian, 1989, "The International Monetary Fund and the Developing Countries: A Critical Evaluation," *IMF Policy Advice, Market Volatility, Commodity Price Rules, and Other Essays*, ed. by Karl Brunner and Allan H. Meltzer, Carnegie-Rochester Conference Series on Public Policy (New York; Amsterdam: North-Holland), pp. 7–68.

Gerster, Richard, 1982, "The IMF and Basic Needs Conditionality," *Journal of World Trade Law*, Vol. 16 (November/December), pp. 497–517.

Gotur, Padma, 1991, "Bangladesh: Economic Reform Measures and the Poor," IMF Working Paper 91/39 (Washington: International Monetary Fund).

Graham, Carol, 1992, "Politics of Protecting the Poor During Adjustment: Bolivia's Emergency Social Fund," *World Development*, Vol. 20 (September), pp. 1233–51.

Gulde, Anne-Marie, 1991, "Sri Lanka: Price Changes and the Poor," IMF Working Paper 91/46 (Washington: International Monetary Fund).

Gupta, Sanjeev, and Karim Nashashibi, 1990, "Poverty Concerns in Fund-Supported Programs," *Finance & Development*, Vol. 27 (September), pp. 12–14.

Hadjimichael, Michael T., Thomas Rumbaugh, Eric Verreydt, and others, 1992, *The Gambia: Economic Adjustment in a Small Open Economy*, IMF Occasional Paper No. 100 (Washington: International Monetary Fund).

Haggard, Stephan, 1985, "The Politics of Adjustment: Lessons from the IMF's Extended Fund Facility," *International Organization*, Vol. 39 (summer), pp. 505–34.

Hajnal, Peter I., ed., 1989, *The Seven-Power Summit: Documents from the Summits of Industrialized Countries, 1975–1989* (Millwood, New York: Kraus International Publications).

Helleiner, Gerald K., 1987, "Stabilization, Adjustment, and the Poor," *World Development*, Vol. 15 (December), pp. 1499–1513.

———, G.A. Cornia, and R. Jolly, 1991, "IMF Adjustment Policies and Approaches and the Needs of Children," *World Development*, Vol. 19 (December), pp. 1823–34.

Heller, Peter S., and others, 1988, *The Implications of Fund-Supported Adjustment Programs for Poverty: Experiences in Selected Countries*, IMF Occasional Paper No. 58 (Washington: International Monetary Fund).

Hicks, Ronald P., and Odd Per Brekk, 1991, "Assessing the Impact of Structural Adjustment on the Poor: The Case of Malawi," IMF Working Paper 91/112 (Washington: International Monetary Fund).

International Bank for Reconstruction and Development, 1984, *World Development Report 1984* (New York: Oxford University Press).

———, 1990, *World Development Report 1990* (New York: Oxford University Press).

International Monetary Fund, *Annual Report* (Washington: International Moneraty Fund, various issues).

———, 1986, *Fund-Supported Programs, Fiscal Policy, and Income Distribution,* IMF Occasional Paper No. 46 (Washington: International Monetary Fund).

James, Harold, 1996, *International Monetary Cooperation Since Bretton Woods* (New York: Oxford University Press; Washington: International Monetary Fund)

Johnson, Omotunde, 1977, "Use of Fund Resources and Stand-By Arrangements," *Finance & Development,* Vol. 14 (March), pp. 19–21.

———, and Joanne Salop, 1980, "Distributional Aspects of Stabilization Programs in Developing Countries," *Staff Papers,* International Monetary Fund, Vol. 27 (March), pp. 1–23.

Jolly, Richard, 1991, "Adjustment with a Human Face: A UNICEF Record and Perspective on the 1980s," *World Development,* Vol. 19 (December), pp. 1807–21.

Jones, Christine W., and Miguel A. Kiguel, 1994, *Adjustment in Africa: Reforms, Results, and the Road Ahead,* World Bank Policy Research Report (New York: Oxford University Press).

Kanbur, S.M. Ravi, 1987, "Measurement and Alleviation of Poverty: With an Application to the Effects of Macroeconomic Adjustment," *Staff Papers,* International Monetary Fund, Vol. 34 (March), pp. 60–85.

Kapur, Ishan, and others, 1991, *Ghana: Adjustment and Growth, 1983–91,* IMF Occasional Paper No. 86 (Washington: International Monetary Fund).

Keller, Peter M., with Nissanke E. Weerasinghe, 1988, *Multilateral Official Debt Rescheduling: Recent Experience* (Washington: International Monetary Fund).

Killick, Tony, ed., 1984, *The Quest for Economic Stabilization: The IMF and the Third World* (London: Heinemann Educational Books).

———, and Moazzam Malik, 1991, "Country Experiences with IMF Programmes in the 1980s," *World Economy,* Vol. 15 (September), pp. 599–632.

Landell-Mills, Joslin, 1992, *Helping the Poor: The IMF's New Facilities for Structural Adjustment* (Washington: International Monetary Fund).

Lawson, Nigel, 1992, *The View from No. 11: Memoirs of a Tory Radical* (London: Bantam Press).

Lippman, Thomas W., 1989, *After Nasser: Sadat, Peace, and the Mirage of Prosperity* (New York: Paragon House).

Liuksila, Claire, 1991, "Colombia: Economic Adjustment and the Poor," IMF Working Paper 91/81 (August).

Lopes, Paulo S., and Emilio Sacerdoti, 1991, "Mozambique: Economic Rehabilitation and the Poor," IMF Working Paper 91/101 (Washington: International Monetary Fund).

Museveni, Yoweri Kaguta, 1997, *Sowing the Mustard Seed: The Struggle for Freedom and Democracy in Uganda* (London: Macmillan).

Nashashibi, Karim, and others, 1992, *The Fiscal Dimensions of Adjustment in Low-Income Countries,* IMF Occasional Paper No. 95 (Washington: International Monetary Fund).

Nelson, Joan M., 1989, "The Politics of Pro-Poor Adjustment," in *Fragile Coalitions: The Politics of Economic Adjustment,* ed. by Joan M. Nelson (New Brunswick, New Jersey: Transaction Books).

Nowak, Michael, and others, 1996, "Ghana, 1983–91," in *Adjustment for Growth: The African Experience,* ed. by Michael T. Hadjimichael, Michael Nowak, Robert Sharer, and Amor Tahari, IMF Occasional Paper No. 143 (Washington: International Monetary Fund), pp. 22–47.

Nsouli, Saleh M., and others, 1995, *Resilience and Growth Through Sustained Adjustment: The Mo-roccan Experience*, IMF Occasional Paper No. 117 (Washington: International Monetary Fund).

Organisation for Economic Cooperation and Development (OECD), 1990, *Financing and External Debt of Developing Countries: 1989 Survey* (Paris, OECD).

Organization of African Unity, 1986, "Africa's Submission to the Special Session of the United Nations General Assembly on Africa's Economic and Social Crisis, Fifteenth Extraordinary Session of the OAU Council of Ministers, Addis Ababa, March 30–31," United Nations General Assembly document A/AC.229/2 (April 23).

Polak, Jacques J., 1991, *The Changing Nature of IMF Conditionality*, Essays in International Finance, No. 184 (Princeton, New Jersey: International Finance Section, Economics Department, Princeton University).

———, 1995, *The World Bank and the International Monetary Fund: A Changing Relationship* (Washington: Brookings Institution).

Sachs, Jeffrey D., 1989, "Strengthening IMF Programs in Highly Indebted Countries," in *Pulling Together: The International Monetary Fund in a Multipolar World*, ed. by Catherine Gwin and Richard E. Feinberg (New Brunswick, New Jersey: Transaction Books), pp. 101–22.

Schadler, Susan, Franek Rozwadowski, Siddharth Tiwari, and David O. Robinson, 1993, *Economic Adjustment in Low-Income Countries: Experience Under the Enhanced Structural Adjustment Facility*, IMF Occasional Paper No. 106 (Washington: International Monetary Fund).

Sharer, Robert, and Calvin McDonald, 1996, "Uganda, 1987–94," in *Adjustment for Growth: The African Experience*, ed. by Michael T. Hadjimichael, Michael Nowak, Robert Sharer, and Amor Tahari, IMF Occasional Paper No. 143 (Washington: International Monetary Fund), pp. 67–82.

Sidell, Scott R., 1988, *The IMF and Third-World Political Instability: Is There a Connection?* (New York: St. Martin's Press).

Sisson, Charles A., 1986, "Fund-Supported Programs and Income Distribution in LDCs," *Finance & Development*, Vol. 23 (March), pp. 33–36.

Uganda Economic Study Team, 1987, *Economic Adjustment and Long-Term Development in Uganda*, Manuscript Report IDRC-MR166e (Ottawa: International Development Research Centre, November).

United Nations General Assembly, 1986, "United Nations Programme of Action for African Economic Recovery and Development 1986–1990," Annex to United Nations General Assembly document A/S-13/15 (June).

United Nations, Secretary-General, 1987, *Africa: One Year Later*, Report of the Secretary-General on the Economic Crisis in Africa a Year after the U.N. Special Session (New York: United Nations).

15

Extended and Specialized Lending

The IMF's primary purpose in lending to its member countries is to provide short-term balance of payments assistance. The preceding two chapters have described how the Fund's policies evolved to help ensure that borrowers would adjust their policies to restore viability to their economies and external accounts, and how special lending operations were developed to handle the problems of low-income countries. Now the focus shifts to the other special windows that provided assistance in particular circumstances during the 1980s.

First, the Extended Fund Facility (EFF)—the most general of these windows, established in 1974—offered countries the option of longer-term credits. Second, the Compensatory Financing Facility (CFF)—the oldest special window, established in 1963—offered credits to compensate for the effects of temporary fluctuations in the value of exports or imports. The 1988 successor to the CFF, the Compensatory and Contingency Financing Facility (CCFF), also provided incremental financing in case of certain unforeseeable events. Third, the Buffer Stock Financing Facility (BSFF) began in 1969 to offer credits to assist countries participating in specified international arrangements for marketing primary commodities. Fourth, although no separate facility was ever created for the purpose, the Fund has on numerous occasions since the early 1960s provided emergency financing to countries hit by natural disasters. Each of these operations is reviewed in the following sections of this chapter. (For a complete summary of the Fund's lending operations in the 1980s, see Chapter 1, Table 1.1.)

Extended Fund Facility

The EFF was established in 1974 as a vehicle for longer-term lending to countries in need of structural economic reforms. It offered larger credits and longer repayment periods than ordinary stand-by arrangements, but in return it required more stringent commitments to adjust and reform economic policies. The Fund struggled to get the balance right: how much to require and how much to offer in return. As it did so, demand for EFF credits went through some wide cycles.

During the first four years of operation up to the start of the present History (see de Vries, 1985, Chapter 19), the Fund completed just six arrangements through the EFF, accounting for less than 10 percent of total Fund lending in 1975–78 (Fig-

Figure 15.1. Extended Arrangements Approved, 1975–95

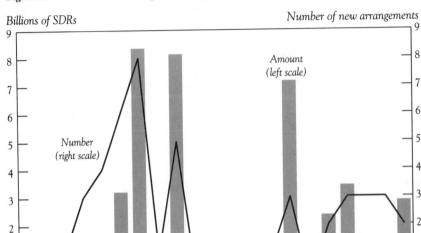

ure 15.1).[1] The next five years (1979–83) were the real heyday of the facility: 24 new arrangements were approved, and more than 40 percent of Fund conditional lending was made through the facility. A fallow period then ensued, with just three new arrangements in more than five years, before the facility was given new life in 1989 as an adjunct to the Brady Plan (Chapter 11).

When the EFF was first established, a typical ordinary stand-by arrangement—which was still intended to be the normal vehicle for the Fund's conditional lending—lasted one year. That is, the country borrowed in quarterly installments spaced over 12 months and committed itself to carrying out specified policy adjustments through that year. The money was to be repaid in quarterly installments beginning after the end of the third year and concluding two years later. EFF programs, in contrast, typically lasted three years, and credits initially were to be fully repaid within eight years (i.e., five years after the end of the program, which normally coincided approximately with the final disbursement). The maximum size of an extended arrangement was larger than for a stand-by arrangement (initially 140 percent of quota rather than 75 per-

---

[1]The amounts graphed in Figure 15.1 represent the initial value of arrangements approved in the indicated year, plus any augmentation of previously approved arrangements. (In 1990, for example, the chart shows that no new arrangements were approved, but a positive amount is shown, which reflects augmentation of two arrangements approved in 1989.) These are gross totals that do not reflect early cancellations or reductions in size. The indicated number of new arrangements does not include three cases in which an existing arrangement was canceled and replaced by a new one covering the remaining period of its predecessor.

cent).[2] The only formal difference in conditionality was that to apply for an extended arrangement, the country had to submit a policy plan for the full three years, but the Fund also expected EFF borrowers to be making structural as well as stabilizing improvements. Charges on credits were the same under both facilities.

The EFF was given a boost in 1979 when the Supplementary Financing or "Witteveen" Facility (SFF) finally came into effect after a long delay (Chapter 17). Although the provisions on the use of the SFF were rather Byzantine, in essence it enabled countries to roughly double the amounts they could borrow by supplementing the Fund's own resources with money borrowed from a group of official creditors. Under a standard three-year EFF arrangement, a country now could borrow up to 280 percent of quota: 140 in "ordinary resources" and 140 in borrowed resources. If the first credit tranche was still available as well, total access could reach 305 percent of quota. (The SFF was available for regular stand-by arrangements as well; in that case, the maximum level of access rose from 100 percent of quota to just over 200 percent.) Just as important, the SFF decision included a "special circumstances" clause under which the Fund could lend even larger amounts, in which case the excess would be funded entirely out of borrowed resources. First informally, and later through an explicit policy, the effective ceiling on access became 450 percent of quota for countries with three-year programs and with no outstanding obligations from earlier stand-by arrangements.

The extra money was a little more expensive, since the interest rate on borrowed resources was equal to the Fund's own borrowing rate plus a markup, and those funds had to be repaid in seven years rather than eight.[3] Nonetheless, potential borrowers now had a greater incentive to formulate the lengthier and more detailed programs that were needed to qualify for extended rather than ordinary stand-by arrangements. Although the resources of the SFF were fully lent out by March 1981, the Fund arranged to borrow a substantial amount of additional money (see Chapter 17) that it used to finance a new "enlarged access" policy, which worked in much the same way as the SFF.

When the Executive Board conducted its second review of the EFF in June 1979, it declined to make any changes in the way the facility operated. Almost immediately afterward, however, the world economy—and many developing countries in particular—suffered a shock when world oil prices were raised sharply by the major exporters. When the Fund's governors convened in Belgrade at the end of September, the Development Committee asked the Executive Board to extend the maximum repayment period from 8 years to 10 and to try to find some means of reducing the cost of supplementary financing. The Interim Committee endorsed the request the next day, and the Board approved the extension to 10 years before

---

[2]In both cases, for a country with no outstanding obligations, an additional 25 percent of quota could be borrowed by drawing on the "first credit tranche." For an introduction to the Fund's "tranche policies," see the Preface. The complex and shifting limits on overall access in relation to quotas resulted from political compromises in the Executive Board. For a detailed review, see Chapter 17.

[3]Beginning in December 1980, low-income countries were eligible to receive a subsidy to reduce or eliminate the excess over the Fund's regular interest rate.

the end of the year. It was not a momentous change, but it did stretch out the average maturity of EFF arrangements by a little over one year.[4]

While the Fund was making the EFF more attractive to borrowers, it also was introducing changes in the rules on ordinary stand-by arrangements that resulted in a blurring of the distinctions between the two. To be eligible for supplementary or enlarged financing, a stand-by arrangement had to be longer than one year and could be as long as three years "in exceptional cases." With that change, a country could obtain a commitment for three years of financing, up to a maximum of at least 165 percent of quota (and possibly as much as under an EFF arrangement), without having to specify a detailed multiyear program of structural adjustment.[5] Although a larger ceiling nominally applied to the EFF, in either case the ceiling could be waived if the Board was prepared to invoke the "special circumstances" clause. In practice, however, the Board approved only three three-year stand-by arrangements: for Turkey, in June 1980 (SDR 1.25 billion, which was 625 percent of the quota that was then in effect and 417 percent of the quota that had been approved to take effect in December; equivalent to $1.7 billion), for Yugoslavia in January 1981 (SDR 1.66 billion, or 400 percent of quota; $2.1 billion), and for Romania in June 1981 (SDR 1.1 billion, or 300 percent of quota; $1.3 billion). Most stand-by arrangements in 1980–81 (the peak period for longer-term stand-by arrangements) provided well under 200 percent of quota. In contrast, for countries borrowing through the EFF, by 1980 nearly all arrangements were for more than 280 percent of quota and several totaled more than 400 percent.[6]

Besides being larger, EFF arrangements were intended to support structural reforms. By the second half of the 1980s, structural reforms also were included in many of the programs supported by ordinary stand-by arrangements, but in the

---

[4]The two committee reports may be found in *Annual Report 1980*, Appendix III. The amendment to the EFF decision is on p. 145 of the same publication. For the original decision on repayments, see de Vries (1985), Vol. 3, p. 505. In addition to making the maximum repayment period 10 years, the amendment provided for repayments to be made at six-month rather than quarterly intervals. For further details, see "Extended Fund Facility—Extension of the Maximum Repurchases Period," SM/79/270 (November 14, 1979) and the minutes of EBM/79/179 (December 3, 1979).

[5]The provisions of the SFF and the enlarged access policy specified a higher ratio of borrowed to ordinary resources for stand-by arrangements than for extended arrangements. Because the seven-year maturity on borrowed resources was higher than the standard maturity on stand-by arrangements but lower than the standard maturity on extended arrangements, these policies lengthened stand-by arrangements and shortened extended arrangements. Under the access rules that were in effect through most of the 1980s, an EFF credit had an average maturity of just under 6 years, compared with just under 5 years for a stand-by arrangement. Without the use of borrowed resources, those figures would have been 7¼ and 4⅛ years, respectively. "Reconsideration of the Extended Fund Facility," EBS/88/7 (January 20, 1988), p. 5.

[6]In 1981, the Fund approved 17 stand-by arrangements, for a total commitment of SDR 4.75 billion ($5.6 billion). Commitments in relation to quota ranged from 25 to 400 percent, with a median of 125 percent. In the same year, the Fund approved 10 EFF arrangements totaling SDR 9.53 billion ($11.2 billion). Those commitments ranged from 213 to 450 percent of quota, with a median of 358 percent.

early 1980s, this special requirement of the EFF was still a distinguishing feature. Sri Lanka, which borrowed SDR 260 million ($325 million; 291 percent of the initial quota) in 1979–81, was a classic example.

For several years prior to 1979, the Sri Lankan economy suffered from serious economic mismanagement characterized by nationalization, an inward-looking development strategy, a highly distorted price system, and extensive subsidization of consumer goods. A new government, headed by J.R. Jayewardene, took power in 1977 and set out to introduce market-oriented reforms. The Fund responded quickly with a one-year stand-by arrangement approved in December 1977, but it was obvious that reforms would have to be introduced and sustained over several years. Consequently, while the stand-by arrangement was in place in 1978, the staff negotiated a three-year extended arrangement aimed specifically at supporting the liberalization of prices and the associated reduction of subsidies. Those reforms were carried out successfully, and—with some delays—the arrangement was fully drawn through 1981.[7]

The role of the EFF in supporting reform was not always so straightforward. One of the more controversial cases was also the largest: the arrangement for Sri Lanka's northern neighbor, India. An examination of this case illustrates the difficulty of setting standards for EFF arrangements that differ enough from conventional stand-by arrangements to warrant running it as a separate facility.

India

The government of India approached the Fund for assistance in November 1980, after a severe drought, the sharp rise in international oil prices, and a generally weak global economy had brought both a sharp setback to the balance of payments and a surge in inflation. When the drought ended, output did not rebound, and the rains thus uncovered the structural weaknesses in the economy, notably bottlenecks in essential industries and in infrastructure. These problems had been masked through much of the 1970s by favorable weather and external conditions. The authorities recognized that the solution lay in a major overhaul of the public investment program, aimed at greatly increasing its efficiency. (See Joshi and Little, 1994, pp. 58–62 and 143–169.) As the government developed its Sixth Five-Year Plan (to cover 1981–85), it decided to supplement its already large use of World Bank resources (then roughly $2 billion a year, of which some 80 percent was in very long-term concessional loans from the International Development Association) with a major macroeconomic adjustment program to be supported by an extended arrangement from the IMF.[8]

---

[7]See "Sri Lanka—Use of Fund Resources—Extended Fund Facility," EBS/79/16 (January 11, 1979) and "Sri Lanka—Mid-Term Review of the Extended Arrangement, 1981," EBS/81/210 (October 20, 1981).

[8]For further background, see memorandum from Tun Thin (Director of the Asian Department) to the Managing Director, and attached draft briefing paper (December 31, 1980); IMF/CF (C/India/810 "Mission, Tun Thin and Staff, January 1981").

The decision to request the use of Fund resources was controversial and highly political in India. The prime minister, Indira Gandhi, was personally active in (and would later become the chairperson of) the Non-Aligned Movement, which was officially opposed to IMF conditionality. Drawing on the Fund would subject her government to criticism from leftist parties in parliament (see Mansingh, 1984, esp. pp. 335–37). The key for overcoming the opposition would be to ensure that the government was not required to alter the economic policies already envisaged under the Five-Year Plan. Officials in the finance ministry and the reserve bank were convinced that the existing Plan was strong enough to meet the Fund's conditions for an extended arrangement, and on that basis, the prime minister gave the go-ahead to enter into secret negotiations. Accordingly, on November 25, 1980, R.N. Malhotra (Secretary for Economic Affairs in the Ministry of Finance) visited the Managing Director at the Fund to signal his country's interest in obtaining a credit arrangement under the EFF.[9]

The requested EFF arrangement was controversial at the Fund as well. India faced enormous structural as well as macroeconomic problems, associated with longstanding traditions of developing indigenous production for domestic consumption, of relying on state enterprises for industrial development, and of shunning the liberalization of policies and markets that was essential for the promotion of international trade.[10] Despite the role of the EFF, a program that was *primarily* structural was still seen in Washington as fundamentally the province of the World Bank, not the IMF. On the macroeconomic side, it was not clear that India had a balance of payments problem that justified drawing on a substantial volume of Fund resources. Because the quota increases envisaged under the Eighth General Review had been delayed (see Chapter 17), those resources were already scarce and would be further squeezed by a program with one of the world's largest developing countries. If India faced a balance of payments need, the Fund was prepared to help finance it, but the case would have to be strong.

Another controversy concerned whether the program, as measured by the performance criteria being imposed, was sufficiently strong to warrant such a large commitment of Fund resources. To a large extent, the Indian government preempted the Fund's conditionality by anticipating the standard requirements for an extended arrangement and incorporating a substantial macroeconomic adjustment

---

[9]IMF/RD, Asian Department file "India—Correspondence, F.O., 1979–1980" (Accession 82/37, Box 2, Section 139); file memorandum by P.R. Narvekar (Deputy Director of the Asian Department).

[10]It is impossible to understand Indian economic policy in the 1970s and 1980s without relating it to the experience of the preceding three centuries. When Mohandas K. Gandhi led India to independence in 1947, a major economic goal was to reverse the trade deficit that had developed under colonial rule by redeveloping traditional labor-intensive trades and industry. Even Adam Smith described the dominant economic role of Britain's East India Company as in direct conflict with India's interests; Erik Erikson described it as "hit-and-run exploitation"; and Jawaharlal Nehru described British economic power in a letter to his daughter, Indira Gandhi, as "the foundation and the basis of the Indian problem of poverty." To Gandhi and his successors, import substitution was an essential means of restoring India's identity as a nation. See Erikson (1969), pp. 268–74.

both in the government budget and in the five-year plan. The staff in the area department were content to develop a program that did little more than require India to carry out its own intentions, but the reviewing staff in some other departments—notably the Exchange and Trade Relations Department (ETR) but also Fiscal Affairs—strenuously objected. ETR staff members in particular insisted on stronger adjustment before they would support the program.[11] Some observers later concluded that the Indian program epitomized the weakness of the Fund's conditionality in that period,[12] while others saw it as a shining example of a government's willingness and ability to design and carry out its own adjustment program. Jacques J. Polak (Executive Director for the Netherlands), for example, concluded later that the "Fund could wish no more than to exercise its leverage with all prospective borrowers in the way it did in the Indian case" (Polak, 1991, p. 13n).

The first negotiating mission went to New Delhi in January 1981, led by Tun Thin, Director of the Asian Department. Because India's proposed program was linked to a detailed capital investment program under the Sixth Plan, the staff consulted extensively with their counterparts in the World Bank before going to India.[13] Subsequently, World Bank staff were asked (exceptionally, for that period) to join the Fund missions and to provide advice on those issues. Because the Fund did not believe that it had either a mandate or the expertise to evaluate some of the main structural measures, the staff deferred to the Bank in that field.

Under the access limits then in effect, India could draw up to SDR 7.7 billion ($9 billion) from the Fund over a three-year period (equivalent to 450 percent of its quota). Of that amount, up to SDR 2.4 billion (140 percent of quota) could be drawn from the Fund's own resources; the remainder would come from borrowed funds. The initial informal request by the authorities was to draw only the portion available from the Fund's own resources, but the staff was concerned that the medium-term outlook for the balance of payments was bleak enough to warrant a larger program.[14] That plan was feasible because India's long run of good years in the 1970s had left it with a quite modest debt burden (less than 15 percent of

---

[11]IMF/CF (C/India/840 "Fund/Bank Mission, Tun Thin and Staff, April 1981"); memorandums from Donald K. Palmer (Deputy Director, ETR) and Richard Goode (Director, Fiscal Affairs Department) to management (both dated May 14, 1981). This relationship between ETR and the area departments was a regular feature of the internal process of evaluating adjustment programs, but the strains were more severe in this case than in most. For an account of the controversy from the ETR perspective, see Finch (1997), pp. 215–16.

[12]In the congressional testimony mentioned below (p. 714), the U.S. Executive Director expressed the concern of his authorities that the program lacked specificity on structural reforms. Joshi and Little (1994, p. 60) described the credit ceilings in the program as "rather generous" and "well within reach." The Executive Director for India, M. Narasimham, took an intermediate view and later wrote that "one cannot say that the Fund was unduly considerate or that India got off lightly" (Narasimham, 1988, p. 72). Many contemporary observers in India, however, viewed the program as a heavy-handed interference with the country's policies. See Gwin (1983) for a balanced assessment of various criticisms of the arrangement.

[13]Memorandum from Tun Thin to the Managing Director (January 15, 1981); IMF/CF (C/India/810 "Mission, Tun Thin and Staff, January 1981").

[14]See p. 9 of the briefing paper for the January 1981 mission (December 31, 1980); IMF/CF (C/India/810 "Mission, Tun Thin and Staff, January 1981").

GDP). Although the requested financial support was not unusually large relative to India's quota, at SDR 5 billion ($6 billion) it was at the time the largest commitment for the use of Fund resources in history.[15]

The starting point for negotiations was that macroeconomic performance was poor and was aggravated by the very closed economic system. Although economic growth was beginning to recover by the time discussions started with the Fund, everyone agreed that production and distribution bottlenecks and bureaucratic rigidities were preventing the Indian economy from living up to its potential. From the beginning, the authorities sought to implement both stabilization and liberalization measures, though the Fund staff pressed for more boldness on both fronts. Because domestic political opposition was strong, the authorities were particularly eager to ensure that the program would be seen as homegrown. On its side, the staff was concerned that reforms be lasting, so that the balance of payments would be sustainable beyond the end of the three-year program period.

Following the first two missions (January and April), several key issues related to the specification of monetary, fiscal, and liberalization measures remained to be resolved before the program could be sent to the Executive Board for approval. Four more negotiating sessions then were held during the spring and summer of 1981. Because of concerns about news leaks on these sensitive negotiations, the meetings were held at various locations outside India: in Libreville (Gabon), Paris, London, and Washington. The atmosphere at these sessions was unusually collegial, reflecting the authorities' commitment to a strong adjustment aimed at avoiding pressures on the balance of payments. Finally, the finance minister, R. Venkataraman, met with the Managing Director, Jacques de Larosière, in Washington just before the 1981 Annual Meetings, and resolved the final outstanding issue, namely the phasing of purchases. Venkataraman then signed and submitted the Letter of Intent on September 28.[16]

Approval of the program by the Board was not to be easy. The amount was large at a time when the Fund's liquidity position was still coming under pressure because of the slow pace of the general quota review. Although India faced a large external deficit, it was a creditworthy country that some Executive Directors felt could have tapped commercial creditors to a greater extent. Also, the program negotiations had brought the Fund more heavily into structural issues than in earlier cases, and some Directors worried that the Fund was financing development rather than helping to correct a balance of payments problem. The Board meeting was scheduled for November 9, 1981, and both de Larosière and the Deputy

---

[15]The arrangement for India held the size record until the Fund approved a 12-month stand-by arrangement for Mexico in February 1995, under which Mexico could draw up to SDR 12.1 billion ($17.9 billion). Over the next four years, the Fund then approved four more arrangements totaling the equivalent of $10 billion or more: for Russia, Indonesia, Korea, and Brazil. As of 1999, the record commitment was a December 1997 stand-by arrangement for Korea totaling SDR 15.5 billion ($21 billion).

[16]See "India—Use of Fund Resources—Extended Fund Facility." EBS/81/198 (October 7, 1981) and Sup. 1 (October 8). Additional information in this paragraph is from background interviews.

Managing Director, William B. Dale, set out to determine the likely degree of support among Directors, through informal meetings and bilateral contacts. Management felt that the nature of the program was appropriate, because the use of EFF resources to promote a specific investment program was seen as essential if the balance of payments was to be sustainable in the longer run. Furthermore, India was planning to obtain substantial additional resources from both commercial and official sources. The Fund was playing a catalytic role as well as providing direct financing.

Curiously, the content of the program—the conditionality—was not especially controversial at the Board meeting. Curious, not only because of the intense internecine battles that accompanied the negotiations but also because the structural elements of the program were at once more detailed than had been customary and yet much less than what was required if India was to break loose from the inward-looking policies of its past. The structural policies described in the arrangement were not specific performance criteria but rather were commitments by the government that were to be reviewed as part of the background for developing the criteria for the second and subsequent years of borrowing. Though that treatment was customary, it did open the door for criticism that the Fund would have little control over the most important elements of the program.

The risks in this process were high, because the Indian government had staked its own prestige on the program, and because the Fund's commitment of resources was so large. In the midst of the effort to line up support within the Board, the staff report was leaked to the Indian press. The reporter indicated that he had obtained a copy from an Executive Director,[17] but an internal investigation at the Fund did not clarify the source. Because of the sensitivity of the information and the delicacy of the negotiations, management regarded this leak as "quite possibly the most serious and damaging . . . in the history of the Fund."[18]

Meanwhile, even the phasing of scheduled drawings had become a political issue, because of concerns that the backloading would be seen as a concession and a sign of weakness on the part of the authorities. The full schedule was not included in the staff report, as it normally would have been, but it was agreed upon separately. Consequently, it became necessary to be sure that everyone understood and agreed.

When the Board met, Richard D. Erb (United States) abstained on the grounds that India did not need as much money as it had requested and could meet its financing needs through borrowing from commercial banks. Other Directors also expressed misgivings. A.R.G. Prowse (Australia), for example, concurred with the United States that there was no real balance of payments need to justify the EFF arrangement. Prowse and others worried that the request was a disguised effort by the authorities to get the Fund to provide medium-term financing for their capital investments. The staff noted, however, that the balance of payments deficit was related to structural imbalances in production and trade and thus qualified for sup-

---

[17]See articles by N. Ram in *The Hindu* (Madras), October 16 through October 21, 1981.
[18]See statement by Dale at EBM/81/133 (October 21, 1981), p. 3.

port under the 1974 EFF decision. That argument carried the day, and the program was approved, with only the United States abstaining.[19]

The U.S. abstention subsequently became a political issue in the United States, as some legislators insisted that the program should have been rejected because of India's commitment to spend $3 billion buying Mirage fighter jets from France. Perhaps piqued because the contract did not go to an American company, they called a hearing in the House of Representatives and asked Erb to testify (see Erb, 1981). Erb insisted in his testimony that military spending was a matter of national sovereignty and was outside the purview of the Fund. That was also the Fund's official position, although the staff was already beginning to view large and rising military spending by countries with serious balance of payments problems as an economic problem. A decade later, such issues would be treated much more openly, and the question of whether such a large increment to the military budget was appropriate when the country was requesting a major use of Fund resources might have been a key issue in the negotiations and the Board's deliberation. At the time, however, India successfully insisted that the purchase be kept out of the picture.

Following the Fund's approval, the Indian government continued to be attacked in parliament for subjecting itself to Fund conditionality. The authorities successfully argued, however, that the EFF arrangement did not impose conditionality at all, because it was fully consistent with the policies that were already incorporated in the Sixth Five-Year Plan. As the prime minister put it in a parliamentary speech that December, the arrangement

> does not force us to borrow, nor shall we borrow unless it is for the national interest. There is absolutely no question of our accepting any programme which is incompatible with our policy, declared and accepted by Parliament. It is inconceivable that anybody should think that we would accept assistance from any external agency which dictates terms which are not in consonance with such policies.[20]

When the Executive Board met a few months later, in April 1982, to conduct the first program review, the program was going well, but the same concerns surfaced that had been raised in November. Erb repeated his view that part of the arrangement should have been put on a contingent basis, to be available only if the balance of payments turned out to be bad enough to warrant it. Robert K. Joyce (Canada) was concerned that there was too little financing from commercial sources. Prowse was worried that there was too much overlap with the Bank. In response, the Managing Director noted the high level of commercial financing, the staff stressed that the Fund relied entirely on the Bank for structural advice, and M. Narasimham (India) argued that reluctance to borrow had not constrained the investment program.[21] In addition to those concerns, Jon Sigurdsson (Iceland) raised the question of whether India could really afford the jets, but he was a decade ahead of time in suggesting that the Fund should concern itself with the viability of mili-

---

[19]Minutes of EBM/81/138–139 (November 9, 1981).
[20]Quoted in Mukherjee (1984), pp. 61–62.
[21]Minutes of EBM/82/48–49 (April 15, 1982).

tary spending. No other Director backed him up when his concerns were criticized by Narasimham, who "was surprised and concerned . . . that the question of India's military expenditures had been raised in the Executive Board. Discussions of such an issue in the Board would open a veritable Pandora's box, and could have significant implications for the Fund's relations with member countries."[22]

The next two reviews (July 1982 and February 1983) went smoothly, as both the balance of payments and economic growth stayed roughly in line with expectations. Much of this success—on both fronts—was attributable to the unexpectedly rapid development of the Bombay High and other offshore oil fields. In addition, the boom in economic development in the nearby oil-exporting regions of the Middle East had spilled over into a boom in workers' remittances in India. More generally, the central bank (the Reserve Bank of India) had quietly shifted to a more flexible exchange rate policy, gradually devaluing the rupee against a basket of currencies without any public announcement or political debate.[23] Otherwise, liberalization was minimal: there were no new takeovers of ailing industries, but also no privatization, and much of the capital investment program was in the hands of state enterprises; some quantitative trade barriers were replaced by tariffs, but the tariffs were set high enough to effectively limit trade; fertilizer prices were raised substantially, but they remained well below economic levels.

India continued to meet all of the performance criteria for the EFF arrangement and to make each drawing on time. The tone of the Board meetings gradually shifted, as the earlier concerns were outweighed more and more by admiration for the success of the adjustment program. By April 1983, when a staff mission visited India to negotiate the third year of the program, economic growth had slowed sharply, but overall the program was still on track and the prospects for a recovery were good. The Executive Board met in July, and although Erb still expressed "major reservations" over the handling of the arrangement, he joined other Directors in supporting it.[24]

By the end of 1983, India had drawn SDR 3.3 billion of the original SDR 5 billion. Another 600 million would become available upon completion of the January 1984 review, and the final 1.1 billion would be subject to negotiation of the fourth year of the program. By that point, however, the authorities were seriously questioning whether they needed the rest of the money. Renouncing it would have several advantages: it would demonstrate both to the population at home and to

---

[22]Minutes of EBM/82/48 (April 15, 1982), pp. 29–30 (Sigurdsson); and EBM/82/49 (same date), p. 15 (Narasimham). The Fund first took a formal position on the role of military spending in national economic policy in October 1991. At that time, Executive Directors concluded that, "as military expenditure can have an important bearing on a member's fiscal policy and external position, information about such expenditure may be necessary to permit a full and internally consistent assessment of the member's economic position and policies" (*Annual Report 1992*, p. 53).

[23]From 1927 until the 1970s, the rupee was pegged to the pound sterling, with one devaluation in 1966 and one effective revaluation when sterling (but not the rupee) was devalued against the dollar in 1967. That link was temporarily abandoned during the turmoil in currency markets in the second half of 1971 and was broken for good in September 1975 when India shifted to the practice of managing the rupee against a basket of currencies without announcing the composition of the basket.

[24]Minutes of EBM/83/108–109 (July 22, 1983).

the world at large that India was in control of its own finances and had undertaken a successful adjustment program; and it would release scarce IMF resources for use by other developing countries. On January 15, 1984, Prime Minister Gandhi announced in a nationwide radio broadcast that the country's balance of payments was now strong enough that the government could forgo the final year's drawings from the Fund. Two weeks later, the Executive Board met for the last time on this issue. The drawing of SDR 600 million was approved, and the Board welcomed India's decision to continue with the adjustment program while forgoing the rest of the money.[25] Finally, on April 6, 1984, Mukherjee wrote to de Larosière requesting cancellation of the arrangement, effective May 1.[26]

Collaboration with the World Bank

The EFF arrangement for India was only one example of how the Fund and the World Bank tried to coordinate their efforts in supporting structural reforms in countries that were borrowing for that purpose from both institutions. From the beginning of EFF lending in 1975, the evaluation of borrowers' longer-term policy plans required Fund staff members to consult frequently with their counterparts in the Bank. The difficulty was to decide just how far to go in deferring to the Bank on structural issues.

In June 1980, as part of a general review of collaboration between the Fund and the Bank (see Chapter 20), the Executive Board agreed that the Fund should continue to look to the Bank for views "on development priorities as reflected in the size and composition of the investment program, recurrent outlays, the efficiency of resource use, and individual pricing decisions."[27] Yet no specific rules or policy governed collaboration on the ground, and no formal distinction was made between the handling of stand-by and extended arrangements.

Through March 1981, in the absence of a general policy, actual practice varied from case to case. During 1980 and the first quarter of 1981, in the context of the Fund's consideration or review of EFF programs for 12 countries, the Bank provided detailed appraisals of investment programs in four cases (Côte d'Ivoire, Honduras, Senegal, and Sudan). In four others, the Bank agreed to provide assessments at a later stage (Guyana, Morocco, Pakistan, and Sierra Leone). In the remaining four cases, the Bank declined to provide an evaluation, either because it was not actively lending to the country or because the government was slow in preparing its investment plans (Dominica, Gabon, Grenada, and Sri Lanka).[28]

The Fund staff was not unhappy with this diversity, because it provided a welcome measure of flexibility. Reviewing the experience with Bank approvals in March 1981, a staff paper concluded as follows: "While there are clear benefits to

---

[25]Minutes of EBM/84/16–17 (January 27, 1984).

[26]Letter of April 6, 1984; IMF/CF (C/India/1791 "Extended Fund Facility, 1984–").

[27]"Fund Collaboration with the Bank in Assisting Member Countries," EBD/80/161 (June 9, 1980), paragraph 5 of Attachment A.

[28]"Progress Report on Fund Collaboration with the Bank in Assisting Member Countries," SM/81/62 (March 19, 1981), p. 6.

be gained by establishing such links [with Bank approval of investment programs], in some cases there may be a need for the Fund staff to adopt a more flexible approach to its operations to take advantage of these benefits." Executive Directors, not surprisingly, had mixed views. In general, creditor countries preferred to require Bank approval as a precondition for EFF arrangements, while borrowers and potential borrowers preferred more flexibility and strongly feared what they perceived as cross-conditionality. At the end of the day, the Managing Director carved out a compromise in which the general rule would be to require only a broad signal from the Bank: "In no case where there is an investment program should we engage in an extended arrangement without having an indication from the World Bank that the thrust of the investment program is in the right direction." In specific cases, however, a stronger and more specific endorsement would be required:

> Another case is one in which a country, generally a small country, has a very large project that really dominates the scene—a big hydroelectric project or very large public works project, for example. I think in that case, if we want to enter into an extended arrangement, we have to have an indication from World Bank experts that this very heavy investment seems appropriate.

Although the reference to a "small country" with a "big project" was intended as a general reference to the dependence of narrowly based economies on the success of single capital investments, the injunction closely followed and had a major impact on an application from one country in particular.

Grenada

The requirement that the World Bank certify a country's investment program created special problems when the Bank was not one of the country's creditors. In such cases, the Bank was being asked to put its own credibility at risk without any direct financial or other incentive to do so. A particularly acute problem arose in the early 1980s when this general difficulty collided against the geopolitical interests of a powerful member country. The World Bank at the time was not heavily involved with direct lending to the small island countries in the Eastern Caribbean; when Grenada applied for an EFF arrangement in 1980, it ran into unexpected problems. Although those problems were unique, the Fund's difficulties in responding to them illustrate the complexities of running a program that requires close collaboration between the two Bretton Woods institutions.

Grenada—the southern tip of the Windward Islands, a tiny country with a population of not much more than 100,000—had been a member of the Fund only since 1975, the year after it obtained its independence from the United Kingdom. Within a year, Grenada took out two stand-by arrangements within its first credit tranche and drew twice on the Oil Facility.[29] Beginning in 1977, Grenada also bor-

---

[29]Total indebtedness from this activity amounted to SDR 1.2 million (61 percent of quota; $1.4 million), of which SDR 0.5 million ($0.6 million) was through the Oil Facility. Under the tranche policies then in effect, the non-oil drawings (36.5 percent of quota) all counted as the first credit tranche. For footnote lovers only: the second stand-by arrangement, for SDR 225,000 ($260,000) in June 1976, was the smallest ever granted by the Fund.

rowed from the Trust Fund. In March 1979, the government that had assumed power with independence in 1974 was overthrown by the New Jewel Movement, which formed the People's Revolutionary Government. The new authorities soon applied for a stand-by arrangement (still within the first credit tranche), which the Executive Board approved in November 1979. Two developments then led the government to request more substantial support from the Fund. First, a series of major storms produced severe crop damage, especially to major export commodities such as bananas and cocoa. Second, in a bid to boost tourism, the government decided to implement a long-standing plan to build a new airport capable of handling modern passenger jets. In November 1980, a staff team headed by Samuel J. Stephens (Deputy Chief of the Caribbean Division in the Western Hemisphere Department) headed for Grenada's capital, St. George's, to negotiate terms for an EFF arrangement.

The main complication in the negotiations was that Grenada's balance of payments problem was unusual, in that it stemmed entirely from a planned increase in capital expenditures associated in substantial part with the proposed new airport. Although the EFF arrangement would not be linked directly to any project, the Fund was in effect being asked to finance Grenada's development plan. If the request had been made several years later, it might have been treated favorably as an example of "growth-oriented adjustment"; in 1980 (even accepting the economic justification of the airport), it was well ahead of its time. Nonetheless, both the staff and management readily approved the request. Although the program was considered "ambitious and unusual,"[30] the request was only for 140 percent of Grenada's modest quota,[31] and it appeared that the Fund's support could assist a troubled economy at a critical juncture. The staff report was circulated to Executive Directors, and a Board meeting was scheduled for March 27, 1981.

De Larosière's approval masked a nagging concern about the absence of an endorsement from the World Bank, which he regarded as "particularly important" in view of the central role of capital formation in the Grenada program.[32] In fact he signed off on sending the request to the Board only after he received assurances from the staff that the Bank's reticence was purely technical and only on the condition that the staff report be amended to include an explicit statement on the Bank's position. The added statement read, ". . . the World Bank is not yet in a position to endorse the investment program, and it has indicated that Grenada would

---

[30]Cover note by the Deputy Managing Director, William B. Dale, forwarding the staff report to the Managing Director (March 2, 1981); IMF/RD Managing Director file "Grenada, 1980–1981" (Accession 83/89, Box 1, Section 378).

[31]The rules in effect at the time permitted EFF arrangements for as much as 300 percent of quota. The interest rate, however, was higher for arrangements in excess of 140 percent, because they had to be financed partly with borrowed resources. (A subsidy scheme to alleviate the burden had been approved but was not yet operational; see Chapter 17.) The Grenadian authorities therefore decided to limit their request to the amount that could be financed entirely from the Fund's own resources.

[32]Handwritten note by the Managing Director, on the March 2 cover note referenced in footnote 30.

need to prepare a comprehensive technical and financial feasibility study of the airport complex to provide the basis for such an endorsement." After the paper was issued, the Bank staff requested—and the Fund staff and management agreed—that this sentence be strengthened. The new version, which was not circulated for the reason explained below, was to read, "The program . . . does not carry the endorsement of the World Bank, mainly because the [investment] program is dominated by a project [the airport], which, according to the information available to the Bank, was undertaken without the benefit of a technical, economic, and financial feasibility study."[33] That wording certainly would have raised eyebrows and probably would have killed the request if it had been presented to the Board.

Three days before the Board meeting, the Alternate Executive Director for the United States, Donald E. Syvrud,[34] asked management to withdraw the Grenadian request from the agenda, principally because the World Bank had not indicated its approval of the country's investment program.[35] De Larosière now realized that the Bank's reticence could not be papered over, and he consented to Syvrud's request. At first, the meeting was merely to be postponed, and the staff were divided on whether to try to resuscitate the proposal. Within a few days, however, the Managing Director decided not to go ahead with the EFF arrangement but to try to persuade the authorities to accept a 12-month stand-by arrangement for a smaller amount (i.e., smaller than the first year of the abandoned three-year program).

The Grenadian authorities reacted with bitter vehemence. The finance minister, Bernard Coard, threatened to take his request directly to the Interim Committee and even to withdraw from Fund membership if the EFF arrangement was not eventually approved. Stephens was hastily dispatched to St. George's with a personal message from de Larosière, and a compromise was soon reached under which the full amount of the original first-year program would be approved (the equivalent of 76 percent of Grenada's quota), but only as a 12-month stand-by arrangement. The Executive Board then met on May 11 and approved the request over the objections of the United States.[36] De Larosière and Coard met 10 days later in Libreville, Gabon, in the margins of the Interim Committee meeting. Afterward, Coard—a U.S.-educated and highly competent economic manager but an advocate of extreme leftist political views—held a press conference to say that his quarrel was not with the Fund: it was with the United States, for politicizing the institution.

---

[33]The staff report, as circulated, was "Grenada—Use of Fund Resources—First Credit Tranche, and Request for Extended Arrangement," EBS/81/55 (March 13, 1981). The first revision was based on a March 11 memorandum from Sterie T. Beza to the Managing Director; the intended second revision was to be based on a March 25 memorandum from Walter E. Robichek to the Managing Director; IMF/RD Managing Director file "Grenada, 1980–1981" (Accession 83/89, Box 1, Section 378).

[34] The Executive Director position was vacant. Sam Cross had resigned in January, and Richard Erb did not take up the position until July.

[35]Syvrud's oral request was made privately, but he later explained his rationale at EBM/81/79 (May 11, 1981).

[36]Minutes of EBM/81/79 (May 11, 1981).

This contretemps would have signified little had it not been a gambit in a much larger game. At the same time that the U.S. authorities were asking the Fund to withhold the EFF arrangement from Grenada, they were asking the European Communities not to provide financial support for the airport. The airport itself had little relevance for the Fund (and none at all for the World Bank), because most of its cost was being paid for by foreign grants. Those grants, however, were coming not only from the former colonial power (Great Britain), its European allies, and Grenada's closest mainland neighbor (Venezuela), but also from such nontraditional and far-flung benefactors as Cuba (which also was providing much of the labor), Iraq, Libya, and Syria. The source of financing was of no matter to the Fund, but it was to the U.S. government. Building an international airport as a foundation for tourism had been a Grenadian goal since before independence, but the U.S. administration in 1981 saw it as a potential base for Cuban military intervention in Angola, Ethiopia, and possibly in the Western Hemisphere.

The final drawing under the stand-by arrangement was eventually disallowed when no agreement could be reached on fiscal targets for the first quarter of 1982. Negotiations on a replacement program then dragged on throughout 1982. The World Bank continued to refuse to endorse the investment program, and Coard continued to press the case that Grenada was being subjected inappropriately to cross-conditionality between the two Bretton Woods institutions. Finally, after several negotiating sessions in St. George's and in Washington, agreement was reached on a three-year EFF arrangement for SDR 13.5 million ($14 million, or 300 percent of quota). Erb opposed the request at the August 24 Board meeting, and he was joined by three other Directors: from Germany, the United Kingdom, and the Netherlands. The Dutch Alternate Director, Tom de Vries, argued that the economic program was too weak to justify such large and extended support, and he moved to amend the proposal by again substituting a one-year arrangement. The majority of the Board, however, approved the full EFF arrangement.[37]

Tragically, Grenada was to make only one drawing under the EFF. On October 19, 1983, while a Fund mission was in St. George's reviewing implementation of the program, the government was overthrown in a violent coup aimed at installing Coard as prime minister. The Organization of Eastern Caribbean States, fearing that the coup would advance expansionist plans of the Soviet Union and Cuba in the region, asked the United States to intervene militarily. Despite widespread pleas to the contrary, including from the British government,[38] President Reagan sent U.S. forces to invade Grenada on October 25—the day after the Fund mission was finally evacuated. Coard and other coup leaders were captured and imprisoned. The new government would face massive rebuilding problems, and for now the Fund had no alternative but to cancel the EFF arrangement and wait for better times.

---

[37]Minutes of EBM/83/121–122 (August 24, 1983).
[38]See Thatcher (1993), pp. 328–33, for the British perspective.

Death and Rebirth of the EFF

No sooner had the Fund begun to succeed in encouraging countries to take advantage of the larger and longer-term resources of the EFF than it began to have second thoughts. As early as 1980, the staff expressed concerns that programs were being approved in cases where the authorities had done no more than the minimum to correct the course of economic policy and had not developed a plan to revitalize growth over the longer term. For the January 1981 review of the operation of the facility, the staff proposed—and the Board agreed—that the criteria for qualifying for an EFF arrangement should be applied more rigorously: countries should be required to put forward a "program with a clearly delineated adjustment path for a medium-term period."[39] That injunction had little direct impact, first because several extended arrangements were already in the pipeline and later because the international debt crisis made large extended arrangements essential, especially for the two most heavily indebted countries, Brazil and Mexico. (As discussed in Chapter 9, Argentina—the third largest—could not develop a medium-term program because it was in the middle of a transition from military to democratic rule.) After 1983, however, the Fund began scrutinizing potential EFF cases much more closely, and few countries were willing even to consider asking for extended arrangements. One-year stand-by arrangements again became the norm, even if they had to be repeated annually to enable borrowers to cope with deep-seated problems. During a period of nearly five years, between September 1983 and June 1988, the Fund approved only two extended arrangements: for Chile, in August 1985, and for Ghana, in November 1987.

Throughout the middle 1980s, the prevailing view in the Fund (and outside; see Killick, 1984, pp. 209–10) was that the EFF had little if any role to play. The gradual liberalization of access terms for stand-by arrangements had given countries a continuum of options, ranging right up to the three-year programs and large size of EFF arrangements. As the economic policy programs supported by stand-by arrangements became more structural and as the specification of medium-term objectives and plans became more nearly universal, the distinction between stand-by and extended arrangements became difficult to discern. The 1985 EFF arrangement for Chile was based on a quite standard set of policy intentions designed to "reduce the external current account deficit, achieve moderate economic growth, and lower inflation."[40] Moreover, low-income countries—a major segment of the original target clientele for the facility—now had a much more attractive alternative in the Fund's concessional lending arms, the structural adjustment and enhanced structural adjustment facilities (SAF and ESAF). As explained in Chapter 14, the EFF arrangement for Ghana was canceled after its first year and replaced by an ESAF arrangement on more favorable terms.

---

[39]"Review of the Extended Fund Facility," SM/80/278 (December 29, 1980), p. 19.

[40]"Chile—Staff Report for the 1985 Article IV Consultation and Request for an Extended Arrangement," EBS/85/122 (May 13, 1985), p. 14.

What breathed new life into the EFF was the need to resuscitate the international debt strategy in 1988. By then, the 1985 Baker Plan had failed, and the Fund was searching for a means to promote growth more seriously in heavily indebted countries. It was still too early to deal directly with the huge stock of outstanding debt, but the time had come for one last effort to find a way for countries to grow out of their debt.

The Executive Board agonized over whether and how to revitalize the EFF, holding four days of meetings on the subject during the first half of 1988.[41] If the facility still had a role, it had two aspects: credits should be larger than those available under ordinary stand-by arrangements, and programs should include deeper structural reforms. The first dimension raised questions of financial prudence, and the second raised questions of the Fund's mandate and competency. Finally, the Board agreed to make three modest changes, which taken together would carve out a niche for new extended arrangements.

First, the Board agreed informally to approve somewhat larger credits within the existing access limits. The two EFF arrangements approved in the preceding five years had been small in relation to the maximum credits the Fund could have extended, and everyone agreed that this trend should be reversed. However, the Board rejected a management proposal to raise the access limits. Arguing for an increase in the three-year ceiling from 270 percent of quota to 330 percent, the Managing Director, Michel Camdessus, noted that net lending by the Fund had been negative for the past two years. Continuing that pattern would not be "an appropriate stance for the Fund at this juncture," and the most effective way to reverse it would be to raise the ceilings.[42] Directors generally accepted the goal but preferred to be cautious in pursuing it.

Second, the Board agreed that countries could get a fourth year of access. The Board still would approve only three-year credits, but once a track record was established, the borrower could apply for an extension.[43] This change introduced two types of flexibility. In one case, if a program went temporarily off track and disbursements were delayed, the original arrangement could be stretched into a fourth year to allow the country to make all of the scheduled drawings. In another, if a reform program was going well, the borrower could apply to augment the original arrangement, with additional drawings in the fourth year. To satisfy Directors who were worried that augmentation requests might get out of hand, this change was linked to the decision mentioned above not to raise the access limits. In other

---

[41]Minutes of EBM/88/23–24 (February 22, 1988), EBM/88/46–47 (March 24, 1988), IS/88/1 (March 31, 1988), and EBM/88/89 (June 6, 1988).

[42]Minutes of EBM/88/46 (March 24, 1988), p. 4. For background on the issue, see "Reconsideration of the Extended Fund Facility," EBS/88/7 (January 20, 1988), pp. 16–17. For a table showing actual access in EFF arrangements through 1987, see "Reconsideration of the Extended Fund Facility—Selected Aspects of the Experience with Extended Arrangements," EBS/88/7, Sup. 1 (January 27, 1988), p. 13.

[43]The staff proposal was to allow initial approval of four-year programs. When several Directors objected, the idea of allowing extensions emerged as a compromise. See "Reconsideration of the Extended Fund Facility," EBS/88/7 (January 20, 1988), pp. 12–14.

words, countries could get an extra year's money a little more easily than before, but the cumulative ceiling on how much they could borrow was unchanged.

Third, the Board changed the "mixing ratio" that specified how much of an arrangement was from borrowed rather than the Fund's own resources to make EFF credits a little less expensive. Instead of lending equal amounts of own and borrowed resources up to 280 percent of quota, the Fund would first lend up to 140 percent using its own resources before the borrowed money would kick in.[44] Since the borrowed resources carried a higher interest rate and had to be repaid more quickly, the total cost of servicing the credit was expected to fall. In the event, however, a subsequent drop in the cost of the Fund's borrowings pushed the rate charged on borrowed resources below the Fund's own rate of charge, so the intent of this change was frustrated.

Not surprisingly, this minor liberalization did not immediately lead to a long queue of applications. For all of 1988, only one new EFF arrangement was approved. In July, the Board agreed to lend Tunisia SDR 207.3 million ($270 million; 150 percent of quota), an amount that eventually was fully drawn over four years. The real revitalization came in the spring of 1989, when the Fund sprung into action to support the Brady Plan. To qualify for the extra funds dedicated to paying for debt reduction, borrowers had to submit a medium-term reform program under the terms of the EFF. As recounted in Chapter 11, the Board approved three EFF arrangements (to Mexico, the Philippines, and Venezuela) in quick succession in May and June, totaling SDR 7.2 billion ($9 billion). Two of the three later were augmented and extended into a fourth year, and the Fund's total commitment under the three arrangements rose to SDR 8.2 billion. (Of that, SDR 1.9 billion was earmarked for debt reduction.)

Throughout the next several years, the EFF was a moderately active facility for Fund lending, partly because of a continuing flow of Brady deals and partly because of an increased willingness by many developing countries to commit themselves to longer-term policy programs. From May 1989 through April 1996, the Fund approved 19 new EFF arrangements (10 percent of total arrangements) for a total commitment of SDR 25.2 billion (36 percent of total commitments). For most of that time, until the large stand-by arrangements for Mexico and Russia took effect in 1995–96, credit outstanding under EFF arrangements averaged about one-third of the total stock of Fund credit. The EFF had had a bumpy ride through its first two decades, but it finally had found its place in the Fund's arsenal.

Compensatory and Contingency Financing

When the Compensatory Financing Facility (CFF) was established in 1963, it was an important and controversial response to a serious economic problem that afflicted many countries in almost every region of the globe. A 1960 staff study

---

[44]This change also was a compromise. The original staff proposal was to raise the access limit on the Fund's own resources to 200 percent of quota.

confirmed what many observers had long suspected: for the developing world, fluctuations in the prices of primary commodities were a particularly large and intractable source of the current account deficits that led them to seek the Fund's financial assistance. Specifically, the staff found that commodity prices had a higher variance than industrial prices and that countries whose exports were predominantly commodities experienced greater fluctuations in their current account balances than did countries with diversified or heavily industrial exports. A case therefore could be made that temporary financing to compensate for these fluctuations would be more appropriate than requiring countries to tighten their belts and wait for better times.

After lengthy soul-searching over the wisdom of weakening the institution's conditionality, the Fund responded by establishing special procedures for providing larger credits and making arrangements easier to obtain for countries facing a temporary shortfall in export revenues because of circumstances beyond their control.[45] As originally designed, the CFF enabled arrangements to be larger by giving borrowers access to more than 100 percent of their quota (for regular and CFF credits in the aggregate), although only 25 percent of quota could be in this form. Moreover, it provided both for faster consideration of requests than under the procedures for stand-by arrangements, with lower conditionality, and for immediate rather than phased disbursements. The Fund, however, explicitly rejected proposals to make access to the facility automatic for countries with export shortfalls.[46]

By the 1990s, after thirty years of experience and many revisions, the CFF had become the Compensatory and Contingency Financing Facility (CCFF) but essentially had been stripped of its usefulness. Jacques Polak, who as an Executive Director in the 1980s had fought to retain a role for the facility, concluded in 1991 that it "is only a slight exaggeration . . . to say that the CFF has ceased to exist as a special facility in the Fund" (Polak, 1991, p. 10). At the apex of CFF activity in FY 1983, 29 countries drew a total of SDR 3.7 billion ($4.1 billion; 36 percent of all lending from the Fund's general accounts). Usage then dropped off sharply (Figure 15.2). By 1989–90, only three countries drew on the facility, borrowing SDR 0.8 billion ($1.1 billion; 18 percent of the total).

A smoothed sketch of the rocky history of the CFF shows that from 1966 through 1979, the facility was gradually liberalized until it became a major channel for Fund lending. In 1983, concerns about the overall weakness of the Fund's conditionality led Executive Directors to toughen conditions for compensatory financing quite severely. Beginning in 1988, various changes were introduced at the margin that were intended to resuscitate the facility but did not succeed.

---

[45]Although the intention was to provide credits to exporters of primary commodities, the facility covered overall shortfalls in revenues from the export of primary or manufactured goods.

[46]For the background on the creation of the facility, see Horsefield (1969), Vol. 1, pp. 531–36, and Vol. 2, pp. 417–27. The Executive Board Decision establishing the facility is reproduced in Vol. 3, pp. 238–40. The motivating staff study was published in *IMF Staff Studies*, Vol. 8 (November 1960), pp. 1–76. For a firsthand recollection of the political negotiations preceding the creation of the facility, in which the United States decided to support a proposal that was opposed by European governments, see Dale (1994), pp. 20–21.

Figure 15.2. CFF and CCFF: Drawings, 1964–96

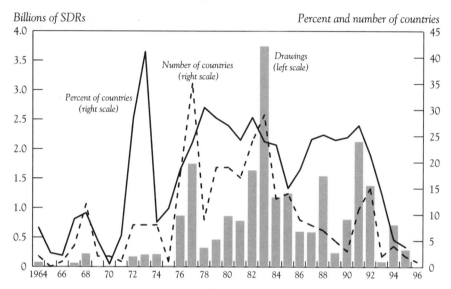

Billions of SDRs   *Percent and number of countries*

Note: Percent of countries is a three-year moving average.

Liberalization, 1966–79

During the first three years after the CFF was established, only three countries took advantage of it. Demand was limited because most commodity prices were strong in the mid-1960s, but potential borrowers also were discouraged by the lending limits. In anticipation of a growing potential demand, the Executive Board liberalized the facility in September 1966 by doubling the cumulative lending limit from 25 percent of quota to 50 percent and by creating the principle of "floating" access. "Floating" meant that borrowing on this facility was treated as independent from borrowings under the Fund's ordinary tranche policies. Before the change, a country with no previously outstanding obligations that borrowed the equivalent of 25 percent of its quota under the CFF rules would then have been subject to full conditionality if it wanted to borrow any more from the Fund. After the change, it could borrow another 25 percent through the CFF *and* would still have its first credit tranche available for a regular low-conditionality arrangement.[47]

From the beginning, the biggest concern of CFF skeptics was that countries that needed to tighten their macroeconomic policies would postpone the inevitable adjustment by relying on compensatory financing from the Fund. That concern was recognized in the official report that the Executive Board approved when it estab-

---

[47]Similarly, if the country had not drawn against its gold tranche, it could borrow through the CFF while leaving its gold tranche intact. The 50 percent limit on cumulative outstanding obligations under the CFF was combined with a 25 percent limitation on drawings in any 12-month period, and the second 25 percent was subjected to a higher level of conditionality. For a more detailed discussion of the 1966 liberalization, see de Vries (1976), Vol. 1, pp. 261–68.

lished the facility in 1963. The report argued that temporary export shortfalls and policy inadequacies were independent phenomena, either of which could lead to a balance of payments problem. The new facility would deal with the former, while the Fund's general tranche policies would continue to deal with the latter. However, *any* proposed drawing, including a CFF credit, that would take the country's obligations above the first credit tranche would trigger an evaluation by the Fund "that a sound set of policies is being followed" (Horsefield, 1969, Vol. 3, p. 447). In other words, the CFF was not to be used to avoid Fund conditionality. Operationally, the rule was that a borrower was expected to "cooperate with the Fund in an effort to find, where required, appropriate solutions for its balance of payments difficulties" (Horsefield, 1969, Vol. 3, p. 239).

When the facility was liberalized in 1966, an additional requirement was introduced for CFF credits above 25 percent of quota. Besides the expectation that the country would cooperate in finding a solution to its problems, the Fund now had to determine that a borrower had already met the test of cooperation with respect to its earlier credits (de Vries, 1976, Vol. 2, p. 199). That is, when a country requested a CFF credit equivalent to 25 percent of its quota, the Fund might ask the authorities to submit a statement of intentions on how they proposed to adjust their macroeconomic policies to put the balance of payments on a sustainable course. If the country requested a second CFF credit a year or so later, the Fund would review the extent to which those policy intentions had been carried out before approving the request.

The 1966 changes stimulated usage of the CFF, even in periods when primary commodity prices were not especially weak. During the 1972–74 boom in commodity prices, more than 40 percent of all Fund lending was to compensate for calculated temporary shortfalls in commodity export receipts.[48] When commodity prices declined anew in 1975, the Fund again turned its attention to a liberalization of the CFF as a way to provide quick but targeted assistance to afflicted countries. In December of that year, the Executive Board agreed to raise the lending limit again, to 50 percent of quota in any year and 75 percent cumulatively; and to introduce some technical modifications designed to cut the lag between a drop in export revenues and the Fund's approval of a credit.[49] These apparently minor changes ushered in a liberality of application that produced an explosion of borrowings over the next two years. Then, in 1978 and 1979, usage dropped off again, owing principally to a renewed cyclical rise in commodity prices.

---

[48]This anomaly resulted partly from the inevitable lag between the actual shortfall and the approval of the credit, and partly from declines in certain commodity prices even while others were rising. The three largest CFF credits in 1972–74 were to Argentina, Bangladesh, and India, which together accounted for nearly one-third of the total. The March 1972 Argentine credit compensated for shortfalls in beef and wheat exports during 1971, which resulted from normal cyclical shifts in production and from adverse weather conditions. The December 1972 credit to Bangladesh compensated for a drop in jute exports during the 12 months through June 1972, which resulted from floods, cyclones, and the 1971 war of independence. The February 1974 credit to India compensated for an overall shortfall in a wide range of exports in the year through mid-1973, some of which (notably jute products) had declined in price during the general boom period.

[49]For the details of the 1975 changes, see de Vries (1985), pp. 399–413.

The third major liberalization came in 1979, at a time when oil-importing developing countries were reeling from the opening moves in the second oil shock. In fact, for several years the governments of concerned industrial countries had been advancing a variety of proposals to compensate developing countries more fully for unavoidable shocks to commodity prices or volumes. In September 1975, the U.S. government tabled a proposal to subsidize CFF credits for low-income countries and to dedicate a portion of Trust Fund resources to compensate eligible countries for declines in the prices of specific commodities. In March 1977, the Swedish government made a similar proposal and suggested somewhat broader coverage. In September 1978, the German government suggested establishing a separate loan fund (outside the IMF) to stabilize developing countries' aggregate earnings from primary commodities and to subsidize loans for the poorest countries.[50] The thrust of these proposals was endorsed by the Group of 77 developing countries and by the Development Committee, and the United Nations Conference on Trade and Development (UNCTAD) initiated a work program aimed at establishing a separate fund along the lines of the German proposal. The Fund staff then responded with a scheme to achieve the basic objectives within the IMF by further expanding the role of the CFF.

As often happens, the staff proposals focused on arcane technical issues, while the effects of the proposed changes had major economic and political implications. The issues included whether to use geometric rather than arithmetic averages of yearly data to calculate temporary shortfalls and whether to make a separate calculation of shortfalls on a list of specified commodities. Though technical in nature, both issues affected whether credits would go primarily to low- or middle-income countries.[51] Several Executive Directors reacted quite negatively and with unusual vehemence to the proposed changes. Robert J. Whitelaw, whose country (Australia) had borrowed the most money from the CFF up to that time but stood to lose under the proposed revisions, suggested that "the staff had ridden rather roughshod over some basic Fund principles" in trying to skew the calculations in

---

[50]The U.S. proposal was introduced at the Fund by the U.S. Executive Director, Sam Y. Cross, during the 1975 CFF review. The Swedish proposal was circulated as a Working Paper of the Royal Ministry of Foreign Affairs (March 31, 1977). The German proposal was circulated as a background paper for the Development Committee meeting of September 6–7, 1978. For summaries of all three proposals, see "Possible Changes in the Compensatory Financing Facility—Annexes I, II, and III," SM/79/24, Sup. 1 (January 23, 1979). The German proposal was circulated at the Fund as "Stabilization of Export Earnings," EBS/78/506 (September 13, 1978).

[51]The basic methodology for calculating a shortfall was to compare merchandise export revenues in the base year with a computed five-year trend, using forecasts for the future years. With an arithmetic average, the trend value was $\bar{X} = (\sum X_i)/5$, $i = t-2, \ldots t+2$. The geometric average used logarithms instead of levels. (For more detailed calculations, see Appendix I to this chapter.) The rationale for using logarithms was that if merchandise export revenues grew at a constant percentage rate, the revised methodology would show a zero shortfall from the calculated trend, whereas the arithmetic average would lie below the calculated trend. Empirically, export revenues for low-income countries tended to have relatively high cyclical rather than trend components. Consequently, switching from arithmetic to geometric averaging would reduce calculated shortfalls more for middle-income (trend-dominant) countries than for low-income (cycle-dominant) countries. For an explanation and illustrative calculations, see "Possible Changes in the Compensatory Financing Facility—A Preliminary Paper," SM/79/24 (January 19, 1979), pp. 6–8.

favor of developing countries. H. Onno Ruding (Netherlands) complained that the staff proposals "would lead to a deliberately arbitrary, discriminatory and unfair shift in eligibility." He favored providing additional support for low-income countries, but not by taking it away from middle-income developing countries.[52]

The Board met several times on these issues from February through April 1979, without resolution. Similarly, an UNCTAD meeting in Manila in May produced no consensus on whether a separate compensatory fund should be established independently from the IMF: an outcome that both the Fund staff and most industrial country governments were quite happy to avoid.[53] Finally, the Executive Board decided in August to keep the basic structure and operation of the CFF unchanged but to liberalize the access rules further. Once again, the lending limits were raised: from 75 to 100 percent of quota, with no sublimit on annual access (previously 50 percent).[54] Moreover, for the first time applicants were permitted to include declines in tourism revenues and in workers' remittances in calculating the shortfall.[55] That change helped several (mostly small) countries to qualify for credits despite a lack of dependence on exporting primary commodities. To improve the timeliness of CFF credits, the Board authorized the staff to use estimated data for calculating shortfalls, with the proviso that drawings would have to be promptly repurchased if the estimates turned out to have been overstated.[56] These various expansions were to be

---

[52]Minutes of EBM/79/18 (February 6, 1979), pp. 3 (Whitelaw) and 9–10 (Ruding).

[53]Two other compensatory funds already existed, aside from the CFF: STABEX, administered by the European Economic Community since 1975, and a scheme established by the Arab Monetary Fund in 1978 to provide financing for its members as a supplement to the CFF.

[54]Gradually increasing the lending limit from 25 percent of quota in 1963 to 100 percent in 1979 did not result in an equally large increase in the portion of export shortfalls compensated by CFF credits, mainly because quotas grew less rapidly than world trade and many countries remained constrained by the ceilings. With the 75 percent quota limit in effect for 1976–79, countries borrowing through the CFF were compensated on average for approximately 50 percent of their calculated export shortfall. With the higher limit in place in 1980–82, the compensation ratio rose to a little over 60 percent. For the 1976–82 compensation ratios, see "Compensatory Financing Facility and Buffer Stock Financing Facility—Review of Experience with Financing Fluctuations in the Cost of Cereal Imports and Selective Policy Issues," SM/83/131 (June 16, 1983), p. 14, fn. 2.

[55]To prevent countries from using data selectively to overstate the case for compensation, this decision specified that if a country chose to include tourism or worker's remittances, it had to continue to do so for the next five years. For the full text of the decision, see *Annual Report 1980*, pp. 136–38.

[56]The general early-repurchase requirement was introduced in 1975, as part of a reform that permitted borrowers to use estimated data for up to six months of the "shortfall year" for export revenues. See de Vries (1985), pp. 409–10. Throughout the 1980s, with the aid of estimated data, some 85 percent of CFF credits were approved within six months of the initial request. In several instances, countries were asked to repay part of the principal early on the basis of revised data. In most cases, that process worked without difficulty. The few exceptions involved countries that were experiencing difficulties staying current on their obligations to the Fund. Notably, in August 1981, the Fund determined that Sudan had to make an early repayment on a CFF drawing, but Sudan asked for a delay on the grounds that it lacked the money. The Managing Director proposed to reschedule the repayment over a period of 2–4 years, subject to lapse-of-time approval by the Executive Board. Ariel Buira (Mexico) objected that the Fund had never before rescheduled an overcompensation repayment, and he called for a meeting. The Board met in October to discuss the proposal and decided to allow only a six-month delay. No general policy was ever formulated on overcompensation delays, because the CFF decision did not give rise to a legal

partially offset by acceptance of the staff recommendation to switch to geometric averaging, which most believed would help to weed out inappropriate credits.

With the extension of the upper lending limit to 100 percent of quota, the Board retained 50 percent as the limit for the "lower tranche," beyond which an applicant would have to demonstrate that it had been cooperating with the Fund to find a solution for its balance of payments problems. In most such cases, the experience had been that countries with that large a problem also had stand-by arrangements in effect, which provided a ready test of cooperation. In the few exceptions, the staff was satisfied that the country could have qualified for a stand-by arrangement at least in the first credit tranche. Therefore, the staff proposed in 1978 that the Fund adopt that standard—first credit tranche conditionality—as a formal test for access to the "upper tranche" of the CFF. Executive Directors, however, rejected that idea as too rigid: if the purpose of the CFF was to compensate for export fluctuations, then the facility should be administered flexibly, and a formal conditionality test would unnecessarily complicate the evaluation of requests.[57]

Throughout the life of the CFF, the Fund applied a liberal interpretation of the condition that an export shortfall must arise largely from "circumstances beyond the control of" the authorities. Political disturbances and wars were obviously matters that the authorities could control, but often only if they were prepared to sacrifice social and political objectives. In April 1982, the Fund acknowledged and reaffirmed that "the question whether a political disturbance could have been avoided is one that the Fund does not address in its relations with members, and consequently, the practice has been to regard shortfalls resulting from such disturbances as being outside the control of the member." This agreement effectively prevented opponents from objecting to CFF requests such as that of Argentina after the war with the United Kingdom, as discussed in Chapter 8.[58]

---

obligation for borrowers to make early repayments. On the Sudan case, see "Sudan—Compensatory Financing Facility—Repurchase under Paragraph 7 of the 1979 Decision" EBS/81/166 (August 7, 1981); "Sudan—Rescheduling of Repurchase," EBS/81/208 (October 19, 1981); and minutes of EBM/81/134–135 (October 30). Additional background materials may be found in IMF/CF (C/Sudan/1750 "Repurchase Obligations, 1979–1984") and IMF/RD Managing Director file "Sudan, 1981" (Accession 83/108, Box 3, Section 376).

[57]"Stabilization of Export Earnings," SM/78/139 (May 23, 1978), p. 31; minutes of EBM/78/93–94 (June 26, 1978); and "Text of Managing Director's Summing Up as Agreed at EBM/78/115 (7/21/78)." Also see "Review of the Compensatory Financing Facility," SM/79/4 (March 15, 1979), pp. 4–6 and 19. Under the terms of the First Amendment of the Articles of Agreement, *all* Fund lending beyond the Gold Tranche had to be conditional rather than automatically available. The issue concerned whether the Fund should specify a particular type or degree of conditionality.

[58]Political disturbances were frequently noted by the staff as one contributing factor leading to requests for CFF drawings, but they were rarely the dominant factor. The clearest case cited in the 1982 review was a July 1981 drawing by El Salvador. In that case, the ongoing civil war between the ruling military junta led by José Napoleón Duarte and leftist guerrilla groups resulted in a sharp decline in export volumes. Even though the staff was unable to forecast exports in those circumstances, the Board agreed that the situation was beyond the authorities' control and approved the request. See "Compensatory Financing Facility—The Meaning of 'Shortfall Attributable to Circumstances Beyond the Control of the Member,'" EBS/82/42 (March 12, 1982), pp. 10–11 and 24–25; and minutes of EBM/82/41–42 (April 5, 1982).

Financing for Food, 1981

The next couple of years saw a continuing flow of financing through the CFF, in amounts that were substantially larger than would have been possible under the pre-1979 rules.[59] Meanwhile, attention turned to a related problem: the increased volatility of food prices in the 1970s, which was creating severe difficulties for many developing countries—especially the poorest—in paying for imports that were needed to feed the population. A 1978 staff paper proposed treating certain food imports as negative exports for purposes of calculating net export shortfalls, but the idea foundered in the Executive Board over concerns that it was inappropriate for the Fund to single out food imports as a balance of payments problem. (If, to tackle the other main issue of the time, fuel imports were also covered, demands on the facility could have become overwhelming.)[60] A few months later, however, the World Food Council and the Food and Agriculture Organization (FAO) of the United Nations asked the Fund to consider establishing a parallel facility to compensate developing countries for temporary increases in the cost of imported food. On receiving the request, the Executive Board agreed to reconsider the idea.[61]

Interest in the idea of a new food facility intensified in 1980, especially after the highly publicized report of the Brandt Commission took up the cudgels (Brandt Commission, 1980, pp. 217–18). De Larosière took a strong interest in the proposal and took extraordinary measures to soften potential opposition by Executive Directors. Three days before the Board was scheduled to discuss the issue in August 1980, he made an impassioned plea to Directors to look well beyond the Fund's usual preoccupations with short-term financial issues. He began in a Malthusian vein by noting that the world's population was expected to grow from 4.4 billion to 6 billion in the next 20 years, a fact that was "one of the most important . . . that any decision-making institution or person should have permanently in mind." Because of that explosion, "the food problem . . . will be one of

---

[59]One year after the 1979 revisions went into effect, the staff calculated that actual drawings in that year would have been reduced by more than half without the liberalization, primarily owing to the elimination of the ceiling on access within a given year. The switch to geometric averaging had a negligible negative impact. "Recent Developments in Programs of Export Earnings Stabilization," SM/80/182, Rev. 1 (August 5, 1980), p. 5. For a detailed description and analysis of how the facility worked after the 1979 revision, and for a complete list of CFF credits from 1963 through March 1980, see Goreux (1980).

[60]"Stabilization of Export Earnings," op. cit., pp. 24–27, and associated minutes and documents cited in footnote 57, p. 729.

[61]The World Food Council's request was included in a report on "World Food Security for the 1980s," adopted in April 1979. In May, the FAO Council adopted a "Plan of Action on World Food Security" in May, which invited the IMF "to consider within the context of its Financing Facilities the feasibility of providing additional balance of payments support for meeting the rise in food import bills of low income food deficit countries, particularly in the event of domestic food shortages and rising import prices" (FAO, 1979, p. F-2). The Director-General of the FAO, Edouard Saouma, formally transmitted the request to the Managing Director in June. "FAO Proposal to the International Monetary Fund," EBD/79/182 (July 17, 1979), and Sup. 1 (July 18). For supporting material, see (under the same title), EBD/80/18 (January 17, 1980). For the Fund's response, see minutes of EBM/79/126 (July 25, 1979).

the main challenges to the survival of man." The Fund, he continued, could not and should not try to solve the problem of how to feed the growing masses in impoverished countries, but it could try to deal with the "much narrower problem . . . of trying to maintain consumption levels in these poorer countries in the face of real but reversible increases of food imports." Finally, he asked the Board "to give weight to the human considerations which are associated with this issue" and to approach the FAO's request with "a considerate, cooperative attitude."[62]

The Executive Board discussed the FAO request on three days of meetings in August and early September 1980, at the end of which a consensus emerged in favor of some mechanism for financing food imports. What remained was a battle over whether and how the proposed financing should be integrated with the existing CFF. That question was not just a technical matter of bureaucracy; at its heart, it was a question of how much money should be put on the table. With a new and separate facility, the Fund would extend credits to cover the cost of a temporary surge in the cost of importing food, regardless of what the borrower's overall trade balance was doing. Alternatively, if the scheme were fully integrated into the CFF, the Fund would provide food-import credits only if the country had a net shortfall in merchandise exports minus food imports. Between these extremes, consideration also was given to "partially integrated schemes," in which countries could borrow either for import excesses or export shortfalls, but with linked limits on the amounts that could be borrowed.[63]

Those favoring a greatly limited scheme did so for a variety of reasons. Bernard J. Drabble (Canada) noted that his Canadian authorities were worried about devoting resources to a "piecemeal approach to balance of payments problems," while the authorities in the small Caribbean island states that he also represented were concerned about the Fund lending money for food imports but not for other emergencies resulting from hurricanes and other natural disasters. Ruding expressed concerns about overlapping with the functions of development banks, which could lead to "double compensation." Heinrich G. Schneider (Alternate—Austria) worried about "stretching or bending the Fund's Articles of Agreement" by lending for problems other than a general balance of payments deficit. Jahangir Amuzegar (Iran) wondered how the Fund, if it approved the FAO request, could possibly refuse a hypothetical request for, say, a "health facility" from the World Health Organization.[64] Nonetheless, the widespread recognition that low-income countries faced a potentially disastrous situation, coupled with the personal persuasion of the Managing Director, carried the day. The Interim Committee endorsed the general idea at its September 1980 meeting and asked the Executive Board to develop a specific proposal.

What finally emerged after several months of further meetings was a scaled-down and partially integrated scheme: a new window within the CFF to compen-

---

[62]Minutes of EBM/80/117 (August 1, 1980), pp. 3–6.

[63]"Possible Assistance to Members Adversely Affected by Higher Food Import Costs," SM/80/264 (November 26, 1980).

[64]Minutes of EBM/80/130 (September 4, 1980), p. 7 (Ruding), p. 8 (Drabble), p. 9 (Schneider), and p. 10 (Amuzegar).

sate countries for temporary increases in the cost of importing cereals (principally wheat, maize, and rice). The idea was to treat the cost of importing these foods as negative exports and to give countries both an extra means of qualifying for a CFF credit and a further small increase in the overall lending limit. A country with no shortfall in merchandise exports but with a surge in the cost of food imports could now apply for a credit of up to 100 percent of its quota through the new "cereals window." A country with a shortfall in exports could continue to apply for a credit of up to 100 percent of quota, as before. And a country with both problems could apply for credits under both windows, subject to an overall limit that was now raised to 125 percent of quota.[65]

These percentages represented a carefully constructed compromise, on which the Board was able to break a deadlock on May 13, 1981, only because Directors were eager to avoid throwing the matter into the hands of the Interim Committee. The committee was scheduled to meet the next week in Libreville, Gabon, and it almost certainly would have recommended at least as large a facility as the one approved by the Board. An extra complexity was introduced in the solution to cover cases in which countries might have (or expect to have) a shortfall in both exports and imports. Under the 1981 decision, if a country had below-trend cereal imports in the same year in which it had below-trend exports, the drop in import costs would be deducted from the export drop to derive a net export shortfall. To avoid penalizing countries in that situation, the option of applying under the 1979 rules (on the basis of the gross shortfall) was retained, and countries choosing that option could still use the cereals window later if necessary. However, once a government chose to borrow under the terms of the 1981 decision, the country was barred from using the 1979 rules for the next three years.[66]

As it happened, the cereals window got very little usage in the 1980s because the cost of importing cereals generally declined after the facility was established. The flip side of the depressed state of world markets for primary commodities in the 1980s was that basic foods were more globally plentiful than before; the problem for most developing countries was the value of exports, not the cost of imports. Consequently, in the first six years of operation (through April 1987), the Fund lent SDR 8.2 billion under the terms of the 1979 rules on compensating for gross export shortfalls, SDR 0.6 billion under the 1981 rules on net export shortfalls, and SDR 0.5 billion for excess cereal imports. Only seven countries borrowed for cereal imports during that period, in amounts ranging from 4 to 59 percent of quota.[67] In all cases, the excess imports resulted from bad weather conditions that

---

[65]In January 1984, after the quota increases under the Eighth General Review came into effect, the CFF lending limits were reduced to 83 percent for each window and to 105 percent for the two windows combined. Since quotas had risen on average by 47.5 percent, the effect was to raise the lending limits in terms of SDRs by 22–24 percent. For the context of that decision, see the discussion of access policies in Chapter 17, pp. 875–84.

[66] For the Decision establishing the cereals window and a few illustrative examples of how these provisions were intended to work, see Appendix I.

[67] The seven countries borrowing for cereals imports through April 1987 were Bangladesh, Ghana, Jordan, Kenya, Korea, Malawi, and Morocco.

cut domestic production and forced countries to import larger quantities of food. In all cases but one (Jordan), these countries also had stand-by arrangements in effect.[68] Some countries that were hit hardest by adverse weather, including much of the African region that suffered from drought and famine in the mid-1980s, either could not afford to take on new debts or could not meet the standards for financial assistance from the Fund.

In the next three years (through April 1990), usage was even lighter, with only two credits for cereal imports (to Algeria and Mexico, both in June 1989, in conjunction with the approval of a stand-by and an extended arrangement, respectively). Nonetheless, although the cereals window benefited few countries in the 1980s, it provided significant and timely assistance for those countries at times when they were hardest hit by external conditions beyond their control. For that reason, the Fund kept it in place through the many changes in the facility that took place in the late 1980s and the 1990s.[69]

Tightening the Conditions, 1983

The two years after the establishment of the cereals window were a golden age for the CFF: 47 countries borrowed a total of SDR 5.4 billion ($6 billion) through the facility in fiscal years 1982–83 (see Figure 15.2). In most cases, those countries also had stand-by or extended arrangements in effect simultaneously. Nonetheless, the question of what "cooperation" meant would not go away. If a country did not have a Fund-supported adjustment program in place, how was the Fund to judge whether the country's policies were appropriate? A continuing trickle of cases kept flowing in, in which countries could not (or would not) put together an acceptable program but otherwise qualified for compensatory financing.[70] In practice, such cases were handled by keeping the country's CFF obligations within the lower 50 percent limit, but the Board was becoming increasingly disenchanted with its own longstanding preference for ambiguity in CFF conditionality. In 1983, the staff responded to those concerns by proposing specific standards for the lower and upper tranches. Those standards were approved by the Executive Board in September, with little change.

The new standard for the lower tranche (up to 50 percent of quota in total CFF obligations) was that the country had to be willing to receive Fund missions and

---

[68]"Review of the Decision on Compensatory Financing of Fluctuations in the Cost of Cereal Imports," SM/87/86 (April 8, 1987), pp. 5–9.

[69]The cereals window initially was established for a fixed term of four years. It was extended without modification in 1985, 1990, and 1994.

[70]For countries facing both a general balance of payments problem and a qualifying "temporary shortfall," the low-conditionality CFF offered an unambiguous advantage over a stand-by arrangement. In 1981, the staff suggested counteracting that advantage by setting the interest rate charged on CFF credits at the prevailing market rate, rather than at the lower rate of charge on stand-by and other credit-tranche drawings. That proposal was supported by a majority of the votes in the Executive Board, but such a change required a 70 percent majority. Directors from developing countries, with a little over 40 percent of the vote, were thus were able to block it from taking effect. Minutes of EBM/81/37–38 (March 9, 1981). The outcome of the debate is summarized at meeting 81/38, p. 26.

discuss its balance of payments problem and possible solutions. If the Fund determined that the country's policies were "seriously deficient" or that its "record of cooperation in the recent past has been unsatisfactory," then the Fund would expect the member to begin a program of corrective action before approval of the request. Those conditions were similar to the requirements for a stand-by arrangement in the first credit tranche. For credits that would take the country's indebtedness into the upper tranche (up to 125 percent of quota), the additional requirement was specified that the country should have a satisfactory balance of payments situation (apart from the calculated temporary export shortfall or excess import costs), or a Fund-supported adjustment program in effect, or a program in effect that would qualify for Fund support "in the credit tranches" if requested.[71] These conditions were similar to those for an upper credit tranche stand-by arrangement, although the quoted phrase deliberately left the door open for situations that would have qualified only for support in the first credit tranche.

On paper, these conditions merely made specific what had long been implicit in the Fund's evaluation of requests for CFF credits. In practice, they would raise the hurdle for countries without stand-by arrangements to qualify for CFF support. During the Board discussion, several speakers (including the Managing Director) maintained that the proposed standard was merely an interpretation, while others worried aloud that the facility was being fundamentally changed. Jacques Polak argued that "compensatory financing should be available promptly" and without "special conditions." It was he who asked that conditionality be imposed in the lower CFF tranche only if policies were "seriously deficient" and not just "deficient." Julius Ismael (Indonesia) garnered the support of several of his colleagues in arguing that "the guidelines constituted a tightening of conditionality that was inconsistent with the objectives of compensatory financing." R.N. Malhotra (India) tried to delay consideration of the proposals on the grounds that they would "change the nature" of the CFF, but the Managing Director assured him and others that "it was not the intention of the staff to formulate a new policy" and that "the proposed guidelines represented the Fund's practice." On that understanding, the proposal was approved, but by a deeply divided Executive Board.[72]

After the new conditionality guidelines were approved, borrowing from the CFF dropped off sharply. More significantly, almost all CFF credits were now made in conjunction with stand-by or extended arrangements.[73] As Polak later observed (in

---

[71]Executive Board Decision No. 7528-(83/140), adopted September 14, 1983; *Annual Report 1984*, p. 137. For the original staff proposal, see "Requirement of Cooperation Under the Compensatory Financial Facility," EBS/83/171 (August 12, 1983).

[72]Minutes of EBM/83/130 (September 6, 1983), p. 17 (Polak); EBM/83/131 (same date), p. 3 (Malhotra) and p. 12 (de Larosière); and EBM/83/140 (September 14, 1983), p. 47 (Ismael) and p. 53 (de Larosière).

[73]From September 1983, when the new guidelines took effect, to the end of 1986, 27 out of 33 credits through the CFF—and all but 1 of the 27 credits in the CFF "upper tranche"—were made in conjunction with a new stand-by or extended arrangement or were to countries with existing arrangements. "Compensatory Financing Facility—Recent Experience and Issues for Consideration," EBS/87/13 (January 26, 1987), pp. 8–9.

the 1991 essay cited above), since the staff considered all sources of finance in determining the appropriate size of a stand-by arrangement, it is reasonable to conclude that auxiliary CFF credits did not provide truly additional resources to the borrower. The borrower got more money up-front, but the later installments of the stand-by arrangement were likely to be smaller as a result. The underlying rationale for this effective downgrading of the facility was that it was rare in practice (at least in the 1980s) for a country to have a temporary and exogenous export shortfall without also having a more persistent balance of payments problem requiring a substantial policy correction. The option of covering a purely compensatory case was never abolished (having a stand-by arrangement was a sufficient, not a necessary, condition for meeting the "cooperation" test), but that option became largely irrelevant.

Tighter conditionality was not the only explanation for the reduced usage of the CFF. Three other reasons were important in the second half of the 1980s.[74] First, the markets for many primary commodities became *permanently* rather than temporarily depressed.[75] The massive and generalized decline in commodity prices in those years was unprecedented in modern history (see Boughton, 1991). Though it seems ironic that the more sustained the decline, the less likely are exporters to qualify for compensation, the effect was to shift the focus to the need for longer-term financial support and for deeper adjustments in economic policies. Second, countries that succeeded in diversifying their economies away from dependence on one or a few primary commodities effectively graduated from the CFF. Although the number of successful cases may have been small, diversification does seem to have had a positive overall effect. Third, many of the countries that are most vul-

---

[74]An additional restrictive factor was introduced more gradually and without a formal decision. Starting in 1983, the Fund occasionally approved stand-by or extended arrangements "in principle," pending completion of financing commitments by other creditors (see Chapter 9). Since Articles I and V of the Fund's Articles of Agreement require the Fund to establish "adequate safeguards" on the use of its resources, the staff considered it appropriate to consider delaying CFF drawings when the Executive Board approved an associated arrangement "in principle." Whether CFF drawings were delayed was determined on a case-by-case basis. (See the discussion in Chapter 10 (pp. 467–71) of a CFF credit for Argentina that was allowed in February 1987 even though the associated stand-by arrangement was approved only in principle, and the discussion in Chapter 13 (pp. 578–85) of a credit for Côte d'Ivoire that was delayed in December 1987 along with the stand-by arrangement.) In such cases, Executive Directors occasionally objected on the grounds that delaying the CFF drawing violated the spirit of the facility. In 1988, however, the Executive Board agreed that the Fund's policy on financing assurances should apply to the CFF as well as to stand-by arrangements. See minutes of EBM/88/16–17 (February 5, 1988).

[75]The impact of this factor was limited, or at least delayed, by the inevitability of forecast errors. Because the calculation of a temporary shortfall required forecasting commodity prices for two years ahead, credits often were extended on a false expectation that a current shortfall would be temporary. A 1987 internal study found that forecast errors from 1976 through 1985 had been frequent and large but not biased. Even so, because many countries with underestimated shortfalls had been constrained by the CFF lending limits, the resulting pattern of credits was biased toward overcompensation. For 1976 through 1985, countries were compensated with SDR 10.8 billion in CFF credits for an estimated SDR 19.3 billion in temporary export shortfalls. With perfect foresight, temporary shortfalls were slightly larger (SDR 19.8 billion), but the Fund would have extended just SDR 7.4 billion in credits. "Review of the Compensatory Financing Facility—Annexes," EBS/87/165, Sup. 1 (July 30, 1987), p. 47.

nerable to the vagaries of world markets for primary commodities also have very low per capita incomes. The establishment of the SAF in 1986, and the ESAF in 1987, provided a much less costly and more appropriate vehicle for providing loans to those countries.

A special case arose when oil prices declined sharply in 1981–82 and again in 1985–86, quite apart from the problem of assessing at the time whether the decline was likely to be temporary or permanent. Because international trade in oil was so large (it accounted for about half of all world trade in primary commodities), potential borrowing to compensate for price declines could have added greatly to total demands on the CFF and could even have put pressure on the Fund's overall liquidity position.[76] Even if the declines had been recognized as permanent, they were large enough that they would have justified large borrowings by exporters.[77] The CFF, however, required that a temporary shortfall in export revenues be beyond the control of the authorities. Since most major oil exporters belonged to the Organization of Petroleum Exporting Countries (OPEC), a central question was whether OPEC determined oil prices or merely set prices in accordance with market conditions.

In May 1983, the Fund staff concluded that there were "doubts as to whether OPEC actions have been consistently determining in respect of export earnings" for its members, and it recommended that requests be considered and evaluated on a case-by-case basis. That conclusion did not dispel the uneasiness felt by a number of Executive Directors, which was perhaps expressed best by Guenter Grosche (Alternate—Germany): ". . . if in certain periods a particular country had cooperated with others to establish a price level that turned out not to be sustainable, it could be considered as having created shortfalls." The Board agreed unanimously that OPEC membership per se was irrelevant, but it reiterated that a country's "output, stockpiling, and price policies" were relevant for deciding whether a shortfall was beyond the authorities' control.[78]

---

[76]Throughout the CFF liberalization phase of 1975–79, calculations of potential use had been made on the assumption that neither industrial countries nor oil exporters would avail themselves of the facility. As discussed in Chapter 7, concerns about opening the floodgates led management to persuade Mexico to drop plans to borrow through the CFF for an oil export shortfall in 1982.

[77]To take a simple numerical example, suppose that a country earns $100 from exports for two years and that exports then drop to $50 for the next three years. The five-year annual average is $70 (or $66, using geometric averaging), and the $20 (or $16) difference between that average and exports in year three counts as a "temporary shortfall." In March 1986, following a major decline in oil prices, the staff calculated that all of the 26 oil-exporting developing countries could qualify for maximum CFF access in the course of the year, based on calculated temporary shortfalls in oil exports, and it estimated that actual requests might come from seven or so countries and total between SDR 2 and 2½ billion through mid-1987. "CFF—Fuel Exporting Countries," memorandum from William C. Hood (Economic Counselor and Director of Research) to the Managing Director (March 27, 1986); IMF/CF (S 1181 "Compensatory Financing of Export Fluctuations, January 1986–March 1987").

[78]The staff conclusion is in "Compensatory Financing Facility—Requests for Drawings by Oil Exporters," SM/83/87 (May 16, 1983), p. 16. For the Executive Board's conclusions, see the Chairman's summing up, minutes of EBM/83/80 (June 2, 1980), pp. 23–25. Grosche's statement was made at EBM/83/79 (same date), p. 22.

In the event, only two requests for CFF drawings related to oil exports were submitted in the 1980s. In August 1986, Ecuador borrowed SDR 39.7 million ($48 million; 26 percent of quota) to compensate for a shortfall in oil export earnings, as an adjunct to a stand-by arrangement approved at the same time. Relevant factors were that Ecuador had consistently produced oil at capacity rates rather than at levels determined by OPEC quotas, and that it was a small enough producer to be regarded as a price taker in international markets.[79] In May 1987, Indonesia borrowed SDR 462.9 million ($602 million; 46 percent of quota) for a shortfall in oil and other exports. Since Indonesia had a good record of cooperation with the Fund and was making only a small drawing that could have been justified without reference to the oil shortfall, that request also was viewed favorably.[80]

Covering Contingencies, 1988

Although the Executive Board generally rejected proposals to include automatic contingency clauses in stand-by arrangements (as discussed in Chapter 13), the broader idea of covering contingencies had an undeniable appeal. In March 1987, the Board considered a proposal for establishing a new window within the CFF to compensate indebted countries in the event of unanticipated increases in interest rates, but that idea also was rejected as inconsistent with the purposes of the facility. What then became clear was that for a contingency mechanism to succeed in generating broad support, it would have to be comprehensive in coverage and symmetric in application. That is, it should relate to the broad determinants of export revenues and should also trigger reductions in the Fund's commitments if developments turned out more favorably than expected. That notion was encapsulated in a June 1987 report by the Deputies of the Group of Twenty-Four developing countries (G-24).[81]

---

[79]Minutes of EBM/86/136 (August 15, 1986).

[80]Ecuador and Indonesia also borrowed through the CFF in 1983, but those drawings were linked to shortfalls in non-oil exports. Indonesia's export shortfall in 1987 was attributable to a wide range of products, but about 70 percent of the total was due to oil (plus 17 percent for liquefied natural gas). The requested CFF drawing, however, was smaller than the calculated shortfall for non-oil exports; that fact was cited by the Executive Directors for the United States, Germany, Italy, and Canada as relevant to their approval of the request. In 1989, the Venezuelan authorities expressed interest in an oil-related CFF drawing, but they did not submit a formal request.
The background to the 1987 credit to Indonesia is given in "Indonesia—Use of Fund Resources—Compensatory Financing Facility," EBS/87/77 (April 13, 1987). For the Board discussion, see the minutes of EBM/87/67 (May 4, 1987). The 1983 shortfall is described in "Indonesia—Use of Fund Resources—Compensatory Financing Facility," EBS/83/145 (July 12, 1983).

[81]Intergovernmental Group of Twenty-Four (1987), paras. 67–71. The specific proposal was that a Letter of Intent for a Fund-supported adjustment program would include projections for key exogenous variables. The stand-by arrangement would include a formula under which the amount of Fund resources available would be increased or decreased by specified amounts if conditions turned out to be less or more favorable. The report was circulated in the Fund as "Report of the Deputies of the Group of Twenty-Four on the Role of the Fund in Adjustment with Growth," EBD/87/196 (July 22, 1987).

In July 1987, the staff responded to the G-24 request by developing a detailed proposal for a contingency mechanism that would operate alongside the CFF but would be activated by deviations from assumptions made at the time that a stand-by arrangement was approved. The member and the Fund would agree at the out-set on projections for export revenues during the life of the arrangement. If a short-fall occurred, the Fund could compensate by extending additional financing; if events turned out favorably, the Fund could reduce its commitment under the stand-by arrangement. Two months later, at the Annual Meetings, U.S. Treasury Secretary James A. Baker III, took that idea a step further and proposed replacing the CFF with a new "external contingency facility" designed to "help cushion the adverse effects on stand-by programs of external, unforeseen developments such as weaker commodity prices, lower export volumes, natural disasters, and sustained higher interest rates."[82] Now the idea had momentum for both creditors and in-debted countries, and the only question was what form it might have. In the view of the developing countries, the goal was to devise a means of providing additional support for countries facing adverse circumstances. In the U.S. view, the goal was to replace the low-conditionality CFF with a new facility that would provide a sim-ilar level of financing but would be linked more firmly to conditional stand-by arrangements.

The next several months were devoted to finding a workable compromise. Al-though this effort technically succeeded, it produced a hydra-headed facility of mind-numbing and self-defeating complexity.

The proposal to scrap the compensatory facility with one designed only to han-dle contingencies for program countries was quickly rejected by the Executive Board in November 1987. Even though the existing facility had fallen into disuse, a large majority of Directors considered that it still had a "vital" role to play in the event of future export shortfalls. Accordingly, Jacques de Groote (Belgium) pro-posed "enhancing" the existing CFF by adding a window for compensating coun-tries in case of adverse external shocks.[83] That general idea quickly gained popular-ity as a possible compromise, and the choice effectively was narrowed to the de Groote proposal (an option that became known as an "external contingency mech-anism," or ECM) and the more general G-24 notion of adapting stand-by arrange-ments to deal with contingencies (an "internal contingency mechanism," or ICM).

In an extraordinarily drawn-out series of 11 meetings in March 1988, the Exec-utive Board agreed that the CFF could be expanded to include a contingency win-dow, but Directors expressed a wide range of views on the implications for the stan-dard compensatory windows. Dallara was pushing to cut access for export shortfalls from a maximum of 83 percent (see footnote 65, p. 732) to 25 percent, while most

---

[82]IMF, *Summary Proceedings*, 1987, pp. 110–11. The U.S. Executive Director, Charles H. Dal-lara, who initiated the idea in the U.S. Treasury, circulated an elaboration of the proposal to his colleagues on the Executive Board shortly after the Annual Meetings. Dallara's statement on "U.S. proposals for Strengthening the Fund's Role in the Debt Strategy" was circulated informally on October 9; an expanded version was presented at EBM/87/156 (November 17, 1987), pp. 17–23.

[83]Chairman's summing up, minutes of EBM/87/157 (November 18, 1987), p. 10, and EBM/87/158 (same date), pp. 65–68. For de Groote's proposal, see EBM/87/157, pp. 68–72.

others insisted on retaining at least 50 percent for that purpose. By the end of March, however, Dallara agreed to consider a 40 percent ceiling for export short-falls, and that move went a long way toward securing an agreement.[84]

The core of the compromise that the Managing Director submitted to the Interim Committee for its April 1988 meeting was that the "essential features" of compensatory financing would be preserved, while access would be further restricted. If a country had an otherwise satisfactory balance of payments and had the capacity to service additional debt, it could still get a CFF credit equivalent to 83 percent of its quota. As before, it could also get a credit for excess cereal imports, subject to an overall ceiling of 105 percent, although the ceiling on access for cereal imports alone was left open for the time being.[85]

In the much more common case where a temporary and exogenous export shortfall came on top of other difficulties, the country could get a credit for 40 percent of its quota if it "was willing to cooperate with the Fund in an effort to find an appropriate solution to its balance of payments problems." If the country had an "unsatisfactory" record of cooperation in the past or if its "existing policies were seriously deficient," the Fund could require "prior actions" before approving the credit and could delay a "second tranche" (half of the 40 percent available) until an approved adjustment program was in place. A country also could apply for an "optional tranche" of up to 25 percent of quota (for a total of 65 percent), if it had an adjustment program in place (either supported by Fund financing or strong enough to qualify); for countries subject to the "prior actions" guideline, the optional tranche would not be made available until the Fund's first review of the program. (These guidelines on the meaning of cooperation were intended to clarify rather than alter existing practices.) In addition, the Board agreed that countries could obtain up to 40 percent of quota under the new contingency mechanism, and up to 25 percent under the "optional tranche" as an alternative to using that 25 percent under the compensatory window. Thus the intention was that total potential access under the new arrangements would remain at 105 percent, but it would be allocated in new and more complex ways.

With the blessing of the Interim Committee,[86] the Board next turned to the difficult task of agreeing on specific operational features (or "modalities," in the preferred jargon of the Fund) of the contingency window. Several of these features were largely technical and need not be reviewed here.[87] Moreover, one central

---

[84]Minutes of EBM/88/30–31 (March 4, 1988), EBM/88/37–38 (March 11, 1988), EBM/88/50–51 (March 28, 1988), and IS/88/1–5 (March 31 through April 7, 1988). Dallara's compromise proposal is on p. 20 of EBM/88/50.

[85]See "Compensatory Financing Facility and External Contingency Mechanisms," ICMS/Doc/88 (April 8, 1988).

[86]See para. 7 of the Interim Committee communiqué (April 15, 1988), in *Annual Report 1988*, p. 148.

[87]For example, decisions were required on issues such as how to phase contingent drawings, especially in multiyear arrangements; how to link drawings with stand-by arrangements that had been approved only in principle; and how to make transitional provisions for countries that had outstanding obligations in excess of the new limits.

question—what contingencies to cover—had already been decided in the preliminary discussions: export earnings, import prices (but not quantities), and the effects of changes in "international benchmark" interest rates. Other components of the current account, notably workers' remittances and tourism earnings, could be covered if they were particularly important for a country.[88] The idea was that a Fund-supported adjustment program[89] would specify assumed values for these variables. If circumstances deteriorated, the Fund would provide additional credits; if circumstances turned out to be better than expected, the amounts available might be reduced, the authorities might be expected to repay credits early, or they might be required to increase the target level of international reserves.

Much debate ensued throughout June and July 1988, on how to delineate the Fund's involvement and how to integrate this contingency mechanism into the existing CFF and create what was now being awkwardly called the Compensatory and Contingency Financing Facility (CCFF).[90] Despite the intricacy of arguments about access limits, thresholds, discount factors, double compensation, etc., the essence of the debate was over how much of the "essential features" of compensatory financing should be retained, and how much (if at all) the Fund's overall potential financial commitment should be expanded.

Advocates of an expanded facility were prepared to accept lower lending limits under the old compensatory windows in exchange for a new contingency mechanism, but they pushed hard for an overall increase in the size of the facility. Adding a contingency window with a ceiling of 40 percent of quota into a facility with a total limit of 105 percent implied reducing access under the export or cereal windows from 83 to 65 percent. Keeping the original ratio of joint access (exports and cereals combined) to access for each window implied setting a joint limit of 82 percent (82/65 = 105/83). That simple mathematics eventually persuaded the Board to agree to raise the overall limit from 105 to 122 percent (82 + 40). Although it was extremely unlikely that any country would ever face such a multiplicity of problems that it could draw anywhere near that limit, at least the theoretical maximum would be higher than before.[91] Within that limit, a country could borrow 40 percent of quota each for export shortfalls and contingencies and 17 percent for excess cereal imports. Any one window could be augmented by up to 25 percent

---

[88]In the event of multiple deviations, the basis for contingency financing was to be the net sum. To qualify, the net deviation had to exceed a specified threshold, which normally was to be 10 percent of the country's quota. The covered amount then was to be reduced uniformly by 4 percent of quota. The associated stand-by arrangement was to specify the portion of the deviation to be covered by additional Fund financing (which could be up to 100 percent).

[89]Programs supported by SAF or ESAF loans also qualified, in addition to those supported by stand-by or extended arrangements.

[90]The name was introduced in "Modalities for the Compensatory and Contingency Financing Facility," EBS/88/100 (May 24, 1988). Until then, the proposal was described even more awkwardly as the "CFF/ECM facility."

[91]A further limiting factor was that contingency financing could not exceed 70 percent of the total amount available under the associated arrangement. As before, drawings under the new facility "floated"; that is, they did not count against the borrower's reserve tranche balance or the overall limits on annual or cumulative access to Fund resources.

of quota (the "optional tranche"). Thus the cereals window was subjected to a much larger reduction than the export window, but since it never had been of much use, its downgrading was little lamented.

Another complication concerned the treatment of unanticipated increases in interest rates. That element of the contingency mechanism was potentially of great value to highly indebted countries, but it worried some creditor countries and raised serious questions about the economic effects of the mechanism. If international interest rates rose, and the Fund responded by providing additional financing to an indebted country, the extra resources might principally benefit other creditors rather than the borrower. To circumscribe this problem, the Board agreed to limit financing for interest rate deviations to no more than 35 percent of quota. It also decided that the Fund should seek to get agreements from other creditors to increase their own exposure in such cases.[92]

The Executive Board reached agreement on all particulars at the beginning of August 1988, and it formally adopted the decision creating the CCFF on August 23. Once the facility became operational, however, demand for it turned out to be quite limited, and almost no money became available to borrowers through the contingency window. During the first 12 months of CCFF operations, the Fund negotiated and approved 29 arrangements,[93] only 12 of which included contingency provisions. In one case, an extended arrangement for the Philippines, the covered variables stayed within bounds, and the contingency provisions were not activated. In the other, a stand-by arrangement for Trinidad and Tobago, an unanticipated increase in oil export revenues triggered the symmetry provisions and resulted in an increase in the target for net international reserves.[94]

Why were borrowing countries so reluctant to request contingency provisions in adjustment programs? At least four reasons seem to have been important in several instances.[95] Certainly the symmetry provisions were a major deterrent. Borrowing countries could always try to deal with adverse developments by requesting modifications or waivers after the fact, and that strategy evaded the symmetry provisions. Second, in some cases the access limits were so small relative to the size of

---

[92]After several years of frustrating experience with concerted lending agreements, no one wanted to make the contingency mechanism inflexibly dependent on cooperation from commercial banks. Consequently, the Decision creating the new facility included only a requirement that the program be "adequately financed, including, if necessary, through the provision of financing from other sources" (para. 24). For the full Decision, see *Annual Report 1989*, pp. 84–89. The Chairman's summing up of the Board discussion on July 6, which provided detailed background on operational features, noted that "parallel contingent financing from commercial banks will be pursued vigorously" but would be required only in cases where "necessary to ensure adequate financing of the program." See minutes of IS/88/8 (July 6, 1988).

[93]This total excludes nine arrangements for which negotiations were essentially complete before the CCFF became operational.

[94]"Trinidad and Tobago—Stand-by Arrangement—Review and Request for Modification of Performance Criteria," EBS/89/135, Sup. 1 (July 13, 1989). The first drawing under the contingency provisions of the CCFF was made by Bulgaria in 1992.

[95]Also see Polak (1991), pp. 11–12, for a discussion of the strengths and weaknesses of the contingency mechanism.

potential shocks that the authorities did not think it worthwhile to negotiate the detailed baseline scenarios and other terms required for contingency clauses. Third, the requirement to seek "parallel financing" from other creditors constituted a potential obstacle and created uncertainties about the value of the Fund's contingent commitments. Fourth, many countries were put off by the CCFF requirement for "broad coverage" in calculating contingencies, which often necessitated detailed and complex calculations. Four programs approved in 1988–89 (extended arrangements for Chile, Mexico, and Venezuela, and a stand-by arrangement for Nigeria) included more narrowly targeted contingency clauses outside the framework of the CCFF.[96] Ironically, the Fund's laborious negotiations to establish the CCFF succeeded to some degree in stimulating interest in contingent financing, but that demand was satisfied primarily through existing channels rather than through the new facility itself.

Other Lending Arrangements

Buffer Stock Financing Facility

Economies that are dependent on selling primary commodities suffer from two interrelated problems: a secular downward trend and high cyclical volatility in world market prices (both measured relative to prices of manufactured goods). Because the trend is difficult to measure and is unlikely to remain constant over time, producers can never know just where they stand in relation to the cycle.[97] Despite the odds, at times of high volatility—beginning in the 1930s but especially in the 1970s and early 1980s—developing countries have tried to form alliances aimed at stabilizing commodity prices near trend levels. Oil exporters formed by far the largest and most visible coalition (OPEC),[98] while less well known groups aimed to stabilize prices of commodities such as cocoa, coffee, rubber, sugar, tea, and tin.[99] In 1969, the IMF established the Buffer Stock Financing Facility (BSFF) to support the stabilization activities of certain of these agreements.

---

[96]The Chilean provisions related to the price of copper, and the other three all were linked to the price of oil exports.

[97]For a discussion of the difficulties in assessing the trend in relative commodity prices, see Boughton (1991).

[98]Although OPEC's initial goal was to raise prices to what participants judged to be equilibrium levels, later activities were aimed at stabilizing output and prices. Its members did not maintain buffer stocks, and it was never considered for inclusion in the BSFF.

[99]During the 1970s, various efforts were made within the United Nations to generalize the goals of the buffer stock agreements that were being established for specific commodities. The Integrated Programme for Commodities was established by UNCTAD in May 1976 to coordinate and promote international commodity agreements. Agreement within UNCTAD to establish the Common Fund for Commodities was reached in June 1980. The intent of the Common Fund was to stabilize commodity prices by providing financial assistance to international commodity organizations. For a summary of developments through mid-1980, see "Recent Developments in Programs of Export Earnings Stabilization," SM/80/182, Rev. 1 (August 5, 1980).

The essence of the BSFF was that the Fund would lend to member countries that were required under specified international agreements to purchase buffer stocks of their exportable commodities at times when prices would otherwise be cyclically depressed. To qualify for such a credit, a country would have to be a participant in a scheme approved by the Fund, and it would have to represent to the Fund that it faced a balance of payments need associated with its financing requirement and would cooperate with the Fund in finding a solution to the problem. A central criterion for an international agreement to qualify was that it had to be directed toward stabilizing the price of a commodity around a medium-term trend. Terms and access limits on credits through the BSFF were broadly similar to those for the CFF, and the pair of facilities were intended to provide two-pronged assistance to developing countries. The buffer stock facility would provide up-front financing to help countries stabilize export prices, and the compensatory facility would provide backup support if export earnings temporarily dropped anyway.[100]

Buffer stock lending began in 1971, some two years after the facility was established. From then through the end of the 1980s, the Fund lent a total of SDR 558 million ($612 million) to 18 countries. In value terms, most of that lending took place in 1982 and 1983; no new lending occurred after the spring of 1984, and by the end of 1988 all BSFF credits had been repaid (Figure 15.3).

Lending for this purpose was highly episodic. All of the credits through 1975 went to five countries participating in the Fourth International Tin Agreement (Bolivia, Indonesia, Malaysia, Nigeria, and Thailand). In the second short burst of activity, the Fund provided credits to six countries (Australia, the Dominican Republic, Guyana, Jamaica, Nicaragua, and the Philippines) to finance their participation in the 1977 International Sugar Agreement. The heyday of the facility then came in 1982–84, when the Fund lent SDR 453 million ($483 million) to 13 countries participating in the tin and sugar agreements and the 1979 International Natural Rubber Agreement.[101] At its peak at the end of 1983, the BSFF accounted for 1.2 percent of total Fund credit and loans outstanding.

The sugar agreement expired at the end of 1984 after producers failed to find an acceptable means of coping with a large increase in world supply engendered by the price support programs of the European Communities and the United States. The tin agreement—the last in a series of international efforts to fix a world price for tin, dating from 1956—was abandoned in 1985 when its managers finally real-

---

[100]For the origins of the BSFF, see de Vries (1976), Vol. 1, pp. 269–86. Developments in the 1970s are covered in de Vries (1985), pp. 417–21. The CFF covered the full value of a country's export earnings, not just those derived from specific commodities.

[101]The 1972 International Cocoa Agreement also was approved by the Fund as a qualifying scheme, but no credits were extended for that purpose, and the agreement lapsed in March 1980. During 1982–84, Indonesia, Malaysia, and Thailand borrowed for both rubber and tin stocks; Côte d'Ivoire and Sri Lanka borrowed for rubber stocks; Australia, Brazil, the Dominican Republic, Malawi, Mauritius, Swaziland, and Zimbabwe borrowed for sugar stocks; and Bolivia borrowed for tin stocks.

Figure 15.3. Buffer Stock Financing, 1969–89

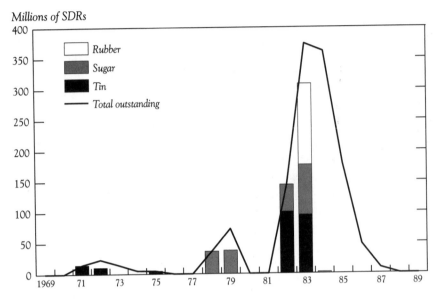

Millions of SDRs

ized that its goals were far out of line with market conditions.[102] After that, only one eligible agreement—rubber—survived. The BSFF remained ready to provide credits if requested, but, at least for the time being, it was not needed.

Emergency Disaster Relief

In January 1962, the Fund agreed to lend Egypt $22.4 million (25 percent of quota) against collateral of an equivalent amount in gold. Although the drawing pushed Egypt's obligations into the third credit tranche, the Fund did not require the authorities to submit an adjustment program. That exception was formally based on the provision of collateral, but the Executive Board also noted that the request was motivated by a dire economic emergency. Much of Egypt's rice crop had been wiped out by flooding in the Nile valley in 1961, and now the cotton crop had been devastated by an infestation of cotton leaf worms. To insist that the usual conditionality be negotiated before approval of the credit would force a deprivation on the country that most Directors felt was unnecessary. (See Horsefield, 1969, Vol. 1, pp. 524–25.) The Fund thus embarked on the practice of occasionally granting emergency relief to countries facing natural disasters.[103]

For 17 years following the assistance to Egypt, the Fund provided emergency relief for natural disasters in just four instances (Table 15.1): following earth-

---

[102]On the sugar agreement, see "Buffer Stock Financing Facility—Report on the 1977 International Sugar Agreement," SM/84/232 (October 19, 1984). On tin, see "Buffer Stock Financing Facility—International Tin Agreement," SM/86/271 (November 5, 1986).

[103]The World Bank also provided emergency loans for disaster relief; see Kapur and others (1997), pp. 341–42.

Table 15.1. Emergency Disaster Relief, 1962–89

Country	Date	Nature of Disaster	Amount (Millions of SDRs)	Amount (Millions of dollars)[a]	Amount (Percent of quota)
Egypt	January 1962	pest infestation		22.4	25
Yugoslavia	September 1963	earthquake		30.0	25
India	April 1966	drought		187.5	25
Nicaragua	May 1973	earthquake	12.0	14.3	44
Chad	May 1974	drought	2.8	3.4	22
Dominican Republic	September 1979	hurricane	23.3	30.4	42[b]
Dominica	December 1979	hurricane	1.0	1.3	50[c]
St. Lucia	November 1980	hurricane	1.8	2.3	50[d]
St. Vincent and the Grenadines	November 1980	hurricane	0.4	0.5	25[e]
Yemen, P.D.R.	July 1982	floods	15.4	16.8	25[f]
Yemen Arab Republic	March 1983	earthquake	9.8	10.6	50
Mexico	January 1986	earthquake	291.4	320.0	25
Madagascar	May 1986	cyclone	16.6	19.4	25[g]
Solomon Islands	September 1986	cyclone	1.3	1.6	25
Ecuador	June 1987	earthquake	37.7	48.5	25
Bangladesh	November 1988	floods	71.9	97.6	25
Jamaica	February 1989	hurricane	36.4	47.9	25

[a]The Fund's accounts have been expressed in SDRs since 1972. Amounts in U.S. dollars shown after that date are converted at prevailing exchange rates.

[b]Plus 50 percent of quota, as a CFF drawing for export shortfalls.

[c]Plus 69 percent of quota, as drawings on the reserve tranche (19 percent) and through the CFF (export shortfalls, 50 percent).

[d]Plus (in March 1981) a CFF drawing equivalent to 50 percent of the enlarged quota (75 percent of the 1980 quota) for export shortfalls related to the hurricane.

[e]Plus 19 percent of quota, as a drawing on the balance of the reserve tranche; and (in March 1981) 50 percent of the enlarged quota (76 percent of the 1980 quota) through the CFF, for export shortfalls related to the hurricane.

[f]Plus 4 percent of quota, as a drawing on the balance of the reserve tranche.

[g]Plus 24 percent of quota, as a CFF drawing for export shortfalls.

quakes in Yugoslavia in 1963 and Nicaragua in 1973, and in response to droughts in India in 1966 and Chad in 1974. Credits ranged from 22 to 44 percent of the borrower's quota. Beginning in 1979, both the frequency and the average size of emergency assistance picked up temporarily. Specifically, in 1979 and again in 1980, the Caribbean region was affected severely by hurricanes. Following Hurricane David, which hit at the end of August 1979, both the Dominican Republic and Dominica obtained emergency assistance from the Fund, amounting directly to 42 and 50 percent of quota, respectively.[104] If associated drawings on the re-

---

[104]Assistance to the Dominican Republic was approved in record time (about two weeks), owing to special circumstances. In July 1979, the authorities requested a drawing through the CFF for export shortfalls, plus a stand-by arrangement for the first credit tranche. A staff mission went to Santo Domingo in August and was concluding negotiations when news came of the approaching storm. The staff managed to leave just ahead of the hurricane. The authorities then requested a drawing for emergency assistance as a substitute for the stand-by arrangement, which the Executive Board approved in September along with the CFF drawing. See minutes of EBM/79/158 (September 17, 1979).

serve tranche and through the CFF are taken into account, financial assistance to those two countries averaged a little over 100 percent of quota (see the notes to Table 15.1). A year later, similar assistance was provided to St. Lucia and to St. Vincent and the Grenadines, to help them cope with the damage from Hurricane Allen.

On several occasions in 1980, during discussions on the proposed "food facility" (which became the cereals window of the CFF), the Executive Director for three of the four hurricane-damaged economies—Bernard J. Drabble (Canada)[105]— proposed that the Fund "formalize" its procedures for granting emergency assistance by establishing a "disaster facility, or disaster tranche" on the understanding that drawings would have to be either repaid quickly or followed by a stand-by arrangement.[106] Neither the staff nor management was particularly eager to attempt to specify conditions for such assistance in advance, and they delayed responding as long as they could. When they finally did submit a paper to the Board, for discussion in February 1982, they urged against creating a new facility and proposed essentially that existing procedures be retained.[107]

The Executive Board agreed with the staff that a formal facility was not needed, and it accepted the idea that emergency assistance should be subjected to a minimal degree of conditionality, essentially equivalent to what was required of countries seeking to draw on their first credit tranche. That is, the authorities would have to submit a statement indicating their willingness to cooperate with the Fund in finding a lasting solution to their balance of payments problems and their intention to implement appropriate policies. By a narrow majority, the Board also agreed that emergency assistance would normally be limited to one credit tranche (25 percent of quota), apart from other non- or low-conditionality drawings that might be available (notably reserve tranche or CFF drawings). On that question, 9 of the Fund's 22 Executive Directors, all of whom spoke for developing countries and who collectively held about 30 percent of the votes on the Board, argued for a larger limit.[108] Others, however, expressed concerns that in most emergency cases up to that time, the borrowing country had not carried out the intentions expressed in its supporting statements; prudence therefore dictated that amounts disbursed quickly should be kept small.[109]

Following adoption of these guidelines, the Fund granted emergency assistance about once a year for the rest of the 1980s, almost always for 25 percent of

---

[105]The Dominican Republic, an original member of the Fund, was in the constituency of Alexandre Kafka (Brazil). Dominica, St. Lucia, and St. Vincent all became members of the Fund after the 1978 election of Executive Directors and were formally in Drabble's constituency only as of November 1980.

[106]See statements by Drabble at EBM/80/119 (August 4, 1980), p. 11 ("formalize"); EBM/80/130 (September 4, 1980), p. 8, where he raises the link with an adjustment program; and EBM/80/179 (December 10, 1980), p. 6 ("disaster facility").

[107]The guidelines adopted by the Executive Board on February 10, 1982, are reproduced in Appendix II to this chapter.

[108]Two of the nine included industrial as well as developing countries in their constituencies: Michael Casey (Alternate—Ireland) and Miguel A. Senior (Alternate—Venezuela).

[109]Minutes of EBM/82/15–16 (February 10, 1982).

quota.[110] In each case, the credits were approved within 2½ to 5 months of the natural disaster. In the majority of cases, the borrowing countries already had a stand-by arrangement in place or were negotiating one, so the question of additional conditionality did not arise. That circumstance applied to the drawing that was by far the largest, by Mexico in January 1986, following the earthquakes of September 1985. As discussed in Chapter 10, Mexico was involved in difficult and prolonged negotiations with the Fund and other creditors, and drawings under its extended arrangement had been disallowed owing to policy excesses. Nonetheless, the Fund responded positively to a request for emergency assistance. In the remaining three cases (the two Yemens and the Solomon Islands), the authorities submitted statements of policy intentions along with their requests for assistance. In 1989, the staff reviewed the guidelines and concluded that the system was working well and could be continued without modification.[111]

Emergency Assistance in Financial Crises

On a few occasions in the early 1980s, the staff considered whether it might be possible to establish procedures for emergency assistance in response to financial crises. In January 1980, the Research Department proposed establishment of a "temporary intermediation facility" to provide low-conditionality loans quickly to countries facing a sudden loss of access to international bank credits. (See Chapter 13, pp. 560–63.) A year later, at the time of the Swedish exchange crisis of January 1981 (see Chapter 2), the European Department toyed with the idea of proposing a credit of up to $1 billion (148 percent of quota) to Sweden for up to six months. Once an adjustment program was negotiated, the credit could be rolled over into a stand-by arrangement. If the crisis passed with no need for an adjustment program, then the balance could be quickly repaid. Around the same time, the Deputy Managing Director, William Dale, proposed using temporary allocations of SDRs on an emergency basis to cope with threats to the stability of the international monetary system arising from debt-servicing problems in one or more

---

[110]The one exception—a credit of 50 percent of quota to the Yemen Arab Republic in March 1983—was made on the spur of the moment and, in a sense, accidentally. Yemen had suffered an estimated $1.8 billion in damages from a severe earthquake in December 1982. In response, the staff and the authorities had discussed a drawing that would be tiny in relation to the damage— approximately $5.3 million, or 25 percent of quota—and the staff report recommended that amount. By the time of the Board meeting, the authorities had not got around to submitting a formal request, so management arranged to ask Directors to approve the drawing in principle. In the course of the discussion, Casey asked whether consideration had been given to 50 percent, in view of the severity of the damage and the unusually small size of Yemen's quota. Mohamed Finaish (speaking for Yemen) quickly asked for 50 percent, and the Board approved that amount over the objections of four Directors. The authorities submitted a formal request a few days later, and the Board confirmed its approval without further discussion. See minutes of EBM/83/35 (February 23, 1983) and EBM/83/40 (February 28).

[111]"Review of Fund Policies with Regard to Emergency Assistance Related to Natural Disasters," EBS/89/69 (April 13, 1989).

large countries. De Larosière, however, reacted negatively to these various proposals, and no action was taken.[112]

In 1982, in the wake of the international debt crisis, the staff noted that "under the Fund's present policies, there are no special facilities that members can use in the event of a financial emergency arising from sudden, severe, and widespread strains in the international financial system." The Executive Board, however, concluded that it would be "inappropriate for the Fund to engage in short-term bridging financing in view of the possible risk of impairing the effectiveness of the Fund's adjustment programs."[113] The idea then was dropped for the remainder of the 1980s.

The general idea of lending to countries before a regular stand-by arrangement could be negotiated was revived in 1993 with the establishment of the Systemic Transformation Facility as a temporary vehicle for assisting economies in transition from central planning systems. The more specific idea of emergency financial assistance was revived in 1995 following the Mexican peso crisis, and interest in it intensified after the onset of the financial crisis in Asia two years later. The New Arrangements to Borrow and the Supplemental Reserve Facility that were approved in 1997 were designed to enable the Fund to respond more effectively in such situations.[114]

Appendix I: The CFF Cereals Window

In May 1981, the Fund established a window within the CFF to compensate countries for the cost of temporary increases in the cost of importing cereals. The text of the Decision is followed by some illustrative examples of how the facility was intended to work.

---

[112]See memorandum from Dale to the Managing Director (January 26, 1981); IMF/CF (S 2110 "Special Drawing Rights, Decisions to Allocate, 4th Basic Period 1981–1982"). De Larosière's disinclination to support these various proposals stemmed from skepticism about their feasibility, not from lack of interest in the general idea. In July 1980, he asked the staff to prepare a confidential report assessing "the role which the Fund could play in the event of a sudden interruption in normal banking flows, whether because of a funding or a lending crisis. . . . This would try to identify where existing arrangements (BIS, national lenders of last resort) might be insufficient to cope with such developments, and suggest a detailed contingency plan for the Fund's possible role." Memorandum (July 10, 1980) to Walter O. Habermeier (Treasurer); IMF/RD (Historian's files). It appears, however, that no such report was prepared.

[113]"The Adequacy of Existing Arrangements to Deal with Major Strains in the International Financial System," EBS/82/194 (October 22, 1982); the quotation is from p. 37. See minutes of EBM/82/150–151 (November 19, 1982); the quotation is from the Chairman's summing up, p. 31 of meeting 82/151.

[114]The New Arrangements to Borrow (NAB) are an agreement by participants to lend to the Fund "when supplementary resources are needed to forestall or cope with an impairment of the international monetary system, or to deal with an exceptional situation that poses a threat to the stability of the system." The Supplemental Reserve Facility (SRF) was adopted "to provide financial assistance to a member country experiencing exceptional balance of payments difficulties due to a large short-term financing need resulting from a sudden and disruptive loss of market confidence reflected in pressure on the capital account and the member's reserves." The quotations are from the Fund's press releases announcing the relevant decisions.

Compensatory Financing of Fluctuations in the Cost of Cereal Imports

1. For an initial period of four years from May 13, 1981, the Fund will be prepared to extend financial assistance in accordance with the terms of this decision to members that encounter a balance of payments difficulty produced by an excess in the cost of their cereal imports. The amount of this financial assistance will be determined in accordance with this decision, which integrates this assistance with that available in accordance with the facility established by the decision on the compensatory financing of export fluctuations (Executive Board Decision No. 6224-(79/135)).

2. For a period of three years from the date of a member's first request for a purchase under this decision, any purchases by the member in respect of its export shortfalls shall be made under this decision instead of under Decision No. 6224.

3. A member with balance of payments difficulties may expect that its request for a purchase under this decision will be met if the Fund is satisfied that

    (a) any shortfall in exports and any excess costs of cereal imports that result in a net shortfall in the member's exports are of a short-term character and are largely attributable to circumstances beyond the control of the member; and

    (b) the member will cooperate with the Fund in an effort to find, where required, appropriate solutions for its balance of payments difficulties.

4. (a) Subject to the limits specified in paragraph 9, a member may request a purchase under this decision for an amount equal to the net shortfall in its exports calculated as the sum of its export shortfall and the excess in its cereal import costs.

    (b)   (i) For the calculation of the net shortfall in exports, an excess in exports shall be considered a negative shortfall in exports and a shortfall in cereal import costs shall be considered a negative excess in cereal import costs.

      (ii) An export shortfall shall be determined in accordance with Decision No. 6224.

      (iii) An excess in cereal import costs shall be determined in accordance with paragraphs 5 and 6.

5. The existence and amount of an excess in the cost of cereal imports shall be determined, for the purpose of purchases under this decision, with respect to the latest 12-month period preceding the request for which the Fund has sufficient statistical data, provided that the Fund may allow a member to make a purchase on the basis of estimated data in respect of a 12-month period ending not later than 12 months after the latest month for which the Fund has sufficient statistical data on the member's cereal import costs. The estimates used for this purpose shall be made in consultation with the member. The calculation of a member's shortfall or excess in exports and its excess or shortfall in the cost of its cereal imports shall be made for the same 12-month period.

6. In order to identify more clearly what are to be regarded as excess costs of cereal imports of a short-term character, the Fund, in consultation with the member concerned, will seek to establish reasonable estimates regarding the medium-term trend of the member's cereal import costs. For the purposes of this decision, the excess in a member's cereal imports for the 12-month period referred to in paragraph 5 shall be the amount by which the member's cereal imports in that 12-month period are more than the arithmetic average of the member's cereal imports for the five-year period centered on that 12-month period.

7. The amount of a purchase under this decision, as defined in paragraph 4, may be either in relation to an export shortfall or to an excess in cereal import costs, or the amount may consist of two components, one relating to an export shortfall and the other relating to

an excess in cereal import costs. The total amount of the purchase and the amount of each component are subject to the limits specified in paragraph 9.

8. (a) The part of the purchase relating to an export shortfall, subject to the limit in paragraph 9(b), shall not exceed the lesser of the export shortfall defined in paragraph 4(b) (ii) and the net shortfall in exports defined in paragraph 4(a).

   (b) The amount of a purchase relating to an excess in cereal import costs, subject to the limit in paragraph 9(c), shall not exceed the lesser of the excess in cereal import costs defined in paragraph 4(b) (iii) and the net shortfall in exports defined in paragraph 4(a).

9. (a) The total amount of a member's purchases outstanding under this decision and Decision No. 6224 shall not exceed an amount equal to 125 per cent of quota, provided that a request for a purchase that would increase the total amount of the member's purchases outstanding under this decision and Decision No. 6224 beyond 50 per cent of quota will be met only if the Fund is satisfied that the member has been cooperating with the Fund in an effort to find, where required, appropriate solutions for its balance of payments difficulties.

   (b) The total amount of a member's purchases outstanding under Decision No. 6224 and this decision that are related to export shortfalls shall not exceed 100 per cent of quota.

   (c) The total amount of a member's purchases outstanding under this decision that are related to the excess in cereal import costs shall not exceed 100 per cent of quota.

10. Where the sum of the export shortfall and cereal import components, as limited by paragraph 9(b) and paragraph 9(c), exceeds the limit specified in paragraph 9(a), the member shall allocate the amount of its purchase as between the two components.

11. Purchases under this decision and holdings resulting from such purchases shall be excluded pursuant to Article XXX(c) for the purpose of the definition of "reserve tranche purchase." For the purpose of applying the Fund's policies on the use of its resources, holdings resulting from the use of the Fund's resources under the policy set forth in this decision shall be considered to be separate from the holdings resulting from the use of the Fund's resources under any other policy, except the policy set forth in Decision No. 6224.

12. When a member requests a purchase on the basis of estimated statistical data the member will be expected to represent that, if the amount of the purchase exceeds the amount that could have been purchased on the basis of actual statistical data, the member will make a prompt repurchase in an amount equivalent to the overcompensation.

13. (a) Subject to paragraph 12, when a reduction in the Fund's holdings of a member's currency is attributed to a purchase under this decision the member shall attribute that reduction between the outstanding cereal import component and export shortfall component of the purchase.

   (b) When the Fund's holdings of a member's currency resulting from a purchase under this decision or Decision No. 6224 are reduced by the member's repurchase or otherwise, the member's access to the Fund's resources under this decision will be restored *pro tanto*, subject to the limits in paragraph 9.

14. (a) After the expiration of the period referred to in paragraph 2, the total amount of the export shortfall components of a member's purchases outstanding under this decision shall be counted as having been purchased under Decision No. 6224, and the resulting total of the amounts outstanding under Decision No. 6224 and the cereal import components outstanding under this decision shall not exceed 125 per cent of quota.

(b) The provisions of Decision No. 6224 shall continue to apply to the export shortfall component of a purchase under this decision after the expiration of the period referred to in paragraph 2 or the expiration of this decision.

15. In order to implement the Fund's policies in connection with the financing of members' cereal import costs and the compensatory financing of export shortfalls, the fund will be prepared to waive the limit on the Fund's holdings of 200 per cent of quota, (i) when necessary to permit purchases to be made under this decision or (ii) to the extent that purchases are outstanding under this decision.

16. The Fund will indicate in an appropriate manner which purchases by a member are made pursuant to this decision, and the export shortfall component and the cereal import component of each.

17. The Executive Board will review this decision not later than June 30, 1983, and when quota increases under the Eighth General Review of Quotas become effective.

Decision No. 6860-(81/81), adopted May 13, 1981

Illustrations of the Functioning of the CFF Cereals Window

As an illustration of how the 1981 cereals window in the CFF handled cereal imports in relation to merchandise exports, consider the following system of equations:[115]

Let

$$S_x \doteq \bar{X} - X_t$$

$$E_m \doteq M_t - \bar{M}$$

$$S_n \doteq S_x - E_m$$

$$\ln\bar{X} = [\ln\bar{X}_{t-2} + \ln\bar{X}_{t-1} + \ln\tilde{X}_t + \varepsilon(\ln X_{t+1} + \ln X_{t+2})]/5$$

$$\bar{M} = [M_{t-2} + M_{t-1} + \tilde{M}_t + \varepsilon(M_{t+1} + M_{t+2})]/5$$

And define the following rules:

$$C_m = \max[0, \min(E_m, S_n, L_m, L - C_x)]$$
and $C_x = \max[0, \min(S_x, S_n, L_x, L - C_m)]$
or $C_x = \min(S_x, L_x)$ under the 1979 Decision;

where $L_m = 100 - L_0$
$L_x = 100 - L_0$
$L = 125 - L_0$
and L_0 = outstanding CFF obligations.

All data are measured in percent of the country's quota in the Fund. $\bar{X}$ and $\bar{M}$ are the calculated trend values of merchandise exports (X) and cereal imports (M); $\tilde{X}$ and $\tilde{M}$ are the estimated values for the shortfall year (t); and ε denotes a forecast value. Note that the trend value of merchandise exports is calculated as a geometric average, while the trend value of cereal imports is calculated as an arithmetic average. S_x and E_m are the calculated export

---

[115]For the detailed mathematical framework of the basic operation of the CFF before the establishment of the cereals window, see Goreux (1980), Appendix III.

shortfall and import excess, respectively; S_n is the calculated net export shortfall; and C_x and C_m are the allowed compensation levels under the export shortfall and cereals windows, respectively.

For illustration, assume $\overline{X} - \overline{M} = 500$ and $L_0 = 0$.

Case #1: The country has both an export shortfall (say, $X_t = 420$) and excess import costs ($M_t = 580$) and is constrained by the lending limits.

Then $S_x = 80$, $E_m = 80$, and $S_n = 160$
and

$$C_x = \min(80, 160, 125 - C_m) \text{ and } C_m = \min(80, 160, 125 - C_x).$$

In this case, the country is entitled to borrow the maximum amount, 125, and can choose how to divide the total between the two windows as long as no more than 80 is borrowed from either window.

Case #2: The country has a sizable export shortfall and a small excess in cereal imports: $X_t = 450$ and $M_t = 510$.

Then $S_x = 50$, $E_m = 10$, and $S_n = 60$
and

$$C_x = \min(50, 100, 125 - C_m) = 50, \text{ and } C_m = \min(10, 100, 125 - C_x) = 10.$$

In this case, the country is entitled to full compensation for the combined shortfall (60), but by doing so it loses the option of using the 1979 rules if it subsequently suffers a gross (but not a net) export shortfall. Alternatively, it can borrow 50 now, using the 1979 rules, and keep open the possibility of using the cereals window at a later date. Now suppose that in the following year, the country has $X_t = 450$ and $M_t = 550$.

Then $S_x = 50$, $E_m = -50$, and $S_n = 0$
and

$$C_m = 0, \text{ and } C_x = \min(50, 100-50) = 50 \text{ under the 1979 Decision.}$$

Thus by limiting its borrowings to 50 in the first year, the country keeps open the possibility of borrowing a larger total amount (100) over two years.

Case #3: The country has an export shortfall, but its cereal imports are below trend by the same amount: $X_t = M_t = 420$.

Then $S_x = 80$, $S_m = -80$, and $S_n = 0$.

In this case, because the net shortfall is zero, the country is entitled to no compensation under the 1981 rules but can still apply for compensation of 80 under the 1979 rules.

Case #4: The country has an export shortfall, but its cereal imports are below trend by a lesser amount: $X_t = 420$ and $M_t = 480$.

Then $S_x = 80$, $S_m = -20$, and $S_n = 60$.

In this case, $C_m = 0$ and the country can choose between $C_x = 60$ (the net shortfall) under the 1981 rules or $C_x = 80$ (the gross shortfall) under the 1979 rules. Since choosing the old rules leaves open the possibility of using the cereals window if $C_m > 0$ for a subsequent year, the country normally will choose the larger amount in this case.

Case #5: The country has above-trend exports that offset its excess costs of cereal imports: $X_t = M_t = 580$.

Then $S_x = -80$, $S_m = 80$, and $S_n = 0$.

In this case, the country is entitled to no compensation, because the 1979 rules do not apply to cereal imports.

Case #6: The country has above-trend exports that only partially offset its excess costs of cereal imports: $X_t = 520$ *and* $M_t = 580$.

Then $S_x = -20$, $S_m = 80$, and $S_n = 60$.

In this case, the country is entitled to compensation for its net excess cereals costs: $C_m = 60$.

Appendix II: Emergency Assistance for Natural Disasters

When the Fund decided in February 1982 not to establish a special facility for disaster relief, it adopted general guidelines for granting assistance to countries hit by natural disasters.

The Managing Director's concluding remarks at EBM/82/16 (February 10, 1982), pp. 17–18, included the following text:

> I think the best thing we can do at this stage is to note the support for the flexible practices that have been used in the past and have been incorporated in the language of Section III of [Fund Policies with Regard to Emergency Assistance Related to Natural Disasters, (SM/82/7, January 8, 1982)] . . .
>
> One of the advantages of the method already in use is that the management is allowed to exercise discretion and judgment on what constitutes a disaster serious enough to make a country eligible for emergency assistance from the Fund. The staff and management might miss some of the important points, but close contact with the Executive Directors concerned would enable them to receive good guidance on whether a given series of events crosses the threshold of disaster. Judgments will have to be made on the gravity of the situation, on the impact on the balance of payments, and on the type of help the Fund can offer the country in question. Such judgments would not fit easily into a set of rigid guidelines. The present language of Section III [below] seems appropriate, because it gives the staff and management general guidance while leaving them the necessary flexibility. In any event, it is the Board that will decide on each particular case. I am sure that the Board will be happy to have, not a legal document, but some guidelines to use as yardsticks in reaching those decisions.

The text to which those remarks referred read as follows:

III. Issues for Consideration by the Executive Board

The review of experience suggests that effective emergency assistance can continue to be provided to members afflicted by natural disasters through a flexible application of the existing policies on use of Fund's resources. There is, therefore, no need in the staff's judgment for establishing a new facility specifically addressed to cases of emergency. Executive Directors may wish to consider the following broad guidelines for the provision of emergency assistance to members afflicted by natural disasters.

(a) In most cases in which a member is afflicted by a natural disaster, effective assistance would continue to be provided by purchases under the compensatory financing facility or by stand-by and extended arrangements. However, in those cases where a member cannot meet its immediate financing needs arising from a major disaster, such as flood, earthquake, or hurricane, without serious depletion of its external reserves, emergency assistance in the form of quick outright purchases would continue, as in the past, to be provided under a flexible application of tranche policies.

(b) Emergency assistance is designed to provide only limited foreign exchange required for immediate relief. In the past, outright purchases for emergency situations were provided for relatively moderate amounts. In half of the cases, such purchases amounted to 25 percent of quota; in the remaining half, purchases ranged from 42–50 percent of quotas. On the basis of experience, the amount of resources would continue to be limited to the equivalent of one credit tranche, though larger amounts could be made exceptionally available. When need for additional financing is present, it would be best provided under the compensatory financing facility and within the framework of stand-by and extended arrangements.

(c) The amount of an emergency purchase would be taken into account in determining the size of any additional support under a subsequent stand-by or extended arrangement. Moreover, in order to avoid double compensation in cases where a member requests a CFF purchase subsequent to an emergency purchase, a determination would be made at the time of the CFF request of the part of export shortfall on which the CFF request is based that has already been compensated by the emergency purchase. In accordance with the procedures suggested in the Appendix, that part would be deducted from the calculated shortfall and an equivalent amount of the emergency purchase would be reclassified as a CFF purchase.

(d) In emergency situations, timing is crucial; quick assistance from the Fund can both provide relief and encourage financing from other sources. While in most instances, balance of payments difficulties will be transitory, understandings are needed to ensure that inappropriate policies do not compound the problems caused by the disaster. As in the past, a flexible and pragmatic approach will be followed to take into account the particular circumstances of the country, the nature and the extent of the disaster and the need to safeguard the revolving character of Fund resources.

(e) For purposes of emergency assistance requests, a member would be required to describe the general policies it plans to pursue, including its intention to avoid introducing or intensifying exchange and trade restrictions. The request will be granted when the Fund is satisfied that the member will cooperate with the Fund in an effort to find, where appropriate, solutions for its balance of payments difficulties. Frequently, at the time of the request of emergency assistance, members expressed an intention to devise adjustment programs in consultation with the Fund, but this intention was seldom carried out. To strengthen this aspect of the Fund's emergency assistance, the member's cooperation with the Fund in designing and adopting, when appropriate and as soon as circumstances permit, necessary adjustment measures would be one of the elements to be considered in the assessment of the requirement of cooperation associated with CFF purchases in the upper tranche. Such an approach would be applied so as to allow the assessment of cooperation to continue to be made on a pragmatic basis in the light of the nature of the difficulties and the circumstances of the member.

References

Boughton, James M., 1991, "Commodity and Manufactures Prices in the Long Run," IMF Working Paper 91/47 (Washington: International Monetary Fund).

Brandt Commission [Independent Commission on International Development Issues under the Chairmanship of Willy Brandt], 1980, *North-South: A Program for Survival* (Cambridge, Massachusetts: MIT Press).

Dale, William B., 1994, "Looking Back," *The Caravan*, IMF Retirees Association, Vol. 13, No. 2 (January), pp. 19–24.

de Vries, Margaret Garritsen, 1976, *The International Monetary Fund, 1966–1971: The System Under Stress*, Vol. 1: *Narrative*; Vol. 2: *Documents* (Washington: International Monetary Fund).

———, 1985, *The International Monetary Fund, 1972–1978: Cooperation on Trial*, Vols. 1 and 2: *Narrative and Analysis*; Vol. 3: *Documents* (Washington: International Monetary Fund).

Erb, Richard D., 1981, testimony before the U.S. House of Representatives, Subcommittee on International Trade, Investment, and Monetary Policy, of the Committee on Banking, Finance and Urban Affairs, in "Oversight Hearings on U.S. International Monetary Policies," Serial 97–38 (December 10), pp. 206–19.

Erikson, Erik H., 1969, *Gandhi's Truth: On the Origins of Militant Nonviolence* (New York: W.W. Norton).

FAO Council, 1979, "Report of the Fourth Session of the Committee on World Food Security," Council Document CL 75/10 (May).

Finch, C. David, 1997, *Werribee to Washington: A Career at the International Monetary Fund* (unpublished; Washington).

Goreux, Louis M., 1980, *Compensatory Financing Facility*, IMF Pamphlet Series, No. 34 (Washington: International Monetary Fund).

Gwin, Catherine, 1983, "Financing India's Structural Adjustment: The Role of the Fund," in *IMF Conditionality*, ed. by John Williamson (Washington: Institute for International Economics) pp. 511–31.

Horsefield, J. Keith, ed., 1969, *The International Monetary Fund, 1945–1965: Twenty Years of International Monetary Cooperation*, Vol. 1: *Chronicle*, by J. Keith Horsefield; Vol. 2: *Analysis*, by Margaret G. de Vries and J. Keith Horsefield with the collaboration of Joseph Gold, Mary H. Gumbart, Gertrud Lovasy, and Emil G. Spitzer; Vol. 3: *Documents* (Washington: International Monetary Fund).

International Monetary Fund, 1992, *Annual Report 1992* (Washington: International Monetary Fund).

———, 1987, *Summary Proceedings* (Washington: International Monetary Fund).

Intergovernmental Group of Twenty-Four on International Monetary Affairs, 1987, *The Role of the IMF in Adjustment with Growth* (Washington).

Joshi, Vijay, and I.M.D. Little, 1994, *India: Macroeconomics and Political Economy, 1964–91* (Washington: World Bank).

Kapur, Devesh, John P. Lewis, and Richard Webb, 1997, *The World Bank: Its First Half Century*, Vol. 1: *History* (Washington: Brookings Institution).

Killick, Tony, 1984, "IMF Stabilisation Programmes," in *The Quest for Economic Stabilisation: The IMF and the Third World*, ed. by Tony Killick (London: Heinemann Educational Books), pp. 183–226.

Mansingh, Surjit, 1984, *India's Search for Power: Indira Gandhi's Foreign Policy 1966–1982* (New Delhi: Sage Publications).

Mukherjee, Pranab, 1984, *Beyond Survival: Emerging Dimensions of Indian Economy* (New Delhi: Vikas Publishing House).

Narasimham, M., 1988, *World Economic Environment and Prospects for India* (New Delhi: Sterling Publishers).

Polak, Jacques J., 1991, *The Changing Nature of IMF Conditionality*, Essays in International Finance, No. 184 (Princeton, New Jersey: International Finance Section, Department of Economics, Princeton University).

Thatcher, Margaret, 1993, *The Downing Street Years* (New York: HarperCollins).

16

Digging a Hole, Filling It In: Payments Arrears to the Fund

An uncomfortable but unavoidable byproduct of the IMF's role as a global financial institution is the necessity of the timely repayment of credits by indebted countries. Delays in repaying either principal or interest threaten the cooperative nature of the membership and can seriously impair the Fund's ability to continue to provide financial assistance to other countries. Although critics have often attacked the IMF for being more interested in getting its money back than in helping its member countries, the vast majority of the Fund's members have always recognized that the institution cannot help unless it preserves its assets as a revolving stock of lendable resources. When arrears to the Fund became substantial in the 1980s, creditor and indebted countries alike insisted on a strong reaction.

This chapter begins with an overview on how the arrears problem at the Fund developed through the 1980s. It then reviews in more detail the cases where countries developed problems serious enough to warrant the Fund declaring them ineligible to borrow any more from the institution. During the 1980s, that was the final step available to the Fund in sanctioning countries, short of compelling them to withdraw from membership. (The lesser action—restricting access to Fund resources until arrears were settled—had a similar effect but imposed less of a stigma on the country, was not a formal step toward compulsory withdrawal, and was intended merely to cut off credits and to pressure the authorities to settle arrears within a limited period.) The practice of publicly declaring countries ineligible to borrow from the Fund was of limited value as a deterrent, and it did nothing to normalize relations with, or restore the economic viability of, the affected countries. The chapter concludes by reviewing the various steps taken by the Fund in the late 1980s and early 1990s to develop new approaches for resolving the arrears problem.

Overview

For most of the Fund's first four decades of operations, arrears were only rarely a problem. Whenever a country had difficulty making a scheduled payment, it was almost always resolved within a few months, after informal consultation between the staff and the authorities. Before 1984, the Executive Board took action in only three cases, each of which resulted to some extent from a major political problem affecting the indebted country.

- Cuba drew its gold tranche and its first credit tranche ($25 million) from the Fund in September 1958, during the final months of the collapsing regime of President Fulgencio Batista. The Fund repeatedly agreed to postpone repayment after Fidel Castro took power in 1959, until the five-year limit on outstanding drawings was about to expire. The Managing Director issued a formal complaint in September 1963 and initiated procedures that could have led to a declaration that Cuba was ineligible to use Fund resources. That process was aborted when Cuba withdrew from the Fund in 1964, and the Castro government eventually repaid the money over the remainder of the decade. (For details, see Horsefield, 1969, Vol. 1, pp. 548–50.)

- Egypt took out a stand-by arrangement in 1962,[1] and a schedule was established for repayment through 1967. In 1966, the authorities requested a new stand-by arrangement, which would have enabled them in effect to reschedule the existing obligations over several more years, but negotiations broke down over the Fund's insistence on a large devaluation. At the end of the year, the authorities stopped paying the Fund, and President Gamal Abdel Nasser publicly linked that decision to the Fund's attempt to impose unacceptable conditionality on new lending. By the time the Executive Board began considering what steps to take in response, the Egyptian economy was hit by new shocks. After the June 1967 war with Israel (the "six-day" war), the Suez Canal was blocked by ships sunk in the fighting, and the economy also was suffering from unrelated problems including a severe drop in the cotton harvest. The authorities again asked for an extension or a new stand-by arrangement, but the Managing Director determined that they should repay their existing obligations before receiving any new credits. The Fund imposed surcharges on the overdue balances starting in July 1967, until the overdue obligations were repaid the following year.[2] No formal steps were taken toward declaring the country ineligible.

- When Pol Pot and the Khmer Rouge took control of Cambodia by overthrowing the government of Lon Nol in April 1975, the country owed the Fund SDR 12.5 million ($15 million) for Compensatory Financing Facility (CFF) drawings made in 1972–73. It also was required under the rules then in effect to restore its gold tranche and reconstitute its holdings of SDRs.

---

[1]At the time, Egypt and Syria constituted the United Arab Republic, which was the member in the Fund. The matter discussed here related to the Egyptian economy.

[2]The standard schedule of interest charges at that time peaked at 5 percent, subject to the provision that the Fund could impose higher charges on obligations outstanding beyond five years. From July 1967 until arrears were settled in February 1968, the obligations of the United Arab Republic that had been outstanding for more than five years were subject to charges at an annual rate of 6 percent. See IMF/CF, C/U.A.R./1750, "United Arab Republic—Charges," EBS/68/16 (January 18, 1968), and "United Arab Republic—Charges," EBS/68/49 (February 23, 1968). For the background documents on which this summary of Egypt's arrears is based, see IMF/RD Middle Eastern Department file "United Arab Republic, 1967" (Accession 71/141, Box 3, Section 118).

Communications between the capital, Phnom Penh, and the outside world were virtually severed during the reign of terror of the next four years (and remained severed after Pol Pot was in turn overthrown by Vietnamese forces in 1978), and the Fund was able to communicate with the government only through Cambodia's ambassador to the United Nations. In December 1975, the ambassador informed the Fund that the new Cambodian government "would not assume the obligations contracted by the Lon Nol Government" and that it "regards all actions taken by the Lon Nol Government as null and void."[3] Subsequently, the ambassador was withdrawn, and the Fund no longer had any reliable channel of communication with the authorities in Phnom Phen.[4] In May 1978, the Executive Board agreed to impose penalty charges on Cambodia's overdue obligations, and in December it restricted access to Fund resources and SDRs.[5]

Arrears to the Fund generalized into an institutional issue in 1984. In April of that year, three countries—Cambodia, Guyana, and Nicaragua—were overdue by more than six months, and eight others were overdue by at least six weeks. Although the Fund had developed practices for dealing with such problems by handling the three isolated cases just described, the Executive Board had not yet adopted formal rules. Several issues had to be resolved.[6]

First, at what stage should Executive Directors get involved? Fund policy from 1946 was that the Managing Director "shall report to the Executive Board any case in which it appears to him that a member [country] is not fulfilling obligations under the Articles."[7] Such reports had been rare until 1981 but had been issued with increasing frequency since then. Normal practice was for the Managing Director

---

[3]"Relations with Government of Cambodia—Performance of Obligations Under the Articles of Agreement," EBS/76/501 (December 4, 1976), p. 3.

[4]In October 1978, the staff delivered a letter of inquiry to Cambodia's deputy prime minister, who was in New York to address the General Assembly of the United Nations. No reply was received. Similar attempts in the following two months also were unsuccessful, after which the Khmer Rouge government was overthrown (although it continued, in exile, to retain its formal representation in the UN). IMF/CF (C/Kampuchea/750 "Obligations Under Fund Agreement"); letter from Leo Van Houtven (Secretary of the IMF) to H.E. Ieng Sary, Deputy Prime Minister in Charge of Foreign Affairs of Democratic Kampuchea (October 11, 1978), with attached cable from the Managing Director, H. Johannes Witteveen; and memorandum from Jan-Maarten Zegers (Special Representative of the IMF to the United Nations) to Van Houtven (October 13, 1978). Also see "Text of Managing Director's Memorandum and Decision—EBM/78/182 (11/17/78)," SM/78/274, Sup. 1 (November 20, 1978), p. 3.

[5]Minutes of EBM/78/72 (May 10, 1978) and EBM/78/200 (December 19, 1978).

[6]See "Overdue Payments to the Fund—Experience and Procedures," EBS/84/46 (March 9, 1984) and minutes of EBM/84/54 (April 5, 1984).

[7]This language is from Rule K-1 of the Fund's Rules and Regulations. Similar language was included in Rule S-1, which was established in 1969 to deal with arrears in settling obligations to the SDR Department. Both rules are reproduced in the Appendix to this chapter. Throughout, this chapter focuses primarily on arrears to the General Resources Account (GRA). While several countries also had arrears to the SDR Department or on loans from the Fund's Administered Accounts, no country developed protracted arrears *only* on those books in the 1980s, and they therefore did not become an independent problem. (Iraq, which had no outstanding obligations to the GRA, went into arrears to the SDR Department in 1991.)

to notify the Board within six weeks after a payment became overdue. The Board, however, did not get involved directly in reviewing or trying to resolve the matter until the Managing Director issued a formal complaint, and there was no standard timetable for him to do so. The Board agreed to set six months as a rough standard, but management was urged to be flexible in applying it.

Second, what steps should be taken to prevent countries in arrears from continuing to borrow? The Fund had no fixed rule prohibiting a country with overdue obligations from drawing on an existing stand-by arrangement. In fact, as long as the performance criteria for the arrangement were met, the Fund had no legal means of denying a request for a drawing. The Board therefore decided to include a standard clause as a performance criterion in all subsequent arrangements, prohibiting drawings by countries in arrears.

Third, should the Fund impose higher penalty charges on overdue obligations? As noted above, the Fund had imposed higher charges in those few cases where amounts had remained outstanding for more than five years. It had not, however, adopted a policy of penalizing countries when obligations became overdue, and it had never gone beyond the 6 percent annual rate specified as a threshold in the Fund's Rules prior to the Second Amendment.[8] The Board agreed that such penalties were unlikely to create an incentive for countries to repay on time and could be counterproductive by adding to a country's financial burden.

Fourth, should the Fund issue public announcements when countries went into arrears? The threat of publicity could help put pressure on countries to settle more promptly, but the Fund still had a culture of secrecy, and the idea made many Directors uneasy. The Board agreed to consider publicizing arrears, but only on an ad hoc basis in extreme cases.

Fifth, should the Fund consider rescheduling obligations as a means of resolving or avoiding arrears? Rescheduling was a standard practice among both commercial and official creditors, but the Fund had made only limited use of it and had generally avoided it since the Second Amendment had gone into effect in 1978.[9] Before 1978, the only firm requirement on repaying Fund credits was the outer limit of five years.[10] Countries typically would agree to a schedule of repayments, but the Fund often agreed later to reschedule within the time limit when countries ran

---

[8]Prior to 1978, charges were imposed at a fixed schedule of rates that increased with the length of time the obligations were outstanding, up to 5 percent on large obligations outstanding for $4\frac{1}{2}$ to 5 years. Beyond five years, the Rules provided that "the Fund may adopt higher maximum rates . . . provided that when the charges . . . have reached 6 per cent the Fund will review the charges to be imposed thereafter." (Rule I-4 (g) as amended through April 24, 1963; de Vries, 1976, Vol. 2, p. 178.) The Second Amendment provided for a system of variable charges linked to the current level of interest rates; see Chapter 17.

[9]Article V of the Fund's Articles of Agreement authorizes the Board to reschedule payments due to the Fund by a simple majority of votes cast, as long as the new payment schedule stays within the normal time limits. By a 70 percent majority of the voting power, the Board can reschedule obligations beyond the normal limits.

[10]As an exception, the Extended Fund Facility (EFF) provided for an eight-year outer limit and specified that "normally," repayments were to be made in 16 quarterly instalments beginning in the fifth year. See Chapter 15.

into difficulties. The Second Amendment, however, called for a standard repayment schedule beginning after three years and ending in five. Only in cases of "exceptional hardship" would the Board consider delaying that schedule. In two cases in 1982 (Guyana and Nicaragua), the Board had decided that the country was facing dire circumstances that made the normal repayment schedule impracticable. In both cases, payments were rescheduled within the five-year outer limit. Unfortunately, both countries failed to meet the revised schedule as well, and they now were the two that had recently become overdue by more than six months.

The decisive point on this issue was that rescheduling of Fund credits was inconsistent with the Fund's role in negotiating new stand-by arrangements as preconditions for reschedulings by the Paris Club and other creditors. Financially, rescheduling is equivalent to providing new credit to the borrower. For the Fund, the provision of new credit is normally subject to the country's agreement to adopt sound economic policies. For other holders of sovereign credits, such an agreement is normally a precondition for a rescheduling. Therefore, negotiating a new stand-by arrangement is almost always the preferred option. Although the Board in 1984 did not completely rule out the possibility of rescheduling, it made it clear that the practice should be reserved for rare cases where policies were already appropriate but where specific circumstances created an exceptional hardship if repayment was to be effected on a particular date.[11]

Sixth, and most controversial, should the staff negotiate terms for adjustment programs that could be supported by new stand-by arrangements once arrears were settled? The staff view was that entering into negotiations on acceptable policy conditions for the use of Fund resources was inappropriate as long as countries were in arrears. The Treasurer of the Fund, Walter O. Habermeier, argued before the Board that the staff's refusal to negotiate "had been one of the most effective instruments in persuading members to settle their overdue payments." That view was supported by the Managing Director, Jacques de Larosière, who added: "We are trying to strengthen this policy, not weaken it."[12] Several Executive Directors from developing countries worried that this policy was counterproductive and could even put indebted countries into a catch-22 situation. If a country could repay the Fund only by borrowing from other international creditors, and if such borrowing depended (as it usually did) on the country first agreeing on economic policies with the Fund, then the refusal to negotiate blocked any possibility of a solution. For the time being, that view was held only by a minority on the Board. Countries could repay if they were willing, the reasoning went, and the key was to create the right incentives.

When the arrears problem arose, the Fund had little available in the way of sanctions. After the initial review in 1984, as soon as a country developed arrears, it could not draw anymore on existing stand-by arrangements and could not even

---

[11]The Board's antipathy toward rescheduling was reiterated and strengthened on several occasions over the next few years, and no payments were rescheduled after 1982. For the evolution of the Fund's policies on rescheduling, see "Repurchase Obligations—Postponement (Article V, Section 7(g))," SM/87/226 (August 25, 1987).

[12]Minutes of EBM/84/54 (April 5, 1984), pp. 33 (Habermeier) and 38 (de Larosière).

Figure 16.1. Protracted Arrears to the Fund, 1978–95

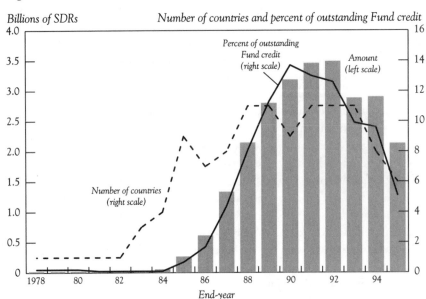

negotiate terms for a new arrangement. Beyond that, all that the Fund could do—short of compelling the country to withdraw from membership—was to issue a series of declarations of increasing displeasure.[13] Typically, those declarations would begin with a suspension (formally, a "limitation") of access to Fund resources until arrears were cleared, and would lead ultimately to a declaration that the country was ineligible to use Fund resources. Neither decision greatly affected the country's immediate borrowing rights, which were already suspended.[14] Nonetheless, they attached an internationally endorsed stigma to the country's refusal to repay the Fund and thus sent a powerful signal to other official creditors. By mid-1985, those sanctions were augmented by the pressure of publicity, as the Fund began releasing information to the public on the most serious arrears cases.

---

[13]Authority to declare a member country ineligible to use the Fund's general resources and to require the country to withdraw from membership are both found in Article XXVI, Section 2. The Third Amendment, which became effective in November 1992, added an intermediate step under which the Fund could suspend the country's voting rights in the Fund. (See the Appendix.)

[14]The Executive Board decisions on arrears refer to a "limitation" with respect to the use of the Fund's general resources and to a "suspension" with respect to the use of SDRs. The term "restriction" is used here to refer to either action, both of which prevented the member from using the specified resources. Restriction on the use of general resources blocked access to any balances otherwise available under the first credit tranche and to credits for emergency assistance or through special facilities such as the CFF, in addition to the already blocked access to credits under the Fund's upper-tranche policies. The right to use SDRs was handled separately and was suspended only in cases where the country had overdue obligations in the SDR Department; see Chapter 18. Arrears on Trust Fund loans were not formally a cause for restriction, but the Board routinely informed countries with Trust Fund arrears that it would take them into account in evaluating requests to use Fund resources.

Table 16.1. Countries with Arrears to the IMF, 1978–89
(*Millions of SDRs*)

Country[a]	Date of Complaint	Date of Ineligibility	Ending Date	Amount of Settlement[b]	Outstanding End-April 1990	Amount in Percent of Quota
Cambodia	11/17/78	...	10/1/93	...	36.3	145
Chad	6/29/84	...	11/8/84	4.1	...	13
Gambia	3/25/85	...	4/25/85	3.7	...	22
	9//85	...	7/25/86	10.4	...	61
Guyana	3/9/84	5/15/85	6/20/90	...	104.8	213
Haiti	7/11/88	...	10/24/88	4.4	...	10
	1/13/89	...	9/8/89	9.4	...	21
Honduras	1/21/88	...	11/9/88	3.4	...	5
	1/30/89	11/30/89	6/28/90	...	25.7	38
Jamaica	6/20/86	...	1/13/87	118		81
Liberia	4/4/85	1/24/86		...	307.8	432
Nicaragua	3/9/84	...	4/26/85	7.5		11
Panama	3/3/88	6/30/89	2/5/92	...	181.5	178
Peru	12/13/85	8/15/86	3/18/93	...	626.2	189
Romania	8/29/86	...	11/21/86	83.5	...	16
Sierra Leone	4/30/85	...	9/18/86	25.1	...	43
	3/17/87	4/25/88	3/28/94	...	70.8	122
Somalia	10/25/85	...	4/22/86	21.9	...	50
	7/22/86	...	9/15/86	12.7	...	29
	2/2/87	...	6/26/87	21.5	...	49
	9/8/87	5/6/88	...	...	103.5	234
Sudan	12/12/84	2/3/86	...	...	889.4	524
Tanzania	6//85	...	7/30/86	22.9	...	21
Vietnam	6/29/84	1/15/85	10/6/93	...	104.6	59
Zaïre	9/2/88	...	5/17/89	115.0	...	40
Zambia	7/31/85	...	1/6/86	115.2	...	43
	7/18/86	9/30/87	12/6/95		800.6	296
Total					3,214.9	

[a]This table excludes cases in which arrears were settled without a formal complaint to Executive Directors, or in which a complaint was outstanding for less than 30 days. The latter category comprises Nicaragua in 1986 and 1987, for SDR charges only; and Uganda in 1987, 1988, and 1989 (see Chapter 14). In addition, a notice was issued in 1989 with respect to overdue Trust Fund repayments by El Salvador. ("Complaints" were issued with respect to overdue obligations in the General Resources Account or the SDR Department; "notices" were issued with respect to overdue Trust Fund obligations.)

[b]As arrears often were cleared in multiple installments, settlement amounts are to some extent arbitrary. The figures given here reflect amounts outstanding prior to the final payment or payments.

As shown in Figure 16.1 and Table 16.1, the arrears problem worsened substantially through the rest of the 1980s and began to taper off during the early 1990s. The origins of the problem, however, lay in the first half of the 1980s, when the Fund was lending heavily to developing countries that were struggling to cope with the international debt crisis, the widespread recession in industrial countries, and the associated withdrawal of commercial and bilateral official loans. The growth in the amount of arrears in the second half of the 1980s resulted primarily from the accumulation of arrears by countries already in difficulty, rather than from new lending. Typically, at the time that a country became overdue on payments to the

Fund, it had a string of future repayments to make. In addition, interest kept accumulating on the overdue balances. Until the country finally settled, the amount in arrears kept growing, often dramatically so.

By 1989, complaints had been issued to the Executive Board with respect to 21 countries, 12 of which had been or soon would be publicly identified as ineligible to use Fund resources. At the peak in 1990, protracted arrears (payments in arrears for six months or more) were equivalent to nearly 14 percent of outstanding Fund credits.[15] In the General Department (the Fund's own resources), total obligations of countries that had protracted arrears then accounted for 11½ percent of total outstanding obligations.

What accounted for the arrears problem? Conventional wisdom suggested that the Fund, under political pressure, was lax in controlling its lending in the early 1980s and that it then had to scramble out of a mess of its own making. (See the first section of Chapter 13.) Instances certainly can be cited where the Fund agreed to support weak or poorly designed adjustment programs that led to an unsustainable accumulation of debts, and some of those instances may have been influenced by political pressure. The prevalence of low-conditionality lending through special facilities in the 1970s certainly raised the magnitude of debts to the Fund by countries that could ill afford to service them; for example, all of the countries declared ineligible to use Fund resources in the 1980s had outstanding obligations deriving from the CFF. But the laxity scenario does not go very far toward explaining the magnitude of the problem. Overall, the reasons for countries failing to repay the Fund were complex, and they varied from case to case. No uniform pattern emerges from either an economic or a political perspective.[16]

In several instances, disastrous shifts in economic or political circumstances after the bulk of the Fund's lending had occurred made it difficult or even impossible for governments to meet the agreed repayment terms. Sudan and Zambia, for example, once had good economic prospects but later were hit by terrible shocks. In other cases, shifts in the political regime led either to a loss of external support or to a populist recalcitrance by the new government, or to both. Peru's arrears resulted largely from a populist governmental policy; Sudan, Somalia, Liberia, and Honduras all suffered significantly from reductions in donor support; Vietnam and Panama were hit by economic sanctions.

In some cases, governments tried to carry out adjustment programs but eventually concluded that the policies recommended by the Fund were either unrealistically austere or technically flawed. The latter argument was made with particular force in cases where a controlled exchange rate regime was replaced by a market-based auction system that resulted in a large and seemingly unstoppable depreciation. Sierra Leone and Somalia are notable examples in that regard. In both Sierra Leone and Zambia, governments tried for a time to undertake a

---

[15]This figure includes obligations that were overdue by less than six months but that were owed by countries that had other obligations overdue by six months or more.

[16]One geographic oddity stands out: no country outside the tropics developed protracted arrears to the Fund until the 1990s.

needed stabilization program but found that they lacked domestic political support.

In at least one case (Honduras), nearly all of these factors were at work to some degree. While no single development was especially severe, the combination created substantial difficulties.

The widespread collapse in commodity prices, the wild cycle in key-currency exchange rates, the debt crisis in Latin America, the final throes of the Cold War and of the efforts of many dictators to hang onto power: the 1980s brought a plague of obstacles to the orderly conduct of international finance. Curiously, however, only a few countries, such as Somalia, completely lacked the means to generate enough foreign exchange to meet their payments to the Fund. The more prevailing problem—most obviously in countries such as Vietnam where the roots of economic difficulties were nurtured in political waters—was that governments had higher priorities than repaying the IMF.

The Fund took a particularly hard line when countries were making payments to other creditors. In the Fund's view, member countries should give the highest priority to repaying the Fund. In other words, the Fund regarded itself as the preferred creditor and expected its member countries to recognize that position (see below, p. 820). Some indebted countries, however, gave preference to repaying creditors from whom a net increase in new lending could be expected. In most such cases, the Fund had already lent heavily, was limited by its policies on exposure relative to the country's quota, and in any case was not prepared to make any promises on new lending until after arrears were cleared. These differences in view created occasional conflicts that prolonged the growth of arrears.

The role of politics in Fund lending and in the evolution of the arrears problem was subtle and complex. Creditor countries occasionally discouraged the Fund, through their Executive Directors or through discreet contacts with management, from lending to countries with whom they were displeased for political reasons. Though perhaps less often, they also pushed the Fund toward lending to countries that were in political favor.[17] Even more subtly, staff judgments unquestionably were occasionally influenced by perceptions of whether countries were in international political favor. In most instances, however, political influences were limited, for three reasons. First, both management and most creditor-country officials placed a high value on the financial integrity and credibility of the Fund and were not willing to take major risks in compromising it. Second, the professional staff of the Fund had built up a very strong reputation for independent technical analysis, and the staff's recommendations therefore were nearly always accorded a dominant weight in the Fund's lending decisions. Third, unless creditor countries all agreed on a particular issue and were all prepared to take a stand on it, their views and votes would not have been decisive in the Executive Board.

---

[17]In 1987, C. David Finch resigned as Director of the Exchange and Trade Relations Department because of what he viewed as inappropriate political pressure on the Fund to lend to certain countries. See Chapter 20, pp. 1046–47.

The decisive role of political considerations in the emergence and settlement of external arrears, including arrears to the Fund, was in the provision or denial of bilateral official assistance to heavily indebted countries. In several cases, as noted above and detailed below, one factor cited by countries in arrears to the Fund was the reduction or withholding of economic assistance by major donors. To some extent, the declines in aid may have been motivated by concerns over whether the recipients were putting the money to effective use, but political factors also were important. Once a country developed arrears, especially when arrears remained outstanding and continued to accumulate for several years, a resumption of foreign aid (or, in less severe cases, a bridging loan) became the sine qua non for resolving the problem. Donor countries then had considerable leverage for affecting the conditions under which arrears might be settled. Such considerations did not directly involve the Fund, but they did set the environment within which the arrears problem was played out.

Digging the Hole: Loans That Went Bad

From 1985 through 1989, the Fund declared 10 countries ineligible to use its resources because of outstanding arrears. One other country, Zaïre, borrowed regularly during the 1980s and later proved unable to repay those debts; Zaïre was declared ineligible in September 1991. The first three cases to reach the stage of ineligibility were all small countries with intractable problems; all south of the Tropic of Cancer, though on three different continents: Vietnam, Guyana, and Liberia.

Vietnam

The Republic of Viet-Nam, as it was then called, became a member of the Fund on September 21, 1956. Under the terms of the July 1954 Geneva Agreements, Viet-Nam was a single political entity with a military demarcation line dividing north and south. The Republic government controlled the south but claimed sovereignty over the entire country. It never drew on Fund resources, although it attempted to do so in the final days before troops supported by the Democratic Republic of Viet-Nam (which controlled the north) captured Saigon (later Ho Chi Minh City) on April 30, 1975. That attempt failed because of fears in the Fund that officials fleeing Saigon would almost certainly abscond with the money. On receiving a request to draw the country's gold tranche, to use the full allocation of SDRs, and to borrow through the Oil Facility, the Managing Director (H. Johannes Witteveen) put the question to the Executive Board as to whether a proper request from a member could be denied. The Fund's Articles of Agreement did not provide for such a refusal, but the Fund's General Counsel (Joseph Gold) observed that the Articles did not cover a situation in which a danger existed that the member state might soon cease to exist. Although a substantial majority of the Board preferred to grant the requests for the gold tranche (SDR 15.5 million) and the use of SDRs (SDR 19.7 million; for a total of $43 million), the Board agreed to a compromise proposal by management to seek further clarification of the continued authenticity of the authorities in Saigon, as a means of buying a little time until the military and political situation became clearer. No response was received to the Managing Director's cables, and the request thus was not pursued.[18] Later that summer, the Fund recognized the Provisional Revolutionary Government as the representative of the renamed Republic of South Viet Nam. The country was formally reunified on July 2, 1976, and the Socialist Republic of Viet Nam succeeded to membership on September 15.

The Socialist Republic moved immediately to draw on the Fund. Within a few months, the authorities drew the country's reserve tranche and nearly all of their allocated SDRs from the Fund, and applied for a CFF drawing for export shortfalls. They obtained that credit (for 50 percent of quota) in January 1977, drew on the first credit tranche in July 1978 and again in January 1981, and got two loans from the Trust Fund, in August 1978 and in March 1981. The authorities also sought a stand-by arrangement, but negotiations dragged on for years without an agreement on the required policy adjustments.

When the Executive Board considered these various requests from Vietnam,[19] the question of whether the government had the financial capacity to service additional debts did not arise. The usual concerns were expressed about the extent of the proposed adjustment measures, and a few Directors raised questions about what they saw as a major waste of scarce resources resulting from Vietnam's military occupation of Democratic Kampuchea (Cambodia).[20] These various concerns probably would have sufficed to defeat a request to borrow in the upper credit tranches, but not the modest amounts that Vietnam requested.

Vietnam serviced its obligations with occasional difficulty through 1983 and then essentially stopped paying. At the end of 1983, Vietnam's obligations totaled approximately SDR 28 million (16 percent of quota; $29 million) to the GRA and SDR 61 million ($64 million) to the Trust Fund (Figure 16.2). Interest charges and rescheduled repayments on those obligations, plus charges due on the use of SDRs, would total a little over SDR 10 million during the first half of 1984.[21]

When the Fund complained about the arrears in February 1984, the authorities responded that they had asked their correspondent banks in the United States to transfer the required funds to the IMF, but that the U.S. government was blocking them from doing so. That blockage dated back nearly a decade, to the day of the capture of Saigon in 1975 and about a year before the Socialist Republic succeeded

[18]See the Secretary's summary of the discussion in restricted session at EBM/75/63 (April 23, 1975) and EBM/75/64 (April 25); and "Special Drawing Account—Restricted Session," EBAP/75/199 (July 24, 1975). For a reasonably accurate contemporaneous account, see Rowan (1975).

[19]The single-word form, "Vietnam," was officially adopted in the Fund in 1995.

[20]See minutes of EBM/81/3 (January 7, 1981). Vietnam engaged in a war against the Khmer Rouge rulers of Cambodia in 1976–78, defeated the Khmer Rouge in 1978, and then ruled the country through a puppet government until September 1989. International opinion widely denounced the occupation, which contributed to Vietnam's difficulties in restoring normal relations with the IMF and other multilateral institutions.

[21]"Viet Nam—Overdue Financial Obligations to the Fund—Report and Complaints Under Rules K-1 and S-1 and Notice of Failure to Repay Trust Fund Loan," EBS/84/142 (June 29, 1984), p. 1.

Figure 16.2. Vietnam: Use of Fund Credit and Arrears, 1976–90

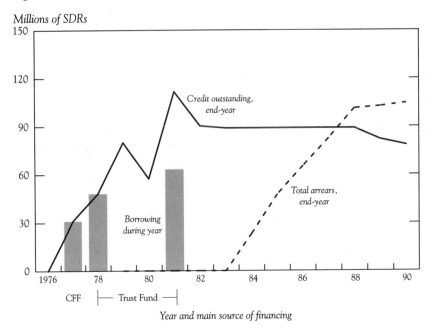

Millions of SDRs

CFF ├── Trust Fund ──┤

Year and main source of financing

to membership.[22] The Fund could do nothing to resolve that political issue, but the Executive Board did note that Vietnam held more than enough unencumbered gold reserves to service its overdue obligations to the Fund without touching the blocked assets in U.S. banks.[23]

---

[22]Blocking the transfer of bank deposits abroad constitutes an exchange restriction that is subject to the jurisdiction of the Fund. If the restriction is imposed for reasons of national security, the member is required to notify the Fund of the restriction, and the Fund may decide that it is not satisfied with the explanation. (See Horsefield, 1969, Vol. 1, pp. 275–76, and Vol. 3, p. 257.) In July 1975, the U.S. authorities represented to the Fund (without objection from the Executive Board) that the restrictions on Vietnam had been imposed for national security purposes. "United States—Restrictions on Payments and Transfers—South Vietnam and Cambodia," EBD/75/173 (July 21, 1975).

[23]Minutes of EBM/84/115 (July 27, 1984). For background information, see "Viet Nam—Overdue Financial Obligations to the Fund—Report and Complaints Under Rules K-1 and S-1 and Notice of Failure to Repay Trust Fund Loan," EBS/84/142 (June 29, 1984) and "Viet Nam—Overdue Financial Obligations to the Fund—Report and Complaints Under Rules K-1 and S-1 and Notice of Failure to Settle Trust Fund Obligations," Sup. 1 (July 25). As of July 1984, when the Executive Board first reviewed Vietnam's arrears, the central bank held a minuscule level of usable foreign exchange reserves: $16 million, which was equivalent to about two weeks' worth of convertible currency imports. Net reserves were negative. The authorities also held $163 million of assets in blocked accounts in U.S. banks, and approximately 735,000 ounces of gold reserves. The portion of gold reserves that was not already pledged as collateral was worth approximately $150 million at the market price. Vietnam's overdue obligations to the Fund totaled only $14 million, but the discounted present value of future obligations was about $100 million. To avoid slipping back into arrears during the next few years while maintaining even a minimum level of reserves would have required either a drastic shift in policies and economic

The origin of Vietnam's arrears problem in 1984 appears to have been frustration by the authorities over their inability to get the Fund to approve a stand-by arrangement on terms that they could accept. The government had been seeking a stand-by arrangement without success since 1977, and since April 1981 had been repaying the Fund without getting any new credits. Beginning in late 1983, the central bank governor, Nguyen Duy Gia, began telling IMF officials that he was even wondering whether Fund membership was worthwhile if the country could not get a stand-by arrangement in the upper credit tranches.[24] The staff view, however, was that Vietnam needed to undertake a serious and comprehensive program of macroeconomic reforms to achieve a sustainable position in its balance of payments.

In April 1984, Gia indicated to the staff that the government was prepared to pay its arrears to the Fund if the Fund would promise to grant a stand-by arrangement soon afterward. Fund policies precluded management from making such a promise, because a stand-by arrangement could be approved only after agreement on an adjustment program and only upon review by the Executive Board. Since the staff was prepared to negotiate a program as soon as arrears were settled, and since the issues that remained outstanding after years of discussion were clearly understood, the distance between the authorities and the institution was not great. Whether the failure to bridge the gap was due to a misunderstanding, or to mutual distrust, or to substantive issues regarding the required degree of economic adjustment, is a matter of interpretation. What is clear is that during this brief period when arrears were small and Vietnam had the resources to settle the balance, the opportunity slipped away.

The Executive Board agreed in July 1984 that Vietnam could and should settle its arrears, and it established August 29 as the date on which it would restrict Vietnam's access to Fund resources if the arrears remained outstanding. Informing the authorities of the deadline, the Deputy Managing Director, Richard D. Erb, suggested that they use their gold holdings for the purpose. Gia ignored that suggestion and responded by stressing the extreme hardships being faced by the population and by requesting a rescheduling of the overdue obligations.[25]

The restriction took effect as scheduled in August 1984. When no further payments were made over the next few months, the Board then took action in December to declare Vietnam formally ineligible to use Fund resources as of January 15, 1985 (the first such declaration to take effect). The Board also considered Vietnam's request to reschedule its overdue obligations, but it declined to do so

---

circumstances, or access to both the gold and the blocked accounts. In the event, Vietnam sold most of its unencumbered gold before the end of 1984 to pay for imports and forfeited the gold that had been pledged as collateral.

[24]See, for example, memorandum of March 23, 1984, by the head of that year's Article IV mission to Vietnam, Willem G.L. Evers (Advisor in the Asian Department); in IMF/RD Managing Director file "Viet Nam" (Accession 85/231, Box 1, Section 177).

[25]See minutes of EBM/84/115 (July 27, 1984); and cables from Erb (August 15) and Gia (August 21 and 22), in IMF/CF (C/Viet Nam/750 "Obligations Under Fund Agreement January 1984–May 1986").

and instead reaffirmed its intention that such action should be held in reserve only for truly exceptional circumstances.[26]

Guyana

The seeds of Guyana's arrears to the Fund were planted in June 1979, when the Executive Board approved a three-year EFF arrangement for SDR 62.75 million (250 percent of quota; $80 million). Guyana had already borrowed heavily from the Fund in the previous three years, but this extended arrangement would be much larger.[27] The economy had been severely and adversely affected by weak international prices for sugar, the principal export crop, and no Executive Director objected to what in retrospect would appear to have been an unrealistic adjustment program.[28]

The economy continued to worsen. Output had declined in 1977 and 1978 but was projected by the authorities to rise by 4½ percent in 1979 as a result of the EFF-supported adjustment program. In the event, output declined again because of a combination of external shocks, poor policy implementation, and a deteriorating domestic political situation. After an initial drawing of SDR 10 million ($13 million) upon approval of the arrangement, Guyana's program quickly went off track.

A year later, the authorities came back to the Fund with a new program and (reflecting the quota increase that was about to take effect) a request to replace the original arrangement with a larger one, for SDR 100 million ($133 million): an amount that would have raised Guyana's obligations to the Fund to nearly 450 percent of the new quota if it had been fully drawn. Moreover, the staff acknowledged that even this amount was not expected to produce a sustainable external balance; a further augmentation would be requested once a better track record on adjustment had been established and the quota increase had taken effect. Guyana had very low foreign exchange reserves and was in arrears to some of its bilateral official creditors; the credit from the Fund would go in part to reduce those arrears. Despite the failure of the previous program, the unusually large scale of the arrangement, and the need to lend into external arrears, the new extended arrangement was approved without objection in July 1980.[29]

The 1980 program also was unrealistic, and the ceilings on domestic credit expansion were soon breached. Concerns on the Board began to escalate a little, es-

---

[26]See minutes of EBM/84/129 (August 29, 1984), on the request to postpone repayments, and EBM/84/173 (December 3, 1984), on the declaration of ineligibility.

[27]Guyana gained independence from the United Kingdom in May 1966 and became a member of the Fund four months later. The Fund approved 11 stand-by arrangements for Guyana from 1967 through 1978, but the government made drawings on only two of the first nine arrangements. Twelve-month arrangements approved in 1976 and 1978 were fully drawn. In June 1979, Guyana had outstanding obligations to the Fund of SDR 32.4 million (130 percent of quota; $41 million).

[28]Minutes of EBM/79/98 (June 25, 1979).

[29]Minutes of EBM/80/110–111 (July 25, 1980).

Figure 16.3. Guyana: Use of Fund Credit and Arrears, 1975–90

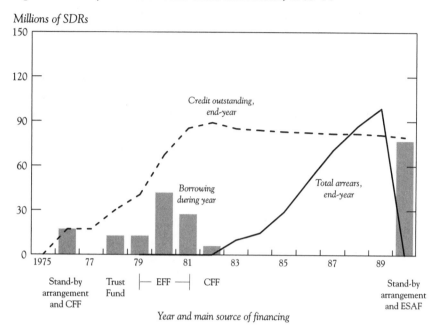

Millions of SDRs

Year and main source of financing

pecially from the Directors for the United States, the United Kingdom, Canada, and the Netherlands. Overall, however, the Board viewed Guyana as having been unlucky ("accident prone"), and most Directors were prepared to give the authorities the benefit of the doubt. A waiver was granted for the missed ceilings, and Guyana made a second drawing.[30]

The situation did not improve. Credit ceilings again were breached at the end of 1980, and no drawings were made during the first half of 1981. Nonetheless, the Board agreed in July to augment the arrangement to SDR 150 million ($170 million) and to allow an immediate drawing of SDR 16.1 million ($18 million), which raised Guyana's obligations to the Fund (Figure 16.3) to approximately SDR 78 million (208 percent of quota; $89 million). All of that, as Donald E. Syvrud (Alternate—United States) remarked with only a slight technical hyperbole, "without a single performance criterion having been met."[31] No further drawings were made under the extended arrangement, and it was canceled a year early, in July 1982.

The record is clear in this case that the Fund recognized (or acknowledged) too late the authorities' inability to carry out their policy intentions. The staff appraisal for the July 1981 review argued that "Guyana's economy has suffered severe setbacks since 1977, partly because of developments beyond the control of the

---

[30]Minutes of EBM/80/163 (November 7, 1980).
[31]Minutes of EBM/81/103 (July 10, 1981), p. 12.

Guyanese authorities."[32] Whatever policy failings were implied by that "partly" were left unspecified, and the report concluded that the "measures already adopted represent a substantial effort, and the authorities have indicated their willingness to consider additional steps should they prove to be necessary." Three years later, with the economy in a complete shambles, the staff reversed the emphasis: "While [external] factors were important, Guyana's poor economic performance is attributable in large measure to inappropriate policies followed over the past several years."[33]

The residue of the failure of Guyana's economic policies to cope with extraordinarily difficult circumstances was an inability to service the additional debts that had accumulated. Beginning in April 1983, the authorities began to fall behind in meeting their payments to the Fund. During the next year, they made a few small payments, but not enough to keep arrears from accumulating. By a year later, arrears (all to the GRA) totaled SDR 14 million ($15 million). The Executive Board then reviewed the situation and set a date in June 1984 to consider taking formal action to restrict Guyana's further access to Fund resources.

Following the April Board meeting, de Larosière wrote directly to the president of Guyana, L.F.S. (Forbes) Burnham, stressing the importance to Guyana of finding a means of settling with the Fund. Burnham, however, responded that "domestic adjustment alone" could not enable the government to repay its arrears, and he requested de Larosière's assistance in securing additional external resources.[34] Without a viable adjustment program in place, however, the Managing Director obviously could not comply with that request.

In taking up the Managing Director's complaint against Guyana under Rule K-1, the Executive Board had to search for the right approach, as this was the first such complaint to reach this stage since approval of the new procedures.[35] Options included (1) declaring Guyana to be ineligible to use Fund resources (in effect, ineligible to borrow), (2) deciding that Guyana may not use Fund resources until it becomes current in its payments on interest and principal, or (3) giving the authorities more time before taking any action. Failure to send a strong signal to the authorities on the essentiality of eliminating arrears could perpetuate the problem;

---

[32]Guyana's leading export was bauxite. Bauxite mining requires large amounts of fuel, virtually all of which had to be imported. Three conditions combined at the beginning of the 1980s to cause the net value added in this sector to plummet: the world price of oil rose sharply, world demand for bauxite dropped, and international competition in supplying bauxite intensified. The government's efforts to adjust to the shocks were hampered by widespread protests and work stoppages.

[33]"Guyana—Consultation Under Extended Arrangement," EBS/81/143 (June 29, 1981), pp. 13–14; and "Guyana—Staff Report for the 1984 Article IV Consultation," SM/84/158 (July 5, 1984), p. 2.

[34]The exchange of letters was circulated as "Guyana—Overdue Obligations," EBS/84/127 (June 4, 1984). On the decline in capital inflows, see "Guyana—Recent Economic Developments," SM/84/169 (July 20, 1984), pp. 45–46. Official development assistance to Guyana had been declining for several years, owing to the government's poor record of implementing projects financed with foreign assistance and to an increasingly objectionable record of human rights abuses. Private capital inflows had dropped sharply after an extensive nationalization program in the mid-1970s.

[35]As noted above, the complaint on Vietnam initially came to the Board the following month, in July 1984.

but without some flexibility and support from the Fund, it was difficult to see how the government could ever take the necessary steps to generate the resources to repay the Fund.[36]

Burnham underscored the seriousness of his own concern by sending his minister of finance, the governor of the central bank, and the ambassador to the United States to participate in the Executive Board meeting on June 6. The minister, Carl B. Greenidge, told the Board that the government "was willing to implement stringent measures" if it could get enough external financing to support them. He requested the "technical assistance" of the staff in designing an adjustment program. Since the Fund's policies prohibited the staff from negotiating a Fund-supported program with a country in arrears, this technical assistance option might offer a way to persuade other creditors and donors that Guyana was trying seriously to put its policies on the right track. Directors responded by taking the middle road and offering a carrot along with the stick. The Board decided that Guyana could not use Fund resources until it was current, offered to provide technical assistance on macroeconomic policies, and agreed to conduct a review within three months.[37]

When the Board reviewed the situation at the end of August 1984, Guyana had made some payments to the Fund, but less than the amount of new payments coming due. Thus the total amount in arrears had risen, from SDR 16 million in June to more than SDR 19 million (and approximately the same in U.S. dollars). Moreover, in the judgment of the staff, little effective change was evident in the conduct of economic policies. The outlook thus was even more bleak than before, but because the authorities were cooperating with the Fund and were actively seeking financial help from other sources, the Board agreed to give them another three months before considering taking stronger action.[38]

For several months, Guyana teetered between progress and relapse. Extremely heavy rains in October severely reduced the sugar harvest and further weakened the balance of payments. Nonetheless, the government paid enough to the Fund to reduce its arrears below SDR 15 million by end-November. With that in mind, the Board again agreed to postpone consideration of ineligibility for another 10 weeks.[39] By that time (mid-February 1985), arrears were rising again even though Guyana was continuing to make whatever payments it could out of its trickle of earnings. The Board accepted the authorities' argument that Guyana's circum-

---

[36]At the end of 1984, Guyana held $5 million in official reserves and had over $600 million in external payments arrears. Although arrears to the Fund were a relatively small portion of the total, the Fund was Guyana's single largest external creditor. See "Guyana—Staff Report for the 1985 Article IV Consultation," SM/85/287 (October 30, 1985), p. 7; and "Overdue Financial Obligations to the Fund—Further Review of the Decision on Complaint Under Rule K-1," EBS/85/36 (February 13, 1985), p. 5.

[37]Minutes of EBM/84/88 (June 6, 1984).

[38]Minutes of EBM/84/131 (August 31, 1984). Also see "Guyana—Review of Decision to Limit Use of the Fund's General Resources," EBS/84/47, Sup. 4 (August 29, 1984).

[39]Minutes of EBM/84/172 and 173 (December 3, 1984). Also see "Guyana—Overdue Financial Obligations to the Fund—Second Review of Decision on Complaint Under Rule K-1," EBS/84/244 (November 28, 1984).

stances were particularly serious at the moment because of a seasonal trough in ex-port receipts, but most Directors also were convinced that Guyana had to make a much stronger effort to put its economic policies on a sustainable course. The Board again agreed to postpone declaring Guyana ineligible, but it tightened the language of its decision a bit.

Although it might seem that the Board was continually putting off the moment of decision on Guyana, it actually was moving inexorably toward it. The process may be seen by comparing the relevant language from these first three reviews of the June 6 decision to restrict access:[40]

- *August 1984*: "The Fund calls upon Guyana . . . to become current on its fi-nancial obligations to the Fund. . . . The Fund shall further review [the June 6 decision] not later than November 30, 1984."
- *December 1984*: "Unless [by February 15, 1985] Guyana is current in its fi-nancial obligations to the Fund, the Fund will consider the appropriateness of further steps, including the possibility of declaring Guyana ineligible to use the general resources of the Fund. . . ."
- *February 1985*: "It is expected that a decision to declare Guyana ineligible to use the Fund's general resources . . . will be taken, with effect on [May 15, 1985] . . . in the absence of full settlement . . . by that date."

Little changed during the next three months. Guyana continued to make small payments, and arrears continued to rise. Overall, in the 14 months since the Man-aging Director issued a formal complaint regarding Guyana's arrears, the authori-ties had paid more than SDR 15 million to the Fund, but arrears had risen from SDR 14 million to SDR 18.7 million. Although the Fund's Executive Directors clearly wanted to encourage Guyana to keep making whatever payments it could, several of them also expressed a need to apply the Fund's principles firmly and evenly and to send clear and proper signals on the need for countries to cooperate fully with the Fund. In a close vote on May 15, 1985, split almost cleanly between creditor and other countries, the Executive Board declared Guyana ineligible to use Fund resources.[41]

Liberia

Liberia's arrears resulted from a nexus of internal and external political difficulties. Although never a colony, Liberia had always had close linkages to the United States and depended heavily on it for financial support. When that support evaporated after 1984, the government was unable to put its policies on a sustainable course.

---

[40]Decision No. 7792-(84/131), adopted August 31, 1984; Decision No. 7854-(84/173), adopted December 3, 1984; and Decision No. 7906-(85/24), adopted February 15, 1985.

[41]All but one of the Directors from the Group of Ten (G-10) industrial countries (the excep-tion being the Belgian chair), plus those from Australia and Saudi Arabia, voted in favor of de-claring Guyana ineligible. The other nine Directors either opposed the proposal outright, or fa-vored a further postponement, or supported a compromise proposal by Alexandre Kafka (whose constituency included Guyana) to negotiate a rescheduling of Guyana's obligations.

Figure 16.4. Liberia: Use of Fund Credit and Arrears, 1977–90

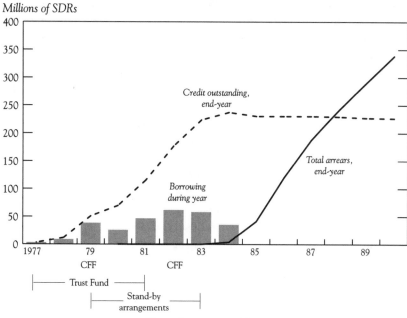

Year and main source of financing

The Fund entered into 13 stand-by arrangements for Liberia between 1963 (one year after Liberia became a member) and 1979. Credits under those arrangements, however, were small, and by the end of 1978, Liberia's only outstanding debts to the Fund were for long-term Trust Fund loans. A new government, led by a young army sergeant, Samuel K. Doe, took power in a violent military coup in April 1980. The Fund then extended sizable credits to Liberia on a regular basis through the end of 1984. During those four and a half years, Liberia's indebtedness to the Fund rose from SDR 29 million ($37 million; 75 percent of quota) to SDR 213 million ($209 million; 298 percent).[42] Throughout, except for a few months in mid-1984, Liberia stayed current on its repayments (Figure 16.4).

The final stand-by arrangement for Liberia was approved by the Executive Board on December 7, 1984. The government made the initial drawing a week later, and on December 17 the Paris Club agreed to reschedule certain of Liberia's debts to official creditors. Two days later, Liberia failed to make a scheduled repayment to the Fund and started down the road to protracted arrears. The sudden shift from cooperation to defiance caught the Fund and other creditors completely by surprise and left them with few options for trying to get relations back on course.

---

[42]In addition, in 1977–81, Liberia borrowed SDR 28.3 million from the Trust Fund. By the end of 1980, Liberia also had used all of its allocated SDRs.

Liberia faced two major fiscal problems at the beginning of 1985. First, with presidential elections scheduled for October, the government was sharply increasing spending. The Fund staff later would estimate that spending was up 22 percent over the previous fiscal year despite a serious decline in revenues. Second, the U.S. government—reportedly upset both with the deterioration in economic management and even more with the dubious progress being made toward restoring democracy[43]—quietly withheld disbursing a substantial portion of an expected $60 million in grants, on which the government had been counting to cover some 17 percent of budgeted spending. Neither development had been anticipated by the staff during the negotiations on the stand-by arrangement, and together they destroyed any hope of either meeting the performance criteria for the arrangement or making the substantial repayments that were now coming due on the earlier Fund stand-by arrangements.

The Managing Director soon issued complaints to the Executive Board regarding Liberia's growing arrears to the GRA and the SDR Department, and a notice on arrears to the Trust Fund.[44] When the Board considered the complaints and notice in May, Liberia's financial situation was evidently hopeless: the central bank held some $2 million in reserves, while payments arrears to all external creditors totaled $58 million. The U.S. Executive Director, Charles H. Dallara, defended his country's withholding of aid on economic grounds, stating that "bilateral creditors could not be expected to provide additional financial support for an adjustment effort that they believed would not succeed." The Board accepted that Liberia's problems were attributable to the government's own failings, and it agreed to restrict the country's access to Fund resources until arrears were cleared.[45]

Three months later, in late August 1985, the Board conducted its first review of the restriction of Liberia's access. Although the Executive Director speaking for Liberia, E.I.M. Mtei (Tanzania), pleaded for flexibility on the grounds that the Fund was asking the government to commit political suicide,[46] that prospect was scarcely viewed with alarm around the table. Following a pattern and a schedule

---

[43]Doe agreed in 1981 to reestablish civilian rule by 1986. A new constitution was approved by plebiscite in 1984, and the initial elections were scheduled for October 1985. Doe announced his candidacy for the presidency in August 1984, and in the following months he sharply limited the number of parties eligible to participate. He won the election with just over 50 percent of the vote and was inaugurated as president on January 6, 1986. For a detailed history of the period, see Liebenow (1987), especially the discussion of the role of U.S. aid and other support (pp. 303–06). Liebenow stressed the limited nature of the U.S. withdrawal of aid, whereas the Fund staff and the authorities were particularly concerned about the delays in disbursing the anticipated aid. For the staff position, see memorandum from Goodall E. Gondwe (Deputy Director of the African Department) to the Managing Director (September 13, 1985); IMF/RD African Department file "Liberia—Correspondence, June 1985–" (Accession 87/051, Room 4843, Section 5-6-9).

[44]"Liberia—Overdue Financial Obligations to the Fund," EBS/85/17 (January 18, 1985).

[45]Minutes of EBM/85/80 (May 24, 1985), pp. 29 (data on reserves and arrears), 31 (Dallara), and 37–38 (decision to restrict access).

[46]Mtei calculated that to generate the required foreign exchange, the government would have to implement tax increases or spending cuts drastic enough to shift the fiscal balance from a deficit equal to 13 percent of GDP to a surplus during the next three months.

similar to that adopted in dealing with Guyana's arrears a few months earlier, Directors decided that they expected to declare Liberia to be ineligible in another three months if arrears to the Fund were not cleared.[47]

During the final few weeks before the elections, the government made two payments to the Fund, totaling SDR 17.7 million ($19 million), which reduced arrears by about one-third. After Doe was narrowly elected president and then fought off an attempted coup in November, he began implementing an adjustment program that included sharp cuts in public sector salaries. This strong and ongoing economic effort put the Executive Board in a bind. It had already decided that it would declare Liberia formally ineligible to use Fund resources if it did not totally clear its arrears by late November. That draconian demand had not been met, but the government clearly was again cooperating and probably was doing as much as it realistically could to contain the problem. So the Board took a Solomonesque stand that it would use in several other cases during the next few years: it declared Liberia ineligible but deferred the effective date to late January to give the authorities a little more time.

The declaration was to take effect on January 24, 1986 without any further action by the Board, unless either the Managing Director or an Executive Director called for a meeting. As the date approached, Liberia had made no further payments to the Fund, and arrears had risen to a new high of SDR 52 million ($58 million; 73 percent of quota). At Mtei's request, the Board did hold a meeting on the subject on January 24, but not a single other Director spoke up on Liberia's behalf. The earlier decision was allowed to stand, and Liberia became ineligible to use Fund resources as of that date.

Sudan

The fourth country to be declared ineligible to borrow involved much larger sums of money than the first three. Sudan's arrears to the Fund ultimately would exceed a billion SDRs and would be larger than those of any other country.

For most of the 1970s, Sudan's economic prospects looked reasonably good. The world market for the major export crop—cotton—was strong and fairly stable, and Sudan had large undeveloped petroleum reserves that became more valuable as the decade progressed. The government undertook three successive one-year stand-by arrangements in 1972–74 and made most of the scheduled drawings. It continued to borrow, through the oil facilities and the CFF, during the next two years, by which point it had outstanding debts of SDR 134 million ($154 million; 186 percent of quota). Those claims initially were serviced without difficulty, and in 1977 and 1978, the Fund's exposure in Sudan was gradually reduced and stabilized (Figure 16.5).

Commercial banks, no doubt eager to gain a foothold in anticipation of future oil production, also lent heavily to Sudan in the 1970s. The ready availability of

---

[47]Minutes of EBM/85/126 (August 26, 1985), pp. 28 (Mtei) and 33 (decision).

Figure 16.5. Sudan: Use of Fund Credit, 1972–90

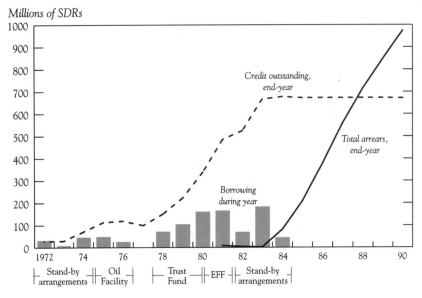

Year and main source of financing

both official and commercial loans induced the government to increase outlays sharply, much of it for current expenditure rather than capital investment. Consequently, loan repayments began to slip as early as 1976, and the banks began to show more caution in increasing their exposure. All external creditors, however, were hamstrung in trying to analyze the extent of the debt problem, because recorded budgetary appropriations covered only the debts incurred directly by the ministry of finance. Government agencies were borrowing independently and without any comprehensive record keeping. Total public sector debts were much larger than anyone realized, and the extent of the underreporting would not become fully known for several more years.[48]

Heavy flooding in this often parched country devastated the cotton harvest in 1978, just as the supply of bank credit was drying up. The Fund tried to help Sudan cope with the natural disaster by negotiating an adjustment program and providing a total of SDR 71 million ($89 million; 81 percent of quota) in credits through the first credit tranche, the CFF, and the Trust Fund. Even that combination of adjustment and financing proved inadequate, and Sudan was unable to eliminate its arrears to the banks. As gradually became apparent over the next several years, a good part of the problem was that cotton production was being weak-

---

[48]The uncovering of the extent of external debt is summarized in an August 16, 1982 memorandum to the Managing Director from A. Shakour Shaalan (Director of the Middle Eastern Department); IMF/RD Managing Director file "Sudan, 1982—Vol. II" (Accession 84/21, Box 5, Section 168).

ened by poor administration, disincentives arising from controls, and other internal problems, not just by unusually bad weather.

In May 1979, the Fund approved a three-year EFF arrangement for Sudan for SDR 200 million ($254 million; 227 percent of quota), under which the government was expected to eliminate its external arrears. (Throughout this period, Sudan was frequently late in making payments to the Fund, but those arrears were settled within several weeks of the due dates.) For the next year and a half, Sudan adhered (with occasional lapses) to the general thrust of its policy intentions, but the settlement of arrears with commercial creditors remained elusive.

During the summer and fall of 1979, the authorities opened negotiations with a group of creditor banks and applied for a rescheduling of official debts through the Paris Club. The latter effort succeeded in November, but negotiations with the banks dragged on for two more years. Meanwhile, the World Bank provided assistance to rehabilitate the agricultural sector and improve export performance, and the Fund granted additional Trust Fund loans. Moreover, in anticipation of the general quota increase that was about to take effect, the Fund augmented the amount of the extended arrangement in November 1980 and supplemented it by a further CFF purchase. Throughout this period, the staff—still working with underestimated debt figures—was led to believe that the financing gap was manageable with a reasonable adjustment effort.

At the beginning of 1981, the economic program went off track, owing to excessive growth of net domestic credit and the authorities' failure to settle arrears that had arisen on official debts rescheduled by the Paris Club.[49] One more drawing on the EFF arrangement was allowed, in June 1981, after Saudi Arabia lent Sudan enough money to settle its arrears to official creditors. Efforts to negotiate the third year of the program then failed, and a second Paris Club rescheduling was repeatedly postponed. In September, Sudan again went into arrears to the Fund, when the authorities failed to make a scheduled repayment for a drawing under the Oil Facility. For the first time, Sudan was unable to settle in a reasonable time, and arrears continued to mount for the next few months. The Managing Director notified the Executive Board in December that Sudan had

---

[49]The efficacy of Fund-supported adjustment programs in Sudan has been much debated. A central element in the programs of the late 1970s and early 1980s was depreciation of the exchange rate, aimed at strengthening international competitiveness of key sectors of the economy. The supply-side elements of the strategy were explained by Nashashibi (1980) and were subsequently criticized by several outside analysts, such as Hussain and Thirwall (1984), Ali (1985), Diwan and Hu (1986), and Branson and Macedo (1989). Brown (1992, pp. 205–207) summarized the criticisms, which dealt both with the likelihood of nominal devaluation depreciating the real exchange rate and with the uncertain linkages between a change in the real exchange rate and competitiveness in the particular markets that were relevant for Sudan. Doubts about the strategy were prevalent in Khartoum and no doubt contributed to the authorities' failure to implement the agreed programs. For an example of the authorities' reluctance to implement the Fund's recommendations, see memorandum from Shaalan to the Managing Director, February 5, 1985; IMF/RD Managing Director file "Sudan" (Accession 87/27, Box 5, Section 535).

some SDR 8 million ($9.3 billion) in overdue obligations, but the authorities brought their payments up to date in February 1982 and no formal complaint was issued.[50]

During the first quarter of 1982, the Fund and other external creditors took an unduly sanguine view of Sudan's prospects. After commercial banks and Paris Club creditors provided enough support to enable Sudan to settle its arrears to the Fund, the Board approved a stand-by arrangement in February for SDR 198 million ($224 million; 150 percent of quota). The Executive Board broke new ground (and qualified its optimism) by requiring the authorities to promise, as a condition for approval of the arrangement, that they would not make any drawings if they had any overdue obligations to the Fund.[51] The practical effect of that prohibition, however, was limited because the stand-by arrangement was unusually front-loaded: Sudan was able to draw SDR 70 million (35 percent of the total) immediately.

Optimism was still being fueled by the prospects for cotton and petroleum exports, by a lack of knowledge about the extent of external debts, and (for bilateral creditors) by respect for Sudan's strategic role in the region. A further Paris Club rescheduling was completed in March, but the apparent equilibrium then quickly came unglued. The adjustment program was not carried out, and no additional drawings could be allowed under the stand-by arrangement; commercial creditors became increasingly wary of maintaining their exposure; and donors became reluctant to provide aid in the absence of supplementary financing from creditors. Without adjustment or external support, Sudan again fell into arrears to the Fund on three separate occasions before the end of the year.[52]

By the time of the Annual Fund-Bank meetings in Toronto in September 1982—the meetings that focused so intently on the debt crisis in Latin America—the full extent of Sudan's external debt had become known. It was now clear that Sudan could not solve its problems through adjustment alone; a broad international program of debt relief would be required if Sudan was to have any hope of servicing all of its debts. De Larosière arranged for André de Lattre, a distinguished French official and banker, to coordinate that effort on behalf of the Fund and the World Bank, while the staff set out to negotiate an economic program that could be supported by yet another Fund stand-by arrangement.

Both the aid coordination and the program negotiations went smoothly, and by early 1983, economic policies and conditions seemed to be getting back on course.

---

[50]See "Sudan—Overdue Financial Obligations to the Fund," EBS/81/244 (December 10, 1981) and "Text of Stand-by Arrangement—EBM/82/19 (2/18/82)," EBS/82/7, Sup. 2 (February 23, 1982).

[51]A similar condition was included in some later stand-by arrangements, and in 1984 it became a routine practice until the Board adopted a general policy prohibiting drawings by countries in arrears. See Chapter 13, footnote 114, p. 603.

[52]"Sudan—Overdue Financial Obligations," EBS/82/147 (August 18, 1982) and "Settlement of Overdue Financial Obligations," Sup. 2 (October 12, 1982); and cables in IMF/CF (C/Sudan/1750 "Repurchase Obligations, 1979–1984").

In February, the Board approved a stand-by arrangement that would turn out to be the only one that was fully drawn by the Sudanese.[53]

The economy was temporarily improving in 1983 in response to a strengthening of structural policies: a new incentive system for farmers that produced a record cotton crop, liberalization of the exchange regime, elimination of many subsidies, and development of infrastructure including the transportation network. This progress, however, was short-lived. A drop in rainfall developed into a major drought that severely reduced agricultural output and exports for the next several years. Chronic disagreements between the dominant Islamic groups in the north and non-Islamic groups in the south erupted in violence in the spring and intensified into civil war in the fall following the imposition of Islamic law across the country.[54] With incomes falling and civil order breaking down, achievement of the political consensus needed to sustain adjustment became all but impossible.

Despite these setbacks and distractions, the authorities completed the 1983 program and entered into one more stand-by arrangement, approved by the Fund in April 1984. Unfortunately, the initial drawing under that arrangement would be Sudan's last from the Fund.[55]

All semblance of stability collapsed in the second half of 1984. In July, Sudan missed another due date and began accumulating what would eventually become the largest stock of arrears to the Fund. Economic conditions deteriorated rapidly, owing to the drought, a lack of foreign exchange to buy essential inputs for production and transportation, falling commodity prices, domestic strife (including a large flow of refugees from the civil war in the south), and budgetary excesses including subsidies effected through an artificial exchange regime. Staff discussions with major donors during the autumn revealed reluctance to provide assistance on the increasing scale that was required, and discussions with the authorities revealed unwillingness to undertake the required policy adjustments.

Until this point, although Sudan had experienced several lapses in paying the Fund on time, the Managing Director had avoided issuing a formal complaint, and the authorities had always found a way to settle arrears within a few months. Time had now run out. A complaint was issued in December 1984, noting that Sudan

---

[53]As discussed in Chapter 9, the Board initially approved the arrangement in principle, pending completion of the financing arrangements by the Paris Club, donor countries, and commercial banks that de Lattre was coordinating. The arrangement was for SDR 170 million ($185 million; 129 percent of quota); when fully drawn, it raised Sudan's overall indebtedness to the Fund to a peak level of 678 million ($720 million; 400 percent of quota).

[54]After Sudan gained its independence from joint British and Egyptian rule in 1956, it had a series of military and coalition governments until Colonel Gaafar Muhmmad al-Nimeiri seized power in a coup in 1969. Ethnic and religious strife quieted down after the southern region was granted partial autonomy in 1972, until it broke out again in 1983. Various efforts at national reconciliation after Nimeiri was overthrown in a 1985 coup were essentially unsuccessful. Brown (1992, Chapter 3) provides a good overview on the sociopolitical background to the economic problems of the 1980s.

[55]The arrangement was approved in principle in April and became effective in June after outside financing agreements were completed. The July drawing raised Sudan's outstanding obligations back to the peak level of SDR 678 million (see Figure 16.5).

already had arrears totaling more than SDR 80 million (approximately 45 percent of quota) and would owe the Fund more than SDR 900 million by 1991 if no further payments were made. The next month, the Director of the Middle Eastern Department, A. Shakour Shaalan, met with President Nimeiri in Khartoum, and tried to make a case for more effective economic management as an essential step toward restoring aid flows and regaining solvency. The president rejected Shaalan's arguments, blamed the Fund for adding to Sudan's problems by increasing the difficulty of obtaining foreign aid, and refused to undertake additional adjustment measures that might raise prices and lead to further social unrest.[56] A week later, on February 8, 1985, the Board restricted Sudan's access to Fund resources.

A military coup in April overthrew Nimeiri while he was en route to Khartoum from meetings with de Larosière and others in Washington. Despite the circumstances, the installation of a new government and a new economic team gave donor countries[57] a new reason for optimism. A resurgence of aid flows then gave the Fund a basis for resuming negotiations on a new adjustment program. When the Managing Director met with the new finance minister, Awad Abdel Magied, at the Annual Meetings in Seoul, Korea, in October 1985, it seemed possible to hope for success. Donor countries, led by the United States, were at least discussing ways to settle Sudan's arrears (which then amounted to SDR 167 million) and to close a massive $3 billion financing gap for the coming year, and Magied was ready to agree to a substantial strengthening of macroeconomic and structural policies. Suddenly, it then all fell apart again.

Although the final collapse came as the culmination of a long and depressing litany of shocks and mistakes, the critical period—the last slight chance to turn the economy around—came in October–November 1985. Magied went from Seoul to Washington for further meetings with the staff and management to put the final touches on a program that could be supported by a new stand-by arrangement in 1986. The Managing Director held two meetings with senior officials from donor countries to secure additional financing pledges. The prime minister, El-Gizouli Dafalla, went to Washington in late October for meetings with U.S. aid officials and with the Managing Director. On October 25, the Executive Board expressed a sense of urgency by giving Sudan only until January 3, 1986, to settle its arrears or to face a possible declaration of ineligibility.[58] The Managing Director,

---

[56]Memorandum from Shaalan to the Managing Director (February 5, 1985); IMF/RD Managing Director file "Sudan" (Accession 87/27, Box 5, Section 535). Also see statement by Shaalan at EBM/85/20 (February 8, 1985), pp. 29–31.

[57]Official aid to Sudan came primarily from the largest industrial countries and from Middle Eastern countries.

[58]Although the decision was widely supported by Executive Directors, different motivations were expressed. The staff had suggested two options: giving the authorities three months to clear arrears, but stating an expectation that the Fund would declare Sudan ineligible at that time if arrears were not cleared; or giving them just over two months (January 3 being the first date when the Board would meet after the elapse of two months on December 25) but stating only that a declaration of ineligibility might be considered at the end of that period. Which option was more severe was open to interpretation. "Sudan—Further Review of Decision to Limit Use of the Fund's General Resources," EBS/85/233 (October 21, 1985), and minutes of EBM/85/156 (October 25, 1985).

though, was anxious to avoid that outcome.[59] To give up on Sudan, with its economic and political importance and the sheer size of its obligations to the Fund, could have disastrous systemic consequences.

By the end of October, two difficulties were beginning to overshadow the progress of the preceding weeks. First, Dafalla did not share Magied's views on adjustment and was reluctant to endorse the package that had been carefully negotiated by the finance minister. Second, a combination of skepticism about economic reforms and concerns about Sudan's international political stance were causing some donors to back away from their plans to provide additional aid.[60] In early December, the cabinet in Khartoum rejected Magied's proposed policy package. Magied promptly resigned in protest, leaving his successor just four weeks to find an exit from a now-hopeless situation.

The Executive Board met as scheduled on January 3, 1986, and decided to give Sudan one more opportunity. Directors declared Sudan ineligible but—as it had for Liberia—deferred the effective date by a month.[61] Negotiations continued both in Khartoum and Washington, but the best that the government could do was to pay SDR 9.1 million ($10 million) out of the SDR 235 million that was then overdue and to propose several policy changes that, in the staff's judgment, fell "far short of" the program negotiated in October.[62] On February 3, at the end of a discussion in which Directors expressed much sympathy for the extreme difficulties faced by Sudan but found no realistic basis for further delay, the declaration of ineligibility took effect.[63]

Peru

The Fund lent heavily to Peru in the late 1970s, when three successive stand-by arrangements and other credits raised Peru's indebtedness to the Fund from zero at the beginning of 1976 to SDR 426 million in mid-1980 ($564 million; 260 percent of the 1980 quota). Under an extended arrangement and a subsequent stand-by arrangement that were active for two years from June 1982, outstanding obligations rose further (Figure 16.6), to SDR 726 million ($750 million; 219 percent of the 1984 quota). By then, however, economic conditions in Peru were badly deteriorating.

---

[59]See memorandum of November 20, 1985, to the Managing Director from Robert M.G. Brown (Personal Assistant to the Managing Director) in IMF/RD Managing Director file "Sudan II" (Accession 87/136, Box 3, Section 168).

[60]During the second half of 1985, Sudan moved to strengthen its relations with certain countries that Nimeiri had shunned, including Libya. The U.S. government accused Sudan of harboring Libyan terrorists, issued a series of warnings, and in November sharply reduced the size of its embassy staff in Khartoum in protest. That response, however, was muted, and the main argument given for restricting aid was the inadequacy of economic policies.

[61]Minutes of EBM/86/1 (January 3, 1986).

[62]The quotation is from a January 31, 1986, memorandum to management from Shaalan; in IMF/RD Managing Director file "Sudan II" (Accession 87/136 , Box 3, Section 168).

[63]Minutes of EBM/86/20 (February 3, 1986).

Figure 16.6. Peru: Use of Fund Credit and Arrears, 1975–90

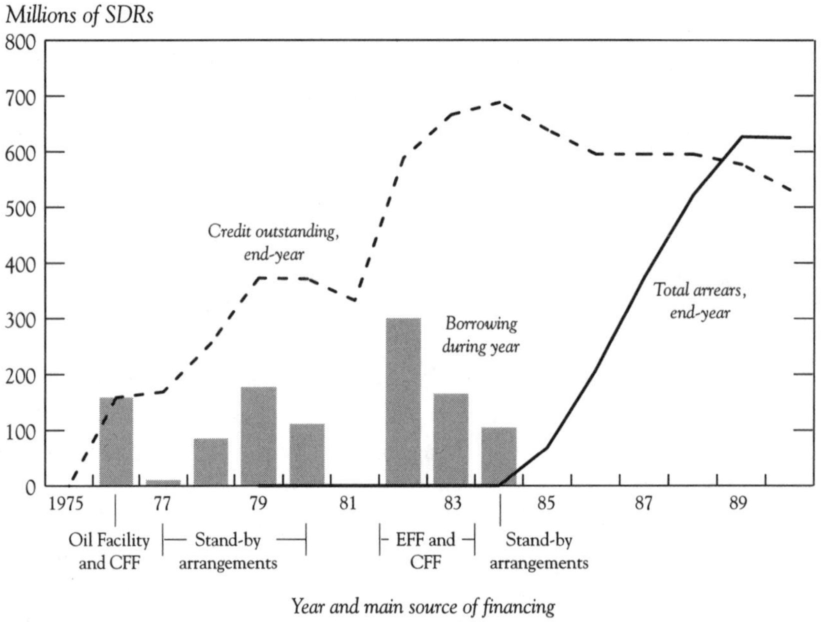

Millions of SDRs

Year and main source of financing

Without question, a large measure of Peru's difficulties derived from natural disasters and other events beyond government control. In 1983 alone, Peru was hit hard by both a drought and severe flooding, communications and manufacturing were disrupted by massive mud slides, and much of the fishing industry was wiped out by the capriciousness of the ocean current known as "el Niño." World market prices for Peruvian mineral exports, particularly petroleum, declined in 1982 and 1983. And the cost and availability of international bank loans deteriorated after the outbreak of the international debt crisis in the second half of 1982.

While acknowledging those factors, the staff nonetheless placed the blame squarely on the government's lax fiscal policy. The March 1984 staff report on the requested stand-by arrangement concluded that "the major factor behind the imbalances in the Peruvian economy and deviations from the economic program during 1982 and 1983 was the large deficit of the nonfinancial public sector."[64] The new arrangement therefore was built around "major tax increases and adjustments of controlled prices" and a "strict public spending policy," aimed at cutting the fiscal deficit from 10 percent of GDP in 1983 to 2 percent in 1985.[65]

---

[64]"Peru—Request for Stand-by Arrangement," EBS/84/57 (March 16, 1984), p. 24. As Webb (1988, p. 251) noted, an abbreviated version of this sentence was included in the Fund's April 26 press release announcing approval of the stand-by arrangement.

[65]"Peru—Request for Stand-by Arrangement," EBS/84/57 (March 16, 1984), pp. 24–25 (the quoted phrases) and 13 (the fiscal target).

The central difficulty with this program was that it required such a severe fiscal contraction that neither the officials who were supposed to implement nor the public at large could fully support it. At first, most government officials disagreed with the strategy and feared that the required fiscal cuts would be counterproductive. Even the central bank governor, Richard C. Webb, who was one of the most diligent in trying to make the program work, later argued that attempting to cut the overall deficit when real spending had already been reduced sharply in real terms was "highly inefficient." It "could not have prevented the eventual breakdown of normal debt service," he argued, and it should have been eschewed in favor of a "more selective approach to adjustment" (Webb, 1988, p. 252). The Fund staff, however, strongly opposed introducing any heterodox elements into the program, such as dual exchange rates, nontariff import barriers, or new controls on wages and prices. Which economic argument was more nearly correct was less important than the fact that a stark austerity program could not possibly be carried out successfully without strong domestic support. The 1984–85 program quickly went off track, and Peru made only two small drawings in April and June 1984. The authorities made a substantial effort to get back on course starting around the end of 1984, but by then Peru was in the midst of a tight presidential election, and they could not recover in time.

When Alan García was elected president of Peru in July 1985, he immediately declared a state of emergency and announced that for the time being Peru would spend no more than 10 percent of its foreign exchange earnings on external debt service. Since scheduled debt service for 1985 exceeded 50 percent of expected export revenues, that declaration was tantamount to a plan to default on a substantial portion of outstanding debts. Priority was to be given to servicing debts to creditors that were willing to reciprocate with new loans or to continue disbursements on existing loans. That policy put obligations to the Fund on a low standing, and by September Peru was in arrears.

The Peruvian case was the clearest one in which arrears to the Fund arose because of unwillingness, rather than inability, to repay the institution. At the end of 1985, Peru's net international reserves, excluding external arrears, totaled about $1.4 billion, and arrears to all external creditors totaled $1.5 billion. Peru could not immediately eliminate all of its arrears without substantial sacrifice,[66] but it could have substantially reduced the total, and it could easily have repaid all of the SDR 68 million ($75 million) that was overdue to the Fund. The government faced a choice between (1) repaying the Fund and then negotiating and implementing a new adjustment program aimed at putting the balance of payments on a sustainable course, and (2) making some repayments to other selected creditors, maintaining existing economic policies, and counting on the continued availability of commercial credits to prevent a ruinous collapse in international trade.

---

[66]For a review and analysis of the economic context of Garcia's populism, see Sachs (1990). Although critical of the overall program, Sachs concludes (p. 167) that "Garcia's declaration in 1985 that Peru needed debt relief, and that the choice for Peru was 'debt or democracy,' was accurate."

Because Peru had the capacity to service its debts to the Fund, de Larosière chose to move cautiously and with the goal of inducing the authorities to cooperate. He issued a formal complaint in mid-December, and the Executive Board held an initial meeting on January 10, 1986, to decide how to proceed. In an unusual gambit for this preliminary stage, Peru was represented at the meeting by its ambassador to the United States, César G. Atala, and by Webb, who now was an advisor to the prime minister. Webb made a lengthy and generally conciliatory statement to the effect that Peru intended to continue to service its debts as best it could and that the government wanted to normalize its relations with the Fund. That desire conflicted with the goal of giving preference to those creditors that were continuing to finance Peruvian investment projects, and Webb was not able to promise much beyond broad intentions. The Board concluded by giving Peru one month to settle arrears before it would consider restricting access to Fund resources.[67]

For the next few months, Peru managed to stave off a formal declaration of ineligibility by making occasional payments and by offering assurances that full settlement was forthcoming. On February 10, the Board restricted Peru's access and set April 16 as the date by which it expected to declare Peru ineligible. This unusually tight deadline (the staff had made a routine recommendation, for a further review in 90 days) reflected a widespread view among Executive Directors from creditor countries that a government that refused to repay the Fund should be dealt with more firmly than those that were willing but unable.[68] Despite an escalation of verbal attacks on the Fund in speeches by García, the authorities made a substantial payment (SDR 30 million) on April 14, and the Board extended the deadline by a few weeks. On May 6, Jaysuño Abramovich (Alternate—Peru) stated on behalf of the government that the "authorities intended to pay the arrears to the Fund by August 15, 1986," that being the deadline suggested earlier by the Managing Director. The Board then declared that Peru would become ineligible on August 15 unless arrears were completely settled. The government continued to make payments, but not enough even to stabilize the level of arrears, and the declaration of ineligibility took effect in August as scheduled.[69]

---

[67]"Peru—Overdue Financial Obligations to the Fund—Report and Complaints Under Rule K-1 and Rule S-1," EBS/85/279 (December 13, 1985); and minutes of EBM/86/5 (January 10, 1986), pp. 29–35 (Webb), and EBM/86/6 (same date), p. 14 (Board decision).

[68]The 45-day deadline for a declaration of ineligibility was requested by Jobarah E. Suraisry (Alternate—Saudi Arabia) and was supported by all of the Directors from G-10 countries. See minutes of EBM/86/22 (February 10, 1986). As a general principle, the staff of the Fund strongly resisted relying on distinctions between willingness and ability to pay. The prevailing staff view was that in most circumstances, any country could gain the ability to pay if it was willing to undertake appropriate adjustment policies. See "Overdue Financial Obligations to the Fund— Six-Monthly Report," EBS/88/243 (November 30, 1988), pp. 3–6.

[69]Minutes of EBM/86/22 (February 10, 1986), EBM/86/62 (April 14), EBM/86/76 (May 6), and EBM/86/135 (August 15). Between the Managing Director's initial complaint in December 1985 and the declaration of ineligibility in August 1986, Peru paid $75 million (SDR 63 million) to the Fund, but an additional SDR 127 million in payments became due. Hence overdue obligations nearly doubled, from SDR 68 million to SDR 132 million.

Zambia

Zambia's arrears to the Fund resulted from a horrific reversal of economic fortunes that cut real incomes by nearly two-thirds in a few years. At times in the 1970s and early 1980s, it appeared that Zambia's mineral wealth—concentrated heavily in copper—could provide a solid base for sustained growth. When copper crashed, this middle-income country (with per capita GNP of $720 in 1981) slipped back into the depths of misery ($250 per capita in 1986) from which no easy path could be climbed.

Zambia gained its independence from Britain in 1964 and joined the IMF the following year. The government of President Kenneth D. Kaunda (who served as head of state from 1964 until 1991) took out its first stand-by arrangement with the Fund in 1973 after its commercial transportation system was severely disrupted by the closing of the border with its southern neighbor, Rhodesia.[70] Foreign currency earnings were heavily dependent on copper exports, and the government took out two more stand-by arrangements, in 1976 and 1978, at times when export prices were weak. By far the largest of those arrangements was approved in April 1978, for SDR 250 million ($310 million), which was fully used over the next two years. That use of Fund credits was the largest ever by a developing country under a single arrangement up to that time.[71] Four more arrangements followed, in 1981, 1983, 1984, and 1986, raising Zambia's total indebtedness to the Fund (Figure 16.7) to about SDR 710 million ($800 million; 263 percent of quota).[72]

With copper prices declining further, Zambia began to have trouble meeting its payments obligations to the Fund in 1982, but the authorities managed to keep the delays short. Then at the end of April 1985, Zambia slipped into more prolonged arrears. Management notified the Executive Board in June, and the Board formally restricted Zambia's access to Fund resources at a meeting held in Seoul, at the end of the Annual Meetings in October.[73]

Oddly enough, by the time of the restriction decision, Zambia was already well on its way toward resolving the problem. For some time, the Fund had been urging the government to replace the pegging arrangement for the exchange rate with an auction system for allocating and pricing foreign currency, as a way of correcting the overvaluation that had crept in after years of deteriorating economic conditions. Fearing a ruinous depreciation, the government had long resisted that ad-

---

[70]Rhodesia (formerly Southern Rhodesia and later Zimbabwe) and Zambia (formerly Northern Rhodesia) battled periodically after the government of Ian Smith attempted to perpetuate minority rule by unilaterally declaring Rhodesia's independence from Britain in 1965.

[71]The 1976–77 stand-by arrangement for Argentina totaled SDR 260 million, but only SDR 160 million of it was drawn. Similarly, the 1977–79 EFF arrangement for Mexico totaled SDR 518 million, but only SDR 100 million was drawn.

[72]Those obligations stemmed both from the stand-by arrangements and from CFF drawings for export shortfalls. In addition, Zambia took out SDR 43 million in Trust Fund loans in 1978–81, of which SDR 27 million remained outstanding at the end of 1986.

[73]See "Zambia—Overdue Financial Obligations to the Fund—Report and Complaints Under Rule K-1 and Rule S-1 and Notice of Failure to Settle Trust Fund Obligations," EBS/85/180 (July 31, 1985) and minutes of EBM/85/153 (October 10, 1985).

Figure 16.7. Zambia: Use of Fund Credit and Arrears, 1971–90

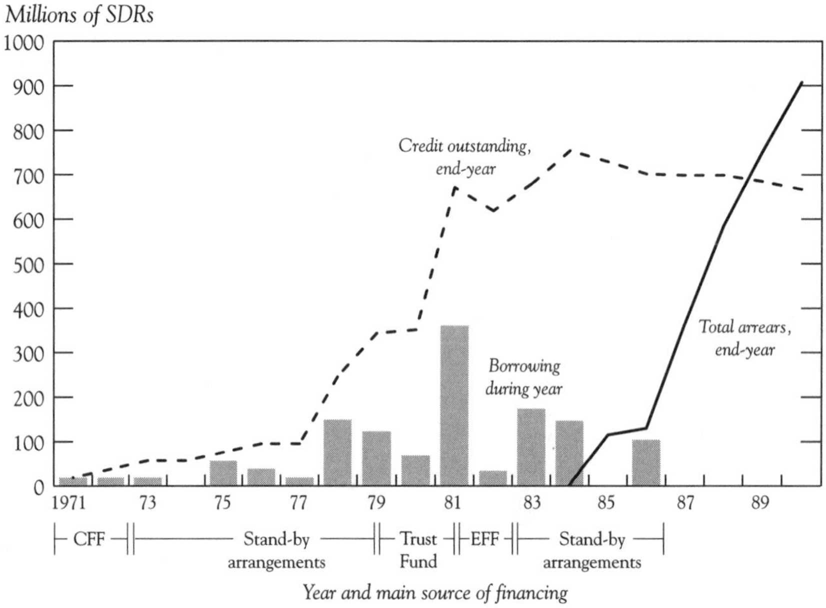

Millions of SDRs

Year and main source of financing

vice, but it finally yielded and implemented the scheme at the beginning of October. Along with some stabilization measures taken around the same time, this
move represented a radical break with earlier piecemeal efforts at reform. Under
the circumstances, the Board's unfortunate decision to restrict access was dictated
primarily by the need to preserve consistency with the way the Fund had handled
the other cases discussed above.

On the strength of its planned adjustment in economic policies, Zambia persuaded donor countries in December 1985 to provide enough additional aid to enable it to pay off its arrears to the Fund, which then amounted to SDR 115 million
($126 million; 43 percent of quota). Arrears were cleared on January 3, 1986, and
on February 21 the Board approved a new stand-by arrangement and a CFF drawing to compensate for a shortfall in export earnings associated with the continued
weakness of copper prices.

The improvement was short-lived: by the end of April 1986, Zambia again was
in arrears. Disbursements under the stand-by arrangement were halted, and in August—with arrears totaling SDR 88 million ($106 million)—the Board restricted
Zambia's access to Fund resources for the second time in ten months. For the next
few months, however, the situation did not seem on the surface to be deteriorating further. The authorities made a few payments and kept the overdue amount
from rising. A meeting of official donors in Paris in December produced some new
aid commitments, albeit not enough to make much of a dent in Zambia's arrears.
By this point, however, the government's scheduled external debt-service payments amounted to more than two-thirds of the country's export earnings, and

domestic opposition to the government's economic policies was turning violent. Riots erupted in December 1986 after Kaunda announced a sharp reduction in subsidies for maize, the mainstay of the diet of many Zambians. Kaunda had to be evacuated from one riot center by helicopter, and unofficial reports placed the death total at about 100 people.[74] (Also see Chapter 14, on the broader context of the riots in Zambia.)

After the riots and the partial failure of the donors' meeting, the government's adherence to the policy program began to waver (for example, the maize subsidy was quickly restored), and arrears began to accumulate more quickly.[75] By March 1987 arrears had more than doubled, to SDR 170 million ($216 million), and the government had stopped making even token payments. The Board then put Zambia on notice that it expected to issue a declaration of ineligibility on May 22 if arrears were not cleared by that date. That prompted a positive response, and the prime minister (who also served as minister of finance), Kebby S.K. Musokotwane, led a delegation to Washington in April to discuss possible reforms.

The April negotiations were successful enough that the Managing Director, Michel Camdessus, agreed to send a mission to Lusaka in May to finalize plans for a new stand-by arrangement, conditional on a successful outcome to an anticipated donors' meeting aimed at settling arrears. He also made a personal appeal for financial support to the G-7 finance ministers and their deputies, during their regular spring meetings.[76]

By all accounts, Zambia's economic troubles resulted from a combination of disastrous external conditions and misguided economic policies. The authorities, of course, stressed the importance of external shocks, while the Fund staff placed greater weight on the policy mistakes. From 1973 (at the height of a worldwide boom in commodity prices) to 1985, Zambia's terms of trade declined by nearly 75 percent, largely because of weakness in the international copper market. Throughout the first half of the 1980s, both the staff and the authorities erred on the high side in forecasting copper prices, which repeatedly left the economic program underfinanced and forced the government to accept greater austerity. Failures by donor countries to disburse aid that they had committed in multilateral meetings further aggravated the decline. For understandable political reasons but with quite predictable and disastrous economic consequences, the government resisted going as far as circumstances demanded.

Throughout the long downward slide, both the Fund and the World Bank offered a range of suggestions on structural reforms aimed at softening the blow and

---

[74]Memorandum for files by Joseph G. Keyes, the Fund's Resident Representative in Lusaka (April 28, 1987); in IMF/RD Managing Director file "Zambia, November 1985–August 1987 (Vol. I)" (Accession 89/164, Box 1, Section 263).

[75]At the time, the maize subsidy was equivalent to nearly 4 percent of the value of annual GDP, so it was large enough by itself to make the difference on whether the fiscal deficit could be financed.

[76]Memorandum for files; in IMF/RD Managing Director file "Zambia, November 1985—August 1987 (Vol. I)" (Accession 89/164, Box 1, Section 263).

restoring long-term growth, but few of those reforms were accepted and implemented. As Kaunda later acknowledged, the government regarded much of the
Fund's advice with a "wide and deep skepticism." The gloomy history of the Zambian economy throughout this period was nonetheless punctuated by occasional
serious efforts to put policies and thus performance on a more favorable and sustainable track.[77]

The April 1987 effort turned out to be the last one of that troubled decade. On
May 1, Kaunda suddenly and unexpectedly broke off negotiations and announced
that Zambia was rejecting "the way of the IMF" and henceforth would "determine
our own destiny."[78] As part of the new program, Zambia (like Peru two years earlier) would limit its debt-service payments to external creditors to 10 percent of export earnings plus certain exceptional payments.[79] In addition, the exchange rate
would be pegged to the dollar at a vastly appreciated rate, and scarce foreign currency would be allocated by a government committee rather than by auction.[80] Although Kaunda and other officials privately reassured the Fund that the government wanted to maintain good and full relations, both their public rhetoric and
their actions suggested a new hard-line stance.[81]

Kaunda's breakaway placed the Fund in an awkward position. If the Board proceeded as scheduled on May 22 to declare Zambia ineligible to use Fund resources

---

[77]See "Zambia—Request for Stand-by Arrangement," EBS/86/24 (February 3, 1986).

[78]"New Economic Recovery Programme," nationwide radio and television broadcast by President Kaunda, May 1, 1987 (official transcript); IMF/CF (C/Zambia/818 "Staff Assignment,
Keyes, Joseph G., November 1985–"). This address is also the source for the "skepticism" quotation in the preceding paragraph.

[79]The 10 percent ceiling excluded payments to service the debts of four key companies: the national airline, the copper company, and the importers of petroleum and fertilizer. Kaunda also indicated that the government would service all new debts on the agreed terms.

[80]The exchange rate was pegged at 8 kwacha per dollar, compared with a market rate that had
been around 21 in late April. "Zambia—Exchange Arrangements," EBS/87/117 (May 28, 1987).

[81]In addition to breaking off negotiations on an adjustment program and canceling the existing stand-by arrangement, the government ordered the Fund's Resident Representative in
Lusaka, Joseph G. Keyes (Advisor in the African Department), to vacate his office immediately;
see memorandum for files by Keyes (May 7, 1987), in IMF/CF (C/Zambia/818 "Staff Assignment,
Keyes, Joseph G., November 1985–"). A few days later, the new finance minister, G.G. Chigaga,
wrote to the Managing Director, saying "it is my country's intention to continue to participate
fully in the affairs of the Fund and that Zambia will continue to play its role as a full member of
the Fund as well as respect the rules of membership under the Articles of Agreement." Cable from
Chigaga dated May 16, 1987, in IMF/CF (C/Zambia/1760 "Stand-by Arrangements, 1986–").
Publicly, however, Chigaga addressed the June 1987 Annual Meeting of the African Development Bank in Cairo by saying that "the IMF programme [in Zambia] became an instrument of
oppression and destruction of human life." Attachment to memorandum from Alassane Ouattara
(Director of the African Department) to the Managing Director (June 12, 1987); in IMF/RD
Managing Director file "Zambia, November 1985 to August 1987 (Vol. I)" (Accession 89/164,
Box 1, Section 263). Kaunda himself reportedly told a group of foreign diplomats that the Fund
was waging a "smear campaign" against Zambia and that the Fund's programs had led directly to
increased deaths from malnutrition; Zambian newspaper report (undated but received in the
Fund on May 6, 1987), in IMF/CF (C/Zambia/818 "Staff Assignment, Keyes, Joseph G., November 1985–").

(which would entail issuing a press release), the move would inevitably be inter-preted as a reprisal. Both Zambia and the Fund would suffer, and restoring normal relations would be made that much more difficult. Not to proceed, however, could be interpreted as special treatment: as greasing the squeaky wheel. Consequently, the Board approved a tortuous declaration to the effect that Zambia would auto-matically be declared ineligible at the end of July unless the Managing Director de-cided that enough progress had been made to reopen the matter:

> Unless by July 31, 1987, Zambia is current in its financial obligations to the Fund in the General Resources Account, or the Managing Director will have called for fur-ther Board consideration of the matter of Zambia's overdue financial obligations, on the basis of contacts with the Zambian authorities that he will initiate and of subse-quent progress by Zambia toward the adoption of comprehensive economic adjust-ment measures, with effect from that date Zambia will be ineligible pursuant to Arti-cle XXVI, Section 2(a) to use the general resources of the Fund.[82]

Although intensive high-level discussions took place throughout June and July 1987 (including lengthy meetings in Lusaka between Goodall E. Gondwe, Deputy Director of the African Department, and President Kaunda), the Managing Direc-tor concluded at the end of July that not enough progress had been made to war-rant reopening the issue. At the last minute, however, the Fund's management de-cided to accommodate a request from the Alternate Executive Director for Zambia, El Tayeb El Kogali (Sudan), to make a plea directly to his colleagues on the Board. With the reluctant but ultimately unanimous consent of Executive Di-rectors at the regular Board meeting on July 31, El Kogali was permitted to request a deferral of the ineligibility declaration even though Zambia was not on the agenda. Deputy Managing Director Richard Erb, the Acting Chairman, explained why management had decided not to recommend a deferral, and a half-dozen Di-rectors from industrial countries spoke up to support that decision. Two G-7 Di-rectors, however, abstained, and the other 13 Directors indicated their support for El Kogali's request. The motion carried on a rare vote, with 47 percent of the vot-ing power in favor and 42 percent opposed. Zambia thus was given two months' re-prieve, to the end of September.[83]

Unfortunately, little changed during those two months, except that arrears con-tinued to accumulate, to more than SDR 290 million ($370 million; 108 percent of quota). Without further ado, the declaration of ineligibility went into effect on September 30. The following week, Kaunda went to Washington and met with Camdessus. Both sides pledged to work cooperatively toward a resolution, but by that time the problem was beyond the reach of the tools at their disposal.

---

[82]Decision No. 8597-(87/78), adopted May 22, 1987, para. 4. Minutes of EBM/87/78, pp. 35–36.

[83]Those opposed (i.e., those favoring management's recommendation to declare Zambia ineli-gible with immediate effect) were Dallara, Bernd Goos (Alternate—Germany), G.P.J. Hogeweg (Alternate—Netherlands), Charles R. Rye (Australia), Masahiro Sugita (Alternate—Japan), and Luc Hubloue (Temporary Alternate—Belgium). Michael Foot (Alternate—United King-dom) abstained, and Salvatore Zecchini (Italy) did not speak on the matter. Minutes of EBM/87/114 (July 31, 1987).

Figure 16.8. Sierra Leone: Use of Fund Credit and Arrears, 1973–90

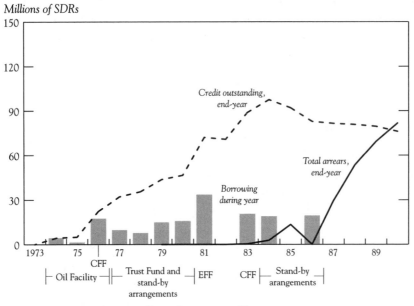

Year and main source of financing

Sierra Leone

The story of Sierra Leone's arrears to the Fund is relatively straightforward. Sierra Leone—a potentially rich country with abundant agricultural and mineral (principally diamonds, rutile, and bauxite) resources—borrowed fairly regularly from the Fund from the mid-1970s through the mid-1980s (Figure 16.8),[84] but the government ran into increasing difficulties in conducting its economic policies. From 1984 on, the government's control over economic activity had deteriorated so badly that it could not prevent smuggling, tax evasion, and black market activity from siphoning off the bulk of potential government revenues.[85] Despite the best of intentions and much goodwill from the international community, the government was unable to muster the resources to pay its bills to the Fund or other ex-

---

[84]Sierra Leone became a member of the Fund on September 20, 1962, about a year and a half after becoming an independent parliamentary republic within the British Commonwealth. The Fund approved three stand-by arrangements in the 1960s, and all of the resulting indebtedness was repaid by 1970. New borrowing commenced in 1974, with drawings on the oil facilities (1974–76) and the CFF (1976 and 1983), Trust Fund loans (1977–81), stand-by arrangements (1977, 1979, and 1984) and an extended arrangement that was approved in 1981 but canceled the following year. Obligations to the GRA peaked in April 1984 at SDR 81.6 million ($86 million; 141 percent of quota), at which time Sierra Leone also had SDR 22.7 million in Trust Fund loans outstanding.

[85]For a detailed study of the pervasiveness of corruption in Sierra Leone in the 1980s, see Reno (1995).

ternal creditors. Nonetheless, it did manage to delay the inevitable declaration of ineligibility until well into 1988.

Serious economic deterioration began in late 1984, several months into an adjustment program supported by a stand-by arrangement with the Fund. In approving the arrangement in February, several industrial country Directors had expressed reservations about the government's ability to manage the economy, though everyone seemed impressed by what Tom de Vries (Alternate—Netherlands) called "the strong sense of commitment on the part of the authorities" to make a major break from the weak policies of the recent past. Costa P. Caranicas (Alternate—Greece) put his reservations most succinctly: "It was an act of faith on the part of management to bring the paper before the Board, and in the final analysis the Executive Board would have to give the member the benefit of the doubt."[86] In less than six months, the program was off track, and the arrangement was abandoned because the authorities were unwilling to accept the staff's recommendations for freeing up the exchange rate to let it reflect market forces. Sierra Leone then fell behind in making payments to the Fund.[87]

Throughout 1985 and the first half of 1986, the Fund responded along the now-standard two tracks. While the staff met regularly with the authorities to devise a strategy for strengthening economic performance, the Executive Board issued a series of escalating decisions. The Managing Director issued a formal complaint in late April 1985, and the Board restricted access to Fund resources at the end of June. In January 1986, the Board put the authorities on notice that it expected to issue a declaration of ineligibility in March if arrears were not cleared by then. Meanwhile, technical discussions were focusing heavily on exchange rate policy, because a major part of the problem was that very little of the foreign currency being earned from exports was reaching the government or even the banking system. In mid-February, the government agreed to switch to a floating rate for the currency (the leone), effective in mid-March. On that basis, the Board agreed to postpone until May its plan to declare the country ineligible to use Fund resources. The government, however, then postponed its own plan to float the leone, until after parliamentary elections scheduled for the end of May,[88] but it compensated partially by making a $3 million payment to the Fund just before the March 12 Board meeting.[89]

Two months later, on May 6, 1986, Sierra Leone won another reprieve, partly because Directors accepted the political necessity of waiting for the new parlia-

---

[86]Minutes of EBM/84/18 (February 3, 1984), pp. 25 (de Vries) and 36 (Caranicas).

[87]See "Sierra Leone—Staff Report for the 1986 Article IV Consultation and Requests for Stand-by Arrangement and for Arrangement Under the Structural Adjustment Facility," EBS/86/243 (November 3, 1986), pp. 1–2.

[88]Sierra Leone introduced a one-party constitution in 1978, with Siaka Stevens continuing as head of state. Stevens, who initially became prime minister in 1967, retired in the fall of 1985 and was replaced by Major General Joseph Saidu Momoh. Momoh then scheduled the election of a new parliament, still under the one-party system.

[89]As of March 12, after the $3 million (SDR 2.6 million) payment, Sierra Leone's arrears to the Fund totaled SDR 14.4 million.

ment to be elected and take office. Floating the currency would result in a large depreciation, which would sharply raise import prices. Without a fresh political mandate, the government expected to be confronted by massive discontent and unrest. Better to wait a few months than to risk a disastrous failure. Furthermore, the finance minister, Joe Amara-Bangali, promised the Fund that the government would make a new payment within a few days, amounting to $4.8 million from the proceeds of an anticipated sale of diamonds in the Antwerp market. That promise also was broken, and arrears continued to mount.[90]

Remarkably, the situation did begin to improve after the elections. In June, the new parliament approved a budget that was in line with the Fund staff's recommendations. The deficit would be curtailed, the leone would finally be floated, import restrictions would be substantially liberalized, and several major subsidies would be reduced or eliminated (most notably on petroleum). Although the Executive Board had already declared Sierra Leone ineligible effective July 16 if it were not current on its payments to the Fund by that date, it now took the unprecedented step of suspending that decision for two months (to September 19) to give the authorities time to negotiate a new adjustment program and to arrange temporary (bridging) financing from commercial banks.[91]

Negotiations proceeded smoothly and succeeded just ahead of the deadline. On September 18, Sierra Leone settled its arrears in full (SDR 25.1 million; $32.5 million), and on November 14 the Fund approved both a new stand-by arrangement for SDR 23.2 million ($31.5 million; 40 percent of quota, of which SDR 8 million would be available at once) and a structural adjustment facility (SAF) loan with an immediate disbursement of SDR 11.6 million ($15.7 million; 20 percent of quota). Sadly, the reform effort then quickly ran out of steam, largely because the government lacked both the political support and the administrative capability to rein in the rampant black market. Virtually no foreign exchange was offered at the official auctions, and the authorities had to fall back on determining the exchange rate administratively.[92] The most pressing consequence of that failure was that the government again could not meet its obligations to foreign creditors. By January 1987, Sierra Leone again was in arrears to the Fund.

In April 1987, the Executive Board restricted Sierra Leone's access for a second time.[93] In the months that followed, the Fund continued to show sympathy and

---

[90]The Alternate Director for Sierra Leone (Ahmed Abdallah—Kenya) later explained that the finance minister had made his promise without approval of the government and that the proceeds had already been committed elsewhere. The nature of the alternative commitment was not explained, and the government made a scapegoat of the minister by sacking him. Minutes of EBM/86/118 (July 16, 1986), p. 28.

[91]Minutes of EBM/86/118 (July 16, 1986).

[92]Weeks (1992), pp. 125–245, argues that the floating rate policy in Sierra Leone was fundamentally flawed, partly because participation in the auctions was limited and more fundamentally because floating was bound to lead to a precipitous and destabilizing depreciation of the currency. He concludes that a crawling peg would have led to greater stability. That solution did not at the time appear feasible to the Fund staff, in view of the government's weak administrative record.

[93]No disbursements were made to Sierra Leone under either the stand-by arrangement or the SAF arrangement after the initial drawings in November 1986.

understanding for the difficult circumstances facing the government, and the inexorable drive toward ineligibility proceeded in as low a gear as possible. In November 1987, shortly after the Board declared its intention to declare Sierra Leone ineligible within three months, the government enacted a state of emergency that included administrative and penal measures aimed at discouraging smuggling. That policy proved ineffective, as the risk of penalty was outweighed by the economic incentive to flout it. Nonetheless, the Board continued to give the authorities the benefit of the doubt. Negotiations on a new adjustment program continued for several more months, but in April 1988—with arrears of SDR 39 million ($54 million; 68 percent of quota)—Sierra Leone was finally declared ineligible to use Fund resources.

Somalia

Somalia developed an adjustment program in late 1984 that depended heavily on foreign aid financing from official donors. In February 1985, the Fund approved a stand-by arrangement to support the program. Everyone knew at the time that the financing was extremely tight and that there was no margin at all for slippages. When slippages did occur, Somalia simply ran out of money. The government tried valiantly to stay current with the Fund, but it lacked the means to do so. Without significant exaggeration, the Executive Director for Somalia, Mohamed Finaish (Libya), reminded his colleagues in April 1986 that the government had used "every last penny of foreign exchange available" to repay the Fund, and he asked for "flexibility and understanding" in handling this difficult case.[94]

For those who remember the political and economic chaos into which Somalia descended in the 1990s, it may be difficult to recall as well that Somalia's economic performance until the mid-1980s was not so bad. After struggling under the effects of several exogenous shocks in the late 1970s (ranging from severe droughts to an invasion by Ethiopian-based insurgents), the government undertook a generally successful adjustment program from 1981 through 1983 that was supported by two fully utilized Fund stand-by arrangements. Those credits raised Somalia's obligations to the Fund from near zero to SDR 116 million ($121 million; 241 percent of quota) by the end of 1983 (Figure 16.9).[95] The success of the adjustment effort up to that point led de Larosière, in a speech to a banking group in Belgium,

---

[94]Minutes of EBM/86/68 (April 23, 1986), p. 26.

[95]Somalia became a member of the Fund in August 1962, two years after becoming an independent and unified republic. (During the 1950s, the territory had been administered partly as British Somaliland and partly—in the southern region once known as Italian Somaliland—as the UN Trust Territory of Somalia under Italian control.) The Fund approved seven consecutive stand-by arrangements from 1964 through 1970. No drawings were made under the last two of those arrangements, and Somalia had no outstanding debts to the Fund from 1969 until a new government took office in 1980. (Major General Mohamed Siad Barre, who had ruled Somalia since taking power in a coup in 1969, was named president in January 1980 by a legislature that had been elected under the terms of a newly drafted constitution.) Only one drawing was made under a relatively small 1980 stand-by arrangement.

Figure 16.9. Somalia: Use of Fund Credit and Arrears, 1979–90

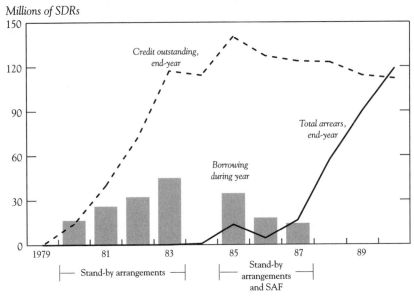

Millions of SDRs

Year and main source of financing

to cite Somalia as a "striking example" of what strong adjustment with Fund support could achieve: agriculture was booming, the growth rate was approaching 10 percent, and all external payments arrears had been eliminated.[96]

Even before that speech, Somalia was encountering a new series of shocks, starting in May 1983 when Saudi Arabia responded to reports of contaminated beef by banning imports of cattle from East Africa. Although the offending parasite was never confirmed to have been present in Somali cattle, the ban closed off the primary market for Somalia's main export for the rest of the decade and beyond. Total exports, measured in U.S. dollars, fell by more than half from 1982 to 1984 before beginning to recover.

The loss in exports was compounded in 1984 by a growing burden of external debt service, as a number of grace periods on official credits began to expire and the government found it difficult to get the major donor countries to provide additional new assistance. The authorities negotiated an ambitious program of liberalizing reforms and macroeconomic stabilization with the Fund staff in late 1984, setting the stage for a new stand-by arrangement if the program could be fully financed. Approval by the Executive Board, however, depended on getting commitments from bilateral donors.

---

[96]"Adjustment Programs Supported by the Fund: Their Logic, Objectives, and Results in the Light of Recent Experience," remarks by Jacques de Larosière before the Centre d'études financières in Brussels (February 6, 1984); in IMF/RD Managing Director file "Centre d'études financières (Bruxelles), February 1984" (Accession 85/231, Box 3, Section 177).

The staff estimated that Somalia would need, in addition to an anticipated $64 million in Fund credits and $33 million in expected debt relief from Paris Club creditors, another $100 million in external assistance to close the financing gap for 1985.[97] A January 1985 meeting of official donors in Paris resulted in just $80 million in pledges, and most of that was to be in the form of commodities rather than cash and was likely to be subjected to lengthy delays before being disbursed. The staff assumed that no more than $55 million of that total would be forthcoming during 1985, which left a gap of some $45 million. By late February, enough pledges of grants and debt relief had been made by Middle Eastern countries to just fill that gap. On that basis, the Executive Board approved the stand-by arrangement and a CFF drawing on February 23, 1985.[98]

Although the program was fully financed on paper, the final commitments gave Somalia far less foreign exchange than had been envisaged during the negotiations. As 1985 unfolded, the cash shortage was compounded by a slowdown in the economies of major Middle Eastern oil producers, which reduced the flow of remittances from Somali workers in that region. By midyear, Somalia was slipping further and further behind in its payments to the Fund.

The Managing Director issued a formal complaint on Somalia's arrears in October, and the Executive Board restricted Somalia's access to Fund resources on December 27, 1985.[99] That restriction was short-lived, but it was quickly followed by new problems. Somalia's official creditors made fresh financing commitments in the first months of 1986, and a group of commercial banks in the United States and Italy provided short-term bridging loans. Somalia repaid all of its arrears in April 1986 with the proceeds from those loans; in May the Fund approved the resumption of drawings under the stand-by arrangement; and on May 16, Somalia borrowed SDR 9.7 million ($11.3 million). That drawing, however, had to be applied immediately to repay the bridge loans, so it did nothing to improve Somalia's cash flow. On the same day, the central bank was scheduled to pay the Fund SDR 0.8 million that was due on the 1981 and 1982 stand-by credits. As it lacked the money, the country immediately went back into the red without so much as a day's respite.[100]

---

[97]The stand-by arrangement was for SDR 22.1 million (50 percent of quota); Somalia also requested a CFF drawing of SDR 33 million (75 percent of quota) to compensate for the shortfall in export revenues.

[98]The Board approved the arrangement in principle on January 25, pending completion of financing commitments. The staff's subsequent finding that financing was sufficient was approved on a lapse-of-time basis. See minutes of EBM/85/11–12 (January 25, 1985); "Somalia—Request for Stand-by Arrangement," EBS/85/1 (January 2, 1985); and "Stand-by Arrangement—Effective Date—Arrangement with Respect to the Financing of 1985 Balance of Payments Deficits," Sup. 2 (February 22, 1985). The Fund's use of "approval in principle" in that period is reviewed in Chapter 9.

[99]"Somalia—Overdue Financial Obligations to the Fund—Report and Complaints under Rule K-1 and Rule S-1," EBS/85/235 (October 25, 1985) and minutes of EBM/85/188 (December 27, 1985).

[100]Minutes of EBM/86/81 (May 12, 1986) and "Somalia—Overdue Financial Obligations to the Fund," EBS/86/136 (June 24, 1986).

Twice more, Somalia managed to settle its arrears to the Fund, using new bridge loans from banks plus grants from the Italian government. After settling in September 1986, Somalia fell behind again the next month. After settling in June 1987 and getting the Fund's approval for a new stand-by arrangement and SAF loan, it fell behind a week later, in early July.[101] As frustrating as this pattern had become, it no longer surprised anyone. The staff report that proposed the new credits projected explicitly that Somalia would continue to go into arrears to the Fund "from time to time,"[102] and the Executive Board approved the arrangement in full understanding of that prospect. The fundamental and chronic shortage of cash was now being aggravated by a weakening of the authorities' ability to govern. Military insurgencies in the northern part of the country were intensifying, and the government itself was torn by reports of internal coup attempts. The prevailing judgment at the Fund was that the country needed and deserved support.

The authorities adhered remarkably well to their economic program throughout 1985–86, despite the interruption of Fund financing and lags in donor support. As a main element of reform, the exchange market was gradually liberalized during those two years, and by the end of 1986 the exchange rate was being determined freely through government-sponsored auctions. Not surprisingly, as economic conditions deteriorated, the rate depreciated sharply. By mid-1987, the government became convinced that it needed greater stability, and in September, it reverted to the earlier practice of determining the rate administratively. What worried the staff and some donors was not so much this technical issue but the possibility that "adjustment fatigue" was setting in. With external assistance continuing to erode, the difficulty of implementing restrictive policies was becoming even greater.

Somalia's economic performance deteriorated rapidly in late 1987 and early 1988. A major reorganization of the government in December 1987 brought in a new finance minister who initially showed little interest in working with the Fund or other external creditors. Financial policies slipped out of control, the exchange rate became increasingly unrealistic, and official aid virtually ceased. By the spring of 1988, the new economic team was beginning to regroup and adopt more constructive policies, but by then what little opportunity might have existed for recovery had been lost. On May 6, 1988, with arrears of SDR 27 million ($33 million; 54 percent of quota) and no prospects for a settlement in sight, the Executive Board declared Somalia ineligible to use Fund resources.

---

[101] Approval of the SDR 33.2 million stand-by arrangement enabled Somalia to draw SDR 5.5 million at once. The SAF loan, for a total of SDR 20.8 million, provided for an immediate disbursement of SDR 8.8 million. All of that and more was needed to repay short-term bank credits. Scheduled repayments to the Fund in July and August totaled SDR 7.4 million, none of which was paid. See "Somalia—Settlement of Overdue Financial Obligations to the Fund and Withdrawal of Complaint Under Rule K-1," EBS/87/113, Sup. 5 (June 26, 1987), and "Somalia—Overdue Obligations to the Fund—Report and Complaint Under Rule K-1," EBS/87/194 (September 8, 1987).

[102] "Somalia—Request for Stand-by Arrangement and Requests for Arrangements Under the Structural Adjustment Facility," EBS/87/122 (June 5, 1987), p. 35.

Panama

Panama's economic problems derived from a political upheaval that erupted in the second half of 1987. An original member of the Fund, Panama had a long series of stand-by arrangements starting in 1965, but it had no difficulty either conducting stable economic policies or servicing its obligations to the Fund until the end of 1987. Over the following months, the economy largely collapsed.

The problem began when the U.S. government turned against the commander in chief of Panama's armed forces, General Manuel Antonio Noriega Morena. Through grand jury and U.S. Senate investigations, charges were raised that Noriega was involved in drug trafficking and a wide range of other serious crimes. Noriega was generally thought to have served previously as an agent of U.S. security interests in Central America and to have amassed both his political power and a considerable personal fortune as a result, and the legal case against him was widely assumed to be part of a concerted effort to oust him from that power and terminate an embarrassing symbiosis.[103] In any event, this development generated substantial political unrest and effectively immobilized the government from formulating economic policies. The indictment of Noriega in the United States in February 1988 was followed by U.S. economic sanctions against Panama, an effective general strike in Panama, a complete shutdown of the banking system for two months, and an escalating degree of economic and political chaos. That situation continued until after U.S. military forces invaded Panama in December 1989, captured Noriega, and eventually restored normal economic relations.[104]

Before the crisis, Panama successfully completed an adjustment program supported by a Fund stand-by arrangement in 1985–87. That arrangement raised Panama's indebtedness to the Fund (Figure 16.10) to SDR 284 million ($360 million; 278 percent of quota). The staff began negotiating terms for a new stand-by arrangement (which would have been the 18th arrangement in 23 years), but the government was unable to formulate a credible program while the economy was crumbling, and the negotiations were postponed.

Panama missed its first payment to the Fund on December 28, 1987. With both its assets in the United States and payments due from U.S. companies frozen, the government soon was unable to make any further payments to the Fund or other external creditors. It was obvious that the government could not surmount this barrier through any shift in economic policies, and it placed the Fund awkwardly in the middle of a noneconomic dispute between two member countries. To tell Panama to take the actions necessary to settle its arrears was, in effect, to tell the government to acquiesce to the United States in the political dispute over the status of General

---

[103]The U.S. secretary of state at that time, James A. Baker, III, hinted at Noriega's earlier role in supporting U.S. interests by describing him as an "erstwhile ally" who had "become increasingly dangerous as his collusion with international drug trafficking deepened" (Baker, 1995, p. 177). For an exploration of the depth of that relationship, see Weeks and Gunson (1991).

[104]Noriega, who functioned as de facto head of state for much of 1988 and 1989, was convicted in the United States on drug trafficking charges in 1992 and was later convicted *in absentia* in Panama for ordering assassinations.

Figure 16.10. Panama: Use of Fund Credit and Arrears, 1980–90

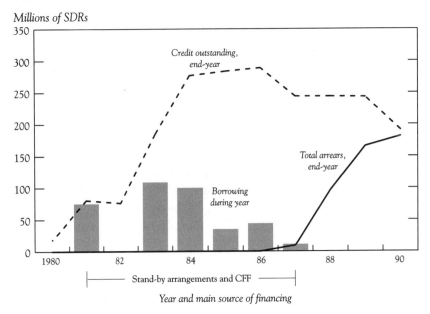

Millions of SDRs

Year and main source of financing

Noriega. To give Panama more lenient treatment than other countries in arrears would open the door to consideration of political excuses in other cases. In the words of the Managing Director, "the Fund was being taken hostage in a conflict in which it had no part."[105] The Executive Board accordingly moved cautiously in responding to the Managing Director's standard complaint on arrears (issued on March 3, 1988) and postponed discussion of the matter until June 8. By that time, the United States had notified the Fund that its restrictions on transfers to Panama constituted an exchange restriction imposed for national security purposes, and the Fund had implicitly approved that restriction by not objecting to it within the allowed time.[106]

The Board discussion was brief, as most Directors chose to stay out of the dispute. The Executive Director for Panama (Alexandre Kafka—Brazil) asked for but did not get a formal vote on the question of whether the Board should find that Panama had failed to fulfill its obligations to the Fund. Leonor Filardo (Venezuela) supported Kafka, Dallara and Guenter Grosche (Germany) spoke in favor of making such a finding, and the Managing Director determined that the sense of the meeting was to approve the decision to restrict Panama's access to Fund resources as long as the country was in arrears.[107]

---

[105]Minutes of EBM/88/126 (August 24, 1988), p. 14.

[106]"Notification Under Executive Board Decision No. 144-(51/52) of Restrictions Relating to Panama," EBD/88/126 (May 9, 1988) and minutes of EBM/88/91 (June 8, 1988), pp. 3–5. For other cases illustrating the Fund's policy on exchange restrictions imposed for national security, see the discussion of Vietnam, pp. 766–70, and Chapter 2, footnote 116, p. 120.

[107]Minutes of EBM/88/91 (June 8, 1988).

When the Board first met to review the restriction decision, in August 1988, Grosche and Charles S. Warner (Alternate—United States) asked for a declaration that Panama would be declared ineligible to use Fund resources if it did not settle its arrears within three months. A consensus of other Directors, however, preferred to wait to see how events unfolded. The decision therefore merely noted that within three months the Fund would "consider the appropriateness of further steps" if arrears were still outstanding.[108]

Three months later, in November 1988, Panama's minister of planning and economic policy, Gustavo R. González, participated in the Board meeting. He impressed Directors by stressing the government's willingness to cooperate with the Fund and by recognizing the Fund's status as a preferred creditor. (Panama had made a token payment to the Fund the day before the meeting and had made no payments to other external creditors since the imposition of sanctions by the United States.) The Board responded by adding an unusually positive sentence to its conclusions: "The Fund welcomes the commitment of the authorities to pursue the adjustment process begun several years ago and to adopt policies aimed at restoring external and internal balance and normalizing Panama's relations with the international financial community."[109] Moreover, since the August review, the Interim Committee—at its Berlin meeting—had "welcomed the intention of the Executive Board to pursue a multifaceted approach to [the arrears] problem involving . . . intensified collaboration where members with overdue obligations are cooperating with the Fund" (communiqué of September 26, 1988, para. 5). With that in mind, the Board agreed merely to repeat the August warning that it would consider unspecified further steps within another three months.[110]

Little changed during that interval. When the next review was held in February 1989, the Board accepted the staff's judgment that Panama should be treated as a special case, owing both to the strong record of performance and cooperation before 1988 and the perception that the authorities were doing about all that they could under present circumstances. The November 1988 decision was repeated word for word.[111] Then in May 1989, the political situation really began to unravel. Presidential elections were internationally denounced as fraudulent, and a prolonged struggle ensued between factions loyal to Noriega and those supporting the apparent winner, Guillermo Endara Galimany. A few weeks later, the Fund finally decided that it could no longer ignore the consequences of Panama's rapidly growing arrears (which then totaled SDR 121 million, or $150 million). The Board accepted a staff suggestion that "Panama could have made more active efforts to settle its overdue obligations," and it gave the

---

[108]Minutes of EBM/88/126 (August 24, 1988).

[109]In drafting this sentence, Directors explicitly rejected a more conventional alternative that would have commended the authorities' commitment to implement an adjustment program; that alternative would have implied a rejection of existing economic policies.

[110]Minutes of EBM/88/171 (November 23, 1988).

[111]Minutes of EBM/89/21 (February 22, 1989).

authorities just one more month to settle their arrears or face a declaration of ineligibility.[112]

The imposed deadline could not possibly be met, and little progress could be reported when the Board met again at the end of June. Kafka again asked for a formal vote on the proposal to declare Panama ineligible, but as had been the rule all along, most Directors declined to express a view. Only two chairs—the United States and Germany—voted in favor, but only four—the constituency that included Panama, the two African constituencies, and China—voted against. The motion carried with 25 percent of the voting power in favor and 10 percent against.[113]

Honduras

The last country to face a declaration of ineligibility in the 1980s was Honduras. An oddity in this case was that Honduras had not borrowed from the Fund for several years and had repaid most of the money it had borrowed in the early 1980s (Figure 16.11).[114] That Honduras fell into arrears to the Fund in the last quarter of 1987 is attributable to several unrelated and coincidental developments. First, the economy suffered from a poorly diversified export base (concentrated in coffee and bananas) that left it heavily dependent on a few international commodity markets. The coffee market weakened severely in 1987; the export price of Honduran coffee fell by 43 percent, and the overall terms of trade fell by 18 percent. Second, foreign assistance declined in 1987, largely as a byproduct of a falloff in covert U.S. support for the Contra rebels based in Honduras.[115] Third, the grace periods expired on many of the loans from official creditors taken out in the early 1980s, resulting in large net outflows to the Fund, other multilateral institutions, and bilateral creditors. Although the amounts coming due to the Fund were a small part of the total, the government adopted a strategy to restrict payments to all external creditors until a coordinated solution to the country's growing payments difficulties could be arranged.

---

[112]Minutes of EBM/89/68 (May 31, 1989). The quotation is from "Panama—Overdue Financial Obligations to the Fund—Further Review of Decisions on Complaints Under Rule K-1 and Rule S-1," EBS/89/109 (May 26, 1989), p. 8.

[113]Minutes of EBM/89/85 (June 30, 1989).

[114]Honduras, an original member of the Fund, began the 1980s with no outstanding debts to the Fund other than a small amount in Trust Fund loans. It then borrowed SDR 140 million in 1980–83 (206 percent of quota; $163 million) from the GRA, mostly under the terms of an extended arrangement, a follow-up stand-by arrangement, and two CFF drawings for export shortfalls. By August 1989, all but SDR 23.3 million had been repaid. Of the SDR 14 million in Trust Fund loans disbursed in 1978–81, all but SDR 3.7 million had been repaid.

[115]The Contras were guerrillas fighting to overthrow the Sandinista government in Nicaragua. In December 1986, it became known that Honduras-based Contras had been financed in part by U.S. government funds diverted from the proceeds of the covert sale of arms to Iran. Following that revelation, U.S. official aid (which accounted for about three-fourths of all official transfers received by Honduras) fell from $108 million in 1986 to $81 million in 1987 and $80 million in 1988.

Figure 16.11. Honduras: Use of Fund Credit and Arrears, 1978–90

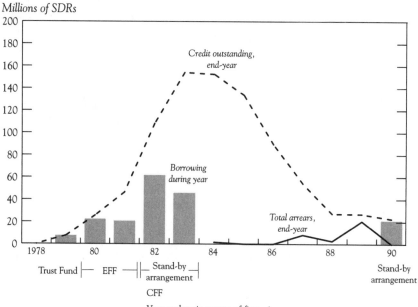

Millions of SDRs

Year and main source of financing

Throughout 1988, Honduras did make several payments to the Fund to limit the rise in arrears, and the authorities negotiated extensively with the staff over the terms of an adjustment program that could be supported by new credits from the Fund once arrears were cleared. The main point of contention in those talks concerned exchange rate policy. The value of the currency had been pegged at two lempira per U.S. dollar for more than half a century, and in recent years the government had been forced to resort increasingly to a variety of restrictions to maintain the exchange rate at that level. The staff argued that action to depreciate the official rate was needed, both to eliminate the restrictions and to create incentives for the expansion of nontraditional exports. The authorities resisted on the grounds that they faced inelastic demand for their products and thus could not realistically expect depreciation to increase export volumes, and that the fixed rate promoted more general economic and social stability.[116]

Although these technical discussions were inconclusive, Honduras managed to obtain fresh loans from the United States and Mexico in August 1988. The authorities used the proceeds from those loans to make a partial payment on their arrears to the Fund and to pay off their arrears to the World Bank completely. The Bank then approved disbursement of a Structural Adjustment Loan to Honduras, which raised an outcry from several Executive Directors at the Fund who felt that the Bank should refuse to lend to countries that were still in arrears to the Fund.

---

[116]Minutes of EBM/88/83 (May 23, 1988).

The Fund's management, however, supported the Bank's action, both because it ultimately was likely to help Honduras repay the Fund and because imposing cross-conditionality between the two institutions seemed inappropriate.[117]

Honduras did settle its arrears, which then amounted to SDR 4.2 million, in November 1988. Although the authorities managed to stay current only for five days, that development succeeded in restarting the clock on the procedures for declaring them ineligible to use Fund resources. Unfortunately, circumstances made it impossible to take advantage of the delay. A tightly contested presidential and legislative election was to be held in November 1989, and for the whole year leading up to it the government felt itself to be incapable of enacting the policy changes that clearly were needed to put the balance of payments on a sustainable course. The Executive Board met three times during 1989, and by the last meeting (on August 30), Directors had run out of patience. Analía Napky (Temporary Alternate—Honduras) explained that the government had agreed to propose fiscal measures, but that the congress would not approve them until after the new government took office in January 1990. Meanwhile, she asked for the forbearance of her colleagues on the Board. A majority, however, insisted that to wait would mean giving Honduras an unwarranted special treatment over other countries in arrears. The Board therefore decided that Honduras would be declared ineligible effective November 30 if arrears were not cleared by that date. Honduras made no more payments that year, and the final ineligibility declaration of the decade took effect as scheduled.[118]

Zaïre

Zaïre[119] borrowed steadily from the Fund for a decade starting in the mid-1970s and was frequently late in repaying those debts when they fell due in the 1980s. Protracted arrears began in 1988 and eventually led to a declaration of ineligibility in 1991. More than in any other case, a persistent subtheme to the growing economic difficulties in Zaïre was the pervasiveness of official corruption and its crushing effect on political and economic activity in the country.

Zaïre's problems began in 1975, when a two-year boom in the world copper market came to an abrupt halt. The price for Zaïre's principal export fell by more than 40 percent that year and remained depressed for the rest of the decade. The government had badly overspent the extra revenues from the boom period and had failed to resolve long-standing problems of inefficient administration and political corruption. These problems were aggravated by sporadic insurgencies against President Mobutu Sese Seko that seriously disrupted mining operations in the Shaba

---

[117]Minutes of EBM/88/138 (September 2, 1988).

[118]The new government quickly adopted a comprehensive adjustment program and allowed the exchange rate to depreciate. Honduras cleared its arrears in June 1990.

[119]The Democratic Republic of Congo, formerly the Belgian Congo, became independent in 1960. It was known as the Republic of Congo during 1960–64 and as the Republic of Zaïre from October 1971 until May 1997.

province for several years. The authorities determined to implement stabilizing policies and to undertake administrative reforms (the "Mobutu Plan"), and they turned to the Fund and other external creditors for help. The Fund responded in 1975–78 with SDR 255 million ($305 million; 226 percent of quota) in mostly low-conditionality credits: from the Oil Facility (SDR 78 million in 1975–76) to compensate for the high cost of importing oil, from the CFF (SDR 84 million in 1976–77) to compensate for the drop in export revenues, low-interest and longer-term loans from the Trust Fund (SDR 47 million in 1977–78), and two higher-conditionality stand-by arrangements (SDR 46 million drawn in 1976–77, out of a total commitment of SDR 86 million).[120] The Fund also assisted in negotiations with bank creditors and in an effort initiated by the Belgian government to improve transparency and reduce official corruption. For the latter effort, the Fund provided technical assistance and nominated external candidates (initially Erwin Blumenthal, a former Bundesbank official, who served in 1978–79, and then a series of successors) to oversee the operations of the central bank.

The reform effort foundered in 1979–80 when a second copper boom weakened the authorities' resolve. World copper prices were cycling wildly: they averaged 57 U.S. cents a pound in 1968–72, 87 cents in 1973–74, 60 cents in 1975–78, 94 cents in 1979–80, and 68 cents in 1981–86. One difficulty, hardly peculiar to Zaïre, was that the authorities treated the peaks as if they were permanent and the troughs as temporary aberrations, so that the fiscal deficit crept up to unsustainable levels. A second and more indigenous difficulty was that inefficient management, lack of oversight, and widespread official corruption devoured much of the potential revenue before it reached the official accounts.

By the late 1970s, the Fund staff was aware of the pervasiveness of corruption and was reasonably knowledgeable on the extent of the drain on the government treasury from what were euphemistically called "the spending habits of the President." In addition to information gleaned directly by staff missions to Zaïre, the Fund received inside reports from Blumenthal and his successors managing the central bank. Blumenthal's role was especially important and has been much discussed and often misinterpreted in the literature on the uncovering of corruption in Mobutu's Zaïre.[121] When appointed by the Fund, Blumenthal was known as an expert on the country and had already worked there briefly in 1964 on behalf of Prime Minister Moïse Tschombe, before Tschombe was overthrown by Mobutu. Although various published reports later claimed that he quit in disgust over the corruption that he found there in 1978–79 and that his reports should have alerted the international community to a pervasive problem, in fact he was personally per-

---

[120]Prior to 1975, Zaïre's only borrowing from the Fund was a CFF drawing of SDR 28.3 million (25 percent of quota) in 1972. A 1967 stand-by arrangement was not drawn upon.

[121]See "Zaïre: Can the IMF Succeed?" *Africa Confidential*, Vol. 20 (January 3, 1979), pp. 1–5; testimony before the Subcommittee on Africa of the Committee on Foreign Affairs, U.S. House of Representatives, by Nguza Karl-I-Bond (a former prime minister of Zaïre), September 15, 1981; interview with Mobutu in *Newsweek* magazine (August 23, 1983, p. 56); Lissakers (1991), p. 106; Callaghy (1993), p. 107; and articles in the *Financial Times*, May 12, 1997, pp. 1 and 2.

suaded by Mobutu to complete his one-year appointment. None of his contemporaneous reports to the Fund raised objections about the activities of the president, who "had always backed [him] up" in his battles with the management of the central bank and who had always shown him "generosity and kindness." Blumenthal did, however, struggle to reduce the extent of corruption at the central bank, of which he understood that the president and his associates were the major beneficiaries. Three years later, in 1982, he prepared a highly critical report, apparently at the request of the Belgian government, that detailed examples of the diversion of central bank assets for Mobutu's personal use.[122]

The Fund's concerns about these problems, however, were outweighed by two factors. First, the Fund in that era scrupulously avoided making judgments about economic or administrative problems that could be construed as deriving from a country's "domestic social and political policies" (in the language of Article IV). Second, Mobutu enjoyed widespread international political support, because of European economic participation in the exploitation of Zaïre's vast mineral wealth, because of the country's strategic importance in the Cold War, and because of a perception that there were no viable alternatives to Mobutu's rule. The staff and management of the Fund repeatedly stressed to the authorities (including Mobutu) the importance of improving transparency and efficiency of the government and of the state-owned mining and trading companies, but the institution had little real influence over the outcome.[123]

A stand-by arrangement (for 78 percent of quota over 18 months) was negotiated laboriously in 1978–79 in the midst of policy slippages and an increasing reluctance by bank creditors to provide new loans. The program twice went off track,

---

[122]For Blumenthal's reports to the Fund from Kinshasa, see correspondence in IMF/CF (S 872 "Zaïre, Blumenthal, Erwin, Principal Manager, 1978–"). For his 1982 report and a letter from Mobutu accusing Blumenthal of waging "a vast campaign of denigration and defamation against Zaïre" (both in French), see IMF/RD Managing Director file "1985—Zaïre I" (Accession 87/136, Box 3, Section 168). For an early example of relevant staff reports to management on the economic and political effects of corruption in Zaïre, see IMF/RD African Department file "Zaire—Correspondence, 1978" (Accession 81/51, Box 1, Section 117): June 9, 1978, memorandum from Justin B. Zulu (Director of the African Department); the "spending habits" quotation given in the text is from that memorandum. Also see IMF/RD Managing Director file "Zaire, 1981" (Accession 83/108, Box 4, Section 376): September 14, 1981, memorandum from Evangelos A. Calamitsis (Senior Advisor in the African Department); September 15, 1981, memorandum from Leif Mutén (also Senior Advisor in the African Department); and November 19, 1981, memorandum from Zulu. Blumenthal also wrote a letter to *Newsweek* (September 7, 1983), challenging claims made against him by Mobutu in the interview cited above, but the magazine apparently did not print it. A copy, attached to a letter (September 20, 1983) sent by Blumenthal to Roland Tenconi (Director of the Administration Department), is in IMF/RD African Department file "Zaire—Correspondence, January–September 1983" (Room 4827, Section 5, Shelf 6, Bin 8).

[123]Mobutu frequently met with Fund missions in Zaïre, and on at least two occasions (in 1979 and 1981) met with the Managing Director in Washington. In addition, he had regular contacts with the Executive Director in the Fund for Belgium, Jacques de Groote, who was also serving on a personal basis as "an expert in the service of Zaïre" and was helping Zaïre design adjustment programs acceptable to the Fund. See note from de Groote to de Larosière (September 11, 1979); IMF/RD African Department file "Zaire—Correspondence, July–December 1979" (Accession 82/13, Box 2, Section 211).

but the authorities made additional efforts. With some modifications, the program was completed, and the stand-by arrangement was fully drawn. The Fund then approved a three-year EFF arrangement in June 1981, on the strength of promises to institute major reforms aimed at making the government's accounts more transparent. When export prices dropped, the government made little effort to restrain spending, and that program was abandoned.

In November 1981, Mobutu went to Washington and asked de Larosière to meet with him at his suite in the Madison Hotel. In response to a request for flexibility in applying the conditionality in the stand-by arrangement, the Managing Director told the president that the Fund would give "no leeway" in assessing compliance and that the finances of the principal state-owned exporting companies would have to be cleaned up and made more transparent if the Fund was to continue to provide financial support.[124] Despite assurances given by Mobutu, little was done on that score. The authorities made no more drawings on the EFF arrangement after that month, and they canceled the arrangement in mid-1982. By then, external arrears (mostly to commercial banks) were beginning to mount.[125] Beginning in the second half of the year, Zaïre also developed short-term arrears to the Fund, and in March 1983 some payments were delayed long enough to warrant a notification to the Executive Board, but the authorities managed to clear the arrears (temporarily) in April without a formal complaint being issued.[126]

For the first half of 1983, Zaïre carried out a "shadow program," with which the authorities complied well enough to lay the groundwork for negotiations on a new stand-by arrangement. A central element in the Fund's strategy was to eliminate the flourishing black market in foreign exchange and reduce the pervasiveness of smuggling by persuading the authorities to dismantle the elaborate system of exchange controls and correct the enormous overvaluation in the exchange rate. That last step, the staff argued, required abandoning the peg against the SDR in favor of a floating rate. The authorities resisted, but the Managing Director—drawing on personal knowledge of the difficulties of operating a system of dual exchange rates, based on his own experience in France—finally convinced them. In September 1983, the official exchange rate of the zaïre was devalued by 78 percent against the SDR (from 6.3 to 28.2 per SDR), a temporary dual rate was established, and plans were made to unify the rate by February 1984. Based on that policy and a wide range of supporting fiscal and structural measures, the Fund approved a 15-month stand-by arrangement in December 1983. That arrangement was almost fully utilized, as Zaïre entered a rare period of economic calm.[127]

---

[124]Memorandum for files by de Larosière (November 30, 1981); IMF/RD Managing Director file "Zaire, 1981" (Accession 83/108, Box 4, Section 376).

[125]For an account of Zaïre's negotiations with external creditors, see Callaghy (1993).

[126]"Zaire—Overdue Financial Obligations," EBS/83/61 (March 22, 1983) and "Zaire—Settlement of Overdue Financial Obligations," Sup. 1 (April 20, 1983).

[127]The 1984–85 stand-by arrangement was for SDR 228 million ($240 million), which was 100 percent of the quota in effect until December 1983 (78 percent of the new quota). Of that, the authorities drew all but SDR 30 million.

The next stand-by arrangement (SDR 162 million) was fully drawn over 12 months in 1985–86, but the economy then turned sour again. Zaïre's terms of trade dropped by 24 percent in 1986, primarily from a 58 percent drop in the price of cobalt, the number two export commodity. The authorities again resisted tightening economic policies commensurately, and the program (supported by yet another stand-by arrangement) quickly went off track.[128] Of the SDR 214 million that was to have been lent to Zaïre through March 1988, only SDR 48 million was drawn.

Once the 1986 program was abandoned, the staff negotiated what has to be seen as an unusually weak program for 1987–88, on the basis of which the Executive Board approved a new stand-by arrangement, a three-year SAF arrangement, and a CFF drawing, for a total additional commitment of SDR 282 million ($367 million; 97 percent of quota).[129] When the program was presented to the Executive Board in May 1987, three Directors (from the United Kingdom, Sweden, and Australia) abstained, and three others (from Ireland, Greece, and the Netherlands) stressed strong concerns over the weakness of the program, but the rest of the Board spoke favorably. Zaïre still enjoyed the goodwill of much of the international community, and that fact formed the basis of the staff's endorsement as well as the Board's. The staff's own appraisal concluded with uncharacteristic bluntness that the program was "unlikely to lead to external viability within the medium term." The staff nonetheless recommended approval, principally on the strength of indications by donor and creditor countries that foreign aid to Zaïre would rise by enough to finance the payments deficit.[130] Unfortunately, that increase did not materialize, and Zaïre was saddled with an ever-increasing burden of external debts over the next few years.

The staff and management continued to express concerns about corruption, but they still lacked an effective means of dealing with it. A 1989 staff report, for ex-

---

[128]On May 30, the same day that Zaïre made the initial drawing on the stand-by arrangement, the government announced a 35 percent increase in public sector wages. The Fund had not been consulted on this policy change, which made observance of the fiscal ceilings extremely unlikely. The Managing Director then called for a "special consultation" under the standard terms of the arrangement, during which the authorities promised to take fiscal measures sufficient to observe the ceilings. The ceilings were not observed, but the Executive Board granted a qualified waiver in September and permitted a delayed second drawing. No further drawings were permitted. "Zaire—Staff Report on the Special Consultation," EBS/86/181 (August 8, 1986) and minutes of EBM/86/137 (August 25, 1986); "Zaire—Request for Waiver and Modification Under Stand-by Arrangement," EBS/86/221 (September 19, 1986) and minutes of EBM/86/162 (September 24, 1986).

[129]The stand-by arrangement provided for SDR 100 million to be drawn over 12 months, of which only SDR 5 million was available immediately. A CFF drawing of SDR 45 million was available immediately, as was a SAF loan of SDR 58 million. The SAF arrangement approved in 1987 provided for an additional SDR 79 million in disbursements through 1990, conditional upon approval of appropriate adjustment programs and structural reforms. The total SAF arrangement was eventually raised to SDR 204 million.

[130]"Zaire—Staff Report for the 1987 Article IV Consultation, Requests for Stand-by Arrangement, and for Arrangement Under the Structural Adjustment Facility," EBS/87/86 (April 22, 1987), p. 42.

Figure 16.12. Zaïre: Use of Fund Credit and Arrears, 1975–92

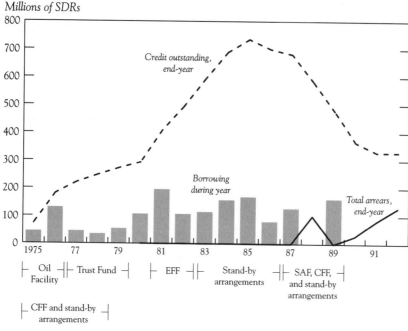

Millions of SDRs

Year and main source of financing

ample, noted that a "key aspect" of the adjustment program that was being supported by a stand-by arrangement with the Fund (the ninth arrangement since 1976) was "the strengthening of expenditure control procedure and monitoring." All expenditures were to be included in the budget and properly accounted for, and controls on overall spending were to be strengthened.[131] Implementation of those intentions, however, was not a condition for drawing under the arrangement, and the Fund had not yet solved the problem of how to refuse to lend to corrupt governments without interfering in domestic politics.[132]

The Fund's lending to Zaïre after 1985 was more than offset by repayments on the earlier credits, and Zaïre's indebtedness fell gradually from a peak of about SDR 750 million ($875 million) in May 1986 to less than SDR 500 million ($700 million) at the end of 1989 (Figure 16.12). In 1988, the government fell seriously behind in making those payments, even though the central bank had sufficient

[131]"Zaire—Staff Report for the 1989 Article IV Consultation and Review Under Stand-by Arrangement," EBS/89/211 (November 2, 1989), p. 15.

[132]In August 1997, the Executive Board adopted a set of guidelines for dealing directly with "governance" problems. Those guidelines provided that "[f]inancial assistance from the IMF . . . could be suspended or delayed on account of poor governance, if there is reason to believe it could have significant macroeconomic implications that threaten the successful implementation of the program, or if it puts in doubt the purpose of the use of Fund resources." *IMF Survey*, Vol. 26 (August 5, 1997), p. 237.

foreign exchange reserves. Zaïre was staying current with some other creditors, including the World Bank, following an announced policy of giving "preferential treatment to creditors that are providing a positive net transfer of resources." Mobutu complained to Fund staff and management that in the first half of the year, Zaïre had paid more than $100 million to the Fund and had received nothing in return. The Fund responded that Zaïre was receiving a substantial net inflow of grants and loans from other official sources, which was possible only by maintaining relations with the Fund.[133] Mobutu rejected that view, publicly accused Camdessus of plotting with the Belgians against Zaïre, and refused to make further payments.[134] In September 1988, the Managing Director issued the first complaint on Zaïre's arrears to the Fund, which then totaled SDR 66 million ($85 million; 23 percent of quota).[135]

The Board met twice to consider the complaint against Zaïre, but Directors were willing to await the outcome of intensive discussions with the authorities that were taking place in Kinshasa, in Berlin (during the Annual Meetings), and in Washington. Finally, a meeting to consider restricting Zaïre's access to Fund resources was scheduled for mid-May 1989, but the authorities obtained a bridge loan from commercial banks and settled their arrears (which then totaled SDR 115 million) in full the day before the meeting was to have been held.[136]

After the 1989–90 stand-by arrangement was approved in June, the longstanding pattern of late payments resumed. Around the same time, the delicate political fabric in Zaïre began to unravel. Mobutu came under increasing pressure from opposition parties to maintain living standards in the face of dwindling international support, pressure from the Fund for stabilization and reform, and continuing weakness in both domestic output and world export markets. The currency collapsed in a hyperinflationary binge, and the central bank could no longer service the country's external debts. In November 1990, the authorities slipped into arrears for the last time. From then on, only limited payments were made to the Fund, and events followed their usual course toward a declaration of ineligibility, which took effect in September 1991.

---

[133]A midyear estimate by the staff (before the break in normal relations) projected net resource transfers to Zaïre totaling SDR 138 million for 1988. That total reflected SDR 544 million in official grants and credits and an anticipated SDR 87 million SAF loan disbursement, less repayments to the Fund of SDR 220 million and SDR 273 million in debt-service payments to other creditors.

[134]See "Mobutu: 'Nous ne céderons pas aux diktats du FMI'," *Jeune Afrique*, No. 1447 (September 28, 1988), pp. 4–9. Also see IMF/RD African Department file "Zaire—Correspondence, 1988" (Accession 91/031, Box 5, Section 526): memorandums of August 29 and October 31, 1988, from John Calvin Williams (IMF Resident Representative in Kinshasa) to Grant B. Taplin (Assistant Director, African Department); and memorandum of June 27, 1988, from Gondwe to the Managing Director.

[135]"Zaire—Overdue Financial Obligations to the Fund—Report and Complaint Under Rule K-1 and Notice of Failure to Settle Trust Fund Obligations," EBS/88/189 (September 2, 1988).

[136]"Zaire—Settlement of Overdue Financial Obligations to the Fund and Withdrawal of Complaint Under Rule K-1," EBS/89/103 (May 17, 1989).

Filling It In: Development of the Arrears Strategy

Balancing the Books

The persistence of arrears had serious financial implications for the Fund. When the Fund began deducting seriously overdue payments from accrued income in 1985, it had to report a net loss for that fiscal year: the first loss in eight years, and a setback for an ongoing effort to strengthen and stabilize the institution's financial position (see Chapter 17). To avoid a further loss in the next year, the Board's standard procedures required it to raise the interest rate charged on outstanding obligations (the "rate of charge") and thereby pass the full cost of arrears onto indebted countries. Those countries that were current—or were trying to stay current—in their payments to the Fund would bear the burden unless a new policy could be adopted. The first step toward a comprehensive strategy for dealing with arrears was thus to develop a means of spreading the burden more equitably.

A mild and not particularly effective attempt was initiated later in 1985 to shift the burden more directly onto the countries that were in arrears, by imposing "special charges" on overdue obligations. Although the imposition of financial penalties was not an appealing or practical proposition in the Fund, a consensus for some such action gradually took hold as the arrears problem worsened during the year. Few Directors were under any illusions about the idea: unless penalty charges were quite steep, they would have little effect on recalcitrant countries (i.e., those that were able but unwilling to repay the Fund), and steep charges could have seriously counterproductive effects on countries that were already in desperate economic straits. For a variety of reasons, the Board rejected the idea of "penalty" charges, but it did support the idea of imposing "special" charges aimed at (eventually) recovering costs.

The stated objective of the special charges was to ensure that the costs of arrears would be borne chiefly by the countries that incurred them and not by the membership at large. Those costs, as viewed by the Fund, arose principally because the standard rate of charge was below the market SDR interest rate and thus included a concessional element. More generally, the cost of arrears could be measured in many ways, but discussions in the Fund focused on this one element.[137] Assuming that the obligations eventually will be settled in full, the cost can be measured most directly as the difference between the institution's cost of funds and the return on the overdue claims. At the margin, that gap is the difference between the SDR interest rate and the rate of charge; the gap times the average overdue balance gives an approximation of the total cost to the institution and thus to its member countries. For given levels of target income, lending activity, and remuneration rate, that cost would normally be allocated among all indebted countries through appropriate adjustments to the rate of charge.

---

[137]Commercial bank loan contracts, including those with sovereign borrowers, typically include clauses requiring the borrower to repay the administrative costs to creditors of rescheduling or otherwise recovering overdue payments. The Fund explicitly rejected the inclusion of administrative costs in this context.

Introduction of a system of special charges required a 70 percent majority of the voting power in the Executive Board, which implied that the indebted countries as a bloc could have vetoed the proposal. Some indebted countries, however, held that countries in arrears should bear the costs themselves and not pass them onto those that stayed current. A preliminary discussion on December 6, 1985, revealed that 14 Executive Directors, holding 76 percent of the votes, were in favor, while the other eight were opposed.[138] After further consideration of several specific options, the Board settled on an approach based on making the total rate of charge on overdue obligations (i.e., the regular plus the special rate of charge) equal to the SDR interest rate. That system had the virtues of simplicity and of fairness, because the effect was to eliminate the concessional element in the interest rate charged on overdue obligations and eventually to recover the increased costs to the membership associated with those arrears.[139]

While the adoption of special charges was effective for its stated purpose of eventually shifting the direct costs of arrears onto the countries incurring them, it had little immediate effect on either recovering those costs or inducing countries to settle arrears more quickly.[140] The system might have been more effective if the special charges had been higher (on an annualized basis, they seldom reached 100 basis points) and if they had been targeted on the most egregious cases instead of being levied routinely on all overdue obligations. Executive Directors, however, were reluctant to approve any scheme that would aggravate the problems of some of the world's poorest countries or, alternatively, would require drawing a line between countries that were unwilling to pay and those that were unable. Consequently, the system of special charges did not evolve into a set of true penalties.[141]

Burden Sharing

The more general question of who should bear the burden of arrears was tackled in 1986. Faced with the prospect of a sudden large increase in the cost of bor-

---

[138]Those voting against were Tariq Alhaimus (Alternate—Iraq), Jiang Hai (Alternate—China), Alexandre Kafka (Brazil), Mawakani Samba (Alternate—Zaïre), E.I.M. Mtei (Tanzania), Fernando L. Nebbia (Argentina), Ghassem Salehkhou (Iran), and Arjun K. Sengupta (India). Minutes of EBM/85/175 (December 6, 1985).

[139]The decision, which took effect on February 1, 1986, and is reproduced in the Appendix, also provided for a separate system of special charges on overdue repayments on Trust Fund loans. Similar charges were imposed on arrears on SAF loans, beginning in 1987.

[140]Through FY 1989, the Fund imposed special charges totaling SDR 87.2 million ($110 million) on 36 countries with overdue obligations; of that total, SDR 4.5 million ($6 million) had been paid as of May 1989. The collection rate improved in FY 1990, when SDR 71.2 million was assessed and SDR 11.7 million was collected (approximately $15 million out of $93 million). The overdue special charges were all owed by the 10 countries that had been declared ineligible. "Overdue Financial Obligations to the Fund—Six-Monthly Report," EBS/89/133 (June 29, 1989), pp. 11–14 and Table 11; and "Review of the Fund's Income Position—Actual Outcome for FY 1990 and the Basic Rate of Charge for FY 1991—And Review of Special Charges and the Interest Rate of the SDR," EBS/90/98 (May 29, 1990), pp. 7–8 and Table 4.

[141]See, for example, minutes of EBM/88/19 (February 10, 1988). A proposal for imposing penalty charges was set out in "Overdue Financial Obligations to the Fund—Six-Monthly Report," EBS/87/252 (December 2, 1987), pp. 11–14.

rowing from the Fund, developing countries objected strenuously. As E.I.M. Mtei (Tanzania) observed during a Board discussion in December 1985, the entire membership had approved the arrangements that had subsequently gone wrong, and equity required that all members share in the cost. Moreover, the indebted countries were the least able to bear the burden, and a sharp increase in the rate of charge could force even more countries into arrears.[142] That argument prevailed, but agreement on an equitable formula did not come easily.

After several months of discussion, a consensus emerged at an informal meeting of Executive Directors on July 17, 1986, and an agreement was formalized in regular Board meetings later that month.[143] The guiding principle for this "burden-sharing" compact (see the Appendix) was that the cost of arrears would be shared equally between debtor and creditor countries through "symmetric and simultaneous" adjustments to the rate of charge to borrowers and the rate of remuneration to creditors. Subject to certain limitations, this policy provided that in each quarter, the rate of charge would be increased, and the rate of remuneration decreased, by amounts sufficient to generate income to the Fund equivalent to the income lost through countries' failure to pay charges when due. When the charges eventually were paid, then these extra amounts were to be returned to the countries that contributed them.[144]

Over the next four fiscal years, nearly SDR 800 million ($1 billion) in charges went uncollected, was treated as deferred income, and was subject to burden sharing. As discussed in more detail in Chapter 17, the rate of charge was raised, and the rate of remuneration lowered, by an average of about 80 basis points to generate an equivalent amount of net income. By the end of FY 1990, about 6 percent (SDR 45 million, or $57 million) of the deferred charges had been paid, and an equivalent amount had been refunded to contributors.[145]

Provisioning

The External Audit Committee, starting in 1985, encouraged the Fund to adopt some formal procedure for accounting for probable losses on overdue obligations.

---

[142]Minutes of EBM/85/180 (December 13, 1985), p. 3.

[143]Minutes of EBM/86/122 (July 25, 1986) and EBM/86/124 (July 30). No record was made of the discussion at IS/86/9 (July 17) except for a summing up by the Chairman, which was attached as an Annex to the minutes of EBM/86/122.

[144]The burden-sharing decision implicitly assumed that the deferred income eventually would be made up, and it did not allow explicitly for the possibility that the overdue charges would be written off. Because the Articles of Agreement make no allowance for writing off claims against a member of the Fund, the only way the Fund could realize a loss on an outstanding obligation (other than liquidating the Fund itself) would be for the country to withdraw from membership. Following withdrawal, the Fund could then attempt to sell its holding of the country's currency, which would almost certainly result in a loss relative to the Fund's claim on the member (denominated in SDRs). That circumstance had never arisen; the four countries that had withdrawn—Poland in 1950, Czechoslovakia in 1954, Cuba in 1964, and Indonesia in 1965—had settled their financial obligations in full.

[145]"Income Position—Burden Sharing—Implementation of FY 1992; and Extended Burden Sharing—Review," EBS/91/47 (March 19, 1991), Attachment I, Tables 1 and 2.

The 1986 audit raised the possibility that the next one might have to be qualified if the Fund did not take clear steps to recognize and acknowledge the poor quality of certain of its assets and claims.[146] Until then, the Fund had resisted taking any actions that might acknowledge the possibility of a permanent loss; it was a cooperative organization, and its membership of sovereign states was expected to fulfill its obligations. When the World Bank decided to introduce procedures for loan-loss provisions in the spring of 1986, the pressure on the Fund to take corresponding measures was increased.

When the Executive Board first formally discussed the idea of provisioning, in April and May 1986, only three chairs (the United States, Germany, and Saudi Arabia) favored it, although several others signaled a willingness to consider it further. (Altogether, 66 percent of the votes and half the chairs were either in favor or willing to consider.) Because of the need to respond positively to the suggestions of the auditors, a revised proposal was taken up again in June 1987. It picked up some additional support (from the constituencies led by the Netherlands, Australia, and Indonesia), but the Board majority still rejected it.[147]

Provisioning against specific probable losses would have raised several problems for the Fund, besides the general anathema mentioned above. First, it could have raised a moral hazard by weakening countries' incentives to repay their debts. Second, it could have sent an unhelpful signal to commercial bank creditors and weakened their determination to work with problem countries to resolve difficulties. Third, because Fund credits are technically and legally distinct from loan contracts, and the Articles do not provide for the recognition of losses on credits to members, provisioning against losses would have raised difficult legal issues.[148] If the general idea made economic and financial sense, the preferred route was to find an alternative to conventional provisioning.

When the Board rejected provisioning, the Managing Director (Camdessus) held open the possibility of establishing a "special reserve" account as a more general way to meet the concerns of the auditors and others. A follow-up meeting of the Executive Board just five days later produced a consensus for that proposal, and the Board agreed to establish a Special Contingent Account (SCA).[149] The SCA was created by transferring SDR 26.5 million ($34 million)—the amount of net in-

---

[146]The primary reporting requirement for the Fund, as for any financial institution in similar circumstances, was to adopt practices consistent with the code known as Generally Accepted Accounting Principles (GAAP). If the auditors of an institution's accounts were to conclude that the financial statements were inconsistent with GAAP, they would be required to qualify their certification. The opinion of the External Audit Committee accompanies the financial statements in each year's *Annual Report*.

[147]Minutes of EBM/86/73–74 (April 30, 1986), EBM/86/84–85 (May 19, 1986), and EBM/87/86–87 (June 12, 1987). Also see "Provisioning Against Loan Losses in the Context of the Fund," EBS/86/82 (April 15, 1986); and "Provisioning in the Context of the Fund—Further Aspects," EBS/87/97 (May 6, 1987).

[148]See "Valuation of Assets in the General Resources Account—Provisioning and Write-Off—Legal Considerations," SM/86/106 (May 16, 1986).

[149]See minutes of EBM/87/89–90 (June 17, 1987).

come for FY 1987 that exceeded the target level for the year—from the Fund's general accounts. The establishing decision provided that the money would be distributed to creditors and debtors in accordance with burden-sharing principles, "when the need for this account disappears." Some months later, that phrase was made more precise: the money in the SCA would be distributed according to specified burden-sharing formulas when all outstanding arrears to the Fund had been settled, unless the Board decided to distribute the funds earlier (see the Appendix).

At the end of each of the next three financial years (through FY 1990), the Fund transferred between SDR 60 million and SDR 65 million to the SCA, and the total balance in the account amounted to SDR 214.8 million ($279 million). The SCA plus the Fund's other reserves (SDR 1.4 billion) then covered about 63 percent of the total credit outstanding to the 11 countries that were overdue by six months or more. That ratio was higher than in the preceding three years, but it was still well below what the staff and the Board felt was comfortable. Additional transfers in fiscal years 1991 and 1992, coupled with the first signs of a resolution of the arrears problem, finally raised the Fund's overall precautionary balances back to a level close to the stock of credit outstanding to countries in protracted arrears (Figure 16.13). Overall, the combined effect of increasing the income target, imposing additional charges, lowering the rate of remuneration, and establishing the SCA was to limit the deterioration in the cover for possible losses during the 1980s and to reverse it in the early 1990s.

Toward a Comprehensive Strategy

In addition to taking these various financial measures, the Fund struggled to develop a comprehensive strategy for eliminating and avoiding arrears. Initially, that effort focused on devising appropriate penalties—financial and nonfinancial—on countries that failed to meet their obligations. Later, it broadened to include cooperative measures to help countries return to a more sustainable course.

The most potent sanction available to the Fund was compulsory withdrawal from membership, but in practice that step could be taken only in hopeless cases. If a country withdrew from membership, whatever chance remained for settling arrears and restoring normal relations with the international community would be lost, perhaps for many years. The Fund could nonetheless take a series of steps in that direction to try to apply pressure for settlement. As described in each of the case studies in the preceding section, the Fund developed a standard path for those steps: preventing the country from drawing on any active stand-by or other arrangements, restricting access to the Fund's resources pending settlement of arrears, and declaring the country ineligible to use the Fund's resources until the Executive Board restored eligibility. Beginning with the *Annual Report* for 1985, declarations of ineligibility were published, and press releases were issued in subsequent cases.[150]

---

[150]The decision to begin publicizing declarations of ineligibility was adopted in March 1985; see the Appendix.

Figure 16.13. Credit to Countries in Protracted Arrears, and Precautionary Balances, 1983–92

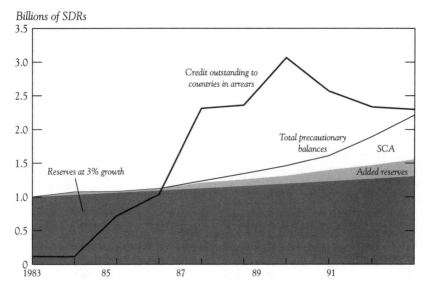

Note: The bottom portion of the reserves plotted in this figure shows the hypothetical level of reserves if the net income target had stayed at 3 percent. The second portion shows the difference between actual reserves and that hypothetical level; that is, the line at the top of that portion represents actual reserves. Transfers to the original SCA continued in the 1990s and were supplemented by a second account (SCA-2) beginning in 1991. Both accounts are included in the plotted data.

On several occasions from 1986 on, Executive Directors from creditor countries asked for consideration of ways to introduce extra steps short of compulsory withdrawal that might continue to tighten the pressure. Most of those suggestions foundered on the obstacle that the Fund did not have the legal power to suspend a member's rights within the institution, such as its voting rights, other than its right to borrow. In June 1986, Yusuf A. Nimatallah (Saudi Arabia) suggested that the Articles of Agreement should be amended to allow the Fund to suspend a country's rights of membership and to prevent participation in quota increases.[151] No action was taken then, but the motion resurfaced a few years later and led to the Third Amendment in 1992.[152] Nimatallah also suggested that the Fund could notify other multilateral lenders when countries were in arrears and should ask the

---

[151]Minutes of EBM/86/92 (June 6, 1986), pp. 8–11.

[152]The Third Amendment of the Articles of Agreement, which became effective in November 1992, authorized the Executive Board to suspend a country's voting rights in the Fund and its participation in the Executive Board and the Board of Governors, as an intermediate step between a declaration of ineligibility and compulsory withdrawal. In 1988, the staff devised a means within the terms of the existing Articles for preventing countries in arrears from participating in quota increases; see below, p. 821.

World Bank to take parallel actions when the Fund restricted a member's access. That and similar proposals were rejected or postponed on the grounds that avoidance of cross-conditionality was too important a principle to compromise for this purpose.

During a February 1989 discussion on ways to make the arrears strategy more effective, Dallara joined Nimatallah in calling for a way to censure recalcitrant debtors more forcefully. Nimatallah argued that the Fund had a right to expect countries in arrears to "come forward and establish an understanding with the Fund on how it intended to resolve its problems." If a country failed to do so, then the Fund should publicly declare the country to be "unwilling to cooperate," take actions to "decatalyze" the flow of funds from other creditors by asking them to stop supporting the country, and initiate steps toward forcing the country to withdraw from the Fund. Dallara suggested issuing a "resolution of censure" in extreme cases and broadening the publicity given to protracted arrears.[153] The staff responded by developing some proposals for "remedial" (pointedly not "punitive") measures, and in July the Managing Director added his voice to the movement. Recalling his personal experiences in dealing regularly with heads of state, Camdessus observed that political leaders were often unaware that their failure to repay the Fund imposed direct costs on other developing countries and threatened their own ability to obtain foreign aid. Publicity was "one of the few instruments available to the Fund" for alerting leaders at the highest level.[154]

Proposals for censure and publicity were bitterly opposed by many on the Board, including a few creditors. Both Hélène Ploix (France) and Johann Prader (Alternate—Austria) argued that a declaration of censure would add nothing by itself to a declaration of ineligibility, and if the Fund failed to follow it up with a move to suspend or terminate the country's membership rights, the institution would appear weak and irresolute. The majority view, however, was that the Fund had to take what measures it could. Several meetings were held throughout July to try to forge a consensus, but Directors' positions barely budged. In the end, over the objections of about half the chairs, the Board agreed to consider issuing and publicizing "declarations of noncooperation" and to authorize the Managing Director to write about arrears problems directly to the Fund's governors and to the heads of certain international financial institutions.[155]

---

[153]Minutes of EBM/89/18 (February 17, 1989), pp. 9 (Nimatallah) and 26 (Dallara).

[154]Minutes of IS/89/15 (July 5, 1989), p. 23.

[155]No vote was taken, and the extent and nature of the opposition varied among speakers. The Acting Chairman (the Deputy Managing Director, Richard Erb) characterized the sense of the Board as follows: "Many Directors had expressed skepticism about the overall approach but at the same time a willingness to go along with it. The opposition to specific parts of the procedures on the part of many Directors had been stated for the record. It could not therefore be said that a consensus had emerged." Minutes of IS/89/15–16 (July 5, 1989), EBM/89/93–94 (July 19), and EBM/89/100–101 (July 27); the quotation from Erb is from meeting 89/101, p. 17. The procedures adopted on July 27, 1989, are reproduced in the Appendix.

During the next few years, the Board declared three countries to be failing to cooperate: Liberia (in March 1990), Sudan (in September 1990), and Zaïre (in February 1992). Four other countries remained ineligible, but they all appeared to be cooperating toward resolving their problems.

Throughout the second half of the 1980s, the Fund came under criticism for focusing more on penalties than assistance. As early as 1986, leaders of developing countries asked the Fund to develop a more cooperative approach, founded on the assumption that countries fell into arrears primarily because of conditions beyond their control. In March of that year, a ministerial meeting of the Group of Twenty-Four (G-24) developing countries called on the Fund and other multilateral institutions to "develop new mechanisms to help those countries which, because of adverse exogenous factors, are not able to repay their obligations to these institutions according to a fixed schedule" (*IMF Survey*, March 17, 1986, p. 91). When the Fund declared Peru ineligible a few months later, the 25 member states of the Latin American Economic System (SELA) complained that the Fund was "causing serious harm to a member state" that was "making intense efforts to meet its financial obligations . . . within an extremely unfavourable international economic climate," and they declared their "complete solidarity with Peru."[156]

Many within the institution also held reservations about the wisdom of prohibiting assistance to countries with overdue obligations. If a country simply was not cooperating, this approach made sense; but if a country needed help in devising an adjustment program and in regaining credibility with donors and creditors, then the Fund's refusal to discuss program requirements became part of the problem rather than part of the solution. Frank Cassell (Executive Director for the United Kingdom) put the issue succinctly: "Where there is full commitment, the Fund must offer a lifeline."[157]

A second, and growing, difficulty with the existing strategy was that the essential level of financing from creditor and donor countries was seldom being attained, even for those indebted countries that were making heroic adjustment efforts. In addition to a widespread deterioration in the willingness of industrial countries to provide foreign aid for economic development, bilateral creditors seemed particularly cool to the idea of providing aid to repay multilateral institutions. Camdessus found that reluctance to be especially galling, and he complained to the Executive Board that "great detriment was done to the Fund's efforts [to resolve the arrears problem] whenever aspersions were cast on major financing arrangements for member countries on the grounds that they were designed to obtain repayment of arrears to the Fund."[158]

---

[156]The quotation is from a statement approved at a preparatory meeting in Caracas (August 18–22, 1986) for the Twelfth Latin American Council that was held in Lima, Peru, in September. Cable from Sebastian Alegrett (Permanent Secretary of SELA) to the Managing Director (September 1, 1986); in IMF/CF (C/Peru/750 "Obligations Under Fund Agreement, 1985–1986").

[157]Minutes of EBM/88/107 (July 19, 1988), p. 4.

[158]Minutes of EBM/88/39 (March 16, 1988), p. 19.

Efforts to find a way out of these impasses began to take hold in 1988, spurred on by concerns expressed by officials from several creditor countries, including the Chairman of the Interim Committee, H. Onno Ruding. At Ruding's suggestion, the Interim Committee held an informal discussion on the arrears strategy over lunch on April 14, 1988, after which it issued a communiqué calling on the Executive Board to prepare a report "on measures to reduce and eventually eliminate arrears" (*IMF Survey*, April 18, 1988, p. 117). Responding to that request in June, the staff bluntly acknowledged the extent of the problem. The existing strategy had kept the problem from worsening but it had "not been adequate to resolve the existing cases of protracted arrears. . . . It is therefore apparent that present measures need to be reconsidered. . . ."[159]

Specifically, the staff report recommended that the Fund's remedial measures be supplemented by an "intensified collaboration" aimed at restoring payments viability for countries that were prepared to cooperate. That collaboration would have three elements. First, the country would show its willingness to implement a comprehensive program of adjustment and reform and establish a track record of sound economic policies. The staff would help the authorities design this "shadow" program, and the Executive Board would approve it. The Fund, however, would not provide financial support until arrears were cleared in full. Second, the country would be expected to pay enough to the Fund during the adjustment period to keep its arrears from increasing. Third, bilateral donors and other creditors would provide enough financial support "to meet the minimum foreign exchange requirements of the adjustment program," including the prevention of additional arrears. To coordinate that assistance, the Fund would help set up a "support group" of creditors and donors. Ultimately, the support group, assisted by a task force of Executive Directors from participating countries, would be expected to provide much of the money for settling the debtor's arrears and clearing the way for renewed financing from the Fund.[160]

The Board readily accepted the general thrust of these recommendations, but it plunged into a summer of marathon meetings before it was prepared to endorse a formal report to the Interim Committee. Establishing a full consensus required detailed attention to the nuances of blame, credit, and responsibilities for both the onset and the resolution of arrears. Much of the debate involved drafting rather than policy. In addition, two substantive issues occupied the floor.

First, since most of the countries in protracted arrears would be eligible for concessional loans from the ESAF Trust once they cleared their arrears, concerns were raised about risks to the Trust.[161] Some ESAF creditors worried that if a country cleared its arrears using funds provided by the proposed support groups, and the Fund then resumed lending by approving a fast-disbursing ESAF arrangement, low-quality assets would simply be transferred from the Fund's own accounts to

---

[159]"Overdue Financial Obligations to the Fund," EBS/88/123 (June 27, 1988), pp. 2–3.

[160]Ibid, pp. 3–7. Also see statement by David Williams (Deputy Treasurer), minutes of EBM/88/107 (July 19, 1988), pp. 3–4.

[161]In the summer of 1988, 13 countries had protracted arrears to the Fund. All but two (Panama and Peru) were otherwise eligible for ESAF loans. (For the eligibility criteria, see Chapter 14.)

those of the Trust.[162] The likely transfer of claims was undeniable, but the prevailing view was that the Fund would retain control over the risks, since the Board would have to approve the country's medium-term adjustment program before any funds could be disbursed.[163]

Second, should countries be expected to treat the Fund as a preferred creditor as a condition for approval of a shadow program? Although it has been argued that the Fund does not have a legal or contractual status as a preferred creditor (see Martha, 1990), the institution had long been accorded a preferred status by most creditors and most indebted countries. Creditor countries agreed as a matter of course not to require or expect the Fund to participate in multilateral Paris Club debt reschedulings and instead made such reschedulings contingent on Fund approval of a stand-by arrangement or similar arrangement. Most debtor countries regarded staying current with the Fund as of primary importance, if only because it was a prerequisite for maintaining normal relations with other creditors and with donors. Nevertheless, as noted in several of the case studies above, some countries with protracted arrears had concluded that the national interest lay in repaying those creditors (including, in some cases, the World Bank) that were willing to provide a positive net flow of resources.

The Managing Director and most Executive Directors were eager to have a clear acknowledgment of the Fund's preferred creditor status placed on the record. Ghassem Salehkhou (Iran) argued persistently against it, on the grounds that many other creditors could be considered preferred and that indebted countries should not be treated less favorably if they chose to repay one rather than the other out of their scarce resources. That view did not prevail, and the final report included the following statement: "Executive Directors have stressed the . . . need for all members, creditors and debtors alike, in practice, to treat the Fund as a preferred creditor."[164]

---

[162]The U.K. Chancellor of the Exchequer, Nigel Lawson, proposed to the Development Committee in April 1988 that ESAF loans be made retroactive for countries that implemented shadow programs prior to clearing arrears. Specifically, under the British proposal, once an ESAF loan was approved for a country that had cleared its arrears, it would be disbursed on a schedule determined as if the loan had been approved at the beginning of implementation of the shadow program. More generally, the June staff report suggested consideration of "some acceleration of disbursements" in such cases.

[163]For the full discussion, see minutes of IS/88/9 (July 12, 1988), EBM/88/107–108 (July 19), EBM/88/110 (July 21), EBM/88/132 (August 30, 1988), and EBM/88/140 (September 6). Also see EBS/88/166 (August 10), Rev. 1 (September 2), and Rev. 2 (September 9). On the Lawson proposal on retroactive ESAF access, see "Retroactive Access to the Enhanced Structural Adjustment Facility (ESAF)," EBD/88/177 (June 28, 1988), statement by Frank Cassell (United Kingdom) at EBM/88/107 (July 19), p. 5, and the related staff suggestion in "Overdue Financial Obligations to the Fund," EBS/88/123 (June 27, 1988), p. 6.

[164]Minutes of EBM/88/132 (August 30, 1988), pp. 9–10, and "Report of the Executive Board to the Interim Committee of the Board of Governors on Overdue Financial Obligations to the Fund," EBS/88/166, Rev. 2 (September 9, 1988), p. 3. This policy was not intended to place the Fund in a preferred position vis-à-vis the World Bank, but only to ensure that countries would not favor the Bank over the Fund. In March 1989, the Managing Director and the World Bank President jointly agreed not to support requests for financial assistance to countries in arrears to the other institution, "when arrears to the Bank [or the Fund] were an indication that the resources of the [other] would not be safeguarded." See Chapter 20, on relations with the World Bank, pp. 995–1005.

In September 1988, the Interim Committee endorsed that position and "urged all members, within the limits of their laws, to treat the Fund as a preferred creditor and to lend their active and tangible support to [the strengthened arrears strategy], so as to bring countries with overdue obligations back into the mainstream of international economic relations" (*IMF Survey*, October 17, 1988, p. 326).

The Committee also endorsed the shift to a three-pronged strategy, combining preventive, remedial, and the collaborative measures described above to reduce and eventually eliminate arrears to the Fund. Measures to prevent countries from getting into situations where arrears might develop were a little vague: better analysis by the Fund of economic conditions before approving lending arrangements, better design of adjustment and reform programs, better cash management by indebted countries. New measures to deter countries from incurring arrears were more specific: withdrawal of technical assistance to countries with protracted arrears, more extensive publicity on specific arrears cases, notification of other creditors, and a prohibition against such countries participating in quota increases.[165]

This "intensified collaborative approach," as it came to be called, became the new standard for the 1990s.[166] Preventive measures gradually were made more specific. Remedial measures, including a tightening of the timetable for the Fund's responses, led also to the Third Amendment of the Articles of Agreement, which enabled the Fund to suspend a country's voting rights after a declaration of noncooperation. Collaborative measures included the "rights accumulation programs," through which countries that were in arrears at the end of 1989 could accrue rights to resume borrowing from the Fund by successfully implementing shadow programs. Despite the generally inhospitable environment for official aid to developing countries—and the consequent difficulty that countries faced in obtaining enough assistance to repay arrears even after completing a shadow program—the adoption of a formal multilateral approach for coordinating assistance to countries that were struggling to implement reforms and settle arrears succeeded in several cases.[167] Indeed, in almost every case in which a country cleared its arrears and regained eligibility to use Fund resources, bridge loans from other creditors made an indispensable contribution to the process.

The first country to normalize its relations with the international community under the new approach was Guyana. Efforts to resolve Guyana's problem had

---

[165]Although a quota increase might be approved as part of a general review of quotas, a country in arrears would be required to discharge its obligations to the GRA before it could pay for the increase. In the absence of payment within the prescribed time, the increase would lapse. See "Report . . . on Overdue Financial Obligations to the Fund," September 14, 1988; in the Appendix.

[166]Because many of these developments took place after the period covered by this History, they are summarized only briefly here. For more detail, see IMF Treasurer's Department (1998), Chapter VI.

[167]The benefits of this coordination effort were particularly evident for contributions from Japan, where legal and institutional barriers prevented the government from providing bilateral assistance to countries with outstanding arrears to the Fund. In March 1989, the Fund established an administered account to receive contributions from Japan and make disbursements for the purpose of clearing arrears. See "The Intensified Collaborative Approach—Establishment of Administered Account—Japan," EBS/89/25 (February 17, 1989) and minutes of EBM/89/16 (February 15) and EBM/89/27 (March 3).

been under way for some months in 1988, without much financial success. During the first half of the year, the authorities negotiated a Policy Framework Paper (PFP) for a medium-term adjustment program with the staffs of the Fund and the World Bank. The Executive Board endorsed that agreement in July, and the Fund transmitted the PFP to Guyana's major official creditors. The initial objective of that exercise was to try to mobilize enough financial support from the donor community to clear arrears, restore balance of payments viability, and enable the Fund to approve an ESAF loan. Fund and World Bank staff and representatives of the Guyanese government then visited most of the large industrial countries but failed to generate anywhere near enough commitments.

After the new arrears strategy was approved by the Interim Committee, the staff set out to negotiate a shadow program for 1989, to be monitored by the Fund, as a means of establishing a track record and regaining credibility. On that basis, the Canadian government agreed to chair an international support group to raise money for debt relief for Guyana. The shadow program was carried out successfully, and the support group finally managed to scrape together the necessary financing in June 1990. By then Guyana's arrears—which had amounted to less than SDR 19 million when the Fund declared the country ineligible in May 1985—had accumulated to more than SDR 107 million ($140 million; 218 percent of quota). To settle arrears to multilateral institutions (the Fund, the World Bank, and the Caribbean Development Bank), the support group obtained just under $50 million in grants from the governments of the G-7 countries, plus a bridge loan through the Bank for International Settlements (BIS) for the remainder. Guyana then used that money (plus a token amount of its own resources) to settle its arrears, and the multilaterals in turn approved new credits that Guyana could use to repay the bridge loan.[168]

Over the next several years, the Fund continued to whittle away at the arrears problem. By December 1998, 8 of the 11 countries that were ineligible at the end of 1989 had cleared their arrears.[169] Four new cases had arisen, of which one—Zaïre (Democratic Republic of Congo)—was particularly serious.[170] That

---

[168]The Executive Board approved a combination of ESAF and stand-by arrangements for Guyana in July 1990. The stand-by arrangement was heavily front-loaded, and immediate disbursements totaled nearly SDR 77 million ($105 million).

[169]As noted above, Honduras cleared its arrears in June 1990, just a week after Guyana. The return of political normalcy to Panama, Vietnam, and (temporarily) Cambodia enabled those countries to settle their arrears in 1992–93. (As a technicality, Cambodia was never formally declared ineligible, because of the lack of an established channel of communication with the Fund from 1975 to 1992.) In the case of Vietnam, economic progress also was an important factor; see Dodsworth and others (1996). Peru, Sierra Leone, and Zambia successfully carried out rights accumulation programs and cleared arrears in 1993–95. Liberia, Somalia, and Sudan made little progress; Liberia and Sudan were declared by the Fund to be noncooperating, as was Zaïre. After the adoption of the Third Amendment, the voting rights of Sudan and Zaïre were suspended, and procedures were initiated toward compulsory withdrawal for Sudan.

[170]Afghanistan, Iraq, the Federal Republic of Yugoslavia (Serbia and Montenegro), and Zaïre developed arrears after 1989 that remained outstanding at the end of 1998. Bosnia and Herzegovina, the Central African Republic, and Haiti also developed protracted arrears temporarily in the early 1990s.

left seven countries in protracted arrears, of which three had been declared to be noncooperating and three others to be ineligible to use Fund resources. Those cases, of course, were the most severe and the most seemingly intractable. Although the total amount of arrears had been greatly reduced and the threat to the institution had been averted, solutions for the remainder were still being developed.

Appendix: Rules and Decisions on Arrears to the Fund

Basic Documents

The Articles of Agreement authorized the Fund, under specified conditions, to declare a member country that was in arrears to be ineligible to use Fund Resources, to suspend the country's right to use SDRs, and to compel it to withdraw from membership:

Article V
Operations and Transactions of the Fund

. . . Section 5. *Ineligibility to use the Fund's general resources*

Whenever the Fund is of the opinion that any member is using the general resources of the Fund in a manner contrary to the purposes of the Fund, it shall present to the member a report setting forth the views of the Fund and prescribing a suitable time for reply. After presenting such a report to a member, the Fund may limit the use of its general resources by the member. If no reply to the report is received from the member within the prescribed time, or if the reply received is unsatisfactory, the Fund may continue to limit the member's use of the general resources of the Fund or may, after giving reasonable notice to the member, declare it ineligible to use the general resources of the Fund.

Article XXIII
Suspension of Operations and Transactions in Special Drawing Rights

. . . Section 2. *Failure to fulfill obligations*

(a) If the Fund finds that a participant has failed to fulfill its obligations under Article XIX, Section 4, the right of the participant to use its special drawing rights shall be suspended unless the Fund otherwise decides.

(b) If the Fund finds that a participant has failed to fulfill any other obligation with respect to special drawing rights, the Fund may suspend the right of the participant to use special drawing rights it acquires after the suspension.

(c) Regulations shall be adopted to ensure that before action is taken against any participant under (a) or (b) above, the participant shall be informed immediately of the complaint against it and given an adequate opportunity for stating its case, both orally and in writing. Whenever the participant is thus informed of a complaint relating to (a) above, it shall not use special drawing rights pending the disposition of the complaint.

(d) Suspension under (a) or (b) above or limitation under (c) above shall not affect a participant's obligation to provide currency in accordance with Article XIX, Section 4.

(e) The Fund may at any time terminate a suspension under (a) or (b) above, provided that a suspension imposed on a participant under (b) above for failure to fulfill the obligations under Article XIX, Section 6(a) shall not be terminated until one hundred eighty days after the end of the first calendar quarter during which the participant complies with the rules for reconstitution.

(*f*) The right of a participant to use its special drawing rights shall not be suspended because it has become ineligible to use the Fund's general resources under Article V, Section 5, Article VI, Section 1, or Article XXVI, Section 2(*a*). Article XXVI, Section 2 shall not apply because a participant has failed to fulfill any obligations with respect to special drawing rights.

Article XXVI
Withdrawal from Membership

. . . Section 2. *Compulsory withdrawal*

(*a*) If a member fails to fulfill any of its obligations under this Agreement, the Fund may declare the member ineligible to use the general resources of the Fund. Nothing in this Section shall be deemed to limit the provisions of Article V, Section 5, or Article VI, Section 1.

(*b*) If, after the expiration of a reasonable period the member persists in its failure to fulfill any of its obligations under this Agreement, that member may be required to withdraw from membership in the Fund by a decision of the Board of Governors carried by a majority of the Governors having eighty-five percent of the total voting power.

(*c*) Regulations shall be adopted to ensure that before action is taken against any member under (*a*) or (*b*) above, the member shall be informed in reasonable time of the complaint against it and given an adequate opportunity for stating its case, both orally and in writing.

Until 1984, the only procedure governing the Fund's response to arrears was that the Managing Director had to notify the Executive Board if he determined that a member country was not in compliance with the Articles. In case of arrears, two sets of rules applied, depending on whether payments were overdue to the General or the SDR Department:

Rules and Regulations of the International Monetary Fund
. . . K—Limatation, Ineligibility, and Suspension of Voting Rights

K-1. The Managing Director shall report to the Executive Board any case in which it appears to him that a member is not fulfilling obligations under the Articles other than obligations referred to in Rule S-1.

Adopted September 25, 1946, amended September 18, 1969, and April 1, 1978

K-2. Whenever the Executive Board is authorized by the Articles to declare a member ineligible to use the general resources of the Fund it may refrain from making the declaration and indicate the circumstances under which, and the extent to which, the member may make use of the general resources.

Adopted September 25, 1946, amended April 1, 1978

K-3. Before any member is declared ineligible to use the general resources of the Fund pursuant to Article XVI, Section 2(*a*), the matter shall be considered by the Executive Board, which shall inform the member in reasonable time of the complaint against it and allow the member an adequate opportunity for stating its case both orally and in writing.

Adopted September 25, 1946, amended April 1, 1978

K-4. When any member that is ineligible to use the general resources of the Fund, or whose use of the general resources has been limited according to Rule K-2 above, requests the Executive Board to permit the resumption of the use of the general resources with or without special limitations and the Executive Board decides not to permit such resumption, a written report shall be presented to the member stating what further action is required before such resumption will be permitted.

Adopted September 25, 1946, corrected October 18, 1950, amended April 1, 1978

K-5. When it is decided to use assets held in the Special Disbursement Account to make a distribution to developing members in accordance with Article V, Section 12(*f*) (*iii*), the Executive Board shall consider whether to permit a member that has been declared ineligible to use the general resources of the Fund under Article V, Section 5 to participate in the distribution before the ineligibility of the member has ceased.

Adopted April 1, 1978

S—Suspension of Use of SDRs

S-1. The Managing Director shall report to the Executive Board any facts on the basis of which it appears to him that a participant is not fulfilling obligations under the Articles that could lead to suspension under Article XXIII, Section 2, and may include a complaint in his report.

Adopted September 18, 1969, amended April 1, 1978

S-2. A participant may complain that another participant is not fulfilling obligations under the Articles that could lead to suspension under Article XXIII, Section 2, and the Managing Director shall transmit the complaint to the Executive Board with his comments. Any complaint shall be made in writing or by any rapid means of communication, and it shall be accompanied by a statement of the facts on which the participant bases its complaint.

Adopted September 18, 1969, amended April 1, 1978

S-3. The Managing Director shall immediately inform a participant of any complaint against it and the statement of the facts on which the complaint is based.

Adopted September 18, 1969

S-4. If the complaint is that the participant has failed to fulfill its obligations under Article XIX, Section 4, the participant shall not use SDRs and this limitation shall continue pending the disposition of the complaint.

Adopted September 18, 1969, amended April 1, 1978, and July 26, 1983

S-5. A participant against which a complaint has been made under Rule S-1 or Rule S-2, the Managing Director, or an Executive Director may request the Executive Board to dismiss the complaint. The Executive Board shall consider the request forthwith.

Adopted September 18, 1969, amended April 1, 1978

S-6. If the right of a participant to use SDRs has been limited under Rule S-4, and a request under Rule S-5 has been made by a participant, the complaint shall be deemed to have been dismissed at the end of ten business days after the request, or at the end of such longer period as the participant states in the request, unless within this time the Executive Board has taken a decision disposing of the complaint.

Adopted September 18, 1969, amended April 1, 1978, and July 26, 1983

S-7. If the right of a participant to use its SDRs has been suspended under Article XXIII, Section 2, the participant may request the Executive Board to terminate the suspension. If the Executive Board decides not to terminate the suspension, a written report shall be made to the participant stating the circumstances under which the suspension would be terminated.

Adopted September 18, 1969, amended April 1, 1978, and July 26, 1983

S-8. All procedures under Rules S-1 through S-7 shall be conducted as expeditiously as possible, and shall allow the participant an adequate opportunity to state its case both orally and in writing.

Adopted September 18, 1969, amended April 1, 1978

Executive Board Decisions, 1984–88

Following notification by the Managing Director under Rule K-1, the Executive Board could prevent the country from drawing on an active stand-by or extended arrangement. In 1984, the Board adopted a general policy:

1. Paragraph 4(*d*) of the form of the stand-by arrangement in Attachment A to Decision No. 6838-(81/70), adopted April 29, 1981, shall be amended to read as follows:

> "during the entire period of this stand-by arrangement, while (member) has any overdue financial obligation to the Fund, or if (member)
>
>> (i) imposes [or intensifies] restrictions on payments and transfers for current international transactions, or
>>
>> (ii) introduces [or modifies] multiple currency practices, or
>>
>> (iii) concludes bilateral payments agreements which are consistent with Article VIII, or
>>
>> (iv) imposes [or intensifies] import restrictions for balance of payments reasons."

2. Paragraph 4(*d*) of the form of the extended arrangement in Attachment B to Decision No. 6838-(81/70), adopted April 29, 1981, shall be amended to read as follows:

> "throughout the duration of the extended arrangement, while (member) has any overdue financial obligation to the Fund, or if (member)
>
>> (i) imposes [or intensifies] restrictions on payments and transfers for current international transactions, or
>>
>> (ii) introduces [or modifies] multiple currency practices, or
>>
>> (iii) concludes bilateral payments agreements which are inconsistent with Article VIII, or
>>
>> (iv) imposes [or intensifies] import restrictions for balance of payments reasons."

3. Other stand-by arrangements involving the use of the Fund's resources in the upper credit tranches and other extended arrangements granted by the Fund after the date of this decision shall also include the provision in 1 or 2 above.

4. The provision in 1 or 2 above shall also be included in an existing stand-by or extended arrangement when the Fund and the member reach understandings regarding the circumstances in which further purchases may be made under the arrangement. (SM/84/82, 4/18/84)

Decision No. 7678-(84/62), adopted April 20, 1984

Ten months later, the Board replaced that decision with a general condition that obviated the need to include a specific clause on arrears in Fund arrangements.

a. Stand-By and Extended Arrangements

1. The following paragraph shall be included, as paragraph 5, in the form of the stand-by arrangement in Attachment A to Decision No. 6838-(81/70), April 29, 1981, as amended, with an appropriate reference to this paragraph to be included in paragraph 1 and the subsequent paragraphs of the form to be renumbered accordingly:

> "(Member) will not make purchases under this stand-by arrangement during any period of the arrangement in which the member has an overdue financial obligation to the Fund or is failing to meet a repurchase expectation pursuant to the Guidelines on Corrective Action in respect of a noncomplying purchase."

2. The following paragraph shall be included, as paragraph 5, in the form of the extended arrangement in Attachment B to Decision No. 6838-(81/70), April 29, 1981, as amended, with an appropriate reference to this paragraph to be included in paragraph 1 and the subsequent paragraphs of the form to be renumbered accordingly:

> "(Member) will not make purchases under this extended arrangement during any period in which the member has an overdue financial obligation to the Fund or is failing to meet a repurchase expectation pursuant to the Guidelines on Corrective Action with respect to a noncomplying purchase."

3. Other stand-by or extended arrangements granted by the Fund after the date of this decision shall include also the provision in 1 or 2 above.

4. The provision in 1 and 2 above shall be included also in an existing stand-by or an extended arrangement when the Fund and the member reach understandings regarding the circumstances in which further purchases may be made under the arrangement.

5. Decision No. 7678-(84/62), April 20, 1984, shall cease to apply in respect of a stand-by or an extended arrangement that includes the provision in 1 or 2 above.

Decision No. 7908-(85/26), adopted February 20, 1985

In March 1985, the Executive Board decided to begin publicizing its declarations of ineligibility:

> The Executive Board decides that overdue financial obligations to the Fund of members having obligations overdue for six months or more will be reported in aggregate by category of obligation but without identifying the members involved, in the Fund's *Annual Report*, quarterly *Financial Statements of the General Department and the SDR Department*, yearbook issue of *Balance of Payments Statistics*, and *International Financial Statistics*.

Declarations of ineligibility to use the Fund's general resources will be reported in the Fund's *Annual Report* and will identify the members concerned, beginning with the 1985 *Annual Report*.

Decision No. 7931-(85/41), adopted March 13, 1985

Effective in February 1986, the Fund began imposing special additional charges on overdue payments:

Overdue Financial Obligations—Special Charges

I. Overdue Repurchases

1. Pursuant to the Rule I-6(8) the Fund has reviewed the rates of charge to be levied under Article V, Section 8(c) on its holdings of a member's currency that have not been repurchased in accordance with the requirements of the Articles or decisions of the Fund.

2. Within three business days after (i) the due date for the repurchase by a member of the Fund's holdings of its currency resulting from purchases of the Fund's ordinary resources or (ii) the effective date of this Decision, whichever is the later, the Fund shall consult with the member on the reduction of the Fund's holdings of the member's currency that should have been repurchased. The consultation shall take place by rapid means of communication.

3. Unless the Fund's holdings of the member's currency are reduced within the period referred to in Section IV below by the amount that should have been repurchased, the rate of charge on the holdings that should have been repurchased shall be increased by a percentage equal to the excess, if any, of the rate of interest on the SDR over the rate of charge levied on the holdings under Rule I-6(4) or (11).

II. Overdue Charges in the General Resources Account

A special charge equal to the rate of interest on the SDR shall be paid by a member on the unpaid amount of charges owed by it under Article V, Section 8(a) and (b).

III. Overdue Interest and Repayments on Trust Fund Loans

The Fund shall levy a special charge on (i) the amount of overdue interest on Trust Fund loans at a rate equal to one-half of the sum of the rate of interest on Trust Fund Loans and the rate of interest on the SDR, and (ii) the overdue amounts of repayments of Trust Fund loans, at a rate equal to one-half of the sum of the rate of interest on Trust Fund loans and the rate of interest on the SDR, less one-half percent.

IV. Waiver of Special Charges

Special charges under Sections I, II, and III above shall be levied in respect of an overdue financial obligation as of the due date or the effective date of this Decision, whichever is the later, unless the obligation is discharged within ten business days after the applicable date.

V. Notification and Payment of Special Charges

1. Special charges levied under this Decision shall be payable following the end of each of the Fund's financial quarters and the member shall be notified promptly of any special charges due. The charges shall be payable on the third business day following the dispatch of the notification.

2. Special charges in respect of overdue repurchases and charges in the General Resources Account shall be paid in SDRs to that Account. Special charges in respect of overdue repayments and interest on Trust Fund loans shall be paid in U.S. dollars to the Special Disbursement Account.

VI. Entry into Effect and Review

This Decision will enter into effect on February 1, 1986. It will be reviewed shortly after October 31, 1986 at the time of the mid-year review of the Fund's income position for the financial year ending April 30, 1987, and thereafter annually in connection with the annual reviews of the Fund's income position.

Decision No. 8165-(85/189) G/TR, adopted December 30, 1985

In July 1986, the Board agreed to adjust rates of charge and remuneration so that the burden of arrears would be shared between debtor and creditor countries:

Principles of "Burden Sharing," Income Target for FY 1987 and FY 1988, Rate of Charge, and Rate of Remuneration

Section I. Principles of "Burden Sharing"

1. The financial consequences for the Fund which stem from the existence of overdue financial obligations shall be shared between debtor and creditor member countries.

2. This sharing shall be applied in a simultaneous and symmetrical fashion.

Section II. Income Target for FY 1987 and FY 1988

1. During financial year 1987 and financial year 1988, the Fund's net income target shall be raised from 5 percent to 7.5 percent of the Fund's reserves at the beginning of each year. The additional net income shall be generated in accordance with the provisions of Section V. It shall be recorded separately in the financial statements of the Fund.

2. For financial year 1988, the Fund may decide to add supplemental income to be generated in accordance with the provisions of Section V. It shall be recorded separately in the financial statements of the Fund.

Section III. Rate of Charge

1. (a) The rate of charge referred to in Rule I-6(4) shall be determined at the beginning of financial year 1987 and financial year 1988. This determination shall be made on the basis of the estimated income and expense of the Fund during the year and the target amount of net and supplemental income for the year, and shall include the adjustment necessary to generate one half of the additional net income and of the supplemental income for the year.

   (b) During financial year 1987 and financial year 1988, when estimating income, no deduction shall be made for projected deferred income.

2. During financial year 1987 and financial year 1988, the rate of charge shall be further adjusted in accordance with the provisions of Section V.

3. The rate of charge in force as of the end of a financial year, as adjusted under Section V, shall continue to apply subsequently unless it is otherwise decided.

Section IV. Rate of Remuneration

1. Effective August 1, 1986, Rule I-10(d) shall cease to apply.

2. Effective February 1, 1987, Rule I-10 shall read as follows:

   I-10. (a) The rate of remuneration shall be equal to 100 percent of the rate on interest on holdings of SDRs under Rule T-1 (hereafter referred to as "SDR interest rate").

(b) The relationship of the rate of remuneration to the SDR interest rate will be referred to as the "remuneration coefficient."

3. During financial year 1987 and financial year 1988, the rate of remuneration shall be adjusted in accordance with the provisions of Section V.

Section V. "Burden Sharing" in FY 1987 and FY 1988

1. In financial year 1987 and financial year 1988, and notwithstanding Rule I-6(4)(a) and (b) and Rule I-10, the rate of charge referred to in Rule I-6(4), and the rate of remuneration prescribed in Rule I-10 shall be adjusted in accordance with the provisions of this Section.

2. (a) In order to generate the additional net income referred to in Section II.1, and the supplemental income referred to in Section II.2, the rate of charge shall be adjusted in accordance with the provisions of Section III.1(a), and the rate of remuneration shall be adjusted, subject to the limitation in (c), in accordance with the provisions of this paragraph, so as to produce equal amounts of income.

(b) If income from charges becomes deferred during an adjustment period as defined in (d), the rate of charge and the rate of remuneration shall be further adjusted, subject to the limitation in (c), in accordance with the provisions of this paragraph, so as to generate, in equal amounts, an additional amount of income equal to the amount of deferred charges. For the purposes of this provision, special charges on overdue financial obligations under Decision No. 8165-(85/189) G/TR, adopted December 30, 1985, shall not be taken into account.

(c) No reduction in the rate of remuneration under this paragraph shall be carried to the point where the average remuneration coefficient would be reduced below 85 percent for an adjustment period.

(d) Subject to the provisions of Section III.1(a), the adjustments under this paragraph shall be made as of May 1 and as of November 1 of each year: shortly after October 31 for the period from May 1 to October 31; shortly after April 30 for the period from November 1 to April 30.

(e) Notwithstanding the provisions of (d), any adjustment made in respect of the first half of financial year 1987 shall affect the rate of remuneration only as of August 1, 1986.

(f) The operation of this decision shall be reviewed when the remuneration coefficient is reduced to 85 percent under (c).

3. A midyear review of the Fund's income position shall be held shortly after October 31 of each year. If, after any adjustment under paragraph 2, the actual net income for the first six months of the financial year, on an annual basis, is below the target amount for the year by an amount equal to, or greater than, 2 percent of the Fund's reserves at the beginning of the financial year, the Executive Board will consider how to deal with the situation. If on December 15 no agreement has been reached as a result of this consideration, the rate of charge shall be increased as of November 1 to the level necessary to reach the target amount of net income for the year.

4. (a) An amount equal to the proceeds of any adjustment made under paragraph 2(a) in order to generate supplemental income in financial year 1988 shall be distributed, in accordance with the provisions of this paragraph, to members that have paid additional charges or have received reduced remuneration as a result of the adjustment, when there are no outstanding overdue charges and repurchases, or at such earlier time as the Fund may decide.

(b) An amount equal to the proceeds of any adjustment made under paragraph 2(b) in financial year 1987 or financial year 1988 shall be distributed, in accordance with the provisions of this paragraph, to members that have paid additional charges or have received reduced remuneration as a result of the adjustment, when, and to the extent that, charges, the deferral of which has given rise to the same adjustment, are paid to the Fund. Distributions under this provision shall be made semiannually.

(c) Distributions under (a) or (b) shall be made in proportion to the amounts that have been made or have not been received by each member as a result of the respective adjustments.

(d) If a member that is entitled to a payment under this paragraph has any overdue obligation to the Fund in the General Department at the time of payment, the member's claim under this paragraph shall be set off against the Fund's claim in accordance with Decision No. 8271-(86/74), adopted April 30, 1986, or any subsequent decision of the Fund.

Decision No. 8348-(86/122), adopted July 25, 1986

In June 1987, the Board established the Special Contingency Account (SCA) as a form of general provisioning against potential losses:

Income Position—Special Contingent Account

In view of the existing overdue obligations, a special contingent account shall be established. It shall be recorded separately in the Fund's financial statements. There shall be placed to that account, for financial year 1987, an amount of SDR 26,547,074. This amount shall be distributed, to creditors and debtors for that year, in accordance with the principles of burden sharing, when the need for this account disappears.

Decision No. 8619-(87/90), adopted June 17, 1987

The terms of the SCA were modified in January 1988:

Special Contingent Account—Additions in FY 1988 and
Disposition of Amounts Placed in FY 1987 and FY 1988

1. An amount equivalent to 2½ percent of the Fund's reserves at the beginning of financial year 1988 already provided for in accordance with Section II.1 of Decision No. 8348-(86/122), adopted July 25, 1986, as amended, shall be placed to the Special Contingent Account at the end of financial year 1988.

2. An additional amount equivalent to 2½ percent of the Fund's reserves at the beginning of financial year 1988 shall be raised in accordance with Section II.2 and Section V.1 and 2(a) of Decision No. 8348-(86/122), as amended, as follows:

(a) effective February 1, 1988 the rate of charge referred to in Rule I-6(4) shall be 6.15 percent;

(b) the rate of remuneration shall be adjusted for the period from February 1 through April 30, 1988 in order to generate an amount of net income equal to the amount generated under (a) subject to the limitation in Section V.2(c) of Decision No. 8348-(86/122), as amended.

That additional amount shall also be placed to the Special Contingent Account at the end of financial year 1988.

3. The amounts placed to the Special Contingent Account, including the amount placed to it in financial year 1987, shall be distributed when there are no outstanding overdue charges and repurchases, or at such earlier time as the Fund may decide, in accordance with subparagraphs (a), (b), and 8 below:

   (a) distributions of the amounts placed to the Special Contingent Account at the end of financial year 1988 shall be made in proportion to the amounts that have been paid, or have not been received, by each member in financial year 1988 as a result of adjustments made under paragraphs 1 and 2 above;

   (b) the amount placed to the Special Contingent Account in financial year 1987 shall be distributed to members that have paid charges referred to in Rule I-6(4) in financial year 1987, in proportion to the amounts that have been paid;

   (c) any distribution shall be made in proportion to the total amount to be distributed to each member under (a) and (b) cumulatively.

4. If any loss is charged against the Account, it shall be recorded in accordance with the principle of proportionality set forth in paragraph 3(c).

Decision No. 8780-(88/12), adopted January 29, 1988

A More Cooperative Approach, 1988

In September 1988, the Board and the Interim Committee approved a tripartite strategy for preventing and dealing with arrears:

**Report of the Executive Board to the
Interim Committee of the Board of Governors
on Overdue Financial Obligations to the Fund**

September 9, 1988
(excerpts)

1. Introduction

. . . In presenting the general framework outlined below, Executive Directors have emphasized that the proposed approach should be viewed in light of the following general principles. First, given the pervasive effects of arrears on the Fund and its membership and the deep difficulties facing many members now having protracted arrears, a positive resolution of the problem must be collaborative in nature, involving not only the member concerned but also the Fund, its membership, and the international community in general. Second, Executive Directors have stressed the unique position of the Fund as an international cooperative institution, its role in the international monetary system, the revolving nature of its resources, and the consequent need for all members, creditors and debtors alike, in practice, to treat the Fund as a preferred creditor. Accordingly, all members should accord the highest priority to the settlement of financial obligations to the Fund. A few Executive Directors suggested that recourse to the provisions of the Articles of Agreement regarding rescheduling of repurchases and payment of charges in local currency would be in order in exceptional cases. The majority of Directors considered, however, that the Fund must avoid opening the way to rescheduling or payment of charges in local currency, which could impair its role in the international monetary system and its effectiveness in the debt strategy. Third, Executive Directors have also emphasized that this approach is to be regarded as a broad strategy and framework for action. The situations and positions of individual countries vary markedly. The strategy may not be applicable to all countries facing protracted arrears, and it is to be expected that the detailed elements of the approach to be taken with respect to each will need to be determined on a case-by-case basis. The Executive Board notes that a number of specific aspects will require further consideration in light of the Committee's guidance.

2. Preventive Actions

. . . Executive Directors will seek further to strengthen policies to prevent the emergence of new cases of arrears in the future. In adapting policies on Fund conditionality, increasing attention will continue to be given to the experience gained with the implementation of programs and to improvements in program design. The design of Fund-supported programs needs to take into account the economic conditions of the country concerned; in this regard, structural aspects of members' adjustment problems and the need for growth-oriented policies have received increased emphasis through the adoption of new policies and the adaptation of existing ones. Directors emphasized the need for the Fund to broaden its assessments of members' capacity to repay and, in this connection, to give close attention to the overall levels of indebtedness of these countries. Where appropriate, and consistent with the case-by-case approach of the debt strategy, the Fund will assist member countries in the arrangement of appropriate debt restructuring and/or debt reduction operations with a view to alleviate excess debt and thus provide better safeguards for the utilization of Fund resources.

Executive Directors stressed the importance of continued and strengthened efforts to prevent the emergence of new cases of overdue obligations to the Fund and to forestall the deterioration of potential or existing arrears problems before they surface or become very difficult to resolve. They have requested the management and staff to give particular attention to strengthening preventive aspects in developing and presenting proposals for the use of Fund resources, which may, on a case-by-case basis, include such reserve management practices as would help ensure that members have on hand sufficient SDRs or other readily available resources to meet forthcoming obligations to the Fund as they fall due. Such practices would be intended to improve the prospects for timely payment to the Fund and help safeguard against possible interruption of the member's program; they would not reduce the need for programs to have adequate underlying strength, design, and financing. Executive Directors emphasized the critical importance of members' implementation of their adjustment programs and noted that, in appropriate cases, prior actions could be required to provide needed assurances regarding implementation.

3. Intensified International Collaboration

While the actions outlined above should help to prevent new cases of arrears from arising, the problems faced by members with sizable overdue obligations to the Fund are of a depth and nature which will require resolution and perseverance by all the parties involved. The Executive Board has considered a framework for organizing an intensified collaborative effort of the international community to resolve problems of protracted arrears to the Fund. This approach would be implemented on a case-by-case basis with adaptations appropriate to the individual circumstances, and would not be expected to apply generally or simultaneously to all members having protracted arrears to the Fund. The principal determinants in each individual case would be the willingness of the member to embark on, and sustain, the required growth-oriented adjustment policies, and the preparedness of donors and creditors, including multilateral institutions, to provide supporting financing on appropriate terms. This approach would consist of three key, integrated elements, all clearly set forth at the outset.

The first element is the adoption and forceful implementation of a medium-term program of strong comprehensive economic reforms by the member with overdue obligations to the Fund. Frequently, the member's poor record of implementation of economic policies would seem to necessitate the establishment of a new track record in order to overcome doubts about the ability of the member to overcome its payments difficulties.

The member's economic program would represent a decisive break with the past, and be part of a medium-term strategy to achieve sustained growth and external viability. The member would develop the program in collaboration with the Fund and, as appropriate, the World Bank, and the program would be submitted to the Executive Board to obtain its endorsement that it meets the Fund's conditionality standards. In this phase, initial external financial assistance would be an important signal of the international community's willingness to support the appropriate foreign exchange requirements of the program. The program would not involve access to Fund resources while arrears remained outstanding. The member would be expected to meet financial obligations to the Fund as they fell due during the program, although this should not be interpreted as relieving it of responsibility for the settlement of all its overdue obligations to the Fund. In presenting programs, the Fund staff would provide an analysis of the factors that had led to the emergence of overdue obligations to the Fund and of the member's prospective debt-servicing capacity.

The second element of this approach, framed in the context of continuing implementation by the member of a strong adjustment effort, would center on the design of financing arrangements needed to mobilize resources for the clearance of overdue obligations to the Fund, and the organization of other financing needed to support the continuing adjustment effort. Such arrangements could include, if appropriate, bridge financing, debt rescheduling, and new money. In addition, where appropriate, an important complement to the member's adjustment program in the initial phase would be the establishment of an escrow account for the purpose of clearing the arrears with the Fund. Contributions to the escrow account should be provided by the debtor member through reserve accumulation, as well as by creditors and donors. The financing arrangements developed should in no way jeopardize any new resources that may be provided by the Fund.

The third element would comprise restoration of normal relations between the member and the Fund in the context of the Executive Board's approval of an arrangement involving use of Fund resources in support of the member's medium-term growth-oriented adjustment program. Many Executive Directors have stressed the need for an appropriate financing role for the Fund following clearance of the arrears. Some, for instance, have considered the possibility of some front-loading of the Fund's general resources, while others have referred to the possibility of some front-loading of ESAF resources. In particular, a number of Executive Directors expressed interest in the proposal of the U.K. Chancellor of the Exchequer that retroactive (or front-loaded) access under the ESAF be considered for low-income countries, once they have established a successful record of policy implementation under an economic program and have become current with the Fund. In some circumstances, where an economic program has yielded satisfactory performance and convincing assurances on the future stance of economic policies, some front-loading of the Fund's regular or ESAF resources may be justified. Directors will give further consideration to this matter in the near future. Use and phasing of any Fund resources would need to be determined on a case-by-case basis and to be consistent with the Fund's policies and practices, including the applicable access limits and the need for satisfactory assurances regarding the overall availability of financing and the member's capacity to repay. In this connection, Executive Directors have reaffirmed that ESAF resources are to be used in support of strong programs of structural reform, and only after the member has re-established a satisfactory track record with the Fund. ESAF resources are not to be used for the purpose of shifting the burden or risk of overdue obligations from the Fund's General Resources Account. This principle would need to be respected in devising financial arrangements for the clearance of arrears to the Fund and for support of the member's continuing adjustment efforts.

The magnitude of financial resources and the degree of cooperation and coordination that will be required for this strategy to succeed is, in some cases, beyond the customary experience of the various parties involved, including, in many instances, agencies and institutions which have not in the past had occasion to work in close collaboration with the Fund. For these reasons, the Executive Board is of the view that, for the collaborative approach to succeed, it will be important in some cases for the Fund to take the initiative to promote the establishment of support groups of major donor and creditor countries for members with substantial arrears to the Fund that are prepared to cooperate in this strategy and willing to implement fundamental economic and financial reforms.

Although the form of such support groups might differ from case to case, they would generally include high-level governmental representatives, and would have a crucial coordinating role with respect to financing. A number of Executive Directors have indicated that their authorities would be prepared, under appropriate conditions and safeguards, to participate in support groups that may be established for individual countries, without implying a commitment to provide financing in any particular amount or form. Further consideration will need to be given as appropriate in particular cases to the possible features of such groups, including, inter alia, their composition, timing of establishment, precise functions, and role of the chairing creditor.

The Fund itself would of course need to play a central role. The management and staff would have an active part in the process of collaboration and coordination, for instance, maintaining contacts with the support group, in particular as regards the process of matching a program's financing requirements with available resources and engaging in dialogue, as appropriate, with the support group on progress under the program. The Executive Board, which would remain solely responsible for any commitment of Fund resources, would be involved from the outset, in considering initial adjustment programs and subsequent Fund arrangements, assessing financing needs, reviewing developments under Fund-endorsed programs, and more broadly in evaluating the overall implementation of the collaborative approach.

4. Remedial Measures

A number of Executive Directors expressed the view that the most effective deterrent against arrears to the Fund is the prospect for a member of increased financial isolation and prolonged economic deterioration. Nonetheless, most Executive Directors considered that, as part of a strategy offering collaborative solutions, the range of remedial measures to be taken or to be considered should be widened in order to demonstrate clearly the membership's determination to deal firmly with any member not prepared to cooperate actively in maintaining or normalizing its relations with the Fund. In considering certain of the actions outlined below, Executive Directors noted that, as a matter of equity, members failing to meet their obligations to the Fund could not expect to receive the same benefits of membership as those that have taken the actions necessary to fulfill their obligations.

In this connection, a number of Executive Directors considered that it would be important to distinguish between members that would seem to be in a position to meet their obligations to the Fund but are unwilling to do so, and those that are willing to pay but unable to do so. To this effect, they have suggested the establishment of objective criteria, and have considered that further analysis of such criteria or indicators could be of assistance to the Executive Board in assessing the relative performance of members in arrears to the Fund and could, indeed, complement more broadly the continuing effort to extend and strengthen the Fund's analyses of capacity to repay in connection with use of Fund resources. The Executive Board is, however, mindful that there are inherent difficulties in making such distinctions and that a considerable element of judgment would be required, including judgment whether a member in arrears is collaborating in an effort to normalize relations with the Fund. The Executive Board will return to this matter in the near future.

The Executive Board has discussed and will give further consideration to the following possibilities for extending the range of remedial actions.

a. Most Executive Directors have agreed in principle that a member must first discharge its overdue obligations to the General Resources Account before it would be permitted to pay for an increase in its quota in connection with the Ninth General Review; and that, in the event the quota payment were not made within a prescribed period, the proposal for an increase in quota would lapse. In the view of these Directors, specific provisions to implement this approach should be incorporated into decisions to be taken in connection with the Ninth General Review of Quotas.

b. Most Executive Directors are agreed that, in the absence of clear willingness on the part of a member to cooperate with the Fund in the resolution of its problems, withdrawal of technical assistance should be considered on a case-by-case basis, paying due regard to the need to maintain a dialogue with these members. A number of Executive Directors noted that the Fund's technical assistance is a scarce resource in heavy demand and that the continued provision of such assistance in such cases, particularly where not directly related to settlement of obligations to the Fund, would inappropriately be at the expense of other members that meet their obligations to the Fund in full.

c. Most Executive Directors also agreed that the Fund's policies regarding the provision of information on individual members in arrears, in the context of the Annual Report and the Fund's financial statements, should be somewhat extended. Some Directors considered that increased use of press releases would be appropriate in some cases, in particular following reviews of ineligible members and where it is concluded that the member is not cooperating actively. Others felt that such increased publicity would not be appropriate.

d. A number of Executive Directors considered that, in certain cases, it would be appropriate for the Fund to inform other multilateral institutions and bilateral official creditors of a member's arrears to the Fund. Some of these Directors also supported adding to such notifications a request that the institutions take the situation into account in their own relations with the member concerned.

e. Executive Directors' views on the efficacy of imposing penalty charges on overdue repurchases continue to differ. Among those Directors favoring such charges, some were attracted by the possibility of holding their application in abeyance if a member was judged to be collaborating actively with the Fund to reduce its arrears.

f. Executive Directors are generally agreed that compulsory withdrawal should be examined only in individual cases and only in the event that all other avenues had been exhausted. Some Directors have asked that possible forms of suspension of membership be examined further, although it appears that the possibilities in this area are quite limited in the absence of an amendment to the Articles of Agreement.

5. Conclusion

The Executive Board believes that a comprehensive initiative to secure the reduction and eventual elimination of arrears to the Fund is urgently needed. Failure or too much delay in the resolution of this problem could well mean that the cost of using the Fund's resources would gradually become more expensive, remuneration to creditors would be eroded, and the Fund's usable resources would be reduced, thereby impairing the possibility for the Fund to discharge its responsibilities. This report has outlined a strategy to avoid such an outcome by addressing the problem of arrears through strengthened preventive actions, intensified international collaboration, and extended remedial measures.

In supporting the broad thrust and outlines of the approach proposed, Executive Directors have stressed that many specific aspects will need to be considered further and that implementation will need to be flexible and determined on a case-by-case basis. They have stressed also that success will require exceptional efforts both by the countries in arrears and by the international community in general. The need to organize and obtain substantial financing in support of members' efforts to fundamentally reform their economies and regularize their relations with the Fund will in many cases necessarily involve institutions such as aid agencies that have their own lending priorities. The Executive Board believes that by supporting this approach these institutions will contribute to restoring conditions in which their own operations in these countries can be most effective. Similarly, the suggested application of preventive and remedial actions will require firmness and determination on the part of the Fund's membership. For both reasons, the Executive Board emphasizes the need for a commitment from all Fund members to the approach to be adopted so as to ensure that all parties involved act together in support of a common interest, and requests the Interim Committee's guidance and endorsement.

Declarations of Noncooperation, 1989

In July 1989, the Board approved procedures for declaring countries not to be cooperating with the Fund. The revised statement reflecting the sense of the meeting, as circulated for approval by Executive Directors prior to the close of business on August 17, 1989, read as follows:

Policy on the Fund's Procedures for Dealing with Members with Overdue Obligations to the Fund, adopted at EBM/89/101 (July 27, 1989)

The Fund, as a cooperative institution, relies on the mutually supportive actions of its membership in all areas of its endeavors. Overdue financial obligations are a breach of obligations to the Fund and are demonstrably a noncooperative action, which imposes financial costs on the Fund's membership, impairs its capacity to assist members, and more generally weakens the Fund's ability to perform its broader responsibilities in the international financial system.

As the experience with arrears demonstrates, countries which accumulate arrears to the Fund also damage themselves, in part through the deterioration which inevitably follows in their financial relations with other creditors. When arrears exist the Fund is not able to provide its own assistance and its effectiveness is diminished as a catalyst for helping the country restore regular financial relations with other creditors.

This statement outlines procedures aimed at preventing the emergence of overdue financial obligations to the Fund and the elimination of existing overdues, including protracted arrears. The need for flexibility in the implementation of the Fund's policies dealing with overdues has been stressed in the past; flexibility must continue to be exercised in order to take account of the specific circumstances of the member. Nonetheless, a balance must be struck between the need for appropriate flexibility and the need for clear and credible procedures that act as a deterrent to members against incurring arrears and to encourage members with overdues to become current.

Arrears preventions

The importance of preventing new cases of arrears has been stressed by the Executive Board. As noted in the past, our best safeguard is the quality of Fund arrangements and we will continue to direct our efforts to ensure that arrangements of the highest quality are placed before the Board. These efforts would include assisting members to design strong and comprehensive economic programs, careful attention to access levels and phasing, explicit assessment of a member's capacity and willingness to repay the Fund, and adequate assurances regarding external financing during the period of the Fund arrangement. Special understandings with creditors and donors may also need to be sought in certain cases to help assure progress toward external viability. In some cases, specific financial or administrative arrangements—designed to ensure that forthcoming obligations to the Fund are settled on time—will be used to increase the assurance that the Fund's resources will be repaid on time. Moreover, the importance of members remaining current on obligations falling due and observing the Fund's preferred creditor status will continue to be stressed.

The Fund's response to overdue obligations

The Fund has developed a set of procedures for dealing with members with overdue financial obligations which are designed to bring about a reduction and the eventual elimination of these overdue obligations. In addition to the procedures set out below, the Fund makes an effort to assist members willing to cooperate to eliminate their arrears through the design and implementation of appropriate policies as well as to help members adopting these policies to secure the necessary financial support.

The procedures initiated immediately after a member falls into arrears provide for a sequence of actions by management, the staff, and the Executive Board.

- Whenever a member fails to settle an obligation on time, the staff immediately sends a cable urging the member to make the payment promptly; this communication is followed up through the office of the Executive Director concerned.
- When an obligation has been outstanding for two weeks, management sends a communication to the Governor for that member stressing the seriousness of the failure to meet obligations to the Fund and urging full and prompt settlement. The Executive Board understands that the Governor will bring this communication and the circumstances that gave rise to it to the attention of his authorities at the highest level. The communication to the Governor would also note that unless payment is received in due course, the Managing Director would intend to raise with the Executive Board the possibility of communicating with Governors of the Fund concerning the situation. The Managing Director has on occasion raised the matter of overdue financial obligations to the Fund directly with the head of government of the member concerned, and he would intend to continue to do so in those cases where he believes it would be a useful procedure.
- The Managing Director notifies the Executive Board normally one month after an obligation has become overdue.
- When the longest overdue obligation has been outstanding for six weeks, the Managing Director informs the member concerned that unless the overdue obligations are settled a complaint will be issued to the Executive Board in two weeks' time. The Managing Director would in each case recommend to the Executive Board whether a

communication should be sent to a selected set of Fund Governors, or to all Fund Governors. If it were considered that it should be sent to a selected set of Fund Governors, an informal meeting of Executive Directors would be held, some six weeks after the emergence of overdues, to consider the thrust of the communication. Alternatively, if it were considered that the communication should be sent to all Fund Governors, a formal Board meeting would be held to consider a draft text and the preferred timing. A sample text for a communication to all Fund Governors is set out in Attachment I.

- A complaint by the Managing Director is issued two months after an obligation has become overdue, and is given substantive consideration by the Executive Board one month later. At that stage, the Executive Board has usually decided to limit the member's use of the general resources, and if the member has overdue obligations in the SDR Department, to suspend its right to use SDRs, and has provided for a subsequent review of the decision. This and subsequent review periods would normally not exceed three months. It would be understood that the Managing Director may recommend advancing the Executive Board's consideration of the complaint regarding the member's overdues.
- The Annual Report and the financial statements identify those members with overdue obligations outstanding for more than six months.

Beyond these procedures, the Executive Board has expressed its intention to provide that a member must first discharge its overdue financial obligations to the General Resources Account before it would be permitted to pay for an increase in its quota under the Ninth General Review, and that, in the event the quota payment were not made within a prescribed period, the proposal for an increase in the member's quota would lapse.

Another measure being considered by the staff relates to the possibility of withholding SDR allocations for members with arrears in the General Department. This measure would require an amendment of the Articles and will be examined further in the next Six-Monthly Report on Overdue Financial Obligations.

Declaration of ineligibility

- If a member persists in its failure to settle its overdue obligations to the Fund, the Executive Board declares the member ineligible to use the general resources of the Fund. The timing of the declaration of ineligibility would vary according to the Board's assessment of the specific circumstances and of the efforts being made by the member to fulfill its financial obligations to the Fund. The procedures for dealing with members with protracted arrears that have been declared ineligible include further reviews at intervals of not more than six months.
- For members with protracted arrears willing to cooperate with the Fund in settling those overdues, the Fund has adopted an intensified collaborative approach, which incorporates exceptional efforts by the international financial community.
- For members that are judged not to be cooperating actively with the Fund, remedial measures would be applied.
- Members not showing a clear willingness to cooperate with the Fund have been informed that in these circumstances the provision of technical assistance would be inappropriate, but the Fund would reconsider providing technical assistance once the member has resumed active cooperation. The Managing Director may also limit technical assistance provided to a member, if in his judgment that assistance was not contributing adequately to the resolution of the problems associated with overdues to the Fund.

- A further remedial measure in cases of protracted arrears would be communications with all Governors of the Fund and with heads of certain international financial institutions. Use of such communications would normally be raised for the Executive Board's consideration at the time of the first post-ineligibility review of the member's arrears. At that time the staff would prepare a draft text of a communication along the lines set out in Attachment II to this statement. It should be noted that the Fund's communication to certain other international financial institutions, such as the three main regional development banks (Asian Development Bank, African Development Bank, Inter-American Development Bank), like its communication to the Governors, would not request the addressee to take specific actions and would leave any action to the institution's discretion. This does not preclude informal contacts with other international financial institutions. The staff would intend to propose to send this latter type of communication on the occasion of the next post-ineligibility review for members that at present have arrears that have been outstanding for a protracted period, in the event the Executive Board judges that the member concerned is not cooperating actively with the Fund in efforts to resolve the problem of its overdue financial obligations to the Fund.

Censure or declaration of noncooperation

- A declaration of censure or noncooperation would come as an intermediate step between a declaration of ineligibility and a resolution on compulsory withdrawal. The decision as to whether to issue such a declaration would be based on an assessment of the member's performance in the settlement of its arrears to the Fund and of its efforts, in consultation with the Fund, to follow appropriate policies for the settlement of its arrears. Three related tests would be germane to this decision regarding (i) the member's performance in meeting its financial obligations to the Fund taking account of exogenous factors that may have affected the member's performance; (ii) whether the member had made payments to other creditors while continuing to be in arrears to the Fund; and (iii) the preparedness of the member to adopt comprehensive adjustment policies. The declaration would follow any communication to Governors after ineligibility and would be considered at a subsequent post-ineligibility review. The period between such communications and the declaration could be about six months, but this time period would be determined on a case-by-case basis.

A draft of the declaration is set out in Attachment III. The actual declaration would be based on this draft text taking account of the circumstances of the individual case. The declaration would be adopted by the Executive Board and published.

Other remedial measures

- On suspension of membership, Directors noted the necessity of amending the Fund's Articles of Agreement to provide for suspension of membership. Some Directors showed an interest in introducing a provision into the Articles of Agreement under which the voting rights of a member that has been declared ineligible to use the Fund's general resources could be suspended. However, most Directors felt that it would not be advisable to propose an amendment of the Fund's Articles of Agreement at this time, but that this matter could be reconsidered in the future.

- Finally, Directors noted the availability to the Fund of procedures under Section 22 of the By-Laws on compulsory withdrawal. These procedures would only be pursued once the Fund has exhausted all other possible avenues to redress the problem of overdue financial obligations and, despite a declaration of noncooperation, the member has not exhibited a willingness to cooperate with the Fund. The Articles of Agreement and the By-Laws provide for procedures for settling claims by the Fund on a member in the event that it withdraws from the Fund. If the procedures were initiated, the staff would prepare an analysis of the effect of the member's withdrawal on the Fund's financial position.

ATTACHMENT I

Draft First Letter to All Governors

Dear   :

The Executive Board has considered the complaint which was recently issued regarding [member]'s overdue financial obligations to the Fund. In considering this complaint the Executive Board has agreed that I write to all Governors of the Fund to draw their attention to this development. Prompt and effective actions now by [member] and the international community would avoid a further deterioration of this situation including the possibility of declaring [member] ineligible to use the general resources of the Fund, would permit these overdues to be cleared before their magnitude makes the problem more intractable, and before they place a financial burden on other members.

[Paragraph on background circumstances of member leading to the emergence of arrears, the views of the member regarding its overdue obligations, and the member's intended approach for addressing the problem of its overdue obligations. This paragraph would be tailored to the specific circumstances of the member concerned.]

The Executive Board is very concerned about these developments which have serious potential implications both for the [member] and for the Fund as a whole, if the problem is not resolved early. The existence of these overdue financial obligations to the Fund precludes the Fund from extending financial assistance to the member. In addition, experience to date indicates that when a country incurs arrears to the Fund its financial relations with other creditors are also likely to deteriorate. These arrears also have an adverse impact on the Fund as an international financial cooperative, which is the central monetary institution in the international monetary system. As you are aware, overdue obligations, if they are not settled, place a financial burden on other members: on the Fund's debtor members in the form of higher charges and the Fund's creditors in the form of reduced remuneration.

The Fund would greatly appreciate any assistance in urging the member to effect the full and prompt settlement of its overdue obligations to the Fund.

Sincerely yours,

Michel Camdessus

Managing Director and

Chairman of the Executive Board

ATTACHMENT II

Draft Second Letter to All Governors
and Certain International Financial Institutions

Dear   :

The Executive Board has reviewed the overdue financial obligations of [member] and its circumstances. In this context it agreed that I write to all Governors of the Fund to seek their assistance in resolving the problem of [member]'s overdue financial obligations to the Fund [and that I inform at the same time the heads of [names of certain international financial institutions]].

As you know, [member] was declared ineligible to use the general resources of the Fund on [date], as it had failed to meet its financial obligations to the Fund. As of [date], [member]'s overdue financial obligations to the Fund amounted to SDR[ ] million and the longest overdue obligation had been outstanding for [ ] months. As you are aware, these overdue obligations reduce Fund resources available to help other members and place a financial burden on debtor members in the form of higher charges and on creditor members in the form of reduced remuneration.

[Paragraph on background circumstances of member leading to the emergence of arrears, the views of the member regarding its overdue obligations, and the member's intended approach for addressing the problem of its overdue obligations. This paragraph would be tailored to the specific circumstances of the member concerned.]

The Fund has developed a set of procedures, including the intensified collaborative approach, for dealing, as appropriate, with members that have overdue financial obligations outstanding for a protracted period. The application of the procedures for members in arrears up to now has not resulted in [member] taking steps that could be expected to resolve promptly the problem of its arrears to the Fund. If, in the period prior to the next review of [member]'s arrears, [member] does not take action to demonstrate its willingness to resume active cooperation with the Fund toward the resolution of the problem of its arrears, [member] may be subject to a declaration of noncooperation. This would be a most serious step that would involve the publication of this declaration, which would refer, inter alia, to the availability to the Fund of procedures under Section 22 of the By-Laws on compulsory withdrawal of [member] from the Fund. The Fund's Executive Board has emphasized the critical stage that has been reached with respect to [member]'s arrears and has stressed its sincere hope that the consideration of further steps will be unnecessary. The Fund would appreciate your [Government/institution] taking whatever actions it considers appropriate to help bring about an early resolution of this situation.

The Executive Board will review again the position of [member] with regard to its arrears to the Fund not later than [date].

Sincerely yours,
Michel Camdessus
Managing Director and
Chairman of the Executive Board

ATTACHMENT III

Draft Declaration on Censure or Noncooperation

The Fund notes that, since the declaration of ineligibility on [date], the member has remained in arrears in its financial obligations to the Fund, thus persisting in its failure to fulfill its obligations under the Articles, and that the level of its arrears has not decreased (or has increased);

[notes that the member has made payments to other creditors while not discharging its financial obligation to the Fund (or not to the same extent), thus ignoring the preferred creditor status that members are expected to give to the Fund;]

- finds that the member is not cooperating with the Fund toward the discharge of its financial obligations to the Fund;
- urges the member to discharge its financial obligations to the Fund promptly and to cooperate with the Fund;
- reminds the member that arrears to the Fund, which is a cooperative institution, are detrimental to the whole membership of the Fund in that they hamper the proper per-

formance by the Fund of its function of assisting members facing balance of payments difficulties;

- reminds the member that members in breach of their obligations to the Fund may be subject to the procedures under Section 22 of the By-Laws leading to compulsory withdrawal.

. . . 5. The Third Amendment, 1992

Finally, in November 1992, the Third Amendment to the Articles of Agreement took effect. That amendment introduced four changes.

First, Article XXVI, Section 2, was rewritten to read as follows:

Section 2. *Compulsory withdrawal*

(a) If a member fails to fulfill any of its obligations under this Agreement, the Fund may declare the member ineligible to use the general resources of the Fund. Nothing in this Section shall be deemed to limit the provisions of Article V, Section 5, or Article VI, Section 1.

(b) If, after the expiration of a reasonable period following a declaration of ineligibility under (a) above, the member persists in its failure to fulfill any of its obligations under this Agreement, the Fund may, by a seventy percent majority of the total voting power, suspend the voting rights of the member. During the period of the suspension, the provisions of Schedule L shall apply. The Fund may, by a seventy percent majority of the total voting power, terminate the suspension at any time.

(c) If, after the expiration of a reasonable period following a decision of suspension under (b) above, the member persists in its failure to fulfill any of its obligations under this Agreement, that member may be required to withdraw from membership in the Fund by a decision of the Board of Governors carried by a majority of the Governors having eighty-five percent of the total voting power.

(d) Regulations shall be adopted to ensure that before action is taken against any member under (a), (b), or (c) above, the member shall be informed in reasonable time of the complaint against it and given an adequate opportunity for stating its case, both orally and in writing.

Second, a new paragraph was added to Article V, Section 3(i), providing for the restoration of voting rights in the Executive Board following the lifting of a suspension:

(v) When the suspension of the voting rights of a member is terminated under Article XXVI, Section 2(b), and the member is not entitled to appoint an Executive Director, the member may agree with all the members that have elected an Executive Director that the number of votes allotted to that member shall be cast by such Executive Director, provided that, if no regular election of Executive Directors has been conducted during the period of the suspension, the Executive Director in whose election the member had participated prior to the suspension, or his successor elected in accordance with paragraph 3(c)(i) of Schedule L or with (f) above, shall be entitled to cast the number of votes allotted to the member. The member shall be deemed to have participated in the election of the Executive Director entitled to cast the number of votes allotted to the member.

Third, a provision was added to Schedule D, governing appointments to the Council:[171]

(f) When an Executive Director is entitled to cast the number of votes allotted to a member pursuant to Article XII, Section 3(i)(v), the Councillor appointed by the group whose members elected such Executive Director shall be entitled to vote and cast the number of votes allotted to such member. The member shall be deemed to have participated in the appointment of the Councillor entitled to vote and cast the number of votes allotted to the member.

Fourth, a new schedule was added to the Articles:

Schedule L
Suspension of Voting Rights

In the case of a suspension of voting rights of a member under Article XXVI, Section 2(b), the following provisions shall apply:

1. The member shall not:

(a) participate in the adoption of a proposed amendment of this Agreement, or be counted in the total number of members for that purpose, except in the case of an amendment requiring acceptance by all members under Article XXVIII(b) or pertaining exclusively to the Special Drawing Rights Department;

(b) appoint a Governor or Alternate Governor, appoint or participate in the appointment of a Councillor or Alternate Councillor, or appoint, elect, or participate in the election of an Executive Director.

2. The number of votes allotted to the member shall not be cast in any organ of the Fund. They shall not be included in the calculation of the total voting power, except for purposes of the acceptance of a proposed amendment pertaining exclusively to the Special Drawing Rights Department.

3. (a) The Governor and Alternate Governor appointed by the member shall cease to hold office.

(b) The Councillor and Alternate Councillor appointed by the member, or in whose appointment the member has participated, shall cease to hold office, provided that, if such Councillor was entitled to cast the number of votes allotted to other members whose voting rights have not been suspended, another Councillor and Alternate Councillor shall be appointed by such other members under Schedule D, and, pending such appointment, the Councillor and Alternate Councillor shall continue to hold office, but for a maximum of thirty days from the date of suspension;

(c) The Executive Director appointed or elected by the member, or in whose election the member has participated, shall cease to hold office, unless such Executive Director was entitled to cast the number of votes allotted to other members whose voting rights have not been suspended. In the latter case:

(i) if more than ninety days remain before the next regular election of Executive Directors, another Executive Director shall be elected for the remainder of the term by such other members by a majority of the votes cast; pending such election, the Executive Director shall continue to hold office, but for a maximum of thirty days from the date of suspension;

---

[171]As discussed in Chapter 20, the Council was embodied in the Second Amendment as an eventual successor to the Interim Committee. As of 1998, it had not been brought into existence.

(ii) if not more than ninety days remain before the next regular election of Executive Directors, the Executive Director shall continue to hold office for the remainder of the term.

4. The member shall be entitled to send a representative to attend any meeting of the Board of Governors, the Council, or the Executive Board, but not any meeting of their committees, when a request made by, or a matter particularly affecting, the member is under consideration.

The Third Amendment also necessitated introducing two new rules:

K-6. Before any member's voting rights are suspended pursuant to Article XVI, Section 2(*b*), the matter shall be considered by the Executive Board, which shall inform the member in reasonable time of the complaint against it and allow the member an adequate opportunity for stating its case both orally and in writing.
Adopted March 10, 1993

K-7. When a member, whose voting rights have been suspended, requests the Executive Board to terminate the suspension and the Executive Board decides not to terminate such suspension, a written report shall be presented to the member stating what further action is required before such suspension will be terminated.
Adopted March 10, 1993

References

Ali, Ali Abdel Gadir, 1985, *The Sudan Economy in Disarray: Essays on the IMF Model* (Khartoum and London: Ithaca Press).

Baker, James A., III, 1995, *The Politics of Diplomacy: Revolution, War and Peace, 1989–1992* (New York: G.B. Putnam's Sons).

Branson, William H., and Jorge B. de Macedo, 1989, "Smuggler's Blues at the Central Bank: Lessons from the Sudan," in *Debt, Stabilization and Development: Essays in Memory of Carlos Diaz-Alejandro*, ed. by Guillermo Calvo and others (Oxford: Basil Blackwell), pp. 191–207.

Brown, Richard P.C., 1992, *Public Debt and Private Wealth: Debt, Capital Flight and the IMF in Sudan* (London: Macmillan).

Callaghy, Thomas M., 1993, "Restructuring Zaïre's Debt, 1979–1982," in *Dealing with Debt: International Financial Negotiations and Adjustment Bargaining*, ed. by Thomas J. Biersteker (Boulder, Colorado: Westview Press), pp. 107–31.

de Vries, Margaret Garritsen, 1976, *The International Monetary Fund, 1966–1971: The System Under Stress*, Vol. 1: *Narrative*; Vol. 2: *Documents* (Washington: International Monetary Fund).

Diwan, Romesh, and Grace Hu, 1986, "Country Objectives and IMF Conditionality: An Empirical Analysis of Sudan Economy," *Indian Journal of Quantitative Economics*, Vol. 2, No. 2, pp. 83–100.

Dodsworth, John R., and others, 1996, *Vietnam: Transition to a Market Economy*, IMF Occasional Paper No. 135 (Washington: International Monetary Fund).

Hussain, M. Nureldin, and A.P. Thirwall, 1984, "The IMF Supply-Side Approach to Devaluation: An Assessment with Reference to the Sudan," *Oxford Bulletin of Economics and Statistics*, Vol. 46 (May), pp. 145–67.

Horsefield, J. Keith, ed., 1969, *The International Monetary Fund, 1945–1965: Twenty Years of International Monetary Cooperation*, Vol. 1: *Chronicle*, by J. Keith Horsefield; Vol. 2: *Analysis*, by Margaret G. de Vries and J. Keith Horsefield with the collaboration of Joseph Gold, Mary H. Gumbart, Gertrud Lovasy, and Emil G. Spitzer; Vol. 3: *Documents* (Washington: International Monetary Fund).

IMF Treasurer's Department, 1998, *Financial Organization and Operations of the IMF*, IMF Pamphlet Series No. 45 (Washington: International Monetary Fund, 5th ed.).

Liebenow, J. Gus, 1987, *Liberia: The Quest for Democracy* (Bloomington, Indiana: Indiana University Press).

Lissakers, Karin, 1991, *Banks, Borrowers, and the Establishment: A Revisionist Account of the International Debt Crisis* (New York: Basic Books).

Martha, Rutsel Silvestre J., 1990, "Preferred Creditor Status under International Law: The Case of the International Monetary Fund," *International and Comparative Law Quarterly*, Vol. 39 (October), pp. 801–26.

Nashashibi, Karim, 1980, "A Supply Framework for Exchange Reform in Developing Countries: The Experience of Sudan," *Staff Papers*, International Monetary Fund, Vol. 27 (March), pp. 24–79.

Reno, William, 1995, *Corruption and State Politics in Sierra Leone* (Cambridge: Cambridge University Press).

Rowan, Hobart, 1975, "IMF Rejected Saigon Request," *Washington Post* (May 12), pp. A1 and A15.

Sachs, Jeffrey D., 1990, "Social Conflict and Populist Policies in Latin America," in *Labour Relations and Economic Performance: Proceedings of a Conference Held by the International Economic Association in Venice, Italy*, ed. by Renato Brunetta and Carlo Dell'Aringa (New York: New York University Press), pp. 137–69.

Webb, Richard C., 1988, "Economic Crisis and Foreign Debt in Peru," in *Development and External Debt in Latin America: Bases for a New Consensus*, ed. by Richard E. Feinberg and Ricardo Ffrench-Davis (Notre Dame, Indiana: University of Notre Dame Press), pp. 241–53.

Weeks, John, 1992, *Development Strategy and the Economy of Sierra Leone* (New York: St. Martin's Press).

Weeks, John, and Phil Gunson, 1991, *Panama: Made in the USA* (London: Latin American Bureau).

IV

Evolution of the Institution

17

Fund Finances: Balancing Demand and Supply

THE IMF IS THE LINCHPIN OF THE INTERNATIONAL financial system. . . . I have an unbreakable commitment to increased funding for the IMF. . . . The stakes are great. This [quota increase] legislation is not only crucial to the recovery of America's trading partners abroad and to the stability of the entire international financial system, it is also necessary to a sustained recovery in the United States.

> Ronald R. Reagan
> President of the United States
> September 27, 1983[1]

The summer of 1983 brought an unprecedented squeezing of the IMF's resources. Demand for Fund lending was at an all-time high as a result of the Fund's efforts to help countries cope with the international debt crisis. To finance that activity, the Fund's governors had agreed to a major increase in quotas and to an enlargement of the pool of resources available to the Fund through the General Arrangements to Borrow (GAB). The effectiveness of both of those increases, however, depended on their approval by the U.S. Congress, which was raising a host of political objections to it and tying it to unrelated domestic issues. The Managing Director, Jacques de Larosière, tried to get the major creditor countries to provide additional short-term loans to the Fund to cover the possibility of a liquidity shortage if the quota and GAB increases continued to be delayed. When that effort failed in September, de Larosière decided that the Fund could no longer conduct business as usual.

The venue for the Managing Director's effort to secure additional loans to the IMF was the Bank for International Settlements (BIS) in Basel, Switzerland. The governors of the BIS included the central bank governors of most of the major creditors, and the BIS would have been the natural intermediary for a short-term loan to the Fund. At the beginning of September, de Larosière was confident enough of success that he told the Executive Board that to prevent a "dramatic" and "worrying" situation from developing—in which the Fund might be unable to meet its own commitments—a loan from the BIS was "of critical importance." Two

---

[1]IMF, *Summary Proceedings*, 1983, pp. 4–5.

weeks later, on returning from Basel, he had to report to the Board that the talks had failed. Although he declined to elaborate on the reasons, it was clearly understood that the BIS governors did not want to take action that would make it easier for the U.S. Congress to continue to delay approving the more permanent increases in the Fund's resources.[2] A political game of cat and mouse was being played, and the Fund's liquidity was the bait.

In response, de Larosière announced that he was immediately instructing the staff not to discuss any new lending arrangements with member countries unless the credits could be financed without the use of borrowed resources. Since most arrangements at the time were drawing heavily on borrowed resources, and strict limits were in effect on the use of the Fund's own money, that decision was nearly tantamount to a moratorium on new lending. Never before had the Fund had to refuse to lend on the grounds that it was running out of money. A more dramatic circumstance could scarcely be imagined for the world's primary source of conditional balance of payments financing.

The impasse induced the president of the United States to endorse the quota increase in the strikingly strong language quoted at the heading to this chapter. Within a few months, the quota-GAB package was approved, the crisis passed, and the backlog of demand for new arrangements was soon cleared.

This episode, although unique in the history of the Fund, illustrates the institution's continuing dependence on timely quota increases. Even though the Fund has occasionally and temporarily met the rising demand for its resources by borrowing, quota subscriptions have provided its permanent assets. The process of increasing quotas, however, requires political commitments that are difficult to secure in the absence of a demonstrable crisis. Consequently, the history of the Fund's resources has taken a bumpy path, marked by long periods of declining liquidity, interrupted by sharp increases. This chapter reviews the major developments of the late 1970s and the 1980s.

Quotas and the Size of the Fund

As a financial institution, the IMF comprises three separate units: the General Department, the SDR Department, and a set of Administered Accounts. The core, and what is usually meant by the "Fund," is the General Department. The SDR Department is the subject of Chapter 18, and the Administered Accounts (such as the Trust Fund and the ESAF Trust) are examined above, in Chapter 14.[3]

---

[2]Minutes of EBM/83/129 (September 2, 1983), pp. 13–14; EBM/83/139 (September 14, 1983), pp. 3–5; and (on the reason for the governors' refusal to lend to the Fund) the statement by Gerhard Laske (Germany) at EBM/83/145 (October 3, 1983).

[3]For a detailed discussion of the Fund's financial accounts, see IMF Treasurer's Department (1998). Appendix I of this chapter gives an alternative presentation that consolidates the two departments and the Administered Accounts into a single table. For another alternative that stresses the potential role of the SDR in Fund operations and criticizes the Fund's liquidity concept, see Polak (1996, 1999).

The overall level of resources in the General Department more than doubled during the period covered by this History, from SDR 46 billion ($60 billion) at the end of 1978 to SDR 99 billion ($130 billion) 11 years later (Table 17.1).[4] That increase resulted almost entirely from increases in members' quotas. The other two major sources of assets—gold and borrowings—declined.[5] This pattern continued the broad pattern since Bretton Woods, in which quotas increased by an average of 5¾ percent a year (aside from the effect of the addition of new members and a few ad hoc increases, which added another 1 percent a year), but in uneven spurts rather than steadily over time (Table 17.2).[6]

A clearer picture of the "size of the Fund"—the amount of lendable resources provided to or available for member countries—is gained by netting out the stock of "currently unusable" currencies held by the Fund and other nonliquid assets. When a country pays in its quota subscription (whether as a new member or in acceptance of a quota increase), it normally pays three-fourths of the total in its own currency. Since many countries have weak balance of payments positions or have currencies that are not fully convertible, the Fund regularly reviews the status of each currency in its portfolio to determine whether it is currently usable for Fund operations. If not, holdings of that currency are excluded from the list of liquid assets. The effective size of the Fund thus varies with the overall quality and distribution of external positions. By this measure (credit outstanding plus cash and other liquid investments), the Fund's usable assets increased at an even faster rate, from SDR 16 billion in 1978 to SDR 51 billion in 1989 ($20 billion to $66 billion).[7]

The 131 percent increase in Fund quotas from the end of 1978 through 1989 reflected two rounds of increases for all members and the addition of 14 new member countries. The Seventh General Review, which took effect in 1980, raised quotas by just over 50 percent, to SDR 60 billion. The Eighth General Review raised quotas by just under 50 percent in 1983, and the total stock of quotas gradually

---

[4]The form of the balance sheet shown in Figure 17.1 on p. 877 differs from the Fund's own presentation in the *Annual Report*, primarily by including the distinction between liquid and nonliquid assets and liabilities. The classification of items as liquid follows the Fund's own practice for the purpose of measuring the "liquidity ratio." (The liquidity ratio was devised by de Larosière in 1980 as a ready reckoner for determining whether the Fund might need to borrow in the near future.) For further details on the balance sheet, see the relevant *Annual Report*.

[5]From 1976 to 1980, the Fund sold or distributed one-third of its stock of gold (initially 150 million ounces). Half of that amount was sold at auction, and the profits were used to finance the Trust Fund (Chapter 14). The other half was sold back to member countries at the official price (SDR 35 per ounce) in proportion to quotas; see de Vries (1985), pp. 625 and 658–59.

[6]The original Articles of Agreement provided for a review of quotas every five years. That provision was modified in the First Amendment (1969) to allow for the possibility of more frequent reviews. The first two reviews were concluded without a general increase.

[7]The category "liquid cash assets" in Table 17.1 comprises currencies, securities, and SDRs held in the General Resources Account (GRA), plus liquid deposits held in the Special Disbursement Account (SDA). The GRA and the SDA are the two principal accounts in the General Department; see IMF Treasurer's Department (1998), pp. 13–15. The sources of the GRA holdings are broadly disaggregated in the table. The SDA also held claims in the form of SAF loans, which are shown separately.

Table 17.1. Balance Sheet of the General Department

(Billions of SDRs; see text for explanatory notes)

	December 31, 1978		December 31, 1989		Change	
Assets						
Liquid cash assets		5.3		26.7		21.4
Quota subscriptions	39.0		90.1		51.1	
Less reserve tranche positions	−8.5		−22.0		(13.5)	
Less nonliquid holdings	−26.4		−43.0		(16.6)	
SDA investments			0.8		0.8	
Nonliquid cash assets		26.4		43.0		16.6
Currently nonqualifying currencies	20.8		28.6		7.8	
Undrawn credit commitments	3.2		4.3		1.1	
Required working balances	2.4		10.1		7.7	
Loans and credits		10.3		23.8		13.5
GRA credits	10.3		22.3		12.0	
SAF loans	0.0		1.5		1.5	
Receivables		0.1		1.4		1.3
Current charges and interest	0.1		0.5		0.4	
Deferred charges			0.9		0.9	
Gold (at SDR 35 per ounce)		4.1		3.6		(0.5)
Other assets		0.1		0.2		0.2
Total assets		46.3		98.7		52.4
Liabilities and Net Worth						
Liquid liabilities		14.9		25.5		10.6
Reserve tranche positions	8.5		22.0		13.5	
Borrowings	6.4		3.5		(2.9)	
Balance of quota subscriptions		30.5		68.1		37.6
SDA resources			2.3			
Other liabilities		0.2		0.4		0.2
Reserves, etc.		0.7		2.4		1.7
Ordinary reserves	0.7		1.4		0.6	
SCA			0.2		0.2	
Deferred charges			0.9		0.9	
Total liabilities and net worth		46.3		98.7		52.4
Memorandum items:						
Gold at market prices		45.9		31.6		−14.4
Unused and available credit lines	5.5		15.3		9.8	
Liquidity ratio (in percent)	36		105			

crept up by a further 4 percent as new members came on board through April 1990.[8] Over the same period, international trade increased at a comparable pace, so the rapid drop in quotas relative to world imports recorded in the 1960s and 1970s was at least interrupted.

Both the Seventh and the Eighth General Reviews brought a few large ad hoc adjustments to the quotas of individual countries. The most notable changes were the increase for China after the People's Republic began representing the country

---

[8]In relation to the initial stock of SDR 39 billion in quotas for 138 member countries, the Seventh and Eighth Reviews represented increases of 52.4 and 74.4 percent, respectively.

Table 17.1 (concluded)

(Billions of U.S. dollars, at end-year exchange rates)

	December 31, 1978		December 31, 1989		Change	
Assets						
Liquid cash assets		6.9		35.1		28.2
Quota subscriptions	50.8		118.4		67.6	
Less reserve tranche positions	−11.1		−28.9		(17.8)	
Less nonliquid holdings	−34.4		−56.5		(22.1)	
SDA investments			1.0		1.0	
Nonliquid cash assets		34.4		56.5		22.1
Currently nonqualifying currencies	27.1		37.6		10.5	
Undrawn credit commitments	4.2		5.7		1.5	
Required working balances	3.1		13.3		10.1	
Loans and credits		13.4		31.3		17.9
GRA credits	13.4		29.3		15.9	
SAF loans	0.0		2.0		2.0	
Receivables		0.1		1.8		1.7
Current charges and interest	0.1		0.6		0.5	
Deferred charges			1.2		1.2	
Gold (at SDR 35 per ounce)		5.4		4.8		(0.6)
Other assets		0.1		0.3		0.2
Total assets		60.4		129.7		69.4
Liabilities and Net Worth						
Liquid liabilities		19.4		33.5		14.1
Reserve tranche positions	11.1		28.9		17.8	
Borrowings	8.3		4.6		(3.7)	
Balance of quota subscriptions		39.7		89.5		49.8
SDA resources				3.0		
Other liabilities		0.2		0.5		0.3
Reserves, etc.		1.0		3.2		2.2
Ordinary reserves	1.0		1.8		0.8	
SCA			0.3		0.3	
Deferred charges			1.2		1.2	
Total liabilities and net worth		60.4		129.7		66.4
Memorandum items:						
Gold at market prices		78.8		54.5		−24.3
Unused and available credit lines		7.2		19.9		12.8

in 1980, and two increases for Saudi Arabia to reflect that country's substantially greater role in the Fund and in the world economy (see below, p. 889).[9] Following

---

[9]Before 1970, the Fund approved several requests for ad hoc quota increases apart from the general reviews. From then on, such requests normally were postponed until they could be considered as part of the next general review. The requests from China (between the Sixth and Seventh Reviews) and Saudi Arabia (between the Seventh and Eighth) were the only exceptions. As explained in Chapter 19, China's quota was increased twice in 1980: an ad hoc increase in August and a further increase in December as part of the Seventh Review. Saudi Arabia's quota also was increased in two large steps: first as part of the Sixth Review (1978) and again in 1981, shortly after the general increases from the Seventh Review took effect.

Table 17.2. General Reviews of Quotas, 1950–92

Review	Originally Scheduled	Effective	Agreed Increase	Number of Members	Stock (Billions of SDRs)	World Imports	Ratio (Days)
		1946		40	7.5	61.7	44
First	1950	1950	0%	49	8.0	62.6	47
Second	1955	1955	0%	58	8.8	93.7	34
Third	1960	1959	61%	69	14.6	129.8	41
Fourth	1965	1966	31%	102	20.9	185.4	41
Fifth	1970	1970	35%	116	28.8	314.0	33
Sixth	1975	1978	34%	133	39.0	715.3	20
Seventh	1980	1980	51%	141	59.6	1537.3	14
Eighth	1985	1983	48%	146	89.2	1909.3	17
Ninth	1990	1992	50%	175	141.4	2561.5	20
Average annual increase:			5.7%		6.6%	8.4%	

Sources: IMF Treasurer's Department (1998), Tables 1 and 2; IFS; and author's calculations. Imports are at five-year intervals, except that the initial datum is for 1948.

the 1979 revolution in Iran (which changed the country's name to the Islamic Republic of Iran), the government became preoccupied with the reconstruction of the economy and the war with Iraq, and Iran declined to accept either of the recommended quota increases in the early 1980s.[10] Consequently, Iran's quota slipped from the fourteenth largest to the twenty-seventh. Other individual changes in rank were generally minor.

The overall distribution of quotas among major groups of countries showed little change during the 1980s (Table 17.3). The share of developing countries rose slightly, but the ad hoc increases for China and Saudi Arabia more than accounted for that shift.[11] Both the large industrial countries and the small low-income countries lost shares, in amounts that roughly offset the large ad hoc increases. Smaller industrial countries and middle-income developing countries approximately maintained their aggregate shares. Quotas for all member countries from 1979 through 1989 are listed in Appendix II to this chapter.

Winning approval for general quota increases has always been a politically contentious task. Several reasons may be cited. First, a country's quota serves four separate functions: it determines the member's voting power in the Fund,[12] its access (bor-

---

[10]See "Ninth General Review of Quotas—Islamic Republic of Iran—Request for an Ad Hoc Increase," EB/CQuota/90/3 (January 12, 1990).

[11]As shown in Table 17.3, the developing country share rose by 1.6 percentage points. Without China and Saudi Arabia, the share declined by 1.7 points (from 32.4 percent to 30.7). For a long-term analysis of the distribution of quotas between industrial and developing countries, see Officer (1991).

[12]The effect of quotas on voting power is modified by the use of "basic votes." Under Article XII, Section 5, each member country has 250 basic votes, plus one vote per SDR 100,000 of quota. This provision was inserted at Bretton Woods as a nod in the direction of the "one member, one vote" principle used in some other international organizations, and to place a floor under the voting power of the smallest member countries (then Liberia and Panama). For the background, see Gold (1972), Chapter 2. Without basic votes, those two members would have held 0.006 percent of the expected voting power; with basic votes, they held 0.258 percent. As the size of the Fund

rowing) limits, its share in any SDR allocations, and its financial contribution to the institution.[13] Each of these functions is important, politically and financially, and the multiplicity leads to intrinsic conflicts. The more quota increases are allotted to potential borrowers, the more that group will obtain in terms of its voting power and its share of access to resources, but the smaller will be the stock of usable resources.

Second, a decision to increase quotas requires an 85 percent majority of the voting power. Quota reviews thus command an extraordinarily high degree of consensus, and resistance by a few major creditors (or even one, since the United States holds more than 15 percent of the voting power) can block action.

Third, despite changes in the Fund's financial structure that eliminated the systematic cost of quota increases, political debates continued to be framed as if costs would be incurred. Before the Second Amendment in 1978, subscription to a quota increase required countries to transfer reserve assets (normally gold or U.S. dollars) to pay the gold tranche portion of the subscription, and the process generated a direct cost to the subscribing country, measured by the lost interest on the unremunerated portion of the increase in the gold tranche. The Amendment froze the absolute level of the unremunerated portion of the reserve tranche (as the former gold tranche was renamed), so that interest would be paid on the entire increase; and it eliminated the requirement that a reserve tranche drawing would have to be repaid, so that countries could immediately offset the transfer of reserve assets.[14] Hence there was no longer any ex ante cost of investing resources in the Fund.[15] Nonetheless, opponents—especially in the U.S. Congress—continued to cite imagined costs as a justification for resistance.

---

increased, the share of basic votes in the total decreased from 11.1 percent as calculated in 1944 to 4 percent in 1989, and the floor sank quite close to the ground. By 1989, the smallest member (Maldives) held 0.029 percent of the voting power, and without basic votes would have held 0.002 percent. To restore the original balance would have required raising the number of basic votes to approximately 740 per member. Since the Articles made no provision for changing the number of basic votes, the perennial effort by small countries to restore or at least maintain their share in total votes centered on the general reviews of quotas (see below, p. 868).

[13]Mikesell (1994), pp. 37–38, discusses and criticizes the background to the decision at Bretton Woods in 1944 to use a single set of quotas for multiple purposes. As complex and lengthy as the quinquennial quota reviews have been, one shudders to imagine the process if the Articles had provided for four independent quotas.

[14]For a country with outstanding debt obligations to the Fund, the requirement was a bit more complex. Rules in effect at the time of the Second Amendment required that payments to the Fund, including quota subscriptions, be applied first to outstanding debts. Assuming that the member had to borrow the foreign exchange or SDRs to pay the reserve tranche portion of its subscription, the net effect was to substitute other external debt for obligations to the Fund. That exchange often involved a significant increase in borrowing costs. In 1981, the Fund modified that rule and allowed countries to apply the payment directly to the reserve tranche. From then on, creditors and debtors had the same options available for eliminating the systematic cost of a quota increase. See also footnote 76, p. 877.

[15]Ex post, for a country that retains its reserve tranche, the marginal cost of a quota subscription is the difference between the country's own borrowing cost and the remuneration rate (both measured in the same currency), which is a function of both interest and exchange rates and could be positive or negative. Aside from differences between the remuneration rate and market interest rates, any risk of a marginal cost can be eliminated by an appropriate reallocation of net foreign exchange reserves or by permanently drawing out the reserve tranche. For a review of the evolution of the remuneration rate in relation to market rates, see below, pp. 900–04.

Table 17.3. Distribution of Quotas, 1979–89
(Billions of SDRs and percent)

Group	Sixth General Review 1979–80			Seventh General Review 1981–83			Eighth General Review 1984–89		
	Countries	Amount	Percent	Countries	Amount	Percent	Countries	Amount	Percent
Industrial countries	22	25,297	64.7	22	37,946	63.2	22	56,866	63.1
G-7	7	19,661	50.3	7	29,492	49.2	7	44,072	48.9
Developing countries	119	13,820	35.3	124	22,054	36.8	130	33,267	36.9
Small low-income	42	1,972	5.0	44	2,954	4.9	45	3,854	4.3
Largest Quotas:									
1	United States	8,405	21.5	United States	12,608	21.0	United States	17,918	19.9
2	United Kingdom	2,925	7.5	United Kingdom	4,388	7.3	United Kingdom	6,194	6.9
3	Germany	2,156	5.5	Germany	3,234	5.4	Germany	5,404	6.0
4	France	1,919	4.9	France	2,879	4.8	France	4,483	5.0
5	Japan	1,659	4.2	Japan	2,489	4.1	Japan	4,223	4.7
6	Canada	1,357	3.5	Canada	2,036	3.4	**Saudi Arabia**	**3,202**	**3.6**
7	Italy	1,240	3.2	Italy	1,860	3.1	*Canada*	2,941	3.3
8	India	1,145	2.9	**China**[a]	**1,800**	**3.0**	Italy	2,909	3.2
9	Netherlands	948	2.4	India	1,718	2.9	China	2,391	2.7
10	Belgium	890	2.3	Netherlands	1,422	2.4	Netherlands	2,265	2.5
11	Australia	790	2.0	*Belgium*	1,335	2.2	*India*	2,208	2.4
12	Brazil	665	1.7	Australia	1,185	2.0	Belgium	2,080	2.3
13	Iran	660	1.7	**Saudi Arabia**[b]	**1,040**	**1.7**	*Australia*	1,619	1.8
14	Venezuela	660	1.7	*Brazil*	998	1.7	Brazil	1,461	1.6
15	Saudi Arabia	600	1.5	*Venezuela*	990	1.7	Venezuela	1,372	1.5
16	Spain	557	1.4	Spain	836	1.4	Spain	1,286	1.4
17	China	550	1.4	Argentina	803	1.3	Mexico	1,166	1.3
18	Argentina	535	1.4	Mexico	803	1.3	*Argentina*	1,113	1.2
19	Mexico	535	1.4	Indonesia	720	1.2	**Sweden**	**1,064**	**1.2**
20	Indonesia	480	1.2	Sweden	675	1.1	Indonesia	1,010	1.1

Note: Countries in bold increased in rank and share from the previous review; those in italics moved down.
[a] The increase in China's quota was approved after the general review but took effect simultaneously.
[b] In September 1981, the quota of Saudi Arabia was raised to SDR 2,100 million.

Fourth, discussion of quota increases became part of the perennial dialogue on the appropriate balance between financing and adjustment for deficit countries. Some creditor countries sought to limit the size of quotas as an indirect way of limiting access to Fund resources and thus forcing stricter adjustment on borrowing countries. Such concerns were mitigated, however, by the reality that reduced financing from the Fund might have to be offset by greater bilateral support to prevent a breakdown in the debtor's economic and social fabric.

Fifth, the level of potential demand for Fund resources is very difficult to assess with any accuracy. Management recommendations for quota increases have been based partly on benchmark relationships between quotas and world economic activity, trade, and reserves; and partly on projections of the balance between demand and available resources. Differences of opinion about the relevance of various indicators can reasonably be, and often have been, quite large.[16]

During the prolonged debates that preceded agreement on general quota increases, the distribution of quotas also excited passions. General reviews of quotas offered an opportunity for countries to try to raise their own relative quotas, with an eye toward increasing their voting power, their borrowing limits, their shares in any SDR allocations, and their prestige among their peers. In addition, both the general reviews and discussions of quotas for new members became an occasion for countries to support their friends and occasionally to punish their enemies; assignments of quotas to new members offered an opportunity to define their position in the international political and economic hierarchy.[17]

One should not strain too hard to rationalize these political pressures on economic grounds. Political battles over quota increases sometimes escalated to dimensions far out of proportion to the economic values at stake. What is important for an understanding of this History is simply that political concerns and economic and financial uncertainties, from whatever source, have combined to prevent Fund resources from increasing *pari passu* with world trade. Even so, the Fund has enjoyed a widespread support from creditor countries, and it generally has been able to secure an essential level of resources when the demand has been most acute.

Quota reviews comprise four distinct stages. First, Executive Directors engage in extensive debates on whether a general increase is warranted, the optimum size of the Fund under current and expected conditions, and how any increase should be allocated among members. Those debates usually focus on technical issues, but political considerations are never far below the surface. That stage concludes with approval of a formal resolution to be submitted to the Board of Governors. Although approval technically requires only a simple majority of votes cast, there would be no point in doing so without an expectation of much broader support. Second, Governors vote on the resolution. When the required majority—85 percent of the total voting power—is achieved, the proposal to increase quotas becomes effective.

---

[16]In 1997, a former Executive Director opined that "the IMF falls from its normally very high analytical standards . . . when the case is made for higher quotas" (Evans, 1997, p. 10).

[17]For a striking example, see the discussion in Chapter 19 (pp. 986–92) of Poland's reaccession to membership.

Third, each member country must consent to its proposed increase. Procedures for doing so vary from country to country and may require parliamentary approval and appropriations. Usually, no member's quota increase can become effective until a critical mass of consents (the "participation requirement") is received. That requirement is specified in the resolution and varies from one review to the next. Fourth, each member's increase becomes effective when it pays in its subscription.

Seventh General Review

Technical preparations for the Seventh General Review, which took place in 1976–77, led to a staff and management recommendation for an increase of 75 to 100 percent. Political discussions then produced a broad consensus for a compromise increase of 50 percent, but the United States and Germany (with a combined vote of just under 25 percent) blocked action for about a year. They dropped their opposition suddenly in the fall of 1978, shortly after the Bonn Summit of major industrial countries highlighted the dangers of sluggish economic growth in many countries around the world. As part of a consensus package negotiated by de Larosière, the Interim Committee agreed in September 1978 to increase quotas by 50 percent, to have a new allocation of SDRs, and to require that the reserve-asset portion of the quota subscription be paid in SDRs. The Board of Governors approved a formal resolution soon thereafter. So as the period of this History began, all that remained was for member countries to ratify the proposed increases.[18]

Although the administration of U.S. President Jimmy Carter supported the quota increase, it failed to get quick action from congress in 1979 and then found the request caught up in the politics of the presidential and congressional election campaigns of 1980.[19] That delay could well have killed the whole process: since the United States held 21.5 percent of the base-period quotas, almost every other member country would have to consent for the increases to take effect without them. No general increase had ever taken effect without the Fund's largest member, and the prospect that this one *could* do so raised interesting possibilities. For one, if quotas were raised for the rest of the membership, the U.S. role in the Fund

---

[18]For a detailed review of the process through 1978, see de Vries (1985), pp. 529–39. The resolution specified that the quota increases would become effective only when members holding not less than 75 percent of the total quotas as of November 1978 consented to them. This participation requirement was set by the Executive Board, as a means of pressuring members to respond quickly and of ensuring that most increases would take effect simultaneously and thus avoiding temporary shifts in voting power.

[19]Although quota payments represent an exchange of assets and do not call for an expenditure by the government, the U.S. Congress demanded that the process involve approval of an appropriations bill. For the administration position on the increase, see the testimony by Anthony M. Solomon, Under Secretary of the U.S. Treasury for Monetary Affairs, before the Subcommittee on International Trade, Investment, and Monetary Policy of the Committee on Banking, Finance, and Urban Affairs; U.S. House of Representatives (February 4, 1980). Solomon's testimony was circulated to the Fund's Executive Directors as "United States—Statement by the Under Secretary of the Treasury for Monetary Affairs," EBD/80/32 (February 6, 1980).

would be greatly diminished until it consented. Its share in the total voting power would drop from nearly 20 percent to about 14 percent, which would imply a loss of veto power over decisions requiring an 85 percent majority (such as future quota increases). Second, the SDR allocation scheduled for January 1981 would be substantially smaller, and no easy remedy was available for making up the gap at a later date. Third, the supply of U.S. dollars for use in Fund operations would be smaller, which could create problems for financing large drawings.

Despite the dangers of these untested waters, de Larosière was eager to push ahead with or without the U.S. increase, and he directed the staff to make an all-out effort to persuade other countries not to wait. An intense lobbying campaign ensued, and it eventually paid off. On November 28, 1980, with the receipt of an official consent from Tunisia, the Fund had the consent of 127 out of 133 eligible countries, accounting for 75.15 percent of the total. The Executive Board approved an implementing decision the same day, and the increases took effect on November 29.

By then, the U.S. elections were over, and congress was in a lame-duck session. That circumstance, coupled with the pressure from the fact that the general quota increase had already taken effect for other countries, created a window of political opportunity. Opposition faded away, and the United States consented to its quota increase in mid-December.

The Seventh Review raised IMF quotas from SDR 39.8 billion to SDR 60 billion ($51 billion to $77 billion), with most of the increment distributed as 50 percent increases in proportion to members' previous quotas.[20] In addition to the large extra increases for China (total increase of 227 percent) and Saudi Arabia (73 percent) mentioned above, eight other countries received bonus increases that reflected a strengthening of their roles in the world economy.[21] Five of those were major oil exporters that received increases ranging from 61 to 69 percent: Iraq, Kuwait, Libya, Qatar, and the United Arab Emirates.[22] Two were East Asian countries that had recorded strong growth in output and exports in the preceding years: Korea (60 percent increase) and Singapore (88 percent). Lebanon, which for many years had declined to accept increases to which it was entitled and whose quota had thus become the lowest relative to calculated values, completed the list with an increase of 133 percent.

Eighth General Review

Work on the next general review began as soon as the 1980 increases took effect. The report completing the Seventh Review had indicated that the next one

---

[20]Increases were rounded upward for several, mostly small, countries. The largest proportional effect from rounding was for the country with the smallest absolute quota (Maldives), which received an increase of 55.6 percent (from SDR 0.9 million to 1.4 million).

[21]No increase was proposed for Cambodia (then known as Democratic Kampuchea), with which the Fund had no formal means of communication at the time (see Chapter 16).

[22]The resolution approved by the Board of Governors also provided selective increases for Iran and Oman, but those recommendations were declined. Iran did not consent to any increase, and Oman consented only to the equiproportional increase.

should include a thorough reexamination of the distribution of quotas to see whether it was still broadly appropriate in the modern world.[23] Consequently, staff preparation for the Eighth Review began with a review of the formulas used to calculate baseline figures for individual and aggregate quotas.

Forty years earlier, the technical staff preparing for the July 1944 Bretton Woods conference had calculated quotas for most prospective members by means of a nonlinear equation based on data for national income, international trade, and official reserves. That equation was calibrated so as to yield an aggregate quota of the size agreed upon during preliminary negotiations among the major countries (about $8 billion for participating countries) and to rank countries in a way that was both politically acceptable and reflective of relative positions in world trade and finance. It was not derived from theory or econometrics, and it was neither discussed nor even officially disclosed during the conference. Nonetheless, it did produce reasonable results for most countries, and no superior alternative was presented. With a few major exceptions, the original quotas of Fund members were set approximately by the Bretton Woods formula.[24]

With technical modifications, the staff continued to use the Bretton Woods formula as a notional device for calculating updated quotas, as a starting point for general reviews of quotas. Beginning with the Fourth Review in the mid-1960s, the coefficients were cut approximately in half to reflect the fact that the actual aggregate stock of quotas was far below the level produced by the original formula. Also, more comprehensive data were introduced, and several auxiliary equations were specified to reflect different views on the relative importance of each determining factor.[25]

---

[23]See section 5 of "Report of the Executive Board to the Board of Governors" (October 25, 1978), in de Vries (1985), Vol. 3, pp. 258–61.

[24]See Horsefield (1969), Vol. 1, pp. 94–98; Altman (1956); Mikesell (1994), pp. 37–38; and "The Working of the Quota Formulas," EB/CQuota/94/2 (February 28, 1994), pp. 53–54. (Raymond Mikesell, as a member of the secretariat preparing for the Bretton Woods conference, derived the quota formula.) The original equation (with all data measured in U.S. dollars) may be written as

$$Q = 0.09 * (0.2Y + 0.5R + M + V) * (1 + X/Y),$$

where Q = the member's quota; Y = national income in 1940; R = gold and dollars held on July 1, 1943; M = average annual imports, 1934–38; and V = maximum variation in exports (X), 1934–38 (i.e., the difference between the highest and lowest of the five annual values).

[25]The revised and reduced Bretton Woods formula was

$$Q = (0.01Y' + 0.025R' + 0.05M' + 0.2276V')*(1 + X'/Y'),$$

where Y' was measured by GDP rather than national income, R' was measured by more comprehensive data on international reserves, M' and X' were expanded to include services and other current account payments and receipts, and variability (V') was redefined to better reflect volatility:

$$V' = \sqrt{\left(\sum_{t=3}^{11} (X'_t - \bar{X}'_t)^2\right)/3}$$

where $\bar{X}'$ is a five-year moving average of X'.

Until the Eighth Review, two versions of the reduced equation were used, one with the original data definitions and the other with these more inclusive variables. See de Vries (1985), pp. 514–17.

What did the Bretton Woods formula, as previously revised and "reduced," imply about the overall adequacy of quotas for the early 1980s? The previous review had been based on data through 1976, and when the staff began its work data were available through 1979. During those three years, world trade had grown by a little over 50 percent, while incomes and reserves had grown by a little less than 50 percent (all measured in SDRs, without adjustment for inflation). The reduced Bretton Woods formula implied that quotas should be raised by 50 to 80 percent to restore the relationship between actual and calculated quotas established for the Seventh Review, depending on the selection of data for the computations; by 140 to nearly 200 percent to make actual quotas equal to the calculated total;[26] and by some 350 percent to make them equal to the total derived from the original 1944 formula.[27]

Even the bottom end of this range of estimates suggested that a substantial increase was in order, and few thought that the calculations overstated the case. As the demand for stand-by and extended credit arrangements grew in 1979 and 1980, the Fund had to borrow from creditor countries to finance its operations (see below, p. 884–85). All those involved in the review agreed that borrowing by the Fund was a temporary expedient, that the debts already incurred should be repaid as quickly as possible, and that quotas should remain the primary source of financing for Fund lending. Assuming that demand for Fund resources would remain strong, management and most Executive Directors viewed an increase in quotas by something close to 100 percent as a high priority that had to be addressed with some urgency.

A second and equally clear message from these initial calculations was that the actual distribution of quotas no longer bore a clear relationship to calculated values. After normalizing the calculated values on the actual total, eight countries had quotas that were less than half the calculated value; eight others had quotas that were more than four times the calculated value; and only 26 countries out of 140 were within 20 percent of the adjusted calculated quota.[28] These massive anomalies resulted from the practice of awarding almost all members at least the agreed minimum percentage increase and making only a limited number of selective increases at each review. Rather than revising the distribution of quotas every five years in response to shifts in the distribution of income, trade, and finance, the Fund had favored inertia.

The Executive Board's work on the Eighth Review began in July 1981, at which time de Larosière set the agenda on the basis of these initial findings. In his view, a "substantial increase in quotas was warranted," and quotas were so "far out of line" with reality that a "significant adjustment in relative positions" was also needed. Although most members of the Executive Board concurred with those assessments from the outset, the opening remark by Donald Syvrud (Alternate—

---

[26]Actual quotas under the Seventh Review were just 59 percent of the total calculated from the reduced Bretton Woods equation.

[27]"Eighth General Review of Quotas—Quota Calculations," SM/81/151 (July 2, 1981), pp. 7–8.

[28]"Present and Calculated Quotas," SM/81/91 (April 23, 1981), pp. 6–10.

United States) was that "the United States does not agree that, at the present time, a substantial increase is warranted."[29]

This initial negotiating position by the United States was noteworthy, because the history of quota reviews shows that the effective constraint on general increases is the consent of the Fund's major shareholders. For most countries, any costs or drawbacks of a quota increase—for themselves, the Fund, or the international monetary system—are greatly outweighed by the benefits. For a few of the largest creditor countries, the calculus is more complex, because they supply the bulk of the Fund's lendable resources. The U.S. position, of course, is predominant in this calculus, because the United States has always held veto power over quota increases (which, as noted above, require an 85 percent majority in the voting by the Board of Governors).

Detailed discussions followed throughout the rest of 1981 and all of 1982,[30] primarily on the two questions of how large the overall increase should be and how it should be distributed. On the question of the optimum overall increase, the staff produced a large number of calculations under different assumptions, which yielded a bewildering array of results. All calculations suggested that quotas should be increased substantially, and a few methods indicated that quotas should be raised severalfold.[31] The bottom line, however, was that the indicators of the determinants of demand for Fund resources had increased, on average, by about 16–17 percent a year. Over five years, quotas would have to rise by about 80 percent to keep pace. Taking account of estimates that the starting point was precariously low added anywhere from 20 to a few hundred percentage points to that figure. Everyone involved understood that a political agreement on doubling the Fund's resources would be extremely difficult, especially since the U.S. administration of President Reagan was then opposing any substantial increase. Technical discussions on whether quotas should rise by 100 percent or by much more took up a lot of staff and Board time in 1981 and 1982 but were essentially meaningless for the eventual outcome.

Technical work on the optimum distribution of quotas focused on the implications of a large number of auxiliary or "derivative" equations.[32] Although the Bretton Woods formula was accorded a central position in the exercise because of its historical role in determining the initial distribution, both the staff and many Directors wanted to examine the consequences of changing the relative weights as-

---

[29]Minutes of the Executive Board Committee of the Whole on Review of Quotas, Meeting 81/1 [hereinafter given in the form EBCQM/81/1] (July 27, 1981), p. 5 (de Larosière); and EBCQM/81/2 (same date), p. 15 (Syvrud).

[30]In May 1981, the Interim Committee asked for "intensified" work on increasing quotas but did not set a date for completion of the review. In July, the Executive Board established a "Committee of the Whole on Review of Quotas," which enabled Directors to debate the issues more freely than in a formal Board meeting. Discussions on the Eighth Review took place in that forum until the time came for final decisions.

[31]See, in particular, "Eighth General Review of Quotas—Quota Calculations," SM/81/151 (July 2, 1981) and "Eighth General Review of Quotas—Calculated Quotas," EB/CQuota/82/4 (April 7, 1982).

[32]The added equations were termed "derivative" because they were normalized to produce the same aggregate result as the Bretton Woods formula.

signed to the various determining factors (income, trade, reserves, and the volatility of trade).[33] After the first few months of discussions, more than 30 equations were being used to generate alternative lists of prospective quotas. Much of the later debate in the Board involved ways to reduce that number. The nature of that process is illustrated by the discussions on the key variable: the role of variability in international trade.

The case for including trade variability as a determinant of quotas was that fluctuations in export receipts affected a country's need for financial assistance from the Fund. Countries with above-average variability might need relatively large quotas to cover their balance of payments requirements. That case had been weakened over time by the establishment of the Compensatory Financing Facility (CFF) as a separate means of covering such fluctuations and by exempting CFF drawings from the conventional limits on access to Fund resources (see Chapter 15 and the section below on access policies). Moreover, in practice the link between variability and demand for Fund resources was not all that strong, and some Directors saw this variable as a source of distortion in the distribution. The staff accordingly specified some equations and generated some alternative quota lists based on a reduced or eliminated role for the variability term. That exercise concluded that the main effect would be to redistribute quotas from major oil-exporting countries to industrial countries.[34] A majority of the Board favored doing so, but the Managing Director attempted to dissuade them from pursuing the idea, primarily on the grounds that the oil-exporting countries at the time were important contributors to the supply of liquid assets to the Fund.[35] After further discussion, Executive Directors accepted a compromise proposed by A.R.G. Prowse (Australia) in which variability played a somewhat smaller role in the derivative equations than it had in previous reviews.[36]

In the end, the Board decided to use four derivative equations along with the reduced Bretton Woods formula (see Appendix III).[37] Relative to the Bretton

---

[33]The use of auxiliary equations began in the early 1960s, when derivative equations with relatively high coefficients on the variability of international trade were used to justify a shift in the distribution of quotas toward developing countries. See Horsefield (1969), Vol. 1, pp. 537–38.

[34]This effect was a consequence of the mathematical property that a large jump in export receipts—such as occurred twice for oil exporters in the 1970s—registered in the formulas as high variability. Variability had the same effect on the calculations regardless of whether it raised or lowered the country's current account balance.

[35]". . . one has to bear in mind the impact of any modification to the definition of variability on the calculated quotas and what effect this would have on the liquidity of the Fund." Minutes of EBCQM/81/4 (October 16, 1981), p. 25.

[36]For the initial review of the issue, see "Variability in the Quota Formulas," EB/CQuota/81/2 (August 11, 1981) and minutes of EBCQM/81/3–4 (October 16, 1981). For the follow-up, see "Variability in the Quota Formulas—Further Considerations," EB/CQuota/82/7 (May 6, 1982) and minutes of EBCQM/82/7–8 (June 4, 1982).

[37]For the five formulas, see "Eighth General Review of Quotas—Calculated Quotas," EB/CQuota/82/11 (November 24, 1982), p. 3. On the discussion and selection of the formulas, see EB/CQuota/82/7, Sup. 1 (June 14, 1982), Appendix I, pp. 19–24; and minutes of EBCQM/82/9–10 (June 23, 1982), EBCQM/82/11–12 (August 4, 1982) and EBCQM/82/13 (August 13, 1982).

Woods equation, the alternatives all gave a smaller weight to GDP and a larger weight to variability. The weights on the other variables were made both smaller and larger in the various equations, and two equations removed the nonlinear term (the ratio of exports to income). The agreed procedure was to compute the notional "calculated quota" as the higher of (1) the quota from the reduced Bretton Woods formula and (2) the simple mean of the two lowest values from the four derivative formulas.

Resolution of the two issues—the size of the overall increase and the distribution of quotas among member countries—was closely linked, since quotas could be changed only in one direction.[38] Without a general increase, no redistribution was possible; the larger the increase, the more (in principle) could be accomplished on improving the distribution by allocating increases selectively. The idea emerged during these discussions of first deciding on the appropriate size of the overall increase and then dividing it between two categories: an equiproportional increase for all members and selective increases for members (or groups of members) with quotas that were particularly low relative to calculated values. Determining those two numbers—the total and the ratio—took the debate beyond technicalities and into politics.

A third, more technical issue, also had to be settled: the form in which members would be required to pay their quota increases. Article III of the Fund's Articles of Agreement specifies that 25 percent of any increase is to be paid in SDRs, unless the Board of Governors prescribes that payment may be made, in whole or in part, in currencies specified by the Fund. For the Sixth General Review, in 1978, members were given the option of paying in currencies, and most did so. For the Seventh, in 1980, in the midst of a series of new allocations of SDRs, members were required to pay in SDRs.[39] The Fund sought to maintain a reasonable balance between SDRs and major currencies in its own portfolio, for reasons related to liquidity, ease of operations, promotion of the SDR as a reserve asset, and avoidance of unusually large or small holdings of a particular currency or of SDRs. In general, the Fund regarded SDRs as more liquid than individual currencies, so the principal issue was whether requiring payment in SDRs would lead to a shortage of SDRs available to member countries. The staff paper on this issue concluded that a shortage could result, and it recommended that countries be given the option to pay in currencies unless a decision was taken to allocate additional SDRs. The Executive Board, however, could not readily reach a consensus on the issue. A majority preferred to use it as a lever to argue for fur-

---

[38]Article III of the Fund's charter specifies that quotas can be changed only with the consent of the member. Normally, countries have no incentive to request or accept a reduction. Even before the Second Amendment of the Articles, when a quota increase required a transfer of real assets, only one country (Honduras in 1948) ever requested a reduction in its quota. See Horsefield (1969), Vol. 1, p. 196; and Gold (1972), p. 17n.

[39]A few member countries at that time were not participants in the SDR Department; they were required to pay in specified currencies. As noted above, the requirement for participants to pay in SDRs was a critical element of the package proposal under which SDR allocations were approved for 1979–81; see de Vries (1985), pp. 880–82.

ther allocations, but others were prepared to resist that linkage strenuously (see Chapter 18).[40]

By the spring of 1982, technical work had proceeded far enough that the locus of the Eighth Review began to shift to the political arena. In the first substantive report on the Review to the Interim Committee, which was to meet in Helsinki in May 1982, the Managing Director noted that the "staff analysis" suggested that "roughly a doubling of present quotas would be required . . . to meet the justified demands on the Fund's resources that are expected to prevail in late 1984." The Executive Board, however, had not reached a consensus on whether that figure was too large (as argued by a few creditor countries) or too small (as argued by some potential borrowers). Similarly, no consensus had been reached on how extensive a redistribution would be desirable, nor on whether to revise the methodology for calculating quotas.[41] In those last few months before the onset of the international debt crisis, some of the largest creditors were still focused primarily on what they perceived to be a need for restraint in the Fund's lending activities, not on the need for additional resources to finance expanded lending.

Divisions ran equally deep in the Interim Committee, and ministers showed no inclination to try to break the impasse by themselves. They issued a communiqué endorsing once more the idea of an adequate increase in quotas, asking the Executive Board to give the matter a high priority, and noting that they "hoped" to be able to resolve the main issues at their next meeting, less than four months hence, in Toronto.

After several more meetings during the summer, the Board reported back to the Interim Committee. The report for the Toronto meeting noted the agreement on the five-formula method for calculating notional quotas, as described above. On the more substantive issues, however, consensus was still elusive.[42] The Committee responded by suggesting more firmly that these issues should be resolved by the time of its next meeting, which was scheduled to take place in April 1983.

By this time the squeezing of the Fund's resources was getting serious. A little more than a year remained before the Board of Governors would have to approve a resolution completing the Eighth Review, but it was not clear whether the Fund could continue to meet the demand for credit without a quota increase or at least new borrowing. The eruption of the debt crisis and the consequent traumas of Toronto (see Chapter 7) had pressed home the fact that creditor countries needed the Fund—and the money they had invested in the Fund—to resolve the crisis. Mexico, Brazil, and Argentina soon would have major Fund-supported programs, and several more sizable credit arrangements were in the pipeline. A quota increase now appeared to be in everyone's interest.

[40]"Eighth General Review of Quotas—Payment for Increases in Quotas," EB/CQuota/82/14 (December 17, 1982); and minutes of EBCQM/82/20 (December 22, 1982).

[41]"Eighth General Review of Quotas—Report of the Executive Board to the Interim Committee," ICMS/Doc/82/2 (April 27, 1982).

[42]"Eighth General Review of Quotas—Report of the Executive Board to the Interim Committee," ICMS/Doc/82/7 (August 25, 1982).

Resolving the problem was still not easy. The Board again took up the question of the appropriate size of the Fund on November 10, 1982. All Directors now agreed that an increase was needed and that the Review should be concluded as quickly as possible. If they could agree on the overall size, it would be desirable to advance the date of the next Interim Committee meeting to bring the review to a successful conclusion. All but three Directors agreed that quotas should be at least doubled, to a minimum of SDR 120 billion, but the three dissidents were among the largest creditors to the Fund. The governments of Germany and the United Kingdom supported the idea of at least a 50 percent increase but were not prepared to commit themselves to a much larger amount, and the U.S. government was unwilling to commit to any figure at all. The U.S. reluctance stemmed from the usual political difficulty, that congress would have to approve legislation to authorize the increase and to appropriate funds for it. The administration was just beginning a long process of lobbying and bargaining with members of congress, and it did not want to set a number that could become a target for opponents.[43]

Within a few weeks of that meeting, the dispute over the size of the increase in quotas began to narrow. When the Deputies of the Group of Ten (G-10) met in Paris just before the end of the month to prepare for a meeting of their finance ministers, they agreed that the issue should be resolved very quickly and that the Interim Committee should meet earlier than next April to reach a final agreement. By December 8, when the ministers of the more exclusive Group of Five (G-5) gathered for an ostensibly secret meeting at the Schloss Friedrichshoff castle in Kronberg, Germany (see Chapter 4, p. 196), the rapidly deteriorating financial status of Brazil further galvanized creditors into action. The U.S. Secretary of the Treasury, Donald T. Regan, was thought by at least some participants to have agreed to support a quota increase of close to 50 percent. In the interest of getting a compromise on the table, those who had been seeking to double the total decided to give up that goal. G-10 ministers met the next day in Paris, confirmed the compromise, and made the agreement known to the press.[44]

Despite the apparent G-10 agreement, the Executive Board continued to be split, with the U.S. chair still unwilling to support an increase larger than around 40 percent (to SDR 85 billion) and several Directors adhering to the goal of doubling quotas to SDR 125 billion. The staff provided additional calculations suggesting that an increase to at least SDR 95 billion was needed to prevent recourse to further borrowing by the Fund. On the distribution, a consensus was forming around the idea of devoting a portion of the overall increase to an equiproportional increase for all members and using the rest to move actual quotas partway toward those calculated on the basis of the agreed formulas. Debate continued, however,

---

[43]That case was set out by Richard D. Erb (Executive Director, United States) at EBCQM/82/14 (November 10, 1982), pp. 4–5.

[44]See Paul Lewis, "Bigger Loan Fund Gets Key Support," *New York Times* (December 11, 1982), p. 42. Regan had mentioned the G-5 meeting to reporters two days before it was to take place, so the usual secrecy was broken. As the host minister, Gerhard Stoltenberg gave a background debriefing for reporters after the meeting. Also see Stoltenberg (1997), pp. 314–15.

on how large the general increase should be and (as a corollary) how large the "adjustment coefficient" (the fraction of the gap to be closed between actual and calculated quotas) should be.[45]

If the Executive Board had taken a decision at the end of 1982 on the basis of a simple majority, it would have voted to raise quotas to SDR 125 billion, with as much as half being distributed equiproportionally among all members and with a small amount being set aside to raise the quotas of countries with extremely small quotas.[46] The final decision, however, rested in the hands of the governors, who had to agree with an 85 percent majority. After 41 meetings over nearly two full years and consideration of some 34 staff papers, the Executive Board still could not reach that degree of consensus.

The February 1983 meeting of the Interim Committee was eventful, even dramatic, in several respects. It was the first time that the committee had scheduled an early meeting to resolve a prickly issue, and it was doing so at a time when many developing countries and even the international financial system were still in crisis. Not only the quota increase but also a major increase in lending to the Fund (see below) was at stake, and the outcome was far from certain. As the meeting progressed on the first day (Thursday, February 10), Regan tried to hold the quota increase to 40 percent, which prompted several governors from indebted countries to revert to their calls for a minimum acceptable increase of 100 percent. To add an extra comedic drama to the scene, that evening Washington was buried under its worst winter blizzard in several years—a storm that de Larosière later remembered in an interview as "of Shakespearean dimensions." Transportation was suddenly frozen, and, for many governors, just getting to and from the meetings was already an achievement. (See, for example, Howe, 1994, pp. 272–73.)

On the quota review, responding to the diplomacy of the chairman—Geoffrey Howe, Chancellor of the Exchequer in the United Kingdom—the governors on the Committee reached agreement on most of the key issues during a snow-bound dinner on Thursday at the F Street Club near Fund headquarters. The next day, at the end of two marathon days of discussions, the Committee formally settled the

---

[45]The agreed procedure imposed the constraint that each member would receive a quota increase composed of an equiproportional increase (i.e., every member would receive this percentage increase) and a selective increase expressed as the product of a constant adjustment coefficient and the ratio of actual to calculated quota. The second term would vary between countries, and the range of possible coefficients was restricted to guarantee that each member would receive an increase in the amount of its quota. As shown mathematically in Appendix III, that constraint implied that a large adjustment coefficient required a large increase in quotas. For the issues in the debate, see minutes of EBCQM/82/18–19 (December 21, 1982) and "Eighth General Review of Quotas—Report of the Executive Board to the Interim Committee," ICMS/Doc/83/2 (January 14, 1983). For the derivation described in Appendix III, see "Ninth General Review of Quotas—Issues Arising in Connection with the Eighth General Review of Quotas," EB/CQuota/87/4 (December 21, 1987), Appendix II.

[46]From 1955 to 1965, the Fund had a policy of setting a minimum level for quotas. That policy eventually was seen as distorting relationships between very small and slightly larger countries, and it eventually was dropped. Restoration of some form of minimum then became a perennial topic during discussions on quota reviews. See "A Review of Fund Policies on Minimum Quotas," EB/CQuota/82/12 (December 13, 1982).

matter. On the overall size, ministers agreed to raise quotas by 47.5 percent, to SDR 90 billion ($99 billion). That amount was not expected to alleviate the Fund from seeking new loans, but it was as much as the U.S. authorities were prepared to ask congress to approve. On distribution, the Committee agreed that 40 percent of the increase (SDR 11.6 billion) was to be allocated in proportion to existing quotas. The remainder (SDR 17.4 billion) was to be allocated in proportion to calculated quotas. Under this compromise, the non-oil developing countries lost about 1.7 percentage points in voting power, but they would have lost another point if all the increase had been allocated according to calculated quotas. Industrial and major oil-exporting countries reaped the gains in roughly equal shares.[47] On the method of payment, they agreed that the reserve-asset portion of the increase (25 percent of the total) was to be paid either in SDRs or in usable currencies.

One issue—minor from a global perspective but very important to a few countries—could not be resolved by the committee, owing to objections from major creditor countries: how to adjust the quotas of the smallest member countries so as to give them a meaningful share in the total without upsetting relative positions. At the suggestion of Cesar E.A. Virata (Prime Minister and Minister of Finance of the Philippines), the issue was remanded to the Executive Board for a decision. In doing so, the committee signaled clearly that it wanted an adjustment that would improve the situation of the smallest countries. Nonetheless, the stalemate in the Board continued. After lengthy discussion spread over two days of meetings, Directors essentially gave up trying to find a substantive solution. Since lip service still had to be given to the problem, de Larosière proposed that the 17 quotas that were below SDR 10 million be rounded up to the next 0.5 million; all other quotas were to be rounded up only to the next 0.1 million. That suggestion was readily embraced, and the matter was closed until the next review.[48]

To expedite the completion of the process and ensure that the increases were likely to take effect before the end of the year, the Board set the participation requirement at 70 percent (reduced from 75 percent in the Seventh Review). That figure would be a little easier to reach without the participation of the United States, and it was hoped that this fact would expedite U.S. approval.[49] By autumn,

---

[47]These effects are based on a starting position in which Saudi Arabia had already received a large ad hoc quota increase after the completion of the Seventh Review. As shown in Table 17.3, the distribution between industrial and developing countries shifted very little from the end of the Seventh to the end of the Eighth Review.

[48]See "Eighth General Review of Quotas—Proposed Maximum Quotas," EB/CQuota/83/4 (February 17, 1983) and the minutes of EBCQM/83/1–2 (February 24) and EBCQM/83/3 (February 25). The effects of the adjustment were distributed randomly among the 17 countries. It raised only 11 quotas, by a total of SDR 2.5 million. The smallest quota (Maldives) was unaffected, as it rose from SDR 1.4 million to 2.0 million both before and after the special adjustment.

[49]As noted above, a participation requirement—consents expressed as a percentage of initial quotas—was normally proposed by the Executive Board for each quota review on the basis of strategic considerations. Of the five general increases prior to the Eighth Review, three required 75 percent, one required 67 percent, and one contained no percentage requirement. On the background of the participation requirement, see "Eighth General Review of Quotas—Draft Report and Resolution," EB/CQuota/83/3 (February 17, 1983), p. 2. The views of Executive Directors are summarized in the minutes of EBCQM/83/2 (February 24), p. 4.

however, it was beginning to look as if the Reagan administration might not be able to muster enough votes to get the quota increase through the U.S. Congress. The proposal was attacked from the left by those who saw it as a bailout for commercial banks that had lent profligately to uncreditworthy developing countries and by those who seized the opportunity to wrest unrelated political concessions from the administration. It was also attacked from the right by those who saw it as a bailout for indebted countries with excessive governmental intervention in their economies. Approval of the quota legislation would require even more political muscle than its 1980 predecessor.

As described in the introduction to this chapter, the impasse in the U.S. Congress led de Larosière to impose a partial freeze on new lending by the Fund, and it spurred President Reagan to undertake a strong personal campaign to elicit support. Finally, the bill won sufficient support in November 1983, after it was attached to legislation authorizing several billion dollars for investments in domestic public housing projects. That linkage created a package of two dissimilar and controversial measures, which as a combination could receive more votes than either measure would have garnered separately.

The quota increases took effect on November 30, 1983, with 122 out of 146 member countries having consented. Those countries held 72 percent of the initial quotas. The United States had not yet formally consented, but congress had approved the necessary legislation several days earlier. As of December 1, consents totaled 131 (96½ percent of the total). Eleven stragglers accepted by the final deadline of mid-March 1984, and the Eighth Review was completed. That left four countries without an increase. As in the Seventh Review, no increase had been proposed for Cambodia (Democratic Kampuchea), with which the Fund still had no formal channel of communications. Three countries—Iran, Singapore, and the United Arab Emirates—declined the increases that had been proposed.

All that remained was for each member to pay in the reserve portion (one-fourth) of its increase, either in SDRs or in currencies acceptable to the Fund. Almost all of that was paid in SDRs, and payments were completed before the end of April 1984. The world still faced a debt crisis, and the Fund was about to be confronted with a quagmire of arrears, but for the moment its liquidity crisis had been resolved.[50]

---

[50]Payments of the reserve-asset portion of the quota increases totaled SDR 7 billion. Of that, less than SDR 1 billion was paid in currencies rather than SDRs; *Annual Report 1984*, p. 75. Out of 142 consenting members, 126 paid entirely in SDRs. Eleven paid in foreign exchange, and five paid in a combination of the two. The bulk of the currency payment was shared equally by the deutsche mark and the Japanese yen, with relatively small amounts paid in U.S. dollars and pounds sterling. A bookkeeping arrangement enabled 39 low-income countries to enlarge their quotas without actually paying in scarce reserves (see above, p. 855). Those countries borrowed SDRs from 11 members with large SDR holdings to cover their reserve-asset subscriptions. They simultaneously drew their reserve tranche position from the Fund and used the proceeds to repay the loan. No interest or commission was charged on those transactions.

Ninth General Review

The quotas established in the Eighth Review were maintained for nearly nine years, the longest period without an increase since the 1950s. Work on the Ninth Review began on schedule in 1987, but it proceeded at a leisurely pace because some of the major creditors again started with a view that the Fund had adequate resources for the near future. Then, in the same way that the international debt crisis spurred creditors to raise the Fund's resources in 1983, the ending of Soviet control over Eastern Europe and then the collapse of the Soviet Union itself provided the impetus for raising Fund quotas in the early 1990s.[51]

Normal Fund procedure called for the Executive Board to appoint a Committee of the Whole to begin work on the review about four years after the governors approved completion of the last one, with the goal of maintaining a five-year cycle. The Board took that first step in March 1987, but it did so without much hope of reaching the end of the path in time. The U.S. governor, Treasury Secretary James A. Baker III, used the occasion of the April Interim Committee meeting to express doubts about the need for an increase. ("We believe it is neither financially necessary nor politically feasible to reach an early conclusion to the Ninth Quota Review.")[52] Most other creditors were also prepared to wait, and neither of the Interim Committee communiqués of 1987 encouraged the Executive Board to give the matter much priority.[53]

Faced with high-level insouciance, the Board confronted a choice between extending its work on the review beyond the deadline—possibly for years—or concluding the review without a recommended increase and waiting for the next five-year cycle. Most Directors wanted to maintain some momentum toward an increase, and they agreed to keep working on that basis. They held meeting after meeting (as the Committee of the Whole) and eventually had to extend their work from the original deadline of March 1988, first to April 1989, then to December, then to the following March, and finally to June 1990 when the governors approved their recommendation for a general increase of 50 percent. Not until November 1992, however, would the increases take effect.

To start the discussion, the staff looked at how the determinants of the notional "calculated quotas" had changed during the interval of five years.[54] Foreign exchange reserves had grown at an annual rate of 3¼ percent, nominal world

---

[51]This pattern was repeated in 1998, when concurrent financial crises throughout East Asia and in Russia finally induced a reluctant U.S. Congress to approve a general quota increase only after a long delay.

[52]IMF/CF; Interim Committee Master File. Verbatim transcript of First Session, p. 31.

[53]"The Committee urged Executive Directors to pursue their work on the Ninth General Review of Quotas so as to be in a position to make appropriate recommendations in due course." Communiqué (September 28, 1987), para. 7.

[54]Collecting macroeconomic and financial data for all member countries inevitably involves lags. The calculated quotas for the Eighth Review were based on 1980 data, and the Ninth Review was based on 1985.

GDP at 7½ percent, trade at 9½ percent, and the variability of trade at 10½ percent.[55] Using the formulas agreed upon for the Eighth Review, these changes—accumulated over five years—increased the aggregate of calculated quotas by 57 percent (from SDR 209 billion to 329 billion) and implied that quotas would have to be nearly quadrupled (from SDR 90 billion) to reach the calculated level.[56]

Notwithstanding the lack of consensus in the Interim Committee, most constituencies responded positively to these findings and favored increasing quotas. As early as September 1987, all but two Executive Directors expressed implicit or explicit support for at least a 50 percent increase, and several argued for a doubling or more. The two exceptions represented the countries with the largest quotas. The U.S. Director (Charles H. Dallara) maintained that the case for a quota increase had not been established, and the U.K. Director (Timothy P. Lankester) maintained that only a minimal increase was warranted.[57]

In addition to citing the obvious fact that quotas had fallen (and were continuing to fall) in relation to world trade and other relevant variables, those who argued for a major increase stressed the implications for the demand for Fund resources of the international debt crisis, the large imbalances among the major industrial countries, and the uncertainties caused by such global imbalances as the sharp declines in primary commodity prices. In response, the U.S. and British resistance stemmed from several arguments. First, these Directors noted that the standard calculations of the Fund's liquidity position allowed for drawings by industrial countries. Since those countries seemed unlikely to draw on Fund resources in the foreseeable future, the Fund could, in their view, take a less conservative approach to its liquidity needs. Second, they wanted the Fund to be more cautious in lending to heavily indebted countries that could ill afford to take on new debts, especially in view of the still-growing problem of arrears to the Fund. Third, they believed that developing countries could obtain more credits from other lenders if the Fund concentrated more on helping countries design adjustment programs and less on lending them money. In other words, the Fund could give greater emphasis to its catalytic role. Fourth, the ESAF—which was just beginning to play a significant role in providing concessional loans to low-income countries—could be

---

[55]The formula for measuring variability of trade (see Appendix III) was not normalized. To a first approximation, with no change in the frequency distribution, trade (X') and variability (V') would rise at the same rate. The increase in the variability of trade from 1980 to 1985 was due primarily to the large declines in prices of many primary commodities, including petroleum. Over the period, this "variability" reduced the trade balances of most developing countries and raised those of most industrial countries. The data, however, were applied symmetrically and served to raise the calculated quotas of both groups.

[56]"Ninth General Review of Quotas—Quota Calculation," EB/CQuota/87/1 (June 5, 1987), pp. 5 and 11.

[57]Executive Directors' positions as of September 1987 were summarized by the Managing Director at EBCQM/87/4 (September 17, 1987), pp. 3–5. Lankester's and Dallara's positions were stated at EBCQM/87/3 (same date), pp. 21–24.

expected to take some of the pressure off the Fund's own resources in coming years.

The first real break in these positions came in March 1989 with the announcement of the Brady Plan for relieving the debt burdens of developing countries (Chapter 11). U.S. Treasury Secretary Nicholas Brady (who had replaced Baker a few months earlier), in announcing the plan, signaled a willingness to consider a quota increase "before the end of the year" to help finance the Fund's role in implementing it. He was, however, still unwilling to propose an amount that the United States would be prepared to accept.

The next movement came in November, within days of the opening of the Berlin Wall. The Fund already was considering stand-by arrangements for Hungary and Poland, and the likelihood was rising that other European countries would soon be joining the Fund and requesting financial support. In recognition of the demands that would be placed on the Fund in that event, the U.S. Director (Thomas C. Dawson II) informed his colleagues that the administration was prepared to support a quota increase of up to 35 percent. That level, though, was well below what most others regarded as a bare minimum under the circumstances. Exceptionally, the Saudi Arabian Director (Yusuf A. Nimatallah) averred that even the U.S. suggestion would be "more than sufficient," and the U.K. Director (Frank Cassell) indicated that it was about as much as his authorities could be persuaded to accept. Everyone else (19 Directors, with 70 percent of the voting power) judged that a doubling of quotas was desirable and that an increase of two-thirds was the minimum that was needed, in view of the new demands on the Fund and the delays in concluding the review.[58]

The third step toward resolving the debate came in March 1990. All three of the holdouts then indicated that they could go along with a 50 percent increase, as did most of those who had wanted a much larger increase. Dawson initially tied his acceptance to a request that the next review be postponed, but that idea was resisted and was dropped from the report sent to the Board of Governors. In June 1990, the governors approved the report, which called for a 50 percent increase in quotas, to SDR 135 billion ($177 billion).[59]

As a general issue, the distribution of the increases across the membership was handled with much less controversy than in the Eighth Review. At the outset, Di-

---

[58]Doubling the stock of quotas would have added SDR 90 billion. An increase of two-thirds represented 60 billion; a 50 percent increase, 45 billion. Dawson's position called for an increase of 32 billion, and Nimatallah expressed a preference for 25 billion. Minutes of EBM/89/154 (November 28, 1989).

[59]The final quid pro quo for U.S. approval of the increase under the Ninth Review was adoption of the Third Amendment of the Articles, which provided for the suspension of voting and related rights of countries with arrears to the Fund that were found not to be cooperating toward resolving the problem (see Chapter 16). Adoption of the Amendment delayed the implementation of the quota increase until November 1992. Work on the Tenth Review eventually was extended beyond its original 1993 deadline. In 1995, the review was concluded without any proposal for an increase, and work began immediately on the Eleventh. A resolution to conclude that review was approved by the Board of Governors in January 1998, with an increase of 45 percent (to SDR 212 billion, approximately $287 billion).

rectors agreed not to fiddle any more with the formulas.[60] They acknowledged that, despite the progress made in the last round, some quotas were still seriously out of line, but they preferred to continue to tackle the problem gradually and with the same tools. The "calculated quotas" therefore were measured as before, and the increases were to be distributed in the same manner but in reversed proportions (60 percent in proportion to existing quotas and 40 percent in proportion to the calculated values).

One new issue had arisen since the previous review: how to treat countries that were in arrears in their payments to the Fund. After some discussion of the possibility of denying increases to such countries (which could have led to complicated procedures after arrears were settled), the Board accepted a staff recommendation to treat the problem as a technical matter involving the prescribed order of payments. That is, a member country would not be allowed to pay for a quota increase until it had repaid any overdue obligations to the Fund's General Resources Account. If arrears were not settled within a limited time frame, the proposed increases would lapse.[61]

The most difficult distributional issue involved a high-profile political battle among the major industrial countries. In January 1988, the Japanese Executive Director (Koji Yamazaki) argued that "the distribution of Fund quotas" was "unjustified" and was "clearly inconsistent with world economic realities."[62] Japan's share in Fund quotas (then 4.7 percent) was among those that were most below calculated levels, and Yamazaki had an unassailable argument that his country's share should be raised substantially. He continued to press the case, as did the finance minister (Kiichi Miyazawa) at the Interim Committee. Japan had begun to play a substantial role as a Fund creditor and provider of official development assistance, which gave the authorities a strong bargaining position. In April 1989, the Interim Committee implicitly acknowledged the point by agreeing that "the size and distribution of any quota increase should take into account changes in . . .

---

[60]The most serious effort to change the formulas was made by Arjun K. Sengupta (India), who made the case that an index of each country's poverty should be included as a determinant of quotas. That argument was resisted on the grounds that the Fund had other means of providing special assistance to low-income countries and that a shift in the distribution of quotas toward poor countries would weaken the benefits of the increase for the Fund's liquidity. See "Some Issues Relating to Criteria for Determining IMF Quotas—A Technical Note," EB/CQuota/88/4 (March 9, 1988), and minutes of EBCQM/88/3–4 (March 14, 1988). Also see the staff evaluation, in "Ninth General Review of Quotas—Review of a Technical Note on Some Issues Relating to Criteria for Determining Fund Quotas," EB/CQuota/88/9 (October 28, 1988), and minutes of EBCQM/88/10–11 (November 18, 1988).

[61]Minutes of EBCQM/88/4 (March 14, 1988), p. 16. In its final form, this rule specified that a country would not be allowed to consent to or pay for the increase until it had settled its arrears to the GRA. See Board of Governors Resolution No. 45–2 (June 28, 1990); in *Annual Report 1990*, p. 103. As a result of that provision, despite multiple extensions of the allowed period, five countries could not consent to the increases proposed under the Ninth Review: Iraq, Liberia, Somalia, Sudan, and Zaïre (Democratic Republic of the Congo). Four others settled their arrears and consented after the general increase took effect: Haiti, Peru, Vietnam, and Zambia.

[62]Minutes of EBCQM/88/1 (January 11, 1988), p. 3.

members' relative positions in the world economy" since the previous review (communiqué, para. 5; also see Chapter 11, footnote 11, p. 480).

Although Japan's request was viewed sympathetically, it raised two interrelated problems. First, the quota shares of all other members would be reduced proportionally, and the size of the shift would have to be substantial to make a real difference to Japan's position in the Fund. Everyone agreed that reducing the aggregate quota share of developing countries to "pay for" the Japanese request should be avoided if possible. Second, raising Japan's share would require downward adjustments to the hierarchical positions of some other major industrial countries. Japan's quota was the fifth largest, but by any measure it should have been second only to the United States. To raise it to that level without other changes would mean lowering the United Kingdom, Germany, and France (then ranked second through fourth) by one notch. The U.K. quota, however, was most clearly overstated, because the British economy had declined in relative importance since Bretton Woods. Discussions therefore focused on ways to adjust quotas among the major industrial countries to achieve a more modern balance.

The key to both issues was for the United Kingdom to absorb the lion's share of the increase in the Japanese quota. In December 1989, Cassell reported that the U.K. authorities were prepared to reduce the increase in the U.K. quota by enough to eliminate the decreases that would otherwise be forced on developing countries.[63] The effect of that concession was that about half of the effect would be absorbed by the United Kingdom and half by other industrial countries. Germany would then remain in third position, Britain would drop to fourth, and France would drop to fifth. That proposal went a long way toward solving the problem, but the French authorities refused to accept the proposed drop in their position.[64]

Trying to resolve what was rapidly becoming an acrimonious and very public fight between two major countries (the United Kingdom and France) placed Executive Directors in an awkward position (to say the least). In January 1990, the Board agreed reluctantly to allow the distribution of G-7 quotas to be decided outside the institution, by that group alone. In effect, the Board would agree on an aggregate G-7 quota, based on the procedures being applied uniformly to all members, and then would ratify an internal G-7 agreement on the distribution. That solution was inelegant, and several Directors worried about setting a precedent for future decisions, but it was the only way out.

The G-7 finance ministers agreed on a solution at the beginning of May 1990. Showing exceptional delicacy, they decided that Germany and Japan should have equal quotas (6.1 percent of total Fund quotas for each country), second to the United States (19.6 percent), and (as a compromise proposed by the French authorities) that France and the United Kingdom should also have equal quotas (5.5

---

[63]Minutes of EBCQM/89/16 (December 20, 1989), p. 5.

[64]Letter from the Pierre Bérégovoy (Minister of Economy, Finance, and Budget for France) to Camdessus (May 2, 1990), in IMF/CF (S 1230 "Ninth General Review of Quotas, February 1990–May 1990").

percent), tied for the fourth spot. With some grumbling about the procedure, the Executive Board accepted that distribution later in the month.[65]

Two other requests for ad hoc increases—from Iran and Korea—failed to muster sufficient support. The request from Iran was intended to compensate for their not having consented to either of the previous two increases (see above, p. 854). In making the case for Korea, Charles R. Rye (Australia) pointed out that the Korean economy had grown very rapidly in the 1980s and that the country's quota was even more out of line with the calculations than Japan's. Creditors who sympathized with Korea found it difficult to support that request without taking the politically awkward step of supporting Iran as well. No one spoke out openly against the specifics of either request, but few creditors were willing to endorse either one.[66]

Access Policies

An increase in quotas does not translate automatically into larger amounts that countries can borrow from the Fund. The other variable in that equation is the "access limit," the ceiling on Fund credits in relation to a member's quota. When the Fund was designed in the early 1940s, quotas were conceived primarily as borrowing rights,[67] and each country's access limit was to be equal to its quota. The 25 percent of quotas that all countries would deposit in gold, plus the 75 percent that the United States and the United Kingdom would deposit in dollars and sterling (respectively), plus whatever other deposited currencies would eventually become usable would provide the liquid assets to finance credits to member countries. No one knew in advance how these ratios would work out in practice, but they were thought to be a safe and conservative starting point.[68] If they turned out to be too conservative, then the Fund could use the flexibility allowed by the Articles to waive the credit ceiling.[69]

---

[65]Minutes of EBM/90/78 (May 21, 1990).

[66]"Ninth General Review of Quotas—Considerations Relating to Special or Ad Hoc Increases in Quotas," EB/CQuota/88/8 (September 16, 1988) and minutes of EBCQM/88/10–11 (November 18, 1988).

[67]The April 1943 version of the British plan for the Fund (the Keynes Plan) put it this way: "Each member State shall have assigned to it a *quota*, which shall determine the measure of its responsibility in the management of the Union and of its right to enjoy the credit facilities provided by the Union" (Horsefield, 1969, Vol. 3, p. 22; original italics).

[68]For example, if the currencies of countries with 50 percent of total quotas were usable for Fund financial operations, then the stock would clearly suffice to finance credits of 100 percent of quota to countries holding the other 50 percent. As a perhaps more realistic initial assumption, if only U.S. dollars were usable, then the stock would suffice to finance credits at that rate to countries holding half of the remainder (since the U.S. quota was just over one-third of original quotas).

[69]Article V, Section 3(b), specifies certain conditions on "purchases" (drawings), one of which is that they "not cause the Fund's holdings of the purchasing member's currency to exceed two hundred percent of its quota." Since holdings equal 100 percent for a country that has drawn its reserve tranche, that provision notionally restricts credit access to 100 percent of the member's quota. Section 4 of the same Article, however, allows the Fund, "in its discretion," to waive that limit.

Policies Before 1980

The history of the Fund's access policies, in a nutshell, shows a loosening of the limits through the early 1980s, in three major steps: the establishment of independent or "floating" facilities in the 1960s and 1970s, the approval of higher limits for extended arrangements in the 1970s, and the use of borrowed funds to finance much larger access beginning in the late 1970s (Figure 17.1).[70] Until that last "enlarged access" policy came into effect, the gradual rise in access limits had roughly compensated for the decline in quotas relative to world trade, so that the amounts that countries could borrow grew *pari passu* with world imports (see the dashed line in the diagram).[71] For a few years in the early 1980s, member countries theoretically could have borrowed up to 775 percent of quota, and potential access in relation to world trade was more than doubled from its historical levels. Access limits then stabilized relative to quotas in the second half of the 1980s and were reduced in the 1990s.

Until 1963, a country's quota placed a binding limit on the amount that it could borrow. When the Fund established the Compensatory Financing Facility (CFF) that year (see Chapter 15), the Executive Board agreed that the 25 percent of quota available under the new facility would not necessarily restrict the member's ability to borrow under ordinary access rules. The rationale was that if borrowing from the CFF was truly to "compensate" countries for temporary declines in export revenues, the facility had to be separate from and additional to any borrowing under the regular tranche policies. Thus the potential use of resources rose from 100 percent to 125 percent. When the CFF was liberalized in 1966, access was raised to 50 percent, drawings were allowed to "float" relative to ordinary usage,[72] and potential total access rose to 150 percent. Three years later, the Buffer Stock Financing Facility (BSFF) was established on similar terms. Although a member could borrow up to 50 percent of quota under either the BSFF or the CFF, the combined limit was set at 75 percent. This decision raised the ceiling on total usage to

---

[70]Data in Figure 17.1, and the discussion in this section, exclude loans made through the Trust Fund, the SAF, and the ESAF. Those loans are financed from administered accounts that are independent from the Fund's general resources. Total ceilings are not strictly commensurate over time, because of overlapping limits, the presence or absence of a cumulative ceiling, and shifting approaches to flexibility in exceeding the limits. Those complexities are discussed below. For years in which access limits changed, the plotted value is the mode for the year.

[71]The normalized aggregate access limit shown in Figure 17.1 has been calculated by dividing aggregate maximum access in SDRs (A) by aggregate world imports (M) rather than by quotas (Q) and then rescaling to give an average value of 100 in the 1960s. That is, if the access limit (L) in percent of quota is $L = A/Q$, the normalized limit is $L' = L \times Q/M$, converted to an index number.

[72]Specifically, "floating" means that borrowing through the facility does not count toward the country's access limits under the Fund's tranche policies. As explained in Chapter 15 (p. 725), the effect of introducing floating in 1966 was that a country with no other outstanding obligations could borrow 25 percent of its quota through the CFF and then borrow another 25 percent under the regular tranche policies without being subjected to the higher conditionality of an upper-tranche arrangement.

Figure 17.1. Potential and Actual Access, 1948–89

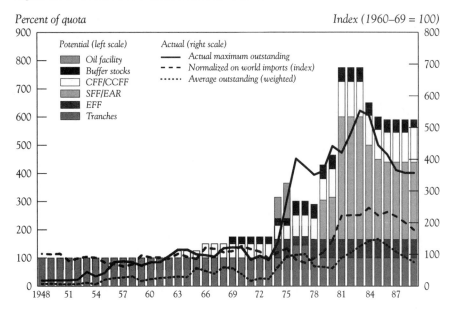

175 percent.[73] As a consequence, the Board began granting waivers of the 100 percent ceiling with increasing frequency.[74]

The oil facilities provided oil-importing countries access to 75 percent of quota in 1974 and 125 percent or more in 1975, in addition to other credits.[75] That access was financed by borrowing from a group of creditor countries (see below). Once those borrowed funds were fully committed, this additional access lapsed.

Under the Extended Fund Facility (EFF), established in 1974, a member country could borrow up to 140 percent of its quota, in addition to drawing on its reserve tranche,[76] the CFF, and the BSFF. Moreover, for two years starting in 1976, the Ex-

---

[73]On the development of access policies for the CFF, see Horsefield (1969), Vol. 2, p. 421, and de Vries (1976), Vol. 1, p. 262. The BSFF limits are discussed in de Vries (1976), Vol. 1, p. 280.

[74]Through 1973, four countries marginally exceeded the ceiling specified in Article V: Egypt in 1963–64, Chile in 1964, and Sri Lanka and Ghana in 1968–70. Beginning in 1974, waivers became routine and covered much larger deviations.

[75]The terms of the 1975 Oil Facility permitted countries to cover up to one-third of the increase in the cost of their oil imports, regardless of the quota-based ceiling (125 percent). In June 1976, Korea's total indebtedness to the Fund peaked at just over 400 percent of quota, of which more than three-fourths was due to drawings through the oil facilities.

[76]Until May 1981, countries were expected to draw their reserve tranche balance before obtaining Fund credits. The Board then dropped that requirement in order to encourage members to retain reserve tranche positions as an important part of their official international reserves. See "Treatment of Reserve Tranche," SM/81/71 (March 30, 1981); minutes of EBM/81/65 (April 22, 1981); and Decision Nos. 6830- and 6831-(81/65), in *Annual Report 1981*, pp. 162–63. The policy change benefited indebted countries in three ways. First, it raised their gross reserves, which

ecutive Board approved a temporary policy that redefined each of the four credit "tranches" to equal 36.25 percent of the member's quota, instead of 25 percent. That change added another 45 percent of access, to a total of about 300 percent of quota, until the Second Amendment became effective in April 1978 (see de Vries, 1985, pp. 527–29).

This gradual augmentation of access to the Fund's resources was matched by an overall increase in demand. By the mid-1970s, the outstanding obligations of countries that had borrowed from the Fund *averaged* about 100 percent, the original ceiling (see Figure 17.1).[77] By then the oil facilities had already been exhausted, and the temporary augmentation of the credit tranches was about to lapse. If a new shock hit the world economy, the Fund would be hard pressed to meet the demand for credits.

The Fund prepared for the next crisis by establishing the Supplementary Financing Facility (SFF) in February 1979, financed by borrowing from official creditors and expected to have a life of just two years.[78] The SFF permitted countries with a stand-by or extended arrangement to obtain supplementary and parallel credits financed by the borrowed resources. That raised maximum access sharply, to more than 450 percent of quota,[79] and established what became known as the "exceptional circumstances clause." Whatever quantitative ceilings were in place could be exceeded, but only after a determination by the Executive Board that the

---

improved liquidity since countries obtained a five-year maturity on their liabilities to the Fund and retained a highly liquid asset in their reserve position. Second, at the time the decision was enacted, the rate of remuneration on reserve positions was above the rate of charge on borrowings (see below, section on "Sharing the Burden: Who Pays for the Fund?" pp. 899–910). A substantial portion of countries with outstanding debit balances took advantage of this provision. Third, as discussed above (footnote 14, p. 855), it gave indebted countries a means of eliminating any cost of increasing their Fund quotas.

[77]"Actual maximum outstanding" is calculated as the maximum value of Fund credit outstanding, expressed as a percentage of quota, for any member during the year. "Average outstanding" is the total amount of credit outstanding, as a percentage of the sum of quotas of countries with outstanding obligations.

[78]For the background to the establishment of the SFF, see de Vries (1985), Chapter 28 and Vol. 3, pp. 512–15. The borrowing arrangements are discussed below (p. 886).

[79]The overall access limit was the sum of several overlapping limits on individual facilities and arrangements. A country could borrow up to 150 percent of quota through a combination of CFF and BSFF credits and 140 percent via an EFF arrangement. Supplementary credits through the SFF could double the size of the arrangement, for a maximum EFF access of 280 percent. All of those amounts were additional to a drawing of the first credit tranche (25 percent), so the total available was 455 percent of quota. If the country had outstanding obligations to the oil facilities, its cumulative stock of indebtedness could be even higher. As part of the activation of the SFF in February 1979, a cumulative limit (excluding CFF and BSFF drawings) was set at 202.5 percent unless the country had an EFF arrangement, in which case it was 305 percent. In September 1979, in response to the oil price increases of that year and the general deterioration in the global economy, the Board accepted an increase in the exclusive cumulative limit to 465 percent (without regard to the type of arrangement). The 465 percent limit was established via a statement issued by the Managing Director at the opening of the Executive Board's discussion of the autumn 1979 World Economic Outlook. See minutes of IS/79/7 (September 12, 1979), pp. 3–4.

borrowing country faced what were then called "special circumstances" warranting the exception.[80]

Enlarged Access

Once the second oil shock hit in 1979, even these limits seemed inadequate, at least until the Seventh Quota Review could take effect. As discussed in Chapter 13, the Fund was encouraged—especially at the Annual Meetings in Belgrade in 1979—to increase its lending so as to help "recycle" the growing surpluses of oil-exporting countries. Meeting in Hamburg in May 1980, the Interim Committee backed up that call and authorized the Managing Director to initiate discussions with potential lenders to further augment the Fund's resources. In response, Executive Directors agreed in July that "we should be prepared to respond on a larger scale than in the past to the needs of our member countries," and that access of 600 percent of quota over three years could be approved.[81] They also set out to establish a policy permitting enlarged access on a more sustained basis than before.[82]

The quota increases that took effect in the last months of 1980 raised the Fund's liquidity, but that result was partially offset by the fact that most of the money borrowed to finance the SFF was already committed. Moreover, the staff was projecting a sharp increase in the demand for stand-by arrangements in response to the 1979–80 increase in oil prices. Either the Fund would have to undertake new borrowing on a large scale, or it would have to scale back its access limits. As a lower extreme, if potential access were to be held constant in absolute value, with no effect from the quota increase, then the cumulative access limit would have to be cut from 600 to 400 percent of quota.[83] To strike a balance between the need to main-

---

[80]Note that the exceptional circumstances clause is separate from the routine waiver that is still required whenever the Fund's holdings of the country's currency will rise above 200 percent of quota. The clause applies both to the size of the arrangement (the flow over a specified period of time) and the cumulative stock of indebtedness, and it relates to excesses of access limits established by the Executive Board rather than to excesses of the limit on the Fund's holdings specified in the Articles. The Executive Board invoked the clause twice in April 1978, in anticipation of the SFF coming into effect: for stand-by arrangements for Turkey (150 percent of quota) and Zambia (177 percent). Under the enlarged access policies of the 1980s, the clause became almost moot. The only time it was invoked during the period covered by this History was for the extended arrangement with Mexico approved in 1989 (see Chapter 11), which had the potential to raise Mexico's obligations to 534 percent of quota while the normal limit on cumulative access was 440 percent.

[81]In addition to limits on total access to Fund credits, the Board has set what might be called "speed limits": ceilings on annual and triennial access. Article V of the original Articles of Agreement limited net annual credit extension to 25 percent of quota, unless waived. That limit was dropped in the 1978 amendments. Thereafter, the Board typically imposed annual limits, triennial limits that were always set at or close to three times the annual limits (and therefore were operationally redundant), and cumulative ceilings that were usually around four times the annual limits.

[82]Chairman's summing up, minutes of EBM/80/107 (July 18, 1980), p. 31.

[83]The Seventh General Review raised quotas by 50 percent; $600 = 400 \times 1.5$. The calculation of potential access, which is the way the matter was presented to the Executive Board, excludes CFF and BSFF drawings, on which the combined access limit of 150 percent was not reduced. To hold total potential access constant would have required reducing the exclusive cumulative limit to 350 percent.

tain liquidity and the desire to meet members' requests for financing, the staff suggested a compromise of 450 percent over three years and 600 percent cumulatively. Since stand-by and extended arrangements were limited to three years, those figures implied that in most cases countries could not add more than 450 percent to existing indebtedness through a single arrangement, but prolonged borrowing could lead to higher indebtedness over time. The Board accepted that proposal in January 1981 and agreed to establish—as a successor to the expiring SFF—the elaborately named and oddly acronymed "Policy on Enlarged Access to the Fund's Resources" (EAR).[84]

At the time the EAR was established, access limits that high could be sustained only through borrowing by the Fund. As discussed below, no one wanted the Fund to become a permanent borrower. The EAR therefore was established as a temporary policy, and the question arose as to how much access the Fund could allow on a sustained basis, without recourse to borrowing. To answer that question, the staff used the Fund's estimated "self-financing ratio": the ratio of potential demand to potential supply of ordinary (nonborrowed) resources. Forward-looking estimates would have been subject to wide margins of error, so the actual calculations were based on past experience. Suppose, for example, that the Fund's "usable" financial assets were equivalent to 50 percent of quotas, and that the demand for those resources came from countries holding 25 percent of total quotas. The Fund could then allow access to average 200 percent of quota (50/25) without having recourse to borrowing. Since average access will always be less than the maximum, the limit could be set somewhat higher, but how much higher is difficult to determine. The applicability of this approach is limited for that reason, and also because neither the level of usable resources nor the demands on them can be accurately forecast. Even so, a retrospective look at the self-financing ratio provides some insight into the range of sustainable figures for access limits.

The calculated ratio, shown in Figure 17.2, is quite volatile over time, mainly on account of fluctuations in the list of countries with outstanding obligations. In the 1970s, the self-financing ratio ranged from a peak of 365 percent in 1972 down to 145 percent four years later.[85] Taking a conservative view, these data suggested that average access of at least 140 percent could be financed by quota resources alone, while much higher access might require recourse to borrowing by the Fund. Since average access was rising at the time and would soon reach that level (refer again to Figure 17.1), the Fund seemed to be driving close

---

[84]"Enlarged Access to Fund Resources," EBS/80/262 (December 4, 1980); and minutes of EBM/80/187–188 (December 19, 1980), EBM/81/5–6 (January 9, 1981), and EBM/81/39 (March 11, 1981). The implementing decision was approved in March 1981; see Appendix IV to this chapter.

[85]See "Review of the Policy on Access to Fund's Resources—Financial Considerations," EBS/83/133 (June 28, 1983), Appendix Table V, p. 28; and "Ninth General Review of Quotas—Consideration Relating to the Increase in Quotas," EB/CQuota/88/1 (February 17, 1988), p. 29. The data cited here are updated staff estimates from those tables.

Figure 17.2. Self-Financing Access Ratio, 1951–90

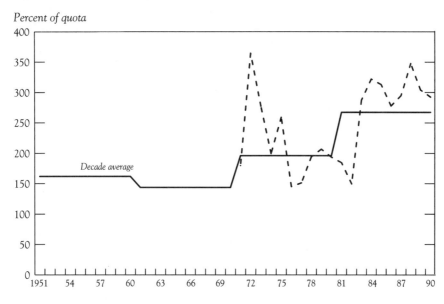

Percent of quota

Note: For definition of self-financing ratio, see text.

to the edge of the prudent range. In fact, however, the average ratio was about to rise sharply because no industrial country would be borrowing from the Fund in the 1980s. In retrospect, the self-financing ratio would average 267 percent in the 1980s and would lie above 200 percent in every year from 1983 on.

After the Eighth Quota Review was completed in 1983, the Executive Board reviewed the EAR, decided to retain the policy, but also decided not to raise access in absolute terms. In other words, the direct effect of the 1983 quota increases was to strengthen the Fund's liquidity but not necessarily to allow it to raise the amount of lending except through the "floating" special facilities.[86]

The first discussion on this issue, in July 1983, revealed a deep split in the Board. Three groups of Directors, each holding approximately one-third of the voting power, favored (1) reducing access in absolute terms to protect the Fund's liquidity, (2) raising it to meet the demands of the membership for new credits, or (3) holding it steady to balance those two considerations. Three more days of discussion in late August and early September produced no material change in those views, and the stalemate was then reported to the Interim Com-

---

[86]Access to credits through the CFF and BSFF was subject to ceilings of 125 percent and 50 percent, respectively, from May 1981 (when the cereals window became effective) through 1983. Those limits were reduced to 105 percent and 45 percent in January 1984, in response to the general increase in quotas. For a country with an average quota increase (47.5 percent) after the Eighth Review, the cut in percentage terms implied an increase of 26 percent in terms of SDRs. See Decision No. 7602-(84/3), January 6, 1984; in *Annual Report 1984*, p. 138.

mittee.[87] The split was not just between creditors and debtors, as one might expect. Within the G-5, the U.S. authorities were holding out for the low end (no increase in absolute terms), while the French were insisting on at least reaching the middle ground with a meaningful increase. The British were trying to craft a compromise under which absolute access would rise but countries would have to meet more difficult conditions to qualify for the increase.

In September 1983, the Interim Committee agreed to the British proposal to establish a temporary two-tier system of access limits, with an upper limit to be applied for countries with particularly serious balance of payments problems and particularly strong adjustment programs.[88] The upper limit permitted cumulative access of 500 percent of quota (reduced from 600 percent), while the lower ceiling was set at 408 percent. The lower limit was set so as to keep access unchanged in absolute terms for countries with an average quota increase.[89] The implication of the two-tier system thus was that countries could get up to 23 percent additional access, or about half the size of the general quota increase, but only by demonstrating that they faced major problems and were implementing strong policies.

The two-tier system was bewildering, especially when viewed in relation to the exceptional circumstances clause, which provided for access above the upper limit. The staff and the Board specifically rejected the idea that access in the upper tier would require a finding of "exceptional circumstances," and they set out to try to define specific criteria for it. Not surprisingly, that attempt failed. What emerged was an agreement that the staff would attempt to provide more detailed justifications for programs with access above the lower limit. In effect, the upper limit would become the operative ceiling, but efforts would be made to keep average access from rising commensurately.[90]

Because the EAR was a temporary expedient, the Board agreed to review the access limits each year. Those reviews became the occasion for a perennial tug-of-war between the defenders of the Fund's liquidity and the advocates for borrowing

---

[87]See minutes of EBM/83/110–111 (July 25, 1983), EBM/83/126–127 (August 31), EBM/83/132–133 (September 7), EBM/83/134–135 (September 8), and "Report to the Interim Committee on the Policy on Access to the Fund's Resources," SM/83/198, Rev. 2 (September 9). Also see "Review of the Policy on Access to the Fund's Resources—General Considerations," EBS/83/132 (June 27, 1983) and "Review of Policy on Access to the Fund's Resources—General Considerations," Sup. 1 (July 18, 1983), "Review of the Policy on Access to the Fund's Resources—Financial Considerations," EBS/83/133 (June 28, 1983), "Enlarged Access—Scale of Access and Limits," EBS/83/172 (August 12, 1983), and "Review of the Policy on Access to the Fund's Resources—Legal and Policy Considerations," SM/83/194 (August 19, 1983).

[88]The proposal was introduced during the July Board meeting by the Executive Director for the United Kingdom, Nigel Wicks. It was advanced within the G-5 by the U.K. Deputy, Geoffrey Littler, and was tabled at the Interim Committee by the Chancellor of the Exchequer, Nigel Lawson. According to Lawson (1992, p. 518), the final compromise numbers were worked out during a meeting of the Commonwealth finance ministers in Trinidad the week before the Interim Committee meeting in Washington.

[89]Quotas were increased by an average of 47.5 percent; $408 \approx 600 \div 1.475$. For the full text, see Decision No. 7600-(84/3), January 6, 1984; in *Annual Report 1984*, p. 135.

[90]Minutes of EBM/83/166–167 (December 2, 1983). Also see "Criteria for the Amount of Access in Individual Cases," EBS/83/233 (October 31, 1983).

countries. When the Board met in September 1984 to consider the limits for 1985, some creditors expressed concerns that enlarged access was enabling many countries to become prolonged users of the Fund's resources (see Chapter 13). In their view, the time had arrived to begin phasing out the policy. Mary K. Bush (Alternate—United States), Hirotake Fujino (Japan), Guenter Grosche (Germany), and T.A. Clark (Alternate—United Kingdom) called for reducing the cumulative limit to the range of 350–400 percent of quota, from the prevailing level of 500 percent. De Larosière, however, made a personal appeal to maintain the existing levels, because otherwise the Fund would have to cut off lending to several major borrowers that were nearing the limits and for which the Fund could continue to play a positive role.[91] As a compromise, the Interim Committee agreed on a small reduction, to 450 percent with no reduction in the lower ceiling (408 percent), a few weeks later. An implementing Board decision was adopted in November.[92]

A year later, staff and management expressed a preference for retaining the ceilings at their 1985 levels but accepted that the cumulative ceiling could be cut to 400 percent of quota or even to 375, as a signal that enlarged access would indeed be phased out over time. To go further would be risky. Three countries would soon reach the existing ceiling of 450 percent, and if it were reduced to 350 percent, more than 30 countries would become ineligible for additional credits by 1986.[93] The major creditors, however, took similar positions as in 1984. Dallara, Grosche, and Fujino asked that the cumulative limit be cut to about 350 percent for 1986, but that position was not supported by the majority of the Board.[94]

Meeting in Seoul, Korea, in early October, the Interim Committee decided that the EAR should be retained with "only modest adjustments" in access limits. The Committee decided that the cumulative limit should be set at 440 percent for 1986, down just slightly from 450 percent in 1985. Nonetheless, several committee members—notably the finance ministers for China, France, India, and Italy—objected strongly on principle to the reduction and went along solely to gain consensus on the extension of the EAR. The finance minister for India, Vishwanath Pratap Singh, went public with his reservations and stated in his Annual Meetings

[91]See "Access Limits for 1985—Preliminary Policy Considerations," EBS/84/168 (August 8, 1984), and the minutes of EBM/84/134–135 (September 5, 1984). At the end of 1984, five countries had outstanding credits (exclusive of CFF and BSFF obligations) in excess of 300 percent of quota: Jamaica (367 percent), Turkey (329 percent), Yugoslavia (321 percent), Côte d'Ivoire (304 percent), and Sudan (303 percent). In addition, existing commitments to Uganda, Mexico, Brazil, and Malawi would carry them above 300 percent if the arrangements then in effect were fully utilized.

[92]Minutes of EBM/84/165 (November 16, 1984), pp. 3–4.

[93]"Access Limits for 1986—Preliminary Policy Considerations," EBS/85/174 (July 23, 1985), p. 16. For the detailed calculations, see the attachment to "Access Limits for 1986," memorandum from C. David Finch (Director of the Exchange and Trade Relations Department) to the Managing Director (September 24, 1985), in IMF/RD Managing Director file "Access Limits, 1985" (Accession 88/274, Box 8, Section 269).

[94]Minutes of EBM/85/137–138 (September 11, 1985). The relevant statements by Fujino, Grosche, and Dallara are on pp. 15, 18, and 22, respectively, of meeting 85/137. For the overall distribution of votes, see the Chairman's summing up at meeting 85/138, p. 14.

speech that he, "along with many others," had objected to the cuts during the Interim Committee meeting (IMF, *Summary Proceedings*, 1985, p. 96). The Board, after some further grumbling, implemented the decision in December.[95]

After that battle, an implicit truce was reached, and no further cuts were made in the access limits. The enlarged access policy remained in force until November 1992, when the quota increases of the Ninth Review took effect.

Borrowing by the Fund

Although the primary source of financing for Fund operations has always been its quotas, it also has the option of borrowing from any source—member countries, other official agencies, or private capital markets. While the option of going to private markets was never exercised, the Fund borrowed from official sources on several occasions. Total indebtedness peaked in 1986, at SDR 14.6 billion (Figure 17.3), the equivalent of 16 percent of quotas or $17 billion.[96]

Borrowing by the Fund began with the establishment of the General Arrangements to Borrow (GAB) in 1962. Under those arrangements, the G-10 (and, later, Switzerland) agreed to lend to the Fund, up to a specified maximum, to help finance drawings by GAB creditors. Because those creditors drew on the Fund only occasionally, the GAB was activated only a few times.[97]

On two occasions prior to the 1980s, the Fund entered into bilateral borrowing arrangements to finance specific drawings. The first occasion was in 1966, when the Fund borrowed $250 million in lire from Italy to lend to the United States through a gold tranche drawing.[98] In 1977, the Swiss National Bank extended credit lines under which the Fund borrowed the equivalent of SDR 154 million to

---

[95]Minutes of EBM/85/177 (December 9, 1985). The Board had a dual decision to take: to extend the EAR for the coming year and to set access limits under that policy. The extension required an 85 percent majority, while the percentage limits required only a simple majority of votes cast. Although Directors with a majority of the votes preferred to keep access limits unchanged, the three chairs that wanted a substantial reduction (the United States, Japan, and Germany) held approximately 30 percent of the votes and thus could have voted down the extension of the EAR and thereby have rendered the second decision moot. The potential impasse from the existence of two blocking coalitions was avoided by a decision to take a single vote on the two elements, with the nominal reduction in access limits.

[96]In addition, the Fund borrowed as a Trustee to finance the Trust Fund, the SAF, and the ESAF. That borrowing is covered in Chapter 14. For the full evolution of the Fund's policies on borrowing, see Gold (1991).

[97]The GAB agreement also specified that it could be activated only after a finding that the international monetary system was threatened with impairment. That restriction, however, was treated as a formality in considering requests for drawings by G-10 countries. Switzerland was not then a member of the Fund and therefore was not eligible to borrow from the Fund.

[98]De Vries (1976), Vol. 1, p. 376, interprets the motivation for the 1966 transaction as a shortage of lire in the Fund's accounts to cover a requested gold tranche drawing by the United States. Polak (1994, pp. 28–29) provides a fuller account and explains the motivation as an accommodation (by the Fund and the United States) to Italy's desire to substitute out of dollar-denominated securities in favor of a gold-guaranteed loan to the Fund.

Figure 17.3. Borrowing by the Fund, 1965–96

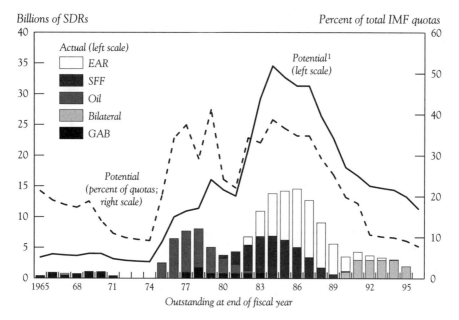

Outstanding at end of fiscal year

[1]Potential = actual + unused and available lines of credit.

help finance stand-by arrangements for Italy and the United Kingdom (de Vries, 1985, pp. 592–93). On that occasion, the purpose was to supplement credits being extended through the GAB.

A third form of borrowing was introduced in 1974–75, when the Fund obtained SDR 6.9 billion ($8.3 billion) in loans from 16 oil-exporting and industrial countries to finance the oil facilities. The facilities were entirely financed with those assets, and the Fund extended an equivalent amount of credit to oil-importing member countries.[99] Both the credits and the Fund's borrowings were repaid from 1979 to 1983.

---

[99]Two sequential oil facilities were established, in 1974 and 1975, but the distinction between them was of only technical significance. The facilities, established with funds borrowed from 16 oil exporting and industrial countries, were the first lending window at the IMF financed entirely outside the Fund's own resources. In that regard, they resembled the later Trust Fund, SAF, and ESAF, although those operations were established as Administered Accounts and thus were further separated from the normal activities of the institution. (As noted in Chapter 14, the Subsidy Account for the oil facilities was the IMF's first Administered Account.) Like the CFF and the BSFF (see Chapter 15), the oil facilities involved only nominal conditionality. Although legally available to all member countries, they were established on the understanding that they would be drawn upon only by oil-importing countries that lacked ready access to international capital on market terms. The origins and early operation of the facilities are covered in de Vries (1985), pp. 305–60; on the linkage between the increase in a country's cost of importing oil and its access to the oil facilities, see pp. 324 and 343n.

By the time covered by this History, the Fund was examining the possibility of other borrowing as a more general way to supplement quotas. These new sources included the SFF, various arrangements to finance the EAR, and an enlargement of the GAB.

Supplementary Financing Facility

The SFF, which provided supplementary credits to countries with a stand-by or extended arrangement, was financed entirely by stand-by loans to the Fund from 14 governments and central banks. A little over half of the money was lent by industrial countries, and the rest came from developing countries (Table 17.4). Of SDR 7.8 billion ($9 billion) in total lines of credit, the largest share came from Saudi Arabia (SDR 1.9 billion, or $2.2 billion), with the United States second (SDR 1.5 billion, or $1.7 billion).[100] These credit lines were drawn upon from 1979 through 1984; loans carried seven-year maturities, and all were repaid by January 1991.

Borrowing to Finance Enlarged Access

Almost as soon as the SFF came into effect, it became clear that its resources would quickly be exhausted and would not suffice to finance Fund lending into the 1980s. In the wake of the 1979–80 oil shock, projections of demand for Fund resources exceeded by a wide margin the supply available from the Seventh Quota Review and the borrowed resources of the SFF. The problem was not just that a lot of countries were likely to seek to borrow from the Fund. It was that those countries faced serious economic imbalances that would take many years to correct, and the Fund would have to prepare itself for a more sustained rise in its lending than in the past.[101] In the first part of 1980, the Fund's management therefore developed a plan to undertake new borrowing on an unprecedented scale.

The first step was to secure political support from the Interim Committee, which was meeting in Hamburg, Germany, in April 1980. The role of the Fund in "recycling" the growing surpluses of oil-exporting countries was on the agenda, and the committee would have to consider whether the Fund had the resources to do

---

[100]Loan commitments were denominated in SDRs, but disbursements were made in the currency indicated in Table 17.4. Half of the money was provided in U.S. dollars, and the rest in the currencies of five of the lending countries. For the background on this financing, see de Vries (1985), Chapter 28. Separate financing was contributed by 12 countries to subsidize interest payments by low-income countries on credits supported by the SFF. The SFF Subsidy Account is discussed above, in Chapter 14.

[101]In June 1980, a staff paper argued that the "current and prospective global imbalances, both in kind and size, are different from those which the Fund has been engaged in financing in the past. . . . An effective role by the Fund in the present situation would involve where necessary both larger and longer financing than in the past." The Executive Board endorsed those conclusions the following month. "Fund Policies for Adjustment Under Current Conditions," EBS/80/146 (June 30, 1980), p. 11. Also see minutes of EBM/80/106–107 (July 18, 1980).

Table 17.4. Borrowing Agreements for the Supplementary Financing Facility, 1979–84

(In millions)

	Currency Provided	Amount in SDRs	U.S. Dollar Equivalent[a]	Share (In percent)
Industrial countries		4,550	5,286	59
United States	U.S. dollars	1,450	1,685	19
Germany (Deutsche Bundesbank)	U.S. dollars	1,050	1,220	13
Japan	yen	900	1,046	12
Switzerland (Swiss National Bank)	U.S. dollars	650	755	8
Canada	U.S. dollars	200	232	3
Belgium (National Bank)	francs	150	174	2
Netherlands (Netherlands Bank)	U.S. dollars	100	116	1
Austria (National Bank)	U.S. dollars	50	58	1
Developing countries		3,234	3,758	42
Saudi Arabia (SAMA)	riyals	1,934	2,247	25
Venezuela (central bank)	bolivares	500	581	6
Kuwait (central bank)	dinars	400	465	5
Nigeria (central bank)	U.S. dollars	220	256	3
Abu Dhabi	U.S. dollars	150	174	2
Guatemala (Banco de Guatemala)	U.S. dollars	30	35	0
Total		7,784	9,044	100

[a]Dollar values are calculated at the average exchange rate for 1979–84.

the job. De Larosière acknowledged that the liquidity position was comfortable for 1980, but he argued that the Fund would have to borrow to meet the demand expected in the next few years. The Committee agreed and "encouraged the Managing Director to start discussions with potential lenders on the terms and conditions under which the Fund could borrow funds to increase its resources, if and when the need arises" (see Appendix IV).

The second step was to develop a specific proposal for a borrowing plan that would be large enough to meet the expected demand but modest enough to secure the support of major creditors. After sounding out the main creditor country Executive Directors, de Larosière suggested to the Board that the Fund might need to borrow SDR 6–7 billion ($8–9 billion) a year for the next few years. The Board endorsed that level of borrowing in July 1980, and de Larosière went public with his proposal in the following months.[102]

Third, from whom could the Fund expect to borrow such large sums? The initial intention was to borrow as much as possible from industrial countries via the BIS and from major oil exporters and then, if necessary, to tap private capital markets for the rest. Borrowing in the open market would have been a radical departure for the Fund and was seen as much less desirable than staying within official

---

[102]See memorandum for files on a meeting of July 11, 1980, in IMF/CF (S 1720 "Use of Fund Resources—Policy, July 1980–November 1980"); and minutes of EBM/80/115 (July 30, 1980), p. 23. For an example of the Managing Director's public advocacy, see his 1980 Annual Meetings speeches, in IMF, *Summary Proceedings*, 1980, pp. 23 and 264.

circles, but it was also thought to be possibly necessary under the circumstances. Few industrial countries had strong enough external balances to be able to lend significant amounts to the Fund in the early 1980s, and the willingness of newly wealthy and still developing oil exporters to take up the slack was still largely untested. As long as the idea was floated as a backup plan and not as a concrete proposal, it received a lukewarm endorsement from most Executive Directors. In the event, even though the amounts raised from official lenders fell short of the expressed goal and the Board continued to discuss the idea on a conceptual level until 1983, no specific proposal for private sector borrowing was ever tabled.[103]

Those who were reluctant to endorse borrowing from the private sector raised several objections. First, it would be more expensive than borrowing from official creditors, because banks and other private creditors would require commitment fees and interest rate spreads as compensation. Second, reliance on private sector borrowing could subject the Fund's lending policies and practices to influence from commercial creditors. Third, the private market for SDR-denominated claims was extremely limited, and the Fund would have to devote considerable effort to the task of developing and sustaining a market for its liabilities. In contrast to the World Bank, for which market borrowing (in currencies) had been a permanent source of financing since 1947, the development of a permanent market for the Fund was seen as incompatible with its quota-based structure. Fourth, raising funds in capital markets would place the Fund in competition with the World Bank, which would further raise borrowing costs for both institutions. Fifth (and most important for the major creditors), the requirement for the Fund to obtain consensus support for quota increases was seen by many as an essential check on the expansion of Fund lending. Large-scale and sustained borrowing could lead to a weakening of that discipline and control. Although those concerns had to be weighed against the obvious advantages, the idea was quietly shelved once the most pressing shortage of resources had passed.[104]

Saudi Arabia

The key to success in this endeavor was Saudi Arabia. In 1980 and 1981, Saudi Arabia had an annual current account surplus of some $40 billion, by far the largest in the world. A loan to the Fund might provide a good investment outlet for part of those assets, and it would help compensate for the difficulty the Fund knew it would face in approaching its traditional industrial country creditors. De Larosière soon found an opportunity to initiate discussions, when he and Sheikh Abdul Aziz Al-Quraishi (governor of Saudi Arabia's central bank, the Saudi Ara-

---

[103]To some extent, talk of borrowing from private markets was a strategic move to secure favorable terms from official creditors. As de Larosière noted, in summing up the first Board discussion on this issue, "borrowing from governments . . . would not be justified if it were not on terms and conditions at least as favorable as could be obtained from the market." Minutes of EBM/80/114–115 (July 30, 1980). The quotation is from meeting 80/115, pp. 23–24.

[104]For the clearest expression of views by Executive Directors, see the minutes of EBM/81/119–120 (September 4, 1981). The final discussion of the subject in the 1980s was at EBM/83/59–60 (April 8, 1983).

bian Monetary Agency or SAMA) were both participating in an international conference in New Orleans, Louisiana, in June 1980. In private discussions, the governor responded favorably to the Managing Director's suggestion, but only if the loan could be structured so as to make it fit in with his country's budgeting and investing strategy. In particular, the Fund had always borrowed by establishing lines of credit on which it could draw when necessary. That enabled the Fund to pass the proceeds directly to a borrowing country and later to unwind the transaction in the same way, without incurring any exchange or interest risks. The lender, however, had no assurance at the outset on the amounts or timing of any drawdowns. For a multibillion-dollar loan, Saudi Arabia would want a more certain investment vehicle. This technical problem was eventually resolved when the Fund agreed to establish a new set of accounts, known as "borrowed resources suspense accounts," for the deposit of borrowed funds pending disbursal.[105]

A more substantive hurdle derived from Saudi Arabia's quota in the Fund. The country had joined the Fund in 1957 with an exceptionally small quota: $10 million, the seventh smallest of the 62 members at that time. That anomaly was marginally reduced in the next general review, and Saudi Arabia's rank rose to thirty-third in 1960. After the first oil shock in the early 1970s, that level became increasingly out of line and increasingly difficult to defend. The case for a sharply higher quota was enhanced starting in 1974, when Saudi Arabia began lending to the Fund for a variety of purposes. That year, the Saudi government lent the equivalent of SDR 1 billion ($1.2 billion) to the Fund as the lion's share of the financing for the first Oil Facility. The next year, they extended an additional SDR 1.25 billion ($1.5 billion) for the second Oil Facility and began a series of contributions that would make them the largest contributor to the facility's Subsidy Account. As noted above (p. 886), they were the largest single contributor to the SFF as well. In 1978, they volunteered to transfer their share of the distribution of profits from the Fund's sale of gold to the Trust Fund, to be used for the benefit of low-income countries. By then, the Saudi currency, the riyal, had become sufficiently strong to be used in Fund transactions and to be included in the 16-currency basket that constituted the SDR until 1981.

The Fund recognized these contributions in 1978 by agreeing to raise Saudi Arabia's quota to the 14th position in the Sixth General Review. Even before that increase took effect, Saudi Arabia was able to appoint an Executive Director to the Fund (rather than participating in the election of Executive Directors along with

---

[105]Assets in these accounts were invested in special depository accounts with the BIS and with the central banks of the G-5 countries (the countries whose currencies constituted the SDR), which were denominated in SDRs and which paid a market-based interest rate approximating the SDR rate. In contrast to other Fund accounts, the Fund, rather than the depositors, was responsible for maintaining the SDR value in the accounts (i.e., for managing the exchange risk). In the early 1980s, the accounts with central banks were used mainly for converting Saudi Arabian riyals into G-5 currencies; the BIS was the primary depository for investments. Subsequently, additional accounts were opened with other central banks. See the Fund's *Annual Reports* from 1981 onward. For the establishment of the policy, see Decision Nos. 6844- and 6845-(81/75), May 5, 1981; in *Annual Report 1981*, pp. 168–69.

most other member countries), as it had become one of the two largest creditors (see the discussion of the Executive Board in Chapter 20, pp. 1031–32). When the second oil shock hit shortly afterward, the new quota was already seriously out of line.

In the course of numerous meetings through the second half of 1980 and into 1981, the authorities insisted that their quota was still "extremely unsatisfactory" and should be raised to the average ratio of actual to calculated quotas for all members.[106] It was clear that a failure to meet this request, which was certainly reasonable on its merits, would threaten the loan negotiations and could thereby undercut the whole enlarged access policy. Saudi Arabia's bargaining position was extremely strong. Even so, a jump of that magnitude—to SDR 2.1 billion, from SDR 1.04 billion under the Seventh Review that was just about to take effect—would place their quota sixth in rank, below all of the G-5 countries but ahead of both Canada and Italy (then ranked sixth and seventh, respectively). Some of the major industrial countries reacted negatively to that prospect, and as a group they tried first to hold the increase below Italy's quota and then to fashion a compromise under which the quota would be raised to a level between Canada and Italy. De Larosière fought off that challenge at the last minute by appealing directly to the U.S. Secretary of the Treasury, Donald Regan.

At the beginning of February 1981, de Larosière met with the Saudi minister of finance, Sheikh Mohammed Abalkhail, in Davos, Switzerland. The quota increase was still uncertain, and a few technical details were still in negotiation, but the two men were able to agree in principle on the terms of a major loan to the Fund. On March 27, the Executive Board approved an ad hoc quota increase to SDR 2.1 billion, the full amount that had been requested. Six weeks later, at Fund headquarters on May 7, de Larosière and Al-Quraishi signed what may then have been the largest loan agreement in history. Saudi Arabia would lend the Fund a total of SDR 8 billion (about $9 billion) in two equal tranches (1981 and 1982), with six-year maturities. The loans would be denominated in SDRs, and the interest rate would be set at the SDR interest rate, with no spread or fees charged to the Fund. It was just over half of the total amount that de Larosière had set out to borrow, but it gave the Fund a strong base of financing on which it could safely launch the enlarged access policy.

Other Oil-Exporting Countries

To begin to raise the rest of the targeted SDR 6–7 billion a year, de Larosière turned his attention to other major oil exporters. Following some initial staff contacts, he decided to make a direct appeal to a few Middle Eastern countries with substantial external surpluses. That appeal would be more difficult than in the case of Saudi Arabia, for three reasons. First, Saudi Arabia was unique in the region in wanting to play a leadership role in international economic policy and in its willingness and ability to reach out to industrial countries. An appeal to other Middle Eastern

---

[106]Letter of December 1, 1980, from Abalkhail to de Larosière; in IMF/CF (E/313 "Executive Directors' Election—19th Regular, 1982").

countries would have to be made on purely financial grounds. Second, because Saudi Arabia was in the midst of a major internal development effort, the authorities were actively seeking good outlets for short- to medium-term liquid investments. Other countries in the region were typically seeking equity and other long-term investments. Lending to the Fund thus would be less attractive to those countries. Third, and ultimately decisively, countries throughout the Middle East were frustrated with the Fund and the World Bank for their failure to get approval for the Palestine Liberation Organization (PLO) to be an official observer at the Annual Meetings of the Board of Governors (see the discussion of the Board of Governors in Chapter 20, pp. 1021–27). Saudi Arabia, as both the largest financial supporter of the PLO and the largest creditor of the Fund, could afford to compartmentalize its support for the two organizations. For others, the two issues were inseparable.

The effort to obtain loans from other surplus countries went forward despite these obstacles and culminated in a personal visit by de Larosière to Kuwait (where he met with the Emir, Sheikh Jaber Al-Hamad Al-Sabah) and Abu Dhabi (where he met with the president of the United Arab Emirates, Sheikh Zaid bin Sultan Al-Nehayan).[107] Although both governments expressed sympathy in principle to the Managing Director's initiative, they responded that they could not lend to the Fund at that time because of the ongoing controversy over the status of the PLO at the Annual Meetings.[108] That impasse persisted throughout the period of heavy borrowing by the Fund and posed an insuperable barrier to what otherwise might have been a significant source of temporary funding.[109]

Industrial Countries

Next on the list were the industrial countries. Although direct lending by governments was precluded in most cases by a combination of economic difficulties resulting from the second oil shock and a growing political reluctance to invest in international assistance, most officials recognized the importance of supporting the Fund's enlarged access policy. Lending by central banks could provide an alternative channel, especially if coordinated and filtered through the BIS. De Larosière again took charge of the negotiations, traveling to Basel in November 1980 to raise the issue with the central bank governors attending the monthly BIS meeting. He got a sympathetic hearing there, and the staff set out to negotiate a specific borrowing arrangement.

---

[107]Officials in Iraq declined a visit on the grounds that responsibility for assistance to developing countries lay with industrial countries and that the Fund already had sufficient resources. A planned stop in Qatar was canceled because the principal authorities were away from the country. Later appeals to several other oil exporters with external surpluses were also unsuccessful.

[108]See materials in "Mission to Middle East—De Larosière and Staff," IMF/CF (S 813); and report by the Managing Director at EBM/80/128 (September 3, 1980).

[109]Although Saudi officials were no less displeased at the handling of the PLO affair, they did not allow it to deflect the negotiations on their loan, for the reasons discussed above. Kapur, Lewis, and Webb (1997), p. 980, describe the effect of the affair on the World Bank's borrowing from Middle Eastern countries but incorrectly attribute the prolonged negotiation of the Saudi loan to the Fund to that problem.

Two technical issues dominated those discussions. First, the Fund wanted to borrow in SDRs, while the BIS preferred to lend in individual currencies. That gap was bridged by an agreement that the loan would be denominated in SDRs, with the U.S. dollar as the normal vehicle currency. The BIS could avoid exchange risk by matching its liabilities to the currency composition of its corresponding claims. Second, the Fund was seeking to borrow for several years, while the BIS normally restricted its lending to short periods. That gap was bridged by an agreement that each drawdown would carry a six-month maturity, but the Fund would have the option to roll over the credit up to a maximum period of 2½ years and to delay the initial drawdown by up to two years. The terms of that agreement—for a loan expected to total SDR 550 million ($650 million)—were approved in May 1981, just a few days after the signing of the loan from Saudi Arabia.[110]

Although the BIS loan was not large, it unlocked the door to parallel agreements with individual industrial country central banks, with the notable absence of the United States. Some countries preferred to lend indirectly to the Fund through the BIS; others preferred to lend directly but were willing to do so on the same terms as the multilateral loan. By August, a series of deals involving 18 industrial countries was completed and signed, for a total amount of just over SDR 1.3 billion ($1.5 billion). All of the G-10 countries except the United States participated in a package deal either through or in parallel with the BIS, along with Austria, Denmark, Norway, Spain, and Switzerland. Four other countries—Australia, Finland, Ireland, and South Africa—entered into similar agreements (see Table 17.5).

In just over a year, the Fund had obtained SDR 9.3 billion (nearly $11 billion) in loan commitments and was well on its way toward covering the expected demand for Fund credits at least into 1983. Before de Larosière could embark on the next round of negotiations, to cover Fund lending in later years, the Board turned its attention to the adoption of a ceiling on overall borrowing. That issue had been raised by Saudi Arabian officials in the course of negotiations on their loan to the Fund, and the Managing Director had promised Al-Quraishi to "assure creditors that the Fund's borrowings will be prudently managed" by setting "a limit on the Fund's total indebtedness expressed as a ratio of its total quotas."[111]

Initial discussions revealed a split in views among major creditor countries on the wisdom of imposing a ceiling on borrowings. While some (notably Japan and Germany) shared the Saudi concerns, others (notably the United Kingdom,

---

[110]Only the initial drawdown could be rolled over for the full 30 months. Subsequent drawdowns were limited to the same ending date as for the first. All loans had to be repaid by that date, which could be no later than January 31, 1985. The Executive Board approved the agreement in principle on May 13, 1981, and the final text (with the amount augmented to SDR 600 million) was approved on June 1. On August 3, the BIS agreement was augmented again, to SDR 675 million, to incorporate a commitment from the Bank of Spain. Pertaining to "Borrowing by the Fund from the Bank for International Settlements (BIS) and from Central Banks and from Monetary Authorities," see "Additional Information," SM/81/109, Sup. 2 (June 2, 1981) and "Additional Information," Sup. 3 (July 30, 1981), and minutes of EBM/81/81 (May 13, 1981) and EBM/81/83 (June 1, 1981).

[111]"Borrowing Agreement with Saudi Arabian Monetary Agency (SAMA)," EBS/81/95 (April 21, 1981), Annex C.

Table 17.5. Borrowing from Industrial Countries to Finance Enlarged Access
(*Millions of SDRs*)

Creditor	Effective Date	Amount
I. 1981–84		
BIS group		1,175
BIS	June 1981[a]	675
National Bank of Belgium	June 1981	50
Swiss National Bank	June 1981	150
Bank of England	July 1981	150
Government of Japan	July 1981	150
Other		130
Bank of Finland	July 1981	30
Reserve Bank of Australia	July 1981	50
Central Bank of Ireland	August 1981	20
Reserve Bank of South Africa	August 1981	30
Total		1,305
II. 1984–86		
BIS	April 1984	2,505
Government of Japan	April 1984	375
National Bank of Belgium	June 1984	120
Total		3,000
III. 1987–90		
Japan	December 1986	3,000

[a]Initially, SDR 600 million; augmented to SDR 675 million in August.

France, and the Netherlands) had reservations. A low ceiling might unnecessarily limit the Fund's flexibility, while a high one would have little meaning and might even encourage the Fund to undertake excessive borrowing. For several months, the staff argued for a ceiling that was much higher than any expected level of borrowing, while Nimatallah, the Saudi Director, insisted on an effective limit. Finally, in January 1982, the Executive Board adopted formal guidelines that were close to those requested by Saudi Arabia.[112] The new rules (see Appendix IV) imposed a ceiling on outstanding indebtedness plus unused lines of credit[113] of 60 percent of total Fund quotas.[114] This ceiling was well in excess of

[112]Decision No. 7040-(82/7), adopted January 13, 1982; in Appendix IV to this chapter. Bruno de Maulde (France) dissented from the decision on the grounds that it could lead to excessive borrowing; minutes of EBM/82/4 (January 11, 1982), pp. 12–13.

[113]Since, at that time, the GAB could be used only for lines to GAB participants and a member's credit line could not be used to support financing for that member, the guidelines recognized that not all GAB credit lines could be activated at the same time. For 1982–83, only 50 percent of GAB credit lines (or the amount outstanding, if higher) counted toward the ceiling. After the GAB was modified in 1983 to permit support for credits to nonparticipants (as discussed below), the portion was raised to two-thirds.

[114] As John Anson (United Kingdom) observed during the debates, the decision to use total Fund quotas as the denominator had the illogical effect of raising the absolute borrowing limit after the Eighth Quota Review took effect and reduced the need for further borrowing. Minutes of EBM/81/119 (September 4, 1981), p. 10.

the actual level (22 percent at the end of FY 1981) but not much above the levels then being discussed (which ranged up to 49 percent).[115] The rules provided further that if borrowings (as defined) exceeded 50 percent of total quotas, the Board would review the status of unused credit lines with an eye toward maintaining a prudent balance. With occasional modification, these guidelines remained in place until 1991, but they had no discernible effect on actual borrowing. When the Fund's potential indebtedness peaked in 1984, the applicable ratio was still below 40 percent.

When the borrowing agreements with industrial countries were nearing expiration in 1984, the Fund negotiated a replacement package extending through 1986 for a much larger amount (SDR 3 billion, compared with the original 1.3 billion). Also in 1984, Saudi Arabia responded to that package by agreeing to a "third tranche" on its loan, for an additional SDR 3 billion. And in December 1986, Japan agreed to lend SDR 3 billion to the Fund, with a five-year maturity. (See Table 17.5, above.) Overall, during these five years of extensive and heavy demands on its resources, the Fund obtained short- to medium-term commitments from 19 countries that made a total of some SDR 14 billion (15½ percent of total Fund quotas) available to finance enlarged access.[116] Although rather less than the Managing Director's ambitious target, this borrowing sufficed to enable the Fund to meet the demand for enlarged-access credits throughout the 1980s.

General Arrangements to Borrow

The GAB was a valuable resource to the Fund, but more as a safety valve than as a direct source of money. The Fund drew on these lines of credit on nine occasions from 1964 through 1978, but not again for the next 20 years (Figure 17.4).[117]

The GAB originated as one of several expedients in the 1960s (including the 1961 Basel Agreement, the establishment of the London Gold Pool, and the creation of swap lines between major central banks) to supplement and protect gold and dollars as official international reserves (see Ainley, 1984, pp. 2–4). It provided a conditional line of credit to the Fund for a renewable period of five years. Throughout the 1960s and 1970s, its provisions were routinely renewed without

---

[115]The quoted percentages are from "Guidelines on Borrowing by the Fund," EBS/81/174 (August 19, 1981), Table 3, p. 19 (as corrected on September 9).

[116]This amount is the sum of the SDR 11 billion in medium-term commitments from Saudi Arabia and the maximum amount (SDR 3 billion) available at any one time from the various shorter-term agreements with industrial countries. During the period of peak usage in the mid-1980s, the equivalent amount in dollars was only slightly larger than the amount in SDRs.

[117]The history of the GAB is covered in Horsefield (1969), Vol. 1, pp. 510–15 and 567–70, and Vol. 2, pp. 373–77; de Vries (1976), Vol. 1, pp. 370–76; de Vries (1985), pp. 587–92; and Ainley (1984). The GAB was next activated in July 1998 to finance the augmentation of an EFF arrangement with the Russian Federation.

Figure 17.4. General Arrangements to Borrow, 1962–96
(Includes associated agreements)

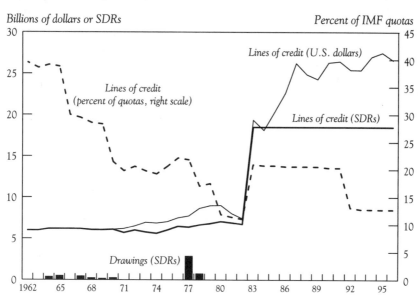

major modification, and the available amount of money gradually declined in relation to quotas and world trade.[118]

Complacency vanished quickly after the debt crisis of 1982 hit while negotiations to increase Fund quotas were at a standstill. At the Interim Committee meeting in Toronto that September, U.S. Treasury Secretary Regan called for creation of "an additional new permanent borrowing arrangement that would be available for use by the Fund only under extraordinary circumstances."[119] Although this general U.S. proposal envisaged creation of a new arrangement, the seed germinated over the next two months into a plan to enlarge the GAB.

Enlarging the GAB was not the obvious choice under the circumstances, because of limitations on its activation. As noted above, the Fund could call on GAB credit lines only to finance a credit arrangement for a GAB participant (i.e., a G-10 country) and even then only if the arrangement was expected to alleviate a problem that threatened the stability of the international monetary system.[120] If

---

[118]The only changes in size or composition before 1983 were the addition of an associated agreement with Switzerland in 1964 and an increase in the credit line from Japan in 1976. Those additions augmented the resources of the GAB by about 19 percent (from $6.3 billion to $7.5 billion, as of 1976).

[119]Minutes of ICMS/Meeting 19, September 4, 1982), p. 15. Regan announced the proposal publicly a few days later in his Annual Meetings speech, in slightly altered language; IMF, *Summary Proceedings*, 1982, p. 51.

[120]For the text of the GAB agreement that was in effect from 1978 through 1982, see de Vries (1985), Vol. 3, pp. 527–33.

creation of a whole new agreement was to be avoided, new flexibility would have to be introduced.

Despite the ambiguities, a broad agreement on the expansion developed quite quickly. The G-10 Deputies, chaired by Lamberto Dini (Italy), met at the Fund office in Paris on November 29, 1982, for a preliminary exchange of views on Regan's proposal. By then, discussions among ministers had already ruled out trying to create a new mechanism. Extension of additional lines of credit to the Fund would have to be made, if at all, through the GAB or possibly the SFF. Oddly, although the proposal was a U.S. initiative and its passage was designed in part to help the U.S. government further its objectives in stabilizing the economies of several countries in Latin America, the U.S. delegates at the November meeting insisted that the expansion be adopted only as part of a package.[121] The complete deal should include a cutback in enlarged access, a tightening of CFF conditionality, and an increase in effective remuneration rates for Fund creditors. Those issues, however, were set aside for the moment, and in a series of meetings through mid-January, the Deputies agreed to expand the GAB almost exactly as proposed by the United States.[122]

The G-10 agreement would expand the GAB in three directions: it would greatly increase its size, from less than SDR 7 billion to 17 billion ($17.8 billion), make it available to support Fund credits to nonparticipants, and open the door for other countries to make associated credit arrangements.[123]

Just how big the GAB should be was debated for several weeks. Most of the G-10 preferred to aim for SDR 20 billion, but the United States fought to keep it closer to 15 billion. The final compromise emerged over lunch at a meeting of G-10 ministers in Paris in mid-January.[124] An equally delicate issue that could have derailed the whole effort concerned how to apportion commitments among the G-10. The existing distribution dated essentially from 1962 and no longer reflected the relative importance of the G-10 countries. Fortunately, a ready meas-

---

[121]IMF/CF (S 371 "Group of Ten Meetings and Studies, 1981–1982"); cable from the U.S. Deputies (December 3, 1982).

[122]The United States eventually obtained substantial victories on all counts. A cutback in enlarged access was agreed upon toward the end of 1983, after substantial debate (see above, p. 881). CFF access and conditionality were tightened around the same time (see Chapter 15), and an increase in remuneration rates was approved in January 1984 (see below, p. 904). The U.S. delegation at the Deputies' meetings was headed by Beryl W. Sprinkel, the Under Secretary of the Treasury for Monetary Affairs, and Henry C. Wallich, Member of the Board of Governors of the Federal Reserve System.

[123]The amendment also introduced three technical changes. First, the denomination of borrowings was changed from individual currencies to SDRs. Second, the interest rate, which had been based on the Fund's rate of charge, was set equal to the SDR rate. Third, the rules were tightened on funds borrowed to finance reserve tranche drawings, since countries were no longer required to repay those drawings. Previously, the Fund's borrowings had carried a five-year maturity. Now, if the purchaser was "included in an operational budget" (i.e., if the Executive Board determined the country's currency to be "sufficiently strong" pursuant to Article V), the Fund had to make repayment equal to the net amount of the purchaser's currency sold in the preceding quarter.

[124]Notes by de Larosière on the January 18 meeting; in IMF/RD Managing Director G-10 Folder (Accession 87/27, Box 19, Section 536).

Table 17.6. Expansion of the GAB, 1983

(In millions)

| Participant | Previous Commitment | | | New Commitment | | | Percentage Increase |
	Local currency	SDR equivalent	Share (In percent)	SDRs	Dollar equivalent	Share (In percent)	
United States	2,000.0	1,910	30	4,250.0	4,450	25	222
Germany (Deutsche Bundesbank)	4,000.0	1,496	23	2,380.0	2,492	14	159
United Kingdom	357.1	517	8	1,700.0	1,780	10	329
France	2,715.4	340	5	1,700.0	1,780	10	500
Italy	343,750.0	216	3	1,105.0	1,157	7	511
Japan	340,000.0	1,367	21	2,125.0	2,225	13	155
Canada	216.2	168	3	892.5	934	5	533
Netherlands	724.0	242	4	850.0	890	5	351
Belgium	7,500.0	140	2	595.0	623	4	425
Sweden (Sveriges Riksbank)	517.3	64	1	382.5	400	2	594
Switzerland (Swiss National Bank)				1,020.0	1,068	6	
Total		6,460	100	17,000.0	17,799	100	263
Associated Agreements: Switzerland (Swiss National Bank)	865.0	394					
Saudi Arabia				1,500.0	1,570		
Total including associated agreements		6,854	18,500.0	19,369.0			

Note: Equivalent values are computed at average exchange rates for 1983.

ure was available, since the shares in the ongoing quota review were viewed as reasonable and were accepted by all participants. The effect, after some smoothing and other adjustments, was to even out the distribution somewhat, as the shares of the three largest creditors all declined (Table 17.6).

On the second issue, the G-10 agreed to drop the requirement that the GAB only be activated to support a drawing by a participant but to retain the requirement that it be used only to cope with a systemic problem and to add a requirement that activation for nonparticipants be restricted to upper-tranche (i.e., high-conditionality) arrangements. From the Fund's vantage, the restriction to systemic problems posed a political problem because it implied that the arrangements could benefit large countries more than small ones. To mitigate the force of this limitation, the agreement was written to permit the Managing Director to initiate a call on the GAB if the Fund's resources were inadequate to deal with "balance of payments problems of *members* of a character or *aggregate* size that could threaten the stability of the international monetary system" (emphasis added). This wording acknowledged that problems affecting several smaller countries could trigger an activation of the borrowing arrangements.

The third issue—allowance for associated agreements—was intended primarily to enable the Fund to negotiate a parallel arrangement with Saudi Arabia. The G-10 Deputies agreed in December 1982 to invite Saudi Arabia to participate in some fashion in the GAB, and the chairman of the G-10 Ministers, Jacques Delors (France), met with senior officials in Riyadh later that month. De Larosière and Geoffrey Howe (who had just been elected chairman of the Interim Committee) then flew to Riyadh in early January for more specific discussions on the matter.[125] Finally, the top Saudi officials—Abalkhail and Al-Quraishi—met with Dini in London at the end of January and then with de Larosière in Washington in early February to complete the deal.[126]

Although the Saudis were responsive from the beginning, negotiations were delicate. Some of the G-10 countries were reluctant to expand their club, and full participation in the GAB also would have created political problems for Saudi Arabia. To support the Fund's lending to developing countries was one thing; to become part of the industrial country establishment was quite another. Moreover, Saudi Arabia's leadership role in the Middle East might require it to opt out if the GAB should ever be activated to support Fund lending to countries with which it or its neighbors had serious conflicts or differences (such as Israel or South Africa). For both the Fund and the G-10, however, a special opt-out clause would have raised questions of equal treatment.

Two possible solutions to this dilemma were considered. First, the discussions during January were predicated on the assumption that the Saudi authorities would accept a parallel status that would require it to be bound by group decisions but would give it voting rights on GAB decisions.[127] Saudi Arabia would not become a member of the group, and the precise nature of its role would remain secret. When that overture was rejected, the G-10 Deputies agreed to consider a much looser relationship. The accepted solution was to negotiate a separate but associated agreement under which some symmetry with the GAB could be retained. Saudi Arabia would have the right to accept or reject any call for activation of the arrangement, independently from the GAB.[128] Saudi officials would not vote or participate in G-10 meetings, but the G-10 would establish regular communication channels for consultations, and the Chairman of the Deputies would debrief senior Saudi officials after each meeting.

A related amendment to the GAB enabled Switzerland to become a full participant. The Swiss National Bank had had an associated creditor agreement since

---

[125]Minutes of EBM/83/10 (January 12, 1983), pp. 3–4.

[126]Reports on the meeting with Dini in London and other G-10 meetings in this period may be found in the Research Department of the Bank of Italy (file H.1.3, "Gruppo dei Dieci, Riunioni"). See in particular Dini's letter of January 28, 1983, to Jacques Delors (Chairman of the G-10); and his February 10 report to G-10 ministers and governors. On Howe's role, see Howe (1994), pp. 270–71.

[127]See January 25, 1983, telex from de Larosière to Abalkhail; in IMF/CF (S 1773 "General Arrangements to Borrow, Participation of Saudi Arabia").

[128]Paragraph 23 of the amended GAB agreement provides either for a closely associated agreement under which calls "shall be treated as if they were calls . . . in respect of a participant" (which would preclude opting out) or for separate agreements "involving an association with participants" without such a provision. The agreement with Saudi Arabia fell in the latter category.

1964, and it now signaled its desire to become a full participant.[129] Since Switzerland was still not a member of the IMF, the GAB could not be used to support lending to it, but Switzerland's financial position was strong enough that this detail had no foreseeable practical consequence. The proposed amendment to the arrangements was hastily revised in February 1983 to incorporate this upgrading of the relationship.

As soon as the Deputies reached agreement on their strategy in December, the Fund got involved both in negotiating the contentious issues just discussed and in drafting the revised agreement. Drafting also proceeded quickly, driven by the early date of the spring 1983 meeting of the Interim Committee. The amended GAB was approved by the G-10 Deputies and then by their Ministers at meetings in Paris on January 17–18, 1983, by the Interim Committee on February 11, and by the Executive Board later that month.[130] The Swiss National Bank became a full participant in April, and an associated arrangement with Saudi Arabia for a credit line of SDR 1.5 billion ($1.6 billion) was finalized in May.

Although the expanded GAB was not activated in the years that followed, it was periodically renewed without substantive change for subsequent five-year terms, beginning in November 1987.

Sharing the Burden: Who Pays for the Fund?

As a cooperative public institution, the IMF has generally sought to manage its finances so as to maintain an adequate reserve to back up its operations and to apportion costs fairly and equitably among its member countries. During the 1980s, the Fund's efforts to achieve these financial goals raised contentious political issues.

Through 1977, the Fund frequently incurred net losses in its operations, including two long streaks of continuous deficits (fiscal years 1949–56 and 1972–77). The early losses, which resulted from a combination of low demand for Fund credits and a low interest rate charged on outstanding balances, were reversed largely because of an investment program carried out from 1957–72 that funded a substantial reserve balance.[131] When increased lending at low interest rates in the

---

[129]IMF/CF (S 1771 "Inclusion of Switzerland in Borrowing Arrangements, 1980–1983"); cable to the Fund from Pierre Languetin, President of the Swiss National Bank (January 28, 1983).

[130]For the original and revised GAB agreements, the associated borrowing agreement with Saudi Arabia, and related documents, see the appendices in Ainley (1984).

[131]In the early years of Fund operations, income from charges on outstanding credits was insufficient to cover administrative expenses. In 1956–60, the Fund sold $800 million worth of gold to the United States, invested the proceeds, and used much of the interest income to establish a Special Reserve account. By 1972, the balance in the account exceeded $400 million, and the Fund had unwound the investment program by repurchasing the gold. Total reserves (the sum of the General Reserve and Special Reserve accounts) peaked in 1971, at SDR 784 million ($784 million), and fell to SDR 687 million in 1977 as a result of the Fund's operating losses in those years (although it rose in U.S. dollar terms, to about $825 million). For an overview, see "Factors Relating to Burden Sharing in the Fund," EBS/85/126 (May 14, 1985), pp. 8–9.

1970s led to renewed problems, the main lever available for stanching the losses was the interest rate (the "rate of charge"), which contained a substantial element of concessionality. The Fund moved cautiously, however, as it was reluctant to force its borrowers to pay higher costs without passing on part of the burden to creditors.[132] Charges had to be not only reasonable and fair, but also low enough to encourage countries to seek early assistance from the Fund when problems arose. Although procedures were put in place to review the rate of charge when necessary, the staff remained uneasy about the prospects for the Fund's financial strength in the 1980s.

Concerns about maintaining an operating surplus came to a head in 1980. After just two years of comfortable surpluses, the Fund barely covered its expenses in FY 1980 (Table 17.7), and the staff projected a deficit for the coming year. Part of the problem was that the Fund was a victim of its own success: because its margin of interest was too low to cover other expenses, the more lending it did, the more it strained its net income. When market interest rates rose sharply, as they did in 1980, income was squeezed further. The problem was compounded even more when the Fund's lending was accelerating, as it did at that time, because the rate of charge rose only gradually with the length of time that credits were outstanding, and the schedule of charges was adjusted infrequently. What was needed, in the absence of some means of subsidizing the gap, was either a reversal of the trend toward paying a high rate of remuneration to creditors or an agreement to set the rate of charge more flexibly so as to cover costs. Neither option, however, was very attractive. Lower remuneration carried the risk that creditors would become less willing to finance the Fund and to hold reserve tranche balances, while higher charges would impose additional costs on borrowers and might decrease the willingness of some countries to seek help from the Fund.

Remuneration to Creditors

The main source of net income to the Fund is the difference between market interest rates and the effective rate of remuneration on member countries' reserve tranche positions. Historically, that difference arose from two sources. First, until 1987 the rate of remuneration was below the market rate on SDR-denominated assets (Figure 17.5). Second, remuneration was paid on only a portion of a country's credit balance in the Fund.

Until 1968, the Fund did not compensate countries for creditor positions, which were considered as being made available by countries in strong balance of payments positions for the benefit of those in need of temporary assistance. In the late 1960s, when the Fund's income and reserve positions were becoming stronger, creditors seized the occasion of the discussion of the First Amendment to the Ar-

---

[132]On the history of the Fund's net income and related policies through 1978, see Horsefield (1969), Vol. 2, pp. 363–73; de Vries (1976), Vol. 1, pp. 383–97; and de Vries (1985), pp. 599–603.

Table 17.7. Income, Expenses, and Reserves: General Resources Account, FY 1979–90
(Millions of SDRs)

	1979	1980	1981	1982	1983	1984	1985	1986	1987	1988	1989	1990
Income												
Periodic (interest) charges	678.1	519.4	592.7	1,092.1	1,545.4	2,363.8	2,969.1	2,739.6	2,088.9	1,865.0	1,719.4	1,825.1
Service charges	6.2	11.1	21.9	34.8	51.3	50.8	30.3	19.7	15.8	20.6	10.6	22.2
Interest on SDRs	57.1	81.8	265.8	657.2	444.3	371.6	478.3	263.2	143.9	66.0	61.3	88.2
Misc. income, net	8.0	1.9	1.8	4.8	4.3	5.7	4.3	6.9	2.1	2.8	2.0	4.8
Total gross income	749.4	614.2	882.2	1,788.9	2,045.3	2,791.9	3,482.0	3,029.4	2,250.7	1,954.4	1,793.3	1,940.3
Expenses												
Remuneration	171.7	241.0	372.8	908.6	981.1	1,286.3	1,721.2	1,452.1	1,020.0	895.2	988.6	1,256.2
Administrative expenses	73.4	86.1	99.9	153.3	191.4	192.8	224.2	223.4	190.9	175.1	172.7	188.6
Interest on borrowing, net	458.1	284.0	329.5	634.9	807.4	1,239.8	1,566.5	1,275.8	927.2	774.6	515.0	345.0
Allocation to SCA									26.5	60.4	62.9	65.0
Total expenses	703.2	611.1	802.2	1,696.8	1,979.9	2,718.9	3,511.9	2,951.3	2,164.6	1,905.3	1,739.2	1,854.8
Net Income	46.1	3.1	80.1	92.0	65.4	73.1	−29.9	78.1	86.1	49.1	54.2	85.5
Reserves, end of period	760.1	763.2	843.3	935.4	1,000.7	1,073.8	1,044.0	1,122.1	1,208.2	1,257.3	1,311.5	1,397.0
Memorandum items:												
Net income as percent of initial reserves												
Target	6.5	0.4	10.5	0.0	3.0	3.0	3.0	5.0	7.5	7.5	5.0	5.7
Outturn				10.9	7.0	7.3	−2.8	7.5	7.7	4.1	4.3	6.5
Reserves as percent of credit outstanding	8.6	9.5	8.8	6.3	4.2	3.4	3.0	3.2	3.8	4.5	5.5	6.3

Source: IMF *Annual Reports*; and IFS.

Figure 17.5. Selected IMF Interest Rates, 1974–90

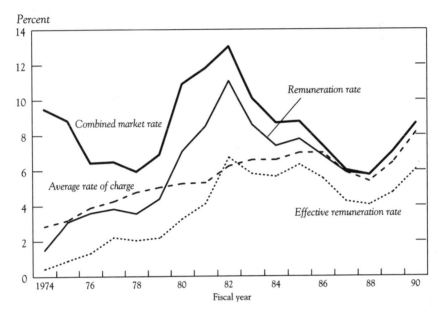

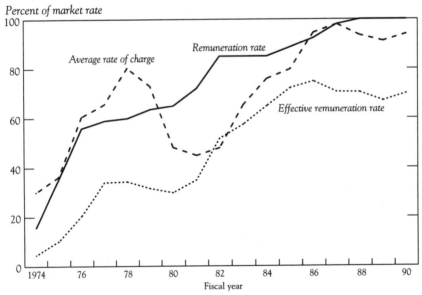

Charges and Remuneration (In percent of market interest rate)

ticles to call for a system of compensation. A discretionary distribution of net in-come was made in 1968 and 1969, and the First Amendment then provided for regular remuneration of creditor positions and established an initial fixed rate of 1½ percent a year. However, no return was paid on the gold tranche (later called the reserve tranche); the base for remuneration was the amount by which the

Fund's holdings of the country's currency were below 75 percent (rather than 100 percent) of quota. The remuneration rate was raised in 1974 to 2½ percent, was set at 3½ to 3¾ percent in 1975–76, and from mid-1975 through 1978 was set equal to the official SDR interest rate (which varied between 3½ and 4½ percent).[133] The 1974 increase thus marked the beginning of remuneration to creditors as a major expense for the Fund.

The Second Amendment to the Articles brought a further major increase, through two changes in the system of remuneration. First, remuneration was to be paid on a portion of the reserve tranche position and not just on creditor positions below 75 percent of quota. The remunerable portion would be determined by reference to a "norm" for each country, as explained below. Second, the rate of remuneration was to be set between 80 and 100 percent of the official SDR rate. Both of these changes were necessary for consistency with other elements in the amendments. Unless the reserve tranche was made into a financially attractive asset to hold, countries with credit positions could be expected to draw on their reserve tranche balance and to hold SDRs or foreign exchange instead, with even more serious adverse effects on the Fund's income and liquidity.

By introducing a norm for determining the base on which remuneration was to be paid, the amendment to Article V fixed the absolute amount of the unremunerated creditor position at the size of a country's reserve tranche in 1978. (For countries joining after the amendment took effect, this amount was to be determined by reference to the average norm for all existing members.) Any subsequent increase in the reserve tranche through enlargement of quotas would be fully remunerated as long as it was retained in the Fund. As a result of this policy shift, the point at which remuneration started rose from 75 percent of quota in 1978 to an average level of nearly 92 percent after the Eighth Quota Review took effect at the end of 1983.[134] Moreover, the amendment also permitted the Executive Board to set the norm at a higher level (as high as 100 percent of quota), in which case it could not be lowered subsequently. The intention was that eventually all or nearly all creditor positions would be fully remunerated, but a possibly lengthy transition period would allow the Fund to absorb the cost increase gradually.[135]

Although the effect of this amendment would be to raise the Fund's remuneration costs over time, it had no immediate effect and therefore raised no

---

[133]In 1974–75, remuneration was paid at 5 percent on any positions below 50 percent of quota. The Second Amendment to the Articles eliminated that possibility by requiring that a single rate be paid on all balances on which remuneration was paid. The official SDR interest rate was set below the market interest rate until May 1981 (see Chapter 18). In 1976–78, the market rate ranged from 5.7 to 6.9 percent, and the official rate was set periodically at 60 percent of the average market rate.

[134]See "'Norm' for Remuneration," EBD/84/51 (February 17, 1984).

[135]For the official commentary on the amendment to Article V, Section 9, on remuneration, see de Vries (1985), Vol. 3, pp. 341–43.

great objections from the developing countries that would eventually be hurt by it.[136] When the debates on the amendment took place, in 1975 and 1976, no one could foretell which countries would be creditors and which ones debtors two or three decades later. Not until the 1980s would the membership become more clearly aligned on that axis.

Tying the remuneration rate to market interest rates had an even greater quantitative effect on remuneration costs. Initially (effective at the beginning of 1979), the Executive Board set the rate at 90 percent of the official SDR rate, which in turn was set equal to 80 percent of the market rate. That raised the remuneration rate to 72 percent of the market rate, from 60 percent previously. Then, throughout the 1980s, the ratio to market rates was steadily raised under pressure from the major creditor countries: to 85 percent in 1981, to 97.5 percent in gradual steps from 1984 to 1986, and to 100 percent in 1987 (Figure 17.5).[137] By the end of the decade, about one-half of the Fund's remuneration costs and one-third of its total expenses were due to the policy changes introduced through the 1978 amendments to Article V. As a result, the Fund had to take measures to generate an equivalent amount of additional income.

Charges to Borrowers

Until 1974, the Fund was able to keep its interest charges quite low and stable. At the beginning of that year, interest on outstanding credits was charged at rates starting at 2 percent a year and rising to 5 percent, depending on the size and duration of the balance.[138] U.S. treasury bills, in contrast, were paying nearly 8 percent. That generous policy was made possible by the Fund's large stock of interest-free resources in the form of unremunerated reserve positions. Later, as remuneration costs rose, so did the rate of charge.

The Fund's initial response to rising costs, in the 1970s, was to try to maintain stability by raising charges selectively and avoiding a direct linkage to changes in market interest rates. By the end of the decade, a complicated and still-rigid system of charges was in place (Table 17.8). As market interest rates rose sharply in 1979–80, the Fund's net income deteriorated, and the Executive Board decided to consider making the system both simpler and more flexible.[139]

The first major step in that direction was to replace the whole sliding scale of charges on credit-tranche drawings with a single unified rate of charge. Al-

---

[136]For a later lament, see Patel (1992), pp. 10–11. Another ameliorating consideration in the late 1970s was the expectation that continuing gold sales by the Fund would generate additional income to help cover the rising cost of remuneration.

[137]For details on the progression during 1984–86, see *Annual Report 1986*, p. 70.

[138]For an overview of the evolution of policies on the rate of charge through 1978, see de Vries (1985), pp. 559–66.

[139]In addition to the interest rates discussed here, the Fund imposes one-time service charges on drawings (other than reserve-tranche drawings) and periodic commitment fees on undrawn balances under stand-by and extended arrangements. See IMF Treasurer's Department (1998), p. 36.

Table 17.8. Rates of Charge on the Use of Fund Resources, 1977–90

(In percent a year; fiscal years)

I. In effect 1977–81: rates vary with the length of time drawings are outstanding[a]

Basic rates	4⅜ to 6⅜
Rates on EFF drawings	4⅜ to 6⅞
Rates on drawings under 1974 Oil Facility	6⅞ to 7⅛
Rates on drawings under 1975 Oil Facility	7⅝ to 7⅞
Rates on drawings financed by SFF borrowings	Rate paid by Fund plus margin of 0.2 to 0.325
Rates on exceptional use of resources	Yield on U.S. treasury securities with five-year maturity, plus margin of 0.25

II. 1981–89: single basic rate

Basic rate, including EFF and other facilities	Set annually in accordance with income target, subject to periodic revision	
Rates on drawings under EAR	Rate paid by Fund plus margin of 0.2	
Rates on Oil Facility drawings and on drawings financed by SFF borrowings	As above; all Oil Facility drawings were repaid by 1983	
Basic rate (before burden-sharing adjustments):	Initial	Final
1982	6.25	
1983–84	6.60	
1985	7.00	
1986	7.00	
second half	7.87	7.00
1987	6.00	5.82
1988	5.80	5.38
1989	5.50	
second half	7.38	

III. 1990

Basic rate (before burden-sharing adjustments)	96.3 percent of the SDR interest rate
Other rates	As above

---

[a]The Second Amendment to the Articles changed the amount on which charges were levied. Prior to the amendment, the base was the amount by which the Fund's holdings of a country's currency exceeded its quota. After April 1978, the base was the amount of holdings resulting from drawings other than those on the reserve tranche. See de Vries (1985), Vol. 3, pp. 339–40.

though obviously desirable, such a move was not easy to make, because the Fund's Articles of Agreement specified that "rates of charge normally shall rise at intervals during the period in which the balances are held" (Article V, Section 8). Moreover, any change in the schedule required a 70 percent majority of the total voting power on the Executive Board.[140] The legal difficulty was finessed by a decision that moving to a more flexible approach created circumstances that were not "normal" in the sense of the Article, and that a sliding scale was

---

[140]Until the 1978 amendments, Article V included a list of specific charges related to the size and duration of outstanding balances, which could be changed by a 75 percent majority.

not required under those circumstances.[141] With that out of the way, consensus was reached in April 1981 on a unified rate, which was set initially at 6¼ percent.[142]

The new unified rate of charge represented an increase in the average rate of about 95 basis points. During the next year, however, because market interest rates continued to rise, the rate of charge actually fell relative to the market. The Board raised the rate again in 1983, to 6.6 percent, and in 1985 to 7 percent. After that, declines in market interest rates and an improvement in the Fund's net income relieved some of the pressure on the rate of charge.

Targeting Net Income

From 1981 on, the major determinant of the rate of charge was the Fund's net income relative to target levels agreed upon by the Executive Board. Toward the end of 1980, the staff circulated a proposal for setting a target for net income each year, which was to be achieved through appropriate adjustments to the interest rates charged on outstanding obligations. The Executive Board held a preliminary discussion of the issue in January 1981 and agreed in principle that the existing system was unsustainable. Without a change in the rules, the Fund was then expected to face an operating deficit in the coming fiscal year of more than SDR 200 million ($250 million). The most troubling aspect of the staff proposal was that charges on Fund credits might have to be set so high as to eliminate the concessional element, discourage countries from borrowing, and aggravate the financial difficulties of already troubled economies. Bernard J. Drabble (Canada) offered an alternative: to set the rate of charge at a fixed percentage of the remuneration rate. That idea generated a lot of interest but foundered on the danger that it could generate volatility and uncertainty in the Fund's charges and still leave the Fund short of revenue. Drabble and some other Directors from creditor countries also offered to support a reduction in the ratio of the remuneration rate to market rates, but the largest creditor countries were reluctant to endorse such a move.

Following two more meetings in March and April, the Board adopted a package that incorporated most of the staff's original proposals. Principally, the Fund would set a target for its net income each year, equivalent to 3 percent of the initial balance of the Fund's reserves. As noted above, the remuneration rate would be raised to 85 percent of the combined market interest rate. The rate of charge would then be determined residually, with the aim of achieving the target in light of the remuneration rate and projections of other relevant data. To achieve a measure of

---

[141]Statement by George Nicoletopoulos (Director of the Legal Department) at EBM/81/4 (January 7, 1981), pp. 28–29. The official commentary on the quoted phrase explains that "it is not mandatory that there shall be a progression of the periodic rates over time, although it is assumed that a progression will be the normal practice." De Vries (1985), Vol. 3, p. 340.

[142]See Decision No. 6834-(81/65), adopted April 22, 1981; in de Vries, 1985, Vol. 3. The unified rate applied only to the use of the Fund's ordinary resources.

stability, the rate of charge would be set for the financial year as a whole, subject to review after six months in the event of a shortfall in income.[143]

For a while, this new system worked well. The Fund's gross income swelled as a result of several years of heavy lending, and modest increases in the rate of charge sufficed to generate unexpectedly large flows of net income (Figure 17.5 and Table 17.7). Nonetheless, by 1985, it became apparent that trouble lay beneath the surface, for two reasons. First, credit outstanding was growing much more rapidly than the Fund's reserves. From a peak of 9½ percent in 1980, reserves fell to just 3 percent of outstanding credit in 1985. Second, the quality of the Fund's claims was deteriorating as a result of the emergence of substantial and prolonged arrears.

Sharing the Burden of Arrears

As soon as the arrears problem[144] emerged, the Fund's external auditors began alerting management to the need to acknowledge the risks in the published financial statements and to take steps to protect the institution from the effects of potential losses. The Executive Board adopted two of the recommended measures quickly. First, in March 1985, Directors agreed to exclude income that was in arrears by six months or more (SDR 56.4 million in FY 1985) from the official figures.[145] That is, overdue charges were to be reported as "deferred" rather than "accrued" income. Consequently, the IMF had its first annual deficit in net income since 1977 (SDR 30 million). Second, in June, the Board raised the target for annual net income, from 3 percent to 5 percent of beginning-of-period reserves. As the amount of arrears continued to pile up (see Chapter 16), the income target was raised further on a temporary basis, to 7½ percent for FY 1987 and FY 1988, and then was pegged again at 5 percent.[146]

The direct effect of these changes in accounting procedures and financial goals was to raise the rate of charge still further, which put an extra burden on indebted countries at a time when many of them could ill afford it. Concerns over that

---

[143]See "Review of the Fund's Charges," SM/80/282 (December 24, 1980), "Revised Pages 24–27," Sup. 1 (January 7, 1981), "Additional Information," Sup. 2 (February 23), and "Charts 1 and 2," Sup. 3 (March 6); "Review of Fund's Charges," SM/81/63 (March 20) and "Additional Information," Sup. 1 (March 27); "Rule 1—Charges on Transactions and Holdings in the General Resources Account," SM/81/89 (April 20); and minutes of EBM/81/3–4 (January 7, 1981), EBM/81/37–38 (March 9), EBM/81/57 (April 15, 1981); and EBM/81/65 (April 22). The new rules also provided for a further review at the end of the financial year and a consideration of how to use or dispose of any excess in net income. For the full set of rules on charges adopted in May 1981, see *Annual Report 1981*, pp. 163–67 and 171.

[144]Also see the final section of Chapter 16, where the development of special charges on overdue obligations, burden-sharing policies, and special reserve accounts is discussed.

[145]Decision No. 7930-(85/41), adopted March 13, 1985; *Annual Report 1985*, p. 115.

[146]The increase to 5 percent was effected through an amendment to Rule I-6(4) adopted on June 5, 1985. The temporary increase to 7.5 percent was implemented as part of the July 1986 decision on burden sharing. For FY 1990, an amount equal to the shortfall in net income for FY 1989 was added to the target, making it 5.7 percent.

prospect came to the fore during the Executive Board's routine review of the Fund's income position in December 1985. The standard calculations implied that the rate of charge would have to be raised immediately from 7 percent to 7.87 percent, which would be above the SDR interest rate.[147] The staff suggested that the burden could be shared in part by creditors if the rate of remuneration were lowered, and in part by the Fund if the target level of net income were lowered. Either action required a 70 percent majority of the votes in the Board. Lowering the income target was widely rejected as financially risky, and creditor countries were split on the prospect of lowering the remuneration rate. Several were sympathetic to the notion of equitable burden sharing, while others argued that even if the rate of charge rose above the SDR rate, borrowers were still getting credits on reasonable and equitable terms (terms that were better than they could obtain from financial markets). Four countries (the United States, Japan, Germany, and the United Kingdom) were opposed to lowering the remuneration rate, and they had enough votes (36 percent) to block it. Consequently, the rate of charge was raised to 7.87 percent, effective November 1, 1985.[148]

Events took an unexpected turn over the next few months. The Fund's net income for FY 1986 turned out to be sharply higher than projected, which made it possible to reverse the increase in the rate of charge and restore it retroactively to 7 percent for the full fiscal year. That action was taken on April 30, 1986, the day the fiscal year ended. The problem of sharing the burden thus was effectively postponed.[149]

A major roadblock in the way of an agreement on burden sharing was that the U.S. Executive Director (then Charles Dallara) was mandated by U.S. law to work toward raising the remuneration rate to the SDR interest rate.[150] Moreover, as Dallara noted during the Board debates, burden sharing by creditors was "anathema" to the U.S. authorities (the Reagan administration).[151] Since no one wanted to impose a solution that would create political problems for the

---

[147]At that time, the Fund's Rule I–10(d) called for a review of the remuneration rate whenever the rate of charge was projected to rise above the SDR interest rate.

[148]Minutes of EBM/85/176 (December 6, 1985) and EBM/85/180 (December 13). The staff's review of the issue and available options is in "Review of the Fund's Income Position," EBS/85/258 (November 20, 1985). Mtei's intervention was at meeting 85/180, p. 3.

[149]Subsequently, net income for FY 1986 turned out to be even higher. The rate of charge could have been reduced retroactively to 6.73 percent for the second half of the fiscal year, but a majority of the Board preferred to add the excess income to the Fund's reserves. Minutes of EBM/86/73–74 (April 30, 1986). On subsequent developments, see "The Fund's Net Income for FY 1986 and FY 1987—Disposition of Net Income for FY 1986 and Determination of the Rate of Charge for FY 1987," EBS/86/116 (May 28, 1986), and minutes of EBM/86/100 (June 20, 1986).

[150]The remuneration rate at the end of FY 1986 was equal to 92 percent of the SDR interest rate. Under Rule I–10(d), it was being raised from 85 percent in FY 1984 to a level between 95 and 97.5 percent by the end of FY 1987.

[151]Minutes of EBM/86/122 (July 25, 1986), p. 75.

Table 17.9. Burden-Sharing Adjustments to the Rates of Charge and Remuneration, FY 1987–90

(In percent, except as noted)

Period Ending[a]	Deferred Charges (SDR millions)	Basic Rate of Charge	Adjust- ment	Adjusted Rate of Charge	Basic Rate of Remu- neration	Adjust- ment	Adjusted Rate of Remu- neration	Remu- neration Coefficient
October 1986	73.1	5.82	0.46	6.28	5.89	0.45	5.44	90.1
January 1987	66.8	5.82	0.77	6.59	5.77	0.76	5.01	85.0
April 1987	41.8	5.81	0.57	6.38	5.87	0.56	5.31	90.5
July 1987	39.8	5.38	0.52	5.90	5.64	0.51	5.13	91.0
October 1987	39.2	5.38	0.52	5.90	6.09	0.52	5.57	91.5
January 1988	47.0	5.38	0.64	6.02	5.70	0.64	5.06	88.8
April 1988	39.3	5.38	0.79	6.17	5.52	0.83	4.69	85.0
July 1988	61.3	5.50	0.92	6.42	5.91	0.88	5.03	85.0
October 1988	46.5	5.50	1.01	6.51	6.86	0.94	5.92	86.3
January 1989	53.9	7.38	0.92	8.30	7.39	0.86	6.53	88.7
April 1989	53.0	7.38	0.96	8.34	8.06	0.90	7.16	88.8
July 1989	59.4	7.67	1.00	8.67	8.17	0.93	7.24	88.6
October 1989	56.9	7.85	0.96	8.81	8.35	0.92	7.43	89.0
January 1990	59.1	8.42	1.00	9.42	8.95	0.92	8.03	89.7
April 1990	59.8	8.62	1.06	9.68	9.16	0.99	8.17	89.2

[a]The initial period ending October 1986 covers six months; all others are three months. For explanation of terms, see text.

Fund's largest member (and one of its largest creditors), a consensus solution was imperative. By July 1986, after a long and occasionally bitter debate, a compromise framework emerged in which the remuneration rate would be raised permanently to 100 percent of the SDR interest rate, subject to a temporary discount as a creditors' contribution toward covering the cost of outstanding arrears.

Beginning in May 1986, the rate of charge on the use of ordinary resources was adjusted upward, and the rate of remuneration was adjusted downward, by roughly equal amounts, to cover the value of deferred charges each quarter (Table 17.9). The burden-sharing agreement provided that half of the required amount was to come from each source, subject to a floor on the adjusted remuneration rate at 85 percent of the SDR interest rate.[152] When the floor was reached (as it was in the first half of 1988), the uncompensated portion of deferred charges would be carried over to the next period. Because the average outstanding amount of balances subject to charges was smaller than the average of remunerable credit balances, the average increase required in the rate of charge (81 basis points through FY 1990) was slightly larger than the average adjustment in the remuneration rate (77 basis points).

---

[152]Decision No. 8348-(86/122), adopted July 25, 1986; in the Appendix to Chapter 16.

This painting, *No More Funds*, by Ernesto Bertani hung in the anteroom of Managing Director Camdessus's office.

Despite the continual accumulation of arrears, the Fund succeeded in raising reserves gradually in relation to outstanding claims, to 6¼ percent in FY 1990, to a level that was in line with historical (pre-1980s) experience. Along with the buildup in special precautionary balances to cover arrears, these measures averted a crisis in the Fund's finances. That achievement, however, had not been costless, because it had required raising the rate of charge to levels close to short-term market interest rates and thus greatly reducing the concessional element in Fund lending. After a decade of struggle and evolution, the Fund had become both a stronger financial institution and a more conventional financial intermediary.

Appendix I: An Alternative Balance Sheet Presentation

The standard presentation of financial accounts by the IMF treats each of the institution's departments and administered accounts as a distinct entity. Separate balance sheets are presented for the General Department, the SDR Department, the Trust Fund, the ESAF Trust, and other administered accounts that have been in use at various times. That practice reflects the legal and financial differences among those units. For analytical purposes, however, it is also of interest to picture the IMF as a conglomerate in which these different operating units are all overseen by a single management and Board of Directors and are all driven by similar goals as defined in the institutional charter (the Articles of Agreement).

Table 17.A1 presents a consolidated balance sheet for all major financial operations controlled by the IMF. As can be readily seen by comparing this table with Table 17.1, the bulk of the assets and liabilities are those of the General Department, but the stock of SDR allocations in 1989 (SDR 21.4 billion) was nearly as large as the total amount of credit extended through the GRA and administered accounts (24.6 billion). A substantial portion of the assets held by the General Department consists of currencies that are judged to be unusable for operations, and other nonliquid claims. Total allocated SDRs are an additional financial claim on the asset side, matched on the other side by the sum of SDRs held by the Fund and outside (by member countries and prescribed holders). ESAF loans and investments and Trust Fund loans, and their corresponding liabilities, round out the picture. Overall, this conglomerate grew somewhat more rapidly than the General Department alone during the 1980s, and at the end of the decade was nearly 25 percent larger than that one department. Whereas the Fund's own resources, provided primarily by quota subscriptions, amounted to SDR 99 billion at the end of FY 1989, the total stock of assets supplied by or through the Fund totaled SDR 122 billion.

Table 17.A1. Consolidated Balance Sheet of the IMF and ESAF Trust

(Billions of SDRs; see text for explanatory notes)

	December 31, 1978	December 31, 1989	Change
Assets			
Liquid cash assets	5.9	27.4	21.5
Quota subscriptions	39.0	90.1	51.1
Less reserve tranche positions	−8.5	−22.0	(13.5)
Less nonliquid holdings	−26.4	−43.0	(16.6)
SDA (Trust Fund) investments	0.6	0.8	0.2
ESAF Trust investments		0.7	0.7
Nonliquid cash assets	26.4	43.0	16.6
Currently unusable currencies	20.8	28.6	7.8
Undrawn credit commitments	3.2	4.3	1.1
Required working balances	2.4	10.1	7.7
Loans and credits	11.1	24.7	13.5
GRA credits	10.3	22.3	12.0
SAF loans	0.0	1.5	1.5
Trust Fund loans	0.8	0.5	(0.4)
ESAF Trust loans		0.4	0.4
SDR allocations	9.3	21.4	12.1
Receivables	0.1	1.4	1.3
Current charges and interest	0.1	0.5	0.4
Deferred charges		0.9	0.9
Gold (at SDR 35 per ounce)	4.1	3.6	(0.5)
Other assets	0.1	0.2	0.1
Total assets	57.1	121.7	64.5
Liabilities and Net Worth			
Liquid liabilities	14.9	25.5	10.6
Reserve tranche positions	8.5	22.0	13.5
Borrowings (General Department)	6.4	3.5	(2.9)
Balance of quota subscriptions	30.5	68.1	37.6
SDRs outside the Fund	8.1	20.5	12.4
Borrowings by the ESAF Trust		0.6	0.6
Dedicated resources	1.5	3.2	1.8
SDA		2.3	2.3
Trust Fund	1.5	0.5	(1.0)
ESAF Trust		0.5	0.5
Other liabilities	0.2	0.4	0.2
Reserves, etc.	2.0	3.4	1.4
Ordinary reserves	0.7	1.4	0.6
SCA	0.0	0.2	0.2
Deferred charges	0.0	0.9	0.9
SDR holdings	1.2	0.9	(0.3)
Total liabilities and net worth	57.1	121.7	64.5
Memorandum items:			
Gold at market prices	45.9	31.6	−14.4
Unused and available credit lines	5.5	19.4	13.9

Appendix II: IMF Quotas, 1979–89

Table 17.A2. IMF Quotas, 1979–89

(Millions of SDRs)

Member[a]	Sixth General Review 1979–80[b]	Seventh General Review 1981–83[c]	Eighth General Review 1984–89[d]
Afghanistan	45.0	67.5	86.7
Algeria	285.0	427.5	623.1
Angola (9/19/89)	. . .	. . .	145.0
Antigua and Barbuda (2/25/82)	. . .	3.6	5.0
Argentina	535.0	802.5	1,113.0
Australia	790.0	1,185.0	1,619.2
Austria	330.0	495.0	775.6
Bahamas, The	33.0	49.5	66.4
Bahrain	20.0	30.0	48.9
Bangladesh	152.0	228.0	287.5
Barbados	17.0	25.5	34.1
Belgium	890.0	1,335.0	2,080.4
Belize (3/16/82)	. . .	7.2	9.5
Benin	16.0	24.0	31.3
Bhutan (9/28/81)	. . .	1.7	2.5**
Bolivia	45.0	67.5	90.7
Botswana	9.0	13.5	22.1
Brazil	665.0	997.5	1,461.3
Burkina Faso	16.0	24.0	31.6**
Burundi	23.0	34.5	42.7
Cambodia (Democratic Kampuchea)[e]	25.0	25.0	25.0
Cameroon	45.0	67.5	92.7
Canada	1,357.0	2,035.5	2,941.0
Cape Verde	2.0	3.0	4.5
Central African Republic	16.0	24.0	30.4
Chad	16.0	24.0	30.6
Chile	217.0	325.5	440.5
China	550.0	1,800.0	2,390.9
Colombia	193.0	289.5	394.2
Comoros	2.3	3.5	4.5**
Congo	17.0	25.5	37.3
Costa Rica	41.0	61.5	84.1
Côte d'Ivoire	76.0	114.0	165.5
Cyprus	34.0	51.0	69.7
Denmark	310.0	465.0	711.0
Djibouti	3.8	5.7	8.0**
Dominica	1.9	2.9	4.0
Dominican Republic	55.0	82.5	112.1
Ecuador	70.0	105.0	150.7
Egypt	228.0	342.0	463.4
El Salvador	43.0	64.5	89.0
Equatorial Guinea	10.0	15.0	18.4
Ethiopia	36.0	54.0	70.6
Fiji	18.0	27.0	36.5
Finland	262.0	393.0	574.9

Table 17.A2 (continued)

Member[a]	Sixth General Review 1979–80[b]	Seventh General Review 1981–83[c]	Eighth General Review 1984–89[d]
France	1,919.0	2,878.5	4,482.8
Gabon	30.0	45.0	73.1
Gambia, The	9.0	13.5	17.1
Germany, Federal Rep. of	2,156.0	3,234.0	5,403.7
Ghana	106.0	159.0	204.5
Greece	185.0	277.5	399.9
Grenada	3.0	4.5	6.0
Guatemala	51.0	76.5	108.0
Guinea	30.0	45.0	57.9
Guinea-Bissau	3.9	5.9	7.5
Guyana	25.0	37.5	49.2
Haiti	23.0	34.5	44.1
Honduras	34.0	51.0	67.8
Hungary (5/6/82)	. . .	375.0	530.7
Iceland	29.0	43.5	59.6
India	1,145.0	1,717.5	2,207.7
Indonesia	480.0	720.0	1,009.7
Iran[f]	660.0	660.0	660.0
Iraq	141.0	234.1	504.0*
Ireland	155.0	232.5	343.4
Israel	205.0	307.5	446.6
Italy	1,240.0	1,860.0	2,909.1
Jamaica	74.0	111.0	145.5*
Japan	1,659.0	2,488.5	4,223.3
Jordan	30.0	45.0	73.9
Kenya	69.0	103.5	142.0
Kiribati (6/3/86)	. . .	. . .	2.5
Korea	160.0	255.9	462.8
Kuwait	235.0	393.3	635.3
Lao People's Dem. Rep.	16.0	24.0	29.3*
Lebanon	12.0	27.9	78.7
Lesotho	7.0	10.5	15.1
Liberia	37.0	55.5	71.3
Libyan Arab Jamahiriya	185.0	298.4	515.7*
Luxembourg	31.0	46.5	77.0
Madagascar	34.0	51.0	66.4
Malawi	19.0	28.5	37.2
Malaysia	253.0	379.5	550.6
Maldives	0.9	1.4	2.0
Mali	27.0	40.5	50.8
Malta	20.0	30.0	45.1
Mauritania	17.0	25.5	33.9
Mauritius	27.0	40.5	53.6
Mexico	535.0	802.5	1,165.5
Morocco	150.0	225.0	306.6
Mozambique (9/24/84)	. . .	. . .	61.0
Myanmar	73.0	109.5	137.0
Nepal	19.0	28.5	37.3
Netherlands	948.0	1,422.0	2,264.8
New Zealand	232.0	348.0	461.6

Table 17.A2 (continued)

Member[a]	Sixth General Review 1979–80[b]	Seventh General Review 1981–83[c]	Eighth General Review 1984–89[d]
Nicaragua	34.0	51.0	68.2*
Niger	16.0	24.0	33.7
Nigeria	360.0	540.0	849.5
Norway	295.0	442.5	699.0
Oman	20.0	30.0*	63.1
Pakistan	285.0	427.5	546.3
Panama	45.0	67.5	102.2
Papua New Guinea	30.0	45.0	65.9
Paraguay	23.0	34.5	48.4
Peru	164.0	246.0	330.9*
Philippines	210.0	315.0	440.4
Poland (6/12/86)[g]	. . .	. . .	680.0
Portugal	172.0	258.0	376.6
Qatar	40.0	66.2	114.9
Romania	245.0	367.5	523.4
Rwanda	23.0	34.5	43.8
St. Kitts and Nevis (8/15/84)	. . .	. . .	4.5
St. Lucia (11/15/79)	3.6	5.4	7.5
St. Vincent and the Grenadines (12/28/79)	1.7	2.6	4.0
São Tomé and Príncipe	2.0	3.0	4.0*
Saudi Arabia	600.0	1,040.1	3,202.4
Senegal	42.0	63.0	85.1
Seychelles	1.3	2.0	3.0
Sierra Leone	31.0	46.5	57.9
Singapore[h]	49.0	92.4	92.4
Solomon Islands	2.1	3.2	5.0
Somalia	23.0	34.5	44.2
South Africa	424.0	636.0	915.7
Spain	557.0	835.5	1,286.0
Sri Lanka	119.0	178.5	223.1
Sudan	88.0	132.0	169.7
Suriname	25.0	37.5	49.3
Swaziland	12.0	18.0	24.7
Sweden	450.0	675.0	1,064.3
Syrian Arab Republic	63.0	94.5	139.1*
Tanzania	55.0	82.5	107.0
Thailand	181.0	271.5	386.6
Togo	19.0	28.5	38.4
Tonga (9/13/85)	. . .	. . .	3.3
Trinidad and Tobago	82.0	123.0	170.1
Tunisia	63.0	94.5	138.2
Turkey	200.0	300.0	429.1
Uganda	50.0	75.0	99.6
United Arab Emirates[i]	120.0	202.6	202.6
United Kingdom	2,925.0	4,387.5	6,194.0
United States	8,405.0	12,607.5	17,918.3
Uruguay	84.0	126.0	163.8
Vanuatu (9/28/81)	. . .	6.9	9.0
Venezuela	660.0	990.0	1,371.5
Vietnam	90.0	135.0	176.8

Table 17.A2 (concluded)

Member[a]	Sixth General Review 1979–80[b]	Seventh General Review 1981–83[c]	Eighth General Review 1984–89[d]
Western Samoa	3.0	4.5	6.0
Yemen Arab Republic	13.0	19.5	43.3
Yemen, People's Dem. Rep. of	41.0	61.5	77.2
Yugoslavia	277.0	415.5	613.0
Zaïre	152.0	228.0	291.0
Zambia	141.0	211.5	270.3
Zimbabwe (9/29/80)	100.0	150.0	191.0*
Total	39,116.5	59,999.9	90,132.6

[a]For countries that became members after 1978, the effective date of membership is given in parentheses.

[b]Quotas under the Sixth General Review came into effect during 1978. Four member countries (Comoros, Guinea-Bissau, São Tomé and Príncipe, and Seychelles) did not participate in that review.

[c]Quotas under the Seventh General Review came into effect during December 1980, except for Oman (February 1981), which is marked with an asterisk. For exact effective dates, see *Annual Report 1981*, pp. 131–33.

[d]Quotas under the Eighth General Review in most cases came into effect during December 1983. Those marked with asterisks came into effect during the first four months of 1984; for exact effective dates, see Annual Report 1984, pp. 106–108.

[e] Democratic Kampuchea did not consent to the quota increases proposed under any of these reviews.

[f]Iran did not consent to the quota increases proposed under the Seventh and Eighth Reviews.

[g]Poland became an Original Member of the Fund in January 1946, withdrew in March 1950, and was readmitted in June 1986.

[h]Singapore did not consent to the quota increase proposed under the Eighth General Review.

[i]United Arab Emirates did not consent to the quota increase proposed under the Eighth General Review.

*See footnote c.

**See footnote d.

Appendix III: Formulas for the Eighth General Review of Quotas

Calculated Quotas

Calculated quotas for the Eighth General Review were computed from a set of five equations, as agreed upon by the Executive Board in August 1982. The general formula for all five equations may be written as

$$Q_c = (\beta_1 Y' + \beta_2 R' + \beta_3 M' + \beta_4 X' + \beta_5 V') \times (1 + \beta_6 X'/Y) \times A, \qquad (1)$$

where Q_c is the calculated quota, the remaining notation is the same as in footnote 25 on p. 860, and all data were measured in SDRs for 1980:

Y' = GDP

R' = total international reserves

M' = imports of goods and services

X' = exports of goods and services ($X' - M'$ = balance on current account)

V' = variability in export receipts: $V' = \sqrt{(\sum_{t-3}^{11}(X'_t - \bar{X}'_t)^2)/3}$.

A is an adjustment factor that makes all five formulas yield the same aggregate quota.

Table 17.A3. Coefficients for Quota Formulas

Formula	$\beta_1(Y')$	$\beta_2(R')$	$\beta_3(M')$	$\beta_4(X')$	$\beta_5(V')$	$\beta_6(X'/Y)$	A
Bretton Woods	.01	.025	.05	0	.2276	1	1
III	.0065	.0205125	.078	0	.4052	1	.87554669
IV	.0045	.0389678	.07	0	.7697	1	.84548032
M4	.005	.042280464	.044	.044	.8352	0	.89703152
M7	.0045	.05281008	.039	.039	1.0432	0	.89568343

Note: As noted in the text, each country's calculated quota was computed as the higher of the quota from the reduced Bretton Woods formula and the simple mean of the two lowest values from the four derivative formulas.

The coefficients for the five formulas, with the designations used in the original presentation, are set out in Table 17.A3.

Actual Quotas

The basic formula used in the Eighth General Review for determining each country's proposed quota may be written as follows:

$$Q = aQ_c + (1 - a)(1 + p)Q_0,\tag{2}$$

where a is the "adjustment coefficient" discussed on p. 867, p is the percentage increase in total quotas, and Q_0 is the country's initial quota.

The adjustment coefficient is determined by the size of the increase (p) and the portion (s) of the total increase allocated to selective increases. To see this relationship, first note that the change in an individual quota may be decomposed into a selective and a general increase:

$$(Q - Q_0) = [s(Q_c/T) + (1 - s)(Q_0/T_0)](T - T_0),\tag{3}$$

where T and T_0 are the new and old magnitudes of total quotas, respectively.

Since $p \equiv T/T_0 - 1$, equation (3) may be rewritten as

$$(Q - Q_0)/T = [s(Q_c/T) + (1 - s)(Q_0/T_0)]p/(1 - p).\tag{4}$$

Successively rearranging terms, one eventually gets to

$$(Q/T - Q_0/T_0) = s\left(\frac{p}{1 + p}\right)(Q_c/T - Q_0/T_0).\tag{5}$$

Now define the adjustment coefficient a as the change in each country's quota share in proportion to the gap between the calculated and initial share:

$$a \equiv (Q/T - Q_0/T_0) \div (Q_c/T - Q_0/T_0).\tag{6}$$

Substituting equation (6) into equation (5) gives

$$a = sp/(1 + p).\tag{7}$$

In the Eighth General Review, the proposed quota increase was 47.5 percent ($p = 0.475$), and 60 percent of the increase was allocated to selective increases ($s = 0.6$). By equation (7), the adjustment coefficient was 19.3 percent ($a = 0.193$). (The highest possible coefficient, with $s = 1$, would have been 32.2 percent.)

Calculation of the U.S. quota illustrates the application of the formula. The initial quota share for the United States was 20.7 percent, and the calculated quota share was 16.8 percent. The adjustment coefficient implies that 19.3 percent of that gap was to be closed, making the new quota share 19.9 percent. Consequently, instead of a 47.5 percent increase (if $s = 0$), the United States got an increase of 42.1 percent. The lowest increase it could have got under this system (if $s = 1$) would have been 38.6 percent.

Appendix IV: Policies on Enlarged Access

In April 1980, the Managing Director alerted the Interim Committee to an expected tightening in the Fund's liquidity position as a result of rising demand for Fund credits.

World Economic Outlook and the Role of the Fund
in Payments Adjustment and Financing
Report to the Interim Committee, April 25, 1980

Mr. Chairman, the world economic picture is decidedly grim. The main difficulties include the severe worldwide problem of inflation, the marked slowdown of economic activity now under way in the industrial countries, the sudden and major worsening of the distribution of current account balances among major groups of countries, and the urgent need for both conservation and new sources of energy.

. . . the outlook for 1980 with respect to the financing of balance of payments imbalances is reasonably reassuring, although this is true only in an overall sense and does not reflect the problems in a number of individual countries that will be difficult to tackle. This relatively "easy" situation we have at present can be explained, in particular, by the existence of cushions of reserve holdings, and by the volume of bank credits which are in the pipeline, having been committed but not yet disbursed.

However, the ability to meet the financing problem in 1980 is not a reason for complacency. The expected further increase in the current account deficit of the non-oil LDCs in 1981, coupled with virtual stagnation in the volume of import growth, foreshadows a very difficult situation. Indeed, even now there are some warning signals in the financial markets: an increase in spreads, a shortening of maturities, and greater selectivity exercised by commercial banks in taking up new risks. And the signals suggest that banks might become more cautious in the recycling process as time goes by, and perhaps less active in this very essential intermediation function. Nevertheless, everyone agrees that, in the years ahead, the commercial banks will continue to play the major role in the recycling process, although perhaps with a more selective touch.

From our discussions in the Fund, I think there is a broad consensus that this institution should stand ready to assume an increasing role in recycling and to continue to promote adjustment. Both these aspects—recycling and adjustment—are closely linked. There was full agreement in our discussions in the Executive Board that the Fund should not undertake recycling on an unconditional basis. Certain elements of the Fund's role in the present situation are crucial. To begin with, in view of the size of the current deficits and of the difficulties that may arise in private intermediation, the Fund must be prepared, when necessary, to lend in larger amounts than in the past. I might summarize the views expressed on this in our discussions as a combination of flexibility and caution, with a readiness to go beyond the existing ceilings in relation to countries' quotas if and when special circumstances arise.

Secondly, the structural problems faced by many countries may require that adjustment take place over a longer period than has been typical in the framework of our programs in the past. In view of the difficulty of predetermining a set of precise corrective measures of a structural nature for a long period in the future, it may well be necessary for our programs to cover periods of one or two years, but accompanied by indications on how the adjustment and the policies are to be completed over the medium term. Our putting forward increased resources for balance of payments financing would of course facilitate adjustment and stretch it over a realistic period. It would also help the Fund to convince borrowing countries to engage in sound adjustment policies at a sufficiently early stage. Moreover, our lending must reflect in practice the sort of flexibility, with an awareness of the circumstances of members, that is called for in the Executive Board's current guidelines on conditionality.

. . . On the question of mustering additional resources for the Fund to use, I think we all recognize that present liquidity in the Fund is adequate for the moment, taking account of the Fund's regular resources and the fact that a large part of the supplementary financing facility resources have not yet been committed. In the longer run, Fund liquidity needs should be satisfied primarily through increases in quotas, which have, relative to international trade, been dramatically reduced since the early days of the Fund. Meanwhile, let me emphasize the importance of early consent to the Seventh Quota Review. In addition, the Fund should be ready to organize borrowing operations on appropriate terms as soon as needed.

The Interim Committee responded positively to the Managing Director's appeal.

. . . 3. In view of the outlook for the world economy and, in particular, the prospect of large and widespread payments imbalances, the Committee agreed that the Fund should stand ready to play a growing role in the adjustment and financing of these imbalances. In this connection the Committee endorsed the views set forth in the Managing Director's statement on the subject and agreed with him that any such financing by the Fund should be made available in conjunction with adjustment policies appropriate to the needs and problems of members in the present economic situation.

The Committee recognized that, in view of the availability of funds under the supplementary financing facility and the expected increase in quotas under the Seventh General Review, the Fund is, under present circumstances, in a relatively liquid position. Nevertheless, in the light of the size and the distribution of payments imbalances, the necessity to phase adjustment over a reasonable period of time, and the time needed for the completion of any borrowing arrangements, the Committee encouraged the Managing Director to start discussions with potential lenders on the terms and conditions under which the Fund could borrow funds to increase its resources, if and when the need arises.

The following year, the Executive Board adopted a policy on enlarged access, allowing for a substantial widening in lending limits on a temporary basis.

Policy on Enlarged Access to the Fund's Resources
Executive Board Decision—March 11, 1981

1. From the date on which the Fund determines that all available supplementary financing has been committed and additional borrowing arrangements have been concluded,

the Fund will be prepared to provide balance of payments assistance to members facing serious payments imbalances that are large in relation to their quotas in accordance with this decision (hereinafter referred to as "Enlarged Access"). Access to the Fund's resources under this decision will be provided under a stand-by or an extended arrangement, and purchases under the arrangement will be financed by resources that the Fund obtains for this purpose by replenishment under Article VII, Section 1(i) (hereinafter referred to as "borrowed resources"), in conjunction with the use of the other resources of the Fund (hereinafter referred to as "ordinary resources").

2. Access to the Fund's resources under other policies of the Fund will remain available in accordance with the terms of those policies.

3. A member contemplating use of the Fund's resources under this decision shall consult the Managing Director before making a request for such use. A request will be met only if the Fund is satisfied: (i) that the member needs financing from the Fund that exceeds the amount available to it in the four credit tranches or under the Extended Fund Facility and its problem requires a relatively long period of adjustment and a maximum period for repurchase longer than the three to five years under the credit tranche policies; and (ii) on the basis of a detailed statement of the economic and financial policies the member will follow and the measures it will apply during the period of the stand-by or extended arrangement, that the member's program will be adequate for the solution of its problem and is compatible with the Fund's policies on the use of its resources beyond the first credit tranche or under the Extended Fund Facility.

4. The Fund may approve a stand-by or extended arrangement that provides for Enlarged Access at any time until the Eighth General Review of Quotas becomes effective, provided that the Fund may extend this period.

5. A stand-by or extended arrangement approved under this decision will be in accordance with the Fund's policies, including the policies on conditionality, phasing and performance criteria.

6. The period of a stand-by arrangement approved under this decision will normally exceed one year, and may extend up to three years in exceptional cases. The period of an extended arrangement will be normally three years.

7. The amounts that will be made available under stand-by or extended arrangements approved under this decision will be determined according to guidelines adopted by the Fund from time to time.

8. The amounts available under a stand-by or extended arrangement approved under this decision will be apportioned between ordinary and borrowed resources as follows:

   (a) Under a stand-by arrangement purchases will be made with ordinary and borrowed resources in the ratio of 2 to 1 in the first credit tranche, and 1 to 1.2 in the next three credit tranches. Thereafter, purchases will be made with borrowed resources only. In the event that a member has already an outstanding use of all or part of its credit tranches because of previous purchases in the credit tranches or under the extended Fund facility, purchases will be made first with borrowed resources until that use of borrowed resources, together with any outstanding use of supplementary financing and exceptional use of the Fund's resources under Decision No. 5732-(78/65), adopted April 24, 1978, as amended on December 27, 1978, equals the amount of borrowed resources that would have been used if the previous purchases had been made under this decision.

   (b) Under an extended arrangement purchases will be made with ordinary and borrowed resources in the ratio of 1 to 1 until the outstanding use of the upper credit tranches and the extended Fund facility equals 140 percent of quota. Thereafter, purchases will be made with borrowed resources only. In the event that a member already has an outstanding use of all or part of its upper credit tranches or the extended Fund facility, purchases will be made with borrowed resources until that use of borrowed resources, together with any outstanding use of supplementary financing and exceptional use of the Fund's resources under Decision No. 5732-(78/65), adopted April 24, 1978, as amended on December 27, 1978, equals the amount of borrowed resources that would have been used if the outstanding use of the upper credit tranches and the extended Fund facility had been made under this decision.

(c) The apportionment in accordance with (a) and (b) above will be made on the basis of the outstanding use by the member of the Fund's resources at the time the arrangement for the member is approved.

(d) From time to time the Fund will review the proportions of ordinary and borrowed resources specified in (a) and (b) above and may modify them, and the modified proportions shall apply uniformly to both arrangements approved after the modification and amounts that may be purchased under existing arrangements after the modification.

9. (a) A stand-by or extended arrangement approved under this decision may provide, in part, for supplementary financing in accordance with Decision No. 5508-(77/127), adopted August 29, 1977, if

 (i) the arrangement replaces an arrangement approved under that decision, or

 (ii) an amount of supplementary financing becomes available because of the cancellation of an arrangement or because it is reasonably certain that an arrangement will not be fully utilized, in which case the arrangement approved under this decision may provide for the utilization of a part or all of the available amount.

(b) When an arrangement under this decision provides for supplementary financing, the supplementary financing will be used before borrowed resources.

10. (a) Repurchases in respect of outstanding purchases under this decision will be made in accordance with the provisions of the Articles of Agreement and decisions of the Fund, including those relating to repurchase as the member's balance of payments and reserve position improves, provided that repurchases in respect of outstanding purchases financed by borrowed resources shall be completed seven years after the purchase, and that the repurchases shall be made in equal semiannual installments during the period beginning three and one half years and ending seven years after the purchase.

(b) If a purchase is financed by ordinary and borrowed resources, a repurchase attributed to the purchase made with borrowed resources in advance of this schedule of installments must be accompanied by a repurchase in respect of the purchase made with ordinary resources at the same time if any part of the latter purchase is still outstanding. The amounts of the two repurchases will be in the same proportions in which ordinary and borrowed resources were used in the purchases, provided, however, that the repurchase in respect of the purchase financed with ordinary resources will not exceed the amount of the purchase still outstanding.

11. In order to carry out the purposes of this decision, the Fund will be prepared to grant a waiver of the limitation in Article V, Section 3(b)(iii) that is necessary to permit purchases under this decision or to permit purchases under other policies that would raise the Fund's holdings of a member's currency above the limits referred to in that provision because of purchases outstanding under this decision.

12. The Fund will apply its credit tranche policies as if the Fund's holdings of a member's currency did not include holdings resulting from purchases under this decision that have been made with borrowed resources. Purchases under this decision with borrowed resources and holdings resulting from these purchases will be excluded under Article XXX(c).

13. The Fund will state which purchases by a member are made under this decision and the amounts of ordinary and borrowed resources used in each purchase.

14. The Fund will determine the charges that it will levy on holdings of a member's currency resulting from purchases outstanding under this decision to the extent that they are made with borrowed resources.

15. The Fund will review this decision not later than June 30, 1983, and annually thereafter as long as the decision remains in effect.

Decision No. 6783-(81/40), adopted March 11, 1981

In 1982, as the Fund's liabilities to finance the enlarged access policy were rising, the Executive Board adopted guidelines that limited the aggregate amounts that the Fund could borrow.

Guidelines for Borrowing by the Fund

Quota subscriptions are and should remain the basic source of the Fund's financing. However, borrowing by the Fund provides an important temporary supplement to its resources. In present circumstances, it facilitates the provision of balance of payments assistance to its members under the Fund's policies of supplementary financing and enlarged access.

The confidence of present and potential creditors in the Fund will depend not only on the prudence and soundness of its financial policies but also on the effective performance of its various responsibilities, including, in particular, its success in promoting adjustment.

Against this background the Executive Board approves the following guidelines on borrowing by the Fund.

1. Fund borrowing shall remain subject to a process of continuous monitoring by the Executive Board in the light of the above considerations. For this purpose, the Executive Board will regularly review the Fund's liquidity and financial position, taking into account all relevant factors of a quantitative and qualitative nature.

2. Subject to paragraph 4 below, the Fund will not allow the total of outstanding borrowing plus unused credit lines to exceed the range of 50–60 per cent of the total of Fund quotas. If the total of outstanding borrowing plus unused credit lines reaches the level of 50 per cent of quotas, the Executive Board shall assess the various technical factors that determine, at that time, the availability of balances of unused lines of credit. While this assessment is being made, the total of outstanding borrowing plus unused credit lines may rise, if necessary, beyond 50 per cent but shall not exceed 60 per cent of total quotas.

3. Recognizing that the credit lines of all participants in the General Arrangements to Borrow (GAB) cannot be used at the same time and that the GAB can be activated only to finance purchases by a GAB participant, the total of outstanding borrowing plus unused credit lines under paragraph 2 above shall include, in respect of the GAB, either outstanding borrowing by the Fund under the GAB or one half of the total of credit lines under the GAB, whichever is the greater.

4. In the case of major developments, the Executive Board shall promptly review, and may adjust, the guidelines. In any event, the guidelines shall be reviewed when the Board of Governors has completed the Eighth General Review of Quotas, and may be adjusted as a result of that review of the guidelines.

5. The percentage limits specified in paragraph 2 above, or any other limits that may be adopted as a result of a review pursuant to paragraph 4 above, are not to be understood, at any time, as targets for borrowing by the Fund.

Decision No. 7040-(82/7), adopted January 13, 1982

These guidelines were amended in December 1983 to take account of new developments, including the expansion and revision of the GAB.

Guidelines for Borrowing by the Fund—Revised

. . . 1. Fund borrowing shall remain subject to a process of continuous monitoring by the Executive Board in the light of the above considerations. For this purpose, the Executive Board will regularly review the Fund's liquidity and financial position, taking into account all relevant factors of a quantitative and qualitative nature.

2. Subject to paragraph 4 below, the Fund will not allow the total of outstanding borrowing plus unused credit lines to exceed the range of 50–60 percent of the total of Fund quotas. If the total of outstanding borrowing plus unused credit lines reaches the level of 50 percent of quotas, the Executive Board shall assess the various technical factors that determine, at that time, the availability of balances of unused lines of credit. While this assessment is being made, the total of outstanding borrowing plus unused credit lines may rise, if necessary, beyond 50 percent, but shall not exceed 60 percent of total quotas.

3. The total of outstanding borrowing plus unused credit lines under paragraph 2 above shall include, in respect of the GAB and borrowing arrangements associated with the GAB, either outstanding borrowing by the Fund under these arrangements, or two thirds of the total of credit lines under these arrangements, whichever is the greater.

4. In the case of major developments, the Executive Board shall promptly review, and may adjust, the guidelines. In any event, the guidelines shall be reviewed when the Board of Governors has completed the Ninth General Review of Quotas, or when there is a significant change in the GAB or associated arrangements, and may be adjusted as a result of such reviews.

5. The percentage limits specified in paragraph 2 above, or any other limits that may be adopted as a result of a review pursuant to paragraph 4 above, are not to be understood, at any time, as targets for borrowing by the Fund.

Decision No. 7589-(83/181), adopted December 23, 1983

Those guidelines remained in effect until November 1991, when they were replaced by a general policy that guidelines could be adopted again in the future as needed; see Annual Report 1992, p. 121.

References

Ainley, Michael, 1984, *The General Arrangements to Borrow*, Pamphlet Series No. 41 (Washington: International Monetary Fund).

Altman, Oscar L., 1956, "Quotas in the International Monetary Fund," *Staff Papers*, International Monetary Fund, Vol. 5 (August), pp. 129–50.

de Vries, Margaret Garritsen, 1976, *The International Monetary Fund, 1966–1971: The System Under Stress*, Vol. 1: *Narrative*; Vol. 2: *Documents* (Washington: International Monetary Fund).

————, 1985, *The International Monetary Fund, 1972–1978: Cooperation on Trial*, Vols. 1 and 2: *Narrative and Analysis;* Vol. 3: *Documents* (Washington: International Monetary Fund).

Evans, Huw, 1997, "The Bretton Woods Institutions: A View from the Boards," Global Economics Institutions Working Paper No. 32, July (London: Centre for Economic Policy Research).

Gold, Joseph, 1972, *Voting and Decisions in the International Monetary Fund: An Essay on the Law and Practice of the Fund* (Washington: International Monetary Fund).

————, 1991, "Borrowing by the IMF: Ultra Vires and Other Problems," in *International Financial Policy: Essays in Honor of Jacques J. Polak*, ed. by Jacob Frenkel and Morris Goldstein (Washington: International Monetary Fund).

Horsefield, J. Keith, ed., 1969, *The International Monetary Fund, 1945–1965: Twenty Years of International Monetary Cooperation*, Vol. 1: *Chronicle*, by J. Keith Horsefield; Vol. 2: *Analysis*, by Margaret G. de Vries and J. Keith Horsefield with the collaboration of Joseph Gold, Mary H. Gumbart, Gertrud Lovasy, and Emil G. Spitzer; Vol. 3: *Documents* (Washington: International Monetary Fund).

Howe, Geoffrey, 1994, *Conflict of Loyalty* (New York: St. Martin's Press).

International Monetary Fund, *Annual Report* (Washington: International Monetary Fund, various issues).

————, *Summary Proceedings* (Washington: International Monetary Fund, various issues).

International Monetary Fund Treasurer's Department, 1998, *Financial Organization and Operations of the IMF*, IMF Pamphlet Series, No. 45 (Washington: International Monetary Fund, 5th ed.).

Kapur, Devesh, John P. Lewis, and Richard Webb, 1997, *The World Bank: Its First Half Century*, Vol. 1: *History* (Washington: Brookings Institution).

Lawson, Nigel, 1992, *The View from No. 11: Memoirs of a Tory Radical* (London: Bantam Press).

Mikesell, Raymond F., 1994, *The Bretton Woods Debates: A Memoir*, Essays in International Finance, No. 192 (Princeton, New Jersey: International Finance Section, Department of Economics, Princeton University).

Officer, Lawrence, 1991, "Are International Monetary Fund Quotas Unfavorable to Less-developed Countries? A Normative Historical Analysis," *Journal of International Money and Finance*, Vol. 10 (June), pp. 193–213.

Patel, I.G., ed., 1992, *Policies for African Development: From the 1980s to the 1990s* (Washington: International Monetary Fund).

Polak, Jacques J., 1994, "The International Monetary Issues of the Bretton Woods Era," in *The International Monetary System: Proceedings of a Conference Organized by the Banca d'Italia*, ed. by Peter B. Kenen, Francesco Papadia, and Fabrizio Saccomanni, (Cambridge, England: Cambridge University Press), pp. 19–34.

————, 1996, "Should the SDR Become the Sole Financing Technique for the Fund?" in *The Future of the SDR in Light of Changes in the International Financial System*, ed. by Michael Mussa, James M. Boughton, and Peter Isard (Washington: International Monetary Fund), pp. 221–39.

————, 1999, "Streamlining the Financial Structure of the International Monetary Fund," Essays in International Finance, No. 216 (Princeton, New Jersey: International Finance Section, Department of Economics, Princeton University).

Stoltenberg, Gerhard, 1997, *Wendepunkte: Stationen deutscher Politik 1947–1990* (Berlin: Siedler Verlag).

18

Evolution of the SDR: Paper Gold or Paper Tiger?

When the IMF amended its Articles of Agreement to create the SDR in 1969, the oddly named newborn soon acquired a more descriptive, though rather pretentious and not very accurate, moniker: "paper gold." The SDR thus quickly came to epitomize both modernity and a traditional solidity and stability. When the Fund again amended the Articles nine years later, it decreed that the SDR was to become the "principal reserve asset in the international monetary system." That description turned out to be equally pretentious and no more accurate, as the SDR played a small and even diminishing role throughout the 1980s and seemed more like a paper tiger. In another twist of phrase, the Dean of the Executive Board, Alexandre Kafka (Brazil), lamented in 1989 that the Fund's "basket currency" had become a "basket case."[1] What had gone wrong?

Background

To understand the strengths and weaknesses of the SDR, one must first tackle the complex question of what the SDR is.[2] That question has four dimensions, corresponding to the four classic properties of money: its service as a unit of account, a medium of exchange, a store of value, and a standard of value.

As a unit of account, the SDR began life as the equivalent of the gold content of the U.S. dollar. The SDR and the dollar were initially equal in value, but when the dollar was devalued against gold and against other major currencies, the SDR retained its nominal gold value: hence its reputation as "paper gold."[3] In 1974, it

---

[1]Minutes of EBM/89/10 (February 1, 1989), p. 4.

[2]Although SDR is formally an abbreviation of "special drawing rights," the asset has little to do with drawing rights in the Fund. The terminology was chosen in 1967 because it seemed less evocative of reserve creation than the more straightforward alternatives. See Gold (1971) and de Vries (1976), p. 154. Later efforts to get agreement on a more palatable name all failed. In an explicit acknowledgment of the lack of meaning in the phrase, the Fund decided in 1983 to make the acronym an official term in its own right.

[3]For the history of the negotiations on the creation of the SDR, see Part One of de Vries (1976), Vol. 1. The reference to "paper gold" is on p. 177. The term "paper gold" was common vernacular usage in the mid-1960s to refer to any scheme to supplement official reserve balances with a fiat monetary asset. Also see Solomon (1982), Chapter 8.

was redefined as a basket of 16 widely used currencies, which was simplified to 5 currencies in 1981. The currencies that composed the simplified SDR basket were those of the Group of Five industrial countries (the G-5): the U.S. dollar, the Japanese yen, the deutsche mark, the pound sterling, and the French franc.[4] This basket was intended to be simple enough to be readily understood in financial markets while still ensuring that the value of the SDR would be fairly stable in the face of wide swings in exchange rates. The Fund's own accounts are maintained in terms of SDRs, and several other international organizations also have adopted the SDR as a unit of account.

By design, the SDR has a very limited role as a medium of exchange. Official SDRs can be created only through an "allocation" or issuance by the Fund to "meet the long-term global need . . . to supplement existing reserve assets," and the stock can be reduced only through a "cancellation" by the Fund. Once created, these assets can be used only in specified transactions involving the Fund, its member countries, and a short list of other "prescribed" holders. Private SDRs (i.e., private sector assets with the same composition as official SDRs) can be created and used for any purpose, but that market never developed any breadth or depth.[5]

As a store of value for a member country, the SDR is the equivalent of foreign exchange reserves. This is really the heart of the issue. An allocation of SDRs by the IMF provides each recipient (a participating member country) with an unconditional and costless line of credit, on which the holder neither earns nor pays interest.[6] That line of credit is an asset for the holder (normally the central bank), and the offsetting entry is only a contingent liability in the event that the Fund cancels SDRs or the member terminates its participation in the SDR Department (IMF, Treasurer's Department, 1995, pp. 41–42). The use of SDRs (i.e., drawing on one's line of credit to settle a financial obligation or to acquire another good or asset) creates a liability to the SDR Department of the Fund, which is exactly offset by a claim held by the counter party to the transaction (another central bank, a prescribed holder, or the Fund). Those net liabilities and claims (i.e., holdings of SDRs below or above allocations) carry a market-based rate of interest, which since 1981 has been equal to the appropriately weighted average of yields on highest-grade short-term securities issued in the corresponding countries.

An allocation of SDRs has little economic value for a country that has ready access to international capital markets on favorable terms. If a country can obtain a line of credit from commercial creditors, then the value of an SDR allocation is measured by the difference between the SDR interest rate and the rate charged by

---

[4]In January 1999, the SDR was redefined as a four-currency basket, with the euro replacing the mark and the franc.

[5]For analyses of the requirements for development of a market for private SDRs, see Coats (1982) and van den Boogaerde (1984). Typical of the period, both papers proved to be overly optimistic in assessing the prospects for the market. For the technical characteristics of the official and private markets for SDRs, see IMF, Treasurer's Department (1995) and Wragg (1984), respectively.

[6]Technically, the recipient earns interest on its holdings and pays interest on its allocations, but the two interest rates are identical and exactly net out. The use of SDRs (reduction of holdings below allocations) is of course not costless.

the market and (less tangibly) by the removal of the risk that the line of credit could be withdrawn if market conditions or the country's financial reputation were to deteriorate.[7] For countries without market access or for which access is expensive and uncertain, an SDR allocation may have substantial value. The standard terminology in the Fund for this phenomenon is that the allocation of SDRs gives rise to a "net transfer of real resources" to countries that lack ready access to capital markets. That terminology is misleading to the extent that the process involves the creation, rather than the transfer, of resources. Allocating SDRs is a positive-sum, not a zero-sum, game.[8]

Finally, as a standard of value, the SDR can serve both as a peg for a country's exchange rate and a means of denominating contracts and other obligations. Pegging currencies to the SDR achieved a measure of popularity in the late 1970s in reaction to uncertainties about the value of the U.S. dollar, but it faded away after that. The SDR has had a more lasting but still limited success as a means of denominating obligations to maintain value over time. Nearly all of the Fund's claims and liabilities are denominated in SDRs,[9] and it is also used by a number of other international organizations, mostly regional development banks.

The SDR was designed originally to vitiate the problem known as the Triffin dilemma.[10] As long as the U.S. dollar was the primary international reserve asset,

---

[7]The SDR has a potential value as a reserve asset for all countries, in comparison with ordinary foreign exchange, in that its value is more stable than any single currency. Any country, however, can replicate that value perfectly by holding the equivalent combination of currencies. Similarly, proposals to enhance the SDR by "hardening" it so as to maintain its value in relation to real goods or assets (see notably Coats, 1990) apply with equal force to other available options and do not directly affect the arguments for or against allocation of SDRs.

[8]Measurement of the extent to which an SDR allocation creates aggregate utility is not straightforward. If other potential creditors price the riskiness of sovereign credits rationally and with complete information, if SDR obligations are de facto senior to other obligations, and if the allocation of SDRs has no effect on any country's creditworthiness, then the value of the allocation will be exactly offset by the increased cost of other lines of credit. If creditors fail to price risk correctly and the other conditions still hold, then the recipient of the allocation will gain utility at the expense of those creditors. If the allocation enhances creditworthiness and confidence by providing a virtually costless liquid asset to the central bank that cannot be withdrawn capriciously by the market or by a bilateral official creditor; or strengthens the international monetary system by improving the distribution, stability, and other qualities of international reserves, then no offsetting costs will arise. The economic value of the stock of outstanding SDRs thus is related only loosely to the size of the stock. For Fund staff views on this issue, see Coats, Furstenberg, and Isard (1990) and Mussa (1996).

[9]As Polak (1979) has stressed, although a large portion of the assets of the Fund's General Department are formally the "currencies" of member countries, the Fund's claims are actually denominated in SDRs. The amounts of currencies held by the Fund are regularly adjusted to maintain their value in terms of SDRs. The accounts of the staff retirement plan and the investment account for benefits for retired staff are maintained in U.S. dollars.

[10]Triffin (1960). For a thorough history of the rationale for creating and developing the SDR as a means of strengthening the international monetary system, see Cumby (1983). Sobol (1982) analyzes the views of European officials in the 1960s and concludes that Europe's primary goal in supporting creation of the SDR was to strengthen the system rather than to supplement the supply of reserves. For the basic history of the evolution of the SDR, see IMF Research Department (1983) and Mussa, Boughton, and Isard (1996), pp. 423–35.

a growing level of world trade and finance required a growing stock of dollars in international supply. That growing stock, however, required persistent deficits in the U.S. balance of payments and thus was a threat to the stable value of the dollar, on which the system depended. The solution to this dilemma lay in creating an international asset to supplement dollars in official reserve holdings. By the late 1970s, however, that problem had vanished from the radar screen, only partially because of the advent of generalized floating of major exchange rates. Most industrial countries and a growing number of developing countries had ready access to international liquidity by drawing on official swap arrangements or by borrowing from official agencies such as the Bank for International Settlements (BIS) or from rapidly expanding private capital markets. Even with no growth in liquid assets, the global demand for liquidity could be satisfied through liability management.

In these new circumstances, the value of official assets such as the SDR was confined to countries with less ready access, as noted above. From about 1976 on, the staff consistently argued that the requirement of a "global need to supplement reserves" did not imply that there had to be a global shortage, but only that the quality and distribution of existing reserve assets had to be so impaired as to be creating serious and widespread economic problems.[11] This shift in the rationale for the SDR led to controversy and ultimately to stalemate between a few of the major industrial countries, who argued against additional allocations on the basis of the original global rationale and who continued to equate "global need" with "global shortage" of reserves; and most other countries, who made the case for expansion (at least implicitly) on the basis of the SDR's ability to improve the quality of the international monetary system and its direct economic value to a subset of the Fund's membership.

Limited Role of the SDR

The history of the SDR, as noted at the outset, is fundamentally a story of the failure of the asset to achieve the dominant position that its designers and defenders imagined for it (see Rhomberg, 1991). It has, however, maintained an important, though limited, role in the Fund and in the international monetary system.

In some respects, the SDR did grow in importance and acceptability during the 1980s. As a glance at the balance sheet of the Fund's SDR Department reveals

---

[11]A September 1978 staff paper put it this way: "There is a strong economic case on the need for additional reserves to deal with potential payments imbalances. . . . The existence of a global need does not require that there be a shortage of reserves; . . . present exchange arrangements and countries' widespread access to international capital markets now virtually preclude the emergence of a global shortage of international reserves." "Revised Draft Report of the Executive Directors to the Interim Committee on Special Drawing Rights, Rev. 1," SM/78/215 (September 7, 1978), p. 5. Also see "Allocations of SDRs—Legislative History of the Concept of "Global Need" to Supplement Existing Reserves," SM/84/148 (June 27, 1984).

Table 18.1. Balance Sheet of the SDR Department
(Millions of SDRs)

	April 30, 1978	April 30, 1990	Change
Allocations			
Net cumulative allocations to participants	9,314.8	21,433.3	12,118.5
Charges due but not paid	0.3	44.7	44.4
Total	9,315.1	21,478.0	12,162.8
Holdings			
Participants with holdings above allocations			
Allocations	2,644.3	11,408.3	8,764.0
Net receipt of SDRs	1,023.3	5,891.0	4,867.7
Total holdings	3,667.6	17,299.3	13,631.8
Participants with holdings below allocations			
Allocations	6,670.6	10,025.0	3,354.5
Net use of SDRs	2,394.1	6,494.1	4,100.0
Total holdings	4,276.5	3,530.9	(745.6)
IMF (General Resources Account)	1,371.1	628.5	(742.6)
Prescribed Holders	. . .	19.3	9.3
Total	9,315.1	21,478.0	12,162.9

Source: *Annual Report*, 1978 and 1990.

(Table 18.1), the total amount of SDRs in existence rose by 130 percent during the 11 financial years, 1979–89.[12] The initial stock (SDR 9.3 billion) was created through a series of allocations in the early 1970s, and the increase (SDR 12.1 billion) resulted from a second round of allocations in 1979–81 (Figure 18.1). After 1981, however, there were no further allocations in the period covered by this History.[13] Nonetheless, the volume of transactions in SDRs rose sharply from 1978 to 1984, especially transactions among participants, and then remained high (Figure 18.2). Also of significance was a marked rise in the apparent acceptability of the SDR as a reserve asset. Until the mid-1980s, less than half of the total stock was held by countries that were net holders of SDRs (i.e., holding SDRs in excess of their allocations). By 1990, about 80 percent was held by net holders (Table 18.1 and Figure 18.3).[14] As the major creditor countries increased their holdings, the large majority of countries that were net users were able to use their allocated balances with greater ease and liquidity.

---

[12]The SDR Department is separate from the accounts in the Fund's General Department, through which the Fund extends credits to member countries. Those accounts are discussed in Chapter 17.

[13]For the history of allocations before 1979, see de Vries (1976), Vol. 1, Part Two; and de Vries (1985), Chapter 45. In 1997, the Fund approved a proposal to amend the Articles of Agreement to permit a one-time special allocation of SDRs, which would double the outstanding stock and equalize the cumulative ratio of allocations to quotas for all member countries.

[14]The IMF's own holdings included both normal working balances and the temporary effects of payments to the Fund in SDRs by member countries. The two large spikes shown in Figure 18.3 reflect members' subscriptions to the quota increases of 1980 and 1983.

Figure 18.1. SDR Allocations, 1970–89

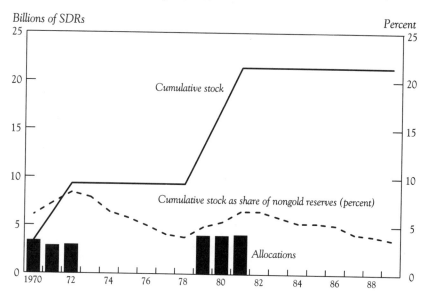

Figure 18.2. Transactions in SDRs, 1970–90

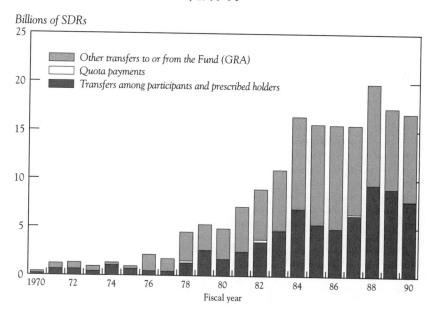

These shifts in the distribution of holdings are not unambiguous indicators of acceptability, and it must be noted that the positive aspects were overshadowed by a persistent concentration of net holdings in a few countries. Throughout the 1980s, about 80 percent of the membership were net users of SDRs, and net hold-

Figure 18.3. Distribution of Holdings of SDRs, 1978–90

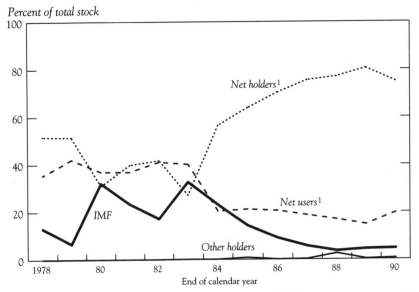

Percent of total stock

¹Percent of total stock held by member countries that are net holders or net users, respectively.

ings were concentrated primarily in the large industrial countries (Table 18.2). At the end of 1989, out of 138 countries that had received allocations, all but 31 were net users. Moreover, most net users had used most of their allocations: 91 countries (two-thirds of the membership) had used at least 75 percent, and 53 countries (three-eighths of the membership) had used at least 99 percent (Table 18.3). Finding ways to encourage or even to compel more countries to hold SDRs had become an important concern of the Fund.

Another positive indicator is that all Fund members chose to become participants in the SDR Department in the 1980s. Participation is voluntary, and in the 1970s a number of countries—including several oil exporters with strong balance of payments positions—chose to opt out. Although participation in general and receipt of allocations in particular are both costless, participants are potentially subject to "designation" to provide currency in exchange for SDRs, and some countries may not have felt comfortable with the transparency of transactions in SDRs.[15] Over time, however, such concerns diminished in importance. All but two countries that joined the Fund from 1970 on became SDR partici-

---

[15]The designation provisions of Article XIX are limited to countries whose "balance of payments and gross reserve position is sufficiently strong." More generally, participants are required by Article XXII "to collaborate with the Fund and other participants in order to facilitate the effective functioning of the Special Drawing Rights Department and the proper use of" SDRs.

Table 18.2. Leading Holders of SDRs, 1978 and 1989

	End-1978			
	Amount held (SDR millions)	Percent of allocation	Percent of total	Cumulative percentage
Germany	1,379	254	17.0	17.0
United States	1,196	52	14.8	31.8
Japan	1,053	279	13.0	44.7
United Kingdom	415	41	5.1	49.9
Belgium	414	198	5.1	55.0
Canada	401	112	4.9	59.9
France	286	59	3.5	63.4
Netherlands	244	103	3.0	66.4
India	226	69	2.8	69.2
Italy	226	71	2.8	72.0
Brazil	184	121	2.3	74.3
Venezuela	167	149	2.1	76.3
Argentina	162	106	2.0	78.3
Sweden	112	105	1.4	79.7
Austria	105	136	1.3	81.0
Spain	103	81	1.3	82.3
Australia	99	44	1.2	83.5
Denmark	98	118	1.2	84.7
Norway	96	126	1.2	85.9
Iran	96	156	1.2	87.1
	End-1989			
United States	7,572	155	37.0	37.0
Japan	1,862	209	9.1	46.1
Germany	1,373	113	6.7	52.8
Canada	1,048	134	5.1	57.9
France	1,011	94	4.9	62.8
United Kingdom	870	45	4.2	67.1
Italy	759	108	3.7	70.8
Netherlands	590	111	2.9	73.6
Spain	523	175	2.6	76.2
Saudi Arabia	467	239	2.3	78.5
Belgium	423	87	2.1	80.5
China	411	174	2.0	82.6
Norway	345	206	1.7	84.2
Iran	305	125	1.5	85.7
Mexico	292	101	1.4	87.1
Sweden	260	105	1.3	88.4
Libya	249	424	1.2	89.6
Australia	234	50	1.1	90.8
Austria	227	127	1.1	91.9
Denmark	213	119	1.0	92.9

Note: Leading holders in this table are those countries holding at least 1 percent of the total stock held by participants.

pants straight away. By April 1980, those two (the United Arab Emirates and Qatar) and all ten of the original holdouts (Ethiopia, Iraq, Kuwait, Lebanon, Libya, Nepal, Portugal, Saudi Arabia, Singapore, and Thailand) had become

Table 18.3. Leading Users of SDRs, 1978 and 1989

	End-1978			
	Amount used (SDR millions)	Percent of allocation	Percent of total	Cumulative percentage
United States	1,098	48	34.6	34.6
United Kingdom	592	59	18.7	53.3
France	199	41	6.3	59.5
Australia	127	56	4.0	63.5
India	100	31	3.2	66.7
Italy	92	29	2.9	69.6
Mexico	82	66	2.6	72.2
Egypt	57	87	1.8	74.0
Pakistan	51	63	1.6	75.6
Turkey	50	100	1.6	77.2
South Africa	50	56	1.6	78.7
Philippines	38	75	1.2	80.0
Peru	36	88	1.1	81.1
Congo, Dem. Rep.	35	89	1.1	82.2
Chile	34	62	1.1	83.3
Greece	33	71	1.0	84.3
Indonesia	33	36	1.0	85.3
	End-1989			
United Kingdom	1,043	55	15.8	15.8
India	595	87	9.0	24.9
Brazil	359	100	5.4	30.3
Argentina	318	100	4.8	35.1
Venezuela	281	89	4.3	39.4
Indonesia	238	100	3.6	43.0
Australia	237	50	3.6	46.6
South Africa	219	99	3.3	49.9
Pakistan	169	99	2.6	52.5
Nigeria	157	100	2.4	54.9
New Zealand	141	100	2.1	57.0
Egypt	136	100	2.1	59.1
Algeria	126	98	1.9	61.0
Philippines	116	99	1.8	62.7
Turkey	112	100	1.7	64.4
Israel	106	100	1.6	66.1
Chile	103	85	1.6	67.6
Greece	103	100	1.6	69.2
Peru	91	100	1.4	70.6
Morocco	85	100	1.3	71.9
Congo, Dem. Rep.	83	96	1.3	73.1
Thailand	72	85	1.1	74.2
Korea	72	98	1.1	75.3
France	69	6	1.0	76.4
Iraq	68	100	1.0	77.4
Zambia	68	100	1.0	78.4

Note: Leading users in this table are countries with net holdings below allocations, with usage of at least 1 percent of the total for all net users.

participants.[16] From then on, all Fund members participated in the SDR Department.

The Fund did take several measures to increase the liquidity and acceptability of the SDR during the 1980s, some of which were effective.[17] One such step was to enable central banks to use SDRs routinely without having to justify or later reverse the transaction. Until the Second Amendment of the Articles took effect, the SDR was conceived as a vehicle for temporarily financing a balance of payments "need." A country using its SDR allocation was generally expected to represent that it had such a need, and it was expected eventually to partially "reconstitute" its holdings.[18] The 1978 amendments deleted the "need" requirement in cases where the transaction was by agreement between the user and the recipient, so that central banks could make more routine use of SDRs in transactions. The reconstitution requirement remained in place, but the rules for reducing or eliminating it were relaxed. The minimum required level of average holdings was reduced from 30 percent of allocations to 15 percent in January 1979, over the objections of some large creditors who argued that it would lead to excessive reliance on SDRs as a permanent source of credit. The requirement then was reduced to zero (and thus "abrogated") in April 1981, as part of a package of measures in which the SDR interest rate was raised to a market level (see the section on Valuing the SDR, pp. 950–54). As is evident from the tables and charts presented above, many countries did begin to use their SDRs more permanently, and the Fund had to look for ways to offset this effect by making the SDR more competitive as an asset to hold.

Because SDRs exist as bookkeeping entries on the Fund's accounts, the range of transactions in which they can be used is limited by rules established by the Fund. Originally, the Fund intended that SDRs be used only in spot (i.e., immediate-settlement) transactions between participating countries or between a participant and the Fund. By the late 1970s, however, that policy conflicted with the broader goal of promoting the SDR as a financial asset. As part of the transition to a more market-oriented role for the SDR, the Executive Board adopted a series of enabling decisions from December 1978 through March 1980. Those decisions specifically permitted participating countries and other holders to use SDRs in swaps, forward transactions, loans, collateralization, and grants (*Annual Report 1979*, pp. 130–34; *Annual Report 1980*, pp. 140–43). Two factors, however, limited the effectiveness

---

[16]Three of the ten initial holdouts (Iraq, Nepal, and Thailand) became participants during 1970, and Portugal did so in 1975. The imminence of a resumption of allocations induced all of the others except Kuwait, as well as the United Arab Emirates and Qatar (both of whom had joined the Fund in 1972), to become participants during 1978. Kuwait became a participant in 1980.

[17]One action that was not taken might have had a major impact. As discussed in Chapter 17, the Fund from time to time considered the possibility of borrowing from private capital markets. Had it done so, the resulting claims would have been denominated in SDRs. It seems likely that commercial banks then would have developed an active market in private financial instruments in equivalent denominations ("private SDRs").

[18]The reconstitution requirement specifies that a country's holdings of SDRs must be at least a designated percentage of its cumulative allocations, averaged over a five-year period.

of this liberalization. First, the decisions were entirely driven by the Fund's desire to promote the SDR, not by a latent demand by others to use SDRs for these purposes. Second, the Fund was unwilling to issue blanket approval for the use of SDRs in any nonproscribed activity. The message therefore was mixed: the Fund wanted to encourage use, but it also wanted to retain a degree of residual control over the types of allowable transactions. For whatever reason, liberalizing the rules stimulated very little new activity. Throughout the 1980s, spot transactions accounted for more than 96 percent of all transfers of SDRs.

Another step by the Fund to broaden the market for SDRs was to create a network of "prescribed holders" among multilateral development banks and regional central banks. The BIS had been named as a prescribed holder in January 1974, to serve as a short-term supplier of currencies to central banks by making temporary exchanges of currencies for SDRs. (See de Vries, 1985, pp. 898–99.) Other than the BIS, only the Fund and participating countries could hold or transact SDRs. The Fund named five more institutions as prescribed holders in April 1980, and over the next five years expanded the list to 16, where it remained.[19] Holdings by these institutions were insignificant (less than $\frac{1}{10}$ of 1 percent of the total stock of SDRs at the end of the 1980s), but they did conduct transactions that helped reduce the illiquidity of the market.

Despite the Fund's multipronged efforts to strengthen the SDR in the first half of the 1980s, the market for it remained illiquid and limited in scope. In 1986, the Fund staff conducted a survey of 27 central banks, representing a broad cross section of the membership, to learn their attitudes about the SDR as a reserve asset. Most respondents indicated that they regarded the SDR as having poor liquidity and that it played only a minor role in their strategy for managing their reserves. The Executive Board lamented this finding and concluded that the qualities of the asset should be improved, but its recommendation did not lead to concrete changes other than a greater emphasis on promoting voluntary exchanges of SDRs.[20]

Perhaps the greatest success of the 1980s was the practical elimination of the need for designation as a means of transacting SDRs. For most transactions through the mid-1980s, a country seeking to use its SDRs would notify the Fund, which would designate a country with a strong balance of payments and reserve position to accept the SDRs in exchange for a reserve currency. To simplify the process and improve the liquidity of the market, several countries made standing commitments to buy and/or sell SDRs when necessary. In addition, the Fund acted as a broker by matching participants for voluntary transactions. After September 1987, no further designations were needed.

One general reason, possibly the main reason, for the limited attractiveness of the SDR as an asset in the 1980s was that concerns about the stability of the U.S.

---

[19]For a complete list of the prescribed holders approved in the 1980s, see *Annual Report 1987*, p. 66n. After Switzerland became a member of the Fund (and a participant in the SDR Department) in 1992, the list was reduced to 15 with the deletion of the Swiss National Bank.

[20]"The SDR in the Reserve Management Practices of Monetary Authorities," SM/87/72 (March 17, 1987) and minutes of EBM/87/55–56 (March 27, 1987).

dollar were greatly reduced in comparison with the 1970s. From 1981 to 1984, while the dollar was appreciating strongly against other major currencies, holders of dollars were more impressed by the currency's strength than by the ever-increasing risk of a reversal. (For example, see Hilliard, 1983.) Subsequently, fears of a collapse in the value of the dollar were tempered by the more cooperative policies of the G-5 (see Chapter 4). More generally, capital markets had developed to a point where central banks and other agents could diversify their risks through a variety of techniques of asset and liability management, which provided far more flexibility than holding SDRs. And to satisfy any remaining demand for a standard multicurrency basket, the ECU (European currency unit)—subject to fewer restrictions, with a broader market, and a cleaner substitute for dollars because the dollar was not a component in the basket—was a generally superior alternative to the SDR.[21]

A second general reason for weak demand, more intrinsic to the SDR, was the absence of a system for pricing the official SDR to market. Since 1981, the interest rate on the SDR has been equal to the weighted average of interest rates on three-month government securities in the countries whose currencies constitute the SDR, with the weights equal to the basket weights recalculated at current exchange rates. (The interest rate is discussed more fully below.) That procedure leads to a possible discrepancy between the SDR interest rate and the rate that would equilibrate an open market for SDRs, because the SDR is not a three-month instrument with the same properties as a government security. As Rudolf Rhomberg (1996, p. 51) has argued, "its maturity seems undefined, and the comparison with specific debts . . . is arbitrary." If the SDR is viewed by market participants as less liquid than the corresponding national securities, the equilibrium interest rate would be above the official SDR rate.

Notwithstanding the efforts made by the Fund to enhance the liquidity and the market characteristics of the SDR, neither management nor the Executive Board was willing to take the final step and relinquish control over the asset's value in financial markets. To the contrary, the Fund felt bound to preserve the "equal value" principle in all SDR transactions and to fix the quantity outstanding.[22] The existence of an official asset that was in fixed supply, had a rate that was imperfectly related to market valuation, and was subject to complex rules discouraged the growth of a commercial market for a similar but more user-friendly private asset. Without official support or even much encouragement from the Fund, private

---

[21]See IMF, Research and Treasurer's Departments (1987), Part Two; Aggarwal and Soenen (1988), and Allen (1993). The ECU was created by the European Communities at the beginning of 1979 to serve as a common unit of account for countries participating in the European Monetary System. It was supplanted by the euro in January 1999.

[22]The "equal value" principle states that, unless the Executive Board adopts policies providing for exceptions, "the exchange rates for transactions between participants . . . shall be such that participants using [SDRs] shall receive the same value whatever currencies might be provided and whichever participants provide those currencies" [Article XIX, Section 7(a)]. The Board recognized that allowing for transactions at different interest rates would be financially equivalent to allowing for different exchange rates.

agents had little incentive to mimic the official SDR in their own instruments. An effective linkage would have required more flexible pricing of the official SDR and the maintenance of a more open market for it.[23] A staff proposal for the Fund to make a market in SDRs was rejected by the Executive Board in 1982, and a proposal to allow for flexible pricing through exceptions to the "equal value" principle was rejected in 1983. Despite the growing evidence that the poor liquidity of the asset was discouraging central banks from holding SDRs, both proposals were rejected again in 1987.[24]

Over time, as countries became less concerned about their ability to diversify their portfolios and more concerned about the poor marketability of the SDR, they gradually lost interest in pegging their currencies to it. Pegging to the SDR peaked around the middle of 1980, when the dollar was at its weakest; 15 currencies were pegged, making that one of the more popular choices among exchange regimes. Over the next few years, several of those countries decided to adopt other (usually more flexible) arrangements, and very few new SDR pegs were introduced. By the end of 1989, only seven countries were officially pegging to the SDR and only four of those were adhering closely to the peg.[25] The number declined further in the early 1990s.

Similarly, interest in the SDR as a unit of account and a standard of value flared up for a few years in the late 1970s and then petered out during the 1980s. From 1975 to 1981, 13 bond issues totaling SDR 563 million, issued mostly by official institutions, were denominated in SDRs. After that, as the market for ECU-denominated bonds began to grow, the market for SDR bonds disappeared.[26] By 1982, 15 international organizations were using the SDR as a unit of account, and 16 international conventions were based on it. The list of such applications, however, showed no further growth.[27]

Proposals for a Substitution Account

Although the original purpose of the SDR was to *supplement* the U.S. dollar as a reserve asset, it quickly became apparent that it could also serve as a *substitute* for a portion of the dollars that central banks were already holding in their portfolios. That realization led the Fund to devote considerable energy to an effort to develop

---

[23]For a discussion of technical issues related to the linkage between official and private SDRs, see Coats (1990).

[24]Minutes of EBM/82/78 (June 7, 1982) and EBM/87/102 (July 10, 1987), p. 30.

[25]Two of the seven countries (Saudi Arabia and Bahrain) had undefined margins against the SDR and were de facto pegged to the U.S. dollar. One country (Libya) maintained unusually wide (±7½ percent) margins.

[26]For the structure and evolution of markets for bonds denominated in SDRs and ECUs, see Wragg (1984), Chapters 5 and 10.

[27]One notable exception occurred: effective August 1984, the International Air Transport Association (IATA) began using the SDR as the basis for changing cargo tariffs. For detailed lists, see *Annual Report 1983*, p. 102; *Annual Report 1988*, p. 78; and IMF, Research and Treasurer's Departments (1987), pp. 56–59.

a workable scheme for promoting reserve diversification into SDRs on a large scale. The story of why that effort failed—first in 1974 and again in 1980—reveals much about the broader weaknesses of the SDR.

When the U.S. dollar first displayed persistent weakness in the late 1960s and early 1970s, analysts both at the Fund and in national central banks began looking for alternatives to the dollar-based system of international reserves. When the U.S. government announced the formal suspension of convertibility of the dollar into gold in August 1971, an estimated 70 percent of all official reserves other than gold was held in dollars. If a central bank wanted to reduce the exchange risk on its reserves, the obvious solution would be to diversify into a balanced portfolio of widely traded currencies. In the 1970s, however, that option was not viable, because both of the countries whose currencies were the main alternatives—Germany and Japan—were reluctant to see their currencies "internationalized" and used as reserves and were actively discouraging central banks from diversifying into marks or yen. Moreover, the prospect of a system of multiple reserve currencies was widely viewed, both inside and outside the Fund, as a potentially destabilizing development that was to be avoided if possible. If central banks held several different currencies, then they would be likely to shift the composition of their portfolios to optimize expected returns. Such speculation could magnify the effects of market shifts in confidence or in expected relative returns.

The SDR offered an alternative channel for diversification. By acquiring SDRs through allocations by the Fund or in exchange for dollars through transactions with other central banks, a country could gain a single asset with a more stable exchange value than the dollar. Several difficulties had to be surmounted, however. First, the SDR was then still a fledgling, and its properties were little understood. Second, the outstanding stock of SDRs was quite small relative to the stock of dollars held in reserve. Third, although SDRs could be readily exchanged among central banks and other official agencies, there was virtually no private market. Fourth, the SDR was not a financially attractive asset, especially because it paid an interest rate well below prevailing market rates on the underlying assets.

Despite these obstacles, the Committee of Twenty (C-20)—as part of its study of possible reforms of the international monetary system in 1972–74—considered proposals to encourage or even to require member countries to replace a portion of their existing foreign exchange reserves with SDRs. Those who favored an obligatory scheme (including notably the French delegation) argued that voluntary substitution could encourage speculation and lead to instability. Others, however, felt that mandatory substitution was unnecessary and excessively costly.[28] The committee's final report provided for the possibility of establishing a substitution account, but it stopped short of endorsing a specific proposal.

The idea of a substitution account lay dormant during the next few years, but it sprang to new life after the dollar again came under heavy selling pressure toward the end of 1977. In the course of an Executive Board meeting on SDR allocations,

---

[28]See de Vries (1985), pp. 180–86 and 248–49, and Sobol (1979).

Jacques de Groote (Belgium) suggested that allocations might be linked with the "consolidation of other reserve assets." That is, countries receiving SDRs through allocations could be expected to exchange dollars or other reserve currencies for them, in order to both promote the SDR as an asset and absorb any inflationary impact of the allocation.[29] De Groote's suggestion piqued the interest of the Managing Director, H. Johannes Witteveen, who asked the staff to look into it. Two requisite differences from the earlier proposal soon became clear. First, a revived substitution account would have to be voluntary to have any chance of being approved, or even to be legally possible under the amended Articles of Agreement that were about to take effect.[30] Second, the inherent asymmetry between the effects on the United States and on all other countries could be minimized if the United States could be excluded or at least discouraged from participating. If any country could deposit dollars in exchange for SDRs, then the United States alone could finance a deficit by issuing its own currency and bypassing the foreign exchange market.

Witteveen was convinced that the problems that had doomed the substitution account four years earlier could be overcome and that the weakening dollar and the prospect of a resumption of SDR allocations made 1978 the right time to put it back on the agenda. When the Interim Committee met in Mexico City in April, he brought up the idea and won a lukewarm mandate to have the Executive Board come back with a more concrete proposal.[31]

Ministerial-level enthusiasm for creating a substitution account was not overwhelming, but some disparate interests were converging to create a general willingness to consider it. Developing countries saw little value in the idea on its own merits; few of them had even comfortable, much less excess, dollar balances, and they had little to gain directly. But they desperately wanted the Fund to start allocating SDRs again, and a substitution account might help promote that objective. At least some U.S. officials saw merit in the idea of promoting the role of the SDR as a means of limiting speculative pressure against the dollar. The most pronounced enthusiasm came from European countries itching to diversify their reserves, though even there the degree of support was quite mixed. Some creditors, including the German authorities, were wary of any initiative that might lead to back-door credit expansion; others, including Japan and Saudi Arabia, argued that stabilizing the dollar required much more fundamental measures than this.

Witteveen's initiative failed to take root, only partly because of these underlying concerns. Another factor was his decision not to seek a second term as Man-

---

[29]Minutes of EBM/77/166 (December 9, 1977), p. 16.

[30]Memorandum from George Nicoletopoulos (Associate General Counsel) to the Managing Director (December 20, 1977), in IMF/CF (S 2040 "Substitution Account, January 1977–October 1978").

[31]"Some members believe that agreement on a substitution account would facilitate an allocation of SDRs. The Committee agreed that this suggestion of the Managing Director should be considered further and that a report should be submitted by the Executive Board for consideration by the Committee at its next meeting," Communiqué (April 30, 1978), para. 5, in de Vries (1985), Vol. 3, p. 237.

aging Director. When he left the Fund in June 1978, the proposal was not yet fleshed out, and its sketch had some troubling features. The most notable problem was that depositors were to be asked to bear the exchange risk for an account that would hold dollar assets and SDR liabilities. In effect, depositors would still be holding dollar-denominated claims, just in a different form. Trying to remedy that defect would dominate much of the subsequent effort to refine the proposal, and the Fund's failure to devise an acceptable solution ultimately would doom the whole enterprise.

The momentum from Mexico City was completely dissipated by the time the Interim Committee next met in Washington that September. The Board's report to the committee concluded gloomily that "an initiative along these lines is not feasible for the moment," and the committee's communiqué merely "noted that the Executive Board intends to keep under review the question of a substitution account." That might have been the end of the story, except that the U.S. dollar was continuing to depreciate in exchange markets and was about to be hit with what the new Managing Director, Jacques de Larosière, would privately call a "crisis of confidence." As soon as the crisis hit its peak, at the beginning of November, de Larosière and the Fund's chief economist, Jacques J. Polak, set out to develop a revised and more detailed plan for a substitution or "reserve diversification" account.

As the revised proposal emerged in the first half of 1979, the Fund would establish and administer an account in which central banks would voluntarily deposit dollars (typically, short-term U.S. treasury bills). In exchange, they would receive SDR-denominated claims, which they could use in the same limited manner as any other SDRs. The account would convert its assets into longer-term dollar-denominated claims on the U.S. Treasury, which would pay a suitably long-term interest rate on them. Interest would be paid to depositors at the official SDR interest rate (which at the time was maintained below the market rate). The intention was that the account's exchange risk would be covered by the difference between the long-term U.S. bond rate and the official SDR interest rate.

De Larosière took this idea to the Interim Committee, which considered it informally over a working lunch in March 1979. Delegates, including the U.S. authorities, indicated an openness to the idea, and they gave the Managing Director their "broad support . . . for active consideration of such an Account."[32]

A more sustainable momentum now was beginning to build, driven both by a general desire to fulfill the objective of the amended Article VIII, to make the SDR "the principal reserve asset in the international monetary system," and a more specific and immediate desire to combat the weakness of the U.S. dollar in exchange markets.

Although Executive Directors from some of the major industrial countries were maintaining a formally noncommittal stance during the Board discussions, their remarks usually focused on technical problems rather than broad issues of principle. Central banks with most of their reserve assets in U.S. dollars were confirming to the Fund that they had a latent demand for diversification and were

---

[32]Press Communiqué, Twelfth Meeting of the Interim Committee, March 7, 1979, para. 6.

prepared to bear some cost in exchange for a more stable investment vehicle. That message was coming not only from developing and smaller industrial countries, but also from the largest surplus countries. By the end of 1979, it was reinforced by the example set by the initial stabilizing success of the EMS and the ECU, and by concerns in some quarters over the freezing of Iranian assets by the U.S. government following the occupation of the U.S. embassy in Tehran in November.

On the other side of the balance sheet, the U.S. government appeared to have an interest in stabilizing the demand for dollars and in removing the overhang in official holdings without depressing the dollar's value. If so, the United States also could be expected to bear some portion of the cost, either by paying a higher interest rate than it was paying on reserve assets or by assuming a contingent liability for covering the account's exchange risk. That positive a view was not widespread in the U.S. Treasury, but it was taking hold. With the active encouragement of Princeton University economist Peter B. Kenen (who was spending the year in Washington as a senior treasury consultant), the Under Secretary for Monetary Affairs, Anthony M. Solomon, became the standard bearer and spokesman for the substitution account within the U.S. administration.[33]

Support continued to spread throughout the summer of 1979, and it culminated in a solid endorsement from the Interim Committee at the beginning of October. The substitution account proposal was the main operational item on the committee's agenda in Belgrade, and the communiqué asked the Executive Board to "continue to direct priority to designing" such an account (para. 7). For the moment, the promise that the SDR would become the principal reserve asset was on the verge of being fulfilled.

Despite the emergence of broad support and this official endorsement, the Polak–de Larosière proposal was soon revealed to be politically unacceptable, for three interconnected reasons. First, the U.S. authorities balked at the idea of converting short-term liabilities to central banks into a long-term liability to the IMF. Since long-term interest rates were normally higher than short-term rates, the conversion could be expensive, and the treasury judged that cost to be higher than the systemic benefit from establishing the substitution account. Second, potential depositors balked at converting U.S. treasury bills into assets paying the lower official SDR interest rate. Whatever benefits they would gain from having claims with a more stable value were seen as outweighed by the direct financial cost. Third, even though the interest differential had been and was expected to be large, the staff

---

[33]The definitive statement of U.S. support for establishing a substitution account was made by Solomon in the course of an address before the Alpbach European Forum in Alpbach, Austria (August 27, 1979). Four weeks later, at a press briefing before departing for the Annual Meetings in Belgrade, Solomon explained that in the U.S. view, the "primary justification" of the account would be to promote "the further evolution of the international monetary system . . . with the focal and primary reserve asset ultimately becoming the SDR. We do not think of it as a dollar support fund even though there would be probably some incidental . . . beneficial side effects in terms of accommodating off-the-market diversification." (Official transcript, U.S. Treasury, September 24, 1979.) The speech and the transcript are in Box 12, Anthony M. Solomon Collection, Jimmy Carter Library, Atlanta, Georgia.

could provide no assurance that it would even be positive in the future or that the scheme would be financially viable.[34] Staff simulations using data from the 1970s revealed that the plan would have fallen far short of covering the exchange risk because of the combination of a declining value of the dollar and low U.S. interest rates.[35] Clearly a more direct method of sharing the risk would have to be devised.

One option that was not seriously considered was to structure the substitution account to reduce its exchange risk or even eliminate it altogether. Instead of holding dollar assets and SDR liabilities, the account could have diversified its own assets to match or approximate the 16-currency composition of the SDR. To avoid a direct effect on exchange rates, this diversification could have been achieved through off-market trades with central banks of countries whose currencies were components of the SDR. The Bundesbank, for example, could have been asked to add to its own holdings of dollars, with a corresponding deutsche mark liability to the substitution account. Even though such an exchange would have been automatically sterilized, the transfer of exchange risk to these central banks would probably not have been politically viable.

When it became clear that neither side wanted to absorb much risk or cost, the staff came up with an alternative plan for the Fund itself to absorb some risk by pledging part of its stock of gold. De Larosière then offered a comprehensive proposal on the further use of the Fund's gold, under which 7–9 million ounces (out of a stock of 103 million ounces) would be sold and another 23–32 million ounces would be transferred to the substitution account.[36] Proceeds from the sale would be invested in interest-bearing assets, and the income would be used partly to subsidize the high cost of credits through the Supplementary Financing Facility (see Chapter 15) and partly to finance the rising cost of remuneration to creditors.[37] The pro-

---

[34]The main risk to the account would arise from a shift toward monetary expansion in the United States, relative to other major countries (or, equivalently, a relative tightening abroad). Such a policy shift, which had in fact prevailed in the 1970s, would generally lead both to a relative weakening of U.S. short-term interest rates and to a depreciation of the dollar. The SDR value of the assets in the substitution account would fall, and the value of interest income would fall relative to interest expense both in dollars and (a fortiori) in SDRs. The shortfall in net interest income would then further reduce the value of the account's assets and reinforce the initial deficit.

[35]From 1971 Q3 through 1979 Q1, the yield on U.S. treasury bills was 6.02 percent, and the full combined SDR market rate was 6.95 percent. Allowing for the depreciation of the dollar during that period, the yield on SDR assets in terms of dollars was 10.64 percent. Subsequent staff estimates generated similar comparisons for longer periods. See "Interest Rate Simulations," SM/79/95, Sup. 3 (June 1, 1979); "A Substitution Account and the Less Developed Countries," SM/79/236 (August 31, 1979); "Substitution Account—Balance Between Interest Received and Interest Paid," SM/79/279 (December 6, 1979); and "Substitution Account—Results of a Simulation Study of the Account's Financial Balance," SM/80/83 (April 2, 1980).

[36]Minutes of EBM/80/5 (January 11, 1980), pp. 3–9, and EBM/80/6 (same date), p. 20.

[37]As discussed in Chapter 17, the Fund was then in the early stages of making both the SDR and countries' reserve tranche positions into competitively structured and priced financial assets. By the late 1980s, that process would sharply raise the Fund's outlays to creditors. In 1981, the Fund began determining the interest rate charged on Fund credits as the residual factor to generate a target level of net income. Although the Managing Director couched the proposal for selling gold in terms of protecting the Fund's financial position, the practical effect after the 1981 policy change would have been to subsidize the basic rate of charge to borrowers.

posal thus had something for everyone, but it depended on a broad consensus in favor of disposing of a substantial portion of the Fund's "crown jewels."

When the Executive Board considered the Managing Director's proposal in March 1980, the discussion revealed that a consensus on disposing of gold would not be easy to achieve. Although most Executive Directors seemed prepared to consider the use of gold to back up the substitution account, many were willing to do so only if the main participants were committed to shouldering a significant share more directly. Notably, H. Onno Ruding (Netherlands) made a plea for a more balanced "tripartite support mechanism," and both Alexandre Kafka (Brazil) and S.D. Deshmukh (India) argued that the Fund should not compromise its ability to reserve its gold for the benefit of low-income developing countries. Sam Y. Cross (United States), however, denied that the account would provide special benefits to his country and insisted that the United States would not be prepared to make a budgetary contribution for this purpose.[38]

While the Board debated these technical problems, de Larosière devoted a considerable amount of personal energy to an effort to secure a final political approval of the proposal. With the assistance of the Interim Committee Chairman, Filippo Maria Pandolfi (finance minister of Italy), he managed to get the developing countries on board by persuading them that their concerns would be outweighed by the systemic benefits.[39] The G-5 finance ministers met in January and agreed on most, though not all, substantive issues. In February, the German finance minister, Hans Matthöfer, further signaled the strong support of his government. In meetings during March with the U.S. Treasury Secretary, G. William Miller, de Larosière got encouraging feedback and saw no reason to doubt that the United States continued to back the idea. But when the Interim Committee met in April, in Hamburg, Germany, support from the United States, Germany, and a few other creditors suddenly vanished, to the surprise and shock of the Managing Director and of those whom he had persuaded to support him.[40] The most that de Larosière could salvage in the communiqué was a bland statement that "some issues remained to be solved" and that the committee "expressed its intention to continue to work on this subject" (para. 6). In fact, however, the proposal to establish a substitution account was dead and would not be revived.

---

[38]Minutes of EBM/80/40–41 (March 10, 1980).

[39]Pandolfi and Polak made a whirlwind tour of several Latin American capitals in late February, 1980. Although they encountered considerable doubts about the value of the proposed scheme for developing countries, they apparently succeeded in defusing overt criticisms. Memorandum from Polak to the Managing Director (March 3, 1980), IMF/CF (S 2040 "Substitution Account, February 16–March 12, 1980").

[40]Miller, Matthöfer, Geoffrey Howe (United Kingdom), and John Howard (Australia) declined to speak on the matter. Those who did speak gave no indication of awareness that the United States and Germany would withhold support. Governors from industrial countries broadly supported the plan on the assumption that the United States was prepared to shoulder part of the potential cost, while most of those from developing countries supported it on condition that it be adopted along with the Program for Immediate Action of the G-24 (on which, see Chapter 20, pp. 1009–10, and references therein). Minutes of the Second Session, pp. 27–56; IMF/CF (ICMS Meeting No. 14—Master File).

As was so often the case where the SDR was concerned, a concerted drive to strengthen its role had come to nothing. Three reasons for the failure stand out. First, on the surface, the withering away of American support can be attributed partly to Solomon's departure from the U.S. Treasury to become president of the Federal Reserve Bank of New York, since he and Kenen had been virtually alone in their willingness to fight for the account.[41] Second, the tightening of U.S. monetary policy that began in late 1979 eased fears of a continuing glut of dollars (see Wijnholds, 1982). Third and more fundamental, however, was the dissatisfaction with the stalemate over how to cover exchange risk. Without a consensus on the use of the Fund's gold as part of an overall burden-sharing plan, the proposal had no hope for success.

It is ironic that the substitution account was doomed by concerns over its potential cost. If the Polak–de Larosière plan had succeeded in 1980, the account would have enjoyed an initial five years in which its dollar-denominated assets would have appreciated by 28 percent against its SDR-denominated liabilities and in which its positive interest margin would have averaged 26 basis points. Its operations in those years would have generated large profits that could have been invested so as to carry it through at least the next decade. Unfortunately, that rosy scenario was unforeseeable in the bleak economic environment of 1980, and it carried no weight in the debate.[42]

SDR Allocations

All of the SDRs in existence through the 1990s were put into circulation through two series of allocations by the Fund to participating countries. The first round of allocations, totaling SDR 9.3 billion, was made in 1970–72 during the "First Basic Period" after the creation of the SDR in 1969.[43] No allocations were made in the quinquennial Second Basic Period (1973–77), but the process resumed in the second year of the Third, which lasted four years (1978–81). Those

---

[41]In August 1979, Michael Blumenthal resigned as Secretary of the Treasury and was replaced by Miller, who had been chairman of the Federal Reserve Board. Paul A. Volcker, who had been president of the New York Federal Reserve, was then named to replace Miller. Solomon remained at the Treasury to cover the transition until February 1980, at which time he moved to New York to fill Volcker's position. For Kenen's views on the substitution account, see Kenen (1981, 1983).

[42]Although the staff recognized that the account might be profitable, the question of how to deal with that contingency was not raised until shortly before the Hamburg debacle and consequently was never considered in detail. An ex post simulation reveals that if the account had been established at the end of 1980, by 1985 it would have generated a net cumulative profit in SDRs equal to more than 40 percent of the initial deposits. Assuming no deposits or withdrawals after the initial setup, that profit would have been gradually offset by losses in the next seven years (through 1992) and would have been of a negligible amount for the following five years.

[43]The 1969 amendment to the Articles of Agreement specified that decisions to allocate SDRs shall be made with reference to "basic periods," normally of five years' duration, and that any allocations shall be made at yearly intervals during such a period. The First Basic Period was shortened to three years, and allocations were made each year at the beginning of January. See de Vries (1976), Vol. 1, Part Two.

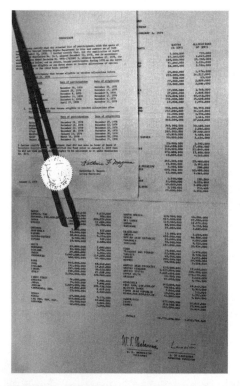

Managing Director Jacques de Larosière signing document authorizing SDR allocation, January 2, 1979. Also in attendance, from left to right: Dhruba Gupta (Treasurer's Department), Sir Joseph Gold (General Counsel), Walter Habermeier (Treasurer), Katherine Magurn (Secretary's Department), Jacques Polak (Economic Counsellor), William Dale (Deputy Managing Director)

allocations, which were equivalent to just over 30 percent of end-1978 quotas for most eligible countries, brought the total stock to SDR 21.4 billion ($27.3 billion).[44] The process then stopped. Throughout the 1980s, countries holding close to two-thirds of the votes in the Executive Board favored making further allocations, but support continually fell short of the required 85 percent.

When the Board first discussed the possibility of allocations in the Fourth Basic Period, in January 1981, most creditor countries seemed open to at least considering the idea. The Alternate Executive Director for Germany, Guenter Winkelmann, noted that his authorities had "some reservations," but he did not preclude their ultimate approval. The U.S. Alternate, Donald Syvrud, was similarly noncommittal and noted that the Reagan administration, which had just taken office, had not developed a position on the issue. John Anson (United Kingdom) concluded that the wisdom of a further allocation was an "open question," and Tiruo Hirao (Japan) urged "prudence." Of the G-5, only Thierry Aulagnon (Alternate—France) expressed clear opposition at the outset, stating that there was "no technical justification" for further allocations. Most other Directors expressed neutral or tentatively positive responses.[45]

Those preliminary views were ambiguous enough to leave room for hope, and they were conveyed in that spirit to the Interim Committee for its May 1981 meeting in Libreville, Gabon. Ministers recognized that developing a consensus on new allocations was going to be difficult, but they urged the Executive Board to develop an acceptable proposal "at the earliest possible date." That order, however, could not be filled. A hard core of opposition was already forming from four countries (all of the G-5 except France, which swam against the current and abandoned its opposition soon after the election of François Mitterrand as president in May 1981), and it would not be reduced through the next decade of debates. Remarkably for a body that thrives on negotiation and compromise, positions on SDR allocations just never evolved and never even inched toward reconciliation.

Those who were opposed were concerned primarily about aggravating inflation and weakening discipline in national monetary policies. They viewed the allocation of SDRs as tantamount to money creation, and they feared that deficit countries would use additional reserves to postpone needed adjustment. This view was reinforced by the unfortunate timing of the first two rounds of allocations, both of which had coincided with major inflationary episodes. In addition, as noted in the introduction to this chapter, opponents argued that the sole criterion for alloca-

---

[44]On January 1, 1979 and 1980, each eligible country, except for a few that opted out, received an allocation equal to 10.4 percent of its quota as of the preceding day. For all but a few countries, quotas were unchanged between those two dates. On January 1, 1981, each country received an allocation equal to 6.8 percent of its quota on December 31, 1980, which reflected the quota increases under the Seventh General Review. This last percentage was calibrated to generate a commensurate aggregate allocation, adjusted upward to allow for new participants. For a country with an average quota increase, total allocations for 1979–81 amounted to 31.2 percent of the end-1978 quota. The agreement to make those allocations, which came at the Interim Committee meeting of September 1978, is covered in de Vries (1985), Chapter 45.

[45]Minutes of EBM/81/10–11 (January 21, 1981).

tion in the Articles of Agreement was the need to supplement the existing stock of reserves, a criterion that they interpreted as quantitative and aggregative. That is, they interpreted the Articles as stating that the existing supply of reserves had to be globally inadequate to satisfy the "need" (and not the possibly larger "demand") for reserves.[46] The strongest position in this regard was taken by the German authorities, who rejected the prevailing view—and the view of the Fund's Legal Department—that a decision to allocate SDRs could be taken even if the global demand for reserves could be met in other (but less satisfactory) ways.[47]

Those in favor of allocations offered several more qualitative arguments, and they generally interpreted the criterion itself as qualitative. That is, an allocation was justified under the Articles if the quality or the distribution of the existing stock of reserves was inadequate, and if an increase in the stock of SDRs could be shown to ameliorate that condition. In addition, they often cited the provision in the Articles that the SDR was to become the principal reserve asset in the system, which in their view could not happen if the stock of SDRs continued to decline in relation to world finance and to total reserves.[48]

This political impasse did not discourage the Fund's management from continuing to place the question on the Board's agenda. After the Fourth Basic Period (1982–86) passed without any agreement, the Board duly began discussing the possibility of resuming allocations in the Fifth. At the first meeting on that question, in March 1987, almost everyone spoke in favor except those in the same four chairs that had steadfastly blocked allocations for the preceding five years.[49]

A year later, the Managing Director, Michel Camdessus, tabled a specific proposal to allocate SDR 20–30 billion "over the next two years." Camdessus cited two factors that together, in his view, constituted a "global need" in the sense of the Articles. First, a large-scale allocation of SDRs would help to prevent a renewal of the disruptive conditions in exchange markets that had characterized the mid-1980s. Second, it would further the resolution of the international debt crisis. The existing level of official reserves, he argued, was inadequate to enable many of the

---

[46]The requirement of a "need" was introduced to convey that a judgment of adequacy was to be made by the Fund. This "need to supplement existing reserve assets" is thus distinct from and does not depend on the economic concept of a shortage in relation to the demand for reserves. The requirement of a "global" need conveys the sense that an allocation of SDRs responds to a problem related to the performance of the world economy and of the international monetary system, not to the need to finance the balance of payments deficits of individual countries or groups of countries. "Allocations of SDRs—Legislative History of the Concept of 'Global Need' to Supplement Existing Reserves," SM/84/148 (June 27, 1984).

[47]See, for example, the statement by Guenter Grosche at EBM/84/131 (August 31, 1984), pp. 25–28.

[48]For a retrospective and evaluation of these views on allocations, see Polak (1988) and the various contributions in Mussa, Boughton, and Isard (1996).

[49]Ian Sliper (Temporary Alternate—New Zealand) noted that his constituency was divided. Australia was opposed to resuming allocations, while most others in the group (which included several developing countries) were in favor. Since no vote on allocations was ever taken, that chair's position was never clarified. (Executive Board rules do not allow Directors to split their votes.) Minutes of EBM/87/55–56 (March 27, 1987).

highly indebted middle-income developing countries to carry out proper adjustment policies.[50]

Camdessus's arguments had virtually no impact on the Executive Board. Discussions on the Fifth Basic Period continued in the same vein through 1989, with no shift in the position of any chair. From then until the period ended in 1991, the Managing Director regularly reported to the Interim Committee that he had determined through informal consultations that the impasse was unchanged.

A Link to Development Finance?

One possibility for reconciling the two opposing camps on allocations would be to dedicate any newly created SDRs to those countries where they are most needed. Since SDRs are valuable primarily to countries without good access to international capital markets, and since the opponents of allocations feared that a global allocation would fuel inflationary pressures, why not target allocations toward developing countries? Targeted allocations could be a valuable addition to foreign aid from scarce budgeted resources and would directly supplement the foreign exchange reserves that developing countries need to sustain growth in international trade. As it happened, however, these arguments hardened rather than softened the opposition to SDR allocations.

The idea of linking SDR allocations to a country's need for development finance was first raised during the earliest discussions of reserve-creation schemes in the 1960s. Some schemes, such as the "Stamp Plan" of 1962, envisioned that reserves would be created only for developing countries, while others aimed only at the main industrial countries. As a compromise, UNCTAD (the United Nations Conference on Trade and Development) and other groups pushed for a scheme that would ensure that any new and deliberate creation of reserves would simultaneously serve to correct the particular shortage of reserves held by developing countries. While most officials and economists from the major industrial (G-10) countries insisted that those two issues—reserve creation and development finance—should be tackled separately, they did come around to the view that newly created reserve assets should be distributed proportionally to all countries. The allocation of SDRs was therefore based on the distribution of quotas in the Fund.[51]

Developing countries continued to raise the issue of linking SDR allocations to development finance—which came to be known simply as "the link"—throughout the 1970s, but as long as support was lacking even for a conventional SDR alloca-

---

[50]Minutes of EBM/88/45 (March 23, 1988), pp. 12–13.

[51]On the discussions in the 1960s leading up to the design of the SDR system, see de Vries (1976), Vol. 1, pp. 61, 72, 84–85, 110–11, and 219–20. The two key reports dealing with this issue were those of the Ossola Group of experts from industrial countries (August 1965) and of an experts group for UNCTAD (November 1965). UNCTAD's proposal was kept alive through the work of the Committee of Twenty in 1972–74, but the Interim Committee failed to agree on any plan to implement it. See the relevant passages of the C-20 Report of June 1974 and the Interim Committee communiqué of January 1975; in de Vries (1985), Vol. 3, pp. 173 and 219, respectively.

tion, the link remained in abeyance. Then in 1979 and 1980, after the Fund resumed allocating SDRs, the link was given a new chance at coming to life. The Group of Twenty-Four developing countries (G-24) renewed its appeal by including link proposals in the September 1979 "Program of Action on International Monetary Reform." The UN General Assembly endorsed that report in January 1980 and asked the Fund to implement its recommendations. At the same time, the report of the Brandt Commission called for further SDR allocations and suggested that the "distribution of such unconditional liquidity should favor the developing countries who presently bear high adjustment burdens" (Brandt Commission, 1980, p. 219). Responding to these appeals, the Interim Committee asked the Fund to "examine in depth" the G-24 recommendations, including the link (communiqué of April 25, 1980, para. 3).

To kick off that examination, a July 1980 staff paper set out six possible linkage schemes. Essentially, the point of the paper was that if a direct link was politically controversial and would require an amendment of the Articles of Agreement, an indirect link could be implemented just as effectively. In its simplest form, an indirect link might involve an agreement by some countries to contribute their allocated SDRs to other countries or to prescribed holders that provide development assistance, such as the World Bank.[52] The Executive Board held a preliminary discussion in August. In general, those who favored further allocations also favored a link (direct or indirect), and vice versa. Overall, however, support for a link was a little below that for proportional allocations. Tom de Vries (Alternate— Netherlands), for example, noted that although his authorities were favorable in principle, they feared that confidence in the monetary quality of the SDR was too low for such a scheme to work at present.[53]

After the Interim Committee asked for a closer examination and the staff refined its proposals a little, the Board gave the link a final hearing in December 1980. Positions did not soften, however, and de Larosière had to conclude that there was "no scope now for agreement on a specific link scheme."[54]

After 1980, the link was effectively abandoned, but related proposals to modify the allocation of SDRs to make the scheme more suitable for developing countries surfaced occasionally. Three notable suggestions were made by Executive Directors in the mid-1980s, each of which aimed to improve the distribution of SDRs without weakening the incentives for developing countries to implement effective adjustment programs. First, Jacques de Groote (Belgium) proposed in 1983 that the Fund allocate SDRs that could be used only conditionally on approval of an adjustment program, and that surplus countries make their own conditional SDRs available to deficit countries by lending them to the Fund. The following year, Bruno de Maulde

---

[52]"Considerations Relating to a Link Between SDR Allocation and Finance for Developing Countries," SM/80/188 (July 25, 1980).

[53]Minutes of EBM/80/125 (August 8, 1980); for de Vries, see p. 11.

[54]Minutes of EBM/80/185–186 (December 17, 1980). The quotation is from meeting 80/186, p. 9. Also see "Further Issues Relating to a Link Between SDR Allocations and Finance for Developing Countries," SM/80/266 (December 1, 1980).

(France) proposed establishment of a scheme under which industrial and certain other creditor countries would agree to lend newly allocated SDRs to developing countries, conditional on approval by the Fund of recipients' policies and the Fund's certification that the loan would strengthen recipients' reserve positions. And in 1986, Arjun Sengupta (India) proposed that industrial countries reallocate their SDRs to developing countries, subject to a requirement that these reallocated SDRs could be used only temporarily (say, for three years). Although these proposals were designed to overcome specific objections raised earlier to a general allocation, opponents concluded that none of the schemes seemed consistent with the original character of the SDR or with reliance on quotas as the basis for financing Fund lending. In July 1986, the Executive Board rejected all three proposals.[55]

One more effort at reform was made in 1988, when consideration was given to resuming SDR allocations as one means of finally resolving the international debt crisis. The main advocacy organization for commercial banks, the Institute for International Finance (IIF), issued an innovative report that year calling for a doubling of the stock of SDRs, on the same order of magnitude as Camdessus's proposal mentioned above. The IIF's intention was that heavily indebted countries would use their increased holdings of SDRs to purchase U.S. treasury securities and would pledge those bonds as collateral for debt conversions or new bank borrowing. Similarly, French President François Mitterrand proposed that industrial countries could set aside their own allocations to guarantee debt payments by qualifying developing countries.[56]

Both of those ideas were overtaken by more direct debt-relief proposals, primarily the 1989 Brady Plan (Chapter 11). Moreover, they were seen by some in the Fund as conflicting with the SDR's basic role as a global monetary asset. The IIF and French proposals, along with other ideas on enhancing the role of the SDR, were on the Executive Board agenda in March 1989, coincidentally just a few days before the Brady Plan was to be introduced by the U.S. Treasury Secretary. Once again, however, no consensus was reached and no action was taken.[57]

In 1989, the U.S. government responded to a request from congress by preparing a study on the possible use of SDRs for financing debt relief for heavily indebted low-income countries. The report, however, concluded that the SDR was an inappropriate vehicle for that purpose, because such usage would compromise the asset's properties as a monetary reserve asset and because debt-relief financing should be made conditional on improved policy performance (U.S. Treasury, 1989).

A central criticism of the early linkage proposals was that development finance should be made conditional on strong policy performance, not unconditional as

---

[55]See "Proposals for Post-Allocation Adjustment in the Distribution of SDRs," SM/86/154 (June 27, 1986), which includes the original proposals in an Annex; and minutes of EBM/86/125 (July 30, 1986).

[56]The IIF proposal, which was circulated as a letter to the Chairman of the Interim Committee, was published in the *IMF Survey*, Vol. 17 (April 4, 1988), pp. 102–06. Mitterrand's proposal was made in a speech to the UN General Assembly in September 1988.

[57]"The SDR and the International Monetary System," SM/89/32 (February 8, 1989); "Further Consideration of Issues Relating to Post-Allocation Adjustment in the Distribution of SDRs," SM/89/45 (February 24, 1989); and minutes of EBM/89/28B29 (March 6, 1989).

would have been the case with SDR allocations. The revised proposals of the 1980s recognized that allocations could also be made conditional, if that was desired. Voluntary redistribution by creditor countries to those in need, as discussed in 1980 and revived for consideration on several later occasions, could also have been made conditional on policy performance. More generally, in February 1989 the staff proposed a two-step procedure in which the Fund could first decide on an aggregate allocation of SDRs and then decide whether countries qualified to receive allocations, based on surveillance criteria. That is, only countries pursuing appropriate economic policies would be certified as eligible to receive SDR allocations. As with the earlier linkage proposals, the Board expressed some uneasiness about that idea and again preferred to reserve the SDR for circumstances related to global liquidity concerns.[58]

Valuing the SDR

The SDR was originally defined in a way that made its value equal to one U.S. dollar. The dollar was convertible into gold at a rate of $35 = 1 fine ounce of gold (or, equivalently, $1 = 0.888671 grams of gold). The SDR was not directly convertible into gold, but it was convertible into dollars or other convertible currencies, at a rate equivalent to 0.888671 grams of gold. After the United States suspended the convertibility of the dollar into gold in August 1971, the relevance of this "unit of value" provision in the Fund's Articles of Agreement became limited to the determination of an exchange rate between the SDR and the dollar.[59] When the dollar was devalued in 1972, the link with the value of the dollar was broken and the formal link to gold was retained. That is, the exchange value of the SDR became approximately $1.09. When the dollar was devalued again in 1973, the rate automatically changed to $1.21. By then, however, the valuation link to gold had become meaningless, because neither the SDR nor any currency was convertible into gold. The Committee of Twenty therefore agreed in 1974 to ignore the official price of gold for this purpose and to determine the value of the SDR by reference to a basket of currencies.[60]

---

[58]"The SDR and the International Monetary System," SM/89/32 (February 8, 1989), pp. 26–27, and minutes of EBM/89/28–29 (March 6, 1989). The Deputy Managing Director, Richard D. Erb, suggested this idea to the staff. Several years later, the proposal to make targeted allocations conditional on policy reforms was reintroduced by Ariel Buira, the Deputy Governor of the Bank of Mexico. See Buira (1996).

[59]Article XXI, Section 2, of the Articles that were in effect from 1969 to 1978. See de Vries (1976), Vol. 2, p. 121.

[60]Joseph Gold, the Fund's General Counsel, described the murky legal situation to the Executive Board as follows: ". . . the legality of adopting the [basket] mode of valuation . . . was derived from the present circumstances of disorder in which the par value system was not operating as it was intended to operate. . . ." Unless the Fund were to suspend all operations, "the only choice left . . . was to attribute gold value in some way, and to select the appropriate mode of valuation. In present circumstances the gold value would become a notion rather than a datum . . ." Minutes of EBM/74/28 (April 1, 1974), p. 17.

Table 18.4. Composition of the SDR, 1969–90
(*In local currency units*)

	July 1969–June 1974 Weight	July 1974–June 1978		July 1978–December 1980		1981–85		1986–90	
		Initial weight	Amount of currency	Initial weight	Amount of currency	Initial weight	Amount of currency	Initial weight	Amount of currency
Gold (grams)	0.888671								
U.S. dollars		0.330	0.4000	0.330	0.400	0.42	0.540	0.42	0.4520
Deutsche marks		0.125	0.3800	0.125	0.320	0.19	0.460	0.19	0.5270
Japanese yen		0.075	26.0000	0.075	21.000	0.13	34.000	0.15	33.4000
French francs		0.075	0.4400	0.075	0.420	0.13	0.740	0.12	1.0200
Pounds sterling		0.090	0.0450	0.075	0.050	0.13	0.071	0.12	0.0893
Canadian dollars		0.060	0.0710	0.050	0.070				
Italian lire		0.060	47.0000	0.050	52.000				
Netherlands guilders		0.045	0.1400	0.050	0.140				
Belgian francs		0.035	1.6000	0.040	1.600				
Swedish krona		0.025	0.1300	0.020	0.110				
Australian dollars		0.015	0.0120	0.015	0.017				
Danish krone		0.015	0.1100						
Norwegian krone		0.015	0.0990	0.015	0.100				
Spanish pesetas		0.015	1.1000	0.015	1.500				
Austrian shillings		0.010	0.2200	0.015	0.280				
South African rand		0.010	0.0082						
Saudi Arabian riyals		0.030	0.1300						
Iranian rials		0.020	1.7000						

In June 1974, the same month that the C-20 Report was issued, the Executive Board redefined the SDR as a basket of the currencies of the 16 countries with the highest share in international trade (see Table 18.4). The number 16 was chosen because it happened to be the cutoff point for countries accounting for at least 1 percent of world exports (see de Vries, 1985, pp. 290–93). It thus had an internal logic, but the large size of the basket eventually would make it difficult for the SDR to become accepted by financial markets. One difficulty was that as economic conditions changed, so would the composition of the basket. In 1978, the Fund dropped the Danish krone and the South African rand from the SDR, added the Saudi Arabian riyal and the Iranian rial, and changed the weights on several other component currencies. Those changes, which were cosmetic and made little difference in how the SDR behaved, were intended to keep the basket up to date and to reflect carefully considered principles on the selection of currencies. In practice, they merely reinforced the perception that the composition of the SDR was elusive and ephemeral.

A second problem was that few of the 16 currencies had a significant role in international finance. At the same time that the Fund adopted the 16-currency basket for valuing the SDR, it defined a much smaller 5-currency basket for determining the SDR interest rate (see below). As the Fund attached an increasingly higher priority to the SDR's acceptability in financial markets, this dichotomy between the interest rate basket and the valuation basket became an obstacle to rational pricing and no longer made sense.

In December 1979, the Executive Board took up the question of whether the SDR interest rate was being calculated in a satisfactory way for purposes of paying interest on the claims to be issued by the proposed substitution account. In the course of that discussion, the Board became attracted to the idea of unifying the two baskets, with something less than 16 currencies in each one.[61] In March 1980, after reviewing a detailed staff analysis on the matter, the Board narrowed the options to a range of five to nine currencies. Only nine currencies had well-developed financial markets (i.e., deep enough spot and forward markets to get efficient pricing on exchange and interest rates). In addition to the G-5 currencies, these included the Italian lira, the Netherlands guilder, the Canadian dollar, and the Belgian franc. As a practical matter, the question was whether to simultaneously raise the interest rate basket from 5 to 9 and reduce the valuation basket from 16 to 9, or to reduce the valuation basket all the way from 16 to 5. The nine-currency option was seen as less radical and as more likely to produce a stable value, while the five-currency option was seen as more sustainable, given the sharp drop-off in the depth and stability of financial markets between the top five and the other four. A clear majority of the Board favored the smaller basket, but some Directors were reluctant to go that far.[62]

Because the Executive Board normally reaches agreement by consensus, it is least effective when confronted with several options. In the spring of 1980, the Board was nearly unanimous in wanting to reduce the size of the basket, but it was far from agreeing on how small to make it. The Fund's management and staff were convinced that a five-currency basket was both the most desirable outcome and the most likely to secure a consensus, but they faced a real danger that the Board would deadlock over details. To focus attention on the preferred outcome, de Larosière proposed making the valuation basket identical to the five-currency basket already used for determining the interest rate, and he took that proposal to the Interim Committee for its Hamburg meeting in April 1980.[63]

The Interim Committee endorsed unification in principle, but as usual it left the details to be worked out by the Executive Board (communiqué of April 25, 1980, para. 7). A decision to change the basket required at least a 70 percent majority (and possibly 85, if a simple majority of the Board judged it to be a "fundamental" change in the valuation scheme),[64] which gave the developing and smaller industrial countries a key role in the decision.

What should have been a straightforward decision got a little ugly that summer, as a few countries objected to having their currencies cut out of the basket and a few others objected to the high weight that the U.S. dollar would have in the shrunken basket. At a Board seminar on the subject in July, some chairs indicated

---

[61]Minutes of EBM/79/188 (December 19, 1979).

[62]Minutes of EBM/80/54 (March 26, 1980). Also see "Substitution Account—Choice of Number of Currencies in SDR Valuation and Interest Rate Baskets and Timing of Change" SM/80/60 (March 13, 1980).

[63]Minutes of EBM/80/68 (April 9, 1980), pp. 17–18.

[64]"SDR Valuation—Majority for Decision," SM/80/180 (July 18, 1980).

that they could go along with a five-currency basket only if the weight on the U.S. dollar was constrained well below the level indicated by the standard formula (which gave equal weight to trade and reserve shares). Lionel D.D. Price (Alternate—United Kingdom) argued that it made little sense to apply a formula that gave the dollar a high weight because of its predominance in reserve balances, "when the major objective of the SDR was to cut back on that predominance." Ruding agreed and asked that the dollar's weight be constrained, perhaps to about 33 percent (its then-current level) instead of the indicated 44 percent.[65] That proposal might well have killed the entire simplification effort, but the staff managed to head it off by determining that artificially lowering the dollar's weight would constitute a "fundamental" change in the method of valuing the SDR.[66]

As late as mid-August 1980, a 70 percent majority appeared unobtainable for any specific reduction in the 16-currency basket, even though all chairs favored or at least said they could accept some sort of reduction. But the staff and the Managing Director kept pushing, and eventually they carried the day by proposing to make a nominal reduction in the weight on the U.S. dollar, from 44 to 42 percent. Although that adjustment was a transparent face-saver, it gave the holdouts something to take home, and the Board approved the implementing decisions on September 17 (see the Appendix to this chapter).[67]

The fuss over small shifts in weights was soon overtaken by events. By January 1, 1981, when the new basket went into effect, exchange rate changes had already pushed the U.S. dollar's weight up to 43 percent (from 31 percent under the old basket). As the dollar appreciated throughout the next four years, its weight continued to rise and reached a peak of 56 percent in February 1985 (Figure 18.4). It then declined again, and by the end of the decade was back to 34 percent.[68]

The correction of the dollar's weight in the SDR after 1985 partly reflected the reversal of the earlier shifts in exchange rates (Figure 18.5), but it resulted more directly and importantly from a revaluation of the basket effective at the beginning of 1986. The decision to convert the SDR into a five-currency basket provided that its composition would be reviewed and revised once every five years. Although it was unlikely that the selection of currencies would change, the amounts of each currency in the basket would be adjusted to restore the weights periodically to levels that reflected each currency's importance in world trade and finance.

---

[65]Minutes of Executive Board Seminar 80/3 (July 10, 1980), pp. 8 (Price) and 12 (Ruding).

[66]Specifically, the Board accepted the view of the Legal Department that reduction of the basket to five currencies would not constitute a fundamental change unless the weight on the dollar were constrained. Thus a five-currency (or a nine-currency) basket could be adopted by a 70 percent majority, but only if the dollar's weight was determined by the previously agreed methodology. Minutes of EBM/80/116 (July 31, 1980).

[67]Minutes of EBM/80/145 (September 17, 1980). Three Directors objected to the decisions and abstained in the voting: Joaquín Muns (Spain), Tom de Vries (Alternate—Netherlands), and Heinrich G. Schneider (Alternate—Austria).

[68]Because the SDR is defined as the sum of specific fixed amounts of each currency, the weights vary daily in response to exchange rate fluctuations. That property gives the SDR a "hard currency" bias, which the Executive Board periodically offsets by revising the basket.

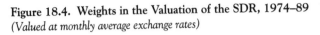

Figure 18.4. Weights in the Valuation of the SDR, 1974–89
(Valued at monthly average exchange rates)

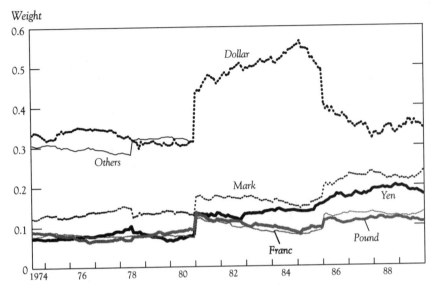

When the first review was held, the Executive Board agreed to drop the weight of the dollar back to 42 percent. Correspondingly, the weight of the deutsche mark would be raised back to 19 percent, and the relative weights of the other three currencies would be shifted slightly (see Table 18.4 and Figure 18.4). To achieve that rebalancing, it was necessary to reduce the amount of U.S. dollars in the SDR by about 16 percent (from 54 cents to 45.2) to compensate for the dollar's appreciation in the intervening years. The amount of yen was reduced marginally so as to yield a slightly higher weight for the yen than in 1981. The amounts of the other three currencies were increased.[69]

The lack of stability in the dollar throughout much of the decade may not have done much to stimulate demand for the SDR as an asset or as a measure of value, but it did enhance the quality of the SDR as a more stable alternative to any single major currency. Partly as a result of the narrowing of the basket but mostly as a result of the increased volatility of the component currencies,[70] each major currency fluctuated markedly against the SDR throughout the 1980s, and the stability of the SDR reflected the offsetting effects of those movements (Figure 18.6).

[69]On the determination of percentage weights, see "Review of the Valuation of the SDR," SM/85/163 (June 7, 1985) and minutes of EBM/85/102 (July 1, 1985).

[70]For a statistical analysis, see Pozo (1984), which rejects the hypothesis that narrowing the basket led to significantly greater variability of the exchange rate of the SDR against major currencies in 1981.

Figure 18.5. Exchange Rate: U.S. Dollars per SDR, 1971–89
(Quarterly average)

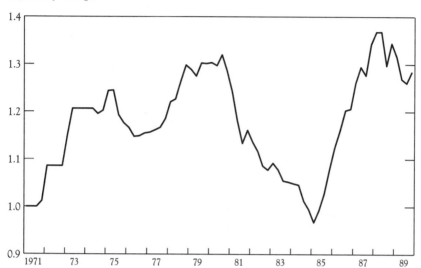

SDR Interest Rate

When the Fund designed the original SDR in the 1960s, the staff did not see the necessity or even the desirability of setting the interest rate at a market-clearing level, because the SDR was seen primarily as a substitute for gold reserves (de Vries, 1976, Vol. 1, p. 182; de Vries, 1985, pp. 282–83). The role of the SDR would be limited to a narrow range of official transactions, and the reconstitution requirement would ensure that participating countries would hold SDRs in reasonable amounts. In those conditions, a stable low interest rate was judged to be both a good means of making it affordable and attractive for countries to use SDRs and a sufficient incentive to induce them to hold SDRs as reserves. The 1969 amendment to the Articles provided that the Fund could set the SDR interest rate between 1 and 2 percent, or outside those limits under certain conditions.[71] In the event, the Board set the rate at 1.5 percent and left it there for 3½ years (Figure 18.7). In June 1974, the rate was raised abruptly to 5 percent, on the understanding that henceforth it would be set periodically at a rate approximately *half* of an appropriately weighted average rate on short-term money market securities in the

---

[71]The rate of remuneration on eligible reserve tranche positions (then known as "super gold tranche" positions) was 1.5 percent in 1969. Article XXVI, Section 3, provided that the Fund could set the SDR interest between 1 and 2 percent without regard to the rate of remuneration. If it set the remuneration rate outside that range, it could also set the SDR rate as high or as low as that rate.

Figure 18.6. SDR Exchange Rates, 1971–89

Index (January 1971 = 100)

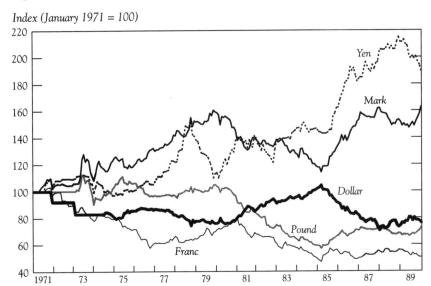

G-5 countries. On that formula, the rate was reduced to 3.75 percent in July 1974 and again to 3.5 percent in January 1976.

Effective in July 1976, the Fund changed this policy again, in three ways. First, the rate was to be set quarterly rather than semiannually. Second, the rate each quarter was to be equal to 60 percent (rather than 50 percent) of the average ("combined") market rate, rounded to the nearest ¼ of 1 percent. Third, the combined market rate was calculated more contemporaneously (based on the average over the six weeks preceding the quarter, rather than over the quarter preceding the semester). Although these changes fell far short of converting the SDR into a market-oriented financial asset, they did represent an initial effort to link the interest rate fairly directly to fluctuations in market rates.

The next step came toward the end of 1978. As of the beginning of 1979, the rate was to be calculated at 80 percent of the combined market rate. Other elements of the calculation were left unchanged, except that the base rate was now to be computed as the average rate over just 15 days prior to the start of the quarter. Ever so cautiously, the Fund was inching toward making the SDR equivalent to a bundle of national short-term securities, but it was still insisting on retaining a discount on the yield, as one component in the Fund's structure of slightly concessional interest rates (de Vries, 1985, pp. 892–95).[72]

---

[72]At that time, the SDR was a 16-currency basket, while the interest rate was calculated with reference to the five leading currencies. That difference, however, does not account for the discount, since interest rates in the excluded countries were not on average lower than those that were included. As noted in the preceding section, the undefined maturity of the SDR implies that the SDR interest rate and the combined market interest rate are not commensurate.

Figure 18.7. SDR Interest Rate, 1970–89

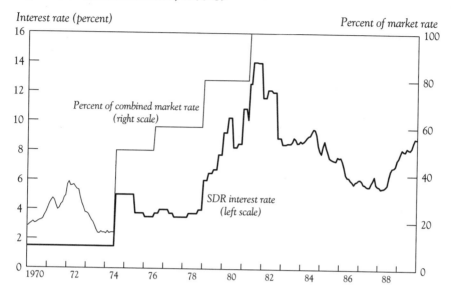

The final major move was to raise the rate to 100 percent of the combined market rate. The Executive Board took that step in December 1980, to be effective the following May, a few months after the conversion of the SDR into a five-currency basket (see the Appendix). By then, the staff and the Executive Board recognized that experience had not borne out the expectation that the SDR's stable capital value would make it attractive enough without a fully competitive yield. In proposing the increase, the staff acknowledged that raising the rate would impose costs on net users, notably on virtually all low-income countries. They argued, however, that the SDR had to be made fully competitive as an asset if it was to fulfill its potential for strengthening the international monetary system. If it was thought desirable to offset the higher costs for developing countries, that could be done by other means.[73] The G-24 followed up on that notion by trying to push the Fund to create a subsidy account for the use of SDRs by low-income countries (ministerial communiqué, April 1980; in *IMF Survey*, May 5, 1980). No action was ever taken on that proposal, and the idea of offsetting the rise in interest costs was allowed to die.

Appendix: Principal Changes in the Valuation of the SDR

In September 1980, the Executive Board agreed to redefine the SDR as a 5-currency rather than a 16-currency basket, effective in January 1981. (For the previous valuation, see de Vries, 1985, Vol. 3, pp. 556–57.) In December, the Board agreed to set the SDR interest rate equal to the com-

---

[73]"The Level of SDR Interest Rate in Relation to the Combined Market Rate," EBS/80/252 (November 24, 1980) and minutes of EBM/80/178 (December 8, 1980).

bined market interest rate in the countries issuing those five currencies, effective in May 1981. The initial decision was as follows.

Method of Valuation

1. Effective January 1, 1981, the value of one special drawing right shall be the sum of the values of specified amounts of the currencies listed in 2 below, the amounts of these currencies to be determined on December 31, 1980 in a manner that will ensure that, at the average exchange rates for the three-month period ending on that date, the shares of the currencies in the value of the special drawing right correspond to the weights specified for each currency in 2 below.

2. On the basis of changes in members' exports of goods and services and in official balances of members' currencies held by other members since the previous review of the method of valuation of the SDR conducted in March 1978, that the currencies and weights referred to in 1 above shall be as follows:

Currency	Weight (In per cent)
U.S. dollar	42
Deutsche mark	19
French franc	13
Japanese yen	13
Pound sterling	13

3. The list of the currencies that determine the value of the special drawing right, and the amounts of these currencies, shall be revised with effect on January 1, 1986 and on the first day of each subsequent period of five years in accordance with the following principles, unless the Fund decides otherwise in connection with a revision:

   a. The currencies determining the value of the special drawing right shall be the currencies of the five members whose exports of goods and services during the five-year period ending 12 months before the effective date of the revision had the largest value, provided that a currency shall not replace another currency included in the list at the time of the determination unless the value of the exports of goods and services of the issuer of the former currency during the relevant period exceeds that of the issuer of the latter currency by at least one per cent.

   b. The amounts of the five currencies referred to in a. above shall be determined on the last working day preceding the effective date of the relevant revision in a manner that will ensure that, at the average exchange rates for the three-month period ending on that date, the shares of these currencies in the value of the special drawing right correspond to percentage weights for these currencies, which shall be established for each currency in accordance with c. below.

   c. The percentage weights shall reflect the value of the balances of that currency held at the end of each year by the monetary authorities of other members and the value of the exports of goods and services of the issuer of the currency over the relevant five-year period referred to in a. above, in a manner that would maintain broadly the relative significance of the factors that underlie the percentage weights in paragraph 2 above. The percentage weights shall be rounded to the nearest 1 per cent or as may be convenient.

4. The determination of the amounts of the currencies in accordance with 1 and 3 above shall be made in a manner that will ensure that the value of the special drawing right in terms of currencies on the last working day preceding the five-year period for which the determination is made will be the same under the valuation in effect before and after revision.

Decision No. 6631-(80/145) G/S, adopted September 17, 1980

Implementation of that decision required amending Rule O-1, and the subsequent decision to equate the combined market and SDR interest rates required amending Rule T-1. Rule O-2, which was not amended, is also reproduced here for convenience. For the previous versions of Rules O-1 and T-1, see de Vries (1985), Vol. 3, pp. 474 and 480.

Valuation of the SDR

O-1. The value of the SDR shall be the sum of the values of the following amounts of the following currencies:

U.S. dollar	0.54
Deutsche mark	0.46
French franc	0.74
Japanese yen	34
Pound sterling	0.071

Valuation of Currencies in Terms of the SDR

O-2. (a) The value of the United States dollar in terms of the SDR shall be equal to the reciprocal of the sum of the equivalents in United States dollars of the amounts of the currencies specified in Rule O-1, calculated on the basis of exchange rates established in accordance with procedures decided from time to time by the Fund.

(b) The value of a currency other than the United States dollar in terms of the SDR shall be determined on the basis of the value of the United States dollar in terms of the SDR in accordance with (a) above and an exchange rate for that other currency determined as follows:

(i) for the currency of a member having an exchange market in which the Fund finds that a representative spot rate for the United States dollar can be readily ascertained, that representative rate;

(ii) for the currency of a member having an exchange market in which the Fund finds that a representative spot rate for the United States dollar cannot be readily ascertained but in which a representative spot rate can be readily ascertained for a currency as described in (i), the rate calculated by reference to the representative spot rate for that currency and the rate ascertained pursuant to (i) above for the United States dollar in terms of that currency;

(iii) for the currency of any other member, a rate determined by the Fund.

(c) Procedures to establish exchange rates under (b) above shall be determined by the Fund in consultation with members.

Interest and Charges in Respect of SDRs

T-1. (a) Interest and charges in respect of SDRs shall accrue daily at the rate referred to in (b) below and shall be paid promptly as of the end of each financial year of the Fund. The accounts of participants shall be credited with the excess of interest due over charges or debited with the excess of charges over the interest due. The accounts of holders that are not participants shall be credited with the interest due.

(b) The rate of interest on holdings of SDRs for each calendar quarter shall be equal to the combined market interest rate as determined in (c) below.

(c) The combined market interest rate shall be the sum of the average yield or rate on each of the respective instruments listed below for the fifteen business days preceding the last two business days of the last month before the calendar quarter for which interest is to be calculated, with each yield or rate multiplied by the number of units of the corresponding currency listed in Rule O-1 and the value in terms of the SDR of a unit of that currency as determined by the Fund under Rule O-2(a) and (b), provided that the combined market interest rate shall be rounded to the two nearest decimal places. The yields and rates for this calculation are:

Market yields for three-month U.S. Treasury bills.

Three-month interbank deposits rate in Germany

Three-month interbank money rate against private paper in France

Discount rate on two-month (private) bills in Japan

Market yields for three-month U.K. Treasury bills.

(d) The Fund will review the rate of interest on holdings of SDRs at the conclusion of each financial year.

References

Aggarwal, R., and L.A. Soenen, 1988, "Private Use of Official Currency Cocktails: The Relative Success of the ECU and the SDR," *Quarterly Review*, Banca Nazionale del Lavoro, No. 167 (December), pp. 425–40.

Allen, Polly Reynolds, 1993, "Artificial Currencies: SDRs and ECUs," *Open Economies Review*, Vol. 4, No. 1, pp. 97–110.

Brandt Commission [Independent Commission on International Development Issues under the Chairmanship of Willy Brandt], 1980, *North-South: A Program for Survival* (Cambridge, Massachusetts: MIT Press).

Buira, Ariel, 1996, "The Potential of the SDR for Improving the International Monetary System," in *The Future of the SDR in Light of Changes in the International Monetary System*, ed. by Michael Mussa, James M. Boughton, and Peter Isard (Washington: International Monetary Fund), pp. 180–202.

Coats, Warren L., 1982, "The SDR as a Means of Payment," *Staff Papers*, International Monetary Fund, Vol. 29 (September), pp. 422–36.

———, 1990, "Enhancing the Attractiveness of the SDR," *World Development*, Vol. 18 (July), pp. 975–88.

———, Reinhard W. Furstenberg, and Peter Isard, 1990, *The SDR System and the Issue of Resource Transfers*, Essays in International Finance, No. 180 (Princeton, New Jersey: International Finance Section, Department of Economics, Princeton University).

Cumby, Robert E., 1983, "Special Drawing Rights and Plans for Reform of the International Monetary System: A Survey," Chapter 10 in *International Money and Credit: The Policy Roles*, ed. by George M. von Furstenberg (Washington: International Monetary Fund), pp. 435–73.

de Vries, Margaret Garritsen, 1976, *The International Monetary Fund, 1966–1971: The System Under Stress*, Vol. 1: *Narrative*; Vol. 2: *Documents* (Washington: International Monetary Fund).

———, 1985, *The International Monetary Fund, 1972–1978: Cooperation on Trial*, Vols. 1 and 2: *Narrative and Analysis*; Vol. 3: *Documents* (Washington: International Monetary Fund).

Gold, Joseph, 1971, *Special Drawing Rights: The Role of Language*, IMF Pamphlet Series, No. 15 (Washington: International Monetary Fund).

Hilliard, Brian, 1983, "The Commercial SDR Since the Simplified Basket," *The Banker*, Vol. 133 (January), pp. 79–81.

International Monetary Fund, Research Department, 1983, "The Evolving Role of the SDR in the International Monetary System," Chapter 11 in *International Money and Credit: The Policy Roles*, ed. by George M. von Furstenberg (Washington: International Monetary Fund), pp. 475–535.

International Monetary Fund, Research and Treasurer's Departments, 1987, *The Role of the SDR in the International Monetary System*, IMF Occasional Paper No. 51 (Washington: International Monetary Fund).

International Monetary Fund, Treasurer's Department, 1995, *User's Guide to the SDR: A Manual of Transactions and Operations in SDRs* (Washington: International Monetary Fund).

Kenen, Peter B., 1981, "The Analytics of a Substitution Account," *Quarterly Review*, Banca Nazionale del Lavoro, Vol. 34 (December), pp. 403–26.

———, 1983, "Use of the SDR to Supplement or Substitute for Other Means of Finance," Chapter 7 in *International Money and Credit: The Policy Roles*, ed. by George M. von Furstenberg (Washington: International Monetary Fund), pp. 327–60.

Mussa, Michael, 1996, "The Rationale for SDR Allocation Under the Present Articles of Agreement of the International Monetary Fund," in *The Future of the SDR in Light of Changes in the International Financial System*, ed. by Michael Mussa, James M. Boughton, and Peter Isard (Washington: International Monetary Fund), pp. 57–87.

———, James M. Boughton, and Peter Isard, eds., 1996, *The Future of the SDR in Light of Changes in the International Financial System* (Washington: International Monetary Fund).

Polak, Jacques J., 1979, *Thoughts on an International Monetary Fund Based Fully on the SDR*, IMF Pamphlet Series, No. 28 (Washington: International Monetary Fund).

———, 1988, "The Impasse Concerning the Role of the SDR," in *The Quest for National and Global Economic Stability: In Honor of Hendrikus Johannes Witteveen*, ed. by Wietze Eizenga, E. Frans Limburg, and Jacques J. Polak (Boston: Kluwer Academic Publishers), pp. 175–89.

Pozo, Susan, 1984, "Composition and Variability of the SDR," *The Review of Economics and Statistics*, Vol. 66 (May), pp. 308–14.

Rhomberg, Rudolf R., 1991, "Failings of the SDR: Lessons from Three Decades," in *International Financial Policy: Essays in Honor of Jacques J. Polak*, ed. by Jacob A. Frenkel and Morris Goldstein (Washington: International Monetary Fund and De Nederlandsche Bank), pp. 150–69.

———, 1996, "The Once and Future SDR?" in *The Future of the SDR in Light of Changes in the International Financial System*, ed. by Michael Mussa, James M. Boughton, and Peter Isard (Washington: International Monetary Fund), pp. 47–54.

Sobol, Dorothy Meadow, 1979, "A Substitution Account: Precedents and Issues," *Quarterly Review*, Federal Reserve Bank of New York (summer), pp. 40–48.

———, 1982, *Europe Confronts the Dollar: The Creation of the SDR, 1963–69* (New York: Garland Publishing, Inc.,).

Solomon, Robert, 1982, *The International Monetary System, 1945–1981* (New York: Harper and Row).

Triffin, Robert, 1960, *Gold and the Dollar Crisis: The Future of Convertibility* (New Haven, Connecticut: Yale University Press).

United States Department of the Treasury, 1989, *Report to the Congress on a Limited Purpose Allocation of Special Drawing Rights for the Poorest Heavily Indebted Countries* (Washington).

van den Boogaerde, Pierre, 1984, "The Private SDR: An Assessment of Its Risk and Return," *Staff Papers*, International Monetary Fund, Vol. 31 (March), pp. 25–61.

von Furstenberg, George M., ed., 1983, *International Money and Credit: The Policy Roles* (Washington: International Monetary Fund).

Wijnholds, J.A.H. de Beaufort, 1982, "Diversification of Reserves and Monetary Stability," *World Economy*, Vol. 5 (November), pp. 303–20.

Wragg, Lawrence de V., ed., 1984, *Composite Currencies: SDRs, ECUs, and Other Instruments* (London: Euromoney Publications).

19

Toward Universal Membership

Global membership for the IMF was not always a widely shared ideal. In the months leading up to the Bretton Woods conference in 1944, Harry Dexter White had to work hard to convince his colleagues in the U.S. government that the Soviet Union and other socialist countries should not be excluded simply because of objections to their economic systems. At the same time, he labored (with only temporary success) to convince Soviet leaders that joining the Fund was in their interests. Meanwhile, the other major proponent of founding the IMF, John Maynard Keynes, was skeptical of the whole idea of bringing developing and small countries into the planning process. The conference, he feared, would be a "most monstrous monkey house" in which delegates with little to contribute would get in the way of the leading men.[1] Remarkably, despite these and other fears that diverse interests would doom an overly broad organization, most of the independent nations allied against the Axis in World War II did come to Bretton Woods, and in the next two years 40 countries became "original members" of the IMF.[2]

Those 40 countries, even without the Soviet Union, were broadly representative of the immediate postwar world economy. More than three-fourths of them would later be classified as "developing" rather than "industrial" countries, so the mix in that dimension was similar to that of the 1980s (77 percent nonindustrial in 1946, and 87 percent in 1986; see Figure 19.1). Half of the original 12 Executive Directors in the Fund came from nonindustrial countries, 2 of which (China and India) were among those with the five largest quotas and thus were

---

[1]White was the de facto leader of the U.S. delegation at Bretton Woods, under Treasury Secretary Henry Morgenthau, Jr. His wartime efforts to foster postwar economic cooperation with the Soviet Union, which were fully supported by the U.S. government, were later interpreted by some critics as disloyal to U.S. interests; see Boughton (2001). For his views on Soviet participation in the Fund and his meetings with Soviet delegates, see the 1942 "White Plan" in Horsefield (1969), Vol. 3, esp. pp. 72–73; Vol. 1, pp. 77–78; and "Pre-Bretton Woods Meetings—Master file; Meetings with the Russian Delegation, Jan.–May 1944," in IMF/CF. The quotation from Keynes (the Chairman of the British delegation) is from a letter of May 30, 1944, to Sir David Walley; see Moggridge (1980), p. 42.

[2]For a thorough discussion of the principles of Fund membership and of the early case history summarized below, see Gold (1974). On the decision by the Soviet Union not to join the Fund, see Mikesell (1951); Bernstein (1993); James and James (1994); and James (1995), pp. 68–71.

Figure 19.1. Membership in the IMF, 1946–97

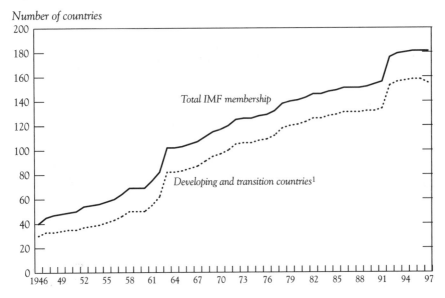

Number of countries

¹See footnote 3 in the text for an explanation of the taxonomy of countries.

entitled to appoint their own Directors (see Chapter 20).[3] Those statistics, however, mask a distinct imbalance of power and some troubling gaps. The six industrial countries with seats on the Executive Board held 69 percent of the voting
power. The United States alone controlled one-third of the vote and thereby had
a veto over the most fundamental decisions. Most of Africa was still colonized and
ineligible for membership. Germany, Japan, and their wartime allies had not been
invited.

The development of the Cold War after the Berlin blockade of 1948 and the
Communist victory in China in 1949 further restricted the scope of Fund membership. China continued to be represented in the Fund by the Nationalist government, which decamped to the island province of Taiwan and no longer controlled the mainland. Poland, another original member, withdrew in March 1950
under pressure from the Soviet Union, claiming that the IMF had become "a sub-

---

[3]This taxonomy of countries, which is also used in Figure 19.1, was adopted by the Fund in
1979 and modified in 1992 and 1997. The 1979 scheme divided countries into two primary categories: industrial and developing. At that time, 21 countries were classified as industrial; in
1989, Greece and Portugal were reclassified from developing to industrial, raising the latter total
to 23. The 1992 revision added a third category: "former centrally planned economies," redubbed
the following year as "countries in transition." No industrial country was reclassified in that shift.
In 1997, the industrial country terminology was replaced by "advanced economies." The new category comprised the 23 industrial countries plus Israel, Korea, Singapore, and two other "territo-
rial entities": Hong Kong and Taiwan Province of China. Here, "nonindustrial" comprises all
member countries that were not classified as industrial or advanced.

missive instrument of the Government of the United States."[4] Czechoslovakia, yet another original member, was required to withdraw at the end of 1954 for its failure to provide the information required for an evaluation of exchange rate policy. At that point, the only member country that lay east of what Winston Churchill had called the Iron Curtain was Yugoslavia. Socialist but largely independent of the Soviet Union, Yugoslavia remained a member throughout the Cold War and developed a large part of its international trade with the non-Socialist west. Romania, the geographic buffer between Yugoslavia and the Soviet Union, joined the Fund in 1972, and the unification of Vietnam in 1975 gave the Fund another Soviet ally as a member. However, no other CMEA or Warsaw Pact country joined the Fund until the 1980s.[5]

Membership in the Fund expanded slowly through the 1950s (Figure 19.1), punctuated most dramatically by the readmission into the world community of most of what the original Articles of Agreement collectively called "the enemy." Italy joined in 1947, followed by Germany and Japan in 1952. Spain, which also had been isolated for its Axis sympathies during the war, joined in 1958. By 1960, the main industrial countries had become an interest group with some cohesion, irrespective of the former conflict. The "Group of Ten," or G-10, still held 66 percent of the voting power in the Fund and took on for itself the role of guiding the evolution of the international monetary system.[6]

---

[4]Letter from Poland's ambassador to the United States, J. Winiewicz, to the Managing Director (Camille Gutt), dated March 13, 1950; circulated as Executive Board Special No. 141 (March 15, 1950), in IMF/CF (C/Poland/780 "Withdrawal from Membership"). Poland had been represented at Bretton Woods by officials of the multiparty Government in Exile, based in London. When the war ended, the Provisional Government of National Unity was formed in which the Communist party played a dominant but not exclusive role. The National Unity government joined the Fund in 1946, but it collapsed in December 1948, when the Soviet Union imposed a single-party system on Poland. It was that Stalinist government that withdrew from the Fund.

[5]The Council for Mutual Economic Assistance (CMEA; also known as COMECON) was established in 1949 to promote economic development through trade between the centrally planned economies of central and eastern Europe and the Soviet Union. It became the main mechanism for organizing trade and settling payments balances within the region until the demise of central planning in the early 1990s. Yugoslavia, an original member of the Fund, was an associate member of the CMEA economic alliance but did not join the Warsaw Treaty Organization (Warsaw Pact) military alliance. Romania was a member of both but did not permit Soviet or other Warsaw Pact troops to be stationed or conduct military exercises on its territory. Because of Romania's stance of independence on foreign policy, any action it took in defiance of Moscow (such as joining the Fund) was likely to entrench Soviet opposition to similar moves by other members of the alliance. For more on Romania's relations with the Fund, see Chapter 8, above, and de Vries (1985), pp. 908–09. Cuba withdrew from Fund membership in 1964, some eight years before it joined the CMEA. The history of Vietnam's relations with the Fund is covered in Chapter 16.

[6]On the composition and origins of the G-10 and other "Groups" discussed here, see Chapter 4. The voting percentage listed here includes the votes of Denmark and Iceland, which were not in the G-10 but were in the same Executive Board constituency as Sweden. For the monetary role of the G-10 in the 1960s, including the "Basel Agreement" on currency stabilization, the General Arrangements to Borrow (GAB), and the creation of the SDR, see Horsefield (1969), Vol. 1, pp. 483–84, 509–14, 543–45, and 587–92; Vol. 2, pp. 518–21; de Vries (1976), Vol. 1, Part One (on SDRs); Solomon (1982), Chapters 4 and 7; and James (1995), pp. 163–74.

Table 19.1. Accession to Fund Membership, 1979–89

Date	Country (Number of members)
November 15, 1979	St. Lucia (139)
December 28, 1979	St. Vincent and the Grenadines (140)
April 17, 1980	(People's Republic of China seated)
September 29, 1980	Zimbabwe (141)
September 28, 1981	Bhutan (142) and Vanuatu (143)
February 25, 1982	Antigua and Barbuda (144)
March 16, 1982	Belize (145)
May 6, 1982	Hungary (146)
August 15, 1984	St. Kitts and Nevis (147)
September 24, 1984	Mozambique (148)
September 13, 1985	Tonga (149)
June 3, 1986	Kiribati (150)
June 12, 1986	Poland (151)
September 19, 1989	Angola (152)

Although the G-10 and its subgroups dominated the scene in and around the Fund in the 1960s and 1970s, the seeds of countervailing influence were beginning to grow. As most of the colonies of European powers gradually gained independence, they all soon joined the Fund. From 1960 to 1978, Fund membership doubled, from 69 to 138 countries. Most of those new members were developing countries in need of financial assistance, and many were newly independent and also in need of technical assistance and training. Developing countries formed their own groups—the G-24, the G-77, and, within the Fund's Executive Board, the G-9—to speak out for their interests and to formulate common responses to G-10 initiatives. Despite their swelling ranks, however, developing countries still held just 36 percent of the voting power at the end of 1978.

From 1980 to 1990, all of the remaining nonmember countries in Africa joined the Fund (Table 19.1).[7] In each of these cases, membership had been delayed by internal or external conflicts. Zimbabwe joined in 1980, shortly after the fall of Ian Smith's minority government and the renaming of the former Rhodesia by the newly elected government of Robert Mugabe. Mozambique joined in 1984 after the government signed a peace accord with South Africa and began to move away from Soviet influence. And Angola (1989) and Namibia (1990) joined after a regional peace accord brought a lull in the Angolan civil war and independence (from South Africa) to Namibia.

This period also brought a wave of new members from very small countries. Four island countries in the Caribbean Sea (St. Lucia, St. Vincent and the Grenadines, Antigua and Barbuda, and St. Kitts and Nevis), three Pacific island countries (Vanuatu, Tonga, and Kiribati), plus Bhutan and Belize; all were smaller than most earlier Fund members, and each one joined with a quota of less than SDR 10 million.

---

[7]Eritrea, which became a member in 1994, was then part of Ethiopia.

The 1980s, like the 1950s, were years of gradually increasing Fund membership. The Soviet Union and most of its satellite countries stayed away, although officials from several countries (including both the Soviet Union and North Korea) made informal inquiries about the requirements of membership. Switzerland also stayed away. Although the Swiss National Bank participated in the G-10, the GAB, and the Enhanced Structural Adjustment Facility (ESAF), and its officials attended even the restricted sessions of the Interim Committee as observers, the Swiss population remained opposed to membership in multilateral organizations.

Not until the 1990s would the IMF become a truly universal institution, with more than 40 new members including Switzerland and all of the countries once in the Soviet Union (more than 180 members in all) and only a handful of isolated countries (notably North Korea and Cuba) remaining outside.[8] The modest expansion of the 1980s, however, belies the importance of the changes that were beginning to occur. In April 1980, China's representation in the Fund moved from the Taiwan Province to Beijing and effectively raised the population of the Fund by more than a billion people. Hungary became a member in 1982, and four years later, Poland rejoined the Fund. Economically, the sphere of Soviet influence was being split openly between the countries that were heavily dependent on the Soviet Union's dwindling resources and the reformers that were turning increasingly to the west. The remainder of this chapter chronicles the events that propelled three key socialist countries into the Fund in the 1980s and that laid the groundwork for the even greater transformations of the 1990s.

China

The IMF's decision in 1980 to recognize the People's Republic of China (PRC), based in Beijing, rather than the Republic of China (ROC), based in Taipei, as the government of China came nine years after that of the United Nations.[9] That delay reflected not just the different roles of the United Nations and the Fund but also an ambivalence about China in the international community and about the Fund in Beijing. To relate the history of China's role in the Fund requires an explanation of that ambivalence, and that in turn requires starting the story at Bretton Woods.

For more than 30 years, the ROC had governed only Taiwan Province of China but had claimed to represent the entire country. The PRC had governed the mainland and had claimed sovereignty over Taiwan as well. The Executive Board of the Fund was of course not called upon to try to resolve that dispute. Its 1980 decision involved neither the admission of a new member nor the termination of an exist-

---

[8]On the entry of Russia and neighboring countries into the Fund following the collapse of the Soviet Union in 1991–92, see James (1995), pp. 576–85.

[9]The terms "Republic of China" and "Taiwan," which were in standard usage in the Fund at the time of the events described here, refer to the government in control of Taiwan Province of China. Their usage here is purely historical and is not intended to imply legitimacy.

ing membership, but only the recognition of a different government to represent the member. It concluded a tangled history of shifting allegiances in the international community, and it began a period of close economic relationships between a once-isolated country and a world that was eager both to trade with it and to understand it more fully.

Nationalist China, 1944–50

China was an original member of the Fund, represented at Bretton Woods by a delegation chaired by the finance minister in the ruling Nationalist government, Hsiang-Hsi Kung. It had the third largest quota until 1959, and thus was one of the five countries entitled to appoint an Executive Director. Yee-Chun Koo, then the vice minister of finance, was appointed in 1946 and served until July 1950. But China's position in the Fund was complicated from the outset, first because of the lingering effects of the Japanese occupation on the Chinese economy, then because of the civil war that resulted in economic chaos, hyperinflation, and finally—following the defeat of the Nationalist army by the Communists—the establishment of the PRC by Mao Zedong on October 1, 1949.

In December 1946, the Executive Board granted China an indefinite delay in reporting a par value for its exchange rate, agreeing that it qualified for such a delay under a provision in Article XX of the Articles of Agreement that covered countries that had been occupied by the enemy during World War II.[10] The effect of this delay, which continued in force until 1970, was that China initially paid in only a token portion of its quota. When the PRC completed taking control over the mainland in October 1949, the former government (the ROC) took up residence at Taipei on the island then known in the west as Formosa and later as Taiwan. From then on, since both the PRC and the ROC claimed to represent all of China, in most cases (with the exception discussed below) they both rejected proposals under which each would be seen as having sovereignty only over the territory that it effectively controlled at the time. Because the majority of the Fund membership did not yet recognize the PRC as the legal government of China, the ROC continued to represent China in the Fund. Koo was succeeded in 1950 by Beue Tann, who served as Executive Director for China for the next 20 years.

Lowering the Profile, 1950–72

The PRC, through its foreign minister, Zhou Enlai, notified the Fund in August 1950 that it considered the PRC to be the sole legal government of China. Zhou, however, did not ask that the PRC be seated, but only that the ROC be

---

[10]This provision was included in the Articles in response to proposals submitted by the Chinese delegation, who did not feel that they would be able to comply immediately with the more general requirements for stable currency values. See Horsefield (1969), Vol. 1, p. 110; and Young (1965), pp. 310–12.

In front of the two negotiating teams in Beijing, Tun Thin (Director, Asian Department), and Wang Weicai (Vice President, People's Bank of China) sign a protocol for transfering representation at the IMF to the People's Republic of China, April 4, 1980

ousted.[11] Within the Fund, on several occasions from 1950 through 1954, Czechoslovakia moved (first in the Executive Board and then through the Board of Governors) to expel China from membership. These overtures, supported on one or more occasions by Poland, India, and Yugoslavia, were all rejected.[12] After Czechoslovakia left the Fund in December 1954, no further formal efforts were made to expel China until the early 1970s.

In spite of the continuing participation by the Taiwan authorities in the work of the Executive Board, and the initiation in 1952 of regular consultations with China (along with other members availing themselves of the transitional provisions of Article XIV; see Chapter 2), in other ways the ROC's role in the Fund was quite limited. In particular, China's quota did not increase along with those of other members, and the country was ineligible to use Fund resources until the authorities paid in its initial subscription.

As for quotas, when the first general augmentation was carried out in 1959, the ROC did not consent to its proposed increase (Horsefield, 1969, Vol. 1, p. 451). Since the original quota had been calculated on the basis of the total size of the Chinese economy, and since the ROC no longer controlled the mainland, an increase would have been difficult to justify. The effect of that decision was that China's quota was no longer in the top five, so it no longer qualified to appoint an Executive Director. Nonetheless, the quota remained large enough to enable the ROC to elect Tann to represent a single-country constituency. That arrangement remained in effect until the authorities again declined to consent to an increase in China's quota as part of the general review of 1966. Korea and Vietnam then joined China's constituency, which continued to be represented by Tann. China's relative quota fell further in 1970, after which the Philippines was brought into the fold. By 1971, China's share in Fund quotas had dropped from 7.2 percent in 1946 to 1.9 percent (twelfth largest).

In 1964 the Taiwan authorities decided to regularize their position in the Fund by communicating a par value and paying in the gold subscription decreed by the Articles of Agreement. This required an assessment of the value of the country's official holdings of gold and U.S. dollars as of September 12, 1946, which turned out to be just under $600 million.[13] China's gold subscription was fixed at 10 per-

---

[11]Reproduced in "China—Relations with the Fund," SM/73/238 (October 15, 1973), Attachment IV. The same document includes a summary of the efforts to expel China in 1950–54, described later in this paragraph.

[12]The 1950 and 1951 episodes are described in Horsefield (1969), p. 258. Also see Gold (1974), pp. 66–68.

[13]In 1942, the United States agreed to lend $500 million to China (i.e., to the Nationalist Government) to help pay for the war effort and to help the government control inflation. This interest-free loan included $220 million in gold that was shipped to China from 1943 to 1947. (More than two-thirds of the gold was shipped after the end of the war.) The rest, aside from a small amount dedicated to pay for textiles imported from the United States, was shipped in U.S. currency and notes. See Young (1965). Although part of the proceeds was used to finance war-related expenses, the bulk of it became the nucleus of China's postwar international reserves. (Most other external aid was linked to shipments of goods or provision of services.) The Nationalists retained possession of the remaining bullion and foreign exchange and removed it to Taiwan at the conclusion of the civil war.

cent of that amount, or $59.7 million.[14] However, no action to pay the subscription was taken at that time. At the end of 1969, China took another step by accepting membership in the newly created SDR Department of the Fund, but it declined to accept the allocation of SDRs to which it would have been entitled. Only in 1970 did the ROC finally activate its financial role in the Fund. That June, the authorities communicated a par value; in August, they paid the gold subscription in full (1.71 million ounces of gold, officially valued at $59.81 million); and in September, they completed the process by crediting the Fund's account with the remainder of the quota in New Taiwan dollars.

Pressure on China and on its position in the Fund mounted in 1971, when the UN General Assembly voted (on October 25) to seat the PRC in place of the ROC. The ROC took the precaution a few days earlier of purchasing its gold tranche and thus withdrawing its reserve assets from the Fund. Although this action meant that China was neither a creditor nor a debtor in the Fund, members were required to repay gold-tranche drawings (i.e., to redeposit equivalent assets) within time limits prescribed in the Articles of Agreement. China thus retained an obligation that would have to be met even if the Fund followed in the UN's footsteps. The Fund, however, as an agency independent from the United Nations, was not legally bound by the action of the General Assembly, and it continued to recognize the ROC as representing China.

The government on Taiwan remained sensitive to the need to maintain a low profile and to recognize the limits to its economic power, as had been evident all along with respect to quota increases. From December 1971 until March 1972—the period surrounding U.S. President Richard M. Nixon's first visit to China—the Taiwan authorities even toyed with the idea of withdrawing from Fund membership and then reapplying as the representative of the much smaller territory over which it retained effective control. In February, the ROC's governor in the Fund, Kuo Hwa Yu, directly informed the Managing Director, Pierre-Paul Schweitzer, of that intention.[15] That maneuver would have given rise to the possibility of a two-China solution under which the PRC could have applied for membership as the mainland government. It seemed, however, extremely unlikely either that the Board of Governors would have readmitted the ROC or that the PRC would have been prepared to apply under those restrictive conditions, and not long afterward the idea was dropped. In March, Peh Yuan Hsu, who in November 1970 had replaced Tann as the Executive Director, suggested that perhaps China's quota could be lowered. That idea also was dropped, since it would have required a formal vote by the Board of Governors and thus

---

[14]Article III required each original member to pay in gold the smaller of 25 percent of its quota (which would have been $137.5 million for China) or 10 percent of its net official holdings of gold and U.S. dollars as of a date when the Fund determined it was ready to begin exchange transactions.

[15]Memorandums for files by Joseph Gold, General Counsel (February 3, 1972) and Frank A. Southard, Jr., Deputy Managing Director (March 14, 1972); in IMF/CF (C/China/000 "Status of China in the Fund").

would have raised the same politically sensitive issues as an application for readmission.[16]

The final step in lowering the profile was the loss of China's representation on the Executive Board. In May 1972, Indonesia indicated that it was prepared to form a constituency of southeast Asian countries. As Vietnam was expected to move to that group, the ROC was unable to retain enough votes to elect an Executive Director in that year's election. Hsu then announced his resignation, and he was replaced on the Board by Placido L. Mapa, Jr., of the Philippines. By the time the election took place that fall, Indonesia had assumed the leadership of a diverse constituency ranging across Asia, North Africa, and southern Europe. The group included all of the countries that had been grouped with China (the Philippines, Korea, and Vietnam), but not China itself. For the rest of the decade, the ROC was without an Executive Director to formally look after its interests in the Fund. Regular Article XIV consultations nonetheless continued. Contacts between the Fund and China during this period normally were through the ROC Embassy (later the Taiwan authorities' representative office) in Washington.

Impasse over Representation, 1973–77

In the fall of 1973, the representation issue was reopened when Ji Pengfei, foreign minister of the PRC,[17] sent a cable to the Managing Director, H. Johannes Witteveen, during the annual meetings of the IMF and the World Bank. The cable reminded the Fund that the PRC was the sole legal representative of China and insisted that the ROC be expelled.[18] Both directly and through member countries, the Fund then made a number of inquiries to the PRC to determine the extent of its interest in representing China in the Fund; that is, the extent to which it would be prepared to assume the obligations as well as the rights of membership.[19] This approach led eventually to a meeting on November 2, 1973, at the United Nations in New York, between the Deputy Managing Director, Frank Southard, and Wang Runsheng, the PRC's ambassador to the United Nations.

These talks failed to resolve the impasse. The PRC authorities continued to insist that the expulsion of the ROC was a prior issue that had to be settled before

---

[16]Memorandum for files by Southard (March 24, 1972); in IMF/CF (C/China/000 "Status of China in the Fund").

[17]Names of PRC officials are given here in the modern Pinyin style, with the surname listed first. Names of ROC officials are given in the form in which they were used in the Fund at that time.

[18]"People's Republic of China—Communication with Managing Director," EBS/73/317 (October 1, 1973).

[19]Jacobson and Oksenberg (1990) conclude, on the basis of interviews with Chinese officials, that Ji's cable had been personally approved by Mao Zedong and that his approval indicated "that he countenanced Chinese participation in the IMF" (p. 63). They also note, however, that in June 1974, the ministry of finance and the ministry of foreign affairs prepared a joint report recommending against joining the Fund, and that the "top leaders agreed with this report" (p. 64). Whatever the authorities' intentions might have been in that period, they were not conveyed directly to the Fund.

discussions could take place on PRC membership, while the Fund maintained that the issue was one of representation rather than membership. In the view of Fund management, since China was already a member, the Executive Board had only to decide which government was entitled to represent the country in the Fund. Management was prepared to discuss representation, but the PRC would first have to indicate its intentions with regard to the requirements for membership, because the expulsion of the ROC as the representative of China would automatically subject the PRC to the Articles of Agreement.

The Fund had no further official contacts with the PRC for three years, until the PRC submitted a new protest against the ROC's credentials in September 1976. This complaint sounded superficially like those that had preceded it in 1950 and again in 1973, but it had a new urgency that reflected a dramatic change in circumstances in China. The economy was in a shambles after ten years of the Cultural Revolution, nearly a quarter of a million people had been killed by devastating earthquakes in July, and on September 9 the death of Mao Zedong had brought an effective end to the rule of the "Gang of Four." Although the extent to which China would now open its doors to trade with the West could not yet be foreseen, the country's new leaders were plainly standing at the sill.

Of even more immediate concern was that at the time of this new overture, the Fund was facing a decision that would materially affect China's financial position in the institution. Implementing an accord reached the preceding year, the Interim Committee agreed in January 1976 to proceed "without delay" (interpreted to mean that it should begin before the end of the year) with the restitution of one-sixth of the Fund's gold holdings to member countries, in proportion to quotas as of August 31, 1975. (See de Vries, 1985, pp. 625, 634, and 658–59.) That formula implied that China would soon receive 470,708 ounces of gold, which at the average price in 1976 (just under $125 an ounce) would have been worth close to $60 million on the open market.[20] Which authorities were to receive that gold, however, was an open question. On September 30, the president of the People's Bank of China, Chen Xiyu, sent a cable to Witteveen, once again protesting the Taiwan authorities' credentials to represent China and demanding on behalf of the PRC that the ROC be expelled from the Fund and not receive restitution of any gold.[21]

The PRC protest was placed on the Executive Board's agenda, in restricted session, on December 3, 1976. By this time the start of gold restitution was imminent—it had been delayed only until January, for technical reasons—and it was clear that the representation issue would have to be resolved before any gold could be restituted to China. The Managing Director proposed sending a reply to Chen,

---

[20]Restitution involved the purchase of the gold by the member country at the official price of gold in the Fund (SDR 35 per ounce), with payment in the member's own currency. If the transaction raised the Fund's holdings of that currency above the quota (as it would in this case), the excess was treated the same as a credit-tranche drawing. That is, the exchange gave rise to an interest-bearing obligation subject to repayment within a specified period of time. Restitution thus was equivalent to a hard currency sale by the Fund to the member at the official price.

[21]The cable is reproduced in "China," EBS/76/465 (October 28, 1976).

seeking further clarification from the PRC as to whether they were prepared to formally accept the obligations of Fund membership. The September 30 cable had laid claim to China's "assets, rights, and interests" in the Fund but had made no mention of obligations.

The omission of any acceptance of obligations appears to have been quite deliberate. In the view of the Beijing authorities, the PRC had a legitimate claim to any assets held in the Fund on behalf of China (for which it was the sole legal representative), but it had no responsibility for any liabilities that might have been incurred (illegally) by the Taiwan authorities. What was less clear was the PRC's intention regarding the ongoing obligations of Fund membership, as set out in the Articles of Agreement. That issue was uppermost in the minds of the Fund's management in determining how best to respond to Chen's initiative, but it was quite subsidiary and well down the road as far as the PRC was concerned. A working group had been established in the central bank to prepare for possible negotiations with the Fund, but the Taiwan issue had to be settled first.[22]

If the PRC was prepared to accept the obligations of membership, the Executive Board could then determine which government was the legitimate representative of China. Although there was little doubt that a definite indication of intentions would ultimately lead to the seating of the PRC,[23] a number of Executive Directors expressed uneasiness at the idea of requiring the PRC to make such a declaration while China was still represented at the Fund by the Taiwan authorities. At the December 3 meeting, the voting power was almost evenly divided between those Directors supporting Witteveen's proposal and those who argued that the Fund should accept the PRC proposal by immediately declaring the Taiwan authorities not to be the legitimate representative of China. But Witteveen managed to avoid bringing the question to a formal vote by agreeing to redraft the proposed reply more positively and to submit the redraft to the Board for further consideration.[24]

The Executive Board met once more to resolve the China question on January 5, 1977, again in restricted session. The first issue on the agenda was whether to authorize the Managing Director to send the redrafted reply to Chen. The draft continued to stress the necessity of "knowing the full intentions" of the PRC government and indicated the desire of the Fund to resolve the matter "in an equitable and satisfactory manner," but it also now emphasized the "positive spirit" in which Executive Directors viewed the PRC's initiative, and it expressed the willingness of the Fund's management "to engage in any further discussions . . . at whatever time and place are convenient to your Government." After some discussion, that course of ac-

---

[22]Based on background interviews with PRC officials.

[23]In September 1976, the Fund had followed a similar procedure when the Socialist Republic of Vietnam had succeeded South Vietnam at the conclusion of the war in that country (see Chapter 16). The Fund first sought and obtained assurances from the new government that it was prepared to assume the obligations of membership, and then recognized it as the representative of the existing member country.

[24]"Restricted Session—China—Relations with the Fund [Secretary's summary of discussion at EBM/76/159 (December 3, 1976)]," EBAP/77/54 (February 28, 1977). Also see the Managing Director's draft letter, in "China," EBS/76/465 (October 28, 1976).

tion was approved by a small majority, with a sizable number of Directors favoring an even more positive response: expulsion of the ROC prior to any further talks.[25]

The Board then turned to the question of restitution of gold to China. The ROC—which, as discussed earlier, had not been represented on the Executive Board since 1972—was represented at this meeting by Martin Wong, minister of the ROC in Washington. On the surface, it would appear to have been easy for the Board to dispose of this question by agreeing to delay restitution until the representation issue was resolved. The barrier to that approach was that the Articles of Agreement require the Fund to provide equal treatment to all members. The Fund could not delay restitution to one country without good cause. If the PRC were to make a claim "of which the Fund could properly take cognizance," in the words of the Managing Director (i.e., a claim made as part of a representation that the PRC wished to assume the obligations of membership on behalf of China), that legal difficulty would be covered. With the voting power still divided too evenly for the outcome of a formal vote to be predictable, the Board once again postponed deciding the matter. Five days later, however, the Board did finally take a decision: to retain the gold that was to be restituted to China until the question of representation was resolved or until April 1, 1977, whichever came earlier.[26] April 1 thus became in effect a deadline for the PRC to indicate its preparedness to assume China's seat at the Fund.

In early March 1977, Chen responded to Witteveen's letter by reiterating the PRC's demands, by insisting that any disposal of China's assets (implicitly referring to gold restitution to the Taiwan authorities) would be illegal, but also by inviting the Managing Director or his representatives to meet with the PRC's delegation at the United Nations. The Fund responded quickly and affirmatively, and a meeting was arranged in New York for March 31.[27]

The New York meeting was cordial, but it still did not resolve the differences of view. Zhou Nan, Counsellor to the PRC delegation at the United Nations, insisted that the Fund should first implement the UN Resolution of October 1971, which called on all UN agencies to expel the ROC.[28] Only then could the PRC enter

---

[25]Nine Directors, with 55 percent of the voting power, expressed support for the Managing Director's proposal; eight Directors, with 31 percent, opposed it. The other three abstained. "Restricted Session— . . . China—Relations with the Fund [Secretary's summary of discussion at EBM/77/3 (January 5, 1977]," EBAP/77/120 (April 26, 1977). Also see the Managing Director's redrafted letter, in "China," EBS/76/465, Sup. 1 (December 14, 1976).

[26]"Restricted Session—China—'Restitution of Gold'," EBAP/77/67 (March 11, 1977) [Secretary's summary of discussion at EBM/77/5 (January 10, 1977)], pp. 7–8.

[27]"China," EBS/77/69 (March 9, 1977); minutes of EBM/77/34 (March 11) and EBM/77/41 (March 30); and letter from William B. Dale (as Acting Managing Director) to Lai Ya-Li (Ambassador from the PRC to the United Nations) (March 22); in IMF/CF (C/China/000 "Status of China in the Fund"). The same file contains the original of Chen's letter, in Chinese.

[28]"The General Assembly . . . [d]ecides to restore all its rights to the People's Republic of China and to recognize the representatives of its Government as the only legitimate representatives of China to the United Nations, and to expel forthwith the representatives of Chiang Kai-shek from the place which they unlawfully occupy at the United Nations *and in all the organizations related to it*" (emphasis added). United Nations General Assembly, A/Res/2758 (XXVI), October 26, 1971.

into membership discussions. The Fund mission—headed by Tun Thin, Director of the Asian Department—pointed out that under the legal obligations of the Fund, if the ROC were expelled without the PRC simultaneously assuming the seat, China would cease to be a member and would have to reapply. In the meantime, the Fund would be obligated to pay any claims of the withdrawing member.[29] At the moment, the only claims were the gold that was to be restituted and an amount in the form of New Taiwan dollars equivalent to China's quota in the Fund. The Chinese delegation agreed to convey this information to the government in Beijing. There the matter would lie for the next three years, as no further initiatives were forthcoming.[30]

Return to Beijing, 1978–80

By the end of the 1970s, several developments were combining to brighten the picture dramatically. First, U.S. President Jimmy Carter announced on December 15, 1978, that the United States was establishing full diplomatic relations with the PRC as of the new year, and would accordingly sever its diplomatic ties with the government on Taiwan. This announcement left the ROC with no effective international support for its claim to represent the people of China.

Second, economic policy in China was being substantially reformed as the country gradually awoke from the nightmare of the Cultural Revolution. Adjustment was proving difficult: the initial drive to expand in 1977 and 1978 had proved to be excessive and, in a number of sectors, misdirected; the authorities, preparing a new program of macroeconomic and structural adjustment, were more open to outside advice and technical assistance than at any time since the founding of the PRC. The Third Plenum of the Central Committee of the Chinese Communist Party, held in December 1978, affirmed this new openness and directed the economy on a course of modernization.

In pursuit of these new policies, Deng Xiaoping, then Vice Chairman of the Central Committee, made a state visit to Washington at the end of January 1979. Shortly thereafter Deng and other leading Chinese officials began speaking publicly about the new outward-looking strategy and about the possibility of PRC representation in the Fund and the World Bank. A month later, an informal mission from the Bank found a receptive environment in Beijing.[31] In April, China established four "special economic zones" to promote exports to market economies. And China's openness was stressed in July 1979 by the PRC delegate speaking at the

---

[29]Memorandum from Tun Thin to the Managing Director, with attached report (April 6, 1977); in IMF/CF (C/China/000 "Status of China in the Fund").

[30]On April 1, 1977 and again on April 11, the Executive Board decided to continue the postponement of gold restitution "for a reasonable time," pending resolution of the representation issue. Minutes of EBM/77/43 (April 1, 1977) and EBM/77/51 (April 11).

[31]See Feeney (1989), pp. 239–40; Hsiung and Kim (1980), p. 239; Jacobson and Oksenberg (1990), pp. 70–74; "China Discusses World Bank Membership," *Journal of Commerce* (February 27, 1979), p. 9; and minutes of EBM/79/35 (February 28, 1979).

annual meeting of the Economic and Social Council of the United Nations (ECOSOC) in Geneva. He noted the "bright prospects" for strengthened cooperation with the "development agencies" of the United Nations, a reference intended to cover the IMF as well as the World Bank.[32] Finally, direct contacts between PRC and Fund officials resumed informally during the Annual Meetings in Belgrade that October.[33]

Third, the Taiwan authorities, doubtless sensing the futility of attempting to hold onto their seat while the stage was being set for a new play, shifted their energies toward making a graceful exit from the scene. In January 1979, Martin Wong volunteered to help the Fund staff in reaching an amicable settlement of the dispute over representation.[34]

The cooperation of the Taiwan authorities was potentially a critical element in the process, because the gold-tranche drawings made in the early 1970s were still subject to repayment. If the drawings remained outstanding when representation shifted to Beijing, then the PRC would have to assume the liability; but it had already indicated its reluctance to do so, on the grounds that the Taiwan government had no right to incur such obligations. One cooperative solution being discussed was for the ROC to repay its gold-tranche drawing and simultaneously redraw an equivalent amount. This new balance would constitute a reserve-tranche drawing under the amended Articles and thus would not be subject to an obligation to repay.[35] The Fund would still hold New Taiwan dollars equal to China's quota, but there would no longer be a legal barrier to simply substituting the PRC's renminbi for them. The Taiwan authorities seemed prepared to take that step, but only if the Fund restituted China's gold to it as part of the deal.

These various threads culminated in a direct approach from the PRC to the Fund in February 1980, in the form of a visit by officials from the new Chinese embassy in Washington to inquire about procedures for their assuming China's seat. From this point on, the representation negotiations would proceed smoothly except for a final hiccup on the restitution of gold. In a matter of just a few weeks, a mission team had been assembled to hold discussions in Beijing to discuss technical issues related to the rights and obligations of membership. These discussions—for which the Fund team was led by Tun Thin and the PRC team by the vice president of the People's Bank, Wang Weicai—led quickly to a memorandum of understanding.[36] But then came the hiccup.

---

[32]Memorandum from Jan-Maarten Zegers (Special Representative of the IMF to the United Nations) to the Managing Director (July 11, 1979), in IMF/CF (C/China/000 "Status of China in the Fund").

[33]Memorandums for files by Zegers (October 4, 1979) and Dale (October 10); in IMF/CF (C/China/000 "Status of China in the Fund"). Also see Jacobson and Oksenberg (1990), p. 72.

[34]Memorandum from Gold and Tun Thin to the Managing Director (January 19, 1979); in IMF/CF (C/China/000 "Status of China in the Fund").

[35]The 1978 amendments replaced the term "gold tranche" with "reserve tranche." The amendment to Article V limited a member's repayment obligation, inter alia to drawings that were subject to periodic charges, which excluded drawings under the reserve tranche.

[36]"China—Notification from the Government of the People's Republic," EBS/80/78 (April 7, 1980).

The agreement between the Fund staff and the Beijing authorities included an understanding that China's gold subscription would be restituted to the PRC, in return for which the PRC would assume the obligation to repay the outstanding gold tranche position. That solution, which required a diplomatic concession by Beijing but was financially favorable, would have bypassed the need for any further involvement by the ROC. On Friday, April 11, one week after the mission concluded its work in Beijing, the U.S. authorities suddenly proposed exactly the opposite combination: the ROC would get the gold in return for repurchasing the gold tranche position.[37] That proposal, which allotted about 40 percent of the net assets to the ROC instead of leaving it all to the PRC, was agreeable to the Taiwan authorities but thoroughly unacceptable to Beijing. As the Executive Board was set to decide the matter on Monday, there was little time to react. On Sunday, the PRC sent a strong message of protest to the Managing Director and to the U.S. Treasury. Nonetheless, the U.S. proposal carried on Monday by a narrow margin, and by Wednesday the ownership of the gold was transferred back to the ROC.[38]

The PRC would have much preferred the earlier agreement, as much for the principle as for the money. Nonetheless, there was a larger principle—and a larger prize—at stake, which was the right of the People's Republic to represent China in the Fund, as it did already elsewhere. After making one final informal protest to the Managing Director about the way the matter was handled, the authorities dropped the issue for good.

The stage was now set for the recognition of the PRC as the representative for China in the Fund. With the gold issue out of the way, the Board's final consideration of the seating decision on April 17, 1980, was anticlimactic. While a few Executive Directors expressed regrets over the effect that the decision would have in isolating the Taiwan authorities, no one voted against it.[39] Cross, supported by a few others, expressed a wistful desire on behalf of the U.S. authorities to maintain "some form of association between Taiwan and the Fund." To that, George P.

---

[37]The net value gold that was to be restituted to the ROC was approximately $224 million, at the prevailing gold price and exchange rates. The increase in the reserve tranche position from repayment of the earlier drawings was about $137 million (SDR 107 million). The effect of the U.S. proposal was to give the PRC the latter amount instead of the former. See attachment to a letter from Tun Thin to the PRC Embassy in Washington (April 23, 1980); in IMF/CF (C/China/652 "Restitution of Gold, 1976–1980").

[38]In this final test of sympathy for the position of the ROC, seven Directors, with 42 percent of the voting power, supported the U.S. proposal: Sam Y. Cross (United States), Teruo Hirao (Japan), Gerhard Laske (Germany), Costa P. Caranicas (Alternate—Greece), Robert J. Whitelaw (Australia), Bernard J. Drabble (Canada), and Mahsoun B. Jalal (Saudi Arabia). Eight Directors, with 31 percent, spoke in favor of postponing a decision (which implied that restitution would be made to the PRC): H. Onno Ruding (Netherlands), Paul Mentré de Loye (France), Gísli Blöndal (Alternate—Iceland), Joaquín Muns (Spain), Kadhim A. Al-Eyd (Alternate—Iraq), Abderrahmane Alfidja (Alternate—Niger), Semyano Kiingi (Alternate—Uganda), and Jacques de Groote (Belgium). Two Directors abstained, and four did not speak on the matter. Minutes of EBM/80/72 (April 14, 1980). Also see memorandum for files by Tun Thin (April 15, 1980); in IMF/CF (C/China/652 "Restitution of Gold, 1976–1980").

[39]Joaquín Muns (Spain) reported that "one member of his constituency, Costa Rica, had expressed opposition."

Nicoletopoulos (Gold's successor as Director of the Legal Department) responded that once the PRC was seated, "all official relations under the Articles of Agreement with the Taiwanese authorities would cease," but "informal arrangements" could be developed. Moreover, it was agreed that the 16 staff members holding ROC passports could continue to work at the Fund.[40]

After so many years of struggle with one of the most delicate diplomatic issues of the time, the Fund concluded by adopting a consensus decision and issuing a two-sentence press release:

> The Executive Board of the International Monetary Fund has decided that the Government of the People's Republic of China represents China in the Fund. China's quota in the Fund is SDR 550 million.

The People's Republic, 1980–89

China moved quickly to strengthen its role in the Fund to a level commensurate with its status in the world economy. The most essential action in that direction was to raise the quota from the SDR 550 million just cited: a level that was unchanged from 1944. If China had received quota increases in the 1960s and 1970s equal to the average of other member countries, its quota would have been nearly four times as large. Even allowing for some initial exaggeration and for China's relatively slow growth in the interim, a major adjustment was clearly warranted.[41] Accordingly, the Fund approved an ad hoc increase to SDR 1.2 billion ($1.6 billion) in August 1980 and then a further increase in 1.8 billion ($2.3 billion) as part of the Seventh General Review in December (amounts that were consistent with staff calculations using the standard quota formulas).[42] With those increases, China had the eighth largest quota in the Fund, exceeded only by those of the Group of Seven (G-7) industrial countries, and had enough votes to elect its own Executive Director without having to form or join a multicountry constituency.[43]

Borrowing from the Fund was not a high priority for China. Fund representation was soon followed by a similar action by the World Bank, and the Chinese authorities focused on obtaining a wide range of development and adjustment loans

---

[40]Minutes of EBM/80/75 (April 17, 1980).

[41]China's initial quota, as agreed at Bretton Woods, reflected pressure from the United States to place China in the top five countries that were authorized to appoint Executive Directors (Mikesell, 1994, p. 37).

[42]For the staff calculations, see memorandum for files of February 25, 1980, by Luc de Wulf (Senior Economist in the Asian Department); in IMF/CF (C/China/1210 "People's Republic, Quota Increase, 1980"). For the key discussion by Executive Directors, see minutes of meeting 80/1 of the "Ad Hoc Committee on Increase in Quotas—China" (August 5, 1980), in the same file.

[43]In September 1980, the Board of Governors agreed to raise the number of seats on the Executive Board from 21 to 22, to accommodate China without squeezing out another developing country. In September 1981, the ad hoc quota increase granted to Saudi Arabia placed that country in eighth place, ahead of China. For the broader issues on quota increases, see Chapter 17.

from the Bank Group.[44] For the first half of the 1980s, China limited its use of Fund resources to a small stand-by arrangement in the first credit tranche and a loan from Trust Fund, both of which the Fund approved in 1981.[45] As economic reforms took hold and output began growing rapidly, China developed a balance of payments problem in the mid-1980s and undertook a second stand-by arrangement (also limited to the first credit tranche) in 1986. For most of the decade, however, China was a creditor in the Fund.

For China, the main benefits from Fund membership—other than access to the World Bank—were the general one of acceptance and recognition in the world community and the more specific one of access to the Fund's information and data, technical assistance, and training. On numerous occasions throughout the 1980s, Chinese officials participated in courses and seminars at the IMF Institute in Washington. From 1982 on, Fund officials conducted several technical assistance and study missions to China on central banking, statistical, and fiscal issues; participated in World Bank seminars, missions, and related activities; held seminars and colloquia there (see, e.g., Hook, 1983); and (in 1983) organized a course in Xian on banking and monetary policy.[46] Although the amount of technical assistance to China was not disproportional in relation to that provided to other countries (see Chapter 20), this activity was particularly important for broadening and deepening the awareness in China of western economic thought and of the best financial and accounting practices in other countries.

Hungary

Knocking at the Door, 1946–80

At the end of the Second World War, Hungary was not yet under complete Soviet domination. The provisional government, established by the Allies with a dominant Soviet presence, sought to establish an independent economic course.

---

[44]During the 1980s, China received 50 loans totaling $5.3 billion from the International Bank for Reconstruction and Development (IBRD, the Bank's regular lending arm) and 28 loans totaling $3.3 billion from the International Development Association (IDA, the Bank's concessional lending operation). For the history of China's relations with the Bank, see Kapur, Lewis, and Webb (1997), pp. 24–25, passim.

[45]The stand-by arrangement was for SDR 450 million ($550 million, or 25 percent of quota) and was fully drawn in March 1981. That same month, the Fund disbursed a loan of just under SDR 310 million ($380 million) from the Trust Fund. Chinese officials requested more substantial assistance from the Fund in 1982, but the Managing Director determined that the data did not meet the requirement for a "balance of payments need." As discussed in Chapter 14, China later volunteered not to draw on the resources of the Fund's concessional structural adjustment facilities. On the handling of the 1982 request, see attachment to note of May 12, 1982, from Donald K. Palmer (Deputy Director, Exchange and Trade Relations Department) to Nigel Carter (Personal Assistant to the Managing Director); in IMF/RD Managing Director file "India" (Accession 84/21, Box 2, Section 168).

[46]See "People's Republic of China—Staff Report for the 1989 Article IV Consultation," SM/90/2 (January 2, 1990), pp. 31–32.

In spite of the Soviet Union's last-minute decision at the end of 1945 not to ratify the Articles of Agreement and join the IMF, Hungary almost immediately (October 1946) expressed interest in initiating discussions with the Fund. Before the Fund staff could pursue that initiative, however, it would have been necessary for the authorities to establish a measure of potential support from the countries who were already members.[47] That support was never likely to materialize, and it became increasingly unlikely as the Stalinist faction in Hungary began to consolidate its power in 1947. With the advent of the Cold War, the political environment of the late 1940s could scarcely have been more hostile to a country regarded as a Soviet satellite. After being told explicitly by officials in the U.S. State Department in 1948 that the United States would not support its application, Hungary dropped the issue and let it lie for nearly 20 years.[48]

By 1966, the Hungarian authorities had determined that the time was ripe to take a few hesitant steps toward economic reform. The mainstays of what would become the "New Economic Mechanism" in 1968 would be modifications to the central planning process, designed to make production decisions driven more by demand, and the unification of the exchange rate near a market level. More generally, some officials—notably the man in charge of foreign exchange matters for the central bank, Janos Fekete—viewed Fund membership as an essential part of the reform process. Without Fund support, they reasoned, they could not maintain a level of international reserves sufficient to sustain the foreign trade without which growth would be stunted. Fekete regularly attended the monthly meetings of the Bank for International Settlements (BIS) in Basel, Switzerland, representing a central bank that had been a shareholder since the BIS was founded in 1930. At such a meeting in June 1966, he approached Joseph Gold, the Fund's General Counsel, to get information on the Fund's operations and policies, and to see if the time had yet come when the membership might be receptive to an application from Hungary. He got the information, but not much encouragement.[49]

The main obstacle continued to be opposition from the United States, but the Soviet Union also was rather less than enthusiastic. Soviet leaders were reluctant to see CMEA member countries pursue independent economic policies that

---

[47]At the time of the Bretton Woods conference in July 1944, Hungary was allied with Germany. The government therefore was not invited to participate and consequently was ineligible to become an "original member" of the Fund.

[48]In October 1946, the Fund informed the Hungarian government that "the entry of Hungary in the International Monetary Fund is a question which would have to be cleared with the Foreign Offices and the Ministries of Foreign Affairs of the member countries," and advised the authorities to make inquiries on their own. A negative response to such an inquiry was made by the United States around the beginning of 1948. See letter of October 17, 1946, from Ernest de Selliers (Alternate Executive Director, Belgium) to A. Szasz (Economic Advisor, Legation of Hungary in Washington); and memorandum of February 4, 1948, from Roman L. Horne (Assistant Secretary) to V. Frank Coe (Secretary); in IMF/CF (C/Hungary/710 "Application for Membership").

[49]See memorandum of July 12, 1966, from Whittome to the Managing Director; in IMF/CF (C/Hungary/710 "Application for Membership"). Additional information is from interviews.

reached out toward the West and that would require divulging data on trade and finance within the CMEA. Romania—always a CMEA maverick—was also considering applying to join the Fund, and Hungarian officials were concerned that a move in that direction by Romania would stiffen Soviet opposition and make it impossible for countries where Soviet troops were stationed to follow (see footnote 5, p. 965). Hungary could not afford to risk having a formal application rejected, but the authorities did decide to develop regular informal contacts with Fund staff.

Over the next 15 years, clandestine meetings took place with irregular frequency and in a variety of locations: normally Basel, Budapest, or Washington, but also anywhere else where discreet conversations could be held. On the Fund side, Whittome would be the key player, often traveling alone and in great secrecy.[50] On the Hungarian side, Fekete was also largely a lone wolf. But whatever the venue and no matter how strong the political opposition on both sides, both men seem to have had the full support of their superiors as they sought a way through the thicket.

Notwithstanding the difficulty of joining the Fund, the New Economic Mechanism was launched at the beginning of 1968, a year that would witness struggles between aspiration and repression in country after country around the globe. The Mechanism itself would be implemented in fits and starts (see Boote and Somogyi, 1991), and in the aftermath of the suppression of the Prague Spring, the program could no longer be seen as the nose of the camel pushing into the tent. Soviet opposition became intense, and Hungarian envoys to Moscow received stern warnings that applying to join the Fund would be inappropriate.

By the late 1970s, the balance of influence had begun to shift in favor of Hungary joining the IMF. On the domestic front, both positive and negative forces drove the country to take bolder steps. Positively, the New Economic Mechanism was replaced by a somewhat bolder reform package in 1978. By 1980, domestic prices of most traded goods—including petroleum—would be determined primarily by prices in world markets, and officials knew that the Fund could play an important role in helping them maintain that policy. Negatively, implementing reforms without external support had required a major increase in external debt, although very few people at the time had a clear picture of the extent of that problem. On the Soviet side, that country's ability to provide even backup economic support to its satellites had gradually weakened, and the invasion of Afghanistan in December 1979 further overextended Soviet resources.

Against this background, the international oil price and interest rate increases of 1979–80 had disastrous effects on the Hungarian economy. By the end of 1980, Hungary had more than $10 billion in external debt, which was becoming more and more expensive to service as world interest rates rose. Without both external

---

[50]Secrecy was not always maintained; on at least two occasions, Whittome's travels were leaked to the press. In April 1971, the *Washington Post* and other newspapers reported that the Fund had sent secret missions to Budapest in the late 1960s, and in March 1978 the *Financial Times* reported that a visit to Warsaw was being planned.

support and a reversal of expansionary domestic policies, the situation would become unsustainable.

Joining the Fund, 1981–82

The reform program that was initiated in 1978, combined with weakening Soviet influence and a deteriorating economic outlook, culminated in a decision in the fall of 1981 to apply for Fund membership. The government knew that an overture to the Fund would be opposed, not only by the Soviet leadership but by most other CMEA countries as well. Some officials also knew that Fund membership would force them to disclose much more economic data than they were accustomed to, and that the existing severe distortions in their national statistics would have to be acknowledged or somehow covered up. They had, however, no other way to avoid default and economic collapse. In September, Janos Kadar (head of the Communist Party since 1956) decided to take a chance and present Hungary's allies with a fait accompli. Fekete and his staff prepared the necessary materials in secret over the next few weeks, while the government took preemptive action to strengthen economic policy by devaluing and unifying the exchange rate (see Boote and Somogyi, 1991, p. 6). On November 4, Fekete arrived in Washington and handed the membership application to William B. Dale (who was serving as Acting Managing Director).[51] On the same day, the government announced the coup by radio broadcast from Budapest, without any prior warning to the Soviets, and the Fund issued a press release in Washington. When no reprisals came, and Poland quickly followed suit (as recounted below), the authorities and the Fund moved quickly to complete the process and secure financial support.

From that point on, no complications or particular controversies arose in handling Hungary's application. Patrick de Fontenay (Senior Adviser in the European Department) led a team of Fund economists and lawyers to Budapest in late November to collect and analyze data, primarily to determine an appropriate quota. After sifting through data on economic activity that were measured partly on market and partly on barter terms, they concluded that "the relative economic position of Hungary would seem to fall between Finland and Romania."[52] That finding suggested that a quota of SDR 375 million ($435 million) would be reasonable, and the Executive Board readily accepted that recommendation in a brief meeting in early April 1982. Meanwhile, the Belgian authorities indicated a willingness to add Hungary to their constituency in the Fund (which then comprised Austria, Belgium, Luxembourg, and Turkey). Jacques de Groote, the Executive Director for Belgium, met with officials in Budapest in December 1981 to get that process under way. Once the Board of Governors completed its voting by mail, the deputy prime minister, Jozsef Marjai, went to Washington for the ceremonial signing of

---

[51]Minutes of EBM/81/136 (November 4, 1981), p. 30.

[52]"Hungary—Calculation of Quota," EB/CM/Hungary/82/1 (February 24, 1982), p. 43.

the Articles at the U.S. State Department. On May 6, Hungary became a member of the IMF.

In Transition, 1982–90

While these steps were being taken, Hungary's economy was deteriorating even more rapidly than before, and the Fund was just beginning to discover how precarious Hungary's external payments position was. In addition to the other problems that had been building up for three or four years, Hungary's access to international bank loans was virtually cut off as the international debt crisis began to spread. Bridge loans from the BIS provided some relief (see Chapter 8), but financial assistance from the Fund was becoming an urgent priority.

De Fontenay returned to Budapest in September 1982, this time to negotiate a stand-by arrangement. Despite the central planning system and the limited role of the private sector and market incentives, the adjustment program was based on the conventional Fund conditionality: restraints on domestic demand through fiscal tightening and monetary control, and strengthening of the external current account through exchange rate depreciation and relaxation of disincentives in the export sectors.[53] In December, the Executive Board approved a stand-by arrangement in support of that program, allowing for SDR 475 million ($520 million; 127 percent of quota) in drawings through the end of 1983. The Board also approved an immediate CFF drawing of SDR 72 million ($79 million; 19 percent of quota) to compensate for a drop in the prices of exported goods. Hungary successfully carried out its policies in 1983 and drew the full amount as planned.

A second stand-by arrangement was successfully completed in 1984, but economic policy in Hungary then began to deteriorate again. Once commercial banks resumed lending to Hungary, the authorities seem to have decided that they did not need the Fund as badly as before. Starting in 1985, they were unwilling to adopt the degree of financial restraint or flexibility in exchange rate policy that would have brought additional Fund support. They did get a third stand-by arrangement in 1988, but they failed to adhere to the agreed policy conditions, and the final drawing was not allowed.[54] By 1989, the economy was on the brink of collapse, just as it had been eight years earlier.

Notwithstanding these difficulties, Hungary was gradually liberalizing the economy and inching along toward holding its first democratic elections in more than 40 years. When a Fund staff team (led by Gerard Bélanger, Division Chief in the European Department) visited Budapest in September 1989 to conduct Article IV

---

[53]"Hungarian People's Republic—Request for Stand-by Arrangement," EBS/82/206 (November 10, 1982).

[54]The second arrangement, approved in January 1984, was for SDR 425 million ($440 million; 80 percent of quota) over 12 months. The third arrangement was approved in May 1988, for SDR 265 million ($365 million; 50 percent of quota), initially over 12 months but later extended by three months. SDR 50 million of that amount was unused. When the last drawing was made in February 1989, Hungary owed the Fund SDR 475 million ($625 million; 89 percent of quota).

consultations and begin discussions on a new stand-by arrangement, they were reasonably upbeat about the prospects. What they learned, however, led to a scandal that would serve as a painful reminder of what the country was trying to leave behind.

Throughout the postwar history of the Hungarian People's Republic, secrecy of economic data had been sacrosanct (or, as one senior official put it during an interview, an "illness"). Although Hungary traded and had extensive financial relations with western companies and banks, the government was not compelled on that basis to reveal the extent of its reserves or of its overall indebtedness to western or CMEA creditors, or even to its own parliament. As debts piled up in the late 1970s and the government sought to minimize the reported size of its burgeoning fiscal deficit, the extent of the underreporting of debt necessarily rose. By joining the IMF in 1982, the government undertook a commitment to disclose such information routinely in the course of consultations with the Fund. In practice, it found that commitment to be both inconvenient and increasingly difficult to meet.

Once the decision was taken in October 1989 to hold democratic elections, officials in the National Bank and the government began to worry that an end to official secrecy would expose the long-standing distortions in the data, that they would be held accountable for it, and that it would damage their electoral prospects. Shortly after Bélanger arrived in Budapest, the governor of the National Bank, Ferenc Bartha, invited him to a Saturday lunch and informed him that the government and the central bank had systematically and deliberately misreported economic data to the Fund from the beginning of its membership negotiations, right up to that time. On Monday morning, Bartha telephoned the Managing Director with the same message. The government, however, was prepared to come clean. He informed Camdessus that the government was going to announce to parliament imminently that data on the country's debts had been underreported since the mid-1970s. He invited the Fund to make a comprehensive reassessment of the country's statistics, and he asked that a new stand-by arrangement be negotiated on the basis of revised data.[55] Camdessus agreed, and Bélanger's team immediately went to work on that basis. Separately, the Fund sent a team of data specialists to try to reconstruct the actual numbers.

As the real data began to emerge, the staff realized that the stand-by arrangements of the 1980s had been based on fraudulent data and that the Fund's ability to assess policies and to determine appropriate conditionality had been seriously impaired. The falsification of data centered on an underreporting of domestic and external debts of the government and an overstatement of reserves and other official assets. Because the government had a long-standing practice of distorting those data publicly and to other creditors, it fell easily into doing so to the Fund as well. The Fund, however, required complete accounting of monetary statistics, and the authorities had to devise a wide variety of compensating adjustments in other accounts, including banking data and the balance of payments. If the data had

---

[55]Minutes of EBM/89/151 (November 20, 1989), pp. 36–37.

been reported correctly at the time, Hungary would not have been eligible to make several of the drawings that it had made under each of the stand-by arrangements of the 1980s.[56]

When the actual data turned out to be inconsistent with the previous stand-by agreements, the Fund required Hungary to repay disputed amounts that were still outstanding before entering into a new arrangement.[57] The authorities agreed, and once the matter was fully resolved, the Fund approved a fourth stand-by arrangement in March 1990. Eleven days later, multiparty elections rejected most of the remnants of the old Communist Party and placed a democratic coalition in charge of Hungary's final transition to an open economic system.

Poland

December 13, 1981

When Alan Whittome awoke at the Victoria Hotel in Warsaw that Sunday morning, he expected to meet with his staff mission team to go over plans for the next several days of meetings with Polish government officials. He and his colleagues then would meet an old friend, Zbigniew Karcz (Director of the Foreign Department in the Ministry of Finance), for an afternoon of sightseeing. After three decades of absence, several years of hesitation, and one month of preparation, the process of getting Poland back into the IMF was finally under way. The rest of the team had arrived on Thursday and had begun collecting data and other information. Whittome (Director of the European Department) had arrived on Saturday and was expecting to take the discussions to the highest levels of government. It was not destined to happen. When he looked out the window, the tanks and armored personnel carriers of the Polish army were rumbling down Krolewska Street and into Ogród Saski park. He could not yet know what was happening—the phones were dead, the state television station was off the air, and CNN was years away from being created—but he had a front-row seat at the latest disastrous setback to Poland's overtures to the West. General Wojciech Jaruzelski had declared martial law in a dramatic suppression of the surge toward democracy that had begun in August 1980 with the recognition of Solidarity as a trade union

---

[56]See "Hungary—Report on Noncomplying Purchases and Recommendation for Corrective Action," EBS/90/31 (February 21, 1990), Sup. 1 (March 6), and minutes of EBM/90/35 (March 14, 1990). Additional information on this episode is from background interviews.

[57]The Fund's Articles of Agreement and supporting Executive Board decisions impose obligations on member countries to provide information that the Fund needs to conduct surveillance, safeguard the use of its resources, and other purposes. In 1984, the Board adopted specific guidelines on the provision of information related to performance criteria and other conditions on the use of the Fund's general resources; "Misreporting and Noncomplying Purchases under Fund Arrangements—Guidelines on Corrective Action"; Decision No. 7842-(84/165), November 16, 1984; published in Selected Decisions. Hungary was not the first member to be out of compliance with that decision, but this case was by far the most extensive and widespread, and it was the first in which the Board declined to grant a waiver for the required early repayment of affected credits.

independent of the Communist Party. Whittome's mission ended before it began, and Poland would not rejoin the Fund for another 4½ years.[58]

Outside the Fund, 1950–80

After withdrawing in 1950 (see above, p. 964), Poland began exploring the possibility of rejoining the IMF as early as 1957, soon after the government of Władysław Gomułka began implementing economic reforms aimed at moving beyond the Stalinist era. At that time, the main obstacle was the opposition of the U.S. government. U.S. officials were sympathetic to Gomułka's tentative overtures, as evidenced by the decision of President Eisenhower to extend grants and credits to Poland for food imports. But when an official delegation raised the question of Fund membership with the U.S. State Department, they were rebuffed.[59] They did not give up, however, and on at least two occasions in 1957 and 1958, Polish officials met with the Managing Director, Per Jacobsson, to obtain information related to membership and to maintain contacts with the institution.[60]

Informal contacts continued occasionally through the 1960s, while Gomułka's regime gradually slipped into repression and eventually crumbled. After Edward Gierek replaced Gomułka at the end of 1970 and initiated new reforms and new openings to the West, Poland began making more serious inquiries at the Fund but still did not attempt to join. Relations with the United States were improving dramatically,[61] but Gierek faced strong opposition from the Soviet Union that he appears to have been unwilling to resist. Meanwhile, Gierek's attempt to link the Polish economy more closely to the West was turning out badly. A large-scale industrial development effort, financed largely by loans from commercial banks, was faltering while increases in international interest rates were making the loans more and more expensive to service. When massive strikes broke out in the summer of 1980 in opposition to long-overdue increases in meat prices and in support of the establishment of Solidarity as an independent trade-union and political force, Gierek could no longer hold onto either the economic or the political reins.[62]

---

[58]Getting home was a small drama in itself: small, at least, in relation to the political background. The airport was closed to commercial flights, and the roads and railways were tightly controlled by the military. The staff spent the next four bitterly cold days confined to their now-unheated hotel while Karcz worked to make diplomatic arrangements for a safe departure. Finally on Thursday, another old friend and dedicated advocate for Polish membership in the Fund, Professor Stanisław Raczkowski of the Warsaw School of Economics, was able to put them on a train (also unheated). After many stops and several inspections by soldiers, the staff team eventually reached Prague, where they were able to board westbound flights.

[59]Throughout this section, unattributed references to internal discussions are based on background interviews with Polish officials.

[60]See "Note for the Files" by Per Jacobsson (May 2, 1958); IMF CF (C/Poland/710). That note also suggests that U.S. Treasury Secretary Robert B. Anderson was more receptive and encouraging than his compatriots in the State Department.

[61]President Nixon went to Warsaw in 1972, and he received Gierek at the White House two years later. In 1977, President Carter visited Poland.

[62]For an overview on Poland's economic difficulties in the 1970s and 1980s, see James (1995), pp. 563–73.

Rejoining, 1981–86

After the riots, General Jaruzelski became the effective head of government and almost immediately intensified the pace of economic decentralization. To further that effort, a group of young economists led by Leszek Balcerowicz issued a highly publicized report advocating wide-ranging reforms within the existing political system.[63] Externally, talks began with official bilateral creditors in Europe on rescheduling debts, and efforts to rejoin the IMF turned serious. Meanwhile, throughout the first half of 1981, the government struggled to keep communication open with both official and private creditors and to avoid defaulting on external debt (see Chapter 8).

Polish officials—at least those in the vanguard of reform—viewed Fund membership as a crucial step for normalizing external relations, but they were receiving mostly negative signals from Soviet leaders on how such a step might be received in Moscow.[64] The U.S. authorities were encouraging them, as were Fund staff. After several months of hesitation, an opportunity suddenly appeared: Hungary was about to submit a formal application to the Fund. If Hungary faced no immediate reprisals from across its eastern border, then perhaps Poland could also move boldly. Hungary's announcement was made on November 4, 1981; two days later, Jaruzelski gave his cabinet ministers the go-ahead for Poland to follow suit. On November 10, Karcz arrived at the IMF and hand-delivered a letter from the minister of foreign affairs to the Managing Director, formally applying for membership for the Polish People's Republic.[65]

The declaration of martial law the following month did not completely halt the membership process. Poland's application remained active, but the Fund postponed plans to send a full membership mission, as it became increasingly clear that the United States and other NATO countries would strongly oppose any move to admit Poland.[66] Whittome wanted to push ahead, but the Managing Director was reluctant. Although admission to membership required only a simple majority of votes cast, and therefore no country held a veto, it was deemed unlikely that other Executive Directors would support an application by Poland as long as the U.S.

---

[63]Balcerowicz (1994) provides a summary and retrospective. Also see Blejer and Coricelli (1995), esp. pp. 33–35.

[64]James (1995, p. 566) cites an account by Jaruzelski indicating that Andrei Gromyko (foreign minister of the Soviet Union) had expressed opposition during a meeting in the Crimea in August 1981. Whittome, however, received secondhand reports that same month suggesting that Soviet officials generally were not opposed to Polish membership. See memorandum from Whittome to the Acting Managing Director (August 28, 1981); in IMF/RD Deputy Managing Director file "Poland, 1982" (Accession 85/99, Box 5, Section 229).

[65]The letter, dated November 6, 1981, is in IMF/CF (C/Poland/710 "Application for Membership").

[66]In January 1982, an emergency meeting of NATO foreign ministers in Brussels endorsed the imposition of sanctions against Poland, including the suspension of trade credits and the postponement of debt rescheduling negotiations. The communiqué made it clear that economic cooperation between Poland and the major western powers depended on an end to what it called the "systematic suppression" of human rights through Soviet intervention.

government objected.[67] Nonetheless, secret talks continued between the staff and the Polish authorities throughout 1982.

The darkness before dawn came in the first half of 1983, when the continuation of martial law, the banning of Solidarity and all trade unions, and the strong reaction of the U.S. government led to the suspension of contacts between the Fund and Poland. Jaruzelski made the first conciliatory gesture in July, by lifting the formal declaration of martial law. Paris Club creditors, including the United States, responded in November by reopening talks on rescheduling debts. The real breakthrough then came in July 1984, when Poland submitted to U.S. pressure and agreed to grant amnesty to Solidarity members and release all political prisoners from jail. The Reagan administration, after much internal debate,[68] finally announced in December that it was informing the Polish government "that an atmosphere has been created that the United States hopes will permit the reactivation of Poland's membership in the International Monetary Fund."

Despite these public assurances, the U.S. authorities were still ambivalent and ideologically divided, and the Managing Director remained reluctant to push strongly for an early resolution. Several staff visits were made to Warsaw in 1985, but Whittome's initial hope that the process could be completed in time for a final approval by the Fund's Governors during the Annual Meetings in Korea was dashed. De Larosière insisted that technical talks be thorough and not be hurried, and the full membership mission did not begin until mid-September, just barely ahead of the meetings in Seoul.[69]

Throughout this period, the United States was far from being alone in its lack of enthusiasm for Poland's membership application. When Polish officials began

---

[67]The Fund's rules are ambiguous regarding procedures for handling controversial membership applications. Applications are submitted to the Managing Director, who places them on the agenda of the Executive Board. The Board recommends quotas and other terms and forwards the application to the Board of Governors for a formal vote. As Gold (1974, pp. 19–24) explains, the Fund's rules include no explicit provision for interrupting that chain of events, but Rule D-1 "seems to authorize the Executive Directors to refuse to go on with the procedure of admitting an applicant, at least for the time being" (p. 21). Rule D-1 includes the following: "When a country applies for membership in the Fund, the application shall be placed promptly before the Executive Board, and a reasonable time shall be allowed for discussion and preliminary investigation by the Executive Board before a decision is reached to proceed with the formal investigation. . . . If the Executive Board decides not to proceed with its formal investigation of an application for membership, it shall report that decision to the Board of Governors with the reasons for the decision." In this case, no decision was taken, but the Board did not object to the Managing Director's strategy of dragging out the process of "preliminary investigation."

[68]U.S. Treasury Secretary Donald T. Regan recounted in his memoirs that he objected that summer when the President's National Security Advisor, Robert C. McFarlane, authorized the State Department to discuss Poland's application with the Managing Director. Regan noted with apparent pride that "Poland did not become a member of the IMF during my tenure" (Regan, 1988, p. 323).

[69]Memorandums from Whittome to the Managing Director (December 21, 1984, and April 2 and April 10, 1985); in IMF/RD Deputy Managing Director file "Poland, 1985" (Accession 90/104, Box 10, Section 415).

approaching western governments regarding the possibility of joining their constituencies on the Fund's Executive Board, they were rebuffed wherever they turned. No one, it seemed, wanted to join forces with the Communist government in Warsaw. Even the Belgian authorities—who had welcomed Hungary into their fold in 1981 and who were Poland's first choice in this regard—and the Dutch, who had represented Romania since 1972, resisted any further tipping of the balance in their seats.[70] It gradually became evident that even if Poland did join soon, it would probably join Cambodia, Egypt, and South Africa in the ranks of members that were not welcome at that time to participate in the election of Executive Directors (see Chapter 20).

At the technical level, the application began to work its way smoothly through the bureaucratic process. The size of Poland's quota became a contentious issue when it turned out that the staff's standard technical calculation yielded an unusually wide range of plausible values—from SDR 630 million to 780 million—owing both to uncertainties about data quality and interdepartmental disputes on how to apply the data. A quota near the high end of the range would have placed Poland near Austria in the Fund hierarchy and well above Hungary, Romania, and Yugoslavia (see Appendix II to Chapter 17). Concerns over the political implications of relative status and over the expectation that Poland would soon request to draw on Fund resources made management reluctant to endorse a figure that high. European Department staff felt that Poland deserved a quota around 750 million, but the final staff paper for consideration by the Executive Board recommended a quota of about 700 million. The membership committee of Executive Directors (chaired by Hans Lundstrom of Sweden) further reduced the recommendation to SDR 680 million ($780 million), which the authorities reluctantly accepted in March 1986.[71]

With that last sensitive issue settled, the Executive Board and then the Board of Governors proceeded quickly to readmit Poland as a member of the Fund. No votes were recorded against the resolution, though the United States—reluctant to the last—abstained. On June 12, 1986, a delegation headed by the minister of finance, Stanisław Niekarcz, signed the Articles of Agreement at the U.S. State

---

[70]Some Fund officials expressed concerns internally that Poland, Hungary, and Romania might band together to form a constituency. That move could have upset the structure of the Board by preventing the Francophone African countries (the existing constituency with the smallest voting power) from garnering enough votes to elect an Executive Director. The Polish authorities, however, sought to reach out to the West, and they never seriously contemplated forming a Socialist constituency. See memorandum from Whittome to the Managing Director (December 12, 1985); in IMF/RD Deputy Managing Director file "Poland, 1985" (Accession 90/104, Box 10, Section 415). In the event, Poland's quota was small enough that the three countries would have fallen just shy of the total required to gain a seat on the Board.

[71]See memorandums from Walter O. Habermeier (Treasurer) and Whittome (December 5, 1985), with responsive notations by de Larosière, in IMF/RD Deputy Managing Director file "Poland, 1985" (Accession 90/104, Box 10, Section 415); EB/CM/Poland/85/1 (December 20, 1985); letter from Lundstrom to Karcz (February 13, 1986), in IMF/RD Deputy Managing Director file "Poland, 1986" (Accession 91/260, Box 5, Section 339); and letter from Karcz to Lundstrom (March 10, 1986), in IMF/CF (C/Poland/710 "Application for Membership").

Department and brought to a successful close one of the longest membership processes in Fund history.[72]

The Last Years of Communism, 1986–89

Joining the Fund brought Poland immediately closer to the West, but another three years would pass before the country was able to fully rejoin the world economy. As expected, Poland did not participate in the 1986 election of Executive Directors. For the next two years, an official from the Polish embassy in Washington was assigned an office at the Fund to serve as a liaison with the government, and an official from the finance ministry represented Poland at the Executive Board meeting concluding the Article IV consultations. That awkward arrangement lasted until 1988, when Italy agreed to accept Poland into its constituency (along with Greece, Malta, and Portugal).[73]

A more concrete result of the limited international acceptance of Poland was that the Fund was not yet willing to provide financial assistance. The U.S. government let it be understood that it would not support a request for a stand-by arrangement, and the Fund's management discouraged the Polish authorities from pursuing the matter. Meanwhile, financial discipline continued to worsen in Poland, and by the end of 1988 the economy was approaching a state of total collapse. With output declining and price inflation escalating, the last Communist-dominated government decided to open the political process to the growing ranks of its opponents. In April 1989, Prime Minister Mieczysław Rakowski agreed to hold open elections. When those elections were won by Solidarity and other non-Communist parties, a newly resurgent Poland wasted no time in moving toward massive reforms.

The incoming prime minister for the newly elected government, Tadeusz Mazowiecki, wrote to Camdessus on September 9, even before his appointment had been confirmed by parliament, to request a stand-by arrangement.[74] Mazowiecki also persuaded Leszek Balcerowicz—the author of the 1980 reform plan mentioned above—to cancel plans to spend the academic year as a visiting professor in England and to become his deputy prime minister and minister of finance. Balcerowicz had a wide range of western academic contacts, including

---

[72]This case involved the longest period in which an application remained active (1981–86). Three countries that participated in the Bretton Woods conference—Liberia, Haiti, and New Zealand—declined to ratify the Articles, did not become original members, and later joined the Fund on the basis of new applications. Liberia applied in 1948, but in 1950 it declined to accept the Fund's offer of membership. A subsequent application was submitted in 1961, and Liberia became a member in 1962; see Gold (1974), p. 32. Similarly, Haiti applied in 1949, but the government decided in 1950 not to join. Haiti reapplied in 1952 and joined the following year. New Zealand applied in April 1961 and joined four months later.

[73]Only one Article IV consultation was held during 1986–89, concluded in October 1986. The second consultation was concluded in 1990, in conjunction with Poland's request for a stand-by arrangement. In 1992, Poland moved to the newly formed constituency headed by Switzerland.

[74]Letter, in IMF/CF (C/Poland/1760 "Stand-by Arrangements, January 1989–January 1990").

Harvard Professor Jeffrey Sachs, who now would become a leading advisor on economic reform.

The Fund also wasted no time in responding. Massimo Russo, who had succeeded Whittome as Director of the European Department, went to Warsaw a few days after Mazowiecki's letter arrived, to begin discussions on how the Fund might help. The following week Camdessus met with Balcerowicz and other officials during the Annual Meetings in Washington. The authorities, especially Balcerowicz, were convinced that a rapid move toward market equilibrium was essential to overcome the endemic rigidities in the economy and to shorten the inevitably painful transition phase. To general skepticism, Balcerowicz publicly set January 1, 1990, as his deadline for getting a comprehensive stabilization and reform program in place. Russo and Peter C. Hole (Assistant Director in the European Department) then returned to Warsaw and negotiated a stand-by arrangement based largely on Balcerowicz's shock treatment for the economy. That program would soon become known famously as the "big bang": rapid adjustment of prices to market-clearing levels, immediate reduction or termination of regulations restricting private sector economic activity, a strong incomes policy aimed at rolling back the excessive wage awards of the preceding two years, and early stabilization of monetary and fiscal policies. Privatization of state enterprises and development of private financial markets were also planned, but those actions were scheduled to be phased in more gradually (see Balcerowicz, 1994, and Sachs, 1993).

In one of the most remarkable and dramatic economic turnarounds of the whole transformation of central and eastern Europe, Balcerowicz and his team succeeded in getting most of these major reforms approved by the end-year deadline. The currency, the zloty, was made convertible at a dramatically high unified rate of 9,500 a dollar (approximately the level recommended by Fund staff).[75] Price controls and the resultant shortages of goods were virtually eliminated, the budget deficit was sharply reduced by cutting or eliminating subsidies on consumer and other goods, monetary discipline was established, and trade barriers were reduced. In three months, the rigidities of the past 40 years, the ambivalent international response of the past three years, and the skepticism of September were all swept aside. On February 5, 1990, the Fund's Executive Directors, in a strong tribute inspired by what was clearly an historic moment, "unanimously expressed their admiration of the Polish authorities for their courage, imagination, and determination in introducing an unprecedented program of radical transformation of the economy," and approved a stand-by arrangement for SDR 545 million ($720 million; 80 percent of quota).[76] Whatever hurdles remained to be cleared, Poland was on a steady course toward market liberalization.

---

[75]The value of the currency was to be supported by a $1 billion stabilization fund, financed by a group of industrial countries and administered through those countries' Executive Directors at the IMF. The fund was established but was never drawn upon.

[76]Minutes of EBM/90/15 (February 5, 1990), p. 13.

References

Balcerowicz, Leszek, 1994, "Poland," in *The Political Economy of Policy Reform*, ed. by John Williamson (Washington: Institute for International Economics), pp. 153–77.

Bernstein, Edward M., 1993, "The Soviet Union and Bretton Woods," in *A Retrospective on the Bretton Woods System: Lessons for International Monetary Reform*, ed. by Michael D. Bordo and Barry Eichengreen (Chicago, Illinois: University of Chicago Press), pp. 195–98.

Blejer, Mario I, and Fabrizio Coricelli, 1995, *The Making of Economic Reform in Eastern Europe: Conversations with Leading Reformers in Poland, Hungary, and the Czech Republic* (Aldershot, England: Edward Elgar).

Boote, Anthony R. and Janos Somogyi, 1991, *Economic Reform in Hungary since 1968*, IMF Occasional Paper No. 83 (Washington: International Monetary Fund).

Boughton, James, 2001, "The Case Against Harry Dexter White: Still Not Proven," *History of Political Economy*, Vol. 33 (summer), pp. 221–41.

de Vries, Margaret Garritsen, 1976, *The International Monetary Fund, 1966–1971: The System Under Stress*, Vol. 1: *Narrative*; Vol. 2: *Documents* (Washington: International Monetary Fund).

———, 1985, *The International Monetary Fund, 1972–1978: Cooperation on Trial*, Vols. 1 and 2: *Narrative and Analysis*; Vol. 3: *Documents* (Washington: International Monetary Fund).

Feeney, William R., 1989, "Chinese Policy Toward Multilateral Economic Institutions," in *China and the World: New Directions in Chinese Foreign Relations*, ed. by Samuel S. Kim (Boulder, Colorado: Westview Press), pp. 237–63.

Gold, Joseph, 1974, *Membership and Nonmembership in the International Monetary Fund: A Study in International Law and Organization* (Washington: International Monetary Fund).

Hook, A.W., ed. 1983, *The Fund and China in the International Monetary System: Papers Presented at a Colloquium Held in Beijing, China, October 20–28, 1982* (Washington: International Monetary Fund).

Horsefield, J. Keith, ed., 1969, *The International Monetary Fund, 1945–1965: Twenty Years of International Monetary Cooperation*, Vol. 1: *Chronicle*, by J. Keith Horsefield; Vol. 2: *Analysis*, by Margaret G. de Vries and J. Keith Horsefield with the collaboration of Joseph Gold, Mary H. Gumbart, Gertrud Lovasy, and Emil G. Spitzer; Vol. 3: *Documents* (Washington: International Monetary Fund).

Hsiung, James C., and Samuel S. Kim, eds., 1980, *China in the Global Community* (New York: Praeger).

Jacobson, Harold Karan, and Michel Oksenberg, 1990, *China's Participation in the IMF, the World Bank, and GATT: Toward a Global Economic Order* (Ann Arbor, Michigan: University of Michigan Press).

James, Harold, 1995, *International Monetary Cooperation since Bretton Woods* (Oxford: Oxford University Press).

———, and Marzenna James, 1994, "The Origins of the Cold War: Some New Documents," *Historical Journal*, Vol. 37, No. 3, pp. 615–22.

Kapur, Devesh, John P. Lewis, and Richard Webb, 1997, *The World Bank: Its First Half Century*, Vol. 1: *History* (Washington: Brookings Institution).

Mikesell, Raymond F., 1951, "Negotiating at Bretton Woods, 1944," in *Negotiating with the Russians*, ed. by Raymond Dennett and Joseph E. Johnson (Boston, Massachusetts: World Peace Foundation).

———, 1994, *The Bretton Woods Debates: A Memoir*, Essays in International Finance, No. 192 (Princeton, New Jersey: International Finance Section, Department of Economics, Princeton University).

Moggridge, Donald, ed., 1980, *The Collected Writings of John Maynard Keynes*, Vol. 26: *Activities 1941–1946; Shaping the Post-War World: Bretton Woods and Reparations* (London: Macmillan).

Regan, Donald T., 1988, *For the Record: From Wall Street to Washington* (San Diego, California: Harcourt Brace Jovanovich).

Sachs, Jeffrey, 1993, *Poland's Jump to the Market Economy* (Cambridge, Massachusetts: MIT Press).

Solomon, Robert. 1982, *The International Monetary System, 1945–1981* (New York: Harper and Row).

Spence, Jonathon D., 1990, *The Search for Modern China* (New York: W.W. Norton).

Young, Arthur N., 1965, *China's Wartime Finance and Inflation, 1937–1945* (Cambridge, Massachusetts: Harvard University Press).

20

Managing the Fund in a Changing World

Previous chapters have examined issues related to the role of the IMF in the world economy. How did the Fund's role evolve in dealing with matters as diverse as the erratic value of the U.S. dollar, the debt crisis in Latin America, and the worsening spiral of poverty in Africa? How did it obtain and manage its resources and deal with a growing membership? This final chapter turns inward for a closer look at the institution itself. As the Fund took on a widening circle of responsibilities, its relations with other multilateral organizations inevitably became more complex. To a much greater extent than before, the Fund saw a need to explain itself and its functions regularly and actively. More subtly, its organizational structure, management, and staff evolved and modernized to cope with a rapidly changing world economy.

Collaboration

In an ideal world, each international organization would serve a unique purpose and would perfectly coordinate its work with others as appropriate. In practice, purposes and activities overlap in ways that change in response to events and require ad hoc rather than resolute coordination. The IMF's relations with other organizations did not change fundamentally during the 1980s, but they did evolve, mainly in response to the debt crisis and the need for structural reforms in many borrowing countries.[1]

World Bank

The most important linkage for the Fund is its relationship with the World Bank. The two have always been known as the "Bretton Woods twins"[2] and more

---

[1]This section gives a selective review of the Fund's relations with other institutions, focusing on the main players. Fund staff and management also had recurring interactions with many other organizations, including notably the regional development banks.

[2]The term originated in a speech by John Maynard Keynes to the inaugural meeting of the Boards of Governors, at Savannah, Georgia, in March 1946: "The gestation has been long; the lusty twins are seriously overdue . . . (and I shall always hold to the view that the christening has been badly done and that the names of the twins should have been reversed)." Quoted in Harrod (1951), p. 631.

mundanely as "sister organizations." The sibling analogy is apt, but it only hints at the nature of the relationship. As the twins have matured, they have continued to live next door (facing each other across 19th Street in Washington, D.C.) and have successfully pursued closely related careers. One is a tidy disciplinarian (both toward itself and others), physically small, nearly devoid of humor, and more interested in gaining respect than in being loved. The other, of course, is a culture apart.[3] They nonetheless manage to accommodate each other's needs most of the time, and their occasional spats are noteworthy enough to make news. During the 1980s, the increasing complexity of the tasks undertaken by both the Fund and the Bank broadened the overlap in their functions and heightened the need for careful coordination in dealing with member countries.

The Fund and the Bank have tried over the years to reduce organizational duplication by forming partnerships on certain administrative operations. Some have succeeded, including their joint library and medical service and joint secretariat for conducting the Annual Meetings of the two Boards of Governors, all of which have been functioning since the 1940s.[4] From 1972 to 1999, the two institutions adopted parallel policies on staff compensation and benefits. Although the two Executive Boards operate independently, a few Executive Directors have always served on both.[5] Other attempts at partnership have eventually failed because the specific needs of the staffs have not meshed, including a joint computer services operation that was started in 1968 and abandoned in 1986 when the operational role of computers (especially desktops) became much more pervasive. Still other ideas have been abandoned after preliminary discussions. For example, consideration was given in the 1980s to producing a single set of Bank-Fund macroeconomic forecasts, and proposals were made to merge the training operations (the IMF Institute and the Bank's Economic Development Institute). In these and other cases, the staff convinced both managements that competition and a continued focus by each organization on its own sphere of expertise would produce better products.

More ambitious proposals to merge the two institutions were never seriously pursued.[6] That reluctance derived only partly from respect for the distinct natures

---

[3]For a good overview on the cultural differences, see Polak (1997). Also see Kapur, Lewis, and Webb (1997), which likens the Fund to the Catholic church and the Bank to "a contentious collection of Protestant sects" (p. 622). Some Fund staff who read drafts of this chapter protested that it underplays the often close and effective collaboration between Fund and Bank staff working on individual countries; others felt that any suggestion of effective collaboration was "Panglossian."

[4]The library and health room were established in 1947. In 1981, the health service was upgraded to a Medical Department, situated within the World Bank but supported by both institutions. From 1946 to 1962, the two Secretaries put together an ad hoc joint staff operation each year to prepare for and service the Annual Meetings. A full-time joint conferences office was established in 1963.

[5]France and the United Kingdom each appointed a single Executive Director throughout the 1980s, and Jacques de Groote (Belgium) was elected to serve on both Boards (1973–94).

[6]See Bergsten (1994), especially the discussion of the value of "functional specificity" on p. 347; the paper by Moisés Naím in Boughton and Lateef (1995), pp. 85–90; and Polak (1994a), p. 155. Krueger (1998) provides a good overview of the distinct and overlapping functions of the two institutions.

of the Bank and the Fund. The Bank was far larger than the Fund (3,400 professional staff members in 1989, compared with 1,100 at the Fund) and had a much broader range of activities and responsibilities. In practice, a merger would therefore have folded the Fund into the Bank, a prospect not viewed positively by most governments, and would most likely have added to rather than alleviated the Bank's already considerable bureaucratic burdens.

When the Fund and the Bank were conceived, in the course of discussions between officials of the United States and Great Britain during the Second World War, their purposes were clearly delineated: financial stabilization for the one and postwar reconstruction and economic development for the other. Their separate specific functions were less clearly defined, and once they began operations in the late 1940s, they found that they would at least occasionally have to coordinate their efforts to help the same countries cope with different manifestations of the same problems. Once they became established as major and permanent participants in the international financial system, formal agreements on responsibilities and procedures for coordination became essential.

The first and most basic agreement was made in 1966, and all subsequent agreements built upon it. At the beginning of that year, the Managing Director and the President of the World Bank issued identical statements to their staffs and Executive Boards outlining procedures for collaboration. Those statements led to several months of discussions in the two Executive Boards and between the two managements and staffs on refinements to the agreements. Finally, a joint document was issued in December, which formally introduced the idea of "primary responsibilities" for each institution in situations where functions overlapped:

> As between the two institutions, the Bank is recognized as having primary responsibility for the composition and appropriateness of development programs and project evaluation, including development priorities. . . . [T]he Fund is recognized as having primary responsibility for exchange rates and restrictive systems, for adjustment of temporary balance of payments disequilibria and for evaluating and assisting members to work out stabilization programs as a sound basis for economic advance. . . . [T]he range of matters which are of interest to both institutions . . . includes . . . the structure and functioning of financial institutions, the adequacy of capital markets, the actual and potential capacity of a member country to generate domestic savings, the financial implications of economic development programs both for the internal financial position of a country and for its external situation, foreign debt problems, and so on.[7]

---

[7]"Fund-Bank Collaboration," memorandum to Members of the Executive Board from the Secretary and to Department Heads from the Managing Director (December 13, 1966); in IMF/CF (B 600 "Bank/Fund Collaboration on Missions and Meetings, 1966"). The initial documents by the heads of the two institutions are in the same file.

These principles were reaffirmed in 1970 and on several occasions in the 1980s, and the procedures for collaboration and avoidance of inconsistent advice were gradually made more specific.[8]

Despite this broad institutional agreement, the staffs of the Fund and the Bank had very different conceptions of their respective roles throughout the 1970s. These differences involved not just where to draw the line, but in what direction it should be drawn. For the Bank, the crucial dimension was stabilization versus development, short- versus long-run. The Fund resisted being squeezed into that pigeon hole and argued that its conditionality had to aim at promoting longer-term balance and providing a proper basis for economic development. For the Fund, the proper demarcation was between macro- and microeconomics, between aggregate performance and the structure of the economy. The Bank resisted being squeezed out of discussions related to the longer-term dimensions of borrowers' macroeconomic policies.[9]

The main line of battle centered on the evaluation of a country's balance of payments prospects over the medium term (i.e., beyond a one- to two-year horizon). Suppose that a country's macroeconomic and exchange rate policies are fundamentally inconsistent with the achievement of equilibrium in the balance of payments over a period of several years. Its problem is not so much a temporary, but more nearly a permanent, external disequilibrium. The Fund and the Bank both

---

[8]See "Fund/Bank Collaboration," EBD/70/38 (February 19, 1970); "Progress Report on Fund Collaboration with the Bank in Assisting Member Countries," SM/81/62 (March 19, 1981) and minutes of EBM/81/62 (April 20, 1981); and "Fund-Bank Collaboration—A Further Progress Report," SM/84/210 (August 27, 1984) and minutes of EBM/84/171 (November 28, 1984). The 1966 agreement is attached to the 1970 document as an appendix. For the legal history of Fund-Bank relations, see Gold (1982). As a matter of principle, the Fund and the Bank affirmed on several occasions that they should not impose cross-conditionality, defined as a requirement that a borrower meet the conditions of one institution in order to qualify for a loan or credit from the other. In practice, the overlapping activities and common purposes of the two institutions occasionally made compromises necessary. See Chapter 14, on the complexities of avoiding cross-conditionality in cases where the Fund and the Bank were both making structural adjustment loans; Chapter 15, on the implications of asking the Bank to certify the quality of a country's investment plans as a condition for approving extended arrangements; and Chapter 16, on the difficulties of developing a coordinated strategy vis-à-vis countries in arrears without resorting to cross-conditionality.

[9]For example, in December 1973, the Bank's Chief Economist, Hollis B. Chenery, submitted a draft memorandum for comments by the Fund staff, which referred to the "Fund's primary interest in questions of short-term balances" and asserted that "it is the difference between short and medium-term approaches, between support for stabilization and development, which provides the rationale for distinct, though overlapping, programs of economic work." In response, Ernest Sturc (Director of the Fund's Exchange and Trade Relations Department, or ETR) objected to this description and noted that "the Fund staff is necessarily concerned with the macro-economic targets and financial aspects of a country's medium-term strategy." The disputed language was deleted from the final memorandum. See memorandum from Sturc to Mahbub ul Haq, Director of the Policy Planning and Program Review Department of the World Bank (December 18, 1973) and attachment; and memorandum from Sturc to the Managing Director (February 28, 1974) and attachment; in IMF/CF (B 600 "Bank/Fund Collaboration on Missions and Meetings, 1972–1979").

felt that resolution of that type of problem was their primary responsibility: the Fund, because the cause was inappropriate macroeconomic policies; the Bank, because it was a longer-term problem of structural imbalance.

When the Bank began making "Structural Adjustment Loans" (SALs) for medium-term balance of payments financing in 1980, it had to reconcile that activity with the Fund's "primary responsibility" for the balance of payments. The Managing Director, Jacques de Larosière, was careful to insist that the Fund would continue to take the lead in advising countries on medium-term balance of payments issues. In an opening statement at a meeting of the Fund's Executive Board on this matter, he noted the importance both of "close collaboration . . . to ensure coordinated action" and of retaining "the distinct character and functions of each institution. For example," he continued, "it is my understanding that if the World Bank were to consider that a country's program of structural adjustment should include a medium-term target for the current account of the balance of payments, the Bank would look to the Fund to develop such a target in close consultation with the national authorities."[10] The Bank did not challenge that understanding, and the management of both institutions issued instructions to the staff on specific procedures for collaborating in countries where both were concerned with medium-term policies. As illustrated most dramatically by the Argentine debacle of 1988 (see Chapter 11 and below), the willingness of staff in the field to defer to their siblings in assessing countries' balance of payments or development requirements was not uniformly high. Nonetheless, most disputes were resolved before they disrupted the provision of assistance to countries.[11]

In addition to problems in defining the boundaries of each institution's territory, important differences in view occasionally arose regarding policy recommendations. As an internal Bank review paper noted in 1986, a common cause of those differences was that the Fund and the Bank focused on different constraints on policymaking.[12] Since the Bank was concerned primarily with determining the requirements for achieving a target growth rate in a country, its staff typically set out to derive the necessary levels of imports, expenditure, and external financial assistance to get the desired result. Since the Fund was concerned primarily with determining the requirements for achieving financial viability and stability for a given level of domestic saving and external assistance, its staff typically set out to derive the corresponding restrictions on imports and other expenditures and treated the growth of output as endogenous. When the resources available to a country were insufficient to produce adequate economic growth, the two ap-

---

[10]Minutes of EBM/80/83 (May 28, 1980), p. 24.

[11]See "Progress Report on Fund Collaboration with the Bank in Assisting Member Countries," SM/81/62 (March 19, 1981), p. 10; "Fund-Bank Collaboration—A Further Progress Report" SM/84/210 (August 27, 1984), pp. 5–8; "World Bank Staff Paper Entitled 'Progress Report on Bank-Fund Collaboration'," EBD/86/163 (June 4, 1986), pp. 4–5; and "Progress Report on Bank-Fund Collaboration," EBS/90/131 (July 12, 1990), pp. 2–3.

[12]Attachment to "World Bank Staff Paper Entitled 'Progress Report on Bank-Fund Collaboration'," EBD/86/163 (June 4, 1986), p. 4.

proaches were bound to generate substantially different outcomes in which the Bank view was relatively optimistic and expansionist. In such cases, each team was likely to view the other's work as irrelevant for the problem it was trying to solve.[13]

To minimize inconsistencies in policy advice, the institutions sought to work more closely together in the 1980s. Proposals to send joint staff missions to countries were usually regarded as unworkable, but more modest tactics—including a Fund staff member on Bank missions, and conversely, and scheduling concurrent missions to countries—were applied with increasing frequency.[14] Staff attendance at relevant meetings of the sister institution's Executive Board also became a more regular practice. Beginning in 1985, the Managing Director and the Bank President began meeting over lunch on a regular monthly schedule, together with a few senior staff, in part to head off possible conflicts in dealing with member countries or on policy issues. In addition, on several occasions the Fund and the Bank held joint seminars and symposia on topics of common interest.[15]

Two other events of the 1980s induced more specific Fund-Bank collaboration: the institutions' foray into structural adjustment lending and the international debt crisis.

The creation of the Structural Adjustment Facility (SAF) in 1986 was an obvious intrusion by the Fund onto the Bank's traditional turf, in that it required borrowers to negotiate medium-term structural reform programs with the Fund. Few objected to the move, on either side of 19th Street, because it was clearly a productive use of the money that the Fund had on hand from the reflows of the old Trust Fund, and it would supplement the resources of the Bank's International Development Association (IDA) for the benefit of low-income countries (Chapter 14). Moreover, the SAF was similar in key respects to the Extended Fund Facility (EFF), through which the Fund had already been making long-term loans for structural adjustment for a decade. The SAF did, however, call for more formal coordination than in the past.

---

[13]Discrepancies also arose naturally in specific cases because of technical or philosophical differences between economic models used in the two institutions, but those differences generally were neither large nor systematic. Informal staff discussions on models and results usually sufficed to narrow the gaps.

[14]In the first five years covered by this History (1979–83), Fund staff participated in 56 World Bank missions; in the last five years (1985–89), 82 missions (up 46 percent). Bank staff participated in 39 Fund missions in the first five years and 102 in the last five (up 162 percent). There were 21 joint missions in the first five years, and 11 in the last five (down 48 percent). These data are compiled from tables in "Fund-Bank Collaboration—A Further Progress Report," SM/84/210 (August 27, 1984); "Fund-Bank Collaboration—Developments in 1985," SM/86/40 (February 25, 1986); and "Progress Report on Bank-Fund Collaboration," EBS/90/131 (July 12, 1990). These figures exclude cases where Policy Framework Papers were involved (see below), since those cases required joint discussions with the authorities.

[15]For examples, see Chapter 13, p. 611, on the 1987 conference on growth-oriented adjustment programs; and Chapter 14, p. 699, on a series of seminars in which Fund and Bank staff exchanged views on ways to limit the adverse effects of adjustment programs on low-income groups.

The principal innovation, as discussed in Chapter 14, was the "Policy Framework Paper" (PFP): a document to be negotiated by the borrowing country with the staffs of both the Fund and the Bank and approved by the Executive Directors of both institutions. The Bank's Executive Board (sitting as a Committee of the Whole) would discuss each PFP first and would naturally focus primarily on the developmental and structural aspects of the paper. The Fund's Board would have the Bank's assessment at hand along with the PFP for its own discussion. It would normally defer to the Bank's judgment on those issues, but it would retain its independence to act as it saw fit. Although most PFPs in the 1980s turned out to be too broadly drafted to have much operational significance, the process did serve to enable the Fund to get the SAF and its "enhanced" sequel (the ESAF) running without provoking internecine warfare or dragging the Fund staff too deeply into unfamiliar waters.

A few countries, notably the United States, argued for more institutional coordination in dealing with PFPs. During the June 1987 SAF review by the Executive Board, the U.S. Director, Charles H. Dallara, argued that the Bank should link its lending decisions explicitly to the PFP and that the Fund and the Bank should "move in tandem" in approving PFPs.[16] At the Annual Meetings in Washington in October 1987, the U.S. Treasury Secretary, James A. Baker III, made a direct appeal for strengthening coordination along these lines. "I . . . call on the Bank and the Fund to undertake joint missions, and to form a joint committee of the two Executive Boards, to review [PFPs]. IDA loans should also be integrated into policy frameworks as closely as loans from the SAF" (IMF, *Summary Proceedings*, 1987, p. 111). Each of those proposals was considered by the Executive Boards, but all were ultimately rejected as impractical, as was a suggestion that joint documents similar to PFPs could be developed for some middle-income as well as low-income countries.

Collaboration in assisting middle-income developing countries did intensify in the second half of the decade. For two years after the debt crisis hit in 1982, the Fund concentrated on negotiating adjustment programs that would justify persuading commercial bank creditors to continue to lend to the affected countries. By 1985, however, the Fund's ability to provide additional credits to several of the most heavily indebted countries was extremely limited. Multiyear rescheduling agreements by other creditors, combined with enhanced surveillance by the Fund, gave some additional life to the strategy, but more systematic relief required both new money and a more structural approach to economic reform. That realization led to the Baker Plan, which called for a coordinated three-pronged effort involving the Fund, the World Bank, and commercial banks (see Chapters 8–10).

Even before the Baker Plan, commercial bank creditors were beginning to insist on World Bank financing as a condition for their continued participation in reschedulings and concerted lending. During 1985 alone, banks required at least six heavily indebted countries—Chile, Colombia, Costa Rica, Côte d'Ivoire,

---

[16]Minutes of EBM/87/91 (June 18, 1987), pp. 8–11.

Panama, and Uruguay—to conclude negotiations with the World Bank as a precondition for reschedulings or new lending (Watson and others, 1986, p. 58). When the Baker Plan was announced that October, the Fund and the Bank built on this ongoing relationship and developed—or at least sketched out—a coordinated strategy for implementing it. Essentially, that strategy involved a commitment by the Bank to make a more concerted effort to direct resources toward the most heavily indebted middle-income countries (the "Baker 15") and a commitment by the Fund to collaborate more closely and systematically with the Bank in helping those countries develop medium-term, growth-oriented adjustment programs (see Chapter 10).

After the Baker Plan failed and was replaced by the Brady Plan in 1989, the two institutions again responded by developing new procedures for collaboration. The central element on that occasion was to ensure that the Fund and the Bank reached coordinated decisions on whether a country qualified for a debt reduction program and that each provided commensurate support for approved programs. A priori, it was not easy to agree on how that coordination would be achieved. The Bank issued a rather vague statement of support for a "concerted effort" in which "the resources from the two institutions would be in aggregate of broadly comparable size and be provided under mutually consistent modalities. However, there was general agreement [among the Bank's Executive Directors] that each institution's contribution would be determined by its own judgments arrived at through established decision-making processes." The Fund's conclusion was similarly equivocal, but the two managements clearly signaled their intention to work together as well as possible.[17]

These various procedures that were initiated in response to the debt crisis did not induce the two institutions to begin working hand in hand on a commonly agreed strategy. Rather, they helped the staffs to keep from tripping over each other's feet when they were both responding to the same fire alarms. When collaboration was effective, as it was in most cases, the Fund continued to defer to the Bank's views on development strategies, the Bank continued to defer to the Fund on macroeconomic policies, and the two kept each other fully informed. The most spectacular exception, as recounted in Chapter 11, occurred in 1988, when the Bank announced at the start of the Annual Meetings in Berlin that it had agreed to lend to Argentina, at a time when Argentina was still negotiating program terms with the Fund. This coup raised the specter of a damaging kind of competition that the Managing Director, Michel Camdessus, had likened to "two shops," where a country could borrow from whichever institution offered easier conditionality.[18]

The substance of the disagreement over policy conditions for lending to Argentina was a prototypical example of the fundamentally different institutional ap-

---

[17]"World Bank Discussion on Operational Guidelines and Procedures for Use of IBRD Resources to Support Debt and Debt Service Reduction," EBD/89/163 (June 2, 1989), p. 2, and minutes of EBM/89/61 (May 23, 1989), p. 29.

[18]Minutes of EBM/88/70 (May 4, 1988), p. 21.

proaches described above, but in this case it was exacerbated by uncharacteristic rashness by Bank staff and coordination failure at the level of management.[19] Even before the dust settled, the Chairman of the Interim Committee, H. Onno Ruding, insisted to Camdessus and to the Bank President, Barber Conable, that they agree on a strategy to avoid a recurrence and submit it to the Committee at its next meeting.

Several months of often acrimonious negotiations ensued, led by management and the most senior staff. Reflecting a long-simmering and still-active resentment at the Bank, Stanley Fischer (Chief Economist at the Bank) seized the opportunity to object to the Fund's assertion of primacy on medium-term macroeconomic policies. The Fund responded by digging in its heels.[20] Finally, an apparent breakthrough was achieved, when Camdessus and Conable agreed on some of the main issues after a long tête-à-tête on a flight back from Tokyo in February 1989, where they had been attending the funeral of Emperor Hirohito.[21] On the basis of that apparent agreement, the Fund staff put the finishing touches on a new statement of principles and procedures for collaboration, which was circulated to the Fund's Executive Directors on March 9.[22]

No sooner was this document circulated than Conable renounced it. The problem was that in trying to forge a compromise, the staff negotiators had introduced a logical contradiction. After listing several specific "primary responsibilities" for each institution, the paper stated: "Primary responsibility . . . does not mean that one organization has a veto power over the other." That seemed to be a pretty open door until one got to the next page: "In the event differences of view persisted even after a thorough common examination of them, the institution which does not have the primary responsibility would need to yield to the judgment of the other institution." After the document was issued, Conable informed Camdessus that he could not accept this latter wording, but Camdessus refused to delete it.

Following three more weeks of intense negotiations, Camdessus and Conable issued a revised statement for consideration by the two sets of Executive Directors (reproduced in the Appendix to this chapter). In this final "Concordat," as it came to be known, the "veto" language was deleted and the "yield" language was soft-

---

[19]The Bank's plan to lend to Argentina was on the agenda for the monthly luncheon between Camdessus and Conable in September, but the staff briefing note did not raise any alarm. Memorandum from L.A. Whittome to the Managing Director (September 2, 1988); in IMF/RD Deputy Managing Director file "Fund/Bank Luncheon, Vol. I" (Accession 91/455, Box 2, Section 489).

[20]See memorandum of February 1, 1989, from L. Alan Whittome and Peter M. Keller to the Managing Director; in IMF/CF (B 600 "Bank/Fund Collaboration on Missions and Meetings, 1989–1994").

[21]Report by the Managing Director at EBM/89/25 (March 1, 1989), p. 3.

[22]"Bank-Fund Collaboration in Assisting Member Countries," circulated in the Fund as SM/89/54 (March 9, 1989) and in the Bank as an attachment to R89–35 (March 10). The Bank document also included a memorandum to Executive Directors from Conable, which noted that although the paper had been issued in the Fund as a joint memorandum from the Managing Director and himself, he had not accepted its key passages.

ened: ". . . the institution which does not have the primary responsibility would, except in exceptional circumstances, yield to the judgment of the other institution." The document then added that exceptions were "expected to be extremely rare." In other words, each one did have a veto, but it could be overridden if the other felt strongly enough and did not abuse its discretion.

To placate those in the Bank who wanted to retain a role in assessing macroeconomic policies, the revised Concordat introduced another ambiguous concept, limiting the Fund's primary responsibility in this sphere to the "*aggregate aspects* of macroeconomic policy and their related instruments—including public sector spending and revenues, aggregate wage and price policies, money and credit, interest rates and the exchange rate" (emphasis added). Correspondingly, the Bank's primary responsibilities included "development strategies; sector project investments, structural adjustment programs; policies which deal with the efficient allocation of resources in both public and private sectors; priorities in government expenditures; reforms of administrative systems, production, trade and financial sectors; the restructuring of state enterprises and sector policies."

If the Concordat had any real meaning as an advance beyond the 1966 guidelines quoted above, it was in the peculiar phrase, "aggregative aspects of macroeconomic policy." That appears to be a subset of macroeconomic policy, but what does it exclude? Prima facie, it could have been interpreted to give the Bank the lead in determining how a Fund-imposed ceiling on credit growth should be allocated between credit to public and private sectors (traditionally a standard part of Fund conditionality). No one could say definitively what it meant, and all efforts to make it more precise failed.[23] It provided the Bank with an excuse for asserting independence with respect to advice or lending conditions on whatever it might characterize as nonaggregative, and it provided the Fund with a reaffirmation of its macro primacy, but in fact it was little more than an implicit acknowledgment that the institutions would continue to disagree.

When the Fund's Executive Board met in May to discuss the Concordat, a few Directors expressed unease about the delineation of responsibilities, but the Board as a whole "welcomed" the agreement.[24] The Bank's Directors, however, expressed greater reservations, and the Bank did not regard the document as institutionally binding (Polak, 1997, p. 515). The Concordat thus took on a semiofficial status, as a management directive to staff but not as a declared institutional policy. Its existence was not mentioned in the Fund's *Annual Report*, and it was not made publicly available until nearly a decade later.[25] It did, however, gradually become an accepted basis for promoting greater collaboration both at headquarters and in the field. The Bank did not attempt to use the "aggregative aspects" phrasing to

---

[23]See Polak (1997), p. 514, for what he suggests was a hilarious effort by Jacob A. Frenkel (Economic Counsellor and Director of Research at the Fund) to make sense of the phrase for the Executive Board.

[24]Minutes of EBM/89/50–51 (May 3, 1989).

[25]The operational guidelines in the Concordat were summarized in the World Bank's *Annual Report 1989*, pp. 96–97.

expand its mandate, and the traditional spheres of influence were essentially restored.

GATT

The General Agreement on Tariffs and Trade (GATT) was another organization with which the Fund had a special relationship, albeit much more distant than that with the Bank. The Geneva-based GATT was founded in 1948, as a compromise solution after the major countries failed to agree on the proposed third leg of the Bretton Woods strategy, the International Trade Organization.[26] It successfully conducted several "rounds" of negotiations to lower trade barriers, including notably the Kennedy Round (1964–67), the Tokyo Round (1973–79), and the Uruguay Round (1986–93). The GATT ceased to exist as a separate entity in 1995, following the establishment of the World Trade Organization as a successor institution.

Relations with the GATT were a byproduct of the Fund's interest in trade policy as an adjunct of exchange rate policy. As a general proposition, trade and exchange restrictions are substitutable means of protecting the balance of payments, so that one cannot be evaluated in isolation of the other. The GATT had jurisdiction over trade restrictions, and the Fund over exchange restrictions, and the two sought to work together to reduce both types of barriers. The Fund also tried to supplement the GATT's multilateral approach by pushing countries to reduce trade barriers on their own, especially when a country was a member of the Fund but not of the GATT.[27]

As noted in Chapter 2, concerns about protectionism were heightened in the first half of the 1980s, as countries tried to shelter their economies from the ef-

---

[26]Largely because of British reluctance to abandon its system of trade preferences with Commonwealth countries, the Bretton Woods conference was unable to deal directly with trade liberalization. As a fallback position, the conference adopted a resolution recommending that participating governments "reach agreement as soon as possible on ways and means [to] . . . reduce obstacles to international trade . . ." (Resolution VII; U.S. Department of State (1948), Vol. 1, p. 941). Consequently, a Preparatory Committee (including representatives from the Executive Board and staff of the Fund) met in London in October–November 1946 and prepared a draft Charter for an "International Trade Organization." Following subsequent more detailed negotiations and drafting, the goal of ratifying the charter was abandoned. The GATT was established in 1947 (effective at the beginning of 1948), with the intention that it would serve as a temporary bridge to the International Trade Organization. For the history of the negotiations, see Gardner (1956); for the Fund's role, see Horsefield (1969), Vol. 1, pp. 171–75.

[27]For an analysis of the logical relationships linking the Fund, the World Bank, and the WTO, see Vines (1997). Horsefield (1969), Vol. 2, Chapter 16, covers the origins and early history of Fund-GATT collaboration. Gold (1986) discusses the legal relationship between exchange and trade restrictions and the history of legal relations between the Fund and the GATT. Eichengreen and Kenen (1994, pp. 6–7) suggest that the GATT was more effective in achieving its goals (reduction of tariffs and other trade barriers) than either the Fund or the World Bank were at achieving theirs, largely because it was relatively free of bureaucratic constraints and thus more adaptable to changing circumstances. As of 1989, 96 countries were members of the GATT, compared with 152 in the Fund.

fects of badly misaligned exchange rates. When Arthur Dunkel became Director-General of the GATT in 1980, he stepped up his organization's crusade against protectionist policies and enlisted the Fund's support in the battle.[28] The Fund responded by paying increased attention to trade issues in various aspects of its work, but it felt the need to do so in a way that recognized its lack of jurisdiction over trade restrictions.[29] Broadly speaking, the Fund's analysis of trade measures complemented the more specific and jurisdictional work of the GATT, and the turf battles that occasionally marred relations with the World Bank were much less of a problem here. Some frictions arose occasionally when the Fund included trade liberalization in its conditions for stand-by or other credit arrangements, since that created at least the potential for a conflict in policy advice in the field of the GATT's jurisdiction. In particular, GATT officials became a little nervous in 1983 when the Managing Director initiated a drive for reduction of trade restrictions in the context of certain Fund-supported adjustment programs.[30] Such concerns, however, turned out to be only light clouds.

In 1980–81, the Fund staff undertook a detailed survey of restrictive trade practices as background for the spring 1981 World Economic Outlook exercise. (See WEO, June 1981, pp. 103–05; and Anjaria and others, 1981.) That study marked the beginning of a gradual rise in Fund activity in the trade sphere. In 1982, the Executive Board held its first separate meeting on trade issues. On that and subsequent occasions, the Board showed its reluctance to get too deeply involved by rejecting a proposal for GATT participation in Fund missions when trade issues were to be discussed in Article IV consultations.[31] The following year, however, the Fund began examining trade policies more systematically through general policy discussions and consultations with individual countries,[32] and the Interim Committee began including occasional expressions of concern on trade issues in its

---

[28]See letter of October 22, 1980, to the Managing Director from Fernando A. Vera (Director of the Geneva Office); memorandum for files (November 6, 1980) by Shailendra J. Anjaria (Chief of the Trade and Payments Division in ETR) on the initial meeting between Dunkel and de Larosière; and letter of November 28, 1980, from Dunkel to de Larosière; in IMF/CF (I 233 "GATT—Contracting Parties, 1977–1981").

[29]In 1974, the Committee of Twenty (the forerunner of the Interim Committee) requested member countries to adhere to a "declaration on trade measures." The declaration would have empowered the Fund to pass judgment on whether a balance of payments justification existed for the adoption of a proposed trade restriction or other measure, and it would have obligated adherents to avoid adopting trade measures without a positive finding by the Fund. Adoption of the declaration required approval by members holding 65 percent of the voting power, which it did not receive. See Gold (1986), pp. 173–79.

[30]See letter from Arthur Dunkel, Director-General of the GATT, to Jacques de Larosière (November 4, 1983); in IMF/CF (I 233 "GATT—Contracting Parties, 1983–1985"). Also see Chapter 9, p. 361, where the Managing Director's initiative on Mexico is discussed.

[31]Minutes of EBM/82/123 (September 20, 1982), pp. 14–15. Also see "Developments in International Trade Policy," SM/82/136 (July 12, 1982), pp. 17–18, and minutes of EBM/88/33 (March 7, 1988), p. 6.

[32]See statement by the Managing Director at EBM/82/162 (December 17, 1982), pp. 28–29.

communiqués.[33] The Fund also published each of its staff studies on trade issues.[34] In 1984, at the request of the GATT, the staff conducted a study of the effects of exchange rate volatility on international trade (IMF Research Department, 1984). And in 1985, the staff began a series of information notices on trade policies for Executive Directors, as a means of keeping track of major changes.

The launch of the Uruguay Round at Punta del Este in September 1986 brought a further expansion of interagency contacts and collaboration, although the Fund still maintained a distinctly subsidiary role on trade issues. C. David Finch (Director of ETR) delivered an address on behalf of the Managing Director at that opening ministerial meeting, and Camdessus participated personally in later ones, notably the midterm review in Montreal in December 1988. Fund staff participated throughout the Round as observers in the technical meetings and negotiations. Their role, however, was limited primarily to providing technical support and information.

On a more active and permanent basis, the staff participated in the GATT Committee on Balance of Payments Restrictions, which consulted with member countries on whether trade restrictions were justified on balance of payments grounds. (If so, the restrictions would be permitted under the GATT's Articles of Agreement.) In that role, which dated from the 1940s and was embodied in the GATT's own rules, the staff provided background macroeconomic information derived from the Fund's Article IV consultations and expressed the Fund's view on the justification for specific restrictions. In the 1980s, the Fund used this forum to argue against the use of trade restrictions for balance of payments purposes, on the grounds that much more positive and efficient methods were available for strengthening a country's external payments position. This position placed the Fund in league with industrial countries, which were trying to overcome the opposition of developing countries to proposals to amend the GATT's Articles on this matter.[35]

In addition to its support of the GATT's effort to liberalize trade policies multilaterally, the Fund gradually adopted a positive view toward regional free-trade agreements. Regional agreements were controversial because they created special preferences for selected countries and in some cases promoted regional import substitution rather than export growth. Potentially at least, the reduction in welfare from trade diversion could wipe out the gains from trade stimulus. Until the late

---

[33]From 1975 on, the Director-General of the GATT (or his Deputy) attended Interim Committee meetings as an observer. Fund staff normally attended the annual meetings of the GATT Contracting Parties when they met at ambassadorial level. ("Contracting Parties" was the legal terminology for the member countries of the GATT. In references to joint actions or meetings, the term was written in all capital letters.) In 1982, the Contracting Parties met exceptionally at ministerial level, and the Managing Director delivered an address at that meeting.

[34]In addition to the 1981 paper cited above, see Anjaria, Iqbal, and others (1982); Anjaria, Kirmani, and Petersen (1985); and Kelly and others (1988).

[35]"The Uruguay Round—Issues of Particular Relevance to the Fund," SM/88/36 (February 5, 1988), p. 15.

1980s, the Fund generally paid little attention to regional agreements.[36] Even such notable examples as the 1982 establishment of the Preferential Trade Area (PTA) for Eastern and Southern African States (the forerunner of the Common Market for Eastern and Southern Africa of 1993) had little immediate impact on trade patterns.[37] Eventually, however, the Fund came to view regional agreements as stepping stones toward multilateral liberalization. Subject to confirmation that a regional agreement did not raise barriers to trading with other countries, the Fund was prepared to express its cautious support. During the 1980s, that support was limited primarily to the U.S.-Canada Free Trade Agreement of 1988 (the forerunner of NAFTA, the North American Free Trade Agreement of 1994).[38]

United Nations

Under the terms of a 1947 agreement, the Fund is a "specialized agency" within the United Nations and functions as an "independent international organization" (Horsefield, 1969, Vol. 3, pp. 215–18.) Because the Fund is essentially a financial rather than a political organization and is governed by a weighted voting system, the major creditor countries have always regarded its independence from the UN as essential for its effective operation. Historically, relations between the two have been limited primarily to liaison functions for the purpose of sharing information and providing occasional assistance in areas of mutual concern.

In 1950, the Fund appointed a Special Representative to the United Nations, and the UN provided an office for the Fund at its headquarters in New York. That office served as a liaison with the Secretary General, his staff, and other UN bodies located in New York; and it monitored and reported on the activities of the General Assembly. In 1967, an additional office was established, in Geneva, to provide liaison with the GATT, UNCTAD,[39] the International Labor Organization (ILO), and other Geneva-based organizations. Beginning in 1987, in recognition

---

[36]The prototypical agreement was the establishment of the European Economic Community (the "Common Market") at the beginning of 1958. The Fund's *Annual Report* for that year (p. 129) noted the founding of the EEC and remarked that the Fund would be following its evolution with interest, but it expressed no view on the merits.

[37]The Fund supported the establishment of the PTA by providing technical assistance on the design of regional clearing and payments arrangements. The staff study of the proposed system concluded "that existing economic structures and physical barriers to intraregional trade militate against any pronounced shift in trade flows in the near future" (Anjaria, Eken, and Laker, 1982, p. 11).

[38]The summing up of the February 1989 Executive Board meeting concluding the Article IV consultation with Canada included the following: "Directors generally supported the Canada-U.S. Free Trade Agreement and agreed with the assessment that it would bring net benefits to Canada. However, several Directors expressed concern about the potential for trade diversion resulting from the FTA." Minutes of EBM/89/20 (February 22, 1989), p. 50.

[39]The United Nations Conference on Trade and Development (UNCTAD) was established in 1964 as the principal UN agency for promoting international trade and economic growth in developing countries. In addition to its regular informal consultations and cooperation with the Fund on development issues, UNCTAD played a role in pushing the Fund to expand and liberalize the Compensatory Financing Facility (CFF) in the late 1970s; see Chapter 15.

of the more active role being played by the staff in Geneva on trade matters, the head of that office was also designated as the Fund's Special Trade Representative.

At the UN, the principal forum for coordinating work among the various specialized agencies is the Administrative Council on Coordination, which meets at least twice each year at the senior (agency head) level under the chairmanship of the Secretary General. Throughout the 1980s, the Managing Director participated actively in this Council's meetings and made an annual address to the UN's Economic and Social Council (ECOSOC). A wide variety of staff contacts and collaboration occurred on an ad hoc but regular and ongoing basis.

The 1947 basic agreement on Fund-UN relations provides that the Fund shall "give due consideration to the inclusion in the agenda [for meetings of the Board of Governors] of items proposed by" the UN. A few proposals were made during the period covered by this History, but none led to the addition of an agenda item at the Annual Meetings. A prominent example was the 1982 General Assembly resolution on the Fund's relations with South Africa, discussed in Chapter 13. In that instance and in several others, the General Assembly opposed or questioned the procedures and even the structure of the Fund.

A major part of the UN criticism of the Fund arose from the relatively limited role of developing countries in governing the Fund. In 1979, for example, the Algerian government gave voice to a long-simmering resentment in the south and developed a proposal for "global negotiations" on creating a "new international economic order."[40] That proposal, which aimed to restructure the IMF to give greater weight to the views of developing countries and place the institution under the authority of the UN General Assembly, was endorsed at a summit meeting of the heads of state of nonaligned countries in Havana in September 1979. A few months later, the UN General Assembly endorsed by consensus Resolution 34/138, calling for global negotiations on international economic issues, including money and finance, to take place "within the United Nations system" (i.e., including the Fund). A special session of the General Assembly met in 1980 to plan such negotiations, but it failed to reach agreement, and the idea was eventually dropped. The Fund took note of the discussions, but it was not asked to take specific actions, and it made no response.[41]

In the autumn 1979 session, the General Assembly also endorsed the "Program of Action on International Monetary Reform," adopted by the Group of Twenty-

---

[40]Voting power in the Fund is determined essentially by quotas, which in turn are determined essentially by economic size (see Chapter 17, pp. 860). In the United Nations, each country has one vote regardless of size. The dream of recreating the international economic order by giving greater voice to developing countries took form in 1974; see Mortimer (1984). It was also manifest in the Arusha Initiative of 1979, discussed in Chapter 13. The prime minister of India, Indira Gandhi, reportedly raised the issue at the North-South Summit in Cancun, Mexico, in 1981 (see Thatcher, 1993, pp. 169–70), and she raised it again at the UN General Assembly in 1983.

[41]Reports on the General Assembly deliberations on Global Negotiations were circulated in the Fund in "United Nations General Assembly—Thirty-Fourth Session," SM/80/11 (January 14, 1980), pp. 7–9, and "United Nations General Assembly—Thirty-Fifth Regular Session," SM/81/3 (January 6, 1981), pp. 1–6. Also see related documents in IMF/CF (I 110), on the 34th and 35th Sessions of the UN General Assembly.

Four (G-24) developing countries at the Annual Meetings in Belgrade. A concerted negotiating effort failed to produce a compromise text that could win consensus support, and all industrial countries opposed or abstained from approving the final text (Resolution 34/216). The Fund considered and acted on various elements of the G-24 program, but it did so at the request of the Development Committee, not the UN (see *Annual Report 1980*, pp. 158–65). The Fund did take what at the time was an unusual step by agreeing to send several pertinent internal documents to the UN Secretariat.[42] However tentatively, that marked a step toward openness regarding the Fund's internal deliberations on current policy issues.

On other occasions, the Fund and the UN at least broadly agreed on the requirements for action and worked together to promote their objectives. In May 1986, while the Fund was beginning to negotiate long-term concessional loans to low-income countries through its newly established SAF, the UN General Assembly held a Special Session on Africa. That session produced a commitment by the "international community" to try in general terms to provide "predictable and assured" resources to support development efforts in African countries. Fund staff participated in preliminary meetings leading up to the special session and provided some logistical support.[43]

In September 1987, the General Assembly passed Resolution 42/198, calling on the international community to provide additional resources to relieve the debt burdens of developing countries. The resolution welcomed several such efforts that were under way at the Fund, including the proposed establishment of the Enhanced Structural Adjustment Facility (ESAF; Chapter 14) and the addition of a contingency mechanism in the Compensatory Financing Facility (CFF; Chapter 15). Although the initiative came at a time when the Fund and some major industrial countries were still reluctant to endorse debt-relief proposals (see Chapter 11), the UN resolution did not endorse any specific debt-relief plan, and only the United States voted against it.

Paris Club

The Paris Club is an informal grouping of governments holding debt claims on other countries, which has met since 1956 when necessary to consider requests to reschedule those claims.[44] During the debt crisis of the 1980s, as described

---

[42]"Transmittal to the United Nations of Certain Fund Documents on the Group of Twenty-Four Program of Immediate Action," EBD/80/279 (October 21, 1980).

[43]See "United Nations General Assembly—Special Session on the Critical Economic Situation in Africa," SM/86/133 (June 13, 1986), p. 3.

[44]A rescheduling of debt claims normally means that creditors agree to defer debt service (interest and principal) for a specified portion of total claims and for a specified period, without reducing the discounted present value of the amounts due. Beginning in 1988, the Paris Club began granting reschedulings on concessional terms to qualifying low-income countries. For an exposition of Paris Club procedures and a history of its work, see Sevigny (1990). For more detailed reviews and complete listings of Paris Club and similar reschedulings through 1989, see the following Fund documents: Nowzad and Williams (1981), Chapter 5; Brau and Williams (1983), Chapter 4; Dillon and others (1985), Chapter 3; Dillon and Oliveros (1987); Keller (1988); and Kuhn and Guzman (1990).

throughout Part Two of this History, the Paris Club faced a nearly continuous demand for reschedulings from a large number of developing countries, and it met on a fairly regular monthly schedule to consider them. It had no formal or legal structure, nor its own secretariat, but it met under the auspices and with the technical support of the French treasury. Because the Paris Club lacked the staff resources to do its own evaluations of sovereign credit risks, it relied heavily on the Fund's assessments of borrowers' economic prospects. Traditionally, it required countries to have an upper-tranche stand-by or extended arrangement in effect before it would consider any request to reschedule outstanding debts. Fund staff participated regularly in Paris Club meetings and explained the status of any ongoing negotiations and of the Fund's assessments. The Fund required member countries to have a plan for eliminating any arrears in debt obligations to other creditors as a condition for borrowing, for which Paris Club agreements provided evidence (see the discussion of "financing assurances" in Chapter 11).

On a few occasions starting in the mid-1970s, Paris Club creditors allowed exceptions to its requirement that countries have an upper-tranche credit arrangement in place with the Fund.[45] Sierra Leone had only low-conditionality drawings outstanding at the time of its 1977 Paris Club rescheduling; Poland (1981) and Cuba (1983) obtained agreements while they were not members of the Fund; and Mozambique got an agreement in 1984 shortly after it joined the Fund. A more complicated situation arose regarding Zaïre (Democratic Republic of the Congo), which was granted a rescheduling in December 1979 while it was out of compliance and ineligible to draw on its Fund stand-by arrangement. That rescheduling was granted on the strength of a positive assessment by the Fund staff that the authorities were formulating additional adjustment measures that would soon bring the program back on track.[46] Zaïre did manage to strengthen its policies enough to complete the stand-by arrangement, but the improvement soon proved illusory (see Chapter 16).

Collaboration between the Fund and the Paris Club intensified in 1980 as a result of the growing debt-servicing difficulties in many developing countries. Responding to a request from the chairman of the Paris Club (Michel Camdessus), the Managing Director (de Larosière) asked the staff to take several steps to help the Paris Club in its work. These steps included providing more information on debt service in background papers for Article IV consultations (which were routinely used by official creditors as a basic source of information on countries re-

---

[45]As discussed in Chapter 13, the Fund's conditionality was increased when a country borrowed "in the upper tranches" (i.e., above its first credit tranche).

[46]Although the Paris Club required countries to have an upper-tranche arrangement, it did not necessarily require that the arrangement be operational. The prepared statement delivered by the staff at the meeting did not mention that Zaïre was out of compliance with the terms of the stand-by arrangement, but the staff did supply that information during the meeting in response to a question from the U.S. delegation. The Paris Club agreement required Zaïre to reactivate its program with the Fund. See memorandum of December 19, 1979, from Evangelos A. Calamitsis (Assistant Director in the African Department) to the Managing Director; in IMF/CF (S 1194 "Zaïre, Debt Renegotiations—Meetings, 1978–1985"). Also see "Yugoslavia—Staff Report for the 1982 Article IV Consultation and Review under Stand-by Arrangement," EBS/83/46 (March 9, 1983), p. 15.

questing reschedulings), offering more extensive assistance to member countries in preparing for meetings with official and private creditors, and upgrading staff participation in Paris Club meetings.[47]

Relations intensified again in 1983, following the outbreak of the international debt crisis. The number and size of rescheduling requests rose sharply (Figure 20.1), which stretched the already limited resources of the Club even further. To keep the process from bogging down and to improve the opportunity for all official creditors to participate in the process, the Club initiated procedures in mid-1984 requiring immediate notification to the Fund whenever a country requested a rescheduling agreement. For its part, the Fund devised procedures to ensure that Executive Directors were promptly notified and that the staff would stand ready to assist both debtors and creditors by providing both data and advice on request.[48]

By the middle of the decade, creditors found themselves facing a gap between the short periods covered by Fund conditionality and the often lengthy periods that debts had to be deferred if indebted countries were to have a realistic chance to repay. The Paris Club was nonetheless insistent on rescheduling only those payments that were coming due during the period covered by a stand-by or extended arrangement. In 1985–86, creditors agreed in principle to continue to reschedule debt obligations of Ecuador and Côte d'Ivoire after they completed their Fund-supported programs, on the basis of "enhanced surveillance" by the Fund. In the event, that procedure was not carried out, because both countries continued to borrow from the Fund.[49] For Yugoslavia in 1986, official creditors (acting outside the aegis of the Paris Club) agreed to implement a multiyear rescheduling agreement (MYRA), also on the basis of enhanced surveillance (see Chapter 10). For that purpose, the Fund provided edited versions of its confidential staff reports on the country to creditors. The monitoring arrangement, unfortunately, was not a success, and it was not repeated.

The Paris Club's luckless experimentation with relaxed procedures for countries under enhanced surveillance suggested that strict compliance with Fund conditionality was usually necessary for a successful rescheduling agreement. With that in mind, Paris Club creditors remained reluctant to accept any proposal that appeared to be a watered-down imitation. Nonetheless, the importance of rescheduling for financial stability in many developing countries forced them to continue to consider alternatives. Most important, creditors agreed to accept SAF and ESAF arrangements as the basis for rescheduling, despite the formal and procedural differences in the way conditionality was applied (see Chapter 14). Through 1989, 18 official rescheduling agreements were approved on that basis for low-income countries.[50]

---

[47]Memorandum to heads of departments from the Managing Director (April 9, 1980); in IMF/RD file on "Paris Club Meetings—1980–83" (Carton RM 5513, Section 13, Shelf 4, Bin 3).

[48]Minutes of EBM/84/98–99 (June 22, 1984) and "Notification to the Fund of Requests for Renegotiation of External Debt Received by the Paris Club," SM/84/236 (October 24, 1984).

[49]See Chapter 9, p. 412, where Ecuador's similar situation vis-à-vis private creditors is discussed; and Dillon and Oliveros (1987), pp. 15–16.

[50]See Kuhn and Guzman, 1990, p. 21. Rescheduling on the basis of an ESAF arrangement was never a major issue, owing to the larger financial commitment and greater conditionality compared with the SAF.

Figure 20.1. Paris Club and Similar Reschedulings, 1975–89

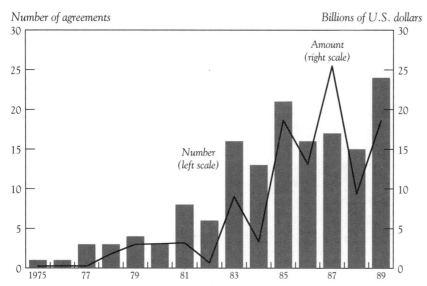

A less satisfactory experience resulted when the Paris Club approved a rescheduling for Brazil in January 1987. As recounted in Chapter 10, Brazil was resisting submitting either to Fund conditionality or to enhanced surveillance, but it had agreed to a monitoring process that it called "enhanced contacts" with the Fund. On that rather weak premise and a personal assessment of progress from the Managing Director, the Paris Club decided to go ahead. Four weeks later, Brazil declared a moratorium on debt-service payments to commercial banks, and the Paris Club had no choice but to scrap a planned second tranche of the deal.

Bank for International Settlements

Uniquely among the organizations discussed in this section, the BIS was established long before the Fund. Relations between the two did not begin propitiously: the Bretton Woods conference adopted a resolution calling for the abolition of the BIS, principally because of the BIS's role in transferring official gold balances to Nazi Germany.[51] Nonetheless, official relations with the BIS were generally cordial, and until the 1980s involved only occasional interaction.[52]

---

[51]The BIS was founded in 1930 as the financial intermediary for handling Germany's reparations payments under the terms of the Versailles peace treaty that ended World War I. Based in Basel, Switzerland, it evolved into a bank for central banks and a forum for central bank governors, especially those of the Group of Ten (G-10). On the Bretton Woods resolution, see James (1995), pp. 49–50. On the early history of the BIS and its relationship to the Fund and the World Bank, see Auboin (1955).

[52]The BIS served as an agent for the Fund's operations in gold, and it was a prescribed holder of SDRs.

The beginning of the 1980s brought both new tensions and a closer working relationship. Since 1948, senior BIS officials had been invited to participate as official observers at the Annual Meetings of Governors of the Fund and the World Bank, and the Fund had been similarly represented at the BIS Annual Meetings in Basel. When the Board of Governors decided in 1980 to end the practice of inviting Observers as a way out of the controversy over inviting Palestinian Liberation Organization (PLO) officials (see below), the BIS argued that it should be exempted from the ban. The Fund's management was sympathetic but was unwilling to reopen Pandora's box. For years afterward, the unintended but ongoing slight continued to irritate many in Basel.[53] This awkward episode was potentially serious, as it came at a time when the Fund and the BIS were becoming bedfellows in managing the strategy for coping with the international debt crisis. The Fund continued to grant the BIS observer status at meetings of the Interim Committee, and, on the whole, the affair does not seem to have seriously soured working relationships.

Before 1982, the BIS occasionally invited the Managing Director to attend its governors' meetings in Basel, when there were specific issues to discuss.[54] A prominent example was the Fund's drive to borrow approximately $1.5 billion from industrial countries in 1981, which was initiated by a presentation to BIS governors by de Larosière in November 1980 (see Chapter 17). In January 1982, the BIS decided to regularize this arrangement by inviting the Managing Director to attend the governors' meetings whenever he found it appropriate. De Larosière accepted and decided to attend the July 1982 meeting, where he made a presentation on how Hungary's economy was responding to the financial support the BIS had recently provided, and on its near-term prospects (see Chapter 8). He also sketched out the Fund's view on the World Economic Outlook and—at the request of Gordon Richardson (governor of the Bank of England and vice-chairman of the BIS)—the role that the Fund might play in the event of a financial crisis. It was just a few weeks before the Mexican crisis would strike, and the systemic effects from the burgeoning external debt in Latin America as well as eastern Europe were beginning to materialize.

From that point on, the BIS frequently provided or arranged for short-term financing as a bridge to Fund support for adjustment programs of the most heavily indebted countries. In doing so, it alleviated the need for the Fund to compress even more severely the time available for negotiating stand-by and extended arrangements, and it helped forestall consideration of an emergency financing facility in the Fund (see Chapter 15). The BIS also lent again to the Fund in 1984, as the lion's share of a medium-term SDR 3 billion package from industrial countries (Chapter 17).

---

[53]See letter from Fritz Leutwiler (President of the BIS) to de Larosière (May 10, 1984) and related correspondence in IMF/CF (G 820 "Observers at Annual Meetings, 1946–1990").

[54]The Director of the Fund's Paris office regularly attended (in the margins) and filed reports on the monthly gatherings. Other Fund staff attended occasionally; see, for example, the references in Chapter 19 to the staff's use of this forum to hold clandestine meetings with Hungarian officials in the 1960s and 1970s.

European Community

Relations between the Fund and European economic organizations have occasionally been strained, dating back to the late 1940s. When the U.S.-funded European Recovery Program (ERP, more commonly known as the Marshall Plan) was launched in 1948, the Fund responded by deciding to conserve its own resources and limit assistance to ERP participants to "exceptional or unforeseen circumstances" (see Horsefield, 1969, Vol. 1, pp. 217–20; and Vol. 2, Chapter 15). Although that decision made some economic sense, it engendered a feeling in Europe that the region should be prepared to look out for itself financially and not rely on the Fund. Several European countries subsequently borrowed frequently from the Fund, and the United Kingdom became the largest user of Fund credit for more than a quarter century. Nonetheless, that sense of the need for independence never faded, and it helped feed the drive to develop a succession of European financial arrangements and institutions. In 1950, 18 countries—most of which either already were or soon would become members of the IMF—formed the European Payments Union (EPU) to restore multilateral payments and currency convertibility. The Union, which completed its task and was terminated in 1958, included a set of mechanisms for financing imbalances within the EPU membership rather than externally from the IMF.[55] The EPU was succeeded by the European Monetary Agreement (EMA, 1958); the credit facilities of the European Economic Community (EEC, 1958; shortened in 1968 to European Community, or EC); the European Monetary Cooperation Fund (generally known by its French acronym, FECOM; 1973); and the European Monetary System (EMS, 1979).[56]

The Fund, as discussed in Chapter 2, took a generally favorable and cooperative stance toward the EMS, though with some initial wariness about potential conflicts over turf. More generally, concerns surfaced at the Fund throughout the 1980s about the extent to which European economic and financial integration might turn inward; that is, about whether Europeans were building a "fortress" rather than bridges. Concerns also arose occasionally about the effect of the European basket currency, the ECU, on the SDR. Because the Fund's Articles of Agreement required its members to cooperate toward making the SDR "the principal reserve asset in the international monetary system," the development and promotion of an alternative multicurrency reserve asset raised legitimate questions. In examining these and related questions, however, the Fund took a decidedly cautious attitude. It had little power to influence European policy and therefore no good reason to raise objections to it. Moreover, as the decade progressed, the Fund adopted an increasingly positive perspective on European integration. The EMS, in the prevailing view at the end of the 1980s, had successfully created a "zone of

---

[55]See Horsefield (1969), Vol. 1, pp. 327–30; and James (1995), pp. 95–99. For an inside overview of the EPU, see Kaplan and Schleiminger (1989); for a critique, see Eichengreen (1993).

[56]For a review and chronology of the development of European monetary and financial agreements, see Ungerer (1997). Bobay (1998) gives a broad overview of relations between the Fund and European economic institutions.

monetary stability" in Europe, and it was contributing to a general liberalization of trade and payments in the region.[57]

On an institutional level, relations between the Fund and the EC were initiated in the late 1950s and have included occasional meetings between Fund management and their European counterparts as well as a variety of regular staff contacts. The Fund's Paris office has provided liaison with EC offices in Brussels and elsewhere. Those contacts were particularly relevant for the EC's work with developing countries, beginning with the first Yaoundé Convention in 1963.[58] Broadly speaking, these relations proceeded smoothly and routinely in the 1980s, despite a reluctance by European authorities to have their regional policies discussed explicitly by the Executive Board. EMS developments were covered in detail in the World Economic Outlook, in the course of Article IV consultations with EC members, and in a series of special reports to the Board. In addition, the Fund staff consulted with the European Commission in conjunction with the Fund's periodic reviews of trade-policy developments and a study of the EC's Common Agricultural Policy (Rosenblatt and others, 1988).

After the two great stand-by arrangements of 1977, for Italy and the United Kingdom (see de Vries, 1985, Chapters 23–24), borrowing by western European countries from the Fund was extremely limited. One should not infer too much from that fact alone, because drawings by other industrial countries were also quite limited after 1977. Indeed, EC member countries did call on the Fund when sufficiently pressed: Denmark, Luxembourg, and the Netherlands made drawings on their reserve-tranche balances during the 1980s.[59] Of more direct relevance is the record of borrowing from the alternative credit facilities established by the EC, which suggests that the main reason for the lack of recourse to the Fund was simply that European countries had little need for balance of payments financing.

Unlike other industrial countries, participants in the exchange rate mechanism of the EMS faced a recurring need for very short-term financing to maintain intra-European exchange rates within agreed margins. Other EC member countries, although not formally committed, also generally sought to limit shifts in their exchange rates against their European partners. To that end, the EC provided its own

---

[57]Minutes of EBM/89/9–10 (February 1, 1989); see especially the Chairman's summing up at meeting 89/10, pp. 14–17.

[58]The Yaoundé Convention of July 1963 was an association agreement between the EEC and 17 African countries. It was replaced by a series of Lomé conventions, which covered a broader range of developing countries in Africa, the Caribbean, and the Pacific.

[59]From 1978 through 1987, those three EC countries made a total of 11 reserve-tranche drawings. Portugal made several drawings in 1982–84, but at the time it was classified as a developing country, and it did not become a member of the EC until 1986. As for other industrial countries, Spain (which also did not join the EC until 1986) made several drawings in 1975–78 and took out a precautionary stand-by arrangement in 1978, the United States made a reserve-tranche drawing in 1978, Australia made two drawings on the Buffer Stock Financing Facility in 1979 and 1982, New Zealand made three reserve-tranche drawings in 1979–84, and Iceland made drawings on its reserve tranche and the Compensatory Financing Facility in 1982. Denmark's drawing in March 1987 was (as of 2000) the last by a country that was then classified as industrial.

conditional credit facilities, with a wide range of available maturities, and an EMS facility for short-term intervention both within and at the agreed margins. During the 1980s, although short-term intervention was undertaken routinely, resort to medium-term conditional credits—substitutes for Fund resources—was rare. Only France in 1983 and Greece in 1985–86 drew on the EC credit facilities in that period (Ungerer and others, 1990, pp. 8–9).

Member Countries: Technical Assistance

In the formative years, the Fund occasionally supplemented its standard consultation procedures by providing technical assistance to member countries on matters such as exchange rate management and the conduct of monetary and fiscal policies. When newly independent developing countries began to join the Fund in large numbers in the early 1960s, requests for such assistance grew to the point that the Fund decided to formalize the practice. In 1964, three new bureaucratic units were formed, primarily to provide specific types of technical assistance: the Fiscal Affairs Department, the Central Banking Service, and the IMF Institute. The first two groups provided staff missions to countries to consult on their areas of expertise, while the Institute provided courses for officials on financial analysis and other relevant economic topics. About the same time, the Bureau of Statistics expanded its program of statistical assistance to members.[60] From that point on, provision of technical assistance to members became an increasingly important and structured activity for the Fund.

By 1970, the Fund was providing some 70 staff-years of services in the field a year, and by 1980 the total exceeded 100 staff-years. This activity peaked in 1983–85, about 130 staff-years, and then fell back to about 100 by the end of the decade (Figure 20.2). In contrast to the gradual growth in earlier years, which responded to the need for newly independent countries to develop managerial and technical expertise, the expansion that began in 1983 was associated with the burst in the Fund's lending that followed the onset of the international debt crisis. This additional assistance was especially focused on external debt management and on improving countries' statistics on external debt. The subsequent cutback did not result from a drop in demand; requests for assistance were undiminished. Rather, it reflected a shift toward belt-tightening at the Fund and a decision that provision of longer-term consultants and advisors was not a cost-effective use of Fund resources. Consequently, provision of technical assistance shifted more toward short-term staff missions.

---

[60]The origins of the Fund's technical assistance in the late 1940s are discussed in Horsefield (1969), Vol. 1, pp. 185–87; its further development and coordination with the UN in 1949–51, on pp. 286–87; efforts to place limits and controls on it in the mid-1950s, on pp. 391–94 and 428; and the establishment of the three new units, on pp. 552–55. The expanded work of the Bureau of Statistics is discussed in de Vries (1976), Vol. 1, pp. 584–86. One should note that before the mid-1960s, a wider range of activities was classified as technical assistance, including assignment of resident representatives and release of staff members to undertake extended assignments paid for by member countries. Also see de Vries (1976), Chapter 28, and de Vries (1985), Chapter 47.

Figure 20.2. Technical Assistance by the IMF, 1964–89

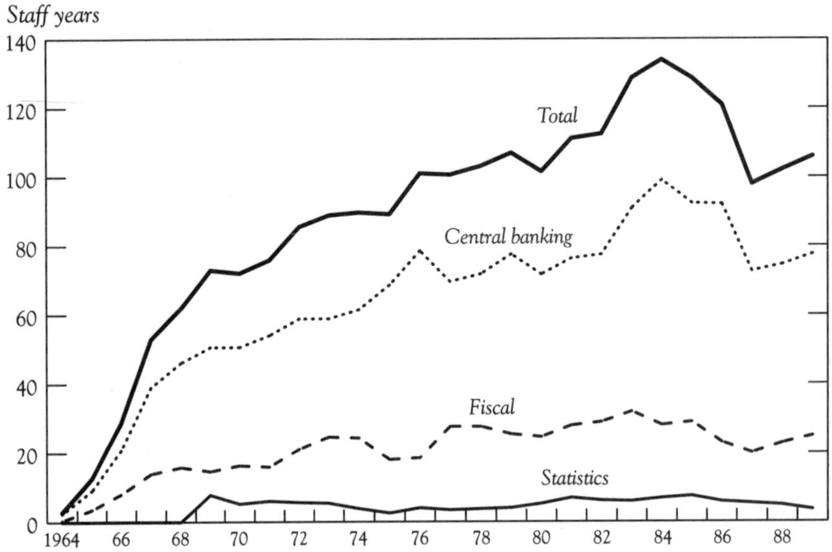

Staff years

Two dozen countries (or, in one case, a regional central bank) received an average of at least one full staff-year of technical assistance a year in the 1980s (Table 20.1).[61] The leading recipient, Zaïre, had been the object of an intensive campaign of assistance dating back to 1960, when the country gained its independence and became known as the Congo (Leopoldville). From the time the Congo—one of the largest and most strategically placed of the newly independent countries in Africa—joined the Fund in 1963, the Fund supported a UN program of special assistance for it. The Fund terminated the special status for the Congo in the late 1960s, but it continued to provide large amounts of technical assistance.[62]

Governance

The organization of the IMF was remarkably stable during the 1980s, especially considering the growth in the institution's role in the world economy. The only major change was that three subsidiary units in the structure were upgraded (Table 20.2). First, in 1980, in recognition of the expanding role of technical assistance to member countries, the Central Banking Service became the Central Banking Department. To head it up, P.N. Kaul, formerly Deputy Director of the Administration Department (see de Vries, 1985, p. 1028), was promoted to Director. Second, in 1980, in recognition of the growing importance of public relations for the Fund, the

---

[61]"Review of Fund Technical Assistance," EBAP/93/78 (December 1, 1993), pp. 34–35.

[62]See Horsefield (1969), Vol. 1, pp. 551–52; de Vries (1976), Vol. 1, p. 588; and the section on Zaïre in Chapter 16 of the present work.

Table 20.1. Top Recipients of Technical Assistance, 1980–89

(Total staff-years)

1. Zaïre	40.0
2. Yemen, Arab Republic	34.5
3. Botswana	29.7
4. Solomon Islands	27.4
5. Papua New Guinea	26.1
6. Vanuatu	25.7
7. Sudan	23.1
8. Uganda	23.1
9. Rwanda	22.7
10. The Bahamas	20.5
11. Oman	20.0
12. Eastern Caribbean	19.0
13. Guinea	18.8
14. Burundi	17.5
15. Fiji	16.4
16. Tanzania	16.1
17. Kuwait	15.6
18. Western Samoa	13.8
19. Bolivia	13.3
20. Costa Rica	13.3
21. Indonesia	13.3
22. Sierra Leone	10.9
23. Cayman Islands	10.2
24. Paraguay	10.1

External Relations Office (formerly the Information Office) was upgraded to the External Relations Department, and Azizali F. Mohammed (see de Vries, 1985, p. 1029) was named to be its first Director. Third, as office technology improved and became more central to the Fund's operations and research activities, several diffused operations were centralized in a Bureau of Computing Services in December 1982, with Warren N. Minami (formerly a local commercial bank official) as its Director.

The size of the staff grew slowly in the 1980s, primarily in the first half of the decade. From a little under 1,400 full-time staff in 1979, the Fund grew to 1,700 staff in 1989 (2 percent a year, or 22 percent overall). That growth reflected the expansion of membership and financial activity of the Fund, but it was not sufficient to keep pressures on staff time and energy from rising. By at least one key measure of activity—the number of stand-by and other financial arrangements in place—the staff grew at a much slower rate than the demands placed on it (Figure 20.3).

The Fund's physical plant—its Washington headquarters—was expanded in the early 1980s, and a few years later the Fund had to begin planning for further expansion in the 1990s. When the headquarters building was originally conceived in the late 1960s, it was designed to be built in stages as the institution grew, on the assumption that the Fund would be able to acquire all of the land in the block bordered by 19th, 20th, G, and H Streets, Northwest.[63] Phase I, which opened in 1973, occupied about two-thirds of the block. The remainder was then owned and occupied by several different parties, including notably The George Washington University and the Western Presbyterian Church. The Fund gradually acquired all

---

[63]For the first few months of the Fund's life in 1946, the staff and Executive Board met in rented rooms at the Washington Hotel on Pennsylvania Avenue. From June 1946 until 1958, the Fund sublet offices from the World Bank in a building at 1818 H Street. In 1958, the Fund moved next door to a new building that it had had constructed on the southeast corner of 19th and H Streets. For the first time, the Fund owned its office space. A few years later, the Fund constructed an addition to that building, extending south on 19th Street to G Street; staff began occupying that building in 1965. See Horsefield (1969), Vol. 1, pp. 137, 145–46, 394–95, 560–61, and 640. When the Fund moved to its new headquarters on the west side of 19th Street in 1973, the World Bank took over all of the east side. See de Vries (1976), Vol. 1, pp. 649–50. The two earliest headquarters, on H Street, were demolished in the 1990s to make room for a new headquarters building for the World Bank.

Table 20.2. Organization Chart, 1979–89

Board of Governors
(Interim Committee)

Executive Board

Managing Director
(and Chairman of Executive Board)
Jacques de Larosière, 1978–87
Michel Camdessus, 1987–2000

Deputy Managing Director
William B. Dale, 1974–84
Richard D. Erb, 1984–94

Area Departments	Functional Departments and Offices	Information and Liaison	Support Services
African	Central Banking Service; Central Banking Department from 1980	Information Office; became External Relations Department in 1980	Administration Department
Justin B. Zulu, 1976–84			
Alassane D. Ouattara, 1984–88			*Kenneth N. Clark, 1976–79*
Mamoudou Touré, 1988–94	*Roland Tenconi, 1978–79*	*Jay H. Reid, 1972–80*	*Roland Tenconi, 1980–85*
	P.N. Kaul, 1980–84	*Azizali F. Mohammed, 1980–90*	*Graeme F. Rea, 1985–95*
Asian	*Justin B. Zulu, 1984–95*		
Tun Thin, 1972–86		Office in Europe (Paris)	Secretary's Department
P.R. Narvekar, 1986–91	Fiscal Affairs Department	*Aldo Guetta, 1977–86*	*Leo Van Houtven, 1977–96*
European	*Richard Goode, 1965–81*	*Andrew J. Beith, 1986–94*	
L. Alan Whittome, 1964–87	*Vito Tanzi, 1981–2000*		Bureau of Computing Services (from 1982)
Massimo Russo, 1987–97	IMF Institute	Office in Geneva	*Warren N. Minami, 1982–*
	Gérard M. Teyssier, 1972–90	*Fernando A. Vera, 1977–82*	
Middle Eastern		*Carlos A. Sansón, 1983–87*	
A. Shakour Shaalan, 1977–92	Legal Department	*Eduardo Wiesner Duran, 1987–88*	Bureau of Language Services
	Joseph Gold, 1960–79	*Helen B. Junz, 1989–94*	*Bernardo T. Rutgers, 1977–81*
	George Nicoletopoulos, 1979–85		*Andrew J. Beith, 1981–86*
Western Hemisphere	*François P. Gianviti, 1985–*	Office at the United Nations (New York)	*Alan Wright, 1986–92*
E. Walter Robichek, 1977–82	Exchange and Trade Relations Department	*Jan-Maarten Zegers, 1973–87*	Office of Internal Audit
Eduardo Wiesner Duran, 1982–87	*Ernest Sturc, 1965–80*	*Rattan Bhatia, 1987–95*	
Sterie T. Beza, 1987–95	*C. David Finch, 1980–87*		*J. William Lowe, 1963–79*
	L. Alan Whittome, 1987–90		*Peter A. Whipple, 1979–85*
			Robert Noë, 1985–90
	Research Department		
	Jacques J. Polak, 1958–79		
	William C. Hood, 1979–86		
	Jacob A. Frenkel, 1987–91		
	Bureau of Statistics		
	Werner Dannemann, 1978–89		
	John B. McLenaghan, 1989–96		
	Treasurer's Department		
	Walter O. Habermeier, 1969–87		
	F. Gerhard Laske, 1987–92		

Figure 20.3. Staff in Relation to Activity, 1979–90

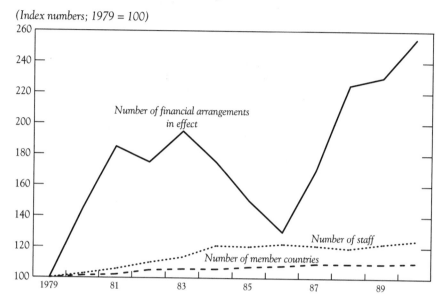

(Index numbers; 1979 = 100)

of the property except the church and built a new wing on the existing building in the early 1980s. That wing, known as Phase II, occupied the northwest section of the block and was completed in 1982.

In 1988, the Executive Board approved expenditure of $30 million to acquire the church property, construct a new building for the church in a new location, and obtain legal permits for constructing Phase III of the Fund headquarters.[64] After several years and some unexpected delays, the building would finally be completed in 1999 with only minor changes from the original design of thirty years earlier.[65]

Board of Governors

> All powers . . . not conferred directly . . . shall be vested in the Board of Governors.
>
> Article XII, Section 2(a)

At the top of the IMF hierarchy sits the Board of Governors. Once a year since 1946, the governors have gathered for two purposes: to conduct the usually routine official business of the Fund and to hold an endless stream of ancillary meetings, bi-

---

[64]Minutes of EBM/88/169 (November 21, 1988).

[65]The delays resulted when residents of the neighborhood where the church was to be rebuilt objected to the relocation of the church's program for feeding homeless and indigent people. Significant design changes included additional setbacks from the principal facade to lessen the apparent bulk of the building, and construction of garden and park features on the broad sidewalk surrounding the building. For a detailed review of the land acquisition and construction of the building, see Thorson (1992–94).

lateral and multilateral, in the margins of the main conference.[66] Every third year, when the Annual Meetings convene away from Washington, a synergy usually develops that spurs the governors beyond routine and impels the Bretton Woods institutions in new directions.[67] At Belgrade in October 1979, governors pushed the Fund to take a more active role in lending to developing countries (Chapter 13). At Toronto in September 1982, a funereal gathering worried about the emerging debt crisis, urged the Fund to avoid panic, and set in motion the case-by-case debt strategy (Chapter 7). At Seoul in October 1985, the U.S. governor, James Baker, called for a new direction to the strategy that would make the World Bank more of an equal partner and would aim the process more effectively at generating economic growth (Chapter 10). At Berlin in October 1988, governors agreed to try a more collaborative strategy for dealing with arrears to the Fund (Chapter 16).

Operationally, the Board of Governors is called upon to vote on major issues such as approval of quota increases, SDR allocations, membership applications, and amendments to the Articles of Agreement or the By-Laws. Most such matters are handled by mail ballot rather than during the Annual Meetings. An exception to the routine conduct of the meetings arose in 1979–80 when developing countries tabled a controversial proposal to invite the PLO to participate as an official observer. The response to this request had important implications for the Fund's relationships with other international organizations.

Some 150 senior officials, representing 42 organizations such as the United Nations and various UN agencies, the BIS, the OECD, OPEC, regional development banks, etc., attended the 1979 Annual Meetings as observers.[68] In June 1979, Mr.

---

[66]The routine business of the Annual Meetings includes approval of the institutions' financial statements, budgets, and changes in the Rules and Regulations; and the biennial election of Executive Directors. Each member country appoints a governor for the Fund and for the Bank. Typically, the finance minister and either a deputy minister or the head of the central bank serve as Governors, but other combinations—including appointment of one governor for both institutions—also occur. The two Boards of Governors have always met jointly. The formal meetings, which are preceded by meetings of the Interim and Development Committees and of various groups of members, are taken up almost entirely by a series of statements delivered by governors.

[67]The inaugural meeting of the Boards of Governors, at which the basic decisions on the location and structure of the two institutions were taken, was held in Savannah, Georgia, in March 1946. The first Annual Meeting was held that autumn in Washington, and the second in London. After meeting in Paris in 1950 and Mexico City in 1952, the governors decided to meet outside of Washington every third year, beginning with Istanbul in 1955. Between then and the period covered here, meetings were held in New Delhi (1958), Vienna (1961), Tokyo (1964), Rio de Janeiro (1967), Copenhagen (1970), Nairobi (1973), and Manila (1976).

[68]For a complete list, see IMF, *Summary Proceedings*, 1979, pp. 365–67. Another 11 institutions were granted observer status but did not send representatives on that occasion. In addition to observers, a large number of individuals attend the meetings with designations such as "guest," "special guest," or "visitor." Only official delegations and observers have access to the plenary sessions. For a complete list and description of organizations invited in 1979, see IMF/CF (G 820 "observers at Annual Meetings, 1946–1990"), "Practice of the Bank and Fund Regarding Invitations to Send observers to Bank/Fund Annual Meetings" (undated). A detailed chronology of invitations to observers from 1946 through 1979, by Milton Chamberlain, "Informal Notes on Observers, November 1979," may be found in IMF/CF (G 820 "Observers at Annual Meetings, 1946–1990"), A longer and more detailed chronology is in IMF/CF "Observers at Annual Meetings 1946–1999 (Mr. Dennison)."

Walid Kamhawi, president of the Palestine National Fund of the PLO, wrote to the Fund and the Bank to express the desire of the PLO to attend as an observer. The request presented the institutions with a major political dilemma, because the PLO was regarded by many countries as a legitimate movement of national liberation and was recognized by the UN as the representative of the Palestinian people, but was regarded by some countries as a terrorist organization. On technical grounds, the request could have been viewed either positively or negatively. The Fund's policies on inviting observers were based generally on Article X of the Articles of Agreement, which requires the Fund to "cooperate . . . with any general international organization and with public international organizations having specialized responsibilities in related fields." Although the applicability of that provision to the PLO was not obvious, the PLO already enjoyed observer status at the United Nations and had the support of the UN General Assembly for similar status in all UN specialized agencies.[69]

After several weeks of quiet negotiations failed to produce a satisfactory response from the Fund, Mohamed Finaish, Executive Director from Libya, asked the Managing Director to put the question to the Executive Board. The Board discussed it in restricted session and approved a decision "not to recommend to the Chairman of the Board of Governors to invite the Palestine Liberation Organization to send an observer to the 1979 Annual Meetings." Seven Directors, all from developing countries and holding a total of 27 percent of the voting power, expressed support for Finaish's proposal to invite the PLO. Nine others, all from industrial countries and holding a total of 56 percent of the vote, expressed opposition. The remaining five abstained, either because they lacked instructions from their authorities or because their consituencies were split.[70] The Bank's Executive Directors reached a similar conclusion. If the PLO had had a lower political profile, that would very probably have settled the matter.

In September 1979, the Group of 77 developing countries (G-77) met in Belgrade just before the meetings were scheduled to begin there, under the chairmanship of Petar Kostić (Yugoslavia's minister of finance). Remarkably for such a large and diverse group, the G-77 reached unanimous agreement to propose to Robert D. Muldoon (prime minister and minister of finance and chairman of that year's Annual Meetings), that the PLO be invited. That level of support forced the governors to take their own concrete steps to deal with the request. Muldoon could

---

[69]"Background Material for Meeting of Informal Working Party of Governors," November 2, 1979; in IMF/CF (G 820 "Informal Notes on Observers, November 1979"), "Palestine Liberation Organization—Request for Observer Status."

[70]Once the motion to invite the PLO as an observer failed, Jacques de Groote (Belgium) proposed a compromise under which the Managing Director would invite the PLO as a special guest, a category conveying only slightly less access and cachet. An informal canvas of Executive Directors revealed that this motion would also fail, albeit by a much smaller margin, and the idea was not pursued further. See Decision No. 6261-(79/156), adopted September 14, 1979; "Restricted Session—Request for Observer Status," EBAP/79/371 (December 20, 1979); and memorandum from Leo Van Houtven (Secretary) to the Managing Director (September 18, 1979), in IMF/CF (G 820 "Informal Notes on Observers, November 1979").

have ruled on the matter on his own authority as chairman, but in view of the evident sensitivity he decided to put the issue to the Joint Procedures Committee.

The Joint Procedures Committee, an advisory group of 21 governors chaired by the Chairman of the Annual Meetings, was convened on an as-needed basis, to decide on issues such as credentials disputes for member countries' delegations. On this occasion, Muldoon called a meeting of the committee for Monday, October 1, on the evening before the Annual Meetings were to start. It quickly became apparent that they would not reach a consensus, as some industrial countries strongly resisted the will of the G-77. As Chairman, Muldoon had full discretion to decide the matter, and he signaled to the committee that he was likely to follow the earlier negative recommendation of the Executive Boards. After a dinner break, the committee agreed by consensus to sidestep its own impasse and ask the Chairman to appoint an informal working party to study the issue. The working party would be asked to report back to the Chairman of the *next* Annual Meetings within three months.[71] That action effectively postponed the issue and prevented the PLO from attending the meetings in Belgrade. It also raised the political stakes, in that a positive decision for 1980 would give a PLO delegation high visibility in Washington in the final weeks of a presidential election campaign.[72]

The working party comprised eight governors or their designated representatives: four each from developing and industrial countries. Although Muldoon hoped to resolve the issue in one meeting, the group had to meet three times: in November 1979 and in February and June 1980.[73] After the first two meetings, positions remained firmly fixed, with all governors from developing countries favoring the request and all others expressing reservations or opposing it. The third meeting failed to change any minds, and the final report concluded by simply reporting the four-four split.[74]

By the time the working party issued its report, the political balance had shifted diametrically. The chairman for the 1980 Meetings was Amir H. Jamal (the minister of finance of Tanzania), an active supporter of the PLO cause. Shortly after receiving the report, Jamal wrote to the Managing Director and the President of the World Bank to say that he wished to extend an invitation to the PLO. The institutions' managements, however, replied that the by-laws required consultation with the Executive Boards, and they insisted on a Board discussion before acting on Jamal's request.[75]

---

[71]"Report on the 1979 Annual Meeting," EBD/79/241 (October 12, 1979), Annex III.

[72]On the relevance of the U.S. presidential campaign, see memorandum from Joseph W. Lang (Deputy Secretary) to the Managing Director (May 5, 1980), with handwritten response from de Larosière; in IMF/CF (G 820 "Informal Notes on Observers, November 1979").

[73]The working party comprised the Governors for Belgium, France, Germany, Indonesia, New Zealand, Nigeria, Pakistan, and Yugoslavia. The first two meetings, which were held at the IMF office in Paris, were chaired by the deputy prime minister and minister of foreign affairs of New Zealand, B.E. Talboys. Muldoon chaired the final meeting in June, at the same venue.

[74]"Report of Informal Working Party of Governors," EBD/80/187 (July 7, 1980).

[75]"Observers to the 1980 Annual Meeting of the Board of Governors—Application of the PLO," EBS/80/163 (July 21, 1980).

The U.S. authorities—supported by the President of the World Bank, Robert S. McNamara—then took the lead in heading off Jamal's intentions, by introducing a resolution to be submitted to the full Board of Governors for a vote. The resolution noted that the by-laws were vague on the procedures for inviting outsiders to the Meetings, called on the Executive Boards to propose amendments to the by-laws, and in the meantime asked that observers be limited to those invited in 1979.[76] Both Boards took up the proposal toward the end of July, and both supported it by small majorities that reflected a clear split between industrial and developing countries. The resolution was then circulated to governors for a mail ballot without meeting.

Without further ado, the U.S. resolution presumably would have carried on a vote similar to that in the Executive Boards. Developing countries, however, used their political and economic leverage to great advantage to postpone and ultimately nullify the process. First, some major oil exporters in the Middle East informed the Managing Director privately that they would not be willing to lend to the Fund as long as the PLO was excluded from the Annual Meetings (see Chapter 17). Second, 16 governors from the Middle East and North Africa submitted formal requests to the Managing Director for the PLO invitation to be placed on the agenda when the governors convened in Washington at the end of September.[77] Those two actions together raised the specter of a public donnybrook that would have damaged the credibility of the Fund and the Bank and could have influenced the U.S. elections and weakened U.S. willingness to finance the institutions. Third, Jamal insisted that an invitation be issued forthwith, without waiting for Governors to vote. When the two heads of institution asked him to refrain, Jamal exploded in frustration. "It is now the whole office of Chairman of Governors which is being humiliated by Executive Directors," he cabled. "Also respect for law being eroded rapidly[;] kindly appreciate matters now beyond me" (IMF, *Summary Proceedings*, 1981, p. 343).[78]

Fourth, and most effectively, most governors who opposed the U.S. resolution declined to vote, in an effort to deny a quorum. That is where the real battle was fought. The resolution required a simple majority of votes cast, provided that a

---

[76] "Observers at the 1980 Annual Meeting," EBS/80/168 (July 28, 1980); also see related materials in IMF/CF (G 820 "Informal Notes on Observers, November 1979"). Section 5(b) of the By-Laws reads as follows: "The Chairman of the Board of Governors, in consultation with the Executive Board, may invite observers to attend any meeting of the Board of Governors." The objection was that the significance of the consultation, the extent of the privileges extended to such observers, and the meaning of "any meeting" were too vague to give appropriate guidance in controversial situations. McNamara introduced the resolution in the Bank. In the Fund, it was introduced by the U.S. Executive Director, Sam Y. Cross, and was neither supported nor opposed by management. See IMF, *Summary Proceedings*, 1981, pp. 339–42. On this and other citations below, IMF, *Summary Proceedings*, 1981 includes references to the original documents that were circulated within the Fund and the Bank.

[77] "1980 Annual Meeting—Observers," EBS/80/204 (September 19, 1980) and "1980 Annual Meetings—Addition of Item to Agenda," EBS/80/212 (September 24). These requests were to become effective if the resolution passed. In retaliation, the U.S. authorities requested that the matter be placed on the agenda if the resolution did *not* pass.

[78] The published text was edited slightly from the original cable.

simple majority of the governors, holding at least two-thirds of the total voting power, cast valid votes. In the final tally, a bare majority of 73 governors voted, out of 140. Of those, 43 voted in favor, 10 voted against, and the rest abstained.[79] Industrial countries and other supporters of the resolution invoked their own parliamentary maneuvers to ensure a quorum, first by extending the deadline and then by denying an effort by four opponents to withdraw their votes. If the more reasonable procedure of allowing withdrawals had been followed, the tally would have fallen two short of a quorum.[80]

Fifth, when the resolution passed in spite of all of these efforts, Jamal invoked his authority as Chairman. The resolution prevented him from inviting any observers other than those invited in 1979, but it left him with the authority to issue invitations within that limit. He responded immediately by announcing that he would not issue *any* observer invitations for the 1980 Meetings (IMF, *Summary Proceedings*, 1981, p. 306).

After more than a year of increasingly acrimonious dispute, this sad episode was not quite ready to fade away. The PLO issue was placed on the Meetings agenda, in the form of a new resolution focusing on the legal procedures for inviting observers. The Joint Procedures Committee held extensive meetings over four days before submitting the resolution to the full Board of Governors for a vote. That resolution (Resolution 35–12; IMF, *Summary Proceedings*, 1980, pp. 318–20), which was passed routinely the next day, created yet another committee of governors, with the specific task of reviewing the provisions in the by-laws regarding consultation and voting on observers. This ad hoc group became known as the Muldoon Committee, after its Chairman.

The Muldoon Committee held two three-day meetings, first in Manila and then in Wellington, New Zealand.[81] It issued a balanced report (IMF, *Summary Proceedings*, 1981, pp. 299–384) that did not change the outcome on this issue but did lay the groundwork for avoiding such procedural battles in the future. Governors should have the right to withdraw votes, as long as they did so before the close of voting, but the Executive Board had acted within its authority in drawing the opposite conclusion in this case. The Chairman had acted within his authority in deciding first to invite the PLO and later to issue no invitations to observers, but Executive Directors were also within their authority in submitting a resolution to the Board of Governors proposing to overrule the Chairman. This report was circulated, published, and discussed at length by the Executive Board and the 1981 Joint Procedures Committee, but no formal action was ever taken on it.

---

[79]Valid replies totaled 72 percent of the voting power; 96 percent of votes cast were in favor.

[80]For the vote tally, see "1980 Annual Meeting—Observers—Results of Voting on Board of Governors Resolution," EBS/80/207 (September 22, 1980). For the tactical debates, see "By-Law 13(E): 'Replies Received'," EBS/80/201 (September 15) and minutes of EBM/80/144 (September 16) and EBM/80/146 (September 23).

[81]The country composition of the Muldoon Committee was the same as that of the earlier Joint Committee, except that Sweden was added as a member and the Chairman (Muldoon) was not given a vote except in case of a tie. That revision avoided the possibility of repeating the deadlock that had stymied the first group. For a personal memoir, see Muldoon (1981), pp. 156–57 and 166.

Throughout the 1980s, each Annual Meetings Chairman followed Jamal's precedent of not inviting any observers.[82] One might well think that observer status at the Annual Meetings would be of small importance, but it grated painfully on the sensibilities of senior officials at the BIS (as mentioned above), the OECD, the Gulf Cooperation Council, and other organizations. The institutions gradually and quietly expanded the privileges granted to officials who came to the meetings anyway, but they moved cautiously out of fear that PLO supporters would accuse them of circumventing the Chairman's order and would reopen the entire issue. Not until 1994, after the PLO signed a provisional agreement with Israel for limited self-rule in Palestine, was the issue finally laid to rest. Invitations were then issued to organizations on the 1979 list, to several new ones, and to the PLO.

Interim Committee

> . . . it is desirable, pending the establishment of the Council, to establish an Interim Committee of the Board of Governors on the International Monetary System with an advisory role, and with a composition similar to that of the Council. . . .
>
> Resolution of the Board of Governors, October 1974[83]

The Interim Committee was a committee of Fund governors established in 1974 as a temporary advisory group that would ultimately be replaced by a formal decision-making body. It replaced the identically structured Committee of Twenty (C-20), which met from 1972 to 1974 for the specific purpose of devising reforms to the international monetary system in the wake of the collapse in the Bretton Woods system of fixed but adjustable exchange rates. The permanent body, to be known as the Council, was not established, and the Interim Committee gradually took on a permanent status as the primary guide and overseer for the work of the Fund. It was reconstituted in 1999 as the International Monetary and Financial Committee (IMFC).

At first glance, establishing a ministerial-level Council would seem to be a natural and even inevitable step for the Fund. The Board of Governors is far too large a body to play an effective operational role on an ongoing basis, and the Executive Board is not constituted at a high enough political level to operate without oversight. The C-20 assumed that the Council would be created soon after the Second Amendment to the Articles became effective, and it established the Interim Committee as a bridge to that point. The Interim Committee was to have the same composition as the C-20: each country or group of countries represented on the Executive Board was to appoint a governor as a member of the Interim Committee. As mandated in the resolution quoted at the head of this section, the new committee would meet a few times each year and would "advise and report to the

---

[82]The only exceptions were for Switzerland, with which the Fund and the Bank had uniquely close financial relationships; the United Nations, with which both institutions had formal reciprocal agreements providing for attendance at each other's meetings; the International Fund for Agricultural Development, a UN agency with which the Bank had a similar formal agreement; and countries with active applications for membership.

[83]The full resolution is reprinted in de Vries (1985), Vol. 3, pp. 213–15.

Board of Governors" on issues related to the international monetary system and on possible amendments to the Articles of Agreement.

The Council, as provided for by the Second Amendment, would differ from the Interim Committee in that it would have the power to take formal decisions, using the same weighted-voting formulas that apply to the Board of Governors and the Executive Board.[84] As an advisory body, the Interim Committee operated instead by consensus and did not take formal votes. Developing and small countries therefore had more leverage in the Interim Committee than they have in the Fund generally and would have in the Council. Replacing the Interim Committee or the IMFC with the Council requires an 85 percent majority, and from the beginning the countries that benefited from the "interim" situation showed little enthusiasm for abandoning it.[85]

A leading advocate of creating the Council was the U.S. government, which formally proposed it at the Belgrade meetings in 1979 as a way to strengthen the legitimacy of Fund surveillance.[86] The Executive Board took up the proposal in February 1980, but the U.S. Executive Director, Sam Y. Cross, failed to generate much support for it. Although Cross anticipated controversy and argued that the Council should not compete with the Executive Board and should deal only with broad policy issues, Directors from a wide range of industrial and developing countries worried that a formal Council would detract from the authority of both the Executive Board and the Board of Governors. Several also expressed concern that the Council would lack the flexibility of the Interim Committee.[87] The proposal was thus shelved, and it was not raised again in the Board during this period of history.[88]

---

[84]The application of voting power differs between the Board of Governors and the Executive Board, in that Executive Directors cast votes in a single bloc. All of the votes for a multicountry constituency are cast as a unit by the Executive Director. Members of the Council, in contrast, would be allowed to split their votes according to the preferences of the individual countries in their constituencies.

[85]The provisions for establishing the Council are found in Article XII, Section 1, and Schedule D, of the Articles as amended in 1978. For the official commentary on the purposes of the Council, see de Vries (1985), Vol. 3, pp. 360–62. When the Managing Director (Johannes Witteveen) proposed creating the Council in 1974, he received unanimous support from the C-20; see especially the minutes of Meeting No. 9 of the C-20 Deputies (January 14–15, 1974), in IMF/CF (C/XX/DEP/Meeting 74/1—Final; Master File). Only later, in light of experience with the Interim Committee, did doubts arise about the wisdom of replacing an advisory with a decision-making body.

[86]The U.S. governor, Treasury Secretary G. William Miller, called in his Annual Meetings speech in Belgrade for "bolder action" to strengthen Fund surveillance. As one step, he suggested that "we might now give serious consideration to the establishment of the Council, as successor to the Interim Committee, and give it a more specific and direct role in the surveillance process." IMF, Summary Proceedings, 1979, p. 116.

[87]Cross was supported by Paul Mentré de Loye (France), Lamberto Dini (Italy), Jacques de Groote (Belgium), and Mohammed Yeganeh (Alternate—Iran). See minutes of EBM/80/19–20 (February 6, 1980).

[88]C. Fred Bergsten raised the issue again during the commemorations of the Fund's fiftieth anniversary, as part of a wider proposal for strengthening the IMF to oversee a system of target zones for exchange rates. See his paper in Boughton and Lateef (1995), especially pp. 51–55. In 1998, the minister of finance of France, Dominique Strauss-Kahn, reopened the proposal for the Council, and Camdessus announced his support in a speech to the Royal Institute of International Affairs in London (IMF Survey, May 25, 1998, p. 163). The 1999 decision to establish the IMFC effectively killed that effort for the time being.

After an initial meeting in October 1974, the Interim Committee began meeting semiannually: each fall (around end-September) as a prelude to the Annual Meetings of the Board of Governors; and each spring along with the Development Committee, usually in April or May.[89] Within a few years, as a high-level advisory body with regularly scheduled meetings, the committee ran into difficulties avoiding being swallowed by its own routine. Meetings would begin with a morning round of formal statements by members, addressing an agenda that had been prepared by the Executive Board in consultation with the staff and the committee Chairman, with several hundred "associates" in attendance.[90] Even in the somewhat smaller "restricted" sessions in the afternoon, spontaneous give and take was difficult to achieve. Consequently, although the Interim Committee served the important function of guiding the Fund's responses to policy initiatives, only rarely was it able to do much more than ratify or discourage initiatives that had been carefully worked out in advance, most often in the Executive Board.

During much of the Interim Committee's first decade, it also suffered from a lack of leadership continuity. The practice was for the Committee to elect one of its members to be Chairman and to allow him to serve as long as he remained in office. For better or worse, finance ministers come and go in response to the vicissitudes of the political parties that they serve; whether a Chairman served for a short or long time was unaffected by how well he served the committee.[91] At the spring 1979 meeting, Denis Healey (United Kingdom) presided over the last of his four meetings as the third Chairman of the Committee.[92] He then resigned following the defeat of the Callaghan government by Margaret Thatcher's Conservatives. That led to the election of Filippo Maria Pandolfi (Italy) to be the fourth Chairman. He presided over two eventful meetings, both on the road: Belgrade in October 1979 and Hamburg the following April. Pandolfi was unable to attend the September 1980 meeting in Washington, and Hannes Androsch (Austria) presided in his absence. The committee then elected René Monory (France) to

---

[89]The only significant exception to this schedule came in 1983, when the Interim Committee met in February to consider the proposed increase in Fund quotas, and the Development Committee met at its regularly scheduled date in April; see Chapter 17. For a general history of the Interim Committee's first decade, see de Vries (1985), pp. 158–68. The communiqués of meetings through 1978 were reprinted in de Vries (1985), Vol. 3, pp. 217–42. For subsequent communiqués, see the Fund's *Annual Report* or the *IMF Survey*. The Development Committee was established at the same time as the Interim Committee, as a committee of governors to advise the Boards of Governors of the Fund and the World Bank on development issues. As a practical matter, the work of the Development Committee related primarily to the Bank rather than the Fund, and it was not given the same degree of operational significance as the Interim Committee. See de Vries (1985), pp. 972–75.

[90]The provision for associates enabled attendance by officials of member countries that were not represented in the membership of the committee, and of additional officials from the represented countries.

[91]Members of the Interim Committee are normally governors of the Fund and are either finance ministers or central bank governors in their home country. By tradition, the Chairman has always been selected from among the ministers on the committee.

[92]John Turner (Canada, 1974–75) had been first, followed by Willy de Clercq (Belgium, 1976–77).

succeed him, but his government was defeated in the Socialist sweep of 1981, and he never presided over a meeting.

Normally, the Interim Committee chose its chair quietly, through a canvass of members during the interval between meetings. Because a meeting was impending at the time of Monoroy's resignation, it was necessary to elect a chairman at that meeting, which was held in Libreville, Gabon. Geoffrey Howe (United Kingdom) allowed his name to be put forward with the expectation that he would be approved by acclamation. To his surprise and disappointment, an unprecedented contest loomed when the Algerian finance minister suddenly proposed Allan J. MacEachen (Canada) as an alternate candidate. To avoid embarrassment, Howe withdrew from contention (see Howe, 1994, pp. 217–18). MacEachen was elected as the sixth Chairman and presided over four meetings, the last being on his home ground, at the Annual Meetings in Toronto in September 1982.

Howe proved himself to be an able tortoise, as he was finally elected Chairman in December 1982. He worked closely with de Larosière to persuade the committee to agree to meet early, in February 1983, so as to approve the Eighth General Review of Quotas (Chapter 17). He presided over that meeting, held in Washington during a major blizzard, and then resigned following a cabinet shuffle in which he became foreign secretary of the United Kingdom.

In addition to his contribution to resolving the political debate on the quota review, Howe had a lasting impact on the committee's meeting practices. Until then, the committee made what Howe called an annual "perambulation" to meet somewhere away from Washington: either in the spring, if the Annual Meetings were being held in Washington that fall, or wherever the Meetings were being held in the fall.[93] Howe regarded that practice as excessively costly, and he decided to terminate it (Howe, 1994, p. 177). From then on, the committee held all of its spring meetings at Fund headquarters in Washington and met outside of Washington only in conjunction with the Annual Meetings.

The committee's second Chairman, Willy de Clercq (Belgium), returned to succeed Howe in 1983 and presided over the next three meetings. When he left office, the committee elected H. Onno Ruding (Netherlands) to take over. As a former Executive Director (1977–80), Ruding knew the Fund intimately. Serendipitously but just as importantly, he was a member of a government that would enjoy several years in office, allowing him to serve as Chairman for five years, through the final meeting of 1989.

Ruding introduced procedural changes to increase the flexibility and spontaneity of the meetings. He allowed each member of the committee just seven minutes to deliver a prepared statement, which freed the afternoon session for an informal and more spontaneous discussion. To further promote interaction among Governors, he sharply reduced the number of people invited in the after-

---

[93]The Committee met outside of Washington on its own on six occasions: in Paris (June 1975), Kingston, Jamaica (January 1976), Mexico City (April 1978), Hamburg (April 1980), Libreville (May 1981), and Helsinki (May 1982).

noon.[94] He made a practice of arriving in Washington several days before the meeting, getting thoroughly briefed, and meeting bilaterally with as many colleagues as possible. Consequently, the Committee began to assume a somewhat more active role in influencing Fund policies such as the establishment of the SAF (see the introduction to Chapter 14), the implementation of the Baker and Brady debt strategies, the intensified strategy for dealing with arrears, and the ninth quota review.

Executive Board

> The Executive Board shall be responsible for conducting the business of the Fund, and for this purpose shall exercise all the powers delegated to it by the Board of Governors.

Article XII, Section 3(a)

It would be easy to fall into the trap of underestimating the influence of the Executive Board during the 1980s. Critics often point to the rarity of rejections of lending proposals put to the Board by management, which is certainly a fact. Three examples of such rejections are described in earlier chapters.[95] Chapter 13 records a battle over a stand-by arrangement for Sierra Leone in 1979, which resulted in a reduction in the size of the initial drawing. Chapter 15 includes the stories of rebellions in 1981 over a proposed EFF arrangement for Grenada, which was approved two months later as a shorter-term stand-by arrangement; and a proposed rescheduling of a CFF repayment for Sudan, which was approved with a much shorter maturity. Otherwise, once requests for financing were approved by management, they faced a fairly smooth passage.

This fact, however, does not imply that the Board was a rubber stamp for management decisions. The Board's influence was exerted far more directly and forcefully on broad policy issues and general procedures than on specific lending decisions. Even on the latter, the Managing Director quite commonly declined to bring requests to the Board after canvassing all or some Executive Directors informally and determining that the proposed action was unlikely to pass. More formally, the Board's regular discussions of the work program, policy decisions, and the World Economic Outlook set the agenda for the institution, while its preliminary discussions of various issues guided the staff in honing policy proposals to a point that could win approval. Management and staff often sought to influence that process by manipulating the range of questions and choices put to the Board, and what

---

[94]The intimacy was only relative. In the morning, there were to be nearly 500 people in the room, including several associates (as many as 30 in some cases) for each of the 22 committee members, plus the 22 Executive Directors and nearly 30 staff and observers. In the afternoon, each member was restricted to 2–4 associates and the Executive Director, and there were to be no more than 7 staff and observers, so that total attendance (including the Chairman and the Managing Director) would be about 100 people.

[95]Also see Chapter 16, which relates the Board's temporary overruling of a management proposal to declare Zambia ineligible to use Fund resources in 1987.

typically followed was a series of parries and thrusts until a satisfactory compromise was reached.

Formal votes were seldom taken, either for financing requests or on policy decisions. Rather, the Secretary would infer from each intervention whether the speaker favored or opposed the proposal, and from that list determined whether the necessary support existed. On that basis, the Chairman would indicate whether "the sense of the meeting" was that the proposal was approved or failed.[96] When objections to a proposal were raised, the nature and extent of the objection would be recorded in the minutes and reflected in the Chairman's summing up of the meeting. The cumulative effect of such comments constituted an additional avenue by which the Board made its influence felt. Alexandre Kafka (1996, p. 327) neatly summed up this process as follows.

> When the Board is dissatisfied . . . it will generally limit itself to expressing doubts and warnings against a repetition of a management proposal similar to the criticized one. There is a sensible basis for this way of proceeding. . . . If the Board refused arrangements negotiated by the staff under authority of the management, it would deprive the staff of the authority . . . of negotiating agreements until they had been approved, at least in outline, by the Executive Board.

The nature of the Executive Board was one of the battlegrounds on which John Maynard Keynes sought to influence the structure of the Fund in the 1940s. Keynes wanted a high-level Board, which would meet infrequently enough that the office could be filled by senior officials whose main responsibilities would still be in their home governments. That structure, he believed, would have given management more leeway to run the Fund as a technocratic rather than a political institution. At Bretton Woods in 1944, he tried unsuccessfully to insert phrasing in the Articles of Agreement stating that Executive Directors "need not be Governors" (i.e., that they normally would be Governors or at least senior deputies) and that they "shall meet not less than once every three months."[97] At the inaugural meeting of the Board of Governors in 1946, he tried—again without success—to write the By-Laws in a way that would ward off full-time Executive Directors. Throughout, the U.S. preference for closer political control prevailed, and the Executive Board became a full-time body resident in Washington.[98]

---

[96]This phrasing was initiated in September 1946, when the Executive Board first adopted Rules and Regulations for the conduct of its meetings. Rule C-10 specified that the "Chairman will ordinarily ascertain the sense of the meeting in lieu of a formal vote" (Horsefield, 1969, Vol. 3, p. 290). The following May, the Board defined the sense of the meeting as "a position supported by Executive Directors having sufficient votes to carry the question were a vote to be taken." For an overview of Executive Board operating procedures, see de Vries (1985), pp. 983–1000.

[97]In a February 1946 letter to R.H. Brand (a member of the British delegation at Bretton Woods), Keynes suggested that "Deputy Governors of central banks" and similar "very responsible people in the heart of their own institutions" would be appropriate choices for Executive Directors under his conception. See Moggridge (1980), pp. 208–9.

[98]See Horsefield (1969), Vol. 1, pp. 130–35. The British proposal at Bretton Woods is in U.S. Department of State (1948), Vol. 1, pp. 45–46.

People

Notwithstanding Keynes's disappointment in the outcome, the Executive Board was sprinkled with prominent names. The first U.S. Director was Harry Dexter White, who had been Assistant Secretary of the U.S. Treasury in charge of international economic policy and who was responsible for much of the design of the Fund.[99] In the Executive Board's first half century, some two dozen Directors had been finance or economy minister in their home country before joining the Board. Notable examples included Camille Gutt (Belgium, 1946, and also the Fund's first Managing Director), Pierre Mendès-France (France, 1946, and also a future prime minister of France),[100] Pieter Lieftinck (Netherlands, 1955–76), Antoine W. Yaméogo (Upper Volta, 1964–76), Erik Brofoss (Norway, 1970–73), Nazih Deif (Egypt, 1970–76), Jahangir Amuzegar (Iran, 1973–80), Abderrahmane Alfidja (Niger, 1978–86), E.I.M. Mtei (Tanzania, 1982–86), and Alejandro Végh (Uruguay, 1990–92).[101] A similar number had served as central bank governors. Louis Rasminsky, a member of the Canadian delegation at Bretton Woods (where he chaired the Drafting Committee of the Fund's Articles of Agreement) and Canada's first Executive Director (1946–62), served simultaneously as governor of the Bank of Canada in the early 1960s; see Muirhead (1999).

In other cases, people who were making their way up through the government hierarchy spent a few years on the Executive Board and reached the pinnacle of their careers somewhat later.[102] Perhaps the two most prominent examples were both Italian: Guido Carli (1947–52), who went on to become governor of the Bank of Italy and later the treasury minister; and Lamberto Dini (1976–80), who later held various ministerial positions, including prime minister in 1995–96. Four U.S. Executive Directors were subsequently appointed Deputy Managing Director of the Fund: Andrew N. Overby in 1949, Frank A. Southard, Jr., in 1962, William B. Dale in 1974, and Richard D. Erb in 1984. Uniquely, Ahmed Zaki Saad (Egypt)—a dominant member of the Board from 1946 until his retirement in 1970—simultaneously held a variety of top-level government positions, including under secretary of state in the Egyptian ministry of finance in the late 1940s and governor of the National Bank of Egypt in the 1950s. Saad also served as governor in the Fund for Saudi Arabia from 1958 to 1977 and as Chairman of the Annual Meetings in both 1955 and 1962.

---

[99]At the time, the assistant secretaries were senior deputies reporting directly to the Secretary. The Secretary is the U.S. equivalent of a finance minister. For an overview of White's role, see Boughton (1998).

[100]Mendès-France, however, served on the Board for only two months and never attended a Board meeting.

[101]Dates in this list are for the period of service on the Executive Board, which in some cases includes a term as Alternate.

[102]In at least one such case, the minister later returned to the Board. After serving as Uganda's first Executive Director in the Fund (1964–66), Semyano Kiingi became governor of the Bank of Uganda (1971–73) and then finance minister (1973–77). He served again on the Executive Board from 1978 to 1982.

Most often, Executive Directors came to the Fund from mid-level government positions one or a few steps below the deputy level.[103] Their status and their role in the Fund was perhaps the economic equivalent of ambassadors in the foreign service. They were expected both to represent the views of their home countries (or of the group of countries that elected them) and to represent the views of the Fund to their constituent governments.

The membership of the Board—Directors and their Alternates—during the period covered by this History is listed in Table 20.3.[104] Evident from this table is a high rate of turnover. Throughout the 1980s, about one-half of the Executive Directors had no more than three years' experience on the Board (including service as Alternates in a few cases). "Institutional memory" thus resided in a few Directors with unusually long service at the Fund, notably Jacques J. Polak, Alexandre Kafka, Byanti Kharmawan, Jacques de Groote, and Mohamed Finaish.

Jacques Polak was without peer as an intellectual force and institutional pillar at the Fund. He became the Executive Director for the Netherlands constituency in January 1981, following a career with the IMF that had carried him from the Dutch delegation at the Bretton Woods conference in July 1944 to senior positions that included Director of Research (1958–79), Economic Counsellor (1966–79), and Advisor to the Managing Director (1979–80).[105] He made his most significant and lasting intellectual contribution in the early 1950s, by developing a model of the monetary approach to the balance of payments that became the foundation for the Fund's approach to conditionality (see Chapter 13). In his last staff role, he oversaw much of the effort to strengthen the SDR as a viable market asset and to try (unsuccessfully) to establish a substitution account for SDRs (Chapter 18). As Executive Director, in addition to continuing to work on broad institutional issues from the "other side of the table," he became closely involved in the development of adjustment programs in Yugoslavia, which was part of his constituency (again see Chapter 13). After retiring from the Board, he was named President of the Per Jacobsson Foundation, which honors the Fund's third Managing Director (1956–1963) by sponsoring annual lectures by prominent economists and policymakers. Ten years later, at the age of 82, having been honored both by his native Netherlands (with the Pierson Medal, awarded at the Netherlands Bank) and by the world economic community (with a festschrift in 1991), Jacques Polak finally

---

[103]Horsefield (1969), Vol. 1, lists the main government positions held by each Executive Director of 1946 and 1968 on pp. 137–38 and 615–16, respectively. De Vries (1976), Vol. 1, lists positions for the Directors of 1971 on pp. 627–30.

[104]For the earlier composition, see Horsefield (1969), Vol. 1, pp. 620–34; de Vries (1976), Vol. 1, pp. 655–62; and de Vries (1985), pp. 1045–55.

[105]The reader will find that Polak is cited often throughout this History in each of his major roles. Also see his summary professional memoirs in the Introduction to Polak (1994b); the profiles in de Vries (1985), p. 1020, and Frenkel and Goldstein (1991, pp. 3–4); and citations throughout the first three Histories.

Table 20.3. Executive Directors and Their Alternates, 1979–89

Part I. Appointed Directors

Country	Executive Director (Alternate)	Dates of Service
United States	Sam Y. Cross	5/3/74–1/10/81
	Thomas Leddy	11/5/75–4/30/79
	Donald Syvrud	5/1/79–10/4/81
	Richard D. Erb	7/18/81–5/31/84
	Charles H. Dallara	8/2/82–9/19/83
	Mary K. Bush	12/13/83–12/24/87
	Charles H. Dallara	10/5/84–5/26/89
	Charles S. Warner	7/15/88–7/14/90
	Thomas C. Dawson II	9/21/89–9/7/93
United Kingdom	William S. Ryrie	10/17/75–1/2/80
	Pendarell Kent	5/3/76–6/22/79
	Lionel D.D. Price	6/23/79–7/31/81
	John Anson	1/3/80–5/1/83
	Christopher Taylor	8/1/81–9/30/83
	Nigel Wicks	5/2/83–8/31/85
	T.A. Clark	10/1/83–11/10/85
	T.P. Lankester	9/1/85–1/24/88
	Michael Foot	11/11/85–10/30/87
	Charles Enoch	10/31/87–7/13/90
	Frank Cassell	1/25/88–7/22/90
Germany, Fed. Rep. of	Eckard Pieske	1/1/75–6/30/79
	Gerhard Laske	1/1/75–6/30/79
	Gerhard Laske	7/1/79–8/31/84
	Guenter Winkelmann	8/1/79–8/31/82
	Guenter Grosche	9/1/82–8/31/84
	Guenter Grosche	9/1/84–12/9/90
	Bernd Goos	9/1/84–12/9/90
France	Paul Mentré de Loye	9/5/78–11/30/81
	Denis Samuel-Lajeunesse	9/5/78–8/31/79
	Thierry Aulagnon	9/1/79–8/31/81
	Anne Le Lorier	9/1/81–8/31/83
	Bruno de Maulde	12/1/81–1/24/86
	Xavier Blandin	9/1/83–8/31/85
	Sylvain de Forges	9/1/85–8/31/87
	Hélène Ploix	2/24/86–10/1/89
	Dominique Marcel	9/1/87–9/20/89
	Jean-François Cirelli	9/21/89–9/25/91
	Jean-Pierre Landau	10/30/89–9/10/93
Japan	Masanao Matsunaga	11/1/76–11/9/79
	Rei Masunaga	7/20/76–6/11/79
	Akira Nagashima	6/12/79–12/24/81
	Teruo Hirao	11/10/79–7/27/84
	Tadaie Yamashita	12/25/81–12/12/84
	Hirotake Fujino	7/28/84–12/21/86
	Masahiro Sugita	12/13/84–12/11/87
	Koji Yamazaki	12/22/86–8/25/91
	Shinichi Yoshikuni	12/12/87–12/24/90
Saudi Arabia	Mahsoun B. Jalal	11/1/78–4/30/81
	Yusuf A. Nimatallah	1/15/79–4/30/81
	Yusuf A. Nimatallah	5/1/81–6/30/90
	Samir El-Khouri	10/10/81–6/2/82
	Jobarah E. Suraisry	6/3/82–10/31/86
	Ibrahim Al-Assaf	11/1/86–10/10/89
	Muhammad Al-Jasser	10/11/89–6/30/90

Table 20.3. (continued)

Constituency[a]	Executive Director (Alternate)[b]	Dates of Service[c]
Part II. Elected Directors		
Greece	Lamberto Dini (Italy)	7/6/76–10/31/80
Italy	*Costa P. Caranicas (Greece)*	11/1/78–4/30/84
Malta	Giovanni Lovato (Italy)	11/1/80–10/31/84
Poland (from 1988)	*Nikolaos Coumbis (Greece)*	11/1/84–4/30/86
Portugal	Salvatore Zecchini (Italy)	11/1/84–1/16/89
	Nikos Kyriazidis (Greece)	5/1/86–1/17/92
	Renato Filosa (Italy)	1/17/89–1/14/93
Costa Rica	Joaquín Muns (Spain)	11/1/78–10/31/80
El Salvador	*Ariel Buira (Mexico)*	11/1/78–10/31/80
Guatemala	Ariel Buira (Mexico)	11/1/80–10/31/82
Honduras	*Miguel A. Senior (Venezuela)*	11/1/80–10/31/82
Mexico	Miguel A. Senior (Venezuela)	11/1/82–10/31/84
Nicaragua	*José Luis Feito (Spain)*	11/1/82–10/31/84
Spain	Pedro Pérez (Spain)	11/1/84–10/31/86
Venezuela	*Guillermo Ortiz (Mexico)*	11/1/84–10/31/86
	Guillermo Ortiz (Mexico)	11/1/86–10/31/88
	Leonor Filardo (Venezuela)	11/1/86–10/31/88
	Leonor Filardo (Venezuela)	11/1/88–10/31/90
	Miguel A. Fernández Ordóñez (Spain)	11/1/88–10/15/90
Cyprus	H.O. Ruding (Netherlands)	1/1/77–12/31/80
Israel	*Tom de Vries (Netherlands)*	1/9/69–1/15/85
Netherlands	J.J. Polak (Netherlands)	1/1/81–10/31/86
Romania	*J. de Beaufort Wijnholds (Netherlands)*	1/16/85–7/15/87
Yugoslavia	G.A. Posthumus (Netherlands)	11/1/86–10/31/94
	G.P.J. Hogeweg (Netherlands)	7/24/87–7/28/91
Austria	Jacques de Groote (Belgium)	11/1/73–3/31/94
Belgium	*Heinrich G. Schneider (Austria)*	12/1/70–6/30/87
Hungary (from 1982)	*Johann Prader (Austria)*	7/1/87–
Luxembourg		
Turkey		
Bahrain	Mohamed Finaish (Libya)	11/1/78–10/31/92
Egypt (from 1986)	*Kadhim A. Al-Eyd (Iraq)*	5/24/77–3/31/81
Iraq	*Tariq Alhaimus (Iraq)*	5/17/81–6/21/87
Jordan	*Abdul Moneim Othman (Iraq)*	6/22/87–12/31/90
Kuwait		
Lebanon		
Libya		
Maldives		
Oman (from 1983)		
Pakistan		
Qatar		
Somalia		
Syrian Arab Republic		
United Arab Emirates		
Yemen Arab Republic		
Yemen, People's Democratic Rep. of		

Table 20.3. *(continued)*

Constituency[a]	Executive Director (Alternate)[b]	Dates of Service[c]
Antigua & Barbuda (from 1982)	Bernard J. Drabble (Canada)	11/1/74–5/7/81
The Bahamas	*Donal Lynch (Ireland)*	11/1/75–3/31/80
Barbados	*Michael Casey (Ireland)*	4/1/80–9/30/83
Belize (from 1982)	Robert K. Joyce (Canada)	5/8/81–10/15/85
Canada	*Luke Leonard (Ireland)*	10/1/83–10/17/86
Dominica	Marcel Massé (Canada)	10/16/85–9/27/89
Grenada	*Dara McCormack (Ireland)*	10/18/86–10/26/89
Ireland	C. Scott Clark (Canada)	9/29/89–11/1/92
Jamaica	*Gabriel C. Noonan (Ireland)*	10/27/89–10/31/92
St. Kitts & Nevis (St. Christopher & Nevis) (from 1984)		
St. Lucia (from 1980)		
St. Vincent (from 1980)		
Australia	Robert J. Whitelaw (Australia)	4/14/75–1/21/81
Kiribati (from 1986)	*R.J. Lang (New Zealand)*	11/1/78–10/31/80
Korea	*Placido L. Mapa, Jr. (Philippines)*	11/1/80–5/31/81
New Zealand	A.R.G. Prowse (Australia)	1/22/81–2/15/85
Papua New Guinea	*Benito Legarda (Philippines)*	6/1/81–10/31/82
Philippines	*Kerry G. Morrell (New Zealand)*	11/1/82–10/31/84
Seychelles	*Antonio V. Romuáldez (Philippines)*	11/1/84–10/31/86
Solomon Islands	Charles R. Rye (Australia)	2/16/85–4/28/89
Vanuatu (from 1982)	*Chang-Yuel Lim (Korea)*	11/1/86–5/31/89
Western Samoa	E.A. Evans (Australia)	4/29/89–4/28/93
	Seung-Woo Kwon (Korea)	6/1/89–10/31/90
Denmark	Matti Vanhala (Finland)	11/1/78–10/31/80
Finland	*Gísli Blöndal (Iceland)*	11/1/78–2/28/81
Iceland	Jon Sigurdsson (Iceland)	11/1/80–1/15/83
Norway	*Leiv Vidvei (Norway)*	3/1/81–3/6/83
Sweden	John Tvedt (Norway)	1/16/83–12/31/84
	Arne Linda (Sweden)	3/7/83–3/10/85
	Hans Lundstrom (Sweden)	1/1/85–6/30/87
	Henrik Fugmann (Denmark)	3/11/85–5/6/87
	Jorgen Ovi (Denmark)	5/7/87–6/30/87
	Jorgen Ovi	7/1/87–6/30/89
	Markus Fogelholm (Finland)	7/1/87–6/30/89
	Markus Fogelholm (Finland)	7/1/89–10/31/91
	Mágnus Pétursson	7/1/89–1/12/90
Bangladesh	S.D. Deshmukh (India)	6/3/77–10/31/80
Bhutan (from 1982)	*Warnasena Rasaputram (Sri Lanka)*	7/1/76–3/20/79
India	*Edmund Eramudugolla (Sri Lanka)*	5/1/79–4/30/80
Sri Lanka	*D. Lakshman Kannangara (Sri Lanka)*	7/1/80–11/30/81
	M. Narasimham (India)	11/1/80–9/30/82
	A.S. Jayawardena (Sri Lanka)	12/1/81–2/31/86
	Ram N. Malhotra (India)	11/1/82–2/3/85
	Arjun K. Sengupta (India)	2/4/85–10/31/88
	L. Eustace N. Fernando (Sri Lanka)	1/1/87–1/2/95
	Bimal Jalan (India)	11/1/88–1/2/90
Brazil	Alexandre Kafka (Brazil)	11/1/66–10/31/98
Colombia	*T. Ainsworth Harewood (Trinidad & Tobago)*	1/1/78–3/14/80
Dominican Republic		
Ecuador (from 1980)	*José R. Gabriel-Peña (Dominican Republic)*	3/15/80–11/27/82
Guyana		
Haiti	*César Robalino (Ecuador)*	11/28/82–2/28/85
Panama	*Hernando A. Arias (Panama)*	3/1/85–3/31/87
Peru (to 1980)	*Jerry Hospedales (Trinidad & Tobago)*	4/1/87–3/31/89
Suriname	*Luis M. Piantini (Dominican Republic)*	4/1/89–3/31/91
Trinidad & Tobago		

Table 20.3. *(continued)*

Constituency[a]	Executive Director (Alternate)[b]	Dates of Service[c]
Fiji	Byanti Kharmawan (Indonesia)	11/1/68–10/5/82
Indonesia	*Savenaca Siwatibau (Fiji)*	11/1/78–10/31/80
Lao People's Democratic	*Vijit Supinit (Thailand)*	12/1/80–11/30/82
Republic	A. Hasnan Habib (Indonesia)	11/4/82–6/30/83
Malaysia	*Jaafar Ahmad (Malaysia)*	12/1/82–10/31/86
Myanmar (Burma)	J.E. Ismael (Indonesia)	7/1/83–10/31/96
Nepal	*Janardana Reddy (Fiji)*	11/1/86–10/31/88
Singapore	*Ekamol Kiriwat (Thailand)*	11/1/88–10/31/89
Thailand	*Tanya Sirivedhin (Thailand)*	11/1/89–10/31/92
Tonga (from 1986)		
Vietnam		
Botswana	Festus G. Mogae (Botswana)	11/1/78–10/31/80
Burundi	*Semyano Kiingi (Uganda)*	11/1/78–10/31/80
Ethiopia	Semyano Kiingi (Uganda)	11/1/80–10/31/82
The Gambia	*Andrew K. Mullei (Kenya)*	11/1/80–4/30/81
Guinea (to 1986)	*N'faly Sangare (Guinea)*	1/5/81–10/31/82
Kenya	N'faly Sangare (Guinea)	11/1/82–10/31/84
Lesotho	*E.I.M. Mtei (Tanzania)*	11/1/82–10/31/84
Liberia	E.I.M. Mtei (Tanzania)	11/1/84–10/31/86
Malawi	*Ahmed Abdallah (Kenya)*	11/1/84–10/31/86
Mozambique (from 1984)	Ahmed Abdallah (Kenya)	11/1/86–10/31/88
Nigeria	*El Tayeb El Kogali (Sudan)*	11/1/86–10/31/88
Sierra Leone	El Tayeb El Kogali (Sudan)	11/1/88–10/31/90
Sudan	*L.B. Monyake (Lesotho)*	11/1/88–10/31/90
Swaziland		
Tanzania		
Uganda		
Zambia		
Zimbabwe (from 1980)		
China (from 1980)	ZHANG Zicun (China)	
	(CHANG Tse Chun)	11/1/80–11/30/85
	TAI Qianding (China)	11/1/80–11/30/82
	WANG Enshao (China)	12/1/82–8/16/85
	JIANG Hai (China)	9/1/85–8/31/88
	HUANG Fanzhang (China)	12/1/85–10/31/86
	DAI Qianding (China)	11/1/86–9/4/91
	ZHANG Zhiziang (China)	9/1/88–12/31/91
Argentina	Francisco Garcés (Chile)	11/1/78–10/31/80
Bolivia	*Julio C. Gutiérrez (Paraguay)*	11/1/78–10/31/80
Chile	Juan Carlos Iarezza (Argentina)	11/1/80–10/31/82
Ecuador (to 1980)	*Raúl T. Salazar (Peru)*	11/1/80–10/31/82
Paraguay	Alvaro Donoso (Chile)	11/1/82–10/31/84
Peru (from 1980)	*Mario Teijeiro (Argentina)*	11/1/82–10/31/84
Uruguay	Fernando L. Nebbia (Argentina)	11/1/84–10/31/86
	Brian Jensen (Peru)	11/1/84–3/25/86
	Jaysuño Abramovich (Peru)	3/26/86–10/31/86
	Alvaro Donoso (Chile)	11/1/86–10/31/88
	Julio Dreizzen (Argentina)	11/1/86–1/14/87
	Ernesto Feldman (Argentina)	1/15/87–10/31/88
	Ernesto Feldman (Argentina)	11/1/88–10/31/90
	Ricardo J. Lombardo (Uruguay)	11/1/88–9/29/90
Afghanistan	Jahangir Amuzegar (Iran)	8/8/73–10/31/80
Algeria	*Mohammed Yeganeh (Iran)*	12/19/78–10/31/80
Ghana	Morteza Abdollahi (Iran)	11/1/80–10/31/82
Iran, Islamic Republic of	*Omar Kabbaj (Morocco)*	11/1/80–1/16/94

Table 20.3. *(concluded)*

Constituency[a]	Executive Director (Alternate)[b]	Dates of Service[c]
Morocco	Ghassem Salehkhou (Iran)	11/1/82–10/31/88
Oman (to 1982)	M.R. Ghasimi (Iran)	11/1/88–10/31/90
Tunisia		
Benin	Samuel Nana-Sinkam (Cameroon)	11/1/76–10/31/82
Burkina Faso (Upper Volta)	*Abderrahmane Alfidja (Niger)*	1/3/78–10/31/82
Cameroon	Abderrahmane Alfidja (Niger)	11/1/82–10/31/86
Cape Verde (from 1980)	*wa Bilenga Tshishimbi (Zaïre)*	12/21/82–3/21/85
Central African Republic	*Lubin K. Doe (Togo)*	5/1/85–8/4/85
Chad	*Mawakani Samba (Zaïre)*	8/5/85–10/31/86
Comoros	Mawakani Samba (Zaïre)	11/1/86–10/31/90
Congo	*Corentino Virgilio Santos (Cape Verde)*	11/15/86–10/31/90
Côte d'Ivoire		
Djibouti (from 1980)		
Equatorial Guinea		
Gabon		
Guinea (from 1986)		
Guinea-Bissau		
Madagascar		
Mali		
Mauritania		
Mauritius		
Niger		
Rwanda		
São Tomé & Príncipe		
Senegal		
Togo		
Zaïre		

[a]"From" dates indicate the year in which the country first participated in the election of the Executive Director for the listed constituency. "To" dates indicate the year that the country moved to a different constituency. Names in parentheses were in effect during the first part of the period.

[b]Alternate Executive Directors are listed under the Director who initially appointed them. Where dates overlap, the Alternate Executive Director was reappointed by the next Director.

[c]Dates are given as month/day/year.

retired from his last official IMF post. He continued to work, however, and was far from fading away.[106]

By tradition, the longest-serving Executive Director is designated as the Dean of the Executive Board. The Dean serves as an informal spokesperson for the Board and chairs certain special meetings of Executive Directors, such as those for the selection of a new Managing Director. From 1973 to 1976, that honor was held by Pieter Lieftinck (Netherlands), who had served on the Board since 1955 and who had assumed the Dean's position following the retirement of André van

---

[106]Polak's research in the 1990s was only partly retrospective (e.g., Polak, 1995, 1997, 2000). Just as often, he was writing on issues such as how the Fund could be restructured financially (Polak, 1996) or whether the Fund's mandate should be extended to cover capital account liberalization (Polak, 1998). His main publications from 1939 to 1991 are collected in Polak (1994b). For an overview of his contributions and a complete bibliography to 1991, see the festschrift volume (Frenkel and Goldstein, 1991).

Campenhout (Belgium). When Lieftinck retired, the deanship passed to Alexandre Kafka (Brazil), who had served on the Board since 1966.

Alexandre Kafka had served on the Fund staff in the late 1940s and at the United Nations in the late 1950s, and had been named Professor of Economics at the University of Virginia in the early 1960s. Originally from Prague, Czechoslovakia; educated in Geneva and Oxford; and an emigré to Brazil at the outset of the 1940s, most of his early career was in a variety of government and other positions in Brazil. Those posts included Director of the Brazilian Institute of Economics at the Getúlio Vargas Foundation and Advisor to the Minister of Finance. He was appointed Alternate Executive Director in June 1966 and was elected that fall for what would turn out to be a record-breaking length of service as Executive Director. In October 1998, at the age of 81, Kafka retired after completing his sixteenth two-year term on the Board.[107] His service and contributions to the Fund, to the Brazilian economy, to his broader constituency in Latin America, to developing countries more generally, and to the professional literature on international economic policy issues were not just lengthy. The exceptional value of those contributions was recognized in the 1990s through special honors and awards from several countries.

Byanti Kharmawan (Indonesia) came to the Fund after a 37-year career in government and private business in Indonesia, the Netherlands, and England, and a two-year period as Executive Director at the Asian Development Bank. He was elected Executive Director in the Fund in 1968 and continued to serve until his sudden death in October 1982.

Two other Directors served throughout the period of this History. Jacques de Groote (Belgium) began his career at the National Bank of Belgium in 1957, worked at the Fund for three years in van Campenhout's office, and participated in many of the discussions on reform of the international monetary system in the early 1960s. After three years with the National Bank of Zaïre, he returned to Belgium and then was elected Executive Director in the Fund in 1973. He retired in 1994. Mohamed Finaish (Libya) was appointed Alternate Executive Director to Deif in 1973, just one year after receiving a Ph.D. in Economics from the University of Southern California. He returned to the Central Bank of Libya in 1977 and then was elected as Executive Director in 1978. Despite occasional challenges to the constituency that he served, he held onto his seat until he was finally defeated in the election of 1992.[108]

Structure

The size of the Executive Board gradually rose from its original 12 members to 20 by 1964 (de Vries, 1985, pp. 764–65). Directors for five seats were appointed by the

---

[107]The deanship then passed to Abbas Mirakhor (Iran), who was first elected in 1990.

[108]In 1978, Syria nominated its existing Director, Muhammad Al-Atrash, for reelection, but several members of the constituency broke away and supported Finaish. Syria, Jordan, and Lebanon voted for Al-Atrash. When that bid failed, they designated Finaish to cast their votes on the Board. Syria nominated Al-Atrash again in 1984, but he withdrew from contention before the balloting. In 1992, Finaish lost out to A. Shakour Shaalan (Egypt).

members with the largest quotas (the United States, the United Kingdom, Germany, Japan, and France),[109] leaving 15 seats to be filled by election by the remaining members. By 1978, the Fund having grown to a membership of 138 countries, the trick was to ensure that the many small countries with low voting power would have appropriate representation. That problem was particularly acute for the African members, which had been joining in large numbers during the 1960s and 1970s and which were able to elect just two Executive Directors to look after the interests of 37 countries. One group of 16 countries was predominantly English-speaking, and a second group of 21 countries was predominantly French-speaking.[110] Even with that large a flock, the Executive Director for the Francophone African countries (Samuel Nana-Sinkam, of Cameroon) had the second-smallest voting power on the Board in 1978. At the very bottom—and thus the most vulnerable constituency—was a group of six Latin American countries headed by Argentina.[111] The Executive Board set its own rules for the biennial election of Directors, and it was widely agreed that the rules had to be structured to ensure that each of the vulnerable groups could continue to elect an Executive Director.[112]

The 1978 election presented a complication, in that Saudi Arabia—which until 1978 had been part of a large constituency of countries in the Middle East and North Africa—had become a large enough creditor to the Fund that it was entitled to appoint its own Executive Director (Chapter 17). The Board of Governors responded by agreeing to increase the size of the Board temporarily to 21 so that the number of elected Directors would not fall.[113]

---

[109]On the original Board in 1946, the five countries entitled to appoint Executive Directors by virtue of having the largest quotas were the United States, the United Kingdom, China, France, and India. Germany replaced China in 1960, and Japan replaced India in 1970 (although India was permitted to appoint a Director in 1970 as a transitional measure).

[110]This division into Anglophone and Francophone constituencies dated from 1964, when the size of the Board was increased to 20 to accommodate the growing number of African members.

[111]The original Articles set aside two elected seats for "the American Republics not entitled to appoint directors." In 1956, following approval of membership for Argentina, the Board of Governors agreed to allow formation of a third constituency for Latin American countries. The special treatment of the region was dropped in 1978 as part of the Second Amendment, but these countries (plus Spain) continued to elect three Executive Directors.

[112]Rules for the election of Executive Directors are set out in Schedule E of the Articles of Agreement, but Article XII, Section 3(d), specifies that those provisions shall be "supplemented by such regulations as the Fund deems appropriate." The governing provision on this issue was from the Commentary on the Second Amendment to the Articles: "the Fund has been guided by the objectives of ensuring that the size of the Executive Board will contribute to the effective despatch of its business, that a desirable balance will be maintained in the composition of the Executive Board, that the size of constituencies will not place undue burdens on Executive Directors and hinder the efficient conduct of . . . business . . . , that members will be as free as possible . . . to form the constituencies of their choice, and that a relative equilibrium will be achieved in the voting power of the constituencies electing Executive Directors" (de Vries, 1985, Vol. 3, p. 358).

[113]Article XII, Section 3(c), provides for an increase in the number of appointed Directors by one or two, if the countries with the largest absolute creditor positions in the Fund are not otherwise entitled to appoint a Director. This provision enabled Canada to appoint a Director for the period 1958–60, Italy for 1968–70, and Saudi Arabia for 1978–92.

In 1980, following the large increase in China's quota described in Chapter 19, the election rules had to take into account that China—for several years not represented on the Board—now intended to elect its own Director and not to join or form a constituency with other members. That prospect raised the possibility that several other countries might attempt to form a new constituency by combining to garner the minimum number of required votes (4 percent of the eligible total, under the standard rules).[114] The two smaller Latin American constituencies protected themselves by reallocating countries between them, but that shifted the Francophone African countries onto the hot seat.[115] Without some preemptive action, all of sub-Saharan Africa might have to be represented by a single Executive Director.

In July, the Board's election committee (chaired by Canada's Executive Director, Bernard J. Drabble) recommended that the number of elected Directors be raised again, but only to 16 (implying that formation of a new constituency in addition to the China seat would squeeze out an existing group), and that the minimum number of votes for first-ballot election be raised to 4.2 percent of the total eligible votes.[116] That raised the bar high enough to discourage formation of a competing group while enabling the Francophone Africans to retain their seat.[117]

For the rest of the 1980s, the Executive Board comprised 22 Directors: 6 appointed and 16 elected, and half of the total from developing countries.[118] Not every member country was represented on the Board. Only a few members had large enough quotas to appoint or elect their own Directors, and the rest had to be welcomed into a multicountry constituency. Those constituencies were usually geographically oriented, but in essence they were voluntarily formed groups with common economic and political interests. At various times in this period, the doors were closed temporarily to five member countries. Four of those cases have

---

[114]Schedule E of the Articles specifies 4 percent as the minimum requirement for electing an Executive Director on the first ballot.

[115]Ecuador, with 1,300 votes, moved from the Argentinean constituency to that of Brazil, in a swap with Peru, which had 2,710 votes. That raised the Argentine group from the bottom (fifteenth) position to fourteenth and lowered the nine-country Brazilian group from the ninth position to eleventh.

[116]"Interim Report on 1980 Regular Election of Executive Directors," EBD/80/199 (July 30, 1980).

[117]The constituency had just over 4.5 percent of the eligible vote, but allowance had to be made for the possibility that some countries might fail to cast a valid ballot on the day of the election. As it happened, Rwanda declined to vote in 1980, but Nana-Sinkam was reelected by a comfortable margin. For the rest of the decade, the Board was able to revert to the 4 percent threshold. The number of elected Directors was set repeatedly at 16, through a series of biennial approvals by the Board of Governors. As discussed in Chapter 19 (footnote 70), the arrival of Poland in the Fund in 1986 could have threatened the Francophone African seat if Poland had obtained a slightly higher quota and had joined with Hungary and Romania to form a socialist constituency.

[118]Beginning with the 1992 election, in response to the large increase in membership that year and the end of Saudi Arabia's eligibility to appoint a Director, the number of elected Directors was raised to 19, and the total size of the Board was set at 24. The three additional elected Directors that year were from Russia, Saudi Arabia, and Switzerland.

been discussed in earlier chapters: Cambodia in the elections from 1976 through 1992 (Chapter 16), China from 1972 through 1978 (Chapter 19), Poland in 1986 (Chapter 19), and South Africa from 1974 through 1994 (Chapter 13).[119] In addition, Egypt was shunned by most other Arab countries and did not participate in elections from 1978 through 1986, as a result of its having signed the bilateral Camp David accords with Israel in 1978.

Management

> The Executive Board shall select a Managing Director who shall not be a Governor or an Executive Director. The Managing Director shall be chairman of the Executive Board . . . [and] chief of the operating staff of the Fund and shall conduct, under the direction of the Executive Board, the ordinary business of the Fund.
>
> Article XII, Section 4

The chief executive officer of the Fund is the Managing Director, who is selected by the Executive Board but has effectively been chosen by agreement among the European member countries.[120] The one election during this period occurred in 1986, to name a successor to the sixth Managing Director, Jacques de Larosière, who was resigning after eight years for personal reasons. After some initial discussions, two candidates were strongly and openly supported by competing groups of countries: H. Onno Ruding (finance minister of the Netherlands and chairman of the Interim Committee) and Michel Camdessus (governor of the Banque de France). The British government proposed Jeremy Morse, the chairman of Lloyds Bank and the former Chairman of the Deputies of the C-20, as a compromise candidate, but that strategem failed when the French refused to withdraw Camdessus's name (see Lawson, 1992, pp. 550–52). When a consensus seemed impossible to secure, the U.S. authorities remained officially neutral but quietly let it be known that they were displeased with Ruding's opposition to their macroeconomic policies and to the G-7 policy coordination exercise. While industrial countries were divided, most developing countries lined up behind Camdessus, who thus gained

---

[119]To summarize, Cambodia (then known as Democratic Kampuchea) was isolated because of international rejection of the government forcibly installed by Vietnam. China was isolated while it was represented in the Fund by the Taiwan authorities and in the United Nations by the People's Republic. When Poland joined in 1986, it had difficulty finding a European constituency willing to take in a socialist state. South Africa was subject to widespread international sanctions because of the practice of apartheid.

[120]The U.S. authorities decided in 1946 that their top staffing priority was to name an American to be president of the World Bank. See Horsefield (1969), Vol. 1, p. 135; Harrod (1951), p. 629; and Moggridge (1980), p. 213. (Moggridge reprints a letter written by Keynes at Savannah in March 1946, reporting that he and the U.S. Treasury Secretary, Frederick M. Vinson, agreed that Harry Dexter White would have been "ideally suited" for the job except for this restriction.) The other major members, who at the time were predominantly European, were thus able to name one of their own as Managing Director. That division was maintained throughout the next fifty years. The five Managing Directors prior to 1978 were Camille Gutt (Belgium; 1946–51), Ivar Rooth (Sweden; 1951–56), Per Jacobsson (Sweden; 1956–63), Pierre-Paul Schweitzer (France; 1963–73), and H. Johannes Witteveen (Netherlands; 1973–78).

enough support that Ruding was persuaded to withdraw. In December the Executive Board confirmed Camdessus as the Fund's seventh Managing Director. (Both de Larosière and Camdessus are profiled in Chapter 1.)

The other top member of the management team was the Deputy Managing Director.[121] Two Deputies served during this period: William Dale (1974–84) and Richard Erb (1984–94). Dale, who was appointed to a second term in 1979 and served until 1984, was profiled in de Vries (1985), pp. 1009–10. During his second term, he spent a great deal of time on the debt crisis in Latin America and served frequently as liaison between the Fund and commercial bank creditors. In that role, his expertise on the economic situation in indebted countries enabled the Managing Director to concentrate more on the overall strategy.

Richard Erb received a Ph.D. in Economics from Stanford University and then began his career with a mix of public sector (staff of the Federal Reserve Board) and private business positions. In 1971, he left the Salomon Brothers investment banking firm to become Staff Assistant to U.S. President Richard Nixon and Assistant Director for International Monetary Affairs of the Council on International Economic Policy. From 1974 to 1981, he alternated between the U.S. Treasury Department and the private sector American Enterprise Institute, until he was tapped to replace Sam Cross as the U.S. Executive Director in the Fund. After being named Deputy Managing Director in 1984, he followed in Dale's footsteps by serving as a liaison between the Fund and the commercial banks that were major creditors of the most heavily indebted developing countries. His primary responsibility, however, like each of his four predecessors, was to oversee the administrative operation of the institution and, when the Managing Director was absent, to chair meetings of the Executive Board and serve as Acting Managing Director.

Staff

> In appointing the staff the Managing Director shall, subject to the paramount importance of securing the highest standards of efficiency and of technical competence, pay due regard to the importance of recruiting personnel on as wide a geographical basis as possible.
>
> Article XII, Section 4(d)

People

Much as the IMF came of age during the 1980s as a player in the international monetary system, the profile of its staff also came of age. Through much of the

---

[121]The Articles of Agreement do not provide explicitly for the position of Deputy Managing Director. It was created as a staff position, appointed by the Managing Director, in 1949. The first Deputy, Andrew N. Overby (1949–52), had been the U.S. Executive Director in the Fund before being named to this post; that began a tradition that the Deputy would normally be from the United States. The second Deputy was H. Merle Cochran (1953–62), and the third was Frank A. Southard, Jr. (1962–74). In 1994, the management structure was expanded to include three Deputies, of which one was to be designated First Deputy Managing Director. The latter post was filled by a U.S. national, Stanley Fischer.

1970s, the Fund was led mainly by people who had joined the staff in its early days and who had developed their careers while the Fund was developing and growing institutionally. Those who moved up into the ranks of senior officers in the 1980s represented not just a new generation but a new vantage point. Having come to a more mature Fund, they were on the whole receptive to and in sync with the changes that were needed to adapt to the complexities of an integrated global economy.

The most noteworthy retirements by members of the Bretton Woods generation were those of Joseph Gold and Jacques J. Polak in 1979. Both had been instrumental in shaping the Fund: Gold from a legal perspective and Polak as an economist. Polak's career is reviewed above, in the context of his service as an Executive Director. Gold's distinguished career at the Fund, which began in 1946, was reviewed in de Vries (1985), pp. 1019–20. Like Polak, Gold continued to pursue an active writing career long after retirement, culminating in a major book on the history of judicial interpretation as it related to the Fund (Gold, 1996).

Six other heads of departments or offices who retired within a few years of Gold and Polak had also been at the Fund since the late 1940s (also see de Vries, 1985, pp. 1021–1026):

- Kenneth N. Clark, a U.S. national and Director of the Administration Department, retired at the end of 1979 after 32 years in that department.
- Ernest Sturc retired as Director of the Exchange and Trade Relations Department (ETR) in January 1980. Sturc had been at Bretton Woods as a member of the delegation of Czechoslovakia and joined the staff in 1946.
- Jay H. Reid, who had been in charge of the Fund's public relations and external information activities since joining the staff in 1948, also retired in 1980.
- E. Walter Robichek, Director of the Western Hemisphere Department and a staff member since 1947, retired in December 1982 to become Advisor to the Managing Director (1983–84).
- Fernando A. Vera, Director of the Geneva Office, also retired toward the end of 1982. Vera joined the staff in 1948, worked primarily on Latin America, and served as Deputy Director of the Western Hemisphere Department (1966–78) before moving to Geneva.
- George Nicoletopoulos joined the staff in 1949, spent 15 years (1964–79) as the Fund's second-highest legal officer under Joseph Gold,[122] and became Director of the Legal Department when Gold retired. Nicoletopoulos retired in 1985.

Three other notable retirements may be mentioned in this context. W. John R. Woodley, a Canadian who joined the staff in 1948 and rose to become Deputy Di-

---

[122]Gold became General Counsel (and head of the Legal Department) in 1960. From 1964 to 1977, Nicoletopoulos was Deputy General Counsel. He was then promoted to Associate General Counsel. The title of "Associate" head of a department is a seldom-used designation in the Fund with the same rank as the department head. The title "Counsellor" is awarded occasionally to a department head who is part of an inner circle of advisers to the Managing Director. Until 1979, only Polak (Economic Counsellor) and Gold held this title. Its use peaked in the late 1980s, when five department heads were designated as Counsellors.

rector of the Asian Department and a leading expert on the Japanese economy, re-tired in 1980. Richard B. Goode served in the Research Department in 1951–59 and then rejoined the staff in 1965 as Director of the newly created Fiscal Affairs Department. He retired from that position in July 1981. (Also see de Vries, 1985, p. 1021.) And the last of the "Class of the 1940s" to retire—and thus the unoffi-cial dean of the staff—was Brian Rose. A native of the United Kingdom, Rose joined the staff in 1947, became Deputy Director of the European Department in 1975, and retired in 1988 with more than 40 years of service to the Fund.

These and other departures meant that the lineup of senior officers was almost entirely changed from 1978 to 1989. Of the 21 heads of departments or offices at the beginning of 1979, only three—A. Shakour Shaalan (Director of the Middle Eastern Department), Gérard M. Teyssier (Director of the IMF Institute), and Leo Van Houtven (Secretary) held the same positions at the end of 1989.[123]

The final retirements of the 1940s class opened the door for new leadership in seven departments: Research, ETR, European, Western Hemisphere, Legal, Fiscal Affairs, and Administration.

Polak was replaced as Director of Research and Economic Counsellor by William C. Hood. Hood had been Professor of Economics at the University of Toronto for many years and was best known in the economics profession as the coauthor of a leading work on econometrics (Koopmans and Hood, 1953). He switched from academics to government in 1964 and eventually became Deputy Minister of Finance in Canada. Hood retired in 1986 and was replaced by an even more well-known economist, Jacob A. Frenkel, the David Rockefeller Professor of International Economics at the University of Chicago. During his academic career, Frenkel made many seminal contributions to the theory and estimation of ex-change rate relationships and the international dimensions of macroeconomic pol-icy.[124] He continued to publish extensively while at the Fund. Frenkel left the Fund in 1991 to become Governor of the Bank of Israel.

Also in the Research Department, Charles F. Schwartz retired as Director of Adjustment Studies and Associate Director of the department in 1983. Schwartz had been on the staff since 1959 and had been instrumental in developing the World Economic Outlook at the Fund (see Chapter 5).

Sturc was replaced as head of ETR in 1980 by an Australian, C. David Finch, who had joined the staff in 1950 and thus had nearly as much experience at the Fund as his predecessor (de Vries, 1985, p. 1026). After being named Counsellor in 1985, Finch abruptly resigned in March 1987 in protest over what he judged to be political interference with the evaluation of proposed stand-by arrangements. Specifically, Finch objected to efforts by major creditor countries to push the Fund into approving financial arrangements for Egypt, Zaïre, and Argentina when the

---

[123]Van Houtven was awarded the additional title of Counsellor in 1987. Teyssier retired in 1990. Shaalan retired in 1992 to become an Executive Director (see footnote 108, p. 1040). Van Houtven retired in 1996 and succeeded Polak as president of the Per Jacobssen Foundation. All three men were profiled in de Vries (1985), p. 1024.

[124]For an overview, see Frenkel and Mussa (1985) and Frenkel and Razin (1987).

staff believed that the proposed economic programs were too weak to justify support.[125] Finch was highly and widely respected as a balanced arbiter on the design of Fund programs, and his resignation (which came less than two years before he would have reached mandatory retirement age) was a clear signal of an incipient threat to the professional integrity of the Fund.

Finch in turn was replaced by L. Alan Whittome, who had been Director of the European Department since joining the Fund staff in 1964, and Counsellor since 1980 (de Vries, 1985, p. 1023). Before moving to the Fund, Whittome had been Deputy Chief Cashier at the Bank of England. In 1991, shortly after retiring from the Fund, he was awarded a knighthood by Queen Elizabeth II.[126]

When Whittome moved to ETR, his old post went to Massimo Russo. Russo had first joined the staff in 1964 as an economist in the African Department. With a two-year hiatus to work at the OECD in Paris, he stayed in the African Department and rose to the position of Assistant Director in 1980. He spent another three years at the Fund as Deputy Director of Administration and then left again to become Director General of the Commission of the European Communities, in Brussels. He returned to the Fund in 1987 as Director of the European Department, a post that he held for the next ten years.

Robichek was replaced as Director of the Western Hemisphere Department by Eduardo Wiesner Duran. Wiesner had held several leading positions in Colombia, ranging from Professor of Economics at the University of the Andes in the 1960s to Minister of Finance in 1981–82. Wiesner directed the department from 1982 to 1987 before becoming the Fund's Special Trade Representative and Director of the Geneva Office. He retired in October 1988.[127] Meanwhile, Sterie T. Beza was named Associate Director of the Western Hemisphere Department in January 1983, shortly after Wiesner became Director. Beza, a U.S. national who had served in that department since 1961 (de Vries, 1985, p. 1028), succeeded Wiesner as Director in July 1987. He was promoted to Counsellor two years later and retired in 1995.

To head the Legal Department, Nicoletopoulos was replaced by François P. Gianviti, who had been Professor of Law at the University of Paris since 1974 and Dean of the School of Law since 1979. Gianviti had previously served in the Fund's Legal Department in 1970–74. A year after returning to the Fund as Direc-

---

[125]See *The Times* (London), March 20, 1987, p. 6; *The Financial Times*, March 21, 1987, p. 2; and Finch (1988, 1997). The two newspaper articles erred in attributing the alleged interference solely to the United States; Finch also cited pressure from French and German officials in his memoirs. Finch's remarks to the Executive Board were not included in the minutes of the meeting at which he announced his resignation.

[126]Sir Alan Whittome was the second Fund retiree, after Sir Joseph Gold in 1979, to be knighted by the Queen of England. In both cases, the Executive Board granted a waiver of Rule N-10, which prohibits Fund staff from accepting "any honor, decoration, favor, gift, or bonus from any government . . . for services rendered during the period of his appointment or service with the Fund."

[127]Wiesner was replaced in May 1989 as Special Trade Representative and Director of the Geneva office by Helen B. Junz, who had been Deputy Director of ETR.

tor of the Department, he was awarded the additional title of General Counsel (which had been vacant since Gold's retirement).

Vito Tanzi, a former Professor and Chairman of the Department of Economics at The American University in Washington, became Director of the Fiscal Affairs Department after Goode's retirement in 1981. Already a noted expert on tax policy, Tanzi joined the Fund in 1974 as Assistant Chief of the Tax Policy Division. After becoming Director of the Department, he continued to conduct and publish extensive research, not only on technical tax issues but increasingly on the growth of tax evasion and the "underground economy" throughout the world.[128] In 1990, Tanzi was elected President of the International Institute of Public Finance. He retired from the Fund in 2000.

Finally, Clark was replaced as head of the Administration Department in 1980 by Roland Tenconi, who had been head of the Central Banking Service (de Vries, 1985, pp. 1023–24). When Tenconi retired five years later, the post was filled by former Rhodes Scholar Graeme F. Rea, who had been Deputy General Counsel since 1979. Prior to that, Rea had worked at the Asian Development Bank for 12 years, the last four as General Counsel. Rea, a native of New Zealand, retired from the Fund in 1995.

In addition to those replacements for the Class of the 1940s, the African, Asian, and Treasurer's Departments also got new directors in the 1980s.[129]

Justin B. Zulu, a former Governor of the Bank of Zambia who had served as Alternate Executive Director for the Anglophone African constituency in 1974–76, headed the African Department from 1976 to 1984. During that time, the department became the Fund's most active in terms of both number of member countries and number of financial arrangements. Zulu then took over the Central Banking Department, which he directed until 1995.

Alassane D. Ouattara was named Director of the African Department in November 1984. Ouattara began his Fund career in 1968, as an economist in the African Department, upon receiving a Ph.D. in Economics from the University of Pennsylvania. He returned to his native Côte d'Ivoire in 1973, where he eventually became Vice-Governor of the Central Bank of West African States (known by its French acronym, the BCEAO). After four years as Director of the Fund's African Department (including a year and a half as Counsellor), he returned home again in 1988 to become Governor of the BCEAO and later (1990–93) the Prime Minister of Côte d'Ivoire. Still in his early fifties, Ouattara then was called back to the Fund one more time, to become Deputy Managing Director in 1994. In 1999, he resigned and returned once again to Côte d'Ivoire to run for president.

---

[128]Tanzi's most well-known contribution to the professional literature was his exposition of the "Tanzi effect," by which a reduction in the inflation rate raises tax revenues; see Chapter 9, footnote 42. On the underground economy, see Tanzi (1983).

[129]The initial leadership of the two new departments of the 1980s—Central Banking and External Relations—has been chronicled above (pp. 1018–19). P.N. Kaul headed the Central Banking Department until his retirement in 1984, and Azizali F. Mohammed directed the External Relations Department until he retired in 1990.

The third head of the African Department in the 1980s was Mamoudou Touré, who took over from Ouattara as both Director and Counsellor in November 1988. This was Touré's second stint as head of the department, the first having been as Zulu's predecessor in 1967–76. He held a number of important positions in between, notably as minister of planning and later as minister of economy and finance in Senegal. Touré retired in 1994.

Tun Thin, a national of Burma (Myanmar), retired in 1986 after 14 years as Director of the Asian Department (de Vries, 1985, p. 1023). He was succeeded by Prabhakar R. Narvekar, who had served as his Deputy during that entire period. Narvekar, a native of India, joined the staff as a Research Assistant in the Asian Department in 1953, after earning a master's degree in economics at Columbia University. He rose to Division Chief in that department in 1963 and to Deputy Director in 1972. He served as Director from 1986 to 1991. At that time, the Managing Director named him to be his Special Advisor. When the management structure was expanded in 1994, Narvekar became one of the three Deputy Managing Directors, a post he held for nearly three years. In 1998, as part of the Fund's effort to handle a major financial and political crisis in Indonesia, he came out of retirement for several months to serve again as Special Advisor.

Walter O. Habermeier, the Fund's Treasurer since 1969 and a Counsellor since 1980, retired in 1987 after 21 years on the staff (de Vries, 1985, pp. 1022–23). He was replaced by F. Gerhard Laske, a former official of the Deutsche Bundesbank and Executive Director for Germany (1975–79 as Alternate and 1979–84 as Director). Laske served as Treasurer for five years and retired in 1992.

Issues

The 36 senior officers mentioned in the preceding section were broadly diversified in most respects. Although 10 (28 percent) were U.S. nationals, altogether they came originally from 24 different countries on all continents, and 12 (33 percent) came from developing countries. Those proportions were similar to those for the staff at large. In 1979, 29 percent of the staff were U.S. nationals, and 33 percent were from developing countries; 10 years later, the U.S. share had dropped to 26 percent, and the developing country share had risen to 41 percent. The striking exception to this diversity is that all but one of the profiled senior officers were men. The Fund's charter, as quoted at the head of this section, mandated geographic but not gender diversity.[130]

The heavily skewed gender distribution of the Fund staff did not evolve significantly during the 1980s. Throughout the decade, the composition of the staff was split almost evenly between men and women, but the female staff were heavily concentrated in the lower-paid support-staff positions. Ninety-five percent of man-

---

[130]It is important to note, however, that geographic diversity is specified as a secondary objective in Article XII and that it was not achieved through quotas. The Fund's Rules, as adopted in 1946, require nondiscrimination in the "employment classification, promotion, and assignment of personnel" on the basis of "sex, race or creed," subject to the goal of achieving geographic diversity (Rule N-2; originally Rule N-1).

agerial positions were filled by men, and all department heads were men. Women constituted 80 percent or more of the support staff and only about 20 percent of the economist-level staff below managerial level. That pattern, which had persisted from the beginning of the Fund in 1946, would finally be bent (though not yet broken) in the 1990s, through a concerted diversity-building program.[131]

The growth in employment of staff from developing countries in the 1980s was also concentrated in support-staff positions. From 1979 to 1989, the number of staff positions held by nationals of developing countries rose by 231. Of those, 87 (38 percent) were additional support staff, and 19 (8 percent) were managers. In contrast, of the 78 additional positions that were filled by nationals of industrial countries, 42 (54 percent) were managers. The number of support-staff positions held by people from industrial countries declined.

The staff of the Fund, as with other international organizations, generally have regarded their position as a privilege, and many outside observers have viewed them as a privileged elite. The reality is rather more complex. As international civil servants, most of the staff are totally dependent on the institution not only for their livelihood but also for their continued right to live in the United States. Many of them have come from countries where the political environment might have changed sharply since they left, making a resumption of their earlier occupations impossible. Many have made their careers at the institution, their spouses may be prohibited by U.S. law from seeking employment in the country, and their children may have grown up with no home other than Washington. Moreover, their employer is immune from prosecution, and labor disputes are not subject to negotiation or arbitration. That dependence and vulnerability have at times made the staff more sensitive to attacks on their position and more resistant to administrative change than might otherwise seem reasonable.

The dominant issue for the staff in both the 1970s and the 1980s was compensation: partly because it was falling in relation to comparable jobs overseas and partly because of what the staff saw as attempts by a few governments—especially the United States—to politicize the compensation system. The real value of staff salaries had been stagnant throughout the 1970s, as the regular adjustments to the pay scale barely kept pace with the accelerating rate of inflation (Figure 20.4).[132]

---

[131]For this purpose, managerial positions are defined as Division Chief, Advisor, or higher. "Economist level" refers roughly to the upper half of the professional grades between support staff and managers. (In terms of the classification of grades in use after 1986, support staff hold grades up to A8; professional staff hold grades of A9 and above; the economist level is defined here as A12 through A15; and managers hold grades of B1 through B5. Department heads normally are B5s.) In 1997, 10 percent of managers, including two department heads, were women. For a table showing the distribution in 1980, 1990, and 1997, see *Annual Report 1998*, p. 101.

[132]The data plotted in Figure 20.4 are derived from the midpoints of the most common grade range for Fund economists. That grade, which lies between the entry level (Young Professional or Economist Program) and that of Senior Economist, was called Range C until 1974, when it became Range H. In 1986, following a major revision of the grading of jobs throughout the Fund, it was reclassified as Grade A13. Nominal salaries are deflated by the U.S. Consumer Price Index based in 1990.

Figure 20.4. Real Fund Salaries, 1970–90
(Deflated by U.S. consumer prices)

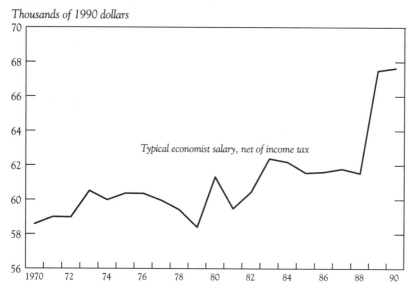

Thousands of 1990 dollars

Typical economist salary, net of income tax

The U.S. federal workforce—by far the dominant economic group in Washington—fared much worse, which created a conflict in perceptions. The staff naturally compared their own salaries with the cost of living and with the pay of other workers in similar jobs around the world. The U.S. authorities focused instead on the immediate comparison with jobs in the U.S. Treasury and the rest of the federal government. A clash was inevitable. In 1976, an attempt by the U.S. authorities to persuade other countries to award a lower pay increase than was called for by the standard cost-of-living adjustment led to a one-day strike by nearly the whole staff (de Vries, 1985, p. 1016). The pay increase was finally awarded over U.S. objections, but the bitterness of the experience persuaded the Fund to review and ultimately to change the compensation system.

The new system was set out in the January 1979 report of the Kafka Committee (the Joint Bank/Fund Committee on Staff Compensation Issues, chaired by Alexandre Kafka).[133] It scrapped the practice of awarding cost-of-living increases and replaced it with a formula linking Fund salaries to a set of market "comparators." These comparators comprised nine financial institutions, nine industrial corporations, and four public sector agencies, all in the United States. The average salaries paid in those markets for jobs that were comparable to Fund jobs became the baseline for Fund salaries. Surveys were to be undertaken of the French and German markets as well, with the intention of modifying the baseline if necessary to maintain international competitiveness. The Fund then agreed to pay a 10 per-

---

[133]"Report of the Joint Committee on Staff Compensation Issues," CSCI/79/1 (January 1979); in IMF/RD "Kafka Committee" files (Accession 79/015, Box 3, Section 149).

cent premium over the baseline to ensure that it could continue to hire staff of "the highest standards," as mandated by the Articles of Agreement.

The staff, through its Staff Association Committee (SAC), initially objected to adoption of the Kafka proposals.[134] The SAC did not object to the shift to a comparator system, but it feared that the stress on the U.S. market, at a time when the U.S. economy and the dollar were weak and the U.S. government was reducing its own salary levels in real terms, would seriously erode the value of Fund salaries. Although the Kafka report explained its U.S. focus on grounds of practicality, the prevailing view among the staff was that the report reflected the political muscle of the host government. The SAC was somewhat mollified by the report's finding that the current level of salaries was not high in relation to the selected comparators, but stressed that the more highly paid European markets should be included more systematically.[135]

The comparator system was adopted in 1979 and was maintained with occasional changes throughout the 1980s. When the first few years of experience exposed several weaknesses in the system, a second Joint Committee was formed in 1984 under the chairmanship of Günter Grosche (Germany). That committee proved fractious, as a minority—particularly Charles H. Dallara (United States)—insisted that salaries were too high, while others came to the opposite conclusion. The battle came to a head in 1986, while the Grosche committee was still trying to reach a consensus. In an apparent effort to pressure the committee to conclude its work quickly, the U.S. governor in the Fund, Secretary of the Treasury James Baker, sent a letter to a number of governors asking them to support a move to postpone any increase in the salary scale until the Grosche committee issued its final report.[136] In response, the SAC also wrote to governors, setting out the case for following the Fund's normal procedures.

The Executive Board delayed considering management's proposed salary increase until late May 1986, some three weeks after the salary scale would normally

---

[134]The Staff Association was formed in the 1940s but was not regularly active until 1979. Its role was formalized that year when the Fund approved a rule giving the staff the right to associate to present views to management and the Executive Board regarding personnel and working conditions (Rule N-14, adopted June 22, 1979). The following month, the Managing Director recognized the SAC as a representative body under the terms of Rule N-14. The SAC, however, was not a collective bargaining agent, and it operated entirely with volunteer staff. Other major issues raised by the SAC during the 1980s included the need for an Administrative Tribunal to rule on the validity of personnel actions taken by the Fund; appeals to the U.S. Congress to liberalize restrictions on the work and immigration status of employees of international organizations; reform of the system relating Fund salaries to U.S. income taxes; and evaluations of proposed reforms of the pensions system, the grading of jobs in the Fund, and various elements of the benefits package for Fund staff. In addition to recognizing the SAC as an avenue for presenting general staff concerns, the Fund established an ombudsman position and a Grievance Committee in 1980 to respond to individual complaints.

[135]The relevant SAC documents are in IMF/CF (A 176.1 "Joint Bank/Fund Committee on Compensation Issues").

[136]Memorandum of April 29, 1986, from Dallara to the Managing Director; in IMF/RD Managing Director "Staff Compensation" file (Accession 88/18, Box 7, Section 485).

have been adjusted.[137] By this time, staff morale was at its lowest point in at least a decade. A major regrading of job classifications had just taken effect, which had resulted in many positions being downgraded to a lower pay range. The Fund's administrative budget was being reduced in nominal terms at a time when the workload was increasing and consumer prices were rising. The reintroduction of political pressure into the compensation system was the final straw. The Managing Director, keenly aware of the problem and convinced that the proposal should be approved, supported the staff position and argued strongly that the salary adjustment should not be further delayed. This time, however, in contrast to 1976, the U.S. lobbying effort paid off, and the Executive Board decided to postpone the increase.[138]

Two days after the Board turned down the increase, the staff heeded an appeal by the SAC and staged a one-day work stoppage. At both the Fund and the World Bank, approximately half of the staff stayed home on May 23. The staff's sense of isolation worsened further in early June, when the Bank's Executive Directors approved a general salary increase for Bank staff.[139] Nearly 90 percent of available staff then signed a petition asking the Fund's Board to reopen the issue. That appeal had no immediate effect on the Board, but it did help to induce de Larosière to shift his position to favor establishing an Administrative Tribunal to protect the staff against arbitrary decisions on personnel matters.[140]

The impasse of 1986 was finally broken by an odd turn of events. In October, Grosche reported to the Managing Director that his committee was expecting to receive new comparator data that would take several months to analyze. Consequently, it could not possibly complete its report before the end of 1987. De Larosière immediately asked the Board to approve the salary increase straightaway, retroactively to May 1. That he would put his personal authority on the line again for this cause, at a time when he had already announced his decision to step down

---

[137]Procedures in effect at the time separated the annual salary adjustment into two components: a merit increase averaging 2.4 percent, included in the administrative budget and distributed selectively to staff on the basis of performance reviews; and a general increase in the overall salary scale. In 1986, the budget with the merit increase included was approved in April. The debate concerned whether to approve an increase in the scale by 1.4 percent for support staff positions and 2.9 percent for higher grades.

[138]Minutes of EBM/86/86–87 (May 21, 1986).

[139]The Bank justified its action on grounds that were outside the scope of the compensation review system, and neither Bank nor Fund management regarded the action as a general salary increase in the usual sense. Needless to say, the Fund staff were not especially impressed by the force of that logic. "Salary Actions in the World Bank," EBAP/86/140 (June 12, 1986) and minutes of EBM/86/96 (June 13).

[140]At a Board meeting in June, in restricted session, the Managing Director recalled that he had earlier opposed establishing an Administrative Tribunal "because he had believed that the institution itself and management could provide the staff the assurance that it would be treated fairly and in accordance with established rules." Now, however, "in light of recent events, he found it extremely difficult to defend the fact that the Fund should be the only international organization whose staff was without access to a body in which the decisions of the institution affecting the staff could be examined to ascertain that they were legal and proper." That epiphany set in motion a long process that culminated in the creation of an Administrative Tribunal in 1993.

as Managing Director and return to France, was widely seen as indicating the depth of his conviction on the wisdom and necessity of granting the increase. With the United States still objecting, the Board approved the request on November 19.[141]

The Grosche committee continued its work through 1987 and well into 1988. After four years of study, its final report recommended retaining the Kafka system in which salaries were based on comparisons with public and private sector jobs, but it proposed several modifications in the methodology. Notably, the committee recommended, and the Board agreed, that the weighting of the still downtrodden U.S. public sector be reduced in the comparator basket and that the procedures for maintaining competitiveness with the French and German markets be made more explicit and transparent.[142] Together, these changes reflected an acknowledgment that Fund salaries were not keeping pace with the market and were no longer competitive either with the U.S. private sector or with European salaries.

The compensation system of the 1980s had succeeded in preserving the real value of Fund salaries, at least when expressed in terms of U.S. dollars. Salaries for Fund economists, which had fallen by 3.5 percent in real terms from 1973 to 1979, rose by 6.8 percent over the next four years before falling back slightly in 1984 and succeeding years (see Figure 20.4). It was less successful in maintaining international competitiveness, as productivity gains brought larger real increases in professional salaries in Europe and other countries. The Grosche committee concluded that Fund compensation had to provide a margin of 10 to 20 percent over comparable pay abroad to induce personnel to accept expatriate positions. When a detailed analysis of the data was completed the next year, it turned out that salaries were well short of that goal; for entry-level professional staff, the margin was substantially negative. Moreover, the Fund was experiencing increasing difficulties recruiting and retaining young professionals. Starting in 1989, therefore, the Fund shifted the salary structure up sharply in relation to the U.S. market in an effort to restore international competitiveness.[143] While the U.S. authorities, and occasionally others, continued to

---

[141]"Reconsideration of Staff Compensation—1986," EBAP/86/266 (October 31, 1986), and minutes of EBM/86/185 (November 19, 1986).

[142]Two other changes were more of a technical nature but still had important effects. First, the 10 percent premium over average comparator salaries was replaced by adoption of the 75th percentile as the baseline. The new benchmarks were at nearly the same level, but the 75th percentile was more stable and reliable. Second, the practice of setting aside 2.4 percentage points of each year's increase for merit increases was abandoned. That practice had led to a steady reduction in the salary scale relative to competitors; salaries of existing staff kept pace with the U.S. market, but the Fund gradually lost its ability to attract new staff. "Report of the Joint Bank-Fund Committee of Executive Directors on Staff Compensation," EBAP/88/190 (August 5, 1988), "Joint Committee on Staff Compensation (JCC)—Principal Elements of Proposed New Compensation System and Proposed Salary Structure," EBAP/89/85 (March 30, 1989), and minutes of IS/89/5–6 (April 14, 1989) and IS/89/7–8 (April 19).

[143]"Joint Committee on Staff Compensation (JCC)—Principal Elements of Proposed New Compensation System and Proposed Salary Structure," EBAP/89/85 (March 30, 1989), pp. 12–20. As shown in Figure 20.4, the salary scale was raised by 15 percent in 1989. Actual salaries, however, rose by much less: an average of 8.8 percent. The difference resulted from the unification of the annual adjustments, as described in the preceding footnote, through which the upward creep of pay within each grade was abruptly reversed.

U.S. President Ronald Reagan addressing the Bank-Fund Annual Meetings, October 1987, with the IMF Secretary Leo Van Houtven and Managing Director Michel Camdessus looking on

complain, the compensation system was now firmly enough rooted in a transparent and accepted methodology that it could more easily weather the controversies.

Compensation, of course, was only a small part of the working environment affecting staff morale. The Fund's ombudsman reported with increasing vehemence around the end of the 1980s about the extent of demoralization in the staff, which resulted from unclear, often arbitrary, and decentralized and thus inconsistent personnel policies at a time of sharply increasing workload. Although few would have concluded that the Fund had ceased being a desirable place to work, signs of strain— which would become increasingly apparent when the countries of eastern Europe and the former Soviet Union became members in the early 1990s—were evident.

For internal management as much as for the response to global economic crises, the 1980s had been a challenging but ultimately rewarding decade for the Fund. In both realms, the 1990s would pose even greater challenges. Assessment of its rewards will be the challenge for the next History.

Appendix: Concordat on Fund-Bank Collaboration

Bank-Fund Collaboration in Assisting Member Countries (SM/89/54, Rev. 1, March 31, 1989)

The President of the World Bank and the Managing Director of the International Monetary Fund have reached agreement on the attached text. This document, jointly prepared by the managements of the Bank and the Fund, reviews the current status of cooperation between the Fund and the Bank and provides for the administrative and procedural steps that are necessary to secure a constructive and stronger collaboration between them.

The purposes and mandates of the Bank and the Fund are defined in their Articles of Agreement, as interpreted by their respective Boards. Operating within the framework of the Articles, the managements of both institutions believe that it is of the utmost importance to ensure the closest possible collaboration and working relations between the two institutions in order to serve member governments with maximum effectiveness in meeting their development needs and in providing support for macroeconomic and structural change.

The guidelines contained in the attached document are intended to achieve this objective and should help avoid administrative friction and facilitate orderly resolution of differences of views. Both of us recognize that the advice, suggestions and support of each institution for the other are essential if they are to discharge their responsibilities effectively and promptly. Smooth and effective working relations between the two institutions have assumed special importance in view of the contribution that both of them are expected to make to policy formulation and sustained economic growth in their member countries.

The staff will be instructed to implement the guidelines embodied in this document in a spirit of close collaboration. . . .

Memorandum to the Executive Board of the International Monetary Fund and the Board of Executive Directors of the World Bank

. . . 1. Guidelines for collaboration between our two institutions have been in place since 1966. They have been reviewed and strengthened on a number of occasions since then.[144] We, and our colleagues in the management of both institutions, have recently reviewed the experience with collaboration under existing policy and practices.

2. The problems faced by our member countries are severe. They are struggling to restore stability, to adjust their economies to a more rapidly changing and less benign international environment, and to restore growth, while they continue to grapple with their massive debt overhangs and limited availability of both concessional funds and commercial capital. The majority of the members of our two organizations face serious problems. Many of them face the urgent need for change in policies, institutions, and the incentive framework. All are entitled, in our view, to the best advice our highly competent staffs can provide—each by drawing on their specialized technical expertise and experience. It is our responsibility, and that of our Boards, to ensure that the procedures in place make possible, to the fullest extent practicable, comprehensive analyses by our staffs, early exchange of views on differences, and a system to refer remaining differences to the appropriate level of management for resolution. Proposals to improve our capacity to achieve these objectives are set forth in this paper.

3. The existing guidelines lay down principles which remain sound and provide a firm basis on which to build. They provide the Bank with ". . . primary responsibility for the composition and appropriateness of development programs and project evaluation, including development priorities." The Fund is assigned ". . . primary responsibility for exchange rates and restrictive systems, for adjustment of temporary balance of payments disequilibria, and for evaluating and assisting members to work out stabilization programs as a sound basis for economic advance." The guidelines further provide that "in between these two clear-cut areas of responsibility . . . there is a broad range of matters which are of interest to both institutions. This range includes such matters as the structure and functioning of financial institutions, the adequacy of money and capital markets, the actual and potential capacity of the member to generate domestic savings, the financial implications of economic development programs, both for the internal financial position of the country and for its external situation, foreign debt problems, and so on."

4. The same guidelines also stipulate that "[on those matters in the area of primary responsibility of the Bank], the Fund, and particularly the field missions of the Fund, should inform themselves of the established views and position of the Bank and adopt those views as a working basis for their own work. This does not preclude discussions between the Bank and the Fund as to those matters, but it does mean that the Fund (and Fund missions) will not engage in a critical review of those matters with member countries unless it is done with the prior consent of the Bank." Corresponding provisions were made for the Bank and Bank missions.

5. While we reaffirm the principles of these guidelines, the overlap of activities of the two institutions has grown rapidly in the 1970s and 1980s as the Bank and the Fund have attempted to respond to the massive financing and adjustment requirements of members in a more difficult economic environment. In recognition of the longer-term and supply-oriented nature of the adjustment process, the Fund increased its consideration of structural issues in stand-by arrangements; extended the repayment period of extended arrangements to 10 years; and introduced the concessional and relatively long-term Structural Adjustment Facility (SAF) and the Enhanced Structural Adjustment Facility (ESAF). In response

---

[144]Additional collaboration procedures were added to the original guidelines in 1970, and guidelines, as expanded, were reviewed and affirmed by managements of both institutions in 1980, and by the Fund in 1984 and the Bank in 1985.

to the serious balance of payments problems affecting many developing countries stemming from the sharp deterioration of the terms of trade and from the weakness in domestic policies and institutions, the Bank introduced Structural Adjustment Loans (SALs) in 1980 that provided financing in support of policies to promote structural, economy-wide changes and, subsequently, Sector Adjustment Loans (SECALs), which focused on structural changes in specific sectors.

6. There is continuous and successful cooperation between the Bank and the Fund. Close contacts between the two staffs contribute to a better understanding of economic problems and policy options, and normally lead to improved and consistent policy advice; better coordination of the amounts, forms, and timing of financial assistance; and a greater effectiveness in mobilizing additional financial support.

7. Yet, given the complexity of the problems faced by our members and the perspectives of the two institutions, it is not unusual that differences of view may sometimes arise. In a few cases, some significant differences about country priorities and policy have emerged. In some cases, they have spilled into discussions by the staff with country authorities. Differences of view have concerned a number of areas, including exchange rate, the level of external assistance sufficient to provide reasonable prospects for sustained and successful adjustment efforts and resumption of growth, the speed of adjustment, and the need to maintain adequate levels of public sector development expenditures. At other times, differences of view between the staffs of the two institutions have centered on the trade-off between efficiency gains from certain structural measures to be accrued over time and balance of payments and budgetary impacts.

8. With the growing contiguity of the activities of the Bank and the Fund, we believe it is essential to strengthen collaboration, to ensure that conflicts of views are resolved at an early stage, do not surface in contacts with country authorities, and do not result in differing policy advice to member countries.

9. The Fund has among its purposes the promotion of economic conditions conducive to growth, price stability, and balance of payments sustainability and is required to exercise surveillance on a continual basis over the performance of its members as defined by Article IV. The Fund is empowered to provide temporary balance of payments financing to members to enable them to correct maladjustments in their balance of payments without resorting to measures destructive of national or international prosperity. Thus, the Fund has focused on the aggregate aspects of macroeconomic policies and their related instruments—including public sector spending and revenues, aggregate wage and price policies, money and credit, interest rates and the exchange rate. The Fund has to discharge responsibilities with respect to surveillance, exchange rate matters, balance of payments, growth-oriented stabilization policies and their related instruments. These are the areas in which the Fund has a mandate, primary responsibility, and a record of expertise and experience.

10. The Bank has the objective of promoting economic growth and conditions conducive to efficient resource allocation, which it pursues through investment lending, sectoral and structural adjustment loans. Thus, the Bank has focused on development strategies; sector and project investments; structural adjustment programs; policies which deal with the efficient allocation of resources in both public and private sectors; priorities in government expenditures; reforms of administrative systems, production, trade and financial sectors; the restructuring of state enterprises and sector policies. Moreover, as a market-based institution, the Bank also concerns itself with issues relating to the creditworthiness of its members. In these areas, except for the aggregate aspects of the economic policies mentioned in the previous paragraph, the Bank has a mandate, primary responsibility, and a record of expertise and experience.

11. While it is important to strengthen the framework for collaboration and to reduce the risk of conflict and duplication, both the Bank and the Fund must be allowed to explore their legitimate concerns with regard to macroeconomic and structural issues and to take them into account in their policy advice and lending operations. The 1966 guidelines stipulate that views on matters clearly within the area of "primary responsibility" of one or the other of the two institutions "should be expressed to members only by or with the consent of that institution." This provision remains appropriate. The procedures for enhanced collaboration spelled out below are designed to assure resolution of issues. It is, of course, equally important that borrowing countries be aware of the responsibility of the institution for policy advice in the areas of its primary responsibility.

12. The objective of the enhanced collaboration procedures is to avoid differing policy advice, but this does not mean that one institution should not engage in analyses in the areas of primary responsibilities of the other institution. On the contrary, the institutions and borrowing members normally stand to benefit from analyses from different perspectives, and thorough discussions between the two staffs are encouraged. In the event differences of view persist at the staff level even after a thorough common examination of them, and should the differences not be resolved by the management, the institution which does not have the primary responsibility would, except in exceptional circumstances, yield to the judgment of the other institution. In those cases, which are expected to be extremely rare, the managements will wish to consult their respective Executive Boards before proceeding. Also, in the interest of efficiency of staff resource use, each institution should rely as much as possible on analyses and monitoring of the other institution in the areas of primary responsibilities of the latter, while safeguarding the independence of institutional decisions.

Procedures for Enhanced Collaboration

13. Given the complexity of the problems handled, the differences in the mandates of the Bank and the Fund and the unique perspectives brought to bear on the assessment of country situations by the staffs of the two institutions, it is expected that differences of view will sometimes arise. Existing procedures and practices of Bank-Fund collaboration are designed to ensure the quality of analysis and policy advice, as well as thorough explorations of any differences of view that may emerge between the staffs. Typically, differences are worked out at the working level and are resolved satisfactorily in the large majority of cases. However, in order to further strengthen existing procedures on Bank-Fund collaboration and to facilitate the resolution of any remaining differences of view, new or more formal steps have been agreed in the following areas:

I. Strengthening Collaboration

14. The daily interactions and ad hoc contacts involving managements and staffs (and monthly, as well as ad hoc, meetings between the Managing Director and the President) will be supplemented with regular meetings of the senior staff of each institution. In particular, there should be regular meetings between Bank Regional Vice Presidents and the corresponding Fund Area Department Directors to review current operational concerns. These meetings should anticipate and thus reduce the differences of view between staffs of the two organizations. In addition, meetings would be held at the senior level as required to review the strategies of each institution for countries of common concern. These meetings would normally be chaired by the Deputy Managing Director of the Fund and the Senior Vice President, Operations, of the Bank supported by a few senior staff on each side.

15. Whenever conditionality or advice to countries on major issues is involved, agreement should be sought promptly, beginning with working level staffs sharing information

and views at the earliest possible stages, and involving their respective superiors when resolution at the working level cannot be achieved. It will be the responsibility of the managers to seek a resolution of any major differences of view between the institutions before the matter is discussed with the member, and before either staff makes proposals to the member. The Deputy Managing Director of the Fund and the Senior Vice President, Operations, of the Bank will meet to discuss any issues not resolved at the Fund Director/Bank Regional Vice President level and advise, if necessary, the Managing Director and the President if any differences remain.

16. Existing procedures should be strengthened by a more systematic exchange of information on future country work and mission plans by country. Area Departments and Regions would be expected to maintain a forward-looking calendar of at least one year that would be updated periodically. Deviations from the work plan or calendar would be communicated to the other institution without delay.

17. We also stand ready to establish, under the direction of the Fund's Director of Research and the Bank's Vice President, Development Economics, ad hoc study groups to examine analytical issues which may arise in the areas of common work between the two institutions.

18. In the low-income countries, PFP discussions should continue to be handled jointly and, whenever possible, with a single mission chief at an appropriate rank, on the basis of pre-agreed terms of reference. The decision on whether the chief of such joint missions should be from the Bank or from the Fund will be determined on a case-by-case basis. When parallel missions are in the field, they would be expected to cooperate fully and meet jointly with the country authorities, following positions clearly agreed on in advance. Assuming members agree, the Fund management could issue an invitation for one or more Bank staff to be attached to missions involving the use of Fund resources in SAF/ESAF-eligible countries where the Bank was also financially active. Comparable provisions would be made to invite Fund staff to participate in Bank appraisal missions for SALs or SECALs in the same countries.

II. Improved Collaboration to Support Adjustment Programs

19. Under existing procedures, the Bank staff includes a discussion of the Fund's financial relations, the status of any negotiations for the use of Fund resources, and the results of any recent Fund reviews in the President's Report to the Bank's Executive Board on a proposed adjustment loan, since adjustment lending operations are not normally undertaken unless an appropriate Fund arrangement is in place. In the absence of a Fund arrangement, the Bank staff should ascertain whether the Fund has any major outstanding concerns about the adequacy of macroeconomic policies prior to formulating its own assessment in connection with the approval of the draft loan documents.[145] The Fund's assessment of macroeconomic policies is also taken into account in the Bank's assessment of its conditions prior to the release of subsequent tranches.

20. While the existing procedure functions well in most cases,[146] it is desirable to strengthen the coordination between the two institutions in this area. Such a need is particularly strong in the context of providing the Fund's assessment of macroeconomic policies for member countries where there are no existing Fund arrangements. Nonetheless, the economic situation or policies of the member may have changed significantly between con-

---

[145]SM/88/249 (11/14/88), pp. 4–6.

[146]Both the staff reports and summings up of Article IV consultations are made available to the Bank staff. Between consultations, the Bank staff is kept aware of the Fund staff's views and the results of other relevant Executive Board discussions on a continuous basis.

sultations. In these cases the Bank will ask the Fund's views, leaving time for consultations with the country authorities as needed. In comparable circumstances, the Fund management will ask the Bank's staff views prior to recommending approval of an adjustment program involving the use of Fund resources.

III. A PFP-Like Document for Middle-Income Countries

21. Some Directors have suggested that consideration be given to preparing PFP-like documents for some middle-income countries requesting the use of Fund resources, particularly those requesting arrangements under the EFF.[147] While the preparation of medium-term plans could be useful for non-SAF-eligible countries where the member seeks a multi-year commitment of resources from its creditors or where structural changes are prominent in the programs (e.g., under the EFF), this matter would be presented to the Executive Boards for consideration after further consultations between the two staffs and managements.

IV. Collaboration in the Context of the Debt Strategy

22. In the context of the debt strategy, the Fund is looked to by the commercial and official financing communities for an assessment of balance of payments prospects and financing requirements of member countries undertaking stabilization programs. Bank views are sought with respect to longer-term external resource requirements and growth prospects. In certain cases menu items play an important role in providing financing and contributing to a viable debt service profile over the medium term. Both institutions have an interest in this aspect of the member's external position as it affects the member's medium-term balance of payments prospects and creditworthiness. Therefore, in order to better coordinate our assistance to debtor countries faced with the need to develop financial menu items and other innovative forms of financing, including those aimed at debt reduction, we will establish a task force to promote cooperation, analysis, and the exchange of information on the financing techniques by our institutions.

V. Collaboration in the Presence of Overdue Obligations

23. Both the Bank and the Fund urge members with overdue obligations to one or both institutions to become current with both. In practice, if a member country has overdue obligations to one institution, this will affect the other institution's assessment of the justification for extending its own financial assistance. Each institution's policies require that it review the ability of a member to meet its financial obligations in light of that member's discharge of its obligations to the other; Fund management would find it difficult to present a request for a Fund arrangement to the Executive Board for a member with overdue obligations to the Bank, both because of its implications for ability to meet Fund obligations and because continued access to Bank or IDA lending is often necessary to ensure that an adjustment program is adequately financed. Fund management, therefore, proposes to seek the views of the Bank in all cases were the use of Fund resources was requested by a member with overdue obligations to the Bank, and would not be prepared to support such a request when arrears to the Bank were an indication that the resources of the Fund would not be safeguarded. Similarly, Bank management would advise its Board with regard to countries with overdue obligations to the Fund and would not be prepared to recommend approval of an IBRD or IDA loan, if the overdue obligations to the Fund were an indication that the

---

[147]See Buff 88/92 (5/13/88), pp. 2–3; and "Proposals for Extending the Policy Framework Paper (PFP) Process to Middle-Income Debtors," (EBD/88/144, 5/31/88).

resources of the Bank would not be safeguarded. Furthermore, the two managements will act in the full spirit of solidarity when one of the institutions is confronted with arrears, as such arrears constitute a major challenge to the cooperative nature of the institutions. They will, in such instances, provide their good offices and support to help eliminate those arrears.

VI. Independence of Institutional Decisions

24. The Executive Directors of the Bank and the Fund have stressed repeatedly the need to avoid cross-conditionality: each institution must continue to proceed with its own financial assistance according to the standards laid down in its Articles of Agreement and the policies adopted by its Executive Board. Thus, although the Bank's assessment of structural and sectoral policies will continue to be an important element in decisions regarding Fund lending, the ultimate decision on whether to support the program rests with the Fund's Executive Board. Similarly, although the Fund's assessments will continue to be an important element in decisions regarding Bank adjustment lending, the ultimate decisions rests with the Bank's Executive Directors.

25. Nevertheless, in the event that Fund management were to decide to submit a program for approval in spite of the Bank's reservations about structural policies or in the presence of arrears to the Bank, Fund management would present the case to an informal meeting of the Fund's Executive Board for discussion prior to communicating its decision to the member concerned. Bank management would adopt the corresponding procedure.

VII. Dealing with Other Institutions

26. Not only have the activities and roles of the Fund and the Bank expanded in relation to their members, coordinating activities to assist member countries in mobilizing resources have grown rapidly, as has the interest of other groups (the OECD, DAC, UN) in matters of debt and the resumption of growth. To avoid conflicting views from being expressed in reports to such organizations, to the maximum extent feasible, the draft reports prepared by either institution will be sent to the other well in advance of the circulation date for review and comments. This will provide an additional opportunity to identify possible problems and to resolve them.

VIII. Longer-Term Promotion of Mutual Understanding

27. To better acquaint staff of the two institutions with the thinking practices and constraints within which each institution operates, we propose to initiate an exchange of staff on two- to three-year secondments at the senior professional levels. During the period of the secondment, staff members would be wholly integrated into the regular staff of the institution to which they have been seconded. For administrative reasons, there might need to be some limit on the number of secondments at any one time.

28. While the measures set out above should go a long way toward resolving emerging differences of view and limiting potential areas of conflict, both the Fund and the Bank remain committed to a process of strengthening their collaboration in a longer-term perspective.

References

Anjaria, Shailendra J., Zubair Iqbal, Lorenzo L. Perez, and Wanda S. Tseng, 1981, *Trade Policy Developments in Industrial Countries*, IMF Occasional Paper No. 5 (Washington: International Monetary Fund).

Anjaria, Shailendra J., Sena Eken, and John F. Laker, 1982, *Payments Arrangements and the Expansion of Trade in Eastern and Southern Africa*, IMF Occasional Paper No. 11 (Washington: International Monetary Fund).

Anjaria, Shailendra J., Zubair Iqbal, Naheed Kirmani, and Lorenzo L. Perez, 1982, *Developments in International Trade Policy*, IMF Occasional Paper No. 16 (Washington: International Monetary Fund).

Anjaria, Shailendra J., Naheed Kirmani, and Arne B. Petersen, 1985, *Trade Policy Issues and Developments*, IMF Occasional Paper No. 38 (Washington: International Monetary Fund).

Auboin, Roger, 1955, *The Bank for International Settlements, 1930–1955*, Essays in International Finance, No. 22 (Princeton, New Jersey: International Finance Section, Department of Economics and Sociology, Princeton University).

Bergsten, C. Fred, 1994, "Managing the World Economy of the Future," in *Managing the World Economy: Fifty Years After Bretton Woods*, ed. by Peter B. Kenen (Washington: Institute for International Economics), pp. 341–74.

Bobay, Frédéric, 1998, "La France, les Institutions Monétaires Européennes et le Fonds Monétaire International 1944–1994," in *La France et les Institutions de Bretton Woods* (Paris: Cómité pour l'Histoire Économique et Financière de la France).

Boughton, James M., 1998, "Harry Dexter White and the International Monetary Fund," *Finance & Development*, Vol. 35 (September), pp. 39–41.

———, and K. Sarwar Lateef, 1995, *Fifty Years After Bretton Woods: The Future of the IMF and the World Bank* (Washington: IMF and World Bank Group).

Brau, Eduard, and Richard C. Williams, 1983, *Recent Multilateral Debt Restructurings with Official and Bank Creditors*, IMF Occasional Paper No. 25 (Washington: International Monetary Fund).

de Vries, Margaret Garritsen, 1976, *The International Monetary Fund, 1966–1971: The System Under Stress*, Vol. 1: *Narrative*; Vol. 2: *Documents* (Washington: International Monetary Fund).

———, 1985, *The International Monetary Fund, 1972–1978: Cooperation on Trial*, Vols. 1 and 2: *Narrative and Analysis*; Vol. 3: *Documents* (Washington: International Monetary Fund).

Dillon, K. Burke, C. Maxwell Watson, G. Russell Kincaid, and Chanpen Puckahtikom, 1985, *Recent Developments in External Debt Restructuring*, IMF Occasional Paper No. 40 (Washington: International Monetary Fund).

Dillon, K. Burke, and Gumersindo Oliveros, 1987, *Recent Experience with Multilateral Official Debt Rescheduling*, World Economic and Financial Surveys (Washington: International Monetary Fund).

Eichengreen, Barry, 1993, *Reconstructing Europe's Trade and Payments: The European Payments Union* (Manchester, United Kingdom: Manchester University Press).

———, and Peter B. Kenen, 1994, "Managing the World Economy under the Bretton Woods System: An Overview," in *Managing the World Economy: Fifty Years After Bretton Woods*, ed. by Peter B. Kenen (Washington: Institute for International Economics), pp. 3–57.

Finch, C. David, 1988, "Let the IMF Be the IMF," *International Economy*, Vol. 1 (January/February), pp. 126–28.

———, 1997, *Werribee to Washington: A Career at the International Monetary Fund* (unpublished; Washington).

Frenkel, Jacob A., and Michael L. Mussa, 1985, "Asset Markets, Exchange Rates and the Balance of Payments," in *Handbook of International Economics*, Vol. 2, ed. by Ronald W. Jones and Peter B. Kenen (Amsterdam: North-Holland), pp. 679–747.

Frenkel, Jacob A., and Assaf Razin, 1987, *Fiscal Policies and the World Economy: An Intertemporal Approach* (Cambridge, Massachusetts: MIT Press).

Frenkel, Jacob A., and Morris Goldstein, eds., 1991, *International Financial Policy: Essays in Honor of Jacques J. Polak* (Washington: International Monetary Fund and De Nederlandsche Bank).

Gardner, Richard N., 1956, *Sterling-Dollar Diplomacy in Current Perspective: Anglo-American Collaboration in the Reconstruction of Multilateral Trade* (Oxford: Oxford University Press).

Gold, Joseph, 1982, "The Relationship between the International Monetary Fund and the World Bank," *Creighton Law Review*, Vol. 15, No. 2, pp. 499–521.

———, 1986, "Some Legal Aspects of the IMF's Activities in Relation to International Trade," *Osterreichische Zeitschrift fur Offentliches Recht und Volkerrecht* (Austria); Vol. 36, pp. 157–217.

———, 1996, *Interpretation: The IMF and International Law* (London: Kluwer Law International).

Harrod, R.F., 1951, *The Life of John Maynard Keynes* (London: Macmillan).

Horsefield, J. Keith, ed., 1969, *The International Monetary Fund 1945–1965: Twenty Years of International Monetary Cooperation*, Vol. 1: *Chronicle*, by J. Keith Horsefield; Vol. 2: *Analysis*, by Margaret G. de Vries and J. Keith Horsefield with the collaboration of Joseph Gold, Mary H. Gumbart, Gertrud Lovasy, and Emil G. Spitzer; Vol. 3: *Documents* (Washington: International Monetary Fund).

Howe, Geoffrey, 1994, *Conflict of Loyalty* (New York: St. Martin's Press).

International Monetary Fund, 1998, *Annual Report 1998* (Washington: International Monetary Fund).

———, *Summary Proceedings* (Washington: International Monetary Fund, various issues).

International Monetary Fund, Research Department, 1984, *Exchange Rate Volatility and World Trade*, IMF Occasional Paper No. 28. (Washington: International Monetary Fund).

James, Harold, 1995, *International Monetary Cooperation since Bretton Woods* (Oxford: Oxford University Press).

Kafka, Alexandre, 1996, "Governance of the Fund," in *The International Monetary and Financial System: Developing-Country Perspectives*, ed. by Gerald K. Helleiner (London: Macmillan).

Kaplan, Jacob J., and Günter Schleiminger, 1989, *The European Payments Union: Financial Diplomacy in the 1950s* (Oxford: Clarendon Press).

Kapur, Devesh, John P. Lewis, and Richard Webb, 1997, *The World Bank: Its First Half Century*, Vol. 1: *History* (Washington: Brookings Institution Press).

Keller, Peter M., 1988, *Multilateral Official Debt Rescheduling: Recent Experience*, World Economic and Financial Surveys (Washington: International Monetary Fund).

Kelly, Margaret, Naheed Kirmani, Miranda Xafa, Clemens Boonekamp, and Peter Winglee, 1988, *Issues and Developments in International Trade Policy*, IMF Occasional Paper No. 63. (Washington: International Monetary Fund).

Koopmans, Tjalling C., and William C. Hood, 1953, "The Estimation of Simultaneous Linear Economic Relationships," in *Studies in Econometric Method*, ed. by William C. Hood and Tjalling C. Koopmans (New York: John Wiley & Sons), pp. 112–99.

Krueger, Anne O., 1998, "Whither the World Bank and the IMF?" *Journal of Economic Literature*, Vol. 36 (December), pp. 1983–2020.

Kuhn, Michael G., and Jorge P. Guzman, 1990, *Multilateral Official Debt Rescheduling: Recent Experience*, World Economic and Financial Surveys (Washington: International Monetary Fund).

Lawson, Nigel, 1992, *The View from No. 11: Memoirs of a Tory Radical* (London: Bantam Press).

Moggridge, Donald, ed., 1980, *The Collected Writings of John Maynard Keynes*, Vol. 26: *Activities 1941–1946; Shaping the Post-War World: Bretton Woods and Reparations* (London: Macmillan).

Mortimer, Robert A., 1984, *The Third World Coalition in International Politics* (Boulder, Colorado; London: Westview Press; 2nd, updated ed.).

Muirhead, Bruce, 1999, *Against the Odds: The Public Life and Times of Louis Rasminsky* (Toronto, Canada: University of Toronto Press).

Muldoon, Robert, 1981, *My Way* (Wellington, New Zealand: Reed).

Nowzad, Bahram, and Richard C. Williams, 1981, *External Indebtedness of Developing Countries*, IMF Occasional Paper No. 3 (Washington: International Monetary Fund).

Polak, Jacques J., 1994a, "The World Bank and the IMF: The Future of their Coexistence," in *Bretton Woods: Looking to the Future*, by the Bretton Woods Commission (Washington: Bretton Woods Commission).

————, 1994b, *Economic Theory and Financial Policy: The Selected Essays of Jacques J. Polak*, Vols. 1 and 2 (Aldershot, England: Edward Elgar).

————, 1995, "Fifty Years of Exchange Rate Research and Policy at the International Monetary Fund," *Staff Papers*, International Monetary Fund, Vol. 42 (December), pp. 734–61.

————, 1996, "Should the SDR Become the Sole Financing Technique for the IMF?" in *The Future of the SDR in Light of Changes in the International Financial System*, ed. by Michael Mussa, James M. Boughton, and Peter Isard (Washington: International Monetary Fund), pp. 221–39.

————, 1997, "The World Bank and the IMF: A Changing Relationship," in *The World Bank: Its First Half Century*, Vol. 2: *Perspectives*, ed. by Devesh Kapur, John P. Lewis, and Richard Webb (Washington: Brookings Institution Press), pp. 473–521.

————, 1998, "The Articles of Agreement of the IMF and the Liberalization of Capital Movements," in *Should the IMF Pursue Capital Account Convertibility?* ed. by Peter B. Kenen, Essays in International Finance, No. 207 (Princeton, New Jersey: International Finance Section, Department of Economics, University of Princeton), pp. 47–54.

————, 2000, "The IMF Model at Forty," in *Empirical Models and Policy Making*, ed. by Frank den Butter and Mary S. Morgan (New York: Routledge).

Rosenblatt, Julius, Thomas Mayer, Kasper Bertholdy, Dimitrios Demekas, Sanjeev Gupta, and Leslie Lipschitz, 1988, *The Common Agricultural Policy of the European Community: Principles and Consequences*, IMF Occasional Paper No. 62 (Washington: International Monetary Fund).

Sevigny, David, 1990, *The Paris Club: An Inside View* (Ottawa: North-South Institute).

Tanzi, Vito, 1983, "The Underground Economy," *Finance and Development*, Vol. 20 (December), pp. 10–13.

Thatcher, Margaret, 1993, *The Downing Street Years* (New York: HarperCollins).

Thorson, Phillip, 1992, 1993, 1994, "The Third Headquarters," *The Caravan: IMF Retirees' Association*, Vol. 12, No. 1 (July 1992), pp. 10–21; Vol. 13, No. 1 (August 1993), pp. 6–17; and Vol. 13, No. 2 (January 1994), pp. 9–17.

Ungerer, Horst, 1997, *A Concise History of European Monetary Integration: From EPU to EMU* (Westport, Connecticut: Quorum Books).

————, Jouko J. Hauvonen, Augusto Lopez-Claros, and Thomas Mayer, 1990, *The European Monetary System: Development and Perspectives*, IMF Occasional Paper No. 73 (Washington: International Monetary Fund).

U.S. Department of State, 1948, *Proceedings and Documents of United Nations Monetary and Financial Conference, Bretton Woods, New Hampshire, July 1–22, 1944* (Washington: United States Government Printing Office).

Vines, David, 1997, "The Fund, the Bank, and the WTO: Functions, Competencies and Reform Agendas," Global Economic Institutions Working Paper No. 26 (London: Centre for Economic Policy Research, April).

Watson, Maxwell, Russell Kincaid, Caroline Atkinson, Eliot Kalter, and David Folkerts-Landau, 1986, *International Capital Markets: Developments and Prospects*, World Economic and Financial Surveys (Washington: International Monetary Fund).

Index

borrowing from the IMF during the 1970s, 17–20

debt crisis of the 1980s, 30–33

econometric models, 259–60

economic conditions in the late 1980s, 33

formation of the G-24, 188

formation of the G-77, 187

IMF approach to exchange rate policy evaluation, 86–87

impact of coffee price fluctuations, 24

impact of exchange rate volatility, 213

oil shocks, 319

policy concerning South Africa, 593

slowdown of economic growth in the late 1980s, 47

support for economic growth in 1987, 612–13

WEO projections of debt burdens, 234–35

Development Assistance Committee (OECD), 684n

Dee, Dewey, 622

Dillon, K. Burke, 360n, 368n, 457, 1010n, 1012n

Dini, Lamberto, 199, 243, 896, 898, 1033

Disaster relief. See Emergency disaster relief

Diwan, Romesh, 779n

Diz, Adolfo, 327

Dobson, Wendy, 186n, 210n, 220n

Dodsworth, John R., 822n

Doe, Samuel K., 775, 776n, 777

Dominguez, Kathryn M., 151n, 192n, 203n, 208

Dominica, emergency disaster relief, 745–46

Dominican Republic
Article VIII status, 120n
buffer-stock drawing, 743
emergency disaster relief, 745–46
protests over IMF programs, 691–92

Donoso, Alvaro, 153, 539n

Dooley, Michael P., 481n, 490n, 499, 541, 544

Dornbusch, Rudiger, 35n, 540

Dornelles, Francisco Neves, 382–84

Drabble, Bernard J., 243, 731, 746, 906, 1042

Droughts. See Emergency disaster relief

Duarte, José Napoleon, 729n

Duisenberg, W.F., 43n

Dunaway, Steven, 32

Duncan, Alex, 598

Dunkel, Arthur, 1006

Duvalier, Jean-Claude, 57

E

EAC. See East African Community

EAR. See Policy on Enlarged Access to the Fund's Resources

Earthquakes. See Emergency disaster relief

East Africa, structural economic reform, 595–602

East African Community, 598

East Germany. See German Democratic Republic

East India Company, 710n

Eastern Caribbean dollar, 76, 78

Eastern Europe
debt crisis of the 1980s, 320–25

Eaton, Jonathan, 313n

EBRD. See European Bank for Reconstruction and Development

EC. See European Community

ECB. See European Central Bank

Echeverría, Luis, 282

ECM. See External contingency mechanism

École Nationale d'Administration, 5

Econometric modeling, 236, 254–60

Economic and Social Council (UN), 977, 1009

Economic Declaration, 173

Economic Outlook, 227–28, 230, 261

Economic Policy Committee (OECD), 187n, 192n

ECOSOC. See Economic and Social Council

Ecuador
in "Baker 15," 419n
CFF drawings, 737
debt crisis, 272
IMF's approval in principle of stand-by arrangements, 410
Paris Club rescheduling, 1012
multiyear rescheduling agreement (MYRA), 412, 416

Edison, Hali J., 192n

Edo, Michael, 682–83

Edwards, Alexandra Cox, 346n

Edwards, Sebastian, 86n, 271n, 286n, 346n, 350n, 539n, 545, 550, 615, 696n

EEC. See European Economic Community

EFF. See Extended Fund Facility